Biographical Encyclopedia:

Chronicling the History of the Church of God Abrahamic Faith 19th & 20th Centuries

by
J. Turner Stilson

Word Edge

Word Edge
315 South Walnut Street
Stillman Valley, IL 61084 USA
www.word-edge.com
Phone 1.815.645.2430

© *2011 J. Turner Stilson*

No part of this book may be reproduced, stored in a retrieval system, or transmitted by any means without the written permission of the author.

Church of God General Conference History Committee:
Kent H. Ross, Chairman
Jan Turner Stilson, Writer
Arlen F. Rankin, Greg Demmitt and Jennifer Winner, Directors

First published by Word Edge in June 2011.

ISBN-13: 978-0-615-46561-6 (pbk.)
ISBN-10: 0-615-46561-7 (pbk.)
ISBN-13: 978-0-615-46562-3 (e-book)
ISBN-10: 0-615-46562-5 (e-book)

Printed in the United States of America

Publisher's Cataloging-in-Publication
(Provided by Quality Books, Inc.)

Biographical encyclopedia : chronicling the history of the Church of God Abrahamic Faith, 19th and 20th centuries / J. Turner Stilson.
  p. cm.
  Includes bibliographical references and index.
  ISBN-13: 978-0-615-46561-6 (pbk.)
  ISBN-10: 0-615-46561-7 (pbk.)
  ISBN-13: 978-0-615-46562-3 (e-book)
  ISBN-10: 0-615-46562-5 (e-book)

  1. Church of God of the Abrahamic Faith--Biography--Encyclopedias. 2. Church of God of the Abrahamic Faith--History--Encyclopedias.   I. Stilson, Jan.

  BX6183.B56 2011   286.7'3'0922
                           QBI11-600074

*This book is dedicated to
the men and women
who have gone before us;
to scholars and historians who have
kept the history alive and fresh,
and to those who labor in the field,
both now and in the future,
to preach the Gospel of the Kingdom
to the world.*

Contents

Preface 1

Foreword 4

19th Century Biographies (Died pre-1950) 9

20th Century Biographies (Died post-1950 or Living) 325

Appendixes, List of 543
    19th Century Appendixes..545
    20th Century Appendixes 580

Index 605

Preface

The Church of God Abrahamic Faith was rooted in British theology, but budded and flowered on American soil. Those familiar with church history have studied the British Conditionalists, British Literalists, British Adventists and British Unitarians. The Church of God has commonality with all those doctrines and some have even accepted British Dispensationalism.

Englishman Joseph Priestley, a theologian and scientist, received wider fame for discovering the role of oxygen in the human body than for his theology, yet he was burned out of his home by persecutors who did not appreciate his dissenting views on the oneness of God.

While it cannot be said that Joseph Priestley was the founder of the Church of God after he came to America, he was a witness for all the above-mentioned ideas and for the premillennial interpretation of prophecy, which included statements by him about the Age to Come. Priestley lived in America only a few years, dying in Pennsylvania in 1804, yet many religious folks paid attention to him. A man like Priestley does not go unnoticed.

About that time, Elias Smith began a loosely organized group of Christians in New England called the Christian Connexion. This man and group of congregations also believed some, if not all, of those same biblical teachings including Age to Come. Smith began to publish these ideas in *The Herald of Gospel Liberty*, the first religious newspaper in America (1808).

By the time William Miller's American Adventist movement was at its zenith (1843), Joseph Marsh, an editor and publisher, moved to the forefront of public attention. He had been ousted as editor of the Christian Connexion's paper, *The Christian Palladium,* because he published too much material about the Second Advent of Christ. This little controversy brought public scrutiny in an unexpected and unwanted manner. Yet, he was able to recover and began to publish *The Voice of Truth*, which at first became the voice of William Miller's movement.

After the Bitter Disappointment and the famed Albany Conference of 1845, Joseph Marsh no longer associated with William Miller. Rather, Marsh became an advocate for the Second Advent of Christ to establish the Kingdom of God on earth during the millennium, to bring restitution of all things, establish the throne of David, send the Jews forth to the nations as missionaries, bring judgment to the unjust and reward to the righteous.

Joseph Marsh was a biblical unitarian, a conditionalist and defender of the promises made to Abraham. He believed the scriptural name of the church should be Church of God. He published journals that reflected his beliefs. Through reader correspondence, he found other believers who believed the same things. Many men stepped forward to assist in spreading the message through camp meetings, church revivals, Bible studies, circuit preaching and publication of tracts and journals.

As the message began to expand and move out of New England, other clusters of believers and congregations were discovered in the Virginias, the Frontier, the South and the Great Plains. After the Civil War, the work to the west grew quickly.

While the published journals of Joseph Marsh and Benjamin Wilson were a somewhat unifying factor, there was additional need for a coalition that would bring believers together from these various regions in fellowship of a common organization. Efforts were made in 1869, 1888, 1910 and 1921 to form a national conference. Finally, the 1921 effort was successful in organizing congregations and state conferences into a national general conference which functions today in McDonough, Georgia.

It was in this setting that the men and women featured in this encyclopedia served the Lord. The dedication of these pastors and leaders cannot be quantitatively measured, but the spirit of their dedication is what inspires and drives us today. The work of the Holy Spirit brought the Church of God Abrahamic Faith into being and continues the work today.

The content gathering for this encyclopedia involved a painstaking process of reading and note taking. Most of the print materials present in the Archives of the Church of God General Conference at McDonough, Georgia, have been read page by page to find names and facts. Note taking was extensive. Archival materials of sister denominations were accessed personally or through online research. The records of the Advent Christians at Aurora University, Seventh-day Adventists at Ann Arbor and Loma Linda, Disciples of Christ at Lincoln Christian College, together with internet materials, were invaluable.

Research also involved hundreds of phone calls, personal interviews and e-mails to Church of God members and friends outside the Church of God. Many librarians were immensely helpful and patient in answering questions and locating sources within their collections. Church of God members have also written and submitted copy. The 20th century portion of this book is primarily from materials donated by family members through a project spearheaded by David Krogh at Atlanta Bible College. Members of the History Committee have also contributed entries and provided editing services.

Those historians who preceded us in research and writing must be given a vast amount of credit for preserving their impressions of Church of God history. Men such as Clyde E. Randall, Paul Hatch, David Graham, Mark Mattison and Terry Ferrell set the benchmark in recording and analyzing the times and events of previous generations. Women who made significant historical contributions, especially in organization of the National Berean Society and the National Bible Institute, include Grace Marsh, Evelyn Austin, Mary Woodward and Emma Railsback. All these historians paved the way for this book.

The History Committee of Kent Ross, Jan Stilson, Arlen Rankin and Greg Demmitt, (Jennifer Winner joined the committee in 2010), initially decided to write biographies of pastors, but as research proceeded, it became clear that laymen served as evangelists and clergy in the early days of the Church of God. Men and women who were humble farmers, carpenters or housewives, took leadership roles to preach and teach—there were no established pastoral classes in the early 19th century. So, the scope of the book was expanded to include more leaders of both genders.

The story of the Church of God is an amazing one. The people in these pages deserve praise, thanks and respect for their sacrificial work to advance the cause of the Gospel of the Kingdom throughout America and Canada in the 19th and 20th centuries. The Church of God has a rich heritage, and it is the prayer of the History Committee that each reader, teacher, pastor and student who reads this book is inspired to step up their commitment to service and to devote their lives to spreading the Gospel of the Kingdom as did the men and women who preceded them.

The book is divided into two parts, 19th century and 20th century. Here are other defining characteristics of each biographical entry:

- If a person died before 1950 the biography is located in the 19th century. Those who died after 1950 or are still living but retired are in the 20th.
- Both sections are organized alphabetically by last names.
- Birth and death dates are given with the name where that information is known.
- At the beginning of each lengthy biography beneath the subject's name, birth and death dates, and prior to the text, is a Table of Contents for major topics within the entry. This allows the reader to see at a glance the direction of the content. The text is organized by the topics in the Table of Contents, allowing for easy reading of the entire entry, or only part of it at one sitting. TOCs are not used with short entries.
- There are no footnotes within the text of each entry, but a bibliography is given after each biography to demonstrate that research was thorough and to document the statements made in the entry. This is not a work of fiction. This is a factual report of the research on each person's life and activities.
- Some historical analysis has been offered especially with the major figures.
- Cross references between entries have been included at the end of a biography to further assist the reader in locating similar information in other entries. For example, in an entry on J. M. Stephenson (19th), "See" references at the bottom include David P. Hall, R. J. Hill, Joseph Marsh and others. This use of cross-references eliminates extreme redundancy.
- There is necessarily some redundancy from entry to entry. For example, background information is repeated as needed so readers unfamiliar with the Church of God can get more information quickly without having to read the whole book.
- Entries of significant figures also include his or her ideas on doctrine. In this manner, as the research came together from many single entries into an encyclopedia, the history and development of thought within the Church of God has also been brought to light. The Appendixes have been designed to supplement the biographies by revealing writings and charts on key events and major doctrines over the past two centuries.
- The Periodicals Timeline and Pathways of Faith graphics in the Appendixes illustrate the timeline of publications and events.

Terms used extensively throughout the book include geographical names such as Oregon, Illinois, and names of churches and organizations such as Church of God, Church of God General Conference, Oregon Bible College, Atlanta Bible College, etc. Such terms are not used in the Subject Index at the back of the book. A few persons are included in the Subject Indies where those names do not have a specific biographical entry but are important to the story. For example, no biographical entry is made for Alexander Campbell or Dr. John Thomas who were never founders of the Church of God, but they are mentioned in the text.

Very short biographies are interspersed with longer biographies in order to shed light upon the life and service of lesser-known individuals who helped make the Church of God great in America. Perhaps such a person was an excellent leader but did not report his activities to one of the journals. This means his or her story has not been discovered either in Church of God literature or in the Archives. If the leaders and pastors did not report their activities to the journals, or if no one mentioned their names in a letter to the editor, there is no economic way for a researcher to discover their life stories.

It is possible to read this book from cover to cover, for the stories of our church heroes are gripping and inspiring and may capture the reader's attention and heart. However, the organizational style also makes it possible to select reading topics to accomplish:

- Quick and ready reference
- Class preparation on topics of history or Bible doctrine
- Sermon illustration
- Life lessons for youth school, church and camp

Assets of this encyclopedia to enhance reading and study are:

- Biographical content
- Alphabetical organization
- Discussion of developing doctrines within an entry
- Subject index at the back
- Tables of contents on major entries
- Inclusion of topical essays in a comprehensive Appendix section
- Dozens of authentic photos and full text of historic documents
- Overview of American church history of the 19th and 20th centuries

The topical essays reflect thinking by Church of God scholars of both the past and present, regarding doctrine, organizational efforts, worship styles and more. One essay by Greg Demmitt so succinctly describes the developing Church of God of the 19th and 20th centuries that it is featured as the Foreword.

This is the story of the Church of God and that history must be celebrated. The content of the book includes the history of thought of additional church organizations including the Christadelphians, Disciples of Christ, Christian Connexion, Unitarians and Advent Christians. The Seventh-day Adventists, Seventh-day Baptists and Seventh-day Church of God are also mentioned. These groups developed beside the Church of God as sister denominations and helped shape its thought and mission. Discussion also includes some of the tangential thoughts labeled "heresy" subsequently excluded from the statement of faith in the Church of God and many of its sister denominations.

Thank you to everyone who assisted with research, writing or editing this book, including the General Conference staff who assisted in the publishing and marketing. Thanks to each reader who purchased a copy.

J. Turner Stilson,
BTh, BS, MALS, MA (Biblical Studies)
Principal Writer
Spring 2011

The author wishes to thank the supporters and critics of this work. Every comment has been helpful. The author does not accept responsibility for errors in the text which may have been initiated by original documents, including variations in spelling of places or names, variation in dates, interpretation of events and omission of details not deemed newsworthy by original editors. If you wish to make a helpful critical comment, or if you wish to donate original materials to the Atlanta Bible College Archives contact the author via **bio-cog.com**.

Front Cover Photos (clockwise from top): Lillie and Thomas Wilson; Oregon, Illinois, Church of God and dormitory, 1963; Benjamin Wilson Home, Geneva, Illinois (photo by Jan Stilson); James Watkins and local boy observe Jerusalem's Eastern Gate; Tanzania Church of God (photo from Rex Cain); Anna Drew portrait; Lawrenceville, Ohio, Church of God, stained glass window (photo from Rex Cain); Sr. Verna Thayer at OBC Chapel, 1960. **Back Cover Photos (from top):** Sylvan Church of God; Paul Hatch, Church of God historian, 1960; Ida Mae and Willis Turner, Rockford, Illinois (photo by Jan Stilson); Left to right J.F. Wagoner, Almus Adams and Jeremiah Hatch–Rules Committee members, first General Conference meeting, Philadelphia 1888.

Foreword

One Way or One Faith?
by Greg Demmitt
Presented at the Second Annual History Conference, North Hills Church of God, Springfield, Ohio, November 8, 2007.

> **Annotation:** *Demmitt explores the early literature of the pre-Church of God to discover commonalities of doctrine divergent from the mainstream churches. Then he examines divergences within the developing Church of God that caused tension over the decades, but which he thinks can be used to advantage in directing the changes that must occur as the General Conference moves forward. This is a very thoughtful and insightful exploration of Church of God roots and trends and serves to inform the reader of the culture into which the biographies in this encyclopedia are nested.*

As a sixth-generation member of the Church of God, five on my mother's side and six generations on my father's side, I've always appreciated my heritage in this movement, and have always thought about how we fit into the greater Christian community. In this paper I will show examples of unity and diversity in our theological history and also show the diverse historical roots of the movement.

Unity and Diversity in Doctrine:

Here's what I can say with a certainty about commonly-held beliefs in all that became the Church of God.

- **The Scriptures are the only authoritative source of Truth**
- **Man is wholly mortal, no immortal soul**
- **The restitution of the earth with the Kingdom located here when Jesus returns**
- **A non-trinitarian Christology**
- **The Imminent return of Christ**
- **Restoration of Israel**

Here are diverse views:

1. **Brotherhood of all Christians.** Joseph Marsh never fully separated himself from the Christian Connexion, which had a strong emphasis on unifying all Christians by getting back to basics. He wrote specifically about the brotherhood of all Christians and refused to join the Adventists when it appeared to him that they were creating a new religious body.

2. **Baptism as essential for salvation.** Marsh argued with Alexander Campbell on this, saying that immersion being essential would negate the faith of nearly all Christians back through history. Quoting:

    It stamps as spurious the many ten thousand experiences of all orders who have lived and now love in our world, who were not baptized for the remission of sins!! And more than this, it ridicules and tauntingly jeers at all Christian experience, except what is obtained in baptism. Hence, the holy of all sects are unchristianized by this modern system of salvation!

    For if God has since the day of Pentecost, ever remitted the sins of the unregenerated heart in any way than baptism, then it must follow that baptism was not instituted for the remission of sins.

    (Source: "Facts are Stubborn Things," *Christian Herald*, Milan, February 19, 1835.)

3. **Nature of Christ.** David Graham wrote that the pre-existence of Christ was held by many in the 1880s. I tend to agree with him, not that I believe in pre-existence, but that many of those in the 1800s did. Jan Stilson is cited as saying that Wiley Jones definitely believed in pre-existence and wrote to *The Gospel Banner* to encourage others to consider it. Henry Grew, who often contributed articles to *The Voice of Truth,* definitely believed in preexistence. The Christian Connexion said that they weren't Arian because they didn't see Jesus as being a created being, that he only had divine nature even after being born as a human. [*Editor's note*: Wiley Jones, a pastor and writer of the Church of God, believed in pre-existence. See Jones, Wiley (19th)]. Go to Google Books and look up *Memoirs of Elder Elijah Shaw*. He tells about sending Marsh as one of several young preachers, and also described his own differences

with the Arian point of view. Also see my paper at *http://homepage.mac.com/gdemmitt/index.htm*, choose iDisk, then Developing Christologies.

Like Marsh, Benjamin Wilson included divergent views in his publications. He was highly influenced by Dr. John Thomas, who had some wild speculations. Here's a summary from Steven Cook on *Cogmail@yahoogroups.com* regarding Dr. Thomas:

John Thomas' view of God-manifestation was later reworked in a book by the then editor of *The Christadelphian* magazine, C.C. Walker, in his work called *Theophany*. In a nutshell, Thomas believed that God was revealed throughout history through various theophanies. Hence, the angel which appeared to Abraham was called YHVH, when Jacob wrestled with an angel he wrestled with El and when Jesus appeared He was God-manifest-in-the-flesh. He was the most prefect representation of God. In fact, in his last published work Thomas referred to Jesus as "the Elohim of the whole earth." He believed that the Divine name, YHVH, from the Hebrew *ehyeh*, meant "He will be" and if asked, what will he be?" the answer would be "Jesus is the One who God would become."

His view of God-manifestation then extended to all believers—so that we become part the Divine family, share in the Divine nature at resurrection, and become manifestations of God.

He once said that the problem with the Trinity was not that it went too far, but that it did not go far enough: God is not three persons, but is manifested in a multitude of persons-first through angels, then through Jesus Christ, and then finally through a multitude of people. At last, God will "be all in all."

Hence, he has been described as neither Unitarian nor Trinitarian–although most Christadelphians these days would think of themselves as Unitarians (although I almost never hear the term in Christadelphian circles).

The variety of Christologies might explain why in the first year of *The Restitution Herald* (1911), there is only one negative comment about the Trinity, and that somewhat obscure, while every issue condemned the teaching of the immortal soul as coming from paganism. (This is also documented in my paper, "Emerging Christologies".)

4. **A Christ-centered theology.** Marsh and the Christian Connexion were very evangelical and focused on Jesus as our Savior. I would characterize their preaching as pointing toward Christ. In the Wilsons, we have a Bible-centered theology—the preaching points toward the Bible as the truth, as the container of all that is needed for salvation. Marsh focused on Christian conversion; Wilson focused on coming to an understanding of the truth. Most of the "One Faith" articles cited below also argue against a Christ-centered Gospel.

Wilson does believe in the atoning work of Christ, although he has qualms about a truly "substitutionary" atonement. See *The Gospel Banner*, February 1, 1868, page 54.

In studying the first year of the *The Restitution Herald*, I see basically an evangelical view of Christ. The article, "Who is Jesus," totally focused on his saving work as the Son of God and included no comments about the Trinity.

Citations of Essays on Bible Doctrines by various authors in chronological order:

Wilson, Benjamin
"Jesus" *Gospel Banner*, Geneva, IL, 4:1 Jan. 1858, 7. There is no anti-trinity in this piece. It mostly focuses on what it means for Jesus to be the Messiah.

"What is the Gospel?" *GB* 4:12, Dec. 1858. 133-135 5:1 January 1, 1859, 12-14.

"Reasons for separating from a Campbellite church" *GB*, 5:5, May 1859. No anti-trinity.

"Peter's Confessions" *GB*, 4:2, Feb. 1858. Focuses on why that is more about being the Christ than being the Son of God.

An early statement of faith may be found in *Gospel Banner* 14:1 Jan. 1, 1868.

Allen, Mark
"The One Body, *GB*, 5:12 Dec. 1859, 129.

"Who are the Brethren?" Dialogue with Levi H. Chase, several articles. *GB* Vol. 4. The Wilsons believed in a specific set of doctrines, which must be believed to be a Christian. This view was consistent with that of John Thomas who left the Stone-Campbell movement and founded the Christadelphians. From Jan Stilson on Cogmail:

> In Geneva, Illinois, under the tutelage and publication genius of Benjamin Wilson, the COGAF

people referred to themselves as Brethren of One Faith or The Faith. Wilson, who had been curious and friendly towards the teachings of John Thomas for awhile, eventually turned emphatically away from him over doctrine and some personal insults cast upon him by Thomas. Just as Wilson did not use "Age to Come" which was popularized by Joseph Marsh in his writings on the United States east coast, using instead the "One Faith" moniker, so he may have also shied away from using "The Truth" because it was used by Dr. Thomas.

Marsh, Joseph

Published an article by Nathaniel Field, which strongly condemned Thomas' arrogance of thinking that he had a corner on essential truth. *Expositor and Advocate,* pgs. 605-7, 627-28 and 663-66.

Woodruff, John O.

"The Great Mystery: God Manifest in Flesh" *The Words of Eternal Life.* Self published, 1901, 356-357. Woodruff does not believe in pre-existence of Jesus but understands key scriptures (John 1:1) as pre-existent Word. In page 347 of this essay Woodruff stated:

> It clearly indicates that the Lord Jesus Christ was a God-development. He was of divine origin. The "Word" was made flesh. The Word was God, the embodiment of God's spirit or His Word personified, if I may speak. We see in Jesus the beginning of the divine creation of God. The divine took hold of the human in Jesus and we partake of the divine nature through Jesus.

McLauchlan, Robert

Addresses and Miscellaneous Papers on Bible Themes, Cleveland, Ohio. 1903. He believed the immortal soul is apostasy but not anti-trinity.

The Church of God has Diverse Roots:

1. **Christian Connexion.** As the original Unitarians in the United States, they became humanistic. Marsh edited one of their papers, *The Christian Palladium*. He was in good standing with the movement at his death. The United Church of Christ and the Congregational Christian church came directly from this movement.

2. **The Adventist Movement.** William Miller began this movement, which represented end-time speculation in American from the late 1700s until 1850. Marsh was also connected with this movement, and he was removed as editor of the *Palladium* because of his constant devotion to prophecy and for including Miller in that publication. [Editor's note: Marsh published the *Voice of Truth*, a Miller instrument, in its early years.]

3. **Stone-Campbell Movement.** This is also known as the Restoration Movement. Barton Stone (the Christians) and Alexander Campbell (the Disciples) coalesced in the early 1800s with Walter Scott who evangelized the Western Reserve. They had the goal of restoring the New Testament church with Christian unity. Several notable things with regard to the Church of God:

    a. Stone was anti-trinitarian, but with a pre-existent Jesus. Campbell's main objection to the Trinity was its non-biblical language, and concepts, and also the dogmatism of the Trinitarians in considering it essential. Campbell denied the eternal Son, saying Jesus came into existence at Bethlehem, although he also saw the LOGOS as a distinct person.

    b. David Lipscomb and James Harding strongly taught the Kingdom of God on this renewed earth. In last year's book, *Kingdom Come*, John Mark Hicks and Bobby Valentine document how what they called the Texas tradition in the churches of Christ, that won out over this view as Texas emphasized that the church was the Kingdom. Texas also was more focused on correct doctrine and required rebaptism for converts.

    This is important for the Church of God as it shows how at least some moved out of the Stone-Campbell movement. Gatesville was originally Church of Christ and left under the leadership of A. S. Bradley, who originally debated in favor of soul sleep while still a Church of Christ preacher against the Baptists, then within the Church of Christ as the Texas church of Christ determined to decide which position was true.

c. John Thomas was originally highly-respected as a protégé of Alexander Campbell but was repudiated as he became dogmatic about things Campbell considered debatable. Thomas took many Disciples into the Christadelphians, and the Wilsons went with him from the Disciples.

Beyond these three distinct movements, in general in the 1800s, publications were the driving forces of various movements. Some have called the publishers "editor-bishops" because of the influence they held over church movements. Anybody with a printing press could advocate any position he wanted and his subscription base was his church. Studies of these subscriptions show that many people were reading a variety of publications, but usually favored one. Jan Stilson and David Graham have documented a great deal of interaction with these publications, including those of Charles Taze Russell of the *Watchtower*, with those that coalesced into the Church of God. The Wilsons were the most influential in bringing together what came to be the Church of God General Conference.

It's my opinion that the followers of these editors became even more sectarian than the editors. While the editors were originally trying to publish alternate viewpoints in what was a discussion about what the Bible teaches, the followers tended to write about how so-and-so contended for the faith. There is an incorrect assumption that the editors were part of a continuous line back to the New Testament and the truth, rather than being truth-seekers. That's somewhat understandable due to the harsh rhetoric of the editors, but most of them were aware they were disagreeing with what had been generally accepted teaching, whether it be baptism, immortal soul or trinity.

Final Thoughts on Historical and Theological Roots:
1. The influence of the Wilsons was felt throughout the Church of God—that's why the General Conference was in Oregon, Illinois. [Editor's note: Wilson's niece, Leila Whitehead lived there.] W.H. Wilson pastored in Louisiana and wrote the *Pine Woods Bible Class*, a catechism that was used throughout the Church of God. Alfred Anthon of Louisiana also knew the Corbaleys (Indiana/Washington) and had some unusual understandings about a lot of things.
2. Different regions show different influences. Ohio is most affected by Marsh and the Christian Connexion. Texas and Arkansas probably reflect a Church of Christ heritage, especially in weekly communion. J.H. Anderson ties together South Carolina, Virginia, Ohio and Indiana. Preaching soul-sleep set him apart from other churches more than anything else.
3. In general, I'd say that soul-sleep is the most distinguishing teaching of the group that became the Church of God General Conference. That seems to be the focus of the first *Restitution Herald*. That seems to be the negative attached to our churches by those who disagreed—along with being the no-hell church. My own experience is that opposition to the Trinity definitely took a second place. In Ohio, our opposition was more along the Church of Christ line that the Trinity isn't in the Bible rather than a Unitarian outlook. Our churches were Christ-centered.
4. The greater focus on the nature of man makes sense in that the Christological disputes are basically technical while a resurrection hope rearranges the time line. Is it possible that a greater understanding of "spiritual development" could create just as great of a contrast between what used to be the conventional wisdom of Christianity and what is truly meant by the Kingdom of God and having the mind of Christ?
5. We have a tension in our group that goes all the way back to the differences between Joseph Marsh and Benjamin Wilson. In a nutshell, some people desire the truth because of what it will do. Others desire truth because you have to have truth. Those concerned about what it will do are usually more concerned about the *application* of truth. Those focused on having the truth are more interested in *accuracy*, and would say, "Without accuracy you don't have anything."

Further, those focused on application are accused of not really caring about truth, of thinking, "Nothing matters as long as you are sincere." Those focused on accuracy are accused of being intellectuals, and that one could believe all the right things and still not be a Christian.

The two sides view change differently. For those focused on application, change is important because they believe the truth will change you. For those focused on the truth, change is bad, except for returning to what has been changed. Change in the individual happens in order to line up with the truth, rather than because the truth is changing the person.

From my historical perspective, Joseph Marsh and the Christian Connexion pursued truth from a pragmatic desire to return to the vitality of the New Testament church. They had a strong emphasis on conversion and saw the Holy Spirit as active in that, more than simply understanding the Word. Dogmatism was viewed as a problem because it created division, and true Christianity was exemplified by unity. Barton Stone also had the emotional fervor, while Campbell thought the Christians were too experiential, but he still wanted the vitality.

Dr. John Thomas had a bent within that unity movement that moved from the pragmatic to the absolute—getting it right isn't just important, it is essential. The Wilsons came out of this movement with their "One True Faith" teaching.

Probably both dynamics were in effect when the General Conference was formed—the movement was declining, and organizing would help preserve it and make it more effective.

The General Conference would be categorized as a conservative movement, but there have always been those in it who are more focused on change. As I understand, F.L. Austin had a strong emphasis upon the spiritual life, as did his students, such as C.E. Lapp. Uncle Clarence always lifted up E. Richard Smith as an example to me, telling me how his ministry was revitalized after spending time at the Pacific Garden Mission in Chicago, and seeing the great need, and the way that the Gospel changed lives. I also see Harold Doan as one who looked for new things in order to make the conference better.

So, we still have the paradox that some of us tend to think change is good because that's the only way things can get better, while others think change is bad because that's how we got so messed up in the first place. Some fear change will lead to a compromise of truth while others fear we'll never be what God wants us to be because we're afraid to change.

There are more than a few ironies here. Our movement would not even exist unless we'd been willing to change from the accepted teaching. Another irony is that dissatisfaction with the current situation is almost essential as a catalyst for change, but I tend to hear more complaint from the people who say they don't like change. To put the shoe on the other foot, some advocating change can be pretty dogmatic about what has to happen, and what the results will look like.

I believe these divergent viewpoints can work together. We need each other. Under no circumstances should we ever compromise our values and conservatives help us remember our values. Things always have to change, and people comfortable with change are usually a lot better at leading it. But you don't want a person who likes being in crisis at the helm, either.

Adams, Almus A.
b. August 12, 1854
d. 1937

A. Evangelistic Reports
B. Debate
C. At Odds with Austin

Almus Adams was born in 1854 to James Crothers and Sarah Ann Piggot Adams in Monmouth, Illinois. He was the oldest of eight children. When Almus was eight months old, his parents moved to Hardin County, Iowa. He was educated there in the common school system. He went on to study more and became a self-made man.

Almus first heard the Gospel from a preacher named Cramer in Gifford, Iowa. Cramer was a "soul sleeper." This term refers to the doctrine of man's nature and states that man's body dies and sleeps in the grave until Christ returns, at which time, if he were a righteous man, he will be resurrected in the first resurrection.

The family of Cyrus Harlan became neighbors to Cramer in Gifford. They were of the same faith. These two families invited J.T. Prime of Nebraska to come to Iowa for a meeting. J.T. Prime was a preacher of the Kingdom of God and his preaching was in high demand. Almus Adam's father immediately accepted the Gospel message.

Another preacher by the name of G.M. Myers was invited to speak to the Gifford group. Myers was challenged to a debate by a Baptist named Barker. Myers accepted the invitation and sent for Mr. Houghawout, an orator and debater from Nebraska.

Minister Houghawout became a mentor to young Almus Adams. After Adams married Elizabeth Jane Wilson on July 27, 1879, he considered how he might best serve the Lord. Almus and Jane called C.C. Ramsay who lived then at Floyd, Iowa. Ramsay was of the faith, also, and had preached formerly in Pennsylvania and Ohio. Elder Ramsay baptized several from the Adams family in one day in 1878.

From that point on, Almus studied the Bible ardently. Their son, William, was born February 27, 1880. The next summer, Almus and Mrs. Adams started a Bible study in their home. Members wanted him to begin preaching. For his first public discourse he tackled a difficult subject, "The Rich Man and Lazarus."

Minister Adams became a great preacher in the Iowa and Nebraska conferences of the Church of God. In 1884 they moved to Nebraska where he homesteaded 160 acres and built a sod house for his family. They lived near Holbrook, Nebraska. Almus helped organize the Nebraska conference, and he was elected its first President in September 1886. The minutes of the Nebraska conference mention his name either as an officer or evangelist every year from the book's inception until its completion in 1911.

Rules Committee, first General Conference meeting, Philadelphia 1888. Almus Adams, second from right.

Adams' ministry was widespread across the nation. In 1888 he was a delegate to the national conference in Philadelphia. He was appointed to the Rules Committee along with J.S Hatch, J.F. Wagoner, A.J. Eychaner and George Elton. He gave the opening prayer at the first session on November 19, 1888. This conference group met again the following year in Chicago, and once again, Almus Adams attended as a delegate. He reported 49 baptisms the previous year. That particular general conference organization never met again. The next attempt to organize a national conference failed at Waterloo, Iowa, in 1910. Almus Adams was present at that meeting also. He believed that having a national conference organization would be beneficial to the local churches. It is interesting to note that Almus Adams, A.J. Eychaner and L.E. Conner were the only ministers in the early denominational work who attended all three organizational meetings: Philadelphia, 1888; Waterloo 1910; and Waterloo, 1921.

In the years after the 1889 conference, Adams preached at Attica, Kansas; Quinlan, Oklahoma; Boise, Idaho; and Omaha. He went everywhere teaching and baptizing.

In 1901, Almus moved his wife and nine children to Omaha by means of a covered wagon. Over winter they resided in the wagon, but in the spring they moved into a big house on Hartman Avenue that covered two city lots. He was advancing in age and Omaha offered a central location within easy reach of his evangelistic tours. He worked hard from one end of the state to the other ministering in homes, schoolhouses and at tent meetings. His salary for 1903 and 1904 was $50 per month or $400 per year. This increased to $75 per month in 1905, and $65 per month in 1906. While he is not listed as an evangelist in the minutes after 1906, evidence that he still served in that capacity comes from the steady stream of reports he sent to the journals.

In 1910 the presidents of the 14 state conferences signed a call for a meeting to consider organizing a national conference at Waterloo. The program for the conference focused on church discipline and the need for a statement of faith. The delegates agreed upon a statement of faith which Adams reported to the conference as follows.

We believe:
1. In one God who is the Maker of heaven and earth (Psa. 146:5) and all things therein (Gen. 1:1, Isa. 40:28 and several more scriptures).
2. That Christ has the right to the literal throne of David, and at his second coming will sit thereon to rule the world, and over the house of Jacob forever (Luke 1:30-33, Isa. 9:6, 7).
3. The literal return of the Jews to the land of Palestine (Jer. 31:Ezek. 36:9, 11, 22, 24, Acts 1:6-8).
4. That man is wholly mortal, and immortality is obtained only through Christ, and put on at the resurrection (Rom. 2:6-7, 8-11, I Cor. 15:53, 54, I Tim. 6:13-16).
5. In the literal resurrection of the dead to a life of everlasting happiness, with Christ upon his throne (Job 19:26, Psa. 17:15, Isa.26:19, Luke 14:14; John 5:28, 29; 11:23 and more).
6. The Church, the Bride of Christ, will rule the world jointly with him on David's throne (Eph. 3:5, Rom. 8:16, 17, Luke 1:31, 33).
7. The earth will be the final and eternal home of the saints (Psa. 37:9, 11, 29, 34; Prov. 2:21, Matt. 5:5).
8. In baptism by immersion for the remission of sins (Acts 2:38, Rom. 6:3, 4, Luke 24:46, Col. 2:12).
9. In the second personal appearing of Christ, at which time will be the restitution of all things. (Dan.7:13-22, Matt. 25:31, Acts 1:9, 11; I Thes. 1:10, and more).
10. The law was done away in Christ, and the law of faith established, in which we stand (Rom. 10:4, 8, 8:1, 4; 7:1-4, Gal. 3:11,12).
11. In the promises made of God unto the fathers Abraham, Isaac and Jacob, as to our future inheritance, and to David as to rule and kingdom. (Gal. 3:8, 16, 29; Acts 26:6, 7; Luke 1:30 and more).
12. In the restitution of all things spoken of by the mouth of all the holy prophets, which includes restoration of life, and the earth from under the curse (Acts 3:19, 21; John 6:35, Rom. 5:17, Rev. 22: 3).
13. And as a prerequisite to salvation, a holy and righteous life (Rom. 6:22, Gal. 5:22, 26; 2 Cor. 7:1).
14. The Bible to be the only rule for our faith and practice (John 3:39, Isa. 66:2).
15. The Bible to be the only true Word of God (Mark 15:20; Col. 1:25; Tit. 1:2, 3; John 17:6; 14:17).
16. In the final destruction of the incorrigible wicked (Mal. 4:13, Psa. 37:10-20, Rom. 6:23).

This list of doctrines became known as the "Articles of Faith" and was approved by the delegates. Each of the state conferences was to approve the Articles along with a statement on church discipline. When all states had ratified the document, it would become the standard by which doctrines could be delineated. To date, the only conferences known to have ratified it were Washington and Texas. Perhaps all of them did, but evidence has not been located. See the biographical entry on Emilus Wilson (Texas) for a complete list of the Texas Articles.

In the final report of the Working Rules of the 1910 Waterloo Conference is the following reminder to officers:

> ...to affirm by print and voice the following biblical truths as are in harmony with, viz.
> - that there is One God and Father of all who is above all, through all and in you all.
> - that Christ died for our sins according to the scriptures, and that he was buried, and that he rose again the third day according to the scriptures.
> - that all scripture is given by inspiration of God, and is profitable for doctrine, for reproof, for correction, for instruction in righteousness.
> - that the gift of God is eternal life through Jesus Christ our Lord.
> - that there shall be a resurrection of the dead.
> - that Christ was once offered to bear the sins of many...as our High Priest he now sits at the right hand of God...and unto them that look for him shall he appear the second time without sin unto salvation. And, that when he shall come in his glory, he shall sit upon the throne of his glory, and before him shall be gathered all nations.
> - that as many as have been baptized into Christ have put on Christ.
> - that all who are new creatures in Christ Jesus "should not henceforth live unto themselves, but unto him which died for them and rose again."

It should be noted that there is no mention here of Jesus as the Messiah, the Son of God, and no mention at all of the Holy Spirit in either one of these lists. In the first list, of the 16 points, fully nine items are prophecy oriented proving that the Church of God continued to highly value correct prophecy interpretation 59 years after Joseph Marsh wrote *Age to Come.*

In 1910, Almus was appointed state evangelist for the Nebraska Conference of the Church of God. In that capacity he visited the Illinois Conference meeting that year in Oregon, Illinois. He led a session at the Illinois Conference on the best means of raising funds for evangelism.

A. Evangelistic Reports

Almus Adams was nothing if not the best correspondent in the Church of God. He reported his circuit travels faithfully to *The Restitution,* the forerunner to *The Restitution Herald.*

Adams' reports to *The Restitution* and *The Restitution Herald* were detailed and bursting at the seams with names of people he visited, preached to and baptized. He was fond of saying in his reports that he "had met so and so, and, we can expect to see them come into the fold before long." He had an expectation of the Lord working in people's lives, and that he was but a conduit through whom the Lord worked to call them into the congregation. The tone of his reports was lively, humorous and sensitive.

One time he wrote, "I am in contact with our people from coast to coast and from Canada to the Gulf in one way or another." He had worked for the Lord for over 30 years and he could tell wonderful stories of God's blessing and protection. He wrote, "Many times it has looked dark and foreboding but in the nick of time help would come." God added the necessary things as He promised. Adams sometimes wrote about his son who was fighting for his life against tuberculosis

In a report from 1920, Adams wrote that the weather was so bad that only a few came to the meeting. One was a Presbyterian minister who was also the undertaker in that town. Astonishingly, when the group met again that afternoon in spite of the bad weather, the undertaker was there again. Elder Adams mused that he was unsure if the man came because he learned something new that satisfied him, or if he was there to find some customers.

Adams' reports also offered his analysis of the state of the Church of God. One time he wrote:

> I can well remember some years ago it was announced that members of orthodox churches had fallen away from their staid principles and were playing progressive euchre. The Church of God people threw up their hands in horror at such doings and recognized that [the word] "progressive" is only used to ease their consciences. In those days it seemed we would never be troubled by such worldly things so, little was said about it and before we were aware of it, these same things began to creep in, and now the problem is, how can we keep them out or eliminate what is already in the church? The church must be pure and clean. Are we passing or sojourning in indifference?

Almus Adams, guest speaker, middle row of adults, left side, among the women, Ohio State Conference (Springfield, circa 1910).

He was speaking of those things which impinged upon the culture in those days: easy travel in the newly invented auto, invention of electricity and the new-fangled air-cooled theaters, speak easies, moving picture shows, development of gambling in Nevada, free-flowing alcohol before and after prohibition, etc. These things and new attitudes about individualism, labor laws and leisure time competed for the attention of the well-intentioned but weak Christian.

Since he carried on his ministry over a span of several decades, and knew many people from their youth through their older years, Adams often saw trends that reflected dedication in some believers, and indifference brought on by isolation in believers who had at first been ardent.

He was greatly influential among the people of the Church of God. Many of the ministers in Iowa, Kansas, Nebraska and westward give credit to Almus Adams for teaching them the Bible. Almus' great-grandson, Warren Sorenson, wrote that Almus taught Grover Gordon the Scriptures, and influenced him to become a pastor on the Great Plains. He also taught and baptized Almus Dimmick (named after Adams), as well as his brother Clarence Dimmick and their wives Hattie and Edith. Almus also married both couples in a double wedding. Sixty years later, Warren Sorenson helped both couples celebrate their anniversaries at Tempe, Arizona, and took great pride in knowing the role his great-grandfather had in their lives. Warren testified that Almus baptized his grandparents on both sides of his family, and that he began churches in western Nebraska and eastern Colorado.

B. Debate

Almus engaged in a twelve-day debate with a member of the Reorganized Latter Day Saints in Laird County, Nebraska, on November 1, 1920. The two men began by exchanging the history of their respective denominations. The opponent told the audience about Joseph Smith. Almus Adams began by handing him a Bible. He said, "Here are the leaders of my church, Jesus and the Apostles." The opponent said the apostles are dead. Adams said, "Their words live on." And so it went, with the Latter Day Saint getting trounced on the subject of man's mortality. Still, Adams was impressed by the fact that Mormon young people took no part in worldly fad or fashion, whereas youth of nominal churches were swept away by worldliness.

He also debated a representative of the International Bible Students in Mitchell, South Dakota, in 1926. They discussed four topics: pre-existence of Christ (Adams opposed), that ancient fathers will not inherit the promises of Christ (Adams opposed), that Christ did not have the same body after the resurrection (Adams opposed) and that the devil is personal (Adams agreed). The reporter said that Adams made it so plain that the International Student contradicted himself several times.

C. At Odds with Austin

Beginning in 1924, Almus Adams directed his evangelism reports to *The Restitution Herald,* which by this time was under the editorial direction of Frederick L. Austin. F.L. Austin returned the report to him and asked that it be shortened. Adams cut the paper in half and returned it saying he did not have time to abbreviate it. This exchange polarized the two men.

In the next issue of *The Restitution Herald*, F.L. Austin made an announcement requesting that all reports from the field be brief, excluding all "temporal" information such as the color of the horse or whether an invitation came by phone or telegram.

In the fall of 1924, Adams came under criticism in the pages of *The Restitution Herald* again. On this occasion, Austin was not initiating criticism but reporting it. Accusations against Elder Adams had made their way to the committee of the General Conference Board that handled ministerial problems and licensure. If a minister's name came to this committee, it might not appear on the List the next year. Ministers on that list were recognized as being in good standing with the General Conference.

Austin reported the accusation against Adams without specifying the details, although it may have been over questions of financial mismanagement. Rumors also circulated that Adams had come to accept Universalism. See the L.E. Conner entry for more complete discussion. Friends and members of churches on the Great Plains took offense at Austin's language in *The Restitution Herald*. Letters of support for Almus Adams poured into *The Restitution*, which was in its last year of publication.

In one letter, L.J. Sweet wrote:

> I have heard so much evil (although unable to be proven) spoken of Bro. Almus Adams, I thought it was high time some good was said of him. I cannot see why the brethren continually focus their attention upon Bro. Adams. Can it be jealousy? Or envy? God forbid. Bro. Adams has forgiven the debt not entirely paid on his annual salary. I remember fifteen or twenty years ago they lacked $800 on an annual salary. He forgave it. He has been the state evangelist continually for forty years and has preached nearly the entire limits of the U.S. from four directions. He has baptized more believers in the U.S. than any other preacher in our faith. He is not perfect nor does he claim to be, but why he is the subject of persecution, is more than I can understand.

The Nebraska conference went on record that same month stating their support of Adams. They knew him. He had been in their homes and they had always found him clean in actions and speech. They called for a meeting with F.L. Austin, and believed that if he failed to arrange it, Almus Adams would be vindicated. It is not known how the matter was settled, as it was not mentioned again in the pages of *The Restitution Herald*. It is thought that Elder Adams was able to clear his name. He carried on ministry for several more years.

In 1929, Almus and Jane celebrated their 50th anniversary at the home of Emory Dixon on Bedford Avenue in Omaha. Robert Anderson, Almus' old friend from Lawn Hill, Iowa, was present to lead a Bible lesson. Guests enjoyed a wedding dinner and cake, after which the Adams received a gift from the group of $182 in gold. Nearly all present had been brought into the Church of God by the preaching of Almus Adams. Almus said he hoped all the guests would be present for the marriage feast of the Lamb. Almus was laid to rest in Mt. Hope Cemetery in Omaha, Nebraska.

See Austin, F.L. (20th)
Conner, L.E.
Gordon, Grover (20th)
Ramsay, C.C.
Prime, J.T.
Myers, G.M.
Wilson, E.M.
For a discussion on Universalism, see
King, Alta (20th)

Stewart, E.O. (20th)
Williams, J.W. (20th)

Bibliography: Ancestry.com. U.S. Census. Iowa. Hardin. Union. 1860; U.S. Census. Iowa. Hardin. Union. 1870; U.S. Census. Iowa. Van Buren. Harrisburg. Dist. 32, 1880; Bender, Edward. "History of Western Nebraska Conference Centennial of the Churches of God Faith of Abraham" from the scrapbook of Icel Steadman, presented to the 2d Annual History Conference at North Hills Church of God, Springfield, Ohio, Nov. 6,7, 2007; Graham, David. *Wisdom and Power* 6:8 November 1992; Magaw, Joyce. Interview regarding Cyrus Harlan, July 9, 2009; Randall, Clyde. Adams and 1910 Statement of Faith. *Historical Waymarks of the Church of God.* Church of God General Conference. Oregon, Il. 1976 21, 24, *Restitution* April 6, 1920; Nov. 1922; Oct. 1924; *Restitution Herald*. Feb. 12, 1924; Aug. 18, 1924; Aug. 25, 1924; Sept. 2, 1924; Sept. 14, 1926. Magaw, Ivan. Notes on Research in Archives, no date; Minute Ledger of the Church of God General Conference, Philadelphia, Pa. 1888 from the Archives of Atlanta Bible College, McDonough, Ga.; PostScript; Pastor Delbert Rankin reported that Almus Adam's son, Ray, accepted the teachings of the Church of God but was not immersed until he was well into his 90s. The service was conducted by both Pastors Kirby Davis and Bill Wachtel in the state of Oregon where Ray lived.

> *For other Statements of Faith see:*
> Huggins, Robert (20th); Magaw, Sydney (20th); Stephenson, J.M.; Wilson, Dr. Emilus; and Wince, John.

Adams, James C.
b. March 10, 1830
d. January 20, 1919

James Adams was the father of noted evangelist, Almus Adams. He was born in Mt. Vernon, Ohio, and died in Gifford, Iowa, where the family had made their home for many decades. He was baptized in 1880 by Elder C.C. Ramsey.

He married Sarah Piggot in Monmouth, Illinois, in 1853. They had four sons and four daughters. When one son moved as far away as Idaho, Almus Adams visited that area to minister to his family. Since there was already a core group living in the region it simplified beginning a ministry there. Pastor G.E. Marsh of Marshalltown, Iowa, officiated at James Adam's funeral service.

See Adams, Almus

Bibliography: Ancestry.com U.S. Census. Iowa. Hardin. Union. Dist. 127. 1880; "Obituary," *Restitution*, Feb. 1919.

Adams, Thomas E.
b. 1832
d. 1904

Thomas E. Adams was an elder at the Little Wild Cat Church in Indiana. He was a friend to J.T. Prime. He may have been born in Indiana and very likely came under

the influence of Ephraim Miller, S.A. Chaplin or Nathaniel Field. Adams and Prime went west and became active in preaching throughout Iowa, Kansas and Nebraska during the 1860s. T.E. Adams resided in Kansas with his wife Nancy and their seven children. He farmed to support his family. He was contemporary with W.P. Shockey, A.J. Eychaner and other pioneers in the work west of the Mississippi. His name appears frequently in the reports of W.P. Shockey to the *Gospel Banner* in Chicago.

According to the "Fragments of Church History" written by Emily Fyfe in *The Restitution Herald*, (date unknown), T.E. Adams lived and worked in the area of Gibbsville, Wisconsin, and was baptized along with James and Jane Fyfe. It is possible, since Newman's name is mentioned in Emily's article, that Thomas G. Newman baptized the Fyfes and the Adams.

It was Elder Adams who first called for the merger of the *Gospel Banner* of Geneva, Illinois, with *Herald of the Coming Kingdom* in Chicago by sending a letter to the *Herald*'s editor in January 1868. The editors of the *Herald* must have agreed with him for they hastened to publish his letter. From then on, the idea of a merger spread and gained a following. The Michigan, Iowa and Illinois Conferences endorsed the merger at their meeting of September 1868. By the end of 1869 the *Gospel Banner* closed its volumes. Later it was said in the *Herald* that "one goal of union was to gain strength." The editors thanked the readers for assisting them in the merger.

Thomas Adams' daughter Laura McAlister continued his legacy of dedicated service to the Lord at the Holbrook, Nebraska, Church of God.

See Chaplin, S.A.
Miller, Ephraim
Newman, Thomas G.
Shockey, W.P.
Wilson, Benjamin
Wilson, Thomas

Bibliography: Ancestry.com U.S. Census Fort Leavenworth, KS, 1880; Various reports by Shockey, *Gospel Banner and Millennial Advocate*, 1868 and 1869; Ferrell, Terry, A Brief History of the Church of God in America. National Berean Youth Conference, Camp Reynoldswood, Illinois Aug. 21-27, 1960; Ferrell, Terry. Interview with Jan Stilson regarding work in Nebraska, July 30, 2009; Fyfe, Emily "Gathering Fragments of Church History" *The Restitution Herald*. Date unknown.; Adams, Thomas E. "Letter to T. Wilson," *Herald of the Kingdom,* Jan 1, 1868; Thank you to Gospel Banner subscribers regarding merger. *Herald of the Coming Kingdom* Jan. 1, 1870; *Michigan State Conference Report 1858-1886*, owned by the Atlanta Bible College Archives, McDonough, Ga.

Adamson, Thomas
b. 1829
d. October 6, 1910

Thomas Adamson was born in Woodborough, Nottinghamshire, England, in 1829 and migrated to Canada in the mid-19th century. He arrived in Guelph, Ontario, with a wife and four children. He had 50¢ in his pocket. He rented a stone house and got a job. Fortunately, he was handy at many trades and found work as a carpenter, machinist, brick maker, cooper and inventor. He invented a washing machine and built a prototype. It is not known if the invention made it to the marketplace.

The Adamson family moved to Doon, Ontario, around 1860. This was a few years after the Bitter Disappointment, but Thomas may not have been tuned in to the Adventist discussion at that time. By this time, their family had grown to seven girls and two boys, John "Jack" and J. Edgar. The family attended the local Methodist church, but Mr. Adamson failed to find exactly what that church was teaching in the Bible. But he was a good member and assisted the congregation in constructing a new church building. It was about half finished when Dr. John Thomas, a Bible scholar, came through.

Dr. Thomas was cordial but could be quite outspoken. He preached directly from the Bible, and Thomas Adamson liked that. All the Methodists went to the meeting to hear the newcomer. By the time the construction was finished, the church was opened as the disciples of Dr. Thomas instead of the Wesleys! However, some of the Methodists held out and would not join the new church, so they were given their money back.

Soon thereafter, a businessman who knew that Mr. Adamson made good bricks persuaded him to move to Walkerton and start making bricks there. Thomas did that and opened a brick yard there around 1875. All the time, he talked to people about the Bible and the Kingdom of God on earth. He had a knack for talking to people about Jesus. Adamson became a very good preacher. A friend of his, Dr. Usher, also assisted with preaching. It was the Ushers who looked after the Adamson grandson, Ezra, who wrote the history of this family.

Ezra's sister, Rachel, became engaged to Donald McLeod, who moved west and became a cowboy in Wyoming. Eventually, the McLeods arrived in Pomona, and the rest is history as they say. Thomas Adamson did not want his daughter Rachel living in isolation in California, so he moved his family west also. By this time, Dr. John Thomas had named his church the Christadelphians, and when the Adamsons arrived in Pomona, they discovered other Christadelphians already there. The newcomers and the existing group members met together to worship, but they had squabbles every meeting over doctrine. The Christadelphians said that Christ had sin within his nature, and his death covered his sin, whereas the newcomers said Christ was sinless and his death covered our sins. Eventually, Adamson and the others moved on. This congregation also believed it was appropriate to seek citizenship, and the record shows that several of them became American citizens around 1900.

In 1902 Thomas Adamson and other members rented a hall for 75¢ a week and purchased an organ for $20. The hall was drab, so when times were better, they rented another place at 2nd and Main Streets for $2.25 per week. After another move, the congregation purchased a lot at 628 Williams Street for $600 and built the first phase of the church called Williams Street Chapel.

Thomas returned to Walkerton, Ontario, and took a second wife. They had two sons both of whom died young. The church work in California carried on through his family.

In 1930, Norman McLeod began to preach at Williams Street Chapel. Also, O.J. Allard came to California with his tent ministry. Allard had meetings in Pomona, Santa Ana, Long Beach and Los Angeles. The congregation found that his message was very much in line with their own biblical understandings. Because of the similarity, they began to use the teaching materials published by the General Conference. In 1938 the congregation incorporated under the name Church of the Open Bible of Pomona. By this time, they were affiliated with the Church of God General Conference.

Thomas Adamson died in his beloved Ontario, but his legacy lived on through the ministries of grandsons and nephews including Pastors Terry Ferrell, Norman and Malcolm McLeod, Dean Moore and church member Pastor Cecil Smead who was in the sixth Bible Training Class at Oregon, Illinois, in 1923.

See Adamson, John "Jack" E. (20th)
    Allard, O.J.
    Dick, William (20th)
    McLeod, Norman
    Smead, Cecil (20th)

Bibliography: Ancestry.com. U.S Census. California. Yolo. Davisville. Dist. 159. 1880; Ancestry.com Selected U. S. Naturalization Records for Thomas Adamson.1790-1974, California Dist. Court. Los Angeles; Ancestry.com. California incorporation document of Church of the Open Bible by Thomas Adamson; Adamson, Ezra, Grandson of Thomas Adamson, a transcribed history from oral comments regarding the formation of the Church of the Open Bible, Pomona, California, as related to Delbert Jones, date unknown. Note: Nearly all the information in this entry came from the Ezra Adamson document. Retired Pastor Terry Ferrell, a great-great nephew to Thomas Adamson remembered that Ezra Adamson was a beekeeper with hundreds of bee hives. He would move them around by truck to various meadows so the bees could benefit from clover, alfalfa, etc. The area farmers "hired" his bees to fertilize their crops; Ferrell, Terry. Interview, June 30, 2010; Hannam, Vicki; Genealogist of Thomas Adamson, via e-mail July 2, 2010.

Addington, Andrew Jackson
b. December 29, 1859
d. November 25, 1919

Andrew Jackson Addington was born in Virginia and married Miss Alpha Owsley on August 11, 1880. Six children were born to the couple: two sons and four daughters.

A.J. Addington obeyed the gospel in 1884 and began to preach the good news of the Gospel of the Kingdom. He preached faithfully for 25 years preceding his death. His ministry area included Texas and Oklahoma. He was popular as a person, but did not enjoy large audiences as people did not like his unique doctrines.

A.S. Bradley said:
Brother Addington was a fine reasoner on the truths of the Bible, and would have been a great preacher if the brethren would have supported him as they should, but as Revelation 14:13 says, 'Blessed are the dead which die in the Lord from henceforth; yea saith the Spirit, that they rest from their labors; and their works do follow them.'

And Bradley said in the Addington obituary:
Truly one of God's noblemen has fallen, but he will rise again at the last day. Jesus has said the gates of hades (the grave) shall not prevail against his church. Brother Addington being a member of that body will burst the grave and come forth to life eternal.

A.S. Bradley conducted the funeral of his friend, and A.J. Addington was laid to rest at the Old Phantom Cemetery in Jones County, Texas.

See Bradley, A.S.
Bibliography: Bradley, A.S., Obituary of Andrew Jackson Addington from the files of the Archives at Atlanta Bible College.

Allard, Alice Thomas
b. April 11, 1841
d. December 17, 1923

Alice Thomas was born in Canada. At age 14, her family moved to Rockford, Illinois. She accepted the gospel message and was baptized by evangelist Thomas Collins. At this writing no information about Elder Collins has been uncovered.

Alice married Isaac Allard in Rockford in 1862. They lived there for ten years before moving to Eagle Point, Iowa. They were the parents of one daughter, Ethelyn, born in 1867. Evidently Alice suffered greatly during the birth as she was incapacitated afterward. Alice was an invalid for many years and bore her suffering patiently.

In time, Alice and Ethelyn went to live with their cousins, the Ourania J. Allard family, whose mother had passed away by that time.

Alice Thomas Allard remained a member of the Church of God until her death. Pastor A.J. Eychaner preached her funeral service and reaffirmed her hope of salvation.

Bibliography: Ancestry.com U.S. Census. Iowa. Pottawatomie. Council Bluffs. 1900; *The Restitution Herald,* Feb. 19, 1924.

Allard, Greenleaf P.
b. August 30, 1883
d. 1927

Greenleaf Pickering Allard was the eldest son of Ourania J. and Belle Allard. He was named after his grandfather Greenleaf Allard. Young Greenleaf grew up in a household without a mother. He was cared for by his elderly cousins, Alice and Ethelyn. In 1910, he and his father were lodgers in the home of Missouri Lathrop in Webster County at Fort Dodge, Iowa.

Greenleaf married Edna Schmidt and became an assistant cashier at the local bank. They never had children. He and Edna were active in church, and they were both noted widely for being good musicians.

The Allards were talented in singing and in leading worship services. They were so well known that they were invited to assist with music at the Southern California conference meeting in 1920. They traveled by train to Pomona and joined James A. Patrick and Joseph W. Williams as speakers for that conference week. These meetings were annual events and that year the meeting was held at the Williams Street Chapel in Pomona, California.

Greenleaf and his father, O.J. Allard, helped to reorganize the Iowa conference in 1888. Greenleaf served as treasurer of the organization for 20 years. He served as treasurer of the newly-organized 1888 General Conference, and he served as circulation manager and later as business manager for *The Day Dawn and Harvest Messenger* during the years it was published from Fort Dodge, Iowa, by James A. Patrick.

Evidence that the newly invented automobile was not always a useful convenience is seen in one story about Greenleaf and his wife traveling to a conference. After embarking on their journey, they suffered two tire blowouts. By the time they arranged for repairs, the conference was over.

Greenleaf died at a young age safe in his knowledge of his resurrection at Christ's return. Following his death, his father, O.J. Allard, and Edna shared a house. At that time Ourania was quite elderly. Greenleaf rests in Oakland Cemetery in Fort Dodge, Iowa.

Arlen Rankin contributed to this entry.

See Allard, O.J.
Patrick, James A.

Bibliography: Ancestry.com U.S. Census. Iowa. Kane. Pottawatomie. 1900. Also. Iowa. Webster. Fort Dodge. 1930; Webster County Grave Record, Ia.; Burnett, Francis et al history committee. *The History of the Iowa Church of God and Conference 1855-1987*, printed at Belle Plaine Union, 1987. Masthead, *The Day Dawn and Harvest Messenger,* June/July 1918; *Restitution*, June 24, 1908; July 13, 1920; *The Restitution Herald* June 8, 1920.

Allard, Orion (or Ourania) John "O.J."

b. December 17, 1860
d. January 16, 1943

A. **The Waterloo Conference of 1910**
B. **Aftermath of a Painful Conference**
   1. **Doctrine**
   2. **The Imperial Ministerial Association**
C. **Camp Director**

O.J. Allard was born in Canada to Greenleaf and Emily (Berry) Allard. He had two half-brothers and four half-sisters. The family moved to Iowa in 1865 and resided in Spring Creek Township, Tama County, at Tama, Iowa. He married Emily about 1880. A son and a daughter blessed this family. O.J. served as Iowa evangelist from 1908 until 1919. He also served as pastor at Koszta along with A.J. Eychaner until 1916. O.J. preached 172 sermons during 1919, a notable accomplishment.

He worked well with the other ministers in Iowa. In 1908, he and G.E. Marsh coordinated a summer of evangelism. G.E. Marsh preceded O.J. Allard by a day to distribute handbills from door to door. This practice was called "billing a town." This method was usually effective for inviting people to a camp meeting. By the time the tent arrived, a crowd was ready to help assemble it and to attend the meetings.

On one occasion at Humboldt, only one isolated member, Bro. Mowlin, and his daughter attended the preaching. The janitor of the hall said people would not come unless you promised them a show. Humboldt was the home of Frank Gotch, a famous wrestler of the day. People of Humboldt wanted a good show. After two nights in a town where people seemed more interested in a good show than the Word of God, G.E. Marsh and O.J. Allard packed their bags and left.

Allard (left) and SJ Lindsay

O.J. often visited and preached up and down the west coast of the United States. He and his wife stayed with his uncle John Allard who lived in Zelzah, California. During one visit, he attended church at the First Day Advent Church where the message was "the same line of thought we can remember hearing as a boy forty-two years ago, and felt to thank God for the light we had received during the past forty years." Since that time he had learned the new message of the Age to Come/One Faith system of prophecy.

As he traveled the coast, O.J. preached in Santa Ana, South Pasadena at Mineral Park, and as far north as Corvallis, Oregon. On one such trip he took a train north from Los Angeles. At each stop he gave a lush description of the beauty of the area and the hazards to the readers of *The Restitution*. He included anecdotes about isolated members with whom he conversed, and general remarks about the lessons he taught or the sermons he preached. On his return trip from Corvallis to Los Angeles, he paid a call on Thomas Wilson, editor of *The Last Days,* and nephew of Benjamin Wilson.

By including this information in his reports to the readers, he offered hope for the future and a rich travelogue to poor and elderly church members who could not travel America. In a report to *The Restitution* he described the challenge of traveling over mountains:

> When one sees three of the large Mogul engines of the Southern Pacific attached to a train of twelve cars taxed to their utmost capacity to pull the train over the mountains it gives some idea as to the steepness of the grade. We traveled about thirty-five miles to get nineteen miles straight across country, and in about twenty miles of the distance we had to take an elevation of two thousand feet. It was the grandest scenery and most enjoyable ride of all my trip since we left Iowa.

After Emily's death, O.J. married his second cousin, Belle Allard. She died in 1900. After her death, he took lodgings with an Iowa banker, Missouri A. Lathrop. In 1928, O.J. married Kate Robinson while he was living in California. She died in 1929. He evidently did not own any land or property for it is recorded in various census data that he resided with various families during the next several years. In 1937 he married Mrs. Mildred Lansing in Cedar Falls, Iowa. She survived him. O.J. Allard rests in the Gladbrook Cemetery in Iowa.

A. The Waterloo Conference of 1910

O.J. was one of the leaders in the Church of God who called for a national organization of a general conference. He endorsed a notice calling delegates to a special summer conference to be held in Waterloo, Iowa. This conference proved to be a watershed in the development of the Church of God as a national movement. It delineated the doctrines that were common among the people, i.e. conditional immortality; oneness of God; Jesus, the Son of God who died, rose and is coming again to establish the Kingdom of God in the age to come; general resurrection of the just and the unjust and the restoration of Israel. Certain doctrines that were deemed unscriptural included teachings such as mortal emergence from the grave and limited resurrection of only the just.

Ministers at the 1910 Waterloo Conference elected OJ Allard, middle back, to follow up by writing a statement of faith. Photo depicts a typical 19th century camp setting.

Other doctrines which were excluded were larger hope, second chance, universal reconciliation, Sabbath keeping, Josephism and Anglo-Israelism. Individuals within the movement *still* privately held to some of these unusual doctrines, but the conference movement rejected them as part of a *commonly believed statement of faith*. The General Conference was not born in 1910, but the discussion served to solidify the body of believers. Within the next ten years the group advanced to form a business organization that would guide state conferences and churches into a denominational effort.

B. Aftermath of a Painful Conference

Nothing is born without pain, and the 1910 Waterloo Conference was the beginning of a period of serious and difficult labor. O.J. Allard took a moderate position in this discussion. When politics reared its ugly head and excluded L.E. Conner, pastor of one of the Cleveland churches, from a vote, O.J. Allard appealed that "every member of the Church here be allowed to vote," believing that a great mistake would be made in limiting voting to delegates. This appeal failed. In spite of Allard's compassionate plea, G.E. Marsh made a motion that no individual church could have a vote. This motion carried. Still not done with the issue of Conner, A.J. Eychaner made a specific motion that L.E. Conner be declared a delegate of the conference with full powers. This motion carried, but the struggle to be seated angered Conner.

After that event Allard committed himself to fulfilling the conference resolution which fell to him as secretary. He was to determine the will of the people concerning commitment to a statement of faith that would be identified solely as belonging to the Church of God Abrahamic Faith. He placed a notice in several issues of *The Restitution* during 1910-1911. He wrote, "I have sent 'Declarations of the Principles of Faith' to each of the delegates, presented to them for action. Do you want to bind the Church to a creed? Or merely [as a tract to] hand to inquirers for enlightenment?"

From this survey, he wrote the "Articles of Faith and Church Discipline." A full rendering of the Articles is given in the biographical entry for E.M. Wilson, for it was he who instructed the people of Texas on this matter and solicited ratification for the Articles. All 14 state conferences were supposed to ratify the document; Texas and Washington succeeded in doing that. There is no evidence that any of the remaining 12 endorsed it, but if they all had, it is thought the General Conference would have become an entity in 1911, but it did not.

1. Doctrine

In doctrinal issues, O.J. stood with believers of the general resurrection. He asked R.G. Huggins, Almus Adams and D.C. Robison in an open letter in *The Restitution* to explain Acts 26:8 "Why is it thought incredible by any of you that God raises the dead?" (RSV) He asked, "Who was Paul talking about? The righteous dead? The unrighteous dead? Or all the dead?"

On other matters of doctrine, he wrote to R.G. Huggins, editor of *The Restitution*, seeking guidance for inquiries about Sabbath-keeping and the Sonship of Christ (Josephism). Huggins gave him a concise exposition from Scripture about weeding out false prophets and heresies. He said it was a vital matter, and "damnable heresies" are false doctrines that will damn. He said Josephism and Sabbatarianism were heresies. He said if men who preached these doctrines were invited to preach at the Iowa conference meeting, then Bro. Allard would not be practicing Titus 3:9 which says to *avoid* them.

2. The Imperial Ministerial Association

The flap between the "Ministerial Five" and A.R. Underwood affected Underwood's publication, *The Restitution*. Allard wrote those actions to be "one of the most preposterous things ever undertaken by any of our brethren." Allard said, "I was born and brought up in the faith of the Gospel, and in my experience, I want to say, that within my province, I have never witnessed the like." He said they were wrong to try to force Underwood to give up his business, and to position themselves as the "voice of the Church of God." He said if they wanted to start another paper, that was within their right, but to place demands upon Underwood was wrong.

C. Camp Director

O.J. Allard was also a leader in maintaining the smooth operation of the Waterloo conferences, which could be best described as a tent camp. Each family was assigned a tent in which to sleep and wash up. They brought their own wash basins and bedding, as there were no public hotels or bathrooms. A community outhouse, located beyond the kitchen, was difficult to reach especially at night.

Each day began with the peal of a big bell. This particular bell had been imported from Belfast, Ireland, in 1874 for use in the Irving church when it was built near Belle Plaine. In 1914, the bell was moved to Colo, Iowa, and, each year thereafter, it was taken to camp. Presently, this bell is located in the Waterloo church building.

The entire campground area, consisting of about two square city blocks, was enclosed by a metal fence. The gate was locked at 10 p.m. each evening. It was approximately five feet high and had sharp points on top. Certain young men decided to test the fence's efficacy one night when they returned to camp after curfew. O.J. Allard patiently waited for them at the gate. He seemed to have anticipated their plan. Anecdotal remarks describe him as a rather large man with a big booming voice, and it seemed the boys preferred not to tangle with him but they did respect him. The next day they scrubbed the kitchen.

Arlen Rankin contributed to this entry.

See Conner, L.E.
Wilson, Benjamin
Wilson, Dr. E.M. - Articles of Faith
Wilson, Thomas

Bibliography: Ancestry.com U.S. Census. Iowa. Wayne. Grand River. Dist. 242 1880 and Iowa. Webster. Fort Dodge. Dist. 41. 1930. In one Census his birth date is given as September 1859; Burnett, Francis et al history committee, *History of the Iowa Church of God and Conference 1855-1987*, printed by Belle Plaine Union, 1987; Graham. David, "Church of God Connexion & Review". *Wisdom and Power*. 6:8 Nov. 1992; Rankin, Arlen F. citing *Iowa History of Church of God*, 49,50; *Restitution*, Feb. 10, 1904; June 24, 1908; Aug. 17, 1910; Sept. 14, 1910; Jan. 1, 1911; Jan. 25, 1911; Feb. 15, 1911; April 15, 1913; May 6, 1913, May 13, 1913; "Linking the past with the present." *Searchlight*. Iowa Berean Society. Feb. 1992; Macy, Emory. "Church History of the Texas Church of God," March 1954; Walker, Betty. Niece of O.J. Allard, interview, May 17, 2011.

Allen, Mark
b. 1814
d. 1889

A. Allen's Western Tour
B. Who are the Brethren?
   1. Marshism
   2. Church of the Blessed Hope

Mark Allen's name appears early in the volumes of the *Voice of Truth*, edited by Joseph Marsh. In the October 10, 1844, issue he revealed that he believed in the Second Coming of Christ and had been out preaching and distributing the literature of George Storrs and the *Voice of Truth*. Allen said he believed he was on his last mission, and that in three week's time, he would be meeting his Lord. But, as history shows, the Lord did not return on the expected date.

Allen was a writer and resided in Woburn, Massachusetts. In 1868, he owned and operated a variety store in that city and boarded in a private home. The store was downtown opposite the Methodist Church.

By 1871 he had become the publisher of the *Woburn Advertiser* and operated this business from the site of his former store. He lived at various times on Broad Street, Spring Street and Green Street. His printing business also produced the *Woburn City Directory* from which much of this personal information was gathered. Through the years as his address changed it reflected upward mobility in his status and prosperity. When he moved to Allen Street in Allenville, his entry in the city directory sported a large print in bold type. Little is known of his family.

Allen taught Millerite principles of Adventism in the Toronto area in 1844, during the date-setting fervor of the Millerite movement. He later joined forces with Joseph Marsh.

Allen was a prolific writer, contributing to Joseph Marsh's *Advent Harbinger and Bible Advocate*, and later to Benjamin Wilson's *Gospel Banner and Millennial Advocate*. He believed strongly in the Gospel of the Kingdom of God. He said the Gospel message was the "glad tidings of something. Of what? Jesus came

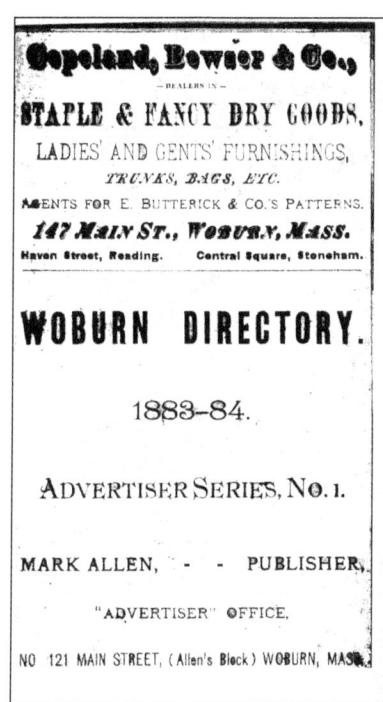

Cover and page from Allen's Woburn Directory.

preaching the Kingdom of God. The good news was about the Kingdom of God."

In defining the church he said:

> We learn from the Scriptures that the Body of Christ is not an aggregation of religious sects, the end and aim of which is the promulgation of certain notions, opinions, thinking of the flesh in regard to religion-getting and saving of immortal souls from hell torments, but a collection of intelligently instructed men and women gathered from among Jews and Gentiles into one body, outcasts from the World, but in the age to come, destined to share with Jesus, our Messiah, the glories of the Kingdom.

A. Allen's Western Tour

When Allen was well into his fifties he made an extensive western tour. He reported his activities later in the *Gospel Banner*. He left his home at Woburn, Massachusetts, and traveled by train to Boston via the Worcester & Boston rail line on the February 16, 1861. He visited an Adventist church in Worcester and stayed with the Gerald family who were staunch defenders of the One Faith. There were nine members at Worcester. He said the numbers in New England had not increased dramatically because "we have not forced the hydraulic pressure system, but have endeavored to intelligently and understandingly instruct men and women for the kingdom before putting them under water, in order that they may understand the relations they are about to assume." He believed in instructing them before immersing them in baptism.

Continuing on to Springfield, he became involved in rousting out the hypocrisy of one Elder George J. Adams, a former Mormon leader, who apparently changed church denominations depending on which part of the country he was in. It was said this notorious liar had been preaching in theaters. In Springfield he had passed himself off as an Age-to-Come preacher, and succeeded in dividing that church. Allen unmasked the scoundrel so that his credentials no longer held up, at least in that place.

Evangelist Allen then preached in the home of Alexander Fisher at Holyoke. He preached the Gospel of the Kingdom there before leaving for Albany, New York. Albany proved to be unreceptive to the ideas of Age to Come, but he preached a few sermons there anyway.

He continued on to Rochester where he stayed with Bro. John Brown. Rochester was the preaching and publishing center of the work managed by Joseph Marsh. Allen said the number at Rochester was small and had come to the truth through the tribulation of "Millerism," "Marshism," "Cookism" and "Storrism" but it had taught them to endure as good soldiers. At Rochester the church met in a brick building on the corner of Stillson and New Main streets. As part of their worship, the choir routinely led the congregation in chanting the Psalms under the direction of Bro. Morse. Mark Allen was very impressed with this recitation.

Having received a letter at Rochester from Dayton, Ohio, Allen traveled south and spent the night at Cleveland, an area he had not previously visited. He stayed at the New England Hotel. When he arrived in Dayton, he was met by George Netts and William Fish. Netts and Fish were from the Springfield, Ohio, Age-to-Come congregation, a short distance from Dayton.

While Allen was in Dayton, rebels fired upon Ft. Sumter on April 10, 1861. He wrote:

> Those wicked men placed themselves in opposition to the Powers that God has ordained, and those whose end is eventually judgment.

The weather was mild and sunny in the south but Allen could not stay to enjoy it. He returned to Cleveland where he was waylaid by a snow storm. He spent the night at a hotel and looked up Bro. Robert McLauchlan who was of the One Faith. He found "him to be an uncompromising believer of the Gospel, and with the wife, I think the only representatives of the Abrahamic faith in Cleveland." This *Gospel Banner* passage appears to be the first use of the phrase "Abrahamic Faith" in print.

At Cleveland, McLauchlan told him of another shady character, John Williams, passing himself off as an Age-to-Come preacher. Williams abandoned Cleveland and returned to Canada after Allen's visit.

While in Cleveland, Mark Allen looked up an old friend who had been a Millerite from a Methodist background.

He was sad to find the man had not made any progress in his faith but was still wandering. Allen's description of the confusion that existed among disillusioned Millerites after the Bitter Disappointment is poignant:

> Some have become Mormons, some Shakers, some Infidels, some have returned back to the old Babylonian folds, and some still wander about blindly in the mazes of Adventism, but a few have had the scales torn from their eyes, and their understandings have been enlightened by the "Word of the Kingdom."

After leaving Cleveland, he proceeded to Toronto where he stayed nearly a week. Here, Allen found that John Williams had lured some brethren away from the faith, but he felt his own preaching had reclaimed those errant brethren. When he left Toronto he expressed regret at leaving old friends behind, but he proceeded home through Rochester after being absent for 11 weeks.

A note in the *Millennial Harbinger and Bible Expositor* said that he also planned a western trip during the summer of 1863. It is not known if he succeeded in making that trip which would have included the states of Iowa, Illinois, Indiana, Ohio, concluding in Pennsylvania and New York.

B. Who are the Brethren?

In another article, Mark Allen responded to the writing of Levi H. Chase of Adrian, Michigan, in which Chase defined brethren as only those who believe in the One Faith, i.e. that faith looking back to the covenant made with Abraham because of the faith which Abraham exhibited. Chase excluded everyone who did not follow a narrow set of Bible doctrines, and he excluded Joseph Marsh because Marsh refused to be rebaptized after he left the Millerite movement. Most of the Age-to-Come leaders had been re-baptized. Dr. John Thomas advocated re-baptism, and Benjamin Wilson recommended it. Wilson was re-baptized in Geneva in 1851.

Chase recommended shunning a person of another denomination by addressing him with a simple, "Greetings, Mr. Marsh," rather than the preferred "Brother." Yet when Chase wrote a letter to Joseph Marsh, he addressed it, "Dear Bro. Marsh." Marsh published this letter in the *Advocate and Expositor,* clearly exposing the inconsistency of L.H. Chase.

In May 1859, Mark Allen responded in the pages of the *Gospel Banner* by saying it would have been better if Bro. Chase had not tried to define "Who is a Brother?" He felt Chase did not make his case but muddied it.

Alfred Malone, a *Gospel Banner* reader from Palestine, Illinois, wrote to call for caution against falling back into Babylon by becoming "heretic detectors," i.e. labeling everyone as heretic who was not of the persuasion of Age to Come or One Faith. He said, "Brethren, let us have charity and forbearance towards others." Malone also stated, "I will not oppose any brother nor think the less of him, nor call him ugly names, because of minor differences upon points not so well understood, provided he oppose not his philosophy or science to the plain declarations of God's word, upon the points at issue, and thereby attempt a schism in the house of God." He concluded with a blessing, "May the grace of Jesus, the love of God, and the communion of the Holy Spirit be with all the holy brothers." Malone was a man of mercy. Later Malone authored a book entitled *Age to Come* which is in the Archives of Atlanta Bible College.

1. Marshism

In a later article, Allen discussed the conversion of Cornelius in Acts 10, and noted that:

> The first fruits of the Gentiles had to hear and believe something more than the *three-fact* [Allen italics] gospel of Campbellism (Alexander Campbell), or the *one-fact* [Allen italics] gospel of the resurrection of the *Expositor* (Joseph Marsh) before they were qualified for immersion into the one Body of Christ. Their salvation depended on something more than their sincerity and piety, as manifested in prayer and good works. It was necessary for them to hear and be instructed in certain doctrines of the Kingdom of the Heavens. By what provision in the scriptures are modern Gentiles exempt?

Therein is the chief complaint, so succinctly stated by Allen, which he and Benjamin Wilson had against the teaching ministry of Joseph Marsh. They felt the Age-to-Come emphasis of Marsh was a "one-fact Gospel." It emphasized the nature of the future resurrection to the exclusion of teaching other major Gospel tenets such as the death and resurrection of Jesus, the name of Jesus, the judging office Jesus will perform, the remission of sins and more. While Marsh may have preached and published all of the above, they felt he pushed his hobby, the Age to Come. This was "Marshism."

Marsh had his ministry. Benjamin Wilson had his. To read more concerning the difference between these two branches of Church of God history stemming from Marsh and from Wilson refer to the *See* references at the end of this entry.

Mark Allen judged men by what they preached and he spoke plainly. He called Edwin Burnham, another Age-to-Come preacher, a "religious circus rider." While it might seem harsh to be judging men in such a way in light of Matthew 7, it is important to remember "by their fruit ye shall know them."

2. Church of the Blessed Hope

David Graham reported that Mark Allen began the Church of the Blessed Hope in 1863, the same year that Ellen G. White began the Seventh-day Adventists and Dr. John Thomas organized and registered the Christadelphians (also known as Nazarines) as a pacifistic denomination. Allen ceased publishing *The Messenger* by 1875 and people heard little from him after that.

While Allen's work did not continue long, it is interesting to note that in 1888 when the Church of God organized a national general conference in Philadelphia, delegates were instructed that their churches could organize under the names of either Church of God in Christ Jesus or Church of the Blessed Hope.

Mark Allen lived to be 75 years old, a distinctive accomplishment in that period.

See Burnham, Edwin
Chase, L.H.
Malone, Alfred
Marsh, Joseph
McLauchlan, Robert
Wilson, Benjamin

Bibliography: Allen, Mark. "A Letter from M. Allen" *Voice of Truth*, Jos. Marsh, ed. Rochester, NY. Oct.10, 1844; Allen, Mark. "What is a Church" *Gospel Banner and Millennial Advocate*, Nov. 1859; Allen, Mark. "Who are the Brethren?" *Gospel Banner*, B. Wilson, ed. Geneva, Il. Sept. 1860; Allen, Mark. "Report of Western Tour," *Gospel Banner and Millennial Advocate*, July 1861 182-185; and August, 1861 212-215; Report. *Millennial Harbinger and Bible Expositor*, June 3, 1863; Allen, Mark. Untitled article signed by Mark Allen. *Gospel Banner and Millennial Advocate*. July, 1859 81-82; Allen, Mark. "Who are the Brethren?" *Gospel Banner and Millennial Advocate*, Sept. 1860 119; Probate records of Mark Allen, Woburn, Mass., retrieved from yeoldwoburn.net, Dec. 2007; Black, Sylvia, E-mail to JStilson regarding correct name of George Netts as the contact person for Allen in Dayton, Jan. 8, 2011; Bond, Newell. Inquiry regarding several old preachers including Allen, *The Restitution*, H.V. Reed, editor, Plymouth, Ind.. Jan. 20, 1875; Graham, David. "The Northwest Christian Association." *Church of God History Newsletter*. JStilson, ed. Wntr 1985; Malone, Alfred. "Letter to Editor". *Gospel Banner and Millennial Advocate*. Jan. 1, 1868; *Voice of Truth*. Oct. 10, 1844; *Woburn City Directory*, Woburn, Mass. 1868-1887, published by Mark Allen.

Alexander, George M.
b. August 20, 1854
d. June 15, 1920

G.M. Alexander was born to Thomas and Rachel Alexander on a farm near Bremen, Indiana. He attended public schools and worked on the family farm. He accepted the Lord and joined the Church of God. He loved the doctrines. In 1887 he married Susie E. Cross. They had one son, George D. Alexander. George moved to Chicago and worked for General Electric in the Monandack building, a good job to have in that day and age. He took ill in Chicago and died at age 66.

G.M. was a friend of John and Roxanna Wince. Through the pages of *The Restitution* G.M. commonly reminded readers to send cards to Auntie Wince on her birthday. Elder Richard C. Railsback of South Bend, Indiana, conducted G.M.'s funeral service in Bremen at the home of Bro. Alexander's brother.

Bibliography: *The Restitution Herald* June 22, 1920; Feb. 8, 1921.

Anderson, Enoch M.
b. July 26, 1842
d. July 9, 1908

A. Baptist Years
B. Preaching for the Church of God

Elder Enoch Anderson was from a prominent family in Henderson County, North Carolina. He was married to Jane and they had four children, two sons, Joshua and John, and two daughters, Adeline and Cordelia. Enoch and John became preachers for the Church of God in the 19th and 20th centuries. Enoch began his ministry near Gallimore Gap, North Carolina. In 1880, he preached in an old church house. The structure was remodeled in 1920 for the brethren to use as a worship center under J.H. Anderson's leadership.

A. Baptist Years

In Enoch's early years, he was a Baptist preacher. He traveled a circuit of four Baptist churches. He learned about the Gospel of the Kingdom from Newell Bond of Cleveland who settled briefly in North Carolina at the end of the Civil War. Enoch Anderson was attracted to the soul sleeping doctrine, but did not yet believe it. He arranged a debate, probably with Newell Bond or perhaps Robert Gresham also an Age-to-Come evangelist in North Carolina. During the debate, the light of the truth apparently moved in Enoch. He accepted it and began preaching it almost immediately.

His Baptist brothers wanted him to renounce his new faith and stay with them, but he said, "No, I must preach the truth." He held services just across the road from the Baptist church from week to week, until he had converted enough Baptist members to control the church building, and then he held services there. He converted nearly every member of that Baptist congregation.

When he left the Baptists, there was a shadow upon his reputation resulting from questionable conduct. Research by Pastor Wally Winner has shown that Elder Enoch Anderson evidently was fond of the ladies and had asked two women to marry him. This information was not well-received by the church elders when they learned of it, nor with the still-very-much-alive Mrs. Anderson. The record shows she requested a letter of dismissal from the congregation, an act which usually meant that she was a member in good standing and wished to place her membership elsewhere. This request was granted.

A month or so later, Enoch Anderson requested a similar letter, which was denied him. After lengthy discussion about this with the elders, Enoch admitted his wandering ways, repented, and was granted his letter of dismissal. It is thought that when Enoch Anderson switched denominations he also improved his conduct.

B. Preaching for the Church of God

God blessed his labors and, evidently, his repentance as well. After he began several Bible studies in North Carolina, Enoch Anderson moved to Pelzer, South Carolina, in 1895. He arranged to preach the Gospel at a local school house with the help of two Advent preachers. Anderson was permitted to use the school just two Sundays and then he had to find other quarters. From Pelzer, he went to Guthrie Grove and organized the Church of God there. He was their pastor until his death.

In a report to *The Restitution* in August 1906, Anderson detailed the greatest meeting they had to date at the Guthrie Grove Church of God. He said, while some pastors did not come who were expected, P.A. Guthrie led the finest singing he had ever heard. Anderson also stated, "We expected only to run the meeting one week, but the interest was so great we were compelled to run it for eleven days." Twenty-one people put on Christ in baptism during those meetings, including the wife of John Anderson, Enoch's daughter-in-law. During that same week, the church met to organize a Sunday school. Joseph Brewer was elected superintendent, and A.N. Durham was elected class leader. Since the majority of the people who were baptized lived in the neighborhood, the leadership made plans to expand the church building.

Two short years later, Elder Enoch M. Anderson died at the home of his only surviving daughter, Cordelia "Dealie" Howard at Pelzer, South Carolina. He was only 65 at the time of death. Emma Pack wrote his eulogy for *The Restitution*:

> Never in the history of my life have I known a mortal man like our brother who has just passed away. He loved everybody, even his enemies, who so despitefully used him. He was always ready to return good for evil. Being persecuted, reproached and evil spoken of by them who obey not the gospel, he bore it all with patience, knowing whom he served, ever looking forward to the time when his Lord should appear the second time without sin unto salvation.

A.N. Durham preached Anderson's funeral service from Revelation 14:13, "Blessed are the dead who died in the Lord ... that they may rest from their labors, and their works do follow them." Anderson was the first to be buried in the newly established cemetery at Guthrie Grove. At the time of his death, Elder Enoch Anderson had baptized nearly 400 believers. His trusted and beloved son, John H. Anderson, succeeded Enoch in the ministry.

Wally Winner contributed to this entry.

See Anderson, J.H.
Bond, Newell
Gresham, Robert
Huggins, Robert (20th)

Bibliography: Isham, Jewely (Craig). Anderson family papers on loan for author's research, Winter 2006; *Restitution* August 5, 1908; Sept. 16, 1913; Nov. 1921; Biggers, Vadie. "E. M. Anderson," by his granddaughter, Vadie for the ABC Biography Project, David Krogh, compiler; Winner, Wally. "Enoch Anderson's Early Ministry", Paper presented at History Conference on Nov. 3-4, 2006. Atlanta Bible College. Morrow, Ga. It was through this paper that we learned of Enoch Anderson's dubious background prior to entering the ministry with the Church of God.

Anderson, John Henry
b. July 20, 1875
d. December 4, 1942

John H. Anderson was born in North Carolina. His father was Enoch M. Anderson, a local preacher who studied the Gospel of the Kingdom. Enoch started the work at Guthrie Grove in a brush arbor. John grew up knowing the life of a circuit rider and learning about the Gospel of the Kingdom, the faith of Abraham, the sleep of the dead, and the coming of Christ to establish the Kingdom.

Elder J.H. Anderson preached his first sermon to 12 people in the grove in South Carolina when he was 18 years old. In 1896, he began to assist his father in the ministry. He also married Lula Wall and she bore him seven children.

He traveled throughout the Carolinas, Virginias, Ohio, Kentucky and Indiana to bring the truth to churches and scattered members. He particularly loved preaching at Roll, Guthrie Grove and Brumsfield.

Guthrie Grove Church of God, Pelzer, South Carolina

John devoted a great deal of his time to working with the brethren at Guthrie Grove Church of God at Pelzer, South Carolina, and Brumsfield, Kentucky. In 1919, he went to Brumsfield and stayed with the Skeels family for several days. Meetings were held in their home. He baptized Mrs. Vernon (Vertie) Carpentar. In his report, he stated that Kentucky was the tenth state he had visited in 23 years. For a while, he lived and worked in Ohio near Dayton and Brush Creek. He also preached throughout Missouri, and conducted special meetings at conferences in Louisiana and Nebraska.

On May 23, 1921, his wife died in childbirth leaving him with several smaller children. He wrote that his plans were suspended for a number of weeks as he tried to determine which course to follow. At the time of her death the Anderson family lived at Maurertown, Virginia.

Anderson's work in Virginia included the ministry at Maurertown in the Shenandoah Valley and at Dry Run in the Fort Valley. It may also have included occasional ministry at the Cool Springs Church of God above Front Royal, the church at Fairfax and another at Baltimore. During the uncertain weeks following his wife's death, he secured the services of Mrs. Cook to watch the children, which allowed him to travel to Gallimore Gap, North Carolina, for meetings from July 28 to August 1.

His daughter, Vadie Biggers, was 15 when her mother died. She wrote through her niece, Nancy Anderson Craig, that her father helped her do the housework. When her mother died there were still five small children at home. Vadie washed clothes, and her father rinsed them and hung them out. The church ladies lent aid as well and made clothes for the family. Vadie said, "We mostly raised ourselves." Her eldest sister Mellie, 19, had married and moved to Winchester, Virginia.

John left Virginia in 1922 and moved north to serve as evangelist in Indiana. He had been in the ministry for 25 years. He left his beloved wife in the Maurertown Cemetery. Later, he married a second time. During this time John preached at North Salem Church of God at Plymouth on a regular basis. After the Plummer Church got its start and changed its name to Hillisburg Church of God, J.H. Anderson preached there for 19 years. It was here that he had his greatest writing ministry. He also made regular visits to the church at Rensselaer.

John Anderson was a prolific writer. He wrote and edited several tracts or booklets, including *God's Two Great Witnesses* or *The Bible and Nature in Harmony*, *The Sunlight of Prophecy* or *Who is the Antichrist*, *The Pathway of Salvation*, *Present Conditions in the Light of Prophecy*, *The Cause and The Remedy*, and *The Great Sabbath* or *What Jesus Will Do When He Comes and Restitution Begins*? These titles were unpublished lesson booklets, often transcribed and mimeographed by Sr. Mabel Edney from sermons J.H. Anderson preached at Hillisburg near Michigantown, Indiana.

JH Anderson (second row, far left) and colleagues at the 1935 annual summer conference in Oregon, Illinois.

John Anderson died in 1942 from complications of diabetes. He was laid to rest at Burnel Cemetery near Frankfort, Indiana.

See Anderson, Enoch M.
　　　Butler, Mellie Anderson (20th)
　　　Randall, Clyde (20th)

Bibliography: Austin, Evelyn. "A Brief Sketch of Indiana Church History", written about 1930; Biggers, Vadie, "J.H. Anderson" for the ABC Biography Project, David Krogh, compiler. *Restitution* Oct. 1919; July 7, 1921; *The Restitution Herald* July 26, 1916; Nov. 4, 1919; Letter from Vadie Biggers, and Nancy Anderson Craig, Phoenix Az., Dec. 2005; Graham, David. *Wisdom and Power*. Nov. 1992; Stilson, Eugene and Janet. Historic footnote: One day during the 1960s when E. Stilson was pastor at the Church of God in Maurertown, Virginia, Mellie Anderson Tronjeau and her husband paid a visit. They had come to get acquainted and to visit her mother's grave on the hilltop overlooking the town. In the course of the afternoon discussion, Mellie shared a great deal of Church of God history that was valuable in researching this encyclopedia.

Anderson, Robert
b. 1892
d. Unknown

Robert Anderson was born and raised in Iowa. He was married to Anna and they had three children. He became an accountant in an oil firm. He became a lay leader and lay pastor of the Church of God at Gifford, Iowa. His hometown was also the hometown of evangelist Almus Adams. Adams and wife visited Gifford occasionally to see old friends and family, and to encourage the brethren. Robert Anderson was single through age 30, and lived with relatives who also looked after his sister. He was an operator at the local depot.

Robert appreciated the friendship and assistance of Almus Adams in

Robert (right) with Almus Adams

church related work. The work at Gifford was small and Anderson expressed discouragement from the members' indifference. Eventually the work increased. Evangelist Adams said of his friend, "Elder Anderson worked hard and at last succeeded."

See Adams, Almus

Bibliography: Ancestry.com U.S. Census. Iowa, Hardin. Union. Dist. 197. 1920; *Restitution,* Jan. 1924.

Andrew, Mary Cordelia
b. September 17, 1848
d. January 24, 1924

Miss Mary Slagle was born in Ogle County, Illinois. She married Daniel Andrew in 1880. Daniel died in 1898. Mary Cordelia raised her children and farmed the family acreage. Her daughter, Alice, was gifted in drawing so Mary sent her to study at the Art Institute in Chicago.

Her son, Charles E. Andrew, graduated from the University of Illinois as an engineer. He was the project design engineer who assisted Charles H. Purcell in the design and construction of the famous San Francisco-Oakland Bay Bridge which opened in 1936.

Mary Cordelia Andrew believed in the Lord and the resurrection, although she remained a faithful Lutheran all her life. Her husband was a Church of God member.

See Carpentar, Alice
Eychaner, A. J.

Bibliography: *The Restitution Herald* Jan. 29, 1924; Virtual Museum of the City of San Francisco. Symphonies in Steel; Bay Bridge and the Golden Gate. http://www.sfmuseum.org/hist9/mcgloin.html.

Andrew, Nicholas
b. 1818
d. Unknown

Nicholas Andrew came from New York and staked a claim at Paynes Point, Illinois, five miles east of Oregon in Ogle County. The land included a farm along Brick Road later owned by Benjamin Carpentar. At the time of this compilation, the property remained in the ownership of Ben's descendants.

Andrew's claim was made in 1854. Competition for land was intense and the claim office was in Dixon, 18 miles south of Paynes Point. Nicholas staked his claim and raced to Dixon to register it before anyone else could. Land sold in those days for $1.25 an acre.

According to Bill Andrew, Nicholas, who was his great-grandfather, built a cabin along Rocky Hollow Road just past the stone quarry on the right side. Nicholas married Margaret Eychaner, the sister of Andrew J. Eychaner. They had four sons, one of whom was Alice Andrew Carpentar's father, Daniel. When A.J. and Margaret's mother died, she and Nicholas took little "Andy" into their home. The Nicholas Andrew family was instrumental in spreading the Gospel in the early days of the Church of God among the pioneers of Illinois.

Margaret Andrew

See Eychaner, A.J.
Carpentar, Benjamin (20th)

Bibliography: Andrew, William. Interview May 2007.

Andrus (Andrew), Erastus C.
b. 1818
d. 1890?

E.C. Andrus was born in Connecticut but migrated to Indiana near Logansport where he became a farmer. He was married with two daughters and one son. During farming's off season, Andrus traveled and preached.

It is not known how he learned of the second advent, but being a native of New England certainly afforded him opportunity to hear the teaching. By the time he relocated to the Indiana frontier he may have already been a staunch advocate of the Gospel of the Kingdom, the second advent of Christ and the Age-to-Come aspect of prophecy. Details of E.C. Andrus' itinerary or schedule for evangelism are scant. Neither is his duration of service known, but the record shows he was active in preaching the Word in 1863 as the evangelist for the Indiana Conference.

He placed a notice in the *Millennial Harbinger and Bible Expositor* asking the readers to identify suitable places for missionary effort. He said the work was arduous and the time was short. In response, J.S. Hatch, as yet an unknown layman in the Church of God movement, wrote and said the work around Crawfordsville, Indiana, had good prospects for accepting the Gospel. Later, Hatch would relocate to Valparaiso and become one of the most outstanding evangelists known to the Church of God in that day or since.

Little more is known of Elder Andrus, but this information demonstrates that there were many more people like him working to spread the Gospel message across the United States and Canada than have become known through Church of God literature. They planted the seeds, and the harvest has been, and is yet to be reaped in America from all ministry activity of the 19th and 20th centuries. Pray the Lord to send forth the workers for the harvest.

Bibliography: Ancestry.com U.S. Census. Indiana. Fulton. Wayne. P.20. 1860; Andrus, E.E. Notice. *Millennial Harbinger and Bible Expositor*, Thos. Newman, editor, Seneca Falls, NY. Sept. 30, 1863; and, Nov. 18, 1863.

Ashcroft, Robert
b. 1842
d. 1921

Robert Ashcroft was a Congregational minister who left that persuasion to become a Christadelphian. He was popular among the brethren in Edinburgh, Scotland, but fell out of favor with Robert Roberts and eventually moved to Toronto where he assumed a publishing career. In one of his books, he named himself as a "minister in the Congregational Church, Rock Ferry, and Liverpool, England."

He believed in the Gospel of the Kingdom of God. In 1891, just as the Church of God was beginning to experience growth pains and had organized a national conference (1888-1892), he wrote a book entitled *The Scriptures Opened*. The subtitle was *Thoughts and Themes for Bible Students*. This book was highly read and endorsed by Church of God pastors, but was not accepted by Christadelphians.

On the page of endorsements, Benjamin Wilson's statement is listed first, followed by other significant recommendations. Ashcroft called Wilson "an old veteran of the truth."

Wilson said of the volume:
The book you sent is at hand. I like it very much. It is written in a kind, attractive, Christ spirit, calculated to win and instruct the reader in the deep things of God as revealed in his Word.

J.L. Wince of Pierceton, Indiana, wrote:
I am well pleased in its style of thought and language. It should be read by all who share with us the faith and hope of the apostolic gospel.

William H. Wilson of Hammond, Louisiana, wrote:
I have read the book with great pleasure and profit. The general scope of the work shows that the writer is a literary man and a scholar, and as a consequence the truth is dressed in a creditable manner. Doctrinally the work voices my own convictions.

Finally, J.F. Wagoner of Rochester, Indiana, noted:
The work breathes throughout the sweet spirit of our Blessed Master. I am irresistibly drawn toward Brother Ashcroft as I read the masterly arguments with which he demolishes the orthodox strongholds. He has the rare faculty of turning their own arguments against them.

In his preface to the second edition Robert Ashcroft wrote, "Indeed, it is abundantly evident that the Kingdom of God is the only Key that will unlock the Sacred Scripture from end to end." The Ashcroft name is seen frequently in the pages of *The Restitution*, but very little is known about his personal life. Ashcroft also published two volumes of *The Truth* from Toronto in 1891 and 1892. He said in December 1892 that it saddened him to cease publishing, but circumstances required it.

Steven Cook, a historian of the Christadelphian movement, has said that Robert Ashcroft had been a student of Robert Roberts and became immensely popular among the members. When he became too popular, Roberts exiled him. Many Christadelphian members to date have never seen the Ashcroft book, of which there are many copies in the Archives of Atlanta Bible College. After Ashcroft left the Christadelphians, there is no record of him joining the Church of God, but many felt a kinship with him and his literary accomplishments, and many bought and read his publications. Ashcroft's book has been scanned to CD for distribution to a new generation of readers.

See Wagoner, J.F.
Wilson, Benjamin
Wilson, W.H.
Wince, J.L.

Bibliography: Ashcroft, Robert. *The Scriptures Opened Thoughts and Themes for Bible Students*. 2nd ed. Self published in Toronto, Canada for distribution in the United States, 1891; Ashcroft, Robert, editor. *The Truth,* Toronto, a monthly theological magazine, Jan. 1891-Dec. 1892. Cook, Steve, Sydney, Australia. Interview regarding the ministry of Robert Ashcroft Rock River Christian College with Jan Stilson. March 2007; Photo from Cook Blog:christadelphian.blogspot.com/search/label/Robert%20Ashcroft.

Aslaksen, Martin
b. December 20, 1851
d. March 26, 1926

Martin Aslaksen was born in Norway. It was said that Martin learned English by comparing the Norwegian Bible with an English Bible. He married an Englishwoman, Mary Henwood, in Chicago in 1876. She arrived in Boston at the same time the Chicago Fire was raging in October 1871. Her parents wrote her to remain in Boston and sent for her later. It is not known how she met Martin. The couple had seven children: Jesse, Martin, Mary, Anna, Emma, Ruth and Grace who died in infancy. It has been reported that Sr. Aslaksen contracted smallpox from a defective vaccination and passed it on to baby Grace.

Someone in Chicago gave a tract to Martin and Mary. Perhaps it was written by H.V. Reed or J.M. Stephenson. They read it, believed it, and both of them accepted the Abrahamic Faith. They were baptized into the Church of God. Martin was a leader in the work to organize the Illinois Conference and, as such, served on the Board of Directors for that conference for several years. He also participated in the formation of the General Conference of Churches of God at Waterloo, Iowa, in 1921.

After Elder Aslaksen retired from his employment, the couple moved west to Ogle County and resided at Adeline. Two of their daughters lived there, Anna Smith at Forreston and Mary Gesin at Oregon. Mary was a teacher at the Bible Training School when it opened in Oregon. Two of her students were Clarence Lapp and Harvey U. Krogh Jr. The family nickname for Sr. Gesin was "Mame." Mame had two daughters, Ruth Gesin Lippert and Alice Gesin Marshall, and a son, Ernest.

Bro. and Sr. Aslaksen and some of their grown family attended the Adeline Church of God. It was a healthy and active congregation before the formation of the Oregon Church of God. It had a dormitory behind the large church so it could host conference meetings and Bible schools. Many Illinois Conference executive board meetings were held here. Martin was a good Bible student and he preached and taught often at Adeline and for the Illinois Conference.

Mary died in 1921. Martin became a resident at the Golden Rule Home in February 1923. He led the First Anniversary service of the Golden Rule Home on January 6, 1924, with a short, earnest and appropriate prayer of "thankfulness for present blessings and a petition for divine guidance in all activities of the Home."

Martin had surgery at the hospital in Dixon, Illinois, and was recuperating nicely. He walked the hall for exercise, sat down and died. The doctor said he had a heart condition unrelated to the surgery. He was interred at the Adeline Cemetery beside his dear wife.

Aslaksen was William Wachtel's grandfather. Bill's mother was childless at nearly 40 years old. Martin told her he would pray for her so she could have a child. At Bill Wachtel's birth in 1927, the year following Martin's death, she felt he was a direct answer to her father's prayer. Bro. Wachtel's mother and other family members are buried beside the Aslaksens in the cemetery across from the old Adeline church campus. At this compilation, the campus was owned by another denomination, but all buildings remained intact.

See Austin, Frederick L. (20th)

Bibliography: Stilson, Jan. Photos of grave monument; *The Restitution Herald,* January 13, 1924; Obituary, *The Restitution Herald*, April 22, 1926; William Wachtel, Stories from the family to Jan Stilson by e-mail, Dec. 7, 2005; Feb. 2, 2006.

Adeline Church of God

Babcock, Amos A.
b. November 26, 1806
d. June 26, 1893

A. Leader in Michigan
B. Abolition

Amos Babcock was born in Otsego County, New York, and migrated to Michigan in 1835. He was the first settler at Albion and built the first log cabin there. For awhile he was the only white settler in that vicinity, Native Americans and wolves being his only neighbors. Over time, his home became a landmark.

Photo from F. Passic, used with permimssion

He married Polly Carr; they had six children, one child, Daniel, lived to inherit the house and land. The other five preceded him in death. They are buried in the family cemetery. a circle of stones surrounds each grave.

It is not known how A.A. Babcock came to understand the Gospel of the Kingdom. It certainly is possible that he studied his Bible well enough to extract Age-to-Come ideas independently, for it is unlikely that he learned of the unique interpretation of prophecy from any evangelist in Michigan who followed the teachings of Joseph Marsh. A.A. Babcock's arrival in Michigan predates Adventist or Age-to-Come activity that is known in the area.

Elias Smith and Abner Jones who started the Christian Connexion in New England also sent men into the frontier wilderness prior to the Millerite movement. There were no, or few, church buildings on the western frontier, so people were hungry for the Word.

It is likely that Babcock was aware of the teachings of William Miller, who began to preach in New England in 1831, saying Christ's second coming would occur in 1844. Babcock must have learned of the Bitter Disappointment when Christ did not return on the appointed date from the various Adventist journals that circulated throughout the frontier states.

These journals included *The Christian Palladium*, owned by the Christian Connexion, edited by Joseph Marsh. When Marsh was ousted from that editorship in 1843, for publishing too much information about the second advent, he began publishing *The Voice of Truth*, and later a new title, *The Advent Harbinger and Bible Advocate*.

It is certain that A.A. Babcock read the *Gospel Banner* and highly prized it. In a letter to the editor in February 1859, he said:

> Enclosed please find fifty cents. I wish you to send the Banner to a friend of mine.... I do highly prize your excellent paper. It is food indeed, next to the Bible. How good it is to be stirred up by way of remembrance, that we be not carried away by spiritualism, which is of the devil, and ends in death. Please give a piece on Spiritualism in the next Banner.

A. Leader in Michigan

Amos A. Babcock's name appears in the minute book of the Michigan State Conference as early as 1860, during the third annual meeting of that new organization. He was appointed to the office of director on the executive board and he held that office for many years. In 1866 the conference meeting was held at his home, which had grown over the years to accommodate a crowd. At this meeting he was appointed to be on a committee regarding the management of the conference.

Reports of the work at Albion appear occasionally in the journals edited by Joseph Marsh with specific mention of A.A. Babcock. He served as pastor of the church at Albion, whose member, J. Byron Jr., reported the activities to the *Voice of Truth*. Very likely, the nature of this work was a house-church which met at the Babcock home.

J. Byron Jr. served as pastor of the church at Climax, Michigan, in 1846. It is understood from these few facts that the message of the Gospel of the Kingdom began to grow in Michigan very soon after the Bitter Disappointment. Byron may have also helped lead the flock at Albion.

B. Abolition

It was rumored around Albion that the Babcock home was a station on the Underground Railroad. There would have been plenty of places to hide runaway slaves as the property had deep woods bordering it. Babcock operated a sorghum mill that also provided hiding places. Babcock's interest in helping slaves may be a clue that he was in touch with Joseph Marsh in the early days. Marsh, a neighbor to Frederick Douglass, accommodated fleeing slaves at his home in Rochester, New York.

The Babcock home may have been an Underground Railroad location.
Photo from F. Passic, used with permission

The brethren associated with the One Faith became known as the Michigan State Conference; they were sympathetic to the cause of abolition. At their meeting in November 1861 they adopted a resolution:

> **The Michigan Conference Resolution on Slavery**
> Resolution for US Congress; adopted at the meeting held November 8-10, 1861:
> *We do therefore pray your honorable body to authorize and require the President of the United States to proclaim the freedom of all the slaves within the United States, and to institute or allow such measures as shall render them efficient supporters of the national cause and qualify them to become useful citizens; accomplishing such act of emancipation with such other provisions as in your judgment, the interest of parties concerned may require, and your petitioners will ever pray.*
> *By order of the Board,*
> *E. Miller, President; O.R.L. Crozier, Secretary*
>
> Ref.: Minute Book, Michigan Conference, Church of God, 1856-1886

The statement of the board leading to this resolution, as recorded in the minute book, is eloquently written in the formal and beautiful language of the day.

The minutes from the Michigan conference show that Elder Babcock was active in that state well into old age. He served as a director in 1861, and being somewhat older, was on the Executive Committee of the Board at their 20th annual meeting in 1877.

Amos died at Albion and was buried at Riverside Cemetery. The Babcock house was maintained for more than 100 years after his death but was demolished in September 1994 due to advanced age and deterioration.

See Crozier, O.R.L.
Marsh, Joseph

Bibliography: Amos Babcock burial record, retrieved from findagrave.com December 29, 2007; *Michigan State Conference Report 1859-1886*, including specific notecards detailing work at Albion and Climax, Michigan from 1846; *Voice of Truth* 10:1,2, 1846; Passic, Frank, Albion Historian, "Historical Albion Michigan. Amos A. Babcock." *Morning Star*, Sept. 8, 1994, 12, retrieved from Albionmich.com December 2007; permission granted to use photos of Babcock and Babcock homestead by Frank Passic, by e-mail December 29, 2007; Babcock, A.A. "Letter to editor", *Gospel Banner*, Benj. Wilson, ed. Geneva, Il., February 1859.

Bacon, Ezra
b. November 12, 1841
d. January 21, 1921

Ezra Bacon was born in Chautauqua County, New York. In 1855, he moved to Ottawa, Minnesota. He married Sophronia Winegar in Ottawa on December 25, 1871. For several years he was an Indian fighter for the government, working among the hostile tribes of the Sioux and the Dakotas.

He was converted in early manhood and was one of the first ministers to affiliate with the Church of God in Minnesota. He relocated to Mora where he met the Randalls. He died and was buried there.

Bibliography: History of the Minnesota Church of God Conference, Sydney Magaw, editor, 1931.

Bailey, Joshua P.
b. November 11, 1815
d. April 7, 1898

Joshua with Lucinda

Joshua Bailey was born in Windfall, Tipton County, Indiana, to Stanton Bailey and Mary Piggot Bailey, both Quakers. Stanton owned considerable acreage in Ohio and Indiana. When Stanton died he left the proceeds of his estate to his sons. After the estate was settled Joshua moved to Tipton County, Indiana. Joshua was baptized there by Fid Plummer who dipped him three times. The Plummers established the present-day Hillisburg Church of God. After his immersion Fid and Joshua began to learn of the Abrahamic Faith from Uncle John Foore. After deliberating about the new Bible teachings, and reading about them in the Bible, Joshua was re-baptized by Elder Foore in 1896.

Joshua married Eliza Plummer who may have been a widow. Joshua became well known to all the Indiana ministers but especially Uncle John Foore and S.A.

Chaplin. Many Church of God conferences were held on Bro. Bailey's property at Little Wild Creek north of Kokomo, Tipton County. Folks came from miles around, pitched tents and stayed for two weeks of meetings.

One problem with camp life during that period was that people often contracted typhoid. The fever was fatal for many. Mrs. Bailey was one such unfortunate.

In 1867, the Baileys, Plummers, Whites and some Coopers traveled by wagon train to Hardin County, Iowa. Joshua Bailey and his family stayed only a couple of years before moving on. He was a land and mineral speculator and when they reached Madison County in Missouri in 1871, he seemed content to settle there.

By this time, Joshua had remarried Lucinda Cooper, a widow with children. Lucinda also was a member of the Church of God. They met at a conference sometime after Eliza's death.

After Joshua Bailey settled on the farm he began to share the Gospel of the Kingdom with his neighbors. He invited ministers of the One Faith to his home to hold services. Ministers who answered the call to help him with the work included John Foore, Kansas; W.H. Wilson, Chicago and Louisiana; J.F. Waggoner, Missouri; J.S. Hatch, Indiana; and J.M. Stephenson of Illinois and Wisconsin. Upon completion of a church building, visiting ministers drew such large crowds that many had to stand or sit outside and listen through the opened windows.

Joshua Bailey offered some of his farmland to build a church. Judge George Plummer, a relative through Eliza, assisted with this. Pleasant Jasper Graham and his seven sons also assisted in the construction.

Blush Church of God

During the planning and construction, Joshua Bailey held meetings at the Piney schoolhouse. The project was completed and dedicated in 1906. Sadly, Elder Bailey died before it was completed. This church became known as the Blush Church of God. Joshua Bailey's daughter was the wife of another Church of God leader in Missouri, Bro. P.J. Graham, also of Blush church. Bailey's stepson, W.A. Cooper became a leader of the work at Fredericktown, Missouri.

Joshua Bailey married four times, giving him numerous stepsons. Altogether, he was the father of 19 children. Joshua died at Madison, Missouri, and left a large family to mourn his death.

He was the grandfather of Elder Ernest Graham Sr.; the great-grandfather of Pastor Ernest Graham Jr.; and the great-great-grandfather of David Graham, a Church of God historian, and Carl Jennings, both graduates of Oregon Bible College.

See Cooper, William
Foore, John
Graham, Ernest (20th)
Stephenson, J.M.
Waggoner, J.F.
Wilson, W.H.

Bibliography: Ancestry.com. Ohio Land Records for Stanton Bailey showing numerous land records for 1820, 1821, 1823, 1832, 1835; Graham, David. *Wisdom and Power* April/May 1993 from the *History of Southeast Missouri* by Goodspeed, 1888; "Family Genealogy." email to Jan Stilson, March 1, 2006, Dec. 7, 2007, July 10, 2009; Photo of Joshua Bailey from David Graham; Williams, Byron. *Abstracts of Obituaries and Weddings from the Restitution.* Self-published. 1994.

Barber, Hannah
b. 1892?
d. Unknown

Hannah Barber was a home missionary. She lived in Pueblo, Colorado. At her own expense she toured to Rocky Ford, Colorado, in October 1920, to meet with the Grimsleys, who had been taught by Bro. Almus Adams the previous year. The Grimsleys were nearly ready to request baptism. She talked with them and answered questions. After leaving their home, she traveled elsewhere to share Church of God tracts and to talk with people. She exemplifies the dedication that many Church of God pioneers had for obedience to the Great Commission.

See Adams, Almus
Bibliography: *The Restitution*, Dec. 3, 1920.

Barber (Robison), Nancy
b. 1856
d. 1940?

Nancy Barber was born in Alabama but relocated to Salem, Ohio. She learned of the Abrahamic Faith and embraced it. She began serving in the Church of God in Ohio in various ways and continued for a number of years. In 1905 she attended a conference at Cleveland and, in an earnest and forceful manner, preached to the congregants regarding the Kingdom of God. All who heard her were convinced that she would be a wonderful evangelist. She was baptized at the Salem Church of God by Pastor Peter Neill in 1906.

Afterward, the Church of God Ohio Conference appointed her state evangelist for the next year and announced the same in the pages of *The Restitution*. She had been filling pulpits for several years throughout Ohio. She may have been a widow, a status that would have given her mobility and means. When she heard there were few preachers in Oklahoma, she spent a year and a half in that state preaching wherever she could. During that time, she may have lived with her daughter and family the Pierce McWaters. She preached so much she damaged her voice. Upon her return to Ohio, the malady healed.

> **Resolution of 1887 Indiana Conference**
>
> The Indiana Conference met in June for their annual meeting and decided to make assignments in order to accomplish the work that needed to be done. They decided to write and publish Bible Readings and invited other state conferences to work with Indiana committees to accomplish this, and then use the materials for Christian education. They also discussed the best method of doing evangelism. They said the new Bible readings could be given to evangelists who would distribute them and teach from them.
>
> They resolved:
> *It is not contrary to teaching of Bible for women to do the work of an evangelist, and we believe it is our duty to encourage all Christian women in this great and glorious work.*
>
> Nancy Barber may have been present at that meeting and taken that invitation to heart, for she went on to become a popular evangelist. Ref.: *The Restitution*, July 4, 1887

When Nancy met Daniel C. Robison, an elder in the Church of God in Cleveland, they struck up a romance. They were married at the home of Brother and Sister Peter Neill. The ceremony was performed on June 26, 1906, less than a year after she preached in Cleveland. The marriage changed her name and her life.

From that time forward, they worked together to be more effective for the Abrahamic Faith, until his death. After Daniel's death, Nancy moved to Arkansas City, Kansas, where she lived with her sister, Martha Randolph, and worked with the Church of God in that city.

See Neill, Peter
Robison, D.C.

Bibliography: Ancestry.com, U.S. Census. Indiana. Boone. Jackson. Dist. 126, 1880; U.S. Census. Ohio. Columbiana. Salem Ward 1. Dist. 41. 1910; and U. S. Census. Oklahoma. Choctaw. Everidge. Dist. 62. 1920; and Kansas. Cowley. Arkansas. Dist. 1. 1930; *Restitution*, Nov. 9, 1887; October 4, 1905; July 4, 1906.

Barnhill, Hugh Sharon
b. March 29, 1809
d. March 3, 1884

Hugh Barnhill was born in Ohio to Robert and Sarah Marvis Barnhill. The family relocated to Marion County, Indiana, in 1820. In 1846 he moved to Marshall County. Here he became active in the Old Pisgah Church. He had already been speaking in public for two years. He and Henry Logan attended this church while it was still a Christian church. They may have learned the message of the Kingdom of God together.

After he and his first wife Phoebe settled on the old Barnhill homestead north of Argos, in 1846, they began their family. By the time their second child was born, a daughter named Bathiel, he was very active in service to the Lord. In subsequent years he fathered 12 more children, ten by a second marriage. He farmed 117 acres and was esteemed by his fellows as a good neighbor and a good farmer.

In 1847, Elders Ephraim Miller and Ed Hoyt of Michigan came and preached at S.A. Chaplin's log cabin at Oswego, Kosciusko County, and at other points, lecturing from charts on the prophecies of Daniel and Revelation. They also came to Old Pisgah and delivered a series of lectures. Almost the whole congregation accepted the message of truth, and a Church of God was organized at that location.

Hugh Barnhill also assisted Stedman A. Chaplin in mentoring other preachers and sending them out to the far west. One of these was John Foore who was ordained as a new Christian preacher at an Indiana conference meeting by Barnhill and Chaplin in 1861.

The early Church of God work in Indiana owes its success largely to Hugh Barnhill. He was pastor of the church at Antioch in Walnut Township for 38 years. He preached for the Church of God until he was fatally injured in a buggy accident on his way to Plymouth.

Hugh S. Barnhill dedicated many years to the Church of God. His son, Hugh W. Barnhill (1850-1920), became a powerhouse for the Lord within the Church of God in Indiana, Kansas and Washington. At the time of this compilation, some of his descendants remained active in the churches at Wenatchee and Cashmere, Washington.

See Chaplain, Stedman
Foore, John
Hoyt, Ed
Logan, Henry
Miller, Ephraim

Bibliography: Ferrell, Terry. *A Brief History of the Church of God in America*. National Berean Youth Conference. Camp Reynoldswood, Dixon, Il, Aug 21-27, 1960; Rankin, Arlen. "The Influence of Old Union in Indiana," citing McDonald, Daniel. *A Twentieth Century History of Marshall County, Indiana*. Chicago. Lewis. 1908; *The Restitution*, April 3, 1907; "Report of NW Christian Conference", *Prophetic Expositor and Bible Advocate*, Joseph Marsh, editor, Rochester, NY, July 15, 1857 and Aug. 21, 1857; *The Restitution Herald*, Oct. 14, 1914; Nov. 4, 1914.

Billingsley, Thomas C.
b. 1844
d. 1934?

T.C. Billingsley's name was among the Arkansas preachers in William H. Wilson's report to *The Restitution* in 1904. At that time he lived and preached at Drigg. Prior to that, he lived at Sallisaw, Oklahoma, where he operated a blacksmith shop. His name is among those recognized by the Arkansas-Oklahoma Conference at the July 1915 meeting. Being "recognized" by a state conference was equivalent to being licensed to preach. Some state conferences gave a license and others noted in the minutes that a certain minister was recognized.

It was at this same meeting that the Arkansas/Oklahoma Conference authorized and challenged the churches to organize with two elders, two deacons and a treasurer. This was to be done wherever there were five or six members. Each member was challenged to pay 10¢ per month. One-third of that went to the state conference treasurer. Isolated members were instructed to send 10¢ a month directly to the state treasurer.

Southern Ministers
Front row, from left: RA Humphreys, TC Billingsley, TA Drinkard, JH Luhman. Back row: EO Stewart, CF Weaver, unknown, LH Shelton, JM Morgan.

Elder Billingsley worked with J.M. Morgan to hold special meetings using a large tabernacle. At Sallisaw, where Billingsley lived, they raised the tent for that purpose. Being a blacksmith, he was well equipped to keep the tent and its hardware in good condition. When the meeting ended, the tent was shipped by rail to Bristow, Oklahoma, so L.H. Shelton could use it.

T.C. Billingsley was highly esteemed by the people of Arkansas and Oklahoma. In 1930, at age 85, he resided in Sallisaw, Oklahoma, with his daughter Anna's family. His exact death date has not been determined.

See Morgan, J.M. (20th)
Shelton, L.H.
Bibliography: Ancestry.com U.S. Census. Oklahoma. Sequoia. Sallisaw. Dist. 210. 1910; U.S. Census. Oklahoma. Sequoia. Sallisaw. 1930; Drinkard, T.A. "A Belated Report," *The Gospel Messenger,* Jan/Feb. 1962. "Report of Wilson" *The Restitution.* Jan. 20. 1904; *The Restitution Herald,* Aug. 25, 1915; Sept. 1, 1915. Thanks to Sherwin Williams, an old "Oklahoma boy" for information on T.C. Billingsley.

Blakely, Frank Vernon
b. March 16, 1880
d. 1949?

Vernon Blakely was born in the village of Torch Lake, Michigan. When he was about three years old, his parents moved to the village of Eastport, at the head of the beautiful Torch Lake. After receiving a good education at home from his mother, he taught school for three years. He left home at age 21 to attend college. He became a bookkeeper, possibly in a band instrument manufactory or retail store.

Blakely met and married Miss Nellie M. Hartman of Athens, Michigan, in 1904, while living in Baldwin, Michigan. It was through Nellie that Vernon first heard about the Gospel of the Kingdom. Her sister, Mrs. A.C. (Lisa) Hartman, also assisted in talking with the young man and was instrumental in scheduling special meetings. She contacted the evangelists to conduct further meetings.

A few months after their marriage, Evangelists B.W. and Sr. M.A. Woodward came to Marlborough to hold meetings. One result of these was Vernon's baptism in the beautiful Pere Marquette River on December 9, 1904.

In 1905, the Blakelys moved to Grand Rapids where he became a credit manager and head accountant for the firm of J.W. York & Sons. Then, in April 1906, Frank Blakely was invited to preach at Dutton, Michigan, which he did. This was his first sermon. The effort was appreciated to the extent that he was asked to come regularly for a few months. Thus, his first lessons in that work were learned on the job.

The following year he was elected secretary of the Michigan State Conference, which position he filled for two years, until he was elected president. In 1908, at that conference, he was ordained to the ministry, and though busy in his vocation found much time to devote to preaching the Gospel. He became president of the Michigan State Conference in 1909 and served in that capacity until 1910.

He attended the 16th Illinois Conference in 1911. In 1913 he preached for that assembly. He also was awarded a ministerial certificate. He preached regularly at Illinois meetings attending annual and quarterly conferences for the next ten years. Shortly after *The Restitution Herald* began to be published, Frank was appointed to the audit committee. He was appointed to the songbook committee in 1914 with L.E. Conner and Mary Elton. He was elected to full directorship of the Restitution Publishing Company in 1914 and 1917. He supported S.J. Lindsay and moved that Lindsay be re-elected as secretary/treasurer of the company in 1918.

In 1912, a Bible Berean Class was organized in Grand Rapids that helped revitalize the work there so that, in 1914, the Church of God Abrahamic Faith and Sunday School was organized with F.V. Blakely as pastor and superintendent of the Sunday school. The work grew slowly but steadily.

Blakely remained active in the work of the Michigan conference and the work of the Church of God General Conference throughout his life.

See Conner, L.E.

Bibliography: Ancestry.com. U.S. Census. Michigan. Kent. Grand Rapids Ward 11. Dist. 111. 1910; Magaw, Ivan. Research notes in Archives Atlanta Bible College, no date; *The Restitution Herald*, June 14, 1916.

Blanchette, Charles Alphonse
b. April 1, 1874
d. November 3, 1930

Charles Blanchette was born in Skowhegan, Maine. He was raised in a Catholic home and studied for the priesthood. However, after he moved to Minnesota and began to learn about the Bible from the Church of God, he changed his faith. He was baptized and began to preach. He was ordained at the Smith Lake Conference on September 22-25, 1898. He became state evangelist the very next year.

He was married to Amanda, but by 1930 she did not reside with him. She may have been in a nursing facility. Instead, his widowed father lived in the household, along with his sons, John and Neil, and son-in-law, Wilbur T. Hyland.

Bibliography: Ancestry.com. Minnesota Death Index 1907-2002 record of Charles Blanchette; *History of the Church of God in Minnesota*, Sydney Magaw, editor, 1931.

Right:
Minnesota Ministers
Mr. and Mrs. EE Thoms,
Charles Blanchette and Amos Randall.

Below: 19th Century Ministers, Minnesota Conference
Top row, from left - CDW Scott, Wm. Parson, Jed. Raymond, SP Matheny; second row - EE Thoms, Mrs. EE Thoms, JL Chadwick, AJ Randall; third row - HA Dingman, JW Dingman, PL Sweany, CA Blanchette; bottom row - JP Driver, C Racy, LR Wood, HH Ranney.

Boice, Harriett E.
b. 1868
d. 1944

Harriett was born to George and Abby Jane Coats in Jamestown, Michigan near Grand Rapids. Her parents were deeply devoted to the teachings of the Church of God. Harriett said the countryside was so wild that deer could graze in the door-yard. Jane came from Quaker background and taught Harriett about quiet and gentle aspects of faith. George's ancestry could be traced to John and Priscilla Alden of "Miles Standish" fame. His mother, Roxana Peabody Coats, was often seen sitting by the stove reading her Bible.

Harriett became an educated woman, and was an advocate for educating the Church of God youth. Harriett was employed at the University of Illinois in Champaign-Urbana, where her family resided for 35 years. She may have been a professor. She felt the pulse of society as she witnessed it in the attitudes and beliefs of the students. She witnessed a slice of society from around the nation as she walked the campus each day.

She was married to L.A. Boice, and they had one son. She was author and editor of *The Visitor,* a small magazine of spiritual encouragement. *The Visitor* dealt with Bible subjects and Sr. Boice concentrated on prophecy, giving "many dates and outlines valuable to the reader." She also wrote a small booklet called *The King's Message.*

She was a prolific writer for *The Restitution* and *The Restitution Herald.* For one article in *The Restitution Herald* she wrote a lengthy defense of the average American college student, entitled, "The Duty of a Watchman." She said not all students are bad because a few are. She challenged parents to take a stand and give their children religious training early in life.

In 1905, a committee was appointed to establish Bible schools and Memorial Homes to represent the Church of God in university towns. This was an Indiana Conference committee. After researching the subject, it was reported in March 1906 that the committee should abandon its appointed mission. Instead, it recommended development of strong leadership in each local church.

In 1910, she made a plea for funds to build a Memorial Home for the elderly. This was the first appeal through the pages of *The Restitution* for such a facility that came a full 11 years before the Church of God organized a national conference to support such a ministry. She said that $100 had been pledged for this purpose in memory of Jeremiah S. Hatch, an Indiana evangelist.

Harriett and her son made a tour of the western United States. She announced her plans for the trip in *The Restitution Herald*, inviting members to meet with her during the trip. In this manner she served as an evangelist meeting many isolated members. Since there was no Church of God in Champaign, Illinois, the closest being Casey or Marshall, she was delighted to meet with isolated members of the Church of God.

Elizabeth Reed, another educated and influential woman in the Illinois Church of God, characterized Mrs. Boice as one of the King's Daughters. Reed said, "She reminds me of the eleventh chapter of Hebrews because of her faith." Mrs. Boice directed the Home Department for the Bereans, a tremendous volunteer effort, which the rest of the Bereans did not or could not do. She was well equipped for it. The Home Department looked after the interests of isolated members, the idea being that they could find a home with the Bereans by studying the principles of the Kingdom conjointly with others who were isolated.

She was a good friend to Elizabeth Reed, Chicago; Clara Chaffee and Mary Woodward, Michigan; and Mrs. Ritenour, Virginia. All of them were educated and capable in writing and preaching. At some point Elizabeth Reed, Clara Chaffee, Harriett Boice, Mary Woodward and Mrs. Ritenour met at Vicksburg, Mississippi, to enjoy each other's company and view the Civil War Memorial Park.

In 1922 Harriett Boice accepted a challenge a reader submitted to *The Restitution Herald*. The newly organized General Conference was trying to raise money to buy equipment for the Golden Rule Home. At the same time, a controversy raged in ministerial discussions about how believers receive the Holy Spirit. One of the more skeptical readers of *The Restitution Herald* made an offer to donate $1,000 if anyone could prove that someone had been healed miraculously. Harriett responded in a column citing the miraculous healing of Elizabeth Reed, stricken ill at the Indian Lake church conference (date unknown), and another example of the healing of a Golden Rule Home resident. (Clara Chaffee testified that she had been amazingly healed while still living in Michigan.) Harriett cited James 5:14 as evidence for healing. It is not known if the challenger delivered the reward he promised.

Mrs. Boice believed the Holy Spirit works in the believer's life and that a believer receives the Comforter from reading the Bible. In an essay published in 1923, she skillfully addressed the question about the Holy Spirit raging throughout the Church of God at that time. Rather than disagreeing with either party, she agreed with both sides of the question, showing true diplomacy and sound Bible interpretation.

Harriett rests at the Woodland Memorial Cemetery, Woodland, Michigan.

See Chaffee, Clara
    Reed, Elizabeth
    Woodward, Mary

Bibliography: Boice, Harriett. *The Voice*, various issues in Atlanta Bible College; Boice, Harriett, Announcement of Bible School Association Convention, *Word and Work*, Minerva Gibbs, editor. Abilene, Texas, July, 1907; Graham, David, "Church of God Connexion & Review", *Wisdom & Power* Nov. 1992; *The Restitution* Dec. 6, 1905; March 7, 1906; *The Restitution Herald* Dec. 8, 1915; May 30, 1922; Aug. 1922; Feb. 27, 1923; March 6, 1923; Oct. 14, 1930.

Bond, Newell
    b. 1798
    d. 1883?

Newell Bond was born in Maine, but located in Cleveland where he became a merchant. Newell and his wife, Mary, lived at 414 Euclid Avenue before selling their home to Mr. and Mrs. Boardman and moving elsewhere in the city in 1835. Newell Bond may have been well-to-do. The *Cleveland City Directory* of 1837 named him as a "Stock Manufacturer". His financial independence helped establish the Church of God in Ohio and North Carolina. The 1870 Census described him as a "Retired Merchant."

Newell and Mrs. Bond were organizing members of the Church of God in Cleveland, Ohio. The work was started as a Bible class as early as the mid-1840s according to a history published by the church. It was not officially organized until October 4, 1863, at the Bond home. The church at Cleveland was among the first to organize into a formal congregation.

Newell Bond was acquainted with Joseph Marsh through his publications, and he knew many of the Adventist men who were Millerites or ex-Millerites, such as Mark Allen, J.V. Himes, J.B. Cook, Stedman Chaplin and Robert McLauchlan. In fact, Newell Bond was elected president of the General Association of the Church of God, Syracuse, New York in June 1863.

While he was president the conference enacted resolutions to provide letters of recommendation to ministers in good standing; that the conference not sustain any responsibility for the character of the professing ministers; that other ecclesiastical bodies do the same for their ministers; that churches with the General Association send letters of recommendation along with members who were relocating to other areas.

It is interesting to realize that these forefathers also contended with unwanted junk mail! Evidence of Newell's frustration with it comes from a letter he wrote in 1850 to Marsh complaining about all the Adventist papers he was receiving, for which he was being charged postage but had not requested. He hoped to narrow down the field a bit, so that he was getting only those he wanted. He wanted Marsh's *Advent Harbinger*.

In this letter, Bond said he believed in the literal interpretation of the scriptures and conditional immortality. He alluded to a scandal brewing in Boston over the ownership details of the *Advent Herald*, a paper owned by J.V. Himes, who had stated that the Adventist movement owned it. Also entangled in this issue was the questionable behavior of a W.J. Johnson who had initiated a petition bearing names of persons *who did not sign it*. Men by the names of Needham and Judson objected to being on the petition.

In 1851, Newell Bond attended the Rochester Union Conference that had been called by Joseph Marsh and several others who believed in the Age to Come. This conference was held following the disastrous New England Conference hosted by J.V. Himes, ostensibly to squash the rumors about his mismanagement of the bookstore, and his editorship of the *Advent Herald*. The effect of the New England Conference was really to cast out anyone who believed in the doctrine of Age to Come. From that point the Age-to-Come movement was definitely separate from the mainline Adventist movement that descended from William Miller. The Adventist branch of Millerism eventually became the Advent Christian denomination (1860).

Newell Bond stood staunchly beside Joseph Marsh, as did Owen R.L Crozier, who first articulated the doctrine of "Jesus cleansing the sanctuary" to explain the Bitter Disappointment. While Crozier withdrew from that idea within a year, the doctrine lingered and was popularized by the Seventh-day Adventists.

As the attendees of the Rochester Union conference prepared to return to their individual homes and congregations, Elder Bond spoke of the blessing of unity that he had experienced with this group. He spoke also of his hope that all had been filled with the spirit of unity so it would sustain them when they returned to their home churches, "where only two or three" would agree with them, understanding that it would be harder to carry on in isolation. Bond emphasized that the Lord would carry them through in the work they were dedicated to do.

Members in attendance at the first organizational meeting of the Cleveland church in addition to the Bonds were Bro. and Sr. Maurice Joblin, Bro. and Sr. George Elton, and Bro. and Sr. Robert McLauchlan. Mark Allen was also there but more as a guest than a regular member. Allen had been a colleague of Joseph Marsh, but had been critical of him for being too liberal.

Newell Bond and the congregation purchased a building in November 1865, and moved it to a lot on old Ohio Street. At some point, the name of this street was changed to Central Avenue.

In 1871 the Bonds relocated to Washington City. Here they may have fellowshipped with Allan Magruder. While in the Capitol, Newell posed a question on prophecy to *The Restitution* which was quoted later in a book by Dr. J.P. Weethee entitled *The Eastern Question*. Bond asked: "What does the drying up of the Euphrates symbolize?" In this scholarly work, Weethee thoroughly discussed the theology of the Age-to-Come movement including the role of the Euphrates.

Shortly thereafter, the Bonds wintered farther south in Hendersonville, North Carolina. Here they fellowshipped with a nucleus of Age-to-Come believers, others of whom were followers of Joseph Marsh and some of the Christadelphian persuasion. Elder Bond baptized Baptist minister Enoch Anderson, father of J.H. Anderson, whose family has remained Church of God. It is an interesting fact that another North Carolina youngster, Robert Huggins, was drawn into the work of the Gospel of the Kingdom during that era. Huggins' parents leaned toward the Christadelphian interpretation of prophecy, and following their lead, Robert began to serve in Christadelphian ministry. He went on to edit *The Restitution*, and to pastor the Church of God in Cleveland that had been started by Newell Bond and Maurice Joblin.

The Bonds lived in the Southeast and worked with that conference for ten years. By 1880 they had declared Hendersonville their permanent address. Daughter Josephine resided with them. Newell reported that he and Mary had ridden 17 miles over rough roads—horse and buggy or horse only being the primary modes of transportation—took their lunch, and stayed the day in order to provide preaching ministry without pay. They then arrived home at sunset.

That kind of ministry demonstrates dedication and endurance. Newell was past 80 when he regularly engaged in that traveling ministry. Details of his death and burial are not known.

See Allen, Mark
Anderson, Enoch
Chaplin, Stedman
Huggins, Robert G. (20th)
Joblin, Maurice
Marsh, Joseph
McLauchlan, Robert
Reed, H.V.
Weethee, J.P.

Bibliography: Ancestry.com U.S. Census. Ohio. Cuyahoga. Cleveland Ward 4. 1870; U.S. Census. Henderson. Hendersonville. District 98. 1880; Cigliano, Jan. *Showplace of America: Cleveland's Euclid Ave.1850-1910*, retrieved from Google Books, Sept. 30, 2010; Graham, David. *Wisdom and Power* July 1992, quoting from various *Restitution* issues; "Letter from Bond to Marsh," *Advent Harbinger and Bible Advocate*, Sept. 21, 1850; "Ohio Name Index", retrieved from LibraryWorld.net Dec. 2007; Conference announcement. *Millennial Harbinger and Bible Expositor.* June 10, 1863; Report. General Association of the Churches of God, Syracuse, New York, *Millennial Harbinger and Bible Expositor*, Thos. Newman, editor, 1863; Weethee, Dr. J.P. *The Eastern Question.* Self-published. J.L. Trauger, printer. Columbus 1887.

Booth, Fannie Collins
b. April 21, 1841
d. February 9, 1919

Fannie Collins was born in England and wed John Booth, an Englishman. The historical record indicates they were not related to John Wilkes Booth, President Lincoln's assassin.

The family farm was located near Chana in Ogle County, Illinois. They attended the rurally located Antioch Church just west of their farm on Flagg Road, about three miles south of Chana. It is thought this church met in the Antioch schoolhouse. This school was used into the early 1950s. After being closed by the school district it was purchased and moved to a nearby farm to be used as a mother-in-law's house.

Fannie was baptized at the Antioch Church of God. Mrs. Booth resided in Aurora but in later years lived with her daughter. At her death, she was buried in the Washington Grove Cemetery a mile west of the old Antioch church site beside her husband. F.E. Siple conducted her funeral service.

See Marsh, Grace (20th)
Stilson, Rolland (20th)

Bibliography: Cline, Lois, Interview with Jan Stilson, July 15, 2009; *The Restitution Herald*. Feb. 19, 1919; Schartz, Marilyn Hardesty was a classmate at Antioch school who furnished information and location of the present building. Spring, 2007.

Booth, Lyman
b. April, 1849
d. 1930?

Lyman Booth was born to John W. and Harriet Booth in Indiana but grew up at Paynes Point, Illinois. He was the eldest son of seven children, three boys and four girls. His father farmed in Pine Rock Township. His sisters included Mrs. John Cross who lived on Flagg Road in Ogle County, and Mrs. J.H. Williams, mother of Grace Marsh Williams.

Lyman probably learned his ABCs and his Bible from the instruction of A.J. Eychaner who was his neighbor at Paynes Point. Eychaner taught at the Slagle School and preached at schoolhouses throughout Ogle County. In adulthood Lyman Booth became a writer. He loved to contribute to the pages of *The Restitution* and *The Restitution Herald*. His name appears in nearly every issue. He wrote well and was reported to be an excellent Bible student.

Lyman married Allie from Lee County, and they chose to reside in Dixon, Illinois, where Lyman engaged in business. As many preachers and writers of the day, Lyman earned his living by means other than as a full-time clergyman. He was a grocery salesman by trade well into his old age. Mrs. Lyman Booth operated a boarding house to supplement the family income. There was a strong congregation of Church of God believers in that city with whom they worshipped. Lyman may have served as pastor of that congregation.

In December 1874, Lyman placed a notice in *The Restitution* telling of the Illinois Conference meeting from December 18th continuing through Sunday the 20th, to be held at the Antioch Church of God south of Chana and North of Ashton, Illinois. People who came to Ashton by train were to wait there to be conveyed to the conference in a carriage. J.M. Stephenson was to be guest speaker at this conference.

Booth wrote several books. The first that we know of was produced from a series of articles written for *The Restitution Herald* in 1921 and 1922. It contained at least 30 articles or chapters. He chose Christian Faith Ministries as his publishing house, which was located in West Lebanon, Indiana. He entitled the book *Acquaintance with God*. A second book, published in paperback, was *The Mystery of Iniquity Explained: Biblical Exposition of the Devil*. The National Bible Institute at Oregon, Illinois, published this book in 1929.

See Cross, John
Eychaner, A.J.

Bibliography: Ancestry.com. U.S. Census. Illinois, Ogle. Pine Rock. Paynes Point. 1870; and, Illinois. Lee. Dixon. Dist. 13. 1900 (verifies birthdate) 1910 and 1930; Booth, Lyman. *Mystery of Iniquity*. NBI. Oregon, Il. 1929; Cline, Lois. Interview with Jan Stilson, July 14, 2009; *Restitution* conference notice, Dec. 9, 1874; and *Restitution Herald*, numerous issues 1911-1930; Rankin, Arlen, general assistance in identifying this Lyman Booth from various other Lyman Booths in America.

Bouk, Peter Henry
b. March 25, 1824
d. January 4, 1916

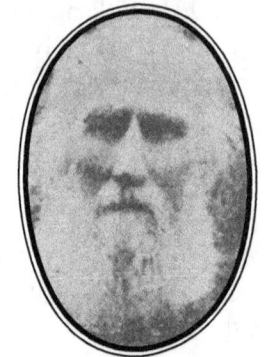

Peter Bouk was from Pelham, Ontario, a Canada West territory. He was the sixth of John and Julia Bouk's seven children. He lived his whole life within ten miles of Thorold Township. He married Mary Ann Damude at age 21. The Bouks had 12 children.

The work at Pelham was the beginning of the work of the Church of God at Fonthill, Ontario. Peter believed in the second coming of Christ, and the establishment of the Kingdom of God on earth. He particularly loved the Age to Come doctrine, which he had never heard explained in the Fonthill Baptist church where he first served as a trustee. When he first heard the Gospel of the Kingdom from Elder J.H. Shipman, Advent clergyman, at the Bouk school house in 1845, he accepted it. The theme of the sermon that evening was, "That the restored earth would be the future home of God's people." From that time on Peter Bouk became a diligent Bible student. He was immersed into the One Faith on February 2, 1846, at age 22.

The 1851 Canadian Census specifically listed Bouk as being "Millerite Clergy." The 1861 Census of Thorold Township listed Peter Bouk, his wife and ten children as "Second Advent." The earliest church record identified itself on July 20, 1862, as "Second Advent Church." The 150th anniversary booklet reported that there were 49 members in the church in 1861. While it might be thought that Peter was firmly in the camp of the Millerites long after the Bitter Disappointment (1844), it can be seen by his association with Joseph Marsh that he was specifically a disciple of Age to Come from 1845 forward.

Peter Bouk wrote occasionally to Joseph Marsh in *The Advent Harbinger* to inform him, "there are still a few faithful here," who loved the Gospel of the Kingdom and rejoiced to hear it.

The congregation at Fonthill met in the Hoover School on Holland Road until 1858. That year a church building was constructed east of Fonthill at Hurricane and Canboro Roads. It was dedicated by C.F. Sweet, of Albion, New York. Sweet also preached there frequently, as did R.V. Lyon, Niagara Falls, New York; O.R.L. Crozier, Rochester, New York; and J.B. Cook, Rochester, New York. Meetings were held there until 1890.

In 1891 the congregation relocated to the upstairs of the Dalton Hall on Route 20. In 1905, Peter issued an invitation to the Advent meeting at Fonthill. At that time, F.L. Austin was living in Niagara Falls, just a few miles from Fonthill. Austin began a study group at Fenwick, 25 miles from Fonthill. He was pastor of the churches in both locations. In the spring of 1908, the work at Fenwick was dropped and the people joined with Fonthill to build a new church in Fonthill. In 1908 a cement block building was constructed across the street from the Hall. There were 56 names on the membership list when the doors were opened on the new church.

Elder Bouk greatly assisted the congregation at Fonthill in building the church house. He reported to *The Restitution* in 1909 regarding the dedication service:

> The Church of God at Fonthill was dedicated on February 14, when despite disagreeable weather, large congregations were present at the services which were conducted in the morning and evening, by Bro. L.E. Conner of Cleveland, and F.L. Austin of Fonthill. Many were present from Niagara Falls and St. Catharine and these stayed for all the services. Meals were served in the basement of the church at noon and six o'clock and even after the evening service. About 250 meals were served throughout the day.
>
> The cost of building the church was about $3,500 and most of this had been previously subscribed, but during the day between $700 and $800 was raised, so that the church is practically free from debt. The money Sunday was raised in fifteen minutes, among the subscriptions being three of $100 each. In design and structure the new church has called forth many expressions of admiration, and the people of Fonthill are to be congratulated on having such a church in their midst.

This was the church home until a new building was built in 1968 on Pancake Lane.

Bouk's daughter, Mary Catherine, married James Albert Railton, a gentleman farmer. He evidently rented his land to farmers and lived off the proceeds. Peter's grandson, young John Railton, moved to Oregon, Illinois, in 1924 to attend Bible Training School.

Peter Bouk died at James A. Railton's home in the full assurance of the triumph of the resurrection. F.L. Austin, pastor at Fonthill, officiated at the service and wrote the obituary.

Elder Peter Bouk was part of a legacy and lineage that has lived on in the Church of God through the Railton, Bolhous and Turner families. Howard Shute, a former director on the Board of the Church of God General Conference, was Peter's great-grandson. Some books from the Bouk library are now part of the archival collection at Atlanta Bible College. Peter Bouk's great-great-great-granddaughter, Jennifer Shute Winner, has agreed to assist in archival preservation of important Church of God materials at the Atlanta Archives. Jennifer is wife of Jesse Winner, producer of the Cogcast.org internet radio program.

In 1996, the Church of God at Fonthill, Ontario, held a 150th Anniversary celebration to celebrate Peter Bouk's baptism. Church records date as far back as 1862.

See Austin, F.L. (20th)
    Cook, J.B.
    Lyon, R.V.
    Marsh, Joseph
    Railton, James A.

Bibliography: Ancestry.com. 1861 Census of Canada, record for Peter Bouk states he was born 1832; Ancestry.com. U.S. Census. New Hampshire. Grafton. Lisbon, 1850 record for J. H. Shipman; Austin, F.L. "Peter Bouk Obituary." *The Restitution Herald.* Jan. 26, 1916; Bolhous, Stephen. Interview in Spring 2005 and 2006; Bolhous, Stephen, *Glad Tidings Church of God Abrahamic Faith, 1846-1996,* published by the church, Fonthill, Ontario, 1996; Letter to Joseph Marsh, *Advent Harbinger and Bible Advocate,* April 17, 1852; Randall, Clyde, *Historical Waymarks of the Church of God,* Oregon, Il. 1976; *The Restitution.* April 6, 1905; March 3, 1909; *The Restitution Herald.* 1948; Fonthill, Ontario, October 7, 1908 History Document, part of the Archives of Atlanta Bible College which gives details of history and people from Peter Bouk's own recollection; Winner, Jennifer. "Peter Bouk", paper presented at 2010 History Conference at North Hills Church of God, Springfield, OH.

Bowman, Peyton Green
    b. September 15, 1809
    d. 1891

Peyton Bowman was born and raised in Shenandoah County, Virginia. He converted to Christ on June 21, 1828, after which he joined the Methodist Episcopal Church. He married Ellen Lartigue Tobin (August 22, 1823-1879)

and they had one daughter, Virginia Caroline Bowman (b. December 16, 1845) and one son, Peyton G. Jr., born in 1854 in South Carolina. Peyton Senior had moved to South Carolina in 1832 and received his exhorter's license the following year. By 1834 he was received in the Methodist Conference in that state as a regular minister.

I.C. Wellcome records in his history that Reverend Bowman was an itinerate preacher who saw "thousands of souls converted and united with the Methodist E. Church." In 1854, Bowman was appointed as a missionary to the plantation slaves across South Carolina. He preached every Sunday to as many as 2,000 slaves, and during his visits he taught children, visited the sick and elderly and gave them Bibles and hymnbooks so they could practice their reading.

On a trip through the North, Bowman was introduced to Second Adventism. He was especially taken with the ideas of Conditional Immortality accompanying that movement. But this doctrine caused trouble among his Methodist colleagues back home, so much so, that in 1871 his presiding officer brought charges against him and Bowman was ousted from the Methodist fellowship.

Bowman continued to minister to Blacks in the south and now he began to teach them about the Second Coming of Christ. He asked for help from the *World's Crisis*, an Advent Christian paper. He asked them to send him a preacher who would accompany Bowman on his rounds of the "colored communities." William Sheldon responded and reported later that Bowman was a man who could not be bound by any theological "hand-cuffs," and "will preach what he believes…fearlessly."

Bowman moved to Pennsylvania and in the early 1880s pastored at the Salem, Pennsylvania, Church of God, a Second Adventist body that may have been affiliated with the Age to Come or One Faith churches. It is thought that he was affiliated with Age to Come, for he was a delegate at the 1888 Philadelphia General Conference and elected to serve on a committee.

Several delegates addressed the Conference body. Peyton spoke about Paul's remarks from I Corinthians 1:30, "But by His doing you are in Christ Jesus, who became to us wisdom from God, and righteousness and sanctification, and redemption." Bowman said the Church of God in Christ has a mighty destiny to come from the east, west, north and south to make a covenant with Christ. Those who overcome will judge and rule and govern with Christ.

Bowman also had early contact with Charles Taze Russell, who commented on Bowman's Second Advent message by saying, "I well remember hearing you speak as a champion of Second Adventism in Philadelphia [probably in 1876]... I then thought you honest and longed to have you see 'the way of God more perfectly.'" Judging from that, Bowman's beliefs did not line up with Russell's, yet Bowman did distribute Russell's book, *The Plan of the Ages*.

At the 1888 Conference, Bowman gave his address as North Carolina, but by January 1889, he relocated to Brooklyn. He was also named honorary vice president of the Board of Directors along with Benjamin Wilson, California; S. A. Chaplin, Indiana; William Brockman, Toronto; and N. J. Morgan, Virginia. Bowman notified the brethren through several successive issues of *The Restitution* in 1889 that he had relocated to Brooklyn and invited correspondence.

Bruce Schulz has recorded two notices from an 1889 *Brooklyn Eagle* indicating that Peyton was the guest speaker at the Church of the Blessed Hope, also an Age to Come or One Faith congregation. This may have been the same congregation in Brooklyn where John D. Donaldson was pastor or it could have been a second group. At the 1888 Philadelphia Conference, the Church of God (inheritors of the Age to Come and One Faith churches) voted to use either Church of the Blessed Hope or Church of God in Christ Jesus for names of local churches.

Shortly thereafter, Peyton began to preach in Blythedale, Maryland, north of Baltimore and south of Lancaster, Pennsylvania, in a Black church, The Household of Faith. This congregation may have been an Age to Come congregation for it was not affiliated with the Advent Christians. Edward and George W. Jackson organized the church on October 2, 1877. George was a former slave who was manumitted by joining a Black regiment during the Civil War.

The circumstances of Peyton Bowman's death, including the location, and his burial details are unknown. He must have been a widower for a number of years as there is no record of his remarrying following his wife's death several years before his own. Even the family genealogies list his death information as "Unknown," although the year 1891 is firm.

See Chaplin, S.A.
Morgan, N.J.
Wilson, Benjamin

Bibliography: Bowman, P.G. Notice of address change, *The Restitution*, Jan. 7, 1889; Bowman, P.G. "Discourse by P.G. Bowman," 1888 Philadelphia Conference address, *The Restitution*, S.A. Chaplin, ed. Plymouth, In. Feb. 6, 1889; Gibson, Steve, "Descendents of Cornelius Tobin" from the website: http://www.bexargenealogy.com, retrieved Oct. 24, 2010; Schulz, Bruce, e-mail to JStilson Oct. 23, 2010, with notes from a forthcoming book with tentative title, *The Development of Identity among Readers of Zion's Watch Tower: 1879-1887*; Salley, A.S. Jr. "The Full Text of the Calhoun Family of South Carolina", retrieved on October 24, 2010 from the website: www.archive.org/stream/calhounfamilyofs00lcsall/calhounfamilyofs00lcsall_djvu.txt; Wellcome, I.C. *History of the Second Advent Message*, self-published. Yarmouth, Me. 1874.

Boyer, Benjamin Franklin
b. July 5, 1835
d. April 10, 1910

Benjamin F. Boyer was born in the heart of Virginia to William and Regina Boyer. He was first married to Isabella Clem. Sylvanus Boyer was their first child. Nine other children followed, six died in infancy. After Isabella died, Benjamin married Julia McInturff (1848-1922) who bore him three more children including Benjamin Franklin, named after his father, Mary Benona, and Charles Chaplin Boyer.

B.F. grew up to become the leader of the work in the Shenandoah Valley from the 1860s forward to late in the 19th century. The Boyer families lived in Boyer's Gap at Dry Run near Seven Fountains in the heart of Fort Valley. The Fort Valley took its name from the Revolutionary War when residents were able to block the entrance of the valley and hold off the British. It was a small narrow valley down the middle of the Massanutten Mountains extending to Harrisburg, Virginia. The Boyer Gap extends west into a ridge of the mountains providing a small valley for settlement.

Benjamin wrote about his home, from which a portion is excerpted here:
> In the year 1898, [these brethren] built a neat and comfortable house of worship at Maurertown, Shenandoah County, Virginia, which they named Immanuel, and in the year 1899 dedicated it to God for the use of the members of the Church of God in Christ Jesus.

The church land was purchased from Robert and Sarah Orndorff of Maurertown and was situated on the hill overlooking the valley. The new building was dedicated by Samuel Wilson of Elizabeth, New Jersey, on June 18, 1899. Wilson was a nephew to Benjamin Wilson of Geneva, Illinois. For his service as dedicatory speaker, Samuel Wilson was paid $25. Following the dedication service, a basket dinner was held on the church lawn. Participants had to sit on the grass or stand to eat. The congregation had invited H.V. Reed for the occasion, but he did not arrive until later in the week.

The first officers of the Maurertown Church were J.E. Boyer, D.S. Boyer and H.F. Boyer, trustees. John D. Boyer was the pastor from the time of its organization until 1915. In 1916 the congregations at Dry Run and Maurertown arranged for J.H. Anderson to preach for the next two years for $750 per year with parsonage and fuel furnished. Anderson continued working in Virginia for three more years receiving additional compensation each year through 1921.

After Benjamin Franklin Boyer's death, his son, Sylvanus (1858-1927) was active in the work at Maurertown. Sylvanus married Mary Rebecca and they had ten children. Their son, David, died on Aug 28, 1924, of complications from a ruptured appendix after six weeks of illness.

See   Anderson, J.H.
  Boyer, John D.
  Boyer, William
  Marsh, G.E. (20th)
  Reed, H.V.
  Wilson, Samuel

Bibliography: Ancestry.com. U.S. Federal Census. Shenandoah. Virginia. 1850; Boyer, Dorothy who furnished the "75th Anniversary and Homecoming of the Maurertown Church of God in Christ Jesus, Oct. 27, 1974," by James Mattison; *The Restitution Herald*. Sept. 16, 1924; Notes about Dedication of Fort Valley Church of God, *The Restitution Herald*, Sydney Magaw, editor, Oregon, Illinois, August 20, 1949.

Boyer, John D.
b. November 1, 1837
d. April 10, 1916

Elder John D. Boyer was born in the Shenandoah Valley to William and Regina Boyer who loved the message of the future Kingdom of God on earth. John learned the Scriptures from an early age, father teaching son, and elder brother teaching younger children. John was one of 11 children, eight boys and three girls. His older brother, Elder Benjamin F. Boyer, baptized him in 1862. He very likely was baptized in the Shenandoah River during the time that the Civil War was raging in that area. He became a member of the Church of God at Seven Fountains in the Fort Valley.

The record indicates that John Boyer was the local minister at Maurertown from its organization until 1915 when his health began to fail. Maurertown is a small village a few miles north of Woodstock. J.D. Boyer lived near Woodstock, Virginia, the county seat, and probably was a farmer of good reputation in his community.

For many years he worked as elder to spread the Gospel in Virginia and West Virginia. His obituary writer said, "His ministry was given as a matter of love for the truth, and there are many who will remember him as the one who taught them the truth and inducted them into Christ by baptism."

Unfortunately, many historical records from the Virginia Conference formation and the growth of the Fort Valley and Maurertown churches were lost long ago to fire. Pastors J.R. LeCrone and James Mattison reconstructed some of that history, and their writings have survived. Added to that are personal comments by Eugene Stilson who was pastor in Virginia from 1963 to 1967.

Richard LeCrone reported that during the mid-19th century the Boyer family learned about the Age to Come through the writings of Joseph Marsh in New York and Benjamin Wilson in Illinois. Further, the passionate preaching of Pilgrim Joseph Thomas who frequently stayed at Peter Boyer's home, William's grandfather, greatly contributed to the spiritual life and growth of the family.

John D. Boyer fell critically ill in the fall of 1915 and prayers were requested in *The Restitution Herald*. Being old and frail, he expired in the spring of 1916.

See   Boyer, Benjamin F.
  Jones, Wiley
  Marsh, Joseph
  Thomas, Joseph

Bibliography: Ancestry.com. U.S. Federal Census. Shenandoah. Virginia. Dist. 58. 1850; and 1910; Boyer, Dorothy from the "75th Anniversary and Homecoming of the Maurertown Church of God in Christ Jesus, Oct. 27, 1974," by James Mattison; *The Restitution Herald*. Nov. 1915, May 17, 1916. Sept. 17, 1946; Thomas, Joseph. *The Life of the Pilgrim*. Self published in Virginia. 1817. Summarized in *The Restitution Herald* by Sydney Magaw, Sept. 17, 1946.

Boyer, William
b. October 13, 1804
d. July 12, 1889

A. The Church in Fort Valley
B. The Influence of the Pilgrim

After his marriage to Regina Stickley (1810-1889), William settled his family at Cedar Creek, Virginia. They joined the Walnut Springs congregation, known as the Christian church. William, his wife and their 11 children were born in Virginia and resided most of their lives in Shenandoah County. The Boyers' had eight sons and three daughters.

William moved the family to Dry Run in the Fort Valley in 1836. This move isolated them from their church, so they initiated family Bible study, from which they realized none of the orthodox churches were following apostolic teaching. This included the Walnut Springs Christian church. They learned from their study that the apostles practiced immersion in the name of Jesus Christ (Acts 2:38), that immortality is not inherent but obtainable at the resurrection, that the earth, not the sky, is the eternal home of the saints, and that the wicked must undergo utter destruction, not eternal suffering.

One of William's sons was Andrew Jackson Boyer, whose son Carmel Boyer provided much of the information for this article.

A. The Church in Fort Valley

When the Dry Run church was organized at the Fort Valley meeting house in November 1878, it chose the name Church of God in Christ Jesus. The statement of faith said:

> We agree to take the Bible, the whole Bible, and nothing but the Bible for our rule of faith, and practice in worship and discipline; therefore, we teach and practice under the Covenant, established at Jerusalem, 33 A.D., with all essential ordinances, exemplified and sustained by the apostles, who delivered to the people the decrees for to keep; and, therefore, we immerse in water in the name of Jesus Christ for the remission of sins all who come to us and confess a willingness to obey the gospel.

The membership agreed that the highest title for teacher should be Elder. An Elder could serve as preacher but he was not to receive a fixed salary. Other church officers would be deacon, treasurer, clerk and sexton. Officers were appointed as follows: William Boyer, B.F. Boyer and John D. Boyer, elders; D.S. Boyer, deacon; Harvey Coverstone, clerk; and Joseph Ritenour, sexton. These appointments were reported to *The Restitution Herald* by J.R. LeCrone nearly 60 years after the document went into effect.

The church board went on record through the organizational statement as being opposed to any kind of military service. The Boyer men shared a strong belief in conscientious objection. In tracing military records in Virginia for the War of 1812 and the Civil War, one notes the obvious absence of the Boyer name.

As there were family and friends throughout the Shenandoah Valley including Fort Valley, in 1898 they joined to build a large church at Maurertown, located between Strasburg and Woodstock. They called it Immanuel. In 1899, the family of believers dedicated it for members of the Church of God in Christ Jesus.

The history of the formation of the Church of God in Virginia is fragmented because many original documents were lost. The information for this encyclopedia entry comes from a summary of historical records sent to Sydney Magaw in 1946 by Pastor J.R. LeCrone, and Carmel Boyer, William Boyer's grandson. It was subsequently printed in *The Restitution Herald* that same year. Pastor James Mattison also wrote an interesting history for the 75th Anniversary and Homecoming at Maurertown in 1974.

B. The Influence of the Pilgrim

The book entitled *The Life of the Pilgrim* is the journal kept by Joseph Thomas during his struggle as a Bible student and preacher from 1806 when he was 16 until 1817 when he was 26.

The writings of The Pilgrim are pertinent because his ministry preceded the Restoration Movement, the Millerite Movement, the Christadelphians and the formation of any Churches of God. He believed that all Christians were part of the Church of God, and he remained separate from any denominational affiliation because his beliefs were different from orthodox teachings.

Thomas initially believed that the Kingdom of God was "present in our hearts." In his early messages one does not find a strong prophetic statement about Jesus coming again to establish the kingdom. Yet his language seems to change after his association with Peter Boyer at Kernstown, Virginia, a small community just south of Winchester.

Thomas visited the Boyer home several times from 1815-1816, during which times he seems to have had satisfactory discussions with Peter Boyer. After this period, Thomas began to write about preaching the biblical messages of "the Gospel of his Kingdom." Other preachers of his day were preaching Revival. For his unusual beliefs, young Thomas faced harsh persecution and was called *Crazy Thomas*.

Study of the US Census data indicates that Peter Boyer of Shenandoah County was William's father. Although there are Boyers throughout the states of Pennsylvania and Virginia during the Revolutionary War, only one Peter Boyer lived near Kernstown.

The strong legacy of the Boyer family in the Shenandoah Valley over the last 200 years illustrates that they espoused earnest Bible study and emphasized the truths therein–truths which were unacceptable to orthodoxy.

William Boyer faithfully raised a family of believers and spread the Word throughout the valley. Due to his steadfastness, the Church of God in that locale became a viable alternative for worship. William and Regina are buried in the Boyer Cemetery on the Samuel H. Boyer farm in Boyer's Gap, Fort Valley, the homestead of the Boyer family.

See Boyer, Benjamin F.
Boyer, Andrew Carmel (20th)
Boyer, W.E. (20th)
LeCrone, J. Richard (20th)
Thomas, Joseph

Bibliography: Ancestry.com. U.S. Census. Virginia. Shenandoah. Eastern District. 1830; Registration Record for World War 2. of Andrew C. Boyer. Stephens City, Va. age 60; Boyer, B.F. "A Return to Apostolic Christianity", as reprinted as "Early Virginia Records." *The Restitution Herald*, April 23, 1946; Boyer Cemetery. www.csonner.net/boyr.html; Boyer, Dorothy by e-mail and correspondence Spring 2007 who forwarded "75th Anniversary and Homecoming of the Maurertown Church of God in Christ Jesus Oct. 27, 1974," by James Mattison; Magaw, Sydney. Review of *The Life of the Pilgrim*. *The Restitution Herald*. Sept. 17, 1946; Thomas, Joseph. *The Life of the Pilgrim*. Full text of this book: www.mun.ca/rels/restmov/texts/Thomas/lpjt/LPJT01.htm.

Bradley, Alfred Seth
b. February 12, 1850
d. October 22, 1928

A. **Church of Christ Affiliation**
B. **The Great Debater**
C. **Bradley's Influence Continues**

Alfred Bradley was born in Caldwell City, Hopkins County, Kentucky, to Enoch Bradley. Alfred's mother likely died at his birth, as she does not appear three months later in the 1850 Census. The family relocated to Missouri and then to Franklin County, Illinois, during Alfred's childhood. Their home was near Rend Lake, a notable landmark in Franklin County in southern Illinois, which is near the present-day Eldorado Church of God.

After a few years, the family relocated to Arkansas where A.S. Bradley spent the remainder of his youth. He met Fannie Sparkman of Independence County, Arkansas. They were married on July 24, 1874. They had nine children, three of whom survived to adulthood. Young Bradley began his adult ministry as a Church of Christ preacher in Arkansas.

He and Fannie moved to Texas where he began preaching the Gospel of the Kingdom and name of Jesus Christ almost immediately. While he was touring Texas to preach, Fannie worked as a hotel manager in Justice Precinct. After a few years, they settled permanently in Mullin, a community in Mills County near Goldwaithe. Mrs. W.H. Reeves of Mullin stated that Bradley began working with the Mullin church in 1899. Early meetings at Mullin were held at the Williams ranch under a tree and beside a stream.

A biographical look at A.S. Bradley's career, published in *The Restitution Herald* in 1922, stated that he had been preaching for the Church of God for 29 years. That would date his conversion to 1893.

A. Church of Christ Affiliation

The history of the Gatesville, Texas, Church of God noted that A.S. Bradley was called by Mr. Robert A. Warren to assist in a debate in or around the year 1890. The debate went to Bradley. As a result, many people came into the new work. Church of Christ scholars believe A.S. Bradley was still affiliated with the *Firm Foundation* at that time.

Bradley may have come to his persuasion on conditional immortality without breaking with his Church of Christ affiliation. One of his more famous debates took place against C.R. Nichol, a Church of Christ man. This heated dialogue was held at Rule, Texas, April 20-22, 1906. Nichol was a Christian and A.S. Bradley was hailed as a materialist. W.W. Golden reported the debate, and Mrs. C.R. Nichol of Clifton, Texas, published his report through McQuiddy Press in Nashville 1907. A copy of the book exists in the Archives of Atlanta Bible College in McDonough, Georgia.

Other men that Bradley debated included J.W. Chisum, W.S. Black, Dr. G.A. Trott, J.D. Tant, W.A. Schultz, Joe S. Warlick, Joe Lockhart, L.W. Davis, Sowell and many others.

The writer of the Gatesville Church of God history says, "A.S. Bradley, known as a power house for the truth, traveled many miles teaching and contending for the truth." His teaching, preaching and writing were popular and effective. He was so influential in what he did, that the Church of Christ editor of *The Eye Opener* from 1904-1908 railed against him for being a "materialist." In brief, materialism is defined as focusing on the mortality of man, the sleep of the dead and the resurrection of the righteous to receive incorruptibility at the coming of Christ.

Because Bradley switched denominations, a lot of people who had loved him followed him into the Church of God conference throughout Arkansas, Oklahoma and northern Texas. He worked with William Gibbs and assisted him with the publication of *The Word and Work*. Like Bradley, Gibbs came out of the Church of Christ. Both were faithful to preaching the Gospel of

Alfred S. Bradley, portraits through the years.
Photo from Hans Rollman, used with permission

the Kingdom of God, and they were persecuted for it week after week through repeated hostile diatribes in the opposing Church of Christ publication, *The Eye Opener*. This did not deter them, however. In fact, it seemed to inspire them to greater and grander efforts to share the Word about the approaching Kingdom of God and the return of Christ to establish it.

In 1903 the congregation built a small church north of Ater on Warren's property and called it Warren Chapel. Warren served as pastor with A.S. Bradley as part-time pastor for a number of years.

B. The Great Debater

In 1900, an editor named Tant reported that the Church of Christ in Texas had been having trouble because of the teaching of conditional immortality (by another group) for 20 years. A.S. Bradley and William Gibbs were responsible for at least *some* of that problem. When they left the Church of Christ, it was a gain for the Church of God.

An interesting story about the ridicule that Bradley endured is illustrated by a comment in the notes about Texas History made by R.B. Taylor. Taylor must have attended several of Bradley's debates. He said:

> Bradley debated with Dr. G.A. Trott, J.D. Tant, S.A. Ribble, Joe Lockhart, W.A. Schultz in Mullin, Tohaka, Tokio, Rule and Glory. With Schultz, a little dog played around the benches during the debate and Schultz said 'Bradley believes when a man dies he will die just like a dog.' He (Bradley) says 'There is no difference in death.'

Because Bradley had intimate knowledge of Church of Christ doctrines and interpretation, he was an excellent debater for the Church of God. He knew what the Bible taught and he knew each denomination's interpretation.

In 1923, he debated T.J. Whitt, a minister from the Church of Christ at San Saba, Texas. Bradley argued *pro* the mortal nature of man (materialism). Whitt argued *con*. They also debated on the topic of the Kingdom of God. Bradley in favor of it being in the future on the earth, and Whitt that it was already present in believers' hearts. The debate continued from March 23 until March 27.

In October 1920, Bro. Bradley preached nightly at the South Texas Conference. A tent was ordered, but it didn't arrive until after the preaching began. He was so effective at that meeting the conference members were inspired to hire him as evangelist the next year. Bro. Bradley was on the list of recognized ministers in the Church of God after the organization of a national General Conference in 1921. He toured Texas in 1922 with Bro. S.J. Lindsay, former editor of *The Restitution Herald*, who had enormous influence throughout the Church of God. Bradley preached at the Texas Conference in the summer of 1922, at age 71. Despite his advanced age, he attended the first General Conference meeting ever to be held at Oregon, Illinois, summer, 1922, which was in the second year of the new national organization. On his return journey, he stopped to attend the Iowa Conference.

C. Bradley's Influence Continues

Recently, Michael W. Casey, a noted scholar at Pepperdine University, said that the Church of Christ experienced difficulties with Adventism during the 1890s. He wrote, "Now it appears that the Adventists among the Churches of Christ may have gone into what became the Church of God Abrahamic Faith." Casey visited the Archives at Atlanta Bible College to copy William Gibbs' *Word and Work* 1904-1907 which speaks extensively about Gibbs and Bradley. This rare volume has since been microfilmed for use by researchers.

After careful study, one can deduce that Church of God preachers and scholars influenced men of all faiths to examine the Scriptures carefully. A.S. Bradley certainly was a man of faith who encouraged others to read the Scriptures with discernment.

Bradley was successful in passing his newfound doctrines to his son-in-law, Tolly Roberts. James Mattison, pastor at Harlingen, Texas, in the 1940s and '50s, related this humorous story in a brief account of Texas history for the *History Newsletter* in 1994. The story concerns a 1948 incident at Ater, Texas:

> ...Brother A.S. Bradley's son-in-law, Warren "Tolly" Roberts, spoke one Sunday afternoon at Ater at the Texas Conference. The benches were on 3 sides of the pulpit. I was sitting on his right side while he faced the middle benches. He was preaching with a lot of vim and vigor. Suddenly his teeth shot out of his mouth; he caught them in mid-air and slapped them back in. I think I was the only one who saw it. From then on his sermon was more subdued.

A.S. Bradley became ill in July 1928 and slipped away quietly. Although his friends and church members knew death was imminent, it did not make the passing easier for them. The funeral service was conducted near Bradley's home in Goldwaithe by T.A. Drinkard of Clyde, Texas. Bradley was interred at Mullin Cemetery. He was survived by his wife, Fannie, and only one of his nine children, Mrs. Ava Moreland of San Antonio.

His obituary writer said, "[He] has been a faithful worker in the vineyard of the Lord. The brethren of Texas, Arkansas and other places owe their Christian hope to his faithful labors."

See Drinkard, T.A. (20th)
   Gibbs, W.L.
   Lindsay, S.J.

Bibliography: Ancestry.com U.S. Census. Kentucky. Caldwell. Dist. 1. 1850; Illinois. Franklin. Township 7 S Range 3 E. 1860; Texas. Fisher. Justice Precinct 1. 1910; U.S. Census Texas. Mills. Mullin. Dist. 170. 1920; and Texas Death Index. 1903-2000; *Eye Opener*. Firm Foundation. 1904-1908. Fragile copies of the *Eye Opener* exist at Atlanta Bible College archives. They are being scanned for use by scholars; *The Restitution Herald*, October, 1920; Jan. and Aug.

1922; Gibbs, William L ed. *The Word and Work*. 1904. The bound volume from this year is owned by Atlanta Bible College archives; Macy, Emory "Church History of the Texas Church of God", March 1954, revised by Seth Ross, February 1991; Mattison, James. Letter to *History Newsletter*, Jan Stilson, editor, May 1994; Nichols, Mrs. C.R., *The Nichols-Bradley Debate*. McQuiddy Press, Nashville, 1907, available in ABC Archives; Obituaries *The Restitution Herald*, Nov. 6, and Nov. 13, 1928; Rollman, Hans, Bradley photo, Used with permission from, Restoration Movement http://www.mun.ca/rels/restmov/restmov.html; Reeves, Mrs. W.H., "History of the Mullin Church of God", circa 1947; Secretary, Mullin Church of God; Taylor, R.B. "Notes on Texas History." This history material is filed with the Texas Conference material in the Archives of Atlanta Bible College.

Bronson, Leroy S.
b. February 17, 1841
d. December 22, 1915

Leroy lived near Buchanan, Michigan, almost his whole life. He married Jennie Barnhill Taber of Argos, Indiana. He was a successful farmer but his heart was in God's work. As a young man he studied under the direction of John Lister, H.V. Reed, J.M. Stephenson and L.H. Chase.

Bronson participated in the organization and stabilization of the fledgling Michigan State Conference. The conference organized in 1858 and held its inaugural meeting in 1859. Bronson's name appears in the minute book at the annual conference held at Prairieville in 1872, where he was appointed to the Executive Committee.

He was a prolific writer on biblical subjects and some of his tracts were widely distributed during the 19th and early 20th centuries. After retirement, in 1910, he particularly enjoyed writing for *The Restitution Herald*. In 1916, he wrote a booklet entitled *Where are the Dead?* published by the Restitution Publishing Co. located in Oregon, Illinois. It dealt with human immortality, the nature of man and future hope through resurrection. By the time this book was published in its third edition, Bro. Bronson had already passed away. This information is noted for the reader on the title page of Bronson's book. In addition to this work, he also published *Evils of the Ballroom Unveiled*, *Is the World Growing Better* and *Table Talk*.

The last article he wrote for *The Restitution Herald* was published at the end of the year on the subject of "Old 1915." He wrote, "one by one the sands have been dropping from the hour glass of time. Good bye, old years, goodbye." It was published December 22, 1915, the day he died.

Mary Woodward, his friend and colleague from Michigan, eulogized him. She stated she was reading his article when the note arrived informing her of his death. In her eulogy, she noted he would forget his own poor health in order to bring sunshine to others. Following his death, his articles continued to run in *The Restitution Herald* under his initials until the supply was finally depleted.

Supplies of Bronson's book, *Where are the Dead?*, were exhausted sometime after his death. Through the pages of *The Restitution Herald* the question was asked, "Shall we print more?" T.A. Drinkard, a southern minister, responded in the next issue with a resounding, "Yes!" He recommended printing at least 2,500 and preferably 5,000. Drinkard challenged readers to send money to S.J. Lindsay for the printing expense.

This fact speaks well of the testimony of the man who wrote the booklet, and the strength of his legacy.
See Chase, L.H.
Reed, H.V.
Stephenson, J.M.
Bibliography: Bronson, LeRoy. *Where are the Dead?* Published posthumously by his friends. 1916; *The Restitution Herald*, Nov. 1915, Jan. 13, 1916; June 15, 1920; *Michigan State Conference Records, 1858-1886*. This ledger is stored in the archives of Atlanta Bible College.

Brooks, Cyrus
b. 1840
d. April 1920

Cyrus Brooks was an English Conditionalist who edited the small paper known as *The Faith*. Notice of his death was placed in *The Last Days*, edited by Thomas Wilson from Oakland, California. The notice itself is interesting.

Mr. F. Madely, from the English Baptist Mission in Tsingehowfu, Shantung, North China, wrote "You will be regretting along with us English Conditionalists, the death of that stalwart champion, the editor of *The Faith*, Mr. Cyrus Brooks, who has passed away at nearly 80 years of age."

Madely then wrote a lengthy piece entitled "How The Great War was Foreseen" in which he quoted a piece written by Cyrus Brooks. He stated that God was raising up among the Methodists those who believed in premillennialism, and that he himself was preaching it. As not everyone in the Methodist church believed it, he came under some criticism. All this because of a piece written by Cyrus Brooks which Madely had come to believe.

Bibliography: Madely, F. "A Message from China," *The Last Days*, T. Wilson, editor, Oakland, Ca. June 1920.

Brown, Benjamin B.
b. 1817
d. October 1880?

Born in New York, B.B. Brown migrated to Waukesha, Wisconsin, in the 1840s. He was married with seven children. His father, William Brown, lived with them and farmed. Benjamin Brown was a carpenter and a joiner by trade.

He was reported to be a poor reader, but he loved the truth and subscribed to the *Advent Harbinger and Bible Advocate*, which he received through the goodness of a friend. It is not clear if reading was difficult for him because he had bad vision or because he never learned to read well.

B.B. Brown began immediately to fellowship with brethren of like faith. He attended the conference at Tyler, Illinois, and preached there twice. His messages were well received, and he was placed squarely in the camp of Age-to-Come advocates.

A letter from Brown to Marsh in the February 5, 1846, edition of the *Voice of Truth and Glad Tidings of the Kingdom* finds the eager circuit rider in Metropolis, Illinois, at the Ohio River across from Paducah, Kentucky. He missed reading *The Voice* and asked Marsh to forward him a copy. To arrive at Metropolis, he probably went to Galena, Illinois, from his home in Wisconsin, bought a ticket on a paddle wheel boat, and cruised down the Mississippi to Metropolis, his intention being to work his way overland back home. We know he remained in Metropolis until spring for Marsh received another letter from him in March, 1846. He said that he found the people hungry for the truth, and that he was preaching in a "bar-room."

In August 1850, he wrote to Marsh praising the paper stating his hunger to hear more of the truth. Brown's was the first invitation from the new frontier to come to the area to preach. He asked if R.V. Lyon could come and bring his tent with him.

Within a year Joseph Marsh came. In 1851 Marsh made a point to meet Bro. Brown when Marsh stopped at Beloit, Wisconsin. Marsh encouraged Brown to continue the work; he was accompanied in it by Bro. Sears of Lake Zurich, Illinois. Brown wrote on July 4, 1851:

> A good impression was made on the minds of this community by your labors here, and I only regret that you could not have remained longer.

> Oh, for the health I once enjoyed, so that I could 'enter into your labors' and preach the Word as formerly. But this pleasure, I fear, is not for me again to enjoy. I did hope, that by rest, I should get recruited; but I find my strength and general health is still declining. To the providence of God I must submit, and wait patiently for that rest which is in reserve for all the saints.

Although poor health hindered B.B. Brown in his pursuit of ministry, it is very evident from this letter that Joseph Marsh had exceptional influence upon the pioneer preachers of Illinois and the Midwest through his journals. This influence is apparent several years before Benjamin Wilson began his prominent ministry upon the brethren through *The Gospel Banner* and his interlitnear translation, *The Emphatic Diaglott*.

In 1870, Brown resided in Van Buren, Michigan, alone except for Amelia, aged 28. It is not known if she was a second wife or his daughter. No further word is heard about his preaching, so perhaps he gave it up due to his advancing age.

He may have died in Burlington, Iowa, in 1880 where he had been residing with one of his married children.

See Marsh, Joseph

Bibliography: Ancestry.com. U.S. Census. Wisconsin. Waukesha. 1850; U.S. Census Federal Mortality Schedules, 1850-1880 about B. Brown; Brown, B.B. "Letter to Joseph Marsh." *Advent Harbinger and Bible Advocate*, Aug. 2, 1850; Oct. 5, 1850; July 5, 1851; Brown, B.B. Reports to Joseph Marsh. *Voice of Truth and Glad Tidings of the Kingdom* April 1, 1846; Jan. 20, 1847 and March 31, 1847.

Brown, William
b. 1852
d. Unknown

William Brown was a native of Scotland. He came to America around 1885 and studied the Bible with his neighbors in Elizabeth, New Jersey, where he settled. His associates included John O. Woodruff and Samuel Wilson. He was married to Sarah and had two children, a son and a daughter.

William Brown testified in *The Restitution* that he first learned about the Kingdom from James Shaw when they were both working in a machine shop. Brown, a practicing Presbyterian, was quietly singing a hymn about heaven. James Shaw stepped up and asked him where in the Bible did it speak of sending men to heaven? Immediately Brown quoted, "in my father's house are many mansions." Shaw pointed out that the rest of that verse (John 14:2) speaks of Jesus coming again. From that point on, William Brown studied, and eventually joined the Church of God.

He reorganized the Church of God at Elizabeth, New Jersey, at the beginning of 1921. Elizabeth was 12 miles from New York City and could be reached by train. A

William Brown and Robert Huggins

group had organized there a few years earlier. Among its congregation were Samuel Wilson, Benjamin's nephew, and John O. Woodruff and his wife, all authors. The church dissolved after the death of Elder Woodruff. The new congregation which formed in 1921 was small but the members were dedicated. Some of the members were Bro. and Sr. Moore. She was a daughter of the Woodruffs. Bro. Jarvis Williams, and Bro. and Sr. Munro completed the group with the Browns.

William Brown said they intended to preach things concerning the Kingdom of God and the name of Jesus Christ. They asked for prayers as they met each Sunday afternoon. They observed communion every Sunday.

When Robert Huggins resigned his editorship of *The Restitution* at Cleveland in early 1922, William Brown, at the age of 70, was called to take over the work. It is reported that he was a Christadelphian. Perhaps because of this change of lifestyle, his wife divorced him. He moved to Cleveland in 1921. At that time, he assumed the pastorate of the church at Cleveland and became well known and beloved by the brethren in Ohio. He published *The Restitution* until it was forced to close due to loss of subscribers and loss of revenue to sustain it. It ceased being published in 1925.

See Huggins, Robert (20th)
Wilson, Samuel
Woodruff, John O.

Bibliography: Ancestry.com U.S. Census. New Jersey. Union. Elizabeth City Ward 4. Dist. 74. 1920; *Restitution* Feb. 21, 1921; March 21, 1923; April 21, 1925; Ferrell, Terry. Interview with Jan Stilson, July 14, 2009.

Burnham, Edwin
b. 1816
d. 1899?

Edwin Burnham was born in Connecticut. When he was still a young man he became convinced, along with thousands of others, that Christ's return was imminent. Mr. Burnham developed a popular following of people who loved to hear him preach the message of salvation. This style of fervent revivalistic preaching was quite popular during the Great Awakenings in New England, Jonathan Edwards being the first and most noteworthy practitioner.

At one time Elder Burnham may have been associated with the *Christ-yun* Baptists. "Christ-yun" is the term generally used to describe the Christian Connexion. These Baptists very likely had some tenets of the Christian Connexion doctrines, i.e. unity of God, baptism by immersion and possibly Age-to-Come emphasis. This is believed because Mark Allen suggested that Elder Burnham was in the camp of the Age to Come.

Mark Allen was harsh in describing people with whom he did not agree and was not overly kind toward Burnham. In relating one of his own evangelistic trips, Allen noticed his preaching consigned the audience to boredom because they were used to Burnham's fervent style of "soul-saving" sermons. Allen's very tame message of the Kingdom of God did not move them.

Allen wrote:
> Among the few who attended there seemed to be some little interest and attention with regard to the things of the kingdom and name. There is a time of great excitement among the people, with regard to the saving of souls. And not among the least popular of the religious *revival* [Mark Allen's italics] teachers was that great gun, whose name is Edwin Burnham, of Millerite and Second Advent notoriety, whom multitudes in Haverhill flocked to hear at the brick *Christ-yun* [Allen italics] Baptist chapel. This individual has for some time been supposed by many to be a thorough convert to age-to-come doctrines. But he has proved himself to be what I have for a long time believed him "a great religious circus rider," who in his endeavors to ride three horses at once (viz. the three classes of people represented by the *Prophetic Expositor* [Editor: Marsh followers], *Advent Herald* ([Editor: William Miller followers] and *World's Crisis* [Editor: Newly formed Advent Christian followers] has fallen off into the confused whirlpool of the sects, and goes from one to the other of them as they choose to call on him.

Mark Allen continued his complaint against Elder Burnham by describing his preaching style. Burnham called himself an "Independent Evangelist belonging to no particular denomination." Allen quoted Burnham as preaching, "You dried-up old bachelors and old maids, I wish God would kick you out." In another article, Allen quoted Burnham, "Miserable green, lazy, lounging backsliders! God would do just right to open the earth and let you down into hell." Also, "Feel down into your pockets; your prayers ain't worth a snap unless they go up with a jingle." He was one of the more lively preachers to be associated with Joseph Marsh.

Along with his attention-getting preaching style, Burnham practiced giving an invitation for sinners to rise up and be prayed for and to come to the inquiring meeting. Allen reported that nothing was said about the Kingdom of God and the one hope of Israel, or salvation by faith or obedience to the plan of salvation or to the name of Jesus. "What folly," Allen concluded.

Elder Burnham's name is seen several times in the pages of the literature produced by Joseph Marsh. There is no evidence that he made evangelistic trips with final reports to Marsh, and it is presumed that, while he considered the idea of Age to Come, he may not have fully embraced the understanding of the Gospel message of the Kingdom and the name of Jesus.

Possibly Edwin was an ancestor of William "Bill" Burnham (formerly of Ohio, Illinois and Florida) and children, Gary Burnham and Karen Fletcher. Bill said, "There are not many Burnhams. This man certainly could have been part of our early family." Bill and Gary have been valued employees of the Church of God General Conference from Illinois to Georgia.

 See Allen, Mark
   Marsh, Joseph

Bibliography: Allen, Mark. "A Communication" *Gospel Banner and Millennial Advocate*. July 1858; Ancestry.com. Storey County Nevada Death and Birth Records, 1862-1903, record for Edwin Burnham; Burnham, William. Telephone conversation, Feb. 17, 2010.

Burr, F.
 b. 1827
 d. Unknown

Mr. Burr was born in Connecticut but spent the majority of his adult years traveling between New York and Ontario. He was a railroad man by trade and may have used that mode of transportation to the advantage of spreading the Gospel of the Kingdom.

In 1863 the Business Committee of the General Association of the Church of God, Syracuse, New York, appointed him evangelist. He served with C.B. Turner, U.S. Algire, A.D. Street and W.S. Finn and preached primarily in Ontario and Livingston County, New York, preaching regularly at Honcoye and Bristol, Ontario, and Danville in Livingston County. In one report Burr noted receipts for a recent evangelistic tour totaled $232.80, and that he had a family of four to support plus a horse. During his travels he baptized five. Some record of Burr's travels is found in *The Millennial Harbinger and Bible Expositor,* edited by Thomas Newman. Nothing more of a personal nature is known about him.

 See Newman, Thomas

Bibliography: *Millennial Harbinger and Bible Expositor,* Thos. Newman, ed. Seneca Falls, New York, 1863 29-30.

Button, Lucius
 b. 1838
 d. March 20, 1919
Button, Emma
 b. 1845
 d. March 24, 1919

Bro. and Sr. Button were a dear couple who exemplified love for the Lord and each other. Emma Wilson was born in England and migrated with her family to Geneva, Illinois, when she was still a child. She married Lucius who was a son of Illinois. After their wedding they resided in Chicago where he pursued carpentry.

The Buttons were original members of the Church of God at Northfield, Illinois, a daughter church of the Geneva, Illinois, Church of God. Emma was the daughter of Bro. James Wilson at Geneva, and Benjamin Wilson's niece. She grew up in the Geneva church where her father was the music master who trained the young to sing.

Sr. Button died only four days after her dear husband, which shocked and saddened the members of the Church of God in Illinois.

Bibliography: Ancestry.com U.S. Census. Illinois. Cook. Chicago Ward 14. 1870; *Restitution Herald* April 9, 1919.

Bywater, John C.
 b. 1813
 d. 1900?

J.C. Bywater was from Lodi, New York. He and his wife had seven children. He evidently relocated his family to Michigan and began there as an evangelist working throughout that state, Indiana and Illinois in the period following the Bitter Disappointment.

J.C. Bywater's name is seen in the journals by Joseph Marsh, and in the minutes of the Michigan Conference of the Church of God as early as 1851. Note cards tucked into the minute book of the Michigan conference reveal that several people, including A.A. Babcock and George Needham, were working in the state as evangelists as early as 1846, a mere two years after the Millerite movement collapsed. Several more people are listed in the note cards as members of local congregations. The Michigan conference minute book is owned by the Atlanta Bible College archives and its cover bears the dates 1859-1886.

From the dates attributed to J.C. Bywater, during which he operated a tent ministry in the Detroit area, evidence suggests the early work was widespread and energetic. It took great amounts of energy and resources to raise a large tent. Generally an evangelist had no money with which to hire workers, so the workforce came from believers and friends who were interested in seeing it succeed. Where rail freight was available it was used to ship tents from one location to another. Most evangelistic sites sprang up around communities big or small that had access to a railroad.

Bywater evidently earned his primary income from his evangelistic work, which meant he lived very humbly. The US Census recorded his occupation as "Clergyman." Most evangelists were forced to work as carpenters, farmers, joiners or teachers to support their families. The small amount of surviving evidence of his life and career indicates that he tried valiantly to spread the Gospel in America.

See Babcock, A.A.
Chandler, Moses
Chittenden, H.A.
Appendix 5–Collaboration in Illinois

Bibliography: "Adventist Newspapers and Periodicals." American Antiquarian Society, Worchester, Massachusetts, J.C. Bywater, *The Watchman*, retrieved on April 30, 2008, from the website: http://www.americanantiquarian.org/Inventories/adventist.htm; Ancestry.com U.S. Census. New York. Oswego. Oswego Ward 3. 1850; U.S. Census. Illinois. Adams. Clayton. 1870; Bywater, J.C. "Politics and Religion" *Voice of Truth*, Nov. 27, 1844; Several note cards from the minute book entitled *Michigan State Conference Records 1859-1886*, specifically one note card entitled "Detroit, Mich. 1851".

Church of God and dormitory at Maurertown, Virginia
Photo provided by Rex Cain

Carter, H. Ralph
b. 1851
d. 1920?

Ralph Carter was born in Ohio and lived near Cleveland. He may have learned of the Kingdom of God from prominent Cleveland Age-to-Come leaders such as Maurice Joblin, Robert McLauchlan, Newell Bond and Mark Allen.

As a faithful believer Carter put feet under his faith by taking the Word far beyond the city limits of Cleveland. Tuttle of Plymouth, Indiana, took the photo which indicates that Elder Carter worked for the Church of God

Portrait found in Atlanta Bible College Archives, inscription on reverse:
HR Carter. Lived in Cleveland. Evangelist. Ranged as far as Kansas. Active 1880-1910.

in that state. Not only did he travel for the purpose of spreading the Gospel of the Kingdom, he also encouraged others, and he encouraged churches to be active. In 1883 he sent a note to *The Restitution* asking the churches to invite preachers to come out to preach.

In 1885 he also served in the evangelistic field at Bitter Creek, Kansas. His permanent address was Ligonier, Indiana. Ralph Carter preached at Old Union church on the Eagle Creek, and at Knox, Indiana, not far from the Eagle Creek church. It became known as "Eagle Creek Church of God" after the orthodox members departed over the issue of soul sleep around 1853. Minister Carter baptized many people there during the later 19th century but the work at Old Union/Eagle Creek went downhill and closed around 1877. J.M. Stephenson spoke of its "dissolution" in *The Restitution*, January 1878.

No other personal information about Elder Carter is known at the time of the compilation of this biography. Perhaps more may come to light to enhance the small amount of detail already known about this evangelist.

See Allen, Mark
     Bond, Newell
     Cochenour, Lewis
     Joblin, Maurice
     McLauchlan, Robert
     Stephenson, J. M.
See Also Wince, John

Bibliography: Carter, H.R. Photo, property of Archives of Atlanta Bible College; *The Restitution* Feb. 14, 1883; Nov. 1909; *The Restitution Herald,* May 5, 1919.

Castle, L'Orient
b. October 1844
d. October 23, 1912

L'Orient Castle was the wife of Asher Castle and the mother of Edith Castle Andrew. The family resided in Oregon, Illinois. S.J. Lindsay baptized L'Orient in the Rock River on August 25, 1907, whereupon she served faithfully in the newly-formed congregation of the Church of God at North Third Street.

Her line of descent includes William Andrew

L'Orient's daughter, Edith Castle Andrew

and son, Jon, of the Oregon Church of God, and daughter, Susan Andrew Lapp, wife of Jon Lapp of Minnesota.

Bibliography: Ancestry.com. U.S. Census. Illinois. Ogle. Oregon. Dist 8. 1900; William Andrew. Interview with Jan Stilson, May 2007.

Catlin, Nicholas Mead

b. 1814
d. Unknown

A. Author and Kingdom Advocate
B. Ministry in Indiana

Mead Catlin lived in Kingsbury, New York, with his parents and younger brother. He was single well into his 40s. His occupation was given as farmer in the 1850 US Federal Census. By 1860 he had married Helen, a young widow with two children.

He was associated with the Church of God at Elizabeth, New Jersey, for a period of time. This congregation was under the leadership of author John O. Woodruff.

Research revealed that Catlin knew Stedman Chaplin and Joseph Marsh in New York. The latter editor spoke of meeting with Catlin during his western tour of 1851 in the pages of *The Advent Harbinger*. Marsh also published Catlin's books.

A. Author and Kingdom Advocate

Catlin became a firm believer in the Gospel of the Kingdom and he began preaching throughout New England. He had been a Millerite but left that persuasion and accepted the teaching Joseph Marsh advocated in *The Voice of Truth* and *Advent Harbinger*. Catlin was an educated man and a good Bible student who often wrote for Marsh's papers. Catlin also wrote a definitive tract entitled *Kingdom of God or the Restoration of David's Throne*, which was heralded by J.B. Cook through the pages of Marsh's *Advent Harbinger and Bible Advocate*. Tracts in most cases were books of less than 100 pages.

Catlin said the kingdom had "oneness." It will be the kingdom of Israel, the kingdom of David, the kingdom of the son of David, the Son of God restored according to the promises. It is always referred to in the Bible as "The Kingdom," not kingdom(s) plural. In reviewing this tract, Cook said, "Its comprehensiveness seems equaled only by its minuteness." It was small but complete. A copy of this booklet is available at the Archives of Atlanta Bible College.

Catlin also authored a series of articles in 1851 for *The Advent Harbinger and Bible Advocate* entitled *The Gospel Contrasted with Protestantism*. He postulated in this series that the protestant churches had wandered away from the teaching of the Bible. To understand the Gospel message they needed but to read and study the Word of God. He discussed a number of key Gospel doctrines in the series that had eight parts. It must be reported that Henry Grew objected to Catlin's title, saying in the *Advent Harbinger* of July 26, 1851, that there should not be correlation of Protestantism to the Gospel, i.e. is Catholicism to be preferred to Protestantism? Grew conceded that some in Protestantism had fallen into error, and said the Gospel of the Kingdom should not be considered part of Protestantism.

The Gospel Banner and Millennial Advocate, published by Benjamin Wilson in Geneva, Illinois, in 1858, featured articles written by Catlin which had appeared in *The Advent Harbinger*. One article, "The Contrast between Protestantism and the Gospel," was published in *The Gospel Banner* during its 1860 edition.

B. Ministry in Indiana

Catlin traveled to central Indiana where he worked side by side with Stedman Chaplin, Ephraim Miller and Ed Hoyt to establish a lasting work there. These men were among the first evangelists in Marshall County, and one of their initial actions was to build a church at Pisgah, an old Indian village. They called this place of worship, the Church of God, and it was open to all faiths to worship there which is generally the characteristic of a Union church. It was the center of the community and offered singing schools that performed many stirring concerts such as Easter cantatas and oratorios.

Trustees of Pisgah Church of God included Patrick Logan, William Thompson and Thomas McDonald. The trustees donated the land for the building. The deed on the land was dated November 11, 1845. It was one of the first Churches of God in the nation. Old Pisgah was located four miles south of Plymouth. A few years later as Pisgah declined, the Antioch church grew to replace it. Antioch was located three miles east of Pisgah. In time, Antioch disbanded in favor of the new North Salem church two miles north of Plymouth.

Some of the research for this encyclopedia used issues of *The Restitution* that had been sent to the McDonalds and the Thompsons. These copies were passed along after many years in someone's attic to the North Salem Church of God at Plymouth. These rare issues were then donated to the Archives of the Rock River Christian College in Beloit, Wisconsin.

The Pisgah church declined as people moved away from Indiana to the west coast. After the building was no longer used as a church for the Lord's harvest, it was used as a corn crib. It can be said that it was still used to hold all the harvest.

See Chaplin, Stedman
Cook, J.B.
Marsh, Joseph
Miller, Ephraim

Bibliography: Ancestry.com U.S. Census. New York. New York Ward 1. Western Division. 1850 and 1860; U.S. Census. New York. Tioga. Tioga. 1870; Cardwell, Darrell. Pastor at N. Salem reported that church documents clarified the decline of Antioch in favor of establishing N. Salem in interview with J Stilson, July 2009; Catlin, N.M. "The

Contrast between Protestantism and the Gospel," published first in *The Advent Harbinger and Bible Advocate,* Joseph Marsh, ed. Rochester, NY. From April 7, 1851 to June 7, 1851. It was subsequently reprinted in *The Gospel Banner and Millennial Advocate,* B. Wilson, editor, Geneva, Il., Vol. 6, 1860; Catlin, N.M. *The Kingdom of God or, The Restoration of David's Throne,* Office of the *Advent Harbinger,* Joseph Marsh, editor, Rochester, NY. 1850. This copy was found and furnished to the Encyclopedia and ABC Archives by Arlen F. Rankin, Fall, 2008; Cook, J.B. "Kingdom of God" book review, *Advent Harbinger and Bible Advocate,* June 22, 1850; Marsh, Joseph. "Western Tour", *Advent Harbinger and Bible Advocate,* July 5, 1851; Advertisement in *Gospel Banner and Millennial Advocate,* Benjamin Wilson, editor Geneva, Il, 1859; *The Restitution Herald,* July 21, 1925. MacDonald, Daniel. *History of Marshall County.* 1908

Chadwick, J.L.
b. August 1834
d. December 1909

J.L. Chadwick was born at Oshkosh, Wisconsin. He first moved to Litchfield, Minnesota, and then to Eden Valley. Elder Chadwick had been a Methodist in his youth, but came over to the Church of God when he learned about the Gospel of the Kingdom on earth. He was baptized and began working earnestly for the Church of God in the Minnesota Conference. As secretary of the conference, he organized many Sunday Schools throughout the state. He also preached at Sunday School meetings.

Chadwick died at the Old Soldier's Home in Minneapolis and is buried in Eden Lake Cemetery.

Bibliography: *History of the Church of God Minnesota Conference,* Sydney Magaw, ed., 1931.

Chaffee, Clara Jane
b. February 6, 1860
d. 1948?

Clara West was born at South Butler, New York, to Clark and Marietta (DeForest) West. Clark, a blacksmith, was a delegate to the 1888 Philadelphia Conference and served on a committee. Clark West married Adaline "Addie" Staley, widow of William Staley after the death of Clara's mother.

Clara had one brother, Charles, and a little sister, Emma. Mr. West's children accepted the new Mrs. West as their mother. Mrs. Staley-West had come from Canada, but it is thought that the Wests lived in New York until they moved to the area near Blanchard, Michigan. Addie West taught her new daughters about the Gospel of the Kingdom and the Age to Come.

Clark West

Addie had been baptized into that faith by Minister John Bowers in 1861, when she was 14. Additional information about Elder Bowers is not known at this time. According to her obituary, Addie's funeral service was conducted by Mary Woodward at East Millbrook, Michigan. Mary was a Church of God pastor.

Clara was baptized at age 23 by O.R.L. Crozier at Millbrook Church. Clara married Charles Chaffee (d. July 3, 1921), and they had one daughter, Lulu Pearl (Danforth). Charles was employed as a track man for the railroad. The family resided at Byron, Michigan. Clara's name appeared many times in *The Restitution Herald* because she preached at various Churches of God and conference meetings. She was a forceful speaker and was asked to participate at meetings throughout the movement. She was active in both the Michigan and Indiana church conferences. She preached at the Indiana conference meeting in 1914. At this particular conference she asked the members for a commitment to live more Christ-like lives.

A severe illness during the winter of 1918-1919, left her bedridden and unable to read or write for nearly eight months. When she improved, she gave glory to God for healing her, and for raising her up to perform simple tasks.

She was highly regarded throughout the movement as an educated woman. She was friends with Mrs. Elizabeth Reed, herself an author of esteem, and Mrs. Harriett Boice, a professor at University of Illinois, Champaign/Urbana. Mrs. Reed referred to Clara as one of "The King's Daughters," a nickname those friends gave themselves.

Clara Chaffee was a supporter of the formation of the General Conference, and after the Golden Rule Home was purchased, she became a resident when it opened December 29, 1922.

She was listed as "Lodger" in the 1930 census for Oregon, Illinois, at 110 South 7th Street. Some of the other residents of the Golden Rule Home included Mary Renner, 86; James Williamson and wife Mary, ages 82 and 78; Elizabeth Scoville, 75; and Alice Kerr, 79. Clara was the youngest resident at 70 years of age. As the correct address of the Golden Rule Home was at 110 N. 7th Street, it must be presumed that construction on the sun porch was underway during the census, requiring residents to be housed temporarily at 110 S. 7th Street, the site of a large and grand mansion that is now the Farrell-Holland-Gale funeral home

Clara continued to reside at the Golden Rule Home well into her old age. Elizabeth Ordnung, a caretaker at Golden Rule, wrote in her diary that Clara was living there in 1942, and six years later notice of a birthday party for her, age 88, and George Loudenslager, age 77, was published in *The Restitution Herald*. Both were born on February 6. Record of her death has not been located, but she is known to God.

See Boice, Harriet,
Netts, Charles (20th) - Golden Rule Home banks
Reed, Elizabeth
West, A. Clark
Woodward, Mary

Bibliography: Ancestry.com: U.S. Census. New York. Wayne. Butler. 1860; U.S. Census. Michigan. Isabella. Blanchard. Dist. 150. 1880; U.S. Census. Michigan. Kent. Byron. Dist. 130. 1880; U.S. Census. Michigan. Mecosta. Milbrook. Dist. 130. Image 15. 1910; U.S. Census. Illinois. Ogle. Oregon. Dist. 28. 1930; *The Restitution Herald* Oct. 21, 1914; July 9, 1919; Feb. 19, 1924; June 2, 1925, Feb. 17, 1948; Records of Golden Rule Residents, Archives, Atlanta Bible College, McDonough, GA.

Chandler, Botilla Z.
b. 1862
d. Unknown

Botilla Z. Chandler was married to Ruth, and they had four daughters and two sons. He named one son Benjamin Franklin Chandler. They resided at Anderson, South Carolina, where he was a farmer. He was an elder at the Guthrie Grove Church of God at Pelzer. J.H. Anderson reported that Botilla preached for a Southeast Conference meeting. Men like Elder Chandler were the main leaders of a local work such as Guthrie Grove. During the era of traveling circuit evangelists including John H. Anderson, local men ministered in the little churches so that the evangelists could do additional teaching and preaching during their short visits. This mirrored the ministry of St. Paul who visited churches and maintained additional contact with them by letter. Local leaders stabilized the work.

In an interesting coincidence, the J.H. Anderson and Botilla Chandler families are recorded on the same page of the 1910 U.S. Census at Anderson, South Carolina. Curiously, this also happened when J.H. Anderson lived in the same neighborhood of Indiana as the Otto E. Dick family in 1930. It is possible that evangelist Anderson rented tenant houses from the church members.

See Anderson, J.H.
Dick, Otto E. (20th)

Bibliography: Ancestry.com: U.S. Census. South Carolina. Anderson. Williamston. Dist. 69. 1910; Anderson, J.H. "Report," *The Restitution*. Sept. 3, 1920.

Chandler, Moses
b. 1812
d. Unknown

Moses Chandler was born in New York and lived near Syracuse. He married Abigail and they had several children. After he accepted the teachings of the Adventists he moved his family to Raisin, Michigan, to preach Age to Come. His evangelistic circuit ranged from the southern line of central Illinois, northward through Wisconsin.

He relocated to Milwaukee in June 1846. He reported later that a few brethren in that city had recently been strengthened in the faith by the preaching of D.I. Robinson (alternately spelled "Robison") of Cleveland.

Chandler's primary means of income came from preaching because he listed his occupation on the US Census as "Christian Minister" instead of "Farmer" as so many other evangelists often did. Many evangelistic preachers had to farm to pay the bills. Donations from church folks paid for the travel, but not much more.

Moses Chandler was excited about preaching on the frontier. In 1847 he wrote a letter to Joseph Marsh at *The Advent Harbinger*. At that time he was writing from Rushville, Illinois, a small town nine miles northeast of the present Ripley Church of God. He said he was 200 miles south of his residence. He was living then either in northern Illinois or southern Wisconsin. He reported that there were a few scattered brethren in this location, and, that he was finding great interest in his preaching. "I have great congregations. This is a great field of labor."

Mrs. E.S. Mansfield wrote in the Schuyler and Brown County's history book: "In 1855… Rev. Moses Chandler came to this county [Brown] to be a gospel laborer."

There is brief mention of him in one issue of *The Voice of Truth* as "being in touch with Evangelist Daniels who was traveling to St. Louis." From this it is seen that while Daniels, Chandler and Mrs. H.A. Parks were riding a circuit in Illinois, Wisconsin, Missouri and Iowa, they were able to stay in touch with each other as a means of coordinating the primitive Christian work.

See Daniels, Daniel J.
Marsh, Joseph
Parks, Mrs. H.A.

See Also Appendix 5–Collaboration in Illinois

Bibliography: Ancestry.com U.S. Census Spring Grove, Il. 1860; Wisconsin Census 1820-1890. gives his residence as 2 W, Milwaukee Township in 1846; Chandler, Moses. "Letter to Joseph Marsh" *Advent Harbinger* June 22, 1847; Chandler, Moses. "Report of relocation" *Voice of Truth* July 1, 1846 and March 31, 1847; Mansfield, E.S. "The Advent Christian Church" *The History of Schuyler and Brown Counties*. 1882.

Chaplin, Stedman Atherton
b. June 2, 1809
d. March 23, 1892

Stedman A. Chaplin was born in Baltimore, Vermont. He became a giant in the Church of God, but many members in today's church are unaware of him. Stedman first learned of the truth under the preaching of Obadiah E. Morrell of New York who later became the chaplain of the Auburn State Prison. At the time Stedman Chaplin was baptized three others were baptized including Mrs. Nancy Royce, his oldest sister.

At the time of his baptism, he maintained membership in the Christian Connexion and resided in Cayuga County, New York. He remained in New York two more years attending several large Christian Connexion conferences. He met several of their best known and most intelligent leaders. These new associates included David Millard, a traveler and writer, who wrote letters to Miller publications in New York; Barzillai H. Miles from the West known by settlers in Marshall County, Indiana; Simon Clough and Joseph Badger.

According to the North Salem history booklet, Chaplin was a school teacher who often walked up to 44 miles in one day to spend his wages on books. He was master of five languages and self-taught in mathematics, history and ancient and modern literature.

Stedman's daughter, Roxanna Wince

Stedman Chaplin was interested in the developing theology of the Adventist movement and frequently wrote to eastern religious papers, making statements and asking questions. He submitted writings to *The Herald of Gospel Liberty*, then edited by Elias Smith of the Christian Connection. His writings included poetry and devotional thought. He also reported Indiana conference activities to *The Advent Harbinger and Bible Advocate*, edited by Joseph Marsh.

Elder Chaplin married Sarah McQuigg who was seven years older than he. They moved to Tennessee because her brother was living there.

Chaplin associated with the Baptists at Oswego, Indiana. Then he met Ephraim Miller and Ed Hoyt, two preachers who explained the Age to Come to him. Chaplin began to consider this doctrine with new awareness. In other areas of doctrine, he did not believe in life only in Christ, so he preached immortality of the soul. Wife Sarah studied her Bible and came to believe in the teachings of Miller and Hoyt. According to David Graham, she chuckled every time she heard Stedman preach otherwise from the Oswego pulpit until finally, she convinced her husband to take another look at these new doctrines.

Mead Catlin also influenced Chaplin at that time. An ex-Millerite, Catlin hailed from Elizabeth, New Jersey, the same city and church which produced John O. Woodruff, a staunch advocate of Age-to-Come millennial teachings. Catlin attempted to organize a church in LaPorte County, Indiana. He congratulated Chaplin when he made the break with the Baptists in 1845 to align himself with the Church of God. To demonstrate his allegiance to his newfound faith Chaplin began preaching at Old Pisgah church often at great hardship to himself. When he didn't have transportation to a preaching appointment, he walked.

Bro. and Sr. Chaplin were greatly sorrowed when their six-year old daughter, *Roxeinia*, died suddenly, probably from typhoid fever so prevalent in those days. The obituary writer, E. Willard, said:

> She was a lovely flower which opened and shed its fragrance all around and then suddenly closed in death. At this early age she had stored her memory with many sweet hymns which she used to sing with great delight in the wilds of Eel River whither her folks had removed from New York.

The Chaplins named their second daughter *Roxanna*.

After Stedman Chaplin and the rest of the Indiana evangelists met with Joseph Marsh at Kingsbury in the summer of 1851, Chaplin focused on building the work in his area. His report to *The Harbinger* of the 1851 autumn conference at Pisgah noted that although some people were caught up with commerce, quarter-sections and gold, there were still many good people who attended. Seymour Stilson was one who had gone west to search for gold. Chaplin reported also that Ephraim Miller was in poor health.

The Chaplins' younger son, Ernest, 21, daughter Roxanna and her husband, John Wince, lived with Stedman and Sarah in 1870. They had relocated to Marshall County, Indiana, by then, possibly because of the influence of his friend, Barzillai H. Miles. Ernest taught school.

Dutton, Michigan, ministers assisted the Indiana Conference work. HV Reed, front right, assisted Stedman Chaplin in editing **The Restitution.**

Stedman Chaplin accepted the duties as editor and publisher of *The Restitution* after the Chicago Fire in 1871. The press was moved to Plymouth in November of 1874 where he assumed the editor's duties the following month. For two years, Hiram V. Reed with Arthur R. Underwood assisted him. Chaplin, who had purchased the paper from Thomas Wilson, took the reins after his "apprenticeship" under the more experienced printers. When Chaplin retired around 1893, A.R. Underwood took over publishing duties. Chaplin left a great legacy when he retired, but due to his severe illness, *The Restitution's* printed quality had declined. Overall quality improved again under Underwood's editorship.

In 1874 Stedman married his second wife, Sarah Logan. She was 30 years younger than he, and became a devoted wife for his remaining years. On August 1, 1874, he met Warren Burch, Nathan Maxay, Cynthia Palmer Stilson, Jeanette Burch McChesney and Joseph Emerson to organize the Fairmount Church of God. They met at the Baker schoolhouse in North Township, Marshall County, Indiana. Additional land was donated in 1881, and more was given to the state conference in 1953. This was the site of the North Salem church, focal point of the Indiana Conference for several years. Many members are buried in the Fairmount cemetery there.

Stedman Chaplin was devoted to God and family. Mrs. Anna B. Eychaner gave meaningful comment about his influence upon her life years after his death:

> Bro. Chaplin, Auntie Wince's father, was a household name in the homes of our childhood, many years ago. My father and mother (who were from Buchanan, Michigan) always entertained him when he came into our neighborhood. Many times have we children listened to the prayers he offered at family worship, for a blessing on the home and its occupants.

Mrs. Eychaner, her cousin, Eva Kinyon, and Roxanna "Auntie" Wince were childhood playmates.

The circumstances of Chaplin's retirement began in 1892 with a cancerous growth in his right foot. The cancer was excised twice leaving him practically immobilized and in great pain with a three-inch crater in his foot. Elder Chaplin died of cancer at Plymouth and was buried near his home.

See Catlin, N. Mead
Marsh, Joseph
Miller, Ephraim
Reed, H.V.
Wickizer, Sarah Logan Chaplin
Wince, Roxanna

Bibliography: Ancestry.com U.S. Census. Marshall Co. Indiana. 1850, 1870; Chaplin, S.A. "Letter to Joseph Marsh" *Advent Harbinger and Bible Advocate,* Oct. 18, 1851; Ferrell, Terry. *A Brief History of the Church of God in America.* Berean Youth Conference at Camp Reynoldswood, Dixon, Il.. Aug 21-27, 1960; Graham, David. E-mail to author, March 21, 2006; May 14, 2006; Kirkley, Iris, Berry, Marilyn and Heyde, Mildred. *North Salem. One Hundred Years.* Aug. 1, 1974; "Obituary Roxeinia Chaplin". *Advent Harbinger and Bible Advocate,* Aug. 3, 1850; *The Restitution,* Jan.-Feb. 1893; Dec. 9, 1908; Feb. 8, 1911; *The Restitution Herald,* Dec. 9, 1908; May 5, 1911; July 15, 1924; March 15, 1921.

Chapman, Samuel
b. 1823
d. Unknown

Chapman, Mary K.
b. 1823
d. Unknown

Samuel and Mary K. Chapman were Adventist missionaries to New England and the frontier. At the beginning of their ministry, their home was in Hartford, Connecticut. Their missionary travels took them to New York, Michigan, Indiana, Pennsylvania, Illinois and Canada West. They may have eventually resided in Illinois. Research indicates that Samuel was an Adventist, but Mary embraced the doctrine of the Age to Come. Like so many others, they earned their living from farming.

Typical of Adventists, Mary did not always accept the Age-to-Come prophetic interpretation. In fact, very few Adventists did. Joseph Marsh took a leap of faith to begin teaching Adventists about this unique aspect of Bible prophecy, and slowly many of them began to understand and began to accept it. Mary was slower to assimilate the new idea. She preached Kingdom of God for nearly two years before she admitted to sitting down with her Bible and studying Age to Come. She said, "I do confess I see things in a different light than formerly. There is a beauty I never discovered before in the plan and economy of God in the glorious restitution."

The difference in those positions hinges on one's view

of prophecy regarding the future of Israel. Adventists say that Israel does not return to its homeland while present-day Jerusalem still exists. The Age-to-Come prophecy stresses the return of Israel to its homeland during the days of "carnal" Jerusalem, prior to Christ's return. The restitution of all things is accomplished by Christ in the millennial age.

The Chapmans preached wherever they were invited. According to Mary, they left home in May of 1851, traveled 100 miles south, and spent several weeks preaching in Baptist, Free-will Baptist and Seventh-day Baptist churches. Samuel Chapman baptized ministers from those congregations. One of those ministers, in turn, baptized 15 people from his congregation.

By May 1851, the Chapmans traveled to Springfield, Illinois, 1,000 miles from their home to preach to a congregation of 12 souls. They also preached in the courthouse to large crowds. They received inquiries from the countryside to come preach. These inquiries could have been from folks at Rushville, Ripley or nearby Camp Point.

The Chapmans went into the rural counties five times during the interval of her report. The people were hungry to hear about the second coming of Christ. She said people came to meeting from eight to ten miles away. She said their health was not strong, and worse, cholera was everywhere. Twelve people had died in Springfield since their arrival.

In July 1851, Mary wrote to *The Harbinger* that she had received word regarding an accident which severely injured her ten-year-old son, Samuel. He was her son by her first husband who had been deceased since the child's birth. Young Samuel lay mortally wounded from injuries in a wagon accident. Samuel Chapman encouraged Mary to return home to be with her son while he remained in Springfield to preach.

Mary reported later that her son lay immobile for five days, but after her return he awakened and was nearly himself after two weeks. Soon thereafter, she was called into the field again to preach about the Gospel of the Kingdom of God around Ulysses, Pennsylvania, where there was a strong center of universalism. She worked at Ulysses for most of the next six months until her husband returned from Springfield in the autumn. In one letter to *The Harbinger* she asked for word of him. She had not heard from him since January 1852.

  See   Bywater, J.C.
      Chandler, Moses
      Chittendon, H.A.

See Also   Appendix 5–Collaboration in Illinois
Bibliography: Chapman, Mary. "Letter to Joseph Marsh" *Advent Harbinger and Bible Advocate* 2: 52, June 14, 1851; Also 3:2, June 28, 1851; Also 3:47, May 1, 1852; Graham, David. *Wisdom and Power* Dec. 1992, Quoting from *History of Schuyler and Brown Counties, Illinois*.1686-1882, Astoria, Il. Stevens Publishing Co. 1970 retrieved from http://www.illinoiscivilwar.org/brown_county.html, December 31, 2007; Marsh, Joseph. "Editorial" *Voice of Truth and Glad Tidings of the Kingdom* Oct. 14, 1846.

Chapman, Dr. L.B.
 b. 1845
 d. July 8, 1913

Dr. L.B. Chapman was born in Darlington, Canada. While a young man, Dr. Chapman went west. In 1870 he met and married Miss Francis T. Thomas in Chicago. They had one son, Irving Lee Chapman, who also became a doctor. H.V. Reed, who worked in the Chicago area at that time, is credited with baptizing Dr. L.B. Chapman into One Faith in 1870.

For many years, L.B. suffered with a disease that doctors could not identify. Eventually he developed Bright's disease. Whether that arose from his first ailment or was a separate problem is not known. Looking for a better climate, he visited Virginia, Oregon and finally Montana where he improved for awhile. In time, he was stricken with paralysis after which he died at his home in Proctor, Montana.

It is doubtful that Dr. Chapman was related to Samuel and Mary Chapman mentioned previously.

Bibliography: *The Restitution*, Sept. 9, 1913

Chase, Levi C.
 b. 1843
 d. July 19, 1926

Levi C. Chase was the son of Levi H. Chase. Levi C. was born in Michigan after his father settled there to do evangelistic work. The family lived for awhile at Raison (Raisin) but relocated to Adrian. Levi had many siblings and probably did not get a lot of attention, but he learned the Word at his father's knees. When he grew up, Levi C. followed in his father's footsteps to advance the cause of the Gospel of the Kingdom.

He served in the Union army during the Civil War for, unless a man had $300 to purchase a replacement, he was required to serve. Levi was assigned to the 11th Cavalry, Company C.

By 1870 at age 27, he married Sarah and began to farm 950 acres valued at $5,500. Sarah's mother, Anna Turner, lived with them in her old age.

One story about him illustrates the respect he had for his father and for his father's friend, Joseph Marsh. Levi C. happened to be at the Tecumseh cemetery near Raisin, Michigan, probably for a funeral. As he left he noticed a tombstone marked "Joseph Marsh." It was old and broken. The stone had sunk into the soil. Levi made inquiries from the Sexton who said there were no Marsh relatives living nearby to tend the grave. So Levi C. Chase took it upon himself to order the repair of the stone, level it, and clear the area of weeds, "so great was his loving respect for the man who had fought for truth amid its pioneer difficulties and died faithful unto death." This information was recorded in a report by O.R.L. Crozier from a story told by Mary Woodward for the Michigan conference.

Levi Chase lived to age 80. He rests at Woodland Cemetery, Barry County, Michigan.

See Chase, Levi H.
Crozier, O.R. L.
Marsh, Joseph
Woodward, Mary

Bibliography: Ancestry.com U.S. Census. Michigan. Lewanee. Adrian. 1870 and 1900; Records of burial at Woodland Cemetery, Barry County, Michigan retrieved from Interment.net/Woodland.htm; Crozier, O.R.L. "Prophetic Day and Hour" *Voice of Truth* April 9, 1845; Crozier, O.R.L. Report to Michigan Conference read by Mary Woodward, circa 1900 prior to Crozier's death, reported in *The Restitution*, date unknown.

Chase, Levi H.
b. March 29, 1806
d. October 5, 1877

Levi H. Chase was born in Providence, New York, and lived east of Rochester. Here he became caught up in the study of the Second Advent of Christ. He moved from New York to Michigan in 1832, just as William Miller was beginning to preach the message of the Second Advent. Elder Levi H. Chase was officially a member of the Society of Friends until 1840, but he also studied the new theology.

After the Bitter Disappointment in 1844, he aligned himself with Joseph Marsh, also of Rochester, who was beginning to advocate a new doctrine of Adventism focused on the prophecies relating to the Age to Come. Elder Chase began to preach wherever he was called. After leaving the Quaker persuasion, he was ordained a Baptist minister, but he repudiated that also and began preaching the Gospel of the Kingdom. He was very likely baptized either by Ephraim Miller who lived nearby, or by Joseph Marsh.

Elder Chase preached the Gospel in Lenawee County, Raisin Township, Michigan, where the people greatly appreciated him. One listener wrote to Joseph Marsh, "I thought it would be cheering to the lovers of truth to hear that Levi Chase is still actively preaching the gospel to the people in this area. He has a place in the heart of this people and the doctrine he has presented will be long remembered, and I know there is not a man who can refute his position."

Here is a description of Levi H. Chase from Dr. Nathaniel Field of Jeffersonville, Indiana as published in *The Prophetic Expositor and Bible Advocate:*
> He has a method peculiar to himself; but well calculated to make a deep impression on his hearers. By nature he is an orator. His manner is grave and dignified, even when caricaturing the follies and absurdities of Methodist revivals, in which he is remarkably expert.

Elder Chase participated in the early Age-to-Come work from his home in Michigan. He attended a conference at Rochester, New York, in May 1852, at which he preached more than once. He engaged in "sincere and deep" conversation with more than 20 other ministers about the future of the work, how to prevent folks (including leaders) from falling away, and other topics of interest. J.B. Cook, conference secretary, noted "the general character of the conference was, as we conceive, in harmony with the example the New Testament furnishes in such cases."

Owen Crozier reported years later that "the Elder Levi [H.] Chase used to come to Rochester. He was a terrible battle ace against sin and error." That was a very apt description of the fiery Levi Chase.

A man by the name of S. Wing reported to Joseph Marsh in 1857 that Elder Chase had spent six months in the vicinity of Brown County, Illinois, and intended to spend the next six months also. The American depression of 1857-1859 greatly hampered ministry opportunities. Dedicated circuit preachers could no longer take several short trips into the field and return home between them. It was too costly. It became necessary to take one trip and remain in the field by staying with folks, and earning what pittance might be available to purchase another train ticket.

Bro. Levi H. Chase made contact with Benjamin Wilson as early as 1859. Levi's letter was published in *The Gospel Banner and Millennial Advocate* in January 1860. He reported that he had chiefly devoted his travels to Ohio the past year, but that he had also been in Indiana and Michigan. He had traveled more than 5,000 miles, preached 310 sermons and baptized 96 people. Records also indicate that he traveled through Pennsylvania and New York before returning home to Adrian.

In the pursuit of introducing people to the Gospel of the Kingdom, Levi encountered many hardships and persecutions "with dangers to life, limb and health to which may be added hard roads, hard fare, hard names, hard times and hard hearts." He expressed his gratitude for the goodness of the people of One Faith and said their generosity had met all his expenses.

In 1860 an article on the question, "Who are Brethren?" was written by Levi H. Chase in *The Gospel Banner*. Should men of the One Faith refer to members of other denominations as "*Brother*"? One or two months later, Bro. Chase wrote the results of his Bible study on this question, and he determined that unless a person believed in the Gospel of the Kingdom and all other aspects of accepted One Faith doctrine, he should not be called a brother.

In a curious departure from his positive report in one letter, Chase said:

> Stacy, Marsh and Fields had no more faith in those promises when they were dipped than wild uncultivated Hottentots. Their little amount of faith, that Jesus Christ is the Son of God, does not comprise the gospel of the glorious kingdom, which Jesus preached and Moses and all the prophets preached. Stacy's, Marsh's and Field's test of faith is in harmony with the Pope of Rome.

These inflammatory remarks certainly propagated and promoted a breech between the leaders of One Faith and Joseph Marsh of the Age to Come. For additional information on the differences between the factions see the entires for Mark Allen and Benjamin Wilson.

In the next issue of *The Gospel Banner*, Mark Allen took exception to Chase's use of "*Brother.*" Chase wrote to Joseph Marsh and called him "Brother" a short time after he had written the scathing article to *The Gospel Banner*. Allen felt it was inconsistent. He said Chase probably addressed him as such because of his kindness toward him as a man. Allen said the greater problem is addressing an editor from the *World's Crisis,* an Advent Christian journal, as a brother. Here he thought the practice should stop, because he did not believe in common with the One Faith.

The exchange of the above comments was an important step in narrowing the fellowship, turning the focus inward instead of outward to include more, and setting up barriers that would further lead the brethren of One Faith into a sectarian stance. Within seven short years, Nathaniel Field of Jeffersonville, Indiana, would break fellowship with the Indiana conference over the question of what should be a test of fellowship: Doctrine or Christian character?

The repudiation of Joseph Marsh over the issue of not being re-baptized may be traced to three men: Dr. John Thomas, Levi Chase and Benjamin Wilson. These leaders from that point on narrowed the focus of the brotherhood to include those who accepted not *one* but *all* of the unique doctrines associated with the One Faith. And while Joseph Marsh did not die until 1863, for all practical purposes, he was to these Midwesterners as already dead. When he died, Benjamin Wilson did not include Marsh's obituary in *The Gospel Banner*.

Questions began to surface among the brethren of One Faith about the role of the Holy Spirit in the life of the believer. "How does one receive the Spirit?" many asked. At a Chicago Conference in 1869, Levi H. Chase spoke for 15 minutes on the subject of God's promises whereby men can attain to the divine nature. He said, "the usual method of calling upon God in revival meetings for the 'power' was all a farce, and that the only power of God for the salvation of men was the Gospel."

Elder L.H. Chase was pastor at the Church of God in Adrian, Michigan, until his death. He reported often to the Michigan State Conference about the work at Raisin. Generally, he had baptized up to 15 persons each year and by 1886 when the Minute book ceases, his congregation had increased to 60 people. This is a large number compared to other Michigan congregations who numbered ten faithful souls.

In August 1888, Levi placed a notice in *The Restitution* regarding the upcoming Michigan Conference. This notice is of particular interest because of the terminology he used. He called for attendance at Dutton, Michigan, for the meeting of both "the Old and the New Conferences." The work had been ongoing four decades by this time so that as the older generation died away, the younger generations saw the need to reorganize their first conference associations. This same phenomenon is recorded in the literature for the Illinois, Iowa, Indiana and Ohio conferences. Minnesota, New York and Virginia may have experienced the same growing pains. The Civil War also interrupted state conference activities in the North and the South. After the War, conferences found it necessary to reorganize.

This is the first time old and new organization were identified, but this nomenclature gives scholars an idea of how leaders of the work reorganized their state conferences as the two fronts of the Church of God began to come together around 1880. Those two fronts, Age-to-Come believers from the East Coast and Midwest, and One-Faith believers from the Midwest and Great Plains, organized nationally in Philadelphia in 1888. This effort failed after four years. It might have been more expedient and nurturing to a young organization if that 1888 meeting had been held in Chicago on the western front.

Location may have been important, but the minutes of the Board of Directors from that conference place the blame for failure at the door of an empty treasury. Financial support was needed to nurture a national work. The National Conference of the Church of God failed in 1892 because the leaders were not experienced in fundraising, and the people were not educated or dedicated to tithing outside of their local churches. It should also be noted that America slipped into a Depression from 1893-1898.

Levi's son, Levi C. Chase, took over the pastorate when his father died, and served faithfully until his own death in 1926. Levi H. Chase died of paralysis at 71. He was buried in Raisin Township, Lewanee County, Michigan.

See Allen, Mark
Chase, Levi C.
Crozier, O.R.L.
Marsh, Joseph
Wilson, Benjamin
Woodward, Mary
Work, George
See Also Hudler, D.M.
Appendix 3–Catalyst for Change: Martyrdom

Bibliography: Allen, Mark. "Discussion of Letter to *Prophetic Expositor*" *Gospel Banner and Millennial Advocate*, Oct. 1860 and 6:11, Nov. 1860; Bezzo. Elder. "Letter to Joseph Marsh" *Advent Harbinger and Bible Advocate*, May 15, 1852; Bolhous, Stephen. Interview with J Stilson at the Holy Spirit Conference, Winnebago New Life Bible Church, May 2005; Chase, L.H. "Letter to Joseph Marsh regarding American Depression" *Prophetic Expositor and Bible Advocate*, Jos. Marsh, ed., Rochester, NY, Jan. 1, 1858; Chase, L.H. "Letter to Benjamin Wilson," *Gospel Banner and Millennial Advocate*, Jan. 1860; Chase, L.H. "What constitutes a Christian?" *Gospel Banner,* Sept. 1860; Chase, L.H., "Report of Travels," *Gospel Banner* Vol. 7, 1861; Cook, J.B. "Report of Rochester Conference," *Advent Harbinger,* June 5, 1852; Crozier, O.R.L. "Report to Michigan Conference." Given by Mary Woodward June 26, 1907; Field, Nathanial. "Description of L.H. Chase" *Prophetic Expositor and Bible Advocate* Jos. Marsh, editor. Jan. 1, 1858; *Church of God History Newsletter,* Jan Stilson, ed. (Aug/Sept 1994); Williams, Byron. *Abstracts of Obituaries and Weddings from the Restitution.* Self-published. 1994; Williams, Byron. "Excerpted works including obituary summary of Levi H. Chase as taken from *The Restitution*" Oct. 24, 1877; Wing. S. "Letter to Joseph Marsh" *The Prophetic Expositor and Bible Advocate* Jos. Marsh, ed. Rochester, NY, Jan. 1, 1858; Work, George. "Minute Book of Board of Directors National Church of God Conference" Philadelphia, 1888, Chicago 1889-1892. This ledger is part of the Atlanta Bible College Library Archives.

Chase, Samuel P.
b. 1851
d. 1895?

The life history of Samuel P. Chase is scant. He does not seem to be descended from the Samuel Chase, Supreme Court Justice, and signer of the Declaration of Independence from Maryland. It is thought that our Samuel P. Chase was born in Rhode Island and made his way into Michigan. He was married to Martha Pollette Chase on November 20, 1878, and three daughters were born to the family. Samuel was a farmer and a practicing clergyman. He believed in the Gospel of the Kingdom.

It is possible that Samuel Chase may have been a brother or cousin to Levi H. Chase, or to his son, Levi C. Chase. Family oral histories have indicated that he officiated at the wedding of his daughter Mary to Frederick L. Austin in May 1896.

F.L. and Mary Austin had four children. Mr. Austin advanced in his ministerial career to become the executive secretary of the Church of God General Conference at Oregon, Illinois, from 1921-1931.

Mrs. Chase died of cancer on November 29, 1895. Their daughters survived her. Samuel P. Chase had predeceased her but his date of death is not known. The heritage of Samuel and Martha Chase lives on in the Church of God today through the generations of Mary Railton Milne, John Railton and Jason Railton, Joyce Bolhous and Marcee Turner, to name a few.

See Austin, F.L.
Chase, Levi C.
Chase, Levi H.

Bibliography: Ancestry.com U.S. Census 1880. Allegan, Michigan. Martin Township; Bolhous, Stephen May 2005 and 2006. Steve's wife, Joyce is a Railton. F.L. Austin was her great grandfather; *The Restitution,* Jan. 8, 1896.

Chittenden (Chittendon), H.A.
b. 1805
d. Unknown

Elder Chittenden was born in New York, but preached throughout the Illinois frontier in 1842. He may have resided in the village of Chicago and worked as a butcher. He is one of the earliest known Adventist preachers, and he may have been the first to represent the Bible in Chicago. In 1850 he also preached in the area of Mt. Sterling, Illinois near the present-day church at Ripley.

He may not have subscribed to the Age-to-Come ideas as Joseph Marsh promoted them because Chittenden believed there would be no mortal subjects in the Kingdom during the millennium whereas Marsh believed that mortal subjects entered the Kingdom on probation.

Even so, Chittenden set the stage in Brown County for Age-to-Come preachers such as Uncle John Foore, D.M Hudler, Mary K. Chapman and J.M. Stephenson, who preached and died at Ripley.

When the Adventist church at Ripley "settled out" over doctrinal issues, the Age-to-Come members stayed at Ripley and the Sabbatarian Adventists and Advent Christians went elsewhere. It is not known if H.A. Chittenden fell among the latter. It is known that the local Disciples church had contended with Seventh-day Adventists at Ripley.

See Appendix 5–Collaboration in Illinois
Appendix 12–Second Adventism in Ripley

Bibliography: "Christian Churches in Brown County *1819-1914,*" retrieved from genealologytrails.com/il/brown/churches.htm Dec.

31, 2007; Graham, David. *Wisdom and Power* Dec. 1992 citing from *The History of Schuyler and Brown Counties, Illinois* 1686-1882, Astoria, Il. Stevens Publishing Co. 1970 retrieved from http://www.illinoiscivilwar.org/brown_county.html, December 31, 2007; Editor, *The Restitution Herald,* Dec'92/Je,'93 p 16, note on Chittenden as the first to preach at Mt. Sterling.

Chown, Robert
b. 1810
d. Unknown

Robert Chown lived at Daysville, Illinois, a burgeoning village along the Rock River just southeast of Oregon in Ogle County. Chown was pastor of the congregation at Paynes Point, five miles east and two miles north of Daysville. Robert was born in England and was married to Margaret who was from Canada. They had four sons and a daughter. Robert Chown also lived for awhile at Plum River, Illinois, where he was pastor of a small Church of God. Plum River's name was changed later to Stockton.

Chown seemed well acquainted with A.J. Eychaner, a Bible scholar from Paynes Point, who went on to become a prominent national figure in the denominational development of Church of God. Perhaps A.J. Eychaner had discipled Robert Chown. Chown is not a prominent figure in Church of God history, but he may be better known by the Iowa members. Knowledge of him was gained from a letter he wrote to the editor of *The Prophetic Expositor and Bible Advocate.* This journal was popularly known as *The Expositor.*

Robert said that he was an avid reader of *The Expositor.* He thought it was so valuable that when he traveled to England, he acted as its agent to gain subscribers there. From this it can be seen that Marsh's publications had an international presence.

Chown was present at the Illinois Conference at Crane's Grove where men were appointed as pastors to congregations. From this report it is seen that J.B. Craton was pastor at Twin Groves church, Elder House at Plum River, T.J. Whitesett at Mt. Pleasant and J. Speers at Crane's Grove. This conference meeting resolved to appoint a traveling preacher for the year and to support him. Benjamin Wilson, translator of the *Emphatic Diaglott,* attended this meeting. Robert Chown reported to Joseph Marsh that Wilson rightly divided the truth.

Chown's comment on Wilson's capabilities is somewhat ironic as Wilson did not have a warm feeling toward Marsh. It is certain that Benjamin Wilson would not have said that Marsh rightly divided the Word. He objected to Marsh's treatment of the Kingdom of God. But, when one reviews Marsh's writings, it is clear that Joseph Marsh's message of the Age to Come also included Benjamin Wilson's emphasis on the biblical teaching of the promises made to Abraham. Wilson's discomfiture with Marsh seemed to be one-sided.

Robert Chown made his way to Iowa and lived near the Irving church. His son George settled in Iowa and continued serving the Lord through the work of the Church of God near Gladbrook.

See Craton, J.B.
Eychaner, A.J.
Marsh, Joseph
Turner, C.B.
Whitesett, Thomas J.
Wilson, Benjamin

Bibliography: Ancestry.com. U.S. Census. Illinois. Ogle. Oregon. 1850; Chown, Robert, "Report," *The Prophetic Expositor and Bible Advocate,* Jos. Marsh, ed. Rochester, NY. Nov. 1, 1857; Chown, G.R. "Notice of Iowa Conference," *The Restitution,* S.A. Chaplin, ed., Plymouth, In., Aug. 15, 1883; Chown, Robert. "Letter to Editor," *The Gospel Banner* Benjamin Wilson, ed., Geneva, Il., March, 1860; Rankin, Delbert. Interview at Iowa Conference Archives, Belle Plaine, Iowa, Nov. 8, 2008; *Place names of Illinois*. Illinois Historical Society, book is located at the Oregon Public Library in the genealogy room.

Clark, Stephen G.
b. May 6, 1818
d. May 13, 1881

Stephen Clark was born in New York and migrated to North Plains, Michigan, with his family. He was married to Caroline and they had several children. He was employed as a furnace man and must have enjoyed a good income. A furnace in those days was a large stone-lined oven located along a stream where ore could be smelted through use of high heat and a bellows operated by the running water. These smelting furnaces were used in industry or for making bullets.

In 1851 he wrote to Joseph Marsh that he preached every Lord's Day the previous year. He reported that his health was improved possibly from winter illnesses. Traveling preachers who worked around the major American rivers such as Ohio and Mississippi often suffered bouts of cholera or malaria. Joseph Marsh, himself, suffered so.

Clark testified that he believed in the God of Abraham, Isaac and Jacob and he looked for an everlasting Kingdom of God and that eternal city which "hath foundations whose builder and maker is God." He said he believed in the Age-to-Come prophecies and in conditional immortality.

Sometime during the early 1860s Clark began to preach throughout the frontier using Baileyville, Illinois, just south of Freeport, as his headquarters. He reported that he and his wife had lost two of their precious children within a week's time to diphtheria. This may have happened while he was on a ministry trip, so that he was not there for the funerals. In spite of his deep grief, he continued in faithful evangelistic service to the Lord. He reported that he had preached at Eagle Point, Black Oak and at Dixon, Illinois. Following that circuit, he returned to Buchanan, Michigan, his next ministry site, staying again at Baileyville along the way. There were several believers at Baileyville. He worked in concert with D.P. Hall.

Stephen Clark died at Windfall, Indiana, of erysipelas, an acute strep infection of the skin. His wife and two sons survived him. It is not known where he was interred.

See Hall, D.P.
Marsh, Joseph

Bibliography: Ancestry.com U.S. Census. Michigan. Livingston. Howell. 1850; Clark, Stephen G. "Letter to Marsh" *The Advent Harbinger and Bible Advocate,* March 1, 1851; Clark, Stephen G. "Letter to Newman," *Millennial Harbinger and Bible Expositor,* Thos. Newman, ed., Seneca Falls, NY, Feb. 18, 1863; Letter, *Millennial Harbinger and Bible Expositor,* Aug. 26, 1863 & Sept. 30, 1863; Millersville University website, "Elizabeth Furnace," www.millersville.edu/~socanth/elizabethfurnace2005.php; Williams, Byron. *Abstracts of Obituaries and Weddings from the Restitution.* Self-published. 1994.

Clover, Lot(t)
b. January 2, 1823
d. April 7, 1903

Lot Clover was one of two Disciple ministers who moved from Indiana to Illinois around 1850, and then to Alden, Hardin County, Iowa, in 1855. He wed Maryett Lewis on December 23, 1844. The couple met Joseph Furry who had also relocated to Iowa from Indiana, and were convinced by him of the message of conditional immortality. They may have been the first converts to One Faith in Hardin County. Lot served in that location as the township Justice of the Peace. Records indicate that he performed marriages in Hardin County in 1857, 1858, 1859, 1862, 1863 and 1864. He built the first house in Alden in 1855 which was destroyed in the great cyclone in 1860.

Soon thereafter, he moved to Nemaha County, Nebraska, then to Walnut Creek, Mitchell County, Kansas. He performed a wedding in Kansas in 1875.

W.J. Orem wrote a letter in *The Gospel Banner and Bible Advocate* in 1869, and mentioned that Lot participated in services in Troy, Kansas. Orem led a series of meetings in the Disciples church in that city. Unbeknownst to the Church of God ministers, the Disciples had not been informed that the Church of God was scheduled to use their building that day. Therefore, when Church of God preachers arrived, the Disciples were already inside and preparing to worship. It fell to Lot Clover to sort out the details. Elder Orem said:

> Lot Clover was there and preached. Our appointment came in conflict with a Campbellite, but he [Lot Clover] very gentlemanly gave way for the 11 o'clock service. The Church of God preached in the afternoon at which Lot Clover, W.P Shockey and W.J. Orem preached and assisted in the Lord's Supper.

A conference announcement in *The Restitution* October 8, 1879, stated:

> There will be a conference of the church of God held at Fairfield school house two miles south of Glen Elder, Mitchell County, Kansas, Nov. 21, 1879. Parties coming from a distance will get off the train at Glen Elder, and shall inquire for Lott Clover. T.E. Cunningham, Sec.

Clover later returned to Southeast Nebraska and was listed in a Nemaha County directory for 1890-1891. He is mentioned in family records as a "traveling preacher" who "moved often." Records indicate that he lived several places in Nemaha County—Brock, Verdon, Howe, Glen Rock—until his death. He is buried in the Linden Cemetery beside his wife.

Arlen Rankin contributed to this entry.

See Orem, W.J.
Shockey, W.P.

Bibliography: Ancestry.com. Indiana Marriage Collection 1800-1941. Record for Lot Clover and Maryett Lewis; Ancestry.com. Hayes Family Tree for Lott Clover; Ancestry.com. U.S. Census. Iowa. Hardin. Union. 1860; Burnett, Francis, et al, *History of the Iowa Church of God and Conference - "Those People Called Restitutionists"* - 1855-1987, published by the Iowa State Conference Directors, 1987; *Clover Family Chronicles,* June Clover Byrne, Editor, Fall 2003, Volume 1, Issue 4. Orem, W.J. "Correspondence," *The Gospel Banner and Bible Advocate,* Benjamin Wilson, editor, Geneva, Illinois, July 15, 1869; Rankin, Arlen F. Personal correspondence with June Byrne, 2007 & 2008; Various issues, *The Gospel Banner & Millennial Advocate,* Benj. Wilson, editor, Geneva, Il. 1854-1869; *The Restitution,* various editors, 1874-1925; Permission to use photo granted by Edus Clover Snyder, great granddaughter of Lott Clover retrieved by e-mail July 15, 2008; [Note: In the literature, the spelling of Lot's name is seen alternately with one T or two Ts.]

Cochenour, Lewis
b. January 4, 1846
d. May 1, 1921

Lewis Cochenour was born in Ohio. He wed Emma Chaplin in 1869. They had five children. Elder Ralph Carter baptized the Cochenours and united then with the Church of God Abrahamic Faith. Lewis Cochenour was largely responsible for the establishment of the Eagle Creek Church of God. He donated the land where it stood, sawed the lumber and superintended the construction. He was a singer, teacher and leader. He was a student of the Gospel of the Kingdom.

When he died, his funeral was held at Eagle's Creek, that "little church in the Wildwood," and he was laid to rest in the adjacent cemetery to sleep in Jesus until the morning of the resurrection. Eagle's Creek was in Kosciusko County, Indiana.

See Carter, H. Ralph
Bibliography: *The Restitution* May 24, 1921

Coffman, Samuel W.
b. 1812
d. November 13, 1887

Samuel Coffman was born and raised in Maryland and wagon-trained to Maryland Township, Ogle County, Illinois, shortly after the conclusion of the Black Hawk War in 1832. He filed a claim on a large tract of land north of the village of Adeline.

At some point he and his family became acquainted with the Age-to-Come teaching, probably through the pages of Joseph Marsh's *Advent Harbinger and Bible Advocate*. This paper was published from around 1848 to 1853. During that time, many different itinerate preachers, such as B.B. Brown, Mrs. H.A. Parker and J.M. Stephenson made a circuit through Stephenson County, Illinois, from Plum River in the north to Adeline south of Freeport.

Evidence indicates that Joseph Marsh visited the area in 1848. Patra Marsh Hepworth, a Marsh genealogist, discovered Joseph Marsh's signature on probate records proving he personally appeared before a judge at Elizabeth, Illinois, in July 1848 to sign a note on his brother's behalf. While this trip has not been mentioned in the writings of Joseph Marsh, it may have occurred between the demise of *The Voice of Truth* and start-up of *The Advent Harbinger*. While on the frontier, Joseph Marsh certainly would have visited some of the subscribers to his paper.

By the time Benjamin Wilson began publishing *The Gospel Banner* from Geneva, Illinois, the Coffmans were well acquainted with the doctrines of the Age to Come, the Kingdom of God on earth, the destiny of the wicked, and certain resurrection issues that were being prominently discussed in the 1850s.

At the seventh semi-annual Conference held in Geneva on July 1-2, 1860, one of the members from the Adeline congregation was present. This is the earliest record we have of involvement by the Adeline church with a Church of God meeting.

Samuel Coffman is important to Ogle County history because of his extensive real estate holdings in the county. He paid a lot of taxes. County records and deeds show many transactions of land by Mr. Coffman and his brothers. The descendents of the Coffman family continue to reside on some of that land in Maryland Township. A Coffman family cemetery located nearby is still being used.

Samuel Coffman is noteworthy for another reason. In 1863 he entertained Dr. John Thomas who was visiting old friends in the West. At that time Dr. Thomas and Benjamin Wilson essentially shepherded the same flock. All isolated Age-to-Come adherents were happy to entertain a passing circuit preacher of the One Faith or the One Truth as Thomas preferred.

In 1863 the Civil War raged across the South. Men who were opposed to war sought exemptions from service. In the Union Army, there were no exemptions for ministers of the Gospel, but the Confederate Army permitted exemptions if the denomination was registered with the Confederate government as being pacifistic. The Union Army allowed an able-bodied man who could not or would not serve in the military to pay $300 for a substitute to serve in his place. Many men could not afford that price. Ministers certainly couldn't afford it.

Dr. Thomas recognized that peace-loving men in the North and the South struggled with this problem. Dr. Thomas registered a new pacifistic denomination with the US War Department and with the Confederacy. The meeting of the Coffmans with Dr. Thomas resulted in a document that was registered with the Union War Department in 1864, just prior to the conclusion of the war.

In the South, a sympathetic judge who was the brother of Allan Magruder of Stephens City, Virginia, assisted Dr. Thomas to meet officials and to grant exemptions to ministers there.

The new denomination was registered as The Nazarines. One author has said, "But the revised Confederate Exemption Act of Oct. 1862 included a national solution, exempting Quakers, Nazarines, Mennonites, and Dunkards, provided they furnished substitutes or paid a $500 exemption tax." In this case, the "Nazarines" meant the Christadelphians to be distinguished from the Pentacostal Nazarenes which did not organize until around 1898.

The meeting at the Coffman farm was the beginning of the Christadelphian denomination, a historic sister of the Church of God. It predated the organization of the Church of God by 58 years.

When the descendants of Samuel Coffman were approached with this story a few years ago they were unfamiliar with the details, although Mr. Coffman acknowledged that Samuel "had been a member of an unusual church group." Evidence suggests that while he was friendly with Dr. Thomas, Samuel Coffman worshipped with the Church of God at Adeline and helped establish that work and the work of the Illinois Conference.

Samuel Coffman is interred in the Coffman family cemetery north of Adeline.

See Marsh, Joseph
Wilson, Benjamin

Bibliography: Report of Seventh Conference. *The Gospel Banner and Millennial Advocate*, Aug. 1860; Coffman phone interview, Summer 2001; Stilson, Jan "An Overview of the Leadership and Development of the Age to Come in the United States 1832-1871" *A Journal from the Radical Reformation*, 10:1, Fall 2001; "Conscientious Objectors in the Civil War", http://www.civilwarhome.com/conscientiousobjectors.htm; Coffman, S.W. Death date from http://www.kristory.com/coffmancem.shtml.

Conner, Lincoln Ellsworth (L.E.)
b. February 9, 1862
d. December 4, 1943

A. Early Years
B. Uncertain Years
C. Politics Leads to Problems
D. Work of the Holy Spirit
E. Universal Reconciliation and Universal Resurrection
F. The Controversy over *The Restitution*
G. 1910 Waterloo Conference
   1. The Ministerial Association
   2. A Split
H. The New General Conference
I. Influential within the Church of God

Lincoln E. Conner was born to Jackson and Nancy Conner near Macy, Indiana, a small town north of Peru. His parents had been born in Ohio but moved to Indiana after their marriage. Lincoln was descended from Scotch-Irish ancestors who settled north of Indianapolis and intermarried with Native Americans. William Conner and his wife, who was an Indian maiden, founded the settlement known as Conner's Prairie.

Jack Conner, Lincoln's grandson, reported that the re-creation of "Conner's Prairie" is just north of Indianapolis near Nora, Indiana. It was one of the first settlements in Indiana while it was still Indian Territory.

Lincoln Conner had a difficult childhood. His father and mother were harsh and quite poor. He had no shoes as a youngster. His clothing was made from gunnysacks, and in winter his feet were wrapped in rags for warmth. He had to walk three miles to school. His feet were frostbitten and bleeding day after day from harsh weather. In summer he went barefoot. He often told the story that when his parents were fortunate enough to have an orange, they gave the peelings to the children to eat. When he was older with a little money in his pocket, he went to town, bought an orange and peeled it. He ate the peeling and threw the fruit away. Conner grew up on a farm, but aspired to leave and have a professional career.

He must have decided that only the Lord and a good education could raise him above such poor means. At his 70th birthday party hosted by the Dixon, Illinois, Church of God, he told his friends about his difficult youth and the events leading to his education. In those days there were three professions: physician, attorney and clergyman. Lincoln succeeded in practicing two of those.

Lincoln graduated from Northern Indiana Normal School which eventually became Indiana University. It is thought that he enrolled directly after completing his secondary education around 1878, at age 16. If he took four years to graduate Normal school he would have graduated in 1882. It is thought that he began to study law at the Normal school.

In one of his classes he was assigned to debate the subject of immortal soul or mortal man. This was to be done in the style of courtroom debate as if one were trying to persuade a jury. He chose the affirmative for immortal soul. He thought it would not be difficult. He went to the Bible to find sources to prove his case. He could not find any. About the same time he became acquainted with Emma Foor whose uncle was a Church of God evangelist. He began to look at immortality in a different light.

On February 27, 1880, he and Emma Alspach Foor, the daughter of David and Ellen Foor, were married. Lincoln was 18 years old and she was 19. "Uncle" John, as he was affectionately known by everyone, spelled his name with a final *e*, as in Foore.

After the wedding Lincoln worked on his father-in-law's farm. Emma bore him his first healthy son, Harvey Earl, in 1884, and a second son, William Estle, in 1887. A third son, Donald, followed later. A daughter, Myrtle (a.k.a. Mertic), was born in 1889.

Emma died of natural causes in 1893. A notice in the *Rochester Sentinel* stated that Emma died after "going to a huckleberry marsh to pick berries," and being "overcome by heat, was carried back, and being critically ill." She improved by the next day so L.E. Conner left home to keep his preaching appointment. She turned worse, however, and died before he could return home. Suddenly Lincoln had four children to raise. Mertic was only four when her mother died.

Mertic Elnora Conner was adopted at age 10 from Danville, Illinois, by Mrs. Sarah Chaplin-Wickizer in Plymouth, Indiana, on November 9, 1900. Mrs. Wickizer was the widow of Stedman A. Chaplin, a noted Church of God preacher. Emma had been deceased over six years when the adoption occurred. Willie went to live with grandparents. A Cronkite family adopted Harvey. Lincoln married Odessa Elliott in 1894. She was 13 years younger than her husband.

Odessa "Dessa" Conner had also been a child of unfortunate means, having been raised as a scullery maid in a family who treated her badly. As such she was forced to live in an unfinished attic where she slept on boards. She was born in Rossville, Illinois, in January 1875. Records show she graduated from Rossville high school in 1894 at age 19. She must have gone back to school to complete her education after she married Lincoln.

Lincoln and Dessa Conner with Robert and Corrine

A. Early Years

Conner's denominational background prior to preaching for the Church of God may have been the Restoration Movement. In addition to John Foore, Conner came to know all the early Church of God evangelists: John Shaffer, Stedman A. Chaplin, J.F. Wagoner and H.V. Reed of Illinois. From the start of his association with the Church of God, L.E. Conner moved forward as a leader within the denomination.

The accompanying "Letter of Recommendation" from the brethren at Macy, Indiana, is dated October 30, 1886. The letter indicates that Lincoln E. Conner was in good standing with the congregation, and they recommended him to be licensed to preach by the Indiana State Conference of the Church of God. If he had not been in good standing with the church, they would have refused to grant him a letter. This letter provides a rare glimpse into the 19th century congregational practices of a minister's licensing procedures.

L.E. Conner began to preach for the Church of God in 1886 through his association with Uncle John and the brethren in the Argos and Plymouth, Indiana, churches. Plymouth is just north of Macy. The two towns were connected by a railroad which simplified travel between them. If a man could not catch a car to ride, he could walk along the railroad tracks. Several Church of God pastors were known to do just that.

Conner, far right, and committee he served on in 1888.

In January 1887 Lincoln was invited by Elder S.T. Hook to assume the preaching assignment in Noblesville near Greensville, Indiana. This was a temporary appointment while Mr. Hook went to court. During Conner's brief tenure there, several were baptized, and it is surmised they had to cut the ice to accomplish this. Elder Hook was an evangelist in Illinois about whom nothing is known.

At the annual June meeting in 1887, the Indiana Conference appointed Lincoln Conner to be delegate to the national organizational conference that was to be held in Philadelphia in 1888. He was thrust into the national limelight then as one of the youngest delegates to that organizational meeting. After that, he cast a larger shadow and began to be recognized for his inspirational preaching and personal warmth as well as for his business acumen. He traveled throughout the Midwest.

In November 1894, shortly after his wedding to Odessa, Lincoln Conner began to preach for the congregation at Rensselaer, Indiana. It is doubtful he continued there longer than a month or two at the most.

His contact there may have come about through Robert S. Dwiggins and D.T. Halstead, two attorneys in the Rensselaer church. Dwiggins had been the second president of the newly formed General Conference which arose from the Chicago meeting in 1889. While at Rensselaer, Conner very likely continued to read law. There is no evidence that he was a member of the bar either in Indiana or Illinois, but he is listed on various census data as "lawyer."

While in Rensselaer he called for evangelists Benjamin and Mary Woodward to come from Michigan to assist him. They spent a week teaching him, and they alternated preaching evening sermons at his request.

Letter of Recommendation for License to Preach from the Congregation at Macy, Indiana, on behalf of Lincoln E. Conner

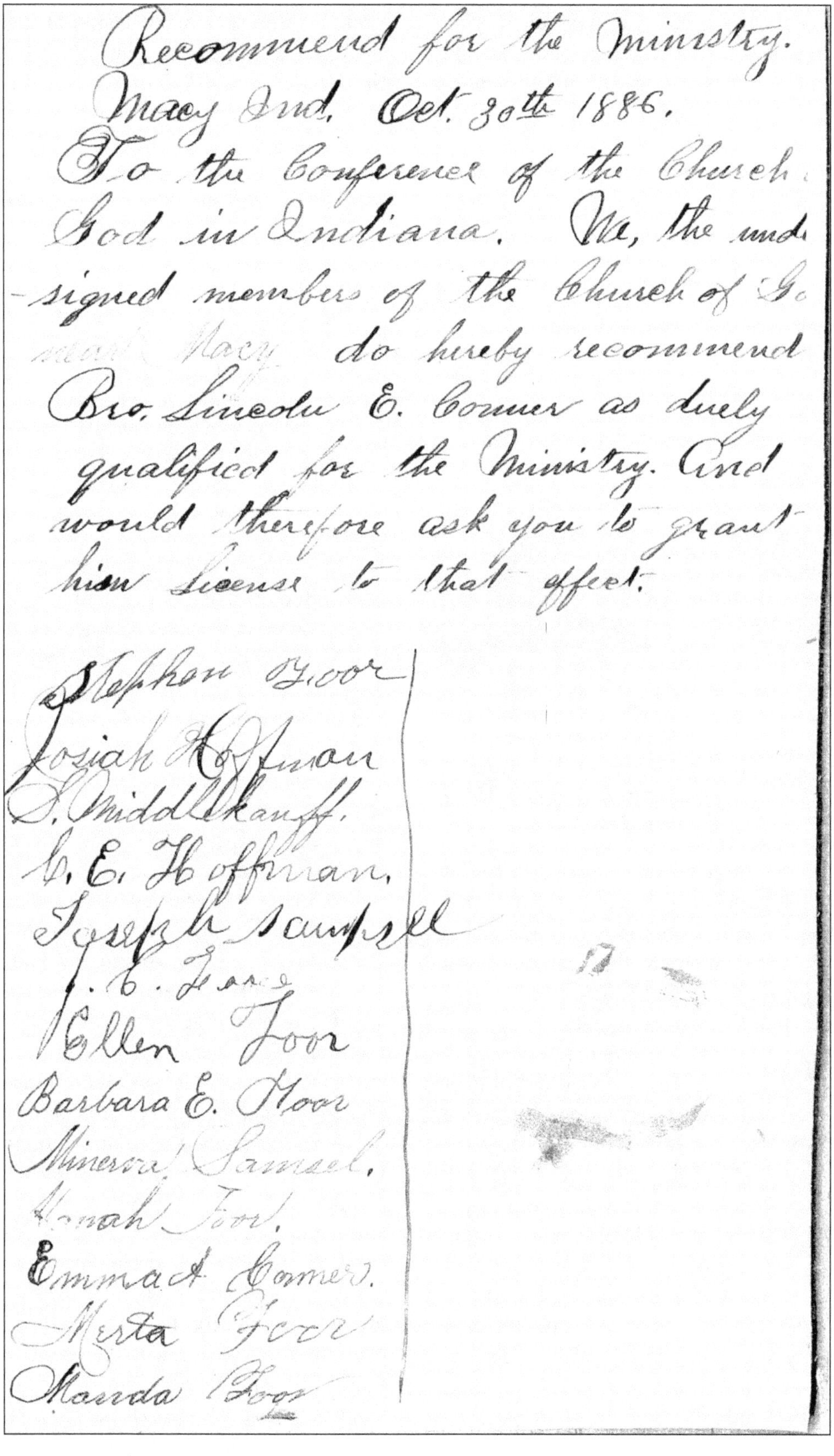

Recommend for the ministry.

Macy Ind. Oct. 30th 1886.

To the Conference of the Church of God in Indiana. We, the undersigned members of the Church of God at Macy do hereby recommend Bro. Lincoln E. Conner as duely qualified for the Ministry. And would therefore ask you to grant him license to that effect.

Stephen Foor
Josiah Hoffman
S. Middlekauff
C. E. Hoffman
Joseph Samsell
J. C. Foor
Ellen Foor
Barbara E. Foor
Minerva Samsell
Hannah Foor
Emma A. Conner
Merta Foor
Maurda Foor

During that same year Conner served as secretary of the Christian Publishing Association, which published *The Restitution* and did job printing for the community.

Records from 1900 indicate that he baptized Mary Cooper in Ripley, Illinois. As with Ripley, he assisted many small churches with special meetings, funerals and conference meetings. Two of these, Casey and Marshall, Illinois, seemed to benefit a great deal from his attention as he resided briefly in Danville, Illinois, just north of those two small towns.

In 1900 Lincoln also worked with folks from Maxenkuckee, Marshall County, Indiana. He assisted Burr Oak in organizing a congregation in a businesslike manner. The Burr Oak brethren had built a building and called a dedication service, but the congregation was in such organizational disarray that the dedication could not be held until the problems were overcome.

B. Uncertain Years

Lincoln and Dessa moved to Oklahoma for unknown reasons, possibly to complete his law education. He may have read law with Horace Speed, an associate of the Indianapolis law firm of Harrison, Haines and Miller. Miller had practiced law in Peru, just down the road from Macy, when Conner was a boy. The Harrison in the firm was Benjamin Harrison who was elected US.. President in 1888.

US President Benjamin Harrison of the lawfirm Harrison, Haines & Miller, Peru, Indiana.

President Harrison assigned Speed to be US District Attorney for Oklahoma in 1889. Conner may have begun reading law with Miller in Peru, and finished up the requirements in Oklahoma with Speed during the years 1896-1898, for we know that Lincoln and Dessa's son, Robert, was born in Oklahoma in 1896.

Conners' Danville home

The family returned to Illinois prior to the birth of their second child, Corrine, in 1898. They rented a home at the east end of Fairchild Street. It was modest in size and style. It was located near the Norfolk Southern railroad tracks. Having grown up with the railroad, Lincoln would have felt at home with the location. Lincoln intended to practice law and to enter politics.

C. Politics Leads to Problems

A.R. Underwood alluded to troubles Conner encountered around Danville, Illinois, when he entered politics. At that time, Conner became involved with "Cannonism," a controversy that Congressional Representative Joseph G. Cannon had with Congress and President Theodore Roosevelt regarding the use of power. Cannon represented the Danville district. His troubles with Congress occurred during his tenure as Speaker of the House from 1903-1911. He held that office longer than any other Speaker except Dennis Hastert who retired from congressional politics in 2007.

During his experiment in politics Lincoln ran into a problem with his wife's friends. The following story appeared in many newspapers:

> **Conner is a prominent Republican politician.**
> L.E. Conner, an attorney, shot five times at J.R. Crews, a prominent furniture dealer of this city Monday, three shots taking effect. After the shooting Conner gave himself up to an officer and sent word to his wife that he had shot Crews and that he would not ruin any more homes. Conner was released on $2,000 bond. It is thought Crews will recover.
> Source: *Fort Wayne News*, July 14, 1903

J.R. Crews was the chairman of the Republican committee for that city or county.

Another newspaper account of that episode stated that Mrs. Conner was acquainted with Mrs. Baumberger, wife of a baker in Fairfield, Illinois. The baker was shot and killed by a third man, O.A. Harvey, two months after the Conner shooting. This second shooting arose from the Conner dispute the previous July. It is surmised that with so many perpetrators, there had been intrigue amongst the ladies and the men. L.E. Conner was determined to clean it up. After that, he had no further incidents regarding his wife. Conner was arrested, tried and acquitted.

Over the years, elderly Church of God historians Grace Marsh, Evelyn Austin and Paul Hatch, friends to Lincoln Conner, privately discussed the shooting. They said it was an incident not commonly known among the brethren. They also said that because Conner was an attorney, he was able to defend himself on the grounds that a man had the right to protect his home.

A.R. Underwood stated in an article in *The Restitution* in 1911, that since living in Danville had not suited Conner well, he left there to return to the ministry in the Church of God where he was received with open arms

L.E. Conner's experiment with politics occurred between 1900 and 1906 because by 1906 Conner had moved his family to Cleveland where he assumed McLauchlan's pastorate at the Church of God Abrahamic Faith, the splintered remnant from Maurice Joblin's Church of the Blessed Hope in 1894. The new church met every Sunday. It rented its building to a Jewish congregation that met on Saturdays, and who turned the pictures of Jesus to the wall.

D. Work of the Holy Spirit

Conner believed that the Holy Spirit was present in believers through the reading of God's Word. The Holy Spirit inspired the men who wrote the Scriptures, and in reading them a believer received that Spirit which is the power of God. This theological idea was not unique to the Church of God. The same doctrine was being taught then by the Restorationists and Adventists. Other denominations went so far as to teach that the Holy Spirit was the third person of the trinity. The Church of God refrained from that teaching.

The discussion about the Spirit that developed in the Church of God is typical of several ongoing discussions of the mid-19th century among Adventists and Age-to-Come ministers. The topics of the other discussions included the place of Israel in prophecy, the time of the re-creation of the new heavens and new earth, and whether there will be probation of mortal nations in the millennium. There were other differences in doctrine, as well, all of which were important details toward the formation of a statement of faith within the Church of God.

Henry Grew, a theologian of the early 19th century, addressed the question of the Holy Spirit in 1851. Grew said, "Some appear to ascribe all our renewal and sanctification exclusively to the Spirit, others exclusively to the Word." Ephraim Miller, noted Indiana preacher, countered, "The truth is found between. We believe that both the Spirit and the Word are concerned in this work." This discussion continued in *The Advent Harbinger*.

Lincoln Conner made a comment about the Spirit that reverberates in the Church of God to this day. The full meaning of his words remains obscure and puzzling. He was quoted by Pastor Francis Burnett as saying, "We don't know what that spirit is, but we don't want it around here." Burnett attended classes with him at the newly formed Oregon Bible College. It was thought that Conner was against Pentecostalism and therefore did not desire to see charismatic tendencies creep into the worship services of the Church of God.

E. Universal Reconciliation and Universal Resurrection

In looking back at the era when universal resurrection was the preferred interpretation in the Church of God, the literature reveals that the term "universal resurrection" apparently had mistakenly become equivalent with the term "universal reconciliation" or "universal salvation" in some people's minds. William Brown, pastor of the Church of the Blessed Hope in Cleveland, wrote a letter to L.E. Conner's congregation, also in Cleveland. In it he explained why the two congregations, once united, could never reunite. L.E. Conner had been accused by Roxanna Wince of believing and teaching universal salvation from the pulpit.

The Brown letter clearly stated the premise that belief in universal resurrection leads to belief in universal salvation. An excerpt of the letter is included on page 66 as proof that misunderstanding of the doctrine led to misuse of the language which, in turn, led to false accusations not only upon L.E. Conner, but also upon the entire organizational effort of the Church of God General Conference at the 1921 conference in Waterloo, Iowa.

The fallacy of Brown's logic is that the Church of God has never taught eternal torment, or eternal life for the wicked.

Conner classed himself with brethren who believed in the "broader hope" or "larger hope"–a term not used much by today's theologians. Broader hope was also sometimes called "second chance," which is language typical of universalism. This teaching also said that sin is temporary to this present evil age and will be set aside in the future so that all men, and even Satan, will be saved. It assumed that the wicked and righteous will be raised at the same time, and during the Millennium the wicked– not only the living of the nations, but also the Adamic dead– will be given a second chance to accept Christ.

Conner believed all men would be raised in the latter days. This idea was known at the time as universal resurrection, also called general resurrection. It is an idea ostensibly taught by Benjamin Wilson early in his life, by S.J. Lindsay and many other prominent leaders in the Church of God. However, while these leaders believed in general resurrection, there is no evidence that they believed in universal salvation or broader hope.

It should be noted that universal or general resurrection means all men will be raised, but it does not mean that all men will be saved. It means the righteous will be saved and the wicked will be condemned. In his later years Benjamin Wilson defined the "wicked" as those who accepted Christ but *backslid and became carnal*. To Wilson, a third category of people were those who never heard of Christ or those who refused to accept him. This class of people would never be raised from the Adamic death. For a full discussion on Benjamin Wilson's understanding of resurrection see the biographical entry under his name.

The majority of the Church of God did not accept the idea of broader hope or second chance. Probation is the term used in the mid-19th century to identify the status of mortal unrighteous nations living at the time that Jesus sets up the millennial kingdom in the Age to Come. These subjects would be respectful to Christ and the Christian rulers appointed by Christ. "Broader hope" and "second chance" were erroneous concepts used to include

The Open Letter
from William Brown, pastor of the Church of the Blessed Hope, to Conner's congregation, Parkwood Church of God

September 9, 1927

Church of God
10623 Lee Avenue
Cleveland, Ohio

To the Official Board, Pastor and Members
Of the Parkwood Church of God

Greetings in Jesus' name;

[The discussion on open/closed communion took six pages. This excerpt commences with page seven.]

Now, we have taken considerable time and space in dealing with the first of the two items of divergence because of the plausibleness of some of the arguments used to support it. The second item of difference between us can be dealt with very briefly. It refers to the Resurrection, which you believe to be universal in its scope, while we believe it to be limited to those responsible to God because of knowledge of His will.

Our position on that point is simply this: Universal Resurrection is an unscriptural doctrine. There is no passage of scripture that undoubtedly teaches universal resurrection. There are numerous passages that undoubtedly teach limited resurrection. We cannot condone a doctrine which, to our mind, is so manifestly unscriptural. Now, as to the question, whether these divergencies are vital, it will be evident to the reader of the foregoing that we consider the first point concerning communion a tremendously important one. And now, with reference to the resurrection, the writer of Hebrews places it among the principles of the doctrine of Christ *and in the foundation*. [editor's note: italics are those of the letter-writer]. Heb. 6:1,2. Now, since the character, safety and security of the Building depends upon the soundness of the foundation, surely anything that affects the foundation must be of vital importance. This [is] well illustrated by considering what the theory of Universal Resurrection leads to. It is the starting point for what I believe to be the distinctive heresy of the church of this generation. I refer to Universalism. It begins with universal resurrection, then, having adopted the theory that all are raised, the mind naturally theorizes on what to do with them, and we have introduced the unscriptural theory of future probation or Russelism which has found its way into the church. It is only a step from Russelism to universal salvation, and many who once held the Truth in its purity and simplicity are now out and out Universalists. They have carried the idea of universal resurrection to its logical conclusion. Of course, if the theory were true, these arguments would have no weight. But being, as we believe, false, and unscriptural, we hold it as being the entering wedge for the destruction of the Faith.

We consider, therefore, that the differences between us are not trivial but tremendous, and therefore, in your present status of belief in open communion and universal resurrection, it is impossible for us to co-operate with you. We would be delighted to see you come back to us as you left us many years ago, to be one with us not only in organization, but in faith and doctrine.

Signed,
W.H. Brown, pastor

The letter was endorsed by Elders Alldridge, Gibbs, Nichols and Pate.
The document was additionally endorsed by Elders Meermans, Huggins, Bell, Miller and Gibbs on July 23, 1944, as the "Statement of Fellowship."

Ref.: *The Open Letter* furnished by Franklyne Ross of Miami, Florida

mortal dead who would be raised to probationary status, a distinctively different idea that promoted universal salvation. Joseph Marsh had emphasized that the biblical teaching of probation focused only on the mortal unsaved nations living at the time of Jesus' return.

F. The Controversy over *The Restitution*

In 1910 Conner took a stand against the editor of *The Restitution*, Arthur R. Underwood, pertaining to his management of the paper. *The Restitution*, as many will recall, was the voice of the Church of God which had descended from the publications of Joseph Marsh and Thomas Newman, *The Prophetic Watchman*, and the merged publications by Benjamin Wilson and Thomas Wilson, *Gospel Banner and Herald of the Coming Kingdom*. *The Restitution* was a highly esteemed publication for many years.

By 1910 private opinion within the Church of God considered *The Restitution* to be less effective than it formerly had been. This attitude is illustrated from an exchange between O.J. Allard of Iowa and Peter Jeffrey of Illinois. Jeffrey related the dialogue in a letter to A.R. Underwood through a special publication called "To Our Brotherhood" which was produced to explain the accusations against *The Restitution*. Jeffrey wrote:

> ...Brother Allard who has complained to myself in his correspondence with me, stated "that the Restitution does not represent the church (of God) in Indiana by any means. It represents two churches is all, and that if a majority of the brethren in Indiana today were called upon to vote they would vote it down.

While the corporate opinion of the brethren seemed to dislike the way in which the Ministerial Association attacked *The Restitution* and its editor, the majority also seemed to agree that the paper was not meeting the needs of the readers as it once had.

The Restitution Herald was begun at the urging of the newly formed Ministerial Association in 1911. With the appearance of *The Restitution Herald* in Oregon, Illinois, the circulation of *The Restitution* began to decline.

The Underwood controversy had reared its head in the autumn of 1910 and raged throughout most of 1911 through the pages of *The Restitution*. Great *Restitution* reader loyalty is seen during this time. *The Restitution* had been highly regarded as the inheritor of the publication legacy initiated by Joseph Marsh many decades before. Readers wrote in and defended Underwood. One made an accusation that Conner believed in universal salvation. Roxanna Wince and her blind female companion both testified that they had heard Conner preach it at a meeting of the Indiana conference. This accusation took the focus off the problems of *The Restitution* for several weeks.

Conner did not deny believing this doctrine, a doctrine which was circulating among some Church of God ministers in those days. Lincoln Conner acknowledged that his belief was outside the norm of Church of God shared doctrines. He declared that he did not preach privately held views from the pulpit, a claim Roxanna Wince disputed. But if he believed it, he was not alone. Other proponents of this doctrine were J.W. Williams, Iowa; G.M. Myers, Nebraska/Kansas; and E.O. Stewart, Arkansas. Elder Stewart reportedly left the Arkansas Conference because of it.

Perhaps the reader can understand how the doctrine of universal salvation might be embedded in a discussion about universal resurrection. Universal salvation was not accepted by the general voting body of delegates of the Church of God at any of its general conferences in the 20th century. It does not seem to be an issue for the postmodern Church of God. As a body, the Church of God repudiated the doctrine of universal salvation, and yet some of the Iowa churches hold universal salvation in high acclaim.

G. 1910 Waterloo Conference

L.E. Conner and D.C. Robison were friends in spite of holding different theological positions. They must have known each other from their common Ohio associations, but the tension of the 1910 summer conference in Waterloo, Iowa, surely must have tested their friendship for they were on opposing sides. The purpose of the conference was to organize a national general conference. The heated debate on doctrinal issues, such as resurrection, Holy Spirit and Sabbath-keeping prevented accord. Conner said later, that while that conference was not a pleasant one, his friendship with Robison was the one good thing that resulted from it.

At the 1910 Waterloo Conference, the credentials committee said individuals could not vote, and individual churches could not have delegates. Only delegates representing state conferences could vote, leaving Lincoln Conner out. He raised the issue during discussions, so O.J. Allard made a motion that all members be allowed to vote. It failed. G.E. Marsh countered with a motion that no individuals or churches be allowed to vote. That carried. A.J. Eychaner moved that the conference grant L.E. Conner delegate status with full conference powers. That passed. Even though Conner was able to vote, the ordeal was humiliating. He went home angry.

Except for the direct intervention of A.J. Eychaner, Conner would have been shunned. Perhaps part of the delegate hostility arose from Conner's involvement in the trouble about *The Restitution*.

After he returned to Cleveland, Conner called a meeting of five ministers. Together they organized a Ministerial Association which continues to this day. The group of ministers that met at Conner's home were

Conner, S. J. Lindsay, Illinois; Joseph W. Williams, Iowa,;F.L. Austin, Ontario; and F.V. Blakely, Michigan.

The purpose of the new association was to promote the general welfare of ministers, to bring churches and brethren into unity and fellowship, to prevent unbecoming conduct on part of members of the Church of God–such as had been exhibited at the 1910 conference just past– and to prevent dissension, discord and divisions within the Church of God on account of agitation on questions of "no good."

1. The Ministerial Association

The Ministerial Association was organized nearly 11 years before the national organization of the General Conference. Like the National Berean Society which organized in 1913, and of which several of those ministers became members, it was visionary in its desire to use organization as a tool of power for the common good of ministers and the brethren. It is doubtful if there would be a national conference today except for the example given by the Bereans led by those who exemplified the Bible study character of Church of God members, and the Ministerial Association led by those who desired to see a business-oriented national general conference.

The organization of the Ministerial Association was very controversial among preachers and church members. Many saw it as a direct attempt to wrest *The Restitution* from A.R. Underwood, its rightful owner. Many readers were aghast at this behavior from the "Ministerial Monopoly" as one reader called it, and all manner of spiteful things were said about it and its founders in the pages of *The Restitution*. The Ministerial Association answered its critics and carried on with its goals.

Because of the Ministerial Association, the ministers of the Church of God were in a prime position to gain recognition as delegates from the credentials committee when the General Conference finally was incorporated in 1921. If they were to have a voice in the development of the new organization, the ministers must have a vote at the annual meeting. They could not assist in conducting the business of the conference if they were not recognized as delegates of it. It seems fitting that one of their ministers, James Patrick, became the first president and another minister, L.E. Conner, was elected vice president in the new General Conference. As an important interest group within the denomination, they had found a way to be heard.

The constitution of the non-profit organization of the Church of God General Conference, doing business as the National Bible Institute at Oregon, Illinois, provided one vote per *member* church for up to 15 members, and one vote thereafter for every 50 members within a local congregation. It allowed one vote per state conference if the delegate were present at a general conference business session, and one vote for each licensed minister in attendance. In the 1950s it was agreed, either by constitutional amendment or policy of the credentials committee, to include each director on the conference Board to have one vote as well.

> **Resolutions from the Minutes of Ministerial Meeting, November 29, 1910, emphasizing three objections:**
>
> Whereas, it is a well recognized fact that a favorably received publication is one of the best means to insure the success of any cause; and whereas, so large a proportion of the members of the Church of God have lost confidence in the management of the paper so long recognized as the official organ of the Church of God as greatly to hinder the cause of truth and impair ministerial and evangelistic effort;
>
> Therefore be it resolved: That this Association hereby recommends the organization of a stock company for the purpose of publishing a weekly paper which shall meet the requirements of a true church organ.
>
> Resolved: That this Association hereby commend the formulation and distribution of concise statements of the more prominent fundamental doctrines of the Church of God for the enlightenment of others; but accept the Bible in its entirety, and the Bible only, as the standard of the members of the church [which] shall be measured and discipline administered.
>
> Ref.: *Present Truth*, St. Paul, Nebraska. 12:3, December 1910

2. A Split

The conference turmoil of 1910 provided the impetus for change and L.E. Conner seized the opportunity to turn things around. He and the "Ministerial Five"–a term coined by historian David Graham–began *The Restitution Herald* shortly after their organization. As a result of the conflict arising out of the 1910 Waterloo Conference, and the disagreement over the church magazines between the forces of S.J. Lindsay and A.R. Underwood, the Church of God split. Five local congregations of the Church of God opted to remain separate from the new general conference. There were too many doctrinal problems to blame Conner for the split.

The Ministerial Association drafted a constitution that encouraged other Church of God clergy to join the group. S.J. Lindsay was made chairman of the new association. It was further resolved that "The Association recommend the organization of a stock company for the purpose of publishing a weekly paper which shall meet the requirements of a true church organ." Further, the new association "heartily" commended the "formulation and distribution of concise statements of the more prominent fundamental doctrines of the Church of God for the enlightenment of others, but accept the Bible in its entirety and only as the standard by which the faith and conduct of the members of the Church shall be measured and discipline administered." This printed statement of faith was not intended to *define* the Church of God, but to be used to *explain* the Bible for purposes of evangelism.

Conner was a member of the new editorial board of *The Restitution Herald*. He began to travel from church to church to offer legal assistance, to teach and preach, and to baptize. He was an outstanding and commanding orator and emissary of the new paper. He reported all his activities in *The Herald* and gained a following.

Conner was a teacher in the newly formed Bible Training School, and an evangelist for the Illinois Conference of the Churches of God. His schedule was even more tightly packed after he became an evangelist for the General Conference in 1922.

L.E. Conner left his pastorate at the Cleveland Church of God in 1929. He had been pastor there for 23 years and the church had relocated twice during his tenure. Lincoln and Dessa moved to Oregon, Illinois, where he became the new business manager of the General Conference, and from there to Dixon in December 1930, where he assumed the pastorate at the Church of God. During his career he also preached in Rockford, Illinois, Tempe, Arizona, and Hammond, Louisiana.

Lincoln replaced Floyd A. Stilson as business manager of the General Conference in 1929. Stilson left to return to teaching in South Bend. As part of his duties with the Conference, Conner preached wherever pulpits were vacant in the Church of God. He helped to strengthen the new church at Rockford, Illinois, by including it in his preaching circuit beginning in 1933.

LE Conner, left front in white, posed with Church of God Ministers at Oregon, Illinois, in 1943.

H. The New General Conference

Conner served as vice president and president of the Board of Directors, a position he was to hold for 12 years from 1930 until his death in 1943. There were no term limits in those days. He was prominent in teaching at the Summer Bible Training School (BTS) held in Oregon from 1922 to 1933 until the formation of the Oregon Bible College in 1941. He continued to preach and to write and to serve wherever he was called.

In 1938, this story circulated among the nation's newspapers:

> **Correspondence School of Religion Proposed by the Church of God Oregon, Il.**
> The establishment of a correspondence school of religious service was proposed Wednesday afternoon by Rev. G.E. Marsh of this city, secretary of the general council of Churches of God, now in annual session here. The plan, to be voted upon at a later meeting, is designed to meet needs of young men and women unable to attend residence schools. Other Church of God pastors who spoke before the council included Rev. L.E. Conner, Dixon, president of the general conference, who presided at a round table discussion of home missions.
> (*Freeport Journal-Standard*, Freeport, IL, Aug. 4, 1938)

For the next several years he enjoyed reasonably good health while he continued in ministry. In 1941, he and Dessa retired from the ministry, having served the pulpits in Dixon and Rockford, Illinois, for at least ten years. They entered the Golden Rule Home with a lifetime membership to live out their days. In 1943, Lincoln's health took a turn for the worse.

His final illness resulted from a blood clot in a foot. He stayed for two weeks at the local hospital, and when released supposed the problem was corrected. He grew ill again near Macy, Indiana, while on a preaching trip to Rensselaer, and was taken to Woodlawn Hospital in Rochester. He had surgery there, possibly for another clot, on July 31, 1943. He underwent surgery again in December, but succumbed during the procedure from bleeding that could not be stopped. Pastor Sydney E. Magaw, editor of *The Restitution Herald*, conducted his funeral service giving words of hope on "death and the promised victory" at the Christian church in Macy.

Ministers present at his funeral were Sydney Magaw, F.L. Austin, G.E. Marsh, F.A. Stilson, A.M. Jones, C.E. Randall, F.E. Siple, A. Weldon McCoy, M.W. Lyon (who sang a beautiful song), Paul C. Johnson, Harvey U. Krogh Jr., Cantwell Drabenstott, C.R. Randall, Emory L. Macy and James Mattison.

After his death, Dessa contemplated moving to California to be near her daughter, but she continued to retain membership and residence at Golden Rule Home until one year before her death. She moved to Peru, Indiana, to be near her son, Robert, and entered the Donut Nursing Home. She died February 13, 1948, at age 63.

A visit to the family plot in Plainview Cemetery at Macy, Indiana, revealed that Lincoln Conner is buried beside his first wife, Emma. His second wife, Odessa, lies beside their son, Robert and wife, Alta, in Row 15.

Robert J. Conner farmed in Macy, Indiana, nearly his whole life except while he served in WWI. "Jack" Conner described his father Robert "who in my objective

judgment is the only man I have known who was truly humble in the divine sense of that word spoken by Jesus." Corrine married Mr. Armstrong and moved to Los Angeles when her parents lived in Cleveland.

I. Influential within the Church of God

L.E. Conner was very much part of the formation of the fabric and literature of the Church of God in the 19th and 20th centuries. He was greatly loved by the people. He wrote for *The Restitution Herald*, and he was the subject of news stories in that same magazine being a person of great interest to readers. He was popular and influential throughout the Churches of God in the nation, so much so that when a rumor circulated that he stood against the formation of the General Conference in 1920, he found it necessary to immediately publish a letter stating his support. He said he was in favor of it and heartily endorsed it.

His obituary, published in *The Restitution Herald*, December 14, 1943, shows that he was loved and highly esteemed:

> Let there be mourning throughout the Church of God. L.E. Conner is dead. His high purpose to live like Christ is stamped upon us, (and we must) press incessantly forward in the work, hard work, he loved and left for us.

See Allard, O.J.
   Brown, William
   Dwiggins, Robert S.
   Halstead, D.T.
   Marsh, Joseph
   McLauchlan, Robert
   Railsback, Emma (20th), for Ezra's motion regarding
      The Restitution
   Robison, D.C.
   Stilson, Floyd A. (20th)
   Wilson. Benjamin
   Lindsay, Samuel J.
   Underwood, Arthur R.
   Wince, Sarah Roxanna

Bibliography: ABC Biography Project, David Krogh, compiler; Brown, William, "An Open Letter to Parkwood Church of God" at Cleveland, L.E. Conner, pastor Sept. 9, 1927; Conner, Jack E. "Memories of L.E. Conner," from a letter by L.E. Conner dated Feb. 3, 1943. *Church of God History Newsletter* 4:1 Summer 1991; "Emma Foor" retrieved from the Foor family genealogy website at www.fooregenealogy.com 11 June 1998, webmaster: Shelly Hallard of Ohio, including several e-mails Summer 2006; "Excerpt" *Fiftieth Anniversary of the Church of God at Burr Oak, Ind. Dec. 12, 1950*; Ferrell, Terry. Interview by phone with Jan Stilson, July 14, 2009; Fonthill, Ontario 50th Anniversary, *The Restitution Herald*, Sydney Magaw, editor, Oregon, Illinois, March 15, 1949; Foreman, Grant. "Horace Speed". *Chronicles of Oklahoma*. Oklahoma Historical Society 25:5 retrieved from the Digital Library of OkState.edu; Graham, David. Several e-mails during Spring and Summer 2006. Discussion from his research notes; Graham, David. Church of God "Connexion & Review," *Wisdom and Power*, Nov. 1992; Indiana Works Progress Administration. *Index to Marriage Record. Miami County 1850-1920 Inclusive*. Vol. 1. Original record located County Clerk's office Peru, Indiana. 1938; Jeffrey, Peter in "To Our Brotherhood" special edition of *The Restitution Herald*, S. J. Lindsay, ed., Oregon, Il., circa June 1911; Ordnung, Elizabeth. Diary. A note there about Conner's blood clot problem, March 10, 1943; "Church of the Blessed Hope" retrieved from www.wikipedia.com, December 30, 2007; "Indiana Conference Report" *The Restitution*, July 4, 1887; Notice of preaching at Noblesville, *The Restitution*, January 19, 1887.

Cook, John B.
b. December 17, 1803
d. October 14, 1888

A. Aberrations
B. Back on Track

Evangelist J.B. Cook was born in Hanover, New Jersey. His family moved to Brooklyn in 1869. After his ordination he accepted a call to preach in Rochester, New York, where one parishioner was becoming famous throughout New England. His name was Joseph Marsh.

Growing up during the Second Great Awakening that spread throughout New England, Cook could not have failed to feel the passion for the Lord's work during his youth. Most likely the Second Advent message of William Miller, so prevalent in that time and place, significantly impacted young Cook. When Cook began to preach, it was an Adventist message.

J.B. Cook began preaching before the Bitter Disappointment. He was pastor in Middletown, Connecticut, at a small Baptist church. He left that pastorate sometime in 1843 "coming out of Babylon" to preach the second coming. He was a noted scholar of Hebrew and Greek. A letter written to Joseph Marsh in *The Voice of Truth* (November 1844) comforted readers after the disillusionment of yet another disappointment.

J.B. Cook preached near Oswego, New York, in February 1845. During that year he planned to publish a series in *The Voice of Truth* about the "Mistakes of Millerism." Up to March 1845, three dates had been set for the return of Christ which did not materialize into a second coming: October 22, 1843; April 10, 1844; October 22, 1844. Just as the second article in Cook's series was to debut, it was held back by Editor Marsh, stating "We think there is a strong probability that the actual coming of the Lord will correct all real and supposed 'mistakes in Millerism' before the close of April" (1845).

Sister Roxanna Wince related later that Cook had been preaching about prophecy and judgment and was stirring up a great deal of interest. This was before and after the Bitter Disappointment and many people and preachers in established non-Adventist churches did not want to disband their organizations. Apparently this meant that while they wished to maintain their denominational identity, they still were open to learning the truths about the second coming of Christ and, therefore, invited preachers in who understood it.

On one occasion, J.B. Cook preached for the Baptists in the home church of David Millard and wife. The Millards accepted the Kingdom message, but Elder Barnes did not accept it. Barnes resisted Cook's teachings. He talked against Cook. Day after day, as J.B. Cook presented his series, tension grew. Cook, being frail, crumbled and said he could not preach there anymore.

After preaching at Oswego, New York, J.B. Cook moved on to appointments at Kingsbury, Indiana, quite a distance away.

This church was jointly led by Elder Barnes and Stedman Chaplin. Even though these pastors stood at opposite ends of belief on the subject of Age to Come, both men were invited to remain as pastors. Chaplin believed in it; Barnes did not. Eventually Elder Chaplin broke with the Baptists.

A. Aberrations

For a little while, J.B. Cook fell under the spell of certain preachers who were saying that Christ had already come. This may have been the result of his acceptance of the theology of the "shut door," or the "cleansing of the sanctuary." An accusation was made by D.I. Robinson (it is thought "Robison" was meant, father of D.C. Robison in Cleveland) in *The Voice of Truth* of December 1845, that Cook and J.D. Pickands had been preaching in Cleveland that Christ had already "come." The former (Pickands) said that the first resurrection had taken place "they are now judging the world, reigning with Christ, riding on white horses and eating and drinking with Christ."

Pickands wrote to *The Voice of Truth* within the next few months and recanted all "his sad departures from the word of the Lord." He said Cook could not give it up until he gave up his interpretation of God's providence having guided him into the shut door theory. Before it was over, William Miller would comment in *The Advent Herald*, "Bro. Cook's head is in the fog." He indicated Cook had held on to '43 and the 7*th* month so fiercely that he left the first principle: the *personal* second advent of Christ.

J.B. Cook's Cleveland publication entitled *Voice of the Fourth Angel* (J.D. Pickands, co-editor) didn't last long. This sheet agreed in some manner with Orlando Squires' *The Voice of the Shepherd*, who was credited with beginning the interpretation of an invisible coming of Christ which ultimately evolved into the doctrine of spiritualism. This new doctrine was sensational and caused major confusion among the people. Cook's paper was not very helpful in explaining the Bible. It must be remembered, however, that good men such as Cook, schooled in Bible and theology, were searching for spiritual explanations of the present realm. Often their search took them into uncharted waters.

The duration of Cook's publication is not known but during that run Joseph Marsh described it as a "small but valuable sheet." One can only speculate that Marsh considered it valuable because it was so blatantly riddled with error. Both Cook and Pickands suffered loss of reputation with the brethren because of spiritualism.

Following the demise of *The Voice of the Fourth Angel,* Cook began to contribute correspondence and articles regularly to Marsh's *Voice of Truth*. It seemed to be a good thing that Cook stayed in touch with Marsh for this editor proved to be a steadying and uplifting force on Cook, a man who for awhile seemed double-minded and unstable in all his ways.

In the April 1846 issue of *The Voice of Truth*, Elon Galusha wrote an open letter to J.B. Cook, where in effect he testified of Cook's love for the Advent message. He said Cook loved it so much so that when he learned of it, he was baptized, as was Galusha also. Galusha said, "I also assent to the truthfulness of your assertion that the spirit and principle which led you to the baptismal stream and into the Advent is the spirit and principle by which you are now governed." Galusha continued by saying that Cook had misfigured the time of the Second Advent in 1846 because he believed that Christ had come in 1843. He then completely laid out a comparison of the prophecies for the readers to show how Cook had been mistaken in this.

Galusha said:
> The difference in our views is as follows. You think the 2300 days have ended, and, therefore the event which characterizes their termination has occurred, while I think the event which characterizes their termination **has not** occurred and therefore, the 2300 days have not ended. Both admit a mistake—you in the manner, I in the time.

Galusha was responding to Cook's article or pamphlet "Doctrine of Providence." Galusha concluded, "I approve your application of those principles until you fly off on the tangent of the bridegroom come and the door shut theory."

If Cook knew about Galusha's letter, he ignored it when corresponding to *The Day Star*, edited by E. Jacobs. Cook's correspondence was subsequently copied to *The Voice of Truth* with nary a word about Galusha's letter. Rather, Cook related to the readers the state of Mrs. Mathewson in Coventry, Connecticut, who 12 years before had died and was revived with a testimony of angels singing and bright lights during her passing. Upon her return to life she fasted for 14 weeks and afterward was not hungry. She was bedridden and was permanently debilitated for the remainder of her life. Some among the spiritualists revered her.

Cook let many weeks go by without contacting Joseph Marsh at *The Voice of Truth*, but when he did in October 1846, it was to discuss the situation and to assure Marsh that he (Cook) had not gone off the deep end with editor Jacobs at *Day Star*. Rather, he still believed in the imminent soon return of Jesus, and Marsh concluded that much of what Cook believed agreed with the rest of the second coming brethren. Cook later submitted his story to the pages of *The Voice of Truth* and that settled the matter.

B. Back on Track

Soon thereafter, J.B. Cook submitted a lengthy article to *The Voice of Truth* entitled, "Return of the Jews." Cook's side-trip into Spiritualism was forgiven. He was back in the fold of the second coming adherents. During his tangential travels he purportedly also accepted the Seventh-day doctrine of Sabbatarianism as preached by Elder Thomas M. Preble. After his departure from Shut Door and Sabbatarianism, Cook continued to preach the Age-to-Come doctrine throughout the Far West and reported his trips in the pages of the new series of the *Advent Harbinger and Bible Advocate*.

So well entrenched was Cook in the good graces of Joseph Marsh, that Marsh entrusted him to debate L.D. Mansfield in *The Harbinger* on Marsh's favorite subject at that time: "The Age to Come." Marsh's book by that title had been published for nearly a year when the debate began. It continued for several issues with Cook making strong arguments. Many considered he won the debate.

Cook had long been an admirer of Marsh, but after Dr. John Thomas entered Marsh's life, the relationship was never the same. The Church of God at Rochester was never the same either. Thomas introduced his notion of re-baptism. That idea demanded that once you have learned of the Gospel of the Kingdom and the Age to Come, you must withdraw from your old church and be re-baptized because for the first time you have learned the truth, and it must be acknowledged with baptism. The issue of re-baptism was prominent in church history through the practice of the Anabaptists in Europe who were re-baptized after their withdrawal from the Catholic Church during the Reformation. Their method of rebaptism was immersion whereas formerly they had been sprinkled.

Thomas also introduced the idea of mortal emergence of Christians from the grave on resurrection morning. Both ideas were abhorrent to Marsh who resisted them through his preaching and writings. Marsh refused to be re-baptized after his repudiation of the Millerite doctrine, and after his study and acceptance of the Age-to-Come doctrine. Marsh felt his faith at the time of conversion and baptism were valid. Dr. Thomas stirred up trouble because of it.

Soon, the Church of God at Rochester nearly imploded from members going over to Thomas and forsaking their friend Joseph Marsh. Even J.B. Cook abandoned Marsh. Marsh left and returned to the Christian Connexion. J.B. Cook continued preaching the Gospel of the Kingdom. It is not known what association, if any, Cook continued to have with Dr. Thomas, but it is known that the Church of God at Rochester continued to be influenced by Dr. Thomas' pet teachings.

The Rochester Church of God began to teach mortal emergence, according to a note that appeared in *The Herald of the Coming Kingdom and Christian Instructor* in January 1868. Thomas Wilson, *The Herald's* editor, learned of the situation at the Rochester church from a report by George Moyer, Wilson's assistant at *The Herald*. The Rochester people did not feel this doctrine was prerequisite to baptism, but rather was for instruction to believers after baptism. It was not an essential item of "saving faith." Moyer said he was not quite prepared to accept the idea of mortal emergence.

J.B. Cook was recognized by scholars as representing the Gospel of the Kingdom. In 1883 he was sent a copy of the book *The Law and the Covenants, and the Sabbath* by Dr. L.C. Thomas, formerly of Wyoming, and recently relocated to Dover, Delaware. Cook reviewed it along with 40 other readers, whose reviews were published in the front pages of the book. Cook, residing in Brooklyn, New York, at the time said, "A very valuable book, written ably, successfully and profitably."

Cook gave up evangelism in his old age, and spent the last few years of his life among his books. His wife died on April 28, 1885.

John Cook died at his home in Brooklyn of heart failure. His memorial service was conducted by Pastor George Kramer of the Church of God. Kramer extolled the ministry and testimony of the beloved Cook who was interred beside his dear wife in the old cemetery of Hartford, Connecticut. His obituary was published in the *Brooklyn Eagle* and *The Restitution*.

See Chaplin, Stedman A.
   Kramer, George R.
   Marsh, Joseph

Bibliography: Chamberlin, E.L.H. "Letter from Chamberlin," *The Voice of Truth*, March 5, 1845; Cook, J.B. "Report of Trip to West."

The Advent Harbinger and Bible Advocate, July 20, 1850; Cook, J. B. "Sister Mathewson" *The Voice of Truth,* as published in the *Day Star.* April 8, 1846; "Letter to Joseph Marsh on Cook's association with *Day Star.*" *The Voice of Truth,* Oct. 21, 1846; "Return of the Jews." *The Voice of Truth,* Nov. 11, 1846; Cook, J.B. and Mansfield, "L.D. Debate on the Age to Come," *The Advent Harbinger and Bible Advocate,* Aug. 10, 1850 intermittently to Nov. 30, 1850; Galusha, Elon. "Letter to Bro. J.B. Cook," *The Voice of Truth,*. April 1, 1846, *The Herald of the Coming Kingdom and Christian Instructor,* Jan. 1, 1868, 57; Marsh, Joseph. "Mistakes in Millerism," (deferred) *The Voice of Truth* March 26, 1845; Editorial Comment on J.B. Cook's position; Dec. 31, 1845; Oct. 14, 1846; Miller, William. "Letter to Advent Herald." Copied in T*he Voice of Truth,* May 13, 1846; Notice of publication of *Voice of the Fourth Angel. The Voice of Truth,* Jan. 1, 1845; Obituary, Mrs. J.B. Cook, *Restitution,* May 13, 1885; Obituary. *Brooklyn Eagle* as republished in the *Restitution,* S.A. Chaplin, editor. Plymouth, Indiana. October 24, 1888; Pickands, "Letter to Joseph Marsh." *The Voice of Truth* ,April 29, 1846; May 6, 1846; Preble, T.M. Sabbatariansim. *Hope of Israel,* Feb. 28, 1845. This source is cited on numerous Seventh-day Adventist websites; *The Restitution,* May 22, 1907; May 29, 1907; Robison, D.I. "Letter to Marsh." *The Voice of Truth,* Dec. 31, 1845; Thomas, Dr. L.C. *The Law, the Covenants and the Sabbath.* Self. Dover, Del. 1883; Williams, Byron. *Abstracts of Obituaries and Weddings from the Restitution,* Self-published. 1994.

Cooper, William S.
b. 1867
d. Unknown

William Cooper was the stepson of Joshua Bailey of the Blush, Missouri, Church of God. Lucinda Cooper Smithson was Bailey's second wife. By the time William was 14, the lad was already earning his living as a farm laborer with the Henry Magill family. Along the way, the Bailey family learned of the Gospel of the Kingdom, possibly from Uncle John Foore who baptized William, or from William H. Wilson, Benjamin Wilson or other itinerant preachers who traveled through the Blush area. As an adult, William Cooper labored in the Fredericktown area to begin another congregation there.

William was an influential man in the community. He had oversight of the schools, essentially, being the Superintendent of Schools.

The Church of God at Fredericktown became known as the Cooper church. Blush Church of God became the Wagganer church and practiced a conservative style of worship. The Blush church never affiliated with the Church of God General Conference.

Bibliography: Ancestry.com U.S. Census. 1870. Cassville, Mo. Barry Co., McDonald Township; Graham, David, e-mail to author. March 1, 2006; *The Restitution,* May 1922; Graham, Jerry. Interview at Pastor Ed Graham's Memorial Serivce, Oregon Church of God, July 13, 2009.

Corbaley, Alvaro Lenhardt
b. January 1, 1862
d. November 12, 1941

A.L. "Allie" Corbaley was born in Marshall County, Indiana, the center of Church of God activities in Indiana. On July 22, 1888, he married Annie Matilda Elizabeth Gard in Waterville, Douglas, Washington Territory. Allie's father, Richard Corbaley, performed the ceremony. Annie was born June 6, 1870, in Kelseyville, Lake, California to George Washington Gard and Eliza Jane Hand Gard.

Allie's journal has this entry from January 1, 1885:

Annie Gard Corbaley

> I came to Badger Mountain Washington Territory May 11, 1884 from California where I had been working with the engineers upon the construction of the SF and SPRR [railroad] for 18 months before. Today is my birthday and I am 23 years of age. There have been six of us at Platt's house.

Platt Corbaley was his older brother. One of those six was Richard Corbaley, Allie's father.

Allie and Annie had eight children, of which William Paul Corbaley was the oldest and became the grandfather of Darlene Mann who presented much of the data for this entry.

Delbert Rankin supplied this interesting information which was related to him by Pastor Lyle Rankin:

> After having left Waterville and riding by horseback through the old stagecoach passes across the Cascades, he settled his family at Puyallup. To find interested parties in Bible matters, he attended (and was not always welcome) at different denominational churches. One—a Christian Church—he found success in that he could answer questions their minister could not and the people began to turn to him. One such question regarded how many kingdoms of God does the Bible speak of? Bro. Corbaley spoke of one, the minister said 13. There were other issues as well.
>
> Out of a split came three groups: the Christian group remaining, some going to Church of Christ (a sister Campbellite group), and some (including the John Rankin family, his wife Emma having recognized the faith from her Kansas baptism) to the Church of God. The Church of God met thereafter in the local library.

A.L. Corbaley's writings appear in the pages of *The Restitution* and *The Restitution Herald* as an organizer and teacher of Bible studies and congregations in that area. In 1922 he preached at the Northwest Conference on the subject of "Creation." At this conference the delegates ratified the new General Conference Constitution and By-laws and became members of the conference.

Corbaley also wrote "Coming Events in the Light of Prophecy." This was published posthumously by the National Bible Institute around 1945. It was a small booklet of 59 pages which clearly and concisely described the events at the end of this age, and the next age. It is well worth reading and may be found in the Archives at Atlanta Bible College.

Throughout his life Allie preached the Gospel of the Kingdom. One relative recalled that Allie knew every verse in the New Testament. Terry Ferrell recalled hearing Scripture "duels" between A.L. Corbaley and Emma Railsback, pastor of the Los Angeles Church. Terry said "It was amazing to hear them recite entire chapters of books of the Bible. One would quote a chapter and the other would pick up and quote the next chapter."

Wherever Allie preached he also sang, for he had a rich bass voice. Aunt Dorothy also loved to play the piano for him for she loved to hear him sing the old hymns.

Annie died a year or so before her husband on August 6, 1940, in Puyallup, Pierce, Washington. She was 70 years old at her death. Allie succumbed to the weakness of old age on November 12, 1941, in Puyallup. On November 15 he was interred beside his wife at Woodbine Cemetery in Puyallup.

See Corbaley, Richard, IV
Railsback, Emma

Bibliography: Corbaley, A.L. *Coming Events in the Light of Prophecy*. NBI, Oregon, Il. circa 1945; Ferrell, Terry. Interview with Jan Stilson, July 14, 2009; *The Restitution Herald*, October 1922.; Mann, Darlene. E-mail to JStilson, 2006; Rankin, Delbert. E-mail to J. Stilson, Oct. 15, 2009.

Corbaley, John
b. 1850?
d. Unknown

John Corbaley was the son of Richard and Jane Corbaley in Marshall County, Indiana. He was one of eight children. Richard was instrumental in spreading the message of the Gospel of the Kingdom throughout Indiana.

Bro. and Sr. John Corbaley were married in Plymouth, Indiana on April 18, 1872. They moved from Plymouth to Los Angeles, California around the turn of the century. The Corbaleys were fortunate enough to celebrate their 50th anniversary on April 18, 1922, in their son Earl's home. Their son, Clarence, was also present. Evangelist Mary Woodward, mother of F.L. Austin, was in California on a ministry trip to isolated members. She attended the anniversary gathering and sent notice of it to the church paper.

See Corbaley, Richard, IV
Woodward, Mary A.

Bibliography: *The Restitution Herald* May 9, 1922.

Corbaley, Richard, IV
b. August 7, 1820
d. July 16, 1903

Richard was the first white child born in Marion County, Indiana. Marion County was part of the New Purchase which was purchased from Native Indians in 1818 and contained about one-third of Indiana including Indianapolis. The area retains that identity to this day.

Richard's parents were Jeremiah James and Jane Barnhill Corbaley. Jeremiah was a farmer, and he was active in helping establish Indianapolis. The family moved to Marshall County near Plymouth in 1839. Jane was the daughter of Adam and Susannah (Goosehorn) Barnhill, and the sister of Hugh Sharon Barnhill. On May 6, 1847, Richard married Jane Croco. She was 20 years old, and he was 27 at the time. Jane was born October 8, 1827, in Holmes County, Indiana. She died March 15, 1915, in San Diego, California. Richard and Jane had six sons and two daughters. Jeremiah died at age three and Ida May died at age eight. The rest of the children lived to adulthood, married and had families.

Paul Hatch reported that Richard became involved in the Old Union Church north of Indianapolis on Eagle Creek originally organized by Patrick Logan in the 1830s. Logan had been a Campbellite in Virginia, but was also familiar with the teachings of Dr. John Thomas. This must have introduced some Christadelphian influence at Old Union. Thomas had also been a Disciple in Virginia, but left them over a doctrinal dispute around 1842. Logan seemed to be a hybrid of Thomas' thinking and Ephraim Miller's Age-to-Come ideas. Miller who also preached at Old Union and Argos was a disciple of Joseph Marsh. Arlen Rankin believes, but cannot yet document, that between Miller's first visit to Indiana (from Michigan) in 1843 and his second visit in 1847, the churches transitioned from Disciples into Age-to-Come thinking. This seems reasonable because the dates fit into a proper sequence. The Eagle Creek church split over doctrine after the Field/Connelly debate in 1851. The rough transition period of this church probably drove the Corbaleys and the Logans to Marshall County near Plymouth. This was especially pertinent to Richard Corbaley after his father, Jeremiah Corbaley, died at Plymouth from a wagon accident in 1844.

David Graham wrote in "The Old Union Church and the Church of God Abrhamic Faith in Indiana" that the turmoil at Old Union over doctrine and politics, which caused so many Age-to-Come families to relocate near Plymouth and Liberty, spread the Age to Come across Indiana, and eventually across western America. The Gladdens, the Longs, the Hornadays, the Corbaleys and the Logans broke away from the Disciples and eventually formed the Indiana Conference of the Church of God.

Richard and Jane arrived in Marshall County, Indiana, in 1848. Here he assisted in organizing the Old Pisgah church near Argos south of Plymouth. He also took an active role in community and county events. He was elected to the office of Clerk of the Marshall Circuit to fill a vacancy. In 1850 he was reelected for a full term which would last until 1855. He studied law and was admitted to the bar as an attorney in Marshall Common Pleas Court on January 22, 1859. During this period he also engaged in the newspaper publishing business. He purchased the *Plymouth Pilot* in March of 1852 and changed the name to *Plymouth Banner*. A year later he sold the paper since he did not have enough experience to operate this business.

He was a gifted speaker, an able Bible student and was given to preaching and discussing the Scriptures with members of other faiths. One story reports that following one such discussion with a preacher from another faith, he baptized the preacher and 13 members of his congregation! Richard preached throughout the state and the record shows he baptized Mary Ann Roose Shaffer in January 1869 and probably many more than that.

Richard was a subscriber to the literature of the Church of God. He reported in *The Millennial Harbinger and Bible Expositor* regarding an upcoming meeting of the Northwest Indiana District of the Church of God at Old Pisgah. He said this church was on the road leading from Plymouth to Wolf Creek Mills, five miles away.

In 1875 the annual conference was held at the Old Antioch church in central Indiana. The former Millerites, under the direction of Joshua Himes, attempted to capture the Indiana conference. There had been cooperation by the Church of God with the Adventists up until that time, but the Church of God desired to withdraw into specific fellowship that recognized and appreciated the doctrine of the Age to Come, especially as it taught the restoration of the Jews to their homeland during the establishment of present-day Jerusalem, and fully during the Millennium. This the Adventists could not tolerate. Nathaniel Field objected to the "sectarian" nature of the Church of God.

Richard Corbaley is credited with preventing the merger of those two groups in Indiana. The effect of this action allowed the Church of God to develop as an autonomous denomination in its own right with doctrines that paralleled Bible teaching and that noticeably diverged from Orthodoxy, Evangelicalism or Pentecostalism. While Field labeled the Church of God "sectarian" due to the narrow aspect of its teachings, the Church of God continued throughout the century to disregard labels and pursue theological depth, educational and evangelistic goals, international publishing projects and growth and development of the body.

Richard was the patriarch of the Indiana Corbaleys many of whom migrated to California and Washington in 1871. They relocated because of Richard's asthma condition. As was his custom, he began talking with his new neighbors about his faith. Arlen Rankin cites a note from Richard to *The Restitution:*

> From the enclosed notice you will learn that we design to have a conference meeting in the Golden state. It is our first effort. When I came here seven years ago last spring, we had not a church in this state. There are now four organizations with a total membership of about seventy.

While living in California, according to Paul Hatch, Richard Corbaley and Benjamin Wilson, living then in Sacramento, organized the California Conference of the Church of God. The scattered members on the west coast held their annual summer conference in the region of the Redwood Forest. They must have used tents and spent a week in the great outdoors. As no journals were emanating from California at that time, there is no written record or photos of the conferences, but Paul Hatch had family who lived in California so his word is reliable.

In May 1884, Richard with his sons Allie and Richard traveled to Washington Territory in a covered wagon where Platt, the eldest son, lived. Sometime later, the women joined them in the new state.

Richard died at his home in Waterville, Washington. It was said that on his deathbed he said, "I thought I would live to see the second coming of Jesus, but I guess not." Jane died in San Diego on March 15, 1915. Both Jane and Richard are buried at Waterville Cemetery. The inscription on the tombstone reads, "Minister of the Gospel for 48 years."

    See Corbaley, A.L.
        Field, Nathaniel
        Hatch, Paul (20th)
        Miller, Ephraim
        Wilson, Benjamin

Bibliography: Richard Corbaley IV information from Darlene Man, the great, great grand-daughter, Feb. 4, 2006. Ferrell, Terry, *A Brief History of the Church of God in America*, National Berean Youth Conference, Camp Reynoldswood, Dixon, IL, Aug. 21-27, 1960; Graham, David. "The Old Union Church and the Church of God Abrahamic Faith in Indiana." *The History Newsletter.* J Stilson, ed.,

1:3 Autumn, 1984 Church of God General Conference, Oregon, IL; Hatch, Paul on Richard Corbaley, From the notes of Ivan Magaw, Archives, Atlanta Bible College n.d.; "New Purchase Boundary Marker" commons.wikimedia.org/wiki/File:New_Purchase_Boundary_marker_%28Delphi,_Indiana%29.png retrieved Nov. 21, 2010; Rankin, Arlen. E-mail regarding Jeremiah Corbaley and Ephraim Miller, Nov. 13, 2010; *The Restitution*, 1878, as cited by Arlen Rankin in a paper prepared for the History Conference at Atlanta Bible College, Nov. 2006, "The Influence of Old Union in Indiana," *The Restitution Herald*, Aug. 26, 1903; Dec. 8, 1915. *Richard Corbaley Diary of 1855* in the archives of Marshall County Historical Society, Plymouth, Indiana, and published serially in their *Quarterly* from 1982 – 1984; Waterville, WA Cemetery, Record of R Corbaley at interment.net.

Cowles, J. Earl
b. 1878
d. Unknown

J.E. Cowles lived at Moorefield, Nebraska, but his influence went beyond that area. Members spoke of him in their letters to the editor in *The Restitution Herald*. He was "an able Bible student who could teach the milk of scriptures, as well as the meat to stronger members." In October 1924 he preached at the Iowa Quarterly Conference. He was included with the licensed Church of God ministers in the 1921 and 1924 lists, which means he was recognized by that organization as a pastor, and that no letters of complaint had been received against him. This list was published annually in *The Restitution Herald*.

He preached at Moorefield, Nebraska, in 1926. The report said, "Bro. Cowles is becoming one of the most efficient speakers and all who hear him know how ably he can conduct his Bible lessons and give his sermons."

J. Earl Cowles also traveled to preach at other Churches of God. The literature reports that he visited and presumably preached in Colorado and Kansas. He was a delegate at general conference in 1921 when the national organization was approved. He was a carpenter by trade.

Bibliography: *The Restitution Herald*, October, 1921; March 1926.

Craton, John B.
b. 1832?
d. 1910?

Elder J.B. Craton was married to Mary and she testified that she came into the knowledge of the Gospel of the Kingdom sometime during the Civil War. John, however, began working within the framework of the developing Church of God across the frontier sometime around 1855. He served as an Illinois pastor in 1857, but in 1870 he lived and farmed in Black Hawk County, Iowa. A report by Robert Chown listed J. Craton as the pastor at Twin Groves, Illinois. This church was at one time led by N.A. Hitchcock, an early circuit preacher on the middle border frontier.

After he migrated west, J.B. Craton published a small paper from Council Grove, Kansas, entitled *The Glad Tidings*. There is only one issue of this paper in the Archives at Atlanta Bible College, making it extremely rare. The message of that single issue clearly taught the Gospel of the Kingdom. There is also mention of several people who donated money or sent letters to the editor. These people were Church of God believers or seekers from Kansas, Illinois, Wisconsin, Michigan, and, as far away as Virginia.

Craton may have originally hailed from Ohio where he first learned of the Gospel of the Kingdom, but it is not known who first taught him about the future Kingdom. While engaged in farming, Craton published *The Glad Tidings* on the side. It is not known how many years he was able to do this. That he had a following of readers is self-evident by the list of names who had contacted him in April 1893, just one month before the opening of the Columbian Exposition in Chicago.

Elder Craton traveled far and wide to preach. In 1905 he was the visiting minister at Seven Fountains (Fort Valley) Church of God which may have been part of the Virginia Conference program. He also preached occasionally at the Cool Spring Church of God in the mountains above Front Royal, Virginia. He was past 70 then, and beginning to slow down.

For a long time J.B. Craton's denominational affiliation could not be proven. After several months of research, his name was discovered in the pages of a Church of God paper published in Abilene, Texas, by Minerva Gibbs who succeeded her husband as editor of the *Word and Work*. In 1893 there were no Church of God denominationally sanctioned newspapers as there was no denomination yet. The best example of a centrally owned and operated press with a strong Church of God readership was *The Restitution* which had passed down the line from Joseph Marsh. All Church of God newspapers were independently published and financed. With that being noted, *The Word and Work* was a professionally printed newspaper which was rapidly gaining readership among the Churches of God across the South. While it was not a denominational publishing house, it had the authority of the developing denomination because it upheld the doctrines. The appearance of Craton's name twice in the body of literature confirms his credibility as a Church of God publisher and evangelist.

In the *Word and Work*, Craton announced that he had sent a circular letter to several Church of God papers, sharing an idea to have a floating mission ship on the Mississippi River. Preaching, music and ministry to stranded travelers would be the focus of onboard missionary activities. Craton organized the Gospel Mission Company to build a floating meetinghouse, and he announced he would sell shares for $25 each through the State of Arkansas. There is no word that he was able to achieve this dream.

In 1893 he moved from Council Bluffs, Kansas, to Fair Haven in Vernon County, Missouri. This was south of Kansas City, perhaps to better implement his mission dreams.

J.B Craton's most interesting inquiry in *The Glad Tidings* came from W.H. Eisenhower in Kansas. Research has determined that Mr. Eisenhower was a member of President Dwight D. Eisenhower's extended family. Eisenhower's inquiry does not necessarily prove he was a Church of God member, but this clearly illustrates that the Gospel message of the Kingdom of God was circulating broadly across the nation, and interested persons responded.

See Chown, Robert
Eisenhower, William Henry
Gibbs, William
Hitchcock, N.A.

Bibliography: Ancestry.com U.S. Census. Kansas. Republic. Norway. Dist. 281. 1880; Craton, J.B. "A Circular Letter," *Word and Work*, Minerva Gibbs, editor. Abilene, Texas, June 1907; *The Glad Tidings*, J.B. Craton, editor. Council Grove, Ks. April 1893; Twin Groves mentioned, *Prophetic Expositor and Bible Advocate*, Jos. Marsh, ed., Rochester, NY. Feb. 1, 1858; Craton, J.B. Letter to Editor. *The Restitution*, A. R. Underwood, ed., Plymouth, In., Dec. 20, 1893; *The Restitution*, July 10, 1905; "We are pleased to honor Cool Spring Church of God" *The Restitution Herald*, Oregon, Il., Nov. 1975; Craton, Mary J. Letter to Editor, *The Restitution*, A.R. Underwood, ed. Plymouth, In., Jan. 3, 1894.

Crockett, Ingram
b. February 10, 1856
d. October 5, 1936

Ingram Crockett was the poet laureate of the state of Kentucky. He may have been related to Davy Crockett of frontier and Alamo fame, but that has not been confirmed. He was the (adopted) son of John W. Henderson who had been a leader in the Confederacy.

Crockett worshipped with brethren from the One Faith at Henderson, Kentucky, and furnished copy to *The Restitution* on several occasions.

He became acquainted with Allan B. Magruder, a fine gentleman from Stephens City, Virginia. Magruder was a writer for several eastern newspapers. It is thought Magruder was an attorney who had considerable influence, especially when he wrote on the subject of Ingersoll and his heresies. Magruder often visited Henderson to preach for the congregation.

Crockett and Magruder became friends. When Magruder died, Ingram wrote a stirring and memorable eulogy for *The Restitution*. Crockett also wrote *A Brother of Christ, a Tale of Western Kentucky*, which was a novel about a Christadelphian believer.

Allan Magruder died in August 1885. In September 1885 Crockett wrote in a letter from Virginia that he believed the truth and wished he could tell more people about it. It was a pensive letter, made sad by the death of a beloved friend. Crockett was a wonderful writer, but he did not have the skill to preach as Magruder had done. Still, he has influenced several generations since his death and perhaps that will continue through his testimony in these pages.

See Magruder, Allan B.

Bibliography: Crockett, Ingram. "Letter to Editor", *The Restitution*, S. A. Chaplin, editor, Plymouth, Ind. Sept. 2, 1885. Crockett, Ingram. Entry from Wikipedia.com retrieved February 15, 2009.

Cronbaugh, Eli
b. October 14, 1835
d. October 23, 1916

Eli Cronbaugh was born at Bucyrus, Ohio. He was one of six sons born to John Cronbaugh. In 1842 the family moved to Michigan and in 1854 they moved a second time to Koszta, Iowa. Here John and three of his sons died.

The remaining sons and their mother developed their farms along the bottomland of Honey Creek at Koszta. They reported the usual trials that pioneers faced in a strange new location. Eli married Abigail Coats. Abigail died on February 7, 1881, leaving Eli with four small children, three daughters and a son.

In 1862 he became a member of the Christian church at Glenwood. Somewhere along the way, he met Minister Ed Houston who began the Church of God in Christ Jesus at Koszta, and was immersed by him in Honey Creek near the location where the church now stands. Nothing more is known about Ed Houston. At that time there was no church building so the congregation met at a schoolhouse. From then on, Eli was a faithful member of the Church of God. His greatest interest in life was to talk about the Word of God.

In the final two years of his life, infirmity kept him close to his chair. He was patient in suffering and was satisfied to lay down the armor, saying that he would not sleep long. He fell peacefully asleep at noon on the day of his death. His funeral was conducted by his friend, J.W. Williams.

He was interred in the Koszta cemetery in Honey Creek Township on the hillside overlooking the Oaklawn Church of God.

See Williams, J.W.

Bibliography: Obituary of Eli Cronbaugh, *The Restitution Herald*, Oregon, Illinois, Nov. 8, 1916.

Crosier (Crozier), Owen Russell Loomis

b. February 2, 1820
d. September 15, 1912

A. The Cleansing of the Heavenly Sanctuary
B. Crozier Launches New Ministries
C. Crozier Repudiates the Shut Door
D. Crozier in Michigan
E. Cleansing of the Sanctuary Revisited

O.R.L. Crosier, as he was popularly known, was born in Ontario County, New York, near the city of Chapin to Archibald and Nancy Loomis Crosier, both of Scottish lineage. He was named Owen after his mother's favorite Methodist preacher, and Russell Loomis after his mother's father. After 1850 for reasons unknown, he began spelling his last name with a "z" and so it shall be here.

His parents died when he was three. He was indentured by the family of Stephan Thatcher from Canandaigua, New York. Crozier spent his childhood in relative contentment, although he did not know until he began preaching that he had a sister, a brother and several cousins, his only close relatives.

He studied the blacksmith trade and quickly moved on from that to academics. Along the way he studied the Bible and began to think about spiritual matters. As a teenager he attended a revival meeting and accepted Christ. He was sprinkled in baptism and eventually joined the Methodist and later, the Baptist church.

In the summer of 1838 he entered the Wesleyan Seminary at Lena, New York. To pay bills he taught school while he was studying theology. He was given a license to preach in the Methodist church.

A friend began to write to him about the Second Advent of Christ. O.R.L. accepted this teaching, and began to search for a church home that would accept the Second Advent. He moved on then to the Baptist denomination in 1843, and in this new setting began to preach the second coming of Christ. This coincided with the times as William Miller and his followers were expecting the return of Christ on October 22, 1844.

Dr. Franklin Hahn supported Crozier's ministry. Crozier held a camp meeting at Hahn's farm on the east side of Lake Canandaigua. This was followed by many Bible studies at Hahn's home. When several other dates passed without the return of Christ, Adventists everywhere were looking for answers. His Bible studies were well attended.

A friend, Hiram Edson, decided to invite O.R.L. to go with him to comfort disappointed Millerites. They and Dr. Hahn began to study the subject of the heavenly sanctuary. They met at Hahn's farm, and O.R.L. was chosen as their spokesman. Crozier wrote brief notes to *The Voice of Truth* early in 1845, but signed his initials only to his notes. Later, Crozier transcribed their discussions about the cleansing of the heavenly sanctuary in a short-lived journal he published with Dr. Hahn, *The Day Dawn*.

The first issue of *The Day Dawn* appeared April 3, 1845. It was published at Canandaigua on an irregular schedule, appearing only a few times, with some issues being as much as a year apart.

A. The Cleansing of the Heavenly Sanctuary

For his explanation of the cleansing of the heavenly sanctuary in *The Day Dawn,* Crozier used hermeneutical principles of typology to examine the Old Testament Holy of Holies to show "that the cleansing of the sanctuary system are [sic] the symbolic representation of the great system of Christ's redemptive work." According to Jane Neuffer in "The Gathering of Israel," Crozier included a section in his article about the Age to Come. Neuffer said that Crozier thought the millennium would be "an age of repair" in keeping with the times of restitution. It was his combination of the shut door theory with the Age to Come that was so appealing to disillusioned Adventists, for it gave an almost indefinite period of time for the transition period. The atonement did not *end* on October 22, 1844, it *began* then and continued for one thousand years.

Crozier said Christ's heavenly ministry had two phases just as the temple had the Holy Place and the Most Holy Place. The first part of Jesus' atonement ministry started at his ascension and continued until 1844. After that, the second phase began. Crozier explained that in Hebrews 9 the Greek word, *hagia,* meant "holy places" and "within the veil" was a reference to the "first veil" in the sanctuary and not the second veil.

Crozier provided six reasons that Christ's atonement was not completed. He said that while the blood of Christ was the sole means for the cleansing of the sanctuary, the cleansing could not be completed until sins were placed on the head of the scapegoat. To Crozier, the scapegoat was a type of Satan, not Christ.

The following year on February 7, 1846, the article appeared in *The Day Star*, a paper that was edited by Enoch Jacobs. This paper effectively advertised the heavenly sanctuary doctrine, which was then favorably accepted by the newly-formed Seventh-day Adventists under the leadership of Ellen G. White. She wrote, "The Lord shewed me that Brother Crosier had the true light on the cleansing of the sanctuary."

His article attempted to explain theologically why Christ had not returned. It seemed definitive to disappointed Adventists and was favorably received by them. LeRoy Froom, Seventh-day Adventist author, said it was a *new* thought that Christ went into the heavenly sanctuary to cleanse it, not to *come out of it*. Professor Ingemar Linden from the University of Uppsala agreed. Linden cited Crozier as saying that the heavenly temple was cleansed when Christ entered the Most Holy Place on October 22, 1844. Crozier said the old dispensation ended, and the new one, the Age of Restitution or Age to Come commenced. He said this dispensation is an age of cleansing.

Yet, a year later, Crozier repudiated Sabbatarianism and began assisting Joseph Marsh in publishing *The Advent Harbinger and Bible Advocate*. Strangely, this did not happen until *after* Crozier and his correspondent Hiram Edson questioned Marsh's ethics in producing *The Voice of Truth* which they did through the pages of one of Crozier's irregular issues of *The Day Dawn*. This happened because Marsh had published a note, "Delinquents, Read This," in the *Voice of Truth* as an attempt to have past due accounts made current. Specifically, Crozier questioned Marsh's financial matters. Marsh was quite surprised by the unexpected attack. In the next issue Marsh published his expenses and gave a good explanation for the means of conducting his business.

Joseph Marsh

While Marsh explained himself, he revealed that he was peeved about the attack in *The Voice of Truth* when he shared the story of Hiram Edson's arrest for beating his son in the woods. Edson had tied his son's hands behind his back. He then whipped the boy with six Beechwood whips that he had cut especially for the task. The boy cried "Murder!" The neighbors heard and reported it, and, Edson was arrested. He appeared before a jury, and paid a $15 fine for his barbarity.

B. Crozier Launches New Ministries

Owen R.L. Crozier reminisced about his work with Marsh from 1846 to 1853 in a report given to the Michigan Conference of the Churches of God in 1907. Crozier was then 87 years of age. He had lived in the Marsh home during the years in question. He must have been almost entirely broken by the adverse fortunes of life that brought him to that status in life. His doctrine of Shut Door was unpopular with nearly everyone; his paper *The Day Dawn* was not a success; and his fortunes were not going well. No wonder he came to have such high regard for Joseph Marsh who helped him recover.

During 1851 while Crozier was assisting Marsh with *The Advent Harbinger*, he published a prospectus for a children's paper, the *Christian Student*. He asked for pledges from 30 people of $10 each. In April 1851, one month after the appearance of the prospectus, the *Advent Harbinger* announced that publication of *The Children's Friend* would begin on a monthly basis out of *The Advent Harbinger* offices, O.R.L. Crozier, editor. He said 30 pledges of $10 each would help get it going.

Publishing the *Children's Friend* cost Crozier a lot. He suffered lack of funds the entire first volume. An appeal was made February 1852 for funds to support the children's paper.

That same year, he joined with Marsh, J.B. Cook, Henry Dingle, Ed Hoyt, L.P. Judson, J. Wilson of New York and J.C. Bywater to attend and participate in the Rochester United Conference.

During the summer of 1851 when Joseph Marsh and wife took a western preaching tour, Crozier continued the business and publishing aspects of the *Advent Harbinger*. That summer he received a letter from G.W. Cherry in Marysville, Ohio, stating that he wished to see Crozier again in that region, and confirming that his preaching of the Age to Come "sets things right before us. Had our brethren seen these great truths at that time, the work of slaughter would not have been so great." Cherry was referring to the "slaughter" of the Adventist movement completed by J.V. Himes at the New England Conference at which he repudiated the Age-to-Come doctrine and all believers of it.

The exchange between Cherry and Crozier indicates that Crozier was completely out of the Adventist movement, including the Seventh-day adherents, whose doctrines he had helped enunciate following the Bitter Disappointment, and that he was solidly in the camp of Joseph Marsh and the Age to Come/Church of God.

C. Crozier Repudiates the Shut Door

Further, in late July 1851, he wrote an article in the *Advent Harbinger and Bible Advocate*, responding to J.V. Himes' assertion that Joseph Turner of Maine had popularized the "shut door theory." Turner had been the editor of the *Hope of Israel* magazine, a Millerite sheet. O.R.L. Crozier took exception to that claim, and stated that "shut door" was first taught by William Miller himself! To prove his point, he cited several incidents where Miller had stated such or written the same.

> Crozier said:
> We have been credibly informed that up to 1839 or 1840 Mr. Miller uniformly taught in 1839 or 1840 at the close of the sounding of the sixth trump, the door of mercy would be closed and during that time, "quickly" from 1840 to 1843, between the sixth and seventh trumpets, would be occupied in separating the good from the bad, at which latter point of time the Lord would come. Here, according to his "original" theory, there were to be about three and a half years before the Advent in which the wicked could not find mercy and the Gospel was not to be preached to them.

Crozier quoted Miller in the September 1840 issue of *Signs of the Times*:

> Your's and Bro. Litch's pieces on the closing of the door of mercy are good. All that I can do in addition is to gather a few passages of Scripture as proof that in the end of the world there must be a little time to gather the wicked from the just.

In an October 1844 letter to Elder Himes published in *The Advent Herald*, William Miller further stated:

> We have done our work in warning sinners and in trying to awake a formal church. God, in his Providence, has shut the door; we can only stir one another up to be patient.

Crozier further asserted that Himes' own *Advent Herald* editorial staff, Elder Apollos Hale, a friend of the aforementioned Joseph Turner, began a new publication, the *Advent Mirror*, for the express purpose of disseminating the theory of the shut door in the fall of 1844. According to Professor Linden, Turner and Hale's shut-door ideas became known as "bridegroom theology." The bridegroom had come invisibly to perform a change in office or work, and he and his followers (the shut door advocates) had moved outside the veil.

Crozier concluded that several were involved in perpetuating the "odious" theory. He further stated in *The Voice of Truth* (March 1845) that most men involved in the error had acknowledged their mistake, but Elder Hale and Elder J. V. Himes had not. He said:

> We find no fault with anyone for having honestly believed in and advocated the theory of the shut door, but to abandon it without a confession and then try to shift off the responsibility upon somebody else, betrays a total want of Christian principle." He said in the same article that Himes had "an unrighteous pride of opinion.

Joseph Marsh, a proponent of open door theory, said that shut door was responsible for promoting prejudice, and spreading the troubling interpretation of spiritualism. The open-door advocates were moderates. Linden said, "According to the open-door brethren nothing at all had happened on October 22, nothing in any historical salvation sense."

In early winter 1851, Crozier and J. Wendell held a series of short conferences in upstate New York because the days were short and they had a burden to preach the news of the Kingdom. Later, Crozier moved his family to Michigan where they fellowshipped with the Church of God, and took leadership to guide that work into a state conference.

As late as 1853, Crozier was still protesting the propagation of his immature theological ideas. In *The Review and Herald*, a Seventh-day Adventist magazine, March 17th, 1853, issue, Crozier complained that he had written the *Day-Star* article of 1846 to prove the shut door. He thought it was not right for the Sabbatarian Adventists to use it, since they no longer believed the shut door. James White stated that Crozier was no longer with the pioneers of the Seventh-day Adventist faith. Linden said in no way could Crozier be considered a pioneer in the formation of the Seventh-day Adventist work.

Fernand Filser's biography of Owen Crozier offers interesting background. Filser learned that Crozier married Maria Polly Alger when he was 33. The census shows that she was born in New York and was 14 years younger than Owen. They had 11 babies, seven of whom predeceased their parents. Owen and Polly Crozier enjoyed 59 years of marriage.

Polly, as she preferred to be called, was a college graduate and an accomplished writer. She wrote for several other secular publications. She wrote also for Marsh's *Advent Harbinger* and for Crozier's paper, *The Children's Friend*. Owen and Polly probably met through *The Children's Friend*.

The couple moved to Michigan by railroad and lived on her father's farm for a year. Her father was John Alger. The next year they moved to a 40-acre farm and began clearing it while both taught school. In 1855 they began to teach school in Grand Rapids. Filser's preface to Crozier's biography noted the school was on the corner of East Bridge and Division streets. During this same time Crozier preached at the Jamestown center in Georgetown, and continued to write for *The Advent Harbinger*.

A state conference of Michigan members was formed at LeRoy, Calhoun County, at a conference, October 16-18, 1858. Ephraim Miller was chosen president; O.R.L. Crozier was chosen vice president; Elder Edwin Hoyt was chosen secretary; and Elder Joel E. Simonds was chosen treasurer. Ephraim Miller was from Mendon, the others were from Grand Rapids. Owen Crozier was chosen to be a delegate from the Michigan conference to conferences in other states. Ephraim Miller and Alva N. Seymour were chosen evangelists.

D. Crozier in Michigan

Crozier preached for the Church of God, but in those days, the churches avoided using a name so as to not be considered sectarian. Filser wrote:

> (Crozier) organized a church State conference in Burlington,

Calhoun Co. in 1856, whose meetings continued every quarter. The church to which Crosier belonged refused to adopt a name in order to avoid 'sectism.' Each congregation was identified by its location. It was "the church," (at such a place). Here the influence of Joseph Marsh was evident. Crozier organized the Michigan Church Conference to unite these churches, and became prominent in its deliberations and its committees.

Early ministers mentioned in Michigan in addition to those already named included J.M. Stephenson, Chesebrough, A.F. Sarvis, Ralph Carter, W.C. Hill, Riley and Sober. First names are not available for some. These men were mentioned as preachers and supporters of the Michigan conference. At one annual meeting at William H. Knapp's farm, 48 people stayed. The hay mow was outfitted with hay to the depth of four feet where the men slept, and the women slept in the house on straw ticks.

In the report to the Michigan Conference in 1907, Elder Crozier had warm words to say for Joseph Marsh. In spite of having wronged Marsh years before, or perhaps because of it, Crozier highly regarded Marsh as the forerunner of the Church of God. He said:

> I was with Elder Marsh in the *Harbinger* from 1846 to '53. He was a good student of the Bible, strong in his opinions and in their defense. [He was] kind in his relations to others "a good man."

Crozier gave Marsh credit for starting *The Restitution*. To him it was clear cut. He said:

> *The Voice of Truth, The Advent Harbinger* and *The Restitution* have been the western organ of the Advent Church, and Joseph Marsh, more than any other man, pitched the key when he objected to the Boston effort to tie up the Advent movement into a new sect on Wm. Miller's views.

Crozier said that in 1860 the *Harbinger* began to drag, and Marsh sold the paper to "Thomas Newman, an Englishman, whom I knew at Rochester. He was a good Adventist but too full of English conceit to be an American citizen." When the slave-holders' rebellion broke out Newman through *The Harbinger*, defended the South. Crozier continued:

> I continued in correspondence with him. I was provoked by the disloyal attitude Newman gave the paper and determined to make it loyal to the United States government. Newman would not dare refuse anything I wrote for the paper. He parlied, and I pushed him and spiked his guns, and published in *The Harbinger*, the true attitude of Christians toward civil government in this age.

Crozier had been an active abolitionist in Kent County, Michigan, before the Civil War. He became the editor of *The Grand Rapids Eagle*, later named *Grand Rapids Herald*. Although he was active in politics, he never ran for office in Grand Rapids. He served as delegate to the Cleveland Mass Convention and as chairman of the Kent County Republican Convention. Crozier continued in political service, and was a good citizen. He was elected eventually as Drain Commissioner for Ottawa County, in Jamestown, Michigan. In this capacity he organized the drainage of several thousand acres of swamp land. He also taught school in Ottawa County and organized a Teacher's Association. He was well known to the best educators of that area.

Filser generously recounts Crozier's preaching experience. He said, "Owen continued preaching in various neighboring counties and in Canada, and writing on subjects of evolution and conditional immortality among others." Other subjects about which he certainly would have written included the Age to Come, Kingdom of God on earth, and repudiation of the shut door theory.

Owen remained relatively quiet in his old age. He baptized young Horace Hammon in Michigan in 1897 when he was 75 years old, though the last 15 years of his life saw weakened health, but not silence. He continued to participate in the Michigan Conference and his local Church of God, but he had stopped writing major pieces years before.

There are a couple of exceptions to that and one of them entails a brief note he sent to Stedman A. Chaplin in February 1889 for inclusion in *The Restitution* after the successful organization of the National Conference in Philadelphia 1888. He said:

> Thank you…for the Report of the National Conference held in Philadelphia last November. I have read [it] with interest and believe that you have made a good start in the right direction. Carefulness, honesty, charity, courage may bring good results.

The other notable article from this period revisited the subject which had lain on his heart for so many years. He hoped to explain the theology of the cleansing of the sanctuary once and for all.

E. Cleansing of the Sanctuary Revisited

In 1905 Owen wrote an article for *The Restitution* entitled "The Christian Sanctuary and its Cleansing." He began by discussing Daniel's vision as given to him on two occasions by Gabriel. Daniel did not understand the interpretation of the vision, and Gabriel returned to him 14 years later to explain the vision so Daniel would understand. In Daniel 9:22-27, he discussed the 70 weeks, broken down as seven weeks and 62 weeks. At the end of 2,300 days, the sanctuary shall be cleansed. Crozier said:

> It is quite possible that the cleansing of the sanctuary might begin, and go on for years unperceived. The work would be as valid if its inspired name were not known. Indeed it is singular that the sanctuary translation itself has been lost under a mistranslation, and men have made awkward attempts to find it.

He demonstrated with the original languages how Greek terms *hieron* and *ho naos*, referring to two aspects of the Sanctuary (i.e., the entire compound for the former and the Levitical sanctuary of the Holy Place and Holy of Holies for *ho naos*), had been lost by translators who substituted the word "Temple" for "Sanctuary." This was corrected in the Revised Version of 1881. He said marginal notes helped him understand this. Crozier explained that the translation of most New Testament verses that speak about the body being the Temple of God clearly show what cleansing the sanctuary means. He said:

> We have found what and where the Christian sanctuary is. The cleansing is easily inferred, and is plainly indicated by the definition of the Hebrew word rendered "cleansed" in Daniel 8:14 i.e. "Justified, made straight, correct, right," just what Paul directed in his letters to the churches at Corinth and Ephesus, and is just what is needed now, and *in fact has been going on for the last half century.*

And:

> The Christian Sanctuary, Hebrews 8, is compared with the type, Hebrews 9. Of the former Jesus fills the priesthood in all its grades. The Sanctuary and its cleansing offer a theme eminently practical in the very last days.

He concluded the article with his very famous initials: "O.R.L.C." It is unmistakably his last attempt to clear up any misunderstandings about his theology of 1845.

Owen Crozier died in his home at 205 Lafayette Avenue in Grand Rapids just nine months after his dear Maria Polly died at age 78 (January 7, 1912).

He summarized his life in 1903, "My eighty three years, though busy have been fairly easy on me. I am happy in the kindness of my children and many friends." If he had ever been unhappy at the turn the Advent movement had taken, or at his inability to explain the Disappointment in such a way as to prevent splits, he did not suffer long. He lived a busy, happy and productive life for his Lord in spite of his early trials.

See Crozier, Hiram P.
Marsh, Joseph
Newman, Thomas

Bibliography: Ancestry.com U.S. Census Rochester, New York. 1850. and U.S. Census 1910. Grand Rapids. Kent; Crozier, O.R.L. "Esdras explains the Time in Daniel." *Voice of Truth* March 19, 1845; Crozier, O.R.L. "Response to Joseph Marsh," *Day Dawn,* Feb. 11, 1847; Crozier, O.R.L. "Appeal for the Children's Friend," Feb. 22, 1851; Crosier, O.R.L. "Shut Door Theory," *Advent Harbinger and Bible Advocate,* Aug. 2, 1851; Crozier, O.R.L. "Call to Conference," *Advent Harbinger and Bible Advocate,* Nov. 1, 1851; Crozier, O.R.L. "The Christian Sanctuary and its Cleansing," *Restitution,* A.R. Underwood, ed. Plymouth, In. Nov. 15, 1905; Crozier, O.R.L. Brief Note, *Restitution,* S.A. Chaplin, ed. Plymouth, In. Feb. 27, 1889; Ferrell, Terry. *A Brief History of the Church of God in America*, National Berean Youth Conference, Camp Reynoldswood, Dixon, Il. Aug. 21-27, 1960, using several citations from early *Restitutions* pertaining to Michigan; Froom, LeRoy. *The Prophetic Faith of our Fathers.* Vol. 4 Review and Herald, Washington, D.C. 1954, 887; Graham, David. Series on O.R.L. Crozier for *Wisdom and Power,* June/July 1993; and 7:3 Sept./Oct. 1993 and 7:4 Nov./Dec. 1993 in which he cited an unpublished manuscript by A.R. Timms of Andrews University for a seminar he completed in 1991; Fisel, Fernand. "Prelude to a Biography of Owen Russell Loomis Crozier," Truthorfables.com/Biography_Crozier.htm. For the reader who wants more detail, Filser's piece contains much background information and an extensive bibliography; "Letter from G.W. Cherry to O.R.L. Crozier," *Advent Harbinger and Bible Advocate,* 3:1, June 21, 1851; Linden, Ingemar. *1844 And the Shut Door Problem.* University of Uppsala, 1982 pages 16-33; Marsh, Joseph "Delinquents to Read," *Voice of Truth,* Feb. 3, 1847; Feb. 24, 1847; Vowless, Monica, ex-sda.com/experience_vowless.htm Crozier left because he was disenchanted with the web of deceptions woven by the Sabbatarian Adventists; Neuffer, Jane. "The Gathering of Israel. A historical study of early writings." *Review and Herald Publishing,* 74-76; *Restitution,* June 26, 1907 Report to Michigan Conference read by Mary Woodward; *The Restitution Herald,* Sept. 30, 1924; Crozier, Polly, Obituary, *The Restitution Herald,* Feb. 1, 1912.

Cross, John Edgar
b. February 1, 1861
d. October 2, 1926

John Cross was born in Pine Rock Township, Ogle County, Illinois, to James L. and Mary Rathburn Cross. He had three sisters and one brother. He lived in the Washington Grove area most of his life on a farm along Flagg Road east of Chana Road. He married Nellie Booth on November 2, 1887. They had two sons, LeRoy and Clarence, and two daughters, Cecile and Maude. Maude married Rolland Stilson of South Bend, Indiana.

John Cross first professed Christ in 1894. He and his family first attended the Antioch Church of God on Flagg Road until the Oregon Church of God organized. When the Oregon church became the foremost congregation in the area around 1910, Antioch experienced a decline in attendance.

John Cross farmed, but enhanced his income as an educator. In 1907 he was appointed Assistant Superintendent of Schools for Ogle County, and in 1910 ascended to the Superintendent's position. He held this position until his death. He was a forceful leader with a quiet manner. He evoked respect and confidence in his approach to people. S.J. Lindsay worked for him at the courthouse.

In 1910, a call went out in *The Restitution* from the organizers to delegates and members to attend the Waterloo Conference "for the purpose of discussing our needs as a body, and, if found necessary, organize a General Conference for the purpose of bringing us into a closer unity of the one Faith and work between the different states and territories."

Each state was urged to send at least one delegate. John Cross added his name to the list of those who endorsed the organizational effort. There were 13 names of Church of God leaders on the list. While the 1910 attempt did not succeed, eventually the organizational attempt of 1921 did succeed, and John became the treasurer of the General Conference board beginning with the 1923 term.

He was a member of the Illinois Conference board for more than one term of office, and became a member and chairman of the National Bible Institute complaint committee. Owing to criticism which the new organization received, efforts were made during the years 1920-1922 to manage the complaints. Service on this committee would require men and women with amazing faith and fortitude. After ratification of the General Conference organization by all the state conferences, the complaint committee turned its attention specifically to complaints that might be initiated against individual pastors.

Pastors applied for recognition from the National Bible Institute at Oregon, Illinois. The NBI was the business operating name of the Church of God General Conference. The process was this: the application of a pastor for recognition by the Conference was published in *The Restitution Herald*. If after the name appeared for a few issues, the complaint committee received no letters of complaint against the applicant, the pastor's name would be added to the list. This was technically not a licensing procedure but it did give ministers certain benefits of travel and authenticity among the membership. The first list was published in *The Restitution Herald* in 1921 with 25 names from 14 states. Later in the 20th century, a License and Ordination Board was created for the purpose of licensing and ordaining ministers.

When S.J. Lindsay resigned as editor of *The Restitution Herald* in 1922, John Cross was named as the new editor. By the time the next issue appeared, the editorial appointment was changed to F.L. Austin who was the new secretary of the General Conference. As if to illustrate that an era had ended, that particular issue of *The Herald* contained a couple of significant typos.

Long after John Cross died, his widow, Nellie Cross, lived on at the farm house. Late into the 1950s she attended church at the Flagg Center Community Church each Sunday morning. Students of Oregon Bible College were worship leaders in this church with Elder Glenn Birkey as a supervisor. William Wachtel, Arnold Johns and other students stopped and escorted elderly Mrs. Cross to church. She was always daintily dressed sometimes with a little hat perched on her head.

Owing to his fame and popularity in Ogle County, John's funeral was held in Oregon's new coliseum to accommodate the crowd of 500 mourners. Members of the community sang and played piano with violin. An article in the *Ogle County Republican* reported that the music was beautiful. His obituary and eulogies were carried in the local papers and *The Restitution Herald* for several issues. The local paper reported:

> Uncle John, as the boys and the girls, the young men and young women loved to call him, has fallen asleep. But though he rests from his labors, his works do follow him, and the influence of John E. Cross will ring down through the ages.

THE RESTITUTION HERALD

VOLUME 16 — OREGON, ILLINOIS, OCTOBER 5, 1926 — NUMBER 1

HE SLEEPS IN DEATH

THE death of John Edgar Cross occurred at his home in Oregon, Illinois, on the evening of October, 2 1926. He had been in failing health for more than two years, though he was regular at his office in the discharge of his duties until early in July, last.

The deceased was born February 1, 1861, in Pine Rock Township and lived his entire life in the county of his birth. He was one of five children, namely, John, Flora, Alice, Jane and Ernest, who were born to James L. and Mary, nee Rathbun, Cross.

On November 2, 1887, he united in marriage with Nellie Booth, to whom were born Leroy, Clarence, Cecile and Maude.

About 1894 Bro. Cross professed a confiding faith in Jesus Christ, uniting with the brethren of the Antioch Church of God, near Chana. Though quiet and reserved his sterling qualities made him one who was sought out for responsibility for church activity — first at Antioch, afterward at Oregon.

Bro. Cross spent his life as an educator. He early began teaching school, continuing till 1907, when he was appointed to be Assistant County Superintendent of Schools. In the election of 1910 he was chosen to the office of Superintendent, which position he held till death — but three months less than twenty years in all.

Bro. Cross was one of the founders of The Restitution Publishing Co., and The Restitution Herald. He was a member of the Executive Board from its incorporation in 1911 until his death, and was one of the few who apportioned and paid the annual deficit.

In 1923 he was sought out for Treasurer of the General Conference of the Church of God. This position he held till, because of his failing health, he was relieved in August 1926.

In the death of Bro. Cross the church and Ogle county must suffer the loss of a capable, worthy, and honored man.

He is survived by his ever faithful widow; by three children — Clarence, of Chilton, Wisconsin; Mrs. Ward Scott, of Lockport, Illinois; and Mrs. Roland Stilson, of 312 E. South St., South Bend, Indiana; by 13 grandchildren; by one sister, Mrs. Jane Rummell, and one brother, Ernest, both of Rochelle, Illinois.

In deference to public wish the funeral services are being held this October 5, at the spacious Coliseum rather than at the Oregon church.

He has fallen asleep under the enemy, death, but for years previous to that fall he was an earnest believer and servant of Him who is the resurrection and the life. Those who knew him sorrow not as those who have no hope.

F. L. Austin.

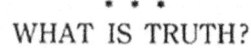
Brother John E. Cross

WHAT IS TRUTH?

THIS question asked by Pilate of the Savior with reference to Himself and the kingdom, John 19: 36-38, pertains with equal force to many of life's problems. The finite mind is brought over and over again to "its wits' end" in trying to fathom the meaning or the reason of life's circumstances. We are prone to reason that because one lives a clean, pure life, exercising careful and faithful trust in God, therefore, he should be particularly relieved from having to endure sin's heavy hand. The record of the Scriptures does not bear out this reasoning. There was no guile in the mouth of our Lord; His finger touched no sin; His lips spake no wickedness — and yet from without sin threw around about Him its steely arms and drew Him down to bitter death. It was because of the *righteousness* and *godliness* of Stephen that sin from without hurled the heavy stones, bruising

(Continued on page 13, Column 3)

The *Ogle County Reporter* reported that "obsequies were in charge of F.L. Austin and F.E. Siple. Rev. Austin's discourse was 'If a Man Die, Shall he Live Again?' from Job 14:14." In honor of the great man, schools in Ogle County were dismissed early and the flag was flown at half staff.

The Reporter quoted King David regarding the death of his captain, Abner, "Know ye not that there is a prince and a great man fallen this day?"

John and Nellie Cross are buried in the Washington Grove Cemetery on Flagg Road with many other members from the Antioch congregation.

See Austin, F.L. (20th)
Birkey, Glenn (20th)
Siple, F.E. (20th)

Bibliography: *The Restitution* Conference issue August 17, 1910; *The Restitution Herald* Sept.12, 1922; Oct. 5, 1926; Oct. 12, 1926.

Crowe, W.L.

b. March 19, 1866
d. November 4, 1924

W.L. Crowe wrote this summary of his life and ministry:

I was born March 19, 1866 near Paisley, Ontario; twenty miles from Lake Huron. We moved to St. Paul, Nebraska in 1881. I was married to Minnie Chambers, Feb. 11, 1892. Wife and I were both members of the Presbyterian Church, and investigated nothing else for years—not even this—for we joined the church of our parents just because invited to do so, and because we wanted to 'be good.'

In the summer of '93 wife and I went to a school house to hear Elder T.G. Bartlett preach a "new and peculiar doctrine." He talked about an hour and a half, on the covenants of promise, the gospel, the nature of man, and baptism. It was all like a new revelation to us, and I had to say I had learned more about the plan of salvation from that one talk than I had learned in all my past life from the flowery orations and lectures in the popular churches. From that time on, the Bible was no longer a book of mysteries to us, but a new book.

Next year, Elder Almus Adams came to St. Paul with the tent, and there apparently conflicting texts were harmonized, and from one [family] in town, believing these precious truths, a church of over 40 members was finally established at St. Paul. I don't know if I was 'called to preach' or not; but I felt that I must tell everyone the good news, and imagined that nearly the whole world would rejoice to hear it as I had done. I lived on a farm six miles from town, but managed, either on foot or in a cart I had made, to get to meeting nearly all the time. After corn husking was over I went to country school houses, preaching the glad-good news free to all.

Finally, Bro. Myers opened a door for me in Iowa, and I came here, and have been State evangelist most of the time since, preaching the best I can, and the best I know, to the few I can get to hear. I think we would have been worth more financially had we kept our farm, but the ambition to acquire earthly possessions has become to me a very secondary matter to the "price of the high calling in Christ Jesus," and the hope of a place in His glorious kingdom when He comes. We have our trials, doubts and fears in the work, and feel the need of the faithful, that our faith fail not, nor our love wax cold, amidst the iniquity and lukewarmness of this waning age. Oh may the King soon come!

Minister Crowe struggled to balance his love for evangelism with his need to earn a living for his family. Not only was he responsible for his own family, but he also looked after his disabled brother, Charles. Charles assisted him in publishing the *Present Truth*, this being his only source of income. Charles had been crippled at 12 years of age by a degenerative disease which had deformed his hip bones and muscles. The disease also claimed his hearing. Yet Charles published the hymnbook *The Glad Tidings* in 1907 which was used throughout the Church of God. Charles also published *The Mormon Waterloo* at St. Paul, Nebraska. This book was written by his brother, and was a discourse that attempted to disprove major doctrines of the Mormon faith. This book is part of the Archives of Atlanta Bible College.

WL Crowe, left, and GE Marsh

In 1902 W.L. Crowe and A.J. Eychaner discussed the idea to establish a Kansas Colony. It was discussed also by the Iowa Conference board, but nothing more is seen of it in the literature. It is not known if they planned to plant a church in Kansas, establish new conference grounds there, or establish a community of believers much like the Oneida Colony.

During 1902 W.L. Crowe preached at the Ripley Adventist Church in Illinois. The Ripley minute book revealed that he baptized Mabel Kindrick Lindsay and Florence Laning Howell in that year. He also worked at Irving, Iowa, and Chanute, Kansas.

In 1910 W.L. Crowe tried to assist in organizing a national general conference for the Churches of God. This movement failed due to unrest over the statement of faith. He commented in his paper, *The Present Truth*, that the 1910 conference was not so successful. There was discord and strife among the ministers who were not able to arrive at solid conclusions leading to national organization.

The Present Truth was widely known among the brethren who lived west of the Mississippi from Minnesota

> **Minutes for the First Conference of the Restitution Church of God for Southern Illinois**
>
> [The Conference] was held at the Restitution Church near Moriah, Clark County, Ills, beginning October 10th and continuing for ten days closing October 20th, 1902.
>
> This conference was presided over by Elder Wm. L. Crowe. By motion and vote the following officers were elected to serve during the conference. President, Wm. L. Crowe, Treasurer, Lewis Weaver, Secretary, John R. Lansbury.
>
> By a motion and vote of the members present it was decided to have a Southern Illinois Conference and upon motion and vote being taken the following officers were elected for the upcoming year viz, President Omnri (?) Brant, Treasurer and Secretary, Lewis Weaver. Also, by motion and vote, the next or second annual conference of the Church was decided to be held in this church in October 1903.
>
> Consideration of local business being next in order, it was decided by the members present that the number of trustees of this church at Moriah shall be three.
>
> Ref.: Photo found on the first page of Minutes at the Archives of Atlanta Bible College, McDonough, Georgia

to Texas. It was not as widely read in the east. When Crowe moved, he took the paper with him. He published it at Irving, Iowa, and St. Paul, Nebraska. Copies of this paper, that was later edited by James Patrick, first president of the Church of God General Conference, are available for researchers at the Archives of the Atlanta Bible College.

Clyde Randall related a story in *Historical Waymarks of the Church of God* about W.L. Crowe at Mora, Minnesota, to demonstrate the preacher's practical nature, and, also his trust in the Lord. Elder Crowe preached in the spring at a rural schoolhouse that was near the confluence of the Snake and Groundhouse rivers. The home at which he was staying throughout these special meetings was three-quarters of a mile from the schoolhouse. Elder Crowe had to cross the rivers on foot just as the ice was breaking up. In order to arrive at a preaching appointment with a dry set of clothes, he removed them from the waist down, forded the flooded river with clothes and Bible held high, and arrived safely on the other side—wet and very cold. He quickly redressed and continued with his calling and preaching. Randall said, "Many were led to believe and obey during the meetings."

In 1915 he went to Hammond, Louisiana, to preach at the Pine Woods Bible Class begun by W.H. Wilson and continued by the Siples and Anthons. This Bible class was rather famous among Church of God members because Wilson had written a book entitled *The Pine Woods Bible Class* so that readers often traveled to Hammond to stay for the winter and to visit the class.

Crowe was greatly shaken in 1918 when he was arrested for subversion against America during WWI. He had mentioned the Kaiser in a sermon. He wrote later in his explanation to the brethren:

> My opinion that the first beast of Rev. 13 with "blasphemy" on his heads, that makes war with the saints, was the German federation reviving the old Roman empire of the Middle Ages, could not have been construed as pro-German, only by those ignorant of history. Germany was the head of the Roman Empire from 962 A.D. under Otto I till the Interregnum, 1253 till 1273. My opinion that the Kaiser was fulfilling the prophecy of Zech. 11:15-17 as to the foolish, idle shepherd who drives his sheep to slaughter, was not flattering to the Kaiser to any who would think on it fairly, yet these two views of prophecy were made the chief cause for my arrest as a "German spy."

There were five witnesses against Crowe at his trial. The court allowed him to defend himself, and when the judge heard his defense, he dismissed the case. Crowe said later, "I thank the Lord that I am of Irish Scotch descent rather than German, and that courts of justice are not so much to be feared as ignorant mobs."

In 1919 W.L. Crowe reported to *The Restitution* that he finally gave up preaching for worldly work because he had to support his family. He had spent $30 of his own funds to preach to poor folks in eastern Kansas, but collected only $3.60 from them towards his expenses. At another location he received $17. He built "a little shack" in Kansas City and worked as a carpenter. Since only by drawing on his own funds could he complete his trips, the time had come to find a little secular work.

WL Crowe Family

Soon after this, someone approached him about writing a book, *The Old and New Covenants* and another on the *Prophecies,* and he agreed to do it. He appealed to the readers to assist him with finances while he put these books together. During 1919 he wrote the content of the prophecies as a series for *The Restitution Herald* entitled "Prophecies of the Last Hour." This series began in November and ran for several weeks. It is doubtful that this series was ever published as a book. The content of the Covenants was published in J.J. Jobe's paper, *The Sower and the Reaper*, from Texarkana, Texas.

In 1920 Minnie was stricken with an ailment of the tonsils so that they had to be removed. Since she was crippled by painful arthritis, she had to be chloroformed before they could transport her to the hospital. Medical expenses were enormous. It is no wonder that in 1921 a western member left $5,000 in his will to be used by Bro.

Iowa Conference delegates and familes, circa 1908

Crowe in his ministry. This donation may have allowed Elder Crowe to publish and distribute the book and to pay medical bills.

He traveled widely throughout the Great Plains, and he reported in *The Restitution* in 1921 that he went to Jordan, Missouri, in his brother's Ford, a distance of 460 miles from Waterloo, Iowa, where he must have been living at the time. He preached regularly in an old Dunkard building that had been abandoned south of Caldwell, Kansas. He preached fearlessly in Mormon and Seventh-day Adventist territory, too. In fact, he wrote his book, *The Mormon Waterloo* to explain the fallacies of that faith as he understood them. He wrote that volume in the home of F.P. Hestand, Anson, Texas. Hestand was one of the editors that helped Mrs. Minerva Gibbs publish the *Word and Work* after the sudden death of her husband, William, in 1906.

Crowe often partnered with Dr. McFarland from Walcott, Kansas, to preach in Kansas City. Since Crowe always struggled to make ends meet, he spoke admiringly of the Mormon and Sabbatarian systems of tithing that seemed plentiful in supporting ministry. He bemoaned the lack of funds throughout the Church of God.

Crowe was a songwriter. He wrote the words and music for "Just Over Eden" and "My Mother's Bible." National Bible Institute published "My Mother's Bible" in the Church of God hymnal *Songs of Truth* in 1947.

W.L. Crowe died at Topeka State Hospital in Chanute, Kansas, at age 58. His medical expenses totaled $90 per week during his final illness, an enormous amount then. Iowa Conference of the Churches of God sent their 25th Anniversary Birthday offerings to assist him. Evangelist Almus Adams visited him in the hospital and reported he was doing poorly and had "nothing to build on."

A noted memorial tribute was written for *The Restitution* of December 31, 1924, by A.J. Eychaner, himself an aging preacher. It is given here in part:

> I first met Bro. Crowe at a state conference in Nebraska. As a farmer, he came fresh from the soil. He was not a preacher at the time, but an earnest student of Bible truth. His progress was rapid and thorough in the things concerning the Kingdom of God and future redemption of man through Jesus Christ. He early recognized obedience in baptism necessary, and sought the guidance of the Holy Spirit, and communion with God in prayer. His petitions were forms of childlike trust and simplicity. Like Elisha, he left the plow in the field and followed the Master in the higher cultivation, the pursuit of which leads to eternal life.
>
> He had the rare ability of quick analysis of the many compounds of thought, to bring out the truth in a simple statement which a child could understand. He had the ready wit of his Irish ancestors and the positiveness of a Scot in the construction of his sentences. He never hesitated, and his sentences were short, given rapidly and accompanied by gestures, peculiarly his own.
>
> He was the author of several books, pamphlets, hymns and tracts, and a volume, *Form Ballads;* he also edited a monthly religious journal known as *The Present Truth*. He also wrote *The Mormon Waterloo*.
>
> His field of evangelistic work extended from Indiana, Illinois, Iowa, Dakota, Minnesota, Missouri, Kansas, Nebraska, Florida, Nevada and California. His converts were many and live in the above named states. It is to them that this is written. Those who read these lines may never fully realize the trials and responsibilities he felt to his family at home, for their needs and for his presence and help. Added to these was the traveling from place to place—many times alone, and on foot, carrying extra clothing and books through snow in winter and the heat in summer. Then he would return home to his family, weary and discouraged,

and take up physical labor on a farm, or in a machine shop, to supply the necessary food and clothing for those depending upon him.

This began to tell on him physically and mentally as the years passed until he had a complete breakdown in health. He finally died in a hospital in Kansas City. Those who knew him loved him most. His readiness to sacrifice time, strength and means, that others might earn the crown of life in the future, was characteristic of his work, freely given. His labors are done. His record is in the Book of Remembrance and a life as useful fills a niche in the economy of the Creator and will be rewarded at the resurrection.

Because Elder Crowe's medical expenses accumulated to nearly $500, members of the Church of God sent donations to Mrs. Crowe. Nearly $300 was collected toward the debt. Dr. McFarland, faithful friend and preaching partner, assisted the widow with expenses. He placed several notices in *The Restitution Herald* so that brethren would know the need.

See Eychaner, A.J.
    Gibbs, W.L.
    McFarland, Dr. Frank

Bibliography: Burnett, Francis et al history committee, *History of the Iowa Church of God and Conference, 1855-1987*, printed at Belle Plaine Union, 1987; Crowe, Chas. E. *The Glad Tidings*, published by the *Present Truth*, 1907; Crowe, W.L.. *The Mormon Waterloo*, Chas. Crowe, St. Paul, Neb. 1917; Crowe, W. L. *The Covenants and Promises*. Self; Crowe, W.L. "Testimony," *Present Truth*, 3:2 May 1901; Report of Waterloo Conference, Oct. 1910; Crowe, W.L. "A Charge of Disloyalty Dismissed," *The Day Dawn and Harvest Messenger*, James A. Patrick, editor, Minneapolis, Minn., June/July 1918; "Photo Copy of Early Records 1900s Ripley Church of God Ripley, IL," copy owned by Rock River Christian College Archives, Beloit, WI, Original Minute book is retained at Ripley Church of God; Rankin, Delbert. Interview in Nov. 2008 at the Belle Plaine Church of God Abrahamic Faith, Iowa Archives by J. Stilson. Randall, Clyde. *Historical Waymarks of the Church of God*, Church of God General Conference, Oregon, Il. 110. 1976; *The Restitution*, July 1919; May 11, 1920; Jan. 25, 1922; March, 1922; Various notes; *The Restitution Herald*, Jan. 6, 1915; Nov. 4, 1919; March 9, 1920; Feb. 10, 1924; April 15, 1924; Nov. 18, 1924; Dec. 23, 1924.

Crozier, Hiram P.
b. 1823
d. Unknown

Hiram P. Crozier was a Unitarian clergyman in Huntington, New York. Hiram was married to Delia Crozier and they had two sons and two daughters. He is believed to be a relative of Owen R.L. Crozier who was raised as an indentured servant and, therefore, didn't know any of his relatives until he was 28.

During the months of O.R.L. Crozier's disrepute brought about by his publication of the doctrine of the cleansing of the heavenly sanctuary, and his attack upon Joseph Marsh over suspected mismanagement of funds at *The Voice of Truth* (a false charge), Hiram Crozier wrote a few pieces for Marsh's new publication, *The Advent Harbinger and Bible Advocate*.

Whether or not Hiram was trying to keep the good name of Crozier before the reading public is not known, but it appears that Hiram became the mouthpiece for Owen in much the same way as Aaron spoke for Moses.

We know from Hiram's writings that he was well-informed about Age to Come and current issues in Adventism. Hiram refuted the doctrine of Sabbatarianism. It is interesting that O.R.L.'s theology of the heavenly sanctuary was accepted and trumpeted by the Seventh-day Adventists as gospel truth even though O.R.L. Crozier, himself, repudiated it. Hiram and many others also strongly abhorred the doctrine.

Hiram wrote a piece for Marsh's new publication, *The Advent Harbinger*, entitled "Persecution of the Saints."

After Owen Crozier made peace with Joseph Marsh regarding his unusual attack upon the editor's character, Marsh took him in as an assistant. For awhile then, he published children's material through the *Advent* office. From that point on, Minister Hiram Crozier's presence is not seen again in *The Advent Harbinger*.

See Crozier, Owen R.L.
     Marsh, Joseph

Bibliography: Ancestry.com. U.S. Federal Census. New York. Suffolk. Huntington. 1860; "Response to Delinquent Readers" *The Voice of Truth* Feb. 24, 1847; "Persecution of the Saints," *The Advent Harbinger and Bible Advocate* Aug. 18, 1850.

Cummings, William J.
b. June 17, 1837
d. December 12, 1915

William Cummings was born near London, England. As a child he migrated to Canada with his parents, Elias and Mary Fielder Cummings. He married Mary J. Tomblin on May 20, 1864. They had nine children. In faith he was a practicing Methodist when he heard the teaching of the Lord's Second Advent. Along with Elder G.W. Wright, of whom nothing more is known, Cummings preached this new doctrine throughout eastern Michigan.

At the time of his death he was a member of the Blanchard Church of God. Elder C.C. Maple preached his funeral at the Decker School House. He rests in the Millbrook Cemetery at Millbrook, Mecosta County, Michigan.

Bibliography: *The Restitution Herald*, Feb. 20, 1915.

Curtis, Rufus A.
b. 1864
d. Unknown

Rufus Curtis lived in Scottsburg, Indiana, from 1914 to 1916. He earned his living from farming with the help of an adult son, Arthur, who lived at home. Rufus Curtis was a prolific writer who kept *The Restitution Herald* well supplied. In 1916 he sent $5 to S.J. Lindsay to publish a new tract, *Inherent Immortality*. The following month he sent an article pleading for the people to support their preachers by paying them for their work. In a denomination that did not have a paid ministry up to this time, except as people felt led to support the itinerant evangelists, paying preachers at a local church was a new concept. He also wrote tracts entitled *The Everlasting Punishment, Conditional Immortality* and *The Sleep of the Dead,* all published in 1921.

See Cooper, John Wesley, discussion on taking an offering
Bibliography: Ancestry.com. U.S. Federal Census for Indiana. Scott Co. Vienna. Dist. 174. 1920; *The Restitution Herald*, January 6, 1915; Feb. 2, 1916.

Ministers at the 1932 Conference (left to right) Front: Sydney Magaw, FL Austin, Mary Woodward, LE Conner, Melville Lyon, Lucille Appleby, Paul Johnson, Frank Siple; Middle: JR LeCrone, J Arlen Marsh, GE Marsh, Harry Sheets, Thomas Savage, Cecil Smead, John Denchfield; Back: Gerry Cooper, Harvey Krogh Jr., CE Lapp, Charles Lapp-?, James McLain, Earl Thayer.

D

Daniel, Dr. Thomas J.
b. December 9, 1857
d. June 4, 1918

Thomas J. Daniel was the son of William and Jane Haney Daniel. He had one brother, John. Thomas became a physician. His medical practice became his principal source of income, but preaching was his first love. He and his wife Elizabeth (December 29, 1850-July 11, 1943) had four sons and  two daughters. One son was named after his father, but two other sons had more interesting names, Scudder and Porsens. Thomas and Elizabeth also raised Dr. Daniel's nephew, Jefferson Thomas Daniel, as their son.

It is not known with which denomination Dr. Daniel was affiliated before he entered the Church of God, but evidence shows he was re-baptized after he heard the teaching of the "One Faith." He may have learned of the faith from W.H. Wilson, who frequented a circuit that included Arkansas and Oklahoma. It would seem reasonable that they may have met when Wilson went to the good doctor for a health problem on his journey. W.H. Wilson listed Dr. Daniel among the Church of God preachers from Arkansas in a report of his travels through that state in 1904.

Dr. T.J. Daniel began editing *The Gospel Trumpet* in 1884 and continued after its name was changed to *The Gospel Messenger* around the turn of the century. He had to change the name due to a complaint of trademark infringement from another paper by the name of *Gospel Trumpet*. Soon after, in 1885 he moved to Waveland, Arkansas. Preachers there persecuted him because they abhorred the teaching of the Gospel of the Kingdom. He preached it in the face of danger.

Dr. Daniel gathered believers and they began to build a house of worship. Before it was finished, he went in and knelt down alone to pray for his Lord's protection, as he feared opposing groups would burn it down. The Lord honored his prayer as the building was used both as a church and a schoolhouse for many years.

In 1894 he moved to Magazine, Arkansas. The Disciples held meetings there but there was no church building at Magazine. Dr. Daniel offered to furnish materials for a building if the Disciples did the construction. The building cost almost $600. To assist with family finances while he was building his practice in a new location, Mrs. Daniels took in boarders. She contributed about $80 toward the construction. Both denominations used the building.

T.J. Daniel labored to teach other ministers about the Gospel of the Kingdom. One he influenced was L.H. Shelton, a young minister.

As part of his educational strategy, Dr. Daniel engaged in many debates with the Baptists. One was entitled "The Great Salvation," and was published in *The Restitution* in 1894. Daniel participated in another debate in which his opponent charged that the Greek word for "one" did not appear in the *Septuagint* in Ecclesiastes 3:19, "They all have *one* breath." The next spring, the same Baptist preacher wanted to debate Daniel on the same subject. In the meantime, however, Dr. Daniel had asked for and received information from A.H. Zilmer who said that "one" was in the *Septuagint*. Dr. Daniel appealed to the readers of *The Restitution* for someone to send him a copy of the *Septuagint* quickly before the next debate.

Another debate for which Dr. Daniel became famous was with John Cargile, a local Advent Christian. The subject of this debate was the "Restoration of Israel." The Advent Christians were the primary inheritors of the Millerite historicist position of prophecy interpretation. This system had a place for Israel in its fulfillment, but placed the restoration *after* the return of Christ, whereas Age to Come and One Faith placed the restoration to Israel *prior* to the Lord's return. This debate was published in a book; the Archives of Atlanta Bible College in McDonough, Georgia, hold a copy.

See Shelton, L.H.
Wilson, W.H.

Zilmer, A.H.

Bibliography: Ancestry.com. Arkansas Death Index. 1914-1950; U.S Census Arkansas. Logan. Revilee. Dist.58. 1900; David Graham in *Wisdom and Power* 6:10, January 1993, quoting from various issues of *The Restitution,* during 1885-1894; Rankin, Arlen F. E-mail from June 11, 2008; Report of W.H. Wilson *The Restitution,* Jan. 20, 1904; Jefferson Daniel. E-mail from FCJackson, citing listsearches. rootsweb.com/th/read/DANIEL/2000-020951247304 retrieved Sept. 23, 2008.

Daniels, (Daniel J.)
b. 1817
d. Unknown

It is believed this man was Daniel J. Daniels, a lawyer from Janesville, Wisconsin, but since his first name is never used in the reports to Joseph Marsh, it is difficult to verify. In that day and age, lawyering and preaching often went hand-in-hand. In the reports it can be seen that he stopped at the home of Joseph St. Johns in Buffalo Grove, Ogle County, Illinois, in 1847. Buffalo Grove to this day is a small settlement one-half mile west of Polo, Illinois. Evangelist Daniels proceeded on a circuit that took him to Springfield, Illinois, and very possibly through Ripley or Camp Point where a nucleus of Adventist members lived. Mrs. H.A. Parks reported to Joseph Marsh in 1847 on the whereabouts of Elder Daniels stating that he was preaching in southern Illinois while she was in northern Illinois.

It is from the early efforts of preachers like Evangelist Daniels, whose particulars are known only to God, that the Age-to-Come One Faith was established on the wild frontier. Without them there would have been no foundation upon which to build when the Wilsons came to Geneva, Illinois.

It was through Evangelist Daniels' association with Joseph Marsh and his publication *The Voice of Truth* that the Word spread across the frontier to the isolated pioneers at risk from Indians, and from the fierce Prairie Banditti operating there. Looking to the blessed hope undoubtedly assuaged their fears of earthly dangers. It was through *The Voice of Truth* that his ministry came to light. Without it, Daniels would be lost to history.

See Chandler, Moses
Marsh, Joseph
Parks, Mrs. H.A.

Bibliography: Ancestry.com U.S. Census. Wisconsin. Rock. Janesville (east side of Rock River.) 1850; "Letters to Editor by Joseph St. Johns." *The Voice of Truth,* Joseph Marsh, editor. Rochester, NY., Sept. 20, 1846, and March 17, 1847.

Drew, Anna E.
b. 1867
d. November 30, 1940

Anna E. Drew was a single woman who helped in the formation of the National Berean Society in 1913. The Berean Societies were formed in Iowa and Illinois as early as 1898. It was in Iowa that Elder C.C. Ramsay suggested the name "Bereans." Anna Drew began to lead the Berean work in 1898 in Illinois. In 1900 she was elected president in that organization, and after that she often took a leadership role to start chapters in local Churches of God throughout the nation. She lived and worked in Dixon, Illinois, with her sister Ada, who was one of the founders of that work.

To help solidify the work of the Church of God to develop leadership among the youth and adults, she developed a three-point program to train in:
1) Organization
2) Leadership
3) Giving

Evelyn Austin said, "She was truly the mother of Berean work." Anna often worked as the member in charge of maintaining contact with isolated members wherever they lived. In those days she did this mostly through correspondence, although she also traveled to homes and conferences to meet people.

As she met with young people in various churches she instructed them on how to conduct a business meeting and how to lead a Bible class. She encouraged every group to organize with officers, meet regularly, conduct lessons in an orderly manner, pay dues and train leaders. She kept in constant touch with the newly formed societies through correspondence and with visitation at least every two years. Her personal touch aided in developing successful groups that shared learning in a pleasant environment.

She was also aware of the people's physical needs and campaigned for better sanitation facilities, sidewalks and other improvements at home and at church that would lead to safer and healthier living.

She and Ada were friends to many of the early organizers of the Berean work including Dr. Leila Whitehead and Evelyn K. Harsh (Austin), Chicago, Illinois; Leota B. Hanson, St. Louis; Esta Lansbury (Starbuck), Casey, Illinois; Idona Romine, South Bend; and many others.

In 1906, Anna wrote a history of the Illinois Berean Society which is summarized here:

> Our organization, the Bereans, was formed at our annual conference in 1899. For sometime we had felt the need of

some special work whereby our young people might become more interested in Bible study, more active in Christian work, and through their influence other people become interested in the truths which God's work teaches. As the years go on, one by one those who hold aloft the cause of truth, fall asleep, and if the light of the glorious gospel is kept shining, the younger ones must carry on the work.

At the meeting held at Lanark, the previous year, work of this kind had been proposed, and Sr. Greenbaum of Chicago, called a meeting, appointed officers, further proceedings were to await orders from her. Four months later, the officers met together, worked out an outline for Bible study, had it printed, and when organized as a society, we had a line of study to enter upon.

Chicago and Dixon, previous to this, had local societies, were finding them so helpful they were anxious for a State organization, that all might be united in one work. Our membership was not limited to young people; many of the older people felt the need of the help gained from such an organization.

The first two years our membership did not increase very rapidly, but our annual meetings were much better attended by our young people, than before, and we found them taking a more active part in the services. In 1901, Bro. W.H. Wilson, who had taken much interest in the work suggested we ask for a column in *The Restitution,* to be filled once a month with articles, reports, letters from the Bereans. Soon after our first column appeared, letters arrived from distant states asking for information, and admittance as members into our society.

In the fall of 1902 a Conference was held in Southern Illinois. It was proposed that the president of our society be sent to that conference to interest the young people there. This was done, and through this effort a society was formed at Moriah, Marshall, and Hazle, Loogootee, and Ingraham. A sister from Oklahoma wrote and a class of nine was started there. Bro. Wilson in his trips throughout the states encouraged the work, and with his help societies were formed in Omor, Wisconsin, Iota, Louisiana, and elsewhere.

Many of our members have put on the name of Christ. Well done, Bereans, well done.

Anna may have moved from Dixon to Indiana, or perhaps preaching at an Indiana Conference was reason enough to issue her a license to preach. Ministerial licenses were commonly granted by local churches or state conferences before the License and Ordination Board of the Church of God was formed.

While her work with the Bereans must be emphasized, it should also be noted that Anna worked tirelessly as a board member of the Illinois State Conference most of her adult life. She served on many committees over the years, and served as treasurer from 1914 until her death. On one occasion she reported in an Illinois Conference meeting that the treasury was empty. J.M. Glotfelty, conference president, immediately called for a collection to be taken, and instructed Anna to send a letter throughout the state soliciting pledges. That solved the problem.

In her old age, Anna was accepted as a resident of the Golden Rule Home at Oregon, Illinois, the facility that had been purchased as the final home of elderly members of the Church of God.

See Austin, Evelyn Harsh (20th)
Glotfelty, J.M.
Hanson, Leota B. (20th)
Ramsay, C.C.
Whitehead, Leila, M.D. (20th)
Wilson, W. H.

Bibliography: Ancestry.com. U.S. Census. Illinois. Lee. Dixon. Dist.65. 1920; Austin, Evelyn. *Impressions and History* (of the Church of God). Unpublished manuscript. 1969; *The Restitution* September 26, 1906; *The Restitution Herald*, 1914-1925; Biography Project of Atlanta Bible College, David Krogh, compiler; Graham, David. Various e-mails to J Stilson. Summer, 2006.

The Berean Society Three-Point Program of Goals

1) to train in organization
2) to train in leadership
3) to train in giving

Drew, Willie D.O.
b. June 6, 1862
d. October 9, 1924

Willie Drew was active in the Church of God at Dixon, Illinois. It is thought he was an uncle to Anna E. Drew who took an active role in organizing the National Berean Society in Illinois in 1913, but family ties are scant. He was married to Mabel, and they had two sons and two daughters. His obituary noted he was engaged in a coal and implement business in Dixon. He was baptized in 1886 when he was 24 years old, but the officiant is unknown. It may have been J.M. Stephenson or W.H. Wilson, each of whom traveled throughout that part of Illinois. Willie Drew's funeral was conducted by

Left to right: Leila Whitehead, Evelyn Austin and Anna Drew helped organize the National Berean Society.

F.E. Siple, a noted Church of God student minister, and a native of Louisiana.

Sadly, the Dixon Church of God which the Drews helped establish early in the history of Illinois, closed in summer 2006. At that time only eight members remained. Shortly thereafter, property and real estate were sold to be used as residences. Dixon church documents have been donated to the Archives at Atlanta Bible College.

See Drew, Anna B.
Siple, F.E.
Wilson, W.H.

Bibliography: Ancestry.com. U.S. Census. Illinois. Lee. Dixon. Dist. 59. 1900; "Obituary". *The Restitution Herald,* Oct. 31, 1924; Stilson, Jan, Interview with Nancy Drew Johnson, Dixon, Illinois, October 29, 2007.

Durham, Andrew N.
b. December 25, 1852
d. May 5, 1926

Andrew Durham was a businessman and the pastor of the Guthrie Grove Church of God in Pelzer, South Carolina. He began preaching as early as 1908 at which time he shared the pulpit with Enoch Anderson. Later he conducted services at three other churches in the area along with two Churches of God in North Carolina. He also held Bible studies wherever he could. In 1920 he shared the pulpit for the Southeast Conference with professor Paran Guthrie, J.H. Anderson and Barzillai Z. Chandler. He baptized his daughter and also B.Z. Chandler's daughter at this conference.

This same preaching team motored to Traveler's Rest and preached several services there and baptized 14 adults. After this the church was reorganized with Bro. Durham as pastor and M.O. Williamson as assistant pastor. M.O. Williamson had been baptized by A.N. Durham in 1908.

Elder Durham was popular with his community and with Church of God members throughout the Southeast conference. For his birthday in 1923, a call was made to readers and subscribers of *The Restitution Herald* to shower him with cards.

Sadly, Elder Durham died in an auto accident, greatly shocking the surrounding community. He was laid to rest beside the Guthrie Grove Church of God at Pelzer.

See Anderson, Enoch
Anderson, J. H.
Chandler, B. Z.
Williamson, M.O.

Bibliography: *The Restitution* June 24, 1908; Sept. 3, 1920; *The Restitution Herald* Dec. 11, 1923; Obituary, *The Restitution Herald* May 18, 1926.

Dwiggins, Robert S.
b. 1835
d 1909?

Attorney Robert Dwiggins was born in Ohio but lived most of his life in Indiana.

Research indicates he began preaching for the Church of God at the new work at Renssalaer, Indiana, in 1860. He studied law and was mustered into war service while residing at Renssalaer. He served in the Civil War with the 9th Indiana Infantry Regiment, Company G. This unit was a volunteer regiment which served around Indianapolis at first, and later in many battles throughout Tennessee and Georgia.

Robert married his sweetheart, Fannie, during the war on December 28, 1862. There is no record of children. Fannie died October 28, 1898, leaving Robert bereaved.

L.E. Conner may have read law with R.S. Dwiggins before he relocated to Oklahoma to read law with Horace Speed. Conner began preaching at Renssalaer while Dwiggins was there, and they served together at the 1888 General Conference.

In 1888, R.S. Dwiggins attended the General Conference organizational meeting at the Church of God in Philadelphia. He was chosen president of the 1889 Chicago board and led the new conference until it closed. Lacking funds to continue, the new effort failed and was disbanded in 1892. The ledger of minutes from this important but immature effort is part of the Archives at Atlanta Bible College

The Restitution reveals that Dwiggins moved around. He was acquainted in California with the Corbaleys, Wilsons, Barnhills and Railsbacks all of whom had moved west from Illinois and Indiana in the 1870s to the 1920s. Voter registration records show Dwiggins registered to vote in Chicago in October 1892.

In 1895, he wrote to *The Restitution* suggesting that all readers send Christmas letters for the next issue containing their testimony about the Kingdom of God. The idea was taken to heart and over the next few issues more than 200 letters from individuals, churches and families were published. These were heart-felt messages of Christian devotion and warmth.

After he retired from practice, he moved to California and began preaching for the Church of God. Since he did not write articles for the church newspapers, it is not known just how active he was in filling pulpits in California.

In 1908 he returned for the annual June conference meeting at the Antioch Church of God near Plymouth,

Indiana. He was 72 years old, but he preached like a young man. He was listed among the ministers and was well respected by all who heard him preach again.

He began to draw a pension from his war duty as an invalid in California in 1904. His travel to old Antioch Church of God was his farewell trip, for he is not listed in the US Census of 1910.

See Conner, L.E.

Bibliography: Ancestry.com. Chicago Voter Registration.1892; Civil War Pension Index 1861-1934 R.S. Dwiggins; U.S. Census. Indiana. Jasper. Rennsalaer. 1860; Minutes of Board of Churches of God in Christ Jesus, 1888-1892. Ledger of Minutes from Conference and Board meetings; *Restitution,* Dec. 25, 1895; June 24, 1908; Williams, Byron. *Abstracts of Obituaries and Weddings from the Restitution* Self-published. 1994.

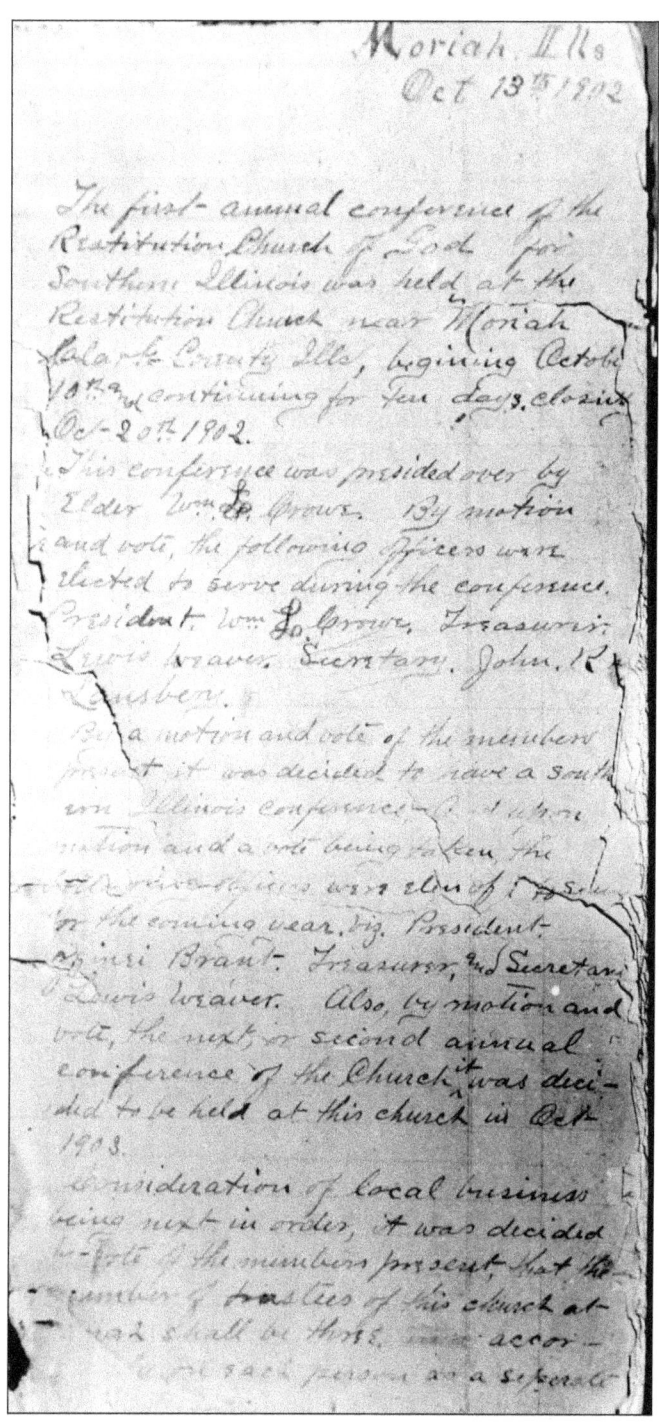

Minutes of Illinois Conference at Moriah Church of God, 1902

Eisenhower, William Henry
b. April 9, 1858
d. January 16, 1926

W.H. Eisenhower was born in Pennsylvania and made his way to Kansas. He settled in the neighborhood near Abilene where other Eisenhower families lived. He was related to President Dwight D. Eisenhower through the President's grandfather, Jacob Frederick Eisenhauer (German spelling). William Henry's father, Samuel Peter Eisenhower, was a brother to Jacob making William Henry and Dwight either first cousins once removed or second cousins.

Roger Cramer, an Illinois genealogist, discovered the relationship between William Henry and the President while researching Dwight's mother's family with the surname of Matter/Motter, While W.H. Eisenhower lived in Abilene, he and another relative, Ferdinand or Frederick Eisenhower, worked for their Aunt Anna Pyke on her farm. William was 23 years old at the time. He married Amanda Hoover on June 16, 1883, in Navarre, Kansas, and they settled on their own farm, residing there the rest of their lives. They had eight boys and two girls. Amanda died on November 11, 1940.

In 1893 William Eisenhower wrote to J.B. Craton, editor of *The Glad Tidings* asking for a list of tracts and back issues. Craton responded that they had been mailed and instructed for payment, "Don't send stamps, especially five cent stamps to pay for subscriptions," because he said he couldn't use them.

Several Church of God members are named in that single issue proving that *The Glad Tidings* was a Church of God paper. Those included are A.J. (Andrew Jackson) Boyer, Stephens City, Virginia; Elder J. T. Prime, Edison, Nebraska; Milton Eychaner, Melbourne, Iowa; and T.H. Lindsay and George Pyper of Adeline, Illinois, all of whom were members or friends of the Church of God. That single issue came into the Archives of the Atlanta Bible College from the collection of Church of God evangelist James W. McClain, who retired to Pine Bluff, Wyoming.

It is thought that W.H. Eisenhower claimed Christ as the Messiah who is coming again to establish the Kingdom, and it is hoped that he shared the message with his extended family. Perhaps the 34th President of the United States learned of the Gospel of the Kingdom on earth sometime during his youth.

See Boyer, Andrew J.
Craton, J.B.
Gibbs, W.L.
Marsh, Joseph

Bibliography: Ancestry.com U.S. Census. Kansas. Abiliene. 1880; Cramer, Roger. "Direct Descendants of Hans Eisenhauer." Sent to JStilson circa 1995; *The Glad Tidings*, J.B. Craton, editor. Council Grove, Ks., April 1893; JStilson Interview with Eisenhower Presidential Library, Librarian, Abilene, Kansas, 1986 at the beginning of research on this family.

Elvey, Charles
b. 1825?
d. November 26, 1919

Charles Elvey arrived in Chicago in 1836 with his family from England. He may have been a small boy at that time. He and the family settled in the wilderness then known as Northfield, Illinois, Cook County. He accepted the Lord and joined the Church of God when he was 20 years old.

He married Frances Sutcliffe, and they moved into Chicago in 1866 after the Civil War. He became engaged in the coal business.

Charles Elvey and his family were neighbors to the Whiteheads. When Dr. Leila Whitehead was growing up, she played with the Elvey children. Several families who belonged to the Church of God in Austin lived on the same street. These families were James and Ruth Whitehead with children, Ralph and Leila; Charles and Frances Elvey and children Minnie, Lilly and Cora; publisher James W. and Sarah Wilson and their son Oliver, and a niece Elsie Pierce; James and Mary Wilson, retired farmers from Geneva, Illinois; Lucien and Emma Button, relatives of Benjamin and James Wilson, with her sons, Henry, Stanley and Rolla and niece Millicent Pierce. This data comes from the 1880 US Census which reveals that Church of God members who were Wilson relatives lived in close proximity, not just in the same town, but on the same street. The Elveys entered into the mainstream of citizenship as we found evidence that Bro. Elvey registered to vote in his precinct for 46 years at 921 Madison Street.

Dr. Leila Whitehead, niece of Benjamin Wilson, wrote Elvey's eulogy; she said he had been devoted to the Lord, and he had guided her in her Christian walk:

> Another of God's noblemen has gone to his rest to await the call of the Savior whom he loved so well. I have known Brother Charles Elvey all my life, and his faithfulness both in attendance at church service and in the performing of the little thankless tasks that must be done by someone. He has had such an influence on my Christian life that I feel I must pass the lesson on to you.
>
> One Sunday when the Bereans had conducted the church service he said to me, "I cannot talk, but I can serve the Lord in being here every Sunday, and being here with thanksgiving." What a lesson to us! What would it mean to the life of the church if every Berean and every church member, young or old, served the Lord by being there every Sunday and serving not with fault-finding but with thanksgiving.
>
> One of my earliest recollections is of seeing Brother and Sister Elvey every Sunday in their seats at church; and the beauty of it is that they loved to come, they did not come from duty. Nothing but sickness ever kept them away.
>
> It was Brother Elvey that passed the hymn books and Bibles every Sunday, and it was Brother Elvey who put them away. It was his work to pay the rent for the hall, to see that the janitor had the steam up in time for services, and a hundred and one little things that we did not realize until sickness held him in its grasp, and he could do them no more. No parade, no fuss, but he just faithfully and quietly did them, and he could not realize how he will be missed.
>
> As deacon of the church his hand was the first to pass me the communion when I entered the Christian fold. He held the position of deacon until he could come no more.
>
> I wish to give one more tribute to Brother Elvey that came from strangers and from the world. One day, when riding on the street car, I heard two men behind me discussing Christians and their failings. One man said, "I tell you there is nothing in it. Christians are like every one else; there is no difference. They will skin you on a deal every time." "Hold on," said the other man, "they are not all like that. There is a Christian coal dealer on Madison St. named Elvey. He is square. If I wanted to test any other coal man I would have that man Elvey deliver a ton of coal and then I would measure every one else by that."
>
> He was a quiet, faithful, loving, unassuming man whose light shone forth in the world.
>
> Written in loving memory, *Leila E. Whitehead*

Charles Elvey's funeral services were held in his daughter's home as was the custom in those days. F.E. Siple conducted the service and wrote the obituary.

See Button, Lucien and Emma
Siple, F.E. (20th)
Whitehead, Leila, M.D. (20th)
Wilson, James

Bibliography: Ancestry.com Voter Registration Record. Chicago. 1888. U.S. Census. Illinois. Cook. Austin. Dist. 212. 1880; Obituary, *The Restitution Herald*, January 27, 1920; Whitehead, Leila, "Eulogy" *The Restitution*, Dec. 10, 1919.

Endsley, Rena
b. 1854
d. Unknown

Rena Endsley was born in Indiana and was married to Charles Endsley. They had one son and a daughter. They lived on the frontier of Nebraska in a log cabin. In 1893 she testified in the pages of *The Restitution* that she had been a member of the Christian Church. She went on to relate how Elder Bebee of the Church of God stopped by her log cabin on the plain, and asked her what her hope was. She replied she hoped to be worthy to go to heaven.

Beebe replied, "Dear sister, you won't find that between the covers of your Bible." He then explained to her the promises made to Abraham, Isaac and Jacob. Rena realized she had never reconciled going to heaven with death and resurrection. She accepted the Gospel of the Kingdom of God and remained a faithful student of it until her death.

Without a first name it is virtually impossible to track a person's identity through the public records. Therefore to date, evangelist Beebe's exact identity is not known. He may have been B.B. Brown. He may have been acquainted with the Church of God through the Ohio, Indiana, Wisconsin or Iowa evangelists. He may have been a friend to Almus Adams, but it is thought he may have pre-dated Adams.

See Brown, B.B.

Bibliography: Ancestry.com. U.S. Census. Nebraska. Cheyenne. Redington. Dist. 55 1900; Council Bluff. Melbeta. Dist. 2 1930; Letter from Rena. *The Restitution* June 8, 1925.

Etheridge, Sympronius R.
b. 1835
d. Unknown

S.R. Etheridge was born in North Carolina and may have heard the Gospel of the Kingdom from the early preaching of Newell Bond. Elder Etheridge became a preacher as well, preaching the good news of the Kingdom of God in the latter part of the 19th century throughout Arkansas especially in the area of Griggs and

Conway. He may have come from a well-to-do family for it is noted in the US Census under the category of occupation that he had his "own income." He may have financed his own ministry and lived comfortably in his old age. He and wife Josephine had nine children, five of whom predeceased their parents.

The McGintytown Church of God is located near Greenbrier, Arkansas. It must be presumed that the steady work and testimony of Elder S.R. Etheridge accounts for the strong heritage of the McGintytown Church of God in the 21st century. In 1883 an announcement of the Arkansas Conference was sent to *The Restitution*. In addition to S.R. Etheridge, the following ministers were present: G.W. Crosby, J.O. Martin, W.J. Dowell, W.N. McCarty, T.J. Dowell, W.T. Roberts, W.H. Porter, C.C. Brown, J.J. Smith, W.W. Corbin, J.D. Dobbs and N.B. Etheridge.

Some of these 13 ministers may have been pastoring the 11 Churches of God that were represented at that conference. Attendance at Arkansas conferences often numbered in the hundreds.

Nothing more is known about Sympronius except he was faithful to the Lord's command to "Go."

Bibliography: Ancestry.com U.S. Census. Arkansas Faulkner. Conway. Ward 1. Dist. 24. 1910; *The Restitution,* July 11, 1883; *The Restitution Herald,* April 26, 1916.

Eychaner, Andrew James
b. September 17, 1842
d. May 26, 1936

A. **Eychaner Becomes a Preacher**
B. **First and Second Attempts to Organize a National Conference**
C. **Foreign Missions**
D. **Getting Older**

Andrew "Andy" James Eychaner was the ninth child of Coonrad and Catherine Eychanner (German spelling). The family came from Steuben, Oneida County, New York, but moved in September 1843, to Paynes Point, Ogle County, Illinois, east of Oregon. A.J.'s mother died when he was four.

Andy grew up in the home of Margaret Andrew. She was either his sister or his aunt, the latter being the better option according to the US Census. He was baptized by Elder A.N. Bostwick in Murphy Millpond, now called Honey Creek, Ogle County, on Sunday, November 2, 1861, being 19 years old at the time. Elder Bostwick may have been Aquel Bostwick from Dupage County, a traveling preacher. Nothing more is known about him. Andy was a member of the Church of God before there was a church building in Illinois. This must have predated the Adeline Church as well. Most likely the Adeline Church of God was built after the Civil War.

Andy, in turn, baptized Margaret. To earn money for school he preached at various schoolhouses in Ogle County including Limerick, Paynes Point and Slagle named after a family to whom Andy was related. He preached at the Antioch Church which was located at the rural intersection of Chana and Flagg Center Roads.

He also converted his older brother, Nathan, who was the father of Delos Andrew and grandfather of William Andrew of the present-day Oregon Church of God.

In 1862, Andy attended conference at Crane's Grove, Illinois, and met J.M. Stephenson; Thomas J. Newman, editor of *The Prophetic Watchman*; H.V. Reed, noted orator from Harvard, Illinois; Benjamin Wilson, translator of *The Emphatic Diaglott* (a work which was then in progress); and Dr. S.J. Jacobs, a veterinarian from Ogle County. These were notable leaders of the early work of the Church of God on the prairie frontier.

Andy was enthusiastic about the future of the Church of God and believed the secret of growth lay in the missionary efforts of its people. In November 1863 he wrote to Thomas Newman, editor of *The Millennial Harbinger and Bible Expositor*, and suggested that readers send offerings to begin a tract fund. This would be used to print and distribute tracts of beloved Bible doctrines. Andy stated that the Church of God at Paynes Point, Illinois, had already adopted a giving plan. Then he sent $5, an enormous donation in those days.

In 1863, Andy moved to Iowa to live, and began preaching there. He had been persuaded to come west by Levi Marsh, a well-to-do merchant at Irving, Iowa. Elder Marsh financed the construction of the church building at Irving.

A. Eychaner Becomes a Preacher

A.J. Eychaner accepted the call and made himself available to do evangelistic work. He often preached at neighboring state conferences. He was evangelist of the Iowa Conference for a number of years, and reported his work faithfully in a diary.

He was a graduate of the Rock River Seminary at Mt. Morris, Illinois, Class of 1867, one of the first advanced schools in Ogle County. Following graduation, he taught school for a number of years in the vicinity.

In 1868 he attended a conference of the Church of God at Waterloo, Iowa. He preached before that conference which was one of the earliest conference organizations to begin meeting regularly in the denomination. Ohio,

Indiana and Michigan conferences also met informally in the 1850s. There is good evidence in the Minutes of the Michigan conference that it was first organized by 1856. It should be noted that evidence exists that those "old" conferences that met early, often reorganized a "new conference" in the 1880s, 1890s or later.

In 1868, Eychaner was appointed President of the Northern Illinois and Southern Wisconsin Conference. This conference also licensed him to preach. The resolution to license said, "Resolved, that the Conference recommend Brother A.J. Eychaner, to the Brethren everywhere as a man of character, and one in whom we can confide as a preacher of the Gospel." In 1870 he preached at a conference in Chicago, where he met Anna Beck. In April 1870, he also worked in the Chicago *Restitution* office to prepare the new hymnbook for publication.

During 1871 and 1872 he traveled in California and Oregon, preaching wherever he could, but he had Anna on his mind so he returned east to marry her.

Andy and Anna married in Buchanan, Michigan, on October 22, 1872. They resided in Buchanan for ten years. In Michigan he certainly would have known Ephraim Miller and O.R.L. Crozier, important evangelists in the Church of God movement. Iowa pulled him home, and they returned there in 1882 to live. He resumed preaching at Irving, Gladbrook, Marshalltown and Belle Plaine on a rotation schedule.

B. First and Second Attempts to Organize a National Conference

In 1869 the first attempt was made to organize a regional conference work. It was called the Northwest Christian Association and was centered on the work of the Wilsons in Geneva and Northfield, Illinois. The endeavor failed. State conferences began then to formally organize their churches so that when their conference was stable with healthy churches, another organizational attempt could be initiated.

In 1887 the Iowa Conference of the Church of God formally organized and held its first conference meeting at Ferguson. A.J. Eychaner helped to ease its birth pains.

The following year, 1888, he was sent as a delegate to the national conference in Philadelphia. Eychaner was against formulating a statement of faith. It was noted by George Work in an open letter in *The Restitution*, that any delegate who opposed such action, should come to the conference anyway, and vote against it!

It was hoped this conference meeting would organize a stable national work. It had been 43 years since the Bitter Disappointment, and the Church of God had not yet successfully organized a lasting national conference. A.J. Eychaner was now 46 years old, and hoped to see that happen while he was still young. He was chosen secretary of the organizing board.

In February 1889, Eychaner met with the executive board of that General Conference in Chicago during which he preached, "Christ is Coming—His Mission." He was re-elected secretary at this meeting. This board of conference officers never hosted another national meeting of delegates. The conference dissolved in 1892. Eychaner, however, was an optimist and was present at the next two attempts to organize a national corporation in 1910 and 1921. The 1921 effort to create a general conference was successful.

By the time the 1890 Iowa state conference was held, the people of that state were planning a tent ministry. Eychaner commented in his diary:

> At the third annual conference of the Church of God in Iowa, held at Ferguson in 1890, the proposition of putting a tent in the field was talked over privately with some of the brethren there. A subscription was started and the amount with which to buy the tent was raised. The cost of the tent and fixtures was $140.
>
> The fourth annual conference was held at Sac City in the new tent June 4-14, 1891. Those who were there will never forget the joy and gladness we had at that meeting, and the Lord blessed our work so that the people were interested and on June 10, I baptized five persons upon their confession of faith in the things of the Kingdom of God and the name of the Lord Jesus. These were followed by others until eleven had put on Christ.
>
> The tent was then sent out to do evangelistic work under a board of managers. Bro. James Prime volunteered to go with me, and we preached the gospel in the cities of Lake View, Iowa, Elk Point, South Dakota, Hawarden, Iowa, and came to Marathon in September where the closing meeting and fall conference were held. During the year I baptized forty-one converts.

Tent ministry is not the only method he tried. One year he reported to *The Restitution* that he was preaching in the McCallsburg Opera House. He had been there five nights in a row.

In 1898 Andy traveled to the State of Washington for 45 days. There he preached numerous sermons and baptized four people. He expected that more fruit would come from that effort. In Wenatchee beginning January 20 he preached on the subject, "What Jesus Preached." By February 6, a congregation met to organize their church. The congregation hired a hall, organized a Sunday School and prayer service.

A.J. Eychaner distributed a copy of Wiley Jones' book, *The Gospel of the Kingdom,* to everyone he baptized. For several years he edited the *Bible Lesson Quarterly* published by James W. Wilson. Eychaner was also a poet, and wrote the lyrics for the hymn in the *Songs of Truth,* "Beautiful Days." One of his more famous undertakings was the series of sermons he wrote for *The Restitution Herald* as a 76-issue series from 1912-1916. "Sermonette" No. 73 was published on his 73rd birthday in 1915.

Sometimes Eychaner's work and teachings were met with stiff opposition from local preachers of mainline churches. They did not want soul sleep being taught in their towns. His diary tells of a time when someone snuck into the tent and stole the clothes out of his trunk while he was out for lunch or dinner. He was unaware of this until it was time to clean up and change clothes for the evening meeting. Without a change of clothes, he was obliged to preach in his daytime attire.

His teachings also met opposition from some members of the Church of God, including preachers. Eychaner came to believe in Josephism, the idea that Jesus was only the human son of Joseph, adopted by God at his resurrection. Most people in the Church of God believed that Jesus, born of the woman and the Holy Spirit, was human with a divine nature. Eychaner was the agreeant in a debate about Josephism against James Patrick of Minnesota opposing the doctrine. Both men were Church of God pastors. Patrick edited *The Day Dawn of the Present Truth* which published the debate in its September 1, 1917, issue.

To illustrate the main emphasis of Eychaner's biblical theology several sermon titles are given: "The Shaking of the Nations," "Plan of the Ages," "Kingdom of God," "Rewards—When and Where?," "The Gospel," "Politics of the Bible," "The Covenants," "The Resurrection," "The Coming of Jesus," "Eternal Life," "What Must I Do to Be Saved?," "The Soul," "The Spirit," "The Inner Man" and "The Return of Israel."

C. Foreign Missions

Eychaner was interested in the Bible Faith Mission owned by the Advent Christians. He spearheaded a fundraising effort on behalf of the American office of the Bible Faith Mission, and was appointed its superintendent under the direction of Mrs. Sarah Taylor, matron of the Bible Faith Mission in India. Mrs. Taylor worked with Pastor Vedantachari, a native pastor. He oversaw the work of 36 churches in India, but he needed a building for central offices.

Sarah Taylor, of the Bible Faith Mission in India

In 1920, A.J. Eychaner began to promote the need in India and to accept donations for foreign missions. Eychaner sent his publicity material for missions to *The Restitution Herald*, and it is through this medium that the details of the mission efforts are known. Eychaner reported that the Bible Faith Mission began in India after Mr. Vedantachari visited the United States and told about the work a "few years back." Mrs. Sarah Taylor took up the challenge and went to India with her husband to assist in the work. The BFM had been operating for ten years and advertised its needs throughout the Church of God and the Advent Christian church. There were 80 workers in India with 36 schools, 1,234 students and 38 churches, totaling 3,150 members. There were 27 conferences with 6,200 attenders in five geographic areas of Madras. The work was 50% sustaining and needed much help.

For this effort Eychaner received severe criticism from Robert Huggins, the editor of *The Restitution*. Huggins said that missions were closed to India by the Lord in Acts 16:6, the charge to Paul to go into Macedonia, and therefore Huggins said this could not be a valid work. In his wrath, he called A.J. Eychaner "a Josephite, a sabbath-keeper and a villifier of God's work." He said that this was known from coast to coast, and he called him "the most noted heretic in America."

Further, Editor Huggins repudiated *The Restitution Herald* as "a so-called Church of God paper." These were harsh words presumably generated because of Eychaner's personal preference for Sabbatarianism, his preaching on the paternity of Jesus, and perhaps some personal animosity by Huggins. The debate on Josephism and an article "A Sabbath Day Necessary" published in *The Bible Advocate* (March 31, 1903, a Seventh-day Church of God paper) was all the evidence Huggins needed before printing his attack on Eychaner in 1920. As there was no formally accepted statement of faith until the General Conference organized in 1921, preachers such as Eychaner who had divergent views could continue to be independent in their belief system because they were not yet violating any formal "creed."

David Graham, Church of God historian, has said that A.J. Eychaner entertained several notions that were

Early ministers, left to right:
Back row - Harry Sheets, Herman Hunt, JW Williams, FE Siple, Melville Lyon, Paul Johnson.
Front row - LE Conner, FL Austin, Mary Woodward (FL Austin's mother), James Patrick, AJ Eychaner.

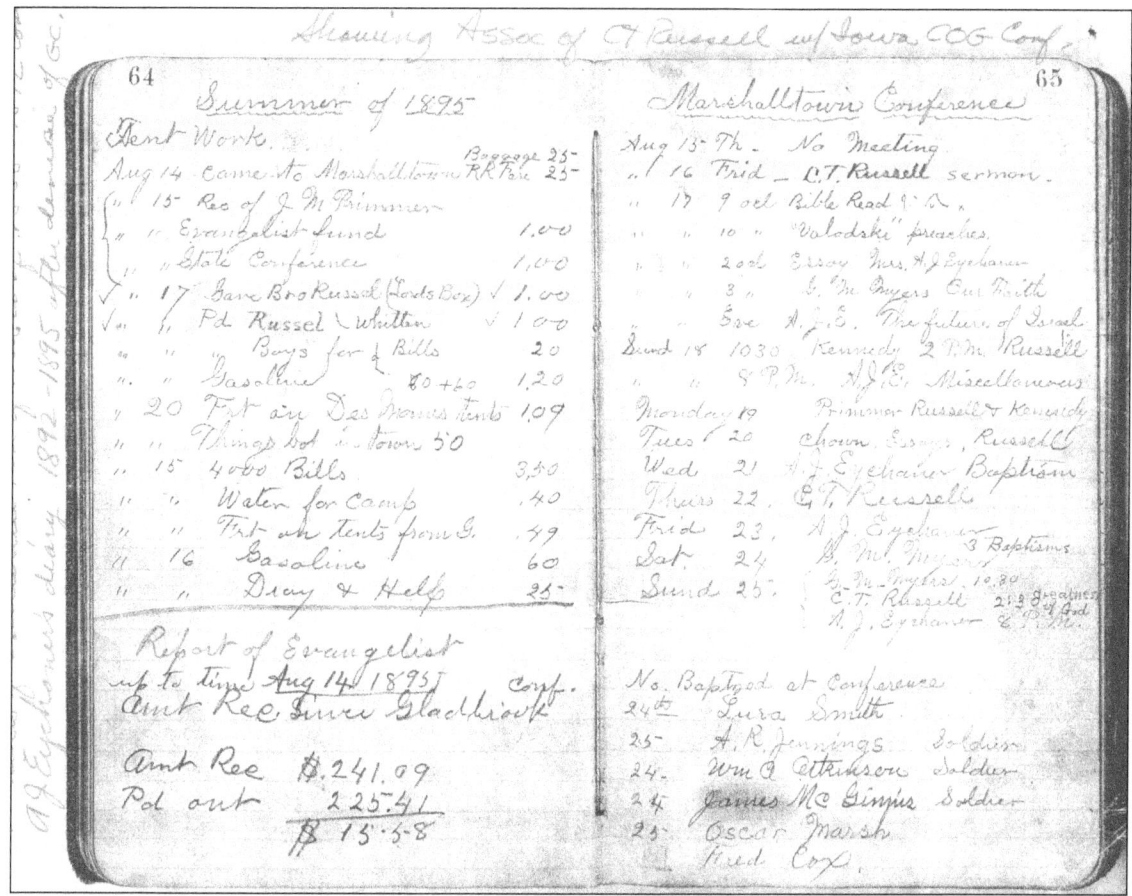

Eychaner's diary noting CT Russell preached at the Iowa State Conference, summer 1895.

common among ministers especially in Iowa. These notions confused believers and frustrated evangelists who were trying to lead men to salvation but who had to spend their time discussing "notions" with confused members. Some of the notions which were swirling about the heads of church leaders and members in those days included the ideas of universal salvation also known as second chance, Sabbatarianism, inspiration of the Bible and Anglo-Israelism; personality or non-personality of Satan; Josephism; and partial or limited resurrection.

The pros and cons of all these issues were being discussed in *The Restitution,* providing another layer of frustration to the evangelists who felt that they should toss the paper away because they could not distribute copies in good conscience to prospective believers. They felt the merit of the paper was compromised by discussing all the heresies and "isms." This is the principal issue that gave rise to the publishing of *The Restitution Herald*. People wanted a pure doctrinal paper that left out the controversies and published the precious truths commonly believed among them.

Andy Eychaner was caught in the middle because of his esteemed position as an elder statesman among the younger ministers and his penchant for encouraging discussion on these controversial matters. Because of the esteem which many churchmen and editors, except Huggins, viewed him, he with W.L. Crowe, J.W. Williams and G.M. Myers were included in the fellowship. And it was definitely to their advantage to discourage a formal statement of faith.

D. Getting older

A.J. and Anna Eychaner began spending winters in Tampa, Florida in the 1920s, returning to Iowa during summer. They attended the 25th Birthday Offering Anniversary celebration at Gladbrook, Iowa, sponsored by the Sunday School. In 1924, Elder Eychaner conducted the funeral of a Christian sister, Anna Marie Brown, at Waterloo.

In his old age, Eychaner wrote several articles for *The Restitution Herald* to strengthen and encourage the brethren. The last of his contributions appeared well after his death; the first of a two-part series beginning in August 1977 was entitled, "A Year in the Life of an Evangelist 1895-1896," taken from his diary. Andy kept a diary that included details of his travels, sermons, finances and names of men who

AJ Eychaner

assisted him with the tent. This series based on the diary provided wonderful insight into the joys and hazards of preaching on a circuit.

The diary entry for the 1895 Iowa Conference mentioned "C.T. Russell" who was paid $1.50 for preaching at the conference on four occasions. Russell was the founder and leader of the Zion's Watch Tower which eventually became known as the Jehovah's Witnesses. There was friendly exchange between Russell and some leaders in the Church of God up to around 1900, but Russell was never part of the development of the Church of God.

A.J. Eychaner died in Tampa, but was interred at Greenwood Cemetery in Cedar Falls Township, Cedar Falls, Iowa. Pastor J.W. Williams conducted the funeral service. Anna, his dear wife, lived to be 108 years old and is buried beside him.

Anna Eychaner

  See Huggins, Robert (20th)
    Taylor, Sarah
    Williams, J.W. (20th)
    Vedantachari, Charles

Bibliography: Ancestry.com. U.S. Census. Illinois. Ogle. Eagle. 1850; and U.S. Census. New York, Oneida, Steuben 1840; and U.S. Census. Illinois. DuPage. Winfield. 1860; Burnett, Francis et al history committee *History of the Iowa Church of God and Conference, 1855-1987,* printed by Belle Plaine Union, 1987. Cline, Lois. "Eychaner's Diary" *History Newsletter of the Church of God General Conference,* Jan Stilson, editor, Oregon, IL., Summer 1992; Eychaner, A.J. "Letter to Editor on Giving Plan," *Millennial Harbinger and Bible Expositor,* Thos. Newman, editor, Nov. 18, 1863; Conference Report at Chicago. *Herald of the Kingdom and Christian Instructor,* Oct. 15, 1868; Eychaner, A.J. "Excerpts from the Diary" Iowa Conference, Summer 1895. This diary is owned by the Archives of Atlanta Bible College, McDonough, Ga; Eychaner, A.J. "History of Tentwork in Iowa" *The Evangelist,* edited by G.M. Myers, April 27, 1898; Interview with Lois Cline in 2005; materials provided by Lois Cline written by her cousin Richard L. Kenyon, "A short biography of Andrew James Eychaner." 3d ed. 2002; Graham, David. Various e-mails to Jan Stilson. Spring 2006; Patrick, James. "Report of Eychaner-Patrick Debate on Josephism," *Day Dawn of the Present Truth,* Sept. 1, 1917; *The Restitution,* June 22, 1920; *The Restitution Herald,* January 27, 1920; Nov. 12, 1924; July 25, 1925; August, 1977; Work, George F. "To the Church of God in the United States and Canadas, and Sister Churches Affiliating with them, by Whatsoever Name they may be Called, Greeting," *The Restitution,* August 15, 1888; Report to Minerva Gibbs, *Word and Work* Abilene, Tx. Oct. 15, 1907.

Field, Dr. Nathaniel (Nathan)
b. November 7, 1805
d. August 28, 1888

A. General Conference at Jeffersonville
B. Christian Liberty versus Sectarianism

Dr. Nathaniel Field was born in Jefferson County, Kentucky, but lived most of his adult life near Jeffersonville, Indiana. He married Sarah Ann Laws at the Grayson house in Louisville, Kentucky, on November 27, 1827. They had one son and three daughters. He was a graduate of Transylvania Medical College, Lexington, Kentucky, after which his family moved to Jeffersonville, Indiana. Dr. Field was a member of the Indiana legislature from 1838-1839. He was a staunch abolitionist, a fact which he denied at the time, but which was well-known. One source said:

> Dr. Field was aggressive and fearless against slavery…and he once had to barricade his house in Jeffersonville against a mob, and tell them to come on, he was ready. The mob did not come on, and Dr. Field became a hero of local history.

During the Civil War, Dr. Field was a surgeon for the 66th Regiment of Indiana Volunteer Infantry. He served in the battles of Richmond, Kentucky, on August 30, 1862, and at Perryville, Kentucky, where, eventually, a Church of God was begun by W.L. Skeels. Nathaniel was president of the Indiana State Medical Society from 1868-1869.

Dr. Field was a leader in the Adventist work in south central Indiana from the beginning of Adventism in that state in the early 1840s. Prior to that he was associated with the Presbyterians, and held a license to preach for them. He became acquainted with Alexander Campbell's Restoration Movement and was baptized at that time. Dr. Field edited *The Journal of Christianity* which was first published in April 1840. In its *Prospectus* Field said, "The paper…shall be devoted to Primitive Christianity and Literature, Bible faith and Bible practice will be taught and insisted on as true orthodoxy, and the only bond of union among Christians."

While Dr. Field was with the Restoration Movement, he wrote to Alexander Campbell and asked him to clarify his position on "destructionism" (conditional immortality). In the written Skinner/Campbell debate published in *The Millennial Harbinger* and *The Evangelical Magazine and Gospel Advocate* between 1837-1839 Campbell said, "Nor would I non-fellowship a destructionist because of his theory, inasmuch as he teaches that it will not be with the righteous as it is with the wicked; nor would I make it a term of Christian union or communion, that a person should agree with me in my exposition of future punishment."

Yet, by the time the July 1850 *Millennial Harbinger* appeared, Campbell called destructionism a "snare of the devil." Campbell asserted that [destructionism] was a "soul-withering delusion" which gives "no consolation, reforms no one, and is a metaphysical tangent" like "trees twice dead plucked up by the roots." He said, "Once deluded by it few are ever rescued from its entanglements."

While Campbell's own ideas seem to have changed over the years, it seems clear from this exchange that Dr. Field was about to accept conditional immortality and future punishment, abandoning the orthodox ideas of immortal soul and eternal torment.

Randall stated in *Historical Waymarks of the Church of God* that Dr. Field became an Advent Christian. In fact, he preached at a large Advent Christian church in Jeffersonville for 17 years. Field was convinced that the Adventists were more nearly correct than the Disciples, but he still had strong leanings toward Christian liberty. He thought that sectarian doctrines should not be a test of fellowship among worshippers. In this he agreed and corresponded with Age-to-Come publisher Joseph Marsh who also believed in freedom to investigate.

In 1851, Nathaniel Field debated T.P. Connelly of the Christian Church at the Old Union Church at Eagle Creek near Indianapolis on the State of the Dead. This was a pivotal event for many who aligned with the Church of God. The debate was originally published in 1853, but had at least one additional edition later: *A Debate on the State of the Dead between Rev. Thomas P. Connelly, A.B., an evangelist of the Christian Church, and Nathaniel Field, M.D., pastor of the Church of God meeting at the Christian Tabernacle in the city of Jefferson, Indiana.* Following this debate several families withdrew from Old Union to form a new Church of God congregation near Argos, Indiana, including the Corbaleys and Logans.

In 1851 Field stood with Marsh and his paper after the Boston Adventist disruptions created by J.V. Himes. Field said he liked Marsh's paper, *The Advent Harbinger and Bible Advocate* and recognized a friend who also believed in Christian liberty.

By Christian liberty he meant:
1. It is the right of every Christian to read the Bible and judge its meaning for himself.
2. It is the right and duty of every man who teaches it to teach it as he understands it.
3. Every man is responsible to God for what he believes and teaches and not to any earthly tribunal.
4. Individuals or churches are responsible to each other for their morality, as far as the question or principle of fellowship; but not for their faith or opinions.
5. Proscription and denunciation for opinion's sake, being essentially popish, we solemnly agree to abstain [from it].
6. As free discussions can do the truth no injury, but is [sic] the only certain corrective of error, we agree to allow every brother associated with us to express his views of scripture and ecclesiastical matters in a decent, respectful and orderly manner. We will encourage a free exchange of opinions in order that we may edify each other, prove all things, and hold fast that which is good.
7. Christian character alone shall be the condition of Christian fellowship.
8. The Bible shall be our creed, our platform, law book and formulary.

A. General Conference at Jeffersonville

Early in 1852, Field sent a letter of invitation to *The Advent Harbinger* for ministers "west of the mountains" (Appalachians) to meet in general conference at Jeffersonville. He said he had already heard from many ministers of the Disciples that they were interested in hearing more than the "Reformation" (Restoration Movement) of Alexander Campbell had given them. He invited all Age-to-Come ministers of the region to come for Bible study and fellowship. Those present at the Jeffersonville conference included:

Dr. Nathaniel Field, Jeffersonville, Clark Co.
John Linville, Laurel, Franklin Co.
Thomas P. Hendric, Laurel, Franklin Co.
Ephraim Miller, Jr. Middlebury, Elkhart Co.
Wm. C. Montgomery, New Franklin, Scott Co.
Benjamin Smith, Bethlehem, Clark Co.
Wm. G. Proctor, Jeffersonville, Clark Co.

Those not present but had indicated a desire to be counted among the brethren of the Age to Come were:
Benjamin Abrams, Laurel, Franklin Co.
Yates Higgins, Kingsbury, LaPorte Co.
D.R. Mansfield, Bigelow Mills, LaPorte Co.
Samuel G. Clark, Middlebury, Elkhart Co.
Henry Logan, Plymouth, Marshall Co.
Hugh Barnhill, Sidney, Marshall Co.
Abijah Hubbell, Middlebury, Elkhart Co.
Nathan Hornaday, Clermont, Marion Co.
Joel Ridge, Ladoga, Montgomery Co.
(Mansfield later left the Age-to-Come movement.)

Dr. Field wrote to Joseph Marsh in the *Prophetic Expositor and Bible Advocate* that he wanted to devote the rest of his life to evangelism. He said the work would support him, and he would never again return to medicine.

During the decade of the 1860s, as the Age-to-Come doctrine became entrenched in Church of God congregations, it stirred up controversy among the other Adventists worshipping with Age-to-Come believers. Joseph Marsh was a pioneer leader for these Age to Comers, and his visit to the 1863 Indiana conference further cemented the idea of coming out from the Adventists to form distinctive congregations which agreed on those unique doctrines. Marsh's visit was his final one before his death in September 1863. It might be interesting to ponder the state of the Church of God today if Marsh had lived to lend his support to Field.

What is Christian Character?

Nathaniel Field felt it was not necessary for Adventists to split from fellowship with Age-to-Come believers. He said Christian character, not doctrine, should be the test of fellowship. In other words, only a man's moral or ethical character should determine if he was a member of Christ's body in good standing with the congregation. He based character upon Christian Liberty which has several main components:

1. A man should study the Bible for himself and teach it as he understands it, for which he is responsible to God.
2. Christians are responsible to each other for morality, but not for faith or opinions.
3. The Bible is the only creed.
4. Christian character is the only test of fellowship.

Ref.: "Christian Liberty" *Advent Harbinger and Bible Expositor* June 14, 1851.

B. Christian Liberty versus Sectarianism

Dr. Field attempted to ward off some of the problems of sectarianism by addressing certain issues of Christian liberty within the pages of *The Advent Harbinger and Bible Advocate,* and later in *The Gospel Banner and Millennial Advocate*. This problem flared in 1867 in the Indiana conference work of which Dr. Field had been a leading voice. Dr. Field discussed these ideas at length in the literature pleading for a return to the position of Christian character, but by the end of 1867 the fate of that particular focus of fellowship was nearly sealed. The Church of God would preach Christian character, but it would primarily emphasize doctrine.

The conflict was all but over when Field wrote his seventh article on the Jewish question for the January 15, 1868, issue of *The Gospel Banner and Millennial Advocate*. He opposed the Age-to-Come idea. He said "no doubt the leaders in the new heresy of making the restoration of the carnal Jews essential to salvation are heartily sick of the debate." H.V. Reed replied in the same issue, "Israel will be converted to the Lord, which will take place when the Redeemer comes to Zion at which time their sins will be taken away."

Up to that time, the church at Argos operated under the principle of Christian character as a test of fellowship. No single doctrinal statement stood out above another. Men of both persuasions about Israel worshipped in common. But to those who were studying their Bibles alongside the works of Joseph Marsh, J.B. Cook, H.V. Reed, Dr. John Thomas and Benjamin Wilson, doctrine began to crystallize into several important categories: life in Christ, Israel in prophecy, Kingdom of God on earth, and the nature and time of the resurrection.

In 1868, Dr. Field wrote to Thomas Wilson, editor of *The Herald of the Coming Kingdom and Christian Instructor* in its debut issue, January 1, 1868, asking, "What is Wilson's plan to unite the brethren in bonds of love? Is it l) upon the basis of Christian character i.e. faith, obedience including baptism, or it is upon 2) Israel of flesh returned or restored to the land of Canaan to be the subjects of the coming Kingdom for one thousand years?" This latter is a definite reference to the Age-to-Come idea whose essential component of doctrine said that Israel would return to old Jerusalem before the Lord returned to earth, and they would be missionaries to the nations, and rule with Christ in the Kingdom.

Field concluded that faith must be the basis of union. Working a specific doctrine is divisive he said. Thomas Wilson answered in editorial comment: "We must unite in One Faith, One Hope." He then defined Christ in terms of his Messiahship, and the Kingdom as the continuation of David's throne. Israel restored is Israel returned to God's favor and all this is in harmony with One Faith. He concluded that one cannot claim faith in Jesus and ridicule his Kingship and Kingdom.

Field's position motivated the One Faith people to organize the Northwest Christian Association, a regional conference with specific doctrines. The new organization did not continue long because the Church of God had not yet worked out issues of local church organization, collection of funds to support it, and methods of educating a ministry, or even the method of offering communion. The conference discontinued within a year, yet the work carried on through local churches and Bible studies and state conferences.

If sectarianism can be defined as narrowing a set of doctrines to create a fellowship that excludes everybody who does not accept that dogma, then the Church of God was moving in that direction. While it did not have a specific written, approved "creed" one was being created in everyone's mind or spirit that included oneness of God, conditional immortality, restoration of Jews to their homeland, second coming of Jesus, Age-to-Come interpretation of prophecy and Kingdom of God on Earth.

Even with diversity, the fellowship was sweet within the group. In August 1868, the first Indiana conference to be held after the debate by Field and Thomas Wilson in *The Herald of the Kingdom* was said to be the best yet with "all united in love." It was not an occasion to "press some particular crochet of his own that would be of no special importance in the great plan of salvation." The Indiana conference had been named by delegates in 1867 as the Association of the Church of God, a name that would eventually go by the wayside.

Old friendships and precious fellowship are hard to forget. Nathaniel Field apparently never lost sight of the Church of God or its newspapers. While he remained Advent Christian until the day of his death, in 1885 Field sent the obituary of his wife to Editor Chaplin. From this it can be seen that in spite of differences, Nathaniel Field always held the Church of God dear in his heart.

Dr. Field died from the painful skin condition known as erysipelas in Jeffersonville. His obituary was sent to *The Restitution*. He was buried in the Eastern Cemetery, Jeffersonville, Clark County.

See Corbaley, Richard
    Logan, Henry
    Marsh, Joseph
    Reed, H.V.
    Wilson, Thomas

Bibliography: Ancestry.com. Field Family Tree. Record for Nathanial [sic] and Sarah Field; Ancestry.com, Indiana Deaths. 1882-1920; Ancestry.com. U.S. Census. Indiana. Clark. Jeffersonville. Dist. 29. 1880; Appleton *Encyclopedia of American Biography*, record for Dr. Nathaniel Field, Appleton & Co. NY, 1892 p 450; Field, Nathaniel. "Prospectus, *The Journal of Christianity*" *The Millennial Harbinger*, Alex. Campbell, ed May, 1840, 240; Field, Nathaniel, "Letter to Joseph Marsh" *Advent Harbinger and Bible Advocate,* April 12, 1851; Field and Connelly: *A Debate on the State of the Dead between Rev. Thomas P. Connelly, A.B., an evangelist of the Christian Church, and Nathaniel Field, M.D., pastor of the Church of God meeting at the Christian Tabernacle in the city of Jefferson, Indiana, Buchanan, Michigan,* Western Advent Christian Publishing Co. 1872 p 308; Field, Nathaniel "Christian Liberty" June 14, 1851; Field, Nathaniel. "A Conference in Jeffersonville, Ia. [Ind]" Jan. 3, 1852; Field, Nathaniel.

"Dr. Field-Destructionism" *Millennial Harbinger,* Alex. Campbell, ed. July, 1850, pg 517; Field, Dr. N. stating place of interment at www.findagrave.com Thanks to Nancy Strickland of the New Albany Floyd County [Indiana] Public Library for locating this information; Field, Nathaniel, "Letter to Joseph Marsh," *Prophetic Expositor and Bible Advocate,* Jos. Marsh, editor, Rochester, NY Oct. 1, 1857; "Judaism Revised" debate with H.V. Reed *The Gospel Banner and Millennial Advocate,* Jan. 15, 1868; Field, Nathaniel. "Letter to Thomas Wilson." *Herald of the Coming Kingdom and Christian Instructor,* Chicago. Jan. 1, 1868; Graham, David. "A Short History of Anti-Sectarianism and the Church of God." *History Newsletter,* Jan Stilson, editor. (Dec 1992/Jan 1993); Linville, John. "Report of Jeffersonville Conference" *Advent Harbinger and Bible Advocate,* May, 15, 1852; "Underground Railroad Indiana!" Dr. Nathaniel Field in *Oldham County History*, Vol. 2 Ch. 18, by Lucien Rule, Filson Club, Louisville, Ky., as retrieved from www.undergroundrailroadindiana.com/Nfield.htm, 2010, Special thanks to the Louisville Free Library, Joe Hardesty, History Librarian for assistance in retrieving this information; "Report of Indiana Conference" *Herald of the Kingdom and Christian Instructor,* Sept. 1, 1868; Obituary Mrs. Nathaniel Field," *The Restitution,* July 8, 1885; Randall, Clyde. *Historical Waymarks of the Church of God,* Church of God General Conference. Oregon, IL., 1976, 12; "The Skinner/Campbell Debate" Series. Published in *The Millennial Harbinger* and *Evangelical Magazine and Gospel Advocate* Utica, NY, 1837-1839 as cited in the *Stone-Campbell Encyclopedia,* retrieved from Google Books, Nov. 26, 2010; Williams, Byron. *Abstracts of Obituaries and Weddings from the Restitution.* Self-published. 1994; *Journal of the Indiana State Medical Society,* Vol. 4, by the Indiana State Medical Society, 1911, record of past presidents, 403.

Fisher, Sarah E.
b. August 8, 1843
d. 1925

Sarah Fisher was baptized in her youth by noted early evangelist J.M. Stephenson in Indiana. She was married to Paul Fisher at Avon, Indiana, on June 10, 1858, at age 15. Twelve children were born to the union. Both Sarah and her husband were devoted to truth and were faithful to their Lord. Her greatest contribution to the Church of God may have been her daughter, Mrs. J.W. Williams, who entered the ministry with her husband. Funeral services for Sarah were conducted in Indiana by Elder J.W. Williams, a Church of God preacher from Iowa, and Sarah's son-in-law. He preached words of comfort from Ezekiel 3 and 9.

Bibliography: *The Restitution Herald,* 1925.

Fisk(e), John R.
b. September 15, 1839
d. February 20, 1923

Fiske, John R., Jr.
b. October 1874
d. Unknown

John R. Fiske Sr. was born in McClain County, Illinois. He married Emma Watters in 1858. They had three children, David, Mary and Wiley. Emma died after which John married Julia Coliver on March 27, 1867. They had nine children including John R. Fisk Jr. John Sr. had been baptized by W.S. Proctor in 1887 presumably while still in Illinois. Nothing more is known about Elder Proctor at this time. In 1893 John homesteaded near Caldwell, Kansas.

Elder John Fiske was a good Bible student as evidenced by his frequent articles throughout the pages of *The Restitution* at the turn of the 20th century, and later, *The Restitution Herald.* He may have been an isolated member, but he got busy and organized Bible meetings with evangelist Almus Adams in order to establish a body of believers. He soon tied in to connections made years earlier by Evangelist Oliver.

One such evangelist trip was noted by Almus Adams in his weekly reports to *The Restitution* in May 1920. This particular meeting was held south of Caldwell, Kansas, over the line in Oklahoma. An old Dunkard building, "commodious" in size, was used by several groups, the Church of God being the largest group. Adams mentioned that evangelist Stephen C. Oliver had preached there for years, but by then was retired, and advanced in age.

Adams also mentioned the names of Ministers J.H. Luhman (Luman), W.L. Crowe, J.J. Heckman and Cleveland as ministers having preached at Caldwell. With all this faithful attention to the area, Church of God views were becoming well known. This indicates the word had gone out there several years before the turn of the century.

After his beloved Julia died, John Sr. resided with his daughter, Hattie Baber, and her family in Kansas. Before his death Fiske authored "Difficult Texts Explained." John Fiske Sr. fell asleep in the Lord, and was buried at Caldwell in Spring Creek Cemetery near that old Dunkard church.

John's son, John R. Fisk Jr., picked up the mantle and carried on the ministry in Kansas that had been his father's for so many years. While a record of his preaching ministry is scant in the literature of the Church of God, his name appears in notable ways by mention of others, and by letters to the editor. In one report Almus Adams described John Fiske Jr. as a capable "young" man whom he had wanted to meet for several years. He was well-versed in Bible and married to the former Mabel Chaplin. It is thought she was a niece of Stedman Chaplin.

One such letter insightfully explains the problem the Church of God had in forming a stable general conference due to lack of unity on doctrinal issues. The date of this letter is unknown, but it certainly must have been printed in *The Restitution* after the disastrous 1910 Waterloo

Conference, for it is addressed to Robert Huggins, and it mentions "Articles of Faith."

> **Reasons Why People Object to Creeds**
>
> Brother Huggins:
>
> I certainly admire the position taken by Brother Adams, and yourself and others on the question of "Articles of Faith." In fact, it is the only right position a believer can take who has the welfare of the truth at heart. Under present conditions one party will assert that Christ is the Deity Himself; others that he is not God, but the "only begotten Son of God;" still others claiming to belong to the one body teach that Christ is the natural son of Joseph.
>
> Besides the above contradictory doctrines, we have advocated here by preachers claiming to belong to the Church of God, Universalism, the fair chance theory, non-resurrection of the wicked, baptism not a saving ordinance, no bodily resurrection, personal devil, etc.
>
> No wonder aliens are bewildered by a people claiming to have the "one faith," yet teaching at the same time so many conflicting ideas.
>
> One thing I have noticed in my short experience is, those who oppose our having "Articles of Faith" usually are afflicted with some heresy, such as that Christians must keep the Jewish Sabbath, universalism, etc. Those who are sound in the faith usually favor the idea.
>
> [I am] praying that the time may soon come when we can "in one mind" tell inquiring aliens what to believe in order to (have) salvation.
>
> Yours in hope of immortality,
> John Fisk, Jr.

From this letter, it is clear that basic issues of doctrine regarding the nature of God and of Jesus had not yet been worked out by the brethren up to 1910. The "Articles of Faith" document (which also contained a lengthy set of resolutions on church discipline) was an attempt to standardize the key doctrines that the majority of Church of God Abrahamic Faith members believed. It would also have the two-fold effect of ignoring or denying various unscriptural doctrines such as Fisk(e) mentioned in his letter. This "Articles" document was to be discussed at the 14 state conferences and ratified by their members at a business meeting. When all 14 conferences had ratified it the Articles of Faith would become the standard statement regarding Church of God doctrines. Two ratifications are known, Washington and Texas.

Greg Demmitt has said at the present-day History Conferences, that the primary interest of the Age-to-Come adherents in Joseph Marsh's era was prophecy, not the nature of God or of Christ. Hence, the Church of God began developing without open discussion regarding the nature of the trinity, Christology or Holy Spirit until around the turn of the 20th century, although oneness of God was commonly believed because of their heritage in the Christian Connexion. The literature of the 19th century seems to support Demmitt's theory, but the "theory" also warrants additional research.

John R. Fiske Jr. accused J.M. Stephenson of introducing the theology of Larger Hope into the Church of God membership in a pamphlet Fiske authored entitled "Partial Resurrection: An Antidote to Larger Hope". Larger hope was shunned by the Church of God, but it was picked up and popularized by C.T. Russell who occasionally fellowshipped in the Church of God, but who later founded the Jehovah's Witnesses. It has not been documented from the writings of J.M. Stephenson if Fiske's accusation has merit. This is also a good subject for research. It should be noted, that most people in the Church of God disagreed with the doctrine of partial resurrection, opting instead for a general resurrection of the righteous and the wicked.

See Adams, Almus
Conner, L.E. - Holy Spirit discussion
Crowe, W.L.
Heckman, J.J.
Huggins, Robert G. (20th) - on Creeds
Luhman, J.H.
Marsh, Joseph
Oliver, Stephen C.
Stephenson, J.M. - Larger Hope
Wilson, Benjamin - Resurrection
Wilson, E.M. - Articles of Faith

Bibliography: Adams, Almus, Report. *The Restitution,* May 11, 1920; May 1923; Ancestry.com. U.S. Census. Missouri. Carroll. Bogart. Dist. 144. 1880; Fiske, John R. Jr., "Partial Resurrection: An Antidote to Larger Hope". Self published; Fiske, John R., Sr. "Difficult Texts Explained." Self published, no date.

Foore, John
b. November 8, 1832
d. March 29, 1915

John Foore was born near Lithopolis, Ohio. His parents were Elizabeth and Frederick Foore. He moved to Indiana when he was 17, and soon thereafter joined the Methodist Episcopal Church of the North Mexico Conference. When he was 21 he married Miss Mahalie Friend, daughter of John and Sarah Friend. They had four children, a son, James Sylvester, and three daughters, Mary Roane, Sarah

E. and Ida M. Mary was the eldest.

John said he first learned of the Word from the preaching of Jacob Shafer, J.F. Wagoner and Richard Corbaley. He was baptized in the new faith in 1861 by Jacob Shafer in Indiana. This new teaching was about the Kingdom of God on earth and other distinctive doctrines put forth by the Church of God Abrahamic Faith. John began preaching for the Church of God that same year, and was ordained at an old Antioch Church of God conference by Elders Hugh Barnhill Sr. and Stedman A. Chaplin. Other ministers who served in Indiana and who witnessed the ceremony were J.M. Stephenson, Richard Corbaley, J.S. Hatch, H. Ralph Carter, Bro. Kimsey, Bro. Orem (possibly the father of W.J. Orem), Bro Gower and Bro. Hicklin.

John Foore preached and baptized regularly at the Ripley Church of God, known in its early days as the Adventist Church. This is known because Foore's name appears in the church minute books beginning in 1887. He may have been at Ripley earlier than that but those records are not available. He baptized members of the Ripley church in 1888 possibly after the death of J.M. Stephenson, the resident pastor. Foore was also present at Ripley in 1889 and 1902. Altogether, he baptized at least ten people at Ripley.

In 1884, he played a role in beginning a work at Arkansas City, Kansas. He first preached in that area at the Sunny Slope Schoolhouse in Sumner County near Millerton. The names of those first listeners are unknown, but records of others who preached there include Isaac Miller, A.H. Zilmer, Almus Adams, A.L. Corbaley, T.A. Drinkard, E.E. Geisler, O.J. Parker, D.C. Robison, and dozens of others in the 20th century.

The church building at Arkansas City in 1932 was located at 709 N. A. Street. Nancy Barber Robison preached there after the death of her husband, and later, Lucille Appleby became the pastor.

Old Antioch Meeting House

John and Mahalie Foore

About that time Uncle John, as he was affectionately called, moved to Parsons, Kansas, and remained there the rest of his life. Francis Burnett reported that Uncle John also worked throughout southeast Missouri. From Parsons John Foore reported his activities to the *Word and Work* in Abilene, Texas.

In one issue of the *Word and Work* Foore wrote his philosophy on forming a national conference. He remembered that men had formed a national conference in 1869 and 1888, and both had failed. Still, there was talk among the people in the churches that a way to unify the work and strengthen the weaker churches must be found. Some thought that the organization of a national work was the means of unification.

Foore said, "Wherever the effort for a national organization has been successful, it has been a death blow for brotherly love, because all such organizations confine it to a sect or parties which says, 'We are holier than others.' Their plea is there is strength in unity." He said that unity must be based on first principles upon which all can agree. He listed them as:
1. Christ the Rock to build on.
2. No life out of Christ.
3. The life lost in Adam will be restored in Christ.
4. God only has immortality.
5. The gospel to be preached, believe, repent, die to sin, be buried and rise to walk in new life.

Elder John Foore preached for 43 years at the Grady School House and later the Rollin Church in Neosha County, Kansas. Throughout his preaching career he traveled a circuit of 16 states. He was a faithful evangelist, preacher and writer representing Missouri and Kansas. He contributed many pieces to *The Restitution* and *The Restitution Herald*. He stopped preaching in September 1913 when he was 81 years old.

In 1914 he and his wife were both under doctor's care with medical bills amounting to $12.50 each month. He said they were joyful and glorified God with their joy.

In the spring of 1915, he became infirmed and soon

John Foore, far right, poses with a family he visited.

died of pneumonia. Delos Johnson, presumably a member of his church, placed his obituary in *The Restitution Herald*. Following his death, Mrs. O.W. Humphreys wrote the editor of *The Restitution Herald* that she regretted he would not write again as she loved reading his pieces.

    See Adams, Almus
           Carter, Ralph
           Corbaley, A.L.
           Corbaley, Richard
           Drinkard,T.A. (20th)
           Geisler,E.E.
           Hatch, J.S.
           Robison, D.C.
           Shaffer, Jacob
           Stephenson, J.M.
           Zilmer, A.H.

Bibliography: Arkansas City, Kansas. Report. *The Restitution Herald,* Dec. 18, 1945; Burnett, Francis. Interview with Jan Stilson from Neighbors Nursing Home, Byron, IL Dec. 2006; "Early Records-1900s Ripley Church of God Ripley, IL" Copy resides in the archives of the Rock River Christian College, Beloit, WI. Original minute book remains at Ripley Church of God; *The Restitution* Dec. 21, 1887; April 3, 1907; Nov. 1915; *The Restitution Herald,* Dec. 23, 1914; April 14, 1915; Foore, John. "Church organizations or sectarian combinations" *Word and Work,* Minerva Gibbs, editor. Abilene, Texas, Oct. 15, 1907; Foore photo, *The Restitution Herald,* S.J. Lindsay, editor. Oregon, IL April 14, 1915; 213.

Frier, Aunt Millie
    b. July 7, 1826
    d. January 9, 1904

Millie Benge Frier was born in Fayette County, Indiana. She was united in marriage to John Frier in February 1842. They had 11 children. They moved to Clinton, Indiana. She united with the Church of God sometime in the 1860s and lived a life that was fully devoted to her Lord Jesus Christ. She had the attributes of a good Christian woman: faithful wife, loving mother, kind, patient, affectionate friend, grateful and charitable. She had a kind word and a pleasant smile. Envy, strife and criticism found no place in her bosom. Of her it can truly be said, "She fought the good fight; she finished the course, she kept the faith; henceforth there is laid up for her a crown of righteousness which the Lord, the righteous Judge shall give her at his appearing and kingdom" (2 Timothy 4:7). Her obituary was written by her relative and Christian brother, William Huffer.

Aunt Millie died at age 77, on January 9, 1904. Elder G.W. Smith preached her funeral sermon to a houseful of relatives and friends. She was laid to rest in Plummer cemetery. The last night of her illness before death overtook her, she said to the vigilant family at her bedside, "Be good children and meet me in the kingdom." The testimony of staunch believers such as Aunt Millie Frier became the backbone of the developing Church of God.

Bibliography: *The Restitution,* January 27, 1904

Furry, Joseph
    b. March 4, 1814
    d. July 24, 1895

Joseph Furry was born in Pennsylvania but moved to Ohio with his parents as a youth, and from there to Rush County, Indiana, in 1822. Joseph Furry married Rosanna Logan in 1836. They had five children. The family moved to Plymouth, Indiana.

After Mrs. Furry died in 1848, Joseph married Sarah Stancliff (June 4, 1822-August 7, 1912) of Elkhart, Indiana. They had four children. They first heard the Gospel of the Kingdom preached at Plymouth from Joseph Marsh in 1851. Marsh made a western tour of the central Indiana churches during that summer. After Marsh's return to New York, Furry wrote him from Plymouth: "We, in this western country, are surrounded by some who sarcastically stigmatize us as 'soul-sleepers'; the more sympathetic look upon us as a deluded people; but we say to all, that immortality must be sought for by all who would attain to it."

The Furry family moved to Eldora, Iowa, in 1854 where he purchased a two-story home. He used the first floor for a general store, and they dwelt on the second floor. He operated the business until 1864 when they moved to Alden, Iowa, and purchased a farm.

Joseph entered immediately into fellowship with the Age-to-Come brethren in Iowa. He began to teach about conditional immortality. The first meetings to discuss how to organize a state conference were held at the Hill home in Alden. Joseph became the president of the first Iowa Conference in 1855.

There were two ministers at Alden, Lot Clover and Philomen Plummer. They were both ministers of the Disciples persuasion. They learned the truth of conditional immortality and all the truths that spring from it, from Joseph and Sarah Furry. Joseph was the first in that community to teach the Gospel of the Kingdom.

Joseph was interred at Alden cemetery.

See Clover, Lot
Hill, R.J.
Marsh, Joseph

Bibliography: Ancestry.com U.S. Census. Iowa. Hardin. Alden. 1880; Burnett, Francis et al of history committee, *The History of the Iowa Church of God and Conference ,1855-1987,* Belle Plaine Union, printer, 1987. "Joseph Furry" as published in *The Advent Harbinger and Bible Advocate,* Jos. Marsh, ed. Rochester, NY. Dec. 7, 1850 and as cited in *The History of the Iowa Church of God and Conference, 1855-1987,* printed at Belle Plaine, Iowa, 1987; "Letter from C.L. Furry, son of Joseph, to A.J. Eychaner" July 26, 1905, cited by Terry Ferrell in *The History of Iowa Church of God Conference;* Furry, Joseph entry from rootsweb.ancestry.com retrieved July 4, 2008.

Fyfe, James Manoah
b. January 30, 1832
d. September 12, 1909

James Fyfe and Emily Jane Cook (April 20, 1839- December 11, 1929) were school teachers in Wisconsin. They married November 29, 1859. They began to study the Bible in a small group that included her brother, Steven Cook. They came to know the teaching of the Church of God Abrahamic Faith. Others who joined the group were Daniel Howard, T.E. Adams and T.G. Newman.

The Fyfe family moved from Wisconsin to Colo, Story County, Iowa, in 1866 where he began preaching the Abrahamic Faith. There they met many people who were "of like precious faith." In the autumn of 1867 a band of these believers settled in Dade County, Missouri. In 1868 S.C. Oliver and James Manoah Fyfe organized the first Church of God Faith of Abraham in Dade County. Both of these men served as elders. Here they met and fellowshipped with Joshua Bailey who became the regular preacher. This freed Oliver and Fyfe to move on and establish other churches. Later James moved to Cedarville where he raised his family. S.C. Oliver settled near Attica, Kansas. Joshua Bailey settled eventually at Fredericktown, Missouri.

Over the years James and Emily had seven children—Arthur James, John, John's twin who died at birth, Mary Elizabeth, Reuben Morris, Joseph David and Daniel.

Joseph David Fyfe (May 21, 1877 to January 30, 1913) was married on March 9, 1909, to Myrtle Collins from Roland, Missouri. They moved to Saskatchewan, Canada, in 1910 where they homesteaded. While in Canada, Emily was born (July 24, 1914 to January 2, 2001). In April 1920 they returned to Cedarville, Missouri, and purchased a home. Joseph David owned and operated a blacksmith shop and mill. He also ran a threshing machine and a gas station. Emily was one of the early students of the Bible Training School in Oregon, Illinois. Emily married David Bender (December 4, 1911 to June 2, 1996). Their son Edward (b. February 15, 1945) graduated from Oregon Bible College and served in the ministry of the Church of God in Illinois, Nebraska, Minnesota, Indiana and South Carolina.

Daniel (August 4, 1878 to May 7, 1902) married Arizona Bays (December 15, 1882 to October 10, 1971). Their son Albert (August 11, 1913 to July 7, 1995) married Ruby Waggoner (May, 7, 1914 to April 19, 1990) in 1934, in Fredericktown, Missouri, who was a member of the Blush Church of God Abrahamic Faith. They had two sons, Daniel W. (b. June 15, 1936) and James A. (b. June 16, 1938). Both Daniel and James graduated from Oregon Bible College and have served in the ministry of the Church of God in Indiana, North Carolina, Texas, Illinois and Missouri. Albert's sister, Ethel, married Lyle Rankin from Cashmere, Washington. Lyle and his extended family have been faithful pastors, evangelists and missionaries for the past several decades.

Arlen Rankin contributed to this entry.

See Adams, Thomas E.
Bailey, Joshua
Newman, Thomas G.
Oliver, Stephen C.

Bibliography: Bender, Ed. "Some of the History of Nebraska Churches of God Faith of Abraham," presented at the 2d Annual History Conference at North Hills Church of God, Springfield, Ohio, Nov. 6, 7, 2007. Burnett, Francis, et. al. of history committee, *The History of the Iowa Church of God and Conference 1855-1987,* Belle Plaine Union, printer, 1987. Family records in the possession Margaret & Abner Fyfe (Son of John Fyfe) and Marilyn and Jim Pirtle (Son of Sarah Jane Fyfe Pirtle); Fyfe, James M. Photo donated by Arlen F. Rankin, July 2008; Fyfe family history assembled by Helen Heisler, Sheboygan, Wisconsin, 1963.

G

Garton, John
b. April 14, 1843
d. April 30, 1913

John Garton was born in Wisconsin where he accepted the Gospel of the Kingdom, and where J.M. Stephenson may have baptized him. John married Emily Latton on March 3, 1860. They had four sons and two daughters; one son and one daughter survived to adulthood.

After John Garton's family moved to Iowa, they resided near Poland, down the road from John's brother, George. Their mother, Phoebe, lived with George and helped manage the farm. John farmed a quarter section of land. T.J. Whitesitt baptized Phoebe Buck Garton, originally a native of Nova Scotia.

John spent most of his adult life as an Iowa minister, working primarily with the Iowa State Conference tent ministry. At each stop on the revival preaching circuit John helped unload the tent from the train and set it up. He certainly also took a turn preaching. Tent circuit preaching thrived during the latter part of the 19th century and early 20th century. John and several other ministers alternated preaching at the Waterloo Church of God from 1908 to 1913. John never forsook the Gospel, and when he died, Pastor G. Eldred Marsh testified that John was a Bible student of great ability. His sermons were clearly expressed and always instructive. Elder Marsh officiated at John Garton's funeral.

See Eychaner, A.J. - Tent ministry
Stephenson, J.M.
Whitesitt, T.J.
Marsh, G.E. (20th)

Bibliography: Ancestry.com. U.S. Census. Iowa. Buena Vista. Poland. Dist. 16. 1880; Rankin, Delbert. E-mail regarding Elder Garton, Oct. 27, 2008; Marsh, G.E. "Obituary of John Garton," *The Restitution Herald,* May 21, 1913.

Gates, John S.
b. September, 1883
d. 1939

John Gates was born in Missouri, south of Kansas City. He was the eldest of five children, two daughters and three sons, born to Donald John and Margaret Gates. In his youth John helped his father on the family farm at Cross Timbers, Missouri. He married Ada Sundwall Driskill in 1908.

After John heard about the teachings of the Church of God, he accepted them. He helped build the Cross Timbers Church of God.

John wrote to the editor of *The Restitution Herald* in the first "Gospel Trumpet" column following the merger of *The Restitution Herald* with *The Gospel Messenger* in 1915. He said that the congregation at Cross Timbers, Missouri, had just finished building a small church costing $600 which they furnished with gas lights. This work was done by 12 men, all poor farmers, paying cash as they could afford it. He called it "a labor of love." He asked the traveling pastors to stop by. In return for a sermon or two, the congregation would host and feed them, and they would send them away with some money. Gates invited people to relocate to Cross Timbers. He called for unity among the readers of both the former *Gospel Trumpet* and larger *The Restitution Herald*.

John Gates died in 1939. Ada lived until 1985. They now rest side by side.

Bibliography: Ancestry.com. U.S. Census. Missouri. Hickory. Cross Timbers. Dist. 95. 1900; *The Restitution Herald,* Summer 1915; Sundwall, Billy and Merle. E-mail to JStilson, April 16, 2008; Merger of *The Gospel Messenger* with *The Restitution Herald,* 75th Anniversary issue centerfold, October 1986.

Gesin, Ernest Frederick
b. August 30, 1846
d. October 16, 1923

Ernest Gesin was born in Baden, Germany, and arrived in America in 1870. He located in Ogle County, Illinois, with other German immigrants. He continued to live there the rest of his life. On November 21, 1878, he married Harriett Koontz also of Ogle County. Four children blessed this marriage. Gesin was baptized in 1878 and united with the Church of God. He became a staunch pioneer of the Gospel faith through the Church of God at Adeline and throughout northern Illinois.

Long before it incorporated in 1898, the Illinois State Conference existed informally in unity of spirit throughout the church fellowship. Gesin worked willingly at the conference meetings held quarterly at local churches but annually at the Adeline church because it had a dormitory. Advance notices of these meetings were published in *The Gospel Banner,* with conference reports following in the next issue.

The conference meetings included Bible classes and preaching, business discussions about the growth of the conference and the worship service format of local churches. Often discussions concentrated on important issues of doctrine. On different occasions the discussions might be a debate, a moderated conversation or a panel discussion involving Bible scholars and ministers in attendance.

Frank Siple conducted Gesin's funeral at the Church of God in Adeline. Gesin was interred in the cemetery there across the street from the church and dormitory campus.

See Gesin, Mary A. (20th)
Bibliography: Obituary. *The Restitution Herald,* Nov. 11, 1923.

Gibbs, William L.
b. March 15, 1851
d. April 4, 1907

William L. Gibbs was born in Hartford, Pike County, Missouri, to John and Martha Gibbs. He was the second of five children, four sons and a daughter. William married Laura in 1873, and they had three children, Annie, Lillian and Willie.

Around 1880 Gibbs moved from Middleton, Missouri, to Coleman, Texas. In 1881, he established a print shop and began to publish a newspaper for that community. Two years later he moved his shop, press and newspaper to Abilene, Texas. In 1883, he began to preach in Abilene for the Disciples because there was no one else available.

Gibbs was a feisty newspaperman. His paper, *The Magnetic Pen,* competed in Abilene with *The Reporter* published by rival editor C.E. Gilbert. Every opinion Gibbs expressed opposed Gilbert's. Gilbert was for unions and against incorporating the town of Abilene. Gilbert favored open-range cowmen and opposed the settlers. An intense rivalry developed that finally erupted into a street duel between the two editors. Five shots were fired but no one was seriously hurt. Following that traumatic event in 1885, Gibbs closed *The Magnetic Pen*, and Gilbert resigned from being the Methodist Sunday School Superintendent.

In spite of the duel, Gibbs was respected as a member of the church

The Golden Rule Home in Oregon, Illinois, offered housing for elderly church members.

Oregon Bible College Campus, Oregon, Illinois

and community. Within a few years the Disciples' congregation had grown to 60 members, and they had constructed a small building. Gibbs became an evangelist and the record of his travels may be found throughout the historic newspapers of Texas. As late as November 1889, he still preached for the Disciples in and near Baird and Eagle Cove, Callahan County, Texas.

In 1892 Gibbs began to edit and publish the *Word and Work*, a religious newspaper, and continued as editor and publisher of that paper until his death in 1907. The *Word and Work* began as a voice of the Disciples movement in Texas, but by the turn of the century it had become a podium for the Church of God Abrahamic Faith. Gibbs published the heated debate between A.S. Bradley and Nichols in the *Word and Work*, and stood staunchly behind Bradley.

In 1898 Gibbs met A.S. Bradley who taught Gibbs about the nature of man (material) and the Gospel of the Kingdom of God. A.S. Bradley also told him about the Abrahamic Faith. Gibbs accepted these distinctive doctrines and began to preach them. The day after Bradley and Gibbs studied together, Gibbs was baptized by A.S. Bradley "into the light of the gospel of the Son of God." Shortly after that, in 1898, W.L. Gibbs began to pastor a small Church of God congregation that had been started at Palava, Texas.

Gibbs may have also studied with W.H. Wilson, Chicago, who often made a circuit into Missouri, Arkansas, Oklahoma and Texas. J.J. Heckman and Uncle John Foore, evangelists of Kansas, also regularly dipped south into Oklahoma and Texas to establish Bible study groups.

A reoccurring theme in the pages of the *Word and Work* included the paternity of Jesus, which had been an ongoing dialogue within the Church of God across the Midwest and Great Plains the previous two decades. Gibbs believed in the virgin birth and Jesus as the begotten Son of God. In fact, he often took swipes at other Church of God preachers and editors who advocated Josephism. If any minister believed both the spurious doctrines of Josephism and universalism, they felt his ire twice over. Church of God ministers who were the subjects of Gibbs' editorial ire included W.L. Crowe, A.J. Eychaner, G.M. Myers and J.W. Williams.

Gibbs defended his new-found distinctive doctrines aggressively. In fact, a great deal of credit is due the *Word and Work* for steering the Church of God into a position to write the Articles of Faith following the 1910 Waterloo Conference. The articles were not endorsed by the all of the state conferences, but they were heartily endorsed by the Texas Conference. This action was foundational to the successful development of the General Conference in 1921 with consensus on a doctrinal statement. (See the Dr. Ephraim Wilson entry for a more thorough discussion on this.)

The *Word and Work* was such an outspoken voice for the Gospel of the Kingdom in Texas that the editors of other religious papers began to speak against it. *The Christian Monitor* repeatedly denounced Gibbs and the message for which he stood. This editor said that Gibbs, A.S. Bradley and T.J. Daniel were "soul sleepers." Editor W.F. Lemmons of *The Eye Opener,* a snappy Church of Christ paper, barraged Gibbs and Bradley repeatedly with criticism. Gibbs contended fervently for his new found faith in the face of stiff opposition, and considering his track record of fighting for principles, that would be expected.

Unfortunately, Gibbs died unexpectedly in April 1907. After his death his widow, Laura, assumed the editorship of the *Word and Work*, the only vehicle in Texas at that time to promote conditional immortality and the Kingdom of God on earth. This was a tremendous burden for her. Research revealed that after William Gibb's sudden death, one of the corresponding editors from the *Word and Work* stepped in to ease the load for a few weeks. Then, Robert Huggins of Oregon, Illinois, began to assist in the effort. His name appears on the masthead as co-editor from 1907-1908.

Huggins lived in Oregon and worked with S.J. Lindsay, a local newspaper man and editor of the monthly *Bible Lessons*. Lindsay founded the Oregon Church of God and conducted the Summer Bible Training school

---

Hans Rollman, Church of Christ historian and educator, provided this feisty poem about William Gibbs which was published by Church of Christ editor, Mr. Burnett:

> He met another preacher,
> Who came upon the scene,
> Who holds the no-soul doctrine,
> And prints at Abilene.
>
> Poor man, you're wholly mortal,
> An earthly sprout or bud,
> And God Almighty made you
> Of atmosphere and mud.
>
> Your washing was delusion,
> Your kingdom's in the sky,
> Your FAITHS not in the gospel,
> But in the 'devil's' lie!
>
> Our worried friend accepted,
> These Sadduceean fibs,
> And in a muddy river
> Was dipped by Wm. Gibbs.

from there. He also founded *The Restitution Herald* in 1911. It is known that Huggins was a student of the school because it was reported in an issue of the *Word and Work* that Huggins had been assigned to do a paper for the Summer Bible Training School on the subject of "The Work of the Holy Spirit, its Nature and Office." Lindsay reported to the *Word and Work* that the Summer Bible school at Oregon was "no longer an experiment, but was now an established instrument for good." Huggins continued with duties in Oregon, and added editing the *Word and Work* to his schedule.

The following is included to illustrate how reports of history do not always tell the full story. Elder Gibbs' obituary was cited in the notes of R.B. Taylor, a Church of God member who wrote *Texas History*. The notes said that within two months after Gibbs' death, the *Word and Work* merged with *The Gospel Trumpet* edited by T.J. Daniel. That action may have been considered as a temporary solution, but there was no permanent merger. While Taylor's notes do not give details, it is known from other sources that Daniel was being forced by the court to shut down *The Gospel Trumpet,* or to change its name. The *Trumpet* may have "resided" in the *Word and Work* only to re-emerge within a few weeks as *The Gospel Messenger*.

A bound volume of the 1904-1908 *Word and Work* is owned by the Atlanta Bible College Archives and is available for use by researchers interested in pursuing this aspect of American church history.

William L. Gibbs rests in Abilene Cedar Hill City Cemetery. Strangely, for a man of such high standing in his city, there is no grave monument. His grave is beneath a tree next to the Bell plot. To find it, enter the cemetery by its third entrance off Cottonwood. Turn right at the first road and look for the Gibbs plot under the tree on the left.

See Bradley, A.S.
Crowe, W.L.
Daniel, T.J.
Eychaner, A.J.
Foore, John
Heckman, J.J.
Huggins, Robert (20th)
Lindsay, S.J.
Miller, Dr. Ephraim
Myers, G.M.
Taylor, Richard B.
Williams, J.W.
Wilson, W.H.

Bibliography: Ancestry.com. U.S. Census. Missouri. Pike. Hartford. 1860. and Texas. Taylor. Abilene. Ward 3. Dist. 150. 1900; "William L. Gibbs", Eckstein, Stephen D Jr. PhD. *History of Churches of Christ In Texas*, 1963. 155, retrieved from restorationmovement.com/gibbs June 2007. The original source was an article in *The Christian Standard*, XXII, (July 23, 1887) 235; "Gibbs Family Genealogy," Posted by Ella Smith July 22, 2000 to answer Hans Rollman. from *Baird Weekly Star*. Sept. 5, 1889; Nov. 14, 1889; Nov. 28, 1889; Gibbs, Wm. Issue of Josephism, *Word and Work*, Feb. 1907; Huggins, Robert. co-editor *Word and Work*. Abilene, Tx., 1907-1908; Lemmons, W.F. editor, *The Eye Opener*, Abilene, Texas, 1904, a few of copies of this are owned by the Archives of the Atlanta Bible College; Rollman, Hans. Dr. Restoration Movement history websites: www.mun.ca/rels/restmov/restmov.html; www.therestorationmovement.com/Gibbs.htm. See also texnews.com/arn/aboutus; Rollman, Hans Dr. August 2006 E-mail to Greg Demmitt with poem, shared with Jan Stilson, March 29, 2008; Macy, Emory. "Church History of the Texas Church of God" March 1954; Taylor, R.B. "Notes about Texas History" These notes were very helpful in filling in gaps of information regarding local church work in Texas. They are part of the Texas Conference collection in the vertical files in the Archives of Atlanta Bible College.

Giesler, Edgar E.
b. 1884
d. 1950?

E.E. Giesler was a recognized minister of the Oklahoma/Texas Conference of the Church of God. He was born in Justice Precinct, Texas, to George A. and Nannie Giesler. He had three sisters and four brothers. He married Novella, and they had four daughters and three sons.

Giesler was a carpenter, working independently where work was available, freeing him to preach at will wherever he could.

It is not known how Giesler learned of the Gospel of the Kingdom, but it is evident that he crossed paths with a Church of God member or evangelist, perhaps J.J. Heckman, Almus Adams or another evangelist in Nebraska.

Giesler's name appears on the 1921 recognition list as one who had applied for, and received, recognition for being a minister in good standing with his denomination. The Constitution of the General Conference said anyone of Christian character could apply for a license from the conference if the notice ran in *The Restitution Herald*. Letters of complaint against an applicant could stall the process, but since no letters of complaint were received at the office, Giesler was included.

Giesler lived in Moorefield, Nebraska, and may have founded that congregation. He preached throughout the Great Plains states, lending a hand wherever he could. He also assisted with preaching at the Nebraska Conference. In 1939 Giesler organized Berean groups in Alliance and Moorefield, Nebraska. Berean societies had already been organized at each of the other Nebraska churches. The Berean societies helped to stabilize a new work by bringing folks together for Bible study and preaching when an evangelist visited on Sundays. Because of the Berean work at Alliance, eventually C. Alan McClain was called to be pastor.

Ed Bender related at the 2007 History Conference at North Hills Church of God, Springfield, Ohio, that E.E. Giesler baptized his father, David R. Bender, before 1940.

Elder Giesler evangelized as far west as Wray, Colorado, where he was responsible for starting and stabilizing a local church. When the Wray work began in 1947, the members began a weekly Sunday school with a monthly preaching service. Giesler visited monthly and if other people stopped by, they were pressed into preaching also. As the Wray congregation grew, its finances stabilized, and they were able to construct a church building. It was dedicated by Elder Giesler on May 9, 1948.

That same summer, Mrs. Verna Thayer, the national children's evangelist of the Church of God, was called to conduct a week-long children's school with teacher training for the members at Wray. It was thought a Vacation Bible School would help with growth of the Sunday school and church.

E.E. Giesler was a member of a new generation at the turn of the 20th century who traveled to his preaching appointments by auto. Driving was a new skill that some people had not mastered. One of those bad drivers ran into the Giesler vehicle, modestly injuring Mrs. Giesler with two broken ribs.

See Adams, Almus
Heckman, J.J.
Thayer, Verna (20th)

Bibliography: Ancestry.com. U.S. Census. Texas. Nolan. Justice Precinct 3. Dist. 118. 1900; U.S. Census. Nebraska. Gage. Beatrice Ward 4. District 52. 1920; Nebraska. Washington. Blair. Dist. 4. 1930; *The Restitution Herald,* Oct. 1921; Oct. 14, 1930; Bender, Ed. "Some of the History of Nebraska Churches of God Faith of Abraham," presented at 2nd Annual History Conference at North Hills Church of God, Springfield, Ohio, Nov. 6, 7, 2007; Various notes in *The Restitution Herald,* including Sept. 30, 1947; Oct. 7, 1947; Oct. 21, 1947; April 3, 1948 and June 6, 1948; Notice of dedication at Wray, Colo. *The Restitution Herald,* Sydney Magaw, ed., Oregon, Illinois, May 9, 1948.

Glotfelty, Joseph M.
b. January 15, 1844
d. May 31, 1920

Joseph M. Glotfelty was born and raised in Pennsylvania. During the Civil War, Joseph Glotfelty attended Normal School, and taught school in Pennsylvania. He may have first learned of the Kingdom of God from John T. Ongley or from the Philadelphia Church of God under the direction of C.C. Ramsay.

When the war raged near the Normal School, the students were commandeered to go out and put up a defense against the Confederate forces. Glotfelty joined a unit sent to Lancaster which was a "deferred" area. Lancaster County was heavily populated by Amish, many of whom were pacifists. Some Amish voluntarily joined the Union cause, but most deferred their enlistment by paying $300. Hence, the term, "deferred area." It is thought that Glotfelty was not an Amish youth who fought with the Union because his "tour of duty" was pressed upon him and of such short duration.

His unit's mission was to resist the Confederate army and prevent them from pushing north. He marched south of town, spent the night in a ditch in the rain, and the next day the unit retreated and burned the bridge. Joseph's military service lasted two days and one night! Then he moved west to Illinois.

Joseph was an early resident of Ogle County, Illinois, first living at Lane (Rochelle). He taught penmanship at Franklin Grove (site of the National Headquarters of the Lincoln Highway Association) where he met his wife, Mary Amanda Mitchell. They moved to Lanark in Carroll County where Joe operated a restaurant. He also prepared meals for the Illinois Conference during the annual meetings at Adeline.

After Mary's death in 1905, Joseph moved in with John Renner and wife, in Lanark. Being only 66 years old, Joseph continued to earn his way as an insurance agent. The Renner's had a source of private income. After Mr. Renner died and Mrs. Renner became a resident of the Golden Rule Home, Joseph married Almeda Glotfelty, 11 years his junior. He was 70. Joseph and Mary A. are buried in the Lanark cemetery south of the city.

See Glotfelty, Mary A.
Ramsay, C.C.

Bibliography: Ancestry.com U.S. Census. Illinois. Carroll. Rock Creek. 1920; *The Restitution Herald.* June 8, 1920; June 15, 1920; Exploring Amish Country retrieved from www.exploring-amish-country.com/amish-history.html on Dec. 3, 2010.

Glotfelty, Mary Amanda
b. 1847
d. 1905?

Mary Amanda Glotfelty was secretary of the congregation at Adeline in northern Illinois. She was married to Joseph M. Glotfelty, who was a fixture of the Church of God and Illinois Conference, a restaurateur and Justice of Peace in Carroll County, Illinois.

The Illinois Conference met at Adeline year to year because it had a large church building with an equally large dormitory at the west edge of the property. Several white frame cabins (12' x 12') housed families. The cabins were arranged neatly in two rows on the edge of the church property beside a cornfield. At the Adeline conference held in November 1915, Elder Ernest F. Gesin preached. Other ministers also took turns preaching.

The Adeline Church of God predated the existence of the Illinois State Conference, the Church of God at Oregon and the General Conference. The Adeline church was formed in the 1850s around the writings of Benjamin Wilson and Dr. John Thomas. It was an older congregation, and from its leadership two denominations were born.

Samuel Coffman lived a few miles north of the church, and it was at the Coffman home that Dr. John Thomas and several other Coffman men developed the idea and plan to create the Christadelphian denomination. This was done in 1863. By 1864 it was recorded with the US War Department that certain individuals in northern Illinois were ministers of the gospel and were pacifists. Strangely, the name Christadelphian is not present in the war documents. The new denomination is listed in government records as "Nazarines" not to be confused with the Pentecostal Nazarene denomination which developed later.

The other denomination that came from the steadfast leadership in the Adeline congregation was the Church of God Abrahamic Faith. Members from this congregation included Samuel J. Lindsay, who not only helped establish the Oregon Church of God, but also established *The Restitution Herald* in 1911. Other notable leaders from Adeline included Martin Aslasken, whose grandson, William Wachtel, served a term as President of Oregon Bible College in Oregon, Illinois, 1961-1968; the Gesin family; the Coffman families; and the Glotfelty family.

Mary Amanda and Joseph Glotfelty took an active role in organizing the church and the Illinois Conference. Joseph was on an early board of the Illinois Conference and the General Conference. Many of these folks and their ancestors are buried across the street from the Adeline church in the cemetery behind the old stone church owned by the Evangelical Brethren.

See Aslasken, M.
Chaffee, Clara
Coffman, Samuel
Gesin, E.F.
Lindsay, S.J.
Wachtel, William (20th)
Wilson, Benjamin

Bibliography: Ancestry.com. U.S. Census. Illinois. Carroll. Rock Creek. Dist. 8 1910; *The Restitution Herald,* December 1915.

Good, John W.
b. 1890
d. Unknown

John Good lived and worked in Rochester, Indiana. He took a preaching tour to the Southeast contacting folks in Harriman, Emory Gap and Rockwood, Tennessee. He also visited throughout South Carolina preaching at several stops. Good reported this information in a brief note to *The Restitution Herald*, April 26, 1916. He was one of many preaching evangelists who neither became famous nor established a large church, but spent his energy on behalf of the Gospel of the Kingdom. Many are grateful to him for the strength exhibited by the congregations in the Southeast Conference today.

Bibliography: Ancestry.com U.S. Census. Indiana. Fulton. Rochester. Ward 1. Dist. 74. 1920; *The Restitution Herald,* April 26, 1916.

Gragg (Gregg?), Grandma
b. 1841
d. Unknown

Grandma Gragg wrote a letter to "our dear little paper," *The Restitution Herald,* on February 20, 1915. She said she was 74 years old and missed being able to get out to preach. Nothing more is known of her, her residence or her home church, but her inclusion here demonstrates the dedication of both men and women to preach the imminent return of Jesus wherever they could even if old or infirmed.

Bibliography: *The Restitution Herald,* Feb. 20, 1915.

Graham, Ernest Edwin, Sr.
b. June 30, 1889
d. November 2, 1918

Ernest was a grandson of Joshua Bailey, the founder of the Church of God in Missouri. Ernest Graham's father was Pleasant Jasper Graham who married one of Bailey's daughters. P.J., as he preferred to be called, was a man of integrity and had the respect of the entire community.

Ernest assisted in building the Church of God known as Blush church near Fredericktown. The church was six and a half miles from the railroad depot, convenient for picking up traveling evangelists. Ernest was a faithful worker in the local church and served as the church secretary. This was a respected position among churchmen, P.J. having held the office before him.

At age 16, Ernest was baptized by Uncle John Foore. While Ernest never became a preacher, he was dedicated to advancing the Gospel. He was a farmer by trade. At age 29 Ernest was married to Maude. They had two children, Alice and Roy, and another child on the way. Unfortunately Ernest was taken suddenly from his family by typhoid fever, a common ailment of the day.

The family sent a telegram to S.J. Lindsay requesting he preach the funeral. Lindsay immediately boarded the train to Missouri, but by his arrival, the family had already buried Ernest. A local church member preached the service. Lindsay remained to comfort the family.

A few months later, Ernest "Ed" Jr. was born. Ed never knew his father, but he grew up to serve his heavenly Father as a dedicated pastor for the Church of God.

See Bailey, Joshua
Graham, Ernest, Jr. (20th)
Lindsay, S.J.

Bibliography: David Graham, "Family Genealogy," E-mail to author, March 1, 2006; *The Restitution Herald* Jan. 22, 1918; Nov. 20, 1918; June 25, 1919; Aug. 6, 1919.

Grant, John
b. November 17, 1823
d. March 30, 1915

John Grant was born in England on the Isle of Thanet. At the adventurous age of 19 he sailed for America, accompanied by his aunt, Sarah Illenden. The ship "Quebec" set sail April 7, 1842, and docked in New York five weeks and three days later. John had learned the carpenter's trade from his father in England, and immediately took up the trade after he settled in Darien, New York, southeast of Rochester. He worked as a pupil in the wagon-building business. He became so proficient in the trade that he bought out his employer and expanded the business to include undertaker services. The 1850 US Census also noted that he was a baker.

He met Elizabeth Rogers of London, England. They were married on May 17, 1845, in Batavia, New York. Three sons and two daughters were born. A son, Thomas, died young. John and his wife were baptized in 1880 by Elder B.W. Woodward, who adhered to the unique doctrines of the Age to Come and conditional immortality. From that time on, John was absorbed with the thought of God's wonderful plan of salvation and the glories of the restitution. He loved to converse on Bible subjects.

The family moved to Alleghany County, Watson Township, Michigan, a dense wilderness. Another daughter was born and died in infancy. In 1909, Elizabeth died and John moved to West Branch, Michigan. John's final illness came upon him on the morning of March 30 at the fine age of 92 years and 6 months. He died before noon. He was laid to rest beside his wife at Watson.

The children who survived him included two sons, Dr. Frederick E. Grant, a noted nerve specialist of Kansas City, Missouri; Dr. William R. Grant, a successful physician of Lyons, Michigan; and two daughters, Mary Austin Woodward of Dutton, Michigan, a preacher and evangelist for the Church of God; and Frances A. Wynne, of West Branch, Michigan.

John Grant was the grandfather of Frederick L. and LeRoy Austin, the great-grandfather of Ruby (Mrs. John Railton), Ethel (Mrs. Paul Johnson) and Mary Austin (Mrs. Leland Hanson). The descendants of John Grant

serving the Church of God in the 21st century include Mrs. Mary Milne, Joyce Railton Bolhous, Pastor John Railton, Louise (Roy) Humphreys and their children and grandchildren.

The family reports that John Grant was related to President Ulysses S. Grant, and he certainly resembled him, but the connection is unconfirmed.

President Grant

Bibliography: Ancestry.com. U.S. Census. New York. Erie. Buffalo Ward 2. 1850; Ancestry.com. U.S. Census. Michigan. Watson. Alleghan. 1870; Interviews with Stephen Bolhous, Spring, 2006; Obituary of John Grant, *The Restitution Herald*, April 14, 1915; Photo of John Grant. *The Restitution.* April 14, 1918. Photo of Ulysses S. Grant from the Archives of Atlanta Bible College, McDonough, Ga.

Gregg, H.C.
b. 1857
d. Unknown

Pastor H.C. Gregg lived in North Folk, Gallatin County, Illinois. He was married to Eva Gregg and they had four children, three sons and a daughter. He was pastor of the Union Chapel which had been a Second Advent church. Through Bible study with Robert G. Huggins, H.C. Gregg came to understand the Abrahamic Faith. It is possible the two men met while Huggins was employed in southern Illinois. Or, perhaps Mr. Gregg received a copy of *The Restitution*, and wrote to its editor, A.R. Underwood, requesting information.

In relating his year-long pulpit exchange program

with Elder Gregg, Huggins said:

> It has been my pleasant lot to preach for this church during the past year alternately with Bro. H. C. Gregg. We both spake as 'oracles of God,' with the result that Adventism was dethroned, and now we all believe, fundamentally, the doctrines of the Church of God. The write [sic] is now identified with you denominationally, and has grounds to believe that ere long Union Chapel Church will belong to our Conference. [He must have meant the Illinois State Conference, as the General Conference was not yet formed.]

During that year, seven members were baptized into truth at Union Chapel. Perhaps Grandma Gragg was related to this family, and her name was misspelled in *The Restitution*.

See Gragg, Grandma
Huggins, Robert (20th)

Bibliography: Ancestry.com. U.S. Census. Illinois. Gallatin. 1900; *The Restitution* September 26, 1906; Feb. 20, 1915.

Gresham (Greshem), Robert H.
b. 1821
d. 1895?

Robert H. Gresham was a real estate agent and merchant in Jeffersonville, Indiana. In 1880 he owned and operated a hardware store in Jeffersonville. He was married to Tryphena and they had one daughter and one son. He first learned of Adventist doctrines from his friend, Dr. Nathaniel Field also of Jeffersonville.

Robert Gresham worshipped with Nathaniel Field at the Jeffersonville church between 1850 and 1870. Robert was instrumental in the formation of the early Indiana conference. He agreed with the Church of God in organizational structure and in doctrinal policy which over time became more narrowly focused. The Church of God began to teach the Age to Come, restitution of all things, Kingdom of God on Earth, the name of Jesus, and the restoration of Israel before the Savior returns as tests of fellowship. The literature indicates that Robert preached the doctrine of limited or partial resurrection.

Gresham also wrote to Robert Roberts, the Christadelphian leader in England who succeeded Dr. John Thomas. Gresham stated in the letter that he had received literature from them, but there was no personal letter enclosed. He sought more literature so he could use it when he preached in the mountains of North Carolina. It was common in the early days of the Age-to-Come movement for men to work for the Church of God, the Advent Christians and the Christadelphians. Everyone cooperated for the advancement of the Gospel.

In the years between 1845 and 1855 when all Adventists were worshipping together for want of church buildings, doctrinal peculiarities were not divisive. "Christian character" seemed to be the glue that held a congregation together. This practice worked well with the ex-Millerites who were searching for a church identity, and with the Disciples of Christ who were stressing the unity of Christians in their budding Restoration Movement.

The Church of God might be part of a larger movement today except in Indiana the movement separated itself from the mainstream, taking a sectarian turn towards a more specific statement of faith. The men of that day and for decades to come shied away from using the terms "statement of faith" or "creed." They wanted to stand on the Bible and Church of God ministers preached the Gospel of the Kingdom.

Joseph Marsh's last evangelistic tour of the Midwest led him to southern Indiana in 1863 just before he grew ill and died. One may speculate that this visit, during which he was hired to be evangelist for the state, firmed ideas of faith that motivated leaders to separate into Church of God congregations outside the parameters of Adventists. The Age-to-Come adherents had never liked the term "Adventist" as it signified theological assumptions about Israel with which they could not agree.

In 1870, Nathaniel Field protested the growing sectarianism and withdrew. These doctrinal issues had been under discussion in Age-to-Come and One Faith literature since at least 1865. Field wrote to Gresham:

> As no one can be a Christian according to your present theory unless he believes in the restoration of the Jews, and as the platform on which we organize the Indiana Conference is for it, there can be no more union between the Indiana Conference and myself unless they retrace their steps, return to the ground from which they strayed, and make Christian Character alone the condition of fellowship and cooperation. The Indiana Conference went on harmoniously until faith in the restoration of the Jews was made a test of fellowship.

The action of the Indiana conference not only alienated Dr. Field, a leader in the work and Marsh's friend up to that point, it effectively alienated the Advent Christians, the Christadelphians and any Campbellites (Disciples of Christ) worshipping there. It also separated friends Nathaniel Field and Robert Gresham.

It is not an easy thing to lose a friend, and Dr. Field had been close. During this upsetting time Gresham moved to Ashville, North Carolina, and continued preaching the Gospel of the Kingdom. In 1876 Gresham signed a Certificate of Baptism administered by him as an elder of the Church of God. But, back in Indiana, Nathaniel Field was entirely out of the Church of God which further cemented the relationship between the Indiana Conference with the Wilsons of Geneva and Chicago, Illinois. It was the published journals and tracts of the Wilsons that helped to stabilize the work from that point on. The other stabilizing force was the diligent work of the evangelists traveling everywhere to proclaim the Word.

Elder Robert H. Gresham was highly esteemed in

Indiana and in North Carolina during that time. Several letters from Gresham and his friend Langford Huggins to *The Restitution* during 1878 indicate the amount of time Gresham spent instructing listeners about the Kingdom of God and the restitution of all things. Langford wrote:

> Editor Restitution: Through the providence of God there was a man sent to this neighborhood, whose name was Robert H. Gresham, of Indiana. He began to teach the gospel of the Kingdom of God, and the name of Jesus Christ, which I verily thought was heresy, and he an Anti-Christ—in the way he taught. So I took down my old Bible—which had been undisturbed for several years…but to my surprise, I was convicted and converted to the whole truth.

Langford Huggins continued his letter by citing the literature he received from Gresham (including the *World's Crisis* an Advent Christian paper); Robert McLauchlan in Cleveland, a Church of God preacher; Nathaniel Field in Jeffersonville, Indiana, thereafter until his death an Advent Christian; and from Alan Magruder, Virginia, a Christadelphian at first and Church of God later.

When Mr. and Mrs. Langford Huggins of North Carolina had a baby boy, they named him Robert Gresham Huggins. He grew up to become the editor of *The Restitution* in Cleveland, 1911-1921.

See Field, Nathaniel
Huggins, Robert G. (20th)
MacLauchlan, Robert
Magruder, Alan B.
Marsh, Joseph
Wilson, Thomas

Bibliography: Ancestry.com U.S. Census. Indiana. Jeffersonville Ward 5. Clark. 1850, 1870, 1880; Graham, David. "Anti-Sectarianism and the Church of God" *History Newsletter of the Church of God General Conference,* Dec/Jan 1992-1993 quoting from "Letter from Nathaniel Field to Robert Gresham" *The Prophetic Watchman*, Thomas Newman, editor August 12, 1867; Gresham, Robert H. "Letter to Bro. Huggins," *Restitution,* Jan. 27, 1920; Gresham, Robert H. "The Truth in North Carolina" *The Christadelphian*, 15:15. Birmingham: Christadelphian Magazine and Publishing Association, 2001 1878. 15:508-509 as furnished by Peter Hemingray; Huggins, Lankford. "A Blessed Conversion," *The Restitution*, S.A. Chaplin, ed. Plymouth, Ind. Oct. 23, 1878.

Grew, Henry
b. 1782
d. August 8, 1862

Henry Grew was born in Birmingham, England, and came to Boston with his parents when he was a teenager. He joined the Baptist church and began to preach for that denomination. Along the way he became acquainted with doctrines that were considered heretical by the Baptists, but he continued to preach wherever he could. Because he was not popular among the clergy of Boston, Grew moved to Philadelphia.

Henry was an educated Bible student whose first acquaintance with Joseph Marsh was through the pages of *The Christian Palladium.* Grew wrote frequently for its columns on all subjects and continued to provide copy even after Marsh left the editorship. In May 1845, Grew wrote about the evils of sectarianism stating that it divides the church asunder, it rejects those whom Christ receives and receives those whom Christ rejects and it deprives the world of one of the appointed means of salvation. He said sectarianism denies union and it substitutes the carnal for spiritual principles. The spiritual principle is simple obedience to Jesus.

Henry Grew began asking questions about the Age to Come and other unique doctrines through the pages of *The Advent Harbinger and Bible Advocate* during the 1850s. He was a friend to Joseph Marsh through the years, and he staunchly believed in life through Christ also known as conditional immortality. Grew was focused on matters of Bible study rather than on questions of loyalty, conduct, procedures and organizational issues. His Bible-based questions and comments stirred up lively discussion in the pages of the *Harbinger*.

The questions Grew discussed during 1850-51 included "How often should the Lord's Supper be observed, weekly, monthly or once a year?" He thought congregations should celebrate communion every Sunday. He also wrote on the benefits of Christian love in accomplishing good, the literal restoration of the Jews to Jerusalem prior to the Second Coming of the Lord, the role of Satan as power and principality of the air, the nature of interest in borrowed money, and atonement.

Grew believed Christ's obedience to death magnified the law and made it honorable (Isaiah 42:21), and is now the end of the law to the righteous and justification to everyone who believes.

He also staunchly defended the resurrection of the just and the unjust, believing it was plainly taught by scripture. He quoted, "The hour is coming in which all that are in their graves shall hear his voice and shall come forth; they that have done good unto the resurrection of life; they that have done evil unto the resurrection of condemnation" (John 5:28, 29).

Grew had a free-ranging ability to discuss many areas of Bible study which he did in a spirit of inquiry and love. In one of the last issues of *The Harbinger* in 1851, Grew wrote to comfort readers who were experiencing conflict during turbulent times. He said, "Let us humble ourselves before the Lord. Let us receive meekly and patiently the correction of the Lord." He said, "Brothers if you are cast down, read the eleventh chapter of Hebrews."

In 1857, he authored a leaflet *An Appeal to Pious Trinitarians* in which he said:

> It plainly appears from 1 Co 2:11, that "the Spirit of God" is

no more a distinct person from God, than the spirit of a man is a distinct person from the man. It would be an anomaly of a most extraordinary character; if there was an infinite intelligent person in the universe, to whom no prophet, priest, apostle, or saint of the sacred Scriptures, ever offered any direct prayer or praise. See the true doxology, Re 5:13. The Spirit of God is "poured out" or "shed forth," Ac 2:17-33; terms inapplicable to personality.

As might be expected this was not a popular work with the mainstream churches. About the same time he also authored *Future Punishment Not Eternal Punishment in Misery but Destruction* in which he firmly presented the case for conditional immortality. In a larger work entitled *The Intermediate State* he laid out the doctrine of conditional immortality in greater detail. At the time of publication full texts of these three works may be found at HarvestHerald.com

Grew was not, nor ever became so far as research shows, a member of the Church of God, yet he served to crystallize thinking on key Bible topics that are found in the statement of faith today.

See Marsh, Joseph

Bibliography: Ancestry.com U.S. Census. Pennsylvania. Philadelphia. Ward 10. 1860; Grew, Henry. Various articles available for print at http://www.harvestherald.com/grewindex.htm; Grew, Henry. "On the Evils of Sectarianism" *The Christian Palladium*, Jasper Hazen et al, eds. Union Mills, NY. May 30, 1845, 1; Grew, Henry. Various articles. *Advent Harbinger and Bible Advocate,* Aug. 31, 1850 -1851; Obituary. *World's Crisis* 17:1. 1863.

Griffiths, Albert E.
b. 1872
d. Unknown

Albert E. Griffiths was the business manager and treasurer of *The Restitution*, a publication that served the readers of the Church of God throughout the nation from 1870 until 1925. It was published at various locations over the 55 years, but when Al Griffiths worked for it, it was being published by Editor Robert Huggins in Cleveland, Ohio. This kind of continuous operation was rare among Church of God papers. *The Restitution* succeeded because of dedicated editors, shrewd business practices and the financial support of its readers When browsing through the older editions one finds very few solicitations for funds.

However, throughout 1920 the cost of paper increased until by summer the price had doubled over the previous year. Finally, Albert Griffiths placed a paragraph in *The Restitution*. It was short and sweet. It asked subscribers to check their labels to see if their subscriptions had expired, and to send in their subscription fees in advance, so *The Restitution* could continue to serve the Lord.

Elder Griffith took the message of the Gospel to Hector, Minnesota, during the latter part of 1920. In Hector, a family by the name of Johnson came into understanding and requested baptism. That was the first family in a core group of five or six families to be baptized at Hector.

Soon this small group wanted a meeting. A.R. Johnson wrote to the editor of *The Restitution*, Robert Huggins, who contacted Almus Adams of Omaha, Nebraska. Johnson traveled to Omaha on business and met evangelist Adams for the first time. When a Johnson daughter was to be married, they called Adams. She requested baptism before marriage. They drove 12miles to Lake Ellie and she became a bride of Christ. The next day she became the bride of her new husband. Then, another lady, Esther Peterson, requested baptism, so after the ceremony, the wedding party returned to Lake Ellie to witness Miss Peterson's baptism. That is how the work began in Hector.

One month after the 1921 General Conference was organized in Waterloo, Albert Griffiths wrote:

> *The Restitution* has never been self-supporting as the subscriber list is too small and of late, still more subscribers have ceased to take the paper--their reason has been they do not approve of certain things contained therein. *The Restitution* has and always will stand unreservedly for the truth.

The paper was not in favor of a general conference and subscribers began to abandon *The Restitution*.

Within a month, the Board of Directors of *The Restitution* announced it was being changed from a weekly to a monthly, "as the shortness of time between issues often forces the editor to use any copy at hand." The board wanted to improve literary merit of the magazine and thought a monthly publication could do that. Griffiths said, "We are convinced that (weeklies) soon deteriorate into light, insipid literature; obits, news items, personal mention and other indifferent things."

The truth behind the business decision is that the paper could no longer support a weekly delivery. Within two years the dimensions were reduced to quarterly size, and by 1925 the great old paper was dead. The people of the Church of God hardly noticed.

See Adams, Almus
Huggins, Robert (20th)

Bibliography: *The Restitution,* June 22, 1920; Dec. 11, 1920; Aug. 30, 1921; Sept. 20, 1921.

Groves, Sterling P.
b. 1862
d. Unknown

S.P. Groves was a faithful member of the Church of God and a reader of *The Restitution*. He was the son of a physician and may have had an income from his father's estate. He resided in Kentucky.

After the organization of the General Conference in 1921, Sterling wrote against it. He spoke out that the fellowship had a "weak creed." He said, [the] "brief statement of biblical teachings" had noticeable defects and omissions. He wrote that the cause to organize in order to unify a house divided was noble, but to depart from biblical truth was "erring against the faith." And, "Why leave out so many of the absolutely essential principles and doctrines of Christ?" he asked. The summary of the effort to organize the General Conference and the short statement of faith were published in the June 21 and 28 issues of 1921 in *The Restitution*. The complete statement of faith is included in the Robert Huggins entry.

See Huggins, Robert (20th)

Bibliography: Ancestry.com U.S. Census. Kentucky. Scott. Georgetown. 1870; *The Restitution* June 21, 1921; June 28, 1921; Aug. 16, 1921.

Gunn, John
b. September 3, 1839
d. September 7, 1920

John Gunn was born in Finry, Scotland. He was married there to Janet Cullen on June 21, 1860, and they had nine children. Being an avid Bible reader, he became a convert to Bible truth in Scotland. When they relocated to America, they settled in Indiana. Gunn became a member of the Eagle Creek Church of God near Knox. Over the years he contributed several articles to *The Restitution*.

Aside from this, little is known about John Gunn except that Pastor D.E. Van Vactor preached his funeral service. Gunn was pre-deceased by his wife and six children. He is buried at Knox Cemetery.

Bibliography: *The Restitution,* Sept. 29, 1920.

Guthrie, Paran
b. 1875
d. February 14, 1936

Paran Guthrie was an elder at what is now the Guthrie Grove Church of God. He was an able preacher and participated in that capacity at the Southeast Conference. He was mentioned frequently in the reports of evangelist J H. Anderson as a staunch and upright leader.

The Guthrie Grove Church of God very likely is named after Paran Guthrie's family.

Bibliography: Ancestry.com. U.S. Census. South Carolina. Anderson. Williamson. Dist. 66. 1900; South Carolina Death Index 1915-1949; *The Restitution,* Sept. 3, 1920.

Guthrie Grove Church of God

Hall, David P.
b. 1805
d. 1865?

David P. Hall was born in Connecticut and became a convert to Second Advent teachings, including conditional immortality, during 1846. One of the earliest reports authored by Hall for an Age-to-Come publication was in *The Advent Harbinger* in 1850. Hall wrote the report from Wisconsin in late October or November of 1850. During the 1850 US Census interviews, Hall resided in New York, but by November of that year Hall had relocated to Wisconsin with his wife and daughter. At that time Wisconsin was still an untamed wilderness.

In the report Hall detailed the expulsion of J.M. Stephenson from the Wesleyan movement in which Stephenson had been a minister. D.P. Hall is important as a worker in the Lord's harvest, but he is also important to historians because he detailed the early career of J.M. Stephenson, his friend. Hall said:

> About three and a half years have elapsed since I first realized the Holy Scriptures were able to make me wise unto salvation through faith which is in Jesus Christ. Prior to this time…I was a Universalist, relying confidently on the doctrine of man's natural immortality.

Early reports about David Hall written by N.A. Hitchcock and Mary Seymour for *The Voice of Truth* in 1848 acknowledged that Hall had been a Universalist but had come out of it into the Gospel of truth. In fact, Hall traveled by stage with Hitchcock, an older evangelist, throughout Wisconsin, and gave stirring testimonies of his departure from Universalism and his hope for salvation. The two of them also met the Seymours in Winnebago County, Illinois, and held meetings together.

Hall attributed his eye-opening conversion experience to George Storr's "Six Sermons," in which Storrs detailed the doctrine of life in Christ, also known as conditional immortality. Hall then acknowledged N.A. Hitchcock for teaching and leading him into understanding of the second coming of Christ to establish the Kingdom of God.

Hall began to talk and preach about his newfound understandings. As a result, he received a great deal of opposition from various denominational preachers. He said:

> In spite of the combined efforts of men and devils, the truth is doing its work in some sections of Wisconsin. But, the field here is large and laborers few; the people intelligent and energetic; and I can add in truth, devout worshippers at the shrine of Mammon.

In 1850, Hall reported working with "Bro. Stephenson" who had just recently left the Wesleyan Connection "on account of having embraced the truth touching man's nature and destiny [conditional immortality]." Before leaving this group, Stephenson met with the president of the Wesleyan organization and tried to teach him the Bible truths. This man said to Stephenson that if he must believe it, he must keep it to himself. When the Methodist annual conference came, Stephenson was summoned to trial without advance notice, and his name was dropped.

During the next eight years Stephenson and Hall became involved in the Sabbath question. Both believed for a while that worship should occur on the Sabbath. However, Stephenson and Hall renounced Sabbatarianism after Stephenson studied with H.V. Reed who was of the Age-to-Come persuasion.

Robert Chown reported to Editor Thomas Newman in *The Millennial Harbinger* that a quarterly conference meeting in 1858 at Mt. Pleasant, Wisconsin, had been interesting. The conference was held in a grove near the Kenner's home, and he reported "it was well attended with perfect harmony." Four people were baptized including Brother and Sister Howe who "had struggled with old teachings for years."

Chown also indicated a resolution had been made "expressing sympathy for 'Bro. Hall'." (Newman said, "D.P. we presume though his given name is omitted. We infer from this that Bro. D.P. Hall has renounced Sabbatarianism, and has consequently been placed in straitened consequences.") The churches in the conference agreed "to do what they can for his support."

Through another of Hall's reports dated five years later in 1863, clearly the churches kept their word. In the report, Hall detailed the various places where he preached, all of which would have paid him for preaching and expenses. He noted preaching appointments at Mt. Carroll's courthouse. Then he dedicated a new barn for Mr. Snarely at Sterling, Illinois. He stayed awhile and held meetings in Sterling. Then he preached three times at Antioch and one time at Paynes Point. Six miles of prairie separated these two locations found east of Oregon.

Hall then returned to Black Oak where a group of six "held the light against the darkness." By this he could have meant Black Walnut near Weld Park between Stillman Valley and Byron. Black Walnut was the site of a gristmill and sawmill, the Trumbull estate and several farmhouses. Following this, a local family asked Hall to preach the funeral service of their nine-year-old daughter who had lost her life to disease.

He concluded his report, "War times open the ears of many in this region to hear what the purpose of God is concerning the nations."

While written evidence of D.P. Hall's life and activities is brief, his contribution to the historical record has been helpful.

See Chown, Robert
Hitchcock, Nelson A.
Newman, Thomas
Reed, H.V.
Stephenson, J.M.

Bibliography: Ancestry.com. U.S. Census. New York. New York. New York Ward 17, p422; Chown, Robert. Report of Mt. Pleasant Quarterly Conference. *Prophetic Expositor and Bible Advocate*, Jos. Marsh, editor. Rochester, NY, Nov. 9, 1858; Hall, D.P., "Report on J.M. Stephenson," *Advent Harbinger and Bible Advocate,* Jos. Marsh, editor. Rochester, NY. Nov. 1850; Hall, D.P. Report of Plum River Conference, *Millennial Harbinger and Bible Expositor*, July 9, 1863; Seymour, Mary. Letter to Editor (included information of D.P. Hall's association with Universalists) *Voice of Truth*, Jos. Marsh, ed., Rochester, NY. June 23, 1848; Hitchcock, N.A. "Letter to Editor" (also including mention of D.P. Hall), *Voice of Truth,* Jos. Marsh, ed., Rochester, NY, June 23, 1848.

Hall, Eugene M.
b. June 1, 1865
d. December 19, 1930

Eugene Hall married Ethel Coats of Coats Grove, Michigan. They farmed 40 acres and gardened. Sale of garden produce contributed to their family income. Their son, Fred Hall, became a Church of God pastor. S.J. Lindsay baptized Eugene in 1909, possibly at a summer Bible school for young adults at Oregon, Illinois.

Eugene's legacy in the Church of God survived through Fred and Fred's son, Pastor Milon Hall (deceased), and his children, Connie Hall Ramsey (Dale), Pastor Ray Hall, Iris Hall (Francis) Burnett (deceased), granddaughters Miriam Burnett Bender and Michal Gigous, and grandson, Larry Townsend.

See Hall, Milon (20th)
Burnett, Francis (20th)

Bibliography: Obituary, *The Restitution Herald*, G.E. Marsh, editor, Oregon, Il. Jan. 13, 1931.

Halstead, David Thorpe
b. May 23, 1826
d. June 22, 1914

David Halstead was the second child of six born to Samuel and Susan Webster Halstead. David married Teresa Webster Reeve and they had three children; two died in childhood. Teresa died in 1880 while she and David were residing in Mississippi. He wed Patience Reed Sharpe on November 3, 1882. They had four children. Patience died on November 22, 1912. After her death, David resided in a boarding house with furnished meals.

In his youth, David Halstead was an energetic and fiery preacher who ministered throughout Indiana and Ohio during most of the 19th century. He believed in the restitution of all things.

In 1863, David Halstead wrote a letter to *The Millennial Harbinger and Bible Expositor* reporting that he had been quite ill with a painful inflammation of the eyes causing him to cancel his preaching appointments. He said he "had been lying prostrate from it barely sustaining life, but was hoping to get back to services." It is not known if this ailment left him with impaired vision. It is thought that even if were blind, he could still preach because he had Scripture committed to memory.

David Halstead wrote to *The Gospel Banner and Millennial Advocate* in July 1868, following receipt of a letter inviting him to a conference of the Brethren of One Faith in Chicago over the Fourth of July. This conference was to include laymen and clergy from Illinois, Wisconsin, Indiana and Ohio. At the time Halstead received the invitation, he was living and working in Rensselaer, Indiana. The church at Rensselaer was organized in 1861, and continued to function well into the 1950s before declining and closing. Halstead continued his ministry in and around Rensselaer until his death.

Halstead's correspondence included a greeting to

the conference delegates expressing the unfortunate circumstance that prevented him from attending. He agreed with having a conference meeting, and realized a great blessing would be received by everyone present. Halstead offered prayers and blessings on behalf of the conference. He wrote in a letter of regret:

> It would be gratifying indeed for me to be present in person and mutually share with you in the joys and benefits arising from such a meeting of the children of the one family, united together by one spirit, called in one hope of your calling, to share in one common inheritance, meeting together for the purpose of exhorting, encouraging, comforting and warning each other. I know it would inspire me with new zeal and courage, to hear your words of cheer.

Within those words is a mission statement, a set of objectives and goals for joining loosely connected churches together in a state or regional organization further uniting in a national conference. The developing Church of God in that day, still calling themselves Brethren of One Faith, was searching for a way to unite all churches in a common organization to accomplish together what one church or one member could not do alone. Thomas Wilson had first published Halstead's letter in *The Herald of the Coming Kingdom and Christian Instructor* following that 1868 Chicago conference. In 1869, the Northwest Christian Association was formed of several Midwestern state conferences to unite the work. Perhaps Halstead's powerful and inspiring letter was the impetus for that action.

In 1874, David T. Halstead was appointed evangelist for the Indiana State Conference. For this responsibility he asked for payment of $800. According to the conference report from *The Restitution* of December 9, 1874, $600 was immediately pledged! Agents were then appointed in each congregation to continue to raise the funds to pay the evangelist.

In 1904, he sent a note to A.J. Eychaner in the pages of *The Restitution* stating he would write an article on Sabbath keeping. Halstead was against worship on the seventh day, and Eychaner practiced it privately.

Halstead preached at Indiana Conference at the Antioch Church in 1908. On this occasion, he preached from 1 Corinthians 4:15, "In Christ Jesus, What and How." This was the famous "June meeting" quite popular with Church of God believers in the Midwest. It drew worshippers from Ohio, Michigan and Illinois, attracting Adventists of all persuasions for miles around.

David Halstead served as mentor for L.E. Conner when he entered the ministry around 1887, and later at Conner's short pastorate at Rensselaer in 1894. Conner said after Uncle David's death:

> The richness of the man lay in his profound honesty, sincerity and integrity of heart. He was a man of truth, in word and in action. I have never known a man in whose Christian character I had greater confidence....

At his death, David Halstead was 88 and still living in Rensselaer. Jessie M. Wilson of Chicago penned these words in tribute: "Bro. Halstead is sleeping in Jesus. It is, as it were, but a night's rest."

After Halstead's death in 1914 Thomas Wilson reintroduced Halstead's 1868 letter to the brethren through the pages of July 15 issue of *The Restitution Herald*. It may have been the inspiration for the formation of the General Conference in 1921.

See Conner, L.E.
Eychaner, A.J.
Wilson, Benjamin

Bibliography: Ancestry.com. U.S. Census. Indiana. Jaspar. Marion. Dist. 20. 1900; Letter to Conference Attendees, *Gospel Banner and Millennial Advocate,* 14:14 July 15, 1868; Letter, *Millennial Harbinger and Bible Expositor,* June 24, 1863; *The Restitution,* June 13, 1904; March 7, 1906; Obituary and Halstead commemorative Issue *Restitution Herald,* July 15, 1914; May 7, 1919.

Hammond, John E.
b. February 6, 1878
d. September 8, 1948

John Hammond was the son of Robert and Martha Hammond, homesteaders in western Nebraska. John was baptized at age 12, and became an ardent Bible student and follower of Christ from that point on. He studied to be a teacher at a Normal school in his area, and later married Abbie Gregg who may have been the daughter of Grandma Gregg (Gragg) also listed in this encyclopedia. They had three daughters.

John E. Hammond focused his ministry on the Great Plains. He was a noted writer who submitted various articles on Bible topics to *The Restitution* and *The Restitution Herald*. He began a humble work at Avery, Nebraska, with a small Bible study group. After several years of assisting this work, like the Apostle Paul, John departed in 1922, and prayed for its stability. John was especially fond of visiting the work at Kennard where the Harvey Krogh family lived in 1921 and 1922.

John became concerned that Church of God people, especially the new members entering from other church backgrounds, might not fully understand the idea of "probation" in the Age to Come. Briefly explained, the Church of God taught that the unrepentant nations living at Christ's return would enter the thousand-year kingdom on probation, subdued by Christ, unsaved, but with the opportunity for salvation. Hammond realized that some new members in the Church of God believed that the *wicked* who had *died* in an unrepentant state during the present evil age would be raised and given probation, or a "second chance," in the Age to Come. He authored an eight-page tract "Future Probation for the Dead Refuted by Reason and Scripture" from his home in Omaha. He explained the doctrine, and he exploded the myth that unsaved dead people would be given probation in the Age to Come.

While short, this tract is interesting in its style but difficult to read. The General Conference printing presses clearly did not produce it, for printing of such bad quality would never be distributed by the Conference. This tract had bleed-through to such an extent, that the text is barely legible on pages six and seven. Still, the gist of his argument is readable and profound. The tract is part of the archival collection at Atlanta Bible College.

Hammond's daughter remembered that whenever he had a spare moment he would read his Bible. She said, "He would rather talk and study the Word of God than do anything else." The last few years of his life were spent in Fullerton, California. Hammond served as an elder in the Church of God at Los Angeles. He died from complications of a stroke and is buried at Fairhaven Cemetery near Orange, California.

See Gragg (Gregg?), Grandma
Krogh, Harvey U., Sr.

Bibliography: Ancestry.com. U.S. Census. Nebraska Avery. Sarpy. 1920; Conference report in *The Restitution Herald*, August 8, 1922; Also, *The Restitution*, June 1921; Hammond, J.E. "Future Probation" self-published from Omaha, Neb. around 1920; *The Restitution Herald*, Dec. 18, 1930; Obituary, *The Restitution Herald*, Sydney Magaw, editor, Oregon, Il. Sept. 28, 1948.

Harrold, Jesse
b. 1880?
d. Unknown

Jesse Harrold wrote to *The Restitution* with a powerful testimony that was very devoted and moving. He said he was a man crippled by rheumatism, and had to walk with crutches when he was able to walk at all. He stated he kept his eye looking Zionward hoping for the happy day when sorrow and pain would be no more.

Harrold spoke of a friendship with a Campbellite preacher who believed the promises made to Abraham but who was unable to preach it or to leave that denomination for the Church of God. "I felt great sorrow for the poor deluded man," Harrold said. Then he concluded, "I am strong in the faith and hope of the soon coming day that will end the pain and sorrow of this world."

There were many people around the world, such as Jesse Harrold, who expressed love for the Lord, and for the simple teachings of the Church of God, and remain unnamed in these pages, known only to the Lord.

Bibliography: *The Restitution,* March, 1923.

Hartman, Mrs. Aurora C. Scott
b. February 18, 1840
d. December 22, 1915

Aurora, wife of John Hartman, was born in Illinois and died in Michigan. Her husband and children survived her. Daughter Nellie married F.V. Blakely, a prominent Michigan preacher and writer.

Aurora's obituary said, "She was a woman of culture and much native ability." She was a teacher for a number of years. She authored *A Letter to A Friend,* which was far longer than your average letter. The letter gave testimony of her great faith and attempted to persuade her friend to accept Jesus as her Savior. Aurora's letter was discovered after her death and published in *The Restitution Herald* of January 19, 1916, with her obituary and picture. In it she said, "I do not claim to be a Bible worshipper but I do claim to worship the God of the Bible." Another memorable quote is, "The Gospel is declared to be the good news or glad tidings concerning the Kingdom of God and the name of Jesus. I believe the Gospel."

See Blakely, Frank V.

Bibliography: Hartman, A.C.S. *Letter to a Friend.* No publication data available. Circa 1916. The book is part of the archival collection at Atlanta Bible College; "Hartman obituary", *The Restitution Herald* Jan. 19, 1916.

Hastings, Horace L.
b. 1804?
d. October 1899

Horace L. Hastings had been a member of the Church of God at Rochester, New York, the same congregation in which Joseph Marsh worshipped. A dispute arose in 1857 between Hastings and Marsh when Marsh refused to publish one of Hastings' articles in *The Expositor,* causing Hastings, the "wounded" party, to leave the church. This episode was reported at length by Marsh in *The Prophetic Expositor and Bible Advocate.*

Miles Grant, publisher of the Advent Christian paper *World's Crisis*, heard about the conflict and published an erroneous statement in his magazine that the church had expelled Marsh. Afterward, Marsh asked, "When a church splits, how can it be said that the one side expelled the other?" It is interesting to note that when Hastings tried working with the Advent Christians, Miles Grant drove him out. Hastings may have been too brilliant and too independent to work within a group.

After the dust settled, Hastings went on to write for the *Voice of the Church,* and supported the Millenarians. He later formed his own church, which brought criticism from his former friends of the Rochester Church of God. He may have found his way into the Advent Christian church after that, but folks in the Church of God still followed his writings. He authored several books which have been well received over the last several decades.

In 1858 he authored *The Great Controversy between God and Man*. A few months later, Ellen G. White, founder of the Seventh-day Adventist movement, authored *The Great Controversy* in which she discussed the tension between God and Satan. It is thought by some that she copied his title. Hastings also authored, *Will the Old Book Stand?*, published in Boston in 1891. This book, while rare, can still be purchased on the Internet.

In 1885 Hastings was arrested in Boston and taken to the police station along with two other protestant pastors. They had violated a city ordinance against preaching on the Commons, a seemingly trivial matter.

H.L. Hastings was helpful to the Advent Christians for a number of years by advancing their awareness of publishing as a means to promote their message. Clyde E. Hewitt, Advent Christian historian, was immensely respectful of Hastings' contribution to their 19th century development. He said:

> One modern scholar has concluded that working independently and in his private capacity Hastings did far more to spread "Advent Christian" truths, though without the label, than he would have been able to do had he continued to work within the conservative-minded Christian Publication Society. At the time of his death and for a dozen years prior, Horace L. Hastings "had become one of the most famous evangelical Christians in the world." And, "The influence of the man, far beyond narrow Advent Christian circles, can be gained in part by the distribution figures of just one of his tracts. "The Inspiration of the Bible or, Will the Old Book Stand?" by the time of his death virtually three million copies had been issued in eighteen or twenty languages."

See **Marsh, Joseph**

Bibliography: Hewitt, Clyde E. *Responsibility and Response,* Venture Books. Charlotte, NC. 1986. p. 45-46, 50-51; Marsh, Joseph. "Report of dispute with H.L. Hastings," *The Prophetic Expositor and Bible Advocate,* Jos. Marsh, editor, Rochester, NY, Sept. 15, 1857; "Report" *The Prophetic Expositor and Bible Advocate,* Jos. Marsh, editor, Rochester, NY., Nov. 15, 1857.

Hatch, A.E.
b. 1862
d. 1920?

Elder A.E. Hatch was the son of a circuit preacher, Jeremiah S. Hatch. He was born near Crawfordsville, Indiana, but as an adult resided in Chicago, Minnesota and Kansas. Hatch was a faithful member of the Church of God and carried on a preaching ministry which included some preaching for the Advent Christians.

He was a member of the Church of God Minnesota Conference Board that worked with Sarah K. Taylor and her husband in the missionary ministry of Charles R. Vedantachari in India. It was unfortunate that by the time Vedantachari could visit the Minnesota Conference in the United States, Elder Hatch had died.

Elder Hatch edited *The Day Dawn and Harvest Messenger* from October 1910 to October 1911. A few years prior to that, it had been edited by James A. Patrick, and Patrick again took up the reins after Elder Hatch resigned. During its years of publication the press of *The Day Dawn* moved from Fort Dodge, Iowa, to Howard Lake, to Minneapolis, and back to Howard Lake.

In his last issue as editor, Elder Hatch indicated there had been some difficulty during his administration. It is not known the exact nature of the problem, but he hinted at a lack of financial support, saying:

> Our reasons for not standing for editorial re-election have been already given, and need not receive another sad recital. Were there co-operation in the church and a brotherly interest in each other's welfare, this cessation of editorial labor might never have been.

Perhaps his difficulty in editing the magazine arose from the fact that he was born completely blind. Information to date indicates he was the only blind pastor and editor in the Church of God. Even with dedicated staff, editing a paper would be difficult without vision.

It is interesting that a year after the attempt to reorganize a national conference at Waterloo in 1910, during which the educational needs of the Church of God were discussed, A.E. Hatch addressed that prospect in the pages of *The Day Dawn*:

> Sometime ago, President Patrick wrote us in regard to a Bible Institute which, he suggested might be conducted by mail. Of course, such an institute would demand a slight expense on the students, but the results would be well worth the while.

James Patrick suggested that Elder Hatch be the instructor. Hatch replied:

> How gladly would we engage in such a venture, were it possible; but our absences from the books in our library

would forever debar us. We are often where there is not even a dictionary, or any literary work.

Even though the Bible Institute did not get underway in 1911, there was in fact summer Bible training being offered in Oregon, Illinois, by S.J. Lindsay. Some of the young men who benefited from these early extended training sessions were Frank E. Siple, Robert G. Huggins, Rolland Stilson, John A. Railton and Maude Cross (Stilson). It would have been good if a formal educational enterprise had been organized in 1911 to fulfill the vision of the Board of Directors from the 1888 Philadelphia Conference. As it was, another decade would pass before the Bible Training Class was formally opened in Oregon, Illinois, with General Conference approval.

Hatch also spoke forcefully in favor of organizing a General Conference. He wrote:

> [The Church of God General Conference] is a subject in which we should all be interested. We have always maintained that the way to church unity was for brethren of widely differing beliefs to be united under the one Bible name, Church of God. When we come to the June conference, let us come prepared to talk over this matter in the spirit of love, and with a desire for progress.

Hatch's positive stance for uniting the churches may also relate to his difficulty as editor. Not everyone in the Church of God of that day agreed with a national organizational effort.

When Elder Hatch completed his editorship with *The Day Dawn,* he moved on in his ministry. C.C. Sweaney reported in a travelogue that he had met him at Kansas City and Elder Hatch had preached four sermons. It is good to know that in the face of discouragement Elder Hatch continued to serve.

See Hatch, Jeremiah
  Hatch, Paul (20th)
  Huggins, Robert (20th)
  Lindsay, S.J.
  Railton, John A.
  Siple, F.E. (20th)
  Sweaney, C.C.
  Taylor, Sarah
  Vedantachari, Charles R.

Bibliography: Ancestry.com. U.S. Census. Indiana. Montgomery. Crawfordsville, 1870; Hatch, A.E. "Editor's Chat," *The Day Dawn and Harvest Messenger,* Howard Lake, Mn. April 1911 and May, 1911; Sweaney, C.C. "A Pleasant Trip," *The Day Dawn and Harvest Messenger,* Jas. A. Patrick, editor, Minneapolis, Mn. Jan. 1918.

Hatch, Jeremiah "Jerry" Stimson
  b. February 28, 1823
  d. October 26, 1905

Evangelist J.S. Hatch was born in Ohio but came into the Church of God in central Indiana. He was baptized into the One Faith in 1861 by A.F. Servis, a preacher  from the Michigan conference. Hatch certainly must have been influenced by S.A. Chaplin, Nathaniel Field and Robert Gresham. By trade, Jeremiah was a blacksmith.

When he and his family lived at Crawfordsville, Indiana, he was not yet involved with the work of the Age to Come. In fact, Jeremiah wrote a letter to E.C. Andrus through the pages of *The Restitution* requesting him to come to southern Indiana and make an effort. He said "The Christian church is nearly gone down, and if some good evangelist could come here they could do a good work." This letter to the editor was probably in response to a previously published letter in *The Restitution* by Andrus asking to be informed of missionary opportunities in Indiana so he could put forth a good effort.

Jeremiah moved his family to La Porte County near Valparaiso, a university town. After the Civil War, J.S. Hatch began preaching at Burgett's Corner in 1866 and was known to have attended the 1870 conference at "old Antioch" in Illinois. Old Antioch was located at the intersection of Flagg and Chana roads in Ogle County. J.S. Hatch was one of the early Church of God circuit riders whose travels included all of Indiana, Illinois, Iowa and Wisconsin.

Hatch traveled in Indiana the fall of 1874. He reported in *The Restitution* that he had meetings at Pierceton with John and Roxanna Wince. People had come out *"en masse"* and mostly represented the United Brethren. They wanted him to debate one of their preachers, but they also wanted him to change the name of the church he represented because it wasn't listed in the *history of the denominations. Hatch said his church was named in the best book around, the Bible. He reported that at the debate, they couldn't hold their proposition. He had stated his proposition as "Resolved: We, the Church of God, are the only people that preach the Gospel of Jesus Christ as preached by the Apostles."

In 1888 he began to work for the Michigan State Conference as their state evangelist. While he served in this capacity J.S. Hatch lived in Berrien County near Buchanan.

He was granted a ministerial Certificate of License by the General Conference of the Churches of God in Christ Jesus which met in Chicago for its second annual meeting in November 1889. It is framed and hanging in the Archives of Atlanta Bible College. The certificate is dated November 17, 1889, and indicates that Evangelist Hatch was qualified with Christian character to preach the Gospel anywhere. Full text of the certificate can be read in a separate excerpt with this entry. The original license is in remarkable condition and offers visual evidence into the ministerial licensing procedures of that era. Having a certificate offered benefits to the evangelist. If a man could produce a ministerial license, he could get discounts on train tickets. Such a document also served as a letter of reference to authorities when he entered a new community of service, indicating he was in good standing with his denomination.

In the decades preceding the practice of issuing Certificates of License, state conferences issued "letters of authority." A note in the minute book of the Michigan State Conference 1858-1886 says, "On motion decided to grant letters of authority to preach to the following, L.C. Chase, E. Hoyt, J.S. Hatch, W. McCrodan, J. Watkins, B.W. Woodward, E. Chesebrough and L.H. Chesebrough.

According to Jeremiah's grandson, Paul Hatch, Jeremiah traveled an arduous circuit by horseback and when feasible, by train. Paul said Jeremiah was dedicated and endured every element of bad weather, as well as bad conduct by men who tried to hinder him or his message. He was faithful to the cause of Christ, and he believed in the Age-to-Come prophecy message.

Jeremiah was contemporary with Joseph Marsh, Benjamin Wilson, J.M. Stephenson, Nathaniel Field, Ephraim Miller, J.B. Cook, H.V. Reed and other influential leaders of the early movement. He also mentored young hopeful preachers and trained them to be evangelists. One report tells of his work in 1863 with the youthful Levi Skeels originally from Columbus, Ohio, then living in Indiana. Skeels gave Hatch full credit for his training.

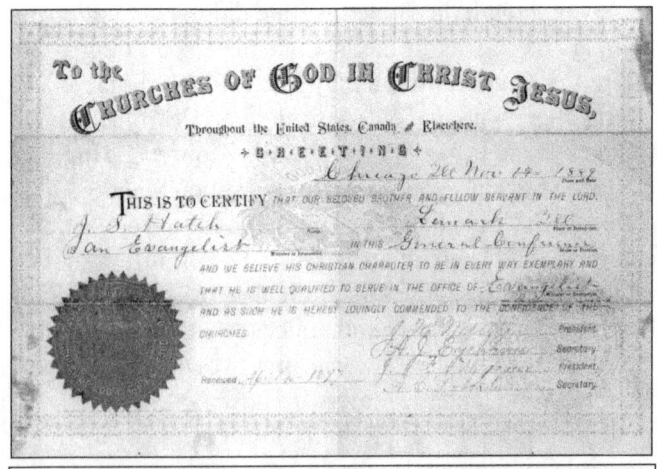

License to preach issued by the General Conference to JS Hatch, dated November 19, 1889.

The license certificate reads:
To the Churches of God in Christ Jesus, Throughout the United States, Canada and Elsewhere. Greetings. Chicago, Ill. Nov. 17, 1889.
This is to certify that our beloved Brother and Fellow Servant in the Lord, J.S. Hatch, Lanark, Ill. is an Evangelist in the General Conference, and we believe his Christian Character to be in every way exemplary and that he is well qualified to serve in the office of Evangelist and as such he is hereby lovingly commended to the confidence of the churches.
Signed,
J.H. Willey, President
A.J. Eychaner, Secretary
J.F. Wagoner, President (Indiana Conference)
A.C. Roberts, Secretary (Indiana Conference)
The license was valid until April 1891. It was secured with a gold seal that read: Churches of God in Christ Jesus General Conference.

Ref.: The certificate is preserved at the Atlanta Bible College Archives

Early Church of God ministers. Left to right: AH Zilmer, John Wince, BW Woodward, JS Hatch, JF Wagoner.

Jeremiah Hatch faithfully attended quarterly and annual conferences of each state in which he visited. In August 1868, he attended the meeting at Cicero, Indiana. It was a good meeting even though poor communications meant that not many people came from out of state. J.S. Hatch was mentioned regarding the discussion wherein all agreed it would not be good to "press some particular crochet of his own that would be of no special importance in the great plan of salvation." A "crochet" such as Anglo-Israelism or second chance was a doctrine on the "fringe" of commonly accepted doctrines.

During this decade, most Churches of God and conferences strove to hammer out a statement of faith describing their unified understanding of biblical truth. None wished to use the phrase, "statement of faith," however, as it sounded like "creed" and all members were anti-creedal. But without a clear statement, they could not distinguish themselves from the Adventists. In many places the advocates of both positions worshipped together as congregations in the same building. However, a break occurred in 1870 between Nathaniel Field and the Indiana Conference over this very issue. The Church of God had begun its list of essentials for salvation, and it required belief in doctrine and Christian character as tests of fellowship, not just character alone.

Elder Hatch's name is mentioned as preaching and baptizing in Crawfordsville, Indiana, in *The Herald of the Coming Kingdom and Christian Instructor,* January 1870. This new publication, edited by Thomas Wilson of Chicago, was the offspring of the merged *Gospel Banner and Millennial Advocate,* B. Wilson, editor, and

The Prophetic Watchman, J.M. Stephenson, editor. Over the next 25 years Hatch often reported statistics similar to those of 1873. In that year, Hatch reported traveling 1,000 miles to preach 300 sermons and organize three churches with 37 baptisms, and two debates.

Elder Hatch continued to faithfully serve the Church of God until his death in 1905. In that same year, he spent two months in Illinois between Peoria, Paris and Marshall where he baptized 11 including a young woman, Martha McClelland of Hollis Township Peoria County, Illinois.

J.F. Wagoner conducted Hatch's funeral service from the Plummer house of worship and wrote Jeremiah's obituary for *The Restitution*. Wagoner wrote: "He died in the faith." Elder Hatch was interred at the Plummer cemetery. Plummer Church was the original name of the Hillisburg Church of God at Frankfort, Indiana.

Jeremiah's legacy lived on through the ministry of his sons, J.E. Hatch of California and A.E. Hatch of Kansas, and his grandchildren, Paul Hatch and Mrs. Sydney Magaw, and great grandson, Ivan Magaw of Oregon, Illinois. Paul assisted the Chicago and Oregon Churches of God most of his life. He was one of the first historians in the Church of God who traveled to research the founding and history of the Church of God in America. Clyde Randall dedicated his book *Historical Waymarks of the Church of God* to Paul Hatch, who laid much of the foundation for the writing of that book.

    See Andrus, E.C.
        Field, Nathaniel
        Gresham, Robert
        Hatch, A.E.
        Hatch, Paul (20th)
        Marsh, Joseph
        Servis (Sarvis), A.F.

Bibliography: Ancestry.com. U.S. Census. Indiana. Montgomery. Crawfordsville. 1870; Hatch, J.S. "Report of Indiana Conference." *Herald of Coming Kingdom and Christian Instructor*, Feb. 1868 and Jan. 1870. Photo of License of J.S. Hatch, owned by Archives of Atlanta Bible College, McDonough, Ga; Hatch, J.S. "Notice to evangelists". *The Millennial Harbinger and Bible Expositor,* Thos. Newman, editor, Seneca Falls, NY 35:25 Nov. 18, 1863; *"History of Denominations" no specific book by that title has been located, but the *Farmer's Almanac* often included a section listing denominations. Also, individual books on church history often listed denominations as in Hurst's *History of the Christian Church*, published 1900; "Notice to Illinois Readers", *The Restitution*, Dec. 9, 1874; "Report of Debate," *The Restitution,* March 28, 1889; Also, May 25, 1904; Nov. 18, 1905; March 20, 1907; *The Restitution Herald*, March 21, 1921; Michigan State Conference Records 1858-1886.

> **Note from Evangelist Hatch published in *The Restitution*, Spring 1889:**
>
> Will all of our brethren in Illinois send me their names and post office address, that I may be able to correspond with you? We want to hear from you all so we can make arrangements to have a conference in June. We want to unite our efforts, and see if we cannot get into better working order.
>
> I was appointed last June in northern Illinois as State Evangelist to preach for one year. I commenced Sept. 15th and have been at work most of the time since. Now brethren, let me hear from you and I will visit as many points as I can between now and the middle of June.
>
> J.S. Hatch, Lanark, Illinois

Haupt, Johannes (John) Gustav
b. February 12, 1855
d. June 9, 1936

J.G. Haupt of Crowley, Louisiana, was born in Prussia. He came to the United States in 1867 with his family and began working as a teacher and librarian at the Davenport Iowa Academy of Natural Sciences. While working there, he resided in Walcott, Iowa. This position allowed him to travel and write during the summer. He prepared a "List of Phaenogamous Plants collected in the vicinity of Davenport" for the *1876 Proceedings of the Academy.* The Women's Centennial Association published this as a twelve-page booklet.

While in Davenport in 1876 he became a naturalized citizen of the United States. He may have left the Academy prior to 1879, perhaps to teach in Cedar County. In late July 1879 he married Alice C. Baker of Aurora, Illinois, at the bride's home. Thomas Wilson, editor of *The Herald of the Coming Kingdom*, conducted the ceremony. It is very likely that the couple first met through their association with Illinois and Iowa Church of God statewide conferences.

In 1882 Haupt put forth his name as a Republican candidate for Superintendent of Schools in Cedar County, but did not receive enough votes on the preliminary ballot to be nominated. That may have ended his experiment with politics.

After he moved to Louisiana, he became bookkeeper in the local bank, possibly a temporary position. In 1896 he became President of the Natchitoches Normal School and lived at Lake Charles. This school developed into Northwestern State University of Louisiana. He was a member of the newly formed National Education Association.

J.G. Haupt was an educated man and loved to write. An article titled simply, "Baptism," appeared in *The*

Restitution on June 20, 1889. He presented a scriptural thesis in favor of baptism by immersion "in" water, not "with" water. He cited the baptism of Jesus by John the Baptist as an example of immersion. He was quite proficient in Greek, and said *baptizo* meant to "immerse" whereas *rhantizo* meant to "sprinkle" and was never used in the scriptures to mean baptism.

A portion of Haupt's history of Miquel Servet or Michael Servetus, the Spaniard who opposed John Calvin during the Reformation.

President Haupt studied church history and wrote about it in his free time. He had the benefit of understanding European culture and history including Reformation history and the development of the church in Europe. In 1922, John wrote a tract about "Miquel Servet" or Michael Servetus, the Spaniard who opposed John Calvin during the Reformation. Servetus, an anti-trinitarian, was also against infant baptism. He was burned at the stake in Geneva on October 27, 1553, with Calvin's approval. Haupt's tract may have been the first look at Servetus by an author from the Church of God. *The Restitution Herald* published it in the April 14 issue.

Elder Haupt also wrote a simple article on the churches of Revelation and the millennial age, as a funeral sermon for a departed Louisiana brother in 1922. John passed away in Natchitoches, Louisiana, and is interred there in the American Cemetery.

Bibliography: Ancestry.com U.S. Census. Iowa. Scott. Blue. Grass. Dist. 264. 1880; U.S. Census Louisiana. Acadia. Crowley. Dist. 13. 1920; Ancestry.com. Selected U.S. Naturalization Record Indexes 1791-1966 about J.G. Haupt; Ancestry.com. Louisiana Statewide Death Index 1900-1949 record for J.G. Haupt; Haupt, J. G. "Miquel Servet" *The Restitution Herald*, April 14, 1922; Williams, Byron. *Abstracts of Obituaries and Weddings from the Restitution*. Self-published.1994; Louisiana Cemeteries, Natchitoches Parish. http://www.la-cemeteries.com/Cemeteries%20Natchitoches%20Table.shtml. *Journal of proceedings and addresses of the ... annual meeting*, Volumes 1-36. Haupt entry from Louisiana. National Educational Association. 1901-1902 retrieved from Google Books, Aug. 1, 2010; *Proceedings of the Davenport Academy of Natural Sciences*, Volume 3. Davenport Academy of Natural Sciences Women's Centennial Association. 1878, record for J.G. Haupt retrieved from Google Books Aug. 1, 2010; "State News and Notes" *The Iowa Normal Monthly* 7:2, Sept. 1883, 88 retrieved from Google Books Aug. 1, 2010. Dec. 9, 1874.

Hayworth, Joel
b. 1826
d. 1888

Joel Hayworth was born in New York and moved west after the Bitter Disappointment 1845-1860. He was married with children and operated a music business is Osage, Kansas. As ladies moved their pianos west, there must have been a significant call for repair parts and printed music.

Joel may have learned of the Second Advent during his youth when Millerism was at its height. He learned of the Gospel of the Kingdom and the Age to Come from Joseph Marsh.

Hayworth was a fixture on the Great Plains before Almus Adams was baptized. He preached the Gospel throughout the state of Kansas where he resided. He was already an established resident in Kansas by the time Uncle John Foore, A.J. Eychaner and John Prime began preaching. It was reported that Hayworth went into homes and sat there "with his Bible on his knees" with the family gathered around him as he taught them from the Word about the Kingdom of God.

By the time a report of Joel Hayworth's evangelistic work reached *The Restitution*, the elderly man had already passed away.

See Adams, Almus
Eychaner, A.J.
Foore, John
Prime, John T.

Bibliography: *The Restitution*, March 27, 1889.

Heckman, J.J. (John Joseph?)
b. 1877
d. October 13, 1939

Elder J.J. Heckman lived and worked in Kansas and Oklahoma. He was a grocery salesman by trade giving him immense travel opportunities. For a number of years he preached where he was needed and for special events such as weddings and funerals. He reported a trip in *The Restitution* that he had made to baptize Mr. Smith and his wife. Smith had known the truth but had delayed being baptized. The Smiths requested that J.J. Heckman help organize the conference in western Nebraska, western

Kansas, Oklahoma and Texas including the selection of officers and collection of funds. They wanted to see the work progress through the efforts of Heckman and other evangelists. This may have been Thomas Smith who became a Church of God evangelist.

Heckman contributed faithfully to *The Restitution* and *The Restitution Herald* after it began. He wrote refuting G.M. Myers' arguments about Joseph being the father of Jesus. Myers published arguments for Josephism saying Scripture spoke of Jesus as Son of God and son of Joseph. Myers said that Jesus could not have been the seminally begotten son of both. "It follows," Myers wrote in *The Present Truth,* "that (Jesus) was the Son of God by the power of the resurrection from the dead."

Heckman wrote an article for *The Restitution* taking exception to Myers' logic. He used the example of Old Testament Joseph being called the son of Rachel and in Genesis 37:10 he is called the son of Leah. Following Myers' logic, Joseph would be made the son of Leah in the resurrection. Heckman said if Myers' logic could not "be overthrown," neither could his own logic about Rachel and Leah be overthrown. Heckman noted the Bible clearly states that Rachel was the mother of Joseph and Leah was his stepmother, and it clearly states that Jesus was the begotten Son of God and Joseph was his stepfather.

See Myers, G.M
   Smith, Thomas

Bibliography: Ancestry.com. U.S. Census. Ark. Poinsett. Marked Tree. Dist. 7. 1920; Arkansas Death Index 1934-1940. *The Present Truth,* Sept. 1915; *The Restitution,* Nov. 2, 1915; June 1, 1920; Nov. 6, 1920.

Heiser, Mary A.
b. August 14, 1871
d. June 2, 1904

Mary was born in Marshall County, Indiana. Mary's mother died when Mary was only five years old. Mary was raised by her father, and within a few years her only brother died. Consequently, Mary wed Joseph D. Heiser of Grant County, Indiana, July 30, 1891. They had three children. She accepted the Lord and joined the Burr Oak Church of God in 1902. Mary died young even for that time. She was survived by her devoted husband and two children. Her funeral service was held at Burr Oak, David E. Van Vactor conducting. She was interred at Burr Oak cemetery.

Bibliography: *The Restitution,* June 8, 1904

Herrick, Frank
b. 1869?
d. Unknown

Frank Herrick was from Iowa where he often served as an assistant to A.J. Eychaner in the tent work undertaken there in 1891. Eychaner and Herrick visited the communities of Lake View, Sac City, Ames, Hickory Grove, Webster City and Ferguson, where the season was brought to a close.

In 1892, the fifth annual conference of Iowa churches was held in Webster City June 9-20, with 63 believers attending that "family reunion." That year Frank assisted in baptizing 28 new members.

The Iowa conference sent young Herrick to Rock River Seminary in Mt. Morris, Illinois. The college was operated by the Methodists who closed it in 1878. This school began as an orthodox college to teach religion and higher education and was A.J. Eychaner's alma mater.

See Eychaner, A.J.

Bibliography: Eychaner, A.J. personal records, Book 4, pg 176 as cited by Terry Ferrell, "History of Iowa Church of God and Conference," History Committee, 1987.

Herrin, S.I. "Si"
b. 1879
d. Unknown

S.I. Herrin was born in the area of Kansas City, Missouri, perhaps near Peculiar where there is a thriving Church of God. He first heard the Gospel of the Kingdom from Elder C.W. Herron, a preacher of the One Faith. Herron had a wonderful resonant preaching voice which captured the boy as the message captured his heart. As Herrin grew up there were no Churches of God around. He drifted into the Campbellite movement and was baptized. He continued among the Disciples for 25 years, but "felt condemned."

After moving to Douglass County, Missouri, with his wife, three sons and two daughters, Herrin began to search the Bible and asked a few questions. Someone told him about *The Restitution*. He wrote to Editor Robert Huggins and subscribed. Huggins told him of J.J. Heckman and Almus Adams, both of whom were evangelists throughout the Great Plains. They wrote Herrin and offered their services. Almus Adams was called, and it became his great joy to baptize Si Herrin and his wife who became faithful workers in the church from that point on.

See Adams, Almus
   Heckman, J.J.

Bibliography: Ancestry.com U.S. Census. Missouri. Douglas. Bryan. Dist. 59. 1920; *The Restitution,* June 22, 1925.

Hicklin, (Josiah)
b. 1820
d. Unknown

Mr. Hicklin is not referred to in the literature by his first name, but it is thought that he was Josiah Hicklin, a farmer from near Terra Haute, Indiana. If this is so, he may have heard the first Word of the Kingdom from Jacob Shaffer, one of the early circuit riders who preached in that area of Indiana. Elder Hicklin began to preach the Gospel of the Kingdom of God in Indiana after the Bitter Disappointment 1845-1860. He was so well known to the readers of *The Restitution* that mentioning personal information about him was unnecessary. It is certainly possible that he was one of the Hicklin uncles of J.M. Stephenson who were or had been Methodist preachers and strict abolitionists. He is only known through testimonies of others in the early literature. Men like Hicklin helped to establish the Church of God in the Midwest.

See Shaffer, Jacob
Stephenson, J.M.

Bibliography: Ancestry.com. U.S. Census. Indiana. Vigo. Sugar Creek. 1870. *The Restitution*, April 3, 1907.

Higgins, Yate
b. 1820
d. 1865?

Yate Higgins was born in Massachusetts. He was a currier who specialized in leather work. Following his acceptance of the Second Advent message, Millerism began to weaken from the effect of the Bitter Disappointment. Yate, however, continued firm in faith and became a circuit preacher. He accepted the teachings of the Kingdom in the Age to Come, as set forth by Joseph Marsh in T*he Advent Harbinger and Bible Advocate*.

Higgins preached for a while in New England, and then relocated to Wisconsin in 1851, a state he felt was ripe for the harvest. His chief mode of travel was walking, for which he used a staff. He visited churches in Indiana, Michigan and Illinois, traveling as far south in Illinois as Brown County, where two men by the names of Penkake and Sweet requested someone to "come and preach." These Mt. Sterling residents frequently wrote to Joseph Marsh and requested that Marsh send someone.

In 1857 Higgins reported in a letter to Marsh that he had been quite ill and feeble most of the year and a doctor out east provided a box of pills that helped immensely; Higgins was back on his feet hoping to travel and preach again.

While it cannot be confirmed, it is thought that Yate Higgin's illness caused his death shortly after his letter to Marsh for his name does not appear in the 1860 U. S. Census. It is known that is wife took in washings to feed the family of three children in his various absences, and after his death may have remarried.

See Marsh, Joseph
Penkake, George
Sweet, Alonzo

Bibliography: Ancestry.com U.S. Census. Massachusetts. Essex. Danvers. 1850; Ancestry.com. Wisconsin. Manitowoc. Buchanan. 1860; "Letter from Penkake and Sweet to Joseph Marsh," *The Advent Harbinger and Bible Advocate,* April 24, 1852; Higgins, Yate, "Letter to Joseph Marsh," *The Prophetic Expositor and Bible Advocate*, Jos. Marsh, editor, Rochester, NY, Oct. 15, 1857.

Hill, R. Judson
b. 1848?
d. Unknown

R.J. Hill was the son of Bezaleel J. Hill (April 2, 1798-August 21, 1872). There is disagreement in the record regarding the year the elder Hill moved his family to Iowa. It is thought that B.J. Hill moved his family there in 1864, but he stayed behind to work the old farm until it could be sold in 1868. R.J. probably worked the new farm. Father B.J. Hill is buried in the Pioneer Cemetery in Alden Township adjoining the Alden Cemetery.

When the Hills came to Iowa they found a fellowship of the Church of God persuasion already there. Joseph Furry had successfully preached the Gospel of the Kingdom in Alden since he and Sarah had arrived from Plymouth, Indiana. In fact, Joseph Furry was president of the Iowa Conference at that time. Before B.J. Hill's death, he occasionally preached at Alden.

When the Hill family finally settled in Iowa, they learned that the conference fellowship had employed Elder Thomas Smith as evangelist. Only scant information is available about Thomas Smith. It is known that he was active in serving the Lord, but no details are available and the only existing picture of him is poor quality. Later that fall, R.J. Hill was appointed evangelist. He was only 17 or 18 at the time.

In 1865, the Iowa conference held an annual meeting at Alden. Thomas G. Newman from Chicago was present as guest evangelist. Newman became editor of *The Millennial Harbinger* after Joseph Marsh relinquished it. Newman then moved the paper to Chicago and changed the name to *The Prophetic Watchman* with J.M. Stephenson as editor. R.J. Hill was appointed state evangelist at this meeting and was to report activities to the paper.

In his role as evangelist R.J. traveled and visited people in Horse's Grove (Rowan), Belmond, Liberty (Goldfield), Dows, Shellrock, Alden and Avon. R.J. Hill is also credited with helping churches already established at Colo and Parkersburg. He often worked with Thomas Smith at Rowan, Belmond and Goldfield in Wright County.

J.M. Stephenson was guest evangelist at a session of the Iowa conference in 1868. A committee was appointed at that time to secure an evangelist and raise the money to support the work for the following year. The work could not grow without the services of a traveling evangelist.

R.J. Hill was mentioned in a letter from Mrs. Amos Gilbert to one of the papers as being an early minister in the Church of God in Blythdale, Missouri. This indicates that he maintained a wide circuit throughout the Midwest.

President A. Hipsher of the Iowa conference announced a two-day winter conference to be held at West Irving, beginning on the evening of Christmas day and continuing through Sunday. That particular conference organization was allowed to lapse for a few years, but was renewed in 1888 possibly because of the organizational meeting of a general conference at Philadelphia that year. A.J. Eychaner, a delegate to that meeting, may have encouraged re-organization in Iowa.

See Furry, Joseph
Heckman, J.J. - regarding Thos. Smith
Palmer, Hannah "Libby"
Smith, Thomas
Stephenson, J.M.

Bibliography: Burnett, Francis et al history committee of the *Iowa Church of God and Conference, 1855-1987*; Belle Plaine Union "Letter by C.L. Furry to A.J. Eychaner" July 26, 1905, cited by Terry Ferrell in "History of Iowa Church of God" p. 9; "Letter by Libbie Palmer to Mrs. A.J. Eychaner." July 17, 1905. Terry Ferrell, *A Brief History of the Church of God in America*. National Berean Youth Conference, Camp Reynoldswood, Dixon, Il. 1960; Randall, Clyde *Historical Waymarks of the Church of God*, Church of God General Conference, Oregon, Il. 1976; Hipsher, A. "Conference announcement," *The Restitution*, H.V. Reed, editor, Plymouth, In., Dec. 9, 1874; *The Restitution Herald*, November 20, 1923; Rankin, Delbert. Information furnished from Iowa Church of God Archives, retrieved by e-mail July 6, 2008.

Hitchcock, Nelson A.
b. 1812
d. 1900?

Nelson A. Hitchcock was born in Vermont. He heard of the second coming of Christ through the ministry of the Millerite movement. When the hope of that movement diminished with the Bitter Disappointment, Hitchcock became aware of the teachings of Joseph Marsh through the pages of *The Christian Palladium* and *The Voice of Truth*, both edited by Marsh.

Hitchcock is first seen in the literature of Joseph Marsh as an evangelist for the Age to Come in New York and New England. Shortly after the Albany Conference in 1845, Hitchcock went to Wisconsin and worked among the people in that frontier territory. He traveled south into Illinois and west to Iowa on a circuit to introduce people to the Gospel of the Kingdom of God. He included the congregation at Twin Groves in Green County, Wisconsin, in his ministry circuit because he lived nearby.

Evangelists who worked with Elder Hitchcock or who knew him were J.M. Stephenson, D.P. Hall, Wm. Howells, B. Brown, Bro. Sears, H.V. Reed, Joseph Marsh, Mary and Samuel Chapman and Benjamin Wilson.

Hitchcock lived in Milwaukee as early as March 1847. He also reported to *The Voice of Truth* in June 1848 that he had been traveling by stage with D.P. Hall, who had shortly before been released from the grip of universalism into the Gospel truth. At an evening meeting just outside Milwaukee, Hitchcock gave Hall time to give his testimony of that release and his hope.

In 1850, Hitchcock sent a notice to *The Advent Harbinger* of an upcoming conference to be held at Tyler, Illinois, in Winnebago County on August 23. this indicates his interest in organizing the various fields of endeavor into a working conference. This makes clear his desire to unite the frontier work with that of Joseph Marsh and his readers because he invited them to the conference. During that time, Benjamin Wilson certainly would have known N.A. Hitchcock for he lived near Geneva, Illinois. This is important since they became leaders in spreading the Age-to-Come message throughout the Midwest.

In 1860 Hitchcock and his wife Matilda, sons Philo and William, and daughter Alvirus lived at Mt. Pleasant in Green County, Wisconsin. The census gives "minister of gospel" as his occupation. They moved at least two more times in Wisconsin before settling in central Illinois at the end of the 19th century. Hitchcock never owned any land, so evidently the land he farmed was rented, and therefore he was subject to moving every March 1.

No records of his death have been found, but he may have lived well into his nineties.

See Brown, B.
Chapman, Mary
Hall, David P.
Howells, Wm.
Marsh, Joseph
Reed, H.V.
Stephenson, J.M.
Wilson, Benjamin

Bibliography: Ancestry.com. U.S. Federal Census. Mt. Pleasant. Green 1860; "Hitchcock report to Joseph Marsh" *The Voice of Truth*, March 10, 1847; Hitchcock, N.A. "Call to Conference" *The Advent Harbinger*, July 6, 1850. Location of Twin Groves *The Prophetic Expositor and Bible Advocate*, Jos. Marsh, ed., Rochester, NY., Feb. 1, 1858.

Hoffner, Christian or Charles?
b. 1818
d. Unknown

Elder Hoffner was a member of the Church of God from Philadelphia. His first name may have been Christian or Charles. He relocated to Austin, Illinois, near Chicago and preached for the Church of God there. During the 1870s he agreed to preach on alternate Sundays with Thomas Wilson.

Clearly, the Church of God at Philadelphia was active and healthy in 1888 as that church was the leader of a successful attempt to organize a national general conference. The national work that began at Philadelphia continued until it was disbanded in 1892 due to lack of money and interest. It is not known how long the local Philadelphia church continued to meet.

See Ramsay, C.C.
Wilson, Thomas
Work, George

Bibliography: Graham, David. *Wisdom and Power*, Oct. 1992; Ledger of the Board of Directors of the Church of God General Conference Philadelphia, 1888. This ledger is housed at the Atlanta Bible College Archives and tells the story of the gradual demise of the new organization.

Hogarth, Annie
b. 1847
d. February 19, 1916

Annie Hogarth lived and died in the area of Fonthill, Ontario, Canada. She was 69 years of age when she expired in an old folks' home. Pastor F.L. Austin reported in her obituary, "She was one of the remaining members of the Church of God at Salina which flourished in the days of R.V. Lyon, noted evangelist to Canada West territory, and also J.M. Stephenson and Joseph Marsh." She presumably was the sister or cousin of Jabez Hogarth.

See Austin, F.L. (20th)
Hogarth, Jabez E.
Lyon, Ralph Vinton

Bibliography: *The Restitution Herald*, March 22, 1916.

Hogarth, Jabez D.
b. 1853
d. December 1, 1920

Jabez D. Hogarth, his father Daniel, and four of his brothers were pioneers in Ontario, Canada, east of Toronto, both in clearing the land and in proclaiming the Lord's coming. They built a chapel in Salina, Ontario, before Jabez was born, about 1852. He was J.E. Hogarth's cousin.

Jabez grew up in this church among pioneer preachers in the Church of God movement. The Salina Church stood as a "beacon in a superstitious neighborhood." Those pioneer preachers included O.R.L. Crozier, who published *The Day Dawn* in 1845; R.V. Lyon, who preached in the Canada West territory; J.M. Stephenson, who preached throughout the Midwest; Joseph Marsh, who popularized the Age-to-Come doctrine after the Bitter Disappointment; Thomas Newman, who preached and published *The Millennial Harbinger* after Joseph Marsh retired from it; and Joshua V. Himes, the noted public relations man of the Millerite movement. Others included Peter Hough, John Bower and James Evans.

Jabez was reared in the truth and read and supported Joseph Marsh's publications and *The Restitution* after Marsh's death.

See Crozier, O.R.L
Hogarth, Jabez E.
Hough, Peter
Huggins, Robert (20th)
Lyon, R.V.
Marsh, Joseph
Newman, Thomas
Stephenson, J.M.

Bibliography: *The Restitution*, January 25, 1921.

Hogarth, Jabez E.
b. 1855
d. 1922

Jabez E. Hogarth was a member of a Church of God in Cleveland. He formerly lived in Salina, Ontario, Canada, but moved south to be near his daughter. He was the father-in-law of Robert Huggins, editor of *The Restitution* and pastor of the Blessed Hope Church of God, 1911-1922.

In 1922 at age 77, J.E. Hogarth was struck by an automobile and killed. Shortly thereafter, Pastor Huggins resigned from the pulpit and from publishing *The Restitution*. He moved his family to Connecticut where he became pastor. It is thought that J.E. Hogarth's tragic death was not the sole reason for Huggin's departure, but it was the final blow at the end of a discouraging few years following the decline of the beloved *Restitution*.

A member of the church sent a note to *The Restitution Herald* of Hogarth's accident, stating that the driver was brought before the court on manslaughter charges. Jabez Hogarth died in St. Alexis Hospital and was buried at Salina, Ontario, in the little cemetery next to the Church of God. The membership of the Church of God throughout the nation found comfort in their faith when they heard the upsetting news of the accidental death.

See Hogarth, Jabez D.
   Huggins, Robert G. (20th)
Bibliography: *The Restitution* June 1922. *The Restitution Herald*, July 1922.

Hornaday, William T.
b. 1841
d. November 24, 1874

William Hornaday was a member of the Church of God and active in the meetings of the Indiana State Conference. He died suddenly at his home in Hartford, Indiana, from typhoid fever while still a young man. He left his wife, Rachel, with several children including a set of twins. D.T. Halstead conducted the funeral service and accompanied the family to Tipton, Indiana, for the burial.

Jonah Pierce, a dear and Christian friend, paid homage to William in a eulogy written a few weeks after the funeral. He said William was a husband, father and teacher of the good news. In his daily conversation with Christ, William showed great respect for God and the truth. He was the life of a meeting, a great example in overcoming evil and a good friend. William died so quickly people grieved for his death and because they were unable to comfort him during his illness.

Members of the Hornaday family moved west near Holbrook, Nebraska, and continued to serve the Lord through the Church of God in that state.
   See Halstead, D.T.
Bibliography: Ancestry.com. U.S. Census. Indiana. Tipton. Wildcat. 1870; Obituary, *The Restitution*, Dec. 9, 1874; Jan. 20, 1875.

Hough, Peter
b. 1810
d. Unknown

Peter Hough was an evangelist who assisted J.C. Bywater and Joseph Marsh in the upstate New York and Canada West (C.W.) tent ministry. He resided at Kingston, C.W. A notice sent to Marsh indicated that Hough and Bywater were able to schedule the tent tightly and move it frequently and fairly rapidly by train or steamboat. The notice announced a four-day meeting at Canandaigua, New York, and another eight-day meeting eight miles west of Niagara Falls on the John Shaver farm. One interesting point to note concerning these two meetings is that Peter Hough invited believers to "come in the name of Jesus, enjoying his spirit, and pray in the Holy Ghost." Then he added, "Sinners may also come. We want your precious souls saved from the wrath to come."

He asked for volunteers to meet him and Dillabaugh at the steamboat landing to assist with moving the tent. He said the next meeting at St. Catharine's would begin *immediately* after the last one closed. Transporting the tent and setting it up in new locations did not seem to present any serious problems or delays.
   See Bywater, J.C.
      Hogarth, Jabez D.
      Marsh, Joseph
Bibliography: Hough, Peter. "The Canada Tent" *The Advent Harbinger and Bible Advocate,* J. Marsh, ed. Aug. 30, 1851; Hough, Peter. "Letter to the Editor" *The Voice of Truth* J Marsh, ed., Nov. 19, 1845.

Houston (Huston), Edward
b. 1842
d. Unknown

Minister Houston is credited with beginning the Church of God Abrahamic Faith near Koszta, Iowa, in 1872. He and his family lived at Belle Plaine where they operated a grocery store. It is not known who first taught him about the Kingdom of God on Earth. Houston hailed from Ohio and may have been part of the Adventist movement in his youth.

Houston most likely knew Levi Marsh, who began the Church of God at Irving, Iowa. In fact, Marsh platted the layout of Irving and operated a mercantile business there. Irving is a few miles north of Belle Plaine.

Eli Cronbaugh's obituary stated Ed Houston was the first to preach the Word south of Belle Plaine. Mr. Cronbaugh left the Christian church to be immersed in the saving faith of the Gospel of the Kingdom. Eli's brother, Van Cronbaugh, was also baptized by Minister Houston.

Ed Houston preached first at the Dayton schoolhouse and later at the Koszta schoolhouse for ten years. Soon the growing congregation built a church. It stands to this day and is known as the Oak Lawn Church of God.

Ed Houston's history is found in the Belle Plaine Church of God Abrahamic Faith Archives.
   See Cronbaugh, Eli
      Marsh, Levi
Bibliography: Ancestry.com U.S. Census. Iowa. Benton. Belle Plaine. 1870. Kiger, Lanie Mabel. Friendly letter to unknown recipient which speaks of Edward Houston, May 18, 1942. This is part of the archives of Iowa Church of God Conference at Belle Plaine. It is part of the material donated to the archives by Terry Ferrell, Iowa historian.

Howard, Susan A.
b. 1853
d. September 23, 1925

Little is known about Susan Howard, but she was a great letter writer. The National Berean Society encouraged its members to write letters to isolated members and to the publications of the Church of God, *The Restitution* and *The Restitution Herald*.

While searching for information through the pages of those volumes one cannot help but notice letters from Susan Howard appearing in issue after issue. Once she wrote to S.J. Lindsay in *The Restitution Herald* asking someone to come to Canada to baptize her. It seemed that no preacher in the States was able to go. The editor asked T.A. Drinkard, a fiery preacher from Arkansas, to make the trip. Drinkard went. People raised money to pay for his round trip train ticket.

Susan Howard was a resident of Chinook Cove, British Columbia, truly an isolated member of the Church of God. In 1921, she was instrumental in organizing a card shower when Auntie Roxanna Wince turned 83 on February 10. In 1924, Susan wrote to *The Restitution Herald* to notify them she was having health problems.

Susan predeceased her husband, dying at home. She was buried in Mt. Olive Cemetery near Chinook Cove.

    See Drinkard, T.A.
         Lindsay, S.J.
Bibliography: *The Restitution*, Oct. 1925; Obituary *The Restitution Herald*, Oct. 6, 1924.

Howell, Benjamin Franklin
b. April, 1848
d. 1933?

Benjamin Howell was born on the Isle of Wight, United Kingdom, to Benjamin and Anne Cribb Howell. Benjamin and wife, Elisa S., came to America in 1869. They had seven children and were members of the first group in Springfield, Ohio, who preached Age to Come and One Faith. Benjamin was Superintendent of The Whitely Manufacturing Company in Springfield.

Benjamin's daughter, Mabel, married Charles L. Netts, and his other daughter, Carrie Maude, married George N.H. Peters who wrote the highly acclaimed three-volume set on prophecy, *The Theocratic Kingdom*. Peters was a Lutheran minister who certainly must have heard the sure word of the Age to Come from his wife and her family. Peters referred to the still-developing Church of God in his books as "The One Faith People," a name made popular by Benjamin Wilson of Geneva, Illinois. Peters wrote that the One Faith People had the best explanation for pre-millennial prophecy of any group that he knew.

Benjamin's legacy continued through his family from Mabel and Carrie, to granddaughter, Margaret Ballentine, and great-granddaughter, Sylvia (Don) Black, Springfield, Ohio.

    See Ballentine, Clark (20th)
         Netts, Charles L.
         Wilson, Benjamin
Bibliography: Ancestry.com U.S. Census. Ohio. Clark. Springfield Ward 6. Dist. 47. 1900; Peters, George *The Theocratic Kingdom*, 3 vols. Springfield, Ohio. 1891. Photo donated by Pastor Alan Cain, Lawrenceville, Oh.

Howell, L.M.
b. 1830
d. Unknown

L.M. Howell was mentioned briefly in *The Restitution* as being one who frequented the June Conference meeting at Antioch Church of God near Plymouth, Indiana.

L.M. Howell took pictures for his own collection. He may have been a printer from Kentucky at one time, who attended the "June meeting" as many did from the Church of God. The Archives reveal that Howell also worked in the Tuttle photo studio in Plymouth, Indiana. Tuttle and Howell took many pictures for the Church of God but little is known about them. Many of the Indiana photos in the Archives at Atlanta Bible College were the excellent work of Tuttle and Howell.

The evangelistic efforts of the Church of God advanced as much by means of the printing press and photography as by horse and buggy or train. The strength of the Church of God has always been its good printers, editors and publishers who made themselves available to proclaim the true Word of God in print.

While little is known about L.M. Howell, the name "Howell" shows up several times in Church of God literature. There are not enough facts to identify each individual Howell or how they might be interrelated. L.M. Howell may have been related to Benjamin F. Howell, of Springfield, Ohio.

    See Howell, Benjamin F.
         Howell, William W.
Bibliography: Ancestry.com. U.S. Census. Kentucky. Montgomery. Dist. 1. 1850; *The Restitution*, 59:25, July 6, 1910.

Howell, William W.
b. 1825
d. Unknown

W.W. Howell was a Welshman from New York. He preached in both Welsh and English. A contemporary of Joseph Marsh, he emerged from the Millerite movement. Soon after the Bitter Disappointment Howell moved to Rockford, Illinois, and began a pioneer ministry throughout the frontier states of Wisconsin, Illinois and Iowa. The Census lists his occupation as "joiner" or cabinetmaker. Rockford was a furniture manufacturing center for nearly a century. Little is known about Howell's ministry. His name appears in the literature, so it is evident that he was known to the editors and ministers of the Age-to-Come movement, and that they recognized his ministry.

H.V. Reed's reports mentioned him. Howell's name first appears in *The Gospel Banner* in 1867. He had organized a small congregation at Big Rock, Illinois, which he said was part of the congregation at Aurora. Thereafter, Howell sent several reports to Benjamin Wilson in *The Gospel Banner*. In an 1868 report Howell mentioned that some "gospel preachers" had passed among the brethren of Mt. Morris and Silver Creek, Illinois, and tried to cause divisions among them. Howell said the preachers expected to find "basswood men," meaning they would be soft and easy to "hew and shape as they pleased to suit their own notions." Instead they found men who "boldly defended the truth and soon silenced the little pop gun." The identity of the "little pop gun" is unknown.

Howell said in another report that he had traveled 200 miles, and had the privilege of preaching in several places about the Kingdom of God. He visited the Palmers in Lettsville, Iowa, and spoke there seven times, having good reception each time. At that time he had been absent from home for a month and planned to spend another four weeks in Iowa. Another report noted that in the winter of 1869-70, he had been preaching in Dade County, Missouri, where there was a congregation of 25.

See Hill, R.J.
   Marsh, Joseph
   Palmer, Libby
   Reed, H.V.
   Wilson, Benjamin

Bibliography: Ancestry.com. U.S. Census. Il. Winnebago. Rockford. 1850; Pierce, H.B. "Report of Twentieth Semi-Annual Conference", *The Gospel Banner*, Vol. 13, B. Wilson, ed. Geneva, Il. Aug. 1, 1867; Howell, Wm. "Letter to B. Wilson," *The Gospel Banner and Millennial Advocate*, April 8, 1868 and Nov. 15, 1868; Howell, Wm. "Report." *The Herald of the Coming Kingdom and Christian Instructor*, T. Wilson, ed., Chicago, Il., Jan. 1870.

Hoyt, Edward
b. 1810?
d. Unknown

Elder Edward Hoyt was a founding preacher of the work in Michigan. He was present at the organizational meeting of the Michigan State Conference in 1858. Hoyt had moved into the state from Indiana the previous year. Ephraim Miller, O.R.L. Crozier and Joel A. Simonds joined Hoyt in that first Michigan Conference. Elder Miller was elected president, Crozier vice president and Simonds treasurer. Hoyt became secretary of the conference. A.N. Seymour and Ephraim Miller were appointed evangelists.

The record indicates this organizing group asked the question voiced by O.R.L. Crozier, "Is it advisable for the churches and brethren in this State to try to unite in some common work for evangelical efforts?" Many comments favoring the proposition led them to appointment of committees to bring this effort into being.

Elder Hoyt served the churches in the Michigan conference the rest of his life by promoting the unifying work of the conference and bringing the truth to new believers. He authored a tract or pamphlet in 1890, "Discourse: Some things the Bible says and Some things it Does not Say." This item was in the library collection of Maurice Joblin, a founding pastor of the Cleveland work, and is now part of the Atlanta Bible College Archives.

See Crozier, O.R.L.
   Joblin, Maurice
   Miller, Ephraim
   Simonds, Joel

Bibliography: Minutes of Michigan State Conference 1858-1920 located in Archives of Atlanta Bible College, McDonough, Ga.; Hoyt, Ed, "Report of relocation to Michigan," *The Millennial Harbinger and Bible Expositor*, Thomas Newman, editor, Seneca Falls, NY, July 15, 1857.

Hudler, David (Daniel?) Maynard
b. August 5, 1837
d. October 30, 1909

David M. Hudler was born in Newbern, Craven County, North Carolina, to Lemuel and Mary Anna (Debruhie) Hudler. He was one of 12 children. David's sister, Mary Ann, married Dr. Palmer, who began the Palmer Chiropractic College in Davenport, Iowa, and Portland, Oregon.

It is not known how David first heard of the Gospel of the Kingdom, but Newell Bond of Cleveland and Elder Enoch Anderson were prominent Church of God evangelists in that region. By the time David moved to Fredonia, Iowa, in 1861, where he met and married Christina T. Riggs-Hudler, he sought to serve the Lord. In Fredonia, they attended a Methodist church where David regularly preached. David and Christina raised eight children. By occupation, he was an insurance salesman.

Hudler reported later that he preached in that same Methodist church in 1906 where people hungered for the Word. He said that year he also preached at Hopguard, North Carolina, where he had previously preached in 1898 or 1899. He reported expecting to preach throughout the South through the summer and longer if his health allowed it, but the climate was adverse to his health and he could not remain.

By the late 1890s, Hudler preached throughout the Midwest to spread the Gospel of the Kingdom. This fact was reported to *The Restitution*. When the Illinois Conference officially organized at Plum River in 1898, David Hudler was hired to be the evangelist of the newly organized conference. He served in that position at least one year and very likely for several years. He preached throughout Tennessee, Kentucky, Missouri, Iowa and at Cashmere, Washington, during the remaining years of his pastoral career.

The Siple family at Happy Woods, Louisiana, knew D.M. Hudler when they all lived and worked together in the Iowa Conference. After Siples moved to Louisiana they arranged for various evangelists to visit them. This was especially important after the death of W.H. Wilson who had begun the Louisiana work. They called upon Elder Hudler to assist them with the work at Pine Woods Bible Class.

The current Iowa conference published a history book featuring information about Hudler. He was licensed to preach by the Iowa Conference in 1896. In the 1900 US Federal Census, his occupation is given as "Clergyman." He was still in active duty, yet no mention is made of him receiving an Iowa license again until 1904. At that time there was no national organization to license ministers for the Church of God, but a man or woman in the Church of God could be licensed to preach either by the local church or by the state conference. A license may have been good for two to four years if the minister remained in good standing.

The minutes of the Ripley (Illinois) Church of God show that David Hudler made regular visits to that congregation, laying the groundwork for many other Church of God ministers. In June 1900, he baptized three women at Ripley. Conference reports and obituaries indicate that David Hudler baptized many. For example, Hudler baptized Ethel Capps Stinman, a young woman in Tennessee. Later, after being married only three years, Mrs. Stinman died suddenly. This was one of the saddest obituaries to be reported to *The Restitution*. It is believed he visited Ripley more regularly after the 1888 death of J.M. Stephenson, Ripley's resident minister.

Elder Hudler escaped the limelight in the Church of God because he did not write for either *The Restitution* or *The Restitution Herald*, nor did he write any books. Yet, he had a powerful and influential ministry. It is known that he worked primarily in the southern Midwest from 1890 to 1909. Fragments of his evangelistic career can be traced because his name is mentioned in the minutes of church and conference meetings. One brother, perhaps a Hudler relative, stated in a letter to *The Restitution* that he had been steeped in the writings of Robert Ingersoll and was not thinking about sin. D.M. Hudler taught him about the Gospel and lifted him to life in Christ. He then burned "Bob's" books.

Martyr's Death?

Another sister wrote that D.M. Hudler had been with them in February for a week. The meetings were held in the schoolhouse and he received great opposition from sectarians and Seventh-day worshippers "who pitched battle on him." Hudler had no trouble defending his position and some apologized to him. She said, "I am not able to express myself on paper but perhaps I have added a mite which will count in the world to come." There was no signature except "A sister in Christ." The letter revealed a clue that may indicate not only how he died, but who brought about his death.

Pastor Harry Goekler, a Church of God pastor whose family roots came from the Casey (Illinois) Church of God, said that it was widely known among his grandfather Claypool's generation that D.M. Hudler's death was due to mob attack while he was preaching in Tennessee. While he was not murdered outright, his injuries caused him to die of gastritis or gangrene. The story, which to date cannot be verified, said that David died at the Elizabeth Sanitarium in Harriman, Tennessee, a few days after being severely beaten. He was 72 years old. His body was shipped to Muscatine, Iowa, where he was interred at Greenwood Cemetery and rests beside his wife among the peonies.

O.J. Allard wrote Elder Hudler's obituary and said, "He died with the armor on and the sword of the Spirit in his hand. He died in active work for the Master at Harriman, Tennessee, as he was holding a series of meetings."

The story of David Hudler's life and death impressed the writers and producers of the Church of God Internet radio broadcast, Cogcast.org. Mark DeYoung wrote a script to depict Hudler's final days. It was produced as a radio play by the Cogcast Theater at the 2010 History Conference at North Hills Church of God, Springfield, Ohio, and was streamed live over Cogcast.org. The play is moving and suitable for production by youth groups for special services.

See   Allard, O.J.
         Goekler, Harry (20th)
See Also   Appendix 3–Catalyst for Change: Matyrdom
Bibliography: Ancestry.com. U.S. Census. Iowa. Muscatine. Muscatine. Dist. 103. 1900; Ancestry.com. Iowa State Census 1895 Record for David M. Hudler; Ancestry.com. Iowa Cemetery Records, record for David M. Hudler at Greenwood Cemetery, Muscatine, Ia.; Interview with Harry Goekler by Jan Stilson in the early 1990s; Hudler, James, Arkansas, "Modified Register for Lemuel Hudler" genealogy furnished by Delbert Rankin, March 30, 2010; "Early Records-1900s Ripley Church of God, Ripley, Il." Original records reside at Ripley Church of God; Rankin, Delbert. *History of the Church of God in Iowa*, published by the History Committee 1987; *The Restitution*, April 18, 1894; March 28, 1906; *The Restitution Herald* March 19, 1919; "Testimony of George Siple," *The Restitution Herald*, Sydney Magaw, editor, Oregon, Illinois. January 6, 1948. Rootsweb, www.rootsweb.ancestry.com/~iamusca2 for D.M. Hudler interment. This was called to our attention courtesy of Delbert Rankin; Grave Monument Photo Credit. Delbert Rankin, Summer, 2010 at Greenwood Cemetery, Muscatine, Iowa; "Obituary of David Hudler," *Muscatine Journal*, Nov. 1, 1909, 7; State Historical Society of Iowa Site Inventory of Thomas Binnie House which mentions "Daniel M. Hudler as owner from 1891 to 1909 retrieved from http://www.musserpubliclibrary.org/MusserPublicLibrary/files/b5/b52ad050-f6c3-4743-ab1e-716d21acec4a.pdf on Nov. 20, 2010. [Note: It is thought the name "Daniel" was used by mistake, but the record is accurate with other names and reflects that Anna, as widow, was owner in 1910, a year after David Hudler's death. Clyde Randall in *Waymarks* called him David Hudler.]

Huffer, Andrew
b. October 17, 1845
d. 1922

Andrew Huffer was an early member of the Church of God in central Indiana. He was married twice. His first wife was Martha Fuer. They had nine children. Later he married Mrs. Cripe and two more sons were born. He was a veteran of the Civil War serving in Company I of the 151st Indiana Volunteers.

He became a member of the Church of God in the 1880's in Clinton County, Indiana. He died in 1922 at age 78.

Bibliography: *The Restitution Herald,* May 1922.

Huffer, Otto
b. June 24, 1895
d. July 17, 1931

Otto was the son of Andrew and Mary Huffer. He was born in Kirklin, Indiana. The family attended the Church of God at Hillisburg, Indiana. He married Bessie Finney in 1916, and they had six children. He died suddenly leaving a large family of children including half-brothers and -sisters.

See   Huffer, Alva (20th)
Bibliography: John Anderson, "Obituary", *The Restitution Herald*, G.E. Marsh, editor, Oregon, Il. July 28, 1931.

Humphreys, Richard Alexander
b. 1854
d. August 15, 1935

Richard A. Humphreys was the son of John and Martha Muncrief Humphreys. Richard grew up in Mississippi and taught himself to read from a small New Testament when he was 15 years old. He was baptized at 17 by a Methodist preacher and later by a Campbellite preacher. At age 23, J.R. Ham from Donaldson, Arkansas, came to town and preached the message of the Kingdom of God. Minister Ham resided in the Humphreys household during the 1860s. When J.R. Ham shared the message with the Humphreys family in Mississippi, it was the first they had heard about the Kingdom of God on earth. Richard asked Elder Ham, "What church preaches that?" "Church of God," was the reply. Richard was re-baptized. They had to cut through the winter ice to conduct the baptism, but Richard went home with a healthy conscience.

After he left the Humphreys home, J.R. Ham traveled a few miles west to the home of Martha's father, Dr. Muncrief, and studied the Bible with him. Muncrief later moved to Arkansas and was said to be the first Church of God evangelist in that state. In 1883, Ham wrote a letter to the editor of *The Restitution* "Does one need to be re-baptized into the Gospel of the Kingdom?" Benjamin Wilson answered the question affirmatively for both the condition of having been baptized previously into some other faith and if the baptismal candidate had never been baptized before.

Richard and Stephen William Humphreys' father, John, had fought in the Civil War as a private in the Confederate army. He was captured and sent to the military prison at the abandoned penitentiary near Alton, Illinois, where he died. Disease so ravaged this prison camp that infected prisoners were quarantined on an island in the Mississippi River. This island may have taken the name "Goat Island" as mentioned in a Humphreys' document.

The Humphreys brothers, Richard and Stephen, were young when their father died. They were raised by their mother who "sang and prayed for peace and worked hard to raise us," said Richard. In a testimony about his conversion, he tenderly quoted, "Would God I had died for thee," from 2 Samuel 18:33. Stephen Humphreys died at age 58 in 1922. He had been an Arkansas Legislator.

Richard exhibited tenderness and affection through the pages of *The Restitution* when writing about his family, but he also had a fiery nature. Whenever he could, Richard denounced the teachings of Charles Taze Russell, who began the Bible Students in 1872, later known as the Watch Tower.

Richard Humphreys spoke well of D.C. Robison, a leader in the Cleveland, Ohio, Church of God, who believed in partial resurrection, i.e. limited resurrection. This teaching said the wicked would die the Adamic death and never live again. It is not thought that Richard Humphreys believed this, but D.C. Robison was such a friendly personality that many people loved him in spite of his assertions.

Richard traveled extensively throughout Arkansas, Tennessee and Missouri, preaching the Kingdom and baptizing wherever he went. He held meetings at Fredericktown, Missouri, as well as Blush Church of God. His contact for those meetings was W.S. Cooper, stepson of Blush's founder, Elder Joshua Bailey. Records indicate that Richard traveled to Hammond, Louisiana, to preach at Pine Woods Bible Class during Christmas where, due to the season, he had very small turnouts, but he succeeded in baptizing four new converts.

His family reported that Richard attended the 1888 Philadelphia General Conference. William H. Wilson listed Richard with other Arkansas ministers in a report to *The Restitution* in 1904.

See Bailey, Joshua
Muncrief, Dr. James L.
Robison, D.C.
Wilson, Benjamin
Wilson, W.H.

Bibliography: Ancestry.com. U.S. Federal Census. Mississippi. DeSoto. 1860; U.S. Census. Arkansas. Yell. Crawford. Dist. 223. 1880; Ancestry.com Arkansas Death Index 1914-1950 record of Richard Humphreys; Bregninge, Poul. *Judgment Can Wait,* unpublished manuscript in English, forthcoming in 2011, regarding the formation of the Russellites and the Watch Tower; Graham, David. "Letter from R.A. Humphrey's daughter" *Wisdom & Power,* Feb. 1993; Report of W.H. Wilson *The Restitution,* Jan. 20, 1904; *The Restitution,* Dec. 25, 1895; Nov. 1919; Jan. 6, 1992; June 22, 1922; May 1925; *The Restitution Herald,* Nov. 4, 1919; Kraft, Ginnie Humphreys, Interview with author Sept. 2008; Wilson, Benjamin. "Question on Baptism." *The Restitution,* S.A. Chaplin, editor, Plymouth, Indiana. Oct. 10, 1883; McCaslin, Ruby. Letter to Jan Stilson sometime during 2009 with information about Muncrief and Humphrey family genealogy. See also the website for the Alton prison: http://www.censusdiggins.com/prison_alton.html.

There are no biographical entries for this letter.

Jacobs, Dr. Samuel J.
b. 1809
d. Unknown

Dr. Jacobs was a pioneer who traversed the northern Illinois wilderness in the 1840s. There were few roads in those days, only animal trails or Indian paths. Travelers often broke their own trails through the thick prairie grasses. Dr. Jacobs desired to teach settlers about the Kingdom of God. When he baptized a new believer, he directed him into membership in the Church of One Faith (what is now Church of God). The fact that the local churches at Oregon and Adeline were known as Church of One Faith tells researchers that they were securely in the camp of Benjamin Wilson and not with Dr. Thomas. It can be seen from their respective literature that Thomas used the phrase "One Truth," and Wilson, "One Faith."

Dr. Jacobs lived in Maryland Township, Ogle County, in or near the small village of Adeline. He was a physician and often traveled bad roads to visit his patients. He married Elizabeth who bore him two children, Henry and Lucinda.

Dr. Jacobs participated in the meetings and fellowship of the Church of One Faith in Illinois. *The History of Iowa Church of God and Conference 1855-1987* mentions him as influencing A.J. Eychaner, also from Ogle County, and says they met each other for the first time at the 1862 Crane's Grove conference in Illinois.

It is understood that Dr. Jacobs was successful in advancing the Kingdom of God, and laying a sure foundation for the work in Northern Illinois from his local travels and his willing nature to talk about his faith. His life's work demonstrates how the work of one dedicated physician in obedience to the Great Physician changed the lives of many people for generations after his demise.

See Andrew, William N. (20th)
Eychaner, A.J.
Knodle, Martha Wagner

Bibliography: Ancestry.com. U.S. Census. Illinois. Ogle. Maryland. 1860; Ancestry.com U.S. Census. Illinois. Ogle. Maryland. 1870; Burnett, Francis et al history committee, *The History of Iowa Church of God and Conference 1855-1987*, printed at Belle Plaine Union, 1987; *The Restitution,* Nov. 2, 1920.

Jeffrey, Peter
b. March 25, 1887
d. Unknown

In 1910, Peter Jeffrey was head of household in a family that included George and Nancy, his father and mother. Peter remained single into middle age, and after he married and had children and grandchildren, he and his wife raised their granddaughter, Miss Ethel Jeffrey, for unknown reasons. Peter may have been related to the Jeffrey family that owned Jeffrey Manufacturing Company in the coal mining country of southern Ohio and West Virginia. This company purchased the rights to and began using the first underground machine that undercut the coal.

The family resided in West Virginia, but after the death of his father, Peter and his mother moved to Murphysboro, Illinois. Murphysboro is west of Carbondale and south of St. Louis. Peter's work included farming, preaching and coalmining at Herron, Illinois. In fact, in the coal industry he held a service certificate indicating he had managed a mine for five years which produced more than 1800 tons of coal a month and had at least 150 employees. There were several other Jeffrey families in the area, but it is not known if they owned the coalmining operation or if they worked there. Peter was tall and lean and sported sideburns. He was financially conservative.

Peter may have learned of the Kingdom of God in West Virginia from traveling evangelists C.C. Ramsey or J.W. Niles. After moving to Illinois, Jeffrey would have

Back row, left to right: Peter Jeffrey, Lyman Booth, LS Bronson, Martin Aslaksen, JM Glotfelty. Front: unknown, Thomas Wilson.

met and studied with W.H. Wilson, who frequently went through Illinois on his southern evangelistic travels.

Peter Jeffrey was a good Bible student and loved searching for truth. He was loyal to the Church of God. Peter participated in the Illinois Conference, which met annually for a few years at Adeline, Lanark and Oregon, Illinois. Churches took turns hosting the quarterly conferences, sometimes meeting at Antioch, Dixon, Casey or Marshall. Peter led classes, preached and held office, all capably and eagerly. He served for many years on the Illinois Conference Board of Directors. He received his ministerial certificate from that board in 1913.

As a supporter of W.H. Wilson's work, Peter hosted meetings when Wilson was in town. As host, Peter retrieved Wilson from the train and held meetings in his home for a few nights. This was a frequent routine for isolated members across the Great Plains as the Word went west. In 1911, W.H. Wilson made his way south into Missouri, Oklahoma, Texas and finally to Louisiana, his winter home. Wilson and Jeffrey often spent several days in Bible study and conversation. When he left, both men were inspired and renewed to carry on the work.

Peter attended the noisy and rambunctious 1910 Waterloo, Iowa, summer conference. This conference, while turbulent, was necessary in order to identify two important elements: 1) *What were the doctrines necessary for salvation?* and 2) *Who believed in them, and who believed in tangential doctrines?* This conference was probably the best thing that could have happened within the Church of God at that time. It defined the denomination by its unique statement of faith. It also defined organizational goals by allowing those who wished to organize a national general conference to do so with assurance that the brotherhood supported the move without fearing that it would collapse.

Peter Jeffrey was the Illinois delegate at the 1910 meeting, and at the meeting, he was assigned to raise funds for future expenses in forming a general conference. He was appointed to the Board of the General Conference in 1910, which was to continue meeting in an effort to successfully motivate the membership to organize a national work. Fitting to his interests, he was made treasurer of the general conference board and served on newly formed Restitution Publishing Company's board, which began to publish *The Restitution Herald* in 1911.

After Elder Jeffrey returned home from the 1910 conference, he received a letter that L.E. Conner and some fellow ministers had formed a Ministerial Association. Peter immediately agreed to support the new organization. His actions indicate that he endorsed the formation of a national general conference; he believed in general resurrection and not limited resurrection; he did not identify with any of the suspicious doctrines that some people investigated such as Anglo-Israelism, larger hope, Sabbath keeping, and universal salvation; and he agreed that a new direction was needed in regard to the editorial policy of *The Restitution*, the "Voice of the Church of God," at that time.

In 1920, Peter turned the $20 treasury over to the committee assigned to study the organizational effort. While that sum might not seem like a significant amount, it very likely paid for the postage and all the carbon copies used by F.L. Austin to conduct the correspondence of the Committee of Ten from 1920-1921.

In 1920, Peter Jeffrey and his wife visited Scotland, the homeland of his ancestors. Curiously, at the 1921 Waterloo Conference, where the General Conference was born, Peter presented his ideas to the delegates about the "flat-earth" theory, but they did not take him seriously.

See Conner, L.E.
Niles, J.W.
Willey, J.H.
Wilson, W.H.

Bibliography: Ancestry.com. U.S. Census. WV. Ritchie. Clay. Dist. 68. 1910 and 1920; *Annual Coal Report of Illinois,* No. 34. State Mining Board, Springfield, Il., 1914/15 Record for John Jeffreys, Murphysboro retrieved from Google Books, Jan. 17, 2011, Also, *Annual Coal Report,* No. 35, 1916; Ledger of Minutes. Illinois Conference of the Churches of God. 1898-1915, Archives of the Atlanta Bible College, McDonough, Ga.; *The Restitution*, March 22, 1911; May 5, 1911; *The Restitution Herald,* May 4, 1920; Hatch, P., Austin, E.A. "Impressions and History of the Church of God," 1975; E. Jeffrey: oregonpioneers.com/family/EdwardLeoFoehr_G6.htm, retrieved Jan. 17, 2011.

Joblin, Maurice
b. 1832
d. October 4, 1907

Maurice Joblin was born in the Isle of Wight, England, and made his way to America as an adult. He learned of the second coming of Christ while living at

Seneca Falls, New York. His initial contact may have been Thomas Newman who edited *The Millennial Harbinger and Bible Expositor* at Seneca Falls. J.B. Cook baptized Maurice in 1860, and along with Thomas Newman dedicated Maurice to the ministry in Seneca Falls.

In 1862, Joblin moved to Cleveland and began to hold meetings in the Temperance Hall; meetings continued there for seven years. Newell Bond, a local merchant, and Robert McLauchlan, a large Scotsman formerly of Presbyterian background, joined in the effort.

In 1873, Joblin's work as a printer took him to Cincinnati where he helped print a book of photography: *Cincinnati, Past and Present.* When the book was finished, Joblin moved to Murphreesboro, Tennessee, where he engaged in farming and continued to preach. He returned to Cleveland sometime before 1888, and was elected elder and evangelist by the congregation.

Construction of the Blessed Hope church building at East 40th Street on Woodland Avenue in Cleveland was completed in 1888 and dedicated November 11, 1888. Robert McLauchlan financed this building. The congregation incorporated as The Church of the Blessed Hope because Ohio government officials would not allow the name "Church of God." They said all churches were churches of God. Joblin served as pastor.

Robert McLauchlan, one of the founding members and world-renowned Bible scholar and author, left the fellowship in 1894 when he and Joblin disagreed. McLauchlan provided a trust fund for the new congregation and church building at East 105th Street at the corner of Columbus Avenue. J.N. Shourds was pastor at the new Church of God in 1900 until L.E. Conner arrived. L.E. Conner became the pastor of the new congregation in 1906 and stayed until 1929.

After the split, Joblin's congregation sought a strong pastor for two years and finally found Robert Huggins, who was single at the time. Huggins began working in Cleveland in 1908. In 1911 he became editor of *The Restitution* and continued until 1921.

The new building constructed by Joblin's congregation was sold in 1917 and became a Jewish Community Hall. Joblin's group then purchased a lot on Garfield Boulevard in the Southeast section of Cleveland but no church was built; the undeveloped lot was sold in 1948. A church was purchased on Lee Avenue and West 125th Street. This building was sold in 1927. Clearly, the congregation never hesitated to pick up and move if the situation demanded it. The members recognized that the body of Christ is not identified with one single church building.

It is speculated that either of the Cleveland congregations could easily have formed the first Church of God general conference because they were strong and powerful, had wealth, published the highly esteemed *Restitution* and were centrally located among all the local Churches of God. However, the conflicts in doctrine and personalities prevented that outcome, and so the center of the work moved west to Chicago.

Maurice Joblin made the acquaintance of A.H. Zilmer of Wisconsin. Zilmer had been a pastor in an orthodox denomination but had come out of that background into the Church of God. Eventually, Joblin baptized Zilmer in Cleveland, the immersion occurring December 12, 1897. A.H. Zilmer subsequently preached for the Church of God across the Midwest only a few years before leaving it to embrace his interests in the Christadelphian fellowship in 1906.

Maurice Joblin was a prodigious writer. He wrote sermons in longhand in 3" x 4" booklets. It was said that to compensate for being so short, he sat on a high stool to preach. He read the sermons, but delivered them so well, no one could tell he was reading. The collection of Joblin sermons is owned by the Atlanta Bible College Archives, having been received and catalogued into the collection at Oregon Bible College in the mid-1980s. They were donated by Mrs. Ruth Tomlinson Hall Overholser, a child in the Golden Rule Church of God (McLauchlan split-off) and a member of long-standing within the Church of God in Ohio.

In 1905, Maurice was still writing and preaching at the Church of the Blessed Hope on Woodland, the original church in Cleveland. He authored a tract in German entitled "What Must I do to be Saved?" It is unknown if it was well received among the German community then or if any copies of this tract exist today.

Maurice Joblin also authored Bible studies for *The Restitution* before his death in 1907. Thereafter, his works were published posthumously for nearly as long as *The Restitution* continued to publish. He authored *Scripture Searcher's Assistant*, a study booklet that was reprinted by *The Restitution Herald* in 1945.

L.E. Conner served in the younger church until 1929 when G.E. Marsh came for a year. Melville Lyon served as pastor at Diane Avenue from the 1930 until 1943; Grover Gordon, a Nebraska native, succeeded him. In 1941, the Golden Rule Church of God was reinvigorated from the remnants of McLauchlan's congregation. Curiously, at that time many members transferred to Golden Rule from the old Blessed Hope Church of God. G.E. Marsh returned from 1948 until 1955. C.F. Pryor, a southern pastor from North Carolina, followed him. Pastor Pryor served until

1964 when Ernest Graham arrived. He served until 1967; his successors were J.R LeCrone, J. Arlen Marsh and David Cheatwood.

While Evangelist Joblin did not intend there be two congregations in Cleveland when he began the work in the 1860s, two were born. After Robert Huggins left Cleveland, the Blessed Hope church had no pastor for two years. Finally, the group called a Christadelphian leader, W.H. Brown. When Brown resigned a few years later, Robert Huggins was again available and returned to Cleveland. He retired in 1955 about the same time that C.F. Pryor came to Golden Rule. Alan Greif was called to pastor the Church of the Blessed Hope from within their own membership.

The churches in Cleveland were vigorous and feisty due to dialogue on doctrine. Joblin believed in limited resurrection, something controversial within the Church of God. In his pamphlet, "Partial Resurrection, and Antidote to Larger Hope," John R. Fiske identified Joblin with this doctrine.

After Robert Huggins left Cleveland, the new congregation pastored by L.E. Conner appealed to the Church of the Blessed Hope for reconciliation. This was during Brown's tenure. In an open letter, Brown abruptly stopped the effort. The elders of the older congregation returned a letter that said they could not reunite because the newer group held two errant doctrines: open communion and universal resurrection.

Communion, they believed, should reflect only members who have been immersed into the belief of the Gospel of the Kingdom. The emblems should not be offered to any other persons outside that local congregation. Their worship service was described by Harry Stadden as beginning with a discourse led by an elder after which members joined at the communion table. The gathering for communion was called "second meeting" where members partook from one chalice, sang a song and departed without a word more.

Universal resurrection, W.H. Brown wrote, was unscriptural. Quoting from Brown's "Open Letter" to the younger congregation:

> The writer of Hebrews places resurrection among the principles of the doctrine of Christ *and in the foundation* (Heb. 6: 1, 2). Now since the character, safety and security of the Building depends upon the soundness of the foundation, surely anything that affects the foundation must be of vital importance. *This is well illustrated by considering what the theory of Universal Resurrection leads to. It is the starting point...to the distinctive heresy of this generation. Universalism.*
>
> It begins with universal resurrection, then, having adopted the theory that all are raised, the mind naturally theorizes on what to do with them, and we have introduced the unscriptural theory of future probation or Russellism which has found its way into the church. It is only a step from Russellism to universal salvation, and many who held the Truth in its purity and simplicity are now out and out Universalists. They have carried the idea of Universal Resurrection to its logical conclusion. We hold it (universal resurrection) as being the entering wedge for the destruction of the Faith.

For additional explanation of the doctrinal confusion caused within the Church of God because of the misunderstanding on both sides about universal resurrection, read the entries for Benjamin Wilson and L.E. Conner.

Today, several Church of God congregations exist in the Cleveland area. Those churches descending through Maurice Joblin meet at Unionville and Salem. In addition, within the general fellowship of The Church of the Blessed Hope, their incorporated name, are the Churches of God at Roll, Indiana; Perryville, Kentucky; and Miami, Florida. The Church of God descending from Robert McLauchlan's congregation in Cleveland no longer meets at the Golden Rule Church of God on Strawberry Lane in Willoughby. The building was sold a few years ago due to decline in the neighborhood.

In 1959, members who lived southeast of Cleveland formed the Bedford congregation. The Bedford Church of God celebrated its 50th Anniversary in September 2009, and is the only congregation in Cleveland affiliated with the Church of God General Conference, McDonough, Georgia. Pastor Rex Cain pastored the Bedford church twice during his career and retired there in 2011. Another congregation coming out of the Golden Rule Church of God was formed in the western suburb of Columbia Station in 1963. Columbia Station has since closed its doors and sold the church building to another group.

See Allen, Mark
    Bond, Newell
    Brown, W.H.
    Conner, L.E.
    Cook, J.B.
    Fiske, John R.
    Huggins, Robert (20th)
    Lyon, Melville (20th)
    McLauchlan, Robert
    Marsh, G.E. (20th)
    Newman, Thomas
    Shourds, Jessie N.
    Wilson, Benjamin

Bibliography: Brown, W.H. "An Open Letter, September 8, 1927 to the congregation of the Parkwood Church of God"; Graham, David. *Wisdom and Power* Sept. 1992; Hearp, Jack. "Memories of Growing up in the Golden Rule Church at Cleveland: Its History." Presentation at the 2d Annual History Conference at North Hills Church of God at Springfield, Ohio, Nov. 6, 7, 2007; Landry. J. *Cincinnati, Past and Present.* 1873. This book of photographs of the American West was highly acclaimed. *The Restitution.* Nov. 1, 1905.

Jones, Abner
b. 1772
d. 1841

Abner Jones co-founded a small New England group called Christian Connection (also spelled Connexion). These congregations were called "Christ-yans." The other co-founder was Elias Smith. Smith believed in conditional immortality and preached an Age-to-Come view of prophecy, including a tenet that the Jews would return to the homeland before the return of Christ, but Abner Jones did not believe all of that. In 1808, Smith began *The Herald of Gospel Liberty*, the first religious newspaper published in America which discussed these ideas and also shared news.

It was to *The Herald* that Stedman A. Chaplin contributed his letters, poems and devotionals. Chaplin later settled in Indiana and became a vibrant force in the growth and development of the work there.

Eventually, Joseph Marsh, former editor of *The Christian Palladium*, left the Christian Connection and began preaching and publishing the second coming. From Marsh's association with Jones and Smith, the Church of God began to take root in America.

Most men who began their pursuit of truth began like Abner Jones, not seeing all the truth at once, but seeing *something* of it and, being led by good mentors, eventually saw the rest.

See Chaplin, Stedman A.
Marsh, Joseph
Smith, Elias

Bibliography: *The Restitution*. December 9, 1908.

Jones, Robert
b. May, 1872
d. December 1, 1949

Robert Jones was a Church of God preacher from Conway, Arkansas, who preached to the congregation at Driggs. William H. Wilson listed Elder Jones among the Arkansas preachers in one of his reports. Robert was a farmer and known as "Bob" to his family and friends.

Nothing more is known of him, but his willingness to serve contributed to the stability of the work in Arkansas.

Bibliography: Ancestry.com: U.S. Census. Arkansas. Conway. Union. Dist. 11. 1900; Arkansas Death Index 1914-1950, Report of Robert A. Jones; Wilson, W.H., "Report" *The Restitution* Jan. 20, 1904.

Jones, Wiley
b. October 18, 1835
d. December 7, 1898

Wiley Jones was the son of William Wiley and Ann E. Hudgins Jones of Richmond, Virginia. He was the middle child with an older sister and younger brother. His family lived first at Richmond, but they moved to Norfolk during his youth. The family then moved to Illinois, but returned later to Virginia.

Wiley was raised in a Christian family and immersed at age 16. Wiley's obituary said it would be hard to determine when he embraced the faith for he loved the Scriptures, "and strove to shape his life by that model." His father believed in the Age to Come and wrote an article, "The Heavens Above the Skies" for *The Advent Harbinger* in March 1851. In this article, William Jones espoused the teaching of conditional immortality, resurrection and the second coming of Christ to establish his kingdom.

When Wiley was grown he married Roxanna Harding from Virginia, who was two years his junior, and they lived in Norfolk. Records are sketchy, but it appears they had two daughters and both died in childhood. From that point on, the couple devoted themselves to Bible study and their retail shop. Wiley owned and managed a bookshop in Norfolk. He also sold shoes there. It is not known if he owned one shop and sold many things or if he owned a series of shops.

Wiley was an author of several works that Bible students consider important. He authored *Evangelism Concerning the Reign of Christ Over Israel and the Nations*, while in Norfolk, Virginia, and *Meditations on the Parables*. *The Restitution* in Chicago published both books, the former in 1872 and the latter in 1874. This seems unusual since *The Restitution* office burned in the Chicago fire of 1871 and was relocated to Plymouth soon thereafter. The books, however, were probably printed on the new presses at the Lakeside building in Chicago at which H.V. Reed worked.

Jones also corresponded with Benjamin Wilson through the pages of *The Gospel Banner and Millennial Harbinger*. One letter to Benjamin Wilson in *The Gospel Banner* featured the topic of pre-existence of Christ. Jones seemed to be in favor of it, yet he cautioned readers that Bible writers did not always understand what they were being taught. He quoted, "the secret things belong unto the Lord our God" (Deuteronomy 29:29), and he cited Job, a man "perfect and upright" who confessed he had uttered things "he did not understand" which were "too wonderful for him" (Job 42:3, 6). Then Wiley Jones concluded, "I am yet constrained to say, that, in my humble judgment, it seems very unscriptural to deny either directly or by implication, 'the pre-existence of Christ'."

He stated in *The Advent Harbinger*:
And when Jesus the Christ, vanquished death in himself, he thus brought to light how life and immortality shall be obtained by the Gospel. He is the first fruit; his saints will rise when he comes in his kingdom. They are now in their graves, not gone to heaven, for they had no immortal souls, and if they never rise, they all perish.

This latter phrase is the strongest evidence seen to date that Wiley Jones was acquainted with the teachings of Dr. John Thomas. The latter statement, "they all perish" coincides with the Thomas teaching of limited resurrection, that the wicked dead do not rise again to judgment. Their judgment is the Adamic death.

Jones regularly corresponded with Thomas Wilson in *The Herald of the Coming Kingdom and Christian Instructor* in 1870. In that year, Jones wrote an article for *The Herald* entitled, "The King of the Jews." Wiley Jones also wrote numerous tracts such as "Who are led by the Spirit" and "The Past and Future Kingdom of God." In 1883 he wrote an article for *The Restitution* entitled, "Speaking and Hearing," which had six main points. An information box accompanying this entry identifies the six points of Wiley Jones' speaking tips.

Regarding his system of interpretation of prophecy, Jones classed himself in *The Restitution* as a prophetic-historicist. He referred to the Mosaic dispensation as defining that. By this he meant that the majority of prophecy has been fulfilled historically but the 70th week of Daniel is still in the future.

Jones authored *The Gospel of the Kingdom of God*. This book became well known through the pages of *The Advent Harbinger* and later in the pages of *The Restitution*, which continued even after his death. The book was registered with the Library of Congress in 1879 and may have enjoyed several printings, for it was still being offered for sale through the pages of *The Restitution* in 1910. It was a compilation of ten sermons, which Jones had preached, with embellishments for publication. The work was highly quoted. Advent Christian authors I.C. Wellcome and C. Goud quoted it in their book, *The Plan of Redemption*, and G.E. Marsh quoted it often in *The Restitution Herald* while he edited it during the 1930s. Minister A.J. Eychaner of Iowa valued this book so much that he gave a copy to everyone he baptized.

Wiley wrote a book or booklet on the topic of *The Great Commission, Or, the Original and Only True Gospel, as Preached by our Lord and His Apostles, a short and plain view*. This work was published as a series in *The Gospel Banner* of 1869.

In a short, beautiful article written from Norfolk for *The Gospel Banner*, Wiley Jones testified of the covenants of God and how wonderful they are. He began with:

'The First Verse of the New Testament.' What a volume of thought and heart-warming meditation is suggested by this verse! With sublime and hieroglyphic brevity far surpassing the most laboriously composed human aphorism, this divinely inspired writing is a gold mine of Gospel doctrine.

He then discussed the plan of redemption in light of the Abrahamic and Davidic covenants, and the impetus the covenants give us to carry out the Great Commission. He also discussed Christ's lineage as evidenced from Matthew 1:1, "The book of the genealogy of Jesus Christ, the son of David, the son of Abraham."

Jones also wrote a small treatise, *Key Words*. It was published in serial form in *The Restitution* from Plymouth, Indiana, beginning in 1883. He described it as an "Englishman's Hebrew and Greek Concordance to certain words which throw important light on great doctrines." It was published as a book in 1891. It is an excellent handbook, including discussion of terms such as repentance, baptism, sprinkling, church, soul, spirit, act of dying, death state, immortality, paradise, Kingdom of God and more. Clyde Randall, author of *Historical Waymarks of the Church of God*, said, "It is a scholarly work, and those who possess such copies should preserve them with affectionate care."

Wiley Jones on Preaching

In "Speaking and Hearing," published in the *The Restitution* in 1883, Wiley Jones taught the readers several key points about speaking and listening. He said speaking should exhibit these characteristics:

1. We should speak to please God
2. We should speak to save ourselves and our hearers.
3. We should speak faithfully
4. We should speak the same doctrine which Jesus spoke
5. We should avoid human doctrines [heresies]
6. We should speak plainly and boldly.

Ref: *The Restitution*, Plymouth, Indiana, January 3, 1883

Other works authored by Wiley Jones include *The Past and Future Kingdom of God*, *The Restitution*, Plymouth, 1890; *Evangelism Concerning the Reign of Christ over Israel and the Nations*, *The Restitution*, Chicago, 1872.

Arlen Rankin published an anthology, *The Ancient and True Gospel: Select Writings of Wiley Jones*, not long before this encyclopedia was produced. Copies of the anthology are in the Archives of Atlanta Bible College.

Jones wrote many tracts and books in addition to those listed here. Recently, Arlen Rankin secured copies of two Wiley Jones' books never before seen in the Church of God and furnished copies for the Archives:

- *Songs of Zion*, published by Jones in 1877, a songbook of 101 songs.
- *Thanatopsis: A Scriptural View of the First and Second Death*, published by Jones in 1881.

In 1890, Elder Wiley Jones visited the Church of God at Salem, Ohio, for special meetings and stayed three months to preach and pastor the flock. During his time at Salem, two more members joined the church.

In his later years, Jones suffered with rheumatism. It slowed him down, but he didn't let the pain stop him. He kept an appointment to preach at Burkeville, Virginia, on December 4, despite inclement weather, knowing exposure would be difficult on him. He told his wife, "I must work 'til I die!" After arriving home, his sufferings increased and he died suddenly of "rheumatism of the heart."

Wiley Jones preached Bible doctrines that were near and dear to Church of God hearts. He believed the Gospel of the Kingdom, and he knew how to research and publish books in order to promote the gospel. He was a good missionary of the Word, and his works live on today.

A.R. Underwood, who wrote Jones' obituary for *The Restitution* said:

> Our earliest recollections go back to the time when his name was a household word at my father's home. We learned to respect him, and later when years brought us acquaintance with him by correspondence and through his works, we grew to love the man who was so earnest and fearless in his defense of the truth. Now he is dead [and] has gone the way of all mankind, but the world and the household of faith have been benefited by his life. Verily, 'his works do follow him.'

Clyde Randall, quoting Longfellow, said, "'When a great man dies, for years the light he leaves behind him, lies on the paths of men.' The light which Wiley Jones left still shines."

Many of Jones' writings are available in the Archives of the Atlanta Bible College in McDonough, Georgia.

See Marsh, Joseph
  Underwood, A.R.
  Wilson, Benjamin
  Wilson, Thomas

Bibliography: Ancestry.com various U.S. Census in Virginia and Illinois 1870-1900; Graham, David. "Of Jesus Concerning His True Nature" *History Newsletter* Church of God General Conference Jan Stilson, ed. Morrow, Ga. Feb/Mar 1993. Graham cites several writers in the Age-to-Come movement on the subject of Christ's nature, including Wiley Jones on the pre-existence; Jones, Wiley, *Evangelism Concerning the Reign of Christ The Restitution.* Chicago. 1872; Jones, Wiley "The First Verse of the New Testament" *Gospel Banner and Millennial Advocate,* March 15, 1869; Jones, Wiley. "The King of the Jews" *The Herald of the Coming Kingdom and Christian Instructor* January 1870. 179; Jones, Wiley, "The Great Commission", as published in the *Gospel Banner*, B. Wilson, editor, Geneva, Il. April 15, 1869 145, and May 1, 1869, 167; Jones, Wiley, "Speaking and Hearing" *The Restitution* S.A. Chaplin, ed. Plymouth, Indiana January 24, 1883; Randall, Clyde. "The Gospel of the Kingdom" *The Restitution Herald* Jan. 13, 1942; Rankin, Arlen. "Wiley Jones "*Church of God History Online Newsletter* Kent Ross, editor. Vol. 2006 No.9: 7,8; Jones, William Wiley, "The Heavens Above the Skies," *The Advent Harbinger and Bible Advocate* Jos. Marsh, ed. Rochester, NY, March 29, 1851; *The Restitution* Jan. 1870; Sept. 29, 1920; June 27, 1921; Underwood, "Obituary of Wiley Jones" *The Restitution* Feb. 8, 1899 furnished for this article by Arlen F. Rankin by e-mail Sept. 17, 2006; *The Church of God of the Abrahamic Faith Salem, Ohio, Dedication Service*, "History Section," June 28, 1970. This booklet was furnished by Franklyne Ross; For further reading on Wiley Jones, see Rankin, A.F. *The Ancient and True Gospel* a compilation of writings by Wiley Jones, Bible Faith Ministries, Wenatchee, Wa. 2009.

K

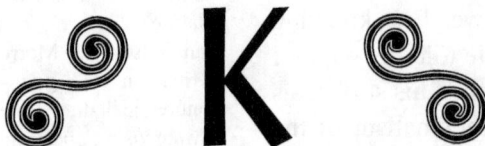

Kendall, Dr. H.R.
b. 1830
d. Unknown

H.R. Kendall was born in Indiana and married Lorinda F. Thompson (January 24, 1852-January 24, 1894) in Portage County, Ohio, on June 28, 1876. They had one son and one daughter. Kendall was a physician and a member of the Christian church in 1876, but he began working with the Age-to-Come movement in Indiana and Michigan, possibly because of the Thompsons' witness in Indiana.

In 1877, Kendall participated in the 19th annual meeting of the Michigan Conference, and was well received by the people. He accepted the teachings of the Bible as presented at this conference, and he preached there on the prophecies of Christ. The conference delegates engaged him as an evangelist in Michigan for that summer. Because of his short acquaintance with the fellowship, the conference secretary noted in the minutes that Dr. Kendall was "comparatively a stranger here."

Kendall lived at Galesburg, Kalamazoo County. He was described as: "a live, energetic defender of the truth [who] never fails to awaken an interest wherever he preaches." The members of the conference were encouraged to make a place in their vicinity for him to preach.

The Kendall family relocated to Belmont, Kansas, in Rooks County where Dr. Kendall established a new medical practice. His brother, F. Kendall, a dentist, resided with the family. Lorinda died on her birthday at age 42. Her death was reported to *The Restitution*.

Bibliography: Ancestry.com. Kansas State Census Collection 1825-1925, Record for L.F. Kendall; Minutes of Michigan Conference of Church of God 1858-1915 owned by the Archives of Atlanta Bible College; Williams, Byron. *Abstracts of Obituaries and Verbatim Marriage Announcements printed in The Restitution, 1874-1900*, self published. 1993, Record for Lorinda F. Kendall, p 55.

Kennedy, J.R.
b. 1810?
d. Unknown

The honorable J.R. Kennedy and his wife established the Asylum for the Deaf and Dumb in downtown Olathe, Kansas. They held the offices of Steward and Matron there. Their temperaments were perfect for working in that noble cause as they were broadly philanthropic, intelligent and compassionate. Mr. and Mrs. Kennedy accepted the new message of the Gospel of the Kingdom, and they were baptized along with eight other adults by J.K. Speer in 1868.

The school was renamed the Kansas School for the Deaf and exists to this day. It is the largest in the state for educating deaf students.

Bibliography: Speer, J.K. "Taking out a People for His Name in Kansas" *The Gospel Banner and Millennial Advocate*, Benjamin Wilson, editor. Jan. 15, 1868; Wikipedia.com Entry for Kansas School of the Deaf, retrieved Dec. 20, 2010.

Knapp, Edgar W.
b. July 23, 1843
d. August 11, 1923

Edgar W. Knapp was born in New York to William H. and Eliza Knapp. The family moved to Michigan when Edgar was a teenager; in 1863, he was baptized there by an elder of the Church of God. In Edgar's testimony years later, he reported that he had been a faithful reader of *The Restitution* since it began in 1852. Edgar Knapp could not have read *The Restitution* in 1852; it was not yet being published. However, he could have read *The Advent Harbinger* (1847-1854), which was published during his childhood and featured a children's column.

Like many others in the Church of God, Edgar Knapp moved west and became active in the ministry through the work of the Northwest Conference, which included churches in the states of Oregon and Washington. He lived in Scholls, Oregon, and served as conference treasurer there. His name appeared numerous times in the pages of *The Restitution* during that era.

At Elder Knapp's death, his obituary writer described his faithful service and explained that his widow, Flora, had no source of income. A call went forth for financial assistance. This method of benevolence was practiced many times through the pages of *The Restitution* as people reached out to help one another.

See Chaplin, S.A.
  Newman, Thomas
  Reed, H.V.
  Wilson, Benjamin
  Wilson, Thomas

Bibliography: Ancestry.com U.S. Census. Michigan. Kalamazoo. Charleston. 1860. *The Restitution,* Aug. 8, 1909; Aug. 23, 1909; *The Restitution Herald,* August 23, 1923. For more information on the succession of Age-to-Come periodicals during the 19th and 20th centuries, see the Appendix.

A Brief History of Church of God Publications

When Joseph Marsh ceased publishing *The Harbinger*, he began a new paper and changed the name to *The Prophetic Expositor and Bible Advocate,* 1854-August 13, 1860. This was followed by *The Bible Expositor* in 1860 only. Marsh started *The Millennial Harbinger and Bible Expositor* 1860-1864, and sold it to Thomas Newman in 1862. Newman moved this title and its press to Chicago and changed the name to *The Prophetic Watchman.* In 1868 it was absorbed by *The Herald of the Coming Kingdom and Christian Instructor*, Thomas Wilson, editor. *The Restitution,* under the editorship of Thomas Wilson, began in 1870 after it absorbed *The Herald* and Benjamin Wilson's *Gospel Banner.*

The Chicago publications used the Marsh mailing list providing a continuous publishing history of Church of God titles to American and English readers for nearly 80 years. After the Great Chicago Fire of 1871, during which many past volumes of *The Herald of the Coming Kingdom* and *Gospel Banner* were lost, *The Restitution* moved to Plymouth, Indiana, and was published from 1872 to 1874 by H.V. Reed with S.A. Chaplin as assistant editor. It ceased publishing in Cleveland in 1925. The history of publishing in the Church of God is interesting and complex.

For more on this topic, see Appendix 13.

Knodle, Martha J. Wagner
b. May 2, 1839
d. April 21, 1920

Martha J. Wagner was reared on the prairies of Rockvale Township in Ogle County, Illinois. At age 18

she met a local veterinarian, Dr. William Swingley, who talked to her about the Kingdom of God. The good doctor was courting Martha's sister, Mary Wagner Swingley. Martha was immersed in a near-by stream, possibly Mosquito Creek. After that time she may have resided temporarily with William and Mary, until her wedding on November 16, 1865, to William Knodle (pronounced K-nodel). Mr. Knodle had just returned from the Civil War where he had served in the 74th I.V. Infantry. He was wounded at the battle of Adairsville in Georgia when a bullet passed through both legs, leaving him disabled.

Martha and William had six children. Two may have died in childhood. Her home in Oregon was always open to guests. Often they were ministers and delegates attending conference meetings at the Oregon Church of God. People loved visiting her at home.

In 1900, Martha was one of the founding members of the Church of God on North Third Street in Oregon, Illinois. Ketts' *History of Ogle County* states that William and Martha were members of the "Church of One Faith" at Oregon. This nomenclature for the church name was typically used in the 19th century by the faithful who followed the teachings of Benjamin Wilson through his publication, *The Gospel Banner.*

Martha contributed generously to her beloved church, making it possible to purchase the old stone church that had been vacated by the Catholic congregation on North Third Street. She furnished cash and took a mortgage of $600 to pay the remainder of the purchase price. Either Martha or her daughter, Mina Knodle, executor of Martha's estate, was the probable donor of funds to renovate the two-story building at 110 North Third Street. Purchase funds were donated by Emmy Harris of Rensselaer, Indiana. The new building became the print shop and classroom of the newly formed General Conference organization in 1921.

See Austin, F.L. (20th)
  Swingley, William
  Wilson, Benjamin

Bibliography: Ancestry.com. U.S. Census. Illinois. Ogle. Rockvale. 1860; Andrew, Wm. Interview with Jan Stilson, May 2007; Ketts. *History of Ogle County,* 1878 p 758; *The Restitution,* Nov. 2, 1920; *The Restitution Herald,* Oct. 21, 1921; War of the Rebellion retrieved from: http://digital.library.cornell.edu/m/moawar/waro.html.

Kramer, George R.
b. 1830?
d. Unknown

George R. Kramer was pastor at the Brooklyn, New York, Church of God. His name is mentioned several times by Stedman A. Chaplin, editor of *The Restitution*, as a recognized pastor of the late 19th century. In February 1889, Chaplin wrote, "Bro. Kramer is eminently qualified for the work to which he has consecrated himself—the gospel ministry."

Pastor Kramer conducted the funeral service for John B. Cook's wife in early May 1885, and in 1888 for evangelist John B. Cook as well. Elder Cook was a lifelong servant with a somewhat unstable and unpredictable nature. He and his wife had been missionaries to Siam (Thailand) in the 1830s. When they returned to New England the Millerite movement was at its height. Elder Cook had been Joseph Marsh's colleague at the Rochester Church of God, but Cook left the Church of God at least once to pursue spiritualism, and after returning to the Age to Come fellowship colluded with his friend, Horace L. Hastings, against Joseph Marsh. Despite these aberrations in his Christian service, Cook was evidently a member in good standing with the Church of God at the time of his death.

The ministry of Pastor Kramer became known through the obituaries of the Cooks, and other notices printed in *The Restitution* in 1888. A pastor's history of service is often preserved through church members' reports. These reports are important to historians tracing a pastor's ministry; often the report of just one family is the only primary source.

There were at least six George Kramer's residing in Brooklyn during Pastor Kramer's life, making it nearly impossible to positively determine a date of birth or death for this well-respected pastor. Presumption is that he was born around 1830 in Germany and came to America around 1850, at the height of the fervor over the Second Advent.

George Kramer wrote an article in *The Bible Banner*, a Seventh-day Church of God periodical (Stanberry, Missouri) on the subject of communion. This sermon was exchanged and reprinted in journals, making its way into *The Restitution* on May 27, 1888.

A few months after Cook's funeral, George Kramer placed a notice in *The Restitution* that he would be available "to preach for any churches who may need my services" and said, "I have been a pastor for seven years, and the work has not been unfruitful. I thank the people for their kindness." It is not known if he had resigned his Brooklyn charge, or if he wished to do evangelistic preaching during the summer.

See Cook, J.B.
Marsh, Joseph

Bibliography: Ancestry.com. New York. Kings. Brooklyn Ward 16; Dist. 278. 1900; Nickels, Richard, *History of the Seventh-day Church of God*, "Independent Church of God Splits—1905," Chapter VII, 1977, Giving and Sharing retrieved from http://www.friendsofsabbath.org/Further_Research/History%20of%20the%20Sabbatarian%20Movement/historysdcog/index.html. This source mentioned *The Bible Banner*; "Obituary Mrs. J.B. Cook," *The Restitution*, May 13, 1885; Kramer, George R. "Communion" *The Restitution*, May 27, 1888; "To the Readers of *The Restitution*" Feb. 27, 1889.

Krogh, Birdie
b. October 27, 1888
d. August 15, 1938

Birdie Krogh was born into a Church of God family. Her father, Herman Mehrens, was baptized in 1860 by W.P. Shockey. Herman and his family were active in the Church of God until his death in 1911. Elder Almus Adams preached his funeral.

Birdie was the youngest of eight children born to Herman and Josephine Mehrens. Birdie was a strong believer in the Church of God's distinctive message, and she was responsible for the conversion of her husband Harvey U. Krogh Sr. (born December 30, 1885), and his father, Carl O. Krogh.

Harvey and Birdie had five children whom they raised to be faithful and dedicated Christians. The Kroghs helped establish the Blair, Nebraska, Church of God and were active in its service. Harvey was treasurer and deacon. Birdie was secretary of the congregation. Her reports of church and conference activities were published in *The Restitution* and *The Restitution Herald*.

Church of God Blair, Nebraska

The Kroghs were close to Almus Adams who often stayed with them while holding evangelistic meetings in Blair. They hosted other visiting preachers as well. Blair was a new congregation blessed with action-oriented members. They built a new church in 1925, which was the site for many revivals by visiting evangelists. In addition to Almus Adams, other evangelists visited the Krogh household, including F.L. Austin of Oregon, Illinois, and John Hammond who lived near Avery, Nebraska.

Birdie also reported the activities of the Sunday School at Kennard. In the summer of 1921, Kennard hosted a picnic attended by many brethren from around the state and even as far away as Iowa. A collection was taken after the meal was finished, and someone went to town to buy ten gallons of ice cream. Later, after the sweet dessert soothed everyone, several ministers including John Hammond gave devotional talks.

Birdie reported to *The Restitution Herald* in November 1925, that several women gathered for an all-day meeting at the church building. Sr. Fannie LeCrone came from a distance. A lunch of coffee, sandwiches and cake was served. Birdie remarked, "all went home feeling thankful we were privileged to meet together and talk over the work that is being done. It gives us incentive to try to push on and do more."

Her husband, Harvey U. Krogh Sr., was born in Deerfield, Wisconsin, several miles from Kroghville, which had been founded by his grandfather who came from Norway. David Krogh wrote, "at one time the village was a thriving town, but when the railroad passed through a neighboring town it went down hill, and today is an unincorporated village."

Birdie's brother, George Washington Mehrens, married a member of the Johns family, descendants of whom are known among 21st century Church of God members: Arnold Johns, a Church of God pastor; Russell Johns, a General Conference Board Member; Janice Johns Haberer; and Ruby of Greenbrier, Arkansas. Arnold and Janice attended Oregon Bible College. Arnold's daughter, Eileen, is a member at East Oregon Church of God.

Members of Harvey and Birdie's family who have served Jesus faithfully in the Church of God include their son, pastor Harvey U. Krogh Jr.; Harvey's wife, Mary Krogh, a volunteer proofreader at the General Conference until the day before her death in 2006. Krogh children, David and Rachel (Carr), continue, at this writing, to be active servants of the General Conference, both serving on home and foreign mission fields, particularly Mexico, Peru and Bolivia.

See Austin, F.L. (20th)
Hammond, John
Johns, Arnold (20th)
Krogh, Carl O.

Krogh, Harvey U., Jr. (20th)

Bibliography: Birdie, Krogh, Various Reports, *The Restitution;* Krogh, David, E-mail to Jan Stilson, Feb. 16, 2006; *The Restitution Herald,* June 1921; March 21, 1922; Nov. 10, 1925.

Krogh, Carl Otto
b. October 11, 1850
d. April 8, 1931

Krogh, Casper
b. 1820
d. 1883

Carl Krogh

Carl Krogh was born to Casper and Catherine Krogh in Kroghville, Dane County, Wisconsin. He married Clara C. Johnson on January 10, 1873. They had four children, Harvey, Raymond, Edwin and Everett. One-year-old Edwin died in 1896 at Newman Grove. Everett died December 31, 1924, at age 26.

Casper Krogh was born around 1820 to Casper Hermann von Krogh (1764-1866) in Krogpl, Osfoldt, Norway. The younger Casper emigrated from Norway and founded Kroghville, Wisconsin, in 1848. He bought 227 acres near Koshkonong Creek, erected a dam and built a sawmill. Casper was Lutheran, and he believed religious freedom was a right. He helped establish several congregations. On religious holidays such as Sunday, Holy Thursday and Good Friday all factories in Kroghville were closed. Casper's faith served as a good example to his descendants many of whom have been faithful members in the Church of God.

Casper Krogh

When Casper demonstrated an invention to the government, he became acquainted with Ulysses S. Grant. Casper developed an arm prosthesis which was well received by returning Civil War veterans. It was made of wax and covered in rubber and so well designed the hand could hold a pen. While Casper perfected the prosthesis during the Civil War, two of his sons, Bernhard and Peter Gustav, joined the Union effort. A third son, Albert, ran off to join when he was only 15.

Casper wrote U.S. Grant and asked him to locate Albert. Grant found him and assigned Albert to be his orderly, thereby protecting the young man. When the war ended, Grant visited Casper at Kroghville. Later, Casper

Krogh home in Kroghville, Wisconsin

visited President Grant at the White House. In 1865, Casper began manufacturing the artificial limb in his factory, which was later managed by Albert Krogh.

Casper also invented a waterpower system for his mill; it generated power by the movement of horizontal wheels rotating on a flat plane, a unique design. Casper also opened a textile mill that also used his waterpower system. His laboratory and machine shop facilitated invention of more products. He operated a Patent Cultivator and other farm equipment in Kroghville and became known throughout the area for his mechanical abilities with iron and steel. John Deere, the inventor of the steel plow, turned to Casper for help with a piece of iron that needed a special lathe. Deere operated a blacksmith shop in Grand Detour, Illinois, where he invented the steel plow that opened the black soil of Illinois prairies.

Both mechanically adept and prolifically inventive, Casper developed many useful products; he had patents on so many items, they cannot all be named here. His mechanical and scientific aptitude passed to subsequent Krogh generations, including Harvey U. Krogh Jr., a watchmaker.

Casper's son, Carl, and his wife, Clara, moved to Blair, Nebraska, in 1878. In time, Carl's brothers left Wisconsin, too. By 1882, Kroghville was in serious decline, and after Casper's death a year later, the US Post Office closed.

In Nebraska, Carl worked in Omaha but returned later to Blair. He worked in the mercantile business in Newman Center and later in Oakland. In 1899, he purchased a farm south of Blair and resided there. He engaged in the hardware business from 1902-1906 moving to Omaha in 1907, where he operated a grocery store. In time, he retired to Blair.

On November 15, 1910, Carl suffered a crippling fall which left him confined to a wheelchair the remainder of his life, just over 20 years. He was never free from pain, but he was a patient sufferer. He turned his thoughts to helping others and tried not to be a burden to anyone.

After the death of his wife on October 11, 1911, Carl and his son, Everett, shared the family home. After Everett died, Carl divided his time between the homes of his two sons, Harvey and Raymond. Carl joined the Church of God in 1916 partly from the influence of his daughter-in-law, Birdie. Elder Almus Adams immersed him.

Carl died at Harvey's home in April 1931. He was survived by two sons and their wives, nine grandchildren, one sister, Caspara Lund of Glendale, California, and a host of nephews and nieces. F.L. Austin conducted the funeral service.

See Adams, Almus
    Austin, F.L. (20th)
    Krogh, Birdie
    Krogh, Harvey U., Jr. (20th)
    Krogh, Harvey U., Sr. (20th)

Bibliography: Krogh family for the Atlanta Bible College Biography Project, David Krogh, compiler; Obituary, *The Restitution Herald*, G.E. Marsh, editor, Oregon, Il. April 28, 1931; Kroghville was in Dane County originally, but county lines may have changed as that village is now in Jefferson County; Carr, Rachel. "The Story of Alfred and U.S. Grant," donated via e-mail October 15, 2010; O'Conner, Pat. "The Historic Minute featuring Kroghville" WFAW and WKCH, March 24, 2008, retrieved on Nov. 5, 2010 from web http://www.hoardmuseum.org/generator/assets/newsletters/2008_spring.pdf; Spencer, Jeffrey. "Historical Account of Casper Krogh" excerpted from *The Cambridge News* no date. Used with permission.

Lapp, Lucy Jane Steadman
b. September 16, 1872
d. August 26, 1949

Lapp, Daniel
b. Unknown
d. 1917

Lucy Steadman grew up in the Church of God. She married Daniel Lapp in 1896, and they farmed in Moorefield, Nebraska. Of their seven children, three died in infancy. The surviving children were Paul, Clarence E. (C.E.), Ida and Charles. Due to drought, the Lapp family moved to Sunnyside, Washington, in April 1912. Their Nebraska farm was in the middle of the Dust Bowl.

Mrs. C.E. (Louise) Lapp recalled the story of the Lapp family's travel across the prairie and over the mountains in a covered wagon. At the time of the relocation, Clarence Lapp was five years old. After Daniel died in 1917, Lucy never remarried; she raised her children alone.

After moving to Washington, Mrs. Lapp became an isolated Church of God member. Nevertheless, she was devoted to teaching her children the promises about eternal life. She attended regional conferences when she could, and in between, her family attended the Brethren church. Daniel had been a member of that fellowship. Some Church of God members criticized those who attended other churches as that influence could dilute the message of the kingdom and lead their children away from the Church of God.

When the Lapps were able to worship with members of the One Faith it was generally with Martha McClelland, Sister Argent and Sister Sullivan. Daniel Lapp would rent a building for Almus Adams, and the women spread the word about special meetings. On one special occasion, they attended conference in Felida so that the Lapp children could be baptized. Charles, Ida and Clarence were baptized at the Felida conference meeting on June 14, 1919.

According to C.E. Lapp, the Lapp farm outside of Moorefield, Nebraska, was never occupied again after

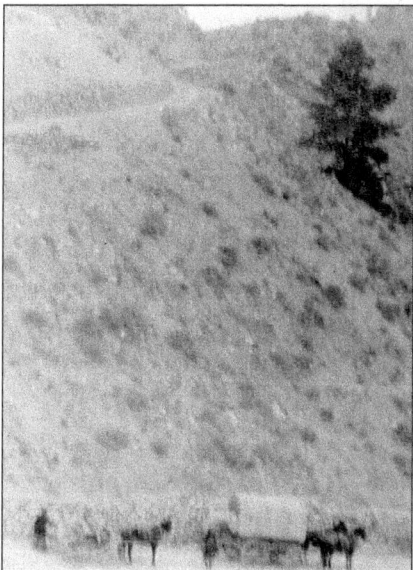

The Lapps left Nebraska and the Dust Bowl by covered wagon, heading west. Enroute to Washington they traversed Blewett Pass (above) and ascended Knapp Hill (left).

the family abandoned it. In 1961, the Gospelettes trio of Oregon Bible College toured the United States with the Lapps, and together they visited the old homestead. The farmhouse stood stark against a still-dusty landscape. When Clarence pushed open the squeaky kitchen door of his childhood home, it was a walk back in time. Everything was faded but still intact. There was no color; all was dusty and gray, lifeless after 50 years of abandonment until visitors stepped through the door.

Clarence conducted a tour of the old house. The kitchen never had running water, but a rusty pump stood in the yard, neglected and overgrown by sage brush. A stuffed chair sat in the parlor where torn lace curtains swayed in the afternoon breeze gusting through a broken

A typical prairie home abandoned during the Dust Bowl.

window. Old postcards still graced the top of a parlor table. A kerosene lamp sat on another table with oil still in it. It had the appearance of an ill-kept home, but still a home simply neglected for several decades.

This little house, while simple, was elegant compared to Lucy's childhood home near Moorefield. According to *The Restitution Herald*, when Lucy was 13, the Steadmans lived in a sod house, with a brush roof and dirt floor.

Lucy became bedfast in 1948. When she died, her surviving children brought her home to Moorefield for burial. She rests not far from the old homestead.

See Adams, Almus
    Lapp, C.E. (20th)
    McClelland, Martha

Bibliography: *The Restitution*, A.R. Underwood, ed., Plymouth, In., p 6, April 22, 1913; July 15, 1913; May 18, 1920. *The Restitution Herald*, S.J. Lindsay, ed., Oregon, Illinois, July 30, 1919. Obituary, *The Restitution Herald*, Sydney Magaw, ed., Oregon, Illinois, June 6, 1949; Stilson, J., Gospelettes Tour, Summer 1961.

Lawrence, Mrs.
Leasley, Mrs.
Fugate, Mrs.

Three sisters by birth, they lived in Raymore, Missouri, near Kansas City and faithfully assisted evangelist Almus Adams in his circuit ministry. They were born in the 19th century, but neither their birth dates nor their first names are known. They are included here for their inspirational testimony.

Almus Adams reported that he first met them at a meeting at Elder "Si" Herrin's house in Kansas City. They learned of the truth at this first meeting and were baptized then. On Adam's next trip through, he stopped to visit Mrs. Lawrence, and stayed there a few nights. Mrs. Leasley called their sister, Mrs. Fugate, who came from another town along with more friends and relatives. Adams held meetings at the Lawrence house several days. Adams said of these women, "It would be hard to find three more earnest workers than these." Desiring that her family come to know the Lord, Mrs. Lawrence rented a hall since the local community church was unavailable to her. This nucleus of women may have been the beginning of the present work at Peculiar, Missouri.

See Adams, Almus
    Herrin, S.I.

Bibliography: *The Restitution,* July 4, 1920.

LeCrone, Fannie
b. 1876
d. Unknown

Fannie was married to John LeCrone, and they lived near Helena, Oklahoma, and Kennard, Nebraska. Her father, G.R. Stewart, was a believer who lived at Kennard. He died August 26, 1925. Fannie fellowshipped with members of the Nebraska Church of God and eventually her descendants settled near Blair, Nebraska.

At Kennard evangelists Almus Adams and T.A. Drinkard visited the LeCrones regularly. The LeCrone family is mentioned frequently in Adams' reports to *The Restitution*.

Fannie and her family eventually left Kennard and became isolated members. Fannie reported in *The Restitution*, "I hadn't heard a sermon in years." When time availed, John and Fannie took a three-month trip in their Ford auto, a welcome respite from five years of hard work. They visited church friends throughout Missouri and Arkansas and found some members who had gone back to their old denominations and others with indifferent attitudes. This troubled Fannie greatly. She wrote to *The Restitution* asking for members who would become involved in the work. Would someone pray; would someone write a letter to an isolated member; would someone go visit a friend or say a cheery word to someone in need? She admonished, "Be faithful, be ready."

Fannie conducted a ministry with her pen. She wrote letters to members, the ill, and to any prospect. Evangelist Almus Adams commended her letter-writing service. He said she was not idle as her pen encouraged many weary people. He said, "I believe this system of writing is doing more good than we think. Letters are the responses of one true soul to another. It was God's way of having the New Testament written."

In 1930, Fannie finally attended a General Conference and met people she had read about in *The Restitution* and *The Restitution Herald*. While there, she heard numerous sermons and also met some people who had exchanged letters with her. She found the experience very uplifting.

Fannie and John were the grandparents of Richard LeCrone and Lucille LeCrone Appleby. Both attended the Bible Training School at Oregon, Illinois, in 1930-31 and became Church of God ministers.

    See Adams, Almus
           Boyer, Lucille Appleby (20th)
           Drinkard, T.A. (20th)
           LeCrone, Richard (20th)

Bibliography: *The Restitution,* Jan. 1920 and June 21, 1921; *The Restitution Herald.* Sept. 25, 1925 and July 28, 1931.

Lehman, Henry L.
    b. October 1, 1829
    d. January 21, 1902

Henry Lehman was born in Lancaster County, Pennsylvania, to Daniel and Elizabeth Lehman. Lancaster County is famous for its Amish culture. Henry moved to West Milton, Ohio, in June 1852 at age 22. In June 1854, he married Catharine Kellar (August 17, 1834-November 21, 1901.) They had seven children, four sons and three daughters. One child died. Their son, David, moved to Marshall County, Indiana, where there was a strong nucleus of Church of God believers.

Shortly after their wedding, Henry worked as a millwright and did well enough for them to purchase a 135-acre farm in 1856. He also maintained an orchard of small fruits, in every variety known to southern Ohio, and grew sorghum. Henry continued as a miller, operating a sorghum mill. He had the latest and best machinery. As Henry grew older, his sons cultivated the farm while he leaned back to enjoy the comforts of his labors.

Henry and Catharine were members of the Church of God, where he was considered one of the best theologians in the county and a great asset to his church. He was active in community affairs, serving as the School Director in his district for three elected terms being noted for his knowledge of current events.

Details of Henry's life are found in a local history book from 1880, but additional information survives in Henry's reports for *The Restitution*, which confirmed his commitment to the Gospel of the Kingdom. Henry sent an invitation to "protracted meetings" from October 17-November 2, 1890. He said guest speakers would be J.F. Wagoner of Rochester, Indiana, and George Elton of Collinswood, Ohio. Both Wagoner and Elton had been delegates to the 1888 Philadelphia Conference and were appointed to a committee. Certainly they would have given reports of the conference to the local congregation.

The Age to Come/Church of God movement was very active in southern Ohio prior to the Civil War. When he learned of Joseph Marsh's Age to Come, Dr. J.P. Weethee left the Millerite movement and began to actively preach it. Dr. Weethee taught at other colleges and eventually started Weethee College and became its president. He wrote extensively. It is also seen that Pilgrim Joseph Thomas of Virginia made frequent circuit trips into the Brush Creek area as early as 1819. He is credited by Church of God members in Virginia for influencing their early members to avoid mainstream churches and to dare to stand up for Bible doctrine in the face of criticism.

Frank Taylor, an Indiana Church of God historian, wrote that the Ohio Conference of the Church of God Abrahamic Faith was first organized in 1828. That has yet to be documented, but it is known that men such as Pilgrim Thomas had been preaching the Gospel of the Kingdom in that region for several years before the Millerite movement. Louise Lapp recalled that the original church at Brush Creek was interdenominational. So, while it cannot be conclusively proven that Brush Creek was always Church of God Abrahamic Faith, it is known that Henry was Church of God in the 19th century.

Henry Lehman passed his devotion for truth-seeking to his son, Daniel. Daniel Lehman was the father of Edna Brewer. His mother, Mary Burns Ludy Lehman, became a member of the Christian Church in 1837 when she moved to Ohio. She believed in the resurrection and was converted at a camp meeting, similar to the Cane Ridge revival of 1801. She probably died as a member in good standing of the Christian church, which also believed in the oneness of God as taught by its leader, Barton Stone.

Mary rests at the Thomas Cemetery, Concord Township, Miami County, Ohio. Her granddaughter, Edna Lehman Brewer, was a member of the Brush Creek Church of God Abrahamic Faith. After the death of Edna's husband, Rollie S. Brewer (d. April 8, 1931), she became dormitory Matron at Oregon Bible College. Rollie was descended from the Curtis family who founded the Brush Creek Church and donated land for the church and cemetery. Rollie's mother was Lucinda Complete Curtis (b. January 1853). Rollie and Edna had two sons, Byron and Kenneth, and two daughters, Dorothy Demmitt, Greg Demmitt's grandmother, and Louise Lapp, Music Instructor at Oregon Bible College in the 1950s and 1960s and mother of Jon and Elaine (Poole).

    See Thomas, Joseph
           Wagoner, J.F. - Curtis Family
           Weethee, J.P.

Bibliography: Ancestry.com. U.S. Census. Ohio. Miami. Union. Dist. 86. 1870; U.S. Census. Ohio. Miami. Monroe. Dist. 136. 1880; Ancestry.com. Lehman Family Tree, retrieved July 18, 2010; Brewer, Daniel, Eulogy of Mary Burns Ludy, March 11, 1890, sent by Jon Lapp, July 25, 2010; Demmitt, Greg. E-mail regarding Henry Lehman, Feb. 5, 2010; Biographical Sketches and Stories of Miami County Ohio http://www.tdn-net.com/genealogy/stories/biograph/biogfl/1486.htm retrieved July 18, 2010; Lehman, Henry L. "Invitation to Revival Meetings," *The Restitution*, S.A. Chaplin, ed. Plymouth, IN. Oct. 1, 1890.

Lewis, Eric
b. 1865?
d. 1941

Eric Lewis was born in England, graduated Eton, and attended Corpus Christi College at Cambridge from which he graduated in 1887. He was ordained in the Church of England by Bishop Crowther, who was famed in missionary annals as the black slave boy who became the first Bishop to Niger. Lewis was sent to the mission field to pioneer a new work in the Sudan. He also worked as a missionary in Hawaii and India.

After returning to England from India, Lewis authored *Black Opium,* an exposé on opium trafficking, published in 1910. In 1912, he immigrated to Canada and settled in Toronto where he came to know R.H. Judd, a neighbor and fellow missionary from the China Inland Mission.

Judd and Lewis exchanged many ideas on the biblical notion of eternal torment. Judd, being part of the Church of God, did not believe in it. He preached eternal punishment of the wicked. Lewis began to depend upon the Word of God to teach him. The jacket of his book, *Life and Immortality,* explained the dilemma he faced:

> The Bible was to this man both the lamp and compass by which he guided his life. Once he saw the fresh light of the Scriptures he did not hesitate or turn back, but dared to follow all the way, even though it led him out from his former associations, and along a road beset with trials.
>
> As he traveled on, he reached various cross-roads of Christian controversy which challenged and invited a change of direction but with single heart he guided his course by that which he had made his pole-star—the Word of God Written.
>
> Finally, he came up with the problem of eternal destinies. Applying his search light to the doctrine of Eternal Torment, questionings began to shape themselves within him. When he began to express his doubts, most evangelical pulpits became closed against him. Consequently an intensive study of the Scriptures followed, which drove him into the position as expounded in this book, "Life and Immortality."

Life and Immortality was reviewed in *The Restitution Herald* on September 30, 1924. R.H. Judd sent a copy of the review to his friend Eric Lewis. In return, Lewis wrote F.L. Austin, editor of *The Herald,* commenting that the book had been favorably reviewed in other publications also and noting that the editor had omitted the title of the book from the review.

A copy of this book is in the Archives at Atlanta Bible College and at Rock River Christian College, Beloit, Wisconsin. It thoroughly investigates the biblical teachings of the destiny of the righteous and of the wicked, the intermediate state between death and resurrection and the problem of eternal torment.

While Eric Lewis was not a member of the Church of God Abrahamic Faith nor any sister denomination that is known, he greatly influenced the thought and message of the Church of God.

See Austin, F.L. (20th)
Judd, R.H. (20th)

Bibliography: Lewis, Eric. *Life and Immortality,* Self published. 1924. Roller, Dr. John, Interview with Jan Stilson, 2005.

Lindsay, Samuel J.
b. January 21, 1866
d. October 10, 1941

A. Relocation to Oregon
B. The Work of the Illinois Conference
C. Solution to a Doctrinal Problem
D. A Problem within the Ranks
E. Preaching and Writing in Retirement

Samuel J. Lindsay was born in Illinois to Thomas and Margaret Lindsay. He had two brothers and four sisters. The family moved to Iowa when Samuel was about two. Shortly thereafter, around the mid-1880s they returned to Adeline, Ogle County, Illinois, 20 miles south of Freeport. They bought a farm for $11,500 from Samuel Coffman, an early settler to Maryland Township.

Samuel and Nellie Lindsay

Sam Lindsay grew up on the farm and developed a love for books. Samuel Coffman also appreciated good books, and being friends with Dr. John Thomas and Benjamin Wilson, had access to the journals and books they published. These were passed along to Sam Lindsay. Titles included *The Gospel Banner* (B. Wilson), *The Herald of the Coming Kingdom and Age to Come* (J. Thomas) and *The Herald of the Kingdom and Christian*

Instructor (T. Wilson), not to mention the *Emphatic Diaglott*, a New Testament interlinear translation by Benjamin Wilson, highly esteemed, not only by frontier believers, but Bible scholars worldwide.

By the time Lindsay graduated from the Adeline School in 1886, he was already knowledgeable on a myriad of theological subjects that some men spend a lifetime studying.

Young Samuel married Nellie Ward in the Methodist Church at 209 South Second Street in Rockford on July 22, 1887, and they became a happy and contented couple. They had three children, Nellie Etta (Val) Mattison, Hazel (Henry) Mattison and Ward Lindsay. Samuel began to teach at the Adeline School in the next term following their wedding. Years later, in 1916, he returned to Adeline as baccalaureate speaker for the graduating class in the newly refurbished two-story, four-room, limestone school. Today that school building is a museum.

Samuel Lindsay was baptized at the Church of God conference campground in Adeline in the early 1890s. Some of the families who were active with the Lindsays in that congregation included the Aslaksens, Gesins, Coffmans and Glotfeltys.

A. Relocation to Oregon

In the late 1890s, Samuel moved his family to Oregon, Illinois, where he became the Ogle County Assistant Superintendent of Schools. John Cross was Superintendent. Samuel held that position for nine years until he left to enter the ministry.

At Oregon, the Lindsays first worshipped at the local Methodist church because there was no Church of God in town. Samuel taught the women's Sunday Bible class and instructed in Age to Come and One Faith. In time, the women's class disagreed with the Methodist message, so the class felt they must leave the denomination to begin a Church of God. This may be the only time a Methodist class planted a Church of God.

The small group purchased the old stone church on North Third Street that had been vacated a few years earlier by St. Mary's Catholic Church. At the time the Church of God purchased it, a merchant had been using the building as a warehouse for animals and supplies.

S.J. Lindsay assumed the pastoral leadership and invited the community to attend. The church work began very humbly with just a handful of believers, but the congregation eventually grew strong enough to support the ministry. Under Lindsay's leadership the church immediately began hosting the Illinois Conference and summer Bible schools. These activities also became a witness in the community; some were drawn into membership because of all the visitors coming to Oregon. At first, guests and students in Oregon resided in the homes of members or community residents, but as their presence became such a regular occurrence, the local church and the Illinois Conference built a dormitory behind the church to house visitors.

Among his other duties, Lindsay also traveled to preach the Word. *The History of the Iowa Churches and Conference* notes: "S.J. Lindsay's name first appears in Iowa conference minutes on August 18, 1902. He preached that evening and the next morning." In 1903, the Iowa Conference granted him a ministerial license as they did for several succeeding years. It can be surmised that he also had a license from the Illinois Conference, which had issued them since 1889, as evidenced by an Illinois license granted to Jeremiah S. Hatch (preserved in the Archives of Atlanta Bible College).

In the summer of 1910, Lindsay baptized Martha Knodle's daughter, Bernice Rogers, and Martha's sister, Mary Swingley, in the Rock River. Mrs. Swingley had been baptized as a Methodist, but after she learned the truth, she felt uncomfortable with her former baptism. Samuel Lindsay said, "(I) have always insisted that baptism does not consist simply of being dipped in water. Unless the knowledge of the first principles of the Gospel precede, the dipping in water is useless." Baptisms always took place north of the damn, usually on the east side of the river, but later on the west side just below the Conover Piano factory.

From 1908-1911, S.J. Lindsay published *Bible Lessons*, a monthly correspondence course with subscribers in many states. He must have been learning the printer's trade nights and Saturdays while he was employed in the Superintendent's office. The record shows he purchased a share of the local newspaper. The experience prepared him to publish a Church of God religious newspaper. While Lindsay learned the printing trade, he brought Robert Huggins to Oregon to assist him. The door to publishing a new magazine opened when the new Ministerial Association asked him to publish and edit *The Restitution Herald* in the autumn of 1911.

The Ministerial Association assumed leadership of the Church of God. In addition to organizing the ministers, they supported and promoted the new magazine, a bold and controversial move. This action came out of the unsuccessful attempt by the ministers and state conference delegates to organize a national conference headquarters in Waterloo the summer of 1910. The division among the ministers and the delegates over the statement of faith and the status of *The Restitution* had to be healed to avoid compounding confusion among the membership.

The first issue of *The Restitution Herald* appeared on October 12, 1911. Copy included articles from pastors and lay writers, editorials, correspondence from Lindsay's students, and in subsequent issues, their answers or essays. This kind of exposure further advertised Lindsay's excellent lesson books. Copies of these lesson books are available to researchers in the Archives of Atlanta Bible College.

S.J. Lindsay published *The Restitution Herald* from the small print shop behind his home on North Sixth Street in Oregon in 1911. Randall wrote:

> The print shop was in the rear of S.J. Lindsay's home in Oregon Illinois. It had been a barn, where Bro. Lindsay kept his horse when he was Assistant Superintendent of Schools. In March, 1922, the print shop and office were moved to a brick building on North Third Street.

B. The Work of the Illinois Conference

S.J. Lindsay was dedicated to strengthening the work of the Illinois Conference whose role, in turn, was to strengthen the churches. To accomplish this, an evangelist had to be hired; this required donations from the churches. To have churches, the evangelist needed to be in the field. It was a delicate structure to implement, and even more difficult to maintain. It began with preaching across the state and the Midwest. Literature shows Samuel Lindsay filled pulpits throughout Illinois on various occasions. Sometimes he assumed a pastorate on a regular basis. In 1915, he preached once a month at Rushville and Camden, Illinois. Both communities are close to the site of the present-day Ripley Church of God in Brown County, Illinois.

The rest of the month, he preached the third Sunday at Rensselaer, Indiana, both morning and evening, the second Sunday at Adeline, Illinois, and, the fourth Sunday at the Oregon Church of God where he was pastor. During the week, he put out *The Restitution Herald* and the local paper. By traveling as he did, he always had fresh church news, births, deaths and marriages, and he kept current on what people were thinking, and what they believed. This provided copy for the paper, and he could address their questions and doubts through its pages as well.

Lindsay assisted the Ripley church in its effort to reorganize. The record shows the William Densmores of Rushville, Illinois, hosted S.J. Lindsay to discuss that matter. At a meeting with members from Ripley and Camden, a new congregation was born into the Church of God out of the remnants of the former work.

Another aspect of Lindsay's leadership was the initial Summer Bible class. When Robert Huggins arrived in Oregon in 1906, he not only assisted Lindsay in the print shop, he was the first student for mentoring and instruction in Bible. In fact, Huggins may have assisted in writing and editing the *Bible Lessons*. Others who were early participants in the summer classes included Frank Siple, Rolland Stilson, Leland Hanson, Clyde Randall, Paul Hatch and John Railton. These young adults were members of the yet unformed denomination, and they became the leadership of the new denomination which would be organized in 1921. After that year, for up to six weeks each summer, young adults came to Oregon from all over the United States to study the Bible.

The educational imperative in the Church of God first appeared at the 1888 Philadelphia Conference through a directive from the Education Committee to the Board of Directors. Evidence for this is found in the minutes. When the conference failed in 1892 due to lack of funds, it must have left a hole in the hearts of pastors and leaders such as Lindsay. Still, Lindsay took the reins and began a grass-roots education movement centered around publishing *The Bible Lessons* and *The Restitution Herald*. It was a mostly one-on-one kind of internship, but it trained leaders before the establishment of the Bible Training Class in 1923. For a summary of the documents regarding education, refer to Eugene Stilson's paper, Appendix 16.

Lindsay and the Oregon congregation were leaders in sculpting a small-town agrarian movement into a national work of publishing and education within the Church of God. People within the community looked to the Church of God for solid preaching, good music and good citizenship. Members from the national Church of God looked to Oregon for direction, with S.J. Lindsay and some of his students taking leadership of the publishing and educational components of the movement. After the organization of the General Conference in 1921, delegates approved formalizing the Bible Training Class as a year-long college-level instructional program. The school opened in 1923 and became Oregon Bible College in 1941.

Students Harry Sheets, Melville Lyon, Cedric Pope and others worked behind the pulpit or the press from almost the first week they arrived in Oregon for the training classes. The need for preachers was so great among the churches and small Bible study groups throughout the country, that it was necessary for the young preachers to get "on-the-job" training. Men who trained them were L.E. Conner, F.L. Austin, S.J. Lindsay and F.E. Siple. Lindsay directed everything and quickly rose to prominence within the Church of God. Each student had a "rotation" of preaching services, so that in a month's time, each man often had visited four to six congregations.

Evelyn Austin said, "S.J. Lindsay, Oregon, Illinois, was the father of vacation Bible school work" in the Church of God. Through his efforts, and those of Anna E. Drew, Dixon, Illinois, youth work and college training began among Church of God congregations from the new church at Oregon; Lindsay pioneered that effort.

After the completion of the dormitory, which had a dining hall in the basement, the church grounds took on the look of a "campus" suited to handle the crowds coming to study. With the additional facilities, programming was increased to educate and sustain the movement. Other church campuses in the Church of God movement included Maurertown for the Virginia conference and Adeline for the early Illinois conference. The Oregon campus eventually replaced the rural Adeline campus.

Through the years, the Oregon congregation has sent out a strong beacon testifying of the Gospel of the Kingdom, and for nearly 70 years, was the headquarters church of the General Conference and Bible College. Through the years, it has published many small historical booklets relating the story of the church.

C. Solution to a Doctrinal Problem

Prior to 1910 the local churches and members of the Church of God recognized *The Restitution* as the leading voice of the denomination, but that would soon change.

The problem centered on the statement of faith, especially resurrection. Readers of *The Restitution* did believe in resurrection, but they felt it was only for believers. Briefly, this doctrine stated that the wicked dying the Adamic death would never again be raised for judgment. This form of belief was labeled limited resurrection which differed with their brethren who believed the just and the unjust would be raised at Christ's second coming, the unjust being the Adamic wicked. The latter is labeled general resurrection.

However, the limited-resurrection members even put conditions on this resurrection. A baptized believer who sinned, or worse fell back into a lifestyle of sin, would not automatically receive immortality at his resurrection. About half *The Restitution*'s readers felt carnal Christians were not responsible Christians and thus did not merit the same reward, if any, as faithful Christians. To reconcile the issue of carnal Christians, they accepted the Christadelphian explanation of mortal emergence from the grave, so that only the righteous would be "changed in the twinkling of an eye." The carnal had to wait for judgment before being changed, if then. The Christadelphians have since modified the doctrine of mortal emergence.

This debate came to a head at the heated 1910 Waterloo Conference. The purpose of this conference was twofold: to organize a national conference and make a statement on church discipline. Debates were so heated and feelings ran so hot that great criticism and damage to the movement resulted. Samuel Lindsay was criticized for not attending, but he had been committed to preaching at the Michigan Conference scheduled that same week. In Michigan, he baptized five people. In a letter to Robert Huggins, Lindsay chastised him severely for trying to split the brethren over a statement of faith when the Bible was all that was needed. Lindsay wrote

Lindsay and fellow ministers, circa 1908, left to right: LE Conner, Joseph W. Williams, Rolla Hightower, SJ Lindsay, GE Marsh, Peter Jeffrey, Robert Huggins.

in a special edition of *The Restitution Herald* entitled "To Our Brotherhood":

> You went there [to Waterloo] with a creed made before hand with the intention of driving from the fellowship all who do not indorse [sic] all you there set forth. Because such extremes met, what was the result of the general conference? *A blot and a shame upon the church!*

Following the conference, S.J. Lindsay, L.E. Conner, J.W. Williams, F.V. Blakely and F.L. Austin organized the Ministerial Association in Cleveland in 1910. This group attempted to wrest control of *The Restitution* from its publisher and owner, A.R. Underwood of Plymouth, Indiana. They alleged certain irregularities in the financial management of the magazine. Underwood took exception to their accusations and defended himself and his paper.

Being unable to gain control of the newspaper, and with the message of *The Restitution* leaning increasingly toward the Christadelphian point of view, the ministers planned to begin a new publication. S.J. Lindsay was named editor. When the new paper rolled off the presses in October 1911, the Church of God was ready to pursue a course separate from the Christadelphians, the same action Benjamin Wilson had taken 50 years earlier.

S.J. Lindsay wanted a paper that represented pure interpretation of biblical prophecy. It represented the biblical position of general resurrection, which teaches that the just and the unjust will be raised for reward or for judgment. No one stays in the grave with the Adamic death. The new paper was well received, and the membership tried for a time to subscribe to both newspapers. Both publications contained wonderful scriptural and inspirational articles with news from the evangelists and members in the field. By 1921, *The Restitution Herald* had gained enough influence to be named the official voice of the Church of God, but *The Restitution* had lost subscribers, a fact that led to its demise in 1925.

D. A Problem within the Ranks

Samuel Lindsay remained as editor and publisher of *The Restitution Herald* until September 5, 1922. After F.L. Austin moved to Oregon to assume management of the new conference, sparks flew in the print shop, and not from the presses. Austin was in charge, and he and Lindsay were at odds almost immediately. S.J. Lindsay relinquished the paper to Austin who was appointed general manager of the publishing department and editor of *The Restitution Herald*.

Randall wrote in *Historical Waymarks* that the board of *The Restitution Herald* Stock Company gave the assets to the General Conference. Shortly thereafter, *The Restitution Herald* began to be published under the banner of the National Bible Institute.

The Lindsays moved to California in the fall of 1922. *The Ogle County Reporter* stated that the Lindsays were taking a much-needed rest and that Reverend Lindsay was going to California to preach. *The Restitution Herald* would be published by John E. Cross of Oregon and Val Mattison, Lindsay's son-in-law. Even though they moved away from Oregon, the Lindsays returned to their two-story home on North Sixth Street each summer and remained active in conference work.

The first print shop was a small barn that sat behind the Lindsay home. After the printing equipment was moved to North Third Street in 1921, the barn was used for storage. Later, it was converted into a small house and, in 1939, rented to newlyweds Willis and Ida Mae Turner. Ida put a rug over the concrete slab in the living room where the press once sat and set up housekeeping. The Turners were baptized into Christ in the Rock River by J.R. LeCrone in 1950. Willis became President of the Board of Directors of the Church of God General Conference a few years later.

E. Preaching and Writing in Retirement

On his way to Los Angeles, Lindsay stopped to preach in Bosworth, Missouri. In Los Angeles, he joined forces with the Railsbacks who had relocated from Indiana a few years earlier. Lindsay pastored in L.A. a number of years, returning to Oregon, Illinois, for summer visits. He also edited a magazine, *The Messenger of Truth*, during his years at the Los Angeles church and engaged in a debate with a man named Fuson, the only debate Lindsay ever had. For 12 years, Lindsay also pastored the Church of God at Tempe, Arizona.

Lindsay remained active in the work of the General Conference from a distance. He served as visiting evangelist in many churches during his "retirement" years. He authored many articles and tracts. Two titles, both from 1921, which bear mentioning as being influential are: "The Resurrection," which took the position of general or universal resurrection, and "The Coming of Christ" in 1921.

Lindsay also authored a short book entitled *God's Covenant with Abraham* where he explored the beginning and meaning of the Abrahamic Faith. It contained three chapters and was easy to read and understand. Lindsay's article entitled "Baptism" originally written for *The Restitution Herald* in 1916 was reprinted in tract form by the National Bible Institute after 1921.

When Lindsay died from complications following surgery, many ministers traveled from all over the United States to attend his funeral. The service was held at the Oregon Church of God, Elder L.E. Conner officiating. Conner preached on the hope that S.J. Lindsay had in the resurrection and the second coming of Christ. Francis Burnett assisted. There was special music by the Hardesty brothers with Bernice Rogers at the organ. S.J. and Nellie Lindsay are interred at Riverview Cemetery north of Oregon.

See   Austin, F.L. (20th)
        Burnett, Francis (20th)
        Coffman, Sam
        Conner, L.E.
        Huggins, Robert (20th)
        Knodle, Martha
        Lindsay, Thomas
        Rogers, Bernice
        Swingley, Dr. William
        Turner, Willis H. (20th)
        Wilson, Benjamin

See Also Appendix 16–Christian Education

Bibliography: Ancestry.com. U.S. Census. Iowa. Deleware. Elk. Dist. 156. 1870 and 1880; Ancestry.com. U.S. Census. Illinois. Ogle. Oregon. Dist. 83. 1910; Austin, Evelyn and Hatch, Paul, *Impressions and History* [of the Church of God] unpublished manuscript, 1969; Burnett, Francis, Interview with Jan Stilson Dec. 2006; Burnett, Francis et al history committee, *History of the Iowa Church of God and Conference 1855-1987*, printed by Belle Plaine Union, 1987; Editorial by A.R. Underwood. *The Restitution*, April 5, 1911; Goekler, Harry, Letter to Editor, *History Newsletter*, Jan Stilson, ed., Oct./Nov. 1993; Interment.net. Riverview Cemetery, Ogle Co. Oregon, Il; Lindsay, John W., *Ward and Marie Lindsay*, self published c2002; Lindsay, Samuel J. *God's Covenant with Abraham*, National Bible Institute, Oregon, Il; Lindsay, S.J. "Baptism" reprinted from *The Restitution Herald*, Feb. 1916, by the NBI, Oregon, Il.; Lindsay, S.J., "To Our Brotherhood" special edition of *The Restitution Herald*, Oregon, Il. circa June 1911. Mattison, Jim. "*Memories of Grandfather S.J. Lindsay*," Correspondence with JStilson. Spring 2006; Randall, Clyde, *Historical Waymarks of the Church of God*, Church of God General Conference, Oregon, Il., 1976, p. 40; *The Restitution Herald*. Oct. 1915; Dec. 8, 1915; Oct. 1921; Nov. 8, 1921; Aug. 29, 1922; June 1925; Oct. 21, 1941.

Lindsay, Thomas
b. May 18, 1841
d. June 25, 1910

Thomas Lindsay was born in eastern Ohio across the Ohio River from Wheeling, West Virginia. When he was four years old, his family moved to Muscatine, Iowa, and when Thomas was about eight years old, he was orphaned to be bound out to strangers. He suffered the common lot of children in such arrangements.

On his eighteenth birthday, Thomas determined he would become his own guardian. He moved to Mt. Morris, Illinois, where he was employed as a farmhand until his marriage on January 5, 1865, to Margaret E. Koontz. Thomas and Margaret moved to Adeline, Illinois, Maryland Township, Ogle County. They had six sons and three daughters. Thomas made the Bible his rule of faith and practice, and he was loyal to every duty in home and neighborhood.

The family returned to Iowa for a few years, and then came back to Adeline where they purchased a farm. Until his retirement, Thomas remained in Adeline. He moved to Oregon only three years before his death and lived with son, Samuel J. Lindsay. It was said Thomas moved to Oregon to enjoy a retired life and the privileges of the church he'd been a member of since his youth. That church was the Church of One Faith, which became known as the Church of God.

Pastor G.E. Marsh of Oregon conducted Thomas Lindsay's funeral in Adeline. Lindsay's six sons served as pallbearers. He was interred in the Adeline cemetery.

John Lindsay contributed to this entry.

See Lindsay, S.J.
Marsh, G.E.

Bibliography: Obituary of Thomas Lindsay, submitted to *The Ogle County Reporter*, June 26th, 1910 as retrieved from Ogle County Genealogy, at rootsweb.com/~iogle/thomaslindsay.htm August 19, 2007.

Logan, Henry
b. 1811
d. Unknown

Henry Logan was an Indiana pioneer. He left Rush County, along with his wife and their daughter, Sarah, and relocated to Marshall County, Indiana, on July 26, 1836, a few days after the county was organized. At that time, Marshall County was still populated with Indians. Sarah was just three. In time, they had several more daughters and a son.

Henry Logan learned of the Abrahamic Faith and the Gospel of the Kingdom from early evangelists; he took up preaching because he loved the doctrines. Arlen Rankin reported to the History Conference in Atlanta in 2006:
> Henry Logan was first an elder in the early Christian Church at "Old Union" and later fulfilled that work in the "Old Pisgah" Christian Church, a church which he, along with Thomas McDonald organized in the winter of 1836-37 near Plymouth, Indiana, between Lake Maxenkuckee and Wolf Creek.

Rankin also noted:
> It was as a result of the evangelistic efforts of Ephraim Miller, Jr., and E. Hoyt in 1843 and 1847 that this congregation espoused the Gospel of the Kingdom and life in Christ, and Henry Logan began his Abrahamic Faith ministry.

Out of the work at Pisgah grew the work known as "Old Antioch" which in turn reorganized later as Argos. Rankin noted in his address that the Argos church building still stands along Michigan Road but is now a private residence.

Logan was contemporary with early Indiana workers Jacob Shafer and Stedman Chaplin, a preacher who had moved to Indiana following the collapse of the Millerite movement. In fact, Logan's daughter, Sarah, later married Stedman Chaplin.

Logan's son, Thomas, remained faithful in the work, and Lottie Logan Pickerl was born into this family. She lived to be 108, and worked faithfully in the Hope Chapel Church of God in South Bend.

See Chaplin, S.A.
Hoyt, E.
Miller, Ephraim
Pickerl, Lottie Logan (20th)
Shafer, Jacob

Bibliography: History of Marshall County, Indiana. Lewis. Chicago. 1908; Rankin, Arlen. "Influence of Old Union in Indiana," paper presented to History Conference at Atlanta Bible College, Nov. 3, 2006; *The Restitution,* May 5, 1911.

Lord, James A.
b. 1849
d. Unknown

James Lord was born in Canada but relocated to Missouri and went down into Texas to preach. In fact, he was the first person to preach the Gospel of the Kingdom in Texas in the early 1880s, predating Warren, Taylor, Bradley and Gibbs. Lord was invited to come from his home in Lafayette County, Missouri, to hold a three-week meeting near Abilene, Texas. He preached about the mortality of man and of the future establishment of the Kingdom of God upon the earth. The year was 1883, well ahead of the ministry of A.S. Bradley and W.L. Gibbs.

Lord must have been engaged in fulltime preaching; the 1880 US Census lists his occupation as "Minister." In those days, unless an established congregation hired them, most evangelists and ministers of the Age-to-Come/One Faith movement were farmers, carpenters or merchants. Preaching was their choice but it provided little or no income.

A.J. Addington and Biggs became the first deacons and leaders of that newly organized church at Abilene. Elder Addington then served as evangelist and preached throughout the area. He held regular meetings at Lythe Cove, New Hope, Iberia and Colony Hill. After this time, no additional information about James Lord is found in church literature.

See Addington, A.J.
Bradley, A.S.
Gibbs, W.L.
Macy, Emory (20th)
Taylor, Richard B.
Warren, Robert

Bibliography: Ancestry.com. U.S. Census. Lafayette. Washington. Dist. 47. Page 26. 1880; Macy, Emory, "Church of God History of the Texas Church of God" March, 1954; Taylor, Richard B., Notes on Texas History upon which Macy based his Texas history. The notes are stored in the Archives of Atlanta Bible College, McDonough, Ga.

Lovesee, Joseph W.
b. 1829
d. Unknown

Elder Lovesee was born in Ohio, but in his adult life resided at Hartford, Kansas. He was married to Cinthia and they had three children. His occupation was millwright, but he also preached the good news of the Gospel of the Kingdom in Kansas wherever he could gain access.

J.W. Lovesee wrote a letter to Benjamin Wilson in February 1868, and said *The Gospel Banner* encouraged him and lightened his load. At that time, Elder Lovesee was working throughout southern Kansas to establish and stabilize three churches. He said these churches had been started in 1862 and *The Gospel Banner* had "assisted me in the organization of a family of God upon the foundation of the apostles and prophets, Christ Jesus being the foundation corner stone."

He referred to the three churches as the upper, center and lower congregations. The upper congregation was located at Middle Creek in Chase County. This congregation elected two elders, Jaspar Balch and Delevan Perry. The central congregation elected a full roster of officers including elders, deacons, deaconesses and a corresponding conference clerk. The lower congregation elected J.W. Lovesee as an elder and elected a deacon and an evangelist. From these descriptions, it is clear that the means and resources of each congregation differed, and Lovesee guided them in their organizational efforts according to needs and qualifications of the members.

Lovesee expressed interest in comments made in the *Gospel Banner* regarding W.P. Shockey's baptism following his exit from the Campbellite ministry. Lovesee supported Shockey in his decision to be re-baptized following his acceptance of the Gospel of the Kingdom.

Having been baptized as a Campbellite, Lovesee wrote eloquently in *The Gospel Banner* that he had not been re-baptized upon learning of the Gospel of the Kingdom because he had been immersed in faith and learned more of the truth following that. This is the same position taken by Joseph Marsh 50 years earlier. Lovesee did not criticize those who wanted to be re-baptized, however. Benjamin Wilson responded that the faith of the believer was more important than the faith of the baptizer, so long as the believer believed in the One Faith.

In time, Lovesee expanded his evangelistic ministry to include the northern counties of Kansas. That was strong Disciples' territory, and a few years earlier, he had engaged in vigorous debates against their pastors in that area. At one place he had the largest congregations they had ever seen in that city. Lovesee said they were very attentive to the word preached from Matthew 11:12, "And from the early days of John the Baptist until now, the kingdom of heaven suffered violence and the violent take it by force."

See Marsh, Joseph
Shockey, W.P.
Wilson, Benjamin

Bibliography: Ancestry.com: Kansas State Census Collection, 1855-1925. 1865. Lyon. Pike; Lovesee, J.W. "Encouraging Letter from Kansas," *The Gospel Banner and Bible Advocate*, B. Wilson, ed., Geneva, Il., Feb. 15, 1868.

Luman (Luhman), James H.
b. 1846
d. Unknown

James Luman was born in Tennessee to parents from North Carolina and Tennessee. He had brothers and sisters, but little is known about his childhood or youth. He was married to Mary, and they had a son and a daughter. They resided in Bristow, Oklahoma, where he served as Justice of the Peace.

At some point he learned about the Kingdom of

God from evangelists who circulated through the South, possibly Uncle John Foore or Dr. James L. Muncrief from Arkansas. Luman concentrated his preaching ministry on Arkansas and Oklahoma, maintaining a preaching circuit throughout those states at the beginning of the 20th century. He preached at Sapula, Oklahoma, once a month for several years. He also preached at Bristow, which seemed to be a focal point of the Oklahoma work.

Luman was one of the first southern preachers to endorse the call to organize a general conference at Waterloo, Iowa, in 1910. James attended the eighteenth annual Illinois State Conference in 1915. He preached two sermons at this conference; they were well received.

See Foore, John
Muncrief, Dr. James L.

Bibliography: Ancestry.com. U.S. Census. Hamilton. Tennessee. Dist. 27. 1850; *The Restitution,* August 8, 1910; *The Restitution Herald,* Oct. 13, 1915; April 12, 1916; Oct. 8, 1918. Minute Book of the Illinois State Conference 1915, p. 201-208.

Lyon, Judd S.
b. May 1872
d. Unknown

Judd Lyon was born in Michigan and died in Citronelle, Alabama, where he led a small Church of God congregation. He married Loulou M. Turney at her parents' home in Chicago on October 25, 1898. Loulou was the daughter of Alexander Turney, originally of Toronto, Canada, but residing then in Chicago. Mr. Turney moved in with the Lyon family when they lived in Hammond, Louisiana, and later, in Citronelle. Judd Lyon and his wife were the parents of Melville, Dorothy (Siple), Margaret (Peg Duvall), and Jean (Hall) Lyon, students at the Bible Training School during the 1920s.

In 1919, the family visited the F.E. Siple family in Hammond, Louisiana, during the holidays. At that time Elder Siple preached at Hammond. During the visit, he baptized all the Lyon teens.

Lyon was active in the national work of the Church of God. In 1920 he was asked to serve on the nationwide committee convened to organize a national headquarters. In fact, Lyon called for a meeting of conference workers to gather information and examine the question for the first time since the failed organizational attempt in 1910. He placed a note in *The Restitution* and *The Restitution Herald* offering to go into the Lord's service. He asked people to write him so he could explain his plan to teach people about the truth. Lyon wanted to gather a group to examine how to organize a lasting national general conference. Subsequently, a small group convened at Oregon, Illinois, November 9-12, 1920. The purpose of this meeting was to examine the needs of the church at large, and the "conditions that confront us."

The group spent two days studying scriptural examples relating to church organizations and governance, planning to design their conference organization in agreement with the scriptural pattern. Frederick L. Austin was appointed conference secretary and instructed to send a report to any Church of God member who asked for one. There was a spirit of love and deference among the 75 members who participated.

Out of this initial meeting the Committee of Ten was appointed to study the matter a full year before recommending a plan at the next annual conference meeting in Waterloo, Iowa. After much study and prayer, an organizational strategy was prepared for the delegates of the upcoming 1921 annual conference. This business strategy included publishing *The Restitution Herald,* setting up central offices in Oregon, future plans for organizing a Bible College, a home for the elderly and a greenhouse business to support the new work financially. This strategy's presentation was visionary and decisive for it resulted in the approval of a General Conference by the delegates in August 1921, which still exists to this day. Ratification by each of the 14 state conferences was needed to activate the corporation; that was accomplished within a few weeks, demonstrating the people's solidarity to organize.

Judd Lyon, who attended the 1921 Waterloo Conference, was elected the second vice president on the new Board of Directors. In fact, it was Lyon who introduced the motion to move the headquarters of the new general conference to Oregon, Illinois, where *The Restitution Herald* was being published.

Lyon wrote a column for *The Restitution Herald* entitled "Wayside Notes" in 1920. The column included general news of Christendom as well as news of Church of God members and churches.

See Austin, F.L. (20th)
Lyon, Melville (20th)
Siple, F.E. (20th)

Bibliography: Ancestry.com. U.S. Census. Illinois. Cook. Chicago Ward 31. Dist. 968. 1900; Hatch, Paul and Austin, Evelyn. "Impressions and History of the Church of God," Oregon, Il., circa 1975; Lyon, J.S. Appeal to Members. *The Restitution* March 2, 1920; *The Restitution Herald,* January 13, 1920; May, 1920; December 1920; Jan. 29, 1924; Woulfe-Schmitt, Thomas. "Our Conference: It's Start and Basis. *History Newsletter* published with the *The 75th Anniversary Issue of The Restitution Herald,* October 1985; Williams, Byron. *Abstracts of Obituaries and Verbatim Marriage Announcements printed in The Restitution 1874-1900,* self-published, 1993. p. 109.

Lyon, Ralph Vinton

b. October 21, 1809
d. 1891

R.V. Lyon was born to Corbin and Rebecca Lyon in Dudley, Massachusetts. He was married to Hester who may have been a second wife. During his lifetime, he resided in various places in Connecticut and Massachusetts, but he ministered primarily in Canada West, Michigan, Wisconsin and Indiana. He often jeopardized his health and suffered fatigue from the exhaustive schedule he maintained. Like Christ, Lyon was a man of sorrows. He signed one letter, "Your brother in sorrow's vale."

Hester Lyon

Lyon was contemporary with Joseph Marsh, and like Marsh, came out of the Millerite movement. He had been ordained a Baptist pastor, but he left that movement when he heard of the second coming of Christ. Lyon was first and foremost a believer in the second advent of Christ, and he accepted the Age-to-Come understanding of Bible prophecy promoted by Joseph Marsh.

Lyon's testimony about his conversion was found in a footnote in *The Glorious Future, The Kingdom of God*:

> The author's attention was called to the doctrine set forth in this discourse, some forty-five years ago, by an objection which Thomas Paine brought against the plan of redemption, as taught by the so-called orthodox world; and, upon embracing the doctrine of 'the age to come,' through the instrumentality of the *lamented* JOSEPH MARSH, he saw how this text [1 Tim. 2:6], and the oath and promise of God made to Abram—Abraham, would be fulfilled in the ages to come, under the reign of Jesus—the Messiah, Gen. 12:3; and about thirteen years ago the substance of this lecture was first given in Borelia, C. W.

Lyon wrote a lot of copy for Joseph Marsh's publications, but he was decidedly non-sectarian. He said he encountered in his travels many "sectarian names of this degenerate age of the world" such as Christian, Methodist, Baptist, Adventist, but he did not want to be known by any of them. He said he was a member of the school of Jesus of Nazareth but had not yet graduated, "Consequently, I am a disciple of his, and a learner and a follower."

R.V. Lyon toured with a tent for evangelistic meetings. Marsh published the meeting schedules for all evangelists weekly, first in *The Voice of Truth* and later in *The Advent Harbinger and Bible Advocate.* People loved hearing Lyon preach so much they would write to Marsh weeks before the tent ministry season began to schedule Lyon to preach.

When Marsh died so did his publishing empire, and R.V. Lyon turned to the most available Age-to-Come medium for reporting his evangelistic efforts. He began writing and reporting for *The Gospel Banner and Millennial Advocate* published by Benjamin Wilson in Geneva, Illinois.

R.V. Lyon lamented in one report that he left his sweet home and traveled 25 hours, probably by stage and train, to the home of P.G. Smith, near Marshfield, Indiana. The trip was tedious, and he was not well. Smith's family cared for Lyon, and he was able to preach at the Church of God at Peach Grove, Jordan Township, Warren County, Indiana, on Sunday. In this report, he mentioned that he had authored two more pamphlets, "The Great Salvation, the One Thing Needful" and "Paul's Commentary on the Penalty of Sin." These pamphlets were available from Mrs. H.M. Lyon, Suspension Bridge, New York, for 12¢ each.

When Lyon left Peach Grove, there was great sadness at his departure. He had preached to large congregations there. After that, he traveled west to Vermillion County, Illinois, where he was well received.

While Lyon lived at Suspension Bridge he wrote another tract entitled "The Gospel of God." He stated the case of God's love for man by sending His Son to die and to be raised. Lyon wrote, "This truth enables us to press with ponderous weight upon the minds of our fellow man, the necessity of Christ's coming and the resurrection." Because Christ was raised, so also shall the faithful be raised from the sleep of death. Speaking of the atonement he said, "Christ cannot represent sinners! For they are compared to thorns and briars!" He added that:

> Christ separated himself from sinners by leading a life of faith and obedience. Sinners will not be made alive at his coming. They will remain in the congregation of the dead. Paul says in 1 Corinthians 15:22 that those who are made alive in Christ will be raised incorruptible! They will sing a victor's song! They will give thanks to God. Verse 56 of chapter 15 says those who died in their sins will be held in a state of death eternally!

R.V. Lyon did not fully agree with Joseph Marsh, since Lyon also agreed with Dr. John Thomas that there will be no resurrection of the wicked, a doctrine Marsh found unbiblical. This doctrine, annihilationism, states that when a man dies in his Adamic sins without acknowledging Christ as his Savior, he will be dead forever. Thus, the righteous only will be raised from the graves; the result of annihilationism is limited resurrection.

R.V. Lyon was the first to admit that Christadelphian uproar over annihilationism had been the undoing of the once-flourishing church at Liberty, Indiana. Even Old Union church had been upset by it, and he said, "Yes, Indiana has felt the shock and an age will not repair it!" While he accepted annihilationism, he believed it should not be a reason to split a church.

One subscriber wrote to Benjamin Wilson that the errors of R.V. Lyon were as great as those of Dr. Thomas. One complaint against Lyon covered the topic of Anglo-Israelism. Some have thought that because he preached a strong message of the restoration of Israel to its homeland *before* the coming of Christ that he was connected with John Wilson (1799-1870) who wrote *Our Israelitish Origins*. John Wilson taught Anglo-Israelism. Yet, R.V. Lyon was not associated with that Wilson or with his doctrine.

In 1861, Lyon wrote, *The Scattering and Restoration of Israel* in which he clearly explained the three reasons that Israel and Judah would be united again as one nation. These reasons are 1) *That the prophet (Ezekiel 21:25-27) takes the position that this kingdom will be overthrown.* 2) *That it should be no more until its rightful heir shall come.* 3) *That it would then be given him.* The rest of the tract is devoted to explaining the teaching of the restoration of Israel to its homeland before the return of Christ. In no way does it suggest the teaching of Anglo-Israelism. A copy of this tract is in the Archives of the Atlanta Bible College.

The emerging Church of God Abrahamic Faith was embryonic following the Bitter Disappointment. Joseph Marsh attempted to clarify doctrines by focusing on interpretation of prophecies regarding the return of Christ. The Age-to-Come doctrine necessarily involved discussion of Israel. John Wilson's book debuted in England in 1840, with a reprint in 1844, and made its way to America soon after. Many American editors advertised it through their pages, as did Joseph Marsh, but neither he nor any other Age-to-Come editors aligned themselves with Anglo-Israelism.

Ralph G. Orr, a Seventh-day Church of God writer has written:

> So strongly did this group emphasize their belief in Israel's restoration, that they have also been known as the Restoration Church of God. While restorationism creates a receptive atmosphere for Anglo-Israelism, *we know of no one from among the Church of God (Abrahamic Faith) who was Anglo-Israelite.* [Orr's emphasis.] Lyon came close. As we will see, it is but a short step from Lyon's restorationism to classic Anglo-Israelism.

R.V. Lyon wrote a tract, "The Sanctuary," in which he discussed the Sabbath question and pointed out weaknesses in the theology of both the first-day Adventists and the Seventh-day Adventists. He said the sanctuary will be on earth where the throne of God will be. God will return to earth when the New Jerusalem comes down from heaven in the new heavens and new earth, at the beginning of the eternal age.

In 1863, Lyon served as the evangelist for the General Association of the Church of God in Syracuse, New York. This association may have been the first formal regional Age-to-Come organization on record. It covered New York and New England, Ohio and Canada West. During the first eight months of the year, Lyon worked in Canada West, and for shorter periods in Vermont, New Hampshire, Massachusetts, Connecticut and New York. In that year, he preached 350 sermons, baptized 43 members and brought one church into existence. He furnished copy for five religious papers. It's not known which titles, but certainly one of them must have been Newman's *Millennial Harbinger*. Lyon also published three tracts, wrote or revised three more works (a total of 218,000 pages) and received $3 for his work from Newman.

R.V. Lyon took a western tour during the autumn of 1866 that brought him south into Indiana and Illinois. He spent time in Vermillion County, Illinois, and met many fine people to whom he preached. This neighborhood is south of Danville near the Casey and Marshall Churches of God. In 1867 Lyon reported to *The Prophetic Watchman* that he had spent ten weeks in Indiana, Illinois and Michigan "presenting the truth, the Gospel, the Good News, the Word of reconciliation, which he has commanded to be proclaimed among all nations, in order to the obedience of the 'Faith'."

When Lyon reported his preaching activities and the results of the Gospel upon the hearts of his listeners, one of his favorite phrases was, "Truth took effect." In one case in Illinois, four persons were baptized after a funeral service. In another case, three were baptized in a nearby river. Men working in the field expected to reap a harvest of souls for Christ.

Lyon submitted a lecture to *The Gospel Banner* in 1869 in which he stated that he did not accept the pre-existence of Christ. Lyon said:

> Neither did he pre-exist previous to his conception and birth, as a conscious being; for this would trample underfoot organic law, and contradict the teachings of the whole Bible. It is true, that in the beginning was the Logos—the Word—the promise—the seed of the woman, "the seed of Abraham" (Gen. 1:3, 3:15, 22:17, 18). And the Logos—the Word,—the promise—"was with God", and the Logos—the Word—the promise—"was God", because it is his Language or thoughts expressed—the development of the plan of redemption—the person named who is to bruise

effectually the head of the serpent, and thereby remove the effects of the fall from the universe of God! "And the Logos was made flesh and dwelt among us"; And Luke informs us how it was done: "And the angel said to Mary, the Holy Spirit shall come upon thee, and the power of the Highest shall overshadow thee; therefore also that holy thing which shall be born of thee, shall be called the Son of God."

Ralph and Hester Lyon resided at Niagara Falls and worshipped at the Fonthill, Ontario, Church of God organized by Peter Bouk. The circumstances of R.V. Lyon's old age and death remain unknown, except that he predeceased Hester by seven years. They were laid to rest at the Oakwood Cemetery at Niagara, New York. Possibly, Pastor Melville Lyon was R.V. Lyon's descendent.

See Bouk, Peter
Lyon, Melville (20th)
Marsh, Joseph
Reed, H.V.
Wilson, Benjamin

Bibliography: Ancestry.com. U.S. Census. New York. Niagara. Dist. 187; Graham, David, Compiled writings of Church of God founders, "Of Jesus Christ Concerning his True Nature," *Church of God General Conference History Newsletter*, JStilson ed, Morrow, Ga. Feb./March 1993; "Letter to Joseph Marsh from Wm. D. Groslin," *The Advent Harbinger and Bible Advocate*, March 22, 1851; and Nov. 1, 1851; Lyon, R.V. *The Glorious Future, the Kingdom of God* 3d ed., corrected by the author, self-published Suspension Bridge, NY circa 1868; Lyon, R.V. "Report" *The Millennial Harbinger and Bible Advocate*, Thos. Newman, ed., Seneca Falls, NY., 1863. Lyon. R.V., Report of evangelistic meetings, *The Gospel Banner and Millennial Advocate*, Oct. 1, 1868; Letter to B. Wilson. *The Gospel Banner and Millennial Advocate* 15:1 Jan. 1, 1869; Lyon, Ralph V. "Atonement," *The Millennial Harbinger and Bible Expositor*, Thomas Newman, ed., Seneca Falls, NY, Oct. 7, 1863; Lyon, R.V. "Beloved Brethren of the Watchman," *The Prophetic Watchman*, J.M. Stephenson and H.V. Reed, co-editors, Harvard, Il., Oct. 19, 1866; Lyon, R.V. The Scattering and Restoration of Israel Office of *The Millennial Harbinger*, Thos. Newman, ed., Seneca Falls, NY. 1861. This copy was furnished by Arlen Rankin; Lyon, R.V. *The Gospel of God*, Suspension Bridge, N.Y., circa 1863; Lyon, R.V., *The Sanctuary,* office of *The Millennial Harbinger,* Thos. Newman, ed., Seneca Falls, N.Y., 1863; Lyon, R.V. Correspondence, *The Prophetic Watchman and Herald of the Kingdom*, J.M. Stephenson, ed., Harvard, Il. Oct. 12, 1867. Orr, Ralph G. "How Anglo-Israelism Entered into the Seventh-day Churches of God a history of the doctrine from John Wilson to Joseph W. Tkach," retrieved in April 1999. http://www.wcg.org This website has been replaced with www.cgi.org and does not presently contain Orr's article; Reference to Lyon, *The Restitution Herald* March 22, 1916; Williams, Byron, *Abstracts of Obituaries and Verbatim Marriage Announcements printed in The Restitution 1874-1900*, self-published, 1993 p. 83.

Magruder, Allan Bowie
b. September 9, 1810
d. August 24, 1885

Allan Magruder lived in Virginia and was well known throughout the state, especially at Washington. He was a prominent attorney who shared his name with the legislator from Louisiana who served in Congress 1812-1813, although the legislator was a generation older and died in 1822. The Allan B. Magruder in this entry may have been named after the earlier Allan Bowie Magruder who was already prominent at the time of the younger Magruder's birth. The names of these two men have become confused in Internet resources; this entry will clear up that confusion.

At the time that the younger Allan B. Magruder entered the social and political scene of Washington, he would have had name recognition because of the previous Allan Magruder whose reputation may have helped the younger gain an immediate audience for his writings. The younger Magruder never served in Congress, but he established his own name by preaching, debating and penning newspaper articles. From this point forward, this entry discusses only the younger Magruder, unless otherwise noted.

Allan B. Magruder married Sarah, and they had one son and five daughters. Allan lived in an elite society but accepted and followed the meek and humble Jesus. Magruder was affiliated with the Disciples of Christ early in his adult life, and later, he joined with the Christadelphians. He edited *The Virginia Advocate*, a Disciples paper, in 1836. When he took interest in the Age-to-Come message, he was forced out of the Disciples' church at Charlottesville. Because of this, he sued Alexander Campbell (1788-1866), the founder of the Disciples. Allan turned his support to Dr. John Thomas, who preached the future Kingdom of God on earth. Peter Hemingray credits Magruder with keeping the work alive in Virginia during Dr. Thomas' absences.

General John Magruder, Allan's brother, assisted Dr. Thomas through Confederate battle lines in order to visit southern churches. John Magruder commanded Confederate defensive lines from Richmond to Fort Monroe. He helped smooth the way for Dr. Thomas on his preaching trips. Yet, after the Civil War, Allan Magruder and Dr. Thomas became estranged, possibly because Magruder objected to Dr. Thomas' teaching of mortal emergence. Magruder argued for immortal emergence from the grave, "changed in a twinkling of an eye."

Allan Magruder was a highly respected lawyer who practiced in Charlottesville, Virginia. His skills in arguing cases equipped him to engage in debates. In 1859, he debated with Mr. E.E. Orvis on two subjects: "Punishment of the Wicked" and "Kingdom of God." Magruder affirmed the wicked would be punished in the lake of fire, and Orvis denied. Magruder affirmed the Kingdom of God is yet in the future and will be established on earth. Orvis again denied. E.E. Orvis was an attorney in the capitol city who was also skilled in debate. The events may have been heated.

Magruder distributed printed copies of the 435-page Orvis debate, which he sold through *The Gospel Banner and Millennial Advocate.* Throughout these years, while conversing with Dr. Thomas, Magruder also communicated with Benjamin Wilson of the One Faith people in Geneva, Illinois. Benjamin Wilson featured an excerpt from the debate in *The Gospel Banner.*

Transferring to the Age to Come/Church of God for doctrinal reasons would have been a comfortable move for Magruder. The doctrines were nearly identical except for mortal emergence. Magruder believed in the oneness of God, sleep of the dead, destruction of the wicked, the second coming of Christ and the Kingdom of God on earth, all Bible teachings emphasized in the Church of God. He began preaching for the Church of God in the Fort Valley at Seven Fountains, Virginia, at Baltimore, and as far away as Kentucky. He wrote for *The Restitution*, the successor to *The Gospel Banner*, both Church of God papers.

One of Magruder's most notable accomplishments

was his book, *Reply to Ingersoll*. Robert "Colonel Bob" Ingersoll was a famous and articulate atheist of that day. Magruder invited him to debate, but Ingersoll refused the offer. One theologian had written a rebuttal to Ingersoll, but Magruder felt he had botched it badly because of questionable theology. Magruder decided to write a rebuttal to Ingersoll's arguments against God, and the result was *Reply to Ingersoll*. It received significant notice. The second edition of *Reply* was published in 1880 and announced in *The Restitution*. A copy of the book is contained in the Archives of Atlanta Bible College. *Reply to Ingersoll* is still highly acclaimed and found in libraries across the nation, especially wherever Ingersoll special collections are housed. The error that some librarians have made is that they attribute *Reply to Ingersoll* to the older A.B. Magruder who died in 1822. It is surprising that they are unable to reconcile the death date of the older gentleman with a publishing date nearly 60 years after his death!

Allan Magruder of Virginia traveled to do evangelistic preaching. He visited Henderson County, Kentucky, and became well acquainted with the congregation. When Magruder died, Ingram Crockett (1856-1934) wrote an eloquent tribute: "Magruder sleeps with full assurance of a joyful resurrection to glory, honor and immortality." Crockett sent the obituary to *The Restitution*.

Crockett, a relative of Davy Crockett, was the Poet Laureate of Kentucky. Ingram Crockett authored *A Year Book of Kentucky Woods and Fields* and *The Magic of the Woods and other Poems* (1908). He was highly esteemed among his peers as Allan Magruder had been among his. Crockett also believed in the Age to Come and wrote several articles for *The Restitution*.

It is entirely possible that the congregation with whom Magruder had worshipped was split over the question of Jesus' paternity. Mr. Nevius of Washington, D.C., wrote to *The Gospel Banner* in September 1860, stating that while most believed in the virgin birth of Jesus, he had come to accept that Joseph was the father of Jesus. Benjamin Wilson responded to Nevius by citing both Matthew and Luke's genealogy and stating that Christ was to be the seed of the woman and was called the *Son of God*. Wilson further stated he was sorry this issue had split the church in Washington, D.C.

As an aside, Wilson's language shows that the seeds of Josephism were planted in his mind also. Generally, if a man says Jesus was "called" the Son of God, he is not willing to say he was the "begotten" Son of God. Rather, he will say Jesus "became" the Son of God at his baptism or resurrection. Rather than use terminology such as begotten, they will refer to his "Sonship." This paternity issue was discussed in *The Banner* several times. Before his death, Benjamin Wilson took an open stand supporting Joseph as the father of Jesus. (See the Benjamin Wilson entry for a thorough discussion on Josephism.)

In 1883, two years before his death, Magruder wrote a series of articles for *The Restitution* on "Bible Baptism." Magruder strongly advocated using the baptismal formula in Matthew 28:19: "in the name of the Father, the Son, and the Holy Spirit." He said Jesus used those words, why shouldn't the church? Wouldn't it even be *wrong* to avoid citing Scripture? In a subsequent article, Magruder stated that the Holy Spirit may be hindered when the Matthew formula is not used. At that time most Church of God members believed the Holy Spirit is received through the reading of the Word, so Magruder felt that the consequences of not citing a portion of the Scripture could be significant.

The question of the role of the Holy Spirit is interesting due to the conflict in Magruder's church over the virgin birth. To deny the Holy Spirit in the conception of Christ opens the door to denying the work of the Holy Spirit elsewhere in Scripture, and in the life of the believer. Magruder clearly believed in the work and power of the Holy Spirit.

Allan B. Magruder died and was laid to rest in a cemetery at Stephens City, Virginia.

See Crockett, Ingram
Malone, Dr. Alfred
Wilson, Benjamin

Bibliography: Ancestry.com. U.S. Census. D.C. Washington. Washington Ward 4. 1850; Ancestry.com. U.S. Census. Maryland. Baltimore (Independent city). Baltimore Ward 19. 1870; "Announcement," *The Gospel Banner and Millennial Advocate*, B. Wilson, ed., Geneva, Il., May, 1860; Nevius, and others, "Paternity of Jesus," *The Gospel Banner and Millennial Advocate*, B. Wilson, ed., Geneva, Il., Sept. 1860, Jan. 1861 "Genealogy of Wyatt Ingram Crockett" retrieved May 11, 2008 from website: http://www.cumberland.org/hfcpc/McGreFAM.htm; Crockett, Ingram. Euology of Allan Magruder, *The Restitution*, Plymouth, Indiana. Sept. 1885; Hemingray, Peter. *John Thomas. His Friends and His Faith*. Christadelphian Tidings. Canton, Mi., 2003; Hemingray's book has detailed information about Allan B. Magruder in Chapter 22. The book may be purchased from author; Magruder, Alan and E.E. Orvis, Debate. *The Gospel Banner*, Vol. 6, 1860 p. 56; Magruder, Allan B. "Bible Baptism," *The Restitution,* Plymouth, In., April 25, 1883; "Announcement of *Reply to Ingersoll*," 2d ed. *The Restitution*, Plymouth, In., Jan. 1880; Report of History of Magruder Preaching at Seven Fountains, *The Restitution Herald*, July 10, 1912; Montgomery, David B. *A Genealogical History of the Montgomery's and their Descendants*, Owensville, Ind. 1903, Ch. 13, retrieved Googlebooks. com Dec. 25, 2010; Williams, Byron. *Abstracts of Obituaries and Verbatim Marriage Announcements printed in The Restitution, 1874-1900*, self-published, 1993, record of Magruder's death p. 29.

Malone, Dr. John Alfred
b. 1835
d. February 16, 1893

Alfred Malone was born in Indiana. He and wife Hattie had one son. Dr. Malone preached the Gospel of the Kingdom. He had come out of the Disciples, and he said when he preached about the kingdom, they listened. In his hometown of Palestine, however, people were not interested. Malone was a physician who operated a drug store. He said his change of beliefs did not adversely affect his business, but he prayed he could preach more, and that people in Palestine would listen.

Malone went south into Clark County, Illinois, for three days in 1860. He preached at the Moriah church that was experiencing conflict. Membership had fallen from 40 to six. He baptized the second wife of John Partlowe, the congregation's preacher for the previous 12 years. Malone told the congregation if they could settle their dispute, he would be back. Malone wrote to Benjamin Wilson that he prayed he would hear from them again.

Dr. Malone also preached in Indiana at the Old Union and New Liberty Churches of God north of Indianapolis. He reported in August 1868 to Benjamin Wilson in the *Gospel Banner* that he encouraged members to subscribe to the *Banner*. He reported having found "not one copy of the *Gospel Banner* in either church." Some members said, "We are taking the *Herald*" (Thomas Wilson's *Herald of the Coming Kingdom and Christian Instructor*). Malone believed they should take *two* papers about One Faith, to have *variety* in reading matter. Some said, "*The Herald* and *The Banner* should be united." Malone replied, "I think not unless they are enlarged and both editors are retained." He definitely supported *The Gospel Banner.*

In the later years of 1868 and 1869, Dr. Malone's writing on the subject, "Do the Dead Live until the Coming of Christ in His Kingdom?" appeared regularly in *The Gospel Banner.* This title is not as unusual as it seems, for the series was a discourse on the orthodox teaching of natural immortality versus the doctrine of conditional immortality. The series indicated Malone's roots in the development of early thought (doctrine) of the Church of God in America, especially in the Midwest.

He wrote once asking for grace and moderation in remarks made about people who did not believe in One Faith or Age to Come. Although Benjamin Wilson did not emphasize the doctrine and phrase "Age to Come," people in the field believed it, and Malone's words echoed the sentiments of the readers. Malone thought some comments on the subject were too caustic and might delay new readers from accepting the Gospel of the Kingdom.

In addition to receiving the Spirit through the reading of the Word, Dr. Malone believed in the indwelling of the Holy Spirit that enables one to serve the Lord through the gifts of the Spirit. He said in the pages of *The Gospel Banner*:

> We believe in all that the scriptures teach, when rightly applied, and "in the words of the Spirit." We believe in the indwelling of the Holy Spirit, in prayer in the church, in the family, and in secret.
>
> And though we may not be able to show *how* the Spirit is received and enjoyed by the believer, yet *we know that this is the case.* We are not commanded to preach the Spirit, but we are commanded to "*preach the word*"—to preach "Christ and him crucified." The *word believed and obeyed* will bring the Spirit into the heart, and exhibit him in the life, and lead to God.

He published a book in 1879 titled *The Age to Come* with a subtitle, *Embracing some of The Things Concerning the Kingdom of God and the name of Jesus Christ, as well as The Future and Eternal Age.* This book was published by *The Restitution* in Plymouth, Indiana, identifying it and its author within the fellowship of the Church of God.

Dr. Malone's premise stated that the King James Bible did not accurately render some of the biblical ideas of the Age to Come. In his introductory remarks he noted:

> There are some words and phrases in the King James' version [that] seemingly oppose this doctrine, and indeed to the veracity of the Bible itself.
>
> For example, King James' version makes Paul say that Jesus died in the *end* of the world. Yet more than eighteen centuries since that event have been rolled back into the ages past, and still the material world is standing. Either Paul was wrong or the King James' version does not fairly represent the original. Heb. 9:26, "But now once in *the end* of the world hath he appeared to put away sin by the sacrifice of himself." The word rendered world here is *aioonoon* in the plural, and should be rendered *ages—not* world or worlds. But it is true that Christ died in the end of the ages—the Jewish ages.

Because of Malone's medical background, his comments regarding scriptural interpretation are full of medical ideas. To illustrate the "sleep of the dead" concept, he noted:

> Chloroform or other anaesthetics may be so used that all thought, feeling and action, other than the involuntary action of the heart and arteries, may be arrested as profoundly as in death; so that capital surgical operations may be performed, and the patient not know it, not feel it. If in natural and profound sleep nothing is known; if the cataleptic may know nothing for days, weeks and months; if those under the influence of anaesthetics know not anything, feel not anything; is it strange that God takes away man's breath or spirit, and that man shall know nothing, feel nothing, until God shall have raised him from the dead? Surely not, and as the Bible is full of such teaching, we cannot be a believer unless we believe it.

Dr. Malone's approach when explaining the Age to Come was different than Joseph Marsh's. Since no evidence exists to indicate Malone quoted Marsh, it must be assumed that during the 28 years since Marsh's book was published, copies of it had become scarce. While Marsh explained the Age to Come by comparing the prophecy systems of the Millerites, the Catholics and other denominations to Marsh's interpretation of biblical prophecy, Malone began immediately to do word studies on Greek terms relating to the ages, and then he discussed the theology. The result is a scholarly and powerful work. Whatever his formal education had been, he certainly had been trained in Greek and Hebrew.

Malone also discussed another topic of interest to Church of God pastors: resurrection and the sequence of those being raised. He said under the heading "Eclectic Resurrection":

> The chosen dead only are to be then raised. I Thess. 4:16, 17: "For the Lord himself shall descend from heaven with a shout, with the voice of the archangel, and with the trump of God. And the dead in Christ shall rise first. Then we which are alive and remain shall be caught up together with them in the clouds, to meet the Lord in the air; and so shall we ever be with the Lord."
>
> It is only those in Christ, not sinners that are to come up in "the first resurrection." There cannot be a "first" without a second or general one. But the second does not take place then, but "a thousand years afterward". I Cor. 15:21-23: "For since by man came death, by man came also the resurrection of the dead. For as in Adam all die, even so in Christ shall all be made alive, afterward they that are Christ's at his coming." This epistle was written to Christians only, but does the phrase "As in Adam all die, so in Christ shall all be made alive," embrace the whole human family? By no means. Whosoever dies in Adam and who are also in Christ will be made alive in this resurrection, but none others.

These comments clearly prove that Malone was not a universalist. He believed that only those who express belief and commitment to Christ will be raised and rewarded, not all humans on earth.

Malone wrote frequently for the pages of *The Restitution*. In 1883, he authored an article, "One Fair Chance for All?" that discussed aspects of the Age to Come, resurrection and probation of the nations.

The Archives of Atlanta Bible College in McDonough, Georgia, received a copy of Malone's book from the library of A.R. Underwood, editor and publisher of *The Restitution* at Plymouth, Indiana. Perhaps some day this book can be scanned and made available once again to researchers.

See Magruder, Allan B. - Holy Spirit
    Marsh, Joseph
    Underwood, A.R.
    Wilson, Benjamin

Bibliography: Ancestry.com. U.S. Census. Indiana. Gibson. Patoka. 1870; Ancestry.com. Indiana Deaths 1882-1920, record for John A. Malone, Gibson County; Malone, Alfred; "Report on trip to Clark County," *Gospel Banner*, Vol. 6, 1860; Malone, A., M.D. *Age to Come*, Office of Restitution, Plymouth, In. 1879; Malone, Alfred, "Letter to Editor," *Gospel Banner and Millennial Advocate*, Jan. 1, 1868; Malone, A. "The Banner-The Cause of Christ," *Gospel Banner*, B. Wilson, ed., Geneva, Il., Aug. 1, 1868; Malone, A. "Do the Dead live until the Coming of Christ in his Kingdom?" No. 3. *Gospel Banner*, B. Wilson, ed., Geneva, Il.. Feb. 1, 1869, p. 47-49; Malone, A. "Spiritual Gifts," *Gospel Banner*, Dec. 1, 1868; p 450-453; Marsh, Joseph, *Age to Come*, self-published, Advent Harbinger Office, Rochester, NY. 1851.

Marsh, Edgar A.
b. 1849
d. 1891?

Edgar Marsh was the son of Julius W. (1802-1861) and Harriett A. Cox Marsh. Julius was Joseph Marsh's brother. Edgar was born in Detroit, Michigan, while the family resided in Buchanan where a strong Church of God nucleus was located. Patra Marsh Hepworth noted "that the family moved around quite a bit." Julius moved the family to Greenfield, Illinois, then to Wisconsin to live with in-laws, returned to Buchanan in 1850, and then back to Illinois by 1851. Joseph Marsh and his wife visited Julius and his family at Cherry Valley, Illinois, on Joseph's western tour in 1851. Edgar was two.

Julius died soon after he moved his family to Iowa. Harriett eventually remarried to George Fischer who was a photographer. They had one child, Lillian. Edgar's sister, Sylvia married and divorced, an unusual thing in those days. Edgar married Josephine Snow, and they had three children, Oscar, George Eldred and Orrisa. From 1870 until 1891, Edgar preached in Iowa and Missouri. Some said he preached for the Advent Christians but that was not an unusual assumption. Pulpit sharing was common. Yet, it is thought that even though Edgar preached for the Advent Christians, he was Church of God since he served as the secretary of the Iowa Conference in 1889. He was a printer by trade as his Uncle Joseph had been.

The Archives of Atlanta Bible College yielded additional information about the generations of this family. Several books had been donated by George Eldred (G.E.) Marsh, and they revealed the lineage through notes made by Marsh and via stickers on the inside front cover. This implies that Edgar passed his books to sons Oscar and G.E. The date in the front of one book, though partly illegible, is May 3, 1847 or 1848. As Edgar Marsh wasn't born until 1849, this book must have first belonged to Julius Marsh or perhaps to Joseph Marsh himself!

For a time, Edgar Marsh lived at Manchester, Iowa, a fact discovered from the front cover of *Our Hope, Why Are we Adventists?* published in 1884. This book also has a second note "Found by G.E. Marsh at Manchester, Iowa 10/20/1906." Additional evidence of family lineage is seen from a sticker in the frontpiece of *The Unspeakable Gift* by J.H. Pettingill, a famous author of the 19th century, who may have been related to the Marsh family.

After Edgar died, Josephine moved to Marshalltown, Iowa, to live near her family. The 1900 US Census notes that her three children were still living at home. The whereabouts of Edgar and Josephine's graves are unknown at this writing.

   See Marsh, Joseph
       Marsh, Oscar J.
       Marsh, G.E. (20th)
       Priestley, Joseph
       Smith, Elias

Bibliography: Ancestry.com U.S. Census. Michigan. Berrien. Buchanan. 1850; U.S. Census. Wisconsin. Walworth, Whitewater. 1860; Ancestry.com, U.S. Census. Iowa. Bremer. Waverly. Ward 3 1870; Ancestry.com, U.S. Census. Iowa. Fayette. Windsor. 1880; Ancestry.com, U.S. Census. Iowa. Marshall. Marshall Dist. 117. 1900; Marsh Library books from Archives of Atlanta Bible College, examined Feb. 2008; "Minutes of the Executive Board of the General Conference 1888-1892," which fell into the hands of A.J. Eychaner after the conference failed, and which also contains Eychaner's diary owned by ABC Archives, McDonough, Ga.; Hepworth, Patra Marsh. "Genealogy of Marsh Family" at http://www.ninetravelers.com; Marsh, E.A. "Report of Iowa Conference." *The Restitution*, S.A. Chaplin, ed. Plymouth, In. June 20, 1889.

Marsh, Joseph
   b. December 6, 1802
   d. September 13, 1863

A. **Attempts to Unify the Movement**
B. **Influence of Charles Beecher in Understanding Time**
C. **Criticisms of Marsh**
D. **Marsh publishes** *Age to Come*
E. **Persecutions Begin**
F. **Another Western Tour**
G. **The Kingsbury Meetings**
H. **Principle of Literal Interpretation**
I. **Age to Come and Anglo-Israelism**
J. **Disagreeing with Colleagues**
K. **Literal Interpretation and the Sabbath Question**
L. **Line of Periodical Succession**
M. **His Last Western Tour**

Joseph Marsh was born in St. Albans, Vermont, to Lemuel and Rosanna Marsh. The family moved to LeRoy, New York, when Joseph was still young. They joined the Methodist church, but then they became acquainted with the teaching of the oneness of God. They rejected the trinity, and were eventually forced to leave the Methodist fellowship.

At 16, Joseph's mother died, forcing Joseph to move in with his older brother James. Sadly, James died soon after from cholera. Joseph's father remarried and moved west. Joseph became a carpenter to support himself. In Rochester, he learned of the Christians (Christ-yans). Joseph testified then that he was emancipated from sin, forgiven and called to preach. Because of his newfound faith, he was baptized in 1823. Joseph entered the ministry in 1824, quickly gaining the reputation of "The Boy Preacher."

On August 4, 1830, Joseph married Sarah Adams in her hometown, Sennet, New York. Joseph's friend, Joseph Badger, performed the ceremony. Joseph and Sarah had three daughters, Sarah E., Mary M. and Parmelia J. (nicknamed Jane or Jennie). For the next 13 years, Joseph pastored Christian churches in New York at Milan, Sennett, Union Mills and Clay. At that same time, he also undertook his first arduous journey through the Midwest wilderness. Possibly during this trip he first encountered typhoid; it plagued him the rest of his life.

Jospeh was an avid Bible student, searching out all avenues of doctrine to satisfy his mind and heart. He stated in the December 1846 issue of *The Voice of Truth* that he had studied the state of the dead in his "early ministry" 20 years before. From his study he determined the Bible was silent on the subject of disembodied spirits. The body goes to the grave to await resurrection. The doctrine of Hades as a site for disembodied spirits, he wrote, "is of heathen origin."

Shortly after Marsh assumed editorial responsibility for *The Christian Palladium* which he held from May 1839 until December 1843, he began the series entitled "Church of God"—a defense of that name as being the scriptural name for the church. Marsh later published the booklet, *Church of God,* a copy of which is in the Archives of Atlanta Bible College in McDonough, Georgia.

During this same time period, Alexander Campbell's group also debated their choice of denominational name. Some wanted "Christians," but the Christian Connexion objected to the confusion it would cause. Campbell wanted "Disciples," which was scriptural and had been used in the first century by the disciples even before believers were called Christians. Disciples of Christ became the official name, but people still referred to them as Campbellites, an easy appellation to recall.

Joseph Badger, editor of *The Christian Palladium,* began a diatribe against the growing Campbellite movement through its pages. Badger founded *The Palladium* in 1832 and edited it until May 1839. His editorial stance did not endear him with Alexander Campbell. Thomas Olbricht, a scholar of the Disciples of Christ, wrote:

> About 1834 the Christians began to recognize Alexander Campbell as the new enemy in the West.... The views concerning Campbell, expressed in the Christian Palladium in 1834, were mixed. In March of that year (p.322) he was mentioned and called a sectarian. In the very same issue, however, L.D. Fleming sent in a report, following a visit to Bethany, which is quite favorable (p.342). In September, an article appeared opposing Campbell's view of the Holy Spirit, and Badger wrote on the subject in the same issue.

David Graham said, "Badger maintained a war of words with Campbell for several years." Graham noted that Joseph Badger challenged Campbell repeatedly, and that Marsh's jabs were "trivial" compared to Badger's.

When Marsh became editor of *The Palladium,* he continued Badger's initiative of "jabbing" Campbell. Marsh had two pet peeves regarding the work of the Disciples. One was Campbell's teaching on baptism for the remission of sin. Marsh said baptism is often used as an entry into church membership. Marsh felt that men could be saved who did not have an opportunity for baptism. The issue of baptism was to haunt Marsh later in his dealings with Dr. John Thomas.

Marsh's second pet peeve with the Campbellites was the emphasis by Barton Stone and Alexander Campbell to unite the eastern Christians with the western Christians. Marsh objected to the close association of Stone's Christians to Campbell's Disciples. Furthermore, Marsh stated that Stone had become one with them, and any Christians who united with Stone must also become Disciples. In the June 1841 *Christian Messenger* Stone attempted to answer Marsh's objection, but he was not too successful. Marsh's objection was significant. Any Christian believing oneness of God in agreement with Barton Stone could not only be a Stoneite Christian as Stone was also a Disciple. So there could be no merging of Oneness people with the Disciples.

During his tenure at *The Palladium,* Marsh and his wife were responsible for managing the Christian Book Concern, which not only published *The Palladium* but made other printed materials available to members of the Christian Connexion.

By the 1840s, Marsh was involved in the Adventist movement and began to publish articles in *The Palladium* on the second coming. David Rowe, Adventist historian, has suggested that, under Marsh's editorial direction, *The Palladium* was so influential in its Adventist message it very likely was the means by which Joshua V. Himes became informed of the message and the activities of William Miller.

The Palladium's editorial board asked Marsh to resign. Surviving reports on the incident are mixed. It must have been painful to Marsh for he mentioned it years later, but at the time, he complied. Marsh's own writings confuse the issue. In 1842 he wrote: "I am bound here [at *The Palladium*] and long to be free, and mean to have my liberty as soon as circumstances will admit." Marsh wrote to Miller: "I am fully convinced of the time [of Jesus' return] and mean to proclaim it fearlessly from the pulpit and the press. My course is fixed, let the consequences follow."

Soon, Marsh was ousted from *The Palladium*, perhaps sooner than he had planned to leave, and not long after that, he turned away from the Christian Connexion. Reflecting on his discontent with the editorial board, Marsh concluded later they were corrupt in 1843 when they asked him to leave; they were corrupt in 1845 also.

After Marsh's death in 1863, his friend R.V. Lyon responded to a story the Christian Connexion published in *The Herald of Gospel Liberty* about "Marsh leaving *The Palladium* of his own free will." Lyon said:

> This is a mistake. They turned him out because he had embraced the doctrine of the soon coming of Christ to reign on the earth—sleep of the saints, and destruction of the wicked, etc." Further Lyon said, "It must be obvious to all that the Christian Church had modified their views and feelings, instead of Elder Marsh.

William Miller set the final date for Christ's return to earth as October 22, 1844. When Christ did not return, there was a great disillusionment among Second Adventist believers. This period describing their pain has come to be known as the "Great Disappointment" or "Bitter Disappointment" which cast the Miller-led Adventist movement into chaos.

Others set additional dates for the Second Advent over the next few years, and the followers were disappointed again. Marsh set at least two dates. But, the ever-present feeling of caution was there even if unheeded. Today, people outside the Church of God are still setting dates. The Church of God has refrained from date-setting for the past 150 years so as to avoid bringing disrepute upon the soon return of the Lord and upon the denomination. No one knows the day or hour because even Christ does not know when He will return. It is said the Lord will reveal it to Him, and the church is told to "watch."

In 1845, due to financial struggles with *The Voice of Truth*, Joseph Marsh determined to save the paper by doubling the amount of news and publishing bi-weekly instead of weekly. While the readers loved having more news and letters, they really wanted to see it weekly.

Page one of The Voice of Truth *from October 17, 1844, just prior to the Bitter Disappointment.*

O.R.L. Crozier wrote a note to this effect in the April 9, 1845, edition. He said, "Let us have it weekly. The crisis demands the change." At this time, Adventists were looking once more for the return of Christ before the end of the month.

A. Attempts to Unify the Movement

William Miller - Marsh first began publishing The Voice of Truth *for Miller to broadcast the message of the Second Coming.*

After the Bitter Disappointment, Marsh began to question the Millerite movement, a fact that became apparent by his absence at the Albany Conference in New York on April 29, 1845. Marsh said politely he could not make the trip due to expenses and that his business was "too urgent." Miller had called for the conference at Albany intending to unite all Adventist leaders behind the collapsing movement, but that goal did not succeed.

In spite of his disillusionment with Miller, Marsh called a unity conference in Rochester for April 2-5, 1846. Among those who continued to walk with Marsh were Peter and Phillip Hough from Canada, D.C. Robison from Ohio and John Grant from New York. Joshua Himes and William Miller also attended. At this conference, Miller addressed the members and offered this statement of faith from which, it can be seen, Marsh gradually departed. Miller advocated a resurrection with mortal emergence before the change to immortality for the righteous, and a split resurrection with no clear statement about the Time factor. Time would become an important issue for Marsh. Here is Miller's statement of faith as Marsh published it in *Voice of Truth,* April 1846:
- The second Advent
- The resurrection of the just (John 5: 28, 29), and the second resurrection, but the time is not given between them.
- Literal resurrection of *mortal* bodies from corruption to eternal life.
- Reign of Christ on renovated earth to be fulfilled in the future.
- Return of Jews to land of Canaan according to the flesh.
- New heaven and new earth will be the territory for the Kingdom.
- Historic interpretation of prophecy, Babylon, Medo-Persia, etc., in the 1260 years.
- Time of Second Advent of the Lord had been mistaken but Miller felt Christ was nigh, even at the door.

In 1847, Marsh mentioned that William Miller was not as strong or as healthy as he had once been, but Miller continued to give fatherly counsel and expressed his sorrow for miscalculating a date. Marsh reported that Miller believed conferences were a waste of time and money, a burden on the local church and not a place to engage in deep Bible research. Miller recommended against having conferences.

In 1851, Marsh said the result of the Albany conference was to "check the spirit of free investigation, free thought and free speech, but the Word of God could not be bound, hence the good cause of the Bible triumphed." The happenings at Albany affirmed Marsh's quest toward understanding the prophecies of the Age to Come. Even though Marsh did not attend, he certainly knew what had happened at that meeting and continued to digest the affects from it for years to come.

By 1851, when Marsh published *Age to Come*, his prophetic interpretation was nowhere similar to Miller's. Joseph Marsh's interpretation of prophecy set him apart from all other Adventists because of his understanding of the last days, the future of the Jews, the times of restitution, the establishment of the throne of David, the destiny of the wicked, the nature of resurrection of believers and the time of that resurrection, and the nature of the thousand year reign of Christ known as the Millennium.

Other Millenarians covered many of the topics stressed by Marsh, but no one understood the Time factor as he did. Marsh and his followers were nicknamed "Judaizers," "Restorationists," "Soul Sleepers," and later, "Restitutionists." One of the chief critics was J.V. Himes, the director of public relations for the Millerite movement.

B. Influence of Charles Beecher in Understanding Time

Upon stating that Marsh had a unique understanding of the chronology and time factor, one must also note that at first he did not understand it. In fact, Marsh refrained from publishing his own ideas about Age to Come because he was uncertain about the Time. Marsh came to believe that the millennial kingdom would be set up using man's time. Perusal of *The Advent Harbinger* reveals his many articles on this subject. Marsh's friend, Charles Beecher of Fort Wayne, Indiana, helped Marsh clarify his thoughts on the amount of time required for Christ to establish the millennial kingdom.

Beecher wrote a lengthy article for *The Advent Harbinger* on the topic Age to Come. He said Christ will work through the Jews to teach the nations; to bring order to the throne of David; to bring about restitution of all things; to judge the wicked living and reward the righteous living using 24-hour days to which man is accustomed.

In June 1847, Beecher elaborated on his views of the first resurrection in an article for Marsh's *The Voice of Truth*. He wrote to explain five components of premillennialism. These included the Millennium, Day of Judgment, Resurrection, Parousia and the Conflagration. In each case he explained the common view and another view (his view). First, he explained the common view: "At the end of the millennium the saints from glory and the lost from torment are summoned to receive bodies, which earth being no more their abode, they carry back respectively to Heaven or to Hell."

A better view, he said, is:

> In the millennial morning Christ, the second Adam, descends and stands in Eden restored. The Elect, their numbers complete, rise from Hades [the grave] and stand the second Eve by His side. Sons of God by resurrection in a regenerate earth, they are married. This is the Exanastasis of the righteous. This is the First Resurrection or the resurrection from the dead of Luke 20:35. The simple Anastasis or resurrection of the rest of the dead is different in origin, nature and end. It begins in no spiritual renewal, confers no eternal life, occurs in the evening of the great day and ends in the second death.

Marsh may not have agreed with his friend on every aspect of this view of resurrection, for Marsh said that Jesus restored Eden after he returned to earth. Christ is to be the Creator of the new heavens and new earth. Christ would not just return and find Eden already restored.

Like Beecher, Marsh was anti-creedal. The Adventists left orthodox churches, repudiated their creeds, and were not anxious to adopt new ones. Marsh said creeds were of human origin and imperfect. Truth never changes but creeds do. They can be set aside; they are divisive; they imply implicit faith; they prevent increase of the knowledge of Christ.

Marsh persevered in his studies and influenced some notable Adventists who became avid exponents of Age to Come. J.B. Cook, former missionary to Siam in the 1830s, was Marsh's friend in Rochester and a member of the Church of God there. Later, Cook became the pastor of that church. R.V. Lyon, a noted preacher in Canada West, was solidly behind Marsh. Mark Allen, Newell Bond, Levi Chase and Dr. J.P. Weethee agreed with Marsh.

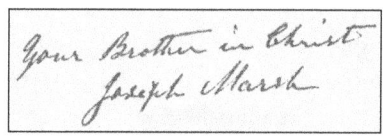
Marsh's signature

C. Criticisms of Marsh

In reading early issues of *The Voice of Truth* one discovers that Marsh's understanding of the Age to Come had not completely "jelled," but by the end of the last volume, his thoughts were coming together. In an article in the April 1, 1846, issue of *The Voice of Truth*, Marsh refuted the argument of a spiritualist woman who said that the first resurrection was the regeneration of the Christian from his sins. Marsh wrote:

> The word of truth teaches that the first resurrection is the dead in Christ rise first (1 Thessalonians 4:16). Nothing is said about the resurrection of the wicked following next, for a very good reason, viz. the living saints were next to be changed; all caught up to meet Christ. All this, cleansing the earth, the reign of Christ and his saints a thousand years, were to intervene between the resurrection of the dead in Christ and the resurrection of the wicked."

In that simple statement is the premise that became the foundation for Marsh's preaching of the Age to Come. The concept denies limited resurrection. It states the unjust will be raised and not remain in the grave resulting from the Adamic death. This is the concept on which Benjamin Wilson and Dr. John Thomas disagreed with Marsh. It is one of the reasons the Church of God split in 1921 and *The Restitution* ceased in 1925.

The last year that Marsh edited *The Voice of Truth and Glad Tidings of the Kingdom at Hand,* 1847, he published a note entitled, "Delinquents Read This." It asked those who were behind in accounts to please pay. O.R.L. Crozier and Hiram Edson raised a question about how much Marsh spent to publish *The Voice,* and how much he earned week to week. In fact, they criticized Marsh's handling of the financial affairs of *The Voice of Truth,* and printed the criticism in *The Day Dawn,* the paper they co-edited. *The Day Dawn* had an irregular publishing schedule; it did not survive past a few issues.

Marsh was stung by the unexpected criticism, and in the next issue of *The Voice,* he gave full disclosure of his accounts, including a statement from his printer verifying everything Marsh said. Still, by the end of July, Marsh settled his accounts and ceased to publish *The Voice of Truth*. Within the year, having suffered some disrepute for his doctrine on the cleansing of the heavenly sanctuary and his attacks on Marsh, O.R.L. Crozier sank into the background, only to re-emerge later as an assistant in Marsh's print shop. Evidently, the two men worked well from that point on. This surely must demonstrate Marsh's attitude of forgiveness.

In 1848, Marsh began to publish *The Advent Harbinger*. He had completely broken with William Miller at this point. Within the year, *The Bible Advocate* merged with *The Harbinger*. By June 1849, Marsh changed the name to *The Advent Harbinger and Bible Advocate* and numbered it volume one.

By the time he began *The Advent Harbinger*, Marsh was fully convinced of the prophetic accuracy of the Age to Come. He began discussing it in the pages of *The Harbinger*, and slowly but surely readers began to respond, some to agree, others to question.

Marsh was never to be completely free of critics. His life would have been much sweeter if he could have preached tirelessly for the Lord without being cut down by those who disagreed so vehemently with him.

D. Marsh publishes *Age to Come*

When Marsh was able to fully verbalize and write about the Time factor, he began writing his definitive work on the prophecies. He had wrestled with the issue of Time since 1842 or before, but intense study of the Time problem helped set his understanding of the Age to Come. In that sense, he was already on the path to understanding before the Bitter Disappointment on October 22, 1844. Previous to the Disappointment, he believed in general or universal resurrection, but he did not believe that the righteous and wicked would be raised simultaneously. He believed the rest of the dead, referred to in Revelation 20:5, were the wicked. He cited John 5:28, 29 "all who hear his voice will rise from the tomb" and Acts 24:15 "there is going to be a resurrection of both the righteous and the unrighteous" (*Emphatic Diaglott*). He did not fully grasp the *Time* in which the Lord would accomplish the work of setting up the kingdom in the Age to Come.

Marsh was puzzled also about Israel. Again, Charles Beecher was very helpful to Marsh in sorting out the issues on Israel's restoration. Like it had on the issue of Time, Beecher's separate series on Israel challenged Marsh's thinking. He published Beecher's articles at first without agreeing with them. Beecher separated Revelation 20 from Revelation 21 so that they were interpreted as a chronology and not a restatement of chapter 20 by chapter 21. Marsh promised to study this matter. By 1849, Marsh acknowledged that he concluded Beecher was right.

Marsh began to fully discuss the Age to Come in his paper, agreeing finally, that Israel would be restored to the land in the flesh prior to the return of Christ. Mattison wrote, "This doctrinal shift…represents the most crucial point in Marsh's career." From the very beginning of Marsh's inquiries into the subject, the doctrine of Israel's restoration received extreme criticism from "Father Miller" and J.V. Himes. They called Marsh's readers "Judaizers." William Miller wrote to *The Voice of Truth*:

> Will some of our Judaizing brethren tell us how any stones can be added to the building, of which Christ laid the foundations and is builded by the Spirit, after the cap or headstone is brought in when he shall descend from heaven with a shout (I Thessalonians 4:16) and finish it. Can carnal Jew and heathen be converted and placed in the same after the headstone is brought in and the building is finished at the second coming of Christ?

By the time Marsh published his book, *Age to Come* in 1851, he had put the puzzle together. In it Marsh clearly defined the doctrine which became so important to the future leaders in the Church of God namely R.V. Lyon, J.M. Stephenson, Thomas Wilson and L.E. Conner.

Christadelphian founder Dr. John Thomas, who was outside the Age to Come and acquainted with but never part of the movement, certainly took notice. Peter Hemingray noted that Thomas and Marsh discussed Age to Come in 1847 and disagreed. At that point, Marsh did not have the Time factor or Israel's restoration worked out. When Thomas returned from England in 1850, Marsh inquired about merging *The Prophetic Expositor* (the successor to The *Advent Harbinger*) with *Herald of the Future Age*. Thomas declined the offer. Marsh subsequently published his book *Age to Come* in 1851, and Thomas changed the title of his journal to *Herald of the Coming Kingdom and Age to Come* the same year. Age to Come was in the news.

The doctrine of the Age to Come represented a shift in the established paradigm of Adventist thought. It certainly was a shift away from orthodox teaching. It would not be easy for Marsh to promote this new teaching, but he was well suited to do it. He owned his own printing press.

One story in *The Harbinger* referred to the accusations of "Judaism" brought against Marsh and his teachings of the Age to Come. A lady invited her husband to hear Elder Marsh preach but the man, a reader of J.V. Himes' *Advent Herald*, said, "No. He didn't want to hear about Judaism." After the meeting, she went home and said there was not one word about Judaism or Age to Come. The husband did not believe her. She went back in the afternoon, and asked Elder Marsh why he had not preached any discourse on either subject. She was informed, in fact, he had. The two discourses he gave were the fundamental Bible arguments about the Age to Come that Joseph Marsh routinely preached. She said, "If that is Age to Come, then I believe it, for it is the Bible."

Marsh's book, *Age to Come*, went through its first printing in a little over a month. For the second printing, Marsh lowered the price to 9.5 cents apiece or 90 cents per 100 copies. The book was more than 100-pages long, and he was practically giving it away.

David Graham has conjectured that Marsh borrowed his ideas about the Age to Come from Elias Smith, the founder of the Christian Connexion. The Age to Come, however, was being proclaimed earlier in England and America by Joseph Priestley, indicating it would have been difficult for Smith or Marsh *not* to be acquainted with that controversial prophetic idea. But since it took Marsh so long to deliberate over the issues of Time and the Restoration of the Jews, it seems more accurate to say that Marsh studied these subjects with Beecher's help.

Some scholars might conclude that Smith, Beecher and Marsh borrowed ideas from Joseph Priestley since Priestley predated them all. Yet, Priestley did not have all his ideas about the millennium clearly in place by the time of his death in 1804. Priestley believed the Age to Come, but he did not fully understand the identity of the subjects in the Kingdom, indicating he did not fully understand the Jewish question.

Age to Come clearly was a new teaching that men on both sides of the Atlantic struggled to interpret over several decades that came to a head in the 19th century.

E. Persecutions Begin

In 1851, two events occurred that were important to Marsh and to the Age-to-Come movement. First, a situation brewed in Boston regarding J.V. Himes' management of his paper, *The Advent Herald*, and the book store associated with it. Himes stated that he did not own the paper or the bookstore. He said that they belonged to the Adventist brethren. When Dr. J.P. Weethee was called from Cincinnati to Boston as pastor of the Chardon Street church, he became acquainted with Himes. Weethee and several others noted that Himes did indeed own the paper and the bookstore and profited from them. They thought Himes was not being forthright in explaining the situation, and they disclosed this information to the brethren.

Himes called a New England Union Conference to unite Adventists and to explain the situation. The purpose was to lay aside all issues and unite in spreading the message of the Second Advent. In a turn-about, Himes began his remarks at the Union Conference by attacking the Age-to-Come believers. Ultimately 16 people were banned from joining the Conference including Marsh and several others. One Adventist was so confounded at being voted out of the conference, and even being refused recognition from the floor, that he stood adamantly in place for 30 minutes until Himes called the sheriff to intimidate him with arrest. The meeting deteriorated into a brouhaha.

Marsh called a Union Conference at Rochester in April 1851. About 24 men attended from New England, New York, Ohio, Pennsylvania, Wisconsin and elsewhere. This proved to be a unifying meeting of Age-to-Come believers. And so now it appeared there were two camps: the Second Adventists and the Age-to-Come believers.

Hence, these issues were discussed pro and con through the pages of each camp's papers, with Bible interpretation mixed with mudslinging and name-calling. While Marsh printed the articles and letters of others, he personally took the high ground. Marsh was already in disrepute because he advocated the Age to Come and because he was an abolitionist; it would not benefit him or his paper to brawl over doctrine.

The second issue important to the Age-to-Come movement involved Dr. Thomas' insistence that Joseph Marsh should be re-immersed. It was presumptuous of Thomas to take such a position with a man who was not of his own fellowship. And Marsh, no doubt feeling the same way, simply refused–an expected reaction if one recalls Marsh's indignation with Barton Stone over the issue of baptism for church membership. Re-baptism was of paramount importance to Thomas, but not to Marsh. The problem escalated until it caused the Rochester Church of God to expel Marsh. He returned to worship for a while with the Christian Connexion. While this was a local church issue, it was broadcast across most of America in the various papers. This problem is more fully explained in the J section of this entry, "Disagreeing with Colleagues."

F. Another Western Tour

The summer of 1851, after the successful conclusion of the Rochester Union Conference, Marsh and his wife departed on a western and southern trip, one he expected would be long and arduous. While in Rochester, Joseph Marsh had received a letter from George Penkake and A. Lonzo Sweet of Mt. Sterling, Illinois. (The letter was published in *The Advent Harbinger* July 26, 1851.) The two men wrote they would take his paper on six-month trial. If they saw any spirit of contention in it, they would not continue. They believed in dealing with contentious people in meekness. They asked him to send someone. Perhaps the letter motivated Marsh to go himself, for he wanted to acquaint people in the field with the doctrine of the Age to Come. He left *The Advent Harbinger* in the capable hands of O.R.L. Crozier.

Marsh planned to visit throughout Ohio; Jeffersonville, Indiana; Alton, Illinois, near St. Louis; Elizabeth, Illinois, where his brother Lorenzo resided; and Beloit, Wisconsin, being the northern most point on the frontier. On Marsh's return east, he planned to stop in Indiana at Kingsbury, Hudson and Middlebury. He then planned to go north to Nankin and Detroit, Michigan, to visit the Seymours at Nankin. The trip spanned May 7 to July 8.

While in Cleveland, Marsh stayed with Newell Bond who had attended the Rochester Union Conference. Throughout this trip, people were friendly, and his subscription list for *The Harbinger* and *The Children's Friend* increased. He also sold many copies of his new hymnal, *The Millennial Harp* (1854).

Marsh noted that the principle of Christian liberty had taken root in Indiana and elsewhere. He said, "They will not bind men's minds, nor be bound. They are free in Christ."

One evening in May, as Marsh preached, a horrific thunderstorm blew up with a tornado in it. It blew all about him as it struck the barn and the schoolhouse, collapsing both. The meeting broke up and people went to find their children. The Lord brought them all safely through that ordeal. It is not known if they were meeting in the schoolhouse or in a home.

From Indiana the Marshes traveled by riverboat down the Ohio River and up the Mississippi River to St. Louis. At St. Louis, Sarah Adams Marsh visited her brother, Washington Franklin Adams, who assisted them greatly in their journey. Having not seen W.F. Adams for 20 years, this trip was especially meaningful to Sarah. W.F. Adams certainly must have been well to do, as he manufactured castor oil in St. Louis.

Joseph preached three times in large halls at St. Louis. He said while there were no congregations of followers in that city, a great interest was awakened. He noted that St. Louis was a great and bustling city, yet slavery was practiced there. This grieved Marsh for he was a neighbor and friend to Frederick Douglass, and as an abolitionist, Joseph participated in the Underground Railroad. Joseph assisted Frederick Douglass in purchasing a home in Rochester, New York.

Marsh related this interesting incident:
> In order to have more time with her relatives at Alton, Mrs. Marsh left St. Louis one day before we did. As the Tempest, the boat on which she took passage, passed the Lady Franklin, (the boat which brought us to St. Louis) the waiters, seeing Mrs. Marsh, swung their hats, caps, aprons and handkerchiefs, and loudly cheered her in token of their high regards and good wishes for her, for having so interested herself in their behalf and the cause of emancipation of their race from bondage, while on the Lady Franklin. This unpolished, yet warm gush of feeling and token of friendship on the part of these poor down-trodden enslaved Africans, more than compensated us both for the odium and contempt which had been cast upon us for advocating their unpopular cause.

At Alton, Marsh took Sarah to stay with her brother, Orlean Miles Adams, whom she had never met until that time. As the Marshes passed through Alton, they couldn't know its future, but it was there that Owen Lovejoy, the Congregational minister turned abolitionist newspaper publisher, would be murdered by a mob over the cause of slavery. At the time the Marshes visited, tensions were already brewing.

The Mississippi River was in flood stage, making the upstream cruise dangerous. Near Galena, Illinois, the river breached its banks, flooding as far as the eye could see. After they landed safely, and Marsh looked around at the rich farmland, and the quaint city of Galena, and its obvious wealth from the lead mining there, he thought Illinois had a prosperous look. He felt this was because Illinois was a free state. He said slave states were less prosperous and seemed to be operating in the past.

Elizabeth, Illinois, was 15 miles east of Galena and to travel there by coach meant traversing the highest unglaciated ridge in northwestern Illinois on dirt roads. Marsh hired a private coach at the rate of $4, but it was well worth the cost for the scenic enjoyment it offered. At Elizabeth, Joseph had a joyous reunion with Lorenzo, his younger brother whom he had not seen for 14 years. When last they were together, Lorenzo was a young lad, and now he was head of his family.

The meetings at Elizabeth were very successful. Marsh baptized 13 people including Lorenzo. He said the field there was ripe for harvest and challenged readers, "Who will come work here?"

In the company of his brother they left for Beloit by private conveyance, a distance of 65 miles. Their carriage was quickly and frequently bogged down in muddy roads made nearly impassable by floods which had swept bridges away. Marsh said the slews of Illinois made a black mould which stained the soil.

At Beloit, the Marshes met with evangelist B. Brown and M.A. Sears of Lake Zurich, Illinois. These two evangelists formerly of New York had become leading Age to Come preachers in that region of northern Illinois. Another leader, Elder N.L. Thayer, took the lead to spread the word among his neighbors in Beloit. Many people came from the countryside around to hear him preach. Nothing more is known about Thayer.

From Beloit, the party traveled to Cherry Valley, Illinois, south of Rockford, to visit with Julius W. Marsh, another of Joseph's brothers. Julius was a believer in the Gospel of Christ. He had recently moved to Cherry Valley where Joseph preached that evening to a small meeting that gathered quickly. Julius later moved his family to Waverly, Iowa.

By the time the Marshes left Julius' home, they were exhausted. The whole trip from Elizabeth to Chicago their coach had been mired in muddy roads that lengthened the journey. Joseph commented later that he had not been able to continue with his journal, from which copy for the weekly *Advent Harbinger* was taken, because of extreme fatigue and muddy roads. Railroads did not yet cross Northern Illinois, and would not for a few more years.

At Chicago they spent one night at the Tremont House and the next morning sailed across Lake Michigan to Michigan City. They arrived in LaPorte, Indiana, and traveled to Kingsbury where they met with Joseph Catlin, the brother of N. Mead Catlin of Kingsbury, New York, a frequent contributor to *The Advent Harbinger*. Evidently the Catlins named the new town in Indiana after their former hometown in New York.

G. The Kingsbury Meetings

Marsh stayed at Kingsbury three days and met with Indiana ministers, including Hugh Barnhill and Henry Logan of Plymouth, Indiana; Ephraim Miller of Middlebury, Indiana; Joseph Catlin, W. Brink and A.F. Servis all of Kingsbury. Marsh said the brethren there were united in faith and believed in the Age to Come. He explained that unity came because people believed in the *literal* interpretation of scripture, and so they were building upon the same foundation.

At Hudson, they visited with more family: Joseph's sister, Mrs. Freedom Green White, and another Marsh brother, William, lived there. Joseph Marsh wrote later that his aged father and stepmother were buried at Hudson, awaiting the resurrection, and he longed to see them again some day. Lemuel had lived with William in Berrien, Michigan, and then just before his death on June 3, 1850, in Hudson, Indiana.

From Hudson the Marshes traveled to Middlebury where they met Ephraim Miller again, along with Stedman A. Chaplin and A. Hubbel. There Marsh preached the Age to Come, which was received with hearty agreement by those in attendance. S.A. Chaplin also preached at that conference, and his message was gladly received. Chaplin was largely responsible for stabilizing the Church of God work in that area.

J.M. Judson, of Norwalk, Ohio, was also there. He was well known to Marsh and it was a glad reunion. At this conference there was a great deal of interest in reprinting N. Mead Catlin's article from *The Advent Harbinger* on the "Contrast Between Protestantism and the Gospel" as a tract. This article discussed the Gospel of the Kingdom. More than $40 was pledged, and Ephraim Miller was appointed to collect the funds so *The Advent Harbinger* could publish the tract.

The Marshes loved their reception at the Middlebury conference so much that Mrs. Marsh composed a thank you poem. Prior to departure, Elder Judson sang a song from Mrs. Marsh's poem. It was called "The Parting" and was printed in *The Advent Harbinger* under her initials only. Two verses are quoted here:

> Farewell, Bro. Judson; be faithful be firm;
> Go sound the glad tidings; the Master will come.
> On you, Brother Miller, a duty must rest,
> The truth to be spreading, in wilds of the west.
>
> The Lord in great mercy, his cause has sustained;
> While Chaplin and others, his truth have proclaimed.
> Farewell, Sister Miller; be patient and strong;
> We'll rest from our labor, I trust before long.

Mrs. Marsh explained later, the poem was hastily written, and she was quite moved when Judson sang it.

Ephraim Miller reported in the next issue of *The Advent Harbinger* that he had felt unity at the Middlebury conference. He appreciated the ministry of Joseph Marsh and "while we have been edified and instructed by the labors of Elder Marsh in the field, we also rejoiced to learn that there existed so general an agreement with our faith. The writer had several points where he expected disagreement, but found none when they came up."

It is obvious from these reports in the field that Elder Joseph Marsh was able to lead people, unite them behind the Gospel of the Kingdom and encourage them to preach the word everywhere. He was a well-respected evangelist, preacher and publisher. A visit from him was like a touch from heaven. People felt refreshed and renewed by the message of hope that he brought.

H. Principle of Literal Interpretation

Marsh explained in the next issue of *The Advent Harbinger*, July 19, 1851, that "the great mass of religious papers of the day are wedded to some abstract doctrine or exclusive sect." *The Harbinger,* he went on to discuss, stood on the side of representing THE WHOLE BIBLE. He had no ulterior motive in becoming sectarian as other Adventists' sheets were doing. *The Harbinger* would continue to follow the principles of literal interpretation, such as "Father Miller" had set forth during the Millerite movement to explain the second coming, the Kingdom of God, the return of Israel, etc.

Marsh's Explanation of the Principles of Literal Interpretation of the Bible

Joseph Marsh discussed literal interpretation while preaching at the Dansville, New York, Conference. He based his comments on 1 Cor. 1:10, saying:

1. Whenever a person, place or thing is the direct subject of a discourse, it is always used in a literal sense.
2. Don't confuse the terms "Zion," "Judah," "Jerusalem" with the Church.

Ref.: *Prophetic Expositor and Bible Advocate*, July 15, 1857

Mark Mattison wrote in *Sharpening Steel* that Marsh was a historicist, however, his system of interpretation also had a futurist component. LeRoy Froom, 20th century Seventh-day Adventist author, discussed in *The Prophetic Faith of our Fathers* that futurists were literalists, and named Joseph Marsh as an example. Joseph Marsh himself explained in *The Voice of Truth* of May 1847:

> But the coming of the Son of Man introduced [in] Matt. 24 could not apply to Jerusalem's ruin [70 A.D.] for the Jews did not then *see* him [Marsh's italics] nor say to him, 'Blessed be he that comes in the name of the Lord.' which he declared would be the case when he would next come."

Henry Grew, a scholar of the Age to Come said this in *The Advent Harbinger*, 1850:

> Now I ask, is it not manifest that this gathering of 'all nations against Jerusalem to battle,' is to *precede* [Grew's italics] the personal coming with the resurrected saints?" Is it not manifest that this prophecy of the gathering of all nations against Jerusalem has not been fulfilled? All the facts ... forbid the application of this prophecy to the past destruction of Jerusalem by the Roman army of Titus.

Regarding pre-existence of Christ, some Church of God historians have thought Marsh approved of it. But it seems obvious from his writings that Joseph Marsh was clearly not Arian and was against the doctrine of the pre-existence of Christ. He authored an article series in *The Prophetic Expositor and Bible Advocate* entitled "The Nature and Origin of Jesus." He argued Christ could not have pre-existed his birth except in the plan or mind of God. In defending himself against one of Dr. Thomas's attacks, Marsh said the "Eternal God, Christ Messiah and the Second Coming" were fundamental truths. He said the "eternal Son" was not a Bible truth.

Eugene Stilson has written that with the Jewish interpretation of the Age to Come, came also the Jewish interpretation of the oneness of God based upon Deuteronomy 6:4, "Here, O Israel, the Lord our God is one." The Church of God has believed the oneness of God from the beginning, but this doctrine, while present in the Marsh literature, is not emphasized. In fact, oneness does not appear in emphasis until the turn of the 20th century. The doctrine of oneness was accepted by Marsh and many others in the Christian Connexion, but it was not a test of fellowship in the Age-to-Come movement until after the Church of God sorted out the nuances of the Age to Come and the Abrahamic Faith, after 1870.

In the 19th century an eclectic doctrinal soup was brewing among Christian leaders. In fact, one member of the editorial board of *The Christian Palladium,* Elder C. Morgridge, wrote this about the doctrinal diversity in the Christian Connexion:

> I know of one Christian church in which there are those who believe in Trinitarianism, Unitarianism, Calvinism, Arminianism, Free and Close communion, immersion, sprinkling, Universalism and the annihilation of the wicked. In this I rejoice—not that there is such diversity; but that with such diversity, pious people can be members of the same Christian church. Each of the above dogmas may still be found in ... the Christian connection. Much has been done of late in the way of reform ... Let us reform as fast as we can by the inculcation of truth ... Let us not reject whom Christ accepts."

Morgridge went on to say that success in church building could not be had without some test of fellowship besides holiness. But sectarianism builds walls which divide the great family. Therein is described the struggle that emerging Christian denominations faced in America as they were challenged by developing dogmas that led eventually to creeds and statements of faith, but who wished to include everyone in their fellowships. The Age-to-Come movement faced some of these same challenges throughout the 19th and 20th centuries.

The doctrine of the Holy Spirit was a key topic of discussion. Marsh wrote in *The Advent Harbinger* that the Holy Spirit was the mind of God. In the next issue Henry Grew responded by saying that the Holy Spirit is the Spirit of God as seen in Genesis 1:2 and Zechariah 4:6, "Not by might, nor by power, but by my Spirit." Grew said, "God's work of mercy toward a fallen world commenced with the work of his Holy Spirit." While Marsh did not disagree with that, he said that Grew failed to prove that the Spirit is imparted independently from the Word!

I. Age to Come and Anglo Israelism

Throughout 1851, discussion in *The Harbinger* pursued the questions raised by *Our Israelitish Origins*. Professor John Wilson of Great Britain wrote the book stating that the Anglo Saxons were part of the lost tribes of Israel. He claimed that other European nations also were. Denmark for example was "Dan's mark." While this piqued men's interests, most Bible scholars did not accept it. Joseph Marsh certainly didn't. There are still theorists today who suggest that the Cherokee Indians were an early tribe of Jews who arrived in America before Columbus.

When one reader asked about Dr. John Thomas' position against Anglo-Israelism, Marsh replied:

> We consider much of the foregoing article founded in assumption with no Bible evidence to sustain it. And besides, the writer has not in the least validated Dr. Thomas' criticism of Genesis 35. Until this is done, the Dr. is correct and *Our Israelitish Origins* is incorrect.

In January 1852, Marsh advertised *The Herald of the Kingdom and Age to Come*, published by Dr. John Thomas of Richmond, Virginia, for $2 a year. This title reflected a slight name change from the publication's former name: *Herald of the Kingdom and Future Age*. At the same time, Marsh became an agent for George Storr's *Bible Examiner*. The men of like faith promoted each other's works. So it would not have been unusual to promote *Our Israelitish Origins* without endorsing its contents.

Excerpt from *Age to Come* by Joseph Marsh, Rochester, New York, 1851

Twelve Thrones will be prepared for the twelve apostles of the Lamb. It seems like they will be intimately associated with Christ in the government of his kingdom; and will eat and drink at his table. They may constitute a part of his wise cabinet.

Is this too literal for you? Then listen to the plain words of the Savior. Speaking to his apostles, he says:

Matt. 19:28: "When the Son of man shall sit in the throne of his glory, ye also shall sit upon twelve thrones, judging the twelve tribes of Israel."

Here it is clearly proved, that the apostles will sit on twelve literal thrones, as it is that Christ will actually sit on the throne of his glory. Both, doubtless, will be most literally and gloriously fulfilled.

Age to Come is available at
http://www.mun.ca/rels/restmov/people/jmarsh.html

J. Disagreeing with Colleagues

Throughout 1852, Joseph Marsh reprinted certain notices from Dr. Thomas' paper, *Herald of the Coming Kingdom and Age to Come*. Marsh viewed these issues and topics in a somewhat favorable light. At the end of May, however, he read an article by Dr. Thomas entitled "What is the Gospel?" Marsh agreed with almost everything except the idea that before baptism, candidates must believe the entire Gospel first. Marsh contended that newcomers to the faith might not have all the points of doctrine in their heart. Not even the Apostles knew all about the Kingdom when they followed Jesus. Marsh wrote a detailed, courteous response.

From this discussion on immersion came negative comments by Dr. Thomas about Marsh in his paper, *Herald of the Coming Kingdom*. The rebaptism controversy raged vehemently during 1853, lapping over into the work of the Church of God at Rochester, so that even Marsh's friend and pastor of the church, J.B. Cook, turned against him. Cook, one of the first evangelists to preach conditional immortality in tent meetings with J.C. Bywater and Jonas Wendall, was highly respected as a former missionary; his repudiation of Marsh was impactful.

Thomas wanted Marsh to be re-baptized. Marsh refused saying his first baptism was valid. He based his first baptism upon faith, rather than being baptized into a movement such as Thomas had been. When Dr. Thomas left the Restoration Movement, he felt it necessary to be re-baptized, but Joseph Marsh did not, because he felt one's faith continues to grow after his obedience to immersion. Marsh was asked to leave the church.

Marsh clarified later in *The Prophetic Expositor and Bible Advocate* that he had been disfellowshipped by Dr. Thomas *not* because he had made errors, but because he had refused to be re-baptized. The errors to which Marsh referred involved his repudiation of the prophecy system advocated by William Miller. Marsh's faith had not altered; his belief in oneness of God had not changed; he still believed in conditional immortality; he still believed in the second coming of Jesus. He had changed his mind on the place of Israel in prophecy, and on who the subjects of the millennial age would be. He saw no need for rebaptism. Marsh said, "We believe that Dr. Thomas' test of baptism to be unscriptural and calculated to divide the flock of Christ."

Marsh capably defended his position noting that Dr. Thomas had an error in judgment by stating the recent Russian war would be the last Great War before the coming of Christ, as he published it in *Elpis Israel* and *Anatolia*. The inconsistency was that Dr. Thomas did not admit his errors, but he expected others to admit theirs!

Marsh believed that one learned about truth by studying. One came to the Lord in faith without knowing many of the answers and having only a few of the questions. Discipleship was a process. Marsh's position opposed the general feeling among followers of Dr. Thomas.

Dr. Thomas was an inveterate and formidable adversary. He had quarreled with Alexander Campbell over points of doctrine and had been cast out. He had stirred up trouble for Joseph Marsh, and later on, Dr. Thomas attacked Benjamin Wilson's reputation in Geneva, Illinois, as well, but Thomas was rebuked.

Things were not going too well for Marsh in New York. Prior to closing *The Prophetic Expositor*, President Hugh Barnhill of the Northwest Christian Conference invited Joseph Marsh to move the publication to Indiana. Under the circumstances, Marsh seriously considered it. He said it was a ripe field and it would be cheaper to publish it there. He had family in the area. He felt it would have been an easy transition. He said he could not afford the move but invited the brethren to help fund it so the press could be shipped. He wanted a little piece of land big enough to have a horse and cow, but he did not want to farm it. He was considering a location between LaPorte, Indiana, and Freeport, Illinois. Evidently, the Midwestern brethren could not raise the money.

The move might have extricated Marsh from a controversy that began in 1857 when he slighted Horace L. Hastings, noted author. Because of the abusive tone of Hastings' article for *The Prophetic Expositor*, Marsh would not publish it. Hastings took offense and stirred up a ruckus. Being a Christian man, and distressed by the sudden turn of events, Marsh sought to manage the problem through channels of church discipline. But this was not a matter of the church. Even so, a council was called to which Marsh came but Hastings did not. The council exonerated Marsh. Both of them being members of the Church of God at Rochester, the church split. Half the church sided with Hastings, and half with Marsh. Marsh published details of the controversy, opening it to scrutiny by his readers and researchers today.

Hastings went on to associate primarily with the Adventists, and the two men apparently never fellowshipped again. Marsh continued to publish *The Prophetic Expositor*. Miles Grant, editor of the Advent Christian's *World's Crisis*, published that Marsh had been cast out of the church. Marsh wondered how it could be said that he had been cast out when the church split.

While it might seem that Marsh made a career of being cast out of fellowships, it should be remembered that the man was persecuted nearly everywhere he went outside of Age to Come circles, because *he didn't fit in anywhere else.* He was not Orthodox, Adventist, nor Christian Connexion. He was unique, and he cut his own path in a jungle of controversy. His daughter Jenny wrote about the constant persecution the Marsh family endured, particularly her father. When persecution came from inside his own congregation it really stung.

K. Literal Interpretation and the Sabbath Question

During the years Marsh published *The Prophetic Expositor and Bible Advocate*, he often said the paper stood by the literal interpretation of the Word. He claimed his paper was the only religious paper following this method, and therefore, its editor occupied the position as a teacher of the Word. He said, "This word he should fully understand. If he knows what truth is, he should publish it."

Marsh followed this particular hermeneutic in the discussion between A.N. Seymour and J.F. Wagoner regarding the Christian's obligation, if any, to keep the Sabbath. For a time Wagoner had believed it was obligatory, but had repudiated that position. Wagoner and Seymour now were advocates of the Age to Come.

Seymour agreed with Joseph Marsh on the Sabbath question. While some believed the seventh-day observance was obligatory, Seymour and Marsh denied it. Sabbath keepers placed the Sabbath in the Gospel age but extended offerings and sacrifices into the millennial age. Seymour urged Sabbath believers to study more. Joseph Marsh said the literal interpretation of the Bible did not allow for Sabbath keeping.

During these years, Marsh studied from Alexander Campbell's *Translation of the New Testament* from the Greek. These were the days before Benjamin Wilson published the *Emphatic Diaglott*, also a Greek translation, but with added interlinear English. Wilson's translation greatly added to the literature of Bible translation and was one of a kind, but until it came along many Bible scholars used Campbell's translation.

L. Line of Periodical Succession

By the time Marsh began publishing *The Advent Harbinger and Bible Advocate*, 1848-1854, his views on the Age to Come were clearly entrenched in his mind. Wanting to remove his movement from being identified with the Adventists, he began another title, *The Prophetic Expositor and Bible Advocate* in 1854. In *The Expositor and Advocate* Marsh explored other topics such as "The Nature and Origin of Jesus," "Baptism," "Church Organization," and "Thomasism." This publication also emphasized the Age to Come. In 1860, he began a short-lived title *The Bible Expositor* with Thomas Newman as his printing assistant. Newman worked with Marsh on *The Bible Expositor* in 1860, then bought it and changed the name to *The Millennial Harbinger and Bible Expositor*.

Newman used Marsh's mailing list, probably less than 1,500 names. The small subscription list may be explained by the special focus of the Age to Come, the consequent small number of congregations and readers who accepted it, the scarcity of population in the newly developing Midwestern states, and possibly the numerous title changes.

The relationship between Marsh and Newman became quite strained. Those close to them knew something of their problem. Not having that knowledge, it is surmised that a technical issue Newman pursued, which differed from the way Marsh had taught him, disturbed Marsh. For example, Newman began numbering his paper with volume 1 instead of volume 33 following Marsh's count from previous titles, but by the third year, Newman's volume count mysteriously jumped to volume 33, probably reflecting Marsh's influence. Also, Newman took a pro-slavery position in a Union setting. Marsh was an abolitionist; Newman was not. (See the O.R.L. Crozier entry for more discussion on Newman's position.)

After he sold his paper to Newman in 1860, Marsh immediately began a new one, *The Bible Teacher* (1860-1863). *The Bible Teacher* and Newman's *Harbinger* competed for the same subscription list. This new title may have caused part of the conflict between the two men. It is thought that Marsh's competition with Newman was a strategy to cause Newman to "knuckle under" regarding their misunderstanding. It must have worked for when Newman increased his paper's volume count to 33, Marsh stopped publishing the competing title.

Joseph wrote to *The Millennial Harbinger and Bible Expositor* that the two had been reconciled over a basic misunderstanding, and that Marsh was discontinuing his work with *The Bible Teacher* as he was now free to write for *The Millennial Harbinger*. He was still living in Oshawa, Canada West, at the time of the dispute and reconciliation. His "obligation" to *The Bible Teacher* ended with the August 12, 1863, issue. Joseph Marsh's life ended with that issue as well, for by the end of September 1863, he was dead. Joseph had said that no further explanation of their differences was needed. To date, no copies of *The Bible Teacher* have been seen by Church of God historians.

If it seems odd that Marsh made sudden decisions to change titles and to sell his publishing business. Such impetuous behavior may be explained by the rapid deterioration of his health.

Before his death, Marsh began another book, *The Light of Life*. It is thought this title was never published. Marsh gave his hymnal and copies of *Age to Come* to Newman for distribution and moved to Canada where he worked with R.V. Lyon for a while. Lyon reviewed *Age to Come* and said, "[This book] has done more good than any other work ever published on the subject in this country."

During 1863 or 1864 Benjamin Wilson in Geneva, Illinois, acquired Marsh's old mailing list from Thomas Newman, who by then had retired from publishing. In 1869, *The Gospel Banner*, Benjamin Wilson, editor, merged with *The Herald of the Coming Kingdom and Christian Instructor*, edited by Thomas Wilson, Benjamin's nephew. In January 1870, Wilson changed the name to *The Restitution*. *The Prophetic Watchman and Herald of the Kingdom* of Harvard, J.M. Stephenson, editor, ceased publishing. (For more on the history of these publications, see Appendix 13.)

In the space of 30 years, the center of publishing for the Age-to-Come movement had moved from the east coast to Chicago, the bustling center of the west. Thomas Wilson was editor of *The Restitution*, but it was of short duration. During the great Chicago Fire of 1871 the office of *The Restitution* burned and, possibly, Joseph Marsh's press with it. The paper did not die, however, as it was passed on to several other editors and continued publishing in Indiana and Ohio until 1925.

In this manner, Joseph Marsh's heritage was passed along to other faithful believers who carried on the work that had burdened Joseph Marsh with controversy. While the Wilsons in Geneva, Illinois, preferred to emphasize the Abrahamic covenant and faith, calling it "One Faith," the ultimate result of that theological system is its rightful inclusion in the Age-to-Come prophetic system.

M. His Last Western Tour

In 1863, while the Civil War raged, Marsh began a western trip to the frontier, especially to south-central Indiana where a fervent dispute brewed between Nathaniel Field and several other Adventists, some of them being of Church of God persuasion. It should be mentioned that Joseph Marsh firmly advocated that the name "Church of God" was the only scriptural name given in the New Testament, but he also believed in free investigation and was therefore against sectarian tendencies.

While in Indiana, Marsh again became ill with typhoid fever. He quickly cancelled his evangelism trip and returned to his daughter's home in Michigan where he died. Descendants of the Joseph Marsh family state that he was trying to reach his home in Canada but was too ill. He is interred at the Brookside Cemetery in Tecumseh in section M, lot 26. It is hoped that interested persons can restore the Marsh gravesite and place a suitable monument there. The 150th anniversary of his death will be marked in 2013.

Thomas Newman received news of Marsh's death after *The Millennial Harbinger* went to press on September 16, 1863. Newman stopped the presses and inserted a one-paragraph notice. The next week a full obituary appeared which was reprinted from *The Rochester Democrat*.

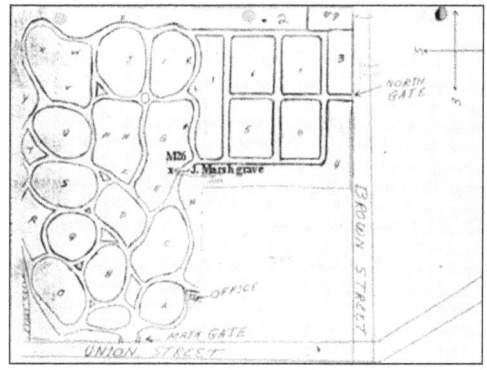

Above: **Cemetery schematic shows the location of Joseph Marsh's grave.**
Below: **Record of Internment at Brookside Cemetery, Tecumseh, Michigan. This indicates Marsh was buried in his son-in-law's family lot.**

Source: E-mail of Sept. 12, 2008, from Austin, Dale, Researcher at Brookside Cemetery.

A few issues later, R.V. Lyon supplied Joseph's last itinerary. After Joseph left the Indiana Conference, he traveled to Cicero, Indiana, where he gave two sermons. This church pledged $70 if he would come to Indiana as their evangelist. From Cicero he went to Liberty, Indiana, and gave five sermons. From Liberty, he went to Old Union. It was here that R.V. Lyon met with him and heard him preach "the best Gospel discourse that I ever listened to." Lyon reported, "but he was sick with his old complaint. [He] gave up the idea of moving to Indiana, on account of his health."

From Old Union, Marsh traveled to Jeffersonville again and intended to cross through Kentucky to Tennessee, but he could not. Lyon concluded that Marsh did not contract typhoid; he carried his fatal illness with him as an "old" illness.

The developing Church of God suffered at the death of Joseph Marsh. Mrs. Marsh must have suffered as well. A note from her in *The Millennial Harbinger and Bible Expositor* said:

> My P.O. address will in future be Rochester, New York. I desire to say to my friends that I should be happy to hear from them. Also, if any who are indebted to my late husband for books, or on account, will pay the amount due, no matter how trifling the sum, it will be most gladly and gratefully received.
>
> Signed: Sarah M. Marsh

Benjamin Wilson did not pay Marsh the respect of publishing an obituary in *The Gospel Banner*. Wilson profited from Marsh's death by receiving the bulk of his mailing list, but he did not deign to honor Marsh in his pages.

Not all Church of God people felt as Wilson did. A few years later Levi C. Chase visited the Tecumseh cemetery near Raisin, Michigan, probably for a funeral. As he left, he noticed a tombstone marked "Joseph Marsh." It was old and broken. The stone was sinking. Written on the stone was "Waiting for the Coming of Our Lord Jesus Christ." Chase made inquiries from the sexton who said there were no Marsh relatives living anywhere nearby. Elder L.C. Chase took it upon himself to order the repair of the stone, have it leveled and the weeds cleared from the area, "So great was the loving respect for the man who had fought for truth amid its pioneer difficulties and died faithful unto death." Mary Woodward who read a report written by aging O.R.L. Crozier related this story to the Michigan conference.

Joseph Marsh served the Lord in the face of extreme opposition during times of crisis and chaos in America's secular and religious culture. His daughter, Jenny, wrote of his dedication to evangelism in her magazine article, *The Little Millerite*. She said, speaking of their move from one home to another in the cold of winter, "They left leaflets at many of the houses we passed, and father preached at the inns where we stopped at night." He expected the Lord's soon return. His answer to questions pertaining to future events was, "if time lasts."

He set his course toward the second coming and Age to Come in the midst of hardship and did not turn back.

See Bond, Newell
Bywater, J.C.
Cook, J.B.
Crozier, O.R.L.
Field, Nathaniel
Higgins, Yate
Newman, Thomas
Marsh, Levi
Parker, Parmelia Jane "Jenny" Marsh
Stephenson, J.M.
Storrs, George
Wilson, Benjamin
Wilson, Thomas

Bibliography: Ancestry.com, U.S. Census, Rochester, New York. 1850, Joseph Marsh is listed in this Census as a "2d Adventist Clergyman"; U.S. Census. Missouri. St Louis. Saint Louis. 1870; Albany Conference Report, *The Voice of Truth*, Joseph Marsh, ed., Rochester. New York, June 16, 1847; Austin, Dale, Photo of Interment Record of Elder Joseph Marsh retrieved from sexton Brookside Cemetery, Tecumseh, Michigan and furnished to author on September 11, 2008; Beecher, Charles. "Premillennialism", *The Voice of Truth*, Joseph Marsh, ed. June 2, 1847, p. 73; Cook, Steven; "Christadelphian Blogspot," E-mail June 2006; Crozier, O.R.L. "Prophetic Day and Hour," *The Voice of Truth*, April 9, 1845; Crozier, O.R.L. Report to Michigan Conference read by Mary Woodward, circa 1900 prior to Crozier's death, reported in *The Restitution*, date unknown; Froom, LeRoy. *The Prophetic Faith of our Fathers*, Vol. 4 Review and Herald. Paperback 2009, Appendix on Literalist interpretation; Graham, David. "Elder Joseph Marsh, A Biographical Sketch," *Wisdom and Power*, July 1991 and, E-mail Feb. 21, 2006, June 6, 2006. Graham, David, "Excerpts from the Western Tour, May-July 1851," *Church of God General Conference History Newsletter,* Jan Stilson, ed., Oregon, Il, Fall 1991/Winter 1992; Graham, David, "A Short History of Anti-Sectarianism and the Church of God," *Church of God History Newsletter,* Jan Stilson, ed., Dec/Jan 1993; Graham, David. E-mail with inscription on Marsh's original headstone, August 26, 2009; Grew, Henry. "The Coming of the Lord," *The Advent Harbinger and Bible Advocate*, Jos. Marsh, ed. Rochester, NY. Sept. 21, 1850; Hemingray, Peter, *John Thomas His Friends & His Faith,* Chapter 21, Christadelphian Tidings, Canton, Mi., 2003; Hepworth, Patra Ann, "The Family of Lemuel Marsh and Rosanna Warner," including discovery of family papers in 2008 which Patra posted on the website: http:www.ninetravelers.com/index; Hepworth, Patra Marsh, E-mails passing along information from descendants of Jane Marsh Parker regarding Frederick Douglass and Joseph Marsh; Higgins, Yate, "Letter regarding his health," *The Prophetic Expositor and Bible Advocate*, Joseph Marsh, editor, Rochester, NY, Oct. 15, 1857; Holland, Elihu Goodwin, *Memoirs of Rev. Joseph Badger* 4th ed., New York. C.S. Francis & Co., 1854; Lyon, R.V., "Letters regarding circumstances of Joseph Marsh's death," *The Millennial Harbinger and Bible Expositor*, Nov. 11, 1863 and, Nov. 18, 1863; Marsh, Joseph, "Church of God" series, *The Christian Palladium*, Union Mills, NY. 1839; Marsh, Joseph, "Not Retreated Yet," *Voice of Truth*, August 13, 1845; "Creeds," *The Voice of Truth*, Dec. 16, 1846 and "When Christ Comes," *Voice of Truth*, April 29, 1846; Miller, William. "Address to Conference at Rochester," April 2-5, 1846, *Voice of Truth and Glad Tiding of the Kingdom*, Jos. Marsh, ed. Rochester, NY, 1:4, April 22, 1846, p 26; Comments on *The Palladium*. *Voice of Truth*, Nov. 4, 1846; "State of the Dead," *Voice of Truth*, Dec. 30, 1846; Marsh, Joseph, "Questions and Answers," *The Advent Harbinger and Bible Advocate*, J. Marsh, ed. Rochester, NY. The following dates of citations indicate that Marsh did not accept pre-existence of Christ: Aug. 3, 1847, Nov. 16, 1847, Feb. 5, 1848, March 11, 1848; Marsh, Joseph, "Editorial on the New England Conference [of 1851,]" *The Advent Harbinger and Bible Advocate*, March 22, 1851 Also, *The Advent Harbinger*, various issues from 1850 and summer of 1851. "Time of Restitution," Pamphlet announcement in *The Advent Harbinger and Bible Advocate* March 15, 1851; Marsh, Joseph, Editorial Response to Comments from *The Herald of the Kingdom and Age to Come*, regarding baptism, J. Thomas, ed., Richmond, Va. in *The Advent Harbinger*, J. Marsh, ed., Rochester, NY. May 22, 1852; Marsh, Joseph, "Report of Difficulty with H.L. Hastings," *The Prophetic Expositor and Bible Advocate*, Jos. Marsh, ed., Rochester, NY, Sept. 15, 1857; Marsh, Joseph. "Explanation of dispute with Dr. Thomas on Baptism," *The Prophetic Expositor and Bible Advocate,* Jos. Marsh, ed., Rochester, NY Nov. 1, 1857; Marsh, Joseph, "Letters regarding dispute with Thomas Newman," *The Millennial Harbinger and Bible Expositor*, July 8, 1863; Aug. 8, 1863; Marsh, Joseph, "The Nature and Origin of Jesus," *The Prophetic Expositor and Bible Advocate*. Series: Feb.15,1859 p 502-504, March 1, 1859 p. 513-516, March 15, 1859 p. 541-543, April 1, 1859 p. 567-569, April 15, 1859 p. 606-610, May 1, 1859 p. 622-626; Marsh, Mrs. Sarah, "Parting" a poem for song. *The Advent Harbinger and Bible Advocate*, July 5, 1851; Mattison, Mark, E-mail on the Pre-existence question, April 2006; Mattison, Mark. "Joseph Marsh's Doctrinal Development and Conflict with Christadelphianism," *Church of God History Newsletter*, Jan Stilson, ed.; Part one (April-May 1993) Part two (Je/Jy) 1993; Mattison, Mark. "The Prophecy Debate in the Church of God of the Abrahamic Faith," Aug. 1990, *Sharpening Steel*, Special Issue. Chuck Jones, ed., Wyoming, Mi. Spring 1991; Miller, William, "Letter to Editor," responding to an article by S. Bliss on Israel. *The Voice of Truth,* Oct. 22, 1845; Morrill, Milo True, *A history of the Christian denomination in America, 1794-1911*, Christian Publishing Assoc. Dayton, 1912, p. 329, retrieved from googlebooks.com; Nichol, Francis *The Midnight Cry*, Review and Herald. Washington, D.C., 1944; Neuffer, Jane. "The Gathering of Israel, a Study of Early Writitngs," may be located at whitestate.org; Newman, Thomas. "Obituary of Joseph Marsh," *The Millennial Harbinger and Bible Expositor,* Sept. 16, 1863; Olbricht, Thomas, "Christian Connexion and Unitarian Relations 1800-1844," *Restoration Quarterly,* 9:3 1966 as retrieved from the website: http://www.acu.edu/sponsored/restoration_quarterly/archives/1960s/vol_9_no_3_contents/olbricht.html; Parker, Parmelia "Jenny" Marsh, "The Little Millerite," *Century Magazine,* Dec. 1886; Marsh, Sarah M. "Notice", *The Millennial Harbinger and Bible Expositor,* October 14, 1863; Morgridge, C., "Principles of the Christian Connection," *The Christian Palladium,* Jasper Hazen et al, eds. Union Mills, NY. July 23, 1845, p. 81; Ross, Kent, "When Time Was Supposed to Be No More," Part one and two. Paper to Theological Conference published in *Journal from the Radical Reformation,* Spg/Sr 2003; Rowe, David L. *Thunder and Trumpets Millerites and Dissenting Religion in Upstate New York 1800-1850,* Scholars Press. Chico, Ca. 1985; "Rochester'sFrederickDouglass,"retrieved4/3/08,workforcediversitynetwork.com/docs/Rochester's FrederickDouglass.pdf; Stilson, Jan, "The Publishing Heritage in the Age to Come Movement," 1800-1985. *75th Anniversary Issue of Restitution Herald,* Russell Magaw, ed., October 1985; Stone, Barton W., "Cause of Disunion a reply to Joseph Marsh," *The Christian Messenger,* Jacksonville, Il., June 1841, p 336-342; Storrs, George. "Northwestern Tour," *Bible Examiner.* Oct. 1851, p 155, [Note] Bruce Schulz alerted us to this reference from research he did with deVienne for their forthcoming book *A Separate Identity: Zion's Watch Tower Congregations 1870-1887* [title subject to change]; Wilson, Benjamin, "Various editorial comments on baptism", *The Gospel Banner and Millennial Advocate,* March 1, 1868; Seymour, A.N. "Discussion on Sabbath-keeping," *The Prophetic Expositor and Bible Advocate,* Joseph Marsh, ed., Rochester, NY., August 11, 1857; "Invitation by NW Christian Conference," *The Prophetic Expositor and Bible Advocate*, Joseph Marsh, ed., Rochester, NY., Sept. 1, 1857; Wilson, George, "Farewell Poem by John Wilson," *The Prophetic Expositor and Bible Advocate,* Jos. Marsh, ed., Rochester, NY, June 15, 1857. For a chronology of Church of God periodicals, please see the Appendix.

Marsh, Lemuel
b. 1770
d. June 3, 1850

Lemuel Marsh married Rosanna Warner. They had 16 children; so many that Lemuel forgot to record some of their births. Among their children were Joseph Marsh and several other sons. Lemuel was a native of Vermont and baptized as a Methodist. The family moved to LeRoy, New York, sometime in 1817. While the family lived in LeRoy, they became acquainted with the teaching of the oneness of God. Lemuel and his wife and sons accepted that doctrine, and because of it, were turned out of the Methodist church.

Joseph described his mother as pious, and after her death, he left home. Rosanna was buried at LeRoy. After that, Lemuel remarried and moved to Randolph, Canandaigua County, New York, where in short succession he buried three sons.

After a few years, perhaps in Lemuel's old age, he and his second wife relocated with William, a son, first to Berrien, Michigan, and then to Hudson, Indiana, in 1850. His daughter, Mrs. Freedom Green White, also lived at Hudson. At Hudson, the elderly Mr. Marsh died and was interred. Joseph published a sweet and loving obituary for his father in *The Advent Harbinger* in July 1850.

Joseph passed through Hudson on a ministry trip in July 1851, and visited his father's grave. He believed that Lemuel believed the truth, and that he would see him again on resurrection morning.

See Marsh, Joseph

Bibliography: Hepworth, Patra Ann, "The Family of Lemuel Marsh and Rosanna Warner," See http:www.ninetravelers.com/index; Lemuel Marsh Obituary. *The Advent Harbinger and Bible Advocate,* July 6, 1850.

Marsh, Levi
b. May 16, 1817
d. June 5, 1910

Levi Marsh was born in Berre, Worcester County, Massachusetts. Church of God historians think he was *not* related to Joseph Marsh, but research is ongoing.

Levi was the fifth son of Lewis and Hannah Marsh. He married Matilda H. Whiting of Rochester, New York, on August 19, 1848. They had four children; three died in infancy. Only George F. lived to adulthood and survived his father. Matilda preceded Levi in death in November 1858. At Worcester, Levi worshipped with the Methodists as a member of a Bible study group.

As a young man, Levi took up the carpenter trade until 1847 when he moved west. He and Matilda settled in Plainfield, Illinois, in Will County south of Aurora. He found work as a carpenter. So far as can be determined, while in Plainfield Levi first learned of the message of the Age to Come. He was familiar with the writings of Joseph Marsh, but at Plainfield it was made clear to him probably by J.M. Stephenson, H.V. Reed (who lived at Harvard, Illinois), or one of the early evangelists, Elder Howell or Elder Sears of Zurich, Illinois.

Levi moved to Tama County, Iowa, in 1853. He established the town of Irving where he built the first frame house in the county. Soon another Church of God family named Root moved to Irving from Plainfield. By this time, a small nucleus of believers allowed the work to continue in that area. There probably had been preaching in the vicinity before the Marshes and Roots arrived, as historic record shows speakers from Illinois and Wisconsin mentioned earlier, J.M. Stephenson (Wisconsin) and H.V. Reed (Illinois), frequented the area.

Two years after Matilda's passing, Levi remarried to Emma Elvira Royce at Tama, Iowa, on September 9, 1860. She lived in the household before marriage, boarding there as the teacher in the common school. Levi was 41. The couple had two sons and two daughters, one of whom died in infancy and the other, Carrie, died at age 6. Living in the household in 1860 were Levi's son, G.F. Marsh, age 9; M. Warfield, a girl of unknown parentage, age 10; L. Fisk, age 53; Fisk's son, F.L. Fisk, age 17; and, E.E. Royce, age 24, who was to become Levi's second wife. A.J. Eychaner baptized Emma.

In 1874, because of persecution by other denominations in the vicinity, Levi erected a church building at his own expense. Unlike a great many men, he deemed it necessary to have a house for the worship of God. The description of the church building from the *History of the Iowa Churches of God* is quite interesting; it is included here to illustrate the architecture often used by early church builders:

> The church home consisted of one room, 32 by 72 feet with 12 foot ceilings. The entrance porch was on the east. All seats were 12 feet long, had fine cushions and faced south. The raised rostrum reached 14 feet from the south and with space for pulpit and organ, three 12 foot choir seats (southwest corner) and stove (southeast corner). Three large windows of plain glass with shutters graced both the north and south ends of the structure. As reported, it could conceivably "seat four or five hundred people." The bell for the cupola was imported from Belfast, Ireland.

H.V. Reed came from Chicago to dedicate the building. There was standing room only.

Levi Marsh retired from managing the mercantile business at age 52 (circa 1870), but he continued to own the business until 1886 when he completely retired. He spent the rest of his days on the old homestead at Irving with his sons Frank and Elmond.

Levi's obituary included the following:
> His life has been a living epistle, known and read of all men. Strictly honest in all his dealings with all men he closed a life that fulfilled the Scripture in Proverbs 8:22; 21:1. He left a name unsullied, both as a business man and a Christian, leaving his sons and grandsons a name to be proud of.

Levi lived to age 93. O.J. Allard conducted his funeral service.

Bibliography: Allard, O.J. "Obituary of Levi Marsh," *The Restitution*, A.R. Underwood, ed. Plymouth, In., June 1910; Ancestry.com. U.S. Census. Iowa. Tama. Salt Creek. 1860. Ancestry.com. U.S. Census. Iowa. Tama. Salt Creek. Dist. 322. 1880; Burnett, Francis. "Firm Unto the End," from sermons by Burnett, part of the archival collection of Rock River Christian College, Beloit, Wisconsin; Burnett, Francis et al of history committee *History of the Iowa Church of God and Conference 1855-1987*, Belle Plaine Union, 1987; Hepworth, Patra Marsh, "The Family of Lemuel Marsh and Rosanna Warner," showing no direct connection of Levi to Joseph Marsh or his family retrieved from http://www.ninetravelers.com.

Marsh, Lorenzo Dewitt
b. 1820
d. 1852

Lorenzo, younger brother of Joseph Marsh, lived in Elizabeth, Illinois, and believed in the Age to Come. He married Maria Jane Kellogg on February 27, 1843. Mr. and Mrs. Joseph Marsh visited the young couple in 1851 while traveling across the Midwest. Joseph must have also visited him in Elizabeth during 1847 and signed a note on land. The transaction record can be found in probate court and states Joseph appeared before the judge.

Elizabeth, Illinois, lies west of Freeport and east of the Mississippi River. It is in unglaciated country with large rolling hills and great beauty. Mr. and Mrs. Joseph Marsh traveled by wagon or stagecoach cross-country to Beloit, Wisconsin, on roads that were rain-soaked and muddy. It was a difficult trip.

After sale of the Elizabeth property, Lorenzo and Maria moved west by covered wagon. During the trip cholera spread through the wagon train and evidently both died at Laramie.

See Marsh, Joseph
Bibliography: Hepworth, Patra Ann, "The Family of Lemuel Marsh and Rosanna Warner", http:www.ninetravelers.com/index; Joseph Marsh, "Report of Western Tour," *The Advent Harbinger and Bible Advocate*, July 1851.

Mason (Railton), Sarah
b. March 1, 1868
d. May 1, 1949

Sarah Mason was born to Dr. Wallace and Jane Mason in McDuff, Scotland. In her adult years, Sarah taught Kindergarten at Lillian near Winnipeg, Saskatchewan. She married James Albert Railton in Toronto on May 24, 1916. She was widowed when he died in February 1925.

They were members of the Church of God at Fonthill, Ontario. She was Mr. Railton's second wife and stepmother of John A. Railton, Austin and Mary Railton Milne's father.

In her senior years, Sarah resided at the Golden Rule Home in Oregon, Illinois. She died at her stepson's home in Rockford, Illinois, and was interred beside her husband at Fonthill. Pastor Grover J. Gordon officiated her funeral service.

See Gordon, G.J.
　　　Mason, Wallace, Dr.
　　　Railton (Bouk), Mary
　　　Railton, Austin (20th)
　　　Railton, James A.

Bibliography: Obituary, *The Restitution Herald*, Sydney Magaw, ed., Oregon, Illinois, May 15, 1949.

Mason, Dr. A. Wallace

　　b. 1840?
　　d. Unknown

Dr. Mason was a Christadelphian who preached a message of unity to flocks in England and Scotland. He lived in Toronto and was Sarah Mason Railton's father. He wanted to unify the Christadelphian and Church of God denominations. During the winter of 1914, he preached every week from October until the end of March on the continent. People were frightened by the war, and thought it might be Armageddon. His announcements indicated he had studied prophecy for 50 years. His advice was, "Be patient, be watchful. Don't be in too big of a hurry. God is working with the nations."

In the fall of 1915, this notice appeared in *The Restitution Herald*:

> I am now disengaged 'til April and can (D.V.) go anywhere in the U.S. to preach the gospel. I have had long experience in preaching the gospel and can speak every night when necessary. I am also an old hygienic physician. Address: Fredonia, NY.

Dr. Mason was active in the Fonthill, Ontario, Church of God.

See Mason (Railton), Sarah

Bibliography: Notices by Dr. Mason, *The Restitution Herald*, Oct. 21, 1914; Nov. 24, 1915.

Matheny, Hiram King

　　b. December 25, 1847
　　d. September 23, 1901

Hiram Matheny was the son of William and Elizabeth Matheny, and the older brother of Simon Peter Matheny. Hiram was born in Queensville, Jennings County, Indiana. His family to Minnesota when he was 13. They crossed the Mississippi River from Prairie du Chien, Wisconsin, to McGregor's landing. From there, they journeyed to Pleasant Grove, Olmstead County, Minnesota, where they remained until after the Dakota War of 1862. They then relocated to Meeker County. William Matheny remained there while Hiram and Peter took homesteads between Dassel and Kingston. Hiram married Aletha Z. Smith at nearby Swan Lake on April 4, 1871. They resided there until 1882. Hiram was a blacksmith as was his father, and they operated a blacksmith shop.

The family moved to Eden Valley in 1883. Hiram farmed 40 acres, 3.5 miles north, near the shores of Eden Lake. It was here that they raised their six children.

Hiram and Aletha's children included Harley, who died in a train accident; Clifford, who died in 1936; and six daughters including Esther who married John Jones and was described by family as being a fierce and mean woman; Maude who wed James A. Patrick on February 27, 1901, and to whom were born Merle, twins Cecil and Cedrick, Carrol and Ione. James was a Church of God pastor in Minnesota and Brush Creek, Ohio. He was also the first president of the Church of God General Conference in 1921. Continuing with Hiram and Aletha's daughters, next is Sarah who married Lester Kirkpatrick. They had five children with one infant death. Their second child, Vivian, was born in 1911; he married Walcie Smith of Arkansas. Vivian and Walcie had five children all of whom continue in ministry today. Daughter Judy (Myers) is chairman of Lord's Harvest International, the Church of God mission-sending agency.

Hiram's fourth daughter was Bertha Alda who married Herman Ruhn on September 27, 1909. They lived in Eden Valley until Herman died; Bertha moved to Litchfield. They had two daughters and one son. Elna Gail "Peg" Ruhn married Stanley O. Ross in Litchfield on December 15, 1939. Stan and Peg had three children, Kent, Scott and Connie. Kent and Scott trained at Oregon Bible College and became Chuch of God pastors and leaders. Their children continue in ministry as well.

Hiram and Aletha's next daughter, Marjorie, married Willard Wood. Willard's grandfather Loxley Wood was a pioneer minister, about whom nothing more is known. They had four children: Joy Ann, Merridee, Mark and Gaye. Gaye Wood is a leader in the Litchfield church and president of the Minnesota Conference of the Churches of God. Hiram's last child was Lois who married Andy Allen. They had two children, Dawn and Dana. Hiram King Matheny's lineage illustrates that godly men raise godly families.

Kent Ross contributed to this entry.

See Matheny, Simon Peter
　　　Patrick, James A.
　　　Ross, Stanley O. (20th)
　　　Smith, H. Scott

Bibliography: Ross, Kent. "The Matheny Family: One Family's Record in the Church of God," a paper presented at the History Conference, North Hills, Ohio, Oct. 5-7, 2008; "The Dakota Uprising" also known as the Minnesota Indian War Retrieved Dec.22, 2010 from *wikipedia.org/wiki/Dakota_War_of_1862*.

Matheny, Simon Peter
b. August 21, 1849
d. September 21, 1901

Simon Matheny was born in Jackson County, Indiana, and eventually took up farming in Minnesota. He claimed a homestead near Swan Lake northeast of Darwin. Through the preaching of two men named Scott and Parsons, Matheny became devoted to the doctrine of the second coming of Christ. He was converted and immersed.

On December 18, 1874, Matheny was ordained a preacher at the Minnesota Conference, which included members of the Advent Christian denomination and the Church of God. This meeting was the very first session of the newly organized Church of God Minnesota Conference. Matheny had been aware that two other preachers had been teaching that the scriptural name of the church should be Church of God for nearly a year. These two ministers were members of the Advent Christian Minnesota Conference. This information survived in a report by Stanley O. Ross, a member of the Litchfield Church of God, who probably used Sydney Magaw's *History of Minnesota* as his reference.

Elder Matheny died and is buried at Eden Valley.
See Kirkpatrick, Vivian (20th)
Magaw, Sydney (20th)
Matheny, Hiram
Parsons, William
Patrick, James A.
Ross, Stanley O. (20th)
Scott, C.D.W.

Bibliography: Ancestry.com U.S. Census. Minnesota. Blue Earth. Mankato. Dist. 6. 1880; Ross, Kent H. E-mail to JStilson June 22, 2008; Ross, Stanley O. "History of Minnesota," *The Restitution Herald*, Sydney Magaw, editor, Oregon, Illinois, May 24, 1949; *History of the Church of God in Minnesota*, Sydney Magaw, ed., 1931.

Matheny, William
b. 1858
d. Unknown

Elder William Matheny was one of the first officers in the newly formed Minnesota State Conference of the Churches of God. The conference was organized at Dassel on December 18, 1874. William Parsons, a former Advent Christian preacher, became the first president; E.D. Thoms became secretary and William Matheny the treasurer. Six churches reported to that first conference. Most of these churches had been former Advent Christian churches who had broken with the fellowship.

In 1873, Elders C.D.W. Scott and William Parsons began to believe that "Church of God" was the only scriptural name for the church, and believing that, they began to organize churches under the name. Eventually, the break with the Advent Christians was complete. In 1875, the conference admitted the Eden Lake Church and a year after that the St. Cloud Church was added.

Other early Minnesota ministers were Jedediah Raymond, Simon Peter Matheny, E.D. Thoms, J.L. Chadwick, Amos Randall, Henry Dingman, John Dingman, P.L. Sweany, Charles Blanchette (an ex-Catholic priest), J.P. Driver and others.
See Magaw, Sydney (20th)
Matheny, Simon Peter
Sweany, Press L.
Thoms, E.D. (20th)
See Also Appendix 10–Lost Saints

Bibliography: Magaw, S.E. *History of the Minnesota Church of God Conference*, circa 1930, cited by Terry Ferrell in *A Brief History of the Church of God in America*, National Berean Youth Conference, Camp Reynoldswood, Dixon, Il. 1960; Minnesota Territorial and State Census 1849-1905, census taken May 1, 1885. Hennepin. Minneapolis.

McAlister, Frank
b. October 1880
d. May 24, 1929

Frank McAlister is listed as an Arkansas minister by William Henry Wilson in his report to *The Restitution Herald* in 1904. Minister McAlister lived at Red River, as did his colleague Elder Jacobs. McAlister was a servant in the farm household of Robert E. Swan. Beyond that, nothing more is known about him, but he is given an entry because he represents the myriad of people who worked to spread the Gospel message across the Southland and the Great Plains.

W.H. Wilson, Almus Adams or other evangelists recognized these servants as doing good work for the Lord in one brief sentence, offering no personal information about them. Frank McAlister is known only to the Lord.

Bibliography: Ancestry.com U.S. Census. Arkansas. White. Red River. Dist. 154. 1900; Ancestry.com. Arkansas Death Index, 1914-1950 record for Frank McAlister; "Report of Wilson," *The Restitution*, Jan. 20, 1904.

McClary, Judge John Hannibal
b. November 13, 1832
d. July 6, 1906

Judge John McClary was born in Piqua, Ohio. In 1857, at age 25, he married Emma Stinchcomb at her parents' home in Grandville, Indiana. The couple moved to southern Indiana where they resided in Taney County for the next 36 years. The McClarys had 11 children, three of whom died in infancy.

John McClary was a well-known and respected citizen, serving his county ably and faithfully as presiding judge for two terms and as county surveyor for three terms. He also made a county plat after a fire destroyed the courthouse and records. He kept quite busy.

When not serving the county, he made improvements on his farm. He always made time to read the Bible and practice his religious duties. McClary first united with the Christian church, but afterward changed his belief, and accepted the doctrines emphasized by the Church of God.

When Judge McClary realized he was dying, he called his family to him, declared he was ready to go and bade them good-bye—words of comfort to his sorrowing relatives.

Elder Speers conducted the funeral service in the presence of sympathizing friends and neighbors. The Judge was laid to rest in the Kirbyville cemetery.

Bibliography: *The Restitution,* Sept. 9, 1906.

McClelland, Martha?
b. 1880?
d. Unknown

Mrs. McClelland lived in Boise, Idaho. Personal information about her is unknown as there were several McClelland families in Boise at that time. She rented a hall across the street from the capitol building and held a series of meetings. Any of the McClellands who were Boise merchants might have had access to downtown facilities for purposes of meetings.

Research shows Mrs. McClelland learned the truth from Almus Adams and desired others in Boise to hear it also. The Boise work was a successful mission effort as Evangelist Adams preached and baptized several people there. Before he left Boise, a Berean class was organized with Mrs. McClelland as its leader and Edna Turner, a new member, as secretary-treasurer.

Mr. McClelland became a Christian because of his wife's testimony. They were friends of Daniel and Lucy Lapp of Sunnyside, Washington. Sometimes the two families worshipped together.

See Turner Family
Lapp, Lucy
Bibliography: *The Restitution,* April 1913; Nov. 2, 1920.

McCory, John
b. December 18, 1834
d. March 3, 1913

John McCory lived near Bridgeport, Indiana. He was united with the Christian church when he was quite young and identified with it until about 1868. He then learned of the Second Advent and became a member of the Advent Christian church at Bridgeport, being one of its charter members. He was an elder in this church for many years, but then moved his membership in 1903 to the Hillisburg Church of God where he remained a "true Christian" until death. He served on the board of the Indiana State Conference as president in 1911.

He was married twice and fathered eight children. He served in the Grand Army of the Republic at Sheridan, Indiana, and was buried in a military funeral. He was laid to rest in Miller cemetery to await the second coming. His last words during his final illness were "Tell all my friends good bye. I hope to meet them at the resurrection at the second coming of our Lord and Savior, where partings and good byes will be no more."

Bibliography: *The Restitution,* Oct. 28, 1911; April 22, 1913.

McDonald, Mary J.
b. 1830
d. December 28, 1895

Mary was born in Waltenborough, New Hampshire, to Mr. and Mrs. Jedediah Witham. She said her father instructed her in Bible doctrine by using the articles from *The Restitution* as a guide. This is another example of members encapsulating all the titles published by Church of God editors in America into one historical concept and calling them *"The Restitution."* The paper from which she was instructed would have been *The Advent Harbinger and Bible Advocate.* Of interesting note is that people of the 19th century referred to the early Church of God papers published by both Joseph Marsh and Benjamin Wilson as *The Restitution,* despite each having distinctive names and years of publication. For a visual depiction of the succession of Church of God periodicals, please see Appendix 13.

To the readers of subsequent generations, all titles were *The Restitution.* In fact, *The Restitution* began in 1870 as the successor to *The Herald of the Coming Kingdom* which had recently absorbed *The Gospel Banner* in 1869, and which had inherited Joseph Marsh's mailing list. This connection of the various titles with Joseph Marsh links the work in the East with the work in the Midwest. This is the greatest evidence available to scholars that the Church of God Abrahamic Faith did not unilaterally begin with Benjamin Wilson.

Mary believed the truth and enjoyed *The Restitution*.

See Marsh, Joseph
　　Wilson, Benjamin

Bibliography: *The Restitution*, Jan. 8, 1896

McDonald, Thomas
b. January 10, 1808
d. March 28, 1875

Thomas McDonald was born in Butler County, Ohio, and moved to Marshall County, Indiana, on March 28, 1836. He embraced the Gospel hope and was baptized by Evangelist Ephraim Miller in 1848. S.A. Chaplin testified to meeting Thomas McDonald on Chaplin's first visit to Marshall County in January 1850. Chaplin said no one in the congregation at Old Pisgah impressed him more that day than Thomas.

In Chaplin's remarks at Elder McDonald's funeral, Chaplin said that over the years the congregation dwindled as people died or departed, but Thomas remained faithful. He said Thomas was a "tireless worker for its welfare" and "with his death the church has sustained a severe loss." Thomas was able to bring peace when dissension occurred. He was a loving parent and a good friend.

Chaplin said:
> The hope of future and eternal life through Jesus Christ to be attained through the resurrection from the dead was the hope that inspired him in life and sustained him as his footsteps neared the dark waters of death. Faith had fixed his view upon the incorruptible, and we trust that his deep repose is only that sweet sleep in Jesus from which none awakes to weep.

Editor H.V. Reed spoke words of comfort at Elder McDonald's funeral in which he described the hope of the Gospel in future life that motivates Christian men to serve.

See Chaplin, S.A.
　　Reed, H.V.

Bibliography: Chaplin, S.A. "Eulogy," and Reed, H.V. "The Christian's Hope," *The Restitution*, H.V. Reed, ed., Plymouth, In., March 30, 1875.

McFarlane, Dr. Frank
b. 1880
d. Unknown

Dr. McFarlane was a dentist who also loved to preach. He partnered with Elder W.L. Crowe to preach in Kansas. McFarlane was married with two sons. When W.L. Crowe became ill, McFarlane looked after his health and assisted in raising funds to pay for his medical bills.

Dr. McFarlane was a leader in the Kansas City church work. He advertised upcoming revival meetings in the spring and summer issues of *The Restitution Herald*. He said the meetings would continue as long as he was able to stand up under the strain.

This ministry developed into the "Eternal Life Mission of the Church of God in Christ Jesus" in Kansas City. Dr. McFarlane also assisted evangelist C.C. Maple in the evangelistic work of the Nebraska conference during 1924.

See Crowe, W.L.
　　Maple, C.C.

Bibliography: Ancestry.com U.S. Census. Kansas. Douglas. Lawrence Ward. Dist. 66. 1920; *The Restitution Herald*, April 11, 1924; Sept. 30, 1924.

McGinty, Thomas
b. August 1, 1845
d. February 26, 1916

Tom McGinty was born near Grand DeTour, Ogle County, Illinois, and, served the Union army in an Illinois regiment during the Civil War. He learned about the Gospel of the Kingdom from Elder Sympronius R. Etheridge around 1890 in Arkansas.

After settling in Arkansas, Tom ran a gristmill and a cotton gin. Eventually, the area came to be known as McGintytown. In the early days of the church, members gathered in the groves for worship for there was no church building. Meetings were held when a circuit preacher came through. Families also gathered at McGintytown for special singing schools. Here they learned to read music using shaped notes; by reading shapes, one could learn to sing harmony. Some also learned to read words from studying the lyrics and to compute math by learning about rhythm.

Several preachers honored each other's schedules by alternating preaching Sundays so that church members could have regular spiritual nourishment, and so that all preachers could be out preaching without overlapping Sunday appointments.

Early churchmen of the McGintytown settlement were F.J. Snow who did a little preaching, and Uncle Frank Utley, about whom nothing is known.

The first church building was constructed in 1918. While it was under construction, members began to meet at John W. McGinty's house for worship. John was the eldest son of Tom McGinty. While the lumber for the church was milled, they met on the bare floor of McGinty's house. John was a believer and often summoned the preachers, housed them and paid for them himself. In fact, members donated $71 for the construction of the church building, and John McGinty paid the rest. In those days, a decent wood frame church building could be built for $600 or less.

The reporter of Tom McGinty's obituary said, "He contended earnestly for the faith."

See Etheridge, Sympronius R.

Bibliography: Interview with Pete and Arlie McGinty, by Stilson for *Church of God History Newsletter*, J.Stilson, ed. 1:4 Winter, 1985; *The Restitution Herald*, April 26, 1916; "We are pleased to honor McGintytown Church of God," *The Restitution Herald*, Oregon, IL, Oct. 1974.

McInturff, Hugh M.
b. February 10, 1876
d. January 31, 1931

McInturff, Esta
b. July 29, 1883
d. April 26, 1976

Hugh M. and Esta V. McInturff were both members of the Maurertown Church of God in Christ Jesus in Maurertown, Shenandoah County, Virginia. Both were baptized as young adults. Hugh was elected deacon in 1908. In 1916, he and two other members were appointed trustees of the Maurertown church and the dormitory behind the church, owned by the Virginia State Conference.

In 1919, he was elected elder and held that office until his death.

Hugh and Esta had three daughters, Gertrude, Eunice and Helen, and one son, Robert. Hugh was a farmer and faithfully taught his children Christian principles of working the land and working in the church.

Hugh died at age 55, leaving Esta a widow until her death. She resided with her daughter, Gertrude, and son-in-law, Frank Morrison, in Woodstock, Virginia. Esta was faithful to the Lord and to service at Maurertown all the years of her life.

Well into her 70s "Miss Esta" was active in the state conference work and the women's ministry at Maurertown. Her sweet and gracious manner of work and communication was a refreshing lesson in peaceful service to the Lord. She heeded well Paul's words, paraphrased, "Let the older women be an example to the younger women" (Titus 2:3-5).

Bibliography: ABC Biography project, David Krogh, compiler; J. Stilson, Memories of Esta McInturff.

McLauchlan, Robert
b. 1826
d. 1904

Robert McLauchlan may have been born, baptized and christened in Perth, Scotland, but he resided in Cleveland, Ohio, as an adult. He joined Maurice Joblin, Mark Allen, Newell Bond and several others to establish a Cleveland congregation of Age to Come believers, which preached the second coming of Christ. In his book, *Addresses and Miscellaneous Papers on Bible Themes,* McLauchlan reported that the Cleveland church organized in 1863 with a core congregation of 14. In a year's time, their numbers had grown to 26. McLauchlan was probably immersed by his friend Joblin.

Joblin was pastor of the church in 1893; McLauchlan had donated the funds for its construction. There may have been disagreement over the building project because a dispute between Joblin and McLauchlan caused a split. McLauchlan's book indicates that his dear friend Joblin accused him wrongly and injured their friendship to the point of an irreparable breach. McLauchlan said:

> When a man who has knelt with you in prayer, and for months and years has sat with you at the same communion table, becomes your false accuser, and the traducer of your reputation in order to make merchandise of you. it is the recollection of these past associations, that gives venom to the sting of your accuser, and poison to the arrows that are aimed at your heart" (Addresses, 411).

In 1894, McLauchlan and his second wife joined with Mr. and Mrs. Jessie N. Shourd to rent a hall in the Pythian Temple building on Huron Road near E. 9th Street. The first Mrs. McLauchlan had died in North Carolina in March 1886. Elder McLauchlan established a trust fund used to carry on the work by Jessie Shourd after McLauchlan's death. L.E. Conner came to pastor the new church in 1906 and served there until 1929.

Churchmen and businessmen recognized Robert McLauchlan as an educated and esteemed Bible scholar. In fact, he was recognized as a scholar by international religious and scholastic associations. McLauchlin was invited to speak at Waverly Hall before the Men's Union Religious Mutual Improvement Association which might be likened to the YMCA. He spoke on the topic of "Reformation and Restoration," two religious ideas made whole through the redemption brought by the blood of Christ.

Rumors circulated that McLauchlan believed in the doctrine of Larger Hope. The idea of Larger Hope was circulating among other denominations and defined Universalism—the belief that sin is temporary and God will destroy sin in the Age to Come and save all men.

The editor of *The Restitution* pointed out that McLauchlan's own writings proved he did *not* believe in the Larger Hope. The key to understanding this doctrine hinged on one's belief of the resurrection. Robert McLauchlan said many denominations were currently preaching Larger Hope. Methodists, Congregationalists and members of all churches believed it. He wrote in *Addresses* that nowhere in God's Word does it says that God will destroy wickedness and save the wicked. He said the term "Larger Hope" indicated multiple hopes, some greater than others. But, he said, the Bible teaches One Hope (Ephesians 4:4). And that hope is the hope of the Gospel (Colossians 1:22, 23). His essay elaborated on the hope for the Christian as well as the final destiny of the wicked. Clearly, McLauchlin did not believe in Larger Hope or Universalism.

McLauchlan stated in *Addresses* that all men would not be raised. By this he meant that when the wicked died, they remained dead in Adam. They would never be raised for judgment again. Dr. John Thomas held this doctrine, and it had come to be called limited resurrection or partial resurrection. The conclusion is, if the heathen are never raised again, there can be *no* Larger Hope or Second Chance, or probationary period for them in the Kingdom. McLauchlan cited "The soul that sinneth, it shall die" as a proof text. It should be noted that followers of Dr. Thomas in the 21st century no longer hold strictly to the doctrine of limited resurrection.

Many readers of *The Restitution,* published from 1870 to 1925, believed in limited resurrection. Some of these members referred to the larger Church of God as "universalists," because in spite of Robert McLauchlan's excellent preaching and writing, some came to believe in Larger Hope.

Benjamin Wilson, editor and publisher of *The Gospel Banner,* believed all Christians would be raised at the Lord's coming, some to reward, the carnal to judgment. He believed this would happen within a single period, as in the sheep and goat judgment as discussed in Matthew 24. Around 1869 others in the Church of God who also believed in general resurrection began to teach a separation, or process, of the first resurrection. They began to teach contrary to Benjamin Wilson's teachings. They said that the righteous were raised and judged at Christ's return, but the wicked lived not until the 1000 years were finished. Then, they were raised to judgment.

This is the second death. Wilson said the Greek text did not support this idea. It may have been largely for this reason that Benjamin Wilson moved his family to California and lived in semi-seclusion the rest of his days.

It should be noted that Benjamin Wilson declared in later years that by the wicked he was referring to Christians who lived a carnal life. The Adamic wicked or unbelievers would never be resurrected. (See the Benjamin Wilson entry for further discussion.) *The Gospel Banner,* in which Wilson discussed this, especially in the year 1869, is also available on CD.

In the early period those leaders who joined Joseph Marsh in advocating the thousand years of transition in the Age-to-Come included Thomas Wilson, a young and dynamic editor, and S.J. Lindsay one of the first influential editors of the 20th century. By the time Lindsay published the first issue of *The Restitution Herald* in 1911, universal resurrection with an interval of 1,000 years between the first resurrection and the second death was widely believed. Some people called it the "second resurrection," but Lindsay pointed out the Bible taught "second death." The believers in limited resurrection were mostly those who admired the doctrines of the Christadelphians.

Themes to which McLauchlan returned several times in *Addresses* include his refuting of the "false doctrine" of Josephism believed by Benjamin Wilson; mortal emergence from the grave believed by Dr. John Thomas; larger hope and invisible coming of Christ taught by Russell; and doctrines taught by Orthodoxy: eternal torment, infant sprinkling, heaven as reward and immortal soul.

McLauchlin said when *Addresses* was first written it wasn't intended for publication. It was written in short snatches from a busy life, "filled with many cares," and this may account for some of it repetitious content.

A book that may have been his final work was published in 1888. It was entitled *An Earnest Appeal on the Chief Points of a Discourse.* This book was published by Lippincott (New York) and discussed the hope of salvation through the Son of God. In this work McLauchlan would have addressed concerns about the Church of God during his lifetime. A copy of the book is in the archival collection at Atlanta Bible College. McLauchlan's portrait also hangs in the Archives beside those of F.L. Austin and Sydney E. Magaw.

When the aged Robert McLauchlan died, *Addresses and Themes* was donated to the National Berean Society for sale. The proceeds went to the Bereans. A copy of *Addresses and Miscellaneous Papers on Bible Themes* is in the Archives at Atlanta Bible College.

See Austin, F.L. (20th)
    Conner, L.E.
    Joblin, Maurice

Lindsay, S.J.
Magaw, S.E. (20th)
Shourds, J.N.
Wilson, Benjamin
Wilson, Thomas

Bibliography: Ancestry.com. Scottish-American Gravestones, Record of Robert McLauchlan, Cleveland, Ohio; Harsh, Evelyn, Berean Column. *The Restitution Herald,* Oct. 9, 1918; McLauchlan, Robert, *Addresses and Miscellaneous Papers on Bible Themes,* Cleveland, 1903 for remarks against Josephism, and in favor of virgin birth p. 91, and p. 352, for doctrines cast down, p. 263, false doctrines p. 93-94, squabble with a friend p 411; McLauchlan, Robert. "Letter to the Editor," B. Wilson, ed., *The Gospel Banner* Geneva, Il., Dec. 1, 1864 p 267,268; McLauchlan, Robert, *An Earnest Appeal on the Chief Points of a Discourse,* Lippincott, NY, 1887; *The Restitution,* June 22, 1920; *The Restitution Herald,* June 4, 1946; Wilson, Benjamin, *The Gospel Banner,* Geneva, Il., 1869; Williams, Byron, *Abstracts of Obituaries and Verbatim Marriage Announcements printed in The Restitution, 1874-1900* Self-published, 1993 p. 31 [Mrs. McLauchlan].

Mehrens, Herman

b. September 27, 1840
d. June 19, 1914

Herman Mehrens was born in Germany and migrated to Iowa with his parents in 1854. Herman's father died there, and two years later the remaining family settled in Cumming City, Nebraska. In 1854, the sparsely populated area had 1,000 settlers north of the Platte River in Nebraska, and nearly 2,000 settlers south of the Platte River.

In June 1861, Herman enlisted in the First Nebraska Co. E. and served three years and five months in the Civil War. In 1865, he filed claim on a homestead five miles north of Blair, where he resided until his death. He farmed there for nearly 50 years.

Herman was baptized by W.P. Shockey and united with the Church of God in 1868 (one source gives the date as 1860). He not only believed the truth but contended for it and supported it with his means.

Herman married Josephine Boice at Omaha on March 28, 1866. They had eight children, seven of whom survived to mourn his death. In addition to the children, 25 grandchildren survived Herman, as did three brothers, Henry, Gerhardt and Chris, all living near Blair.

Eighteen months after his wife died, Herman succumbed to stomach cancer. At the funeral, a group of "trained voices" sang the old hymn

Josephine Mehrens

"Asleep in Jesus." Almus Adams preached Herman's funeral, speaking from Job 14, "If a man die, shall he live again?" On Herman's tombstone in Blair, Nebraska, is written "Asleep in Jesus," testimony to his belief in the sleep of the dead until the second coming of Jesus.

The Blair *Pilot* of June 24, 1914, printed an obituary:

> Herman Mehrens, one of the old, well known and highly respected pioneers of Washington County passed peacefully away at his home north of Blair, Friday June 19th at 4:15 p.m., surrounded by many friends and loved ones. He was a great sufferer for five weeks before the end came, with that terrible malady, cancer of the stomach. He realized death was near and expressed his readiness and willingness to go.

His family filed legal papers at the County Court which stated that Herman had no will or testament, but that he owned real and personal estate estimated at $34,000; no small amount in those days.

Obituaries were published in Church of God papers, as Elder Mehrens was well known throughout the developing denomination. One was printed in *The Restitution* July 14, 1914, as reported by Almus Adams. It credited Herman with being "a loving and wise father, a noble member of the [church] and a fine citizen of the community." Adams said, "He died in the belief that he would triumph in Jesus."

Nell Mead sent an obituary to *The Present Truth,* a Nebraska Church of God paper. The *World's Hope* and *The Last Days,* published by Thomas Wilson in Oakland, California, also published obituaries.

Dedicated men like Herman Mehrens braved the hardships of pioneer life and succeeded in founding the Church of God Abrahamic Faith west of the Mississippi in the 19th and early 20th centuries. These dedicated men, both laymen and evangelists, pushed the message westward and helped to establish the denomination that was organized at Waterloo, Iowa, in 1921.

Men and women of the current century who descended from this hardy soul include Harvey U. Krogh Jr., and his children Rachel Carr and David Krogh.

See Adams, Almus
Krogh, Harvey U., Jr. (20th)
Krogh, Birdie
Shockey, W.P.

Bibliography: ABC Biography Project, compiled by David Krogh.

Miller, Ephraim, Jr.

b. December 1811
d. April 5, 1882

Ephraim Miller was an ardent proponent of the second coming of Christ. He left his denomination to preach within the framework of the Millerite movement.

While he still lived in Massachusetts, his first preaching circuit was southern New York State.

In 1845, when he lived in Chester, Massachusetts, Ephraim Miller's name began appearing regularly in the pages of *The Voice of Truth* and *The Advent Harbinger*. At that time he was 33 years old, married, and his wife's parents, Chris and Amy S. Bowen, lived with them. Ephraim and wife, Amy S. (named after her mother) had two children, Emily and Herbert.

Following the Bitter Disappointment, Ephraim Miller was solidly in the camp of the Gospel of the Kingdom of God. In 1846, he relocated his family to LaPorte, Indiana. It was said he moved there to be near his father, and he viewed the West as a harvest field for the Lord.

In February 1852, a letter published in *The Advent Harbinger and Bible Advocate*, greeted Miller and recalled the wonderful work he had done in New York. The letter writer, A.H. Eggleston of Independence, New York, said, "And I would say to Bro. E. Miller, Jr., we have not forgotten him, and should he ever return to the State of New York, we invite him to come this way and preach to us once more the gospel of the Kingdom."

When Marsh considered his western tour of 1850, he was looking forward to meeting with Miller in central Indiana and Michigan. That particular tour was cancelled as logistics could not be worked out until 1851. In that year, Joseph Marsh and his wife made a western tour, and on their way home from Wisconsin, Marsh finally met Miller at Kingsbury, Indiana.

Several gathered at Kingsbury for a short ministers' conference. Miller went forth from that meeting renewed and energized to preach the Gospel of the Kingdom throughout Indiana, Ohio and Michigan.

Between then and the end of 1852 Ephraim Miller traveled from one end of Michigan to the opposite end of Indiana proclaiming the Word. Within a few years his ministry centered on Michigan, but occasionally he covered other states. Miller was president of the first Michigan Church Conference organized in 1858.

The Archives at Atlanta Bible College own the Minute book of the Michigan Conference. Research in it revealed that Ephraim Miller was elected president of the conference the first few years of its existence. Subsequent to his term as president, he was on the executive board for many years. Miller assumed the secretarial duties from O.R.L. Crozier in 1863, and served in that office until 1875. A note is recorded in the 1875 minutes that Bro. Miller baptized Sister Hopkins for the "remission of sins." He also reported that due to the harsh winter not much had been done with the evangelistic work. He hoped "that more evangelistic work will be done within our bounds during the present year." In August, the executive board appointed Bro. Wilcox as evangelist.

Ephraim Miller was slowing down, but he took an active role in planning the 1877 conference at Mendon and in preaching throughout 1878.

In the period before his death, Miller traveled with A.N. Seymour to talk with folks about the Sabbath question. The two evangelists challenged a congregation of Seventh-day Adventists who had formerly been with the Church of God. These people were very unfriendly toward the two old evangelists, and refused to let them preach in their church building. The evangelists solved that problem by visiting the families in their homes, and attempting to persuade them that Christ's law of love fulfills the Law of Moses.

When Ephraim Miller had passed his prime for serving as evangelist and as secretary of the Michigan Conference, the task passed to his son, Herbert S. As far as is known, Herbert did not take up the challenge of preaching. Ephraim died at his home in Mendon, Michigan. It is not known where he was interred.

See Crozier, O.R.L.
Marsh, Joseph
Seymour, Alva N.

Bibliography: Ancestry.com. U.S. Census. Michigan. St. Joseph. Mendon. 1870; "Letter to Joseph Marsh," *The Advent Harbinger and Bible Advocate,* March 6, 1852; and June 5, 1852; Morley, Butler, "Letter to Marsh," *The Voice of Truth,* June 23, 1847; Notice of change of address. *The Voice of Truth*, May 27, 1846; Michigan State Conference Records 1859 [1858]-1886. Despite its title, the record book begins in 1858; Remittances including one from E. Miller; *The Millenarian*, H.V. Reed, ed., Chicago, Il., March-April, 1874; Seymour, Alva N., "My Seventh Sabbath-day Experience," *The Restitution.* May 2, 1888; Williams, Byron, *Abstracts of Obituaries and Verbatim Marriage Announcements printed in The Restitution 1874-1900.* Self-published. 1993.

Moore, Reuben P.
b. 1799
d. Unknown

Joseph Marsh mentioned Reuben Moore in his report of the Western Tour at Elizabeth, Illinois, noting Moore as "the only minister of our faith who resides about twelve miles distance, and who is doing much good in the cause of truth." Marsh's evidence for his conclusion was that many came in from miles around who seemed "engaged and grounded in the truth." These folks accepted Christ and understood the Age to Come, so that Marsh baptized 13 people there, including his own brother, Lorenzo D. Marsh.

Reuben was a farmer who resided at Plum River and helped establish a thriving church there. He and his wife, Mary, had seven children. In addition to that, they provided shelter and care to a young widow and her three children.

Marsh said Reuben Moore would do what he could for the region but more help was needed. "Who will go to Elizabeth and assist with this work?" he asked.

Within six months Bro. Moore reported to *The Advent Harbinger* that he had been traveling throughout southern Iowa preaching where he could, giving discourses on the second coming of Christ, life only in Christ and the destiny of the wicked.

He spoke of an ailment called "flax" which took the life of a young mother he had baptized the preceding April at Mill Grove in Stephenson County, and later, her young baby, leaving the father, Mr. Barnes bereft.

Bibliography: Ancestry.com U.S. Census. Illinois. Jo Daviess. Plum River. 1850. *The Advent Harbinger and Bible Advocate*, July 5, 1851; Letter to *Harbinger*, Dec. 13, 1851.

Moore, W.A.
b. 1860?
d. Unknown

W.A. Moore and wife were Nebraska pioneers who studied with evangelist Eddie A. Adams at Rathburn School. They may have migrated west from Philadelphia. "Eddie" preached 19 sermons that were "ably handled." He was a workman, but no shame comes from such a livelihood. It is thought that Eddie A. Adams was related to Almus Adams, noted evangelist of the Great Plains.

No additional facts about W.A. Moore are available except that he was faithful to his call.

See Adams, Almus
Bibliography: *The Restitution*, Jan. 8, 1896.

Morgan, N. Jackson
b. March 16, 1824
d. Unknown

Elder N.J. Morgan was the son of William and Mary Reeder Morgan. He was born in Lexington, Kentucky, but moved to Warren County, Virginia, at age 32. He was educated in the common school of the district and from home study. His Bible knowledge was profound. Perhaps it was his Bible knowledge more than his age that earned him the respectful title of "Elder." He may have been a boot maker in Lexington, but in Virginia he was a farmer and evangelist. *The History of the Lower Shenandoah* cites him as a minister at Highview.

Morgan organized Bible study groups that met for preaching and worship in schoolhouses and groves. He began preaching in 1856, married Frances Rudacille in 1859, and continued to preach in Warren County. He purchased the Mountain View farm and lived there 15 years. He farmed 134 acres, a good-sized farm in those days. His preaching in Warren County was a predecessor to the formation of a congregation at Browntown where a Church of God currently thrives.

In 1890, *The History of the Lower Shenandoah Valley* described Elder Morgan as a general elder of the Church of God in both the United States and Canada. Information indicates he founded the House of the Brethren where the association for the promotion of Christian knowledge had its beginning as a Church of God auxiliary in the United States and Canada. The 1890 history concludes, "He now resides in the midst of one of the first congregations established in the Valley of Virginia."

This somewhat cryptic historical account may have been an attempt to describe the 1888 Philadelphia General Conference to which N.J. Morgan was appointed as the Virginia delegate. Also, he was honored to be appointed to one of the committees at the conference for organizing the national work in the United States and Canada. As the recording secretary of the Virginia Conference, he made a general report to the Philadelphia delegates of the annual Virginia conference, which met that year at Browntown. Morgan reported to *The Restitution* in the November 4 issue:

> The time was taken up by consideration of the National Conference as one of the most important movements or steps ever taken by us as a people. Why, the very thought of a goodly number of the true and tried ones who have been toiling on a portion of their time almost alone, in sounding out the midnight cry, "Behold the bridegroom cometh, go ye out to meet him." Of having an opportunity offered them of meeting together by the good and generous-hearted brethren of Philadelphia; when and whence we can talk our trial, sorrows and joys over, fill our little cups to overflowing, and the hope of the good resulting from such a meeting like Benjamin's [word not clear in text; perhaps "blessing"] a double portion.

The Virginia history book detailed the work of Elder Morgan and described the attitudes of the Church of God regarding pacifism. Quoting:

> Such were his Scriptural convictions of Christian character that he refused to take any part in the Civil War of this country. This caused him to go through quite an ordeal with the military element of that day. He threw his life on the altar as a sacrifice for his conviction of truth. Such as in his own words, that 'a true Christian could not be a sectionalist.' For the saints of the Most High will in the great and notable day of the Lord come from the east and the west, the north and the south, and sit down with Abraham, Isaac, and Jacob in the Kingdom of God.

G.E. Marsh published information about Elder Morgan in *The Restitution Herald* after an interview with Carmel Boyer of Stephens City, Virginia, in September 1940. Carmel Boyer showed *The History of*

Lower Shenandoah Valley to Marsh and discussed Elder Morgan's influence on the valley.

Elder Morgan's whereabouts after the Civil War are unknown.

See Boyer, Carmel (20th)
Marsh, G.E. (20th)
Thomas, Joseph

Bibliography: LeCrone, J.R. "Life Sketch of Elder Morgan", citing, Norris, J.E., ed., *History of the Lower Shenandoah Valley* Chicago. A. Warner and Co. 1890. *The Restitution Herald,* April 22, 1946; Marsh, G.E. Interview with Carmel Boyer, Stephens City, Virginia, *The Restitution Herald,* Sept. 24, 1940; Randall, Clyde, *Historical Waymarks of the Church of God,* Church of God General Conference. Oregon, Il., 1976, p 96. Morgan, N.J. "Conference Report," *The Restitution,* S.A. Chaplin, ed., Plymouth, In., Nov. 4, 1888.

Moses, E. Wilfred
b. 1867
d. 1948?

Wilfred Moses was from Houston and a leader in the work of the South Texas Conference. In 1920, he was elected president of the first Texas Conference. In 1922, he wrote a report to *The Restitution Herald* on the work of the South Texas Conference and the work of E.O. Stewart there. The report was positive and included a note that Stewart was working with visiting evangelist F.E. Siple at the time.

In addition to Siple, visiting evangelists who worked in Texas but who did not reside there were W.H. Wilson, Almus Adams, Uncle John Foore and E.O. Stewart. These men laid the foundation that James Mattison and Emory Macy built upon in the 20th century. Early resident Texas evangelists were Robert Warren, Richard B. Taylor, A.S. Bradley and William Gibbs.

As conference president in 1926, E.W. Moses sent notices to the church newspapers inviting people to the campgrounds at Goldwaithe. He said Dr. E.M. Wilson was taking reservations for camping space that summer.

Moses may have known A.S. Bradley and William Gibbs. These men had been Church of Christ preachers but learned of life through Christ and began preaching for the Church of God. They faced a great deal of persecution and obstruction from a certain Church of Christ editor who published the *Eye Opener*. Gibbs published the *Word and Work* in 1904 and presented Age to Come, conditional immortality and Kingdom of God through its pages.

In 1950, James Mattison left Gatesville and became the first paid pastor at Riviera and Harlingen. He received $40 a month from the National Berean Society. Emory Macy succeeded Mattison at Gatesville in 1950.

Mattison said that universalists came into Texas and influenced the president. That president probably was not E.W. Moses. Mattison said from that time on, the work declined. By the time Elder Emory Macy arrived, he had to nearly start over.

See Adams, Almus
Bradley, A.S.
Foore, John
Gibbs, William
Macy, Emory (20th)
Mattison, James (20th)
Siple, F.E. (20th)
Stewart, E.O.
Wilson, W.H.

Bibliography: Mattison, Jim. E-mail, April 2006; *The Restitution,* Sept. 29, 1920; *The Restitution Herald,* Aug. 24, 1920; July 23, 1922; June 2, 1926.

Moyer, George
b. 1829
d. 1920?

George Moyer was born in Germany, the son of Gesper S. Moyer, a One-Faith believer. The family arrived in LaPorte, Indiana, from Germany in 1839. George co-edited *The Herald of the Coming Kingdom and Christian Instructor* with Thomas Wilson in Chicago from 1868-1870. Following the Chicago Fire of 1871, Moyer relocated to Iowa.

In the January 1, 1868, issue of *The Herald*, Moyer noted that since Marsh had left the Church of God at Rochester, that church now believed in mortal emergence, a characteristic doctrine of the Christadelphians. George Moyer said he was not prepared to accept that idea. The Rochester people did not feel their doctrine was a prerequisite to baptism, but rather instruction to believers after baptism. It was not an essential item of "saving faith."

A Moyer editorial in *The Herald* referred to "dispensations." This does not bear the assumption that men who believed in the Age to Come were disciples of Irving and Darby of Great Britain, for Church of God interpretation of the restoration of the Jews and the establishment of the Kingdom differed greatly from Irving's system. Irving said that when the Jews return to their homeland at Christ's return, they will reign in the Kingdom on earth, while the Christians receive their eternal reward in heaven. The Church of God said that all believers will inherit the Kingdom on earth.

Joseph Marsh, George Moyer and others teaching Age-to-Come interpretation of prophecy, believed the restoration of the Jews would be fulfilled in the days of *old* Jerusalem before Christ's return. There they will be subject to the great tribulation, which unless Christ returns all would die. At Christ's return, they will accept him, be rewarded with entry into the Kingdom and sent into the mortal unsaved nations to be missionaries to them during the Age to Come. The nations will be the mortal subjects of the Kingdom bowing the knee but not the heart. Some will accept Christ. Some will not and will die without Christ. They will be raised when the 1000 years are over and will be judged for the second death. The Church will rule with Christ on earth as its reward for being faithful. The church is the bride of Christ; Israel is the restored wife of Jehovah, as taught in the book of Hosea.

Moyer explained the four dispensations he accepted. They are the Patriarchal, realized in family worship; the Jewish, realized in state worship; the Christian, paralleled to the church; and the Millennial which will bind all moral elements together so that the immortal host of redeemed, atoned people become a spiritual family.

George Moyer believed in the non-personality of Satan. He may have been one of the first in the Church of God to verbalize this idea. Dr. John Thomas was a firm believer in non-personality, but generally, most people believed Satan was manifest as some sort of material entity. Moyer said that belief in a "fancied invisible personal devil is evidence of deception. How a man can bring himself to believe there is a pre-Adamic invisible, immortal Satan wielding almost omnipotent power over men can only be accounted for that in childhood they were taught to believe it." He said, "Whatever opposes God is a satan." He said that binding Satan in Revelation 20:1-3 is symbolic of binding sin. When sin is bound, the earth can be restored.

In other areas of doctrine, Moyer's writings in *The Restitution* show he believed in general resurrection as taught by Benjamin Wilson, but not as George Storrs taught it. Moyer refuted Storrs' teaching on general resurrection or universal resurrection. Storrs said universal resurrection was of all men anywhere anytime. (See the Benjamin Wilson entry for a fuller discussion on resurrection issues.)

Moyer also wrote an article for *The Restitution Herald* based on Luke 16:16. He said that Jesus preached the Gospel of the Kingdom of God. It was a standard message within the Church of God, although orthodox churches of the day were not preaching it.

When Moyer left the employ of the Wilsons, he moved to Iowa permanently to be near his father. He lived at Clarksville where he preached, wrote tracts and published a book, *Anthropos*. Moyer's name is seen often in the diary of A.J. Eychaner as someone who assisted in the Iowa Conference. He also assisted in the work throughout Northern Illinois, particularly in Geneva and Chicago. His father, Gesper, died at Clarksville in 1893.

Moyer traveled and preached as often as he could. He is known to have preached at the Michigan conference August 23-25, 1861, and in Iowa as early as 1868. He indicated in his notes in *The Herald* that those he met in Iowa firmly believed in the Age to Come.

See Eychaner, A.J.
Wilson, Benjamin
Wilson, Thomas

Bibliography: Moyer, George, "Report of Rochester," *The Herald of the Coming Kingdom and Christian Instructor,* Jan. 1, 1868; "Notes by the Way" *The Herald of the Coming Kingdom and Christian Instructor,* Feb. 1, 1868; Report of Geneva Conference. *The Gospel Banner and Millennial Advocate* 15:1 Jan. 1, 1869; *The Restitution,* May 11, 1904; *The Restitution Herald,* May 14, 1919; Nov. 4, 1919; Minutes of the Michigan Conference of the Church of God 1858-1886, Aug. 23-25, 1861; Williams, Byron. *Abstracts of Obituaries and Verbatim Marriage Announcements printed in The Restitution 1874-1900*; self published, 1993. p.54.

Muncrief (Moncrief), Dr. James Leonides
b. April 10, 1832
d. September 21, 1921

James Leonides (pronounced *lee-o-need-ees*) Muncrief married Sarah Ann Stroud; they celebrated 59 years together. The couple had five daughters, Martha and Sackie lived to adulthood, three died in childhood. Martha married John Humphreys. Sackie married James Doris. Dr. Muncrief originally resided in Tennessee and moved to Mississippi where he was a slave owner. He was an avid Bible scholar and taught a Bible class for his slaves every Saturday morning.

Dr. Muncrief may have learned "doctoring" from Dr. James W. Red in 1860, with whom he lived in Dark Corner Beat, Mississippi, when he was 28. In those days when a person couldn't attend a medical college, he learned medicine by apprenticing with a physician. Muncrief may have practiced a little folk medicine, because his licensing as a physician is unverified. In fact, the 1910 US Census listed his occupation as "General Farmer." It is known, however, that Dr. Muncrief moved to Arkansas to practice medicine. Although he had three trunks packed with medicines, he soon learned his patients were too poor to pay for it. He gave it away, and soon it was gone.

James was said to have formal training in doctrine, and it is thought that he learned from a mentor named J.R. Ham. It may have been during this instructional period that the doctor contacted Church of God editor J.B. Craton of *The Glad Tidings* in Council Grove, Kansas. In April 1893, Craton replied, "Jas. L. Muncrief, Bear, Arkansas, glad to hear of the interest you take in the things of God and the soon coming of His Son to commence the work of Restitution of all things."

John Humphreys, husband of Muncrief's daughter

Martha, fought in the Civil War for the South, and may have been held in the Union military prison at Alton, Illinois, dying there. John and Martha had several children of which two sons distinguished themselves. Stephen William became a Legislator in Arkansas, and Richard A. became a leading voice in the Arkansas Church of God. To date several families of Humphreys descended from this union still serve in the Churches of God.

Sarah Muncrief predeceased her husband on December 20, 1920; nine months later her husband died also. In his final illness with his family around him, James Leonides Muncrief said that he should have given his farewell speech 17 years earlier when his mind was better! His last words were, "Well I guess I'll go now." Richard Humphreys submitted his obituary to *The Restitution Herald*.

Dr. Muncrief was interred beside his wife. Sarah had kept their home, looking after the welfare of her husband and family, while he looked after the spiritual welfare of his family and others in the Arkansas family of God.

    See Craton, J.B.
         Humphreys, Richard A.
         Ham, J.R.
         Warren, Robert A.

Bibliography: Ancestry.com. U.S. Census. Mississippi. Holmes. Dark Corner Beat. 1860; U.S. Census. Arkansas. Garland. Lee. Dist. 70. 1910; Ancestry.com. Arkansas Death Index. Record for James Leo[nides] Muncrief of Garland, Arkansas, Sept. 21, 1921; *The Glad Tidings*, 1:4 April 1893; *The Restitution*, June 11, 1921; Sept. 23, 1921; Obituary, *The Restitution Herald*, Oct. 4, 1921; Report by Wm. H. Wilson, *The Restitution*, Jan. 20, 1904; Kraft, Virginia Humphreys, Interview, August 2008. The Arkansas Humphrey Sisters. Interview with Jan Stilson, 1986; McCaslin, Ruby. Letter to Jan Stilson, 2009, with information about Muncrief and Humphrey family genealogy; See also: http://www.censusdiggins.com/prison_alton.html.

Myers, G.M.B.
    b. March 23, 1842
    d. 1908

A. The Beginning of Pastoral Ministry
B. The Presence of C.T. Russell
C. Editor and Publisher
D. Dialogue on Atonement
E. Myers Wanders

George M. Myers was born near Plymouth, Indiana, to Joseph and Elizabeth Myers. The family moved to Wapello, Iowa, when George was eight. Joseph was a merchant who trained his sons in the business; George operated the family grocery store after Joseph retired. In their old age, Joseph and Elizabeth lived with George and his wife Mary. The grocery business afforded young George the way and means of preaching. He was able to support preaching trips and may have combined them with buying trips to the city.

Myers must have relinquished the grocery business when he returned to live in Indiana. He preached throughout that state as reported in the minutes of the Michigan State Conference. He lived at Plymouth in 1876 and spoke to the 19th Annual Michigan Conference on the subject of Daniel 2. It is not known if he also lived temporarily in Michigan while pursuing an extended preaching circuit. By preaching in Michigan, he was qualified to receive a license from that conference.

A. The Beginning of Pastoral Ministry

In 1878 Myers was pastor of the Restitution Church of God at Irving, Iowa, and resided at Belle Plaine, Iowa, but he traveled back and forth to attend and preach at the Michigan conference.

G.M. Myers sometimes used a third initial, "B." The minute ledger of the Michigan Conference refers to G.M. Myers and G.B. Myers in notes from the conference held at Mendon May 31 to June 3, 1888. It is thought that different secretaries recorded an alternate set of initials, but that it was intended in both instances to refer to the George M. Myers herein.

During the aforementioned Michigan conference, several ministers were licensed, including George Myers. The minutes recorded: "On motion it was agreed that all ministers recognized by this conference be furnished with letters of authority to preach by the Executive Board. Also those Evangelists be furnished with credentials." This language and subsequent letter is what enabled ministers to travel using rail discount. It may have afforded them discounts at hotels and restaurants as well. Men in Michigan who received these letters included G.M. Myers and L.C. Chase, L.H. Cheseborough, S.A. Chaplin, J.S. Hatch, B.W. Woodward, H. Ralph Carter and more. The letters of authority also served to give a good reference to a minister as he entered a new community as a stranger.

Leaving Michigan, Elder Myers worked throughout the Great Plains during the late 1800s. He worked where opportunities arose. He lived and preached in Lanark, Illinois, in 1882. While there he published a journal similar in name only to *The Millenarian* of H.V. Reed. About that same time, Myers also published *The Covenants and Their Relationships*, a highly esteemed book.

B. The Presence of C.T. Russell

There is some thought that G.M. Myers fellowshipped with The Bible Students begun by C.T. Russell. The name of evangelist "Myers" appears in *Zion's Watch Tower* in May 1886 and February 1887 as being a Watch Tower evangelist active in Iowa. Since no given name or initials are included, it cannot be proven that this evangelist was the G.M. Myers of this entry, but Watch Tower historian Bruce Schulz believes that he is the same Myers. With all the initials G. M. Myers used during his mysterious life, it would be more conclusive if he had used some to identify himself if/while preaching for Russell. The fact that no initials were noted leaves open the possibility that it was another Myers preaching for Russell. If this *is* G.M.B. Myers, at least in Iowa, it seems either that Church of God members fellowshipped with Watch Tower adherents for a while, or Myers went off on his own.

Further evidence of a relationship between the two groups comes in the exchange of articles in the *Zion's Watch Tower* by H.V. Reed, and by his wife, Elizabeth. Bruce Schulz noted:

> Peters in *Theocratic Kingdom* lists H.V. Reed with some of Russell's associates. An article by H.V. Reed is copied in part from *The Restitution* in the July/August 1881 double issue of *Zion's Watch Tower*. *Zion's Watch Tower* also has an article by his wife in the February 1884, issue. Its title is "Infidels not Martyrs."

Another association with the Watch Tower was identified by Schulz. Schulz wrote: "Myers entered into an active Watch Tower affiliated ministry…with the publication [by the Watch Tower] of *Food for Thinking Christians* in 1881."

Elder Myers authored *Meat in Due Season*. He appealed to readers of *The Millenarian* to assist him in paying for printing 2,000 copies. He said in effect, "If Pastor Russell can raise $60,000 to publish *Food for Thinking Christians* then the Church of God can do it too." Daniel Smead reports from his own research that most of the publication cost of *Food for Thinking Christians* came from Russell's own pocket. Smead speculates that Myers did not understand this when he appealed for funds for *Meat in Due Season*.

Exchange of articles between publishers was quite common among magazines and newspapers of the day. Having these publications in a Russellite newspaper does not affirm that the Reeds were part of that organization, but it does demonstrate that their point of view was well-received by Charles T. Russell, editor and publisher of *Zion's Watch Tower*.

Myers included a somewhat favorable review of C.T. Russell's book, *Millennial Dawn* in an issue of *The Millenarian*. He said "it contains a great deal of good and advanced thought calculated to interest the reader, while it has in it some things, *we think,* hardly correct. But we say, buy the book and read it."

Russell's presence can be seen in the Church of God in Iowa, but as a friend of the Church of God, not as a member. Evidence reveals that C.T. Russell preached at the Iowa Conference of 1895, as it is noted in A.J. Eychaner's diary. Russell preached four sermons for which he was paid a small amount.

C. Editor and Publisher

G.M. Myers lived in Lanark, Illinois, from 1882 to 1887. These are the years his name is mentioned in the Watch Tower literature. Mobile as he is known to have been, it is certainly possible that he traveled throughout Iowa during those years. Prior to that time G.M. Myers authored *The Covenants and Their Relationships* in 1882. During that period, Myers edited and published *The Millenarian* in Lanark (1885-1890). Research revealed that G.M. Myers also edited a paper known as *The Lever* in Belle Plaine in 1888. This evidently was a trade paper and not pertinent to the Church of God.

Myers also edited *The Christian Enquirer* from 1890 until 1895 after which it became *The Evangelist* in Belle Plaine, Iowa, a fact noted in the 1897 Belle Plaine city directory.

Quoting from the *History of the Iowa Church of God and Conference 1855-1987*, "the first edition of *The Evangelist* rolled off the press in Belle Plaine in October, 1895." Iowa historians wrote:

> First it was a monthly, later semi-monthly, but for eight months in 1898 it ran as a weekly. On June 28, 1896 the office of *The Evangelist* burned. This left an uninsured debt of $500. Soliciting subscriptions and running advertisements were attempts to recover the loss. In September that year the Iowa State Conference agreed to buy 75 subscriptions for a year to help offset indebtedness. The directors would become an advisory committee and fiscal management would shift to G.M. Myers.

In the issues that are available for examination, *The Evangelist* was at least 50% general and world news, tips for farming, housekeeping and cooking. One recipe for Corn Pudding detailed its ingredients and the method of baking and stated, "This should be eaten as a vegetable." In the first issue only, the front and back pages had Church of God news. Libbie Palmer wrote an article, "Women in the Sunday School." Edith Anderson wrote "Thanksgiving." The next issue included more Bible articles and the Constitution of the Church of God in Nebraska, which described the duties of the officers. The Nebraska state evangelist was instructed to work under the direction of the president and to report any sudden changes in the work to him, as well as reporting the details of his work at each quarterly conference. The inside page included four Sunday School lessons written by A.J. Eychaner.

> **Directors Listed in *The Evangelist* showing that this paper represented the Church of God.**
>
> | | |
> |---|---|
> | A.J. Eychaner | Gladbrook, Iowa |
> | Geo. Moyer | Clarksville, Iowa |
> | W.J. Orem | Baileyville, Kansas |
> | J.L. Wince | Pierceton, Indiana |
> | L.C. Chase | Adrian, Michigan |
> | E.C. Lavish | Stroudsburg, Pennsylvania |
>
> Ref: *The Evangelist*, masthead, Belle Plaine, Iowa, Nov. 1895
>
> Except for Elder Lavish, each of these men is listed in this Encyclopedia. See entries under their names.

By autumn 1897, its second year, *The Evangelist* had shrunk from newspaper format to magazine size. It was eight pages and two of them contained an article about G.M. Myers, whom the reporter called "Dr. Myers." The occasion was a Spiritualists' camp meeting in Marshalltown where Myers was guest speaker on the subject of psychology. Myers' comments on psychology were outlined. Psychology may have been his area of expertise, and the discipline for which he received acclaim. A reporter from the local community paper wrote a positive story about the sermon. Myers later copied the article in *The Evangelist*. The reporter reviewed Myers' sermon and featured the major doctrines of the Church of God. The reporter thought G.M. Myers had a Ph.D. If this is a fact, it has not been verified. This same lecture was given at a General Conference of the Stanberry Seventh-day Church of God on December 14, 1902, and was published in two parts in their paper, *The Bible Advocate*, on March 31, 1903, and a subsequent issue.

Time eventually ran out for *The Evangelist*. It was sold to W.L. Crowe in 1898 and became known as *The Present Truth*, which was eventually absorbed into *The Restitution Herald* in 1915. Atlanta Bible College Archives owns the first two issues of *The Evangelist* but no bound volumes of it.

D. Dialogue on Atonement

Myers published articles refuting Russell's interpretation of the atonement. Briefly summarized, C.T. Russell advocated the ransom theory of atonement and Myers did not. Russell taught that the ransom theory contained these tenets, which he listed in *Zion's Watch Tower* July 1884:

1. Why did Jesus die? Jesus gave his life a ransom for many. Matt. 20:28
2. How did Jesus' death affect our sins? His death and resurrection gives us the victory through Jesus over sin and death. I Cor. 15:57; Rom. 14:9
3. How did Jesus put away sin by sacrifice of himself? Christ the perfect man bought back the rights which Adam lost. Rom. 5:18, 19
4. In what way did he give himself a ransom for all? He voluntarily gave his life and paid the price of condemnation so many could be made righteous. Rom. 5:17
5. In what way was he a propitiation (satisfaction) for our sins? Jesus paid our ransom by paying the death penalty and justifying us to life. Rom. 3:25, 26
6. In what sense were we "bought with a price?" Jesus is our substitute and his death redeemed us.

According to Bruce Schulz, Russell later dropped the use of the word "substitute." Myers responded to Russell in an article which answered the six areas and explained his view of At-one-ment which he considered to be the correct view.

According to Maurice Joblin in his book, *Paternity of Jesus*, Myers barely believed in atonement, because he denied original sin, and he taught that the blood of Christ had no value for the remission of sin because Christ was merely a man. Myers and others who denied the virgin birth believed that Christ had sin and was baptized for remission of his own mistakes and faults; that atonement was not important and Christ's death was not necessary, but His resurrection was necessary; that man could avoid sinning and lead a righteous life by making a decision to turn away from sin and to stop sinning; and that there was no Church of God because man baptizing man could not impart the Holy Spirit. The Church of God would not come into existence until Christ returns.

Yet in 1898 Myers in *Ek Nekron Anastasis* presented a biblical model of atonement which Joblin said Myers himself did not believe. Joblin said Myers' was beguiling believers and called him a fraud. Joblin said:

> ...It is not difficult to think of a greater pious fraud than this, to obscure the glorious provision made by a God of love and mercy, that like Abraham we can have our faith reckoned to us for righteousness if our hearts be right, although our ways be not perfect—yes; justification by faith is rejected in the late deliverance of our writer; and instead of this, we are bidden to do what ONLY ONE of all the countless millions of Adam's children ever did, live without sin, as Jesus did.

Joblin said, "We have incontrovertible evidence that for years Mr. Myers taught publicly what he did not really himself believe; and has at last been PROVOKED to admit it." Joblin's book is the best evidence to date of a direct attack upon a minister's false teachings in order to root heresy out of the Church of God fellowship. Denial of the virgin birth was an insidious doctrine that denied nearly every aspect of Christology that the developing Church of God had come to hold dear.

The Church of God bases its model of atonement on the relationship of God the Father to Christ the Son, and the relationship of Christ to believers. Christ mediates for them. He advocates on their behalf before the Father's throne. The Church of God doctrine of atonement is based on Jesus, the Messiah of the Old Testament, the perfect, anointed, obedient Son of God who is coming again to fulfill the promises to believers. To the man who has never accepted Christ, there can be no atonement unless, and until, he repents. "For as in Adam all die, so also in Christ shall all be made alive" (I Corinthians 15:22) does not mean universal salvation for all men regardless of their belief or their lifestyle. Atonement is for those who accept the gift and are obedient believers. Reconciliation is fulfilled at Christ's coming.

Myers and C.T. Russell exchanged dialogue on atonement through their respective papers, *Zion's Watch Tower* and *The Millenarian*. Russell charged in the *Watch Tower*'s June 1883 issue that Myers believed "that no-ransom" theory. Russell called it "blasting and blighting heresies." Myers defended his interpretations and answered Russell's attacks. Enough on the subject could not be said in dialogue between the papers causing Myers to author a tract entitled "At-one-ment" to refute Russell's ideas, but no copy is known to exist. The Archives in Atlanta would appreciate a copy of that tract.

E. Myers Wanders

The Iowa history book mentioned earlier reveals that G.M. Myers did not attend the Iowa Conference in 1900. He was in Prescott, Kansas, at the time.

He began to investigate Sabbath keeping, and possibly came to believe in it as he studied the question. In 1902, the Stanberry Seventh-day Church of God said that he had joined with them. The Seventh-day Church of God developed alongside the Church of God Abrahamic Faith with similar beliefs except for the Sabbath question.

Copies of *The Bible Advocate* published by the Seventh-day Church of God from 1903 reveal articles by G.M. Myers in which he refuted statements made by James Wilson of the Chicago Church of God as published in *The Present Truth*. The Wilson Bible class had itself previously refuted an article which supported keeping the Sabbath, published by Myers in *The Advocate,* and in a subsequent issue Myers responded:

> So you think it foolish and faddish for us to keep the commandments of God. But what care we for this friendship and approval of men, when the friendship and approval of God are better.... We intend to do our duty religiously as we read it in the Bible, even if every human on earth should denounce us.

Articles by A.J. Eychaner and J.W. Niles, Church of God evangelists with interests tangential to Church of God teaching, appeared in the same issue. Eychaner wrote "A Sabbath Day Necessary" in which he stated in five paragraphs that man needs a seventh day of rest. Niles wrote "The Gospel from the Jews and Gentiles, and the Gospel from the Gentiles to the Jews" number three in a series.

George M.B. Myers fell into disfavor with the Stanberry group within a year or so. He was not granted a license to preach at the proceedings of their General Conference in 1903. He asked that his name be removed from their roll. That request was granted. Their papers reported "Elder G.M. Myers came among us about one year ago of his own free will, and has left us of his own free will, and that is the end of a very short chapter."

W.H. Wilson, an esteemed Church of God Abrahamic Faith evangelist, reported these facts through the pages of *The Restitution*, the Abrahamic Faith paper, and appealed to the brethren not to allow Myers to "re-connect" with "our" Church of God. That is a sad commentary on Myers' ministry. Wilson also informed Abrahamic Faith readers that Stanberry had voted Myers out of their conference. Myers objected to this description in the December issue of *The Restitution*.

Myers must have re-connected with the Church of God for he published *The Investigator* for an unknown number of issues. It was discontinued but the editor resumed publishing in 1904. Myers said then, it was not to be bound by any creed, confession or association whatever.

Joblin's book mentioned above was published in 1905 shedding further light upon the Josephite problem and Myers' role in it. Apparently all this came to light and provoked W.H. Wilson's ire because Myers had published an article by Benjamin Wilson in *The Investigator* which endorsed the doctrine of Josephism. Myers had come to believe it also, but still claimed to believe Jesus was the Son of God. Benjamin Wilson's nephew, W.H. Wilson, took up his aged uncle's cause through the pages of *The Restitution* to clear his name since he could not now defend himself.

Regardless of Myers' affiliations, Church of God Abrahamic Faith members read his books and tracts, for

---

"The Gospel" Tract

This tract was published by the office of *The Present Truth*, St. Paul, Nebraska. There is no date and no author, but presumably G.M. Myers was responsible for this short work. It presents the concept of the Gospel message in six points.

1. The Life of Jesus is our example.
2. The Death of Jesus is for our sins.
3. The Burial of Jesus for three days is to fulfill the prophets.
4. The Resurrection of Jesus by which he received the key of Hades and Death.
5. The Ascension of Jesus to heaven, and His work there as our high priest and advocate.
6. His Coming and the resurrection of the dead, judgment of the world, binding of satan and establishment of the Kingdom of God on earth.

Ref.: "The Gospel" from Archives of Atlanta Bible College

they are part of the archival collection at Atlanta Bible College in Georgia.

Elder A.J. Eychaner visited the home of Myers' daughter in 1924, and wrote of her and Myers: "Much of the success of the Iowa Conference and gospel work is due to these workers."

See Allard, O.J.
    Crowe, W.L.
    Eychaner, A.J.
    Joblin, Maurice
    Niles, J.W.
    Wilson, Benjamin
    Wilson, W.H.

Bibliography: Ancestry.com U.S. Census. Iowa. Wapello. Agency City. Dist. 13. 1850, 1860 and 1870; *Belle Plaine, Iowa City Directory*, G.W. Myers, publisher, 1897, entry for G.M. Myers and family. The name of "G.M. Myers" seems to be the preferred style although the use of G.M.B. Myers is also seen in the record of his cemetery gravesite in Eldon, Iowa; Burnett, Francis et al history committee, *History of the Iowa Church of God and Conference 1855-1987*, printed at Belle Plaine Union, 1987; *The Evangelist*, G.M. Myers, ed., Belle Plaine, Iowa, Vol. 1, #1,2, Oct./Nov. 1895 and Sept. 1, 1897 housed at Atlanta Bible College Archives in the files; *The Millenarian*. Lanark, Il., Feb. 1887; Eychaner, A. J. "A Sabbath Day Necessary," *The Bible Advocate*, Stanberry, Mo., March 31, 1903; Joblin, Maurice, *The Paternity of Jesus*. Self-published, Cleveland, 1905. Here Joblin cites Myers' confession as Josephite as revealed in *Independent*. Nov/Dec.1904 p. 308; Myers, G. M., "Bro. Wilson's Bible Class," *The Bible Advocate,* Stanberry, Mo., March 21, 1903; Niles, J. W. "The Gospel from the Jews to the Gentiles," *The Bible Advocate*, Stanberry, Mo., March 31, 1903; Myers, G.M. "A Lecture on Psychology," Part 1 *The Bible Advocate,* Stanberry, Mo., March 21,1903; Rankin, D. Minutes Iowa Church of God Abrahamic Faith Conference, 1907, 1908 E-mail to JStilson, Jun 26, 2008; *The Restitution* Dec. 3, 1903; Jan. 6, 1904; March 23, 1904; *The Restitution Herald* Sept. 7, 1919; March 25, 1924; Michigan State Conference Records 1859-1886 "Minutes of Twenty-Fifth Annual Conference June 1-4, 1882," Herbert S. Miller, Secretary and "Mendon Conference, May 31-June 1, 1888"; Schulz, Bruce, E-mail discussing role of G.M. Myers if any in Watch Tower activities in Iowa, citing C.T. Russell's *Zion's Watch Tower*, June 1883, May 1886 and June 1887, retrieved e-mail March 25, 2008; Smead, Daniel, Reflections on Myers' fundraising plea, retrieved from e-mail, Dec. 19, 2010. Schulz, Bruce, Pertaining to Reed in *Zion's Watch Tower,* July/Aug 1881 and Feb. 1884 retrieved e-mail March 25, 2008; Nickels, Richard C., "History of the Seventh Day Church of God," Giving and Sharing. Neck City, Mo., 1999, retrieved July 1, 2008 at giveshare.org/churchhistory/historysdcog/index.html; Wilson, W.H. "Pine Woods Bible Class"*The Restitution*. A.R. Underwood, ed., Plymouth, In., March 2, 1904; Wilson, W.H. "Discussion of Myer's *Independent* article," *The Restitution*, A.R. Underwood, ed., Plymouth, In., March 28, 1904.

Neill, Peter
b. 1844
d. December 12, 1909

Peter Neill was born in Scotland and had a good sense for commerce. He was a salesman in a dry goods business in Salem, Ohio, but his avocation was preaching the Word. Peter Neill and his wife Martha were Church of God evangelists in Ohio and Indiana during the late 19th and the early 20th centuries.

In 1902 the Church of God at Salem invited him to become their pastor. He and the family moved from Cleveland to take up that ministry. Regular services were begun at Salem in October 1902. Elder Neill's ministry program greatly assisted the church's growth. Sunday school was offered each Sunday morning, with worship both Sunday morning and evening. Communion was served each Sunday morning. They also held midweek services and hosted the Ohio Conference on several occasions.

Pastor Neill baptized the Barber sisters in 1906. Nancy Barber became a powerful evangelist for the Church of God in Ohio and later in Arkansas City, Kansas.

Peter was cited in a pamphlet written by John R. Fiske for believing in limited or partial resurrection. The pamphlet was entitled "Partial Resurrection an Antidote to Larger Hope," and was published by Fiske from Kansas. At that time Church of God membership was not united on their understanding of resurrection, but Peter did not let that deter him from preaching. Peter believed in partial resurrection, which many members of the Church of God accepted as being scriptural, while many other Church of God ministers and members refuted.

Peter Neill firmly believed that people should study their Bibles, and so he was an avid organizer of Berean classes. The Bereans of the New Testament studied the scriptural documents of their day to see if St. Paul taught the truth. In 1908 Peter began Berean groups across Indiana, initiating classes at South Bend, Plymouth, Argos, North Salem, Pleasant View, Hillisburg and Burr Oak. During this same year he also edited the Berean column for *The Restitution* and wrote the Sunday school lessons which appeared in it. That was quite a load. It can be seen from this activity that Indiana was certainly a leader in promoting and organizing state and local Berean classes. The National Berean Society was not organized until 1913.

At the end of 1908 Peter announced he was slowing down and handed over the work to Evelyn Harsh, a school teacher who was not able to travel much. She feared the work would suffer, but evidently Peter had laid a good foundation in Indiana for some of those Berean classes became churches which are still active.

Peter Neill served as pastor of the Salem church the final seven years of his life. His death meant a terrible loss for the congregation. Martha, his widow, was appointed pastor and served in that office until October 1912.

See Barber, Nancy (Robison)
Fiske, John R.
Austin, Evelyn Harsh (20th)

Bibliography: *The Restitution,* Feb. 7, 1906, and June 24, 1908; Fiske, Jr. John R., "Partial Resurrection an Antidote to Larger Hope," Milan, Kansas, no date; "*The Church of God of the Abrahamic Faith Salem, Ohio Dedication Service,*" "History Section" June 28, 1970. This booklet was furnished by Franklyne Ross.

Newman, Thomas Gabriel
b. 1834
d. 1903

Thomas Newman was born in Ireland and came to the United States as a young man. He arrived in New York Port on the ship Rappahannock on June 15, 1851, when he was 17. He was a farmer. It is thought that he or his parents may have been British Adventists, so that when he heard the Age to Come message of Joseph Marsh, he was already somewhat familiar with it. He participated in the American prophecy fervor that dominated New England around the Finger Lakes area of New York during the 19th century.

When Marsh's *The Prophetic Expositor and Bible Advocate* (1855-1860) ceased publishing, Newman served as assistant editor under Marsh for *The Bible Expositor*, a short-lived publication from Seneca Falls. This title was published for a few months in 1860 only. This brief "internship" prepared Newman as an editor. It is clear that Marsh trained a younger man to replace him, and when Newman was ready, *The Bible Expositor* merged with *The Millennial Harbinger* to become *The Millennial Harbinger and Bible Expositor*, which Newman purchased from Marsh.

Newman served as editor and publisher of *The Millennial Harbinger and Bible Expositor* from 1860 to 1864 taking control when he was only 26. The first issue of *The Millennial Harbinger and Bible Advocate* debuted in September 1860 in Seneca Falls. Joseph Marsh was nearby for editorial advice, which he offered freely. The first two volumes were numbered volume 1 and volume 2. Then in 1862-1864 volumes were numbered 33-37, a rather significant jump in volume count.

It is somewhat speculative, but it is conjectured that Newman began with volume 1, and Marsh interrupted to insist on continuing the volume count with 33, thereby having an unbroken line of succession beginning with *The Voice of Truth* and continuing through all of Marsh's publications. This may have been the cause of an ongoing feud between Marsh and Newman from 1860 until June 1863. If the Newman numbering sequence had been continued, there would not have been a continuous volume count through the century until the beginning of *The Restitution Herald*.

While Newman operated the print shop for *The Millennial Harbinger* it became a major publishing house for Age to Come and Kingdom of God booklets. R.V. Lyon and H.V. Reed used the presses extensively to publish small booklets with less than 100 pages. Newman also published a study help he entitled, *What is Truth? Or, Divine Instruction to the Inquirer after Truth*. This short work was essentially an index of Scriptures by key topics to assist a Bible learner in study.

The Millennial Harbinger and Bible Expositor advanced an editorial position on the War Between the States in favor of slavery—or so it seemed to O.R.L. Crozier. Newman's position on this was especially significant when the reader remembers that Joseph Marsh, Newman's consulting editor, was a staunch abolitionist, and a friend and neighbor to Frederick Douglass in Rochester.

Crozier, himself a noted early Adventist, Age-to-Come leader and former editor, may be credited with keeping Newman's publication on track in favor of the Union effort. Crozier stated years later that he was aghast at Newman's editorial position, and therefore, Crozier kept up a barrage of letters to Newman discussing the issues of the war, and thereby influencing him to stay loyal to the Union. Crozier said that his own national profile within the Age-to-Come movement, and within the Adventist movement in general, was strong enough that Newman dared not refuse to publish any of Crozier's letters or articles.

In 1863, in the middle of the war, Newman resigned the editor's role, reason unknown. Speculation says he may have resigned because of Crozier or possibly because of the dispute with Joseph Marsh mentioned earlier. Marsh had aired his grievances against Newman in a new paper Marsh entitled *The Bible Teacher*. This paper was drawing readers away from Newman.

Marsh announced in June 1863 that the dispute had been amicably settled, that he would discontinue *The Bible Teacher*, and that its subscription list would merge with that of Newman's *Millennial Harbinger*. But Newman had already turned the reins over to H.V. Reed of Chicago for a year. Joseph Marsh left then on an evangelistic trip, and in fact was soon to die. Reed published the paper under Newman's proprietorship until June 1, 1864, and after that it was published by Judson Austin, G.W. Green and J.M. Stephenson for a few months each. That must have been a difficult year as it took so many men to continue the effort.

Newman was engaged as an evangelist for the General Association of the Church of God from Syracuse, New York, in 1863. During this year he preached 101 sermons, traveled over 3,000 miles, baptized 21 new members and "spent more than he received." Newman was elected vice president and secretary/treasurer of the association.

During that time Newman traveled extensively and probably had very little to do with editing except to send in a notice of the semi-annual meeting of the New York Association of Church of God meeting in Syracuse on November 27, 1863, to *The Harbinger*. This Association was to furnish credentials to the New York evangelists, "commending them to the brethren."

Exiting from New York, Thomas Newman appeared in Chicago before the end of 1863. It is thought that Newman also preached Age to Come across Wisconsin, as indicated in an essay by Emily Fyfe during this time. She noted that Thomas Newman baptized several Age to Come believers there.

There are indications in literature that Thomas Newman assisted with preaching duties throughout Illinois, Wisconsin and Iowa after he stopped being an editor. The people seemed to receive him and his message well. It is thought that he settled briefly in Cedar Rapids, Iowa, where he published the city newspaper. He may have been influential in helping to begin the work at Waterloo. After that his whereabouts are unknown.

See Adams, Thomas E.
   Crozier, O.R.L.
   Marsh, Joseph
   Reed, H.V.
   Stephenson, J.M.

Bibliography: Adventist Newspapers and Periodicals Inventory. American Antiquarian Society, Worchester, Mass., retrieved April 30, 2008 from http://www.americanantiquarian.org/ Inventories/adventist.htm; Ancestry.com. Iowa. Linn. Cedar Rapids, Ward 1. 1870; Ancestry.com. Irish Immigrants: New York Port Arrival Records 1846-1851, Record for Thomas Newman; Fyfe, Emily. "Fragments of History," *The Restitution Herald*, Oregon, Illinois, date unknown; Newman, Thomas. "Conference Announcement," *The Millennial Harbinger and Bible Expositor*, Nov. 18, 1863; Newman, Thos. "What is Truth?" Office of *The Millennial Harbinger*, Thos. Newman, ed., Seneca Falls, NY. 1861; Report of a meeting of New York Assoc. of Church of God., *The Millennial Harbinger and Bible Expositor*, June 10, 1863; Marsh and Newman disputed settled. *The Millennial Harbinger and Bible Expositor*, June 10, 1863;

Niles, John W.
   b. June, 1832
   d. 1904

J.W. Niles was born in New York, but preferred to reside in the more southern states. While still single he taught at a common school in Tyler County, Virginia. In 1862 he married Desdemmonia Wait, the daughter of Adin and Phebe Wait and granddaughter of Arvah Austin, all of New York. J.W. and Desdemmonia had two daughters. The family resided for a while in Ohio and later in Edinborough, Pennsylvania, where John was a farmer. In the spring, summer and fall he farmed, and in the winter, he preached. John traveled throughout Pennsylvania, Ohio and West Virginia on evangelistic tours after he returned from duty in the Civil War. He served as a private in the 56th Regiment Pennsylvania Infantry, Company C for three years. The 56th Regiment fought at Antietam, and opened the battle of Gettysburg under the command of Col. J. William Hofmann for which it was given special notice. Niles was mustered out at Charleston, South Carolina.

John W. Niles may have been related to Hezekiah Niles, famous editor of *Niles Weekly Register* in Baltimore, who tried valiantly to thwart the coming Civil War through his editorial opinions on slavery and abolition 30 years before the War began.

J.W. Niles was active in the ministry throughout Pennsylvania. He was a younger man than Joseph Marsh, but word of him is found in Marsh's *Prophetic Expositor and Bible Advocate* in 1858. He was known to work with John T. Ongley, a fellow evangelist from Ohio and Pennsylvania. Ongley reported that Elder Niles of Hayfield, Pennsylvania, preached at the September 1858 Northwest Pennsylvania Conference meeting from Hebrews 11:6 that "without faith it is impossible to please God" from which he fully explained the Abrahamic Faith.

Throughout the pages of Marsh's *Prophetic Expositor and Bible Advocate* it can be seen repeatedly that Marsh and his evangelist colleagues preached one faith, meaning, the Abrahamic Faith. To them, the Gospel of the Kingdom was an understanding of the promises to believers who are made heirs to the promises made to Abraham through belief and acceptance of Christ. It cannot and should not be said that Abrahamic Faith began with the Wilson influence in Geneva, Illinois. The Age-to-Come movement always included a component of One Faith. The difference was, Marsh pushed the phrase "Age to Come" while Benjamin Wilson pushed the phrase "One Faith." It was a difference of emphasis, not belief.

Not only was J.W. Niles a man of One Faith/Age to Come, he was also a man in favor of a national organization. In March 1889, evangelist Niles wrote to the secretary of the newly formed National Conference in Philadelphia (1888) to report his evangelistic efforts. He was inspired by and in agreement with the Church of God's attempt to organize a National Conference in Philadelphia, and he was impressed with Christ and the Gospel of the Kingdom.

Niles wrote from North Bend, West Virginia, that he had been working around Washington, Pennsylvania and Shirley, West Virginia, on that circuit. It was tough going. He preached to the poor mountain people of West Virginia. He said the people were fine folks and friendly, but they did not have homes that afforded comfort to guests. They usually did not have guests. He said the houses were small and the beds were hard. The roads were twisty, steep and often muddy. His progress was slow and congregations were usually few in number.

J.W. Niles said in one report to *The Restitution* that he had heard Elder C.C. Ramsay preach at Philadelphia during the general conference in November 1888. Niles remarked he was not fluent like Ramsay, but he was slow of speech and deliberate in his delivery. He had preached for many years and had baptized many. He gathered groups of 50 or more people to his preaching services around Shirley.

On evangelistic tours Niles was separated from his family and often had no place to sleep. If he found one, he often slept with cold feet in a strange place. In one place, Niles suffered with cold feet so badly that it made his throat hoarse. He developed laryngitis and could not preach, but still the people came. He held meetings and whispered to a local brother who became his voice that night. Because of his ailment, attendance picked up.

People were curious to see the duo-preachers, and finally after several large meetings, he was able to speak again.

Niles pursued a difficult ministry so that folks might come to know the love and peace which Christ's message could bring to a thankless existence. He usually preached in small houses crowded with listeners, because there were very few church buildings in the mountains, and communities did not like to let out their schoolhouse for meetings. He often traveled on foot. He said, "Mud was in abundance."

Niles may have been the first evangelist to be supported by the new General Conference. The congregation of L.C. Chase of Raisin, Michigan, had sent in donations to the national office to begin an evangelist's fund. It is thought this money was used to underwrite some of Niles' expenses. The editor wrote in April 1889 that money intended for Bro. Rice had been sent instead to Bro. Niles! It is supposed money was also sent then to Bro. Rice.

Richard Nickels, noted historian of the Seventh-day Church of God, said that in 1887, Niles was associated with their fellowship. Enemies of Niles' preaching called his West Virginia followers, "Nilesites." Evidence in *The Bible Advocate* indicates that Niles had at one time been a Sabbatarian. He wrote a series in that paper during 1903. So it is not known if he came out of the Church of God and into the Seventh-day or the other way around.

It should be noted that Nickels' made the point that the Age to Come and the Seventh-day Church of God were, and still are, amazingly alike in doctrine. Their chief point of difference is first-day worship versus seventh-day worship. For Niles to write for either paper does not deny his belief in the Kingdom of God on earth, oneness of God or conditional immortality.

It is thought that Niles came out of Seventh-day into the Church of God/Age to Come movement as had J.M. Stephenson and D.P. Hall, both of whom repudiated it. Since John Ongley mentioned Niles positively as early as 1858, it is probable that Niles was a believer in the Abrahamic covenant and the Age to Come. And since Niles spoke glowingly of Church of God organizational efforts in 1888, it seems possible the Nickels' history reflects a short period in Niles' career. This is an area of future research.

John Niles wrote a series of articles for *The Restitution* in 1893 on the Covenants. He submitted something for publication at least once a month and sometimes more often. He was quite a good theologian and writer. He wrote another series in the 1893 *Restitution* entitled, "Was Jesus the Son of Joseph?" He argued against Joseph being Jesus' earthly father. He said:

> [If] Jesus were the son of Joseph then there is no new covenant, no salvation from sin, Jesus has not been exalted as a prince and a savior to grant…remission of sins. The amount of the whole matter is if Jesus were the natural son of Joseph he could not be the Christ.

John died at home and was interred at the Edinboro Cemetery.

In 1965, Eugene Stilson, pastor of Fort Valley and Maurertown Churches of God in Shenandoah County, Virginia, was called to a mountain community of West Virginia to preach a funeral for a lady who had been a baptized member of the Church of God. There were no Churches of God in that locale, but the funeral was well attended by family and friends. When it was over, her daughter came forward and said, "Thanks, that sounded like a Church of God sermon. Mother wanted to be buried by a Church of God pastor."

Earl Poland of Skelton, West Virginia, attended

The Church of God at Skelton, West Virginia, under the direction of Elder JW Niles.

Oregon Bible College and served the Lord in ministry at Hedrick, Indiana, for a number of years. The ministry of J.W. Niles may still be bearing fruit in West Virginia.

See Hall, D.P.
　　Marsh, Joseph
　　Ongley, John T.
　　Poland, Earl (20th)
　　Ramsay, C.C.
　　Stephenson, J.M.
　　Stilson, Eugene (20th)
　　Wilson, Benjamin

Bibliography: Ancestry.com. U.S. Census. Virginia. Tyler. Wick, 1860; U.S. Census. Ohio. Ashtabula. Saybrook. 1870; U.S. Census. Pennsylvania. Erie. Edinborough. Dist. 157. 1880; U.S. Census. Pennsylvania. Erie. Washington. 60. 1900; U.S. Civil War Soldiers 1862-1865 record for John Niles, Pennsylvania; FindaGrave.com record for John W. Niles, Edinboro, Pa.; Bates, Samuel Penniman, *History of Pennsylvania Volunteers 1861-1865,* Historical Society of Pa. Harrisburg. Pa., State Printer. 1869 p 218, 220; Nickels, Richard C., *History of the Seventh Day Church of God,* Neck City, Mo. Giving and Sharing. Reprint, 1999 quoting A.N. Dugger, and C.O. Dodd. *A History of True Religion.* Jerusalem. 2d ed. Pacific Press. 1970. 311-316; Niles, Hezekiah (1777-1839,) *Niles Weekly Register,* 1811-1836, Balitmore, Md.; Niles, J.W. "Report," *The Restitution,* March 28, 1889; Niles, J.W. "The Covenants" series, *The Restitution,* S.A. Chaplin, ed. Plymouth, In., February 8, 15, 22, 1893; Niles, J.W. "The Gospel from the Jews to the Gentiles," No. 3 *The Bible Advocate,* Stanberry, Mo. March 31, 1903; Niles, J.W. "Was Jesus the Son of Joseph?" The *Restitution* A. R. Underwood, ed., Plymouth, In., Oct. 23, 1893; Ongley, J.T. "Report of Conference in Northwest Pa.," *The Prophetic Expositor and Bible Advocate,* Jos. Marsh, ed. Dec. 1, 1858; Chaplin, S.A. Note about funds to Niles. *The Restitution,* April 10, 1889; Williams, Byron. *Abstracts of Obituaries and Verbatim Marriage Announcements printed in The Restitution, 1874-1900.* self published 1993, records for Adin and Phebe Wait.

Nokes, Clarence A.
b. 1859
d. Unknown

Clarence Nokes was well known by his church and community as an excellent Bible student. It is recorded only once in *The Restitution Herald* that he preached at Los Angeles using a prophecy chart. He was elected president of the California Conference in 1922.

He was born in Canada and married Elsie. They had one son and one daughter who were still living at home, unmarried, in their thirties. The family operated a greenhouse and a floral shop.

Bibliography: Ancestry.com. U.S. Census. California. Los Angeles. Dist 3. 1920; *The Restitution Herald,* August 8, 1922.

Norris, William Lewis
b. December 16, 1842
d. September 24, 1916

William Norris was a servant of the Lord and a member of the Argos, Indiana, Church of God. He married Adelia Baldwin on January 7, 1864. They had eight children. H.V. Reed, noted Illinois orator, baptized William Norris. Norris died at the home of his daughter, Mrs. Lewis Schafer, in Argos, Indiana. Pastor F.L. Austin conducted the funeral and wrote Norris' obituary for *The Restitution Herald.* He said of Norris, "he was an exemplary worker of the Lord."

See Austin, F.L. (20th)
　　Reed, H.V.

Bibliography: Obituary, *The Restitution Herald,* Oct. 1916.

Oliver, Stephen C.
b. July 1, 1837
d. September 13, 1924

Stephen Oliver was born in Valparaiso, Indiana. He moved to Iowa with his parents in 1853. He married Elizabeth B. Connell on April 23, 1862. They had four sons, Abner M., Charles P., Emory (in Attica, Iowa) and Frank (in Reno, Nevada).

In 1866, Stephen moved his family to Osage Claim, Kansas, later known as St. Paul, Kansas. They sold their claim early in 1867 and moved to Jasper County, Missouri, near the little town of Arvilla. From there they moved to Dade County, Missouri, near Greenfield early in 1868. They moved several more times in Missouri and finally to Harper County, Kansas, where they settled on a farm and built a home in November 1882.

The frequent moves were extremely difficult as pioneers made their way in covered wagons over hundreds of miles of unsettled and inhospitable country with all its toils, privations, hardships and dangers in bad weather on muddy roads. For long moves of entire households, covered wagons were used well into the 20th century. Stephen moved to Attica, Kansas, in 1906, and Elizabeth died there in 1911 at age 67, leaving Stephen and her four sons.

Stephen Oliver was a member of the Church of God and a minister who preached the second coming and the restitution of all things. He primarily preached in the area of Oklahoma south of Caldwell, Kansas. He and his student group took over an abandoned Dunkard church in that location and renovated it. They made repairs, painted, built pews and altar furniture and landscaped the outside. When they were finished, it looked like new. Stephen also preached for the Church of God that met at the Flint schoolhouse in Grant County, Oklahoma, where he placed J.R. Fiske Sr. in charge as elder and evangelist.

According to one of Almus Adam's reports, Stephen Oliver worked in the Oklahoma ministry for many years. His name is not included in the list of licensed ministers compiled by the General Conference because his service predated the conference. He probably was licensed by the Missouri/Kansas state conference, but that record is not available.

In May 1906 when Elder Oliver was nearly 80, he stepped onto a train and departed for Attica, Kansas. The railroad surpassed the covered wagon as the chief means of transportation on the Great Plains in those days. Even though the automobile had been invented and people were buying them for personal use, they were unreliable and problematic for long trips. Usually they were left at home in favor of the train. On this particular trip Stephen preached, baptized and served communion along the way to isolated members.

His ministry spanned more than 50 years beginning in the 1870s while he still lived in Missouri. It is through the efforts of this man that a work was established in Oklahoma and southern Kansas. It was upon this foundation that the evangelistic work of Almus Adams was built.

See Adams, Almus
Fiske, John R., Sr.
Lapp, Lucy (20th) - Covered Wagons

Bibliography: *The Restitution,* Jan. 25, 1911; Nov. 15, 1911; June, 1916; 1920. *The Restitution Herald,* Sept. 20, 1924.

Ongley, John T.
b. June 1819
d. 1905?

John T. Ongley was born in England but moved to New York. In 1841, he married Adah "Addie" Ann (d. August 16, 1889). They resided at Bloomfield in Crawford County, Pennsylvania. By occupation, he was a shingle maker. John wrote that they "embraced the blessed hope in 1844, and soon after that, the glorious restitution and the hope of Israel." This language clearly placed him in the camp of Joseph Marsh and Age-to-Come teachings. John preached the Gospel throughout the region of Pennsylvania, Ohio and the Mid-Atlantic States.

John Ongley was also one of the first Age-to-Come evangelists to partner with George Storrs in preaching conditional immortality. Storrs conducted a tent ministry throughout New York explaining the nature of man and life only in Christ. Other men who worked with him in this tent ministry were J.B. Cook and J.C. Bywater. Historian Bruce Schulz wrote:

> In September 1851, Storrs went on a tent-preaching tour with [J.C.] Bywater, J.B. Cook, and John T. Ongley, who along with Wendell had been the principals in the 1850 Movement. Their itinerary took them to Honeoye, New York, where Bywater and Wendell had preached the year before. Storrs reported 'A Tent Meeting was held in this place last year, and the doctrine of Immortality and Endless Life through Jesus Christ *alone* was proclaimed for the first time by Brethren Bywater and Wendell, who traveled with the Tent together at that time. The seed which they sowed had sprung up, and much good was the result: not only were numbers, at the time, led to confess the truth, but the word of truth grew during the year.'

John T. Ongley did not have a strong presence in the Atlanta Bible College Archives' research materials; he is known primarily from brief notes to the editors of *The Millennial Harbinger and Bible Expositor* and *The Restitution*. Ongley's name is also mentioned in connection with John W. Niles. They shared some preaching services in Pennsylvania and West Virginia. This indicates that he preached a circuit but little more is known about him. The record shows, however, that he was present at the dedication service of the new church at Salem, Ohio, in 1887.

It is also known that he preached the Word of the

End of Tent Ministry in Pennsylvania

In a letter to *The Restitution* Elder Ongley discussed the lack of opportunities in the field because he preached Age to Come. He said if he had set dates or preached no age to come, he would still be using the tent. As it was, he relinquished it to two others in Kansas.

Source: *The Restitution* September 8, 1875, courtesy of Bruce Schulz

---

Gospel around Cowdersport, Pennsylvania, and had some success there. In his old age, he toured with D.C. Robison of Cleveland and Salem, Ohio, to carry on evangelistic ministry. Robison reported that on one tour Elder Ongley, (also seen as Ongl) preached 14 times. He was active in the ministry when the Church of God organized a national conference at Philadelphia in 1888.

John wrote in Adah's obituary that they had been married for 49 years and she always supported him when he went out to "preach the precious truths." They enjoyed a total of 32 children *and* grandchildren many of whom were gathered at her side when she died. Mollie Grove of Plum, Pennsylvania, preached Adah's funeral sermon. Nothing more is known about Mollie Grove.

See Bywater, J.C.
    Cook, J.B.
    Niles, John W.
    Robison, D.C.
    Storrs, George

Bibliography: Ancestry.com. U.S. Census. Pennsylvania. Crawford. Athens. 1870; U.S. Census. Pennsylvania. Crawford. Bloomfield. Dist. 3 1900; *The Restitution*, Thomas Wilson, editor. Chicago, Il., November 1874; Ongley, John. "Letter to Thomas Newman," *The Millennial Harbinger and Bible Expositor*, Nov. 18, 1863; *The Church of God of the Abrahamic Faith Salem, Ohio Dedication Service*, "History Section" June 28, 1970. This booklet was furnished by Franklyne Ross; Williams, Byron. *Abstracts of Obituaries and Verbatim Marriage Announcements printed in The Restitution 1874-1900*, Self-published. 1993; Ongley, John. Obituary for Ada Ongley, *The Restitution*, S.A. Chaplin, ed. Plymouth, Ind. Sept. 4, 1889; Storrs, George. "Report of Tent," *The Bible Examiner*, Oct. 1851, p. 155 Bruce Schulz furnished this quote from a book he is presently writing due to be published in 2011, tentative title *A Separate Identity: Zion's Watch Tower Congregations 1870-1887*; Williams, Byron. *Abstracts of Obituaries and Verbatim Marriage Announcements printed in The Restitution. 1874-1900*, self-published. 1993 record for Ada Ann Ongley, p 44.

Orem, William J.
b. June 1836
d. 1923?

William J. Orem was born in Maryland but made his way west. He passed through Indiana, Missouri and resided finally at Wolf River, Doniphan County, Kansas, with his widowed mother, Martha. He helped to support several siblings. He was a painter by trade. He fought in the Civil War as a private in the 6th Regiment Missouri State Militia Cavalry Company E, and he received a small pension from that service. He returned to serve a term in the Kansas Legislature representing his district at Doniphan.

His introduction to the Gospel of the Kingdom came through Church of God influence in Indiana. *The Restitution* noted Orem began to preach in that state shortly after the Bitter Disappointment in 1844 and remained in the area until around 1860. He may have studied the Bible with John Shafer, Uncle John Foore, J.F. Wagoner or Joshua Bailey who settled in Missouri. Orem and W.P. Shockey worked together throughout Kansas.

The younger Orem greatly assisted William Shockey during his frail and failing years in Kansas. A letter from Orem to *The Gospel Banner* on July 15, 1869, detailed his plan to take up preaching from Elder Shockey. Both men were present at a service where Shockey felt too weak and at the last minute, Orem preached in his place. W.J. Orem went on to say that the "brethren of the West with whom Bro. S. has labored so incessantly the last few years, by which he has shattered his health, should not forget him in his affliction."

The service for which Elder Orem preached followed a misunderstanding with a Disciples preacher over the use of the building. On the Sunday in question, the Church of God was scheduled to use the building, but the Disciples showed up by mistake. Most of the congregation came primarily to hear Shockey and Orem but some Disciples sat in as well.

Orem spoke to them of the Kingdom of God from Daniel 2:44. They received it gladly, and participated in the Lord's Supper following the afternoon service at which Elder Shockey was well enough to preach.

W.J. Orem is infrequently mentioned in the literature, but he must have continued steadfastly in ministry across the Great Plains because his name is seen in a reports published in *The Restitution* in 1905 and 1907 indicating that he was loved by the people. Another letter of gratitude by Mrs. Amos Gilbert of Blythedale, Missouri, to *The Restitution Herald* in 1923 indicated the time-span of Orem's ministry to be from age 16 in Indiana to well into his 90s.

Orem once reported to Benjamin Wilson in *The Gospel Banner* that he greatly appreciated "the press and highly prized *The Gospel Banner, The Herald of Life, The Herald of the Coming Kingdom, The World's Crisis* and *The Marturion.*"

William remained single most of his life and cared for his mother. He married Ida Ordnung in 1891. She was 24 years younger than her husband. They had one daughter, Wilma. In her old age, she became a resident of the Golden Rule Home in Oregon, Illinois. Ida was Miss Elizabeth Ordnung's sister; Elizabeth also lived at the Home. Ida was visited once by her daughter who traveled by air to Illinois from California in 1946.

Elder Shockey, his protégé W.J. Orem and wife Ida rest in peace.

See Bailey, Joshua
Ordnung, Elizabeth (20th)
Shockey, W.P.

Wilson, Benjamin

Bibliography: Ancestry.com U.S. Census. Kansas. Allen. Iola. Dist. 9. 1880; Ancestry.com. U.S. Census. Kansas. Marion. Nemaha. 1900; Ancestry.com. U.S. Civil War Soldiers 1861-1865 about William J. Orem; Ancestry.com. Wilder, Daniel W. *The Annals of Kansas*, Topeka, Ks., 1875 p 428; Orem, W.J. "Correspondence," *The Gospel Banner and Millennial Advocate,* July 15, 1869*;* and, *"*Report of Wolf River Conference," *The Gospel Banner and Millennial Advocate,* September 1, 1869; *The Restitution*, May 24, 1905; April 3, 1907; *The Restitution Herald,* Nov. 20. 1923; *The Restitution Herald,* July 28, 1931; June 1, 1948.

Osborn, Samuel
b. 1840
d. 1932

Samuel Osborn was born in Ohio. His family moved to Indiana when he was four. The family settled at Eagle Lake near Knox, Indiana. Both of his parents died that same year. He was the youngest child, and was raised by the oldest brother.

After serving in the Civil War, Samuel returned to Indiana, married and settled near the site of the present Burr Oak Church of God. He cleared the land so that he might engage in farming and raising cattle.

Samuel was largely responsible for building the Burr Oak Church of God following the conflagration of the first building shortly after its construction. The first church was called the North Union Church of God.

A son, Oren, died at age four, but three daughters, Olive, Cora and Carrie were faithful members of the Church of God at Burr Oak. Cora married Benjamin Fetters at her father's home on March 25, 1894.

Samuel Osborn remained a faithful member of the Church until his death.

Bibliography: Atlanta Bible College Biography Project, David Krogh, compiler. Williams, Byron. *Abstracts of Obituaries and Verbatim Marriage Announcements printed in The Restitution 1874-1900*, self-published, 1993, p 107.

Palmer, Hannah Elizabeth "Libby" (Hill)
b. March 1840
d. 1915?

Libby Hill Palmer was born in Ohio, a daughter of Bazaleel Hill. The family moved to Michigan in her youth. In 1855, she and her brother, R.J. Hill, helped to begin a church in Iowa. She returned to Michigan to wed Hiram D. Palmer (b. August 27, 1831) at Veray in 1857.

Libby became a leader in the Iowa ministry, and was noted for teaching, preaching and organizing conferences. She was still serving in a leadership capacity when the Iowa Conference reorganized in 1888. *The History of the Iowa Church of God and Conference* by the history committee of that conference states, "Women took an initial place of leadership in the work among church members. Libby Palmer was the first conference president and Anna Eychaner was secretary."

To emphasize her belief that godly women should be about the Lord's business she wrote a column in *The Evangelist*'s very first issue. It was entitled "Women in the Sunday School." She said:

> As woman's capabilities have come to be appreciated, one by one, have the barriers been removed until to-day we find them side by side with men almost everywhere but in the pulpit. Even there she is beginning to be appreciated, while along the lines of educational work and social reform me thinks she is almost taking the lead.

Her premise was that since women have largely taken the lead in the Sunday School, "they hold much of the destiny of the nation in their hands." Teachers for the Sunday School should first be Christian and qualified to teach. They should teach "the simple rational plan of God for the future salvation of man, and redemption in Christ through the resurrection, and the benefits of a pure life here and hereafter."

Libby worked faithfully for the Lord throughout her life and was granted a pastoral license by the Iowa conference at their annual meeting in 1896, and was one of "eleven ministers present who aided in the public preaching" at the 1899 conference. She also helped organize the first Berean Society at that conference. Through service on several committees within the Conference and the Berean society, Libby set a good example for women in their service to the Lord.

The Women's Christian Temperance Union was a national organization of women dedicated to eliminating or moderating the drinking patterns that interrupted and ruined families. Libby was a member. Delbert Rankin, Iowa pastor and historian, has said, "she was active in the WCTU and took her program as far away as Washington State."

Repeatedly throughout the history of the Church of God, the Christian service of women was highly esteemed, and Libby Palmer led the way.

See Lucille Boyer (20th)
Hill, R. J.
Myers, G.M.B.

Bibliography: Ancestry.com. U.S. Census. Iowa. Hardin. Alden. Dist. 142. 1900; Burnett, Francis et al of history committee, *History of the Iowa Church of God and Conference 1855-1987*, printed by Belle Plaine Union, 1987; Palmer, Libbie, "Woman in the Sunday School," *The Evangelist*, G.M. Myers, editor. Belle Plaine, Iowa, October, 1895; Rankin, Delbert, Information from Iowa Church of God Archives retrieved from e-mail July 6, 2008.

Parker, Ann Alice
b. March 4, 1849
d. October 31, 1915

Ann Parker was a woman of great faith. She was born near Vicksburg, Michigan, into a hardy pioneer family. Soon after she married, she began to experience ill health. Nearly all her 66 years were spent in pain. Perhaps she suffered from debilitating arthritis or fibromyalgia for which at that time, there was no relief. She turned to

Spiritualism, but felt there was something missing in that system. Various ministers were called to her home and asked to read the Bible and explain it. Two of them were F.L. Austin and Mary Woodward. Mary wrote Mrs. Parker's obituary. When Austin shared the Gospel message with Mrs. Parker, she accepted it. At this time, she was already dying and the family felt that baptism was out of the question. She died in the glorious hope of the resurrection. Sr. Woodward and Bro. Austin preached her funeral from the text of John 11:21, "Lord, if thou hadst been here my brother had not died."

Bibliography: Obituary, *The Restitution Herald*, Dec. 8, 1915.

Parker, Parmelia Jane "Jenny" Marsh
b. June 16, 1836
d. 1913

Parmelia Jane Marsh was the daughter of Joseph and Sarah Marsh. When she was eight, the family moved to Rochester, New York, where she grew up. Her father preached and worshipped at the Rochester Church of God, one of the first churches in New England to take that name which Joseph believed was scriptural. Joseph was a leading voice in the Christian Connexion, and later, the Millerite movement. After the Bitter Disappointment in October 22, 1844, he became the main proponent of a new interpretation of prophecy, which he aptly named the Age to Come. He was highly persecuted for his ideas. Her father's beliefs and persecution impacted Jane.

In New England, the frenetic days preceding the Bitter Disappointment were traumatic for children. Jane and her two sisters were deeply affected by it. Because of the uncertainty of the times, they were not allowed to go to school. They spent their days at home being schooled by their mother who was a poet. They spent a great deal of time in meetings learning about being true believers, so they would not be left behind when the Savior returned to earth. To quote a website originating out of Rochester, New York, "it was a frightening life for a sensitive eight-year-old child." When Jane was in her forties and fifties she began writing about those frightful days. In "The Littlest Millerite," published in the *Century*, Jane related how after the day passed as usual, children began taunting her with "Hi, there, Millerite! When are you going up?" The book details the persecution her father and the family endured at the hands of men who could not accept Marsh's Age-to-Come ideas.

After 1843, Jenny's parents put her into school. She attended Dr. Chester Dewey's Collegiate Institute, Clover Street Seminary and finally the schools of Professors Wetherill and Peck. In 1847, Frederick Douglass moved in next door to the Marshes, and Jenny befriended the family. Her friendship with them lasted a lifetime. This raised her social conscience for the plight of her black neighbors.

Her introduction to abolitionist feelings may have precipitated a religious crisis after her turmoil over the Millerite frenzy. Sometime during this period she joined the Episcopal Church and continued that affiliation her whole lifetime.

Joseph Marsh helped launch his daughter's publishing career. At age 16, she wrote a poem for the *Expositor* which he gladly published. The following year a poem and seven short stories were published in *Waverly* magazine. Fifty of her poems were eventually published in the *Rural New Yorker*. Her first novel, *Toiling and Hoping, the story of a Little Hunchback* was published in 1856.

Jane was part of a devout Christian family. She referred in her writings to having been raised in the doctrine of Christ's Second Coming for "forty-three" years. In spite of a lifetime of scars from that experience, she retained many of the values she was taught throughout her life, being of a conservative nature. Like her father, she loved to write, and like her mother she liked writing poetry. Jane was a freelance journalist and novelist. In 1886, she wrote *The Midnight Cry* depicting the religious enthusiasm that swept over New York. She also wrote "A Story Historical" which depicted the semi-centennial of Rochester. In this book she said, "Millerism was the logical outcome of the theological teaching of the centuries." She must have heard her father say that often enough over the years.

Jane married Rochester attorney, George T. Parker. They had four children. The web site mentioned earlier notes: "Church and family were her themes (in writing and teaching art) as when she founded the magazine." Jane wrote for the Episcopal Church magazine and wrote several Sunday school books, as well. She was a journalistic powerhouse.

In effect, Jane became her father in Episcopalian garb and even wrote a novel which was a polemic seeking to turn people toward her adopted church. This novel *Barley Wood, or, Building on the Rock* was published in 1860. It was the story of a Presbyterian girl who turned from her background towards the Episcopal Church, a story that closely mirrored her own life.

Sadly, according to her descendants, Jane did not associate with her mother and sisters again after her father's death in 1863. No reasons for this are given.

In the 1870s, Jane again demonstrated her concern for social issues—a consciousness awakened so many years before by the abolition movement. Now she focused on women's rights. Jane was active in the women's movements of the day and a suffragette, with a high regard for Susan B. Anthony. Still, Jane distanced herself from the very aggressive women in the movement. She did not like their anti-male rhetoric.

In 1881, she organized the Ignorance Club with Dr. Sarah R. Adamson Dolley. This was the first club organized for women in Rochester. Like Margaret Fuller from Massachusetts, who advanced the cause for women in the 19th century, a half-century earlier, Jenny organized the ladies to discuss the major issues of the day so the club "became a major cultural force in the city."

Throughout the rest of her life, Jane devoted herself to writing about theology, social concerns, history and many more topics. She was a cultural force in her own right. Sadly, though, she is considered a little-known writer. Had the times been different, she may have attracted more national attention for her talented efforts.

In 1889 Frederick Douglass had just been appointed the US Ambassador to Haiti, and he invited her to sail with him to visit that island. She stayed there three months and studied Haitian history, social and racial conditions, women's conditions and Catholic and protestant missionary efforts. All these topics were written and published when she returned home.

After her husband's death in 1895, Jane lived with her children in Milwaukee and Detroit. She spent her summers in Rochester and lived for a while with another daughter in California. There she continued to write about millennialism.

Her biographer, Marcelle LeMenager Lane, wrote *The Life and Work of Jane Marsh Parker*. Some of the information in this entry has been summarized from Lane's book as posted on the website.

Jane Marsh Parker rests beside her husband at Mount Hope Cemetery in Rochester, New York.

See Marsh, Joseph

Bibliography: Ancestry.com. U.S. Census 1850 Rochester, New York; "The History of Rochester, NY at Mt. Hope Cemetery, Stories in Stone. Famous Women in Mount Hope Cemetery," http://www.fomh.org/Stories/Parker.htm summarizing from a book by Marcelle LeMenager Lane, *The Life and Work of Jane Marsh Parker, 1836-1913*. See also www.gutenburg.org/files/31125/31125-h/31125-h.htm#FNanchor_95_95; Hepworth, Patra Marsh, Various e-mails, particularly, May 31, 2008 which stated that Jane distanced herself from her family after Joseph's death; Parker, Jane Marsh. *Rochester, A Story Historical.* 1884 p. 253; Parker, Jane Marsh. *The Littlest Millerite*, New York. 1886; Stilson, Jan. *Art and Beauty in the Heartland, the Story of Eagle's Nest Camp at Oregon, Illinois 1898-1942.* Authorhouse, 2006. This book contains a detailed chapter on the life of Margaret Fuller who visited Oregon, Illinois in 1843.

Parks, Mrs. H.A.
b. 1815
d. Unknown

Mrs. Parks was a circuit preacher who traveled throughout the Illinois and Wisconsin frontier declaring the imminent return of Christ. She may have lived in the Waukesha, Wisconsin, area. If she did indeed live there, records show she had four children. Letters to Joseph Marsh indicate that he knew her. One report mentioned that she preached at Buffalo Grove, Illinois, near Polo, and that she remained in the area to preach "several times" at the Rock River Seminary at Mt. Morris, Illinois, which the Methodists owned at the time. She also preached to the quite-liberal Freewill Baptists; they were astonished at her Bible doctrine. Reports also show she preached in Freeport. She must have been well educated and certainly was an outstanding Bible student.

Dixon, Illinois, Church of God Mrs. Parks preached in Ogle and Lee Counties (Illinois) and helped begin the work at Dixon.

Mrs. Parks wrote to Joseph Marsh in April 1847 that she was in Buffalo Grove, Illinois, and had been talking with believer William Putnam. She requested a speaker come in the spring and bring a chart with him "because it excites great interest." She suggested the speaker follow a circuit which she herself very likely followed: Milwaukee to Illinois locations of Rock Prairie, Buffalo Grove, Springfield, and from there, to Indiana. She mentioned that Bro. Daniel Daniels was in southern Illinois.

Beyond that small amount of information, nothing more is known about this courageous woman.

See Chandler, Moses
    Daniels, Daniel J.

Bibliography: Ancestry.com. U.S. Census. Wisconsin. Waukesha. Summit. 1850; Parks, Mrs., Report of work in Ogle County, Il., *Voice of Truth*, Joseph Marsh, ed., Sept. 20, 1846, Jan. 20, 1847 and April 8, 1847.

Parson, William
b. March 6, 1819
d. July 2, 1895

Elder Parson was born in Fountain County, Indiana. At age 12, he converted to the teachings of the Christian church but later affiliated with the Advent Christians. In the early 1870s he became convinced that the correct name of the church should be Church of God and began to preach that, working with C.D.W. Scott to organize several churches.

On December 18, 1874, the Minnesota Church of God Conference ordained Elder Parson at its very first session. He was also made president of the conference at that meeting.

Parson lived at Fort Ripley and died by drowning in the Crow Wing River. He had been driving his horse and buggy through the water on his way home from the Minnesota Conference which met at Bergen that year. It saddened the whole brotherhood. He was buried in the cemetery six miles east of Fort Ripley.

See Scott, C.D.W.
Bibliography: *History of the Minnesota Church of God Conference*, Sydney Magaw, ed., 1931.

Pascoe, James
b. 1835
d. December 18, 1921

James Pascoe was born in England. He moved to Canada and married Margaret Hogarth. They had four sons and five daughters. As a young man, James Pascoe embraced the Gospel of the Kingdom. Elder R.V. Lyon baptized him. Pascoe remained faithful to his calling his whole life.

While little is known of his life, it is clear he raised his family to love the Lord for the Hogarth name remained in the Church of God for several generations. Pascoe died at his home in Ontario.

See Hogarth, Annie
Hogarth, Jabez D.
Hogarth, Jabez E.
Bibliography: *The Restitution*, Feb., 1922

Patrick, James A.
b. July 23, 1870
d. August 12, 1948

James Patrick was born to Solomon and Nancy Massy Patrick who resided in Howard Lake, Minnesota. Elder James Martin baptized James in 1896.

Elder Patrick remained in Minnesota and attended church with the Randalls in Stearns County, Eden Lake Township. He began to preach in 1899 and farmed for income. Ordained into the ministry on March 5, 1899, at the Ellsworth Church of God, Elder Patrick served churches in Minnesota for more than 20 years. He is listed in the 1910 US Census as a teacher in a country school. He was married to Maude Matheny and they had three sons, Merle, Cecil and Carrol, and a daughter, Iona. Cecil "Pat" Patrick and Merle excelled in distinguished and dedicated Christian service throughout their lives just as their father did.

Elder Patrick edited *The Day Dawn and Harvest Messenger* during most of its publication. The editor's position was elected by the delegates at the Minnesota Conference. As long as a man was willing to serve and the people read the paper, it was likely he would be re-elected. Patrick shared the editorial responsibilities with E.D. Thoms, who began the paper in 1898, and with A.E. Hatch who edited it from 1910 to 1911.

Church of God Ministers (left to right)
Standing: HA Sheets, WS Hunt, JH Williams, FE Siple, MW Lyon, Paul Johnson. Seated: LE Conner, FL Austin, Mary Woodward, JA Patrick, AJ Eychaner.

Elder Patrick was a good Bible scholar and published well-written articles to explain difficult Bible topics. He published J.W. Williams' paper, which took a conservative position on the subject of the Holy Spirit. Williams stated that the Spirit had not been given to present-day generations. He felt it was poured out only on the first century church, which needed it to plant and grow Christianity in a hostile Roman world. This seems to have been the majority opinion in the Church of God at that time.

In 1940, Patrick authored a twelve-page tract on the subject, "What is Man?" The author and the National Bible Institute distributed the tract from the NBI's offices in Oregon, Illinois.

Patrick had been on the Committee of Ten responsible for designing and organizing a General Conference and bringing the plan to the delegates at the annual Waterloo, Iowa, conference in 1921. This committee worked throughout the year via correspondence and a few meetings to prepare and publicize the plan for a national headquarters organization. During this year, Elder Patrick and his family resided in Michigan. After the General Conference was organized and ratified by each of the state conferences, Elder Patrick joined several other men in having his name added to a list of recognized and certified ministers of the Church of God. He was on the first list in 1921.

James Patrick became the president of the Church of God General Conference Board of Directors in 1921; he was still the evangelist for the Michigan state conference at that time. Patrick also pastored the Church of God at Blanchard, Michigan, while he was Michigan evangelist. He also pastored at Brush Creek, Ohio, and Southlawn in Grand Rapids, Michigan. His travel ministry took him into Indiana and Ohio as well. Patrick served as interim pastor at Fonthill Church of God in Ontario and at Niagara from 1928 to 1929 following the resignation of G.E. Marsh.

James Patrick had been active in church and conference work long before the actual organized effort was successfully voted upon. He preached wherever he was called, and literature shows him at the Iowa Conference in 1916. He also assumed the editorship of *The Present Truth* from W.L. Crowe who gave up the work to publish a book. Patrick's service to the Lord was tireless. G.E. Marsh conducted his funeral service at Ashland, Ohio.

Elder Patrick's heritage lives on in the Church of God through the dedicated service of Gayle Patrick Reye Guthrie and her family, who serve at East Oregon Chapel Church of God in Oregon, Illinois.

   See Crowe, W.L.
       Hatch, A.E.
       Marsh, G.E.
       Martin, Joseph
       Thoms, E.D. (20th)

Bibliography: Ancestry.com: U.S. Census. Minnesota. Beltrami. Taylor. Dist. 30. 1910; U.S. Census. Minnesota. Stearns. Eden Lake. Dist. 185. 1920. Patrick, James A. "What is Man?" National Bible Institute, Oregon, Il., 1940; *The Restitution Herald*, Sept. 22, 1916; Jan. 20, 1925; Files from Committee of Ten, Archives, Atlanta Bible College, McDonough, Georgia; Williams, J.W. "The Comforter No. 6 The Gift of the Holy Ghost," *The Day Dawn and Harvest Messenger*, Jas. A. Patrick, ed., Fort Dodge, Iowa, Nov. 1919; Patrick at Blanchard, *The Restitution Herald*, Nov. 10, 1925; Obituary, *The Restitution Herald*, Sydney Magaw, ed., Oregon, Il., Aug. 17, 1948.

Peck, William J.
   b. 1858
   d. Unknown

William J. Peck preached throughout the southwest, especially in Texas. Prior to affiliating with the Church of God, he had been a Disciples of Christ minister. When he came into the Church of God around the turn of the 20th century, he engaged in several debates with Campbellites and Baptists. In 1902, he debated W.S. Miller at Oakdale on the nature of man. Peck was "pro" conditional immortality and Miller was "con."

Elder Peck also debated champion Baptist debater J.K.P. Williams in 1900. The debate's result was published in *The Firm Foundation*. Peck witnessed to the One Faith, which is the Faith of Abraham, wherever he had the chance and contributed to *The Restitution* as well.

A copy of *The Firm Foundation* is in the Archives at Atlanta Bible College.

Bibliography: Ancestry.com U.S. Census. Texas. Justice. Throckmorton. Dist. 133. 1920. *The Restitution*, April 15, 1913.

Pencake (Penkake), George
   b. 1822
   d. Unknown

George Pencake lived in Mt. Sterling, Illinois, west of the present-day Church of God at Ripley. Pencake and a man named Alonso "A.L." Sweet were wagon and carriage makers who also partnered for Bible study. They wrote two letters, six months apart, to Joseph Marsh in 1851. The first stated they wanted to take a six-month subscription to *The Advent Harbinger* so they could study it. They warned Marsh at that time that if the paper began to name-call and stifle free investigation, they would not take it any longer.

The second letter stated that they were satisfied that *The Harbinger* was like the *Advent Herald* used to be. *The Harbinger* supported free investigation, did not subscribe to creeds, was not sectarian and did not appear to be involved in name-calling, although its editor had experienced some persecution.

Overall, they liked what they read, and they did not part company with the paper. They even said they had no objection to the Age-to-Come doctrine, for they could see the teachings of it plainly in the Bible.

In this second letter of December 1851, they also requested that a Church of God minister come to Illinois. They requested that Jonathan Wilson, evangelist from New York, or Evangelist R.V. Lyon be sent to preach near Mt. Sterling.

At the time, Elder Chapman was preaching at Springfield, Illinois, just a few miles south of Mt. Sterling. He had reported in a letter to Marsh that he was covering territory between the Illinois River and the Mississippi River, which would have been the area north of Beardstown.

In April of 1852, Pencake and Sweet wrote another letter to Joseph Marsh. Here they stated that they had studied the *Age to Come* thoroughly, and completely believed it. They sent out a notice to all the Advent believers around Mt. Sterling and Ripley who had followed "Father Miller" saying, "If the unfulfilled prophecies are to have as literal fulfillment as those already fulfilled, this work is as true as the author represents it to be, however contrary it may be to our former teachings." They told Marsh they might be dis-fellowshipped for that statement, but if so, so be it.

In this same letter they mentioned that Yate Higgins would be coming to town for a conference meeting. His usual "mode of travel was walking with a staff."

See Higgins, Yate
Marsh, Joseph
Sweet, A. Lonzo

Bibliography: Ancestry.com. U.S. Census. Illinois. Brown. Mt. Sterling. 1850. Letters to Joseph Marsh by Pencake and Sweet, *Advent Harbinger and Bible Advocate*, Dec. 13, 1851; April 24, 1852.

Pinney, E.R.
b. 1801
d. 1855?

Elder E.R. Pinney served the Lord in Rochester, New York, and helped Joseph Marsh publish the first hymnbook in the Age-to-Come movement, *The Millennial Harp*. It was a collection of scriptural hymns, original and selected, for social and family worship. The prospectus said it was adapted for all Christians, and the cost was 69-½ cents each or 50 cents wholesale from the *Advent Harbinger* office.

It was a small 2" x 3" black leather bound book, containing mostly words of hymns and a few lines of written melody for some of the songs. The Archives of the Church of God General Conference at Atlanta Bible College has a copy of this rare hymnal.

E.R. Pinney may also have served as Joseph Marsh's bookkeeper, and maintained a correspondence with Marsh over the years. Pinney sent several communications to Joseph Marsh during 1851 stating he had health problems with skin cancer. Pinney had one cancer removed, but it had reappeared. He said he expected to die and looked forward to seeing Jesus soon and to reign with him in the Kingdom of God.

Bibliography: Ancestry.com U.S. Census. New York. Monroe. Rochester Ward 6. 1850. Letter to Joseph Marsh, *Advent Harbinger and Bible Advocate*, March 8, 1851.

Priestley, Joseph
b. March 13, 1733
d. February 6, 1804

Joseph Priestley was born near Leeds, Yorkshire, England. He was one of six children born to Jonas and Mary Swift Priestley. There were four boys and two girls; Joseph was the eldest. Mary died when Joseph was nine. He was adopted by a childless aunt, Mrs. John Keighley, his father's sister. He lived with this family until his aunt's death.

The Keighley home was a meeting place for vigorous discussion. In that day any religious topic outside the orthodox teaching was considered liberal. Joseph took part in the many theological discussions advanced by the dissenting pastors of the day. Joseph's education included classical languages, and he became proficient in Hebrew and Greek, preparing him to examine the scriptures in their original form. During a bout of illness in his teens he was forced to drop out of school; he used the recovery period to teach himself several more languages including Italian, French, German, Syriac, Chaldean and Arabic.

Joseph also had a talent for mathematics and science, but he decided to pursue education for the ministry. Since he was a dissenter, or "liberal," he could not be admitted to university as that would require him to confirm ten statements of orthodox faith and reconfirm them every six months. He enrolled instead in the liberal Daventry Academy in Northhampton. Such academies arose for dissenters to become the centers liberal education.

Priestley was already demonstrating unitarian ideas, and for that reason his first pastorate was not too successful. In addition to his unorthodox theology was the problem of his speech impediment, an inherited stammering which made preaching difficult. Priestley viewed it as his "thorn in the flesh." His second pastorate at Nantwich went better, and he used the income to purchase equipment he needed for his scientific inquiries.

During the happy time of this pastorate, Joseph became a tutor at a newly opened dissenting academy at Warrington. He was ordained in the dissenting ministry just before he wed Mary Wilkinson. While at Warrington, Priestley began to study and write about political theory, and he led his students in these studies. He became rather well known because of his contribution to utilitarianism. Priestley believed in using the reason of Common Sense in matters of philosophy.

In London, he associated with Benjamin Franklin and Richard Price who wrote the book *Civil Liberty*, which was attributed with influencing the writers of America's Declaration of Independence. As Priestley's friendship with Franklin continued his interest in the science of electricity expanded. Priestly wrote *The History and*

Present State of Electricity for which he was elected as a Fellow of the Royal Society. Soon thereafter, he accepted the pastorate of a church in Leeds, close to his birthplace.

Priestley experimented with "fixed air" or carbon dioxide. He impregnated water with the fixed air creating soda water and from his work emerged today's carbonated drinks including champagne. His experiments earned him the coveted Copley Medal from the Royal Society.

Priestley conducted more experiments in oxygen. He discovered that depleted or injured air was replaced by green plants and that "good air," which he called dephlogisticated air (oxygen), was five times heavier than common air. Ironically, when he told his friend, Lavoisier, about his experiments, Lavoisier recognized good air as the missing element in his own research and was able to overthrow Priestley's ideas about it. Not only did Priestley discover the importance of oxygen to human life, he identified eight other gases, including ammonia.

By this time several well known men underwrote the costs of Priestley's experiments, and he lived in a provided home in Birmingham with his family, now numbering three sons and a daughter. He enjoyed the fellowship of several men who, like him, were becoming experts in natural philosophy.

In Birmingham Priestley joined the Lunar Society, a small group of scientists and philosophers who discussed natural religion and philosophy. This group became known as "The Lunatics" because they met once a month near the time of the full moon. Benjamin Franklin was frequently a guest of the group. Priestley's thinking contributed to the discussion begun by David Hume the skeptic, but Priestley refuted Hume in his work, *Letters to a Philosophical Unbeliever*, *A History of the Corruptions of Christianity*, and in, *History of the Early Opinions Concerning Jesus Christ,* which was anti-trinitarian.

Priestley's books not only identified him as a dissenter, but as a non-trinitarian dissenter. They set off a fire-storm of controversy. Dissenters were not granted citizenship and unitarians were not even tolerated. Some English dissenters had been granted rights under the Act of Toleration of 1689, but unitarian dissenters fell outside the bounds of toleration. When the French Revolution came to a head, the dissenters sympathized with the downtrodden of France, another unpopular move. On the second anniversary of Bastille Day, July 14, 1791, a drunken party got out of hand and partiers burned Priestley's home and church. Warned in advance, Priestley and his family fled, only to look back and see his house and laboratory going up in flames.

Persecution continued in England, and Priestley was forced to resign his membership in the Royal Society. On April 7, 1794, the family sailed for America. They landed in New York, and traveled to Pennsylvania where they settled with a colony of English Dissenters, away from the heavily traveled highways of the cities, and free to be unitarian.

He was invited to teach at the University of Pennsylvania, but he declined. Thomas Jefferson consulted Priestley about the curriculum at the University of Virginia. Priestley continued to write, even when he was so ill he could not lift his arms. In fact, so much is known about him today because he wrote a prodigious number of books and letters dialoguing with their recipients on topics of theology and science.

The importance of Joseph Priestley to the Church of God is not that he was involved in founding it, for he was not. His importance is his understanding of Bible doctrine that so nearly encompassed everything the Church of God came to stand for. Examination of his Bible commentaries, *Notes on All the Books of the Scriptures,* indicates he believed essentially the same combination of doctrines as the Church of God later collected into a statement under the guidance of Joseph Marsh, Benjamin Wilson and others. According to Scholfield, Priestley relied upon 30 different biblical scholars in gathering his *Notes*. He referred to Johannes J. Griesbach's New Testament translation, the same source Benjamin Wilson used in translating *The Emphatic Diaglott*. Priestley also cited Isaac Newton regarding 1 Timothy 3:16, "And without controversy great is the mystery of godliness: God was manifest in the flesh, justified in the Spirit, seen of angels, preached unto the Gentiles, believed on in the world, received up into glory." (KJV) Newton wrote:

> The word Deity imports exercise of dominion over subordinate beings and the word God most frequently signifies Lord. Every lord is not God. The exercise of dominion in a spiritual being constitutes a God. If that dominion be real that being is the real God; if it be fictitious, a false God; if it be supreme, a supreme God. (Wallace)

Priestley's writings are important because he arrived at his belief about the unity of God separate from the Unitarians in America. He accepted the mortality of man long before George Storrs popularized it. Priestley believed Jesus was the Son of God born of a virgin despite stiff opposition by orthodoxy. He believed in the second coming of Christ to earth to establish the millennial Kingdom long before the American Adventist movement began. He set a precedent to be honest enough with the Bible to dare to be labeled a liberal, reviled and ridiculed by every orthodox theologian. Priestley believed in speaking out and in starting churches.

In Priestley's sixth letter to his neighbors in Northumberland, Pennsylvania, "To the Professors of Christianity," he spoke of his religion:

> Be not backward or afraid, my brethren to use your reason in matters of religion or where the scriptures are concerned.

Both of them (reason and scriptures) proceed from the God and Father of us all who is the giver of every good and perfect gift.

He also said:
Whereas unitarians deny, indeed, a trinity in God, but they believe in one God, the Father, and in the divine mission of Christ. They believe that he worked miracles by the power of God, that God raised him from the dead, and that he will come again to raise all the dead, and judge the world.

Further, in explaining his views on Christ, in whom he saw no divinity, he said:
Christ may be supposed to have pre-existed, or to have had a being before he was born of the virgin Mary, without supposing him to be the eternal God; but it appears to me that the apostles considered Christ as being, with respect to his nature, truly and properly a man, consisting of the same constituent parts, and of the same rank with ourselves, "in all things like unto his brethren" and the texts which are thought to speak of him as having existed before he came into this world, appear to me to bear other interpretations very well.

Regarding his understanding of the atonement he said:
There will be nothing left but the simple belief that the merciful Parent of the Universe, who never meant anything but the happiness of his creatures, sent his well-beloved Son, "the Man Christ Jesus" to reclaim men from their wickedness, and to teach them the way of righteousness; assuring them for their encouragement, of the free and unbought pardon of their sins, and promising a life of endless happiness to all that receive and obey the gospel, by repenting of their sins, and bringing forth fruits for repentance. This is the essence of what is called Socinianism.

Priestley said in *Notes* about Ephesians 1:14, "by redemption of the purchased possession" that redemption or reconciliation will be completed when Jesus returns. Notice that he was not a universalist, for he called for repentance and for Christians to bring forth fruit.

Priestley believed in a future state of life as revealed in Revelation. In volume 2 of *Theological and Miscellaneous Works* (346) he described the resurrection of the righteous as such:
We are informed [in I Thessalonians 4:13-17] that, at the second coming of Christ, the virtuous shall be raised first and immediately after that, *a change* which shall supersede death, will take place upon all who are alive; in consequence of which, their bodies, as well as those who are raised from the dead, will become incorruptible, and not subject to die any more.

While the happiness of the righteous is expressed as a state of rest in their future state, the sorrow of the wicked must be expressed as exclusion from happiness. Priestley said if the scriptures were taken literally, it must be determined that the future state of the wicked is eternal punishment. There is no reprieve, no reversion of it. The wicked will be cast into the fire. This he speculates may be the fire that cleanses the earth as Peter indicates the righteous will inhabit the earth after their resurrection. In *Notes on All the Books of the Scriptures* specific to Revelation 21, Priestley wrote, "By 'lake burning with fire and brimstone' we have seen that annihilation, or extinction of being, is intended."

Priestley also believed in the commencement of the Millennium after the return of Christ, and of the restoration of the Jews to their homeland.

At the time Priestley wrote the *Notes* in England, he had not yet worked out the millennial order of things. He understood some aspects of the millennial kingdom, but he did not yet understand who the subjects would be or the timeline. Regarding Revelation 22:5, he wrote: "A reign naturally implies subjects. But who they will be, or how those who are called kings and priests will be employed, we cannot tell."

He also seemed unsure of the duration of the millennium. LeRoy Froom wrote:
He now affirmed the literal, visible return of Christ and the literal resurrection of the righteous at the beginning of the millennial kingdom on earth, during which Christ will reign over restored Israel and the world for a long and unknown period, followed by the general resurrection and judgment, with probably the annihilation of the wicked, and finally the renovation of the earth.

Joseph Priestley's life ended prior to the end of the first decade in the 19th century, but he is included here because his influence lived throughout that century and into the next two centuries. The lives of earlier theological giants, men of thought and devotion who read and interpreted the Scriptures independent of orthodox thought prior to the 19th century, can only be mentioned here; men such as John Milton, Robert Burns, Sir Isaac Newton, Michael Servetus, Faustus Socinus and William of Occam felt the call of God, studied and developed dissenting beliefs. Some of them recorded their studies for our benefit. Some stepped forward to voice their beliefs and gave up their lives.

The Church of God has not stood alone in preaching its unique message in the 19th, 20th and 21st centuries, for faithful men have preached God's promises of old since the days of Abraham.

As Joseph Priestley neared death he called his family to him and uttered this now famous quote from his memoirs, "I am going to sleep as well as you for death is only a good long sleep in the grave and we shall meet again." He then finished some corrections on his writings, and half an hour later, he died.

See Marsh, Joseph
     Smith, Elias
     Storrs, George
     Wilson, Benjamin

Bibliography: Ancestry.com. U.S. Census. Pennsylvania. Northumberland. Point. Page 3. 1800; Froom, LeRoy. *The Prophetic Faith of our Fathers*. 4 Vols. Washington, D.C. Review and Herald Press. 1950-1954; Huffer, Dr. Alva. Telephone Conversation with Jan Stilson, November 29, 2009; *Dictionary of Scientific Biography*, C. C. Gillispie, Editor-in-chief, Vol XI, Scribner Publications, New York, New York, 1975; Schofield, Robert E. *The Enlightenment of*

Joseph Priestly: A Study of his Life and Work from 1733 to 1773, Penn State Press, 1975; Schofield, Robert E. *The Enlightenment of Joseph Priestley, his life and work from 1773 to 1804*. Penn State Press, 2004; "Joseph Priestley" as retrieved from www.woodrow.org/teachers/chemistry/institutes/1992/Priestley.html; Priestley, Joseph. *Autobiography of Joseph Priestley* with an introduction by J. Lindsay, Associated University Presses, Cranbury, New Jersey, 1970; Priestley, Joseph. *The Theological and Miscellaneous Works of Joseph Priestley*. Vol. 2 Geo. Smallfield, printer, Hackney. See especially "To the Professors of Christianity" in Vol. 2, p. 384; Priestley, Joseph. *Notes on the Scriptures,* Vol. 4 "Ephesians." p. 344, also "Revelation 21," p. 664; Wallace, A. "Anti-Trinitarian Biographies," Vol. III, 1850 regarding Newton's theological position, retrieved on December 11, 2009 from http://www.answering-christianity.com/timothy3_16.htm.

Prime, Dr. James Mark
b. July 15, 1872
d. June 22, 1948

James Prime was the son of John and Martha Prime. The family moved from Indiana to Edison, Nebraska, by wagon when James was a boy. The first year on the prairie, they lived in a dugout. A.J. Eychaner baptized him, which may be how he met his future wife.

Prime studied for the ministry prior to the founding of the Bible Training School or Oregon Bible College. He studied by learning Greek from an unknown scholar in Dixon, Illinois. Prime may have had trouble mastering the language, for he gave up his dream to preach and became a dentist instead.

The Holbrook Church of God at Dr. James Prime's house

He began his practice at Oxford, Nebraska, in 1900 and married Pauline Eychaner, daughter of A.J. Eychaner. Prime remained active in the Church of God all his life. He practiced dentistry in Omaha for 34 years.

The ministry's loss of this young man and others like him may have goaded the Church of God leadership to plan and begin a regular program of college-level classes for training ministers. Shortly after the turn of the 20th century, S.J. Lindsay began having summer Bible school classes for young adults at the Oregon Church of God for two to six weeks each year.

James M. Prime visited Oregon, Illinois, where his wife's relatives lived, and attended the Illinois Conference. He was struck by the beauty of the area, saying he had seen charming places, but "Oregon was one of the most charming places on Earth." Prime spoke of the monolithic statue designed by Lorado Taft:

> [Black Hawk] stands there undaunted, unafraid. As the sun hides his face behind the western hills, the placid waters at his feet, his great form seems to raise itself like a phantom, symbolic of the great spirit of Indian mythology.

Robert Hardesty, pastor at Omaha, and C.E. Lapp conducted Dr. Prime's funeral service

See Eychaner, A.J.
   Lindsay, S.J.
   Hardesty, Robert (20th)
   Lapp, C.E. (20th)
   Prime, John T.

Bibliography: Obituary, *The Restitution Herald*, Sydney Magaw, ed., Oregon, Il., June 22, 1948.

Prime, John Thomas
b. March 27, 1834
d. December 29, 1917

J.T. Prime was associated with the Little Wild Cat church in Indiana during the 1860s. He was baptized by A.N. Seymour, an Age-to-Come evangelist. During that time Prime wrote a letter to the editor of the *Millennial Harbinger and Bible Expositor*, indicating he was an avid reader of Church of God periodicals.

His name is in the minutes from a conference held near Windfall, Tipton County, Indiana, in 1863. He and T.E. Adams were elders of the Little Wild Cat church named for the river on whose bank it rested.

Prime's wife, Martha Ann, and his father-in-law, James Carr, were also members of the Little Wild Cat church. The Carrs were hospitable people and always kept an open table for those working for the Lord's cause. John Thomas and Martha Ann were the parents of James M. Prime. When James grew up, he married Pauline Eychaner, daughter of Andrew and Anna Eychaner, and he became a dentist.

Elder John T. Prime must have learned to preach at Little Wild Cat, for in 1874 he was called to assume the pastorate at Irving, Iowa, Church of God. At that time there were only three families in the faith at Irving. These were Levi Marsh, the founder of the work, John Fitz and Elek Marshman. Levi Marsh was the most prosperous of the three. He funded the church construction at Irving. When finished, the building seated 400 or 500 people. That showed a lot of faith.

J.T. Prime remained at Irving for two years, speaking twice every first day, unless called away to preach elsewhere. Elder Prime was proud that the church members supported the work so well. He said he "thinks he is safe in saying that a public collection has never been seen in that good old Restitution church to this day." Many able men spoke there and Levi Marsh generally gave them each $50 for their time and preaching. These men included R.J. Hill, J.M. Stephenson, W.F. Wilcox, George Moyer, William Braton, A.F. Dugger, A.J. Eychaner and H.V. Reed.

During J.T. Prime's ministry, the church at Irving hosted a debate between George Moyer, the associate editor of *The Gospel Banner*, and a Methodist minister. George Moyer made it so hot for the other debater that the Methodists sent for a second man who was appointed to debate with G.M. Myers. The church could hardly hold the people who came to hear. Because of unbelief it appeared that the people could not endure "sound doctrine."

The Primes returned to their farm in Story County, Iowa, where he continued to accept invitations to preach in other counties such as Furnas and Red Willow, Nebraska. Records from 1894 show he preached throughout Nebraska.

John T. Prime is interred at Nevada Cemetery, Story County, Iowa.

See Eychaner, A.J.
   Prime, Dr. James Mark
   Seymour, A.N.

Bibliography: Ancestry.com. Iowa Cemetery Records about John T. Prime; "History of the Iowa Church of God and Conference 1855-1987," by the History Committee of the Iowa Conference, Belle Plaine, Ia., 1987; Ferrell, Terry. "A Brief History of the Church of God in America," National Berean Youth Conference, Camp Reynoldswood, Illinois, Aug. 21-27, 1960; Kenyon, Richard L. *A short biography of Andrew James Eychaner.* 3d ed. Sept. 14, 2002; Prime, J.T. Letter to editor. *Millennial Harbinger and Bible Advocate*, June 24, 1863. *The Restitution,* Nov. 28, 1894; *The Restitution Herald,* Nov. 17, 1925; Wince, Roxanna "Story of a Happy Christian Life," *The Restitution 57:28* no date.

Prosser, W.A.
b. February 1863
d. Unknown

W.A. Prosser participated in the Church of God conference work in the state of Washington and may have been its evangelist at the turn of the century. He preached at the 1909 Washington Conference even though no records have yet been found to show he lived in that region. It is possible he preached as an invited guest. Prosser received a letter of commendation from the church conference for his service, clearly indicating he was a faithful and dedicated servant of the Lord.

Evangelist Prosser may have resided in Chicago. The 1900 US Census reveals that a William Prosser lived in Hyde Park, a wealthy neighborhood on the south Lakeshore, where many professors and professionals from the University of Chicago lived. Mr. Prosser was a buyer which certainly meant that he traveled extensively to purchase materials for whatever business he represented. It is possible that W.A. Prosser learned about the Gospel of the Kingdom from his association with H.V. Reed and other educated Church of God preachers. Reed was a well-known publisher in Chicago; he participated in the Columbian Exposition of 1893 which was largely responsible for the birth of the University of Chicago. Mrs. H.V. Reed wrote books to refute eastern religions, which was a topic she discussed in conference during the World's Fair. The doctrines of the Church of God were publicized in Chicago during this era.

See Reed, Elizabeth
   Reed, Hiram Vaughn

Bibliography: Ancestry.com. U.S. Census. Illinois. Cook. Chicago Ward 34. Dist. 1086. 1900; *The Restitution,* Aug. 9, 1909; Stilson, Jan. Interview with Mrs. Philip Miller, daughter of Illinois Governor Frank O. Lowden, and resident of Hyde Park, at her home, 1983. Stilson's book, *Art and Beauty in the Heartland,* AuthorHouse, 2006, has much on Hyde Park and the development of the University of Chicago.

Racy, Christopher
b. February 3, 1849
d. October 23, 1927

Christopher Racy was born in Germany and came to America at age three. As a young man he went to Minnesota; Elder E.E. Thoms baptized him into the Abrahamic Faith near Watkins in 1881. Racy was ordained to preach in 1885. He spent his retirement years in Idaho. Almus Adams, the evangelist across the Great Plains, visited him occasionally. Racy is interred at Spirit Lake.

See Thoms, E.E.
Bibliography: *History of the Church of God in Minnesota*, Sydney Magaw, ed., 1931.

Railsback, Caleb
b. July 7, 1805
d. July 9, 1895

Caleb Railsback was among the pioneers who settled near what later became Indianapolis. McDonald's *History* relates that Railsback was born in Roan County, North Carolina, on July 7, 1805. His parents, David (1768-1856) and Sarah (Stevens) Railsback (1773-1858), moved the family to the Whitewater River area in Wayne County, Indiana, in 1807. Caleb grew up there and married Nancy Barnhill in 1828. They moved to Marshall County, east of Plymouth in 1834 where he developed approximately 700 acres of timber into farm land around Argos, Indiana.

Nancy died April 26, 1875, at age 63. "She was a true wife, a kind mother, and a devoted member of the Church of God," said her obituary writer, initialed only as S.A.C. Caleb's second wife, Rebecca, may have been a native of Ohio. She died at their home in Argos in 1882 and was interred in Wooster, Ohio.

Caleb was a member of a Christian church until he learned about the Church of God in 1847. When he learned about life only in Christ and the glad tidings of the Kingdom, he embraced them as truths to live by and united with the Church of God at Pisgah, Indiana. He and 17 others organized a Church of God at Argos in 1869.

For many years Caleb served as Road Commissioner for Marshall County. He divided his land to his children as they reached adulthood. He died on July 9, 1895. Elder J.S. Hatch conducted his funeral service.

Caleb Railsback was the patriarch of an extended family which has reached down through generations of the Church of God to the present. Caleb's son, Richard C., married Christina Swafford and later, Lydia Evans. Caleb and Christina's son Ezra Caleb Railsback married Emma Weeks. Ezra and Emma moved from South Bend, Indiana, to Los Angeles, California, in 1919 and began the Church of God work in California. Also from this faithful family came Dean Moore, long-time pastor and missionary to Mexico.

Arlen Rankin contributed to this entry.

See Moore, Dean (20th)
Railsback, Emma (20th)

Bibliography: McDonald, Daniel. *The History of Marshall County, Indiana 1836 to 1880*. Chicago: Kingman Bros. 1881. p. 49, p. 584. McDonald and his father Thomas McDonald were members of the Church of God. "Nancy Railsback Obituary," from *The Restitution*, 1875, and "Rebecca Railsback Obituary," from *The Restitution*, 1882, as furnished by Dean Moore Family Papers January 9, 2008; Rankin, Arlen. "Influence of Old Union in Indiana," Paper for History Conference, Nov. 2006; Atlanta; Moore, Dean, "Family Tree of David Railsback" and other family papers furnished to Jan Stilson January 9, 2008.

Railsback's descendents ready to depart Indiana in 1919.

Railsback, William
b. December 3, 1830
d. November 24, 1915

Will Railsback was born in Marion County, Indiana, the son of Caleb and Nancy Barnhill Railsback. The family moved to Marshall County in 1846. He married 21-year-old Melissa Brown who was born in Jefferson County, New York, in February 1853. They lived in a hewed cabin in Marshall County for three years then moved to Argos, Indiana, where they began a sawmill. Will continued in the mill business until 1885. In April 1885 he and several other men, including Thomas O. Taber of the Church of God, organized the Exchange Bank of Argos of which Will Railsback was president until 1907.

Will sat on the committee that drafted the Declaration of Principles and Constitution for the 1886 Church of God Indiana Conference. He and his brother Robert contributed as editorial board members of *The Restitution* in Plymouth.

William died at Argos, a faithful and dedicated member of the Church of God. Elder J.F. Wagoner officiated his funeral at the Argos Church of God. Will rests in the Maple Grove Cemetery near Argos.

Bibliography: Moore, Dean, "Family Tree of William Railsback," and other family papers furnished to Jan Stilson January 9, 2008; "Obituary," *The Restitution Herald*. Dec. 8, 1915; Randall, Clyde, *Historical Waymarks of the Church of God*, Church of God General Conference, Oregon Il., as cited by Arlen Rankin in "The Influence of Old Union in Indiana," a paper presented at the Second Adventist History Conference, Atlanta Bible College, Nov. 3-4, 2006.

Railton, James Albert
b. January 29, 1860
d. February 15, 1925

James Albert Railton married Mary Bouk of Fonthill, Ontario. James and Mary were parents of John Albert Railton (b. January 23, 1896). James and Mary traveled to Oregon in 1924 to visit young John who was a student at the newly opened Bible Training School. They traveled by train via Jackson, Michigan, and stopped in Grand Rapids to attend the Michigan quarterly conference. John worked for the General Conference in the greenhouse business and operated a brick-making machine that turned out cement blocks. He operated that business from his home at 503 South 5th Street in Oregon. John married Ruby Austin, F.L. Austin's daughter.

Through the pages of *The Restitution Herald*, James Railton appealed to the people to help raise funds for the two-year-old General Conference organization. To pay employees' salaries, cover the rising cost of printing paper, and expand ministries through the Golden Rule Home and the Greenhouse at Oregon, the conference needed $15,000. Shortly after authoring this appeal, James Railton's health took a turn for the worse, and he died following an operation in Welland, Ontario.

James' family continues to serve the Lord through the ministry of Mary Milne, sister of Austin Railton, now deceased, and through Austin's children, Joyce (Bolhous) and John Railton, and their families. From the Bouk descendants, the children and grandchildren of Howard Shute, now deceased, continue to serve.

See Austin, Frederick L. (20th)
Bibliography: Ancestry.com. Ontario. Canada. Deaths 1869-1936, and Deaths Overseas, 1939-1947, Welland. 1925, record for James A. Railton. *The Restitution Herald,* Dec. 16, 1924; March 1925; Winner, Jennifer, great, great, great granddaughter of Peter Bouk, presented "History of Peter Bouk" at 2010 History Conference, North Hills Church of God, Springfield, Ohio, including data about James Albert Railton and Mary Bouk Railton.

Railton, Mary C. Bouk
b. December 10, 1857
d. September 21, 1913

Mary was the daughter of Peter Bouk, leader of the early work in Fonthill, Ontario, near Niagara Falls. R.V. Lyon, the circuit preacher to Canada West during the early 1800s, baptized her.

Mary married James Albert Railton. They had two children, John and Mattie. She predeceased them all in 1913 at age 56. F.L. Austin wrote her obituary; he was her pastor at the time.

See Bouk, Peter
    Lyon, R.V.
    Railton, James Albert
Bibliography: *The Restitution*, Oct. 21, 1913.

Ramsay (Ramsey), Charles C.
b. December 13, 1830
d. September 15, 1908

According to his obituary, Charles C. Ramsay was born in Lowell, Massachusetts, to Cyrus and Ellen Ramsay. Eventually the family relocated to Pennsylvania where Cyrus and Charles worked for the railroad, possibly the Coudersport and Port Allegheny Railroad which connected the two communities. Cyrus was an engineer; Charles was a clerk. As early Church of God evangelists traveled by train, it is entirely possible that young Ramsay first heard the Gospel of the Kingdom while on duty. By 1850 Charles Ramsay was working as a hostler, defined as a workman who runs train engines back and forth within the train yard but never on the open track. He was still single at this time.

Charles began traveling between Pennsylvania and Iowa and eventually married his first wife in Iowa where they began a family, probably at Floyd. After Charles' first wife died, leaving him with two children, he married a widow, Martha "Mattie" Branson, in March 1885; she was nine years younger than her new husband. This was also Martha's second marriage, and she brought one son, Edwin, into the family. The Philadelphia Bransons owned a large coal business. Mattie may have brought a little money into the union with Charles. For a short time, they lived in Stroudsburg in the heart of the Pocono Mountains, west of New York City and north of Philadelphia.

Charles and Mattie also traveled extensively to Iowa and to Virginia where he enjoyed preaching. They had many friends in Virginia, and in fact, it was Emily R. Boyer, a Virginia friend, who provided obituaries for both Mr. and Mrs. Ramsay.

Charles was a summertime evangelist in Iowa during the 1870s and 1880s. He lived at Floyd, Iowa—the same town where Iowa's evangelist R.J. Hill resided during the early 1880s. From this community Charles was called to Gifford, Iowa, to baptize young Almus Adams. When Almus was first chosen to be the state evangelist at the 1887 Iowa Conference, Charles was in attendance as a guest speaker. His association with Adams continued through the years. This relationship may account for Adams being an invited delegate at the organizational meeting of the 1888 General Conference in Philadelphia.

In the winter of 1882-1883, Elder Ramsay became ill and unable to preach the whole season. After he recovered, he announced his intention to live in Chicago. A notice in *The Restitution* stated his interest in doing mission work there. He invited any who could or would to help him establish a church, which he called "The Blessed Hope Mission." He appealed for prayers and financial support, telling readers to reply to 259 Randolph Street in Chicago.

Charles appeared to have been actively involved in evangelism ministry on the frontier. Evidence shows him visiting new territories in the west and preaching. His name appears in the Kansas work as early as 1885, and he may have resided there briefly. Both Charles and John Foore were present at one Kansas Conference where both men assisted with preaching.

Elder Ramsay was the pastor of the Philadelphia church at the time the General Conference was reorganized there on November 16, 1888. Charles took a leading role in hosting and helping organize the conference. The Philadelphia City Directory of 1890 listed Ramsay's occupation as Reverend, confirming he was pastor of the Church of God. The church, known as the Blessed Hope Mission, was on the corner of 12th and Dickinson. In 1900 C.C. Ramsay, Mattie and Edwin resided at 1726 French Street. For a larger picture on the National Conference's formation see the George F. Work entry.

In the October 10, 1888, issue of *The Restitution* two calls to conference were issued. In the first, Ramsay and Levi Patterson, pastor at Perryville, Maryland, issued a call to conference for delegates of all the Churches of God on the eastern seaboard. The meeting's purpose was to organize a regional conference to assist churches and replace individual state conferences. Instead, they organized a national conference. The second call was issued to delegates and friends in 1889 to attend a National Conference in Chicago, the second annual meeting of the new general conference.

In 1894, Ramsay visited Dodge City (later known as Fort Dodge), Iowa. Despite his age, he was evidently healthy enough to travel.

How long he stayed to work in Iowa is not known, but he was present at the Iowa Conference in 1898. Discussion at that conference focused on the best means to distribute leaflets and tracts. This led to the idea of forming a new organization chiefly for the youth and young adults that would serve as a mission and education arm of the conference. C.C. Ramsay coined its name: "Berean Society."

Several women in Illinois, Evelyn Harsh and Leila Whitehead from Chicago and Anna Drew from Dixon, developed the Berean Society into a growing and vital organization in every state where Church of God evangelists preached. Its aim was Christian education and evangelism. From their efforts came a national work, formally organized as the National Berean Society by 1913, eight years ahead of the organization of the national general conference. The Berean Society became an organization of great influence as it helped to begin and stabilize new Bible study groups across the Great Plains over the next 40 years or so.

Elder Ramsay became ill in 1907, but he was nursed to health sufficiently to enable him and Mattie to travel to Iowa to visit his children. The next summer, while Martha visited friends in Virginia, Charles visited his children at Mason City one more time before his death in September. He and Mattie had first traveled to Virginia in 1889, and they loved visiting the brethren there.

Charles was interred at the Oakwood Cemetery in Floyd Township beside his first wife Emily T. Ramsay. His dear Mattie outlived her husband by 15 years. Because of this connection to the Church of God through

Emily Boyer in Virginia, there is possibly some family connection between C.C. Ramsay and the Fulton Ramsey family in Fort Valley. Fulton Ramsey was born and raised in Pennsylvania. Fulton and Ellen (Van Fleet) and sons Dale, Gary, Chris and Jay have been faithful servants in the Fort Valley Church of God. Dale served as Music Director at Oregon Bible College and Atlanta Bible College for many years. Chris served on the Board of Directors 1988-1992. Jay served on the Youth Caravan to Fonthill in 1970.

See Adams, Almus
  Austin, Evelyn Harsh (20th)
  Drew, Anna
  Foore, John
  Work, George F.

Bibliography: Ancestry.com: U.S. Census. Pennsylvania. Allegheny. Pittsburgh Ward 4, 1850; U.S. Census. Pennsylvania. Allegheny. Allegheny. Dist. 7. 1880; Bender, Ed. "History of the Western Nebraska Conference," Paper for History Conf. North Hills Church of God. Springfield, Ohio. November 2007; Boyer, Emily R. Charles Ramsay's Obituary, *The Restitution,* Sept. 22, 1908; Boyer, Emily R. Martha Ramsay's Obituary *The Restitution Herald,* July 14, 1925; Burnett, Francis et al history committee, *History of the Iowa Church of God and Conference 1855-1987,* printed at Belle Plaine Union, 1987; "Report of Kansas Conference," *The Restitution,* Nov. 4, 1885; Ramsay, C.C. "Notice of Work Starting in Chicago," *The Restitution,* June 27, 1883 and Aug. 1, 1883; *The Restitution,* April 8, 1894; "Information about the National Conference," *The Restitution,* Oct. 6, 1888; Nov. 2, 1915; Oct. 12, 1920; *The Restitution Herald,* July 14, 1925; Ramsay, C.C. "Call to Conference," *The Restitution,* S.A. Chaplin, ed., Plymouth, In., Oct. 9, 1889; Oakwood Cemetery http://iagenweb.org/floyd/Cemetery/oakwood.htm.

Randall, Amos J.
b. January 22, 1835
d. January 24, 1911

Randall, "Auntie" Susan
b. February 6, 1841
d. December 5, 1927

A.J. Randall was born in New York. When he was a small boy, his family moved to Ohio. He accepted the Lord and joined the Methodist church. On December 23, 1859, A.J. married Susan Elizabeth Dean of Ottawa County. Amos and Susan had three sons, George, Clyde and Harlow. Several years later, they moved to Minnesota and united with the Church of God at Silver Lake. Amos was ordained at the Rice Lake church. Amos and Susan lived near Eden Valley for more than 30 years. Susan was credited in *The Restitution* of 1925 with starting the Church of God work in Minnesota.

In 1925, at age 84, Susan was well respected by her family and friends. Her vision was failing, and she

Left to right: George Randall; his mother, Susan Randall; her grandson, Walter; and his daughter, Ruby (Bennett).

suffered from rheumatism, but she still loved the Lord. A year later severe pain confined her to a wheelchair. Her church family had a big birthday celebration for her. Her grandsons, Clyde, Ernest and Walter Randall, were all active in the work of the Mora Church of God. Clyde E. Randall was the pastor. Susan was the last charter member of the Church of God in Minnesota. She died at Mora. Afterward, the Randall men escorted her remains on the train to Eden Valley, where she rests beside Amos.

See Randall, Clyde (20th)

Bibliography: Ancestry.com. U.S. Census. Minnesota. Stearns. Eden Lake. Dist. 146. 1900; Letter by Muriel Randall Haas to Julie Craig, Jan. 23, 1995; *The Restitution Herald,* Feb. 3, 1925; Sept. 14, 1926; *History of the Church of God in Minnesota,* Sydney Magaw, ed., 1931.

Randall, George
b. January 3, 1861
d. February 27, 1944

George Randall was the son of Amos and Susan Randall and father of Clyde Randall. Amos was one of the first men in Minnesota to preach the Adventist truth. The Randall family may be credited with helping to begin the Church of God in Minnesota.

Left to right: Walter Randall, Ruby Bennett holding Sharon Jean Bennett, and grandfather, George Randall.

George was a farmer in Stearns County, Eden Lake Township. His wife Lilly died with three children still at home: Grace (19) and two sons, Ernest (17) and Clyde (12). Two other sons, Walter and Arthur, had already left home. Clyde remained at home with his father until around age 22. By this time, his father had remarried to a woman with a child, so Clyde departed for the Bible

Training School in Oregon, Illinois. Clyde went on to a leadership role within the National Berean Society organized in Chicago (1913), and later within the Church of God national conference. George and his new wife had a son, Lyndon Cole Randall.

A solid family man, George was also a faithful and well-versed teacher of the Word. Every year on his birthday, the family gathered for oyster stew and had a big celebration.

See Randall, Amos and "Auntie" Susan
Randall, Clyde (20th)

Bibliography: Ancestry.com. U.S. Census. Minnesota. Stearns. Eden Lake. Dist. 146. 1900 and 1910; Bennett, Ruby. Randall descendant supplied information for the Randall entries, Jan. 25, 2011; Haas, Muriel Randall, Letter to Julie Craig Isham, Jan. 23, 1995; *The Restitution Herald*, Feb. 3, 1925.

Raymond, Jedediah
b. October 3, 1807
d. December 2, 1900

Jedediah Raymond was born in Newberg, New York. He became a skillful sea captain crossing the Atlantic 12 times and spending a number of years on the Great Lakes.

He preached for the Church of God in Minnesota shortly after it began in 1874. He loved to preach about prophecy. The Minnesota Conference considered him one of its most loyal ministers; working with him was a privilege. He was an excellent Bible student and very adept with the Scriptures. He died at Eden Valley and rests in Eden Lake Cemetery.

Bibliography: *History of the Church of God in Minnesota*, Sydney Magaw, ed., 1931.

Reed, Hiram Vaughn
b. November 4, 1836
d. July 11, 1920

A. The Reed Debates
B. Aspects of Ministry
C. The Chicago Fire Changes Things
D. The Pains of Old Age

Hiram Vaughn Reed was born in Utica, New York. In his childhood, the family moved to Waupausee, Walworth County, Wisconsin. Hiram had few opportunities for education while growing up. When he could, he walked 3-1/2 miles across fields to a rough country school.

He attended church and listened to points of doctrine, but found the thought of eternal torment revolting, he became a skeptic for a while. His mother continued to pray for him. At age 15, Hiram met with Walter Lee, a man with considerable Bible knowledge. Lee believed in conditional immortality, and it made sense to Hiram Reed. He became an earnest and enthusiastic student of the Bible from that point on, carrying his copy to the fields with him to study it on his rest breaks.

When he was only 16, Hiram invited friends to his father's house to hear his first sermon on matters related to the Kingdom of God and the name of Jesus Christ. Almost immediately, he began holding meetings around Wisconsin, baptizing as he went. Some of the churches he organized were at LeRoy, Waupauca, Stephen's Point, Farmington, Palfreyville and Oshkosh.

He also rode a preaching circuit during the 1850s, extending south into Illinois and including the towns or villages of Forreston, Buffalo Grove, Dixon, Amboy, Harvard, Elizabeth and Adeline. He was so well known in these communities that when people accepted the Gospel message, they were known as "Reedites."

Hiram was of medium height, well proportioned, with fine appearance. He had a commanding presence in the pulpit, was eloquent and flowery in speech with the power to fix his thoughts in the memories of his hearers.

At age 26, Hiram attended a conference at Twin Groves, Wisconsin, west of Beloit. He arrived late and gave the closing address. He remained in Twin Groves for three months to sow seeds of the Gospel. His words impressed people and the following illustrates that point: A noted physician approached H.V. Reed about 45 years later, in 1907 at Buchanan, Michigan, and said he had been in the Twin Groves conference meeting when the doctor was a boy, and heard the youthful Reed preach there. The doctor testified that he "had never forgotten the influence which then obtained over his mind and heart."

A. The Reed Debates

Hiram Reed's first debate was in 1857 in Omro (near Oshkosh, Wisconsin) against Congregational clergyman Edward Reynolds on the subject of conditional immortality. The debate was supposed to last ten days. But clergyman Reynolds was so baffled by the effort to sustain his arguments that he abandoned the discussion on the second day. In fact, *The Runnels and Reynolds Genealogy* described him as "former Congregational minister," so perhaps after that debate he became an Age-to-Come minister.

In another debate with a Baptist minister named Smith, Hiram Reed argued for four nights on the issue, "The Scriptures Do Not Teach the Natural Immortality of Man." On the last night a vote was taken and nine-tenths of the audience voted that Reed had fairly sustained his position. More than 800 people attended that debate.

Hiram Reed held a third debate in Forreston, Illinois, with Methodist ministers Ely and Williams on the same topic. This debate lasted three days and much came from it. The Church of God at Adeline grew out of this rich climate of dialogue on conditionalism. Reed excelled in debating conditionalism and, in 1858, debated once more on the topic of conditional immortality in LeRoy, Wisconsin, against Universalist J.C. Crawford.

Reed also engaged in a debate that brought national interest. The opposition was represented by Vernon Hull, who had been chosen by Harvard ministers. Hull determined to champion the cause of the doctrine of eternal suffering for the wicked. The discussion continued for eight evenings, with four speeches (pro and con) each day, 32 sessions in all. The report of the exchanges was published in a book, and the entire edition was soon exhausted. The friends of truth were satisfied, and an account of this debate is given in Alger's *History of the Doctrine of Future Life* published in Boston by the Unitarian Association.

H.V. Reed engaged in a debate at Buchanan, Michigan, with P.S. Russell concerning whether the Kingdom of God spoken of in Daniel 7 was set up in the days of Caesar. Russell said, "Yes." Reed said, "No." The other question asserted that in death there is a complete cessation of existence until resurrection. Reed said, "Yes." Russell said, "No." The debate lasted three days. Elder Russell was considered the "Champion of the Reformation in the Western States." It was a good debate, attended by many people of Buchanan, most of whom were well acquainted with the arguments on both sides.

The debate with P.S. Russell was published in *The Prophetic Expositor* and copied by the *Gospel Banner*. During this debate, Hiram met Sophia Elizabeth Armstrong, a Buchanan member, and she became his bride in 1860. He brought her back to Chemung, Illinois (near Harvard), where he conducted a Bible study with 12 members.

While Reed resided in Harvard, Illinois, he debated Dr. Nathaniel Field in Cicero, Indiana. This discussion was published in the pages of *The Prophetic Watchman*. The subject was "Restoration of Israel." Reed contended for the natural return of the Jews to present-day Jerusalem, and Field argued against.

When H.V. Reed returned to Harvard, he was asked to be the church pastor. Dr. John Howell, the old pastor, returned east to continue his ministry. He was later taken ill with tuberculosis, ending his work. H.V. Reed remained as Harvard's pastor for 12 years, using it as a center to launch other works. During this time, he dedicated a church building at Eureka, Wisconsin, and raised $900 to pay off its mortgage. He was active in Aurora, Geneva, Chemung and Dunham. He also traveled throughout New York. In Iowa he helped establish the Church of God at Belle Plaine.

The 1860 US Census listed H.V. Reed's occupation as "2d Advent Clg. (Clergy)." In addition to ministry, he operated a secular business in Chicago and published a newspaper, tracts and books at Harvard.

B. Aspects of Ministry

In 1860 Hiram Reed traveled north from Harvard and went throughout Wisconsin. Here he met J.M. Stephenson for the first time. He pronounced Stephenson sound in doctrine as believing in the "one faith once for all delivered to the saints." After visiting a couple of communities he reached Eureka where Stephenson resided with his family.

The Stephensons' son had recently died, and they were grief-stricken at the time of Reed's visit. He preached there to a small crowd, where five people were baptized. This greatly encouraged J.M. Stephenson in his sorrow. Reed continued his journey dipping south into Illinois and returning to Harvard by way of Eureka, where once again he visited the Stephenson family.

Elder Reed also took his ministry to Rockford, Illinois. A member by the name of Woods lived at Burritt north of Rockford, and a brother Keeling lived at Manchester northeast of Rockford. There are no churches in those locations today.

In 1860 Benjamin Wilson visited Harvard and described H.V. Reed as a young man who has earnestly contended for the "faith once for all delivered to the saints." He said Reed had considerable ability with a plain and forceful manner in presenting the truths of the Gospel. This manner aroused much opposition among the sects, and he was invited to debate frequently.

Wilson's visit coincided with Reed's preaching tour. Also at that time Reed was scheduled to debate a member

L: O.J. Allard, F.E. Siple, A.J. Eychaner, H.V. Reed, C.C. Maple, F.L. Austin, G.E. Marsh

of the Seventh-day Baptists. The debate was to go five evenings on the topic of the final punishment of the wicked, but the fifth evening's discourse was canceled because it was the beginning of Sabbath and the other gentleman was not willing to debate.

H.V. Reed also traveled to Waterloo, Iowa, to preach to the people of the Church of God there in 1863. He preached "the good news of the Kingdom." This ministry trip is recorded in the *Millennial Harbinger*.

The Kingdom was one of his favorite subjects. He wrote a small book about it, published through the *Millennial Harbinger* office in 1861. In *The Kingdom of God or Reign of Christ on Earth,* he clearly laid out the theology of Christ's message of the Kingdom. The book is a joy to read; a copy is available at the Archives of Atlanta Bible College.

While living at Harvard, Hiram Reed became editorially connected with the *Millennial Harbinger and Bible Expositor,* edited by Marsh from 1860 to 1862 and from 1862 to 1863 by Thomas Newman at Seneca Falls, New York. Reed contributed articles and wrote editorials for this publication. He prepared books and pamphlets. In fact, Newman was absent most of 1863 leaving the publishing details to Reed and three others.

The *Millennial Harbinger and Bible Expositor* was published concurrently with the *Gospel Banner* (1853-1869) in Geneva, Illinois, edited by Benjamin Wilson, and *The Prophetic Watchman & Herald of the Kingdom* (1860-1867) published by H.V. Reed and J.M. Stephenson in Harvard. According to David Graham, when Marsh died in 1863, Newman moved The *Millennial Harbinger* subscription list and press from New York to Harvard, Illinois, where it merged with *The Prophetic Watchman*. After a couple of years, the press was moved to Chicago. When Thomas Wilson began publishing the *Herald of the Coming Kingdom* (1867-1870), *The Prophetic Watchman* ceased and its subscription list and Marsh's press went to the *Herald*. In 1870, Thomas Wilson changed the name of *The Herald* to *The Restitution*. Marsh's press, used for *The Watchman/Herald/Restitution* in succession, was destroyed in the Chicago Fire of 1871.

Hiram Reed was a busy man. The 1870 US Census listed his occupation as Minister, Editor and Publisher. William H. Hornaday of Indiana also resided in Harvard, Illinois, and assisted Reed with printing and publishing duties. Hiram's work often took him to Chicago so a reliable man was needed. In 1872, H.V. Reed moved his family to Norwood Park on Chicago's west side. He was a trustee of an insurance company, the Life Association of America, and a member of the Board of the Donnelly Corporation. The *Lakeside Monthly* and the *Western Monthly* were managed by him at the downtown Tribune building. Reed probably gained enough wealth from his secular employment to be comfortable.

C. The Chicago Fire Changes Things

After the Chicago Fire in 1871, Thomas Wilson continued to publish *The Restitution* from Chicago until November 1874, possibly through the auspices of the Wilson, Pierce Publishing house or at the office of *The Evening Post* where Wilson worked. In December 1874, the paper relocated to Plymouth, Indiana. Hiram edited the December issue with S.A. Chaplin as associate editor. J.M. Stephenson, Chaplin and Thomas Wilson were contributing editors from the Plymouth location. In that issue, Reed acknowledged that as the new editor he had goals for the paper. He said he had been associated with the paper's publishing operation for the past 12 years, which takes his association back to 1862.

Before relocating in 1874, Reed had published the Church of God's *The Millenarian* in Room #27 at the Lakeside Press. In the December 1874 issue of *The Restitution*, Reed announced that *The Millenarian* would be increased to 24 pages and produced by Wilson, Pierce Publishing in Chicago. When Reed moved to Plymouth he turned *The Millenarian* over to Thomas Wilson with Reed's assistance, but it did not continue long in that format. Wilson changed the name to *Our Rest*.

Since Reed mentioned being associated with the paper for 12 years, explanation should be made. The mergers noted above make it difficult to track the volume numbers, but the intent of each succeeding editor was to continue numbering each new title in the same manner as Joseph Marsh had. This is easy enough to recall by remembering that in 1874 (the earliest known copy), *The Restitution* began at Volume 22; it ended with Volume 78 in 1925. Errors in numbering of volumes abound among printers. For example, *The Restitution's* Volume 29 seems to be two years long.

Reed continued to manage the Chicago publications at the new Lakeside Press building at 187 Clark Street until 1874. He also began publishing *The Chicago Record*. Reed also produced numerous tracts including "Age to Come, not a Heresy," "The Coming Nation," "The Word of God vs. the Word of Man," "Baptism–Not in Three Names," "Sprinkling–Not Baptism" and others. He also composed a song, "The Millennial Day."

After the Plymouth relocation, Reed assisted the Argos congregation, where he helped build a comfortable church building and a loyal congregation. He also helped begin a work at Goodland where 50 people were baptized. He made many friends in Indiana and records show he baptized several believers, including Melissa Vance of Argos in 1877.

Elder Levi Marsh of Irving, Iowa, called on H.V. Reed to assist in discussions with opponents of the One Faith in

Irving. Reed joined Marsh in working with people in the community, and assisted in the construction of another church building. He dedicated that building and several others in various communities.

Within three years of *The Restitution's* relocation to Plymouth, H.V. Reed was able to move his family back to Chicago because the work at *The Restitution* was stable. Chaplin became editor-in-chief November 10, 1877, and continued there until September 1889, just two years before he died.

After the Reeds returned to Chicago, Hiram assisted Thomas Wilson in publishing Church of God journals. One title that did not endure was *Our Rest and Signs of the Times*, formerly *The Millenarian*. Reed formed the Christian Publishing Association and operated the company from his home. It was a tract and book publishing house, which proved to be very helpful to the Church of God in the next two decades.

Reed gained notice across denominational lines. George Peters writing *The Theocratic Kingdom* in the early 1880s cited Reed's position on Colossians 1:13, "Who hath delivered us from the power of darkness and hath translated us into the Kingdom of His dear Son," to refute the idea that the Church equaled the Kingdom. Peters cited Reed as translating that verse as, "Who has delivered us from the power of darkness and changed us for," while R.V. Lyon translated it as, "and hath transferred us over unto the Kingdom." Peters may have heard Reed utter that interpretation when Reed preached at the Church of God/One Faith in Springfield, Ohio, Peters' hometown. Also, Peters' wife, Carrie Howell, was raised in the One Faith, so Peters certainly was acquainted with Church of God teachings. From the arguments in his book, it is clear he believed them.

In 1885, Joel A. Simonds questioned Reed on his understanding of Jesus as the only begotten Son of God through the pages of *The Restitution*. Josephism positioned Christ as son of Joseph and was prominently discussed throughout the Church of God that year and into the 20th century.

Reed responded by defending the Bible account of the Virgin birth. From this it's clear Reed never entertained notions of Josephism. In fact, he wrote: "Josephism advocates natural generation which in order to accept that view, the first chapter of Matthew and the third chapter of Luke have to be rejected as spurious."

Reed believed the first resurrection was for righteous Christians only. The creedal statement as given in the June 1874 issue is repeated in nearly every issue of *The Millenarian*:

> *The Millenarian* advocates the personal return of Christ to our earth, his literal reign over Israel and the nations, the resurrection of the holy dead at the commencement of the Millennium, and their reign with Christ during the Millennium and beyond. It also advocates the necessity of a life of trust and obedience in order to a participation in that kingdom which shall stand forever. The literal fulfillment of Prophecy, and the signs which foreshadow the nearness and certainly of His coming who is the Desire of Nations are also specially examined.

While this might lead readers to believe Reed advocated limited resurrection as did the Christadelphians of that day, it should be noted he believed and preached that all men would be raised, the holy ones at the beginning of the Age to come and the wicked at its end.

HV Reed (seated, far right) with Dutton, Michigan, Group.

D. The Pains of Old Age

The Reeds retired to Magnolia Springs, Alabama, where the Boyle family probably first heard the Word preached by that eloquent old gentleman. When Gladys Boyle moved to South Bend, Indiana, she attended the Bible Study group at the YMCA taught by the Railsbacks, where she met and married Everett Stilson. This study group became the Hope Chapel. H.V. Reed was active in preaching and assisting many churches and conferences. In 1910 he traveled from Alabama to Virginia to preach, and while there obliged the bereaved to preach a funeral.

In 1913, the Reeds returned from Alabama to visit the Indiana and Michigan conferences. They were aging and soon such travel would end. In fact, Mrs. Reed grew ill and died in June 1915. The aging orator keenly felt her loss. He wrote to F.L. Austin on June 21, 1915:

> It is with a sad heart that I send the word of sorrow which pervades my whole being. My wife has passed into the shadow and is at rest in a beautiful little spot in Rose Hill Cemetery. All is Cloud! I am in my little home desolate and without any one to cheer my returning footsteps. May God keep her in the silence of Rest until the Voice of our Absent Lord shall ring in Resurrectional power and give Life eternal in the Kingdom of Immortality.

Accompanying the letter was a poem, "The Millennial Day," penned by Elder Reed in which his sorrow and his hope are deeply felt.

The following year, the elderly Reed returned alone to preach at Indiana conference. Reports in *The Restitution* stated that his preaching was eloquent and that his presence and preaching were a rare treat to the younger generation of conference attendees.

Hiram married Sarah Bethel, a physician engaged in research. Sarah was a widow and half Hiram's age. She became a prominent worker in the Child Conservation League. The couple rented a bungalow in Winter Park, Florida. Eleven months before his death Hiram fell and broke a leg. His sons, Mr. Earl Reed and Dr. Charles Reed, informed the church in Chicago of their father's accident and his admission to Wesley hospital in Florida. Hiram was hospitalized for five weeks with the fracture. Even with good medical attention, he never fully recovered from the accident. He died at age 84 from a heart ailment.

Aware that the end was near and that he would not see his Church of God friends again while he lived, Hiram requested that 1 Thessalonians 4 be read at his funeral to reflect the hope of resurrection in which he believed. Rev. Ezra T. Riggs, a retired, prominent pastor of the Congregational Church, conducted the service. Hiram was interred temporarily at the Palm Cemetery, Winter Park, Florida, but it is believed he still rests there. The Church of God mourned the loss of the Lord's old warrior who had fought the good fight and finished the course.

See Chaplin, S.A.
Newman, Thomas
Reed, Sophia Elizabeth "Lizzie" Armstrong
Simonds, Joel A.
Stephenson, J.M.
Wilson, Benjamin
Wilson, Thomas

Bibliography: Ancestry.com. U.S. Census. Illinois. McHenry, Chemung, 1860; U.S. Census. Illinois. McHenry. Harvard. Image 1, 1870. U.S. Census. Illinois. Cook. Chicago. Dist. 116; 1880; U.S. Census. Illinois Cook. Chicago Ward 7. Dist. 422, 1910 [this gives information about Widow Sarah Bethel]; Black, Sylvia. Paper at 2010 COG History Conference, North Hills COG, Springfield, Ohio, at which she said George Peters was the brother-in-law of her grandmother, Mabel Howell Netts; Peters, George. Footnote #1 detailing Reed and Lyon's position on Col. 1:13 in *The Theocratic Kingdom* Vol. 2, NY. Funk & Wagnalls, 1884, p. 36; Reed, H.V. *Proceeds of Discussion at Buchanan, Michigan,* reported in *Gospel Banner and Millennial Advocate* March, 1860; Reed, H,V. Report of Travels, *Gospel Banner,* May, 1860; Report of travels, *Millennial Harbinger,* Joseph Marsh, ed., July 8, 1863; Reed, H.V. "Letter of Sorrow to F. L. Austin, June 21, 1915, owned by Archives of Atlanta Bible College, McDonough, Ga.; Reed on Josephism, *Restitution*, July 8, 1885; Reed, H.V. *The Millenarian* creedal statement, Chicago, Il., Feb. 1874, May 1874, June 1874; Reed, H.V. *The Kingdom of God,* Office of the *Millennial Harbinger,* Thos. Newman, ed., Seneca Falls, NY. 1861; Various issues: *The Restitution,* Dec. 16, 1874; "Our Rest" Jan. 20, 1875; Aug. 19, 1885; July 6, 1910; August 1913; October 1919; August 2, 1920; *The Restitution Herald,* April 12, 1916; July 26, 1916; Oct. 8, 1919; Obituary, July 27. 1920; Jan. 17, 1922; Runnels, Moses T, *A Genealogy of the Runnels and Reynold Families,* Boston, 1873 p. 258 Thanks to Bruce Schulz for this citation; Zimmerman, Angela. "The H.V. Reed Story," unpublished paper for Church History at Oregon Bible College, housed in the Archives of Atlanta Bible College; "Death of Mr. Reed" *Winter Park [Florida] Post,* Aug. 8, 1920 as retrieved Dec. 30, 2009 from wppl.org/wphistory/newspapers/1920/08-05-1920.pdf and Aug.7, 1919 regarding retirement of Rev. Riggs.

Reed, Sophia Elizabeth "Lizzie"
b. 1842
d. June 16, 1915

Sophia Elizabeth Armstrong was born in Winthrop, Maine, to Alvin and Sylvia Armstrong. The family moved first to Georgia and then to Buchanan County, Michigan, which is adjacent to Lake Michigan north of the Indiana state line. This area was a Church of God stronghold. As a young woman, she met a dashing young clergyman who served a circuit across Illinois and Wisconsin. After Hiram V. Reed courted her, they were married in 1860 in Buchanan—she was 18 and he was 23.

Soon after the wedding, the Reeds moved to Chemung, Illinois, near Hiram's hometown of Harvard. Alvin and Sylvia moved with them. Alvin opened a grocery store. For a while at least, they all shared a home.

Within a short time "Lizzie" as she preferred to be called, became an educated woman, her exact credentials being unknown. She was granted honorary degrees from Northwestern and Illinois Wesleyan universities and Bethany College and became an accomplished author. She wrote *The Bible Triumphant* in 1866 while they lived in Harvard. She certainly must have gained knowledge of writing, editing and publishing a book from her husband, who was knowledgeable in the field. Her first book was republished in 1882 by H.L. Hastings in Boston. Lizzie received acclaim for her writings.

She and Hiram raised two sons, Charles B. and Earl H, and a daughter, Myrtle (MCullough). Charles became a physician. Myrtle matured into a fine author and poet. She authored a humorous novel entitled *Lavender and Old Lace* and many other works that were well received. Sadly, in 1911, Myrtle committed suicide by drug overdose at age 37. Church of God members who knew the Reed family felt Lizzie never recovered from the loss of her daughter.

Lizzie chaired the Women's Congress of Philology which was held just prior to the opening of the Columbian Exposition in Chicago in 1893. She was a student of eastern religions–not for the sake of being an advocate, but to understand them in order to refute them.

She edited a curriculum on Universal Literature and served four terms as president of the Illinois Women's Press Association. She authored several books, *Earnest Words for Honest Skeptics* in 1874; *Hindu Literature or the Ancient Books of India* in 1891; *Persian Literature, Ancient and Modern* in 1893; *Primitive Buddhism, The Origins and Teachings* in 1896 by Scott Foresman Co.; and *Hinduism in Europe and America* published in 1914. This latter work was published in New York and London by G.P. Putnam Co. She said she wrote this title because of active proselytizing by Asiatics in Europe and America using "roseate misrepresentations of 'hideous beliefs.'" She was anxious to teach American women about the errors of eastern religions.

In 1899, Lizzie wrote a biography entitled *Daniel Webster*. This was advertised as a character sketch with anecdotes and chronology. In 1903 a Milwaukee publishing house reissued the book with an additional essay by G. Mercer Adam. In 1915, the University of Chicago published a book by Elizabeth Reed entitled *Progress*.

After the 1871 Chicago Fire the Reed family lived briefly in Plymouth, Indiana, where Hiram edited *The Restitution*, a church paper owned by S.A. Chaplin, who was ill-equipped to manage it alone. The Reeds remained in Plymouth from 1872 to 1874 assisting Chaplin as he learned the editing and publishing business.

When they returned to Chicago, Lizzy resumed her studies and writings, and Hiram resumed his evangelistic work for the Church of God. He traveled throughout the states already mentioned, adding Iowa, Michigan and New York to his speaking engagement calendar.

Mrs. Reed was active in the Church of God mission. She so fervently believed the doctrines emphasized by the Church of God that she wrote to isolated members encouraging them in their separation from regular fellowship with like-minded believers.

She was friends with Harriett Boice and Clara Chaffee and called them Daughters of the King. The three took trips together, met for Bible study and carried on correspondence with isolated members.

Elizabeth died after a short illness. A bishop of the Episcopal Church in Chicago conducted her service, there being no Church of God pastor present. Elizabeth was interred at Rosehill Cemetery in Chicago's Edgewater neighborhood. Hiram was interred at Palm Cemetery in Winter Park, Florida.

    See Boice, Harriett
          Chaffee, Clara
          Hastings, H.L
          Reed, Hiram V.

Bibliography: Ancestry.com U.S. Census. Georgia. Walker. East Chicamauga. Image 54, 1850; U.S. Census. Illinois. McHenry, Chemung, 1860; U.S. Census. Illinois. McHenry. Harvard. Image 1. 1870; U.S. Census. Illinois. Cook. Chicago. Dist. 116. 1880; Graham, David, "The Northwest Christian Association," *History Newsletter of the Church of God General Conference*, JStilson, ed., Oregon, Il., Winter, 1985 p.9; *The Restitution Herald*, Dec. 9, 1914; July 7, 1915; Zimmerman, Angela, "The H.V. Reed Story," a student paper for OBC research class, with contributions by Terry Ferrell and David Graham, Feb. 1991. This story identifies Elizabeth's location in Rosehill at Lot 106 Section 107; "Elizabeth Armstrong Reed," Wikipedia.com.

Rennie, William
    b. May 14, 1846
    d. December 15, 1921

William Rennie was born in Cumberland, Scotland. He came to America to work for the Glascow Point Washington Iron and Coal Company, in Port Washington, Ohio. In Ohio he learned the truth of the Kingdom of God and united with the Church of God. In his lifetime, he baptized more than 100 members including his eight sons and two daughters. He delighted in talking about the Bible and wrote many pamphlets on Bible subjects. He finished his last book, *Our Faith*, just before he died.

William may have been the one who contacted William Farley of West Virginia. Farley reported that a man from the Church of God in Ohio, whose name Farley could not remember, came down the Ohio River to baptize him.

Rennie died at Staten Island, New York, where presumably he was living with one of his children. None of Rennie's pamphlets are known to be part of the archival collection of Atlanta Bible College.

    See Farley, William (20th)
Bibliography: *The Restitution*, March 1922

Renner, Elizabeth
    b. August 10, 1830
    d. February 14, 1904

Elizabeth Swope was born in Maryland and moved with her family to northern Illinois, Ogle County. She wed Samuel P. Renner on December 21, 1843. They had two girls and three boys. At the time of her death only one child was still living. Elizabeth embraced the precious Abrahamic faith and tried to live a Christian life in peace and harmony with all whom she met.

She and her mother moved to Mt. Morris in 1873, and then she moved to Plum River with her stepfather. Elizabeth fell ill while caring for her mother, age 94, who ultimately survived Elizabeth. Elizabeth's husband also survived her. Her funeral was conducted in the new building of the Plum River Church of God. Pastor O.J. Allard conducted the service. She was laid to rest beside the four children who preceded her in death.

Bibliography: *The Restitution*, March 1904; April 13, 1904.

Renner, Samuel P.
b. 1831
d. 1910?

Samuel Renner was married to Elizabeth Swope on December 21, 1843, in northern Illinois. They became involved in study with the Church of God as its members were calling it. The Abrahamic Faith particularly intrigued them. The Renners served the Lord in the Plum River church near Savanna, Illinois, and were active in the Illinois state conference work. Here is S.P. Renner's brief history of the formation of the Illinois State Conference as told to J.M. Glotfelty:

> I am informed by Bro. S.P. Renner that early in the year 1852 regular preaching began at Plum River, Illinois by one Collins, and in the year 1858, a conference was held at this place, a union of the brethren of southern Wisconsin and northern Illinois. Dr. Jacobs and Bro. Collins were the preachers, and from that time on, regular yearly conference was held at Plum River and other places. Bros. Chown, Collins, McGinnis, Arnold, Mitchell, Whitesitt, and Gains being the local preachers until J.M. Stephenson and H.V. Reed and Bro. [D.M.] Hudler came in to fill up.

This passage lists church members about whom little is known, except all the men assisted with preaching and sharing the Word. If not for men who passed along oral history in this manner, little would be known about the early frontier work.

See Chown, Robert
Hudler, D.M.
Renner, Elizabeth
Stephenson, J.M.

Bibliography: *The Restitution*, April 13, 1904

Robison (Robinson), Daniel C.
b. 1846
d. January 16, 1925

A. Ultra-Conservative
B. Infamous Waterloo Conference of 1910

Daniel C. Robison was a conservative member of the Church of God. He may have been the son of Daniel I. Robison, an Evangelical Adventist preacher and editor who is known to have had a son named Daniel. The name is seen in literature alternately as Robison or Robinson. The names of both men appear in early Church of God literature, serving as far west as Wisconsin.

Maurice Joblin baptized young Daniel Robison in 1875 in Cleveland. From that point on, Daniel traveled to preach the Gospel of the Kingdom and reported to *The Restitution* in 1887 that he had been traveling through Ohio. He toured with Evangelist John T. Ongley (or Ongl), also of the Faith, who preached to the Disciples. Robison reported that Ongley was an elderly man from Lincolnsville, Crawford County, Pennsylvania. At one meeting Robison was scheduled to preach, he became ill and could not. The Disciples paid him $5 anyway. Robison's favorite theme was the Age to Come. At one time, when Robison and Ongley were working the field together, Ongley preached 14 sermons.

When Robison lived at Bladensburg, Ohio, northeast of Columbus in 1887, no Church of God congregation was active in that vicinity. Robison was considered an isolated member of the fellowship at that point.

In 1910, Robison wed Nancy Barber who by then had been an evangelist for the Church of God since 1906, the year of her baptism. He was 64 and Nancy was 52; possibly this was a second marriage for both of them. They met at a conference meeting of all the Ohio churches and got on well right from the start. After the wedding, Nancy moved to his home in Salem. Robison served as pastor at Salem until 1916 when he asked to be released so he could continue his evangelistic tours.

A. Ultra-Conservative

Robison lived in or near Cleveland, Ohio, and grew up under the leadership of Maurice Joblin, who was descended from the original Adventist movement in New England, as were Newell Bond and Robert McLauchlan, two leaders in the work. Many of the leaders in Cleveland were scholarly and well respected. If the work had not organized in Waterloo, Iowa, with headquarters to be in Oregon (Illinois), it is likely that the leaders of the Cleveland work would have organized a federation of churches that believed the statement of faith as described in the Robert Huggins entry.

Briefly stated, the Cleveland church preferred some Christadelphian doctrines not usually recognized by the rest of the Church of God. The most noteworthy exception to Church of God teaching included the idea of limited resurrection, i.e. the wicked who died in their sins would never be raised again for judgment; the Adamic death was their judgment.

The Cleveland members also believed that Christians must be responsible in order to receive immortality at the resurrection. In other words, if a Christian backslid by engaging in a carnal or worldly lifestyle, he was not being responsible and would not be rewarded at the resurrection. This gave rise to the 12 principles of responsible Christian living, which were outlined in a book of the same name written by Robert Huggins. These principles are scriptural and involve practicing holy Christian living and service. They pondered the dilemma of carnal Christians who might be raised and changed to immortality in the twinkling of an eye but were unworthy to enter the Kingdom. How could this dilemma be solved?

The solution had the Cleveland members siding with the Christadelphian doctrine of mortal emergence. They said all Christians are raised mortal, judged first, and then the righteous receive immortality but the carnal are condemned. Most Church of God members found this idea unscriptural because it could not be reconciled with "changed in a twinkling."

Many of those who adhered to these ideas disagreed with the initiative to form a national organization of a general conference. They felt the churches should be independent, operating within the framework of state conferences. On that basis, D.C. Robison was against the organization of the General Conference in 1910 and 1921.

B. Infamous Waterloo Conference of 1910

Daniel was an Ohio state delegate to the annual conference held at Waterloo in 1910, and there he again met the other Cleveland pastor, Lincoln E. Conner. Conner was in favor of the national organization but he was not a delegate so he couldn't vote on the issue. At that time ministers did not have a vote unless previously selected as a state delegate. Conner's cause to obtain a vote seemed lost. After several failed attempts, the conference finally voted special privilege for Conner to vote. The feud created tension at the meeting and illustrated the tension in Cleveland between the Church of the Blessed Hope and the Lee Avenue Church of God stemming from the split in 1900.

Elder Robison sincerely felt that the strength of the Church of God movement lay in its state conferences. Each conference monitored the work of the individual churches through regular quarterly conferences. Churches took turns hosting the conference. This meant that each church in the fellowship gained experience in planning class sessions, preaching services, music, food planning and serving and hosting attendees in their homes. It was a plan that worked—a plan designed by Joseph Marsh.

Robison said at the 1910 Waterloo Conference if a general conference were created:

1910 Conference, Waterloo, Iowa
Standing, left to right: Peter Jeffrey, GE Marsh, JW Williams, JH Williams, JA Patrick, LE Conner, OJ Allard, Robert Huggins, WL Crowe, MD Newell, AR Underwood, John Garton. Seated: JH Moore, AJ Eychaner, JH Willey, Nancy Tichenal, unknown, Almus Adams, DC Robison.

There will be none of our [state] conferences, at the expense of the cause in general. Conferences, and Conference work will be arranged that the great good can be done. Brethren, let this thought sink deeply into every mind and let all work for the general good. Less than 10 years ago the churches in Ohio were strangers. A few at Salem labored courageously and unselfishly and called a conference in which all the churches might mingle and become spiritually strengthened. Today we are a band of loving brothers and sisters and we have been greatly built up and strengthened.

As a result of the heated dialogue about doctrine and delegates on both sides of the question, a general conference was not organized in 1910.

One positive result of the 1910 Waterloo conference was the conference attendees' endorsement of the value in having and promoting a Sunday school at the local church. Several people were involved in conducting Sunday schools in their home churches and gave testimonials about the worth of it. D.C. Robison said, "Sunday School must be made attractive, strong that the pupil may feel drawn and interested." He said, "The Sunday School was the strongest influence in the Church—the main factor in bringing members into the Church."

In 1919 and 1920, Robison wrote a series of Sunday School lessons for the *Truth Seeker's Quarterlies*, and doctrinal articles for *The Restitution*. These articles were published at the rate of one per month for several months well into 1921 and covered the nature of God, heaven, the Kingdom, creeds, death and immortality and more. Daniel co-authored a tract with L.E. Conner entitled *Death Reigned from Adam to Moses* in 1921. He also authored a tract entitled *Man is Mortal*.

While his greatest contributions to the Church of God were his dedication to seeking the truth and to thinking and writing about it, Robison also contributed his time and service to evangelism. He spent time in Louisiana working with the congregation at Hammond during April 1916. The members' report after his departure noted he had greatly assisted the church and the congregation.

After completing his series of doctrinal articles, D.C. Robison wrote a letter to *The Restitution* that he was ill with the flu and laying down his pen. He had written for *The Restitution* since 1878, nearly 50 years. He died in 1925 and was buried near his hometown of Mt. Vernon, Ohio. Robison was known throughout the brotherhood as a writer and speaker of considerable ability. He had a keen appreciation of the truth and earnest desire to know God's great promises. W.S. Tomlinson of Cleveland furnished his obituary for *The Restitution Herald*.

See Conner, L.E.
Ongley, John T.
Robison, Nancy Barber

Bibliography: Ancestry.com. U.S. Census. Ohio. Columbiana. Salem ward 1. Dist. 126. 1920. Raum, John O. *History of the City of Trenton*, W.T. Nicholson. Trenton. 1871 p. 184, Bruce Shulz furnished this citation; *The Restitution*, "Report of Travels," April 6, 1887; *The Restitution,* Dec. 9, 1908; Sept. 14, 1910; May 1, 1920; November 22, 1921; *The Restitution Herald,* April 12, 1916; March 20, 1920; Feb. 3, 1925; *The Church of God of the Abrahamic Faith Salem, Ohio Dedication Service*, "History Section," June 28, 1970, Franklyne Ross furnished this booklet.

Roll, Ruth Anne
b. 1867
d. July 1948

Roll, Ward "Wardie"
b. September 17, 1853
d. July 17, 1930

Ruth Roll was the widow of Ward Roll. Ward Roll had been previously married to Eliza Brotherton with whom he had three children. Eliza died on February 23, 1879. He then married Ruth Anne Roby, and they had three children. Ward was baptized in 1898 at Blackford County, Roll Township, Indiana.

The Rolls established the Roll Church of God in Marion, Indiana. L.E. Conner baptized Ruth. She was diabetic and suffered loss of health and mobility because of it, yet according to Ruth's friend, Eleanor Rogan, "She took great pleasure in reading the *Restitution Herald* and discovering the Bible and its teachings with other members of the church."

Ward died in Marion and was buried in a nearby cemetery. Cantwell Drabenstott conducted the service.

In 1987, members of the Roll Church of God assisted the General Conference archival staff in microfilming *The Restitution* copies from the 19th and 20th centuries. Much gratitude goes to those members who assisted in preserving the history of the Church of God and made it more accessible to all members. The microfilm has recently been transferred to digital format and is available through the Church of God History Committee.

See Drabenstott, Cantwell (20th)

Bibliography: Obituary, *The Restitution Herald*, Sydney Magaw, ed., Oregon, Il., Aug. 3, 1948.

Ohio State Conference (Springfield, circa 1910)

Ruhn, Herman Paul
b. 1879
d. 1936

Herman Paul Ruhn was born in Germany but grew up in Eden Valley, Minnesota. As a young man he met and married Alda Matheny, a steadfast Church of God member. Shortly after their marriage, Herman was baptized into Christ and remained a dedicated member of the Church of God throughout his life.

Herman Ruhn was a member Eden Valley Church of God board in various capacities, and he was the Sunday School superintendent for many years.

The Ruhns had five children, all of whom became active church workers: Vernice Hamilton, Elton Ruhn, Elna (Peggy) Ross, Marjorie Wood and Lois Allen. Most of their grandchildren are baptized and active in the church as well, including two full-time Church of God ministers: Kent H. Ross and Scott Ross. In addition, Kent's son, Seth O. Ross, is in ministry.

Herman Ruhn always put the Lord's work first in his life and remained active until his death in 1936. Both his and Alda's influence greatly impacted the lives of the generations following them, as well as many others whose lives they have touched.

See Ross, Stan O. and Elna (20th)

Bibliography: Ancestry.com. U.S. Census. Minnesota. Stearns. Eden Lake. Dist. 136. 1910; Information written by family members and sent to Atlanta Bible College Biography project, David Krogh, compiler.

> *2 Peter 3:10-11, 13*
>
> "But the day of the Lord will come as a Thief, in which the HEAVENS shall pass away with a rushing sound, and the Elements burning intensely shall be dissolved, and the Earth and the WORKS in it shall be burned up. All These things, therefore, being dissolved, what persons ought we to be in Holy Conduct and Piety?
>
> But we, according to his PROMISE. are looking for New Heavens and a new Earth, in which dwells Righteousness."
>
> *- The Emphatic Diaglott*

Jaynes Street Church of God, Omaha, Nebraska
Photo provided by Rex Cain

S

Salley, D.F.
b. 1821
d. March 2, 1892

D.F. Salley was a lay preacher who lived in Princeton, Arkansas. He preached to his neighbors and traveled to reach many who were far from his home. He reported that preaching to his neighbors added 20 believers to the family of God.

In 1857, Salley reported 1856's expenses had been so great he had to stay home in 1857 to pay bills. He agreed to preach in 1858 for a specified sum furnished by pledges from a few supporters. He said, "preachers and their families cannot live on wind." When not preaching, Salley earned his living as a jobber (job printer).

Salley wrote to *The Prophetic Expositor and Bible Advocate* in December 1857, stating that lately he had been working to pay bills, but he wanted to return to preaching, and planned for that in the upcoming year. He reported that he had recently baptized 20 new members.

After D.F. Salley died his son David S. Salley became a lay preacher. In William H. Wilson's 1904 report to the brethren, he listed David among the Arkansas ministers.

Bibliography: Ancestry.com. U.S. Census. Arkansas. Ouchita. Carroll. 1870. Letter by Salley to Joseph Marsh in *Advent Harbinger* Oct. 23, 1857; Obituary of D.F. Salley, by son, *The Restitution*, S.A. Chaplin, ed., Plymouth, In., April 13, 1892; Report of Wilson, *The Restitution*, Jan. 20, 1904; Salley, D.F. Report, *The Prophetic Expositor and Bible Advocate*, Joseph Marsh, ed., Rochester, NY. Dec. 1, 1857.

Samuelson, Selma
b. November 9, 1868
d. January 27, 1921

Selma was born in Sweden and came to America, settling in New York, as a young girl. She united with the Church of God in Brooklyn, New York, where her brother was a member. She subscribed to *The Restitution* until she could no longer see to read. From then on, she passed along her copies to others so they could learn of the truths she loved. Selma remained a loyal and self-sacrificing servant until her death.

Bibliography: *The Restitution*, Feb. 15, 1921

Sarvis (Servis), A. F. (Arthur)
b. 1800?
d. Unknown

A.F. Sarvis may have been born near Ashland, Ohio, and made his way into Indiana as a youth. He may have heard about the Kingdom of God through Age-to-Come evangelists in Ohio, such as J.P. Weethee. Sarvis' name is seen in the literature with the alternate spelling of A. Servis.

Sarvis lived at Kingsbury, Indiana, and was one of the early ministers in that state. He and the other Indiana and Michigan ministers met with Joseph Marsh in 1851 when the Marshes completed their western tour.

The Kingsbury meetings are discussed more fully in the Joseph Marsh entry. They were a time of reunion for some in attendance: S.A. Chaplin had known Joseph Marsh and Ephraim Miller in New York. Others made new acquaintances. The meeting united the men and their wives in fellowship, unity of spirit and hope for the future of the Age-to-Come work.

Terry Ferrell refers to A.F. Sarvis as a minister in Indiana about whom little is known. Evidence does show Sarvis participated in the work of the Michigan Church of God. He attended the Michigan churches' conference meetings and participated there as an evangelist, having been appointed to the position from 1865 through 1869. During the 11th annual meeting of the Michigan Conference, 1868, he preached on the Age to Come "on the place *where*, and the time *when* of the reward."

At a recent History Conference, it was reported that Sarvis placed his flag among the Advent Christians, but available evidence indicates that in his early years in Michigan he was respected and worked faithfully in the arms of the Church of God. From the ministry of A.F. Sarvis came the ministry of Jeremiah Hatch. Sarvis baptized Jeremiah S. Hatch in Indiana giving the Church of God movement one of the greatest circuit riders in the Midwest.

    See Chaplin, Stedman A.
          Hatch, Jeremiah S.
          Marsh, Joseph
          Miller, Ephraim
          Weethee, J.P

Bibliography: Ancestry.com. U.S. Census. Ohio. Ashland. Vermillion. 1850. Terry Ferrell. *A Brief History of the Church of God in America*, National Berean Youth Fellowship. Camp Reynoldswood, Dixon, Il., 1960; Minutes of Michigan Conference of Church of God, 1858-1886, 11th Annual Meeting entry, June 4-7, 1868.

Savage, T.M.
    b. April 5, 1862
    d. Unknown

T.M. Savage was born in Newcastle, New Brunswick, Canada. He moved to Winnepeg in 1881 where he worked for the Canadian Pacific Railway. In 1887, he moved to St. Paul, Minnesota, and in 1891 to St. Cloud where he worked for the Great Northern Railway.

Savage married Mamie Dell Bowers on May 17, 1893. They established their first home in Waite Park, Minnesota. Elder Savage was baptized by Elder E.E. Thoms. T.M. Savage began serving the Lord in the pulpit at St. Cloud and served beside Elder Fred Daubanton for 16 years following the death of Elder Thoms. The church had an organized Sunday School, a Berean Society and a Ladies Aid group.

Although details are not available about this loyal servant's work, his heritage lived on through the life of his granddaughters, Ruth Dell Savage Lewis and Sara Savage See. His great-granddaughter Tracy Savage, daughter of Bill Savage, served as a missionary in Russia for a number of years in the 20th century.

    See Daubanton, Fred (20th)
          Lewis, John and Ruth (20th)
          Savage, Thomas (20th)
          Thoms, E.E.

Bibliography: *History of the Minnesota Church of God Conference*, Sydney Magaw, ed., 1931. E-mail from Sara See, 2009 and 2010.

Scott, C.D.W.
    b. 1814?
    d. January 10, 1878

Charles D.W. Scott was born in Pennsylvania but resided in Indiana. He was reportedly a direct descendant of Walter Scott who had been highly esteemed by Alexander Campbell in the Restoration Movement. In fact, Walter Scott first baptized Dr. John Thomas. Thomas later repudiated that baptism, was re-baptized, and went on to form the Christadelphians.

Charley Scott left the Christian church in Indiana and moved to Ottawa, Minnesota. For some time he affiliated with the Advent Christians there. He was greatly enthusiastic for the work of the Lord and affiliated with the Church of God in its early days in Minnesota, helping found and stabilize it.

Scott was particularly fond of working with William Parson who, like Scott, had come out of the Christian church and affiliated with the Advent Christians. The two men may have met in this work. They became convinced that the correct name of the church should be Church of God and began to preach it in 1873. Sydney Magaw noted Elder Scott was a man of unimpeachable character.

He was considered an earnest worker, and it is believed he converted hundreds of people. Evidence shows he organized many churches. Scott died suddenly after an illness lasting just 2-1/2 hours. He was buried at his home in Ottawa. His death was a serious blow to the work for he was deeply loved by the members.

    See Parson, William

Bibliography: Ancestry.com. Minnesota Territorial and State Census. 1849-1905, record for Charles D. Scott from 1857 Census; *History of the Minnesota Church of God Conference*, Sydney Magaw, ed., 1931.

Sears, M.A.
    b. 1800?
    d. Unknown

The names of M.A. and Mrs. Sears are seen in the literature from time to time, but details of their ministry are scant. It is known that the Sears lived in or near Lake Zurich, Illinois, and that M.A. believed and preached the "gospel of the Kingdom." He was looking for the "glorious restitution of all things."

Mrs. Sears wrote a letter to Joseph Marsh in the *Voice of Truth*, and from this it can be seen that her husband was one of the earliest men to teach the Age to Come on the Illinois frontier in 1846.

When Joseph Marsh made a tour of the frontier in 1851, he met B.B. Brown and M.A. Sears in Beloit to discuss the work. He left the work in the hands of Bro.

Sears. Whether Sears served as a circuit rider is not known, but Marsh must have considered him quite capable.

See Brown, B.B.
Marsh, Joseph
Parks, H.A.

Bibliography: "Letter to Joseph Marsh from Mrs. Sears." *Voice of Truth,* April 1846. Marsh, Joseph, Report of Western Tour, *Advent Harbinger and Bible Advocate,* Aug. 1851.

Self, J.H.
b. 1862
d. Unknown

J.H. Self was a southern preacher, born in Arkansas, who traveled throughout Arkansas and Oklahoma. He was married with six sons and one daughter. Information about his conversion and first encounter with the Gospel of the Kingdom is not available, except for this testimony about his ministry from J.M. Morgan. Morgan said, "Bro. Self is a good preacher, and we all love to hear him preach."

In 1926, J.M. Morgan and J.H. Self preached together at a series of meetings in Bristow, Oklahoma.

See Morgan, J.M. (20th)

Bibliography: *The Restitution Herald,* April 12, 1916.

Seymour, Alva N.
b. 1818
d. 1900?

Seymour, Mary A.
b. 1819
d. Unknown

Alva N. Seymour, a noted preacher of the day, was married to Mary. They had one son. The Seymours resided at Clarkson, New York. Before joining the Age-to-Come movement with Joseph Marsh, Alva was a Christian Connexion clergyman. The 1850 Census specifies his denomination as "Clergyman, Christ'n." It is thought this was a general designation for anyone coming out of the Christian Connexion, a loosely organized group of churches in New England that were predominantly unitarian. Joseph Marsh also came from the Christian Connexion.

While still living in New York, Alva and Mary traveled widely across eastern United States, dipping south and moving into the frontier to minister. In 1846, she wrote that they had been working in Nashville, and they sent their greetings to many friends across the states. She wanted to go west but was prevented from working there because of the fevers. Moving to Michigan afforded them a new territory for evangelism.

At first, Alva Seymour resided temporarily with the Fitzgeralds at Nankin, Michigan, while he worked an evangelism circuit. When the Seymours moved west, they took up permanent residence in Nankin.

They were highly esteemed evangelists who often reported their travels in Joseph Marsh's *Voice of Truth* and later, in the new paper, *Advent Harbinger and Bible Advocate.* Their reports are also prevalent in Benjamin Wilson's *Gospel Banner* and later *The Restitution.*

A.N. Seymour wrote very little in the journals, but one article mentioned his opinions on Sabbath-keeping. He said, "Before the crucifixion it was obligatory to keep the Sabbath and all laws. Now there is no law that holds the Jews or Gentiles to the Sabbath." Alva also testified years later that he began to study prophecy in 1842, and he thanked God that he opened his eyes to the wonder of Jesus' Second Coming. He also believed that the Church of God would be placed in the power of the little horn on the fourth beast in Daniel 7:7, 8, "That plucks up three kings." This would endure for 1260 days or 3-1/2 years. He asked, "Is the bride of Christ ready for the translation? Are your lamps trimmed and lights brilliantly burning? Is she discharging every duty and obligation that rests upon her? May all the family of God hold themselves in constant readiness."

Mary was able to aptly express her opinion. In one issue of the *Voice of Truth,* she wrote a letter to the editor about the skeptics ridiculing the Adventists. She said:

> The despisers of our blessed hope relate, to their own amusement, many anecdotes about the ascension robes of the poor 'insane Millerites'. They say that they are made of drab cloth, and laid aside, ready to robe ourselves when we go up. As to the charge of having robes ready for the ascension, we do not deny; but our enemies are looking through a glass darkly.

By this she did not mean they sewed actual garments, for she said, "moths would soon devour them." She meant that all Christians should be clothed in robes of righteousness to be ready to meet the Lord, and "when Jesus comes, he will give us ascension robes. Then we shall assuredly be caught up." In the same issue a second letter appeared from Mary entitled "Charity, Charity" in which she called for forbearance, humility and charity among brethren while the Lord delays his coming.

During the spring of 1851 a controversy over women's ministry brewed in the *Harbinger* fueled by Henry Grew's and Sylvester Bliss' comments that women should be silent in church. Hence, they could not preach. Some contributors on the subject took a softer approach, but others took a hard line that women should be silent in church. Of course, Mary Seymour did not accept this.

She wrote that Paul said, "Everyone of us shall give an account to God." She said, "If women are included in *everyone,* she cannot give an account to God by proxy through her husband." Mary pointed out that Paul directed Titus to teach men and women to be ready for every good work. In 1 Corinthians 11:5 women are instructed to have their head covered when they prophesy, and in 14:3 they are included in prophesying for the purpose of edifying, exhorting and comforting. Mary said, "If women thus prophesied, then they preached."

Also, she pointed out that Joel and Peter said, "I will pour out my spirit upon all flesh and your sons and daughters shall prophesy." She also pointed out that at Pentecost when the Holy Ghost fell upon them the church at Jerusalem had 120 men and women. When persecution broke out, they all were scattered abroad, and *they went everywhere preaching the gospel.*

She further stated that commentaries and history have proof that women were active in preaching in the church until the Papacy stepped in and stopped it.

Mary stated it would be a curious gospel if women only mended socks. She encouraged women, saying:

> I would say to my sisters who have sound heads, hearts and speech, that cannot be condemned, arouse yourselves to action. Go out in the name and strength of Jesus Christ, and sound aloud the last notes of warning to a perishing world, and try, if possible, to gather in souls from the broad road that leads to perdition.

In a curious turn of events, a note in Thomas Wilson's *Herald of the Kingdom* early in 1870 stated Mary Seymour turned away from the Age to Come. Why she left is unknown. Perhaps she felt that some Age-to-Come publishers disrespected the role of women in ministry.

Alva remained faithful to the cause, however. He worked beside Ephraim Miller, and together they fought the damaging influence Sabbatarianism was having in Michigan and Wisconsin. Many believers of the Age to Come had been led away by Seventh-day adherents.

Alva Seymour wrote in *The Restitution* in 1888 that he had not changed his mind about the gospel, a significant statement since Mary had changed her mind about it. He said Sabbatarianism had stolen many people from the Jackson, Michigan, church but he had been sealed with the Holy Spirit after believing in the Gospel of the God revealed through Jesus Christ, "for when we receive that seal we are dead, delivered from the law which made nothing perfect, but the bringing of a better hope, did."

See Grew, Henry
     Marsh, Joseph
     Miller, Ephraim

Bibliography: Ancestry.com. U.S. Census. Michigan. Wayne Co. Nankin. 1850; "Report on M. Seymour" *Herald of the Kingdom and Christian Instructor*, 1868; Seymour, Mary. "Millerites and the Ascension Robes," *Voice of Truth*, Jan. 29, 1845; Seymour, Alva N. "Report," *Voice of Truth*, Nov. 26, 1845; Oct. 21, 1846; Seymour, Alva N. "Sabbath-keeping," *Expositor and Advocate*, Issue 28, 1857-58; Seymour, Alva N. "The Glorious Light of Truth," *The Restitution*, S.A. Chaplin, ed., Plymouth, In., March 20, 1889; Seymour, Mary, "Letter from Sister M.A. Seymour, *Voice of Truth and Glad Tidings of the Kingdom*, Rochester, NY., Jan. 6, 1847. Seymour, Mary, "Letter to Joseph Marsh," *Advent Harbinger and Bible Advocate*, April 4, 1851; Seymour, Mary, "Leaves the age to come." *Herald of the Coming Kingdom*, Jan. 1, 1870; *The Restitution*, April 18, 1888.

Shafer, Hugh Marion
    b. June 20. 1863
    d. June 19, 1936

Hugh Shafer was the son of John Shafer. His grandfather's name was John also, but personal information on the older John is unknown. Hugh was married twice. His first wife was Mich. He wed the second, Mary Angeline Long, on November 25, 1886. Mary was born February 7, 1869, and died in January 1929. Hugh and Mary had three daughters; the eldest, Lulu (Stilson), was born in 1888; Verna (Thayer) was the middle child; and Bessie, the youngest. Lulu and Verna were active in Church of God ministry their entire lives.

See Shafer, John
     Stilson, Floyd and Lulu (20th)
     Thayer, Verna (20th)

Bibliography: Ancestry.com U.S. Census. Indiana. Marshall. Center. 1900. *Voice of Truth*, Oct. 10, 1844.

Shaffer (Shafer), Jacob
    b. April 20, 1803
    d. April 4, 1887

Elder Jacob Shaffer was a pioneer advent preacher in central Indiana who came from Pennsylvania. He was contemporary with S.A. Chaplin, and according to his own account in *The Restitution*, baptized several other notable early preachers, including J.F. Waggoner, "Uncle" John Foore and Joshua Bailey during the 1860s.

Jacob was a landowner, a farmer and a taxpayer. He married Mary who was born in Maryland in 1802. They had three sons and two daughters. Mary joined the Church of God at Antioch in 1876, and served the Lord faithfully all her life. She died March 24, 1904.

Many baptisms occurred after Jacob shared his view of atonement. He preached that Christianity falsely teaches that believers receive their reward prior to Christ's second coming. J.F. Wagoner, for example, could not defend from Scripture that it taught the Kingdom of God is within the believer. He asked Shafer to explain it to him. When Jacob laid out the doctrine, stating our atonement comes when Christ returns to set up his Kingdom, *if* we are believers who have been immersed in the Gospel of the Kingdom, Wagoner accepted it and was baptized.

> **The Church of God view of atonement**... has been based upon the model from the Old Testament. Jesus has become the propitiation and covers our sin as the mercy seat covered the Ark of the Covenant. Believers in Christ receive salvation because they have been justified by his death. It was necessary for Christ to die, so that believers can be reconciled to God through Christ. Redemption allows believers to approach God through Christ in prayer, and is the guarantee or down payment for a place in the Kingdom of God, which is to be established literally when Christ returns. Christ's death was necessary so he could become the first fruits of the resurrection to immortality, and believers will be raised from the grave if they believe.

Shaffer described his work in Rochester, Indiana, saying:

> I preached east of Rochester at a school house and said (among other things) that I couldn't find anywhere in the Bible where it says that believers receive immortality before the resurrection. J.F. Wagoner went home, took his Bible down from the shelf where it had rested for 15 years, and asked for more.

Shaffer studied with them, and baptized Wagoner, Foore and their wives. These men went on to become two of the greatest evangelists the Church of God has seen in the Midwest. Likewise, following similar discussions, other baptisms happened in the late 1850s and 1860s. Shaffer baptized over 70 men, many of whom left Indiana to carry on evangelistic ministries west of the Mississippi River.

For awhile, Jacob lived in Fulton County, Kewanna Township, Indiana, near Burr Oak. He continued to preach and reported he had baptized six after preaching on the Gospel of hope in September 1863. He also mentioned that he was at the Indiana Conference the previous August; this was the last conference Joseph Marsh attended.

Shaffer loved the Word of God so much that he never stopped rejoicing in it even when circumstances turned against him. In his last years he was a resident of the County Farm in Adams County, where he enjoyed fellowship with many others. The US Census listed his status as "Pauper." At that time in American history Social Security did not exist, nor was there a welfare program for old ministers except county homes. It is not known where he and Mary are interred, possibly at Burr Oak.

See Foore, John "Uncle"
Marsh, Joseph
Wagoner, J.F.

Bibliography: Ancestry.com. Indiana. Adams. Washington. Dist. 138. 1880; Graham, David. E-mail to author. Feb. 21, 2006 and March 1, 2006; *The Restitution,* April 13, 1904; Harrison, Bert. E-mail about Hugh Shafer from Stilson family genealogy, July 14, 2007; Obituary. *The Restitution,* May 11, 1887; Shafer, Jacob. Letter to Editor, *The Restitution,* S.A. Chaplin, ed., Plymouth, In., Oct. 10, 1883; Dec. 12, 1883; Shafer, Jacob; Report, *Millennial Harbinger and Bible Expositor,* Thos. Newman, ed., Seneca Falls, NY, Sept. 23, 1863; Shafer, Jacob, Testimony of his evangelism and baptisms, *The Restitution,* Jan. 7, 1885.

Shaw, A.E.
b. January 27, 1861
d. Unknown

A.E. Shaw wrote this about his life and ministry:

"A hundred years hence, what a change will be made in politics, morals, religion, and trade!" Thus are the words of a familiar hymn. If changes continue for the next hundred years as they have since we first heard the hymn, we trust that God's Kingdom will have been ushered in. Since the day of my birth, I have seen a great change, but not as a whole for the better. To have real peace, the Prince of Peace first must come.

I was born January 27, 1861 in Allen County, Ohio, at the beginning of the Civil War, the third child of a family of four. My youngest brother W.H. Shaw is still living in Stroud, Oklahoma. We lived in a log house of which the floors were logs split in half with the split side up. There was no varnish on them and no rugs. I remember my father bringing in the back log for the fireplace by horse, where for several years our meals were cooked before we had a cook stove.

At the age of fourteen years, together with my parents I moved to Western Iowa where I met the girl of my choice. I found it was a wise choice, for her life always has been an influence for good in solving hard problems and for helping over many difficult and rough places down through the path of life. We were married at Logan, Iowa, April 12, 1883. Mrs. Shaw was 21 years of age and I was 22.

Mrs. Shaw was the eldest of a family of eight of which one sister, Mrs. Minnie Carr of Logan, Iowa, and one brother, John C. Owens of Bentonville, Arkansas, are yet living, was born April 5, 1862, and reared in Harrison County near Logan, Iowa.

In 1910 we moved to western Nebraska, where we lived until 1920. In 1915, our oldest daughter died following surgery in an Omaha hospital.

In 1914 we united with the Church of God of the Abrahamic Faith under the evangelistic meetings of Bro. Almus Adams in Frontier County, Nebraska, together with Brother and Sister Frank Lakin. For lack of water necessary, we were baptized in a stock tank. About that time, Sister James Halley, mother of Harry Halley who now lives in Wray, Colorado, was baptized by Brother Adams. Previous to this, we were affiliated with the Church of Christ.

Having been isolated, we knew the publishers and writers of the Church of God through tracts and church papers. Some of these publications were: *The Restitution*, published by Elder R.G. Huggins, for which we subscribed until it was discontinued; *The Restitution Herald*, from the time it was first edited by Bro. S.J. Lindsay until the present; *The Gospel Trumpet*, edited by Bro. W.H. Luhman. This same paper underwent a title change to *The Gospel Messenger* under the editorship of Bro. T.A. Drinkard; *The Last Days* by Bro. Thomas Wilson, and *The Present Truth*, by the Crowe brothers (Charles and Will) and Bro. James A. Patrick; the book, *The Pinewoods Bible Class*, and a tract written by Bro. W.H. Wilson (father of Sr. Jessie Wilson, who now resides at the Golden Rule Home, Oregon, Illinois).

In 1920, we located on a homestead in western Colorado, where we lived until 1931, when we came to Denver to make our home with our son at the present address, 4703 W. Fifty-Second Street.

On March 31, 1943, our daughter Nellie (Mrs. A.E. Mock of Grand Valley) was killed in an automobile grade-crossing accident near her home on her husband's birthday. She and her son Floyd were baptized by Bro. S.J. Lindsay.

Our four living children are: Clark of Clifton, Donald and John of Denver, and Clyde of Croker, Arkansas, formerly of Tempe, Arizona, where he and his wife and two daughters were baptized by Bro. Lindsay. We have eighteen grandchildren and seven great-grandchildren living.

Since the time of our conversion, we have been isolated except for an occasional visit from the late Bro. S.J. Lindsay, Bro. T.A. Drinkard, and now we are rejoicing that Bro. Ernest Graham and wife have located in Golden. We appreciate the privilege of being able to have the blessed truths taught as they are recorded in God's Word, and trust that many may be brought to a knowledge of the truth through their teaching.

We commend Oregon Bible College for training such able young ministers. We do not know many of them personally, but feel that we know them through their articles in the *Restitution Herald*, and by the recommendations of others, we feel that we can highly recommend them because of their work. May God bless them for their every effort to preach His Word, that many may be brought to a knowledge of the truth and be saved through their teaching.

We want to live until the coming of Christ.

See Adams, Almus
Drinkard, T.A. (20th)
Graham, Ernest (20th)
Lindsay, S.J.

Bibliography: Shaw, A.E. "Our Life" *The Restitution Herald*, April 16, 1946.

Shearer, Carrie
b. 1875
d. 1941

Carrie D. Shearer was the youngest daughter of Mr. and Mrs. Samuel Osborn. F.L. Austin baptized her in 1900. She was a faithful member of the Burr Oak Church of God all her life. Her faith and works are known to the Lord.

Bibliography: Atlanta Bible College Biography Project, compiled by David Krogh.

Shelton, Lovett Holland
b. 1868
d. Unknown

L.H. Shelton was a popular pastor from the Arkansas-Oklahoma conference. He lived at Driggs with his wife, Rebbeca, and their eight children. His preaching tours across two states resulted in long absences from home. In the early 20th century there were numerous rural congregations to visit, including meetings and conferences held in open fields or under arbors for protection from the sun. People came from all over for the Church of God meetings with sometimes as many as

Illinois Conference, August 19-22, 1915
Left to right: LE Conner, Cleveland, OH; LH Shelton, Driggs, AR; SJ Lindsay, Oregon, IL; JH Anderson, Troy, OH; JH Luman, Sapulpa, OK.

Photo by Roland Stilson, South Bend, IN

several thousand in attendance. They arrived by buggy or carriage, parking vehicles in one field while the meeting was held in another.

Meetings often had a camp meeting format with generous doses of music and Holy Spirit. Attendees included Adventists, Church of God, Campbellites and anyone else who wanted to hear a good revival sermon. Shelton was particularly fond of preaching on the baptism of the Holy Spirit. He preached that subject in a sermon at the Illinois Conference in 1915 as their invited guest speaker.

L.H. Shelton was an exceptional debater. Well known throughout the South, he was often invited to debate Church of Christ and Methodist preachers. They were no match for him. One time he intercepted colleague J.H. Luhman as he was about to run an errand and asked him to moderate a debate between him and a man named Bailey. Bailey lost. A second debate ensued a few days later with a man name Lawrence, again with Luhman as moderator. Luhman said later he had moderated many debates of different faiths, and Lawrence was the weakest of them all.

In that day singing schools were held at churches to teach and to provide music. No one knew how to read music, so music masters taught people the shaped note method of recognizing harmony parts. Each note in a musical scale had a different shape, so that one could learn to read music and harmonize by recognizing the shapes of the notes. Notes were shaped as triangles, diamonds, squares, circles, etc.

Shaped notes have long been used to teach people to read music and sing harmony. Seven shapes are used including circle, square, triangle, diamond and oval.

Elder Shelton worked closely with Dr. T.J. Daniels, who mentored the younger man. Bro. R. Jones also lived and worked in Drigg where Shelton lived.

Members of the 1923 Arkansas/Oklahoma state conference chose L.H. Shelton to edit *The Gospel Messenger*. *The Gospel Trumpet*, predecessor to *The Messenger*, merged with *The Restitution Herald* in 1915, but evidently the southern members wanted their own publication so *The Messenger* re-emerged a few years later, with the new title of *The Gospel Messenger*, and continued in publication as a mimeographed paper well into the 1960s. A few copies of *The Gospel Messenger* and *The Gospel Trumpet* are on file in the Archives of Atlanta Bible College, McDonough, Georgia.

W.H. Wilson reported L.H. Shelton among the list of ministers to the brethren. Shelton's ministry lived on through his family's testimony, including his daughter, Blanch Shelton Hays, who was a lifelong member of the Church of God in Arkansas.

See Turner, R.O.
  Gates, John S

Bibliography: Bynum, Elda. E-mail to Kent Ross, JStilson, January 22, 2006; Report of Wilson, *The Restitution* Jan. 20, 1904; *The Restitution Herald*, July 14, 1915; May, 1915; Oct. 23, 1923; Sherwin Williams loaned many copies of *The Gospel Messenger* for research on the encyclopedia publishing project.

Shockey, William P.
b. 1814
d. Unknown

Evangelist William Shockey was contemporary with the organization of the One Faith in Geneva, Illinois. An Indiana clergyman from Campbellite background, he became convinced that he needed to make a change.

Once he accepted the Gospel of the Kingdom of God, Shockey moved to the frontier. He began around Rensselaer, Indiana, during the pioneer days of that region. He very likely studied the Gospel through the outreach of the Rensselaer Church of God. On the frontier he lived and worked throughout Iowa, Nebraska, Kansas and Missouri. In one report to *The Gospel Banner and Millennial Advocate*, Shockey said 150 people were with the One Faith across those three states. He had traveled over 3000 miles, and baptized 38 believers in and around the state of Kansas. In the six months since his previous report, he had preached 273 times. His ministry was self-supporting, showing a $483 profit one year. At the annual conference in Nebraska, it was decided to return Bros. Shockey and S.E. Adams to the field to increase the growth.

William Shockey was a good Bible student, and he was interested in helping others study as well. He wrote a series of lessons entitled "Bible Instruction and Analysis." The first one appeared in *The Gospel Banner*, and fittingly enough, was on the topic of the "Abrahamic Covenant and the Kingdom of God on Earth."

In an 1867 letter to *The Gospel Banner* Shockey reported being unable to go into Missouri because of a very deep snow. He stated he lived near Hillsdale, Kansas. Also, one reader requested that Shockey ask Benjamin Wilson to please avoid using statements in *The Gospel Banner* that discussed non-resurrection of children because it was too upsetting to frontier folks.

In 1868, Shockey reported in *The Gospel Banner* that he still struggled for the truth in the far west. He wrote then from Aspinwall, Nebraska, located on the banks of the Missouri River, only three miles from his residence. His two sons had settled there also and a community was springing up. A gristmill had been erected recently, and soon it would begin grinding food. He invited folks considering emigration to do so since unimproved homesteads could be purchased for $3 per acre and improved homesteads with homes for $10 to $25 per acre. His two sons had just settled North Nemaha City, and he was headed there as well. Shockey preached the Gospel in Aspinwall and Nemaha even though he battled illness most of the winter and spring.

Also in 1868, a Kansas believer wrote to *The Gospel Banner* questioning if William Shockey had been baptized at the hand of an elder from the Campbellite persuasion and asking whether the faith of the person being baptized was as important as the faith persuasion of the one doing the baptizing. Shockey answered two weeks later in the March 1 issue that while he did not understand the Gospel of the Kingdom at the time of his baptism, he did understand and believe the Abrahamic faith and covenant then, and he learned of the Kingdom on earth later. Benjamin Wilson, editor of *The Gospel Banner* endorsed Shockey's comments and said he did not think it necessary for everyone to have full understanding at baptism as growth comes after baptism also.

During an era when ministers of the Church of God and other denominations haggled over the Sabbath question, William Shockey weighed in on the side of serving communion on the Lord's Day. Without making it an issue, he told readers of *The Millennial Harbinger and Bible Expositor* that he believed in Sunday worship.

In the winter of 1869, Shockey and his wife took ill. Her ailment made her lame, requiring a crutch, and he suffered with "lung fever." Shockey wrote expressing his gratitude to people in Hoboken, New Jersey; Cleveland, Ohio; and Rensselaer, Indiana, who had sent monetary gifts totaling $48.60 on one occasion and $40 on another. When he was slightly recovered, he preached again throughout Nebraska. When she was a little better, Mrs. Shockey accompanied him on two three-week trips through Harrison County, Iowa.

William Cook reported that the Lord had blessed the labors of Bro. Shockey for he had baptized five women in Mr. Cook's family. William Cook was sure there were others waiting for Bro. Shockey to baptize them as well.

Benjamin Wilson supported Shockey's position on baptism in 1868. Yet, his nephew Thomas Wilson, editor of *The Herald of the Coming Kingdom*, was not so charitable. In 1870 Shockey had submitted an article for the *Herald*. When Wilson did not publish it, Shockey wrote asking why. Wilson replied tersely, "Your view on the restoration of Israel is Adventist and conflicts with ours." As the developing Church of God narrowed its view on eschatology, separating itself from other Adventist groups during 1870 and beyond, Wilson spared no feelings in sorting truth from what he considered half-truth. For a related discussion, see the Nathaniel Field entry regarding his separation from the Chicago brethren.

See Field, Nathaniel
Wilson, Benjamin
Wilson, Thomas

Bibliography: Ancestry.com. U.S. Census. Indiana. Wabash. Noble. 1850. Cook. William. Correspondence, *The Gospel Banner and Millennial Advocate*, Benjamin Wilson, ed., June 15, 1868; *The Restitution*, Sept. 3, 1920; Shockey, W.P., "Report to Chicago Conference," *The Gospel Banner and Millennial Advocate*, Jan 15, 1868; "Letter to Editor" *The Gospel Banner and Millennial Advocate*, Vol. 13, April 1, 1867; Correspondence and Reports, March 1, 1868; May 1, 1868; Oct. 1, 1868; Shockey, W.P., "Bible Instruction and Analysis No. 1," *The Gospel Banner and Millennial Advocate*, Dec. 15, 1868; "Letter of Gratitude, *The Gospel Banner and Millennial Advocate*, April 15, 1869; "From Bro. Shockey," *The Gospel Banner and Millennial Advocate* June 1, 1869; Shockey, W.P., "Letter," *The Millennial Harbinger and Bible Expositor*, June 24, 1863; Wilson, Thomas, "Response to W.P. Shockey," Dec. 1870.

Shourds, Jessie N.
b. September, 1836
d. 1920?

In 1900, Jessie N. Shourds was co-organizer of a new Church of God in Cleveland, the Church of the Blessed Hope. Many years later it became the Golden Rule Church of God. In 1888 the constitution and by-laws of the newly formed General Conference at Philadelphia stated that when churches organized they should take the name Church of the Blessed Hope, or Church of God in Christ Jesus. Both names were popular among Abrahamic Faith churches during the 19th and early 20th centuries.

After the new church at Cleveland was organized, Robert McLauchlan provided a trust fund, and J.N. Shourds preached for all the regular worship services. In the early days, most services were held in Shourd's home at 45 Outhwaite Avenue. In 1903, the small congregation decided to rent a hall in the Pythian Temple building on

Huron Road and E. 9th Street. Jessie Shourds, an attorney by profession, served as pastor there until 1906 when L.E. Conner came to carry on the work. Conner was also trained in law. Research revealed Jessie Shourds had his own law firm at 511 New England.

Jessie and his wife, Harriett L., divided their time between Cleveland and Florida at the time he was church pastor. While they wintered in the south, someone else must have filled the pulpit, perhaps Robert McLauchlan or one of the elders. Sometime before 1910 Jesse and Harriett moved to San Diego, possibly for their health.

Because L.E. Conner shared a similar interest in the law, he fit well into that professional-level congregation. So far as can be determined, Conner never practiced law in Ohio after he became pastor at Blessed Hope.

See Conner, L.E.
McLauchlan, Robert
Robison, D.C.

Bibliography: Ancestry.com. U.S. Census. Florida. Alachua. Micanopy. Dist. 10. 1900; U.S. Census. California. San Diego Ward 7 Dist. 159. 1910; Hearp, Jack. Paper presented at the 2nd annual History Conference at North Hills Church of God, Springfield, Ohio, Nov.6-7, 2007 based on a paper "Summary of Historical Records from Golden Rule Church of God at Cleveland, Ohio, reported by Dorothy Robertson, (1976) and Martha Hobbs (1998)"; Cleveland City Directory 1900, page 1003, found at www.http://distantcousin.com/Directories/OH/Cleveland/1900/Pages.asp?Pages=1003; *Church of God General Conference Minute Book Ledger of the Board of Directors*, Philadelphia Conference 1888 and Chicago Conference 1889 through 1892, owned by Atlanta Bible College Archives, McDonough, GA.

Early conferences included meetings and discussions, the camaraderie of camping and outdoor activities. Here the Woodwards pose in front of a typical tent.

Simonds, Joel A.
b. July 24, 1812
d. December 21, 1892

Joel Simonds was born in Pawlet, Vermont. He wed Emily Toby there in 1838. They had three children; one died at birth. They moved to New York where he farmed until he was around 30. Emily died in 1851. Simonds married Widow Harriet Garfield on June 9, 1852. They had three children, and again, one died at birth. During winter when a farmer's work was greatly diminished, Joel taught school. He had a scholarly mind and was especially apt at mathematics. He had built a good library before age 21. Simonds was an avid advocate of abolition and temperance.

He began Bible study and joined the Baptist church. Many thought he should preach but he did not feel that he had been called to it. When Joel heard about conditional immortality as it was being preached by George Storrs in 1848, he found it in the Bible and studied it. It revolutionized his Bible views, and he took up preaching. His message was "Behold the bridegroom cometh." He preached life in Christ through his coming and resurrection of believers.

Simonds is often associated with the Age-to-Come work in Michigan and Indiana. He moved to Grand Rapids in 1854, putting him in the proximity of Michigan, Indiana, Illinois, Ohio and Wisconsin. He continued to study the Bible and came to realize that the Gospel of the Kingdom uncovered the hidden truths of the Bible that had been covered by a "fog of mysticism." His letters and articles may be seen frequently in the pages of *The Gospel Banner* and later *The Herald of the Kingdom*. In one article, Simonds called for the brethren of One Faith to meet the challenge to study and work.

As the Michigan Conference was becoming organized in 1858, Joel Simonds was elected treasurer of the first conference board. This board wrote the first constitution and by-laws that are found in the minute book. At this same October conference, Ephraim Miller and A.N. Seymour were appointed to be state evangelists.

In the late 1860s the question of Anglo-Israelism was debated among the brethren. The literature offered little exposure to the topic, but people talked about it. This question arose from the works of Jonathan Wilson of England who wrote *Our Israelitish Origins*. This book, written around 1840, was advertised in the pages of Joseph Marsh and Benjamin Wilson's publications and was still being discussed 20 years later. In fact, some sources note that F.L. Austin, also from Michigan, was fascinated by the topic nearly his whole life. He is credited for giving impetus to the movement in America even yet today although, except for one vague phone call, Austin's leadership on the subject has not been documented.

Another issue hotly debated in *The Herald* at the time was that of mortal emergence. The Christadelphians advanced the spurious idea that the righteous would be raised mortal as Christ had been; the Church of God disregarded that teaching. Simonds, however, believed in limited resurrection. He defended that position in a letter to Thomas Wilson through the pages of *The Herald*, offering the arguments for a righteous-only resurrection in 1870. Thomas Wilson refuted the arguments, and concluded, "There is no difference in the death of the righteous or the wicked, but there is a big difference in their future."

The time and nature of general resurrection was a third issue discussed or debated. The Church of God adhered to general, i.e., "universal resurrection," meaning the just would be raised at Christ's coming and changed, and the unjust would be raised to receive judgment after the thousand years ended (Rev. 20:5), while the Christadelphians said the righteous and the carnal would be raised for reward or judgment at the coming of Christ. Those who believed the latter also tended to believe in mortal emergence.

The resurrection argument within the Church of God divided the Wilson family. Thomas Wilson said the first resurrection was a process encompassing the whole of the Age to Come. The righteous would be raised and rewarded when Christ comes again, while the wicked would be raised at the end of the thousand years after the consignment of Satan to the Lake of Fire. Benjamin said the Greek did not support that and believed all the righteous, including the carnal, would be raised and judged when Christ returned. Benjamin believed the wicked would never be resurrected, and the two classes of people included in the general resurrection would be the righteous and the carnal backsliders, i.e., the sheep and the goats.

The Gospel Banner and *The Herald* frequently included such arguments or discussions. Men such as Joel Simonds wrote letters asking questions or stating an objection. This would generate another comment or article from the editors, and in this manner the Church of God theologians of the 19th century learned and discussed important Bible truths.

This same function continues today in two ways: l. The Theological conference which meets annually sponsored by Restoration Fellowship and Atlanta Bible College; and 2. The Church of God Pastors list (Cogpastors@googlegroups.com), an online e-mail list to proliferate discussion of theological and pastoral topics. Theologians in any denomination need a medium by which they can dissect topics of Bible, theology, ethics and prophecy, and rebuild them. This has been the way scholars and clergy shared during the past centuries of church history, although not always so civil as the discussion groups have been. Internet resources and programs add a new dimension for the 21st century. The Theological conference has been running annually since 1990. The Cogpastors has been running daily since 1998.

Joel and Harriett Simond's second son, Ossian Cole Simonds, lived in Chicago and was Superintendent of Graceland Cemetery. In 1880, Joel and Harriett moved to Chicago to be near their son.

Elder Simonds served faithfully in the Michigan conference until, finally, this notice appeared in the minutes: "The president read a communication from Bro. Joel Simonds of Chicago formerly of this conference. A vote of thanks was extended to Bro. S. for the same." The faithful warrior was slowing down and could no longer attend conference. Joel and Harriett are interred at Oak Hill in Grand Rapids, Michigan.

See Marsh, Joseph
    Miller, Ephraim
    Seymour, Alva N.
    Wilson, Benjamin

Bibliography: "Letter by Simonds to T. Wilson," *The Herald of the Kingdom and Christian Instructor*, Jan. 1, 1868 and "Objection to Resurrection of Wicked," *The Herald of the Kingdom and Christian Instructor*, Nov. 1868 and Jan. 1870; "Comments by Moderator," *Cogmail*, March 7, 2006; *Michigan State Conference Records 1859-1886*, owned by Archives of Atlanta Bible College, McDonough, Ga.; Wilson, Benjamin. *Thy Kingdom Come*, John O. Woodruff, compiler and editor, Elizabeth, NJ, 1901; Simonds, Joel, Obituary, *The Restitution*, Jan. 25, 1893; "Genealogy of Joel A. Simonds," Source unknown. Retrieved from savingforestpark.org/wp-content/uploads/2010/08/Genealogy-of-Joel-A-Simonds.pdf, Jan. 17, 2011; Williams, Byron P. *Abstracts of Obituaries and Verbatim Marriage Announcements printed in The Restitution 1873-1900*, self-published, 1993 p.45.

Skeels, Levi
    b. March 27, 1831
    d. June 14, 1893

Levi Skeels was born in Franklin County, Ohio, to Harvey (1796-1867) and Huldah May Vining Skeels (1804-1869) who had nine children, eight sons and one daughter. Levi married Ann H. Martin on July 7, 1852. They had four daughters and one son, Benjamin F.

In 1869, Levi entered the ministry and promised that he would always preach the Gospel of the Kingdom. To finance his evangelistic travels, he sold the family farm in Mansfield, Ohio. He then built a mobile home on wheels and took the family on the road. In those days, such a vehicle was horse-drawn. This was probably not a recreational vehicle but a residence to support his trade as a "tinker." A tinker traveled from town to town, home to home, repairing a housewife's or farmer's tin goods that may have rusted through. The technique was to place a circular piece of flat tin against the pot on the outside of a rusted hole, and another on the inside, and meld them together probably by heat.

It is surmised that Levi was a tinker because he is known to have been skilled in working tin. The fact that he fabricated a mobile home proves his skill. In fact, he invented Tinner's Shears for which he registered and received a US Patent in December 1856. These shears were especially designed to cut circles too large to be stamped by machine. The manufacture and sale of this product may have helped finance his ministry.

On April 3, 1869, he and the family began their travels through Indiana, Ohio and Illinois. In July 1876, they traveled south to the Ohio River and crossed into Kentucky in September. Along the way Levi stopped to preach in schoolhouses, groves, parks, wherever he could. His family provided music for the services.

Levi's journeys took him near Perryville, Kentucky. Perryville is just a few miles north of where the old Mackville battle was fought on October 8, 1862. Levi settled at Dixville where he bought another farm. At first, people would gather at his house. He would stand on the porch and preach by kerosene light to a congregation seated or standing in the yard. They used the pond on the Skeels-Bradley farm for baptisms. Many people were immersed there. The area quickly became a stopping point for other Age-to-Come evangelists including J.F. Wagoner, W.H. Wilson, J.H. Anderson and many more.

As the crowds grew larger it became evident that they needed a meeting place. In 1915, the Skeels' heirs deeded a half acre of land for a church. The first church was a small frame building that was difficult to heat in the winter. Later, the congregation built a 30' x 40' brick building to serve the needs of their growth.

When Levi faced death, he said the greatest tribute that could be paid to his life were the words, "He died in the Lord."

    See Anderson, J. H.
        Skeels, W. L.
        Wagoner, J. F.
        Wilson, W. H.

Bibliography: Ancestry.com. U.S. Census. Ohio. Union. Leesburg. 1850; Ancestry.com. Kentucky. Mercer. Dixville. Dist. 131. 1880; Ancestry.com. "Tinner's Shears", U.S. Patent and Trademark Office Patents 1790-1909 Patent No. 16,290, Dec. 23, 1856; Long, Elsie Bradley, "Perryville, Kentucky Church of God" no date; Weyrauch, Rosalie, Carpentar; Edited version of Elsie Long's history. Cline, Lois, Interview with Jan Stilson, July 2009.

Skeels, William Levi
b. June 1844
d. February 12, 1912

William Skeels was the son of Simeon and Anna Skeels. He may have been related to Levi Skeels, but a connection has not been proven. William wed Maggie Phipps Skeels on February 22, 1866. The couple moved from Worthington, Ohio, to Hendersonville, Kentucky. They had one son and three daughters.

Elder Skeels was a faithful Church of God preacher throughout the South, across Kentucky, Kansas, and up and down the West Coast. His first name is seldom used in the literature which at first made it difficult to identify him. He evidently was so well known by everyone of his day that it was not necessary to use his full name. He is usually referred to as W.L. Skeels. His full name was revealed through the letters of his trip to San Francisco in the spring of 1906.

By his own account Skeels learned the "preachin' trade" from Elder Jeremiah Hatch, a colleague from Indiana. They spent 1863 studying together until Skeels was able to launch out on his own. Three years later, Hatch also began to preach and became one of the greatest evangelists known to the Church of God.

Skeels, in turn, taught W.H. Earles about the Gospel. Over the years Skeels made numerous trips from his home in Perryville, Kentucky, to meet with the Earles family and others who cared to listen. In winter he preached in homes; in summer he preached in groves.

After Maggie's death (May 25, 1895), Skeels married again on August 15, 1896, to *Nancy (Nannie) M. Titchenal (b. January 1870) who had previously lived in Missouri. She was the daughter of David and Mary Moore Titchenal. William was 52, and she was 26. Richard Corbaley officiated the ceremony. A.L. and Annie Gard Corbaley were witnesses. They had one child, Aletha.

In 1904 Skeels preached in Felida, Washington, and while there he performed a funeral. He was the evangelist for the Washington conference during that year. Skeels summered in Washington or Oregon and wintered in Arizona where his older daughter lived. The history of the Lakeshore Church of God in Tempe lists him as pastor from 1900 until 1901. During this decade, he must have split his time between the Northwest and the Southwest. The 1905 Yearbook lists him as evangelist in the state of Oregon. He was pastor of the Scholls Ferry, Oregon, Church of God.

Skeels mother died in Ohio in 1906. Her obituary appeared in *The Restitution,* and it reveals that William settled her estate in the Midwest and returned to his family on the West coast.

The 1906 earthquake devastated San Francisco.

Skeels arrived in San Francisco just in time for the great earthquake of 1906, but he was unhurt. The story goes that he nearly fell into the gaping sinkhole that opened up in the earth just ahead of him. After the quake had passed, he found Thomas and Mrs. Wilson at their home at Oakland. They were quite shaken but unscathed by the catastrophe. Skeels was supposed to meet his daughter, Grace Tarrance, during this visit, but she had to leave the city before he was able to arrive. She had cancer and sought treatment up the coast. They met later.

In 1906, Skeels continued up the coast to Oregon and Washington and preached wherever he was received. In the winter he lived in Phoenix and in the summer he traveled "from just north of Mexico to just south of 'the Brit territories'" at Puget Sound, evangelizing everywhere he went. He did not own a home in Arizona for a notice appeared in *The Restitution* in 1907 that he was staying with Bro. J.M. Pike in Phoenix.

W.L. Skeels often preached at his own peril and usually at his own expense. He made one appointment at a schoolhouse. His intention was to preach on soul sleeping. People were not avidly interested in this, but a few showed up out of curiosity. Some who heard it complained, but others believed.

Nannie Skeels may have died, making Skeels a widower, for the record seems to indicate that he married again to a woman named Laura who divorced him. He returned to Phoenix where daughter Grace resided.

During the hubbub surrounding the Conner/Underwood accusations in 1910, many people wrote to support A.R. Underwood. W.L. Skeels sent a letter asking the brotherhood to seek self-purification. He said he stood by *The Restitution* and that he was still active in the work and available for Bible studies or preaching. Within one short month someone had accused him of believing in universal salvation. He denied this accusation vehemently in the pages of *The Restitution*.

In 1910, a notice appeared in *The Restitution* that Skeels had relocated to Maricopa County, Arizona, a fact confirmed by the US Census. He was 65 years old. In 1911, he reported baptizing Caleb Deming. Then Skeels and Deming organized a meeting with other new members of the Church of God in the Arlington, Arizona, area. Together, they helped Skeels organize a church. William Miller and Caleb Deming were elders with A. Anderson and William Perry as deacons. L. Anderson was appointed treasurer. This was the beginning of the formal work in Arizona. Skeels had toiled many years in that state to get the work to the point of a formal organization.

After he laid the groundwork in Arizona, other ministers came to stabilize it. When Skeels left the pastorate in Tempe, Elder Clinton Wilson filled the pulpit from 1917-1919; O.J. Allard from 1920-1921; J.W. Williams in 1921; S.J. Lindsay from 1928-1941; and L.E. Conner, 1941-1942. In addition to these early ministers Clarence Lapp, Gerald Cooper, C.E. Randall, Vernis Wolfe, Warren Sorenson, Hollis Partlowe, Kent Ross, Alva Huffer, Joseph Myers and Greg Demmitt have served at Tempe/Lakeshore.

It is thought that Skeels died while on an evangelistic trip to Oregon state. His burial location is unknown.

See Allard, O.J.
    Conner, L.E.
    Hatch, Jeremiah S.
    Lindsay, S.J.
    Underwood, A.R.
    Williams, J.W.

Bibliography: Ancestry.com. U.S. Census. Oregon. Washington. South Tualatin. Dist. 152. 1900; U.S. Census. Arizona. Maricopa Co. 1910; Oregon Death Index 1903-1998, Record for W.L. Skeels; Washington Death Index 1940-1996, record Nannie M. Skiles (Skeels) d. Sept. 29, 1949; Cline, Lois, Interview with Jan Stilson. Lois has family roots at Perryville, Ky. through her father Ben Carpentar. She was able to give details of Skeels in Kentucky, July 15, 2009; *The Restitution* August 3, 1904; Nov. 22, 1904; May 2, 1906; "Obituary of Anna Skeels," *The Restitution*, Dec. 5, 1906; Jan. 1, 1911; Feb. 2, 1911; March 5, 1911; Sept. 16, 1913; David, Graham. "Letter from Mrs. Weyrauch," E-mail to author. March 24, 2006; Rankin, Arlen, E-mail with vital data regarding W.L. Skeels to author, Feb. 10, 2007. "Skeels," *The Restitution Herald*, Jan. 18, 1949; *Regarding the date of Skeel's marriage to Nannie, Arlen Rankin cites a wedding date of June 1897 in a paper, "The Influence of Old Union in Indiana," for the History Conference of November 2006; Skeels, W.L. "Obituary and Eulogy of Mattie Skeels," *The Restitution*. June 19, 1895.

Smith, Elias
b. June 19, 1769
d. June 29, 1846

Elias Smith was born in Lyme, Connecticut. His family relocated to Woodstock, Vermont, while Elias was still a boy. When Elias was about 20 he became a member of the Baptist church in Woodstock and began to preach for them. The Calvinist Baptists ordained him to preach as an evangelist when he was only 23 years old.

He tired of denominational affiliation for he withdrew from that fellowship within 12 years. This occurred in 1804. The previous year he had met Abner Jones, and the two became friends in the faith deciding to work together teaching and preaching the cause of Christian Liberty.

Elias published extensively on religious subjects of faith and prophecy. He published *Twenty-Two Sermons on Prophecy* in 1808 which discussed the Age to Come, meaning the millennial age. He also wrote tracts, a New Testament dictionary and more.

Many forefathers of the Abrahamic Faith such as Joseph Marsh, Owen R.L. Crozier, J.B. Cook and E.R. Pinney were doubtlessly acquainted with the contributions of Elias Smith through his doctrinal writings and songbooks, and his attendance and preaching at Christian Connexion conferences. Such conferences were an important part of the movement he began, and they set the model for organization within the Age-to-Come movement under Joseph Marsh decades later. In fact, of interesting note is that when Joseph Marsh published his book, *The Age to Come,* in 1851, it was a mere five years after the death of his friend and mentor, Elias Smith.

As co-founders of the Christians in New England, Smith and Jones were two of its most prominent representatives during the American Restoration Period. Tom Olbricht wrote that the Christian Connexion was a "feeder" movement in New England to the Restoration Movement. One can also say it was a feeder movement to the Age-to-Come movement introduced by Elias Smith and Joseph Marsh, and therefore to the Church of God.

Smith was a prolific writer and a brilliant preacher who focused his spiritual energy and intellectual ability towards his Christian audience. According to David Graham, Age-to-Come Adventism, one of several unpopular beliefs at the time, was Smith's most cherished belief. He wrote and preached profusely to defend it. Graham wrote, "This is how the message of the Gospel of the Kingdom found its way into America."

Smith knew from experience the bitterness of doctrinal and political dissent. He knew the issues of dissent that could lead to conflict. One small issue for example, was the correct, biblical name of the church. "Chrīst-yans" indicated that those members were followers of Christ. From 1801 until 1816 he and Abner Jones formed several congregations known as "Chrīst-yans," "Christ" pronounced with a long "i." But Smith thought the name should be "Church of God" because it was the scriptural name for the church. So, both names are seen frequently in the Christian Connexion's literature, apparently being synonymous. An interesting feature of the Chrīst-yans was their cherished belief in unitarianism, that is, the oneness of God. This was opposite the accepted teaching of trinity by orthodox denominations, but unitarianism had a biblical basis.

One example of extreme action is seen in the Dartmouth Baptist Church which boasted 600 members from the Groton Conference. Having heard Smith preach of the corruptions and absurdities of the Baptist Sect during a Sunday morning service, the entire church went over *en masse* to the Smith and Jones Church of God movement. Such a drastic change received notice.

Within that period, Smith published more than 60 books, pamphlets and songbooks, including a religious periodical *Herald of the Gospel Liberty*. In fact, in 1808 the *Herald* was the first religious newspaper journal ever to appear in print in America. All its articles dealt with the premillennial advent of Christ, his millennial reign on earth, political and religious freedom, religious curiosities and doctrines, and personal struggles in promoting a spiritual movement. To emphasize this subject, Smith wrote *The Whole World Governed by a Jew; or the Government of the Second Adam, as King and Priest* delivered from a pulpit on the eve of the presidential inauguration on March 4, 1805.

Smith wrote in an issue of volume seven that his *Herald* had been received in nearly every state of the Union, numbering 18 in 1815, for the previous seven years. The presence of *The Herald of Gospel Liberty* in so many states, including territories on the frontier, explains why households were prepared to accept Adventism, and the Age-to-Come ideas of Joseph Marsh.

In between studies and writings, Smith made preaching tours throughout New England and the coastal states including Georgia and the Carolinas in the South, and Virginia, Pennsylvania and New York in the Mid-Atlantic States.

While in Virginia, Smith influenced the heart of a young Joseph Thomas, known as the White Pilgrim. At 16, Thomas felt the call to accept Jesus as his Lord at a country preaching service and to preach the Gospel throughout Virginia. Thomas began to preach in 1808 at the very height of the Second Great Awakening fervor across the southland, the same year that Elias Smith launched *Herald of the Gospel Liberty*. Thomas was contemporary with Elias Smith in preaching a unique doctrine before the onset of the Adventist movement in

New England spawned by William Miller.

Smith withdrew from publishing *The Herald* with the December 1815 issue and challenged someone else to pick up editorial duties. When no one came forward, Smith's list went to *The Christian Palladium*. In the last *Herald* issue, he published the things dearest to his heart which he preached and published. They are quoted here:

- One God
- One Mediator
- One Lawgiver
- One perfect Law of Liberty
- One name for the Children of God, to the seclusion of sectarian names
- A Republican government, free from religious establishments and state clergy
- Free Inquiry
- Life and immortality brought to light through the Gospel (conditional immortality)
- The reign of Christ on earth one thousand years (Age to Come)
- The new heavens and earth at last
- The utter destruction of all who at the last day are found enemies of Christ.

Smith concluded:

All these are precious to me at the present time and are truly worth contending for, and striving to obtain with eternal life. May the Lord enable us to shine as lights in the world, and prepare us to meet in that world to come, which is without end. Amen.

By 1816 Smith was instrumental in bringing more than 50 converted clergymen from other denominations scattered across the new democracy into the Chrı́st-yan movement. Some of these important converts sold all of their worldly possessions and moved out West with the tide of emigration to the frontier; some of these missionaries were well educated. All of them knew the Bible. These particular converts knew and realized that beyond the Allegheny Mountains lived American pioneers whose families had no church wherein to worship.

From the desire to assist these families came circuit riders such as Jeremiah S. Hatch, Ephraim Miller Jr., N.A. Hitchcock, Alva N. Seymour, E. Hoyt, Stedman A. Chaplin and John Walworth, who rushed to preach the Age to Come. These men were "Smith-ites." The Gospel of the Kingdom was being planted everywhere by the influence of Elias Smith prior to 1845 when Joseph Marsh continued the development of that prophecy movement across America.

Smith was reported to have been a Universalist from 1816 to 1823, however, after teaching this doctrine, he concluded that he should search the scriptures for truth. In 1846 Jaspar Hazen, editor of *The Christian Palladium*, said, "Elder Smith openly embraced and published the doctrine of Universalism. After preaching the doctrine for a time, he again renounced it, finessed, and desired to be restored again to the confidence of his brethren."

Smith died in Lynn, Massachusetts, just a few months after the Bitter Disappointment of William Miller's collapsed Adventist movement.

David Graham contributed to this entry.

See Chaplin, Stedman A.
Cook, J.B.
Crozier, O.R.L.
Hatch, Jeremiah S.
Hitchcock, N.A.
Hoyt, E.
Jones, Abner
Marsh, Joseph
Miller, Ephraim
Thomas, Joseph

Bibliography: Graham, David. "The Age to Come Influence of Elias Smith," *Church of God General Conference History Newsletter*, J. Stilson, ed., Oregon, Il. Summer 1984; Hazen, Jaspar, ed., "Elder Elias Smith," *The Christian Palladium* June 3, 1846; Morrill, Milo True, *A history of the Christian denomination in America, 1794-1911*, Christian Publishing Assoc. Dayton, 1912, pp. 329-335 retr'vd googlebooks.com; Olbricht, Thomas. "Christian Connexion and Unitarian Relations 1800-1844," *Restoration Quarterly*, 1966, retrieved from the website: acu.edu/sponsored/restoration_quarterly/archives/1960s/vol_9_no_3_contents/olbricht.html; Thomas, Joseph. *The Life of the Pilgrim*, 1817. This work was excerpted by Sydney Magaw for the Sept. 17, 1946 issue of *The Restitution Herald*; "Summary of Life of Elias Smith," *The Restitution*, Dec. 9, 1908; Smith, Elias, Address. *The Herald of the Gospel Liberty*, Portsmouth, Me., December 22, 1815; Smith, Elias, "Introduction," *Twenty-Two Sermons*, Portsmouth, Feb. 8, 1808.

Smith, Thomas
b. 1868?
d. Unknown

Thomas Smith lived at Colo, Iowa, and labored for the work of the Kingdom with R.J. Hill, the Iowa evangelist, as an elder in 1865. Little beyond this is known about Smith. In those days, elders assumed both preacher and pastor duties in the absence of the evangelist. They baptized, performed weddings and conducted church-member funerals. Elder Thomas Smith is included among the Midwest ministers. The label for the archival picture of the ministers at Indiana conference prior to 1906 indicates Thomas Smith is on the left end, front.

The picture below has been dated before 1906 because A.H. Zilmer is among them (second from left back row)—Zilmer left the Church of God in 1906 due to disagreement with doctrinal and organizational issues. Zilmer and Smith seem to be among the younger preachers. Also in the photo are: F.L. Austin, front center,

standing next to his first wife, Mary Austin before illness overtook her. Others in the photo include J.S Hatch next to Smith; J.H. Willey in front of Zilmer; A.R. Underwood far right, front; and R.S. Dwiggins, first President of the 1888 General Conference, far right, back row. To the left of F.L. Austin, front middle, stands David Van Vactor of Indiana with his Bible tucked under his arm. The gentleman standing between Van Vactor and Underwood is O.J. Allard from Iowa, always identifiable by his mustache.

    See Allard, O.J.
        Austin, F.L.
        Dwiggins, R.S.
        Hatch, J.S.
        Hill, R.J.
        Underwood, A.R.
        Van Vactor, David
        Willey, J.H.
        Zilmer, A.H.

Bibliography: Ferrell, Terry. "A Brief History of the Church of God in America," National Berean Youth Conference, Camp Reynoldswood, Illinois. Aug. 21-17, 1960; Photo from Archives of Atlanta Bible College, Cornerstone Church of God, McDonough, GA.

Smith, W.C.
    b. 1810?
    d. Unknown

W.C. Smith began serving the Lord as a preacher at the old Christian church in Indiana; he also preached for the Disciples. Smith "preached the Bethany gospel," but having heard about the Age to Come he, like Apollos, accepted it and was immediately immersed, probably by J.K. Speer. Speer met with Bro. Smith in Kansas where he worked with F.E. Henderson and several others in a group near Olathe. Speer endorsed Smith by saying "His standing is above reproach; but his old friends will of course hunt him out, if possible," ostensibly to persuade him to come back.

    See Speer, J.K.

Bibliography: Speer, J.K. "Taking out a People for His Name in Kansas," *The Gospel Banner and Millennial Advocate*, Benjamin Wilson, ed., Jan. 15, 1868.

Snowden, Dr. James H.
    b. 1846
    d. Unknown

Dr. James Snowden lived at Center Ridge, Arkansas. He was a medical doctor who also preached. He wed Nannie J., who was nine years his junior. They had one son. W.H. Wilson said of Snowden, "He was an able Minister of the gospel and a zealous defender of the faith." Snowden did not compromise with the Adventists or the Campbellites, which he demonstrated through many debates. He was a former Disciples of Christ minister. Little is known about this dedicated brother.

    See Wilson, W.H.

Bibliography: Ancestry.com U.S. Census. Arkansas. Conway. Center Ridge. Dist. 8 1900; Report of Wilson, *The Restitution,* Jan. 20, 1904.

Sowell, W.J.
    b. 1881
    d. Unknown

W.J. Sowell lived at Beebe, Arkansas. W.H. Wilson noted him as an Arkansas minister in a report to *The Restitution's* readers. Sowell may have been born in Alabama, but he lived in Arkansas when he began his ministry. Nothing more is known of him.

Bibliography: Ancestry.com U.S. Census Report. Alabama. Conecuh. Jamestown. Dist. 51. 1900. Report of Wilson, *The Restitution* Jan. 20, 1904

Speer, J.K.
    b. 1810?
    d. Unknown

J.K. Speer was from Sweetwater, Illinois. He heard of the Gospel of the Kingdom from One Faith preachers and came into the conference movement at the meeting of the Northern Illinois and Southern Wisconsin Christians held at Daysville in September 1867. Speer was welcomed with open arms and preached on the subject of the "Kingdom of God" at that meeting. When he realized he had not understood the Gospel at the time of his immersion, Speer was re-baptized.

Benjamin Wilson did not fully appreciate the ministry of J.K. Speer, for in 1866 Speer had been working with Nathaniel Field in Jeffersonville, Indiana. Wilson wrote, "Instead of going to Jeffersonville to care for the church of God and build it up, he has led unsuspecting men over to Dr. Field's faction." It seems Speer did not take offense, or perhaps he had not read that issue of *The Banner* yet when he wrote in the February 1 issue that he had debated Mr. Linn of the Reformers. Linn had slandered Benjamin Wilson by stating he had mistakenly translated Matthew 10:28, "Be not afraid of those who kill the body, but cannot destroy the [future] life; but rather fear Him who can utterly destroy both Life and Body in Gehenna" (*Emphatic Diaglott*). The accusation allegedly came from men who believed in natural immortality; they felt Wilson had added the word "future" to the English translation. The Greek, however, was translated word for word.

Once Speer turned his attention away from Dr. Field in Jeffersonville, the light of Benjamin Wilson shone upon him. Wilson said that Speer was doing excellent work in Sweetwater, Illinois. Speer had been preaching in a Campbellite church and had drawn 40 members into the teaching of the Gospel of the Kingdom, causing church elders to rule that Speer could no longer preach there. Then, they elicited the help of the aforementioned Mr. Linn who came from Ohio to debate J.K. Speer for four days. Linn failed to make his scriptural points.

Speer wrote a statement of faith, "We are all agreed," for *The Gospel Banner;* it included 21 points of doctrine. Among them was a statement which indicated Jesus was a man, anointed to reign on David's throne. Speer also said the congregation agreed that man would be raised mortal, changed instantly if righteous or returned instantly to death if unjust. Those three doctrines were not accepted by the majority of Church of God biblical students.

J.K. Speer preached the Word in Kansas and was surprised to find ten people at Olathe, Kansas, who had studied God's Word and believed in mortality of man, that resurrection must take place before immortality is granted, and that God is to establish His Kingdom upon the Earth. Speer said, "They had the word of the Kingdom as well as the kingdom of God in their hearts."

He spoke of F.E. Henderson, W.S. Speer, W.C. Smith and J.R. Kennedy who believed these things and fellowshipped together. The first three men had been preachers with the Campbellite organization for several years and highly respected among its members. Some continued to preach among the Campbellites but now preached about the Kingdom of God. All had been immersed into the new truths they had discovered and ceased preaching about the Reformation or Restoration.

Speer authored *The Great Reconstruction Question Settled: An Exposition of the Kingdom of David Under Jesus.* Benjamin Wilson published this booklet at the *Gospel Banner* office in Geneva, Illinois, in 1866.

Literature indicates Speer became a bit hostile over nuances of doctrine regarding the Age to Come. He eventually left the Church of God to fellowship exclusively with the Christadelphians.

See Kennedy, J.R.
Smith, W.C.
Stephenson, J.M.
Wilson, Benjamin

Bibliography: "Conference Report," *The Prophetic Watchman and Herald of the Kingdom,* J.M. Stephenson, ed., Harvard, Il., Oct. 19, 1867; Speer, J.K. *The Great Reconstruction Question Settled,* Gospel Banner Office, Geneva, Il., 1866. This booklet is bound with *The Millenarian,* H.V. Reed, ed., Chicago, Il., 1874, in the Atlanta Bible College Archives; Speer, J.K. "We are all Agreed," *The Gospel Banner,* Vol. 13, B. Wilson, ed., Geneva, Il., Dec. 1, 1867; Author Unknown, "Elder Benjamin Franklin," *The Gospel Banner,* vol. 13, B. Wilson, ed., Geneva, Il., Jan. 1, 1867. This article discusses J. K. Speer, and a few pages are unreadable; Speer, J.K. "Taking out a People for His Name in Kansas," The *Gospel Banner and Millennial Advocate.* Benjamin Wilson, ed., 14:2 Jan. 15, 1868; Speer, J.K. "The Reformers have gone over to Rome and Egypt," *The Gospel Banner,* Vol. 13, B. Wilson, ed., Geneva, Il., Feb. 1, 1867, p. 48; Wilson, Benjamin. "The Gospel at Sweetwater, Il.," *The Gospel Banner,* B. Wilson, ed., June 1, 1867.

Spencer, D.M.
b. 1893?
d. Unknown

D.M. Spencer was an evangelist who served in Iowa and surrounding states. During the 1918 flu epidemic he ceased his ministry temporarily due to the public health order closing public meetings. He returned home by rail after an absence of 26 days. In Des Moines he saw 25 deceased soldiers stacked on the railroad platform awaiting shipment home. They had died from the flu.

When things quieted down, Spencer received train fare and an invitation to return to the preaching circuit. He traveled to Brooklyn Ridge and Pleasanton, Kansas, to preach to families there.

Bibliography: *The Restitution Herald,* Nov. 6, 1918.

Stephenson, James M.
b. March 5, 1822
d. June 1, 1888

A. **The Studied Path**
B. **Beginning a New Era**
C. **Return of the Jewish Nation**
D. **J.M. Stephenson, a Leader in One Faith**
E. **Criticism**
F. **Ripley, Illinois, Church of God**

J.M. Stephenson was born in Jennings County, Indiana, near Madison to Lawson Stephenson and wife. James had six brothers. His parents died when he was 15, and he was placed in the care of Thomas and Lewis Hicklin, his uncles. They were Methodist ministers and ardent abolitionists.

The Hicklin brothers participated in the Underground Railroad, concealing slaves on their journey from the South into Canada to freedom. Young J.M. Stephenson escorted several groups of refugees into the northlands. When he was 18, the Lawrenceburg Academy (Danville, Kentucky) invited him to give an oration. Through this experience James realized he enjoyed public speaking. It was a turning point in his life even though the audience did not like his spirited anti-slavery comments, and battered him with rotten eggs and the like. James became an abolitionist spokesperson for the Methodists and was soon made president of their conference.

JM Stephenson

When James learned about Adventism he accepted it and began preaching it. The church fathers did not approve of that doctrine. He left that fellowship in 1845, and fellowshipped with D.P. Hall. Hall advocated the Age-to-Come doctrine of prophecy but also dabbled in Sabbatarianism.

The first written record of J.M. Stephenson in Church of God material is found in Joseph Marsh's *Advent Harbinger and Bible Advocate* in June 1850. A report appeared there stating James attended a Bible conference at Rochester, New York. Within a year D.P. Hall wrote to Marsh about 14 souls who were baptized into Christ, including himself and Stephenson. This was published in the April 1851 issue of *The Advent Harbinger*.

David Hall further stated that James Stephenson became disaffected with his Wesleyan baptism, choosing to be re-baptized into the faith of the Gospel. "To use his own language he wished to wash away the stains of the mother of harlots." That comment may seem offensive to readers, but keep in mind, in the 19th century "Come out from Babylon!" was a common cry of the Adventist movement indicating repudiation of orthodoxy in order to embrace the Second Advent teaching.

Hall and Stephenson were then chosen as evangelists. Elders Moses Chandler and Yate Higgins laid hands upon them to ordain them to the ministry.

Following this baptism, Yate Higgins moved his family to Wisconsin, a new territory that needed preachers. J.M. Stephenson also moved to Wisconsin and worked throughout that state, Illinois and Indiana. During that period, Stephenson considered the Sabbath issue. For a time, he went in the direction of the Seventh-day worship but left that movement in 1855. This so aggravated Ellen White, the prophetess of the movement, that she predicted his "immediate destruction" in her *Testimony No. 1*, page 15. This was unfulfilled prophecy because for more than 30 years J.M. Stephenson continued to serve within the Age-to-Come/One Faith movement that eventually became the Church of God.

A. The Studied Path

J.M. Stephenson's journey into the Church of God took a roundabout course. After his baptism, he became convinced of the Sabbatarian view because of the fourth commandment, "Remember the Sabbath day to keep it holy" (Exodus 20:7). He felt that to observe that commandment was a moral law, and he believed the gospel was a law of faith. Stephenson was re-baptized three times; his first re-baptism was to accept Adventism, the second to repent because he had not been observing the fourth commandment, and the third to acknowledge his mistake in adopting the Sabbath. His account of this is detailed in the *Gospel Banner* on June 1, 1864. In an article for Thomas Wilson's *Herald of the Kingdom*, Stephenson wrote a lengthy piece refuting Sabbatarianism. He repudiated Sabbatarianism while he preached the Age to Come throughout the Midwestern frontier.

Julia Neuffer writing from a Seventh-day Adventist perspective states in her paper, "The Gathering of Israel," that Stephenson and D.P. Hall broke away from the Seventh-day Adventists and formed their own "party" called the Messenger Party. For the interest of the reader, the following quote comes from the paper written by Nickels for the Seventh-day Church of God. It is an interesting perspective:

> Associated with the Messenger Party were J.M. Stephenson and D.P. Hall, some of the first converts of Adventist preacher J.H. Waggoner in Wisconsin. Stephenson and Hall soon became prominent Adventist preachers in their own right. At a conference in Jackson, Michigan, in April 1855, they appeared to be against the Messenger Party and said they would go back to Wisconsin to overcome the Messenger Party's opposition to the Review. Yet later they came out for the "age-to-come" doctrine, that of believing in a probationary period after Christ's coming.
>
> At conferences in Eldorado and Koskonong, Wisconsin on October 5th and 12th, 1855, they denounced the Review as sectarian and resolved to withdraw support from it. Soon Stephenson and Hall began to write for the Messenger and associated themselves with the people they had said they would oppose. Yet in a few weeks, they gave up the Sabbath and opposed it, attempting to form an "age-to-come" party with themselves as its leaders.

There is much discussion among the Seventh-day scholars about Stephenson during this time, but it is outside the scope of this publication.

The Messenger Party is not mentioned anywhere in the writings of the Church of God, and evidence demonstrates that Stephenson continued to work with this group the rest of his Christian life, and indeed, he put himself on the front lines. He wrote for the papers; he traveled as evangelist; he worked in Canada in tent meetings with R.V. Lyon; and he served as example, pastor, and friend of many people and churches. It was reported in one local church history that Stephenson kept a diary or journal of his travels. To date, no one has seen a copy of it, and it is presumed lost.

Stephenson debated J.H. Waggoner on the question of the Sabbath at Crane's Grove, Illinois, in 1860. *J.H. Waggoner* was a Seventh-day Adventist and should not be confused with *J.F. Waggoner* from the Church of God. Both J.H. Waggoner and J.M. Stephenson had once believed in Sabbath-keeping. In fact, Nickels stated that Waggoner converted Stephenson to Sabbatarianism. In the debate, Waggoner took the "pro" position and Stephenson argued "con." That would certainly have been a dynamic debate since Stephenson knew all the "pro" arguments and could undoubtedly anticipate Elder Waggoner's next point!

In 1857, H.V. Reed wrote in *The Prophetic Expositor and Bible Advocate* that Stephenson had been editing *The Bible Investigator*, a Sabbatarian paper. Stephenson lived in Omro, Wisconsin, and had just renounced the Seventh-day doctrine. H.V. Reed was responsible for persuading him to reconsider that position based on their mutual study in the Scriptures. Stephenson recanted the position in December 1857, and ceased publication of *The Investigator.* He wrote "The Law and the Sabbath" for the *Expositor*.

Marsh honored Stephenson's subscribers with issues of *The Expositor*, an anti-Sabbatarian paper, beginning with the January 1, 1858, issue, and continuing until their subscriptions expired! This was a costly proposition for Marsh, and the first of the year he made a fund-raising trip across Canada to raise $2100 for expenses on *The Expositor and Advocate*.

During the Wisconsin years, J.M. Stephenson and his wife suffered the death of their son. Circumstances are not known, but H.V. Reed testified to their anguish. The death happened sometime in the winter or spring of 1860 while the family lived at Eureka, Wisconsin. Stephenson and his wife eventually lived separate lives.

B. Beginning a New Era

After Stephenson laid the doctrine of Sabbath-keeping to rest, a strong relationship between him and H.V. Reed began to develop. It would be appropriate to conclude that Reed mentored Stephenson, having brought him out of Sabbatarianism.

By 1865 the two men joined forces to edit *The Prophetic Watchman*. This was a beautiful magazine-sized paper. The masthead featured the publication's title in elegant script. The paper stock was rich and velvety to the touch. The content was deep but easy to read. However, the paper suffered the same dilemma that other religious papers of the day faced: too little money to pay printing bills.

The two editors differed on their approach to collecting the funds. Stephenson chose to face the situation and pay the bills himself instead of informing the people of their financial need. Eventually the unpaid bills accrued to $1000, which jeopardized the effort. In one issue, H.V. Reed stated that, since Stephenson was away, he would inform the people of the need. He said:

> It costs $35 per number to print the Watchman, and we must pay this amount out of our own pocket, or the printer must go unpaid. It occurs to us as a very strange state of affairs, that a people who are looking for the immediate coming of the Son of God, cannot afford to assist the paper which is edited for nothing, and all that is asked, is to keep it out of debt.

The paper operated out of funds received from purchase of books on hand. J.M. Stephenson reported in the next issue that Reed had purchased all the books, and that they had decided to form a stock company with pledges of $10 each. He solicited readers to send in pledges so that a board could be formed to manage the paper. He said all the live papers of the day were funded and managed in this manner.

In 1867 the paper's format increased to magazine size, and H.V. Reed no longer edited it. This does not infer that the two men could not get along, for they were dear friends. H.V. Reed was noted for stepping in to help stabilize a floundering paper. He had assisted Thomas Newman with *The Millennial Harbinger* in 1863, and he was a contributing editor to *The Restitution* in Plymouth, Indiana, in 1873-1874. When Reed stepped away from *The Prophetic Watchman* it was likely because he thought the paper could stand on its own. In fact, Newman's *Millennial Harbinger* had moved to Harvard in 1864, and with it came Marsh's press, so with that subscription list and equipment, the paper should have been in a strong position to thrive. But, it didn't. The paper was merged with *The Herald of the Coming Kingdom and Christian Instructor* in Chicago in 1868.

C. Return of the Jewish Nation

In an 1866 issue of *The Prophetic Watchman*, an interesting article appeared concerning the restoration of the Jewish nation. Under the headline "The Holy Land" was this description:

Organization of the International Society of the Orient—Project to re-establish the Jewish Nation in Palestine—Grants of Land to be Made by Turkey to the Society—Jewish Immigration to the Orient to be Encouraged.

This kind of information excited people who had, for

22 years, taught that the Jewish people would return to their homeland prior to Christ's return. This doctrine is a principle of the Age-to-Come prophecy system. One quote is worthy of mention:

> It is known that Palestine needs only labor in order to produce abundantly. It is one of the most remarkable and most fertile [nations] of the globe.

The Society was headquartered in Turkey, and wanted to see "the transformation of the ancient Jerusalem into a new city, which will rival in importance the finest cities of the World." Henry Dunant, founder of the International Convention, authored the project and article. This seemed to be the beginning of the clamor for Jewish restoration. The process would be painful and would take another 82 years, culminating in 1948 when Israel became a nation.

Church journals were often the topic of discussion at the quarterly and annual conference meetings of the Age-to-Come movement. One conference was reported in *The Watchman* of September 1867. The Northern Illinois and Southern Wisconsin Christian association met at Daysville, Illinois. Several baptisms were performed in the Kyte Creek which flows into the Rock River north of Daysville. There was a very good spirit at this meeting, which came from inspired preaching, teaching and election of officers. J.K. Speer of Sweetwater, Illinois, was welcomed into the fellowship and preached for the conference, as did Stephenson, Tompkins and Jacobs. C.W. Tompkins was appointed president; A.J. Eychaner, secretary; J. Tilton, J. Booth and S. Nohe became the committee to plan the next conference. This meeting's attendance was so large the rented hall became too small. Everyone found this encouraging. Teaching classes often took subjects published in the journals, in this case, restoration of Israel, as their topic of discussion.

D. J.M. Stephenson, a Leader in One Faith

J.M. Stephenson became well-known to the Wilsons in Geneva, and his letters and articles may be seen in *The Gospel Banner*, *The Herald of the Coming Kingdom*, and *The Restitution*. Stephenson continued to work throughout Illinois, Iowa, Indiana and Wisconsin to spread the Gospel message. He also lived in the state of Oregon from 1871-1874. Randall stated in *Waymarks* that Oregon's first Gospel seed was sown near Jefferson where Stephenson's cousin lived. Stephenson preached wherever he could, but found the people unreceptive. While in Oregon he began writing the manuscript of *God's Plan of Salvation*.

A.D. Eshelman, Canton, Ohio, published *God's Plan of Salvation, or, His Purpose Concerning Man and Earth*. Stephenson had baptized Eshelman's wife and daughter in Canton in 1860. While in Canton, he was invited to hold a series of meetings. Printed posters announcing the meeting were hung throughout the city, but someone removed the posters and burned them. This happened three days in a row. Stephenson held the meetings anyway, and three people were baptized, one for each day of persecution! This illustrates the kind of menace circuit preachers faced from the opposition.

Stephenson was a good writer, easy to read and to understand. C.E. Randall, noted Church of God historian said, "he was the most lucid writer the church ever produced." Randall also credited *God's Plan of Salvation* with totally rooting out the false doctrine of limited resurrection, which set the Church of God on a different course than the Christadelphians. That would mean that Stephenson, perhaps more than any other person, had great influence upon members who organized the Church of God General Conference in 1921. A copy of *God's Plan* is contained in the Archives of Atlanta Bible College, McDonough, Georgia.

In January 1868, Stephenson traveled to Waterloo, Iowa, and preached for a week. This trip was reported in *The Herald of the Coming Kingdom and Christian Instructor*, and it was said that Stephenson "preached the Word of the Kingdom acceptably." If there were any problem with his early Sabbatarian ideas, this was not considered a test of fellowship. Lots of men came into the Church of God from backgrounds of divergent doctrines.

During 1868, Stephenson also published a book, *The Herald of Messiah's Reign, or The Kingdom of Glad Tidings, or, the Kingdom of God*. The Archives of Atlanta Bible College, McDonough, Georgia, also holds a copy of this book.

At Dixon, Illinois, in 1869, Stephenson held a series of meetings with George Moyer of Geneva, Illinois. An advertisement was placed in the *Dixon Evening Telegraph*. In it the congregation is described as "congregation of believers" and "disciples of Christ." At that time, Church of God congregations in the Midwest were still following Benjamin Wilson's lead and calling themselves Brethren of One Faith or disciples of Christ (with a small "d" to prevent confusion with Alexander Campbell's Disciples). The use of the name Church of God, specific to Joseph Marsh, had not caught on with the Geneva Wilsons. In fact, if Alexander Campbell had not chosen the name Disciples to define his arm of the Restoration Movement, it is highly likely the Church of God would today be known as the Disciples.

What is interesting about the 1869 advertisement is the statement of faith that accompanied it. This is the earliest and most detailed statement of faith of any from that period found to date. (To compare 19th century statements of faith, see the entries herein for Benjamin Wilson, Ephraim Wilson and Robert Huggins.)

Stephenson's statement (see below) is missing only one component that would seem important today: a statement on the Holy Spirit. Up to this time, early leaders in the Age to Come/One Faith movement did not articulate the nature of God, Christ or the Holy Spirit in a statement of faith, so Stephenson's statement is elegant, concise and the most comprehensive of all statements in this volume.

Stephenson wrote:

> We, the disciples of Christ in Dixon, Illinois, in order to prevent any misinterpretation of our views, and to show that we are followers of no men who have lived since the days of Christ and his apostles, would set forth the following declaration of things believed by us:
> 1. There is one Supreme God, who is Infinite in all his attributes.
> 2. That Christ, the Savior, is His Son.
> 3. That man is wholly mortal, having no distinct spiritual or intelligent nature, apart from the material organization, formed out of the dust of the ground.
> 4. That all consciousness and intelligence cease with man's life; and that he is absolutely and exclusively dependent upon a resurrection from the dead, for all future life, intelligence and reward.
> 5. That such resurrection and rewards will take place when Christ shall return the second time, without sin unto salvation.
> 6. That eternal life will be bestowed upon the obedient alone, through the medium of a resurrection, if dead, or a change to immortality, if living, in a moment, when our Lord shall return to earth.
> 7. That all incorrigible sinners shall be punished with everlasting destruction.
> 8. That the advent of Christ will be premillennial, and that Christ and the saints will reign conjointly over the nations, which will be mortal, for one thousand years.
> 9. That the metropolis of the Kingdom will be located upon Mount Zion, in Palestine, from whence all laws shall radiate for the government of all nations of the earth.
> 10. That the Kingdom of God will be as literal a government as ever existed upon the face of the earth.
> 11. That through the instrumentality of this government, all the nations of the earth shall ultimately be blessed.
> 12. That the conditions on which any person may share the glory and honor of this kingdom, when established, together with incorruptibility and immortality, are faith in the Gospel of the Kingdom of God, repentance of all their sins and baptism in the name of Christ for the remission of all past sins, and subsequent obedience to all the commandments of God, as taught by Christ and his apostles.
> 13. We take the Bible as our only creed, make it its own interpreter, and are governed by the literal rule of interpretation in all matters pertaining to doctrine and practice.
> 14. We acknowledge no man, or men, as our leaders, except Christ and his inspired apostles.

This statement was reprinted in *The Herald of the Coming Kingdom and Christian Instructor* in Chicago in February 1869. Point 14 categorically denies not only Joseph Marsh as leader and founder of the Church of God, but Benjamin Wilson as well.

Stephenson was a prolific writer, and he was well-known throughout the entire Adventist world. He was bold and plain-spoken. For example, he entered into vigorous debate at the Old Union Church with the intention of dividing the congregation so the Christadelphians would leave. He was so vocal at the 1867 meeting of the Indiana Conference that he had to be shushed up several times by the officers. Here follows the account from "The Story of a Happy Christian" in *The Restitution*:

> This Conference was held at Old Union: Brother David T. Halstead was chosen as the Conference Chairman. As chairman, he had to calm down the spirited debate between J.K. Speer, Dr. Reeve and J.M. Stephenson several times. (The former were Christadelphians, trying to sway the Conference to their Philosophy.) Stephenson had to be called to order several times also due to conflicting issues arising between the three of them.

In the years that followed, this debate was further expanded by Stephenson, H.V. Reed and Richard Corbaley to oust the Advent Christians from Indiana Conference.

When Stephenson wrote, people read it and considered his ideas. He furnished copy for the *Millenarian* when H.V. Reed published it in Chicago, and for the *Evangelist* when G.M. Myers edited it in Lanark, Illinois, and Belle Plaine, Iowa.

J.M. Stephenson traveled to Miami County, Ohio, in 1870 to preach a series of sermons at the Brush Creek Church of God. Only a dozen people attended, six men and six women, but his preaching must have stirred

---

Doctrinal Statement

Atlanta Bible College Advocates:

- The oneness of God (1 Cor. 8:6)
- That the Holy Spirit is God's Power (Acts 1:8)
- Jesus Christ is God's only begotten Son. (Mt. 16:16), and is our Mediator (1 Tim. 2:5)
- The Bible is the inspired Word of God (2 Tim. 3:16)
- The mortality of man (Job 4:17; Psa. 146:4)
- The near return of Christ (Acts 1:11), and life only through Him (Col. 3:3)
- The literal resurrection of the dead (John 5:28, 29)
- The immortalization of those in Christ (1 Cor. 15:53, 54)
- The destruction of the wicked (Rev. 21:8)
- The final restoration of Israel as the Kingdom of God under the kingship of Christ (Rom.8:17), and Israel to be made head over Gentile nations (Isa. 60:13)
- The "restitution of all things which God hath spoken by the mouth of His holy prophets since the world began" (Acts 3:21)
- The repentance and immersion in the name of Jesus Christ for the remission of sins (Acts 2:38), and a consecrated life as essential to salvation (Heb. 12:14)

Source: abc-coggc.org. Copyright 2009. Used with permission.

interest, for on Sunday that week J.F. Wagoner preached to a full house, "the largest congregation that had ever been at the church before," according to the history of Brush Creek. Wagoner was related to the founder of Brush Creek, Rufus Curtis.

E. Criticism

John R. Fisk criticized Stephenson, stating in his pamphlet "Partial Resurrection an Antidote to Larger Hope," that Stephenson introduced the heresy of larger hope into the Church of God's theological discussion at that time. Fisk reported that in time C.T. Russell adopted this doctrine, showing again, there was dialogue between some Age-to-Come preachers and C.T. Russell. Larger hope taught that the wicked dead would be raised and given a second chance, i.e., probation, during the millennial kingdom of Christ. This teaching was contrary to probation taught by Age to Come which said the wicked *living* nations would enter the kingdom on probation. If Stephenson at one time believed in larger hope or universalism, it needs to be additionally documented; it is thought he may have considered it, and repudiated it.

In 1874, J.M. Stephenson led the congregation at Lanark. He informed *The Restitution* that he intended to spend some time preaching in Canada over the winter season. Before making that trip, however, he was keynote speaker at the Iowa Conference held in West Irving. During this conference he preached on the design of the Gospel "in this and in the ages to come." R.J. Hill was elected president of the Conference at this meeting.

Also, Stephenson was scheduled to attend the December 1874 conference of the Antioch Church of God (near Plymouth, Indiana). From there, he traveled to Buchanan, Michigan, and on to Canada by February 1, 1875.

J.H. Waggoner, the Seventh-day Adventist, wrote in *Refutation of the Age to Come* that Stephenson criticized Dr. John Thomas for teaching the New Jerusalem was not in heaven, but "is above only in the sense of being exalted which denotes the position it will occupy in the Age to Come. And, if this is so, when the New Jerusalem descends, it must indicate an abasement and deprivation." Waggoner said Stephenson's criticism of Thomas was not correct. This anecdote is cited by George N.H. Peters, author of *The Theocratic Kingdom*. Peters explained that New Jerusalem must be on earth because of the location of David's Throne, and the necessity of the nations needing to access it. Peters mistakenly identified Stephenson as I.M. Stephenson, possibly a printer's error.

F. Ripley, Illinois, Church of God

In 1880 Stephenson lived in Chicago, as shown by the US Census listing him as a boarder at the Jerome Turnkey home. By this time, Stephenson and his wife had certainly parted company. His occupation was given as "Minister," so it is thought he prepared the field in Chicago for the arrival of C.C. Ramsay, after which Stephenson moved south to Brown County, Illinois, in 1883, settling in Ripley to pastor the Church of God there until his death in 1888. Scanning the history books, newspapers and other resources from Brown County for Stephenson's name, one finds he performed marriages and officiated at funerals and baptisms until April 1888, just two months before his death. Yet, during that five-year period, he wrote no additional articles or books that are known of today.

Several possible reasons exist for this lapse in authorship. Perhaps his eyesight failed and the aging scholar could no longer see well enough to write. It seems his health may have been failing during his last year of life, because Uncle John Foore went to Ripley occasionally to preach in 1887.

One source from a sister denomination said Stephenson went crazy. No information about his mental health has been found in Church of God sources, but J.N. Loughborough, a Seventh-day Adventist historian, said Stephenson was of unsound mind, and divorced his virtuous wife to marry a younger woman. Because of this, together with being of unsound mind, Loughborogh said, his own people in the Age to Come would not allow him to preach. Yet, it can be proven that he preached at Ripley Church of God, and baptized five young women just weeks before his death. The last baptisms Stephenson performed for the Church of God are recorded in the Ripley church minutes. He is buried at Ripley. Stephenson must have been in good standing with the Church of God at the time of his death, for his writings were still being reprinted in *The Restitution* several years later.

In November 1888, the Church of God held a General Conference meeting in Philadelphia. J.M. Stephenson had been in favor of a national organization, and he believed that once the congregations agreed upon a statement of essential faith, it would be a fact. It is unfortunate he died before this meeting occurred.

J.M. Stephenson's grave is in the Ripley cemetery. The gravestone reads, "James M. Stephenson (1822-1888) He is Waiting for the King." On the stone is an engraving of gates that are opening, bidding one to enter. At first glance, one might think these are the pearly gates of heaven, yet Stephenson did not believe in heaven at death. Behind the gates in the engraving is the rising sun. The gates depict the *Eastern Gate* through which the Prince will enter Jerusalem when He comes again (Ezekiel 44:1-3).

A point of interest, possibly more to historians than to readers, is about J.W. Williams of Belle Plaine, Iowa, moving to Ripley to be the Church of God pastor in 1920. The minute book notes that Williams lived in the house where J.M. Stephenson had resided years before. This parallels Stephenson's actions in 1862 when he lived in Buchanan, Michigan, an early center of Church of God activities. He sold his home to J.V. Himes, the great coordinator of William Miller's Adventist movement.

See Hall, David P.
Hill, R.J.
Marsh, Joseph
Newman, Thomas G.
Peters, G.N.H. - *Also see* Appendix 25
Reed, H.V.
Wagoner, J.F.
Williams, J.W. (20th)
Wilson, Benjamin
Wilson, Thomas

Bibliography: Ancestry.com. U.S. Census. Illinois. Cook. Chicago. Dist. 128; "Brush Creek Church of God History 1833-1969," author unknown. This paper states that the Brush Creek congregation began as a Union church in 1833 and it taught soul sleep. The paper is part of the Archives of Atlanta Bible College in McDonough, Ga.; Dunant, Henry. "The Holy Land," excerpted by *The Prophetic Watchman*, J.M. Stephenson, ed., Oct. 12, 1866, from the *New York World*, Sept. 8, 1866; Fiske, John R. "Partial Resurrection: An Antidote to Larger Hope," self published, no date. A copy of this pamphlet is in the Archives of Atlanta Bible College; Hall, D.P. "Letter to Joseph Marsh," *Advent Harbinger and Bible Advocate*, April 19,1851; "Photo Copy of Early Record. Ripley Church of God, Ripley, Il., 1900s." Original documents owned by Ripley Church of God. Here can be found baptismal records, lists of officers, minutes, lists of pastors and notes about church business; Marsh, Joseph. "Notice of Tour through Canada," *The Prophetic Expositor and Bible Advocate*, Joseph Marsh, ed., Rochester, NY. Jan. 1, 1858 and, *The Restitution*, Jan.27, 1875, March 17, 1875; Report of George Moyer, *The Herald of the Kingdom and Christian Instructor*. April 15, 1868; *The Restitution*. Nov. 28, 1894; Nickels, Richard C. *History of the Seventh Day Church of God*, Giving and Sharing. 1999, chapter 2 discusses the Messenger Party, retrieved on May 3, 2008 from website: giveshare.org/churchhistory/historysdcog/index.html; Neuffer, Julia, ed., "The Gathering, a Historical Study of Early Writings," from the Biblical Research Institute, Silver Spring, Md., retrieved May 3, 2008 from website http://www.whiteestate.org/issues/gather.html; Peters, George, *The Theocratic Kingdom*, Vol. 3, NY Funk & Wagnalls, 1884, p. 50 citing J. H. Waggoner's *Refutation of the Age to Come*, p. 63; Randall, Clyde, *Historical Waymarks of the Church of God*. General Conference. Oregon, Il., 1976, pps. 45,46 and, Captions on pps. 83, 85, 102; Reed, H.V. "Report on Stephenson recanting of Sabbatarianism," *The Prophetic Expositor and Bible Advocate*, Joseph Marsh, ed., Rochester, NY, Nov. 1, 1857 and Dec. 15, 1857; Reed, H.V. "Wisconsin Tour," *The Gospel Banner*, B. Wilson, ed., Geneva, Il., April 1860; Stephenson, J.M. "Correspondence," *The Gospel Banner*, Geneva, Il., June 1, 1864; Stephenson, J.M. "Refuting Sabbatarianism," *The Herald of the Kingdom* Jan. 1, 1868; Stephenson, J.M. "Report," *The Restitution*. Dec. 16, 1874; Stephenson, J.M. "Conference Report," *The Restitution* Jan. 6, 1875; Stephenson, J.M."Duties Devolving Upon Disciples After Faith, Repentance and Baptism," *The Restitution*. A.R. Underwood, ed., Plymouth, In., Oct. 18, 1893; Stilson, Jan, *History Newsletter of the Church of God*. Heritage Sunday Bulletin Insert. October 6, 1985; Visit to gravesite with photos. April 22, 2007 and Nov. 22, 2009; Wince, Roxanna. "Story of a Happy Christian #64," *The Restitution*, A.R. Underwood, ed. Plymouth, In., Nov. 4, 1908.

Stetson, Dr. George W.
b. 1815
d. October 9, 1879

George W. Stetson was born to Reuben and Lois Smedley Stetson in Champlain, New York. He had 12 brothers and sisters; one died in childhood. Because of the family's size, an older brother raised George. George married Mary Porter in 1846, and they had five children. After Mary died in 1855, George later married Anne Elizabeth Barlow. They had three children.

As a boy, George attended a Calvinist church with his family. One day, he was upset by a sermon that included comments about the destiny of un-baptized babies. He said later in life that this experience may have predisposed him to believe in the Arminian system of free choice (to accept Christ or not).

George became a physician either through education or internship; his first practice may have been in New York. He moved to Ohio early in the 1850s and practiced medicine there as well. He even took on a student and mentored him in medicine, perhaps as someone had mentored Stetson in his youth. During this time George's young daughters died, possibly from the diseases associated with hot wetland such as malaria, cholera or typhoid.

While in Ohio, records indicate Stetson preached for an Age-to-Come congregation at Fairfield between Cincinnati and Dayton. This group followed the teachings of Benjamin Wilson, but Adventists from other backgrounds also worshipped together as was common in that day. J.M. Judson mentioned the Fairfield church in a letter to Joseph Marsh published in *The Advent Harbinger* in 1857. Judson was a member of that congregation. He reported baptizing five believers the previous Sunday, and he expected more. He said their little group was receiving considerable "thundering…anathemas" from an orthodox church in the area.

In October 1857, Joseph Marsh attended a conference held at Norwalk. That December Hiram Reed came to preach. This was definitely an Age-to-Come congregation. George Stetson must have preached there on a regular basis. He circulated among Age-to-Come ministers, and he wrote for Age-to-Come journals. Although his earliest article was written first for the *World's Crisis* (an Advent Christian paper), it was picked up in exchange and published later in *The Gospel Banner* (May 15, 1869) in one of the last issues Benjamin Wilson published before moving to California. In the "Gathering of the Nations" Stetson made the point that Christ had not yet been given the power to rule nations.

Evidence shows Stetson was a member in C.T. Russell's Bible study group in Allegheny, Pennsylvania, in 1869. Russell himself referred to Stetson and George Storrs who had both been with the Advent Christians. Beyond this there is little evidence that Stetson was ever a disciple of Russell's, but he may have "passed through" Russell's sphere of influence briefly.

Stetson wrote regularly for *The Restitution* during the 1870s usually on prophecy or Israel's restoration. By the mid 1870s, Stetson seemed to fully understand the restoration issue as Joseph Marsh and Benjamin Wilson taught it. In his 1876 book review about Joseph Frey's *Restoration of Judah and Israel*, Stetson said someone had asked him, following his remarks in class, if he had read Frey. Stetson said, "No." The man expressed surprise because Stetson's position was nearly exactly like Frey's. So Stetson purchased a copy of Frey's book, read it and wrote his book review. In the review he said, "There, Brother Reed, that comes the nearest to Bible teaching of anything I have seen of human production." Therefore, it can be concluded that Stetson liked Frey.

Stetson said he had been teaching restoration for 15 years and believed the 12 tribes would return to Jerusalem before their conversion. That would date his first understandings of the doctrine to 1861, prior to his association with Russell. One month later, Stetson wrote another article for *The Restitution* saying the earth would be restored to more than its Eden state, for paradise would encompass the whole world whereas the Garden of Eden had not. This short piece came in response to criticism leveled against Stetson by Ephraim Miller of Michigan.

Stetson continued to write for *The Restitution* until shortly before his death. In May 1876 part one of a new series on New Jerusalem was published; part two has not been found yet. It is thought that his health may have prevented him from completing the series. Still, in March 1879, just six months before his death, Stetson authored another article for *The Restitution* regarding questions about Revelation 13:1 "...And I saw a wild beast ascending from the sea having ten horns and seven heads..." (*Emphatic Diaglott*). Stetson said he did not see the seven heads to be the papacy.

He died of spinal fever (possibly meningitis) in Edinboro, Pennsylvania, the same community in which John T. Ongley resided.

Bruce Schulz contributed most of this entry.

See Marsh, Joseph
　　Miller, Ephraim
　　Ongley, John T.
　　Reed, H.V.
　　Storrs, George
　　Wilson, Benjamin

Bibliography: Ancestry.com. U.S. Federal Census Mortality Schedules. 1850-1885 record for George W. Stetson; Judson, J.M. Letter to Marsh, *The Prophetic Expositor and Bible Advocate*, Jos. Marsh, ed., Rochester, NY, Oct. 1, 1857; "Conference at Fairfield," *The Prophetic Expositor and Bible Advocate*, Jos. Marsh, ed., Rochester, NY, Nov. 15, 1857; Schulz, Bruce, From *A Separate Identity: Zion's Watch Tower Congregations 1870-1887* [tentative title], the chapter on "George W. Stetson," E-mail Jan. 17, 2011; Stetson, G. W. "The Gathering of the Nations," *The Gospel Banner*, B. Wilson, ed., Geneva, Il., May 15, 1869; Stetson, G.W. "Book Review on Frey's *Restoration of Judah and Israel*," *The Restitution*, Plymouth, In., S.A. Chaplin, H.V. Reed, co-editors, March 1, 1876; Stetson, G.W., Reply to E. Miller, *The Restitution*, April 19, 1876; Stetson, G.W. "The New Jerusalem," Pt. 1, *The Restitution*, May 24, 1876. If other parts of this series exist please forward them; Stetson, G.W. "Queries on Revelation 13:1" *The Restitution*, March 13, 1879.

Stilson, Alexander Fremont
b. March 13, 1855
d. January 21, 1911

Alexander Stilson was born to Seymour and Cynthia Stillson in Marshall County, Indiana; he lived there nearly his whole life. He married Eva Armena McChesney (September 11, 1857-September 24, 1911) on November 23, 1878, in Marshall County. Alexander was a farmer. He and Eva had five children, Floyd, Myrtle (Houser), Rolland, Iris (Kirkley) and Forrest. Except for Forrest, the Stilson children married within the Church of God and raised families in the church.

Stilson was baptized into Christ in September 1878. He helped define the doctrines of the Age to Come at the Argos church and was an avid reader of all the religious papers of the day including *The Gospel Banner, The Prophetic Watchman* and *The Herald of the Coming Kingdom*.

A short illness resulting from the common cold led to Stilson's death. He and Eva rest at Fairmount Cemetery north of Plymouth, Indiana. Their gravesites are located in the south central portion along the driveway.

See Houser, Graceton (20th)
　　Kirkley, Iris (20th)
　　Stilson, Eugene (20th)
　　Stilson, Floyd (20th)
　　Stilson, Rolland (20th)

Bibliography: Harrison, Bert, Stilson family genealogy; Stilson, Christie, Stilson/Stillson Family Genealogy/Addendum. Fairmount Cemetery List of gravesites of Stilson/McChesney families furnished by Iris Kirkley at Rootsweb.com.

Stilson (Stillson), Asher
b. September 16, 1835
d. May 8, 1916

Asher Stilson was the son of Seymour and Cynthia Palmer Stillson and a brother of Alexander Fremont Stilson. Seymour's family moved to northern Indiana from New York in 1832. Asher was born on Palmer Prairie, known later as Sumption Prairie, just south of South Bend, Indiana. The family spelled the name with a double "L" at this time, but it is thought Seymour himself began to use one "L". Asher was the second of nine children. As a young man, Asher was baptized by Mead Catlin, a member of the Church of God. Asher married Helen Burch in May 1859. She died in March 1872. They had five children, two of whom died in childhood. Sons Charles and Dennis survived their father.

In his youth, Asher mustered into Company A of the 73rd Indiana Regiment of Volunteers in the Civil War. His obituary noted he received a slight wound in the hand at the battle of Stone River. Another account said his regiment was captured in Georgia and Asher was severely mistreated. He attained the rank of First Sergeant and was discharged in 1865.

After the war, Asher and Helen returned to Georgia. In January 1866, he wrote a letter to his brother stating his progress in getting settled, buying horses and supplies as he planned on a spring planting. A drought in that state forced them to move back to Indiana. Soon after that, Helen became ill and died.

On December 28, 1874, Asher married Mariah (Maria) Dysert (Dipert) (1864-1914). Mariah had been Helen's nurse. She and Asher had five children. A boy, Andrew, died at age five from an accidental gunshot by a neighbor child. Martha Jane Jackson, Walkerton, Indiana; Mary Elsie Von Dieck of Chicago; James Asher Stilson of Plymouth, Indiana; and Bertha Ethel Hentz of Marshall, Texas, survived their father. Two of Asher's sisters, Mrs. Charles Kanaare and Mrs. J.D. Fields of Plymouth, survived him. James was a member of the North Salem Church of God at Plymouth.

Asher died while visiting his daughter in Texas. His funeral was at Plymouth. A second service was held at Grovertown, his old home, and he was buried at Grovertown Cemetery. The bodies of Asher and Maria were moved to the new Walkerton Cemetery on the south side of Plymouth, Indiana, in the 1950s.

See Catlin, Mead
Stilson, Floyd (20th)
Stilson, Seymour

Bibliography: Ancestry.com. U.S. Census. Indiana. Marshall. North. 1860; U.S. Census. Indiana. Marshall. Plymouth Ward 2. 1910; Obituary of Asher Stilson, *The Restitution Herald*. May 24, 1916; Stilson, Christie. Stilson/Stillson Family Genealogy/Addendum, Rootsweb.com; Harrison, Bert. [Sylvia Stilson] E-mail regarding Stilson family genealogy July 2009.

Stilson (Stillson), Seymour
b. March 24, 1808
d. January 25, 1873

Seymour Stilson married Cynthia Ann Palmer (1814 to March 8, 1896) in New York on March 8, 1832. They were from Onondaga County, New York, and traveled to Marshall County, Indiana, in 1833 by oxcart. The *Marshall County, Indiana History* relates this interesting story about Seymour.

> They settled about two miles south of LaPaz on Michigan Road. He worked in construction and was involved in community and civic affairs. He was a member of the Church of God Abrahamic Faith. He was a stone dresser and helped make the grinding stones for the mill. Although Seymour had made friends with the Indians, he volunteered to remove them from Marshall County. Getting as far south as Southern Indiana, he deplored the mistreatment of the Indians and came back home. Seymour went to the gold rush in California in 1849 but found no gold. He used his remaining money to buy horses and a wagon and went into the draying business. He sent what he could to Cynthia. When he saved enough money, he bought Cynthia six silver spoons and journeyed back home.

The story concluded with Seymour's fascination for Indian lore. The information in the Marshall County history came from Iris Stilson Kirkley as told to Alethea "Lee" Stillson Lanphier. Iris owned the silver spoons and gave one to Lee.

Seymour and Cynthia's son Asher was born on Palmer Prairie, also called Sumption Prairie. The Stilsons had an early presence in Marshall County. Seymour and Cynthia may have been the first Stilsons to bring Church of God influence in the state of Indiana north of Jeffersonville. If this is so, presumably, since they were from New York, they had acquaintance with S.A. Chaplin, Joseph Marsh, Ephraim Miller and Mead Catlin before they migrated west. Mead Catlin may have baptized them.

Seymour knew J.F. Wagoner, Hugh Barnhill, Richard Corbaley, Uncle John Foore and Jacob Shafer. Seymour died in 1873, leaving Cynthia a widow until her death in 1896. She had an injured leg and was called "Crippled Grandma." Cynthia and Seymour are buried at Fairmount Cemetery north of Plymouth, Indiana, along old Route 31, in the south central part of the cemetery.

See Catlin, Mead
Chaplin, S.A.
Kirkley, Iris (20th)
Marsh, Joseph
Miller, Ephraim
Stilson, Asher

Bibliography: Graham, David, E-mail to Jan Stilson. March 13, 2006;

Harrison, Bert. "Stilson genealogy," E-mail to Jan Stilson, Spring 2006; *The Restitution Herald,* May 24, 1916; Stilson, Christie, Stilson/Stillson Family Genealogy/Addendum, Rootsweb.com; Fairmount Cemetery List of gravesites furnished by Iris Kirkley at http://www.rootsweb.com/~inmarsha/3/fairmoun.pdf.

Storrs, George
b. 1796
d. 1879

George Storrs was born in New Hampshire, the youngest of eight children. His father, Constant Storrs, was an army colonel in the American Revolution. His wife, Lucinda Howe was a half-sister to Richard Storrs, a minister. They had seven sons and a daughter and taught them the things of Christ and his Gospel.

George was an individualist and a very good Bible student. He was a Presbyterian before becoming involved with William Miller in the Adventist movement. Later, at age 19, he turned away from Calvinism and became a member of the Congregational Church. George had never been fond of the doctrine of eternal torment. Still unhappy, he later joined the Methodist Traveling Connection after the death of his beloved wife. He was highly esteemed by the Methodists and chosen as delegate to at least two of their general conferences in 1832 and 1836.

During this same period, George became passionate about the Abolitionist movement, paralleling the interest of Joseph Marsh. The Methodist church censured him for his involvement.

George was the first Bible scholar in America to verbalize the doctrine of conditional immortality. He preached six sermons on the subject near the beginning of the Millerite movement. From that point on, George Storrs and the doctrine of life only through Christ, known as the Life and Death issue, were co-opted into the Millerite movement.

After the Adventist movement broke into splinter groups, George Storrs worked with Joseph Marsh in the tent ministry of the Age-to-Come preachers. For that period, by his involvement, he participated in the formation of the Church of God. J.B. Cook, J.C. Bywater and John T. Ongley, also part of Marsh's Age-to-Come movement, assisted Storrs.

From 1848-1852, while Joseph Marsh published *The Advent Harbinger,* and later *The Advent Harbinger and Bible Advocate,* George Storrs published *The Bible Examiner.* This work had begun as an occasional journal, but by 1847 was being published twice a month. This work was dedicated to the issues of conditional immortality as well as other topics discussed by the Adventists and Age-to-Come believers.

The *Examiner* carried ads for various drugs, which indicated George Storrs manufactured these tonics. Storrs as editor may have supported his paper through the means of advertising and sales of drug goods, and some have said he was a druggist or pharmacist.

The October 18, 1851, issue of *The Advent Harbinger and Bible Advocate* included full text of one of Storrs' discourses at a tent meeting. He preached on Matthew 16:21-27 in which Peter said, "Thou art the Christ, the Son of the living God." Jesus said upon that confession he would build his church. Storrs said many people do not favor the cross anymore. It does not have value to them because they think they have immortal souls, and they will have endless life. Storrs pointed out the Bible said, "The soul that sinneth, it shall die." Men out of Christ have no life. He then explained the tenets of conditional immortality and the value of atonement to believers.

In that same issue, George Storrs announced he had 200 sets of *The Bible Examiner* on hand for the years 1850 and 1851, and 50 sets for the year 1849. He wanted to sell them for $2 per set with an extension of the subscription through 1852. He said he really needed the money more than the sets. The life of a publisher and preacher guaranteed a life without luxury and often without even the necessities. In 1874, Storrs published a second book, *A Vindication of the Government of God, or The Promise and Oath of God to Abraham.*

During this time, Elder Storrs pastored the church at Philadelphia which J.P. Weethee pronounced in "excellent" condition. The Life and Death issue was "exciting an unusual interest" there. Later Storrs returned to New Hampshire, fell ill and died. He had established a small sect known as the Life and Advent Union, an offshoot of the Advent Christian denomination. The two groups continued to cooperate with each other until the Life and Advent Union was finally absorbed by the larger group in the 20th century.

See Bywater, J.C.
Cook, J.B.
Marsh, Joseph
Ongley, John T.
Weethee, J.P.

Bibliography: Amazingforums.com/Storrs, discussion regarding possibility of Storrs being a druggist. Ancestry.com. U.S. Census. New York. Kings. Brooklyn Ward 1 District 1, 1860; Storrs, George, "Discourse at the Buffalo Tent Meeting," *The Advent Harbinger and Bible Advocate,* Oct. 18, 1851; Weethee's report, *The Advent Harbinger and Bible Advocate,* Oct. 25, 1851; Heinzman, David J. "Storrs Biography," seen at Harvestherald.com/storrs-sermons.com; Storrs, George. "Report of Tent," *The Bible Examiner,* Oct. 1851, p. 155. Bruce Schulz furnished this quote from a book he is presently writing due to be published in 2011, tentative title *A Separate Identity: Zion's Watch Tower Congregations 1870-1887*; Storrs, George, Several volumes of *The Bible Examiner* are available for researchers at the Archives of the Atlanta Bible College, McDonough, Georgia.

Story, Reuben Pliny
b. April 11, 1851
d. Unknown

Reuben Pliny Story was born in Iowa to Amos and Elizabeth David Carson Story. Amos was from Ohio and Elizabeth from Pennsylvania. It is thought this was Elizabeth's second marriage and that her mother, Jane David, lived with the Storys until her death. Amos and Elizabeth had four sons: David, Reuben Pliny, Stephen A. and James R. The family lived in Center, Cedar County, Iowa, but when Pliny was 15, they moved to Hardin County, Iowa. There he met Eleanor Scott whom he married on February 25, 1872. Eleanor was the sister of Jesse Scott Harlan and John Scott. Pliny and Eleanor lived just north of Gifford, Iowa.

Evangelist C.C. Ramsay baptized Pliny and Eleanor in 1882. They became members of the Church of God Abrahamic Faith. They were faithful workers in the church, and Pliny was an excellent Bible student. He liked to discuss Scriptures. In fact, aside from a little history, the Bible was nearly all he ever read. He thought Eleanor wasted her time if she read a novel.

In the spring of 1884, Pliny's family, along with other farm families, moved to farmland southeast of Holbrook, Nebraska. These families were Church of God members, and they planned to begin a new church at Holbrook. This group included the families of Almus Adams and John Adams, both of Gifford. John Scott, Eleanor's brother, wed Elizabeth Harlan after the move to Nebraska in 1886. Si Harlan, Elizabeth's brother, and his wife, Jesse Scott Harlan, also accompanied the caravan as did the Nathan Hornaday family. The latter families may have migrated to Nebraska as a second caravan.

Pliny registered a tree claim five and a half miles northeast of Hendley, Nebraska. He settled the land in March, and his wife and the children came by train in April. They lived in a dugout that summer and built a sod house in the fall. They had to haul drinking water from the Republican River about seven miles away. They didn't have pens for the hogs, so they turned them out to freely range. When the hogs were ready for market Pliny drove them six miles to sell.

Farm duties included shucking and shelling corn by hand. Eleanor made shucking mittens to protect the hands from this damaging work; they may have been the first work gloves on the great prairies. She also knitted their socks. The two oldest children, Mary, 10 and Warren 6 or 7, herded the cattle to pastureland that summer, since they had no ground feed for them. Every member of the family had a job.

In 1886 Stephen Story (Pliny's brother), his wife Cora and their one-year-old son Andrew came from Iowa to join the Nebraska group. Andrew grew to be a big man and married Goldie Herman in 1912. They had five sons: Lowell, Leland, Gerald, Bernell and Kermit, and a daughter, Audrey. This family contributed significantly to the stability of the Holbrook Church of God.

All the families mentioned in this entry were active in establishing and stabilizing the work at Holbrook. For a while there was a Church of God on the north side of town and another one south of town. Why there were two is unclear, but it must be remembered that travel was difficult at that time, and if families settled near each other, it was easier to meet nearby, perhaps on family land, for worship than to travel, unless of course they were traveling to spend a weekend at a quarterly conference.

The congregation on the south side of Holbrook met in an abandoned schoolhouse which they remodeled. Eventually both congregations came to town and united to buy an existing church building. This effort may have happened at the beginning of the 20th century. E.E. Geisler assisted them in this effort, although most of his preaching was focused on the congregation at Moorefield. Other ministers at Holbrook included Leon Driskill, Terry Ferrell, James Rencontre, Vivian Kirkpatrick Sr., Grover Gordon and Clyde Long.

The Bereans organized at Iowa Conference in 1913.

Reuben Pliny Story became vice-president of the Nebraska conference of the Church of God Abrahamic Faith and served in that capacity in 1912 and 1916. This conference group met in a tent borrowed from the Iowa conference and pitched on Reuben and Eleanor's land. The picture accompanying this entry depicts the delegates present at the 1913 Iowa Conference where the Bereans were first organized. Notice the tent in the background. This conference may have been held at the campground in Cedar Falls or the Waterloo church property.

Joyce Wilson Magaw contributed to this entry.

See Adams, Almus
Geisler, E.E. (20th)
Ramsay, C.C.

Bibliography: Ancestry.com. U.S. Census. Iowa. Cedar. Center. 1850; and Iowa, Hardin. Union. Dist. 127, 1880; U.S. Census. Iowa. Hardin. Eldora. Dist. 122. 1880, Record for Stephen Story; Magaw, Joyce. Reuben Pliny Story, Summer 2008. Joyce is the great-granddaughter of R.P. Story.

Sweany, Press L.
b. December 17, 1863
d. Unknown

Press Sweany was born in Jackson County, Indiana, and moved to Swan Lake, Minnesota, as a boy. An enthusiastic worker, Press was ordained to preach for the Church of God at the Eden Lake Conference on March 10, 1895.

Sweany was a leading member of the Church of God in Minnesota during the early 20th century. He preached throughout the region and pastored at the Sylvan Church of God. He became president of the state conference.

Sylvan Church of God

In 1904 he gave this description of the work for *The Day Dawn and Harvest Messenger*:

> The Sylvan Church began on July 11, 1900 when Elders James A. Patrick, Blanchette and Sweany pitched the mission tent in B.T. Wicker's grove and began a series of meetings. The residents in the neighborhood did not want a tent in the area but Bro. Wicker agreed and helped in various ways to accomplish that.
>
> Meetings were conducted for about three weeks with the result that fourteen came forward and were baptized. The tent was left standing so that meetings could be held there for a longer period of time. That fall, the President of the Minnesota Conference, Elder S.P. Matheny set the church in order by helping them to elect officers. James Patrick was selected to serve as pastor the remainder of the year.
>
> When the tent was removed church worship services were held in a vacant house in the neighborhood which was too small. Soon members wanted to build a church. Early in March Elder Sweany was called to be pastor and work was begun on a church building. It was built on land donated by Mr. Douglas Oliver. E.D. Thoms was engaged to do the carpenter work. The building was finished in the fall of 1901. [Paraphrased]

Pastor Sweany had served for at least four years at the time he wrote the article. He left the Church of God for several years, but returned to serve at the 1924 Minnesota Conference.

For a while in 1924, Sweany assisted Evangelist C.C. Maple who conducted meetings in Ohio. Sweany was guest evangelist and traveled to meetings with James A. Patrick, a fellow Minnesotan and one of the Church of God General Conference board of directors. Sweany baptized Lila Kirkpatrick (Giles) the young daughter of Lester and Sarah Kirkpatrick. From this baptism came the distinguished pastoral ministry of Sharon Giles Cain, second wife of Pastor Rex Cain, their son, Dan (Rachel) Cain, and daughter and husband, Sarah and Sam An.

When Pastor Sweany relocated to Grove, Oklahoma, to begin a pastorate, he stayed for three years. No further information is available.

Bibliography: "Report of C.C. Maple," *The Restitution Herald*, Feb, 20, 1924; Sweany, P.L. "Report of the Church of God at Sylvan," *The Day Dawn and Harvest Messenger*, Jas. A. Patrick, ed., June 1904; *History of the Minnesota Church of God Conference*. Sydney Magaw, ed., 1931.

Sweet, A. Lonson "A.L." (Alonson)
b. 1823
d. Unknown

A.L. Sweet was a Bible student from Mt. Sterling, Illinois, who read Joseph Marsh's *Advent Harbinger and Bible Advocate*, but he was suspicious of it. Sweet was a well-known wagon maker and employed several craftsmen in his shop.

George Penkake, a carriage maker in Mt. Sterling, was Sweet's friend and neighbor. Both men were aware of the controversies encircling the Adventist movement in the East, but they believed in the Second Advent. Being isolated residents in the newly developing Middle Border, they attempted to sort it all out by studying the Bible and learning what they could from the publications. This was typical of many folks in the 1850s who tried to discover the truth following the Bitter Disappointment.

Penkake and Sweet wrote a letter to Joseph Marsh and said they would subscribe to his paper for six months to see if he became embroiled in controversies and mud slinging. If not, they would continue their subscriptions. When they wrote that letter, they were young married men ages 28 and 27 respectively.

Sweet and Penkake's investigations into Bible truths may be the first inquiries that resulted in the organization of the Church of God at Ripley, Illinois.

Bibliography: Ancestry.com. U.S. Census. Illinois. Brown. Mt. Sterling. 1850. "Letter to Joseph Marsh," *The Advent Harbinger and Bible Advocate*, Dec. 13, 1851; April 24, 1852.

Swingley, Dr. William
b. March 20, 1833
d. March 26, 1904

William Swingley was born in Washington County, Maryland. The family moved to Maryland Township of Ogle County, Illinois. The Swingleys were part of a migration of several families from Maryland, including the Coffmans and the Lindsays, to northern Ogle County; they named their township Maryland.

Swingley spent 18 years helping his father on the farm, after which he spent three years learning carpentry. He wed Mary E. Wagner on December 8, 1853. They had three children, Oscar, Benjamin and Jacob.

William was skillful in treating diseases of horses, and as an animal lover, he turned his skill toward veterinary surgery. This became the vocation he followed until within the last few years of his life. Failing health compelled him to retire from active work.

Church of God members and friends in the Adeline area knew Swingley well. He was interred in the family cemetery at Silver Creek, Illinois, to "await the judgment of that great day." S.J. Lindsay preached his funeral and wrote his obituary.

See Lindsay, S.J.

Bibliography: Andrew, William. Interview with Jan Stilson, May 2007; *The Restitution*. April 13, 1904.

Taylor, Sarah K.
b. 1867
d. May 1920

Sarah K. Taylor was president and correspondent of the Bible Faith Mission of India. She lived at Friendship, Maine, and traveled to India annually. Her husband, Dr. Austin Taylor, often stayed in India while she returned to America for fundraising. The Taylors lived humbly, neither having a home of their own, nor having enough money to rent a home. They boarded with the Burkhardt family, so while Mr. Taylor was away, Mrs. Taylor had a family around her. The Taylors had immigrated to America from England in 1901.

The Minnesota Conference of the Church of God supported Sarah's work in India with Charles Vedantachari. Sarah wrote articles for *The Day Dawn and Harvest Messenger* explaining the work and sharing the good news of the India-based ministry. In June 1912, she wrote an article, "Reasons why the Bible Faith Mission is needed in India," and listed 17 points including information about the Hindus' need for Christian faith, the lack of prejudice there which made working there inviting, the participation of native Indians in the work, the democratic nature of Bible Faith Mission which gave everyone a voice, and many others.

Sarah visited the Church of God conference in Waterloo, Iowa, in 1916. *The Day Dawn and Harvest Messenger* of June 1920 said, "Sister Taylor was ordained to the ministry by the Church of God in Minnesota, as was Chas. R. Vedantachari, the Superintendent of missions of which Sister Taylor was the head in this country."

A.J. Eychaner, 74 years old at the time, reported to *The Restitution Herald* that Mrs. Taylor was "an earnest, faithful and intelligent worker in missions." He referred to her great work as "the Church of God in India."

Mrs. Taylor appointed Eychaner as superintendent of the Church of God's Indian missionary work. He spearheaded a fundraising effort on its behalf. For this work he was severely criticized by Robert Huggins, who called him the chief heretic in America.

In 1920, the National Bible Institute received word of Mrs. Taylor's death. The Bible Faith Mission expressed great grief at her passing. The Bible Faith Mission was under the direction of the Advent Christian denomination.

See Eychaner, A.J.
Huggins, Robert (20th)
Vedantachari, Charles

Bibliography: Ancestry.com Maine. Sagadahoc. Bath Ward 7 Dist. 140. 1920; "Editorial Mention: Mrs. Sarah Taylor," *The Day Dawn and Harvest Messenger*, James A. Patrick, ed., Fort Dodge, Iowa, June, 1912 and June 1920; *The Restitution Herald,* May 10, 1916; Aug. 24, 1920.

Taylor, Richard B.
b. 1854
d. 1913

Richard Taylor was born in Coosey County, Alabama. He married Francis Ray on December 14, 1875. They moved to Texas in 1890, settling in Comanche County. When they arrived in Texas, Richard had already been baptized into the Gospel of the Kingdom of God, and the name of Jesus Christ. Soon after their arrival, he began preaching throughout the state of Texas, traveling by horseback, buggy and train. He baptized the family of W.L. Robbins of Riviera, Texas.

Richard also was interested in Texas history. The Archives at Atlanta Bible College contain his notes on Texas Church of God history, from which Emory Macy took his outline for "Church History of the Texas Church of God" in 1954. A paper by Seth Ross, also preserved in the Archives, is also based on previously written Texas histories.

See Bradley, A.S.
Gibbs, William L.
Macy, Emory (20th)

Bibliography: Macy, Emory, "Church History of Texas Church of God," March 1954. Ross, Seth, "Texas History," for revised Macy content, February 1991.

Thomas, Joseph
b. March 17, 1791
d. April 9, 1835

Joseph Thomas was an early 19th century preacher who prepared the way for the Church of God in Virginia, Ohio, Pennsylvania and New Jersey. He felt the call to preach before he even adequately knew what he should preach or how to preach it. He just went out, and given an opportunity to preach, stammered a bit and sat down quickly, pouring out his agony to the Lord in prayer. Fortunately, in his travels, he met many good neighbors from the Methodists, Presbyterians and Baptists, whose preachers helped him find his "preaching" voice.

As he wandered from town to town and church to church on his broken-down nag, he studied his Bible along the way and practiced preaching to his horse. Thomas became aware that what he preached was different than what the Presbyterians preached so he would not join them. His message also differed from the Methodists, Baptists, Quakers and other orthodox churches.

Thomas wanted to preach the Gospel, so he preached a message of faith and repentance much as John the Baptist had done. Along the way he recognized he did not hold to infant baptism or sprinkling of adults. Because he could not baptize himself, he was immersed by a Baptist. He preached throughout Virginia, and began to say all Christians are disciples. Themes of gospel liberty and Christian character are seen in his writings—the same themes preached by the Christian Connexion. Like them, he said he believed all Christians were members of the Church of God. He was one of the first to carry the unique message of the Christian Connexion across the south.

Frank L. Greenagel confirmed Pilgrim Thomas' alignment with the Christian Connexion, a biblical unitarian group of New England:

> Thomas spurned the entreaties and advice of more experienced itinerant preachers and allied himself with the Christian Connexion and traveled extensively preaching to any who would listen. He had a wife and children in Ohio, but nevertheless traveled most of the year.

Pilgrim Thomas preached at Fort Valley, Virginia, and Kernstown in Frederick County south of Winchester, Virginia, where the Boyers lived. He married Carolina Christiana Rittenour near Kernstown in 1812, and they began a family. The pair had met through Bible studies at Kernstown. Thomas' autobiography detailed their trials and tribulations while he traveled the road for the Lord. After he had traversed Virginia for several years, he went west into Tennessee and up to Ohio. He preached several meetings at Brush Creek, where eventually a Church of God was formed

An interesting and humorous anecdote grew from Thomas' meeting with an unnamed man. Thomas told him he had been directing sinners to repentance, and he was going to New Jerusalem. The man said, "New Jerusalem. I have heard of that place but I never was there; I believe it is a great distance to that place." Thomas told him he did not know precisely the distance but he firmly believed it was not so great that he could not get there. "Why," said the man, "by what I have heard of New Jerusalem, you are not in the right course. Is there a big road all the way in this direction?" Thomas said it was "very peculiar that all who started for New Jerusalem and kept on straight forward would arrive safely." The man asked if it were a newly settled place. Thomas said that he had not been there but he heard it contained 144,000 inhabitants." The man said he believed it was a lie for that would be larger than Philadelphia, and he heard Philadelphia was the largest city in America. He continued that he thought New Jerusalem stood on the banks of the Ohio River, but Thomas said, "No, it stands on the banks of the river of the water of life…that proceeds out of the throne of God and the Lamb." "Ah!" the man said, "Now I understand you."

Thomas recorded this story in his diary, which he published as a book after he'd been on the road nine years. He preached in various denominational buildings. By 1817 Thomas had established himself as an independent circuit preacher and earned two nicknames: "Crazy Thomas" and "The White Pilgrim." Instead of dressing in black garb like other circuit preachers, Thomas dressed all in white. In his book, Thomas stated he believed in the coming of the Lord, the resurrection, the Kingdom of God, and that the name for believers should be Church of God. He said he preached the "Gospel of his Kingdom."

In 1946 Carmel Boyer, son or grandson of the Mr. Boyer who hosted Elder Thomas, gave an old copy of *The Life of the Pilgrim* to Sydney Magaw, editor of *The Restitution Herald*, who reviewed it for readers in the September 17, 1946, issue. Carmel wouldn't have remembered Elder Thomas, but retained that old book which had been passed down through his family. The Thomas ministry in Virginia preceded the Age-to-Come doctrine of Joseph Marsh and the development of the Church of God as a denomination. Thomas is an important figure because he laid the groundwork in Virginia and southern Ohio prior to the Adventist message of William Miller or the Christadelphian message of Dr. John Thomas.

While it cannot be said Joseph Thomas founded Churches of God as they're known today, in either Virginia or Ohio, it can be said he preached in places where Churches of God were later established, and which remain to this day. That he came from the same religious background as Joseph Marsh identifies him more closely with the foundations of the Church of God than would otherwise be thought at first glance. It is beneficial to look closely at this man and his early influence, and his book is entertaining reading.

Pilgrim Thomas rests in the cemetery beside Old Stone Church, Johnsonburg, New Jersey.

Photo by Dr. Frank Greenagel, used with permission.

The White Pilgrim died suddenly while preaching at an Episcopalian house of worship in Johnsonburg, Warren County, New Jersey. He was buried beside the Stone Church, which still stands. Frank Greenagel cites a verse from Bob Dylan who recorded "The Lone Pilgrim" based on a poem written about The White Pilgrim after his death:

> I came to the place where the lone pilgrim lay
> And pensively stood by his tomb,
> When in a low whisper I heard something say
> "How sweetly I sleep here alone."

Historians of the Brush Creek Church of God trace their congregation to 1833. Frank Taylor, an Indiana Church of God historian, used 1828 to date the Ohio work. Either of these dates predates the pinnacle of the Millerite movement: 1844. Clyde Randall made the point in *Historical Waymarks* that Old Union, an Adventist church in Indiana that became a Church of God, held services in 1828. Old Union evidently was not the only community Adventist church to predate the Millerite movement. Brush Creek historians describe their 1833 congregation as "Second Adventist or Soul Sleepers." Soul Sleepers believe in conditional immortality, an important biblical teaching of the Church of God. Therefore, it seems that the soil cultivated by Joseph Thomas may have given rise to at least one of the earliest Churches of God on record.

Church of God preachers who served in Virginia, as cited by J.R. LeCrone in *The Restitution Herald* (April 23, 1946) included Samuel Wilson, Elizabeth, New Jersey; H. Dauterich, Baltimore, about whom nothing is known; J.F. Wagoner, Rochester, Indiana, the grandson of Brush Creek's founder and one of the earliest Church of God preachers to circuit the area; H.V. Reed, Harvard and Chicago, Illinois, who was active in the Church of God from 1850 until his death; Allan Magruder, Virginia; C.C. Ramsay, Philadelphia, who went west and concentrated his work in Iowa and Kansas; and many, many others. Except for Dauterich all these men have biographical entries in this encyclopedia, and like Joseph Thomas, all became circuit preachers.

See Boyer, Carmel (20th)
    LeCrone, J.R. (20th)
    Magaw, Sydney (20th)
    Magruder, Allan B.
    Marsh, Joseph
    Ramsay, C.C.
    Reed, H.V.
    Wagoner, J.F.
    Wilson, Samuel

Bibliography: "Brush Creek Church of God History 1833-1869," author unknown. This paper is part of the Archives of Atlanta Bible College, McDonough, Ga.; Greenagel, Frank L. *The New Jersey Churchscape: Encountering the 18th and 19th Century Churches*, Rutgers Univ. Press. Dec. 2010, retrieved Dec. 12, 2010 from: http://www.njchurchscape.com/about.html; LeCrone, J.R., "Ministers Who Have Served in Virginia," *The Restitution Herald*, April 23, 1946; Magaw, Sydney, Editorial on The Life of the Pilgrim. *The Restitution Herald*, Sept. 17, 1946; Morrill, Milo True, *A history of the Christian denomination in America, 1794-1911*, Christian Publishing Assoc. Dayton, 1912, p.329, retrieved from googlebooks.com; Thomas, Joseph. *The Life of the Pilgrim*, Winchester, Virginia, J. Foster, 1817.

Thompson, William
b. December 24, 1825
d. September 1, 1897

William Thompson was born in Fayette County, Indiana, and moved to Argos, Marshall County in 1837. He married Christine Lowe, in Warren County, New Jersey, on January 22, 1857. Perhaps they were married in the Old Stone Church at Johnsonburg; Pilgrim Joseph Thomas rests in the cemetery there. They had one son, John, and one daughter, Josie. They were Church of God members. Christine died in 1885.

Thompson's ancestors were Scottish and members first of the Old Christian church, presumed to be part of the Christian Connexion. This same congregation became Campbellite and then Church of God. As they studied their Bibles, they came into richer understanding of its precious teachings.

William Thompson was one of the first preachers at the Old Pisgah church, which was organized in 1846. After Stedman A. Chaplin came out of the Baptist denomination he also preached at this church, about the same time that Thompson came into the Church of God. Old Pisgah, a community church that had strong Adventist teachings, was located about five miles east of Plymouth, Indiana. It pre-dated the Old Antioch church at Argos, and many of its members moved there from Old Union at Eagle Creek after the confusion there over doctrine in 1851.

Many of *The Restitution* issues used in researching this encyclopedia bore the subscription label of William Thompson. Thompson must have shared a sense of history with his children because his papers were passed down and saved for the Church of God archival collection. Julia Harsh (May 7, 1845 to Feb. 3, 1926) was Elder Thompson's granddaughter; Julie was Evelyn Harsh Austin's adoptive mother. Julia died in Chicago at Evelyn's home.

See Austin, Evelyn Harsh (20th)
Chaplin, Stedman A.
Thomas, Joseph

Bibliography: *The Restitution Herald,* February 16, 1926; Williams, Byron. *Abstracts of Obituaries and Verbatim Marriage Announcements printed in The Restitution 1874-1900,* self-published, 1993 pp 30, 75.

Thoms, Egbert E.
b. January 12, 1838
d. January 7, 1924

E.E. Thoms was born in Wheatland, New York, to Charles and Phebe Thoms. The family moved to Indiana in Egbert's youth. In 1857, he married Mary L. Trousdart (Trousdail), "Aunt Lyde" as she came to be known. They established a homestead after moving to Minnesota in 1868. They had four sons and three daughters. In 1874, Thoms began preaching in St. Cloud, Minnesota. He preached and Aunt Lyde sang.

The Minnesota Conference also licensed Aunt Lyde to preach. She and Sarah Taylor of the Bible Faith Mission were the only women ever licensed by the Minnesota Conference. E.E. Thoms was ordained at the Ottawa Church of God conference on September 15, 1877. During Elder E.E. Thoms' old age and final illness T. M Savage and Fred Daubanton, both of St. Cloud, assisted him. Both entered the ministry of the Church of God at that time and carried on the work after Thoms' death.

Aunt Lyde preceded her husband in death by two years on June 12, 1922, at St. Cloud at age 79. They rest beside each other awaiting the resurrection.

See Daubanton, Fred (20th)
Savage, T.M.

Bibliography: Ancestry.com U.S. Census. Indiana. Jennings. Geneva. 1850; *History of the Minnesota Church of God Conference.* Sydney Magaw, ed., June 1, 1931; Ancestry.com, Minnesota Death Index, 1908-2002, record for Egbert E. Thoms; U.S. Census. Minnesota. Stearns. Eden Lake Township. Dist. 146. 1900.

EE and Mary Thoms

Litchfield and Eden Valley are cities within Forest Prairie, a township in Meeker County, Minnesota. Forest Prairie was misnamed: It had no prairie and was covered with woods. The church was located either within Forest City or a distance outside the city. Forest Prairie is south of Clear Lake near Eden Valley. The Church of God at Forest Prairie was eventually abandoned in favor of the larger congregation at Eden Valley.

Thoms, Mary L. Trousdail
b. September 9, 1842
d. June 12, 1922

Mary Lyde Trousdail was married to Egbert E. Thoms on September 9, 1857—her 15th birthday. They had eleven children some of whom may have died in childhood. The Thoms family moved to Minnesota in 1868 and became charter members of the Church of God. E.E. Thoms began to preach the Kingdom of God and may have been the first minister to take the message throughout the state. Mary and the children accompanied him. She organized the music and led the singing with her lovely voice.

Mary was granted a minister's license because she was so active in the evangelistic effort. Many said "her singing did as much good as his preaching." When she was elderly, her voice failed; everyone missed hearing her sing.

She was laid to rest two years before her husband. James A. Patrick conducted the funeral service.
See Thoms, E.E.
   Thoms, E.D. (20th)
Bibliography: Mary Thoms Obituary. *The Restitution Herald*, Oct. 10, 1922.

Titchenal, Nimrod D.
b. January 20, 1865
d. March 27, 1949

Nimrod "Nim" Titchenal was an early preacher in the Northwest at the turn of the 20th century. He was born in Illinois, the son of Davis and Mary Jane Titchenal. Nim was one of six children, four boys and two girls. Nim's sister, Nancy or Nannie, married William L. Skeels, a Church of God minister.

In 1882, the family crossed the Great Plains to the State of Washington in a covered wagon. When the family arrived, they homesteaded in Titchenal Canyon, Douglas County, Washington. Nim lived at home with his parents, working as a farm laborer until nearly 40 years old. He never attended school but he could read and write, so his mother must have taught him at home. Nim married Myrtle Patterson on August 14, 1902. They had no children but they raised Myrtle's niece. They lived in Wenatchee, Washington, and served the Lord in the Church of God in that city. He was a real estate salesman. Nim served as pastor of the Church of God at Wenatchee. He was interred at Renton Cemetery.

Bibliography: Ancestry.com Washington Death Index. 1940-1996 record for Nimrod D. Titchenal; U.S. Census. Washington. Douglas. Mountain. Dist. 11. 1900; U.S. Census. Washington. Chelan. West Wenatchee. Dist. 313. 1910; U.S. Census. Washington. Chelan. Wenatchee. Dist. 46. 1930; Graham, David. Titchenal Information by email, Oct. 2, 2009; *The Restitution,* Robert Huggins, ed., Cleveland, Ohio, Sept. 29, 1920; Obituary by Bessie Lawrence, *The Restitution Herald,* Sydney Magaw, ed., Oregon, Il., May 3, 1949.

Titus, Inez
b. 1878
d. Unknown

Inez's parents, Mr. and Mrs. W.H. Garton, raised her in the Church of God. She may have been born in Wisconsin, but if so, the family moved to Iowa in her childhood. As a child, she learned about the Kingdom of God through traveling evangelists who visted their area. Elder and Mrs. T.J. Whitesitt visited on preaching tours, and often stayed as long as two weeks. T.J. Whitesitt preached at Inez's schoolhouse in the 1890s.

When Inez was 14, the Iowa believers held special meetings at Marathon, Iowa. Inez knew she wanted to be baptized because she had been studying. When she made it known, Bro. Almus Adams questioned her on points of faith. It was the first time she had met him. A.J. Eychaner baptized her in 1890. She was an isolated member, and she strove to remain faithful.

Inez wrote an article for *The Restitution Herald*, October 1938, the first issue edited by Sydney Magaw. In her article, "When Faith Was Pure," she said, "If we humble ourselves before God, He will lift us up."
See Adams, Almus
   Eychaner, A.J.
   Magaw, Sydney (20th)
   Whitesitt, T.J.
Bibliography: Ancestry.com. Iowa State Census Collection, 1836-1925. Linn. Cedar Rapids. 1885; Iowa State Census Collection, 1836-1925. Pocahontas. Dover. 1885 ; *The Restitution,* July 8, 1925; *The Restitution Herald,* October 18, 1938.

Tomlinson, Walter S.
b. 1871
d. 1940?

W.S. Tomlinson was born in England, but lived in Cuyahoga, Ohio, near Cleveland. He married Mattie Sutherland on July 27, 1893. Maurice Joblin baptized Walter and Mattie. Their daughter Ruth was born in 1907. Mattie died in 1931 leaving Ruth to care for her father.

In his youth, Walter heard an older man talk about man's nature and the resurrection. It seemed reasonable, and Walter thought about it. Later, he learned about the hope of salvation and the need to be ready to give an answer for the hope that lies within us. (1 Peter 3:15). Walter considered that too.

Later, someone gave him a tract about the Kingdom of God, which he found favorable. His family moved to Cleveland, as it happened, just down the street from a Church of God pastored by Maurice Joblin. Tomlinson attended a Baptist church on Sunday mornings and the Church of God on Sunday evenings. He thought the Church of God had more to offer. He talked with Elder Joblin who helped him settle some questions. Tomlinson, still a teenager, was baptized in March 1899.

Walter Tomlinson was a diligent Bible student and dedicated Christian servant. He saw spiritual carelessness emerging in the modern Church of God and called for "constant vigilance in teaching the doctrine to the people." He served in the Church of God for 50 more years. Ruth was an only child; she became a teacher. Ruth remained single until her mid 50s when she married Will Hall, a widower. After his death, she married another widower, Paul Overholser from Lawrenceville.

See Joblin, Maurice
Overholser, Ruth Tomlinson Hall (20th)

Bibliography: Ancestry.com U.S. Census. Ohio. Cuyahoga. Cleveland Ward 26. Dist. 403. 1910 and 1920; U.S. Census. Ohio. Cuyahoga. Orange. Dist. 682. 1930; Ancestry.com. Ohio Deaths, 1908-1932 record for Mattie Tomlinson; *The Restitution Herald*, March 2, 1931; Jan. 20, 1948; May 11, 1948.

Turner, C.B.
b. 1800
d. Unknown

C.B. Turner was an evangelist of the early Age-to-Come movement in New York. In spring of 1863, he attended the General Association of the Church of God in New York. He reported traveling 3,872 miles and preaching 223 times. He baptized 23 new believers, and from his travels, he received $377.06, an outstanding amount in those days. Turner contacted *The Millennial Harbinger and Bible Expositor* to inform readers that he was calling a special conference at Westbury, Cuyahoga County, New York, at the "Grove" on June 26, 1863.

Turner served on the General Association's business committee with T. Burr, U.S. Algire, A.D. Street and U.S. Finn; nothing else is known of his fellow committeemen. This association should not be considered a national effort to organize a headquarters. It was equivalent to a state conference.

Elder Turner left New York and moved to Ogle County, Illinois, sometime before 1860. He may have traveled from Illinois to New England in the summer to meet his evangelistic appointments. He resided in Ogle County with his son-in-law, Francis McCamley, to help him raise six children. Turner certainly would have been involved in the developing Church of God work at Daysville, where Elder Chown and J.B. Craton resided, or at Paynes Point, the home of A.J. Eychaner, however, evidence of his activity in Illinois is not available, and he cannot be traced in subsequent census data.

See Chown, Robert
Craton, J.B.
Eychaner, A.J.

Bibliography: Ancestry.com U.S. Census. Illinois. Ogle. Rockvale. 1860; Report. *Millennial Harbinger and Bible Expositor*, June 4, 1863; June 10, 1863; June 17, 1863, July 20, 1863.

Turner, George W.
b. 1820?
d. Unknown

Elder Turner was a member of the L.D. Mansfield congregation in New York. When Mansfield and his wife became missionaries in the Caribbean, this small congregation carried on. Turner wrote to Joseph Marsh that they continued meeting for fellowship and occasional preaching. Turner noted how they missed Elder Mansfield but tried to develop the work. The group obtained a meeting hall they were cleaning up for meetings.

George Turner believed the Age-to-Come doctrine should not divide Adventists. He said if there were divisions, it was because it hearkened back to some believed Paul, some Apollo, and not to the Age to Come. Ironically, it was the Mansfields who were partial to the Advent Christians' message that spoke disparagingly of the Age-to-Come movement. A few years later, when the Mansfields departed the Adventist fellowship to preach for the Methodists, a subtle but disparaging remark "for the good of all," appeared in an Age-to-Come paper.

George Turner confessed that he believed he would receive immortality when the Age to Come begins at Jesus' return to earth.

See Marsh, Joseph

Bibliography: Letter to Joseph Marsh, *Advent Harbinger and Bible Advocate*, May 3, 1851.

Turner, Harry
b. 1890?
d. Unknown

Harry Turner lived on a farm outside of Boise, Idaho. He learned of the truth through the missionary efforts of Sr. McClelland of Boise during an autumn revival series in 1920. Almus Adams was invited to Boise to conduct meetings during October that year. Mrs. McClelland and Evangelist Adams were brother and sister.

Almus Adams reported later that Harry Turner was a genius. Turner built a concrete fountain on his farm with pipes in it that were fed by a spring. It forced water 24' upwards into a water tower. Using this same spring, he also invented a dynamo-powered water wheel to power electric lights. Turner operated a ranch with 17 varieties of cherries he sold for produce. His mother composed music. Almus Adams said, "If you cannot enjoy this home you are hard to please."

At the revival meetings, Harry Turner was so taken with the Gospel of the Kingdom that he brought his wife, daughter and son to be baptized.

Adams visited Turner's home more than once to disciple its residents. Today an Advent Christian church exists at Weiser which, until recently, was pastored by Church of God pastor, Emory Macy. Perhaps the seeds of this Idaho work were sown by Martha McClelland, Almus Adams and Harry Turner.

See Adams, Almus
Macy, Emory (20th)
McClelland, Martha

Bibliography: Ancestry.com. U.S. Census. Idaho. Canyon. Nampa. Dist. 60. 1920. *Restitution*, Nov. 2, 1920; August 1922.

Turner, Robert Oscar
b. November 4, 1870
d. May 15, 1946

R.O. Turner was born in Calhoun County, Arkansas, the son of Middleton and Eliza Turner. Robert may have learned of the Abrahamic Faith in his youth from Dr. Moncrief or Thomas McGinty in Arkansas, both of whom were early evangelists in that state. Robert accepted the Lord and One Faith in his youth and moved to Oklahoma in 1890.

Robert married Margaret Elizabeth Turner, and they had one son and four daughters. He operated a real estate business in Boynton, Oklahoma, and served as cashier at the Sallisaw Bank & Trust Company. In his spare time, Turner published *The Gospel Trumpet*. He was the last editor to manage it before it merged with *The Restitution Herald*. It was a sad duty to shut down operations and give the mailing list to the editor of the *Herald*.

Correspondence about combining the papers by December 1 began with Samuel J. Lindsay to Turner sometime in the autumn of 1914. A letter written from Turner to Lindsay indicated he was late in answering due to the time it took to gain information from the Managing Board of *The Trumpet*. Lindsay replied on November 24, 1914, and said that if Turner would provide the list, "we would do the right thing by your people in giving them a paper of eight pages weekly to the end of the time for which they had subscribed with you."

On January 6, 1915, the readers of *The Gospel Trumpet* learned of the merger through a column in *The Restitution Herald*. There was to be a *Trumpet* column each issue to accommodate news and letters to the editor from those readers. Samuel J. Lindsay, *Herald* editor, assured *Trumpet* readers that the two papers' doctrines were identical, and they were all of One Faith. Lindsay appealed to them to renew their subscriptions to *The Restitution Herald* and to find even more readers throughout Texas and Oklahoma.

Afterward, the merger was approved by the Arkansas-Oklahoma conference board at their July meeting in 1915. If *Trumpet* readers were upset about the sudden change, it is not indicated in the literature. However, evidently the response from the readers in the Southwest was less favorable, for a letter from R.O. Turner to Lindsay on March 12, 1916, answering a Lindsay inquiry, indicated the people were non-responsive to publications in general due to their lack of education, feelings of inequality and lack of interest in maintaining the faith. Turner said he coped with these problems when he had been editor of the *Trumpet*.

The arrangement continued for a few years. In 1923 a revival of *The Gospel Trumpet* was approved by the Arkansas-Oklahoma conference board with Minister L.H. Shelton appointed editor. It re-emerged with a title change and became *The Gospel Messenger,* but did not continue long as a published paper. As a four-page mimeographed newsletter *The Gospel Messenger* continued for several years with Elder T.A. Drinkard as its fiery editor.

Sherwin Williams of the Blessed Hope Bible Church in Rockford, a native of Oklahoma, remembers R.O. Turner as a dedicated Christian and a mighty preacher.

See Drinkard, T.A. (20th)
Lindsay, S. J.
Shelton, L.H.

Bibliography: *The Restitution Herald,* Jan. 6, 1915; Aug. 25, 1918; Obituary, 1946; Williams, Sherwin. Interview by Jan Stilson. April 2007. Sherwin Williams, pastor of Blessed Hope in Rockford, Il. and Ripley, Il., is an Oklahoma boy who knew many of the Church of God evangelists in Arkansas and Oklahoma.

1910 Summer Bible School at Oregon, Illinois. SJ Lindsay is on the far left with the bow tie.

Black Hawk Statue by Lorado Taft at Oregon, Illinois. While the statue is called Black Hawk, it does not look like the noted war chief of the Sac and Fox. Rather, Taft's sculpture is his respectful tribute to the eternal Indian.

Underwood, Arthur R.
b. December 23, 1853
d. July 22, 1919

A.R. Underwood was the son of Edwin Underwood who moved his family from England to America in 1849. Edwin Underwood and Maria Raggett Underwood settled in St. Charles, Illinois. Mr. Underwood owned and operated a flourmill and was an avid Bible student. He became quite proficient in prophecy. Arthur went to school there and grew up among the believers of the Geneva, Illinois, Church of God. He knew all the Wilsons. As a young man, he learned the printer's trade from them in Chicago at *The Restitution* office under the guidance of Thomas Wilson.

During the Chicago Fire of 1871, Arthur saved the record books and valuable mail lists. If not for him, the abundance of archival material used as background material for historical research might not exist today. The extra bound volumes of *The Herald of the Kingdom and Christian Instructor*, and several years of bound volumes of *The Gospel Banner* that had merged with *The Herald* in 1869 were lost in the fire, as was the press. Both of those titles, however, are preserved in the Atlanta Bible College Archives.

When the remains of *The Restitution* were moved to Plymouth, Indiana, Hiram V. Reed accompanied it as editor and as S.A. Chaplin's editorial mentor and publisher. Reed was paid $1,000 the first year for his editorial work. The second year he received $700 and Chaplin $300. Chaplin owned *The Restitution* and gradually accumulated the majority of stock in the company. The next year Hiram Reed returned to Chicago, and Stedman Chaplin became editor.

During this transition, A.R. Underwood also moved to Plymouth. In 1887, he became the editor and manager, continuing until 1911 when *The Restitution* was sold to Church of God Publishing Company at Cleveland, Ohio. Underwood's editorial mission was clear: he offered a pure Gospel message that explained simple Bible truths and avoided "contentions that lead to mischief and strife." He was able to carry out this mission in an admirable fashion until 1910 when the "Ministerial Monopoly" as someone has called it, came into being. For the full story, see the Lincoln E. Conner entry.

Arthur Underwood was baptized in 1875, probably by Thomas Wilson, and remained faithful to the Church of God until his death. He held various church offices and edited *The Restitution*, the official organ of the denomination until 1911. In that capacity, he knew many people throughout the United States and Canada.

Arthur was a strong advocate of Sunday School at the local church. He once said that the success of a Sunday school depends upon a thoroughly prepared teacher, "who should teach self sacrifice as the only practical way of, in a measure, showing our appreciation of Christ's sacrifice." For teaching material, he advocated using the "International Lessons as a uniformity of lessons is desirable, in order that pupils may meet others on common ground." He published lesson materials within the pages of *The Restitution* but missed the opportunity to publish separate lesson books which would have been easier to transport between home and church. Instead, W.H. Wilson began publishing various little lesson books for Bible students.

Underwood took an active role in Plymouth's community affairs, including fire protection as leader of the Wide Awake Hose Company and later assistant chief. His experience fighting the Chicago Fire served him well. He knew the significance of saving one's home, business or valuables. Upon the fire chief's death, Underwood received the post. He was also a city water works trustee. Eventually he became superintendent of the water works. After he sold *The Restitution* he became a reporter for *The Plymouth Republican*.

A.R. Underwood was present at the infamous 1910 Waterloo conference where a national general conference organization was attempted. There was so much discord at the conference that organization was impossible. However, from the contentious meetings came unity of purpose regarding the definition of doctrines, both those commonly accepted and those considered heresy by most, and who believed what. See the O.J. Allard entry for a more on the outcome of the doctrine discussion.

At the 1910 conference L.E. Conner and D.C. Robison became better acquainted. Both men were pastors from Cleveland. At the conference they observed A.R. Underwood, editor of *The Restitution*, the most powerful voice in the Church of God at that time. This conference also saw the battle lines drawn for doctrinal squabbles over the next ten years until the General Conference of the Church of God was formed in 1921 and until the death of *The Restitution* in 1925. Robison sided with Underwood and Conner with the ministers and the new paper, *The Restitution Herald*. (Additional details on this era are found in the L.E. Conner entry.)

When the Ministerial Association began *The Restitution Herald* in Oregon, Illinois, in 1911, Samuel J. Lindsay became the editor. The new paper began small but grew steadily in popularity and readership. This paper emphasized the resurrection view held by Joseph Marsh and Thomas Wilson, i.e., general resurrection with "split" scenes: the righteous rewarded at Christ's return, and the wicked judged at the end of the thousand years. *The Restitution* strongly advocated limited resurrection, especially after it moved to Cleveland under the editorship of Robert Huggins.

Unknown parties made accusations against A.R. Underwood, stating *The Restitution* was being mismanaged. Special editions of *The Restitution* and *The Restitution Herald* were published to air their dirty laundry. Details of the disagreement are unclear, but those who remember the ordeal are still pained by it. As with any old feud, old hurts die slowly and pass on from generation to generation even after the first disagreement is forgotten. Still, it's never too late to forgive.

Arthur Underwood died of a heart ailment. Pastor D.E. Van Vactor conducted his funeral service. Underwood, a good and faithful servant of the Lord, was interred in Oak Hill Cemetery.

See Allard, O.J.
  Conner, L.E.
  Marsh, Joseph
  Robison, D.C.
  Wilson, Thomas

Bibliography: Allen, Mrs. Margaret, "History First Congregation of Disciples of Christ Geneva, IL. 1844-1893," *The Restitution Herald*, Jan. 3, 1956; "Church of God Roots" citing a article by W.H. Wilson "How, When, Where, and by Whom Was the Gospel of the Kingdom First Introduced into the Western States?" in *Progress Journal*. Oregon. Il. April 1981 and more recently Jan. 28, 2011; *The Restitution*, Jan. 13, 1904; Sept.14, 1910; Dec. 14, 1910; *The Restitution Herald*, Aug. 13, 1919.

Updike, Alice
b. July 7, 1865
d. April 12, 1949

Alice Updike was born in Virginia and married Henry Ashby Updike on September 8, 1892. They moved to Winchester from Front Royal and Browntown, Virginia. Benjamin Boyer baptized Alice in 1900 at the Ammon Updike dam in Browntown. She was an active worker in the Church of God after her baptism and until her health failed.

Howard Beemer, pastor at Maurertown Church of God, performed her funeral service. She was interred at Mt. Hebron Cemetery outside of Winchester.

Alice was Cecil Baggarly Railton's grandmother; the family lineage continues through Joyce Railton Bolhous and Marcee Bolhous Turner.

See Boyer, Benjamin
  Railton, Austin (20th)

Bibliography: Obituary, *The Restitution Herald*, Sydney Magaw, ed., Oregon, Il., May 3, 1949.

Updike, John J.
b. May 24, 1826
d. June 11, 1920

In 1844, Elder J.F. Wagoner, an Indiana evangelist, baptized an 18-year-old John Updike. A few years later, Updike married Elizabeth Rudacille and built a house in the mountains above Front Royal, Virginia, at Cool Springs. They had 11 children. His wife and six children predeceased him. The Church of God congregation at Cool Springs met at the Updike home. Updike died at age 94, survived by five children, 22 grandchildren and 53 great-grandchildren. Five of his grandchildren were Church of God members at the time of his death. Pastor J.H. Anderson conducted Updike's funeral from the home of Bro. Updike's daughter. Anderson offered comfort through Job 14:14-15 which speaks of the hope of the resurrection: "If a man dies, will he live again? All the days of my struggle I will wait until my change comes. You will call, and I will answer you" (NAS).

Bibliography: Obituary *The Restitution*, July 4, 1920.

Vanzandt, James C.
b. 1845?
d. September 7, 1943

James C. Vanzandt was born in Missouri but moved north after marrying Miss Alice Gruber on October 7, 1891. He learned the printing trade and earned his income from setting type. He said in one letter that he had set millions of pages of Christian literature. Vanzandt, a Church of God Bible scholar, is credited with planting a work in Portland, Oregon. He had strong associations with the brethren in the Minnesota Conference, and his name appears frequently in *The Day Dawn and Harvest Messenger*. In 1904 he wrote:

> I am spending my entire time in evangelistic work, and the Lord has been giving me some good meetings during the winter. I started in the work nearly eighteen years ago. I stand squarely committed to the doctrine of conditional immortality, holiness and healing through Divine power. I believe that the baptism and the Lord's Supper are ordinances in the Church, and that none but those saved from sin have any right to them. I believe that the Church in each locality is made of saved people, and that in God's eyes all the Christians in each locality are members of that local church. I am sure we should take the name that God himself gave the Church, letting all others pass out of use. I feel sure that Christ will manifest himself to the world in a very short time, and we need to be found in his name, and in his order in all things.

When he entered the evangelistic ministry, Vanzandt sold all his possessions and paid his own way. He said:

> During the summer season I often held two or three open air services daily, leading in the singing, as well as doing much talking in private, etc. During different winters when mercury was 15 to 20 below zero, I went without any overcoat, and without socks on my feet, laboring among people who were financially well off. This intense labor and exposure wrecked my voice and health until I had a real breakdown. Finally, I got hold on the Lord for a restoration of voice and strength and entered the work again. I am now in the reclining years of life, and the days of intense exposure in the past are now telling on me physically.

He shed interesting light on the subject of ministerial-discounted rail travel. He said, "Since October 1912, I have paid for more than 10,000 miles of car fare—full fare because I could not have rates when not devoting my whole time to gospel service—besides I have almost wholly earned our support at manual labor."

Vanzandt described Portland as a busy shipping and shipbuilding center. Because of its prosperity and demand for housing, rents had increased. He purchased a house for $1,000 on installment because it was more economical than renting.

His striking article on sanctification noted sanctification has two meanings: God makes us holy through our acceptance of the sacrifice of Christ, but we also have a responsibility to make ourselves sanctified, or consecrated to the work. God will do His part in sanctifying us. Vanzandt said that we must do our part to remain consecrated to the work.

He wrote frequently of errors Charles Taze Russell published in his papers, *The Millennial Dawn* and *The Scripture Studies*. Russell wrote that the four angels of Revelation 7:1-2 were "Russell's Little Flock, and that the loud voice to the four angels was Russell himself!" Vanzandt skillfully refuted all of Russell's teachings.

Vanzandt's writings sound somewhat discouraged because financial support for the ministry had not come from the people, but people everywhere were struggling at the turn of the 20th century. The economy was just recovering from a depression, and disease was rampant across the Midwest, taking breadwinners from many families. It is a miracle that people had the resources to support their own ministries in the face of such hardship. Vanzandt was a stalwart individual committed to serving despite the difficulties. This kind of dedication is profoundly important to Church of God's great legacy.

Bibliography: Ancestry.com. U.S. Census. Oregon. Multnomah. Portland (Dist. 1-219) Dist. 195; Ancestry.com. Missouri Marriage Record 1805-2002 James C. Vanzandt record; Vanzandt, J.C., "Sanctification—Two Kinds," *The Day Dawn and Harvest Messenger*, Jas. A Patrick, ed., Howard Lake, Minn. June 1904; Vanzandt, J.C. "What I am doing and Why I am doing it," *The Day Dawn and Harvest Messenger*, Jas. A. Patrick, ed., Minneapolis, Minn. June/July 1918; Vanzandt, J.C. "Some Russellism," *The Day Dawn and Harvest Messenger*, Minneapolis, Minn. Jas. A. Patrick, ed., Jan. 1918.

Van Vactor, David E.
b. October 1863
d. Unknown

Elder David E. Van Vactor was an Indiana preacher who devoted his life to ministry. His father, Hiram, was from Virginia, and his mother, Catharine, from Germany. David grew up in Walnut Township, Marshall County, Indiana. Hiram was a farmer and David worked with him. They very likely attended the Church of God at Argos. Young David would have had the benefit of knowing the old preachers, H.V. Reed, S.A. Chaplin, Ephraim Miller and J.M. Stephenson. He might have known Nathaniel Field of Jeffersonville, Indiana. As these great figures passed away, David would have encountered Jacob Shafer, Uncle John Foore and J.F. Waggoner. David Van Vactor was contemporary with F.L. Austin, L.E. Conner, J.W. Williams, J.S. Hatch and Mary and B.W. Woodward. He was in good company, for they were all dedicated evangelists.

David Van Vactor seemed to be an at-home man. He married Matilda ("Matty" or "May") around 1889, and they settled in Argos. From that point, he worked as a machinist at a local factory. A daughter, Janice (Venna), was born in 1892 followed by three more children, Anna, Evelyn Emma and David Glen. Lloyd Miller, a 15-year-old ward, lived with them until 1900. By this time, David had been promoted to manager at the factory.

On Sundays, David preached at Argos, Plymouth, Burr Oak at Culver, Rensselaer and elsewhere as needed. He did not write tracts or articles to any great extent, making it difficult to learn details of this dedicated preacher through *The Restitution*. His name appears there, however, in the obituaries, for he was called to do nearly every funeral of a Church of God member or a neighbor in Marshall County. Since the evangelists traveled on preaching tours, it fell to David to conduct the funerals and weddings back home. He did not always remain in Indiana, however. He was invited to participate in the Nebraska conference, and when he retired, he moved out of state.

This humble man served on one of the most important committees appointed in the Church of God movement. In 1920, the conference delegates at Waterloo, Iowa, selected him to conduct a study by August 1921 and return a recommendation detailing the best method for organizing a national general conference that would last. The Committee of Ten, as it was called, had a serious assignment. They were charged with creating something that had twice before been achieved but did not endure (1869 and 1888), and nearly achieved (1910), but had not yet succeeded. It was hoped that something positive and enduring would happen in 1921.

In addition to Van Vactor, the Committee of Ten consisted of J.W. Williams, an Iowa preacher; Grace Marsh, a minister's wife from Iowa; businesswoman, Leota B. Hanson, St. Louis; layman Rolla Hightower, Macomb, Illinois; F.L. Austin, Fonthill, Ontario; Alta King, a librarian from Nebraska and California; Pastor James A. Patrick; and Evangelist F.E. Siple who was still in good standing with the state conferences and the people at that time. J.W. Williams was appointed chairman, but he left the committee over a doctrinal issue before it finished its work. Elder Van Vactor and the remaining colleagues on the committee accomplished the mission as directed.

The Church of God General Conference formed at the 1921 conference by vote of the delegates, and afterward by ratification of the member state conferences.

Van Vactor believed in having a national organization of the Church of God. Such an organization would serve the needs of the pastors and churches, and it would unite the work behind a denominational goal. He also believed the new headquarters would thrive in Argos, Indiana. At the 1921 Waterloo Conference, he pleaded with the delegates to name Argos as the new General Conference's headquarters doing business as the National Bible Institute. His pleas passed over unhearing ears. Oregon, Illinois, was chosen as the headquarters since *The Restitution Herald* was already being published there.

Van Vactor was one of the first to have his name added to the 1921 General Conference list of recognized ministers. By then, he was preaching at Michigantown, Indiana, once a month and rotated Sundays with Argos and Burr Oak. He had worked with this latter group since it was a new work at the turn of the century. Van Vactor was the architect of the first church (it burned later), and he built the pulpit. It is not known if the pulpit survived the fire. He preached once monthly at the new church work in South Bend from 1916-1921.

D.E. Van Vactor always preached at "June meeting" at Old Antioch Church of God at Argos. For several years after this church ceased having regular meetings, the Church of God Indiana Conference still met there the second Sunday of every June. People came from all over Indiana and beyond. Some preached, but most came to listen and share fellowship. The Antioch church was sold in 1915 and razed in 1920 in favor of attendance at the newly built North Salem Church along Route 31. David Van Vactor preached regularly at North Salem also.

In his retirement, David moved to Evanston, Illinois, possibly to be near his daughter Janice. The rest of the children, all in their twenties, remained at home. Daughter Anna, son-in-law Walter Meloy and Meloy's brother lived with the Van Vactors in Evanston. Nothing is known of his death or interment.

See Austin, F.L.
  King, Alta
  Patrick, James A.
  Siple, Frank (20th)
  Williams, J.W. (20th)

Bibliography: Ancestry.com. U.S. Census. Indiana. Marshall. Argos. 1910; U.S. Census. llinois. Cook. Evanston. District 2138. 1930; Austin, Evelyn. "A Brief Sketch of Indiana Church History" written from South Bend, around 1930. *The Restitution*. Numerous obituaries from *The Restitution,* and *The Restitution Herald*; Burr Oak 50th *Anniversary of the Church of God.* Booklet. Dec. 10, 1950.

Vedantachari, Charles
  b. 1850?
  d. Unknown

Pastor Charles Vedantachari was the native Indian pastor in the Bible Faith Mission. Dr. Austin and Mrs. Sarah K. Taylor operated this mission work for the Advent Christian denomination. The mission work had close association with the Church of God through the Minnesota Conference.

It is important to note that many of the Minnesota churches, which became Church of God, had emerged from the Advent Christian work there. This friendly association continued through the decades as members of each other's denominations visited their state conference meetings.

One outcome of this association was the joint effort at foreign missions. Through the example of the Minnesota conference, foreign missions were introduced into the Church of God General Conference in the 1950s. The first such mission work was in India with Pastor John Manoah, the successor to Charles Vedantachari.

In 1912, Pastor Charles Vedantachari visited the mission-oriented Churches of God in Minnesota with Mrs. Sarah Taylor. Mrs. Taylor and Charles Vedantachari were ordained into the ministry through the Minnesota Church of God conference at the St. Cloud conference meeting. Elder Vedantachari's ordination service was held on June 24, 1912. Ministers E.E. Thoms, Henry Dingman and James Patrick served at the ordination. Vedantachari returned to his home in Madras, India. Mrs. Taylor was ordained at the 1914 Minnesota summer conference.

The organized Church of God in India predated its fellowship with the Church of God Minnesota Conference. James Patrick wrote in *The Day Dawn*, July 1912, that the mission work in India "up to a short time ago, had but thirty members."

Charles Vedantachari also wrote eloquently of his first impressions of the Church of God. He first read of the Church of God through *The Day Dawn and Harvest Messenger*. He liked the message presented in the pages of this magazine, but he wondered, "Who are these people?" He thought they might be "a set of cranks like myself and friends." He wondered if he would ever meet them. Then the Bible Faith Mission sent him tickets for a steamer and he made his way to the United States and to Minnesota.

See Patrick, James
  Taylor, Mrs. Sarah K.
  Thoms, Egbert E.

Bibliography: "Editorial Mention," *The Day Dawn and Harvest Messenger*, James A Patrick, ed., Fort Dodge, Iowa, June 1920; Vedantachari, Charles, "Home and Foreign Mission Work," *The Day Dawn and Harvest Messenger*, James Patrick, ed., Howard Lake, Minn. Oct., 1912. Taylor, Sarah, "The Reason Why the Bible Faith Mission is Needed in India." *The Day Dawn and Harvest Messenger*, June 1912; *History of the Church of God in Minnesota,* Sydney Magaw, ed., 1931.

Wagoner (Waggoner), James F.
b. January 30, 1834
d. February 19, 1917

J.F. Wagoner was born in Miami County, Ohio. The family moved to Fulton County, Indiana, when he was a small boy. He was the grandson of James Curtis in Miami, who donated land for Brush Creek Church of God's first building. James married Rebecca Sample and together they farmed. He also preached for most of their lives. From their farm, James, his sons and brothers operated a water-powered sawmill on a lively creek.

The *Rochester Union* reported in April 1874, that Frank, Wagoner's 13-year-old son, was injured at the mill when his thumb was caught between a rolling log and the skid. They anticipated it might require amputation.

At one time Elder J.F. Wagoner was a pioneer Adventist minister who fell away, possibly after the Bitter Disappointment in 1844, but then took it up again to become a Church of God preacher. He was well known in Ohio and Indiana. Wagoner did not understand the message of the Gospel of the Kingdom and its subsequent interpretation of atonement. But, when he heard Jacob Shafer preach on the subject of atonement, it got him to thinking. One story recounts that Wagoner went home, dusted off his Bible, which he hadn't used in 15 years, and began to study. That would place his interaction with Shafer around 1860.

Shafer stated that atonement is fulfilled in the future when Christ returns. Wagoner had not yet heard that idea, so he asked Shafer about it. Shafer said that Christendom has incorrectly taught that Christians receive their reward before the second coming of Christ. Wagoner had believed that also, but couldn't defend his position from Scripture, so he invited Shafer to his home to discuss it.

Shafer explained that believers are saved when they accept Christ. Salvation is conditional upon man's acceptance of it. Christ's death covers sin in the same way the mercy seat covered the ark. The Jewish Day of Atonement is *Yom Kippur*. *Kippur* means a cover or lid. In the Old Testament on the Day of Atonement, the priest carried the blood of the sacrifice into the Holy of Holies, and the sin passed to him. When he exited, he laid hands upon the scapegoat and sent it out into the wilderness, casting sin (Satan) out of the camp. Numerous atonement metaphors in orthodox Christendom try to explain the issue but fall short. Christ's death means little to someone who never accepts Him. His shed blood covers our sin. There is no reconciliation to a sinner who doesn't repent, has not accepted the Lord, or has not been immersed.

Anything less than this understanding leads into universalism which states that all men will be saved. Reconciliation is for believers who are reconciled now by receiving the earnest (down payment) of our inheritance (Ephesians 1:14), with assurance of salvation when Jesus comes. J.F. Wagoner did not believe in universal salvation.

When Elder Shafer laid out the truth of reconciliation for believers in Christ, and the promises relating to the future, James Wagoner gladly accepted it, and was baptized by Elder Shafer. Wagoner then introduced this idea of atonement to the members of the church he had been attending, and they all accepted it. This became the Church of God at Rochester, Indiana.

When J.F. Wagoner went to Brush Creek to visit his Curtis relatives, he preached the Gospel of the Kingdom. The early Brush Creek congregation was a mixture of Adventists, Christians and Conditionalists. The first members in that rural community of Ohio who believed the Gospel of the Kingdom were baptized in 1869, and the present congregation was formally organized in 1897.

Wagoner preached in Florida in 1886, perhaps for the winter, and while there introduced Mrs. Frances Hambreck to the Gospel message. She remained faithful to the Faith until her death in 1904. Wagoner wrote a thoughtful eulogy for *The Restitution*.

Wagoner also preached at the Church of God in Argos, Indiana. S.A. Chaplin had served as pastor there for 15 years, but when he died, J.F. Wagoner stepped up to serve for the next ten years. This congregation was organized on January 1, 1869, with 18 members. The membership included the Caleb Railsback family with their six sons and their wives. Wagoner resigned early in 1900 possibly to explore the new field opening on the Great Plains.

J.F. Wagoner baptized one outstanding Indiana member, Joshua Bailey; after baptism Bailey moved his family to Missouri and began the work at the Blush Church of God.

In his later years, Wagoner preached throughout Kansas and the eastern part of Oklahoma, a poverty-stricken area after the Depression of 1893, and rented old log houses. If area residents had a mortgage, they couldn't afford to pay it. One farmer offered all his stock to the bank in return for canceling his farm mortgage. The bank refused the offer. Life was difficult on the Plains. The life and times were tough on preachers, too. But men and women took comfort from preaching the Gospel and from hearing it. William L. Crowe worked with Wagoner in this area where times were tough for preachers, too. The record states that Crowe spent $30 traveling to join Wagoner and received only $3.60 to cover his expenses.

In 1904, J.F. Wagoner was secretary of the Indiana Conference. He recorded details of business meetings and sent them to *The Restitution*. He also preached at that conference on "Signs of the Times." He preached again at Indiana conferences in 1913 and 1914. He was old a frail at the time. As a "pioneer of the faith," he preached on prophecy—the very topic that made the Church of God Abrahamic Faith distinctive.

Two years after Rebecca's death, Elder Wagoner combined his home with his sister, Mrs. Mark Richter, near Argos. He was feeble, and finally, hypo-static pneumonia led to his death. His obituary said he was "well-known in the county as a preacher and author of religious tracts." Pastor David Van Vactor preached the funeral from the Richter home. James was interred at the Odd Fellows Cemetery in Rochester, Indiana.

See Bailey, Joshua
Crowe, W.L.
Marsh, Joseph
Shafer, Jacob
Thomas, Joseph
Wilson, Benjamin

Bibliography: Ancestry.com. U.S. Census. Indiana. Miami. Allen. 1870; "Brush Creek Church of God History 1833-1969," author unknown, 1969. This paper states that the first Brusk Creek congregation was formed in 1833 which predates the Millerite movement; Ferrell, Terry. *A Brief History of the Church of God in America*, National Berean Youth Conference, Camp Reynoldswood, Dixon, Il., Aug. 21-27, 1960; Graham, David. E-mail to author, March 1, 2006 and January 2009; *The Restitution*, Feb. 2, 1904; April 6, 1904; July 6, 1913; *The Restitution Herald*, October 4, 1921; March 1922; J.F. Wagoner Obituary, *Fulton County Indiana Obituaries*. Year 1917,

Jean. C. and Wendell C. Tombaugh, Rochester, In., 1908; "Church of God" *Argos Reflector,* Argos, Indiana, August 30, 1900 furnished by Arlen Rankin.

Walke, Dr. William H.
b. 1839
d. Unknown

Dr. Walke was a member of a Church of God in California. At age 83, he preached at the Southern California Conference for one and one-half hours on "the Judgments." The secretary who sent the report said, "The gracious words which fell from the lips of this grand old soldier of the cross were prompted by the Holy Spirit."

Bibliography: *The Restitution Herald,* August 1922.

Warren, Robert A. "Bob"
b. 1858
d. Unknown

Robert Warren was the son of Alexander and Nancy A. Warren, originally from DeQueen, Arkansas. The Warren family moved to Coryell County in Texas when Bob was a teen. He engaged in farming with his father and brothers until he left home.

He may have learned of the Age to Come and conditional immortality while growing up in Arkansas. In those years, Dr. Muncrief and J.R. Ham preached in arbor groves across Arkansas. When Robert went out on his own, he worked for the Church of God in Texas. While evidence suggests James Lord began the first Church of God in Texas, the Warren work was a close second. Warren may have been responsible for teaching conditional immortality to A.S. Bradley. The specific issue of conditional immortality (materialism) brought A.S. Bradley out of the Church of Christ and into the Church of God.

A Texas history written in 1976 declared, "He [Warren] invited A.S. Bradley of DeQueen, Arkansas to join him about 1890." He invited Bradley to assist him in a debate within the church he was attending. The two of them ably defended their position, and a number of conversions and immersions resulted. Warren Chapel was built on the Warren farm north of Ater, Texas, near Gatesville in 1903, and Warren served as pastor.

Elder Warren was a catalyst for action in the South Texas Conference which included the Riviera Church of God, comprised of the W.L. Robbins family, and the Kingsville Church of God. There may have been some work organized at Gonzalez, and later, Harlingen.

That conference elected Robert Warren editor of *The Gospel Trumpet* throughout Texas. It is unknown if he became a corresponding editor who fed news to the editor in chief or if he were sole editor. Also unknown is how long he served in that role, for T.A. Drinkard is principally known as its editor. It is thought that Warren handed the paper off to R.O. Turner who merged it with *The Restitution Herald* in 1915 from which *The Gospel Trumpet* re-emerged around 1923.

See Bradley, A.S.
    Drinkard, T.A. (20th)
    Ham, J.R.
    Lord, James
    Muncrief, Dr. James
    Turner, R.O.

Bibliography: Ancestry.com U.S. Census. Texas. Jefferson. Beaumont. Dist. 11. 1930. *The Restitution*, January 27, 1920; Nov. 2, 1920; "History of Texas," 1976, author unknown, though the writings of Emory Macy and James Mattison have been helpful in identifying the growth of the work in Texas.

Weeks, John
b. 1850?
d. Unknown

John Weeks became a member of the Church of God in 1871, and served the Lord faithfully for 50 years. He may have lived in Arkansas or Oklahoma at the time of his baptism. In 1921 he wrote to S.J. Lindsay at *The Restitution Herald* and to Robert Huggins at *The Restitution* that he was living with his son in Waco, Texas, and that he was ill.

Weeks had rheumatism and a cancer on his ear. There was no government welfare in those days, and he could not pay his doctor bills. He appealed to the brethren of the Church of God for help. He thanked them for the prayers and assistance they had already offered. This sort of letter from needy subscribers is seen occasionally in Church of God papers. Members responded by lovingly sending whatever they could afford to assist a brother or widow with unexpected expenses.

The Church of God General Conference put a formal structure in place for the elderly generations of the early 20th century by opening the Golden Rule Home in Oregon, Illinois, in February 1923. The facility played an important role for isolated and elderly members. It was through the services at the Home that the physical and spiritual needs of many Church of God senior citizens were met. A problem that could not be overcome, however, was the exclusion of impecunious seniors who had no way of paying for their keep. The newly formed General Conference could not afford to subsidize the residents, and people could not be admitted until they had funds to cover the costs. Such members often lived their final years at a county farm.

See Shafer, Jacob

Bibliography: *The Restitution* Oct. 1921; *The Restitution Herald*, Report Oct. 25, 1921; March 28, 1922.

Weethee, Dr. Jonathan Perkins
b. 1812
d. August 8, 1889

A. A Former Millerite
B. Theologian and Academician
C. Weethee and Himes

Jonathan Weethee was born near Millfield in Athens County, Ohio, and grew up on a farm where he gained an appreciation for the earth and nature. His parents were Daniel Weethee of New Hampshire and Lucy Wilkins of Virginia. He married Anna K. Krepps of Philadelphia in 1840. They were married for 24 years when she died, childless. In 1886, he married Miss Ella Barber of Salem, Ohio. Miss Ella may have been the sister or sister-in-law of Nancy Barber, the well-known Ohio evangelist for the Church of God.

J.P. Weethee was a physician and a professor. He had been an unenthusiastic student at Ohio University; nevertheless, he earned his bachelor's degree in 1833. Next, he studied medicine with a private physician. He often returned home from college by walking a path through a dense forest atop a two-mile ridge. One day in that beautiful setting, he had a vision of God's glory which drew him to the Lord and resulted in his conversion. He testified that he wanted to see the Lord's return and the restitution of all things from that day forward.

Within a year after his graduation, true to his conversion experience, he became interested in the teachings about the Second Advent. He placed himself under the tutelage of the Presbyterian Church in Pittsburgh and Uniontown in 1834. Dr. Weethee studied eschatology and believed in the coming of Christ to establish His Kingdom. Unlike "Father Miller," he never set any dates, but he wrote about the times and the seasons in which to expect the return of Christ. He became aware of the work and writings of Joseph Marsh.

A. A Former Millerite

Some scholars say Weethee was never part of the Millerite movement, but evidence seems to indicate that he was. An article in *Ohio History* said:

> J.P. Weethee...was the most influential Millerite in the Muskingum Valley. Professor Weethee, President of an academy at Beverly, Ohio, was already a powerful voice in the area and had lectured up and down the Muskingum

River valley. He was an enthusiastic worker for the Advent cause from the day he read a copy of *The Midnight Cry*.

He wrote then to Miller explaining how he had become converted. When Miller and Himes journeyed to Cincinnati in August 1844, J.P. Weethee, Mr. Boggs and Mr. E. Marsh met them at the train and encouraged Miller to begin preaching right away.

A letter to Joseph Marsh by E. Marsh in *The Voice of Truth* May 7, 1845, offered details of the preaching ministry of Weethee and Boggs at McConnellsville, Morgan County, Ohio. E. Marsh then invited Elon Galusha to come to Ohio and advised him to give Dr. Weethee about three weeks notice so he could prepare for the meetings.

Weethee reported to Marsh's *Advent Harbinger* that he had been traveling throughout the east to preach the glad tidings of the kingdom at hand. He had traveled through New Hampshire, Maine, New Brunswick and Nova Scotia as far as Halifax. He also pastored churches in Cincinnati and Boston. Joseph Marsh mentioned Weethee's ministry in Ohio in 1851 during his western tour which included Cincinnati.

In 1876, Weethee began writing a column for adult Christians in *The Sunshine*, a paper edited by J.F. Wilcox from Plymouth, Indiana. This paper was primarily a children's periodical with stories, puzzles and activities. It was a good idea and greatly needed, but it is doubtful that the paper was supported by subscriptions. It probably did not continue to be published past that year. A copy of a single issue, Volume 1:11, is in the Archives of Atlanta Bible College.

Dr. Weethee was present at the dedication service of the Salem Church of God, Salem, Ohio, on November 13, 1887. Other Ohio pastors present at that service included G. Elton of Cleveland, and J.T. Ongl (Ongley) of Pennsylvania. Dr. Weethee lived in Athens at this time.

B. Theologian and Academician

While engaged in preaching and writing about the doctrine of the Age to Come, Weethee became president of Madison and Waynesburg colleges in Pennsylvania, and Marietta College in Ohio. After a brief disagreement at Waynesburg over aspects of being a co-educational college, Dr. Weethee left and formed Weethee College at Sunday Creek near his home a few miles from Ohio University. He operated the college from 1861 until his death.

Dr. Weethee was a dynamic speaker and in much demand throughout the East. He was so busy, he could not accommodate every appointment demanded of him. He authored several books of interest to miners regarding Ohio's geology. His books on these topics are preserved in the collection of Ohio University at Athens.

He also authored three books on eschatology, including *Armageddon*, *The Coming Age Its Nature and Proximity*, and *The Egyptian Phase of the Eastern Question* which discussed the Egyptian empire and those of Britain, Ottoman, Hebrew, American and the Messianic kingdom. This last title was first published as a 35-article series in *The Restitution* throughout 1883 and as a book the following January.

The Coming Age is preserved in the archival collection of Atlanta Bible College in McDonough, Georgia, and at Ohio University Library at Athens. *The Coming Age* is also mentioned in a bibliography of the famous *Schaff-Herzog Encyclopedia of Religious Knowledge*, Volume One, under an article about Adventists. This book was still being advertised in the pages of *The Restitution* in 1888 just one year before the great professor's demise. It was advertised as being "a religious book of surpassing excellence." It had over 500 pages and sold for $3—a large price in those days.

C. Weethee and Himes

J.P. Weethee may be well known for his role in exposing the doubletalk of Joshua V. Himes following the Union Conference of 1851. Himes was William Miller's lieutenant who expertly promoted the Millerite movement. As Miller aged and declined in health, Himes' star rose brightly. Himes traveled widely and published *The Advent Herald* following the Albany Conference of 1845. Himes mistakenly told his followers that he did not own *The Advent Herald* or the Advent bookstore associated with that publication's office. He said the Adventist movement owned it. People accepted that and supported the paper and the bookstore handsomely.

During the year 1850-1851, Joseph Marsh felt heat from the Adventists over his growing verbalization of that strange doctrine, Age to Come. Himes certainly was not taken with it. Evidence of discontent filtered through the pages of Marsh's *Advent Harbinger* and tempers flared. Yet, Marsh was discreet, and did not fully disclose the problem.

In the meantime, the congregation on Chardon Street in Boston invited J.P. Weethee to become their pastor. Weethee accepted and moved to Boston. Himes attended this church. Over the weeks and months of his association with Himes, Weethee discovered that the latter indeed *was* the owner of *The Advent Herald* and the bookstore, and singularly profited from it. Himes' apparent contradiction was widely publicized; both Adventist members and evangelists in the field disapproved.

Weethee authored a pamphlet, "Vindication," about the commotion at Boston regarding Himes. Marsh wrote that reform was needed. A copy of "Vindication" is preserved in the collection of the Library at Ohio University at Athens.

In 1851, Weethee submitted a letter to Marsh in which he stated that investigators into the Boston matter had decided to withdraw from fellowship with Himes. To quiet the raging turmoil among Adventists, Himes called a union meeting in New England, ostensibly to unite them all into one movement as it had been under Miller.

Himes announced at the beginning of the meeting that it had been called to take immediate measures for the general union and cooperation of Adventists throughout the country and to choose a corresponding committee to contact all Adventists and report the meeting's outcomes.

Then in a sudden turn, Himes and a few colleagues decided to expel anyone who had persecuted him over the Boston problem in 1850. He immediately drew up a list with 16 names including a gentleman from Lenyart, who was so astounded at the punitive action he defiantly refused to relinquish his stance on the floor until Himes explained why his name was on the list. The offended man was still standing after Himes called in the sheriff, the constable and some officers to bring about order. One man was so incensed, he said, "Let us dismiss not for prayer to God, but to Caesar!" Men lost reason. It was a raucous scene. Weethee reported these events to *The Advent Harbinger*, and Marsh published it.

To smooth things over, Joseph Marsh, J.B. Cook, E.E. Pinney, George A. Avery, J.H. Hayes and James McMillan called a Union Conference at Rochester in spring of 1851. At the same time Weethee and 46 others called another Union Conference in New York City the same weekend.

Joseph Marsh asked if Weethee's group would delay their conference by one or two weekends for the sake of the meeting in Rochester, and so they could all attend. This he did. Both meetings were held. The Rochester meeting was well attended by local evangelists and several men from the West, and the work went forward.

When the conflict with Himes settled down, Dr. Weethee returned to Ohio.

In addition to teaching school at the Ames Academy in Ohio from 1854-1856, Weethee participated in the development of the railroad infrastructure in Ohio. He was a member of the Board of Directors who brought the railroad through the Athens area. The first one ran from Michigan to Virginia, but he also helped bring the Atlantic and Lake Erie Railroad to the state.

Dr. Weethee died in 1889. He was interred in Nye Cemetery near Chauncey, Ohio.

See Barber, Nancy
Cook, J.B.
Marsh, Joseph
Ongley, John

Bibliography: Chew, Tim. *The Chew Family Tree*, Rootsweb.com. This was a valuable source in detailing portions of Dr. Weethee's life. "Report of New England Union Conference," and, "Call for Union Conference," *Advent Harbinger and Bible Advocate*, March 1, 1851 and March 8, 1851 Also, *Advent Harbinger and Bible Advocate*, June 7, 1851; "Letter by Weethee to Marsh," *Advent Harbinger and Bible Advocate*, Nov. 2, 1850; "Boston Difficulties" *Advent Harbinger and Bible Advocate*, Jan. 18, 1851; Gordon, Thomas N, "The Millerite Movement in Ohio," *Ohio History*. Ohio Historical Society, Columbus, Oh., Spring 1972, pps. 102-104; Marsh, E., "Letter to Joseph Marsh," *The Voice of Truth*, May 7, 1845; *The Restitution*, Feb. 1, 1888; Weethee, J.P., *Sunday creek valley: its mineral resources and prospective wealth*. Athens, Oh., 1892; Weethee, J.P. *The Salina and Chauncey Mineral district: description, history and geological analysis*. Athens, Oh., 1892; Weethee, J.P., *The Eastern Question, in its various phases: Egyptian, British, Russian, Ottoman, Hebrew, American and Messianic*, Trauger. Columbus, Oh., 1887; Weethee, J.P. *The Coming Age, Its Nature and Proximity*, C.H. Jones. *Chicago. 1884*; Weethee, J.P., *The Trial of Elder JV Himes before the Chardon St. Church, A report which vindicated the course taken by Prof. J.P. Weethee and Elder George Needham*, Damrell and Moore. Boston. 1850; Weethee, J.P., "Experience," *The Restitution*, A.R. Underwood, ed., Plymouth, In., Jan. 10, 1894. This piece about Weethee's conversion must have been published posthumously; Wilcox, J.F., *The Sunshine*, vol. 1:11, Archives, ABC as noted in *The History Newsletter*, JStilson, ed., Oregon, Il., Summer, 1984; Wince, Roxanna, Obituary of J.P. Weethee, *The Restitution* [front page], Sept. 6, 1899; *The Church of God of the Abrahamic Faith, Salem, Ohio. Dedication Service*. "History Section" June 28, 1970. Material was sent by Franklyne Ross.

West, A. Clark
b. 1836
d. 1920?

Clark West was born in New York. He married Marietta "Mary" DeForest West and they had three children, Charles, Clara and Emma. He was a blacksmith, tall and strong, handsome and dignified. It is presumed that Clark was acquainted with the Second Advent message, because he lived in upstate New York where Adventism was popular, but he may not have known at first about the Age to Come.

The family moved to Blanchard, Michigan, around 1869. Sometime within the next decade Marietta died, leaving Clark to raise Emma alone. The older children had already moved out. He married Adaline "Addie" Staley (July 24, 1847-May 20, 1925), the widow of William Staley. Addie was well liked and easily accepted into the family. It is thought that Addie Staley-West had come from Canada, and she taught the children about the Gospel of the Kingdom. Possibly at this time Clark began to study it also. Minister John Bowers had baptized Addie into the Gospel in 1861 when she was only 14. No additional information is known about Elder Bowers.

Clark was a delegate to the 1888 Philadelphia Conference, and served on one of the committees.

Addie was laid to rest in the Decker Cemetery,

Millbrook Township, Blanchard, Michigan. Mary Woodward officiated at the funeral service. It is thought that Clark was laid to rest beside his first wife, Marietta, at an unknown location.

See Chaffee, Clara
  Marsh, Joseph

Bibliography: Ancestry.com. U.S. Census. New York. Wayne. Butler. 1860; U.S. Census. Michigan. Isabella. Blanchard. Dist. 150. 1880; Randall, Clyde, *Historical Waymarks of the Church of God,* Oregon, Il., 1976 p. 15, shows West's photo but gives little information.

Westcott, J.M.
  b. 1800?
  d. Unknown

Elder Westcott of Dundee, New York, was an old friend of Joseph Marsh. Dundee is in the heart of Finger Lakes country in upstate New York, south and east of Rochester. Elder Westcott, like Joseph Marsh, was a member of the Christian Connexion, a spectator of the Adventist movement, including the William Miller years, and a reader of Marsh's religious papers. Apparently, Westcott did not disagree with the Adventists about the return of Christ, and in a letter to Joseph Marsh indicated he thought they were progressing in their thought.

Yet, to Westcott, history was repeating itself.

Having come through the beginnings of the Christian Connexion and knowing and being known by Elias Smith, Abner Jones and several other early leaders and publishers, Westcott recognized that what Joseph Marsh was introducing into the Adventist movement, i.e., the Age to Come, was in fact what Elias Smith had taught 40 years before.

Westcott wrote:
> You have not reached one whit beyond the positions held by E. Smith, A. Jones, C.W. Martin and others 40 or 45 years ago. See Smith's *22 Sermons on the Prophecies*, published, if I mistake not, in 1807. It is a fact that the Christian Connexion, with whom you and I stood and labored for 20 years and upwards were started on the very grounds in which you assume in your articles on the 'Age to come' and while they, as a body, have proclaimed the right of free discussion, they have applied the GAG, and by the aid of their conference organizations, and their trammels upon the press, have succeeded in smothering the most solemn truths which were committed to them and thus have thrown themselves 50 years behind the times.

This was an indictment of the Christian Connexion by Westcott on two issues: for silencing the message of their people about Christ's second coming and the Age to Come, and for criticizing Joseph Marsh for teaching it. Westcott saw their problem as twofold. When *The Christian Palladium* voted to expel Marsh from its editorship for teaching the second coming, Marsh had only been reviving the historical message of the Christian Connexion. Elder Westcott further indicted the Adventist movement under J.V. Himes' direction by exposing their 1851 "Union" conference in New England and New York as a device to stymie free discussion. He encouraged Marsh to keep his paper free by not squelching free investigation as only sectarianism could.

See Marsh, Joseph
  Smith, Elias

Bibliography: Westcott, J.M. "Letter to Joseph Marsh," The *Advent Harbinger and Bible Advocate,* Aug. 9, 1851.

Whitesitt (Whitesett), Thomas F.
  b. 1829
  d. June 1895

Elder T.F. Whitesitt was born in Indiana. He embraced the faith in 1865 and became a preacher shortly thereafter. He married Betsy Larkheart in Vermillion County, Illinois, and they had 11 children. He may have been a circuit preacher in the Danville area after he moved to Illinois. The record shows that the Illinois Conference appointed him pastor at the Twin Groves congregation in northern Illinois in November 1857.

He is known to have baptized Phoebe Buck Garton in 1870. She was the mother of John Garton, an early Iowa and Wisconsin preacher. Whitesitt was appointed the first Iowa evangelist at Watkin's Wells at the June 1888 Iowa Conference. He was hired for $1 a day plus expenses on scheduled workdays. People who invited him to work in their area were to pay railroad expenses. Twenty-six conference attendees pledged $62.65 toward Elder Whitesitt's services which paid for at least 62 days a year. The first year he baptized 23 people; the second year his converts numbered 15; in the third year, despite ill health, he baptized 11. From his evangelistic work, he organized a congregation at Marathon, Iowa, where the Garton families including George, John and Phoebe were members.

In 1887, Whitesitt lived at Broadhead, Wisconsin, but served throughout northern Illinois and Iowa. He had been a church planter and organizer. He said a national conference could help unify the work. He lived to see the organization of a national conference in 1888, and its demise in 1892.

In 1888, a General Conference of the Churches of God in Christ Jesus was organized in Philadelphia. One of the conference programs encouraged the state conferences to organize ten new churches in every state. Whitesitt tried to fulfill that goal. He organized a church at Marathon, Buena Vista County, Iowa, on June 14, 1889, and another at Levey, Polk County, Iowa, on July 4, 1889. As he aged, he was forced to slow down and unable to work fulltime anymore. He continued as evangelist until 1891 when his health prevented it. Thomas Whitesitt died suddenly in Iowa four years later. Inez Garton wrote his obituary, and said, "He died without pain." He is interred at Garfield Cemetery in Calhoun County, Iowa.

See Garton, John
See Also Booth, Lyman
Brown, B.
Chown, Robert
Stephenson, J.M.

Bibliography:Ancestry.com. Illinois Marriages 1790-1860 record of Thomas Whitesitt; Ancestry.com. Iowa Cemetery Records for T.F. Whitesitt; A.J. Eychaner, *History of the Iowa Conference of the Church of God*, 1900, written from notes in his scrapbook. Waterloo, Iowa Annual Conference report Burnett, Francis et al, history committee. *History of the Iowa Church of God and Conference 1855-1987* printed at Belle Plaine Union, 1987; Garton, Inez. Obituary. *The Restitution*, June 19, 1895; *The Restitution*, June 29, 1895; Evangelist report, *The Present Truth*; Rankin, Delbert. E-mail about Elder Whitesitt, Oct. 27, 2008; Whitesitt, T.F., "Report" *The Restitution*, S.A. Chaplin, ed., Plymouth, In., June 1, 1887.

Whittey, John
b. 1870
d. Unknown

John Whittey was a leader in the conference work of South Texas. Nothing more is known about him, although his work may have been recorded in copies of *The Gospel Trumpet*; a few loose copies exist in the Archives of Atlanta Bible College.

Bibliography: *The Restitution*, Nov. 2, 1920.

Wickizer, Sarah Logan Chaplin
b. 1833
d. May 4, 1911

Sarah Logan moved to Marshall County, Indiana, with her parents at age three. The area was still an unsettled wilderness. She grew up as a pioneer child, seeing Indians and learning the hardships of living off the land.

Her father, Henry Logan, was one of the first settlers in Marshall County, arriving only a few days after it became a county. He was a preacher of the Gospel message, and Sarah grew up as a believer. She married Stedman A. Chaplin who, like Logan, became a preacher of righteousness.

Sarah Logan was Chaplin's second wife. She raised his children, Roxanna and Henrietta. Sarah's belief in eternal life through Christ was firm. She could argue a point capably, having learned the art from her father and her husband.

In her older years, after Stedman's death in 1892, she married James M. Wickizer. In 1900, she adopted Mertic Conner, ten-year old daughter of L.E. Conner who had remarried and could not care for her. Sarah and Myrtle, as the girl came to be called, lived as companions until Myrtle grew up and moved to California where she married.

Sarah suffered from asthma in her old age and was cared for by her stepdaughters. David E. Van Vactor conducted her funeral at the Plymouth, Indiana, Church of God. She was laid to rest in Oak Hill Cemetery. She left a good witness to her love for truth, and she rests in peace.

See Chaplin, Stedman A.
Logan, Henry
Bibliography: *The Restitution*, May 17, 1911.

Willey, Joseph H.
b. November 23, 1840
d. Unknown

J.H. Willey from Indiana lived through the formative adolescent years of the Church of God. He was born too late to be part of the Millerite movement, and he was raised in the church as it became established in Indiana before the departure of the Advent Christians from the Indiana conference in 1870.

At age 48 he was appointed a delegate to the 1888 General Conference organizational meeting in Philadelphia. This was not the first attempt to organize a national work, but it was an important time in the life of the church. Many state conferences had already organized. Many new churches were being started across the Great Plains and the South, and members were calling for missions, ministerial education and lesson materials for the church. People wanted doctrine, but they also wanted help for their church programs and ministries. It was hoped a conference organization would help accomplish what the churches had not done and could not do alone. Willey was elected president of that conference board. A.J. Eychaner was elected secretary. Samuel Wilson was vice president, and George F. Work of Philadelphia was elected treasurer.

The following year another general conference was held in Chicago. At this meeting R.S. Dwiggins was elected president, and J.H. Willey was elected member at large of the board. A motion was made to try to secure the ownership of *The Restitution*, published at that time by S.A. Chaplin in Plymouth, Indiana. The attempt was unsuccessful. Without ownership of a nationally distributed newspaper, there would be no way of communicating conference activities with the hundreds of isolated members out west. If the conference could have negotiated the paper's purchase at that time, it is entirely possible that a national conference could have become a viable enterprise. Without a paper and without a press, it was doomed. The board of directors met a few more times between 1889 and 1892, but no additional general conference meetings with delegates were held. Finally, George F. Work made a note in the treasurer's ledger in 1892 that the conference was dissolved due to lack of funds and activities.

Perhaps the lack of financial backing is too simple an answer. According to Lyman Booth, the Church of God nearly died from lack of interest in the decade before 1892. It seems at odds that, while delegates were trying to build something national through the creation of a general conference, a minister who lived through the era would say the church was nearly dead. In 1892, Booth said when D.M. Hudler appeared on the scene revival swept across the churches, beginning in Illinois. For years, historians focused on the national effort in 1888 and beyond, but research of local churches' activities in that era might reveal that Booth's analysis was correct.

Eleven years passed before a national organization was attempted again in 1910, however, it too failed. The 1920 action at Waterloo, Iowa, finally succeeded in birthing a conference in 1921; it still exists today.

The 1910 Waterloo conference's intent was to organize a permanent national organization. The meetings were filled with wrathful dialogue mostly focused on disagreements over doctrine, but also fueled with disagreements about who could be a delegate. L.E. Conner seemed to be the focus of the latter problem.

From this organizational effort, a general conference board was elected. This board continued to meet at least throughout 1911, and tried to salvage the organizational effort towards having a successful vote at the 1911 summer conference. J.H. Willey, was elected president; O.J. Allard, secretary; Peter Jeffreys, treasurer; and J.H. Morse, general director.

This board met in St. Louis in March 1911 to make recommendations to the delegates in August. They recommended that each church send a delegate to the next conference to decide the general conference question. This recommendation satisfied the complaint of the 1910 conference, which had nearly ousted L.E. Conner who was not a recognized delegate but who insisted upon representation. The board also recommended a plan to pay expenses for delegates attending the general conference.

A.E. Hatch, editor of *The Day Dawn* during 1910-1911, commented on the change pertaining to delegates and said:

> The personnel of the gathering this year will be different than last as it will be composed of a delegation of the brethren and not of leaders. Therefore, the apparent desire to be dictators eliminated, and no occasion for the voice of any but the delegates, and by deciding on Waterloo, the board felt we were putting all factions on the same footing as last year, so there could be no occasion to accuse one another of unfairness by moving the place of meeting east or west.

However good the intent was, the general conference organization was not approved in 1911 either, and would not be for another ten years. Hatch also did not continue as editor beyond 1911, possibly because of his candid editorials.

On J.H. Willey's 84th birthday in 1924, a party was held at the Plymouth, Indiana, Church of God. He was the long-standing president of the powerful Indiana Church of God conference. In 1908 he presided over an annual meeting at Antioch church and gave the opening address entitled, "Antioch." He said this name was a sacred name and took his comments from Hebrews 1.

J.H. Willey's name appears frequently in Church of God literature as a writer, preacher and officer, declaring by his writings that he remained faithful to the task.

> See Allard, O.J.
> Conner, L.E.
> Hatch, A.E.
> Hudler, D.M.
> Jeffrey, Peter

See Also Appendix 3–Catalyst for Change, re: D.M. Hudler
Bibliography: Ferrell, Terry, *A Brief History of the Church of God in America*, National Berean Youth Conference, Camp Reynoldswood, Dixon, Il.. 1960; Hatch, A.E., Editorial Comment to "Meeting of General Conference Board Announcement," *The Day Dawn and Harvest Messenger*, A.E. Hatch, ed., 1910-1911, April 1911; *The Restitution.* June 24, 1908; *The Restitution Herald*, Dec. 2, 1924; Work, George, *Ledger of Board of Directors*, General Conference 1888, 1889-1892. This ledger is housed with the archival collection at Atlanta Bible College, McDonough, Georgia.

Williams, Charles
b. January 8, 1837
d. June 22, 1916

Charles Williams was born near Washington Grove, in Ogle County, Illinois. He married Susan Moats on February 9, 1860. He learned of the truth while attending the small rural Antioch Church of God, located two miles east of Washington Grove on Flagg Center Road. Antioch enjoyed quite a nice congregation for a number of years, meeting weekly, hosting the Illinois quarterly conference meetings, and welcoming a number of auspicious preachers such as Benjamin Wilson, H.V. Reed, J.M. Stephenson, D.M. Hudler and J.S. Hatch.

H.V. Reed baptized Charles on July 10, 1898, and Charles devoted the rest of his life to training his family and telling his neighbors about the Abrahamic Faith. Charles and his wife were the parents of Joseph H.

Williams who was the father of Grace Williams Marsh.

Grace described the Antioch Church of God as a wood frame building with a single room. Located on the southwest side of Flagg Center Road where it intersects with Chana Road, this likely was also the Antioch schoolhouse. It had a wood-burning stove for heat. The building sat back from the road a bit so there was room for everyone's horse and buggy to tie up to the hitch. The cut into the field can still be seen, but they stopped using the building after the Oregon Church of God was begun at the Old Stone Church on North Third Street around 1900. People had autos by then, and it was easier to travel to town to worship with a larger congregation.

When Grandfather Charles died, Pastor L.E. Conner preached the funeral at the Washington Grove Congregational Church which sat adjacent to the neighborhood's most prominent cemetery. Charles had helped organize and beautify that cemetery, and it was fitting that he should be interred there. The Washington Grove Church was demolished in September 2010.

See Conner, L.E.
Marsh, Grace (20th)

Bibliography: Marsh, Grace. Interview with Jan Stilson. 1980s at her residence at Pinecrest Manor, Mt. Morris, Illinois; *The Restitution Herald,* July 19, 1916.

Wilson, Addison Bennett
b. February 9, 1875
d. June 4, 1944

Addison Wilson was born in Jefferson, Iowa. He married Elma Mason on November 25, 1903; they were members of the Methodist church. Addison made a commitment to Christ when an evangelist came to town; he likely was not a Church of God evangelist. When the preacher asked for Addison's confession, he also asked Addison to promise he "Won't swear, won't dance, won't work on Sunday." Addison refused to be baptized. He felt he should not have to answer to any man. According to his daughter, Carol, word of it spread through Holbrook, Nebraska, "as if someone's house had burned."

Eva Phelps, Grover Gordon's sister, visited Addison and promised to bring a preacher from Omaha if Addison would hear him preach. He agreed, and she called for evangelist Almus Adams. Adams stayed "two or three weeks, and about 20 in the community were baptized," including Addison and his son, Wayne. This was in 1916, and it is thought Adams baptized them all. That is how the north side Holbrook Church of God began, with meetings held at the local schoolhouse.

The congregation south of Holbrook relocated there years earlier with friends and Church of God members from Gifford, Iowa. Reuben Pliny Story and wife Eleanor moved from Gifford with several families who were members of the Church of God.

Addison Wilson with Wayne and Byrce

Another of these members was John Adams, brother of Almus Adams. This group owned a large tent which they often pitched on Story's land for revival meetings and summer conferences. At some point the tent was moved south to the Republican River where there were more trees to offer shade.

Eventually both congregations became one. The formation of the Holbrook Church of God was interesting. The members from the south side and the north side of Holbrook got together and decided to build a church in town. Ladies from the church went around town and collected money from townsfolk to help finance the construction. When the building was finished, the congregation was debt-free. It was dedicated at Nebraska Conference in August 1927.

All of Addison and Elma's chldren and nearly all their grandchildren were baptized members of the Church of God. As they all lived in the Nebraska panhandle they were unable to attend church regularly except during Nebraska Conference. Carol Wilson (Burton) Smith helped begin a new church at Chappell, Nebraska, because she wanted her children brought up in the faith.

Addison was a good Bible student, and a firm believer in the Abrahamic Faith. His family said that the Bible was the only book he ever read. Until the Holbrook Church of God was able to hire a pastor, Grover Gordon and Addison Wilson served as lay pastors. Grover Gordon preached and Addison assisted with teaching.

One time Addison had a discussion with a local preacher who believed in predestination. Evidently they had discussed the subject more than once, and the preacher was a little exasperated with Wilson's position. He slammed his fist against his hand, and said "Why don't you see what I am telling you?" Addison replied, "If your theory is true it must be because God won't let me." The minister turned and walked away.

Addison Wilson suffered a big loss over a swindle by the local bank. He had taken out a loan to plant his crop, and the bank called in the loan before the crop came in.

Addison lost the farm. It seemed to be a deliberate act to take over his land. He never recovered the loss, but he never lost his faith.

Addison's legacy lives on through the ministry of his granddaughters, Joyce (Russell) Magaw and Carol Smith and their children.

Joyce Magaw contributed to this entry.

See Adams, Almus
   Gordon, Grover (20th)
   Story, Reuben Pliny

Bibliography: Gordon, Grover. "Predestination," 1950. Magaw, Joyce Elma (Wilson). "The Story of Addison Wilson and family," E-mail to author. 2005; Smith, Carol Wilson. "Letter from Aunt Carol," no date, furnished by Joyce Magaw.

Wilson, Benjamin F.
b. February 17, 1817
d. May 8, 1900

A. *The Emphatic Diaglott*
  1. Critics
B. **Wilson's Affiliations**
  1. **Wilson, Campbell and Thomas**
  2. **Wilson and Joseph Marsh**
C. **Wilson and Campbell Stop Communicating**
D. **Discussion on Resurrection**
E. **Western Tour Brings Troubles**
  1. **Dr. Thomas Brings Accusations**
F. **Wilson on Re-baptism**
G. **Wilson on the Holy Spirit**
H. **Health Issues**
I. **Second Western Tour**
J. **Relocation**
K. **The Problem of Josephism**
  1. **Josephism Question Re-Emerges**

James W. (1783-1852) and Sarah Wilson were married in the region of Halifax, West Ridings, Yorkshire, England, in 1816. Benjamin Wilson, their youngest son, and his brothers were born at Halifax, but Benjamin and John, the eldest brother, relocated to the United States in 1844. James and Joseph Wilson followed in 1849. The brothers and their families settled in Geneva, Illinois, a small village with English architectural characteristics and beautiful scenery along the Fox River.

Benjamin and Alice Wilson

Benjamin and Alice arrived in America with daughter Sarah. They had two more daughters, Mary and Rescue, and three sons, Benjamin Edwin, Charles Henry and

Albert S. after settling in Geneva. Rescue P. Wilson was born in 1864 when Alice was 50. After that birth, Alice's health declined until she died in 1870.

William and Richard Appleyard arrived in 1849 with James and Joseph Wilson. Later Joseph Cockroft and George Westgarth of Halifax relocated to Geneva as well. These men helped Wilson publish the local newspaper and his book, *The Emphatic Diaglott.*

Legend says that James W. Wilson, the family's patriarch, was a printer who passed those skills to his sons. Benjamin learned his lessons in Greek well, for he became a skilled translator, as well as a printer. Within three years of arriving in Geneva, he began printing the local newspaper, *The Western Mercury*, which debuted on January 8, 1847. Benjamin's business also accepted job printing from local businessmen and paid advertising from Fowler and Wells, a publishing company in New York City.

David Graham discovered Benjamin began publishing a journal, *The Guardian and Advocate,* in Geneva in 1852. *The Western Mercury* was suspended from 1851-1856 but re-emerged as *The Kane County Republican;* Wilson was not associated with it as he was already involved in publishing *The Gospel Banner* and translating the *Diaglott.* No copies of *The Guardian* are known to exist.

A. *The Emphatic Diaglott*
From 1847 until 1854 Benjamin wrote occasional articles for Joseph Marsh's *Advent Harbinger.* During this period, Wilson also translated the New Testament for an interlinear edition. This had never been done before, but Wilson planned it to have two columns on each page, one on the left with Greek on one line, and the English word immediately below its Greek counterpart. The right-hand column included an English translation with emphasis on key words through capitalized typography. According to the *The Emphatic Diaglott*'s preface, no other translation up to that time had undertaken such an arduous task. It was the first of its kind in the world, and many translators would emulate it.

Benjamin entitled his new translation, *The Emphatic Diaglott, a New Emphatic Version of the New Testament*. Wilson gave the *Diaglott* a subtitle, the "Interlineary Word for Word English translation, a new Version, with the Signs for Emphasis." It had copious references and footnotes, and an "Alphabetical Appendix" which was a short Bible dictionary. This translation would make him famous to this day.

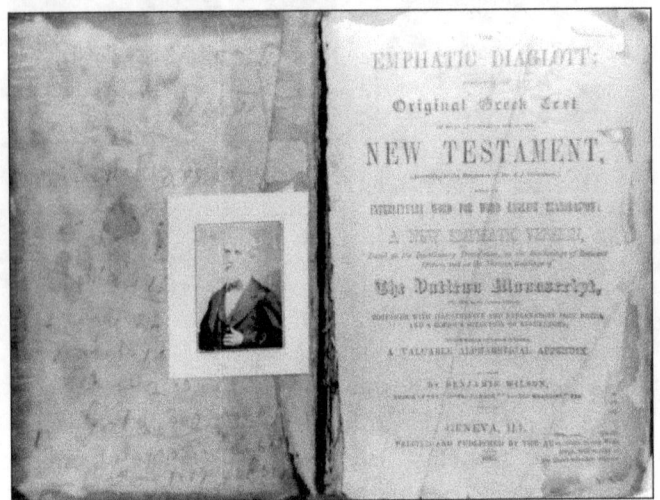

The exercise of translating from Greek was difficult, but Wilson was up to the task. He based the translation upon many texts and manuscripts, but relied principally upon J.J. Griesbach's critical version of the New Testament. Wilson stated on the title page that he also referred to *The Vatican Manuscript*, number 1209 in the Vatican Library. Of all others, Wilson preferred Griesbach's translation. Wilson stated in his introductory essay "History of the Greek Text":

> Griesbach in critical labors excels by far any who preceded him. He *used* the materials others had gathered. His first edition was commenced in 1775; his last was completed in 1806. He combined the results of the collations of Birch, Mattael and others, with those of Wetstein. In his Revision he often preferred the testimony of the *older* MMS to the *mass* of modern copies. [Wilson's italics in all cases.]

Griesbach died before he finished his last version (1806). Others, their names as yet unknown, finished it. John Carras is researching the names of scholars who finished the J.J. Griesbach Greek text, because Revelation 20:5 is also in that 1806 version.

Griesbach had drawn his analysis from *Textus Receptus* printed by Elsevir in Leyden in 1624 which had been based largely upon Robert Stephen's translation in 1549, itself a derivative from Erasmus' 1516 edition. Where Griesbach questioned *Textus Receptus,* he made marginal notes to explain his departures.

The Greek plates for Wilson's *Diaglott* had to be imported from England. Presumably since the Wilson men had been members of the Oxford Printer's Guild in Britain, someone, possibly his father, assisted him with the plates. Although shipping costs were exorbitant, Wilson paid the bill himself. He hoped to recover some costs through the sale of subscriptions to the published book.

Wilson distributed the *Prospectus* for the *Diaglott* in 1853. Of interest to many, a copy of the *Prospectus* was recently discovered bound in the back of Joseph Marsh's *Prophetic Expositor and Bible Advocate.* The Antiquarian Society in Worchester, Massachusetts, owns this copy. This confirms to Church of God historians that Wilson was in communication with Marsh and that they exchanged journals. A note about the *Prospectus* in the inventory of the Antiquarian Society's Advent Newspapers and Periodicals says:

> **Bound after Oct. 15, 1857 is *Prospectus of a New Work, The Original Greek Text, a Word-For-Word Translation, and a New Emphatic Version of The New Testament.* Geneva, IL: Wilson & Cockroft. 8 pages.**

Binding often occurs a few years after receipt of periodicals in a library, hence the difference in the date between the announcement in the *Prospectus* and the binding date.

Wilson translated sections of the New Testament and prepared them for the press. Wilson printed the *Diaglott* in sections, and advertised them through the pages of *The Gospel Banner* and Newman's publication. He distributed each section as it was completed. In 1863, sections 20 and 21 were received by Newman for *The Millennial Harbinger and Bible Expositor* in Syracuse, New York. This brought the project to Hebrews 9:5. The notice said, "This is the most valuable version of the New Testament that has ever been published!"

Each section cost $2. Perhaps modest income from their sales allowed him to proceed. When all sections were printed, the printer sent them to the bindery and they became a book. The first edition of *The Emphatic Diaglott* was copyrighted by Benjamin Wilson in 1864 from Geneva, Illinois; it carries that imprint. A copy of an 1865 *Emphatic Diaglott*, also printed in Geneva, was donated to Oregon Bible College now Atlanta Bible College, by Dr. Leila Whitehead, Wilson's great niece. This rare edition is stored in the Archives.

W.H. Wilson described his Uncle Benjamin's arduous labor in this manner:

> In my mind's eye I still see Uncle Benjamin sitting at his desk making a literal word-for-word translation of the New Testament. I remember seeing the Greek type arrive from England. Many readers of the *Diaglott* may not be aware that my uncle not only translated the *Diaglott* but took charge of the mechanical work as well. He electrotyped the entire book himself.
>
> As each page of the *Diaglott* was put into type, he took an impression of the page of type in wax. This wax mold was then black-leaded with very fine black lead dust. He

had a vat containing acid. In this acid he hung a copper plate and also the wax mold before he went home at night. In the morning, he would find the wax mold covered with a thin sheet of copper. The acid dissolved the copper and the black lead attracted it to the wax mold. He then made metal plates out of melted metal and fastened the copper upon it. He printed the first edition of the book from the plates on a hand press. I used to ink the plate by a soft roller while he worked the press.

Thus from Geneva as the early gospel center, issued one of the most useful aids for Bible study that ever issued from the press, in any section of the county.

Lee Erickson, who wrote about the publishing industry in Great Britain, noted that printing in England was inferior to printed works from the Continent, but the English industry was greatly enhanced when Andrew Wilson, an English printer, invented stereotype. Andrew Wilson was a partner in an ink-making business in Wild Courts, Yorkshire. Stereotype was a process of printing from a plate instead of moveable type. Stereotype increased the printing quality in England so much that it placed England on the international map as a leader in printing technology in 1804. This process was sold to Oxford in 1805 where Andrew Wilson was hired to print Bibles and prayer books at the University Press. Cambridge University was licensed to use the new method in 1809. Electrotype printing, an advancement in stereotype, came later. It is not proven, but is suspected, that Andrew Wilson was known and perhaps related to Benjamin Wilson. Research is ongoing to verify this.

It is certain that Benjamin Wilson was a master of electrotype, and quite gifted in designing and manufacturing high quality printed products. *The Gospel Banner* and *The Emphatic Diaglott* are two of the most beautiful pieces of workmanship to be found anywhere in 19th century printed materials. The printing is crisp and easy to read. The pages are well designed with headings and "white space" to rest the eyes. *The Gospel Banner* is well indexed. The paper is rich to the touch, does not tear easily and has resisted the problem of acid damage so frequent from paper-making techniques in past centuries. The leather binding has held up well even in volumes with heavy use.

1. Critics

Orthodox biblical scholars have not appreciated some of Wilson's translations in the *Diaglott*. One, for

---

Personal Presence

The following article was written by George F. Work, one of the first officers of the Church of God General Conference organized in Philadelphia in 1888. The piece is an explanation of the Greek word *parousia*, as used by Benjamin Wilson in translating the *Emphatic Diaglott*. This is an excerpt of the first portion of the article:

The words used in the Scriptures to denote the second advent of our Lord, make it very certain that it will be a real, personal presence. That "this same Jesus," the same corporeal person, will return to this earth, establish the Kingdom of God here, and reign over the nations with his immortalized saints as kings and priests with him, are truths so plainly taught in the Bible that they become the broad foundation on which we base that faith without which "it is impossible to please God."

"Alas! when the Son of man cometh, will he find this faith in the land?" The word "coming" so often used in the New Testament, is, in seventeen instances used to denote the second advent, or personal coming of our Lord, a translation of the word Parousia, which literally means, "a personal presence," "a being alongside of." Let the reader use the word "presence" in place of the word "coming" in the following texts, and see, as the original text would show him, how much better we realize the idea of a tangible person, whom our eyes can see, and our hands handle, than the myth of a spiritual coming in the hearts of men, or a providential coming in the events of history.

I Thes. 3:15 "We who are alive and remain unto the coming of the Lord."
I Thes. 5:23 "May you be preserved blameless unto the coming of tour Lord Jesus."
2 Thes. 2:1 "We beseech you, therefore, by the coming of our Lord."
James 5:7 "Be patient, brethren, to the coming of the Lord."
James 5:8 "For the coming of the Lord draweth nigh."
2 Pet. 1:16 "Made known unto you the power and coming of our Lord."

Also note how clear examples we have of a visible, personal presence in some cases where the same word is used in connection with other persons, as in

I Cor. 16:17 "I am glad of the coming of Stephanus and Fortunatus and Achaicus."
2 Cor. 7:16 "God comforted us by the coming of Titus, and not by his coming only, but by the consolation," etc.
2 Cor. 10:10 "His bodily presence (coming) is weak."
Eph. 1:26 "By my coming to (presence with) you again."
Phil. 2:12 "Not as in my presence (coming) only, but now much more in my absence."

The same word will be found in such passages as, "the sign of thy coming," The coming of the Son of Man," Christ's at his coming," "At the coming of our Lord," and should always be translated "presence."

Ref.: *The Millenarian* Vol.1:1 January, 1874

example, is John 1:1 in the Greek word-for-word column which reads: "a god was the word" Most scholars do not like the phrase, "a god," but the English translated column reads, "In the beginning was the Logos and the Logos was with God and the Logos was God." Wilson was true to his literal understanding of the Greek.

In another instance, a man criticized *The Diaglott* in a conversation with evangelist J.K. Speer of Illinois. Speer reported the comment to *The Gospel Banner*, writing for the February 1, 1867, issue that he had debated Mr. Linn of Ohio. In the course of the debate, Linn had slandered Benjamin Wilson, saying Wilson had mistakenly translated Matthew 10:28, "Be not afraid of those who kill the body, but cannot destroy the [future] life; but rather fear Him who can utterly destroy both Life and Body in Gehenna" (ED). The accusation was the supposed addition by Wilson of the word "future" in brackets in the English column. It is not present in the Greek column to the left. Speer said the accuser and his friends were "immortalists," "never-dying," and they slandered the Bible.

Another questionable outcome of the translation was Charles Taze Russell's latching onto Wilson's translation of *parouisa* which literally means "presence" instead of "coming" as the King James had translated it. Russell distorted the meaning of the passage because he believed Christ was raised a *Spirit*, therefore His coming in spirit would be an "invisible coming." This is not what the translation meant, but Russell's mistranslation has become more famous than Wilson's correct translation. James Penton, an ex-Jehovah's Witness, wrote in *The Coming Kingdom*, "Thus he [Russell] came to hold that in the last days immediately before his revelation in wrath at the battle of Armageddon, Christ would be *invisibly* present. At that time, only his faithful followers would recognize him."

Many of Wilson's colleagues in theology believed the earth will pass away in fervent heat, and that Christ will create the new heavens and new earth. Wilson used 2 Peter 3:10 to prove that the earth shall not be burned up because it violates the covenant to Abraham, and the promise to David in Psalms 104:5, "The earth shall not be removed for ever."

The Emphatic Diaglott continues to receive praise by scholars who recognize the magnitude of the translation and criticism by other scholars who question certain difficult passages. Because of these passages, the discussion about *The Emphatic Diaglott* will be ongoing. A brief search on the internet will produce many references to this now-famous translation, the first of its kind.

B. Wilson's Affiliations

The Wilsons were cordial towards Alexander Campbell and aligned themselves with Campbell for a year after moving to Geneva, Illinois. Nephew W.H. Wilson, writing years later about the Wilsons' search for truth, said:

> [A] congregation was begun on this partial reformation called "The Disciples of Christ," at Halifax, England. The little light that they received made them (the Wilsons) anxious for more light. The congregation then formed itself into an investigating class, with a firm determination to search carefully the Holy Scriptures. They began with Genesis, and had not gone far before they crossed the Covenants of Promise made to Abraham and repeated unto Isaac and Jacob. You can imagine the golden cord they discovered that those promises permeated and ran through both the Old and the New Testament Scriptures, and constituted the base of the Gospel of the Kingdom. At this point the true light began to shine brighter and brighter until they were led unto obedience of the one true faith and hope of the gospel.

Then later, Thomas Wilson's editorial comments indicate the Wilsons were aware their neighbors in Geneva thought they were Disciples of Christ.

> Our correspondent wishes to know who we are and what church we belong to. We profess to be a believer of the glad tidings the apostles preached, consisting of "the things concerning the Kingdom of God and the name of Jesus Christ, and like the Samaritans who believed Phillip preaching these things, we have been immersed for the remission of sins, calling on the name of the Lord, and hence we belong to the same body or church that they did. We have no sectarian name by which we are known and hence are not recognized or counted among the Christians. The little band of brethren with which we associate, are generally known by our neighbors as Disciples of Christ.

Thomas Wilson explained many years later that they took the name "Disciples" because all Christians are disciples of Christ, and that is the only sense of the word that they had in mind when using this phrase. It is also clear from W.H. Wilson's comments that the Wilsons felt the Abrahamic Faith advanced the Reformation beyond Luther's or Campbell's. It provided the "rest of the story" that had been missing from interpretation since the first century.

While Benjamin was preparing the *Diaglott*, he and the congregation built a small meetinghouse. They called it Disciples Meeting House. It still stands today

Disciples Meeting House, Geneva, Illinois

in Geneva, as does the Wilson home. The name of the church has led Geneva historians to class the Wilson church as Campbellite. Wilson's own words from the January 1, 1861, issue of the *Gospel Banner* explain why they were not Campbellites:

> According to announcement in December No. of the Banner, a Conference of immersed believers in the Kingdom of God and the name of Jesus Christ, was held in the Disciples meeting house in this place commencing on the Lord's day, Dec. 23rd and closing on Wed. evening, Dec. 26th. And here I might observe that some have the idea that the Meeting house referred to belongs to the Campbellite Society, which is erroneous. It was built some years ago by the congregation of believers here and has ever since been occupied by them.

1. Wilson, Campbell and Thomas

After an initial interest in Campbell and Thomas, Wilson took exception to their teachings. The three editors exchanged papers, but it should be noted that while Alexander Campbell published a list of the exchange papers he received every month in the *Millennial Harbinger*, he did not list papers received from the Wilsons, Joseph Marsh after he left *The Palladium*, or Dr. Thomas after he left the Restoration Movement. Alexander Campbell did not list them in the *Harbinger* as it was his custom because these editors no longer followed his doctrinal preferences. Evidence of an exchange between Campbell and Wilson is found in a cancellation request from A. Campbell of Washington in the *Gospel Banner*. See section "C" below.

The Wilsons went from a Baptist affiliation in England to Campbellite affiliation there. Wilson stated in an address he delivered in Edinburgh, printed in the *Messenger of the Churches*, December 1868, that the Wilson family continued with the Disciples fellowship for a year after arriving in America. Yet, even in Halifax they had read and discussed Paul's remarks in Galatians 3:8 about the "gospel preached to Abraham." They thought about this, and as "new light shot across their minds," they finally concluded in America that they must depart from the Disciples.

The Wilson family accepted One Faith by 1849 or 50 after the other two brothers arrived. They believed that fulfillment of the promises to Abraham will occur in the millennium, and they therefore accepted a pre-millennial prophetic system. Campbell was post-millennial, another reason Wilson could not continue in that fellowship. In writing about the future Kingdom of God on earth, Wilson always used his favorite phrase, "One Faith," referring to the faith of Abraham, the same faith mentioned in Jude 3, "the faith once delivered to the saints," who look forward to the Abrahamic covenant being fulfilled when Jesus returns to set up his Kingdom in the millennium. Wilson reported to the brethren in Edinburgh that they were all baptized in 1851. They may have been baptized by local resident, Peter Innes.

Dr. Thomas and Benjamin Wilson did not personally meet until 1856, but Thomas was familiar with Wilson for he referred to Wilson's preaching at Halifax in *Herald of the Future Age*, August 1843. This was prior to Wilson's arrival in America. Benjamin Wilson read Thomas' papers, *The Herald of the Kingdom and Future Age* (1843-1849) and *The Herald of the Kingdom and the Age to Come* (1851-1861). Since Dr. Thomas did not confess that he found the Gospel until 1847, long after he abandoned Campbell and left the St. Charles, Illinois, area, and three years after Wilson settled in Geneva, it cannot be said that Wilson influenced Thomas in One Faith. However, Dr. Thomas was re-baptized in 1847 after he came to believe the Age to Come. Benjamin Wilson read the Thomas materials, so it certainly could be said that Wilson was influenced by Thomas.

Wilson always referred to local congregations as "Brethren of One Faith at (Buchanan, Michigan or Oregon, Illinois)." The One Faith movement became so well known across America by the end of the 19th century that noted men such as George Peters in *The Theocratic Kingdom* referred to it as "The Faith" or "One Faith People."

Peters, a Lutheran minister and author, married Carrie Howell, a Church of God woman from Springfield, Ohio. Being well acquainted with the doctrines of the Church of God, Peters gave a fair mention of the One Faith People as having a good blend of multiple doctrines regarding the Kingdom of God. In contrasting "One Faith People" with groups who spiritualize the Kingdom he wrote:

> "One-Faith People" [are] a mixture as far as we can understand them, of Storrism, Second-Adventism, Christadelphianism, etc... "The No-Age People" some of whom are connected with these and others, while others stand independent. ..They [No-Age People] are characterized by two peculiarities, viz., materialistic views, and denial that the Sec. Advent is to be succeeded by an age to come. All these ignore the fundamental positions upon which Pre-Millenarianism rests, viz., the Davidic Covenant and the resultant Messianic Kingdom, making it (excepting the "One-Faith People") a purely spiritual Kingdom, very different from the one covenanted. [*Note*: brackets are supplied by editor to clarify the statement, but parentheses were supplied by Peters.]

Simply said, with all the groups hashing over various components of pre-millennialism, only the "One-Faith People" seemed to have the best explanation of all the variables, thereby avoiding the trap of spiritualizing the Kingdom during this present church age. It is certainly possible George Peters communicated with Wilson about the One Faith People as their careers overlapped.

Benjamin Wilson never completely agreed with anyone, choosing his interpretations based upon his understanding of the Greek. Wilson sent a letter to Dr.

Thomas in the *Herald* in 1846 stating that he agreed with Thomas on the nature of the soul. He also agreed with rebaptism, but he disagreed with him on the use of wine in communion, and the personality of Satan. Thomas was non-personality, but Wilson stated in the Appendix to the *Emphatic Diaglott*, "*Ho Satanos* and *ho diabolos* are used and applied in several instances to the same being," and "Christ in the temptation, Matt. 4, in his repulse of the tempter, calls him Satan." At least one article in the 1858 *Gospel Banner*, entitled, "Satan" is pro-personality. William Wachtel, Church of God theologian and historian, has concluded that Benjamin Wilson was pro-personality.

Wilson also strongly disagreed with Dr. Thomas on mortal emergence from the grave. Wilson called it the heresy of the 19th century and published an article to that effect. In spite of Wilson's forthright comments, the two men were or continued to be friends, for Dr. Thomas wrote to Wilson in volume 13 of *The Gospel Banner*, and signed his letter, "Your sincere friend."

2. Joseph Marsh

Joseph Marsh had many followers and readers across the Midwest. When Marsh and others called a Union Meeting at Rochester in 1851, people in the Chicago area were subscribers to *The Advent Harbinger and Bible Advocate*. What they read in *The Harbinger* was reinforced by those preaching in northern Illinois/southern Wisconsin including Nathan Sears at Lake Zurich; Mrs. H.A. Parks, Buffalo Grove, and H.V. Reed at Harvard and Chicago, Illinois; and Elder Howell in Wisconsin.

Sometime in 1853 Thomas Wilson, who was assisting his uncle in publishing *The Gospel Banner*, wrote to Marsh requesting a copy of *The Age to Come* (1851). He also indicated they wanted to write for the *Harbinger*. Either Benjamin or Thomas sent several articles to Marsh but didn't sign any of them, making specific authorship unknown. In 1853, the Wilsons furnished articles to *The Advent Harbinger* including "The Faith" based on Jude 3, "Will Jesus Come Again?" the answer to which is, "Yes, Jesus himself taught it," and "The Sure Word of Prophecy" (2 Peter 1:19). In 1854, the Wilsons supplied a series on the Kingdom of God and followed that into 1855 with several short pieces. It is clear from this exchange that the Wilsons had ample opportunity to clarify and strengthen the points they felt Marsh was handling loosely.

At some point they also bought copies of Marsh's hymnbook because the Geneva congregation used *The Millennial Harp* as its songbook for their meetings. This was one of the first hymnbooks published in America.

Wilson began publishing *The Gospel Banner and Millennial Advocate* in Geneva, Illinois, in September 1853 as a monthly paper. In the November 5 issue of *The Advent Harbinger*, Marsh wrote:

> The Gospel Banner...is a small but well-filled monthly sheet published and distributed gratuitously by B. Wilson, Geneva, Illinois. Its object...is the proclamation of the Gospel, and the good news of the Kingdom. It has reached its third number from which we copy "The Faith." It is worthy of being sustained by the benevolent lovers of truth, whose free-will offerings Bro. W. will thankfully receive to aid him in his enterprise. We wish much success to our brother, in his endeavors to proclaim the glad tidings of the kingdom.

Even though Benjamin Wilson and Joseph Marsh believed many points of doctrine in common, their publications differed in emphasis. Benjamin Wilson agreed with Marsh on the restoration of the Jews to Jerusalem prior to the return of Christ. This is known because of Wilson's response to an article written by J.V. Himes in which Himes referred to restoration as "Jewish fables." Wilson took him to task and refuted his position through the pages of *The Gospel Banner*. Wilson said the restoration of Israel is what the Apostles believed and preached. This demonstrates that there was doctrinal agreement between Joseph Marsh and Benjamin Wilson, at least on the issue of the restoration as a key component of the Age-to-Come and The Faith system.

Wilson continued to emphasize One Faith and Marsh certainly did not discount the Abrahamic covenant, but continued to emphasize Age to Come until his final illness and death. After Marsh's death in 1863, writers began sending copy to Wilson for *The Gospel Banner* on the topic of Age to Come. It can be surmised that they missed Marsh's publications. Two examples can be listed: H.V. Reed wrote an article later published as a tract "Age to Come is Not a Heresy." Reed pointed out that Jesus Christ is the appointed King to rule the world to come. Christ will sit upon David's throne and will be King of the Jews when they are restored to their land and to God's favor. Also, Dr. Alfred Malone wrote a book in 1879 entitled, *Age to Come*. See the Malone entry for more discussion on his book.

In 1868, Benjamin described to the Edinburgh brethren why and how he began *The Gospel Banner*:

> ...It was mooted that a small publication would be useful in directing the *minds of others to the things which we believe*. I had in my possession a printing press. I proposed to the brethren that, if they would subscribe and buy a small font of type, I would print a publication of eight pages, per month if possible, containing the things which we believed. They readily acceded to the proposal, and thus commenced the "Gospel Banner." [Editor's italics for emphasis.]

Furthermore, once *The Gospel Banner* was issued, Benjamin Wilson seemed surprised to find little groups of believers popping up out of nowhere. He mentioned in Edinburgh that there were churches "All through Wisconsin, Michigan, Indiana, Minnesota, Nebraska, Arkansas," as well as "Aurora, Chicago, South Northfield and West Northfield, Illinois, and Antioch in Ogle County, Illinois." Across the South were churches in Kentucky and Norfolk, Virginia. There were also congregations in Cleveland, Brooklyn, Canada, and in Elizabeth, New Jersey. It is accurate to say that all these groups were begun and sustained firstly by *The Herald of Gospel Liberty,* Elias Smith, editor, and secondly by the writings and visits of Joseph Marsh and Dr. John Thomas. By the time Benjamin Wilson was in print, his paper went to homes already studying the promises. Wilson inherited those readers and built upon foundations already laid. If this had not been the case, the work might have languished after the death of Marsh never to emerge with strength.

David Graham wrote that Marsh lost subscribers to his *Advent Harbinger* when he included Dr. Thomas and the Wilsons in its pages after 1853. Statistics on loss of subscribers would be impossible to document, yet it seems more reasonable that if Marsh lost subscribers it was because of Dr. John Thomas' attacks on Marsh. The Wilsons benefited from Marsh's loss. When Wilson introduced *The Gospel Banner* in 1853, there was an eastern and midwestern audience ready to read it.

Benjamin Wilson taught that the earth would not be destroyed when Jesus comes to create the new heavens and new earth. Wilson's scriptural reasons:

Eccl. 1:4 - "the earth will endure forever."

Psa. 119:90 - "you have established the earth and it stands fast."

Gen. 8:21, 22 - "I will never again curse the ground...neither will I ever again destroy every creature as I have done." (in the flood.)

II Pet. 3:13 - "according to His promise, we wait for a new heavens and a new earth wherein righteousness dwells." (RSV)

C. Wilson and Campbell Stop Communicating

Alexander Campbell refuted an article by Henry Ward Beecher in *The Gospel Banner* of July 1858 on the subject of baptism. Campbell said, "Jesus had been coronated as head of the church, the Lord of the universe, all authority is in him alone." Wilson disagreed with this idea. He said Campbell "had no proof in God's Word. The Lord Jesus is gone into a far country to receive himself a kingdom and to return and thus, he will be King in Zion, Lord of lords and King of kings."

This is strong evidence that Alexander Campbell and Wilson exchanged papers with each other as has been mentioned briefly in this entry. More evidence is found in Volume 5:4 of *The Gospel Banner and Millennial Advocate,* 1859. Wilson printed an article entitled "Alexander Campbell against Himself" with comments by J.M. Stone of Kentucky. This article was taken from Campbell's notes in his own translation of the New Testament in 1832. Campbell discussed whether the coming of Christ was figurative or literal. He said the question was purely a literary one, making it figurative. He then gave several reasons for his argument, which J.M. Stone quickly refuted.

In the next monthly issue of *The Gospel Banner* a reader from Burritt, Winnebago County, Illinois, wrote "Why I Separated from a Campbellite Church." He said he perceived that to preach the Kingdom of God was to preach the Gospel, and that was not being preached in the Campbellite church. So he left.

A month later, a letter was received from Campbell:
I as a brother feel constrained helping to propagate crochets, as exhibited of late in *The Gospel Banner*; and feel sorry to be obliged to request you to stop sending it to my address. I am, however, leaving Washington. Wishing you all blessings in truth, I am your brother in hope.
(Signed), A. Campbell of Washington

Benjamin Wilson published the letter and expressed dismay over its content. He said, "We have not *knowingly* offended him. As to the charges he made against *The Gospel Banner*, we plead not guilty until it is proven. We cannot divine what he is alluding to."

A Disciples' scholar recently stated, "A. Campbell could not be Alexander Campbell." Yet, it seems that it must be Alexander Campbell for his name is seen more than once in *The Gospel Banner.* For example, Wilson ran an article from Campbell's British *Millennial Harbinger* signed "A. Campbell" on the subject of the Lord's Prayer. It seems conclusive that Wilson and Campbell did professionally recognize each other, but Wilson ended it by leaving the Disciples, and Campbell completely ended it by cutting off the courtesy exchange of periodicals. Additional research on this question would be welcome.

When Benjamin Wilson left the newspaper business and began to publish his religious journal, *The Gospel Banner and Millennial Advocate* in 1853, the name of Wilson's new journal left no doubt that he was not associated with Campbell for Campbell did not preach a message of pre-millennial hope. Campbell's post-millennial interpretation advanced a message of Christian liberty, Christian unity and restoration to first century principles. Campbell taught that the millennium could not be initiated until the whole world was restored to primitive Christianity.

D. Discussion on Resurrection

The brethren of Geneva, Northfield, Aurora, Burritt, and Adeline in northern Illinois met for the Fifth "General Assembly" at Geneva, July 3-4, 1859. During the discussion it became clear there was disagreement over their interpretation of resurrection. Some said the wicked would never be raised, a position of Dr. John Thomas. Others said the righteous would be raised to reward, and the unjust would be raised to condemnation.

After general discussion they came to consensus that all men would be raised, some to life, some to death, a pre-millennial position. But the specifics of resurrection were not settled. In 1869, Benjamin Wilson believed in general resurrection, unlike Dr. John Thomas, but he differed from his brethren by believing the sheep and goat judgment would occur at Christ's coming without a thousand year separation. In this manner, he repudiated the Age-to-Come interpretation of Joseph Marsh. Quite a vigorous discussion was held on this Bible topic at a conference at the Geneva church in Illinois in January 1869. The resurrection issue had been amply discussed but not settled during the previous decade.

The disagreement on the resurrection surrounding Revelation 20:4,5 continued in Geneva and throughout the developing Church of God until after Benjamin Wilson closed his print shop and moved to California in 1870.

Benjamin Wilson maintained the position that the Greek did not support the idea advanced by Marsh followers: "but the rest of the dead lived not again until the thousand years were ended." In a footnote for Revelation 20:4-5 in *The Diaglott*, Wilson noted "these words were probably omitted by oversight in the Vatican manuscript [number 1160]." Wilson said they were in the ABC (A=Codex Alexandricus, B=Vat. MSS 1209, C=Codex Ephraemi Syri Rescriptus), but not the Syriac [Aramaic] manuscript. John Carras, a present-day Greek language, *Diaglott* scholar, and member of the Society of Biblical Literature, examined the ancient Aramaic and Egyptian Coptic texts, and wrote for this entry that those manuscripts include Revelation 20:5. George Homer, a Sahidic Coptic expert, verified and agreed with John Carras regarding that Coptic manuscript.

Analysis of this verse in scholarly writings indicates that all scholars are uncertain about the presence of the first sentence in verse 5 in original Greek manuscripts. There is evidence for and against it being included in the earliest manuscripts available to scholars, none of which are pre-Constantine (4th century). Should something earlier surface, perhaps the discussion on Revelation 20:5 could be reopened and reevaluated. Benjamin Wilson certainly would have been well acquainted with this discussion in his day. Wilson included Revelation 20:5 in the *Diaglott* with a brief footnote, and then continued to protest the "two-phase" or "split" resurrection doctrine among the Church of God ministers through his remaining days. Why include it, and then state "the Greek does not support it?"

Wilson's exact word-for-word Greek translation of Revelation 20:5 in *The Diaglott* reads: "[The but remaining ones the dead ones not lived till should be ended the thousand years.]" In the Greek column, this portion of verse 5 is in brackets, which John Carras said Wilson may have done to link verse 4 with the first part of 5, both of which speak of the living. Carras said, "Both 4 and 5 are not the same group. That is why many [translators] put in parentheses [brackets in the Greek; parentheses in the English]. This may explain why Wilson also put in parentheses." Wilson's English translation is "But the rest of the dead did not live till the thousand years were ended. This is the first resurrection." Wilson did not include the word "again" after live. "But" and "again" are two words that remain at issue in the scholarly discussion of verse 5. For further discussion on Wilson's translation as compared to other later diaglotts on controversial verses download *Appendix I Introduction to Use of the Greek New Testament Manuscripts* at heraldmag.org/rvic/nt/28_NT_Appendix_1.doc

Leaving the discussion of manuscripts and returning to the discussion of resurrection in *The Gospel Banner*, one newcomer to Adventism from Vermont raised a question about death of infants with Benjamin Wilson. He said that George Storrs had recently introduced his group to the idea that the wicked would not be raised to judgment and that infants who died would not be raised. This latter idea particularly upset some of his members, and they appealed to Wilson for his answer.

Wilson answered staunchly: "I do not believe in Geo. Storr's idea of the Non-Resurrection of the Wicked. The Scripture teaches me there will be a resurrection of the Just and the Unjust Acts 24:15." In the August 1860 issue of *The Gospel Banner* Wilson replied to Mr. Beale's question about resurrection. Wilson explained there are *three* classes of people. The people who have never known or accepted Christ will not be raised from the *Adamic* death. The righteous will be raised with the wicked. He defined the righteous as belonging to Christ, and the wicked are those who accepted Christ but disobeyed, namely, the carnal Christians. These he believed were the unjust. The righteous and the carnal will be raised, and the carnal will be condemned. In this respect his teaching at that stage of his life was not unlike what the Christadelphians taught about limited resurrection of the righteous and carnal.

Greg Demmitt has recently pointed out that a belief in annihilation (the eternal sleep of the Adamic man) also led into universalist thinking. Once it had been assumed that only those who were righteous would be raised, then, ALL men who would be raised would be saved. Hence, universal salvation. While this might seem logical, it is not exegetically supported.

Wilson wrote an essay for John O. Woodruff's

book, *The Words of Eternal Life,* on the subject of the resurrection in which he said *only* the righteous will be raised. This article was published posthumously. Wilson also authored a tract on resurrection that was advertised in *The Restitution* in 1894. The ad said, "None but the believers have the promise of resurrection to life." The name of Wilson's tract was "The Way of Salvation." The Archives in Atlanta would like to have a copy of this tract.

Readers became tired and confused by all the rhetoric on the subject of One Faith and resurrection being dialogued in the Wilson papers. John R. Lithgow, a reader from Nova Scotia, a Christadelphian it is thought, wrote to *The Herald* complaining that he thought One Faith was deficient. He complained that there was something missing from Dr. Thomas' theology because not all the brethren have one faith. He said if you sat Dr. Thomas in one room, Robert Roberts in another, and each of the editors of *The Gospel Banner*, *The Herald* and *The Marturion* in separate rooms, and instructed them all to write at length their interpretation of One Faith, they all would have separate interpretations. So that, he thought, was the fallacy of One Faith.

Furthermore, he felt this inadequacy also explained the ongoing argument about resurrection. To his letter he added a postscript:

> P.S. Take the resurrection of the unjust, consider it as an item of the One Faith, and where will you find two leading brethren that agree concerning it. 1. As to who shall be raised. 2. When? 3. With what body shall they come? Again, take the doctrine of the judgment of the quick and the dead. No two can agree as to, 1. The nature of that judgment. 2. The subjects of it. 3. The time of it. Yet this judgment is an item of the One Faith on account of which God justifies sinners. God help us, if it be so.   J.R.L.

Thus it raged in the papers. The resurrection issue was crucial to the doctrinal development of the young Church of God, and no two minds could agree upon it in 1870.

E. Western Tour Brings Troubles

In the autumn of 1860, Benjamin Wilson accepted an invitation of the brethren to visit them. In the company of Mrs. Wilson, he traveled to Harvard by train to meet H.V. Reed. During this time, Reed was engaged in a series of debates with the local Seventh-day Baptist preacher. The evening of arrival, a crowd had started to gather at the Reed home to meet the Wilsons. Guests included James Wood, a tailor formerly of Burritt/Rockford then of Harvard, and A. Barnes of Boone County. A Mr. Keeling of Rockford attended a later meeting at the Fish residence where the Wilsons spent three days.

After the debates, Benjamin and Alice continued west to spend time with Samuel W. Coffman of Adeline. Since in his remarks B. Wilson did not refer to him as "Brother" it should be assumed that Samuel was still a seeker. Coffman invited Wilson to hear a few things that Dr. John Thomas had recently related to him. Dr. Thomas had made a trip into northwestern Illinois while he was a resident in St. Charles in 1842 after Alexander Campbell ousted him from the Restoration Movement. It's not known how far back the association between Coffmans and Dr. Thomas went, but they may have known each other while Coffmans still lived in Maryland.

A few years later in a letter to Robert Roberts in the *Ambassador,* 1865, Dr. Thomas criticized S.W. Coffman and the Church of God for its fragmented leadership, but it is presumed in 1860 that the Coffmans and Dr. Thomas remained on good terms. One source has said Coffman was a Christadelphian as the denomination was formed in his home in 1863 or 1864.

Benjamin Wilson was shocked to learn from "friend" Coffman that, on a recent trip to Adeline, Dr. Thomas had made accusations against Wilson.

1. Dr. Thomas Brings Accusations

After associating with Dr. Thomas for nearly 20 years via exchanges of letters in periodicals, Benjamin Wilson might have expected that Dr. Thomas would try to discredit him since Thomas had previously smeared the reputations of Alexander Campbell and Joseph Marsh. In his initial report to the *Banner,* Benjamin Wilson was not prepared to give details as there was a great deal of investigation to be done on the matter, so he said, "At present we have nothing to publish concerning them, only to say, that if necessary, we are prepared to vindicate our moral integrity and defy anyone to *prove* the contrary."

The story that would unfold within the pages of *The Gospel Banner* over the next year diverted the editor and the readers from the intent of the journal. It involved personalities, "crochets," or negative theological hobbies, accusations and special editions to explain all. In the end, Wilson was exonerated from any wrongdoing.

The incident involved a business relationship between Miss Mary Hayes and Mr. Peter Innes of the Geneva congregation. Innes was a close friend of Dr. John Thomas, and indeed, even provided hospitality to the Thomas family when they were ousted from the Campbellite movement around 1842 before they settled in St. Charles. Benjamin Wilson had no business in the dealings with the lady in question who ostensibly accused him. It was eventually favorably sorted out, and Wilson's honor was preserved. Many readers stood behind him, and repudiated the actions of Dr. Thomas, but other readers fell away.

It is interesting to note that in the issue with the report of the accusation, Benjamin Wilson included an article by George Dowie, a minister and bookbinder from Edinburgh. Dowie was a follower of Dr. Thomas and Robert Roberts, but fell out of favor with both men around 1860 prior to the formation of the Christadelphians. Here follows a quote from Steve Cook, a fellow researcher from Australia, on the subject of George Dowie:

> Dowie edited *The Messenger of the Churches* between 1858 and 1870. He had been converted by John Thomas in 1853, but by the early 1860s they had fallen out. John Thomas published volume one of his exposition of The Revelation (*Eureka*) in 1861 and Dowie wrote some articles in *The Messenger* putting an alternative view. Thomas wasn't happy, and made it clear to his lieutenant in Britain (Robert Roberts, who had been a close friend of Dowie's) that he wasn't happy. In 1864, Dowie wrote an article which mentioned, in passing, his belief in a personal devil. Roberts disfellowshipped him immediately.

Thus is seen the pluralistic religious climate in which Benjamin Wilson functioned. In the report mentioned above, he discussed with considerable passion the "isms" that were swirling around that confused readers and church members. Many of these "isms" were being imposed upon readers of Dr. Thomas' *Herald of the Kingdom* as "tests of fellowship." Some of these "isms" included "porkism," "vegetarianism," "unleavened breadism," "raisinism," "abolitionism" and several more. Wilson said partaking or not partaking of any of the "isms" did not nullify one's Christianity, nor enhance it.

F. Wilson on Rebaptism

Wilson agreed with Dr. John Thomas and George Dowie on the issue of baptism. Dr. Thomas said anyone coming out of any other denomination into acceptance of the Gospel of the Kingdom of God needed to be re-baptized. Dr. Thomas attempted to destroy Joseph Marsh over this issue. Marsh refused to be re-baptized.

Wilson interpreted this question in terms of faith. He said "re-baptism" was a term of accommodation. He said faith, One Faith, comes before baptism. If one did not understand the Gospel of the Kingdom before baptism, it was not valid. The faith of the believer at the time of immersion was therefore important. If he came into the understanding of One Faith, i.e., Gospel of the Kingdom, he should follow it with baptism.

If a candidate for baptism believed in One Faith, it did not make any difference who baptized him. Wilson also upheld the confession and baptism of Elder William Shockey in that issue, stating "it is not necessary to know everything before baptism." In this position Wilson agreed with Joseph Marsh. To contrast, re-baptizers believed that candidates for baptism should know about the Kingdom of God before baptism be performed.

Wilson wrote a terse editorial on baptism in *The Herald of the Coming Kingdom*. It was entitled "Why we cannot fellowship with Immersed Believers in Jesus." Wilson concluded such believers may believe that Jesus is God or Son of God, that he reigns in their hearts or in heaven, that he will judge the world, but:

> ...yet if he does not believe that Jesus is "the Son of God, the King of Israel," he is ignorant of the main truth—the foundation-truth of the Church of God. For Jesus told Peter that on this rock He would build His Church. And if any one ignores this doctrine, or accepts of something else as truth which nullifies it, then he is not on the foundation of the Prophets and Apostles, Jesus the Christ being the foundation corner stone. It makes no difference as to his being baptized, if he is without faith—faith as respects the Messiah and His Kingdom. Or, if he may have learned the true faith since his immersion, that immersion being done in ignorance is of no account. We deem it absolutely necessary to come up to the apostolic platform—to have the true faith first, and then immersion. We must believe that "Jesus is the Christ, the Son of the living God"—we must believe " the things concerning the Kingdom of God, and the name of Jesus Christ"—or ten thousand immersions will avail nothing.

The Gospel Banner of June 15, 1861, clearly stated Wilson believed in re-immersion after a person came to believe the Gospel of the Kingdom. In 1883, he answered a question by J.R. Ham in *The Restitution* by admitting that Wilson had been baptized in (England) as a Campbellite and was re-baptized in Geneva in 1851. In the December 1868 *The Messenger of the Churches* Wilson said he had been re-baptized 17 years before. W.H. Wilson stated in an article on the history of the Church of God in *The Restitution*, later reprinted in *The Progress Journal*, that his father, Joseph Wilson, and his uncle, Benjamin Wilson, were baptized by Dr. John Thomas. This cannot be a fact because the two men did not meet until 1856. It is thought the Wilson brothers may have baptized each other, or perhaps Elder Innes baptized the first Wilson who in turn baptized the others.

In the 1883 "Question/Answer" article, Wilson said that what one believes prior to baptism is essential. One Faith should be understood. A Methodist will believe in saved by faith through God the Son, the trinity, immortality of the soul, eternal torment. Those being baptized into the Gospel of the Kingdom must believe in One Faith, which is the promises made to Abraham given to the Gentiles through Christ, and that Christ is coming again to establish the Kingdom of God on earth.

G. Wilson on the Holy Spirit

On the issue of the Spirit, Wilson said one *is in the Spirit* if he is obeying the teachings of the Spirit. "By the teachings of the Spirit we mean those that are found in Scripture. God spoke to the fathers through the prophets in ancient times, but in these last days by his Son. His Spirit was in the prophets and in his Son." He said, "none who claim to possess the Holy Spirit now can establish their claims like those who wrote the Bible."

Wilson never regarded the work that the believers of One Faith were doing as being "sectarian." Members who preached the Abrahamic Faith and the Gospel of the Kingdom were of One Body. Unlike the Christadelphians, the group organized by Dr. John Thomas, Wilson had no intention of organizing a denomination. He said:

> It is scarcely probable that we will exchange truth for error and become sectarian, for all such organized under the name Christadelphian, we regard so. They have separated from the One Body, follow and glory in a human leader, have taken for themselves a name, have adopted a published a creed, and are deeply imbued with the spirit of their master, bitter and proscriptive, and anything but Christlike.

Notice in the above quote Wilson said the Christadelphians separated from the One Body. That indicates the Wilsons accepted Dr. John Thomas and his friends as members of the One Body up to the point where Thomas began preaching mortal emergence and use of wine in communion. It also offers another reason why Wilson left Illinois in 1870. He didn't wish to be part of any national organizational effort that would have cemented sectarianism within the Church of God, thereby minimizing One Body in his estimation. And yet, strangely in 1888, Benjamin went to Philadelphia as a delegate to the organization of the national general conference.

The acting editor of *The Gospel Banner* in the summer of 1868 repeated this same sentiment when he said:

> Although as a class or sect, the Christadelphians have separated themselves from us, and denounce us not knowing the truth as they teach it, with reference to mortal resurrectionism, we will not follow their example. We look upon them as malinstructed and misguided brethren and would treat them kindly and with great forbearance of love.

Also in 1868, the brethren in assembly at a Chicago conference agreed to organize in a general assembly known as the Northwest Christian Association, the purpose being the advancement of the cause of truth. The organization was to include members from Illinois, Indiana, Ohio, Michigan, Wisconsin and Iowa. As the first acts of business, a financial committee was appointed, and J.M. Stephenson was hired to be evangelist. While this has been defined as the first or second national organizational attempt, it hardly got off the ground and was only intended to be a regional association.

During 1867 there was some trouble in the Geneva church. The nature of the problem is not known unless it was the meddling of Dr. Thomas, but Wilson referred to it in the *Herald's* February 1868 issue. He indicated it had something to do with Thomas Wilson's parents and younger brother, either Samuel Wilson or W.H. Wilson. Benjamin noted that the congregation was now in harmony, and one Sunday after he preached, five persons came forward for baptism.

Early in 1868, Wilson found fault with Joseph Marsh's hymn book, *The Millennial Harp*. He said there were unscriptural hymns in it. He noted that it was advertised in the *Prophetic Watchman*, along with other tracts by Joseph Marsh. Wilson offered to publish a new edition of *The Millennial Harp*. It is doubtful that Wilson had time to do this before he turned over the reigns of publishing to his nephew Thomas Wilson in 1869, but Thomas did publish *The Christian Psalmodist*, although hymnal copper plates certainly were lost in the Chicago Fire. Thomas Wilson must have started over. Copies of the Marsh hymnal and the Wilson hymnal are in the Archives at Atlanta Bible College.

During the turmoil of managing a growing publishing ministry and a frail church organization, Benjamin Wilson did not neglect to stay in touch with the people who were reading *The Gospel Banner*. Located with this entry is a letter written by Wilson which he sent to Joseph R. Cooper in Ripley, Illinois, upon the death of Cooper's father. The letter illustrates Wilson's gracious nature towards his fellowmen. This is the debut of this letter, and it is hoped that it can benefit other Wilson scholars.

H. Health Issues

In July 1868 Benjamin and Alice Wilson toured through New York to visit a health clinic owned by a friend. Both Wilsons were patients, but it was the health of Mrs. Wilson that needed the most attention. The director of the clinic suggested that a sea voyage would benefit Mrs. Wilson, and so they informed readers of the *Gospel Banner* that they would be traveling to England and would be there up to three months. They left the *Banner* in the hands of his brother, Joseph Wilson, and A.R. Underwood.

In correspondence from England, Benjamin Wilson mentioned their visit to Newell Bond in Cleveland on their way to meet the steamer, City of Baltimore, in New York. They were kindly received at the Bond's home, and while there, the Wilsons met the Joblins, McLauchlans and Cherrys of that church. It seems reasonable that the meeting of Wilson with the heads of the Eastern Church of God at that time may have been an effort to explore and perhaps plan a merger of the eastern church with the west. The Northwest Christian Association did not reach to the east coast. To be successful, a larger organization was needed.

Bruce Schulz, a historian familiar with Abrahamic Faith, believes one of the purposes of the 1888 Philadelphia national conference was to merge the Eastern Church of God with Wilson's One Faith movement in the West. The seed for that idea may have been sown at the 1868 meeting of Wilson with Joblin, McLauchlan and Bond.

In Halifax the Wilsons stayed with Benjamin's brother whom he had not seen in 25 years. As they were ill when they arrived they stayed several weeks in order

> **Benjamin Wilson's letter to John Wesley Cooper in Brown County, Illinois**
>
> Geneva, Kane Co., Ill.
> Jan 1st, 1863
>
> Your letter came duly to hand with the sad intelligence of your father's death, and I take the first opportunity which presents itself to reply. I would have done so immediately but have had my time so fully occupied, and attention engrossed by the Conference and the business connected with it, that I could not do so very well. O what have sickness and death made in the world! How many houses are desolate, hopes crushed, and bright prospects dimmed by the cruel tyrant. And death came into the world through sin—and sin is the transgression of the law—"it is appointed unto men once to die," and "there is no discharge in that war." Yet although we know that we all must die, God never designed that any of us should die before our time, viz of old age, with diseases inherited from our forefathers, or from ignorance (of doctors) of the laws of our nature, or of doing what is best for our health, or from indulging our fleshly appetites, disease is entailed or produced, and life is cut short. Oh that mankind in general were wise, that they understood this, that they considered that they ought to honor God by their lives, and in their bodies, and especially Christians.
>
> Remember me to Bro. (Wing?) and any other friend with you, or in the neighborhood whom I know. I shall be glad to hear from you at any time you may feel inclined to write.
>
> Excuse more at present. May God bless you and preserve you for his heavenly Kingdom and glory is the desire of
>
> Your brother in hope,
> B. Wilson

to recuperate. The city of Halifax had doubled in size since Benjamin had last seen it. In 1801, Halifax had little more than 8,000 residents. By 1901, it had over 50,000 residents, so a population estimate of 16,000-20,000 residents in 1868 seems appropriate. There were wider streets and more of them, new buildings and parks, and Beacon Hill overlooking the town had been tunneled for a railroad. When the railroad came through in the 1870s it purchased the church and graveyard that had been the original pulpit of John Wesley.

The Campbellite congregation on Grove Street, which had occupied the building 25 years before, was defunct. Grove Street was merely one block long with storefront buildings on either side of the street. This small neighborhood did not allow a church structure of any great size.

In place of the Restoration church was a "Christadelphian Synagogue" as it was known. The Wilsons attended one worship service with that congregation *incognito*. The congregation had 20 people. Although Wilson could not agree with their understanding of resurrection or the devil, they did believe in One Faith, and the Kingdom of God on earth. He said, "Their peculiar notions are opinions and have no right to be imposed upon the public or the brotherhood as 'first principles' of the gospel." He stated he had done a small part in teaching them about the Kingdom, presumably through his writings in the *Gospel Banner*.

While in Halifax, he accompanied his brother and family to the Baptist Chapel, where he had worshipped and attended Sunday School 25 years earlier, and whose members "were his associates then, but whose faces were now altered."

When beginning the return trip to the states, the Wilsons stopped briefly in Edinburgh. They were met there by his nephew, John Wilson of Dundee. In Edinburgh, the Wilsons met Bro. Laing and his congregation. Benjamin addressed the congregation on Sunday, October 25, 1868, and brought greetings. He gave a brief history of his coming to America and a lengthy report of their travels. This address was published in December 1868 in *The Messenger*, George Dowie, editor. The Wilsons met George Dowie, Bro. Duncan, Bro. Lindsay and several others in Dundee before sailing from Glasgow.

Stephen Cook of Scottish lineage has said that since Dowie broke with Dr. John Thomas before Thomas formed the Christadelphians, Dowie was never a Christadelphian. Cook has written a brief history of the Dowie churches in Scotland at the time Wilson visited:

> [The] Edinburgh church began in March, 1853 with 24 members, meeting at George Dowie's home at 12 Beaumont Street, and calling themselves "Baptised [sic] Believers in the Kingdom of God." By 1862 it had 97 members. The following year numbers went down to 59 due to high unemployment and members moving south (the original members of the London church were expatriate Scots who had moved south to seek work).
>
> The Edinburg church split in 1866 over the Roberts-Dowie conflict and a new church was formed in Leith, near Edinburgh. The Edinburgh church took the name Christadelphian and still exists today. The churches sympathetic to Dowie eventually took the name "Conditional Immortality Mission" and existed under that name in Britain well into the 20th century.
>
> In 1858 a tiny church was established in Berwick, Scotland, through the efforts of William Wilson and Andrew Tait of Halifax, and the following year George Dowie preached in the area and baptized new converts. In 1861 some members of Dowie's Edinburgh church, including Henry Wilson, helped to form a new church south at Jarrow on the border.

The trans-Atlantic homebound cruise was not easy for the Wilsons. West of Ireland the ship developed a mechanical problem and sprang a leak. Passengers had to change ships. The seas were very rough due to inclement weather, and they were sick most of the time. Mrs. Wilson was prostrate most of the trip after that, and was so affected by illness that she did not remember much of the trip for a couple of days after arriving on Staten Island. The cruise home took 16 days and they were grateful to be back in the States.

I. Second Western Tour

Within weeks of returning from Halifax, Benjamin answered the "Macedonian Call" from a reader in Missouri. The reader wrote he had learned a little and wanted to learn more, who could Bro. Wilson send to teach him? Wilson determined he would go. He arranged for friends to meet him at Quincy and took the train to that city, and then on to St. Joseph on a cold, drafty train.

Almost immediately the Lord put men in his path who wanted to converse on issues of truth. He engaged in several one-to-one conversations explaining the Abrahamic faith to them. Many also wanted to discuss the restoration of Israel. When the meetings were finished, he baptized 11 people. Ice had to be cut from the river so the ferry could pass across the channel, and in that ice-free channel, the baptisms were held.

The next morning in worship, Wilson preached about putting on the whole armor of God. A Campbellite preacher, Mr. Fisk, came to the meeting after worship and asked a few questions, as several of his members attended the meeting. Benjamin invited him to write an article for *The Banner*, which he agreed to do, on the Kingdom born at Pentecost. Benjamin promised to respond to it. It is conjectured that this Mr. Fisk was John Fisk who began to preach for the Church of God in Missouri and Kansas around 1890.

In 1869, Benjamin's son, Charles Henry, died of consumption. He was 20 years old. This caused a great deal of grief to the aging editor and his wife.

Wilson continued to publish *The Gospel Banner* until December 1869. At that time future issues were merged with *The Herald of the Coming Kingdom* in Chicago, edited by his nephew, Thomas Wilson. Benjamin explained in his final editorial that the work could not support more than one paper. In the previous year the *Herald* had lost $2500, and the Michigan and Illinois conferences called for the merger of *The Banner* with *The Herald* during that year. Wilson said he was laying down his editorial pen, but he would pick it up to correspond with *The Herald* in the future.

The business end of this action happened because it is what the delegates of the Northwest Christian Association wanted. In one of their meetings the year before, they had voted to take this action. Benjamin was sad, but he was willing. He was older. His health was compromised. He lost ground among the delegates regarding the doctrine of resurrection. He opposed a "split" first resurrection. They didn't. Sentiment and preference went with the younger generation on the issue of general resurrection.

Even Mark Allen, who had been a long-time faithful contributor to *The Gospel Banner* questioned its stand on immortal resurrection versus mortal emergence, accusing him of the latter. In the August 1868 issue the acting editor denied it, saying:

> We think he is a little intolerant. In an age of transition from error to truth, from darkness to light, we ought to be careful lest we be too precipitate, overbearing, and intolerant of brethren who don't see things just as we see them. They may not be as advanced as we are. "Let such receive one another as Christ received us to the glory of God."

J. Relocation

In 1870, Benjamin and Alice relocated to Sacramento, California, with their five-year-old daughter, Rescue, and sons, Albert and Edwin. Sarah was already married and expecting a baby. According to Leila Whitehead, Benjamin gave power of attorney to a merchant to look after his property. When they arrived in Sacramento Benjamin was 53 and Alice was 56. Alice had not been well, and she died from the effort of moving. Her name does not appear in the 1870 California Census. Wilson and his children temporarily resided with a farm family named See. Benjamin took a job as a printer, but later farmed. In 1877, he sold the Geneva property for $1500. The record showed at the time that Benjamin was a widower with Edwin and Rescue still residing with him in Sacramento.

Shortly after arriving in California, Benjamin received word his daughter was critically ill from a hemorrhage. He returned to Geneva to be at her bedside when she died. She left a one-month old baby. When Wilson returned to California, his son-in-law, baby, the baby's nurse and nurse's sister returned with him. One of these women, the nurse or the sister, may have become Benjamin's next wife, Angelina, a native of New York. The 1880 Census shows them as married with Rescue, age 15, still living at home. Wilson and Angelina had three children who died in childhood from birth defect, measles and bronchitis. All are interred in Old City Cemetery.

Benjamin maintained contact with the Church of God for the rest of his life through correspondence with his family, which in turn was published in *The Restitution* when appropriate. He promised to write a series for *The Restitution* entitled, "Bible Truths vs. Bible Myths." This was to be published during the years immediately after the Chicago Fire, but those early Indiana issues of *The Restitution* were lost. However, others written by Wilson from 1874 until 1900 are available to scholars. In fact, he authored several columns in *The Restitution* entitled, "Misunderstood and Misapplied Texts" from 1888 until his death.

In 1883 he wrote "Will the Earth be Burned?" in *The Restitution*. He said the Earth would endure and not be destroyed. He cited Ecclesiastes 1:4 "A generation comes, and a generation goes, but the earth remains forever," and Psalms 119:90 "Thou has established the earth and it stands fast." In Genesis 8:21 "God said, 'I will never again curse the earth…neither will I destroy every living creature as I have done.'" Wilson explained Peter's comments by saying that Peter was writing to Jews before the destruction of Jerusalem, and he was speaking of persecution in their own day. He said, "In 2 Peter 3:13, 'looking for a new heavens and earth' means we are looking for a new order of things."

In other writings, he also provided copy for books published by John O. Woodruff from Elizabeth, New Jersey. Wilson authored "The Last Days" for *The Restitution* in 1888. He said the term is significant and suggestive. "The last days of what?" he asked. Wilson said the Scripture refers to the end of the present evil age (Galatians 1:4). He also said when the Jews rejected Christ and he was cut off, God cut off the Jews. "The dispensation of the Spirit was about to begin, and a new order of priesthood and sacrifice ordained." He said the dispensation of the Spirit was the "Gospel era." He felt the 70th week of Daniel will begin with the resurrection of the just and translation (rapture) of those who are Christ's, and will end with the resurrection of the patriarchal and Mosaic just.

In April 1889 he authored another article for *The Restitution* in which he asked "Is the Church the Kingdom?" The answer was "No," but he said, "The church is on probation during this [present] age, and it is called upon to be faithful, and to suffer for and with Christ. The kingdom is the place of reward for the faithful" (Revelation 2: 10).

However, in another issue of *The Restitution,* Wilson offered to debate someone through its pages on the question of "Shall the dead who never knew Christ be given a chance to enter the Kingdom of God on probation?" He said, "No." This language indicates he was firmly against the infiltrating heresy known as Larger Hope. Only the mortals living at the time of Christ's return will enter the Kingdom on probation.

Benjamin attended the 1888 Philadelphia Conference as a delegate. James Wilson and Samuel Wilson joined their uncle Benjamin to represent the family in Philadelphia and met many old friends there. Benjamin was appointed honorary vice president of the board of directors. Reports of the 1888 conference paint a picture of excitement, hope and anticipation that a lasting national work would emerge. Wilson no doubt hoped his support would result in a national publishing house so he would have a permanent place to deposit the Greek plates of the *Diaglott* insuring that its publication would continue.

The *Diaglott* continued to receive attention as it was being avidly quoted by Church of God scholars in The *Restitution,* by Adventists and Russellite Bible Students, who loved its translation of *parousia* as "presence." Even now, scholars refer to it. It was said that The New World translation of the Bible by the Jehovah's Witnesses was patterned largely on *The Emphatic Diaglott.*

Recently, John Carras, quoted from a piece first written in the *St. Paul Enterprise* in 1916 about Wilson:
> In 1892, J.A. Bohnet of the Watch Tower Society twice visited Benjamin Wilson in Sacramento, California, living there with his wife [Angelina] and family. During Bohnet's second visit, Wilson told him that he was not affiliated with the Christadelphians, but did consider himself a "Resurrectionist." Bohnet wrote that Wilson's biblical ideas reside somewhere between Wilson's personal interpretation, and the friendly criticism of C.T. Russell.

In October 1892 Benjamin Wilson authored a two-page tract entitled "Twenty Important Questions." This was published in *The Restitution* and also made available for distribution. To date copies of that tract have not been seen by researchers because that particular issue of Th*e Restitution* was not available to be microfilmed.

In 1902, an arrangement was made with the Watchtower Publishing Company to publish the *Diaglott*. It is thought Wilson's nephew, Thomas Wilson, made this transaction as Widow Angelina had already relocated to New York to live with family. The reason the Church of God was not chosen to receive this work was because without a national headquarters office, it had no stable publishing house. The only paper representing this yet unorganized conference was *The Restitution*, Plymouth, Indiana, owned and published by a private individual, A.R. Underwood, who had been Wilson's understudy when he was publishing the *Diaglott*.

The Zion's Watch Tower gave a printed statement in their first edition of the *Diaglott:*
> The *Emphatic Diaglott* has been published under the author's copyright by Fowler and Wells Co. New York City, until 1902….For several years a friend, an earnest Bible student, desirous of assisting the readers of our Society's publications, has supplied them through us at a greatly reduced price; now he has purchased the copyright and plates from Fowler and Wells Co., and presented the same to our Society as a gift, under our assurance that the gift will be used for the furthering of the Truth to the extent of our ability….

Over 100 years later, the *Diaglott* copyright expired and was taken up by the Church of the Blessed Hope under the leadership of Franklyne Ross in Florida. This group is unaffiliated with the General Conference, but has made the *Diaglott* available in hard cover and CD.

K. The Problem of Josephism

Questions about the paternity of Jesus surfaced in *The Gospel Banner* as early as 1860. Thomas Churchill of Canada wrote a piece denouncing Josephism entitled, "The Paternity of Jesus." This was not a new issue in

Christianity as the paternity question surfaced at various times in church history dating back to Marcion, but it was a fairly new topic for the Church of God.

Indeed, Stephen Cook has written that Josephism briefly surfaced in England during the 1860s among the Christadelphians. While on a visit to England, Dr. Thomas baptized Charles Dealtry who had formerly been an Adventist. In 1866, Dealtry preached for the Christadelphians and was popular, but by 1868 Robert Roberts had denounced him and ostracized him for preaching that Jesus was the son of Joseph. Cook wrote, "His ostracism demonstrated the swiftness with which Roberts dealt with dissenters. I don't think Josephism was ever an issue for Christadelphians after that."

One would expect that Benjamin Wilson led the way in preaching that Jesus Christ was the begotten Son of God, conceived by the Holy Spirit, born of a virgin. Yet Wilson's language on the subject seems quite flexible. Wilson addressed the issue in a tract entitled "Is It Essential to Believe in the Royalty of Jesus?" Wilson's tract was published by his nephew Thomas Wilson in Chicago at *The Restitution* office, so it can be dated between 1871-1874, while *The Restitution* resided in Chicago after the fire, but prior to its relocation to Plymouth, Indiana.

In this tract Wilson made the point that Jesus was the Christ, the Messiah of the Old Testament, the Son of God, anointed at his baptism. He said Jesus could not be the Anointed until he was anointed. He concluded that Jesus was royalty, and that it is essential to believe it. However, his language that Jesus could not be "the anointed Son of God until he was anointed" is, in fact, adoptionist. Proponents of virgin birth say Jesus was the only begotten Son of God.

However, language analysis is not conclusive, because Wilson also used the word "begotten." In a September 1860 editorial in *The Gospel Banner*, Wilson said Jesus was begotten, but he also said that Jesus was *called* Son of God by John and was only begotten *before* his resurrection. So begotten was not applied to virgin birth, but rather to resurrection.

In an 1893 letter to his niece in response to her question about the doctrine of Josephism, Wilson wrote, "Jesus came in the line of Abraham and David according to the flesh, and therefore was the son of Abraham and David, but he was the only begotten Son of God of a *spiritual* nature." In any of Wilson's writings on this subject, he avoided using "begotten" if he could, and would say Christ was adopted at his baptism and resurrection sometimes using the term "Sonship" of Christ, a clear reference to his adoption rather than begettal.

The subject was discussed by Benjamin Wilson in a tract written from California in January 1885 entitled, "What Think Ye of Christ. Whose son is He?" This was accepted and published by *The Restitution*. In it Wilson said, "Jesus of Nazareth became the Christ of God when he was anointed by the Holy Spirit. Christ or Messiah means anointed. He could not be the anointed one before he was anointed. He was neither prophet, priest, nor king before his anointing." He said, "He proved to be God's son by resurrection of the dead." Then, in plain English he said, "Jesus was the only begotten of the Father not an adopted Son of God begotten by the Word of truth, as we are." The statement denying adoption and endorsing Jesus, the "only begotten of the Father," seemed to settle the matter for the time being.

1. Josephism Question Re-Emerges

The evidence, however, seems compelling that Benjamin Wilson was a Josephite, but it is not clear when he took that position. A brother's testimony in *The Restitution* of February 22, 1893, testified of his agreement with "Brother B. Wilson on the origin of our Savior, the Christ, the only begotten Son of God John 3:16." Wilson was a special contributor to *The Restitution* then. But still, a letter from Benjamin Wilson around that same time was reprinted in a tract written by J.E. Robbins of Los Angeles. Robbins tract is entitled "What Think Ye of Christ? Whose Son is He?" nearly the exact title Wilson had used in 1885 to discuss the topic. Robbins believed that Jesus was the son of Joseph, and if Joseph were removed from the equation, Jesus could not be the Son of David in the flesh. Wilson wrote:

> I am glad that my article in the "Messenger" interested you. I find but few brethren anywhere who sympathize with this view; they rather avoid those who hold it and esteem them as sadly in error. ...For myself I am satisfied from the internal evidence found in the narratives given in Matthew and Luke that those historians never wrote them but have been added by others. And again, the fact that those accounts of the infancy and early life of Jesus, with the miraculous circumstances related as connected therewith, are not once mentioned or alluded to by either Jesus, prophet or apostle, is enough to condemn the whole as fiction. Your espousal of the doctrine will not be received favorably by your brethren. That is the case with myself. I care little what others say, if I know I have the truth.
> Yours in the Anointed, B. Wilson

The Messenger in question seems to be *The Nazarine Messenger* edited by W.L. Kells from Listowel, Ontario. (Readers are reminded that Dr. Thomas registered his followers as pacifists in Washington, D.C. during the Civil War as "Nazarines.") In *The Nazarine Messenger* Wilson clearly wrote, "I have changed my mind on the paternity of Jesus of late, and now believe him to have been the son of Joseph." Maurice Joblin, the reputable pastor of the original Cleveland Church of God, refuted Josephism, as reported in his book, *The Paternity of Jesus* (1905), and said that [Wilson] wrote in the May 1894 issue, "there was no need for Christ's blood,—all one has to do, is to give up his past life, and devote his future life to God." This comment stemmed from the belief that Christ, the son of Joseph had sin in his life, and therefore his blood was of no value for atonement.

Joblin quoted *The Messenger* verbatim:

> Jesus was a man like other men, or, why did He require to be baptized of John. Whose baptism was for the remission of sins? (Luke 3:3); if He did not require it for the purpose for which it was administered,--He did the institution *no honor*. If he had no faults to be remitted, or sins to be washed away, He did *wrong to pretend to comply* with an ordinance given by God, for the purpose of cleansing from sin. If he did not need it, and did it just the same, it was simple mockery, and sham, instead of fulfilling all righteousness, as He did, Matt. 3:15. There could be no moral excellence if there was no moral requirement.
>
> ...but He felt His weakness, FRAILTY, NOTHINGNESS and UNCLEANNESS in the sight of God, and went down into the water *to wash away* His faults and shortcomings, and fulfilled that form of righteousness. He could not be human and have no failings...[Italics and emphatics by Joblin.]

A copy of *The Messenger* article by Wilson would add to the documentation on Wilson's position on Josephism. Research to locate the original article in *The Messenger* will continue, but until then conclusions regarding Wilson's position must of necessity be tenuous.

In the same book by Joblin written five years after Benjamin Wilson's death, the Addendum directly named G.M. Myers as one who also was a Josephite. Joblin quoted from Myers' publication *Ek Nekron Anastasis* and from personally handwritten letters received from Myers that "there is no Church of God" because when men and women are baptized into Christ, the baptizers cannot impart the spirit. The Josephite issue rejected a lot of Bible teachings commonly accepted by Church of God members and became a volatile issue leading up to the 1910 attempt to organize a national general conference. Joblin's book is part of the archival collection at Rock River Christian College, Beloit, Wisconsin.

Even with Wilson's death in 1900 the matter was not to disappear. In 1904 Wilson's name was brought into the Josephite controversy by G.M. Myers himself. Myers had come to accept Josephism, and he published an article, ostensibly by Benjamin Wilson, endorsing the doctrine. When it was brought to W.H. Wilson's attention, he jumped into the foray to defend his deceased uncle in *The Restitution* (March 24, 1904). William H. Wilson said:

> Hence, these Josephites took advantage of his old age and sickness to extract from him what they could gloat in trumpeting it abroad as his sentiments. If they had approached him when he was younger, he would have given them a severe scourging. In true sentiment he was no more a Josephite than he was a follower of the false prophet Dowie. This was attributable to the weakness of his old age and so was the expression of Josephite sentiments.
>
> Signed, W.H. Wilson

Myers reacted to W.H. Wilson's accusation in a subsequent issue of *The Restitution* and upheld his own statement that the article was Benjamin Wilson's. However, Myers' reputation was not sterling, as he had just been cast out of the Seventh-day Church of God in which he had dabbled for a year. As Church of God brethren were questioning Myers and his doctrinal preferences and ethics, members sided with W.H. Wilson. David Graham recently wrote "Anything Myers had was not used [by *The Restitution*] because Myers himself was too controversial."

As to W.H. Wilson's reference of Benjamin's association with George Dowie, the matter cannot easily be settled, for in Edinburgh, Wilson's American followers were called "American Dowieites." So far as can be discovered Wilson's beliefs did not coincide with Dowie's beliefs for Dowie advanced pre-existence, immortal soul, etc. But they had one thing in common: they both disagreed with Dr. Thomas and Robert Roberts. Stephen Genusa described Dowie in an unfavorable light:

> In 1866, [Robert] Roberts held an interview with George Dowie which was published as a supplement in *The Christadelphian* late that same year. It was clear from the recounting of the meeting that Mr. Dowie was evasive and used "elastic language" so as to allow for his and his cohorts' false ideas.

The description of "elastic language" seems also to describe the language method of Benjamin Wilson to weave among controversial issues in an enigmatic way on such doctrines as paternity of Jesus and resurrection. Elastic language may explain why the Church of God could not arrive at a consensus on a statement of faith and could not organize a lasting General Conference until 1921. There was no clear leadership.

In 1887 a series written by Dr. L.C. Thomas entitled "Paternity, Genealogy, Nature and Character of Jesus in Light of the Covenants" was published in *The Restitution*. This series was decidedly opposed to Josephism, and the majority of the developing Church of God also stood opposed to Josephism.

An article in *The Restitution* after Wilson's death entitled "Are the First Few Chapters in Matthew and Luke Authentic?" indicates that the discussion within the Church of God about the paternity of Christ was ongoing for several more months or years.

Until new evidence proves otherwise, in looking back from the present perspective, it would seem that Benjamin Wilson's indictment of Joseph Marsh "for handling the Kingdom of God loosely" proved unmerited. Unlike Marsh, at least on the issues of resurrection and paternity, it seems more likely that Wilson handled them loosely.

Benjamin Wilson died at his home at 1900 J. Street, and was interred in the Old City Cemetery in Sacramento beside his children. As a famous public figure Benjamin

Wilson cast a very long shadow in the Church of God continuing to this day, but the private man and what he believed borders on the enigmatic.

 See Bond, Newell
   Fisk(e), John
   Ham, J.R.
   Huffer, Alva F. (20th)
   Humphreys, Richard A.
   Joblin, Maurice
   Magaw, Sydney (20th)
   Magruder, Allan B.
   Marsh, Joseph
   McLauchlan, Robert
   Myers, G.M.
   Smith, Elias
   Speer, J.K.
   Wilson, Thomas
   Wilson, W.H.
   Woodruff, John O.

Bibliography: "Adventist Newspapers and Periodicals Inventory," American Antiquarian Society, Worchester, Massachusetts, retrieved information on Prospectus from website http://www.americanantiquarian.org/Inventories/adventist.htm on April 30, 2008; Aland, Kurt and Barbara Aland. *The text of the New Testament: an introduction to the critical editions.* 4th ed. Berlin: Walter de Gruyter & Co. 1993; Ancestry.com. U. K. Scotland. Angus. Dundee. 1851-1891, record for George Dowie, displaying birth, address, various occupations inducing bookbinder, and clerk at Jute works; Ancestry.com. U. S. Census. IL Kane. Geneva. 1850, 1860; and, U. S. Census. Calif. Sacramento. Brighton. Dist. 116. 1870, 1880; Ancestry.com. England & Wales Free BMD Death Index, 1837-1983, Record for James Wilson, Halifax, Yorkshire, West Riding, West Yorkshire, March 1852; Beale, B. "Inquiry concerning the "non-resurrection of the wicked" to B. Wilson including Wilson's response," *The Gospel Banner*, August, 1860; Campbell, A. "The Lord's Prayer," *The Gospel Banner*, July, 1858 exchanged with *The British Millennial Harbinger*, and Campbell, A., "Baptism," *The Gospel Banner*, July 1858; Carras, John, member and researcher, Society of Biblical Literature, Anderson, S.C. Mr. Carras located information about the parents of Benjamin Wilson, when they were married and where they lived, Spring 2007; Carras, John, Comments via phone and e-mail to JStilson 2006-2010, about Wilson's use of Greisbach's *Critical Edition of the New Testament*, and about the *Latin Vulgate*. The Vulgate was named from the Latin word *vulgar* meaning common people, and is parallel in meaning to the Greek *hoi polloi*, the people. Go to AmericanBibleSociety.com/BibleResources for more on translations; Carras, John. E-mail to Stilson Nov. 15, 2010 citing Geo. Homer, regarding the Coptic texts, and discussing translators' use of parentheses; "Church of God Roots," citing W.H. Wilson in the *Progress Journal*. Oregon, Il., April 1981, and republished electronically *The Restitution Herald*, Feb. 2011; Chaplin, S.A. Editorial, *The Restitution*, Plymouth, In., S.A. Chaplin, ed., A.R. Underwood, publisher. Jan. 9, 1889. It is here Chaplin reported Benj. Wilson in attendance at the 1888 Philadelphia Conference; Churchill, Thomas. "The Paternity of Jesus," *The Gospel Banner*, Geneva, Il., 1860; Cook, Stephen. E-mail on George Dowie. Spring, 2006. Mr. Cook is interested in identifying the relationship between Benjamin Wilson and George Dowie. Wilson published Dowie's articles and visited him in Edinburgh in 1868; Cook, Stephen, "E-mail with brief history of churches in and around Edinburgh, Scotland during the 1850s and 1860s, Oct. 4, 2010; Demmitt, Greg. Posting on "Universal Ransom" retrieved from Cogmail-l, JStilson, Cogmail Owner, at YahooGroups.com on Feb. 22, 2009; Dover, Paul. citing from David King, "History and Mystery of the Christadelphians," to the Stone-Campbell Archives List, November 4, 1998 on the relationship of Dr. Thomas, B Wilson and Joseph Marsh; Dowie, George. "Animadversions," *The Gospel Banner and Millennial Advocate*, Oct. 1860. Erickson, Lee, *Economy in Literary Form: English Literature and the Industrialization of Publishing 1800-1850.* John Hopkins Press. London; Genusa, Stephen. "Dowieism," Nov. 2004, retrieved from http://genusa.com/truth on Oct. 6, 2010 p. 17; Graham, David, Correspondence with J. Stilson on the question of Wilson and Marsh, Feb. 17, 2006; "Letters to B. Wilson," *Gospel Banner and Millennial Advocate*, May 1859, June 1859 and Jan. 1860; Graham, David. Bibliography of Periodicals in his library, Insert, *History Newsletter*, JStilson, ed., Summer 1984 lists B. Wilson's *Guardian and Advocate*, 1852; Graham, David. Comment on G.M. Myers, March 7, 2011; Griesbach, J.J. *Novum Testamentum Grӕce, Textum ad fidem Codicum Versionem et Patrum recensuit et Lectionis Variatatem adjecit D.* 2nd ed. London and Halle, 1796 and 1806. 2 vols., large octavo; Hemingray, Peter. Information about *The Nazarine Messenger*, e-mail, March 7, 2011; Hooper, Leonard J., County Recorder, Sacramento, "Death Certificate of Benjamin Wilson," May 8, 1900; Herald Magazine, *Appendix I Introduction to Use of the Greek New Testament Manuscripts* no date, retrieved from heraldmag.org/rvic/nt/28_NT_Appendix_1.doc, Jan. 23, 2011; Hoover, Mary. "Queries on the Kingdom," *The Gospel Banner and Millennial Advocate*, April 15, 1869; Joblin, Maurice, *The Paternity of Jesus*, self-published. Cleveland, Oh. 1905; Lithgow, John R. "A Protest," *The Herald of the Coming Kingdom and Christian Instructor*, T. Wilson, ed., Chicago, Il., Jan. 1, 1870; Mattison, Mark. E-mail to Stilson. April 2006; Report of General Assembly at Geneva, July 3-4, 1859. *The Gospel Banner and Millennial Advocate*, Aug. 1859; Peters, George N.H., *The Theocratic Kingdom*, Vol. 3, Funk & Wagnalls, New York, 1884, p. 269; Reed, H.V. "The Age to Come is Not a Heresy," *The Gospel Banner*, B. Wilson, ed. Chicago. April, 1864; "The Heresy of the Nineteenth Century," author unknown. *The Gospel Banner*, B. Wilson, June 15, 1867, p. 177; "Report of Chicago Conference," *The Gospel Banner and Millennial Advocate*, June 15, 1869; Robbins, J.E. "What Think Ye of Christ? Whose Son is He?" and the Appendix, Self-published, Los Angeles, Ca., 1900; "Minutes of the Michigan Conference 1858-1886," specific mention on an index card tucked into the minutes, "conference urged the merger of the semi-monthly publication the *Herald* and the *Banner* into a weekly." September 1868.

Roberts, Robert. *Life of Dr. Thomas* information retrieved from website http://www.christadelphians.com/john_thomas/john_thomas_part_2.htm on February 23, 2009. It should be noted that there is no entry in this encyclopedia for Dr. Thomas because he was never interested in the Church of God, and he tried to destroy the work by debasing Joseph Marsh and Benjamin Wilson through a negative propaganda campaign to ruin their reputations; Ross, Franklyne. Phone conversation with JStilson on the association of Dr. Thomas with B. Wilson in Illinois, Feb. 19, 2009; Rust, Albert D. *Paternity of Jesus Investigated*, 3d ed. Published by W.N. Kerns, Bellingham, Wa., 1850 This tract quotes from *The Nazarene Messenger*, Oct. 1899; Schulz, Bruce. E-mail to Stilson, October 21, 2010 on the merger of the Eastern Church of God with One Faith in the Midwest; Speer, J.K. "The Reformers have gone over to Rome and Egypt," *The Gospel Banner*, Vol. 13, B. Wilson, ed., Geneva, Il., Feb. 1, 1867, p. 48; Stilson, Jan, "An Overview of the Leadership and Development of the Age to Come in the United States: 1832-1871," Herein is discussed more fully Wilson and Campbell's breech in the pages of the *Gospel Banner*, and the Disciples of Christ opinion on the matter. This information is contained in a footnote page 43 in *Journal from the Radical Reformation*, Fall, 2001; John Thomas, M.D., "Visit to

Canada and the West." *Herald of the Kingdom and Age to Come*, Feb., 1857, p. 32. It was in this piece that Dr. Thomas stated he had not met Benjamin Wilson prior to 1856; Thomas, L. D. Dr. *Paternity, Genealogy, Nature and Character of Jesus in Light of the Covenants*, two lectures delivered at Wyoming, Delaware, This was a conclusion of a series. *Restitution, Feb. 23, 1887*-August 3, 1887; Underwood, A.R. "Are the First Chapters of Matthew and Luke Authentic," *The Restitution*, Underwood, ed., Plymouth, In., March 5-23, 1904. In the midst of this three- part series W.H. Wilson's article dispelling the allegations that his uncle Benjamin was a Josephite or Marcionite appeared; Whitehead, Leila. "The History of the Geneva Church of God," *The Restitution Herald*, Harold Doan ed., Oregon, Il., Jan. 3, 1956. Here is discussed the sale of the Geneva Wilson home; Whitehead, Leila, "The Wilson Brothers" a family tree presented to The Geneva Historical Society, Aug. 1963; Whitehead, Leila, "The Story of the *Diaglott*," *The Restitution Herald*, Jan. 3, 1956; Watch Tower Publications. "The Special Terms Under Which This Valuable Work is Now Supplied to Bible Students" *Emphatic Diaglott*. Watch Tower Bible House, Allegheny, Pa. 1902; Full Text of *The Emphatic Diaglott* at http://www.archive.org/stream/emphaticdiaglott00wils/ emphaticdiaglott00wils_djvu.txt

Wilson, Benjamin. "Address Delivered By Brother Benjamin Wilson," *The Messenger of the Churches*, Geo. Dowie, ed., Edinburgh, Dec. 1, 1868, p. 177; Articles from *The Gospel Banner* in exchange with the *Advent Harbinger* presumably by B. Wilson include "The Sure Word of Prophecy," Aug. 1853, "Will Jesus Come Again?" Sept.1, 1853, "The Faith," Nov. 5, 1853, The Kingdom of God Series Nos. 1-3, Feb. 25, 1854, March 25, 1854 and April 3, 1854, and "Mammon of Unrighteousness," Jan. 6, 1855 and "Signs of the Times," presumably also 1855; "Denies Josephism," *The Gospel Banner and Millennial Advocate*, B. Wilson, ed., Geneva, Il., Sept. 1860; Wilson, B. "Report of Western Tour," *Gospel Banner and Millennial Advocate*, Oct. 1860; "Criticism of *The Millennial Harp*," *Herald of the Coming Kingdom and Christian Instructor*, Thomas Wilson, ed., Chicago. Jan. 1, 1868. "Report of Discord," Feb. 1, 1868; "2 Peter 3:10 explanation," Jan. 1870; "Editor's note regarding baptism," and "Bro. Shockey's Position," *The Gospel Banner and Millennial Advocate*, March 1, 1868, and "Editorial Comments on the Spirit," *The Gospel Banner and Millennial Advocate* May 15, 1868; "Refuting J.V. Himes on Jewish Question," *The Gospel Banner and Millennial Advocate*, Geneva, Il., March 15, 1868; "Report of Travels to England," *The Gospel Banner and Millennial Advocate*, Dec. 15, 1868. In this report B. Wilson also mentioned his meeting with George Dowie; "Report of Macedonian Call," *The Gospel Banner and Millennial Advocate*, Jan. 1, 1869; "Re-Immersion," *The Gospel Banner and Millennial Advocate*, March 15, 1869; "Response to Letter, 'Banner Objected To,'" *The Gospel Banner and Millennial Advocate*, April 1, 1869; Wilson, Benj. "History of the Greek Text," *The Emphatic Diaglott*, Geneva, Il., 1864, p.4; Wilson, Benj. "The Time of the Resurrection," *The Gospel Banner and Millennial Advocate*, last issue, Dec. 15, 1869. Wilson refutes Thomas Wilson and Mark Allen's position on "the rest of the dead lived not again until the thousand years were ended" and states Rev. 20:4,5 is a spurious passage, pp. 442-443; *The Emphatic Diaglott*, John 1:1 and 2 Peter 3:10. Rev. 20:4-5; "The Last Days," *The Restitution*, Feb. 1, 1888; "Letter to Joseph R. Cooper at Ripley, Il.," 1863. Letter owned by Helen Burnett Jones, Grand Detour, Il. Copy donated for use, December 2006. A note by an unknown Cooper/Burnett family member at the bottom of the letter says, "This letter from Benjamin Wilson to our parents has been kept through the years. Lola turned it over to me. It is worth keeping by someone in the family partly on account of its age, but more on account of who is the writer. If I understand correctly he is the author of the *Diaglott*." This is a rare letter, indeed. This letter was furnished for the online version of *A History Newsletter*, Kent H. Ross, ed., Dec. 2006; Wilson, Benjamin, "Is it Essential to Believe in the Royalty of Jesus?" Restitution Office, Chicago, Il., circa 1871; Wilson, Benjamin. Special Contributor. *The Restitution*, March 22, 1882 --Others whose names also appeared on the masthead included A.B. Magruder, J.A. Simonds, Wiley Jones, G.M. Myers, J.P. Weethee and D.T. Halstead; Wilson, Benjamin, "What Think Ye of Christ Whose Son is He?" *The Restitution*, Jan. 7, 1885; Wilson, Benjamin. "Why we don't fellowship with Immersed Believers in Jesus," *The Herald of the Coming Kingdom*, T. Wilson, ed., Chicago, Il., Dec. 15, 1870; Wilson, B. "Is the Church the Kingdom?" *The Restitution*, S. A. Chaplin, ed., Plymouth, In., April 10, 1889; "Larger Hope," *The Restitution*, April 18, 1889; Wilson, B. "Memoriam for Richard Appleyard," which explains their childhood together in Halifax. *The Restitution*, S.A. Chaplin, ed., Plymouth, In., Feb. 15, 1893; "The Way of Salvation," *The Restitution*, April 18, 1894; "Letter to a Niece," Dec. 24, 1899 as published in *The Restitution*, March 23, 1904; Wilson, B.F. Record of interment in Old City Cemetery, Sacramento, Lot 7, beside his three sons, Edwin B, 66, Bennie Lewis, 7, Harry Edwin, 1 mo, and a daughter, Nellie Hazel, 3. www. oldcitycemetery.com/images/PDF/CemeteryIndex.pdf;

Wilson, James. Wm. Brockman, S.A. Chaplin, Committee Report of 1888 Philadelphia Committee, *The Restitution*, S.A. Chaplin, ed., Plymouth, In., Dec. 12, 1888; **Wilson, Joseph, interim editor** "Are we Right or Wrong," editorial comment answering Mark Allen's criticism, *The Gospel Banner and Millennial Advocate*, August 1, 1868; "Conference at Geneva," *The Herald of the Coming Kingdom and Christian Instructor*, Jan. 15, 1869, Chicago, Il.; "Letter to Sydney Magaw," as cited in *The Restitution Herald*, Feb. 14, 1922; Wilson, Thomas, "Report of the Eighth Semi-Annual Conference at Geneva, Il.," in which it is stated the Disciples Meeting House was not Campbellite. *The Gospel Banner*, Benj. Wilson, ed., Geneva, Il., Jan. 1, 1861;

Wilson, W. H. "A Josephite Error Corrected," *The Restitution*, A.R. Underwood, ed., Plymouth, In., March 24, 1904; Wilson, W. H. "A short history of the Church of God," *The Restitution Herald*. This article was republished in the *Progress Journal*, Oregon, Il., April 1981, as "Church of God Roots."

Wilson, Dr. Emilus M. "Em"
b. 1864
d. Unknown

E.M. Wilson was born and raised in Alabama. At some point he or his family moved west, for when his name appears in the literature, he is already living in Goldthwaite, Texas. Dr. Wilson was a dentist, but he also led a small nucleus of people in a weekly study of the Scriptures. They were believers in the Gospel of the Kingdom. One wonders if, when he went out on a circuit through Oklahoma and Kansas, he took his little black bag and fixed teeth. Chances are he did. People affectionately referred to him as "Em." In 1920 his elderly father-in-law resided with the Wilsons, as did the doctor's mother, Sarah. Dr. and Mrs. Wilson had four daughters.

He may have learned of the truth from any of the early evangelists, such as James Lord and Robert Warren, who frequented the Texas region where Wilson and his family lived. Elder Joshua Bailey, J.F. Wagoner, Uncle John Foore, and later, E.W. Moses, E.O. Stewart and

W.H. Wilson all preached in Oklahoma and Texas.

Dr. Wilson was an avid Bible student. He wrote a Statement of Faith that was accepted by the Texas Conference in 1917. This same statement was submitted to *The Restitution Herald* in 1922. It had 17 components including one which stated the name of the denomination as Church of Jehovah God and Jesus Christ. A summary of each of the other components follows:

How Organized Select elders, teachers and deacons (Eph. 4:11).

Belief There is one body, one spirit, one hope one Lord, one faith, one baptism, one God (Eph. 4:4-6).

One God One God, the Father whose name is Jehovah. He had body, parts and passion (Ex. 6:3, Ps 83:18, Eph. 4:6, Heb. 1:3).

One Lord Jesus Christ, the Son of God Jesus Christ is Savior, made of woman, came in the flesh, took upon himself the seed of Abraham, was tempted (Matt. 1:21, Luke 1:32, Gal. 4:4).

One Holy Spirit The holy spirit came in the name of Jesus to guide the apostle into all truth (John 14:26, Acts 2:1-4).

One Body Members of the church as members of the mystical body of Christ (Eph. 4:4, Rom. 12:4-5).

One Hope The hope of Israel, the restoration to the land, and the inheritance of the earth for ever by Christ, immortality in the kingdom of God to be received at the Second Coming. (Gen. 12:1,2, Ezek. 38, 39).

Statement of Faith (Acts 26: 6,7, 23:6, Gen. 12:1-4, Heb. 6: 17-20, Rom. 11:11-26, Matt. 5:5).

One Faith Faith comes by hearing the Word of God, (Gospel) (Eph. 1:21-23).

Repentance Bible repentance is turning from evil to do good, a godly sorrow (2 Cor. 7:10).

Confession Confess with the mouth that Christ is Savior (Rom.10:8-10, Matt. 10:32).

One Baptism for the remission of sins (Matt. 28:19).

Obedience to the Commandments required. Avoiding politics; avoiding wars; love your enemy (Matt. 5:44, 2 Cor. 6:14-18).

God will bring peace In the age to come through Jesus. Kingdoms of world will become Kingdoms of our Lord. (Ps. 2:1, 2 Tim. 4:1, Rev. 20:4).

The composition of Man Mortal being unconscious at death (Job. 4:17, Gen. 2:7, Eccl. 9:5).

All Raised from Dead As all go down to death because of Adam's sin, so all will be raised through obedience to Christ. (1 Cor. 15:2, Rom. 5:12-20, John 5:28-29).

Destiny of the Wicked They will be as though they had not been. Mal. 4, Ps. 19:17, Prov. 21:6).

Wilson said he hoped to see this in print again after the General Conference delegates approved it at the first annual Conference meeting.

Compare that statement to one published by F.L. Austin in *The Restitution* and *The Restitution Herald*, October 1921. This is the statement which Robert Huggins adversely critiqued in *The Restitution* because it contained no Scripture, and did not state that Jesus was the Son of God:

a) That there is one God and Father of all, who is above all, and through all.

b) That Christ died for our sins according to the Scriptures; that he was buried, rose again on the third day.

c) That all Scripture is given by inspiration of God, and is profitable for doctrine, for reproof, for correction, for instruction and for righteousness.

d) That the gift of God is eternal life through Jesus Christ our Lord.

e) That there shall be a resurrection of the dead.

f) That Christ was once offered to bear the sins of many, as our high priest he now sits at the right hand of God; and, unto those who look he shall appear a second time without sin unto salvation; and that when he shall come in his glory, he shall set upon the throne of his glory, and before him shall be gathered all nations.

g) That as many as have been baptized into Christ have put on Christ.

h) That all who are new creatures in Christ Jesus should not henceforth live unto themselves, but unto him, which died for them and rose again.

Dr. Wilson and other leaders of the Texas work endorsed the "Articles of Faith" as advanced by the delegates following the 1910 Waterloo Conference. O.J. Allard wrote the articles after the conference delegates appointed him to do so. They were then distributed to each of the state conferences for endorsement. Only the Texas Conference and the Washington State Conference ratified Allard's Articles of Faith. Included here are the ratified Articles as endorsed by the Texas Conference:

We believe that the things concerning the name of Jesus include the name of the Father, Jehovah, Jesus being a contracted form of Jehovah as prophesied by Jer. 15:16 literally came in the Father's name.

We believe that the kingdom of God will be a personal reign of Jesus and his Saints upon the earth. Jer. 23:5.

We believe the Holy Scriptures were originally given by the inspiration of Jehovah God, and reveal one God only. Deut. 6:4.

We believe that the Holy Bible reveals One Lord Jesus, the Christ, the Son of the living God, who was made of a woman, made under the law. Gal. 4:4.

We believe in one Holy Spirit the Divine power emanating from God; sent in the name of Jesus. John 14:15, 16, 17.

We believe that there is but one true Faith—a belief, Dan. 7:26; 2 Tim. 4:1.

We believe that there is One Hope of the Christian, Eph. 4:4.

We believe in One Baptism, Eph. 4:4. An immersion in water for the sins of the past. Matt. 28:19.

We believe that man is mortal subject to death and in the death state, unconscious. Job 4:17.

We believe in a resurrection from the dead, at or in connection with the second coming of Jesus. John 5:28, 29.

We believe that the wages of sin is death, but the gift of God is eternal life. Deut. 30:16, 17, 18, 19; Gal. 6:7, 8.

We believe that God foreordained that his children should be conformed to the image of his Son. Rom. 8:28, 29, 30. That he foreordained and inspired the Prophets, Jesus and the Apostles to give us the plan of salvation; and that we are to be saved by this plan. (But we do not believe that God foreordained any individual to be either saved or lost.) Eph. 1:3, 4, 5.

We believe in faith, repentance and baptism (by immersion in water) and a righteous walk thereafter in order to gain eternal life. Therefore we are opposed to WARS in all forms. We believe in invoking the Golden Rule. We are commanded not to kill. Wars come from fleshly lusts. James 2:10, 11. "He that leadeth into captivity shall go into captivity." Rev. 13:10.

We also go on record as endorsing any and all preachers who preach the foregoing fundamental principles, and who do not go beyond what is written in the Bible--the Word of truth.

This was signed by the Committee of
E.M. Wilson, T.B. Conradt, and A.S. Bradley

The Church of God "Articles of Faith" were issued for consideration in the same year that the Fundamentalist movement was beginning to gain momentum in America. The Church of God was a Bible-based church which did not emphasize its unitarian background until around 1910. Higher criticism from the German schools of theology was beginning to gain influence in American theological scholarship, but it was liberal in approach, and the Church of God reacted against it. By 1917, the conservative evangelical churches answered the liberal threat with a 12-volume work entitled *The Fundamentals*, written by R.A. Torrey, L. Myers and A.C. Dixon. *The Fundamentals* represented the conservative protestant approach to Bible study with emphasis on trinity. John G. Machen, who founded Westminster Theological Seminary, a conservative Presbyterian school, had supported it. Out of this conservative theological climate also came the Bible College movement to educate ministers in a conservative style of Bible study and preaching.

After the 1910 conference, during which the Articles of Faith and Church Discipline were the principle topics of discussion, the Church of God struggled with some of the same conservative biblical issues that were being advocated by the "fundamentalists." They agreed with much of it, but could not agree with the trinity, or natural immortality. By 1917, the Church of God still did not have consensus on doctrine to form a national organization. Since it could not endorse every tenet of Torrey, Myer's and Dixon's *Fundamentals*, the Church of God recognized that as a conservative group with a biblical message, it had to step forward with its own unique statement of fundamentals and a ministerial educational system. Because of this need, it might have organized a stable national work as early as 1914, following the example of the Bereans who organized in 1913, except for the interference of WWI. By 1920, the leaders in the national effort knew that the time had come, and by 1921 a general conference was born from discussion, controversy and prayer. See entries for S.J. Lindsay, F.L. Austin and L.E. Conner for additional information on this topic.

Emilus Wilson was part of the national discussion within the Church of God as the Texas representative who promoted the "Articles of Faith." He was well known to William H. Wilson, the evangelist from Chicago, but

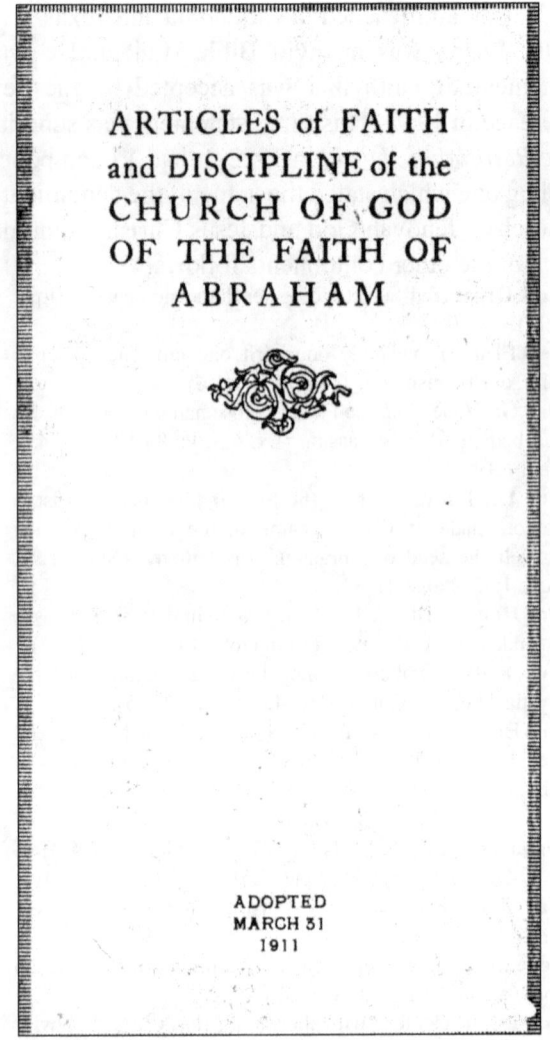

probably was not related to him except through Christ. When W.H. Wilson was in Texas on an evangelistic trip, he often stopped at Goldthwaite to visit the E.M. Wilson family. In one report from 1911 W.H. Wilson said, "We met our brother Dr. E.M. Wilson of Goldthwaite, Texas." He also said E.M. loved the blessed hope. That is a good summary of a man's life.

See Allard, O.J.
Austin, F.L.
Bradley, A.S. (20th)
Conner, L.E.
Huggins, Robert (20th)
Lindsay, S.J.
Lord, James
Warren, Robert
Wilson, W.H.

Bibliography: Ancestry.com U.S. Census. Justice Precinct #1 Goldthwaite. Texas. 1920; *The Restitution,* March 22, 1911, Oct. 1921; *The Restitution Herald*, Oct. 1921; May 9, 1922, July 19, 1922; "Articles of Faith" by the Committee, Wilson, Conradt and Bradley, source unknown. Document is located in the Texas history file of the Archives of Atlanta Bible College; Torrey, R.A., Myers, L., Dixon, A.C., *Fundamentals a Testimony to the Truth.* 12 vols. Chicago. 1917.

Wilson, James W.
b. 1799
d. 1892

James Wilson was born in Halifax, England. He was the third son of five of whom Benjamin Wilson was the youngest. James resided first in St. Charles and later in Northfield, Illinois. He was married to Mary Woodward, Martha Woodward's (Mrs. Joseph Wilson) twin. James and Mary had five children, including Ruth Wilson Whitehead (1838-1918), mother of Dr. Leila Whitehead. James owned a farm, later known as the Evans farm, two miles west of St. Charles. He sold the farm when he moved to Northfield.

James was a member of the One Faith church at Geneva, Illinois. He loved the truth of the Gospel and served as officer of his local congregation and the Illinois State conference in which they fellowshipped. In fact, he and several other families, many of them related to the Wilsons, established a congregation in Geneva in 1844. After 1845 when Mr. and Mrs. Boyes moved to Northfield, they met in each other's homes in Geneva. This congregation was never part of the Millerite movement which experienced its Bitter Disappointment in 1844.

The group grew, and soon Mr. Westgarth built a house with the upper floor finished as a hall, which they used until 1849. After two more Wilson brothers arrived with their families, and Edward Underwood arrived with their five children in 1849, the need to build became evident. They organized and built a small meetinghouse on land donated by Joseph Cockcroft with the understanding that if the church ever disbanded, it would revert to the Cockcroft estate.

They called their new church "The Disciples Meeting House," even though they had not been associated with Alexander Campbell since 1845. Thomas Wilson was to say years later that we are all disciples of Christ, and the name was not meant to indicate any formal association with Alexander Campbell's group

James assisted in the church's construction, but his greatest asset was his fine tenor voice. When the worship meetings began he led the music and assisted in forming a worship style which is still in practice in many Churches of God today. The worship format included an opening service with one or two hymns, prayer, scripture, followed by words of exhortation, concluding with communion and prayer. Communion was observed every Sunday. To lead the singing, he used a tuning fork to set the pitch and proceeded unaccompanied by instruments.

The minute book of the Illinois Conference of the Church of God for the northern district recorded that James held offices with that organization as president in 1898, 1899, 1900 and 1901 and program committee chairman, or member with S.J. Lindsay, 1900 and 1902.

James authored two titles, *Will It Pay to Become a Christian* and *A Textbook for Bible Students*, which were distributed to Chicago businessmen and to prospective church members by W.H. Wilson on his evangelistic travels. The subtitle of *Will it Pay* was "A Prospectus of Christianity, and Manual of Primitive Christian Faith." It is thought that Jessie M. Wilson, James' great niece and daughter of W.H. Wilson, whose publishing business she supervised, published the book posthumously in 1904.

The interesting thing about *Will It Pay* is the simple explanation Wilson gives to his audience of Chicago business readers. He explained One Faith as being seven-fold to agree with the seven candlesticks in Revelation:

> Seven candlesticks (Rev. 1: 12, 13, 20) are representative of the whole church universal in all ages of the world. The Gospel in its seven divisions is the light of the seven candlesticks or churches.

According to James Wilson, the seven components of the Gospel are:

I. Faith in the promise of the forgiveness of sins, through grace, and the sacrificial offering of the Son of God, and in his present mediatorial office as our High Priest at the Court of heaven.
II. Faith in the testimony that God raised Him from the dead.
III. Faith that at His coming the faithful in him shall be raised also.
IV. Faith in the promise of eternal life with eternal joy, peace, prosperity and happiness.
V. Faith that the Lord Jesus Christ will come again to fulfill His mission on the earth.
VI. Faith that on his return as the son and heir of David, he will re-establish the kingdom and reign as King over re-gathered Israel, and as the Son of God, reign as "King of kings," over the whole earth, to restore peace, prosperity, righteousness and happiness to the world.
VII. Faith in the promise that his faithful followers shall receive an eternal inheritance in the Kingdom of God, with positions of honor and trust, each "according to his work."

Wilson concluded by saying:
This is "one faith" (Eph. 4:5). It is the 'doctrine' of which Paul in his first letter to Timothy, spoke. It is the faith kept by Paul who said, "I have kept the faith: henceforth there is laid up for me a crown of righteousness." (2 Tim. 4:7, 8)

See Wilson, Benjamin
Wilson, Thomas
Underwood, Arthur

Bibliography: Magaw, Ivan. Biographical notes from the Minute book of the Illinois Conference on file with Archives in Atlanta Bible College, retrieved March 2008; *The Restitution*, May 17, 1911; Whitehead, Leila. "History of the Geneva Church of God," *The Restitution Herald*, Jan. 3, 1956; Wilson, James. *Will it Pay to Become a Christian?* W.H. Wilson, Publisher, Chicago. 1904. pps. 74-77.

Wilson, Jessie Mae
b. May 6, 1874
d. March 3, 1938

Jessie M. Wilson was from Chicago. She was faithful to the message of the Gospel of the Kingdom all her life. Jessie never married. Her parents were William Henry and Agnes Sutcliffe Wilson, making Jessie a great niece of Benjamin Wilson's, who translated *The Emphatic Diaglott* and published the *Gospel Banner and Millennial Advocate* (1853-1869).

Jessie worked with Leila Whitehead, her cousin, and their mutual friend, Evelyn Harsh Austin from Indiana, who came to reside in Chicago with Dr. Whitehead. In their youth, these women began the National Berean Society with the assistance of Anna Drew from Dixon, Illinois, and other notable women such as Harriett Boice, Champaign, Illinois, and Clara Chaffee of Michigan.

Miss Wilson was a leader not only in organizing the Berean movement, but also in marketing and distributing the Berean's and her father's publications. The Bereans published *Berean Study Books,* each containing 13 weekly lessons. These booklets were among the first formal Christian education materials published and distributed separately from *The Restitution*. As such, they filled a need within the developing Church of God that aided local congregations in their Bible study.

W.H. Wilson wrote several small hard cover study booklets and kept a stock of them at his home. Jessie mailed them to churches and individuals. She was the power behind all publishing efforts in Chicago and undoubtedly prepared the copy, gave it to printers, arranged for binding, and saw to advertising and distribution.

Advertisements for W.H. Wilson's many books and tracts were scattered throughout the pages of *The Herald of the Coming Kingdom and Christian Instructor* (Thomas Wilson, ed.), *The Restitution* (various editors), and *The Restitution Herald* (S.J. Lindsay, ed.).

Even after her father's death, Jessie continued to market his writings, so that most churches had multiple copies of his works, and many church members did as well. A dedicated daughter preserved this notable Church of God publishing heritage single-handedly. Many copies of W.H. Wilson's publications are available for research in the Archives of the Atlanta Bible College and the Rock River Christian College in Beloit, Wisconsin.

Jessie was a capable publishing manager who supervised her father's business while he traveled for evangelistic meetings throughout the Midwest, Great Plains and south into Louisiana. After her mother died, Jessie closed up their Chicago residence and spent her last years at the Golden Rule Home in Oregon, Illinois, however, the record shows she died in Chicago.

See Austin, Evelyn Harsh (20th)
Boice, Harriett
Chaffee, Clara
Drew, Anna E.
Whitehead, Leila, M.D. (20th)
Wilson, William H.
Wilson, Benjamin

Bibliography: Ancestry.com. U.S. Census. Illinois. Cook. Chicago Ward 35. Dist. 1132. 1900. Ancestry.com. Cook County Death Index, 1908-1988, record for Jessie M. Wilson; *The Restitution Herald,* Dec. 15, 1915; Nov. 22, 1921; Whitehead, Leila, "The Wilson Brothers" a family tree. From the Evelyn Austin papers housed at the Atlanta Bible College Archives.

Wilson, John A.
b. July 25, 1832
d. March 29, 1904

John Wilson was born near Worthington, Ohio. He was a Civil War veteran who saw very little service, but who experienced great strain from the conflict. He participated in the Mitchell Raid, the 24-soldier unit ordered to blow up the Georgia State Railroad bridges. They stole a train but for more than 100 miles were hindered by passing trains from blowing up any bridges, as they could not put any distance between them and other trains. Finally, they abandoned their engine after it failed and hid in the woods but were captured. They were first placed in the old "Swim Hole" in Chattanooga from which they tried repeatedly to escape. Their leader, a man named Andrews, was hung as a spy in Atlanta. Seven others were subsequently hung, but the balance of the Raiders broke out and followed the Chattahoochee River to the Gulf of Mexico where they were rescued by a Federal blockade squadron.

Here the exhausted Union men were fed and returned to their homes in broken health, "mere wrecks of their former selves." They were honorably discharged, and Mr. Wilson began a grocery business in Haskins, Ohio. Later, being in better health, John visited his brother-in-law in southern Ohio. John's cousin learned of the Abrahamic Faith from a man named Downer who had been taught it by Levi H. Chase, an evangelist in the area a few years before his death. Being obedient to the Lord, John's cousin wanted his relatives to hear and believe also.

John Wilson learned from his cousin as much as he could in a short visit, and as he was about to return home, the cousin said "John, will you read a paper if I send one to you?" He agreed, and soon *The Restitution* began arriving at his grocery store. He said afterward he "would rather burn the paper than to take the trouble to read it." He did read it, however, and he believed it, too.

He committed to not sell liquor in his store and emptied

the casks into the ditch. He said he had the courage to face the Southern Confederacy so he had the courage to live by what he read in *The Restitution*, and to contend for the truth no matter how unpopular it may be.

See Chase, Levi H.
Bibliography: Testimony of John Wilson, *The Restitution*, April 20, 1904.

Wilson, Jonathan
b. April 1777
d. Unknown

Jonathan was an evangelist across New England, contemporary with Joseph Marsh. Wilson devoted his life to preaching the Gospel of the Kingdom of God, the restoration of the Jews to their homeland, the second advent of Christ to earth and the sleep of the dead.

He joined Joseph Marsh and several others who, by 1851, accepted the new prophecy teaching of Age to Come explained by Joseph Marsh in the pages of *The Advent Harbinger and Bible Advocate*. To show his devotion to this truth he joined Marsh, Dingle, Hoyt, Crozier, Weethee, Cook and others in the Rochester Union Conference in April 1851. Wilson was asked to lead the group in prayer as it was his 74th birthday.

These men from Illinois, Wisconsin, New England, Pennsylvania, Ohio and elsewhere gathered in conference to pray and study together for the advancement of the work. Then, they went back to their home churches and shared the happenings at conference with them.

See Cook, J.B.
Crozier, O.R.L.
Hoyt, Ed
Marsh, Joseph
Weethee, J.P.
Bibliography: Report of Rochester Union Conference. *The Advent Harbinger and Bible Advocate*, April 19, 1851.

Wilson, Joseph
b. 1820?
d. January 15, 1924

Joseph Wilson was born in Halifax, England, and immigrated to Geneva, Illinois, in 1849. He was married to Martha Woodward for 57 years. His brothers were Benjamin, James and John Wilson.

Joseph and Martha had six children, three sons and three daughters. His sons made a name for themselves in the Church of God. Samuel lived in New Jersey and pastored at the Church of God at Elizabeth. Thomas became the noted editor of *The Herald of the Kingdom and Christian Instructor* published in Chicago, as well as *The Last Days* published in Oakland, California. William Henry authored numerous study books and treatises including *Cunningly Devised Fables*, a book exposing the errors of Russellism, and he was an evangelist to the South Central Plains states and Louisiana.

Joseph helped to form the Church at Geneva, Illinois. He was one of the first trustees, along with his brother Benjamin and Henry Pierce, a son-in-law. Their names appear in the records of the Kane County Recorder as charter board members of the new church organization.

All his children attended Joseph's funeral. He rests in Diamond Lake Cemetery near Libertyville, Illinois.

See Button, Lucian and Emma
Wilson, Samuel
Wilson, Thomas
Wilson, W.H.
Bibliography: Obituary, *The Restitution Herald*, Jan. 29, 1924; Incorporation Record. Kane County Recorder's Office. Book 58, p. 524; Whitehead, Leila, "The Wilson Brothers Family Tree," part of Evelyn Austin's papers at the Archives of Atlanta Bible College.

Wilson, Joseph C.
b. 1855
d. Unknown

Joseph Wilson was a carpenter and minister from California who was mentioned by his cousin in a letter to *The Restitution Herald*. He was originally from Missouri and had "come home" to preach for a series of meetings. Wilson was such a good Bible student that Mrs. Gilbert felt he should be pressed into service for the cause of the truth. He was the best preacher she had ever heard.

Joseph married late in life to Rosa, and they had two sons and two daughters. Wilson performed preaching and ministry in Compton, California, baptizing believers in the local Advent Christian church baptistery, which they cheerfully lent him.

Bibliography: Ancestry.com. U.S. Census. California. Colusa. Fresh Water. Dist. 16. 1880. U.S. Census. California. Los Angeles. Compton. Dist. 40. 1920. *The Restitution Herald* Nov. 20, 1923; Jan. 22, 1924.

Wilson, Samuel J.
b. 1840?
d. Unknown

Samuel Wilson lived in Elizabeth, New Jersey, with his wife, Mary, and son, Clarence. Samuel was a nephew to Benjamin Wilson. He was the youngest son of Joseph Wilson, and brother of W.H. Wilson and Thomas Wilson of Chicago. His family came to Geneva from Halifax,

England, in 1849 while Samuel was still a boy.

At age 20, Samuel left home and moved in with Thomas in Chicago to begin work as a clerk in the publishing business. Samuel and wife Mary may have lived in Philadelphia at one time where he worked as a clerk for a railroad company. By that time, the census reveals that they had two sons and a daughter. Daughter Mary Ann died at age 16.

Sadly, Samuel's wife died suddenly September 3, 1913, during a visit to Chicago. The stricken family was astonished. H.V. Reed, a long-time friend of the family, conducted her funeral in Chicago. Mary and Samuel had been married over 40 years at the time of her death, making her about 60 years old. Her friend, Elizabeth Reed, said, "She is sleeping in her armor awaiting that glorious morning when all tears shall be wiped away."

Samuel Wilson advocated universal resurrection, meaning that all men both righteous and wicked would be resurrected. He believed that "the rest of the dead lived not again until the thousand years were over. This is the second death" (Revelation 20:4, 5). His famous uncle, Benjamin Wilson, did not adhere to that interpretation, but believed all would be raised upon Christ's return, some to reward, and some to judgment. Samuel Wilson believed fervently in the establishment of the Kingdom of God upon the earth after Christ returned. He was an author who published many tracts and edited a magazine, *The Rock* (1885-1901), proclaiming the Abrahamic Faith. The Archives in Atlanta have various issues from 1889 and 1890.

Samuel traveled south from Elizabeth to preach at Baltimore and throughout Virginia. He was active in the conference work of the Virginia brethren. He also participated in and was possibly the pastor of the Church of God at Philadelphia in 1874. During that time the church relocated to worship in a hall on Locust Street. Samuel also served as guest speaker at the fifth annual Nebraska Conference in 1890.

The 1888 General Conference organization elected Samuel Wilson vice president during its meetings in Philadelphia. George F. Work of Philadelphia was the treasurer. A.J. Eychaner of Iowa was elected secretary, and J.H. Willey was elected president. The people who cared enough to serve as officers cared enough to set the example for a forward-looking national organization. The members of the Church of God were not ready for it, however. The new organization only met two successive years, and finally was disbanded by the board in 1892 due to the lack of financial support by its members. It is a sad commentary that, historically, the Church of God members have been slow to put financial support behind its national organization, although currently they are gracious and generous in their support.

See Boyer, Benjamin Franklin
Reed, Elizabeth A.
Reed, H.V.
Wilson, Benjamin
Wilson, Joseph
Wilson, Thomas
Wilson, W.H.

Bibliography: Ancestry.com. U.S. Census. Pennsylvania. Philadelphia. Dist. 598. 1880; U.S. Census. New Jersey. Hudson. Jersey City. Ward. 9. Dist. 143. 1900; Bender, Edward, "History of Western Nebraska Conference," paper presented at the History Conference, North Hills Church of God, Springfield, Oh., Nov. 2007; "Church of God Roots," citing an article by W.H. Wilson. *Church of God Progress Journal*. Oregon, Il., April 1981; *The Restitution*, Dec. 22, 1874; Aug. 1913; Sept. 9, 1913; *The Restitution Herald*, July 23, 1922.

Wilson, Thomas
b. June 22, 1835
d. May 8, 1926

A. Chicago the Center of Publishing
B. Holding the Line on Doctrine
C. Not Always in Agreement with Uncle Benjamin
D. Other Accomplishments
E. Published *The Last Days*

Thomas Wilson was born in Halifax, England. He migrated with his parents to Geneva, Illinois, in 1849 where the family became involved in the publishing business. He was the eldest son of Joseph and Martha Cockroft Wilson, a brother of Samuel and William Henry Wilson and the nephew of Benjamin Wilson. Thomas also had three sisters. Thomas Wilson and his brothers learned the publishing and printing business by assisting Benjamin in his publishing house in Geneva. He and William, his brother, worked in printing and real estate in Geneva in the early days. In this manner, they were able to make enough income to support the evangelism work in which they were both interested.

In 1864, Thomas Newman moved to Chicago and brought Joseph Marsh's press and mailing list with him. At that time *The Prophetic Watchman* in Harvard, Illinois, merged with *The Millennial Harbinger*. Then, within two publishing years, operations in Harvard ceased, *The Gospel Banner* in Geneva merged with *The Herald* in Chicago, and the Harvard equipment, including Marsh's press, moved to Chicago. Suddenly Thomas Wilson became very busy.

A. Chicago the Center of Publishing

Wilson had been employed at the *Chicago Evening Post*. He was cashier and business manager. When he began publishing *The Herald of the Coming Kingdom* in 1868, he resigned his position at the *Post* to devote his time to the *Herald*. At his retirement party, the *Post* gave him a gold watch and a gold-knobbed walking stick.

In 1870, Wilson changed the name of *The Herald* to *The Restitution*. This new paper was an immediate hit with readers. It carried the same message that had been handed down from Joseph Marsh, used Marsh's press, and was free from the stigma left behind by the rapid merging of those several titles from 1867-1869.

The 1871 Chicago Fire destroyed The Lakeside Press building with *The Restitution* inventory and two presses, including Marsh's press. Arthur Underwood is credited with saving the records and the mailing list from their sixth floor offices at great risk to himself during the fire; all bound volumes of *The Herald, The Restitution,* and the equipment were lost. Members owned other complete sets of *The Herald* and *The Gospel Banner*, and those copies have been donated and archived at Atlanta Bible College. What remained of the paper was moved to Plymouth, Indiana. Chances are Reed and Wilson donated money for a new or used press.

Thomas and Mary moved to Brookville, Indiana, with their two sons, his brother, Samuel Wilson, and a young lady, Ellen Westgarth. After Mary died, Thomas married Lillie Cockroft on January 6, 1873, in Detroit where she had been teaching school. It was her first marriage. She was 18, and Thomas was 35. They had four children in

Lithograph of Lakeside Press building in ruins after the Chicago Fire.

Lithograph of the rebuilt Lakeside Press building.

Photos in public domain.

> **David Graham on the locational history of *The Restitution* in Chicago before and after the 1871 Chicago Fire**
>
> I have studied the locations where *The Restitution* was situated in Chicago before and after the Great Fire.
>
> First it was located in the McCormick Block at 191 Dearborn. (downtown); then after the Fire, it was moved to Clark and Adams (the Lakeside Press building, downtown just a few blocks away). The Lakeside Press was built exactly on the same spot where it was being erected. (It was not quite finished when the Fire struck.) They used the same exact architectural drawings! Nothing was changed.
>
> Robert Donnelley was a very religious man who made the Wilsons and their team, prominent members of the board of directors. James Wilson was his secretary for a while. Thomas and H.V. Reed were also on the board especially at the new Lakeside building.
>
> I had always thought for some reason the Lakeside Press was out on 22nd street where it is located now, as R.R. DONNELLEY, and the MCCORMICK Bldg too. But in the 1870's and 80's it was in downtown Chicago. I gave you photos or lithographs of the Lakeside Bldg. That bldg was the one they rebuilt on Clark and Adams!! I have all that history.
>
> They had to buy new type and equipment for *The Restitution* and other publications, which they got from Pennsylvania. A.R. Underwood saved all the subscription materials, so they were able to start up immediately at the home of Thomas Wilson on 183 Oakley, which was up town then.
>
> Ref.: David Graham, March 7, 2011

addition to Ira, Thomas' son, who was still living at home, and who survived his father.

B. Holding the Line on Doctrine

While editing the *Herald*, Thomas Wilson refuted many of the spurious doctrines that were swirling about in those days. One of them was mortal emergence, an idea popularized among Christadelphians by Dr. Thomas and others at the Rochester Church of God. This church had been Joseph Marsh's home church but was taken over by opposing factions.

Wilson said the teaching of mortal emergence was that Christ was resurrected mortal and ascended to heaven mortal. He explained the teaching stated if Christ were not mortal when he ascended, He could not be our atonement. It was stated that Christ needed to be human with blood to be our intercession. Hence, man will also rise mortal. Wilson skillfully refuted that argument from Scriptures. He stated, "When I become convinced of the truthfulness of mortal emergence, I shall embrace it." This was not a promise but rather a statement of exaggeration as in, "when cows fly...."

In 1897, Thomas published a small 24-page booklet, "The Jew Question." His opening statement certainly catches the attention of the reader:

The sect known as "Adventists" hold to the view that "as a nation, Israel will never return to Palestine—no never!" We mean, of course, the nation that was expelled from there ages ago, and carried into captivity. This is what their leading ministers and editors affirm....This position is false.

The booklet was a reply to Miles Grant, a noted Advent Christian theologian. From beginning to end, Thomas explained the teaching of the Restoration of Israel to old Jerusalem prior to the second coming of Christ as Age-to-Come advocates always taught it in America, and the Church of God has taught it around the world.

Thomas Wilson, far right, with members of the Los Angeles Church.

C. Not Always in Agreement with Uncle Benjamin

Thomas and Benjamin did not always agree on doctrinal issues. Thomas Wilson agreed with Joseph Marsh in two key areas. He agreed on the issue of Age to Come, and he agreed on the issue of Resurrection. Marsh believed the righteous would be raised when Jesus returns and rewarded at that time with immortality. The wicked dead would not be raised until the end of the thousand years. Uncle Benjamin did not believe in a "split first resurrection." He believed the wicked would not be raised from the Adamic death, but all Christian men (both faithful and carnal) would be raised and rewarded or judged at the time of Christ's return. Benjamin also chose to emphasize the covenant made to Abraham, calling it One Faith, rather than to emphasize the Age to Come.

Thomas Wilson explained the sequence at Christ's coming this way: Based on 1 Thessalonians 4:16, the righteous dead are raised, "snatched quickly" (the idea from Greek) into the clouds so as to protect them from view, i.e., a fog, mist (also idea from Greek) in the air for the meeting with the Savior. Air carries the idea of atmosphere that surrounds the earth. The redeemed meet the Redeemer. The meeting in the air acquaints the saints with the order in which judgment shall proceed. The Lord and his saints will descend to earth. Then the pouring out of judgment begins, the execution of which shall be done by the saints (Psalms 149:5-9). "So shall we ever be with the Lord" means no more partings. The first resurrection judges those saints who have been raised from the grave, and also changes to immortality those saints who are living at his appearing.

Bruce Schulz confirms that the explanation of resurrection "being protected from view" is "classic two-stage partly invisible *parousia* doctrine as promoted by Siess and Schimeal, and for a short few years by Russell. Russell discarded this—some would say more sensible doctrine—for a totally invisible *parousia* in 1881."

In a later issue of *The Herald,* Wilson stated that *The Emphatic Diaglott* translation of 2 Peter 3:10, 11, "The elements will be dissolved (*luthesontai*, i.e., loosened or released) with intense heat, and the earth and its works will be burned up" (NASV), proves that the earth will not be burned up in the re-creation process, because it violates the Abrahamic covenant and the promise to David in Psalms 104:5, "He established the earth upon its foundations, so that it will not totter forever and ever" (NASV). There is a difference between the earth being annihilated by fire (completely destroyed) so that it no longer can be seen in space, versus its elements (that which the world is made of) are dissolved, cleansed, and then re-created by Christ.

The majority of One Faith believers in the Northwest Christian Association or conference preferred to accept the Marsh interpretation of Revelation 20. The wicked would be raised and judged at the end of the thousand years. Thomas Wilson wrote an editorial in *The Last Days* in 1919 indicating he still believed in the truth of the Age to Come. He published *The Last Days* for the last 27 years of his life.

D. Other Accomplishments

In 1869, *The Gospel Banner* was merged with *The Herald*. In 1870 the name changed to *The Restitution*. Thomas continued to edit the paper in Chicago through the November 5, 1874, issue from his home after the Chicago fire. By the December 9, 1874, issue, *The Restitution* had been relocated to Plymouth, Indiana, with H.V. Reed as editor. S.A. Chaplin was associate editor entrenched in learning aspects of the publishing business. When Chaplin understood his job well enough, Reed relinquished his responsibilities as editor and returned his family to Chicago.

It is not known how long Thomas remained in Chicago after the fire, but it was long enough to pick up the pieces of the lost hymnal and to compile and publish another hymnbook, *The Christian Psalmodist*. It contained 342 hymns with emphasis on the Father, the return of the Son, and the establishment of a literal kingdom on earth. It had beautiful leather binding with gold edges and sold at $1.25 per copy.

Thomas Wilson also agreed to continue publishing *The Millenarian* with Reed as co-editor. This began in January 1875 and before the month was over Wilson changed the name to *Our Rest,* but it did not continue much longer than the end of the year. Reed and Wilson's *Millenarian* should not be confused with G.M. Myers' *Millenarian* published in the 1890s in Iowa, although at one time it was thought that the one succeeded the other. They were completely different publications.

After Wilson and Lillie were married, he lost interest in publishing in Chicago. Eventually Thomas and Lillie followed Uncle Benjamin to California where they settled in Oakland possibly around 1875.

E. Published *The Last Days*

In 1897, Thomas began to publish a small monthly paper called *The Last Days* from 1712 E. 20th Street, Oakland. This paper was not an official church paper, but it was filled with topics of prophecy, signs of the times and practical Christianity. It was advertised both in *The Restitution* and later, *The Restitution Herald,* and it was devoted to Church of God interpretation of biblical doctrine. It preached the restoration of Israel to its homeland, the imminent Second Coming of Christ, Conditional Immortality and establishment of the Kingdom of God on earth.

The editor said in June 1920 issue, "We are still hoping to be of the company who will be caught up to meet Him without dying." With that issue, Thomas celebrated his 85th birthday, his wife Lillie beside him in her 67th year.

Church of God readers who supported his work included A.C. Boyer, Virginia; J.E. Adamson, California; Leota B. Hanson, St. Louis; J.L. Muncrief, Arkansas; Roxana Wince, Indiana; Blanche Cox, Arkansas; H. Krogh, Nebraska; and many more.

While publishing *The Last Days*, Thomas Wilson also produced a booklet, "Exposition of the Consecutive Prophecy of Our Lord," which he sold for 10 cents or three for 25 cents; "Israel in Two Phases"; "Dead or Alive, Which?"; "Is the Millennium Past or Future?"; "God's Measuring Rods"; "Does the Bible Teach that the Soul will be Tormented Forever?"; "The End Drawing Near"; "The Terrible Day of the Lord"; "The Greatest Dream on Record"; and "The Seventy Weeks of Daniel." At that time, *The Restitution Herald* advertised several other tracts written by Thomas Wilson: "Dead or Resurrection," "Absent from the Body and Present with the Lord," and "Paul's Desire to Depart and be with Christ." Notice that those titles are all key doctrinal issues. Wilson always sought to hold the line on doctrine.

Thomas was a source of comfort to his aging uncle, Benjamin Wilson, and may have looked after Benjamin's business interests regarding the publishing of the *Emphatic Diaglott* until Benjamin's death in 1900. It is very likely that the *Diaglott* provided Benjamin's retirement income. He probably received royalties from the sales, and when he or his agent purchased the copyright and Greek plates from Fowler and Wells, there weren't any additional royalties to be had for the famous translator. An unknown "earnest Bible student" gave the plates to the Watchtower Publications. The Watchtower published it faithfully for more than 100 years.

Bruce Schulz is doing research for a book on C.T. Russell and has discovered that Thomas Wilson dialogued with some of Russell's former associates, Nelson Barbour and John H. Paton, through their publications. This friendly exchange over a number of years offers another reason *why* the *Emphatic Diaglott* made its way to the Watchtower publishing house instead of to the Church of God.

Thomas died at age 91. His wife, Lillie M.C. Wilson, sent his obituary to *The Restitution Herald*. She reported,

---

Turning Point in Church of God History

Summarizing the major components of three men and their ministry, whom do you think had the greatest influence on the Church of God in the 19th and 20th centuries?

Joseph Marsh
- Distanced himself from the Adventist movement.
- Perfected and proclaimed Age to Come and Restoration of Israel.
- Published the Word everywhere east of the Mississippi and Canada.
- Persecuted but endured.
- Planned organizational structure around local churches and state conferences.
- Promoted free investigation into God's Word.
- Traveled as evangelist.

Benjamin Wilson
- Defended the Abrahamic Faith.
- Translated *The Emphatic Diaglott*.
- Published One Faith widely east and west of the Mississippi and into Canada.
- Traveled to make contacts.
- Modeled worship and communion style.

Thomas Wilson
- Turned the brethren away from doctrine of Limited Resurrection.
- United the Eastern and Western Church of God through Marsh's press.
- Started *The Restitution.*
- Defended the Church of God against Indiana Adventists over the issue of Restoration of Israel.
- Took a sectarian stance in 1870 that led to development of doctrinal thought from which a national organization emerged.

What other men or women could be placed on this list?

"He founded *The Restitution* which later became two papers, [*The Restitution Herald*] and he had helped Benjamin Wilson publish *The Emphatic Diaglott*."

Thomas is interred at the Mount View Cemetery in Oakland. Lillie, his son Ira, and Lillie's children, Mrs. N.T. Turner, Elmer and Irlon, survived him.

 See Adamson, J.E.
   Chaplin, Stedman A.
   Hanson, Leota B. (20th)
   Marsh, Joseph
   Muncrief, J.L.
   Reed, H.V.
   Wilson, Benjamin
   Wilson, William Henry

Bibliography: Ancestry.com. U.S. Census. Indiana. Brookville. 1870; Illinois. Cook. Austin. Dist. 212. 1880; "Church of God Roots," citing an article by W.H. Wilson, *Progress Journal*, Oregon, Il., April 1981; Marsh, Joseph. *Age to Come, Advent Harbinger* Office. Rochester, NY, 1851; Schulz, Bruce, e-mail to JStilson, Oct. 13, 2010; Wilson, Thomas "Mortal Emergence," and "Rapture," *The Herald of the Coming Kingdom*, Jan. 1, 1868; Wilson, Thomas. Editorial, *The Last Days* as cited by *The Restitution Herald* April 30, 1919. June 1920. Louw & Nida, *Greek English Lexicon of the New Testament based on Semantic Domains*. Vols.1, 2. United Bible Societies. 1989. Advertisement for *The Last Days*, *The Restitution Herald* Dec. 23, 1914; *The Restitution*. Jan. 13, 1904; Feb. 3, 1904; Obituary, *The Restitution Herald*, F.L. Austin, ed.,, Oregon, Il., June 15, 1926; Whitehead, Leila, The Wilson Family Tree, part of the Evelyn Austin papers in the Archives of Atlanta Bible College; Ad for "The Christian Psalmodist," *The Restitution*, Thos. Wilson, ed., Chicago, Il., Nov. 5, 1874; Notice of *Our Rest, The Restitution*, Plymouth, In., H.V. Reed, ed., Jan. 20, 1875; Wilson, Lillie. Obituary of Thomas Wilson, *The Restitution Herald*, June 15, 1926.

Wilson, William Henry

 b. September 21, 1841
 d. December 9, 1914

William Henry Wilson was born in Halifax, England, to Joseph and Martha Wilson. The family came to America in 1844, settling in Geneva, Illinois, where they joined with other Wilson families to begin a church work. William married Agnes Sutcliffe on June 2, 1864, and they had two children, daughter Jessie and son Walter. Walter died at age four or five.

Elder Edwin Smith immersed a teenage William in the Fox River in 1857 at which time William united with the Geneva church. That was four years after his uncle Benjamin Wilson began *The Gospel Banner*. William learned the printing trade from his uncle from that point on. When he was grown, in addition to working as a printer, he also sold real estate in Geneva with his older brother, Thomas. In this manner he was able to acquire income that enabled him to move to Chicago, write books and travel for evangelism purposes. William practiced the tent-making example set by missionary St. Paul.

Throughout his life, William served the Lord by writing study books and publishing them. He mailed them himself from his home. At the back of one such book, *The Bible Student's Text Book,* he included a note "For anyone wanting evangelistic services, write to me at home."

Other books he authored included *The Destiny of Russia and the Signs of the Times,* a small book of 96 pages; *The Pine Woods Bible Class*, a clothbound, 480 pages; *Cunningly Devised Fables*, a treatise exposing the weak doctrines of Charles Taze Russell; *The Book of Revelation Made Easy to Understand*; *The Prophetic Word Now Being Fulfilled*; *The Restoration of Israel, An Expose of Russellism,* only 32 pages; and *A Bible Study of Hades,* 20 pages. These were small study books usually less than 100 pages, 4" x 6", just the right size to tuck in a pocket or a purse to take to Bible class.

Wilson and his family moved to Hammond, Louisiana, in 1887 and built a house he called "Happy Woods." Here he also established a Bible class he called "Pine Woods Bible Class," and together they built a church. *The Pine Woods Bible Class* was written specifically as a lesson book for this class. But, of course, the book became very popular throughout the Church of God and sales were good. This booklet shows William believed in the non-personality of Satan. (See Lesson Ten.)

In 1886 William preached at Dixon, Illinois, where he was called to baptize Henry Drew, infirmed and bed-ridden for several months. William asked several men to manufacture a tin tank large enough to hold a man. When it was filled with water, seven men lifted Henry in his blanket and gently lowered him into the waters of baptism without giving him pain or injury. In that same visit, more people requested baptism, but they were baptized in the Rock River.

As William aged he continued to serve the Lord through evangelistic work. He felt the written word was important, but he could be more effective in voice and person. He traveled from Gulf to Canada and from the Atlantic to the Pacific. Everywhere he went he proclaimed the Gospel of the Kingdom. To illustrate a typical preaching circuit, a report from an 1871 *Restitution* demonstrated how rigorous his travel schedule was. This particular report mentioned the Chicago Fire. From Chicago he went to Ripley, Illinois, by train where he had a series of meetings. From Ripley he went to Blush Church of God in Missouri, and from there, south into Arkansas. After Arkansas he went further south into the Oklahoma and Texas Indian reservations. After Texas, he returned to Magazine, Arkansas, where he spent some time at the church pastored by Dr. T.J. Daniel. Staying a week or more in each place, such a tour could easily take two months. From Arkansas William returned home.

In 1911, William took another trip, perhaps his last trip in good health. This trip was as ambitious as the rest had been. Beginning from Chicago, he stopped once in Illinois, then Missouri, Kansas, Oklahoma, Texas and back to Louisiana for the winter. By visiting these favorite places every year or twice a year, he built up several congregations and contacted many isolated members.

He and his wife Agnes were married just short of 50 years. Their daughter, Jessie, remained active in the Lord's work by continuing to oversee the publication business her father had begun and distributing the study books he wrote before his death.

In 1913, William's cousin Dr. Leila Whitehead reported in *The Restitution* that he was gravely ill from appendicitis and peritonitis. He had an operation but the infection was massive. He died at age 72 from that short illness. People everywhere mourned the death of their friend, a giant in the Lord's work.

H.V. Reed preached the funeral service in Chicago where friends and family gathered to respect the old soldier of the cross. They heard the story of the glorious resurrection which brought them great comfort. W.H. Wilson arranged his own funeral service and asked for the hymn, "It is Well With my Soul." Horatio G. Spafford wrote this hymn following the sinking of the Ville du Havre in 1873. Mr. Spafford wrote the hymn to assuage his grief because he lost his four daughters in that tragic sinking. W.H. Wilson said, "It is well with my soul because my life is hid with God in Christ. Tell the church my trust and faith were true. Hold to the faith of the Savior's coming for it is near." Leila Whitehead, wrote the Wilson obituary for *The Restitution*.

Recently one of W.H. Wilson's books was copied and mailed to an author in Denmark, Poul Bregninge, who authored a book on Charles T. Russell. Bregninge's premise was that Russell made a connection with the Age-to-Come movement and was influenced by it. Bregninge wanted evidence that the two organizations were aware of each other during the late 19th century and that Russell had borrowed ideas from the Age to Come. Because of receiving Wilson's *Cunningly Devised Fables*, Mr. Bregninge completed his research before his publication deadline. The book is being published in America under the title *Judgment Day Must Wait* but had not been released at the time of this writing.

See Myers, G.M.
    Reed, H.V.
    Whitehead, Leila, M.D. (20th)
    Wilson, Benjamin
    Wilson, Thomas

Bibliography: Ancestry.com U.S. Census. Illinois. Chicago Ward 35. Cook. Dist. 1132. 1900. Graham, David. "Church of God Connexion," *Wisdom and Power*. Wyoming, Mi., Oct. 1992; Bregninge, Poul *Domedag das Vente (Judgment Day Must Wait)*, 2006; Report at Dixon, *The Restitution*, Illinois, July 21, 1886; Various articles or reports: Jan. 13, 1904; Jan. 1, 1911; Oct. 21, 1913; Dec. 21, 1913; Wilson, W. H. "A short history of the Church of God," *The Restitution*, republished in the *Progress Journal*, Oregon, Il., April 1981, as "Church of God Roots," and electronically in *The Restitution Herald*, Jan. 29, 2011; Wilson, W.H. "Pine Woods Bible Class" *The Restitution*. A.R. Underwood, ed., Plymouth, In., March 2, 1904; Wilson, W.H. "Discussion of Myer's *Independent* article," *The Restitution*, A.R. Underwood, ed., Plymouth, In., March 28, 1904.

Wince, John L.
b. December 24, 1832
d. October 4, 1910

John Wince was born in Culpepper County, Virginia. The family moved west and settled in Illinois. The Baptists baptized him near Zanesville, Illinois, in 1851. In 1853, he moved to Whitley County, Indiana, where he taught school. In Whitley he first heard the doctrine of conditional immortality. He pondered it that night. "Could it be true the soul was not immortal? If the Bible did not speak of it in plain words, it may not be there in any words at all," he thought. He began to study his Bible.

He had visited the area of Claysville, Indiana, with an aunt where he met evangelists who preached this new doctrine. As their visit was very short, they promised to return in order to meet with John Wince again. According to his testimony in *The Restitution* in 1909, these evangelists were Nathan Hornaday, Ephraim Miller, S.A. Chaplin, E.C. Andrews, J.M. Stephenson, Jacob Shaffer, J.S. Hatch, H.V. Reed and J.F. Wagoner. They must have all been in the vicinity at the same time for a quarterly conference at the local Age to Come/One Faith church.

The seed planted in John's mind began to take root. He was especially grateful to Samuel Andrews who took Wince under his wing and mentored him in the unique Bible doctrines he was hungry to learn. With Andrews as mentor, John learned for the first time about the Six Sermons preached by George Storrs that had become so popular among Adventist churchmen. These sermons set forth the eternal principles of conditional immortality. After learning these startling biblical truths, John Wince returned to his Baptist church in Ohio, where he had been living. Talking about this with those members caused quite a stir. Pastor Madden, an elderly gentleman, talked with John and advised him to "let the matter drop."

Eight months later, Wince returned to Indiana where he was re-baptized late in the fall of 1854. In early 1855 he united with the Church of God at Claysville. All the preachers mentioned above preached there often over the years, and Wince preached there for about 40 years.

The first time he stood to speak, John had in mind to give a 30-minute discourse, but exhausted everything he wanted to say in 15 minutes. Ralph Carter, a local member, stood up and led a discussion of the topic for the next 45 minutes. Carter was a skilled speaker who had learned to preach as he rode a circuit through Ohio, Indiana, Illinois, Wisconsin and Iowa. John preached again and preached often, but he felt inferior and greatly embarrassed, "like he would sink through the floor," being painfully conscious of himself. He said constant preaching wore off the embarrassment almost entirely.

Over the years he almost never failed to attend any of the conferences held by the Church of God throughout the state of Indiana. Only illness deterred him from making these trips which on one occasion was due to small pox. John's travels took him to Argos, Plymouth, Salem, Gospel Grove, Eagle Creek and Jeffersonville. He preached wherever he went.

John married Sarah (Sally) Roxanna Chaplin, daughter of Stedman A. Chaplin, on March 13, 1867. Roxanna Wince (also known at Auntie Wince) was as strong a leader in the Church of God as her husband. Throughout John's life, his faithful wife accompanied him and assisted him in the ministry.

At Jeffersonville, he was privileged to witness the debate between Dr. Nathaniel Field and Thomas P. Connelly on the nature of man. This debate was recorded in shorthand and published later in a 308-page book. This book is available for scholarly examination in the Archives of the Atlanta Bible College in McDonough, Georgia.

At Jeffersonville, he also met the famous Joseph Marsh. John's impression was not overly complimentary. He said:

> Marsh, in the estimation of the writer was an indifferent speaker; very slow, lacking in enthusiasm, but clean and logical.

It is thought he met Marsh in 1863 when Marsh was already suffering his fatal ailment, typhoid fever, merely one month before Marsh's death. Marsh left Jeffersonville for his home in Canada but made it only to his daughter's home in Tecumseh, Michigan, where he died.

John was a preacher in the Church of God for nearly as long as he could talk. Being a farmer, he preached at places within his reach. There is no evidence that he traveled outside Indiana or Ohio as an evangelist, but he cut a wide swath within his own territory. He believed all the precious truths that have inspired pioneer preachers and members for the past century.

John Wince may have been a hesitant speaker, but he was a great writer. In 1870, he sent a letter to the editor of *The Herald of the Coming Kingdom and Christian Instructor* in Chicago. He said that people should not put so much emphasis on material matters because doing that takes away from one's spiritual work. To show that he stood behind what he believed, he sent $10 to cover a $2 subscription for the paper. He said the rest was a donation for operating expenses. He suggested that 100 people send $10 each and offered a list of names. Thomas Wilson reported later that other than one other man and Wince, 98 people had not responded. The paper was experiencing financial strain and that may be the reason people called for it to merge with *The Gospel Banner*. The people could not afford to support multiple papers.

Wince continued to write on issues of doctrine throughout his career. When *The Herald* ceased and *The Restitution* began, Wince regularly supplied thoughtful and doctrinal copy. He wrote the profound in a simple style that any reader could understand, one of the benefits of having been a teacher. He was a good communicator. He wrote so many articles, after his death, they were published in *The Restitution* for several months.

The Chicago church sponsored a conference of national scope in 1870. It is thought the Northwest Christian Association, formed in 1868, sponsored this meeting. While the minutes make no mention of any move toward general conference organization, the meeting hosted "representatives," a term used instead of delegates, from 33 churches in six states. Sixteen of those churches were from Illinois, including Oregon, the earliest mention seen to date of activity at Oregon; three from Ohio; six from Indiana; three from Michigan; two from Wisconsin; and one from Massachusetts. In addition to members present, several ministers preached, including John Wince. Other preachers were H.V. Reed, J.M. Stephenson, Benjamin Wilson, James Wilson, David T. Halstead, Richard Appleyard, J.F. Wagoner, L.H. Chase, A.J. Eychaner and Frank Berrick, about whom nothing is known. Andy Eychaner of Paynes Point, Illinois, met his future wife, Anna Beck of Buchanan, Michigan, at this conference.

Elder Wince sat on the committee that helped to reorganize the Indiana State Conference in 1886. Wince submitted this statement of faith, called a Declaration of Principles:

> We, the members of the several churches represented by delegation feeling deeply the necessity of closer cooperation in the proclamation of the Truth, and the promotion of the cause of Christ among us, as preliminary to this end, do set forth the following declaration of principles as the foundation of our faith.
>
> We accept the Bible as the only rule of faith and practice.
>
> We believe in the final "restitution of all things which God hath spoken by all his holy prophets since the world began."
>
> As a means to this end, the establishment of the Kingdom of God on the earth, with the Christ as the King of Kings,

- and the immortal saints as joint-heirs with him in the government of the nations; the restoration of Israel; the literal resurrection of the dead, the immortalization of the righteous, and the final destruction of the wicked, eternal life only through Christ.
- A hearty belief in the Gospel, repentance, and immersion is prerequisite to the forgiveness of sins, and a holy life as essential for final salvation.
- We believe that Jesus Christ is the Son of God.
- And further to secure this end, we reorganize this state conference.

While this declaration was not intended as a statement of faith, it sounds like one. Therefore, it must be noted that there is no statement here about the Unity of God or the nature of the Holy Spirit. This seems to be further evidence that, among the forefathers of the Church of God, these two doctrines were understood by membership consensus, and therefore, were not emphasized in the early days. It would have been ill advised to make oneness of God a test of fellowship when so many Adventist groups worshipped together in the same building.

In fact, Wiley Jones, a well-respected theologian in the Church of God in the 19th century, wrote to *The Herald of the Coming Kingdom* in 1870, the last issue before it became *The Restitution*, and vehemently protested a statement in *The Marturion*, a Christadelphian paper, that slighted Christ by calling him a mere man. Jones wrote:

> **BROTHER WILSON**:—Allow me through the **HERALD**, to earnestly protest against the unscriptural ideas lately set forth in the "Marturion," by a trans-Atlantic writer on the nature of Christ. I think that such language as that writer applies to our Lord is little, if anything, less than the old exploded Socinianism. Did not Thomas call Him "my **LORD** and my **GOD**?" And are not all men commanded to "*honor* the Son, even as they honor the Father?" John xx: 28; v.23.
>
> We may well study to praise and honor the Son when we remember that "in Him dwelleth all the fullness of the Godhead bodily," and that "He thought it not robbery to be equal with God;" as Paul himself has taught.—Col. ii:9; Phil. ii:6. Let us avoid even the remotest approximation to the sentiments of ancient errorists. Read carefully John v:18; Psa. 1:21-23. The Lord Jesus is repeatedly called "**GOD**," in scripture. Isa. ix:6; Matt. i:23; Heb. i:8, *et al*. I admit that in one place He is also called "The *man* Christ Jesus." 1 Tim. ii:5. But this one scripture does not neutralize all others giving Him *higher* attributes. We must get the concentrated and harmonious light of *all* scripture on any subject before we can understand it. Paul does not let this isolated sentence lead his beloved Timothy astray, for although he could not say everything in one breath, yet in the *same* epistle he uses another expression which embodies the two natures, as it were, and the two trains of thought in one, "*God* was "manifest in the *flesh.*" 1 Tim. iii: 16 [bold type and italics by Jones].

Even though the majority of One Faith people stood for biblical unitarianism, clearly a school of thought existed within the membership and leadership of the developing Church of God that Christ had a divine nature, and as such deserved more attention and devotion than some were willing to give Him. This dichotomy of thought lingered into the 20th century.

In 1909 John commented briefly about all those men who taught him doctrinal and preaching principles in his youth, and of the faithful men of the Old Testament who looked forward to Christ:

> About all those who attended these larger gatherings of early days are gone to the house appointed for all the living. Unconsciously they sleep awaiting the trumpet call that will awake Job and all the long line of ancient worthies who saw the fulfillment of the promises from afar.

Wince's tract "Salvation and Resurrection" was published for *The Restitution* by the National Berean Society in 1916. Evelyn Harsh received orders for it in Chicago, and she and Leila Whitehead packaged and mailed them.

Before his death at his home in Pierceton, Indiana, John completed a manuscript published as a series in *The Restitution* in 1920, several years after his death. John's widow gave his manuscript to Robert Huggins who planned to publish it as a book. It is unknown if this was ever accomplished. When John Wince died, a memorial fund was established at the newly organized Church of God General Conference to outfit a room or two at the Golden Rule Home. Many people helped purchase furniture in his honor for the new home for the elderly.

See Carter, Ralph
    Chaplin, Stedman A.
    Chase, Levi H.
    Field, Nathaniel
    Hatch, J.S.
    Huggins, Robert (20th)
    Jones, Wiley
    Marsh, Joseph
    Miller, Ephraim
    Reed, H.V.
    Shafer, Jacob
    Stephenson, J.M.
    Storrs, George
    Wagoner, J.F.
    Wilson, Benjamin
    Wilson, Thomas
    Wince, Sarah Roxanna (Auntie)

Bibliography: Ancestry.com U.S. Census. Marshall Co., Pierceton, Indiana, 1860 and 1870; Eychaner, A.J. "Conference Report," *The Herald of the Coming Kingdom and Christian Instructor*, Sept. 15, 1870; Ferrell, Terry, *A Brief History of the Church of God in America*. National Berean Youth Conf. Camp Reynoldswood, Dixon, Il., Aug. 21-27, 1960; Jones, Wiley, "Protest," *The Herald of the Coming Kingdom*, T. Wilson, ed. Chicago, Il., Dec. 15, 1870; Randall, Clyde, *Historical Waymarks of the Church of God*. Church of God General Conference, Oregon, Il., 1976, p.77; *The Restitution* January 1, 1909; January 27, 1909; October 1910; Sept. 22, 1920; *The Restitution Herald* June 21, 1916; June 1924; Wince, John, "An Exhortation," *The Herald of the Coming Kingdom and Christian Instructor*, T. Wilson, ed., Chicago. Il., Jan.1, 1870.

Wince, Sarah Roxanna (Auntie)
b. February 10, 1836
d. March 27, 1929

Auntie Wince, as she was fondly known by hundreds of Church of God children, lived in Pierceton, Indiana; she was the wife of Elder John Wince. Auntie Wince was active in the Indiana Church of God Conference most of her life. She was noted throughout the Church of God as a teacher and writer of children's material. Auntie Wince wrote a weekly Bible story column and lessons for children in *The Restitution,* and later *The Restitution Herald.* Sometimes she also wrote short pieces of admonition or encouragement for the adults. In 1924, now elderly, she held Sunday School at her home for children of the neighborhood. Sadly, her house burned to the ground in a fire. After she was settled in her new home, she had difficulty coaxing kids to the new place, but she did not give up.

In 1907 she penned a hymn set to the tune written by Dr. N. Jeff Smith. The name of the hymn was "Coming Reign of Messiah." It debuted at the Indiana State Conference at Plymouth, Indiana, and was published later in *The Restitution.* She also wrote the lyrics to the hymn, "How Long, O Lord" sung to the tune "Stand Up, Stand Up for Jesus" by G.J. Webb.

Auntie Wince carried on a letter-writing ministry to isolated members of the Church of God well into her old age. When she was in her mid-80s friends returned the favor, showering her with cards and letters on her birthday. She reported later to *The Restitution* that as she was reading them it was "like being in prayer meeting." She was beloved by members throughout the Church of God regardless of what they believed concerning the resurrection or other controversial subjects. She was able to transcend any controversy and meet the needs of her friends at the heart's level.

She reported in *The Restitution* that her eyesight and strength were failing. Editor Robert Huggins wrote:

> The thought that age will incapacitate Sr. Wince…is a nightmare to us. Her services to the brotherhood exceed estimation. She has always stood at our right hand in defense of the gospel. God forbid that we should lose her cooperation in the gospel of the Kingdom of God before that kingdom comes.

While she was able, she continued to write. Auntie Wince wrote a series of 55 columns for *The Restitution* under the title "The Story of a Happy Christian Life." The series was in the form of letters exchanged between Roxanna, her aunt and a cousin. They encouraged each other, shared stories, sorrows and joys. It was interesting reading and slightly more personal writing than usually found in her articles about topics of Bible and theology. The readers loved it.

Roxanna was the daughter of Stedman A. Chaplin, a noted Baptist preacher who moved to Indiana during the 1840s and learned of the Adventist movement then. He gravitated toward the teachings of Joseph Marsh who promoted a unique point of view of prophecy he called Age to Come. Roxanna was raised in a climate of prophetic importance, and to her the teaching of the Kingdom of God on earth was as important as eating.

She and her sister Henrietta learned of these important truths and passed them on to their children and the children of others in the church and in the community.

Auntie Wince continued in a frail state until her death in 1929. Her obituary listed her as Reverend Mrs. John L. Wince.

See Chaplin, Stedman A.
See Also Huggins, Robert (20th)
Weethee, J.P.
Wince, John L.

Bibliography: Rootsweb.com List of Indiana Obituaries. Kosciusco County; *The Restitution* Jan., 18, 1911; Jan. 27, 1920 and June 18, 1920; This picture was published in the 1924 *The Restitution Herald.* Wince, S. Roxanna, "How Long, O Lord," *Songs of Truth*, National Bible Institute, Oregon, Illinois, 1948.

Woodruff, John O.
b. 1819?
d. 1909

John O. Woodruff was a member and leader of a small congregation at Elizabeth, New Jersey. Samuel Wilson, Benjamin's nephew, also worshipped with this congregation.

John Woodruff's wife, Carrie, authored "A Letter to a Friend on the Covenants of Promises." *The Restitution Herald* offered this piece as a tract for several years due to its popularity and comprehensive message written in simple terms. John also authored *The True Way of Life,* a 400-page book that represented the best writing of the Christadelphians and the Church of God. Essays by Benjamin Wilson are included on the subjects of resurrection in which he states only the righteous will be raised, "The Name of Jesus" in which he indicates Christ was the adopted Son of God (2 Samuel 7:14 and Psalms 89:26, 27), and "Life, what is it?" This particular book was published sometime after Benjamin Wilson's death for Woodruff states at the beginning of one article, "by the late Benjamin Wilson." That would place the date of publication sometime after 1900.

Woodruff also authored *Thy Kingdom Come*, another book of essays. The subjects are Bible-centered but free ranging in topic. It is no wonder Benjamin Wilson admired Woodruff. He was prolific in publishing the Word.

In 1868, Benjamin Wilson and his wife visited the Woodruffs in their home prior to the Wilsons' journey to England. One year later John Woodruff wrote a piece for *The Gospel Banner* on the importance of spreading the truth. He was a firm believer in the promises made to believers of eternal life in the Kingdom. He encouraged readers of *The Gospel Banner* not to grow weary, even if their congregations were small. He admonished readers to continue to hope and spread the One Faith.

After the death of the Woodruffs and Wilsons, the work at Elizabeth declined. It was revived again a few years later, with hopes that it could be sustained.

See Wilson, Benjamin
See Also Brown, William
Wilson, Samuel

Bibliography: Ancestry.com. U.S. Census. New Jersey. Union. Elizabeth. 1870; Woodruff, John, "Interesting Letter," *Gospel Banner and Millennial Advocate,* Sept. 1, 1869; Mrs. J.O. Woodruff, "Letter to a Friend on the Covenants of Promise," advertised in *The Restitution Herald,* April 2, 1919; Woodruff, J.O., *The True Way of Life*, a book of essays compiled by the author at Elizabeth, NJ; Woodruff, J.O., *Thy Kingdom Come*, also *Book of Essays,* Elizabeth, NJ., 1904; John O. Woodruff presented to Roxanna Wince on the anniversary of John Wince's death, a copy of Wiley Jones' book, *Evangelism Concerning the Reign of Christ Over Israel and the Nations,* Chicago. The Restitution Office. 1872; *The Restitution Herald*, Identification of Carrie as author of "Letter to a Friend on the Covenants of Promise," Feb. 23, 1926.

Woodward, Benjamin W.
b. February 19, 1831
d. October 18, 1919

Benjamin W. Woodward was born in Chautauqua, New York; in 1846 at age 14 he moved to Gaines Township near Dutton, Michigan. He lived within a mile of that pioneer homestead most of his life and owned the farm he bought at age 18. It was said he watched Grand Rapids grow from a small fishing village and trading post to a bustling commercial center. Benjamin married Caroline Lavendar Carey in 1853. He continued to provide for his family through farming. Caroline's mother, Cora, lived with them, and they had one son, Kansas. Caroline died July 6, 1881, at Hammond, Michigan.

Benjamin came from a Methodist background. In fact, his grandfather had been a Methodist evangelist. When he was 16, Benjamin was appointed teacher for a Methodist Bible class. About that time, Woodward first heard of the Second Coming at a Seventh-day Adventist meeting. Elder J.B. Frisbie, a Sabbath Adventist, preached a sermon on the mortality of man and the need of the resurrection from the dead. Woodward was very interested in Frisbie's comments, but he couldn't completely accept them. Even so, this sermon spoiled his Methodist views. He began to study the Scriptures and soon embraced the beautiful truth of the coming King to establish a righteous government.

At that time Church of God evangelists Joel A. Simonds and Ed Hoyt preached throughout Wisconsin and Michigan, and they began teaching the young Woodward. In 1856, Woodward was a farmer, member of the Grange and the Masons, and a participant in politics. Evangelist Simonds said to him, "Benjamin, you are successful making Grangers and good Templars and Greenbackers, is it not more important to make Christians?" So Benjamin paid up all his dues on the worldly organizations, and when he was called on to preach, he accepted. From this beginning, Benjamin soon fell deeply in love with the Gospel and began preaching it in distant states.

Benjamin was appointed state evangelist of Michigan at the annual conference in 1880. He succeeded Ephraim Miller in this position and served faithfully until old-age infirmities compelled him to retire from active service. In 1880 most people who were interested in his message were acquainted only with the *World's Crisis* paper published by the Advent Christians. When Benjamin began preaching in Hesperia and Millbrook near Blanchard, his work interested the *Crisis* readers. He introduced them to *The Restitution*. From this they received light on the prophecies they had not learned before.

After Caroline's death, Benjamin married Mary Austin, a widow, in 1883. A small grandson lived with them. Mary traveled with Benjamin for ministry and also developed her own preaching style.

The first time they visited the Indiana Conference in 1883, he was the guest of Stedman A. Chaplin. The conference was held at the Antioch church; Woodward was awed by its size. He didn't know where they would find the people to fill it, but when they all came, they filled the churchyard with rigs and the building with people. He described the building as 40' x 60' filled with "the little flock," probably around 300 people whose faces shone

Evangelism Committee of the 1888 General Conference, Woodward (left) with Samuel Wilson and LE Conner.

with joy at the message they heard.

At one point in reflecting on his preaching career, Benjamin said he had traveled thousands of miles, preached 250 sermons every year and baptized 400-500 people. He ministered to Native Americans who lived in Michigan and who were already loyal Methodists. Out of respect to Benjamin, they attended his preaching services and testified in eloquent fashion with tears in their eyes. He lived among them for 63 years. It was through this association that the Church of God began its work in Baraga and L'Anse. They loved him so much they made him president of their association.

Elder Woodward spent most of his time in nearby Millbrook. Through the work of the Woodwards there were at one time 125 names on the church roll. He was always happy to tell people, "If you want a good spiritual meeting where 75 people will testify or pray in less than an hour, go to Millbrook."

B.W. Woodward made no pretension to eloquence in his public work, but when he announced his subject, listeners knew from start to finish what he was aiming at, and when he said, "Amen," he had made his subject so plain that even the "children could understand it." He preached only one subject at a time.

Woodward celebrated his 80th birthday at a surprise party which began in the afternoon and continued at home with 66 people coming to dinner. Guests came from several states to see him, as he had been the one who baptized them. They presented him with several gifts and wonderful memories of ministry.

As a leader, he weighed in on the 1910 controversy between the Ministerial Association and the irate subscribers to *The Restitution*. He said:

> As some are asking how I stand in regard to the Ministerial Association and their course toward the *Restitution*? Let me say, I have taken our paper for about fifty-five years, since the days of Joseph Marsh, though under different names, and have never failed to pay my subscription promptly, a little before the time expired.
>
> I have had a long and large experience as an evangelist and pastor, and in these thirty-five years more have visited many homes in many states, and have found that many of these homes from one ocean to the other have been helped and made happy by the weekly visits of the dear, old *Restitution*. From several I have asked the question, How did you first learn the truth? The answer was, I picked up a stray *Restitution* years ago, became interested in the doctrines taught, continued to study, and was finally baptized into the Christ. The *Restitution* has proven to be a good missionary and in the day of reckoning many will bless the day they just happened to see the *Restitution*.
>
> This paper has always stood for something, instead of everything. It is clean-cut and has always stood by its principles, never faltered though at times it has seen violent opposition. It has contended earnestly for the faith once delivered to the saints. We have taken several papers that claim to be of "the faith" which we dare not hand to strangers or new converts for we did not want them to think we believed such monstrosities as were printed there.

Woodward mentored F.V. Blakely who eventually conducted Woodward's funeral and wrote his obituary.

See Hoyt, Ed.
    Blakley, F.V.
    Marsh, Joseph
    Simonds, Joel
    Vadnais, Mary (20th)
    Woodward, Mary

Bibliography: Michigan State Conference Record 1859-1886; Obituary, *The Restitution Herald,* Nov. 4, 1919; Various reports, *The Restitution Herald,* Jan. 25, 1911; Feb., 22, 1911; Nov. 18, 1914; June 14, 1916; Wince, Roxanna. "Life of a Happy Christian." #56. *The Restitution,* June 24, 1908; *The Restitution,* June 27, 1883; Williams, Byron, *Abstracts of Obituaries and Verbatim Marriage Announcements printed in The Restitution 1874-1900.* self-published. 1993, p. 18.

Benjamin and Mary camping at the 1908 Michigan Conference.

Old Antioch, Argos, Indiana

Woodward, Mary Alice Grant Austin
b. July 5, 1842
d. August 1, 1935

Mary was the daughter of John Grant, who may have been related to President Ulysses S. Grant. Her family lived in Michigan and Indiana. The details of the lineage are not known. Mary Alice married her first husband, William Austin, in 1869. They had two sons, Frederick Lloyd (F.L.) and LeRoy.

Mary and second husband, Benjamin Woodward

Mary's father, John Grant

Mary was active in Michigan State Conference work, but her name does not appear in the minutes until after Ephraim Miller' death; he had been their dedicated secretary. Her name first appears in the minutes when she was drafted to take them in the absence of Ephraim Miller's son, Herbert Miller, also a faithful stenographer. It is presumed that women attended the conferences of most states, but they tended to teaching the children and preparing the meals for conference guests. It is interesting to note that Mary became a leading worker in the Michigan conference. An interesting passage in the first minutes recorded by Mary of the Quarterly Conference at Hesperia, Michigan, January 12-14, 1883, reads:

> On Sunday when the stage arrived from White Cloud, we were anxiously waiting and wondering who were among the occupants that had come up to help push the car of truth along. As the driver, Mr. J Carlisle (who by the way, is one of those thoughtful large-hearted men) halted with the ominous, "Whoa!" the genial faces of Elders Hoyt and Kendall, Brother and Sister Gatt of Allegan County and Brother Lemon of Vicksburg appeared at the door. We all rejoiced greatly at their coming and as the evening drew near those who were interested in the meeting went up to the hall and Dr. Kendall spoke to a full house from Psa. 107-108.

After Mr. Austin died, Mary married Elder B.W. Woodward of Dutton, Michigan, sometime during 1883. Mary and her new husband were middle-aged and energetic in serving the Lord throughout the Midwest. They traveled from church to church through Michigan and Indiana, going where they were called. They attended the Indiana Conference for the first time the autumn of 1885. Afterward, they remained in Indiana for several weeks to hold meetings.

She learned her lessons from Benjamin and filled the pulpit at Watson in his absence. After a few years, the couple was engaged as joint-state evangelist, a position they shared for 30 years. Mary became the pastor at Coat's Grove, Michigan, in 1914.

Later in life, Mary wrote she and B.W. Woodward began working in ministry around 1897, first in Michigan, and later around and throughout Northern Indiana and Illinois. After Benjamin's death, she said, "While he sleeps from a long life of gospel work, I will try to continue his work and mine, as long as God gives me strength."

Mary was described by her friend Elizabeth Reed, a noted author in her own right, as having "a sweet spirit of consecration, wearing that silvery diadem and blue eyes radiant with love and hope." Reed counted Mary among "The King's Daughters," saying Mary's face was touched with "character lines graven by sorrow."

After Benjamin's death, Mary continued in ministry. Her mother-in-law from her first marriage resided with her, offering company and comfort. People called on Mary to aid with problems and to understand the Gospel. She was a good preacher and good with people. In helping them she found comfort for her grief. She sent a letter of appreciation to *The Restitution Herald*.

In 1921 she wrote *The Restitution Herald* calling the brethren to help organize "a headquarters or association where young people can study to become (strong) in knowledge of the Word of God." Her son, F.L. Austin, became the executive secretary of the Church of God General Conference in 1921. Her son, Leroy, lived and worked in the North Salem Church of God at Plymouth, Indiana.

After the General Conference organized, she applied to be recognized as a minister. In this manner, evangelists were able to receive rail passes for ministry purposes. Soon thereafter, she traveled to California to visit Lydia Railsback. Her reports through *The Restitution Herald* are filled with visits to isolated members up and down the west coast, often to the point of great fatigue for the elderly woman. In this manner she was helpful in the establishment of the church work at Los Angeles under the direction of Emma Railsback.

Inscription from a Friend

Presented to Rev. Mary A. Woodward in Remembrance of her many Christian Courtesies, shown on different occasions, to her friends."

Signed: Marie Wilson Beesley

Ref.: Title page of *The Call of the Carpenter* by Bouck

Mary Woodward settled in Oregon, Illinois, at the Golden Rule Home in her senior years sometime around 1929 or 1930. Her son was close by at the General Conference office but maintained a home in Chicago. She divided her time between Oregon and Chicago and probably accompanied him by train to and from the city. Here the record is unclear, for another source indicates she was the pastor at Dutton, Michigan, from 1930 until her death in 1935. She died in Chicago.

While it seems the old preachers of the Church of God are gone, it may be seen that their ministry lives on through the children and great-grandchildren of granddaughter Ruby (John) Railton, Fonthill, Ontario. Ruby's children included Mary Railton (Milne) and Austin (Cecil) Railton. Austin and Cecil's children included John (Alice Dochstader) Railton, and Joyce Railton (Steve Bolhous), and their children. All of these family members have been pastors or pastor's wives down to the seventh generation.

See Austin, F.L. (20th)
Railsback, Lydia
Woodward, Benjamin

Bibliography: Ancestry.com. Cook County Illinois Death Index 1908-1988. Record for Mary Alice Woodward; Austin, Mary, "Minutes of meeting at Hesperia," *The Restitution*, Feb. 7, 1883; Report of Indiana Conference, *The Restitution*, Oct. 21, 1885; *The Restitution Herald*, Nov. 18, 1914; June 14, 1916; Oct. 25, 1921; Dec. 16, 1921; Sept. 26, 1922; Oct. 28, 1930; Interview with Steve Bolhous at Winnebago New Life Bible Church, May, 2005 and 2006; Wince, Roxanna, "Life of a Happy Christian," #56 *The Restitution*, June 24, 1908.

Work, George F.
b. June 1856
d. 1920?

George Work was the son of Jacob Work. George was a farmer by trade and a member of the Philadelphia Church of God. He was married with a family; his elderly father resided with them. George was elected to the Board of Directors of the newly reorganized Church of God General Conference when it convened in Philadelphia November 16-26, 1888.

Clyde Randall described the organizational effort in *Historical Waymarks of the Church of God:*
> The place of meeting was at the Philadelphia church, corner of 12th and Dickinson. The first session met at 3 p.m. After getting acquainted and enjoying fellowship, the meeting was called to order by R.S. Dwiggins, temporary chairman, and A.J. Eychaner, temporary secretary. The chairman appointed various committees.
> The dispatch with which the conference was organized indicates the professional type of leadership and the serious purpose for which the delegates had assembled.... There were thirty-three churches and thirteen conferences and states represented by twenty-five delegates.

> A permanent organization was brought into being at the morning session, November 17. Officers elected [were] R.S. Dwiggins, Indiana, President; P.B. Bowman, Pennsylvania, Vice President; A.J. Eychaner, Iowa, Secretary; James W. Wilson, Illinois, Corresponding Secretary, and George F. Work, Pennsylvania, Treasurer.

Of 25 delegates, 19 were appointed to committees. Some of the committee members included L.E. Conner, Illinois; S.A. Chaplin, J.F. Wagoner and J.S. Hatch, Indiana; L.C. Chase and A.C. West, Michigan: N.J. Morgan, Virginia; Albert O. Young, Maryland; and Almus Adams, Nebraska. Benjamin Wilson, Eychaner and Adams represented the work west of the Mississippi. Adams, Conner and Young were the youngest delegates.

Randall spoke also of the non-delegates who attended, including Peter Jeffrey, Illinois; J.W. Niles, C.C. Ramsay and John Ongley, Pennsylvania; Benjamin Woodward, Michigan (Mary was a delegate); D.C. Robison and Benjamin Howell, Ohio; George Kramer, Brooklyn; Samuel Wilson, New Jersey; Peter Bouk, Canada; and William Thompson, Indiana.

The men and women who organized the Philadelphia conference were hopeful that a:
> Common Covenant could be accepted by the delegates as a means for churches to remain independent...[but] united in loving bonds pledged to support and sustain each other.

This quote is taken from an invitation issued by Work to A.J. Eychaner and several others. His plea was in effect, "if you can't support a common covenant [statement of faith] then please come up with another idea to accomplish unity."

The reason for interest in formulating a statement of faith was to offset errors which were creeping in. In August 1888, George Work wrote to *The Restitution*, "In many cases churches built up on the doctrines first taught them, have had fatal discords introduced among them by later and unauthorized preachers teaching contrary doctrines."

The Philadelphia Church of God agreed to host the conference and cover the cost of it. They offered sustenance and housing for delegates and agreed to pay delegates west of Philadelphia $10 for travel and those east of Philadelphia $20 for the same. To demonstrate solidarity, several eastern churches joined Philadelphia in the invitation to conference. These churches included Brooklyn, Winchester (Virginia) and Baltimore. C.C. Ramsay, pastor at Philadelphia, and George R. Kramer, pastor at Brooklyn, put their names and reputation behind the effort.

Another conference meeting was held in Chicago in 1889, but no additional meetings were called either by the Board of Directors or the delegates. This General Conference remained in existence on paper until 1892. At that time, the Board felt it necessary to dissolve the

> **Six Issues Discussed by the Delegates of the 1888 Philadelphia National Conference**
>
> 1. Statement of Faith (Common Covenant)
> 2. How to collect money to finance the work of evangelists
> 3. How to help build up weak and needy churches
> 4. How to empower evangelists to represent the Church
> 5. How to govern the new organization and make rules for the future and yearly conference
> 6. Decide when and where it will be and who would be delegates.

organization because there was no money, no staff, no program, no activities and no interest. While it might be thought that members were lazy or lethargic, it should be remembered that America suffered a severe depression that lasted nearly the remainder of that decade with more than 10% unemployment until the Spanish American War in 1898.

Historically, the Church of God had many opponents to organizing a national headquarters. Many leaders opposed having a formal statement of faith for they thought it would lead to sectarianism. Others opposed a national organization as it would make the state conferences weak. Yet there were others who felt that a national office with a board of directors would bring the many local churches into a coalition to cooperate for the advancement of evangelism, Christian education, worship style, fellowship and to support a publishing house.

The ledger book of minutes from the board of directors of this defunct General Conference is part of the Archives of Atlanta Bible College in Georgia.

Little more is known of George Work or his ministry in Philadelphia, but it fell to him, as treasurer of the failed conference, to inform the Church of God members that the Board was ending it. George continued to serve within the Church of God as shown by a letter or an article he sent to R.G. Huggins for *The Restitution*, stating that George remained faithful to the Gospel of the Kingdom well into his old age.

See Bouk, Peter

See Also Appendix 3–Catalyst for Change: Matyrdom
Dwiggins, R.S.
Kramer, George R.
Niles, J.W.
Ongley, John
Ramsay, C.C.
Robison, D.C.
Thompson, William
Woodward, Benjamin
Woodward, Mary

Bibliography: Ancestry.com. U.S. Census. Pennsylvania. Fayette. Franklin. Dist. 24. 1900; Work, George F., "Notice of Conference," *The Restitution.* S.A. Chaplin, ed., Plymouth, In., August 15, 1888, Oct. 17, 1888, Nov. 2, 1915; *Ledger of Minutes*, Church of God General Conference, Board of Directors, 1888-1892, Atlanta Bible College Archives, McDonough, Ga.; Whitten, David., O., "The Depression of 1893," http://eh.net/encyclopedia/article/whitten.panic.1893 retrieved Feb. 10, 2011.

Young, George W.
b. 1843
d. October, 1919

George Young was a good Bible student who hailed from Brooklyn, New York. He was an engineer, and lived at home with his parents, Michael and Johanna Young. George reported Alexander Donaldson's baptism to *The Restitution*. The pastor at Brooklyn at that time was John Donaldson, about whom nothing is known. George was a delegate to the 1888 Philadelphia Conference and appointed to serve on a committee. George reported to the Church of God membership that the Philadelphia Conference was a meeting unlike any before, "and mark my words can never be again if this effort comes to naught!" He told them that their faith must be welded to works. The local churches must put in motion the work that is to be done, and provide the money to support it. He said:

> The history of our church is the history of too many like it; a disposition to settle down and say, What can we do? There are too few of us and the popular mind is engrossed with that which is popular and orthodox. I know living in a city of a million souls, and across the river another city with twice as many, that it seems almost out of the question that we should be able to do what we desire—a revolution in religious belief showing men and women a better hope than is commonly entertained.

He continued by challenging the delegates and all local churches to be unafraid to face giants.

In 1891, George wrote to *The Restitution* and informed the brethren that he had moved to Puget Sound, Washington. He said he had lived in Brooklyn 40 years and endured all kinds of weather, but he loved the weather in Puget Sound.

Nothing more is known of Young, but George was remembered by his friends as "a brother well and favorably known for his staunch faith and deeds of love."

Bibliography: Young, Geo. F. "Present Duty and Privilege," 1888 Philadelphia Conference Report, *The Restitution*, S.A. Chaplin, ed., Plymouth, In., Jan. 9, 1889; Randall, Clyde E., Photos of Committee appointments, *Historical Waymarks of the Church of God*, Church of God General Conference, Oregon, Il., 1976, p.14; Young, George. Announcement of relocation, *The Restitution*, S.A. Chaplin, ed., Plymouth, In., April 13, 1892; Obituary. *The Restitution*, October 1919.

Young, Albert O.
b. 1868
d. Unknown

Albert was married and resided in Frederick County, Maryland. He may have been related to George Young, but if so, it was distant, perhaps as an uncle, nephew or cousin. Albert was only 20 when he became a delegate to the 1888 Philadelphia Conference. He was appointed to serve on a committee.

He accompanied N.J. Morgan of Virginia to the Philadelphia Conference, and both of them participated in the Virginia churches. Nothing more is known of him.

See Adams, Almus
   Conner, L.E.
   Young, George

Bibliography: Ancestry.com. U.S. Census. Maryland. Frederick. Middletown, Dist. 72. 1880, record for Albert O. Young.

Zilmer, Albert Herman
b. July 18, 1868
d. October, 1949

A.H. Zilmer hailed from Wisconsin, and was an ordained elder and minister in the Methodist church. He withdrew from the fellowship of the Evangelical Association in 1897 and wrote a short paper entitled "A Minister's Reasons for Leaving His Church." Elder Maurice Joblin, pastor of the Blessed Hope Church of God baptized Zilmer in Cleveland on December 12, 1897. Zilmer may have learned of the Gospel through *The Restitution,* published at that time in Indiana with prominent contributions to its pages by Elder Joblin and Robert McLauchlan, a forefather in the faith in the Cleveland area.

Zilmer married Anna Timm, and they had four children. He was so involved in ministry he admitted that Anna raised the children. He was highly esteemed within the Church of God, and he was a popular speaker.

While Zilmer was with the Church of God, he was quite active in preaching in various churches and conferences. The minute book of the now-defunct Chicago Church of the late 19th and early 20th centuries revealed that he visited the Chicago church on a regular basis. One of his sermons concerned why he left the Evangelical Association and how he came to the truth. He conducted evangelistic meetings with F.L. Austin in Chicago in 1904.

Another major accomplishment during this time was Zilmer's work to begin a new Bible study group at South Bend, Indiana, in 1901. It began with his visits to several isolated Church of God members from which a nucleus group gathered, resulting in a congregation. Elder Ezra Railsback was placed in charge. With A.H. Zilmer's help, a Sunday School class was begun with preaching services by visiting evangelists when they were available. The group moved from home to home or rented halls until a building was purchased. For a time they met in the YMCA building.

In 1905 Zilmer wrote an article for *The Restitution* entitled "A Consideration of the Doctrine of Universal Salvation," a spurious and injurious idea infiltrating the Church of God on several fronts. Several preachers were coming to believe it, partly because of Age-to-Come eschatology which taught that mortal nations would enter into the millennial reign of Christ on probation. For the righteous to be rulers with Christ meant that there must be subjects, hence, the mortal nations which are brought into subjection when Satan is thrown into the Pit. These nations bow the knee, but not the heart. Some will become believers; some will not. Universalists interpreted probation as the Second Chance or Larger Hope. A.H. Zilmer thought this issue should be addressed and hoped to see change resulting from his article.

In August 1906, Zilmer submitted a column to *The Restitution*, an open letter "To the Church of God." By the time Zilmer got around to writing that letter, his reasons for leaving were the same as when he withdrew from the Methodists: He objected to doctrinal inadequacies, and he objected to organizational inadequacies which allowed "heresies" to proliferate.

Regarding his book of lectures, he wrote, "The addresses contained in this volume are in exposition of what the members of the community known by the name of 'Christadelphians' believe to be foundation principles of saving truth."

After declaring preference for Christadelphian principles, Zilmer lived in Morrilton, Arkansas, and continued preaching and publishing. He may have had some friendly contact with Church of God members at Morrilton and Waterloo, Iowa, where he lived for awhile. It must be remembered that the Church of God and Christadelphians are quite similar in all the major components of Bible doctrine, differing only on a few

Church of God Preachers, left to right: AH Zilmer, John Wince, BW Woodward, JS Hatch and JF Wagoner.

points of interpretation regarding the fate of the wicked and the nature of the righteous man at resurrection. However, evidence seems to indicate Zilmer was re-baptized into the Christadephian fellowship in Chicago in 1906 and stopped working for the Church of God then.

The Universalist issue simmered in the underground Church of God until the 1910 Waterloo Conference, at which time doctrinal issues were discussed. The organizational effort failed at Waterloo because the delegates could not agree, but a statement of faith was clarified following the conference.

The statement of faith and a policy on church discipline came after Zilmer left the organization, and possibly were a result of his departure. If the Church of God continued to lose its rising stars, it could not survive.

Zilmer's departure caused suffering throughout the Church of God for the members had loved him. Further,

---

A.H. Zilmer's open letter to the Church of God stating his principle reasons for leaving the fellowship:

It becomes my duty to inform you that I am no longer in your fellowship, having recently identified myself with the Christadelphian body. I have been forced to take this step, owing to the following conditions in the "Church of God."

1. A want of discipline, resulting in a state of things being intolerable. Looseness in the reception of members, and admitting many who have not been legally baptized according to the standard of the "Church of God."
2. The existence of a number of utterly un-Scriptural theories, such as universal salvation, fair chance, Jesus the son of Joseph, yearly communion, feet washing, and Sabbath keeping.
3. Identification with the present evil world (Gal 1:4) on the part of members in seeking and holding political offices, bearing or approving bearing of arms, and membership in lodges and secret societies.
4. Un-Scriptural means employed by some of the congregations for raising church funds, such as suppers.
5. A paid ministry which is unscriptural and subversive.
6. I believe that all who will be brought forth at the coming of Christ will come forth mortal bodies, to appear at the judgment seat of Christ (2 Cor. 5:10) and that the approved will obtain immortality.

I do not wish by my presence as a member, to add another element of discord to the already confused state of things, and hence, for this and the preceding reasons have identified myself with the Christadelphians, who have convictions upon these questions similar to my own.

Signed A.H. Zilmer

Ref.: *The Restitution*, August 6, 1906

---

by withdrawing from the confusion, he had not been able, or perhaps willing, to participate in the organizational efforts of the Church of God to assist them in their need. His grievances indicated he wanted a better organization in which to work and did not plan to help design the organization. It may be surmised that in Point 3 of the grievances, he referred to L.E. Conner who had dabbled in politics in Danville, Illinois, and was still to receive criticism on that issue from A.R. Underwood, editor of *The Restitution*. L.E. Conner suffered difficulties, but he stayed with the Church of God and channeled his business and legal expertise in helping it become stable.

A.H. Zilmer's grandson, Norm Zilmer, has graciously provided the details of evangelist Zilmer's last years. A.H. Zilmer was strongly in the Christadelphian fellowship from 1906 until his death. He began preaching for them immediately in 1906 after his re-baptism. A.H. estimated that he preached over 2500 sermons throughout America and Canada. He also edited *The Christadelphian Advocate* and *The Faith*. He was responsible for "logging 10,000 miles a year" in order to spread the word and to establish Christadelphian ecclesias.

Steve Genusa reported that A.H. Zilmer made waves within the Christadelphian organization over the doctrinal issue of "clean flesh," but Zilmer was able to weather the storm. In his own defense he authored a booklet, "The Charge Not Sustained." Albert Hall wrote of the exchange between Zilmer and an accuser, that "Zilmer wrote in a thoughtful brotherly way and is particularly good in his exposition of 1 Pet. 2:24." Hall, editor of *The Fraternal Visitor*, said Zilmer's reports would always be welcome.

Arterial problems caused a foot infection and brought about Zilmer's demise in 1949. His friends in the Church of God were saddened to hear of his death.

See Conner, L.E.
    Huggins, Robert (20th)
    Joblin, Maurice
    McLauchlan, Robert
    Underwood, A.R.

Bibliography: Graham, David, "The Cleveland Connexion," Church of God Connexion & Review, *Wisdom & Power,* Sept. 1992; E-mail interview with Mike Casey, Researcher and writer of the Church of Christ, Oct/Nov 2005; *The Restitution*, Jan. 27, 1904; May 18, 1904; May 25, 1904; April 6, 1905; Aug. 22, 1906; Stilson, J. ed., *History Newsletter* Feb/March 1994; Zilmer, A.H. *Ten Lectures.* John Lea, Philadelphia, 1912; Zilmer, A.H. *The New Covenant*, self published, Morrilton, Ark., 1927, p. 77; Zilmer, Norm. E-mail biography of A.H. Zilmer to author from Steve Cook. Used with permission. Oct. 15, 2006; Zilmer, Norm, e-mail to Jan Stilson of various documents regarding A.H. Zilmer's transition into the Christadelphians, Aug. 15, 2008; "Hope Chapel and Parsonage, South Bend, Indiana," *The Restitution Herald*, Sydney Magaw, ed., Oregon, Il., Oct. 11, 1950; Genusa, Steve, www.genusa.com/Truth/ChristadelphianTimeline.pdf retrieved Feb. 7, 2011.

20th Century Biographies

Adamson, John "Jack" Edgar
b. December 31, 1867
d. 1957

J.E. Adamson was a successful scientist, engineer and businessman who helped found the Church of the Open Bible in Pomona, California. He married Grace Steffa, a Church of God member from Iowa.

Jack and a brother, William, were originally Christadelphians. When several families fell out of favor with the Christadelphians in California over doctrinal issues, these families turned to the Church of God and became staunch leaders in the work. The Pomona Church of God was officially launched in 1915. The church joined the General Conference after its national organization in 1921; it was the first local church to ratify the constitution and by-laws of the new organization. This was quite an honor. Jack often preached at Pomona and promoted the General Conference.

Jack was a successful and well-known mechanical engineer for the San Diego Street Railway system. When streetcar service ceased he became the chief installer of the Pomona power plant. For a time he directed the Pomona Fruit Growers Association and witnessed how devastating frost can be to crops. He sought a way to control the problem, and his research led him to found the Frost Protection Association. Part of his duties required him to manage the Pomona Weather Reporting Station. His legacy as a scientist in frost protection of fragile produce is highly respected to this day.

In 1920 the family resided in Des Palmas and enjoyed comfortable living from which the church benefited. Jack was president of the California conference that year.

Norman McLeod and Terry Ferrell, two Church of God pastors originally from California, are J.E. Adamson's nephews. Terry Ferrell now resides in South Carolina and continues to dialogue with church historians on people and events in Church of God history. His classic work on Church of God history for a 1960 Berean Youth Camp has been quoted numerous times in this encyclopedia. Norman McLeod directed one or more Summer Bible Training Classes of six-week duration during the 1940s in Oregon, Illinois.

Norman submitted a report to *The Restitution Herald* about Adamson's 80th birthday party at the Pomona church where Adamson preached a robust sermon as he had done for over 50 years. Jack died at age 90.

See McLeod, Norman
See Also Adamson, Thomas (19th)
Bibliography: Ancestry.com. U.S. Census. California. Los Angeles. Pomona Ward 1. Dist. 588. 1920 and 1930; McLeod, Norman. Report of 80th Birthday, *The Restitution Herald.* June 29, 1920; Sept. 28, 1920; Jan. 6, 1948; Paterson, Alan M., "Oranges, Soot and Science, The Development of Frost Protection in California." *Technology and Culture,* July 1975; Jack Adamson Photo, Pomona Public Library, Photo Collection. Used with permission; *The Restitution,* Sept. 3, 1920; Ferrell, Terry, Interview with J. Stilson, July 14, 2009.

Andrew, William "Bill" N.
b. June 13, 1927
d. September 9, 2009

Bill Andrew was born in Oregon, Illinois, to George D. and Mabel (Canode) Andrew. He graduated from Oregon Community High School in 1945, and then from Coyne Electrical School in Chicago. He was a lifelong resident of Oregon except for a tour of duty in the US Army during WWII. After his military service he took employment with Commonwealth Edison Company and worked there 34 years.

He married June Andersen in Capron, Illinois, on January 22, 1949; they had two children, John (Susan Little) and Susan (Jon Lapp). Bill and June hosted many social events throughout the years.

Bill professed his faith in the Lord in his youth and was a baptized member of the Church of God Abrahamic

Faith at Oregon, Illinois. June professed her faith and was baptized by Harvey U. Krogh Jr. Bill served in the church as Sunday school superintendent, teacher, elder, deacon, trustee and choir member. Bill supervised the construction and electrical work when the new Church of God was built in 1990.

Bill held a post on the board of the Illinois State Conference and served on many committees over the years to plan and direct quarterly and annual conference meetings.

Just a year before his death, Bill and June sat down with this volume's author and reviewed Andrew family generations that had been involved in the Church of God. Bill was descended from Nicholas Andrew who began the work at Paynes Point in which A.J. Eychaner was prominent in his early years.

Bill's ancestors on both sides of his family helped to establish the work of the Church of God in Oregon. Bill followed the example of his family, always demonstrating a strong testimony of dedication to the truth, and love for his country, his community, his church and his neighbors. Bill's life provided the kind of Christian spirit that knits the body of Christ together in love.

Bill died peacefully following a long illness. Pastor Michael Hoffman conducted his funeral service at the Oregon Church of God. Bill was interred at Riverview Cemetery overlooking the Rock River north of Oregon.

 See Andrew, Nicholas (19th)
    Castle, L'Orient (19th)
    Eychaner, A.J. (19th)
Bibliography: Andrew, Bill, Interview with Jan Stilson, June 2007; Obituary, *Rockford Register Star*, Sept. 10, 2009.

Anthon, Alfred
 b. January 15, 1888
 d. August 1972

Alfred Anthon was a spirited preacher from Louisiana. He was a good Bible student who first learned about the Abrahamic Faith from W.H. Wilson, Chicago, a winter resident in Louisiana.

Wilson began the Pine Woods Bible Class in Louisiana from 1890 to the early 1900s. He baptized all of the Anthons in Yellow Creek. The Wilsons, Anthons and Siples came together to form the Happy Woods church. After the Happy Woods Sunday School started at Hammond, Alfred Anthon began a Bible study and Sunday school near Springfield, 12 miles from Hammond at Blood River.

After W. H. Wilson died, brothers George and Frank Siple continued the work with Alfred Anthon as preacher. Gradually, the work grew. They called on preachers across the south to assist with preaching. They received help from R.A. Humphreys of Arkansas, and D.M. Hudler and O.J. Allard of Iowa. Alfred Anthon learned to preach by watching these men and practicing between their visits. Alfred's works may be followed through his correspondence with the editors of *The Restitution* and *The Restitution Herald*. For example, he wrote in 1922 that he baptized several believers at Blood River Church of God.

When the Hammond congregation was able to afford a full-time preacher, the Anthons moved from Louisiana to serve churches in other parts of the nation. During his lifetime, Alfred pastored in Minnesota, Oregon and Louisiana. He attended General Conference at Oregon, Illinois, as often as he could, and late into his senior years supported the students of Oregon Bible College through his presence on campus and in chapel.

He was a forceful speaker who loved the message of the Gospel of the Kingdom. His love for the Word was clearly communicated as he presented his sermons. The influence of his ministry continues today in the older generation of ministers through the Church of God.

Alfred rests near his old home in Carter Cemetery, Springfield, Louisiana.

 See Allard, O.J. (19th)
    Hudler, D.M. (19th)
    Humphreys, R.A. (19th)
    Siple, F.E. (19th)
    Wilson, W.H (19th)
Bibliography: Graham, David. "Church of God Connexion and Review," *Wisdom and Power*, Nov. 1992; *The Restitution Herald*, March, 1922. Siple, George. "Testimony," The *Restitution Herald*, Jan. 6, 1948; Photo from the album of Jessie M. Wilson, owned by Archives of Atlanta Bible College, McDonough, GA.

Austin, Evelyn Harsh (Harsch)
 b. October 9, 1880
 d. September 1975

A. **The National Berean Society**
B. **The Chicago Church**
C. **The Credentials Committee**

Evelyn Thompson was born in Plymouth, Indiana. When she was still a young child, Amos and Julia Thompson Harsh adopted her. Evelyn taught school and remained a spinster most of her adult life; she married widower F.L. Austin in 1928 in Chicago. They had no children.

Evelyn cultivated friendships with Anna Drew, Dixon, Illinois, and Dr. Leila Whitehead, Chicago. These young women were sisters in the One Faith and instrumental in leading many people into the Church of God organization through their part in forming the National Berean Society in 1913 in Chicago.

The Berean Society saw itself as an educational arm of the Church of God, which in 1913 remained decentralized as state conferences with no central publishing house or educational system. The Berean members formed chapters in each local church for home Bible study and Christian service. The local chapters were overseen by the state officers. The Illinois women and other Bereans wrote, published and distributed Berean lesson books that became the foundational literature for educating isolated and new members in the movement.

The Bereans also published tracts and other instructional materials. Dr. Whitehead and Evelyn kept an inventory of educational literature for children and adults in their Chicago home. When an order for literature arrived the bundles were wrapped and mailed usually at the end of the week. The ladies loaded up a red wagon with bundles and pulled it to the local post office for mailing. In the early days the president and the corresponding secretary distributed all the literature. The attic was their storage room. Evelyn described the process this way: "Climb a ladder to the attic, go to the basement for carton wrapping, borrow a neighbor boy's little red wagon, and walk four blocks to the Post Office."

In this manner, they helped pull together local churches, conferences and isolated members through the use of a commonly accepted literature.

FL and Evelyn Austin

A. The National Berean Society

Evelyn described the Berean work:
> The National Berean Society was organized in the summer of 1913 at the Church of God, Oregon, Illinois. The enthusiasm was so great at the time of the actual organization that the Chautauqua "salute", the waving of handkerchiefs, was spontaneous.

Prior to this time, Illinois, Indiana, Iowa and Michigan had state societies. These four states had worked together in the preparation of lesson books and in matters related to ordering and dispensing the Berean pins. The pins were given to members for attendance and accomplishment. Leaders from the Midwestern states became acquainted with each other at the annual summer Bible schools. They talked about the work and the problems in their respective states. They felt the need of unified action. After a while, the urge for a national organization was very keen. A meeting was held in Oregon, Illinois, to consider an organization. Papers were read, discussion followed, and the organization was put into effect. The name "Berean" was selected because of Acts 17:10,11 "searched the scriptures daily." History shows the name was used as early as 1896 by an organized group of young people in Plymouth, Indiana, and prior to 1900 by a state organization in Iowa. The Illinois state society adopted the name in 1900 and as other states organized, they also adopted the name. From 1914 to 1922, 5439 Ohio Street, Chicago, Illinois, served as the headquarters for the Berean Society. This was the home of Leila Whitehead, who acted as president of the group for eight years, while Evelyn K. Harsh (Mrs. F. L. Austin) was corresponding secretary for ten years,.

During some of this time Evelyn lived in South Bend. It is not known why, but it is certainly feasible that she was helping to stabilize a new work begun there by A.H. Zilmer and the Railsbacks.

The Berean work was born out of sweat and tears. Mrs. Austin continued her history by explaining the criticism received by the new organization:
> So many letters from here and there and everywhere severely criticized the Berean organization. The same letters brought eager orders for lesson books printed and financed by the National Society. These much-wanted books were the very thing which organized action had produced. Many of the church leaders across the country opposed the organizational efforts of the Bereans because they felt that the young people of the Church were trying to take away church powers.

Actually, the Bereans were trying to be an "auxiliary" of something that didn't yet exist, but which they hoped would materialize. Ironically, the already existent "auxiliary" first ratified the National Bible Institute because they were present, organized and ready to act.

The National Berean Society preceded the National Bible Institute by eight years. Their motto suggested by G.E. Marsh was "We stand for unity, truth, and righteousness." Evelyn took pride in her role of helping establish the National Berean Society, and she was fond of saying that the Bereans set historical and organizational precedent in the Church of God Abrahamic Faith. While the larger group was unsuccessful in organizing a national headquarters until 1921, the Bereans were able to do so.

Many of the charter Berean members went on to become pastors and leaders in the Church of God in the 20th century. Men such as G.E. Marsh, Clyde Randall, Paul Hatch, Rolland Stilson, Harry Sheets, Leland Hanson, John Cross and many others exemplified the quality of preachers the Bereans had trained.

B. The Chicago Church

Evelyn and Dr. Whitehead were active in reorganizing the church in Chicago and took copious notes in the minute book. The ledger of the Chicago church is in the Archives of the Atlanta Bible College. In it are many anecdotes of church business, visiting speakers, whereabouts of Bible training students, activities of the Illinois and Indiana conferences and much more.

After Evelyn married F.L. Austin, she and Leila Whitehead continued to maintain a home in Chicago. Evelyn taught school, and Fred stayed at home between preaching assignments as a househusband. In 1930 when F.L. Austin was overcome by dental surgery and had to seek sanctuary to recover, he resided quietly at their Chicago home until he recuperated. The Austins and Dr. Whitehead combined their homes, and Dr. Whitehead moved to Oregon, Illinois, around 1943. They lived at 301 S. 4th Street for more than 20 years.

Evelyn assisted her husband in many capacities during these years. She hosted visiting guests in their home, continued to write literature and served as general encourager and errand girl. She worried about his heavy workload such as could be expected in a new organization striving to perform multiple services for their constituency with no budget and little or no help. After his death, she expressed frustration that things had not been easier for him, and he had experienced not only a heavy workload, but often a thankless return from the people and churches he served.

Evelyn loved music, art, history, Bible studies, research and the church. She took young women under her wings and taught them about worship and service by working with them and setting a good example. One of the highlights of a Sunday evening service was Evelyn playing her saw. This was not a typical instrument, but she bent it between her knees and played it with a violin bow while someone accompanied her on the piano.

Dr. Whitehead and Evelyn continued to share a home after the death of Mr. Austin. They invited young people into their home to train them in ministry, crafts, Church of God history and music. Evelyn participated in plays and musical programs at church and the newly organized Oregon Bible College.

Evelyn authored a tract the size of a post card, "Plan of Salvation." This card was a memory device for Bereans and Sunday school children to teach them about important Bible doctrines. It could be carried in a pocket or tucked in the Bible.

C. The Credentials Committee

Mrs. Austin served the General Conference in a volunteer position for years as the chairwoman of the powerful Credentials Committee. Her duties were to accept information from the local churches during the summer months before the annual meeting. Each church designated its delegate(s) depending upon its membership size. She typed the names of the delegates each church appointed and prepared voting cards for them. As each delegate arrived at conference, he or she was issued a delegate card at the beginning of each business meeting. The cards were returned to the credentials table when the meeting was over.

As each vote was called, delegates lifted their cards to be counted by the members of the Credentials Committee and verified against the counts for that business session. This was important business and, before computers, care was needed for accuracy. A resolution could pass or fail on one vote, so accurate counts were important. Evelyn trained Janet Turner and Ruth Tomlinson Hall Overholser on the mechanism of the committee so that upon her retirement a smooth transition on the committee would follow.

As a member of the Women's Christian Temperance Union in Chicago, Evelyn sang its praises. She and Dr. Whitehead gave demonstrations to youth on the detrimental effects of alcoholic beverages on living tissue. Dr. Whitehead's demonstrations were her only acknowledgment of her training in science and medicine.

Evelyn was a member of the New Century club, which was formed at the turn of 1900. This group met throughout the 20th century as long as members lived.

In matters of faith, Evelyn believed in Jesus the Son of God, his return to establish his Kingdom, the return of Israel to its homeland, the signs in the stars that told the Gospel story and sharing the Gospel with others. In matters of conduct, she believed in practicing a moderate and temperate life style, belonging to social and club groups to spread the word and writing letters to encourage others. She was fascinated with Bullinger's system of star study and with Bible numerics. She said when she and Leila moved to Pinecrest Manor that her laundry number was 29 which meant "cleansing" in Bible numbers, and Dr. Whitehead's was 30, three being one of the numbers of God in the Bible.

Evelyn died in Pinecrest Manor, Mt. Morris, Illinois, at nearly 95 years old. She rests beside her husband at West Elm Cemetery in Chicago.

See Austin, F.L.
Overholser, Ruth
Thompson, William (19th)
Whitehead, Leila, M.D.
See Also Drew, Anna E. (19th)
Neill, Peter (19th)
Wilson, Jessie M. (19th)

Bibliography Ancestry.com. Social Security Death Index record for Evelyn H. Austin; Austin, Evelyn and Paul Hatch. *Impressions and*

History [of the Church of God] unpublished manuscript. 1969; Evelyn Austin, Letter to friends upon entering Pinecrest Manor, May 24, 1963; Austin, Evelyn. "Plan of Salvation," National Bible Institute, Oregon, Il., no date; Stilson, Jan. Memories of Evelyn Austin; Minute book of Chicago Church 1870-1925; *The Restitution Herald*, Nov. 1915; Nov. 9, 1924; Oct. 21, 1930.

Austin, Frederick Lloyd
b. September 26, 1870
d. July 2, 1952

A. Family Life
B. Leadership of the Ministers
C. Kingdom of God and Atonement
D. The Resurrection and Other Questions
E. Getting Down to Business
F. Managing Programs and Crises within the New Conference

Frederick L. Austin was born to William and Mary Alice Grant Austin in Otsego, Michigan. The Austins were a Christian family who raised their son in the Church of God. It was expected that Fred would become a preacher, and he did just that. He became popularly known as F.L. Austin.

B.W. Woodward, Fred's future stepfather, baptized Fred in Big Lake, Watson, Michigan; from that day on, Fred tithed his income to the work of the Lord. While still a boy, he purchased a bell for the church at Watson. When Watson closed, this bell was given to the Church of God at Blanchard, Michigan.

FL and Evelyn Austin

F.L. Austin learned to preach at Rensselaer, Indiana, from 1892 until 1900. From Rensselaer he moved to Argos, Indiana, serving the Argos church and the congregation at Burr Oak, Indiana, until 1904. When he lived in Plymouth, he walked along the railroad tracks to preach at the Argos and Burr Oak Churches of God on Sunday mornings. The Burr Oak church historian reported many years later: "This was our well known and beloved F.L. Austin." He then served the Churches of God at Niagara Falls, and Fonthill, Ontario, Canada, until 1922. Fred and his wife Mary built a home in Fonthill, where growth of the congregation led to construction of a new church building in 1908.

A. Family Life

Mary Stone Chase Austin (September 2, 1874 to November 17, 1926) was the daughter of Samuel P. Chase, an early pioneer and Church of God member in Michigan. Samuel wed Fred and Mary in May 1896. The couple had three daughters, Mary (Leland Hanson), Ruby (John Railton), Evelyn (Paul Johnson), and two sons, George and William (Billy).

Mary Austin

Austin was unable to move his family to Oregon, Illinois, at the time the Conference work commenced in 1922. It took several months to set up an office, and to locate a home for his family. With Mary's health in decline, she had special needs. From the time she arrived in Oregon, her health further deteriorated. She died in the spring of 1926; she was interred at the Riverside Cemetery north of the Old Stone Church of God on North Third Street. Her picture and obituary appeared in *The Restitution Herald* November 1926 issue.

Their son Billy worked for the General Conference as manager of the greenhouse. In the fall of 1925, he resigned and went to work for Governor Frank O. Lowden at the Sinnissippi Farms southeast of Oregon. After he left the Governor's employ he moved to Chicago to work as a security guard. Unfortunately, this did not work out well for him as Billy was murdered in Chicago in 1939. After Billy's untimely death he was buried in Oregon at the Riverside Cemetery. It was a sad time for the Austin family.

Following an appropriate mourning period, Fred Austin married Evelyn K. Harsh from Indiana and Chicago. She was noted for helping organize the National Berean Society several years prior to the organization of the General Conference.

Evelyn was a capable matron who was highly esteemed in the Church of God by everyone except F.L. Austin's children and extended family. Simply said, the family did not like Evelyn. They felt she had made her intentions known before the death of their mother, and they could barely tolerate her new position in the family. Mary's LaMoge china was passed along to Mary's eldest daughter, Ruby Railton, so that it could be handed down through the generations. At this compilation, the china has been handed down to a great-granddaughter of the sixth generation.

B. Leadership of the Ministers

During the early years of his pastoral career, F.L. Austin was active in the formation of a national association. He met with four other ministers at L.E. Conner's home in Cleveland in 1910 and assisted in the formation of the Church of God Ministerial Association.

> **Organizing Members of the Church of God Ministerial Association in 1910**
>
> Pastor L.E. Conner, Cleveland, Ohio
> Pastor F.L. Austin, Fonthill, Ontario
> Pastor F.V. Blakely, Grand Rapids, Michigan
> Pastor S.J. Lindsay, Oregon, Illinois
> Pastor J.W. Williams, Koszta, Iowa
>
> Ref.: *The Restitution*, A.R. Underwood, ed., December 14, 1910

This meeting came out of delegates' efforts to form a national conference organization at the ineffective 1910 Waterloo, Iowa, annual conference. There seemed to be two reasons the Waterloo conference effort had failed. First, no one could agree on a statement of faith, and second, the practice of selecting only state conference delegates was not representative of the total population of members and clergy. Ministers and ordinary members did not have a vote unless they were appointed as state conference delegates. They felt frustrated and voiceless.

In August 1920 F.L. Austin met with J.W. Williams to discuss organizing a general conference. Along with 12 other ministers they sent notices to ministers and delegates of state conferences to join them in Oregon, Illinois, in November 1920. Those in attendance at the gathering came from nine states and Canada. They chose a name, "The National Bible Institute," and drew up a constitution and five articles of policy. These articles were evangelism, publication of literature, facilities to aid, unity of spirit and coordinated effort. From this meeting, the Committee of Ten was chosen to direct the preparatory plans for a new general conference organization.

As a member of the Committee of Ten, F.L. Austin was appointed secretary. Most of the workload fell on him. He typed all the letters in multiple carbon copies, sometimes typing them a second time as the carbons were too faint. There were a couple face-to-face meetings that year, at least one at the Marsh home in Marshalltown, Iowa, but the bulk of the business was conducted by correspondence. These documents are part of the archival collection in Atlanta. The collection was preserved and donated by Grace Marsh, a committee member.

While this small group was actively involved in planning an organization of national magnitude, Church of God members were embroiled in a discussion on the nature of resurrection. Readers of *The Restitution Herald* believed in general or universal resurrection, i.e., all men will be raised, the righteous to reward and the wicked to judgment. The readers of *The Restitution* generally believed in limited resurrection, which said the Adamic wicked dead would never be raised and that the just were the righteous and the unjust were the carnal, backslidden Christians. The difference in the two resurrection theories revolved around the *time* when the wicked would be judged. This is discussed more thoroughly in section D.

C. Kingdom of God and Atonement

Frederick Austin believed in the Gospel of the Kingdom as it was commonly taught in the Church of God. He believed in a Kingdom of God on earth following the return of Christ to earth to judge the righteous and establish the peaceful thousand-year reign known as the millennial kingdom.

He believed and preached atonement. Fred cited Hebrews 10:19, 20 "having liberty to enter into the holiest by the blood of Jesus let us draw near with a true heart in full assurance of faith." He said a righteous man died but was quickened at the resurrection. Being raised, he was in the holy of holies with God, a reference to the inner area of the temple where only the High Priests could enter. Through this act, he said, believers are reconciled, not only the individual, but also the whole household of faith. The Church of the firstborn is fashioned into Christ so that at the proper time it may be unveiled to the groaning creation, which also awaits his return. Atonement or reconciliation was begun at the cross but will be completed at Christ's return. Those who are reconciled will be rulers in the Kingdom of God.

D. The Resurrection and Other Questions

Most readers of *The Restitution* believed in partial or limited resurrection, popularly taught by Christadelphians. In 1920, this doctrine taught that the wicked die the Adamic death and are never raised. This idea is also known as limited resurrection or annihilation. The *time* of judgment was a major difference between the two interpretations. Limited resurrectionists believed the wicked who died the Adamic death, to which all men are subjected, receive their judgment at the time of death. They are never raised again for judgment.

Readers of *The Restitution Herald* adhered to general resurrection, and they believed judgment would occur when Christ returns to establish the Kingdom. Christ's judgment would have a two-fold effect. Judgment of punishment would be served upon the unjust, but judgment of reward would go to the just. The rest of the dead would be judged in the Great White Throne judgment at the end of the millennium, those dead being the mortal nations who inhabit the Age to Come as the subjects.

F.L. Austin preached a message of general resurrection of the just and the unjust, the unjust being the wicked from the Adamic death. Those mortals from the nations who died during the millennium will also be raised for judgment at the end of that period. If their names are not found written in the Book of Life, they will die the second death.

There was yet a third position on resurrection. A few universalists within the Church of God believed that all men would be raised, citing, "As in Adam all die, so in Christ shall ALL be made alive" to prove their point. Misunderstanding regarding universalism may have arisen from the teaching of the Age to Come, which instructs that unbelieving nations will enter the millennial kingdom on probation, after Satan is subdued in the pit. Therefore, sin will be eliminated and all men will be saved. This minority position did not track with the majority doctrinal position in the Church of God of conditional immortality.

Eventually, the statement of faith included the doctrine of literal, general resurrection, but the doctrines of limited resurrection and universal salvation were not accepted as the official position of the General Conference.

Still, universal salvation was such a volatile issue that J.W. Williams, chairman of the Committee of Ten, was asked to step down because he wrote an article in *The Restitution Herald* entitled "Saving Faith," which the committee felt supported a position too liberal to coincide with the majority of Church of God beliefs. They evidently interpreted it to be universalist in nature and not supportive of repentance, conversion, immersion and holy living.

F.L. Austin tried to bring the two groups together. He issued a call to unity in the denomination's two weekly papers, *The Restitution* and *The Restitution Herald*. Austin said: "We are one in Christ. One faith. One hope. One baptism. We do not need a creed or statement of faith because all Church of God members know what the basic principles are." He called upon all believers to lay strife, divisions and jealousies aside. His pleas for unity had a positive effect on many, and it was this group of people who supported the formation of the general conference for the purpose of bringing unity. The critics remained aloof and do not participate in the General Conference to this day. See the entry for Robert G. Huggins for additional insight.

Other issues separated believers that year. In fact, the birth of the general conference organization of the Church of God came out of a climate of lethargy, confusion and division. Its birth as a national entity was a miracle.

E. Getting Down to Business

In his capacity of executive secretary of the General Conference, F.L. Austin managed the new greenhouse in Oregon, and after 1922 he organized and managed the new Golden Rule Home for the elderly. The Golden Rule Home was located in the old high school on Sandhill that had been built in 1857. Some years prior, it had been converted into a fine family dwelling and owned by the Gilberts, wealthy merchants of Oregon. The old two-story brick mansion easily converted into a residence for the elderly. It had nine bedrooms and four bathrooms. In addition to these duties, F.L. Austin commenced the delegate-approved Bible Training Class, and became its foundational professor.

Finally, after S.J. Lindsay resigned as editor, a position he had held since 1911, Austin became the new editor of *The Restitution Herald*. Austin and Lindsay may have found it difficult to work together as they had "feuded" a little during 1920 when the Committee of Ten was conducting its feasibility study. Lindsay could not heartily endorse the movement to organize a national conference. He generated several letters to the committee which Austin, as secretary, received. While the Committee was able to look beyond that difficulty, Lindsay was not. Lindsay looked ahead and foresaw that with the organization of the General Conference, ownership of *The Restitution Herald* would have to be surrendered to it, and as the new conference grew in strength, *The Herald* would grow weaker.

As if to counteract that prediction, in 1922 Austin accepted the mailing list of *The Day Dawn*, "faithfully standing for years past." Austin said prophecy and articles "pertaining to the proclamation of the gospel, and walking in newness of life would be addressed in *The Restitution Herald*." James A. Patrick in Howard, Minnesota, had published *The Day Dawn and Harvest Messenger* since 1898. The merger added readers to *The Herald's* subscription list.

At first F.L. Austin's office was in the back of the flower/gift shop in downtown Oregon, and the print shop was behind Lindsay's home in a little barn. The flower shop was on the first floor of the Sinnissippi Hotel at the intersection of Routes 2 and 64. It was stocked with flowers and plants from the greenhouse and with books and Bibles. After a few months, a church member donated a building to the General Conference. At last, Austin could move his desk away from the proximity of the flowers. The new home of General Conference offices and bookstore was at 110 North Third Street, just one block from downtown Oregon and one block south of the Oregon Church of God. The flower shop continued a few years and then closed because it was not cost-effective.

The "new" building was an old two-story historic structure. The print shop for *The Restitution Herald* occupied the basement. The main floor included offices in the front and mailroom in the back. The second floor was briefly Austin's residence until his family could join him. One upstairs room became a classroom and library when the Bible Training Class opened in 1922.

After F.L. Austin moved into his office at the National Bible Institute, he began to give conference reports in *The Restitution Herald*. The tone of his reports was positive and hopeful. He traveled often and spoke well of the new General Conference. One report said the General Conference "caused an entirely different feeling for the better toward the work."

In addition to his many office duties, F.L. Austin traveled in the field to meet members, and to fill pulpits with preaching services. He is cited often in the pages of *The Restitution Herald* as visiting throughout Illinois, Indiana and Michigan. He also served as pastor of the Oregon Church of God. Other issues that concerned believers in that year surfaced during his travels. Such questions as necessity of tithing, pacifism, ministerial conduct, how to write copy for *The Restitution Herald*, management issues at the General Conference and church discipline surfaced over the next decade. In fact, the birth and continuation of the General Conference of the Church of God came out of a climate of confusion and division. If its birth was a miracle, it's continuation was even more so.

F. Managing Programs and Crises within the New Conference

The development of the new General Conference under Austin's direction was generally successful. Programs during his tenure included the greenhouse and flower shop venture, the Golden Rule Home, the publication of *The Restitution Herald*, evangelistic efforts throughout the nation, and the beginning of the Bible Training Class to prepare ministers. A policy to *recognize* ministers was begun almost immediately in 1921. This was not a licensing procedure, but being on "The List" gave the ministers recognition by a national denominational office. It allowed ministers to travel for evangelistic work with discount rail tickets. The idea was that the General Conference would recognize ministers until they were settled in their own state work. After that, it was expected the state conference would license them. This policy was clearly stated in *The Restitution Herald*.

When Austin inherited *The Restitution Herald*, in September 1922, Frank E. Siple came with it. Mr. Siple had been called to Oregon to participate in an early training program around 1906 and to assist Lindsay with the work. Siple worked in the print shop and filled preaching appointments among the churches. Austin and Siple did not get along well, and in looking back, one wonders why Austin did not send the man packing.

For all the duties of managing the General Conference, F.L. Austin earned $175 a month which some thought was a lot. The president of the board of directors defended this *large* amount since "he was doing the work of two men."

One hoped-for program did not materialize, even though the board and the delegates approved it. In 1924 and 1925 efforts were made to collect funds for the publication of a professional journal to be called *The Bible Investigator*. F.L. Austin was behind this effort. This publication was intended for ministers and students to discuss Bible topics in depth. The emphasis would be academic whereby scholars of the new denomination could identify issues of theology and doctrine.

The idea did not catch on with the donors, and accumulated funds proved to be inadequate for the project. Funds were redistributed to donors. It was to be another 70 years before such a journal could be launched in the Church of God. *The Journal from the Radical Reformation* debuted in 1991 under the direction of editorial board Anthony Buzzard, Kent Ross and Mark Mattison, great-grandson of Samuel J. Lindsay. That publication is now in transition and has not produced a printed copy since 2009.

By 1926 several problems had developed. The Bible Training Class was not paying for itself and tuition had to be charged beginning in 1926. The costs of the Golden Rule Home with all its liabilities were great. Many more elderly wanted to be admitted than had funds to pay for their keep. The country experienced a bad depression so donations to the new conference had dropped off. Things were not going well with Frank Siple. Austin was overworked and grieving; in the space of four years, he had lost his beloved wife and son. He was overwrought.

In 1930, he took two months leave for dental surgery and adequate recuperation due to exhaustion. During his absence the students at the Bible Training Class filled the pulpit at the Oregon Church of God. They expressed interest in having him return to class so they could resume their studies. He returned to work but resigned

Ministers at the 1932 Conference (left to right)
Front: Sydney Magaw, FL Austin, Mary Woodward, LE Conner, Melville Lyon, Lucille Appleby, Paul Johnson, Frank Siple; Middle: JR LeCrone, J Arlen Marsh, GE Marsh, Harry Sheets, Thomas Savage, Cecil Smead, John Denchfield; Back: Gerry Cooper, Harvey Krogh Jr., CE Lapp, Charles Lapp-?, James McLain, Earl Thayer.

the editor's position at *The Herald* on October 13, 1931. G.E. Marsh succeeded him as editor.

It was said that Fred made a striking appearance while teaching: "Austin had his coat open and a gold watch chain across his vest. Coats had narrow shoulders for padded shoulders did not come in for another year." He had an intellectual, stylized manner of speaking that included flourishes of eloquent language with rich inflection of tone. He was known to pound the pulpit. He commanded attention and focused his students or his congregation upon the Word.

Austin continued to teach at the Bible Training Class and was grateful for the help. Other ministers came in to teach including G.E. Marsh in Bible and pastoral ministry; Mary Gesin, history and English; and Alice Carpentar, drawing and art. In 1936 when the class was on solid footing, the Austins moved from Oregon to Grand Rapids.

Ensemble practice for Hope Chapel was held at the parsonage. FL Austin is on the left.

Fred was pastor for two years at the new Pennellwood Church of God. This was followed by his pastorate at Hope Chapel in South Bend, Indiana, from 1940 until 1943. In South Bend, he was paid $100 per month and no parsonage was furnished. To make ends meet, Evelyn taught school. In 1942 the salary was raised to $125 per month. Austin returned to Oregon, and assumed the pastorate at the Oregon Church of God from Sydney Magaw on September 1, 1943, serving there until he retired in 1947.

After 1947, F.L. Austin and Sydney Magaw continued to preach intermittently at the Oregon church. In 1948, when J.R. LeCrone was called to be the fulltime pastor at Oregon, a parsonage was built, and the General Conference ministers were free to preach out of town.

FL Austin amidst his congregation at North Salem.

When Austin retired, people stopped contacting him. He put a notice in *The Restitution Herald* that he had retired but was still available for evangelistic services, to fill a pulpit, or to do a series of meetings. Following that announcement, churches were happy to call him to be guest speaker at state conferences until he was unable to serve.

F.L. and Evelyn Austin continued to worship at the Oregon Church of God until he was so infirmed he could no longer leave home. He died peacefully at home and was buried at Mount Elm Cemetery in West Chicago, near Austin, Illinois. His second wife grieved deeply for several years after his death and was eventually buried beside him. Austin's service left a deep imprint on the denomination of the Church of God Abrahamic Faith.

See Austin, Evelyn Harsh (Harsch)
Lindsay, S.J. (19th)
Magaw, Sydney
Siple, Frank
Woodward, Mary (19th)

See Also Adams, Almus (19th)

Bibliography: Ancestry.com. U.S. Census. Indiana. Marshall. Argos. Dist. 84. 1900; U.S. Census. Illinois. Cook. Chicago. Dist. 1294. 1930; Austin, F.L. "Sermon on Atonement," retrieved from Cogcast. org Sunday, Back to the Future broadcast, July 13, 2008; Biography Project of Atlanta Bible College, David Krogh, compiler; Bolhous, Stephen. Interview with Jan Stilson May 2005 and 2006, e-mail, March 13, 2011; Burnett, Francis, Interview with Jan Stilson, October, 2006; *Fiftieth Anniversary of the Church of God at Burr Oak*, Dec. 12, 1950; "Fonthill 50th Anniversary March 13, 1949," *The Restitution Herald*, March 15, 1949; Graham, David. *Wisdom and Power*, Chuck Jones, ed., Southlawn School of Ministry, Grand Rapids, Mi., Nov. 1992; Graham, David. E-mail to Stilson regarding F.L. Austin, Dec. 1, 2005; Obituary. *The Republican-Reporter*, Oregon, Illlinois, July 10, 1952; Ordnung, Elizabeth, Notes from her Diary, September 1, 1943, available to researchers at the Archives of Atlanta Bible College; *The Restitution* Aug. 9, 1921; Sept. 1924; *The Restitution Herald* Oct. 25,1921; March 27, 1923; May 1924; Aug. 18, 1924; Nov. 28, 1924; June 9, 1925; Oct. 20, 1925; May 18, 1926; Dec. 1, 1925; Mary Austin's obituary Nov. 23, 1926; Nov. 18, 1930; Dec. 9, 1930; 75th Anniversary issue, center pull-out "History of Age to Come Periodicals," Oct. 1985; Smead, Cecil, Letters from the Smead estate furnished by John Smead, Summer 2009.

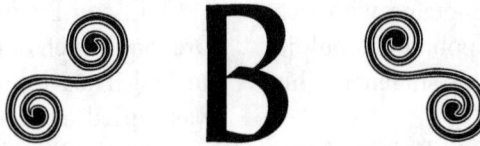

Bagwell, Annie Kate Durham
b. May 21, 1906
d. March 1988

Annie Kate Durham Bagwell was the daughter of George Washington and Bessie Ellenberg Durham. She was born in Anderson County, South Carolina, and graduated from White Plains High School in 1923. Kate attended Furman University in Greenville, South Carolina, after which she taught first grade at White Plains Public School for five years. On December 23, 1926, she married George Furman Bagwell. They had two sons.

According to her family, Kate was a helpful, hard-working wife, a wonderful mother, a dedicated Sunday school teacher and public school teacher. She loved her family. Kate Bagwell attended church regularly, and took her sons and grandchildren to church with her. Her influence on them was great.

Kate was elected teacher of the Guthrie Grove primary department in 1926. She held this position for many years. She also helped with vacation Bible schools, and served as clerk of the church. She was a charter member of the Ladies' Circle of Guthrie Grove Church, serving as both president and treasurer, and providing many inspirational devotions.

Family remembers her as a friend and neighbor to all, a lover of people, a servant of God. She was a defender of truth and very industrious. Her hands were always busy. She crocheted often and gave many pieces to friends. Her cooking skills were unsurpassed. She was faithful to her husband and family and worked outside the home at J.A. Timmerman's Department Store.

Kate Bagwell was laid to rest in the Guthrie Grove Cemetery on March 5, 1988. Today her sons and wives and all of her grandchildren are members of the Guthrie Grove Church of God. Son Lloyd has served as a trustee for over 25 years. Son, Guy, has served as clerk, deacon, and on the building committee.

    See Durham, Bessie E.
             Durham, George W.

Bibliography: Bagwell, Guy for the ABC Biography Project furnished by family members. David Krogh, compiler.

Bender, David R.
b. December 2, 1911
d. June 2, 1996

The Bender family moved from Germany after the Queen of Germany (Catharine the Great) married the Czar of Russia. Edward Bender reported:
> My grandfather, Karl Bender, was in the Russian army signal corps when news came that there was going to be a revolt. He asked for a leave of absence and went home near the Ural Mountains, put everything he owned in a horse-drawn cart, and sold it in town. They received a visa on February 15, 1911, and left for England. They took a ship to America and docked somewhere in Maine.

Karl's wife had a half-sister in Nebraska and for that reason the rest of the family settled there. Shortly after that, David R. Bender was born.

David grew up in Moorefield, Nebraska, and attended the Union church there. The majority of the families attending this community church were Lutherans. The Benders had traditionally been Reformed and Lutheran. When the pastor said communion was the physical flesh and blood of Christ, David could not accept it. David's friend Wilsey McKnight knew E.E. Giesler, the preacher of the Church of God, as both men played the mouth harp and perhaps practiced together. Wilsey told David about the doctrines of the Church of God and sometime later, Giesler baptized David.

David married Emily Fyfe on April 25, 1943, "at high noon" according to the newspaper account. Emily was born on July 24, 1914. After living with David's family until WWII ended, they purchased acreage and began farming. Emily and David had two sons, Edward and James, and a daughter, Esther. Edward "Eddie" entered Oregon Bible College in 1965; after graduation he became pastor at Moorefield, 1969 to 1970.

All his life, David remained faithful to Bible teachings

he had learned from E.E. Giesler. He rests in peace beside Emily.

Edward Bender contributed to this entry.

See Giesler, E.E. (19th)
McKnight, Wilsey

Bibliography: Bender, Edward "Some of the History of Nebraska Churches of God Faith of Abraham," presented at the 2nd Annual History Conference at North Hills Church of God, Springfield, Ohio, Nov. 6-7, 2007.

Biba, Marilee Hummel
b. January 16, 1943
d. November 17, 1987

Marilee Hummel Biba was the daughter of Charles M. Hummel II and Betty B. Hummel. Marilee was a lovely, fine Christian daughter who was an outstanding student. She attended UCLA and received a Bachelor of Arts degree there because she wanted to attend her mother's alma mater. Marilee later said she wished she'd attended Oregon Bible College at least one year.

Marilee loved to travel and became a United Airlines flight attendant. She wed Richard Biba. They had three children, Kristen, Andrew and Paige. Marilee was an outstanding, talented church worker and much loved.

Dignitaries from Apple Computer and United Airlines paid tribute to Marilee at the memorial service.

See Hummel, Betty
Hummel, Charles

Bibliography: ABC Biography Project, David Krogh, compiler.

Birkey, Glenn
b. August 16, 1886
d. January 1977

Glenn Birkey lived in Rochelle, Illinois, and in 1921 wrote to *The Restitution* that he had witnessed for the teachings of the Church of God since he was first connected with it. He had answered many questions about it, some about the name itself. He challenged readers to bear criticism patiently. He said the name Church of God in Christ Jesus was scriptural.

Birkey and his wife were isolated members for many years, attending church at Oregon, Illinois, Church of God when health and weather permitted. In the 1940s, a call was made to the Oregon Bible College to send students to preach at Flagg Center Community Church. The Birkeys lived just down the road from this church.

Soon, there was a regular program of activities in Flagg Center managed by Bible college students with Glenn Birkey providing oversight. Verna Thayer and four young women began a Sunday school at Flagg Center in the fall of 1947. As soon as it was feasible, Oregon Bible College preaching students began preaching Sunday worship. Gradually, attendance increased from the community and surrounding rural area. Glenn Birkey continued to provide oversight at the church and seemed well satisfied with its progress.

On more than one occasion Glenn spoke for Chapel at Oregon Bible College. One time he gave his testimony, recalling he had been a railroad man for 38 years. Specifically, he was a postal employee and supervised the mail car. He was not allowed to talk religion to fellow employees, but they knew that he stood for Christ.

He had been in many train wrecks, but "God guarded him," he said. One time he was rendered unconscious in a derailment and woke up to see workers gathering remains of a fireman into a basket. That was a sobering scene and made him appreciate God's goodness toward him even more.

Eventually, the Flagg Center church was brought into the Church of God General Conference fellowship, and it has remained a member of that denomination with a Church of God pastor always filling the pulpit. For the last two decades of the 20th century, Pastor Gordon Landry filled the pulpit and has seen the church through an extensive remodeling that enlarged the sanctuary and provided a new entrance.

Pastor Landry retired September 1, 2010, and the ministry has been continued by Pastor Brian Froehlich and wife Hannah (Hoffman).

See Landry, Gordon
Thayer, Verna

Bibliography: Memories of Bro. and Sr. Birkey by JStilson; *The Restitution*. Oct. 1921; *The Restitution Herald*, Oct. 14, 1947; Oct. 21, 1947.

Bolhous, Marjorie (Burnett)
b. May 4, 1925
d. March 29, 2005

Marjorie was one of five children born in Brown County, Illinois, to Loren and Mary Cooper Burnett. She was the granddaughter of John Wesley Cooper and a precious treasure to the family. Her brothers Harold and Lozell remained in the Ripley area all their lives, but Marjorie, sister Helen and brother Francis moved to Oregon, Illinois, where they attended Oregon Bible College.

While a student in Oregon Marjorie married Walter Bolhous. She met him when he was a driver for employees at Kable in Mt. Morris. During the war, gasoline was rationed, and it was necessary to carpool. Students noticed that Marjorie was quite taken with Walter, and they encouraged her to sit in the front seat when he drove. Soon they were a couple. He was a staunch Lutheran and remained so most of their married life. Marjorie remained faithful to the teachings of the Abrahamic Faith and raised a son, Stephen, and daughter, Paula, who continue to serve in full-time Christian ministry within the Church of God.

Marjorie worked in the local school system as a playground supervisor and later as secretary to Nash and Jefferson schools. She was involved in several community groups including the Sharing and Caring Widows group, the Ogle County Senior Center and the CHUMS mentoring program.

Marjorie loved missionary work. She was a member of the Mary and Martha ladies' group at Oregon Church of God from its inception. She continued to serve on the Missions Committee well into her old age. Another love was the American Bible Society. She made Bibles available to anyone who needed them and encouraged people to send donations to this auspicious group. For one who could not go to the foreign mission field herself, she made copies of God's Word available to others serving on the mission field.

Due to her Christian witness and the prayers of the Mary and Martha group, Walter began attending church with Marjorie. He accepted the Lord and was baptized. In his senior years, Walter was stricken with leukemia and died on April 24, 1987.

Marjorie never drove a car and was often seen walking in downtown Oregon shopping and carrying packages. In her elderly years she used a cart or a battery-powered mobile chair for shopping. She was a small woman but quite independent and strong.

She sleeps beside Walter at Riverview Cemetery.

   See Burnett, Francis
          Cooper, John Wesley

Bibliography: *The Restitution Herald*, June 1925; May 19, 1946; Marjorie G. Bolhous. Obituary, *Rockford Register Star*, April 2, 2005; Stilson, Jan. Memories of Marjorie Bolhous, 2006.

Boyer, Andrew Carmel
   b. February 17, 1882
   d. February 16, 1964

Carmel Boyer lived on the family acreage where his father and grandfather had lived, south of Stephens City, Virginia. The house was built in 1840 and remained standing at the time of this writing. Carmel's ancestors tended the farm during the difficult days of the Civil War as it raged around Winchester, Virginia. The Kernstown battle was just "up the pike" from the Boyer homestead. "Pike" is a Virginia term for highway stemming from "turnpike."

Carmel's lineage is as follows: Carmel's father was Andrew Jackson Boyer, the son of William Boyer, the son of Peter Boyer, the patriarch from whom the Church of God Boyers descended. Peter Boyer lived at Kernstown prior to the Civil War. The Boyer men were pacifists and, therefore, conscientious objectors. It was difficult being an objector during the Civil War in the South, even though the Confederacy had provision for religious objection and exemptions for clergy. See the entry for N.J. Morgan for more discussion. The North did not allow exemptions but allowed an objector to buy his way out for $300.

In 1963 Carmel Boyer summoned Pastor Eugene Stilson to his home at Kernstown soon after Stilson began the pastorate at Maurertown and Fort Valley. The house was old and stately and so were Carmel and Hilda Boyer. The old couple used kerosene lamps because electric lights were considered a new-fangled invention. During the visit, Carmel discussed his faith and his family. He shared the story of his framed exhibit of Confederate currency. His father, who refused to fight in the Civil War, had collected the money. A hundred years old, this collection was turning yellow in the frame. It was a rare exhibit, equal in quality to museum displays.

Carmel discussed his upcoming funeral service, which he had already planned, and for which he wanted several scriptures read to the congregation. He stressed his belief in the Kingdom of God, and he correlated his love for this doctrine with his firm belief in conscientious objection. He cited Luke 13:29, "they will come from the east, west, north and south, and will sit down in the Kingdom of God." And, in Genesis 28:14, "Your seed... spread to the north and to the south." Carmel explained his position, as the position of his forefathers had been, that one should not fight against other believers for one day all will be assembled in the Kingdom.

At the beginning of the WWII, Carmel registered with the local draft board at age 60. The interesting thing about this particular draft is that it required every man in the United States to register, regardless of age, and is known as "the old man's draft."

In 1946 Carmel forwarded his precious copy of Joseph Thomas' book, *The Life of the Pilgrim*, to Sydney Magaw of *The Restitution Herald*. Magaw summarized the book as a story that clearly demonstrates a young preacher's trials as he traveled through Virginia, Ohio and Pennsylvania to preach the Gospel in the early 1800s.

   See Boyer, Benjamin F. (19th)
          Boyer, John D. (19th)
          Boyer, William (19th)
          Thomas, Joseph (19th)
          Stilson, Eugene

Bibliography: Ancestry.com U.S. Census. Shenandoah. Virginia. Dist. 58. 1850; Ancestry.com. U.S. World War II Draft Registration Cards, 1942 Record for Andrew Carmel Boyer; Boyer, Dorothy, Material provided to author from consultations with Boyer family members, September, 2007; Magaw, Sydney, Editorial on The Life of the Pilgrim, *The Restitution Herald*, Sept. 17, 1946; Stilson, Eugene. "Memories of Carmel Boyer," March, 2007.

Boyer, Lucille A. (Appleby)
b. July 4, 1906
d. April 9, 1993

Lucille was born in Kenard, Nebraska, to Claar J. and Ida Belle Steward LeCrone. Lucille's family first learned of the Church of God from evangelists in Nebraska. Some of those who ministered to her family included: J.J. Heckman, Almus Adams, Uncle John Foore and many others who traversed the Great Plains. Lucille was baptized in August 1919, and found great joy in her faith. On October 28, 1937, she married Clinton Appleby. They had one son, Wayne.

Lucille and Ernest Boyer on their wedding day.

J.R. LeCrone was Lucille's brother, and both became esteemed Church of God pastors. They attended the Bible Training Class at Oregon, Illinois, in 1931. After her studies there, Lucille received a license to preach, joining the ranks of a few Church of God women, including Libby Palmer, Mary Austin Woodward and Anna Drew. Lucille preached for the Church of God at Helen, Oklahoma; Arkansas City, Kansas; and Fremont, Nebraska.

Little LeCrones and Applebys. Appleby relatives shared this photo with Pastor Scott Ross of Omaha.

Clinton died on December 29, 1974, and on January 31, 1976, Lucille married an old friend, Ernest L. Boyer of Fort Valley, Virginia. It was a second marriage for both. While living in Virginia she served as Sunday School Superintendent at Fort Valley.

Lucille was gifted in many areas and loved to work with flowers, cook (especially her angel food cake), garden and can the produce. She also sewed and quilted, creating many quilted masterpieces over the years. She died at 86. Pastor Jon T. Welch conducted the funeral service at Fort Valley Church of God in Christ Jesus. Her love and dedication continue to be greatly missed.

See Adams, Almus (19th)
Drew, Anna (19th)
Foore, John (19th)
Heckman, J.J. (19th)
LeCrone, J.R.
Palmer, Libby (19th)
Woodward, Mary (19th)

Bibliography: Biography project of Atlanta Bible College, David Krogh, compiler.

Boyer, Samuel H.
b. November 24, 1904
d. April 28, 1991

Samuel Herman Boyer was born in Fort Valley, Virginia, to Mr. and Mrs. Samuel E. Boyer. Sam married

---

Devoted Clergywomen

A note card found among Evelyn Austin's papers said, "Women were more active in the Berean Society" indicating that Bereans helped train women desiring to preach and teach. Women clergy within the Church of God included:

19th Century
- Clara West Chaffee, pastor
- Mary Chapman, evangelist
- Anna Drew, evangelist
- Martha Neill, evangelist
- Libby Hill Palmer, pastor
- Mrs. H.A. Parks, evangelist
- Elizabeth Armstrong Reed, evangelist/author
- Nancy Barber Robison, evangelist
- Mary Seymour, evangelist
- Nancy Titchenal Skeels, evangelist
- Thoms, Mary Lyde Trousdail, evangelist
- Roxanna Chaplin Wince, children's pastor
- Mary Austin Woodward, evangelist

20th Century
- Alice Aldrich Badillo, missionary
- Lucille Appleby Boyer, pastor (deceased)
- Deborah Bryant, pastor
- Rachel Krogh Carr, missionary
- Donna Claussen Cooper, pastor
- Rebekah Mattison Martin, missionary nurse
- Judy Kirkpatrick Myers, mission leadership
- Louise Brewer Lapp, ministerial educator
- Merry Peterson, pastor
- Emma Railsback, pastor
- Christy Ross, pastor
- Connie Scott, pastor
- Janet Turner Stilson, archivist/author
- Verna Shafer Thayer, child evangelist (deceased)
- Mary Brown Vadnais, pastor (deceased)
- Tracy Savage Zhykhovich, missionary

Lillian Coverstone on February 4, 1929. The couple had two daughters, Charlotte (Fyfe) of Hendersonville, North Carolina, and Dorothy Boyer of Fort Valley, Virginia.

Sam joined the Fort Valley Church of God in Christ Jesus at his baptism on June 3, 1917. He served the Fort Valley Church in many ways, including as teacher, deacon, church treasurer and elder for numerous years.

One of Sam's greatest loves was music. Throughout his lifetime, he enjoyed singing folk songs and gospel quartets. For years he distributed tapes of songs he had performed. Each Virginia church family has at least one copy of one of his tapes, if not all of them. Sam brought pleasure to those around him as he shared God's love by what he did and said. Sam and Dorothy's tapes are formatted for cogcast.org internet radio and may be enjoyed in streaming format or downloaded.

Sam Boyer fell asleep in Jesus on April 28, 1991, at 86 years. His gentle voice, friendly smile and firm handshake continue to be missed by all who knew and loved him.

Bibliography: Boyer family for the Atlanta Bible College Project, David Krogh, compiler.

Boyer, William Enoch
b. January 20, 1900
d. February 24, 1999

W.E. Boyer was born at Pelton in Fort Valley, Virginia, to Samuel Edward and Charlotte Munch Boyer. He graduated from Woodstock High School in 1920 and attended Dunsmore Business College in Staunton, Virginia. As a young man he worked on the family farm until he became associated with the National Bank of Woodstock, later a part of the NationsBank system. He served as cashier until his retirement in 1970. Afterward, he began to repair and restore old clocks. He moved to Richmond in 1988 to be near his sons.

Bill married Florence Lanes who preceded him in death in 1975. Following his baptism in 1917 by Pastor J.H. Anderson, William was a lifelong member of the Church of God Abrahamic Faith. For many years he was treasurer of his local congregation and the Virginia Conference of the Church of God. His grandfather, William Boyer, is credited with being the founder and first elder of the Fort Valley Church in the late 1870s. W.E. Boyer was a member of many civic organizations, including a charter member of the Woodstock Lions Club.

Boyer was an elder and treasurer of the Maurertown Church of God, and as such, helped Eugene Stilson a few days after the Stilsons arrived in Maurertown, Virginia.

Before the first week was over the new pastor was asked to perform a wedding that weekend. It was then that Eugene and W.E. Boyer realized Virginia law requires a minister be bonded to perform weddings. So, hastily, the banker and the young pastor met at the courthouse and secured a bond for $500. The church covered the cost, and because W.E. was both banker and church treasurer, the process was expedited.

Bill also helped when the pastor's car quit. Another church friend owned the local Plymouth/Dodge dealership. Frank Morrison wrote the loan application, and W.E. Boyer guaranteed the loan. Those were good men and good friends.

As a good and faithful member of the board at Maurertown Church of God, Bill looked after the welfare of the building and the grounds which were used for Virginia Conference. W.E. Boyer served as trustee. Trustees could be expected to maintain the grounds, look after the church and dormitory, replace burned out well pumps, eliminate field mice when they entered the church, repair the organ and arrange repairs at the parsonage. Since he was elder, trustee and treasurer, he could authorize payment.

Bill Boyer was survived by his three sons and their wives, Charles W., Richard L., and Donald E. Boyer, including eight granddaughters and four great-grandchildren. Pastor Dale Ramsey conducted his graveside service in Sunset View Memorial Gardens.

See   Boyer, William (19th)
    Boyer, Sam
    Morrison, Gertrude (Frank)
    Stilson, Eugene

Bibliography: ABC Biography Project, David Krogh, compiler; E. Stilson, Memories of W.E. and Florence Boyer.

Brewer, Edna Lehman
b. August 2, 1885
d. September 26, 1958

Edna Lehman married Rollie S. Brewer near Tipp City, Ohio. They had four children, Mary Louise (Lapp), Byron, Dorothy (Demmit) and Kenneth. After Rollie died from Hodgkin's disease, Edna studied to become a practical nurse in 1931.

When the Church of God General Conference asked her to become Matron of the newly formed Bible Training Class in Oregon, Illinois, she agreed. She moved to Oregon at the start of the reorganized Bible Class in 1939. It was discontinued in 1933 due to unfortunate financial circumstances following the Great Depression. The students who lived on South Third Street during Edna's employment were Emory Macy, Richard "Dick" Smith,

Francis Burnett, Verna Lawrence, Linford Moore and Terry Ferrell. The students called her "Mom Brewer."

Terry Ferrell reported that four people quoted Scripture well enough to impress a person: Emma Railsback and her colleague from Washington, A.L. Corbaley, who had Scripture debates with each other—he could pick up quoting where Emma left off. It was said that he memorized the entire New Testament. Another was T.A. Drinkard who quoted Scripture so fast in debates with members of other denominations he would "snow them under." The fourth was Mom Brewer. She committed long passages to memory and quoted them often.

Edna poses with plaque above the fireplace at Oregon Bible College. The plaque is now on exhibit in the Atlanta Bible College Archives.

Edna served as Matron for nearly eight years. After the college purchased a stately old mansion north of Oregon and moved there in 1946, Edna returned to Ohio. She was presented with a plaque at the end of her service. This plaque is part of the archival collection of Atlanta Bible College in McDonough, Georgia.

Edna and Rollie Brewer's family continues to serve in the Church of God through the ministry of Jon Lapp and Elaine Poole, Jerald Brewer and Pastor Greg Demmitt.

See Burnett, Francis
Lapp, Clarence
Lehman, Henry (19th)
Macy, Emory
Moore, Linford
Smith, E. Richard

Bibliography: Ferrell, Terry. Interview with Jan Stilson July 15, 2009; Lapp, Jon, E-mail to Stilson including the Brewer Family Tree, July 21, 2009.

Brown, Leonard John
b. July 6, 1921
d. May 20, 1992

Leonard Brown was born in Detroit, Michigan, and became a member of the Church of God after he learned of the Gospel of the Kingdom of God. He attended Oregon Bible College during the late 1940s. He and his wife Helen had 12 children, many of whom are still active in the Church of God at the time of this compilation.

Leonard served churches in L'Anse, Michigan, and in Missouri. His family continues to serve in the Missouri Conference of the Churches of God. Raymond Brown, Leonard's younger brother, was pastor in the Nova Scotia mission work in the 1970s. Their sisters, Mary Vadnais and Grace Grant, were active in the Champion Community Church.

As an avid student of history and the Bible, Leonard read many books and commentaries in an attempt to comprehend the vast wisdom, knowledge and power of Almighty God. In his mature years, Leonard studied and hypothesized on such topics as the biblical account of dinosaurs, the shifting and movement of continental plates, prophecies about the return of Christ and the Scriptures regarding the Kingdom of God.

Known as a man who was unafraid of controversy, Leonard was outspoken about anything that might endanger the perception of the church, its people or the conference as a whole. He was equally outspoken within the secular arena. He was opposed to abortion, premarital sex, and promiscuity as displayed by the television networks. He campaigned against politicians whom he felt opposed the basic Judeo-Christian morals upon which this country rose to power.

Leonard believed that he lived in one of the greatest eras of all time because he was allowed to see more prophecy fulfilled than any other generation since Christ's birth. Leonard looked to the return of Christ, which he thought he would see before his death. He died during his pastorate at the Cross Timbers Church of God in Missouri. His legacy continues through the service of son Dale Brown of Missouri who served a term on the General Conference Board of Directors, and John Nelson, grandson, who is a Missouri pastor.

See Brown, Raymond
Vadnais, Mary L.

Bibliography: Biography Project of Atlanta Bible College, David Krogh, compiler; Ancestry.com. Social Security Master Death List, Record for Leonard J. Brown.

Brown, Raymond
b. July 19, 1925
d. November 12, 1974

Raymond was born in Detroit, Michigan. It is not known when he first learned of the message of the Gospel of the Kingdom, but he accepted it as did his brother, Leonard, and sisters, Mary Vadnais and Grace Grant.

Ray and Doris with Dennis

Ray graduated from Oregon Bible College in 1950 and became a licensed minister of the Church of God. He served congregations in Greytown, Wisconsin; St. Cloud, Minnesota; Arkansas City, Kansas; Eldorado, Illinois; Morristown, Tennessee; Hillisburg, Indiana; Waterloo, Iowa; and Digby, Nova Scotia. He was beloved among the congregations of the General Conference.

His beautiful tenor voice was perfect for solos, and his singing brought joy to everyone who listened. Ray participated in musical ensembles with students and ministers, and he loved to sing in male quartets. Ray's rendition of "Ship Ahoy" was a favorite everywhere he went. It still plays occasionally on cogcast.org internet radio. His voice was particularly suited to that song's range and message.

Ray married Doris, and they had two children, Dennis Ray and Laura Lee. Later, Ray and Doris adopted two little girls, Jeanie and Nancy Joy. Doris, a skilled pianist, taught Dennis to play piano, and he became one of the best performance pianists in the Church of God beginning in his youth. Dennis often served as musician for General Conference or Youth Conference. He married Susan Foster, great-granddaughter of S.J. Lindsay.

Lighthouse Mission Church of God, Digby, Nova Scotia

When Ray died unexpectedly while serving the Digby, Nova Scotia, Lighthouse Mission Church, the entire denomination mourned his loss. Pastor C.E. Lapp officiated the service on November 16. Ray is interred at the Digby Cemetery at Prince William and Third Streets.

 See Brown, Leonard
    Lapp, Clarence E.
    Lindsay, S.J (19th)
    Vadnais, Mary L.
Bibliography: ABC Biography Project, David Krogh, compiler.

Burch, Lawrence I.
b. May 10, 1895
d. January 27, 1994

Lawrence "Larry" Burch was born in Tyner, Indiana. He worked for Oliver Tractor at Plant 2. Lawrence married Cuba Stanton in 1919; she died in 1921. Lawrence and his second wife, Mary E. Senff, had three daughters, Evelyn Fisher of Niles, Michigan; Lois Fritz of Plymouth, Indiana, and Martha Ulrey of St. Petersburg, Florida. Mary died in 1960.

Mr. Burch was a loyal and faithful member of the North Salem Church of God at Plymouth. Pastor Stanley Lawrence conducted his funeral service from the Van Gilder Funeral Home. Larry was interred at the Tyner Cemetery.

Bibliography: Burch, Mary Senff, Letter and obituary, April 12, 1994.

Burnett, Francis "Frank"
b. June 2, 1917
d. March 15, 2007

Francis Burnett was born in Brown County, Illinois, to Loren and Mary Burnett. He had two brothers and two sisters. Francis graduated from Mt. Sterling High School in 1935. After graduation, he worked as a farmhand in the area. Francis attended Ripley Church of God. F.E. Siple baptized Francis at age 13. He attended summer Bible schools in Oregon and eventually attended the new Bible college at Oregon.

Francis and a sister, Marjorie (Bolhous), moved to Oregon where they joined the student body in 1940. Later, Helen, another sister, also moved to Oregon to attend college. Francis served as student pastor of the Blessed Hope Church of God in Rockford from 1941 to 1943. At that time the church met in a rented Independent Order of Odd Fellows (IOOF) Hall on North Third Street. Later, the congregation met in a rented church at 2425 West Jefferson. Francis preached two Sundays a month. After several months, this increased to three Sundays. Pastor L.E. Conner, a professor at the college, supervised him.

Francis served on the Board of the Illinois Conference of Churches of God from 1938 to 1943. He graduated from Oregon Bible College in June 1943.

In Oregon, Francis met his future spouse, Iris Hall, from Grand Rapids and married her on June 7, 1941. They had four daughters, Martha, Mary, Michal and Miriam, all Bible names. The story was told at Francis' funeral by spiritual son Dale Swartz that Francis often said it was a

Friends and fellow evangelists, Francis Burnett (left) and James McLain.

good thing he didn't have a son. He would have had to name him Mahershalalhashbaz (Isaiah 8:1). In time, Iris and Francis were blessed with ten grandchildren.

Francis and Iris became National Evangelists for the Church of God General Conference after his graduation. They pulled a trailer home behind their vehicle and worked throughout Missouri, Illinois, Arkansas and Iowa. James McLain and Melville Lyon had used the trailer when they served as National Evangelists. When the Burnetts stopped living in it, it was used for Ed Graham's family at Oregon Bible College; they parked it and lived in it on campus while he was a student.

The Burnetts moved to Missouri in 1945 and remained there as state evangelist until 1956. They lived in a rural area near Cross Timbers, Missouri. After Martha and Mary were born, the family worked a little farm

Morse Mill, Missouri, Church of God

for income. The girls were given chores, and although they were little, they were a big help to their parents.

The church building was located at Jordan, Missouri, a small village with only three homes, a grocery store and post office. In 1947, the congregation built a new parsonage for the Burnetts which increased the size of the village by 25 percent! Francis preached at Jordan two Sundays each month, and once each month at Kansas City and at Bosworth.

Francis answered the call to pastor the Brush Creek Church of God and moved his family to Tipp City, Ohio, where they resided while his daughters grew up. He also served on the Board of Education of Oregon Bible College and the Board of Directors of the General Conference. In November 1968 the Burnetts moved to Grand Rapids, Michigan, where Francis became pastor of the new church at Garden Park.

At the same time, he taught a class at Oregon Bible College. During this time he augmented his education with summer courses at the University of Arizona in Phoenix. He also served as Youth Director for 14 years while teaching classes.

In 1974, Francis became the Sunday School Director of the General Conference. He also served as interim pastor at the mission church in Digby, Nova Scotia, in 1975 while continuing as Sunday school director. In 1976 he resigned his duties with the General Conference and Oregon Bible College and purchased the local Montgomery Ward Catalog store in Oregon. During this time he also was a real estate agent with the Willis Turner Realty Agency in Rockford.

Francis received a call to go to Oak Lawn Church of God at Koszta, Iowa, in October 1976, and preached intermittently there until he was hired to preach fulltime in 1981. Francis and Iris resided at Koszta for over 20 years. After Iris died, Francis continued there alone for a number of years. Finally, a few years before his decline and death, Francis retired and returned to Oregon where he lived independently until he was unable to do so.

His last months were spent at Neighbors' Nursing Home in Byron, where he received many visitors. Many people from the community and the denomination who loved him attended his funeral service. Pastor Michael Hoffman conducted the service. David Krogh represented the staff and students of the Atlanta Bible College and the General Conference. Dale Swartz represented the Ministerial Association, and being nearly an "adopted" son of Francis, told several humorous and loving stories that made the congregation laugh and weep. Francis is interred beside Iris in the Daysville Cemetery.

   See   Bolhous, Marjorie
         Conner, L.E. (19th)
         Graham, Ed
         Lyon, Melville
         McLain, James
         Turner, Willis H.

Bibliography: Atlanta Bible College Biography Project, David Krogh, compiler; Memories of Frances and Iris by Jan Stilson, Spring 2007; Swartz, Dale, Memories of Francis shared at his funeral service and confirmed by e-mail to Jan Stilson, Jan. 22, 2008; Note about Missouri, *The Restitution Herald,* Sydney Magaw, ed., Oregon, Il., Oct. 21, 1947 and Nov. 11, 1947.

Burnett, Loren L.
b. February 4, 1894
d. November 27, 1971

Burnett, Mary Josephine Cooper
b. June 27, 1897
d. March 27, 1972

Loren Burnett was born to Charles and Nora Burnett in Brown County, Illinois. Loren grew up on a farm and attended Brown County schools. At 18 he enrolled in Gem City Business College, Quincy, Illinois. After graduating, he worked for a short time in a bank in Chicago.

Loren married Mary Josephine Cooper on February 16, 1916. They had one son, Francis, and moved to a farm in 1918 after the baby's birth. Mary was a member of the Church of God Abrahamic Faith at Ripley, Illinois, and Loren had been a member of the local Christian congregation. Loren took his Bible to church and followed along during the sermon. Occasionally, he wondered why the pastor didn't quote all of a scripture. He found the answers he sought in Mary's church where Frank E. Siple baptized him and Francis in July 1930.

Loren devoted his life to serving the Lord through the local church. He served on the church board and did his best to live a dedicated life for Jesus. His influence is still found in the lives of his children and grandchildren.

The Burnetts had other children, Marjorie (Bolhous), Harold, Lozell and Helen (Jones). Francis, Marjorie and Helen all attended Oregon Bible College. The daughters married and began families in Oregon. Francis graduated and went on to devote his career to pastoral ministry in the Church of God.

Mary was born to John Wesley and Myrtilla (O'Neal) Cooper, busy members of the Ripley Church of God. Mary was raised by Christian parents who were energetic church workers. She was talented in music, both instrumental and vocal, and performed as a soloist for worship and other church programs. She played piano for Sunday school, morning and evening worship, and was a faithful Sunday school teacher. She was a good Christian mother and passed her love for the Lord to her children.

Loren and Mary were involved in an auto accident the Saturday after Thanksgiving in 1971. Loren lived only four hours. Mary suffered a stroke about ten days after the accident and lived until Easter in the spring. Both rest in the Ripley Cemetery awaiting fulfillment of the "blessed hope."

   See Burnett, Francis
         Cooper, John Wesley
         Siple, Frank E.
Bibliography: ABC Biography project, David Krogh, compiler.

Butler, Mellie Anderson (Rogers, Tronjeau)
   b. October 15, 1903
   d. November 18, 1988

Mellie was the eldest daughter of John H. and Lula Anderson. Lula died in childbirth at Maurertown, Virginia, in 1921 when Mellie was 18. Mellie's health declined that same year possibly from the trauma of losing her mother and having to care for five children.

Mellie married Julian Rogers in February 1921 and moved to Winchester, Virginia, but her health plagued her causing great concern to her father. Mellie began to teach her husband about the Bible, and he accepted it. J.H. Anderson baptized him on March 26, 1922.

After Julian's death, Mellie married twice more. She retired in Indiana and attended Hope Chapel.

   See Anderson, J.H. (19th)
Bibliography: *The Restitution*, November 1921; *The Restitution Herald*, April 1922.

Buzzard, Sir Anthony
   b. June 28, 1935

Anthony Buzzard was born in the United Kingdom, the son of Rear Admiral Sir Anthony Buzzard. Young Anthony graduated with a master's degree in foreign languages from Oxford University. He came to America to study, and became a teacher of Bible and Greek at Oregon Bible College (now Atlanta Bible College) in 1982. He subsequently received a master's in theology from Bethany Theological Seminary in Chicago. Anthony and Barbara, a native of Michigan, were married on June 21, 1970. They have three daughters: Sarah (Jimenez), Claire (Price) and Heather. Anthony and Barbara worship at the Restoration Church of God in Fayettville, Georgia.

Anthony has traveled the world several times to attend meetings and speak at conferences on current issues of theology. He has authored numerous articles and books including: *The Doctrine of the Trinity: Christianity's Self-Inflicted Wound, Jesus was not a Trinitarian, Our Fathers Who Aren't in Heaven, The Law, Sabbath and New Covenant Christianity, The Coming Kingdom of God: A Solution to the Riddle of the New Testament, The Amazing Aims and Claims of Jesus, Who is Jesus? A Plea for a Return to Belief in Jesus the Messiah* and *What Happens When We Die?* Many of these titles are available on Amazon.com. Sir Anthony's books and *Focus on the Kingdom* radio tapes may be fully examined at www.restorationfellowship.org.

Anthony was knighted by Queen Elizabeth. He has been nominated for the prestigious Templeton Award. In 2009 he received an honorary Ph.D. from the Korean Association of Bible Colleges.

                     Rex Cain contributed to this entry.
   See Appendix 23– Resurrection
Bibliography: Buzzard, Anthony. Email January 25, 2011; Cain, Rex, Email April 2, 2011.

C

Cain, Grace
b. July 23, 1939
d. June 7, 1977

Grace Ratering was born in Grand Rapids, Michigan, to Alvin and Lucille Ratering. Lucille had a voice like an angel, and Grace grew up singing as well as or better than her mother. Grace's soprano was clear and vibrant. She sang solos or blended with duets or trios. Watching her sing was a joy as she exuded love for Jesus and her music. From Grace's youth until her untimely death she was known throughout the Church of God as a woman of great Christian character and faith.

Alvin and Lucille Ratering

Grace attended Oregon Bible College, and met her future husband there. She wed Rex Cain on June 4, 1960. He said, "She told me when she was a small child playing with dolls that she always pretended that the male doll was a pastor and the female doll was the minister's wife. That was her dream, to be a minister's wife." The Cains had three children, Laura, Alan and Mark. Rex and Grace served four churches during their married life: Morse Mill, Missouri; Bedford, Ohio; Dayton, Ohio; and Macomb, Illinois.

In Macomb, Grace worked with Dale Ramsey, Oregon Bible College's music instructor, to produce an album of Christian music. A talent scout told Grace in high school that she should pursue a musical career because she had the talent for it, but she wanted to sing for the Lord.

Oregon Bible College classmates of 1960. Grace is standing, third from the left.

In 1977, her dream of completing a solo album slipped away when she died from cancer. She had fought for over five years to overcome the disease but could not win the battle. As a result, some of her music from that never-cut album was included on the 1978 Oregon Bible College Chorale Album and it was dedicated to her.

Rex distributed a tape of some of her favorite songs as a "thank you" to everyone who wrote to him after her death. He said, "Her music touched those who heard her. Her family, her church, her friends, and all those who knew her will not forget the way God moved through her music." Rex entitled the tribute tape "Grace Still Sings in Our Hearts." In 2008, Grace's concert tape was provided to producers of the Church of God Internet radio broadcast, cogcast.org. Grace sings again through MP3 technology, and now the whole world listens.

Grace was interred in Forest Lawn Memory Gardens in Macomb, Illinois. The monument includes the inscription "The dead in Christ shall rise first" (I Thessalonians 4:16).

Bibliography: Ancestry.com Social Security Death Index record for Grace Cain; ABC Biography project from material furnished by Rex Cain, David Krogh, compiler; JStilson, Memories of Grace Ratering Cain; Cain, Grace, Concert tape, Cogcast.org retrieved June 2008.

Cain, Rex
b. July 23, 1938

Rex was born in Kentucky to Lyle and Thelma Cain, but when only a few months old, his family moved to Springfield, Ohio, where he was raised. His parents settled about one mile south of the Lawrenceville Church of God and so, just by geography, he came into the Church of God. He believes it was God's providence.

The late Pastor Richard Smith looked after Rex during his teen years because Rex's homelife was difficult with parents who fought and finally divorced. Indeed the whole church helped care for him, and he said:

> That is no doubt why I am today a Christian. I don't recall consciously thinking about baptism but Richard must have touched me regarding it, because one Sunday in February 1956 I stepped forward to accept Christ. I was baptized in a cow's tank in the church basement before the church built a baptistery.

Rex wrote, "Like so many things in my life it seems God just worked in my life even when I don't consciously recall seeking God's guidance. In my teen years, I wasn't a praying teenager! I was a typical teenager!"

As an example of God's watch care, God changed Rex's mind. As Rex got into the car, planning to go downtown one day to sign up for the Air Force, his stepfather yelled from the house that Richard Smith wanted to see him right away. So, Rex drove right past the recruiting station and out to Richard's home ... and his life was changed. Pastor Smith said Rex needed to try Oregon Bible College for a semester. He did, and he stayed, graduated and entered the ministry where he has been preaching for 50 years! Rex recalls, "I missed going into the military by only seconds – God watching out for me? I give praise to God that Richard was there when I needed him."

While at Oregon Bible College, Rex met Grace Ratering, and they wed on June 4, 1960, at the Grand Rapids, Michigan, Pennellwood Church of God. The late Pastor Milon Hall officiated, assisted by Alva Huffer who currently lives in South Carolina. Grace and Rex had three children: Laura (Shane Varnadore), Alan (Susan Lee) and Mark (Karen Crowcroft). Sadly, Grace died of cancer June 7, 1977, while they were pastoring in Macomb Illinois.

In April of 1978, God led Sharon Guiles—a dedicated Christian woman from East Lansing, Michigan—into Rex's life. Clarence Lapp was a key figure in introducing Rex and Sharon. Their courtship was short, and they married in August 1978. Rex said, "Sometimes, God leads clearly and you just know this was meant to be. God has been so good to me! Sharon and I have two children: Sarah (Sam An) and Daniel (Rachel Cunningham)."

Rex continued:

> As a diversion through the years I've enjoyed photography, motorcycle riding, traveling and reading. This says nothing of enjoying my family including numerous grandchildren–the greatest joy of life outside of the glorious hope of immortality thanks to the vicarious death of the Lamb of God!
>
> These are the churches I have pastored: Morse Mill, Missouri (1961-1964); Bedford, Ohio (1964-1969); Dayton, Ohio (1969-1976); Macomb, Illinois (1976-1991); Bedford, Ohio (1992-2011).
>
> As for any advice to a young pastor, I would say, never give up! My first 2 years in ministry were the worst in my 50 years. A stump in the nearby woods was a close friend of mine where I went alone to sit and talk with God often. I almost quit ministry several times. But finally, it all came together and I proceeded for the next 48 years with God beside me. If I'd had internet then, it might have been easier with the pastoral support we can get daily. But then, I felt very alone in the foothills of the Ozarks!
>
> My greatest joy in ministry was to see people turn their lives over to Christ. The greatest sorrow was to see them turn and walk away. But, I kept in mind that we are commanded to sow the seed and God will give the increase.

Rex and Sharon plan to retire in July 2011; they have purchased a home near Lawrenceville, Ohio, Rex's hometown. Rex plans to continue in ministry (at a slower pace), working with son Alan, the pastor there.

See Huffer, Alva
Lapp, C.E.
Smith, E. Richard

Bibliography: For ABC biography project, Cain, Rex. E-mail, March 9, 2011.

Carpentar, Benjamin
b. September 11, 1888
d. February 1979

Carpentar, Alice Andrew
b. August 30, 1881
d. September 5, 1971

Ben and Alice on their wedding day.

Benjamin Carpentar grew up in Kentucky. He was a member of the Church of God Abrahamic Faith at Perryville. In 1910, he traveled to Oregon, Illinois, to attend Summer Bible School sponsored by S.J. Lindsay at the Church of God. Benjamin remained in Oregon, residing with the Nicholas Andrew family, and took a job at the Schiller Piano Factory. He met Alice Andrew when she came to visit her cousins. She was a member of the Paynes Point Methodist Church at that time. When they became interested in each other, Ben taught her about the Church of God. He returned to Perryville but couldn't forget Alice. He returned to Oregon, and they were married in December 1911.

After the wedding they began farming and raised three girls: Margaret "Peggy" Lois (Greenfield) Cline, Genniel (Anderson) and Rosalie (Weyrauch). The sisters were members of the Flagg Center Church of God.

Ben did a little preaching in his youth. Records show he preached at the Dixon Church of God in 1919. For this occasion his father, J.F. Carpentar, and his sister, Quincy, visited Dixon with him. They resided in Brumfield, Kentucky. This was a small representation of the family of eight brothers. As part of their remarks to the congregation, the Carpentars requested the congregation visit Kentucky and worship with them.

Alice was a great-niece of A.J. Eychaner, noted evangelist in the Church of God. She grew up in Pine Rock Township. As a young woman, she attended the Art Institute in Chicago where noted sculptor Lorado Taft was her teacher. He created the Black Hawk statue at Oregon. During summers, Taft and his friends resided at Oregon at the Eagle's Nest Art Camp. Alice specialized in painting and sculpture. She was equally capable in producing portraits or landscapes. Her portraits of F.L. Austin and Sydney Magaw were donated to the Church of God General Conference and are on exhibit in the Archives in McDonough, Georgia. A painting by Alice of the Old Stone Church of God at Oregon was donated to the Ogle County Historical Society. Alice's brother, Charles E. Andrew, was also a talented artist by nature and an engineer by career. Charles was the project engineer for construction of the Oakland Bay Bridge. This structure was named the seventh Engineering Wonder of the World in 1956.

In the mid-1960s Alice painted a nativity scene on plywood which was lovingly and carefully cut out by Ben. It was used at the Oregon Church of God for many years during the Christmas season. The nativity figures of both humans and animals are nearly life-sized and their expressions evoke the feelings of surprise, awe and reverence that those around the manger must have felt at the birth of Jesus. The art has a compelling quality that it so life-like it seems that one can see their eyes blink and hear the animals shuffling in the straw.

Alice Carpentar

The nativity scene has 15 separate pieces. Originally stored in the church at Oregon, it was moved when more space was needed. Later it was returned to Genniel's farm for storage and, more recently, was temporarily moved to the Flagg Center Church of God where it has been displayed several Christmas seasons.

Ben was known for his beautiful clear-toned tenor voice. He excelled on any choir number with difficult and intricate tenor passages. Ben could sing anything, and a look of joy shone from his face as he sang. One could never forget the choir rendition of "Walk Around Zion," in which he joined and led out in sweet and clear solos.

In addition to choir work, Ben served for years as elder at Oregon. When he was too old to attend meetings regularly, the board voted to retain him as an honorary elder with a lifetime appointment.

Alice died first and was laid to rest at the Mt. Pleasant Cemetery at Paynes Point, Illinois. Ben died several years later and rests beside her. They are just down the road from their beloved farm.

See Carpentar, Quincy
     Eychaner, A.J.

Bibliography: Ancestry.com Social Security Master Death List, Record for Benjamin Carpentar; Cline, Lois. (Margaret) Interview with Jan Stilson, Christmas Eve Day at Flagg Church of God observing the beauty of the Nativity Scene, 2006; Weyrauch, Rosalie and Mary, Letter, April 12, 2006; *The Restitution Herald*, November 11, 1919; June 24, 1920.

Carpentar, Quincy
b. 1891
d. February 14, 1967

Quincy Carpentar lived at Brumfield, Kentucky. She was Benjamin Carpentar's sister and a member of the Church of God Abrahamic Faith. In 1923, Quincy's name appeared several times in *The Restitution Herald* as she submitted reports about church activities, documenting J.H. Anderson's travels to preach and minister in Kentucky. Anderson preached a circuit from Indiana through North and South Carolina and Virginia.

Over the years Quincy and several of her brothers visited Ben and family in Oregon, Illinois. Even today, Quincy's church continues meeting in Perryville, Kentucky, and Carpentar family members attend.

See Anderson, J.H. (19th)
     Carpentar, Benjamin

Bibliography: *The Restitution Herald,* Nov. 23, 1923; Dec. 4, 1923; Cline, Lois. Interview with Jan Stilson, Spring 2007; Weyrauch, Rosalie and Mary, Letter, April 12, 2006.

Claussen, Frederick Mennen
b. June 9, 1906
d. March 24, 1991

Claussen, (Yula) Myrle Hatten
b. September 2, 1908
d. July 12, 1989

Frederick Mennen Claussen was born to Siebolt and Nettie (Jansen) Claussen in White Rock Township, Illinois. Fred grew up on a farm just east of Oregon, Illinois. He noticed on Sunday mornings his neighbor, Ben Carpentar, crossed the old wooden bridge by Claussen's house. Fred got curious about where Ben and his family went every Sunday morning, so one week he followed Ben's car into Oregon. Of course, Ben went to the Oregon Church of God. Fred also knew Paul and Arthur Johnson who attended there. From then on, Fred attended services each week at the church.

Myrle Hatten was born to Dominicus and Minnie Rosabelle Hatten near Burr Oak, Indiana. Myrle was an identical twin to Mrs. Pearl (John) Bloom. C.E. Lapp married Pearl and John.

Before she turned 20, Myrle moved to Oregon, Illinois, to work in the Golden Rule Home. She met Frederick at the Oregon Church of God. F.L. Austin wed the couple on July 27, 1930. At the time of their wedding, Fred worked in the print shop of *The Restitution Herald*. In his later years, he worked as a pressman at Kable in Mt. Morris, Illinois. Fred and Myrle raised four daughters, Barbara (George) Scott, Rockford, Illinois; Betty (Peter) Halpin, Novato, California; Donna (Loyd) Cooper, Farmington, Missouri; and Diane McCormick, Shabbona, Illinois.

The Claussens were very active in the Church of God. Over the years Fred served as a deacon, a trustee and an elder. Since he was deaf he installed hearing aid devices in a number of the churches they attended, including the one at Fredericktown, Missouri. Fred never preached or sang in the choir, but he did almost everything else.

Myrle taught Sunday and Bible school classes at Oregon, and later at the Blessed Hope Church of God in Rockford. When the children were young, if one were sick, Fred would stay home with her while Myrle taught Sunday school, and then Myrle would return home so Fred could usher at church while Myrle taught the Sunday school lesson to the sick child. In this way, none of them ever missed a Sunday school lesson.

The Claussens regularly attended Illinois Church and General Conferences held across the United States. They also attended Indiana Conferences at North Salem where Myrle served as a cook and teacher. Many pastors stayed in the Claussen home during minister and general conferences in Oregon.

In their senior years, Fred and Myrle joined Flagg Center Church of God. Myrle died in 1989, Frederick two years later. Gordon Landry officiated both funerals. Prior to their deaths, Myrle gave Pastor Landry a list of scriptures to include in their services. They wanted people to hear the scriptures they held so dear. Ecclesiastes 9:10 and I Thessalonians 4:16-18 were some of those verses. They rest in the Ebenezer Cemetery east of Oregon.

 See Austin, F.L.
    Carpentar, Benjamin
    Johnson, Paul C.
    Lapp, C.E.

Bibliography: The Claussen biography was submitted by Donna Cooper, Sept. 18, 2009.

Cooper, Gerald Leigh
b. July 27, 1912
d. October 1979

Gerald "Gerry" Cooper was the third of four children born in Ripley, Illinois, to John W. and Lillie May Myrtilia O'Neal Cooper. He attended the Bible Training Class at Oregon from 1929 to 1931 and, years later, reported some of the problems and antics of the students at the BTC in *The Restitution Herald*. The following excerpts are from Gerry's letter during the Camp Mack days of the 1970s:

> Did you ever hear of Cooper Hall? Or, the "Beanery"? You won't be able to locate either for the present for they were names given to the old Illinois Conference Building, which was at the rear of the Oregon church building and which was torn down seven or eight years ago. The "Cooper Hall" name came about because my mother and two sisters came from Ripley to Oregon to cook and keep house for me and five other fellows attending "Bible Training School" during the 1930-31 term. When a telephone was installed "Cooper Hall" became the listing in the directory. The name "The Beanery" followed shortly afterward because as our funds became less and less, we had to eat more beans, and it is the name that is remembered best by those of us who were there. We lived there throughout the seven month term, sometimes wondering if we might freeze, as the building had no insulation of any sort. At one time we had been using so much coal that a decision was made to try burning some wood. As I recall, one truck load of wood lasted only two or three days. Most of the fellows slept upstairs and used all the blankets that could be found. Yet, we never suffered.
>
> The Bible Training School had been a going concern for approximately ten years before my appearance. Classes were held in an upstairs room on the south side of the Restitution Herald building. Our teachers were Bro. F.L. Austin and Sr. Mary Gesin. Our subjects were The Bible, English, Memory Work, and Public Speaking. Classes were held only during morning hours, with afternoons free to work. Only there wasn't much [work].
>
> I was from four to six years younger than the other boys [there were two girls in school also, Lucille LeCrone (Appleby) and Edna Cooper (Hughes)], and even those fellows will admit a conspiracy that they agreed on—not to laugh at any of my jokes. I remember also throwing a pillow at one of the fellows. He dodged and a window was broken. Only a moment before I had told my mother, "You can't break a window with a pillow."
>
> We did many of the things that OBC students do. We assisted with a religious survey of Ogle County, attended Sunday School conventions and other church services, and presented an amateur (VERY amateur) program at least once in a country school house.

Another of Gerry's colorful stories of an Illinois blizzard and what happens when a "gospel team" is caught in it:

Perhaps we were the first to go on a "gospel tour" as a group, an event which is very common at present. It started out on a Thursday morning in early March 1931, as a long weekend, with one carload leaving then, and another to follow on Friday. The destination was Ripley, Ill., and the purpose was to present sermons, musical numbers, etc., from Thursday to Sunday. After the first meeting, it started to snow, but stopped enough that the second car arrived safely and the Friday evening service was held. Then it started to snow again, and never stopped until late Sunday afternoon, the worst blizzard in years. The highways were completely blocked for miles around, but the telephone wires kept intact. Well, Ripley and the vicinity was never the same again. We were scattered about, in six or seven homes, and the only contact we had was by phone. Finally some good local politicians phoned the Governor of Illinois and on Tuesday the highways were finally opened. We had church services on Tuesday and Wednesday evenings, and literally raced back to Oregon. As we (headed north) the accumulation became less and less, until a few miles north of Kewanee there was none at all. People in Oregon were wondering why we were four days late in getting back and found it difficult to believe the "blizzard" tale of woe.

Harvey U. Krogh Jr., Clarence Lapp, John Denchfield, Richard LeCrone and Cecil Smead participated in the gospel team.

Gerry had a sense of humor, and once joked to the students about a man who got a haircut without taking off his hat. No one laughed at this joke (by prior agreement), so he had to explain it. The haircut was the length and shape of his hat.

About those long-ago days, Gerry recounted:
A little over a month later, "The Beanery" days came to an end. Some of us returned that fall for the 1931-32 term. I left at Thanksgiving planning to return when finances became more plentiful. But I never made it. The General Conference finances were no better than mine and in April 1932, the Bible Training School came to its end. When a school to train ministers was opened in September, 1939, it was known as Oregon Bible College, and I was in a sanatorium in Minnesota. Somewhere in my apartment I have a sliver of wood from the Illinois Conference building brought to me by Dr. Alva Huffer at the time it was torn down. This is all I have left of the physical part of "The Beanery" but the memories and recollections are far more than a mere "sliver of wood."

A thin man, Gerry battled illness much of his life. During his pastorate at the Church of God at Tempe, Arizona, he took a leave of absence and entered Good Samaritan hospital for lung surgery. After several months he moved to a local sanatorium to complete his recuperation. His preaching work was necessarily restricted thereafter due to his frail condition.

Gerry participated in Illinois and General Conference business as often as possible. He preached occasionally. He loved a good story and a hearty laugh. He never married, but he was beloved by all who knew him. He is interred in the Ripley Cemetery with his family.

See Huffer, Alva
Krogh, Harvey U., Jr.
Lapp, C.E.
Smead, Cecil
Denchfield, John

Bibliography: Ancestry.com U.S. Census. Illinois. Brown. Ripley. Dist. 9. 1920; Social Security Master Death List Record for Gerald Cooper; Cooper, Gerald. "Letter to *The Restitution Herald*," this material was donated for use by relative, Helen Jones. December 2006; *The Restitution Herald*, Feb. 3, 1948; June 15, 1948; Smead, Cecil. Letters from the Smead collection, furnished by John Smead, Summer, 2008.

Cooper, John Wesley
b. July 20, 1874
d. August 18, 1953

John Wesley Cooper was one of six children born to Philander and Mary (Robbins) Cooper in Cooperstown, Brown County, Illinois. Mary's parents, the Robbins, were among the founding families of the Ripley Church of God; they helped organize it as an Adventist fellowship in 1867. In fact, when John Cooper was born the church had existed for seven years. As a young man, John moved to Ripley. He farmed and did carpentry to support his family.

Cooper family documents supplied by Helen Jones, J.W. Cooper's descendent, tell the story of early settlers. In those days, the Sauk and Fox Indians roamed the Brown County area. One account said that war chief Black Hawk sent braves from their village at Saukenuk near Moline, Illinois, to assist a white settler with building his log cabin. This was before the Black Hawk War of 1832. This is an amazing account, for popular opinion has been that Black Hawk, famed for his aggressive nature, was never friendly toward new settlers and always itched for war. The Cooper family record proves he was friendly enough to help with several days of construction.

J.W. Cooper loved the Gospel message. Though not a founding member of the Ripley Adventist church, he was a leader of it. In the early days at Ripley, believers who favored Age-to-Come ideas met with Adventists. The Age-to-Come believers separated from the Adventists, but they did not have a building for worship. They met on occasion in the Christian Church in Ripley, and later built a wood frame building in the lower part of town. In 1883, this building was moved from the south side of Route 24 to its present location on the hill north of the highway.

A remarkable aspect of the church's interior architecture is the arched ceiling in the original sanctuary.

The story is told that the arch in the ceiling beams occurred naturally in the tree milled specifically for the ceiling. This style of arch replicates the proscenium arches of the canal bridges in Venice and is considered one of the most beautiful curves of architecture.

L.E. Conner baptized John and his wife Myrtilla in March 1902. Eventually John operated a grocery business in Ripley and listed his occupation as "Salesman, Retail trade" in the 1910 census. The editor of *The Restitution Herald* said, "His sunny disposition and upright methods would help him build a good business." The Illinois State Conference licensed elder Cooper to preach in the Church of God in 1911.

In bad weather, Elder John took his family to church early to "stoke the fires." They would wait, and if the weather was too bad, or if the farmers had to make hay and no one came, they'd go home. The congregation hoped that by hiring a regular pastor, people would attend more regularly and be faithful in meeting their pledges. The congregation voted to hire C.E. Lapp, a recent graduate of the Bible Training School at Oregon, Illinois.

During Clarence Lapp's ministry, John Cooper's grandchildren were baptized. John's daughter Mary Josephine had married Loren L. Burnett on Feb. 19, 1916, and they had five children, Marjorie (Bolhous), Francis, Helen (Jones), Harold and Lozell. Marge, Francis and Helen attended Oregon Bible College, and Francis Burnett became one of the leading pastors in the Church of God.

The minute book from Ripley offers a telling insight into the question of church finances. In those days, the offering plate was not passed during the service. Offerings were free will, but they were based on pledges. The funds could be privately deposited in a box at the back of the sanctuary or handed to the pastor. On the occasion noted in the minutes, the church was experiencing severe financial difficulties. People didn't know what to do. "Bro. Howell gave a talk on the taking of a collection, in order to give members who cannot pledge a chance to give to the church work." A motion was made that a collection be taken once a month. The motion lost and pledges were taken. Months later, J.W. Cooper made the same suggestion to the congregation. Wayne Laning remembered that after Cooper's pep talk, someone said, "Guess we'd better pass the plate." The Ripley people have always been a problem-solving congregation, and sometimes they just had to "pass the plate."

The Ripley women made apple butter as a church fund-raising activity. Helen Lewis described the work involved. They all gathered at the Laning farm. The men carried the apples and iron pot, stoked the fire, kept things moving and ran errands. The women peeled apples and added them to the large iron pot heated over an open fire. Everyone continued to peel apples. They cooked them, mashed them and added spices, cooking it down to a thick butter just right for biscuits. They stirred the thick mixture to prevent scorching

The butter was canned in two-quart jars and sold for the church's benefit. They also donated it to the Illinois Conference for conference meals and to Oregon Bible College for dormitory meals. Making apple butter was hard work, but the whole congregation joined in and many hands made the work lighter.

John Wesley Cooper greatly influenced the Ripley Church of God and his children. Son Gerald attended the Bible Training Class in Oregon, Illinois, and went on to preach for many years in spite of poor health. The other son, Wes, was a staunch supporter of the local work.

Helen Jones contributed to this entry.

See Burnett, Francis
   Cooper, Gerald
   Lapp, C.E.
   Wilson, Benjamin (19th)

Bibliography: Ancestry.com U.S. Federal; Cooperstown, Brown Co. Dist 35; 1880; and Brown Co. Ripley Township. 1910; Bolhous, Steve, Interview of Memories of Family at Ripley, Spring 2005 and 2006; Burnett, Francis, Interview with Jan Stilson and Helen Jones, December 2006; Jones, Helen, Interview and documents furnished from family records. Dec. 2006; and May 2007; Lewis, Helen. Interview at Ripley Il., Conference by JStilson about 1985; *The Restitution Herald*. Oct. 13, 1915; March 1, 1916. "John Wesley Cooper," ABC Biography Project, David Krogh compiler.

Coulter, William
b. May 17, 1898
d. July 13, 1986

Coulter, Madge
b. January 31, 1902
d. November 15, 1968

William and Madge Coulter attended Eden Valley Church of God. Elder James A. Patrick baptized them in their youth. Elder E.E. Thoms married them in October 1920. They had five children, Walter, Fern, Wilber, Margaret Norman and Marion Manuel. Bill and Madge held various offices in church and Sunday school.

Bill purchased land for the Minnesota Long Lake Bible Camp and helped construct the original buildings. Bill and Madge remained active members all their lives.

See Thoms, E.E. (19th)
   Patrick, James A. (19th)

Bibliography: ABC Biography project, David Krogh, compiler.

Courtney, (Chas M.?)

b. 1895
d. Unknown

Elder Courtney and Almus Adams were co-workers. Courtney and wife Abbie resided in Kearney, Nebraska, where he managed a creamery station. Courtney, Clyde Anderson and Mrs. Harvey Krogh of Blair, Nebraska, worked together to raise funds for a new meeting tent. Courtney solicited donations through a letter to brethren published in *The Restitution*. Mrs. Krogh received the money. They purchased the tent and shipped it to Gifford, Iowa, Adam's boyhood home. For seating, it was outfitted with benches from a merchant's hall; people filled the tent each evening.

The tent became an evangelism tool for the Iowa and Nebraska state conferences. It was packed when the camp meetings concluded, loaded onto the train and shipped to the next destination. Another crew unpacked and set it up. By the time it was ready, the evangelist had arrived for the meeting in the new location.

See Adams, Almus (19th)

Bibliography: Ancestry.com U.S. Census. Nebraska. Buffalo. Kearney. 1920; *The Restitution*, Dec. 1922.

Coverstone, Perry Garnett

b. August 11, 1900
d. March 28, 1986

Perry Garnett Coverstone was born to J. Edward and Ida Coverstone. Garnett joined Fort Valley Church of God in Christ Jesus when J.H. Anderson baptized him on June 17, 1916. That same day, Garnett's sister (Mary) Catherine was baptized in Dry Run Creek. She had moved away from the valley to McKee Rocks, Pennsylvania, and returned to Fort Valley, Virginia, for meetings.

Garnett married Mary Margaret Burke on July 1, 1922. Mary died on September 21, 1938. they had one child, Reba Marie Harper, of Omaha, Nebraska. On April 15, 1942, Garnett married Alva Virginia Shiley; they had three children, Robert Glenn, Fort Valley; JoAnn Painter, Toms Brook, Virginia; and John Harvey, Fort Valley.

Garnett was the backbone of the Church of God in Fort Valley. He believed the truth and raised two families on it. Garnett served in many capacities. He could talk to people, teach class, sing in the choir, build a church and maintain a farm to earn his income. When the farm didn't produce due to drought, Garnett took money from his savings to donate to the church so the pastor could be paid. Garnett had great dedication. He died at age 85.

His obituary recorded:
> He served the Fort Valley congregation in many ways, including Sunday School Superintendent, and strove to share the love of God to those around him by his kind deeds, words of wisdom, and acts of generosity.

His love for God and people will be remembered and cherished by all whose lives he touched.

Fort Valley Church of God prior to the addition of the fellowship hall across the back. The Massanutten Mountains are in the background. Garnett Coverstone served as elder, teacher and charter member of this church.

Bibliography: Ancestry.com. U.S. Census. Virginia. Shenandoah. Johnston. Dist. 90. 1910; *The Restitution Herald*, June 21, 1916; Coverstone family for the Atlanta Bible College Biography Project, David Krogh, compiler.

D

Daubanton (Dubestein), Fred J.
b. July 1873
d. 1951

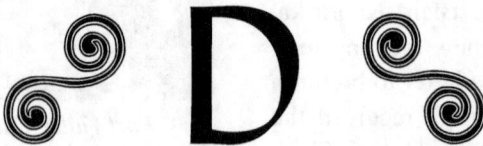

Fred Daubanton was born near St. Cloud, Minnesota, to German immigrants. In 1886, he went to work for the St. Paul, Minnesota and Manitoba Railway. He was promoted to engineer in 1897. The 1900 US Census lists him as a "Ry Engineer."

Fred met someone from the Adventist/Age-to-Come persuasion, and when he heard about it, he believed it. Elder E.E. Thoms baptized him in March 1916. Fred began preaching for the Church of God Minnesota Conference. Fred and T.M. Savage assisted E.E. Thoms at St. Cloud. After Elder Thoms died, Fred Daubanton became the pastor and supervised the church building renovation in 1920.

Fred Daubanton represents the many dedicated servants of the Lord who worked to advance One Faith west of the Mississippi. Additional information about Fred is sketchy, but the newly organized Church of God General Conference recognized him to preach in October 1925. He is mentioned in *The Restitution Herald* as the officiating pastor at little Vivian Savage's funeral about that same time.

   See Thoms, E.E. (19th)
       Savage, T.M.

Bibliography: Ancestry.com U.S. Census. Minnesota. Stearns. Melrose. Dist. 169. 1900; Minnesota. McLeod. Hutchinson. Dist. 91. 1920; Social Security Master Death List has a record for Joseph F. Daubanton of Kanabec, Mn; "Vivian Savage Obituary" *The Restitution Herald*, October, 1925; *History of the Minnesota Church of God Conference.* Sydney Magaw, ed., 1931; See, Sara. E-mail July 30, 2009.

Denchfield, John
b. March 18, 1909
d. August 18, 1996

John Denchfield was born at Thief River Falls, Minnesota, to Albert and Lizzie Denchfield who had three sons and three daughters. Elder Fred Daubanton baptized John, and he became a member of the Church of God in 1929. John married Cleora Randall who preceded him in death on July 28, 1990. They had four children, Darlene, Doris, Roger and Dallas (d. March 5, 1960).

John attended the Church of God Bible Training School at Oregon, Illinois, from 1929-1931. He was the first student from Minnesota to do so. Following his ministerial training, he became pastor of his home church, St. Cloud, Minnesota, Church of God, and later of the Southlawn Church of God at Wyoming, Michigan. After Roddy Pike left the newly established missionary work in Digby, Nova Scotia, John and Cleora accepted the call to that ministry. It was while they lived at Digby that Dallas was killed in an auto accident. Dallas was a student at Oregon Bible College when he died.

Pike, first pastor at Digby

John served the Southlawn Church of God at the same time C.E. Lapp served at Pennellwood. Cecil Smead, a classmate of Lapp and Denchfield at Bible Training Class, lived in Midland, Michigan, and worked at Dow Chemical. Smead filled pulpits as needed. The three men assisted the work in Michigan while the congregation at Pennellwood built a new church building in 1947. During the 1970s John served as the evangelist

Lighthouse Mission Church, Digby, Nova Scotia

for the Illinois Conference of the Churches of God.

After Cleora's death, John married Helen Brown, widow of Pastor Leonard Brown. John died at age 88 with his family surrounding him. Richard Alcumbrack, Roger Denchfield and David Krogh conducted the funeral services at Southlawn, and he was laid to rest beside Cleora and Dallas.

See Brown, Leonard
Lapp, C.E.
Smead, Cecil

Bibliography: Ancestry.com. U.S. Census. Minnesota. Stearns. St. Cloud. Dist. 53, 1930; Social Security Master Death List, Records of John and Cleora Denchfield; Biography Project of Atlanta Bible College, David Krogh, compiler; *The Restitution Herald*, Sydney Magaw, ed., Oregon, Il., Oct. 21, 1947; Smead, Cecil. Letter to Marjorie Overmeyer, June 2, 1970 furnished by John Smead; *History of the Minnesota Church of God Conference*. Sydney Magaw, ed., June 1, 1931.

Dick, Otto E., Sr.
b. March 19, 1901
d. July 1, 1963

Otto E. Dick Sr. was born in Elwood, Indiana, to Joseph and Lulu Matt Dick. Otto had a brother, Ray, and three sisters, Zora, Mabel and Maude. Otto married Blanche Spurgeon, and they had four children, William, Richard, Betty and Otto Jr. They lived in Johnson township, Clinton County, Indiana, on the family farm, and Otto taught school. He was a lifetime member of the National Education Association.

Otto received his undergraduate education at Indiana State Teacher's College and, upon receiving his master's degree at Indiana University, he accepted the principal's position at Scircleville and Kempton, Indiana. He served in that position for 23 years.

Left to right: OBC President Otto Dick, Sydney Magaw and FL Austin

The Dick family joined the Hillisburg Church of God near Frankfort and lived in the same neighborhood as J.H. Anderson. In fact, in 1930 the two family names appear on the same page of the US Census.

When Otto was called to serve as professor at Oregon Bible College (OBC) in 1946, he sold the farm and moved to Oregon, Illinois. In 1949, he became the college's superintendent and served an additional 17 years. Later, that title was changed to President. During his tenure, the college moved from the campus outside of Oregon, which was purchased by the Maxson family to become a restaurant. The new college facility was located in downtown Oregon on North Third Street. Here students met for classes, attended chapel, used the library, worked in the print shop with Paul Johnson and participated in Christian services assignments. Otto Dick supervised the students in their Christian service, and taught Old and New Testament Survey, English, Preaching, Geology, Homiletics and other courses on demand. He was student council and senior class advisor.

Otto Dick had oversight of the OBC Student Council. Standing, left to right - James, Fyfe, Etta Marie Routson (Whetzel), Otto Dick, Becky Barnhill (Peterson), Robert Pike. Seated - Marylyn Holquist (Fyfe), Rex Cain, Russ Magaw, Janet Turner (Stilson).

Otto Dick wrote a series of articles for *The Restitution Herald* in 1948; they guided readers in becoming better Bible teachers. The teacher training articles contained principles of education that could be applied to Sunday school classes for children or adults and to Berean classes.

President Dick suffered ill health the last few years of his employment in Oregon. He sought treatment for a heart condition but died following surgery at St. Mary's Hospital in Rochester, Minnesota. It was a great and sad shock to the college's students and alumni and to the general Church of God membership. Otto never wrote a book, but he built a library. He never entered the mission field, but he trained ministers and missionaries.

William Wachtel, who succeeded Otto as Oregon Bible College President, wrote:

Alumni remember their years here as a time when their thinking and living were molded under the genial and patient guidance of one who was a Christian gentleman, a worthy counselor, and a devoted teacher. The brotherhood at large shared this conception of Otto E Dick, and their confidence in the purpose and program of Oregon Bible College rested in large measure upon their confidence in his leadership.

William Wachtel, Harold Doan and Clyde Randall conducted Otto Dick's funeral service. A few years later, Blanche died and was buried beside Otto at Daysville Cemetery near Oregon, Illinois.

See Anderson, J.H. (19th)
Dick, Richard
Dick, William
Doan, Harold
Wachtel, William

Bibliography: Ancestry.com. U.S. Census. Indiana. Clinton. Johnson. Dist. 11. 1930; *The Restitution Herald*, Jan. 13, 1948; May 31, 1949; July 26, 1949; Wachtel, William, Foreword to OBC Catalog, 1964. Obituary, *Hammond, Louisiana News*, July 4, 1963; Obituary, *Dixon Evening Telegraph*, July 4, 1963.

Dick, Richard S.
b. April 12, 1937
d. January 5, 2005

Richard Dick was one of four children born to Otto and Blanche Dick. He had two brothers, William and Otto Jr., and one sister, Betty, who predeceased them. Richard was born in Indiana, but the family moved to Oregon, Illinois, when his father took a position at Oregon Bible College (OBC). Richard graduated from Oregon High School in 1954 and attended Bible college that fall. He graduated from OBC and went into the pastoral ministry in Front Royal, Virginia, at the Cool Springs Church of God. He also served at Blood River, Louisiana.

Richard was gifted with a pure and sweet tenor voice. In college, he sang with the choir and in several ensemble groups. He traveled extensively on gospel teams because his voice lent so much to the worship service, and he often served as worship leader. He was also a skillful trumpet player. Hearing him perform was always a blessing.

He left the ministry for personal reasons and settled in Arizona, eventually moving to southern Ohio. When he left the ministry, it was a great loss.

See Dick, Otto E., Sr.
Dick, William

Bibliography: Ancestry.com Social Security Master Death List, record for Richard S. Dick; Oregon Church of God History. 1978; ABC Biography Project, David Krogh, compiler.

Dick, William J.
b. July 15, 1929
d. October 29, 2007

"Billy Joe" Dick was born in Indiana to Otto and Blanche Dick. He was the eldest of four children. The family moved to Oregon when Otto assumed a teaching position at Oregon Bible College. William graduated from Oregon High School, and then Oregon Bible College in 1951. He entered the ministry at Pomona, California, soon after. He did not remain in the ministry but continued to reside in the west.

See Dick, Otto E., Sr.
Dick, Richard

Bibliography: Ancestry.com Social Security Master Death List, William J. Dick record; ABC/OBC Alumni Newsletter, David Krogh, compiler February 4, 2008.

Doan, Harold John
b. June 1, 1924
d. January 28, 1983

Harold Doan was born in Kent, Michigan, to Lyle and Martha Lafler Doan. He was the eldest of three sons. Lyle and Martha were Michigan Church of God leaders, and raised Harold in a Christian environment. Martha was a wonderful soloist, and often visited Churches of God to give special programs.

After high school, Harold moved to Oregon, Illinois, to attend Oregon Bible College, planning to enter the ministry. He married Bette Jean Lindsay. Jean was S.J. Lindsay's granddaughter. Jean was beautiful and musically talented. Harold and Jean had two sons, Chris and Greg; Greg predeceased his family.

Harold graduated Oregon Bible College and assumed the pastorate of the church in Chicago. While there, he became the Church of God's radio evangelist. He hosted a radio program, "Truth Seeker's Bible Class," over WAIT every Sunday morning. It debuted on March 21, 1948. The station was so powerful it reached people all over the Midwest. For several of the early programs, guest speakers and guest musicians were featured. Pastor Sydney Magaw, editor of *The Restitution Herald* in Oregon, Illinois, was the first speaker. Eventually Harold broadcast the majority of the fifteen-minute programs.

In *The Restitution Herald* Harold reported the radio broadcasts were well received by the listening public. Many listeners sent letters with questions. To the General

Conference the positive response from listeners was good news; it had been searching for new methods of evangelism.

The program format generally featured introduction and announcements, followed by ten to twelve minutes of preaching. Sometimes there was "live" music, but all programs were pre-recorded. By "live" it is meant that musicians and preachers came to the studio to record the program. For each program, the radio station cut a 16" vinyl record using a diamond needle. These masters could only be played on a unique commercial turntable used by radio stations at that time. The records ran at an especially slow speed, 16 rpm, or half the speed of standard 33-1/3 long playing albums that became popular in the 1950s. The WAIT records are preserved in the Archives of the General Conference in McDonough, Georgia. Cogcast Internet radio plans to transfer the vinyl recordings to MP3 format so once again they can be broadcast to the world.

While Doan was pastor of the Chicago church, the congregation bought a storefront building on West Division Street and renovated it into sanctuary and classrooms. This congregation was the remnant of the congregation that worshipped in Chicago from the days of the Wilsons. Leaders of this group at the time Harold served included Robert and Jean Hall, Margaret "Peg" Duvall and Ruth Wachtel and son William, who was brought into the Chicago Church of God through the ministry of Harold and Jean Doan. Students from Oregon Bible College often attended worship services as part of Christian service preaching assignments. College musicians also helped.

In 1954, Harold and Jean moved to Oregon, Illinois, where he became the executive secretary of the Church of God General Conference; he held the position until 1968. His administration was noted for growth. For 16 years almost steady growth was evident in the number of foreign missions; the number of titles published; an increase in Oregon Bible College's student population and the size of the campus; growth in the youth education and camping programs; increased emphasis in Sunday school development and growth; and steady improvement in pastoral enrichment and church development throughout the Church of God.

The Decade of Development set the pace for ten years of unparalleled activity throughout various ministry departments from 1955-1965. During this time the mission fields of Nova Scotia, Lebanon, Philippine Islands, South Africa, India and Mexico were developed under the supervision of Rachel Krogh (Carr) and Stanley O. Ross, Superintendents of Missions. Contacts came in from Peru and Nigeria. People began to travel for short term mission trips to assist in foreign ministry. First, Harold Doan traveled to the Philippine Islands in 1961. Stanley O. Ross and Merle Patrick made a trip to the islands and around the world in 1966. During this time, Dean Moore moved to Mexico to train and assist Roberto and Lupe Badillo in establishing a work in Labor Vieja, Mexico. Youth teams began making short-term mission trips to Mexico. There were increased inquiries from around the world including England, Australia and New Zealand.

During this time student numbers and graduation numbers increased and pulpits were filled as graduates left Oregon, Illinois, to take up pastorates. In the publishing arena, *The Restitution Herald* became a free publication and went to all parts of the world as a missionary tool. Multiple copies were sent to members who distributed them to libraries, physicians' offices and places of business. *The Progress Journal* began as a separate publication to provide news of the churches to the members. *The Restitution Herald* became the means for spreading the Word. One issue was entitled, "Your Introduction to the Church of God." It was printed in large quantities so it could be distributed one house at a time to entire communities wherever a Church of God was located. A revised edition of *Songs of Truth* was published and distributed throughout member churches in 1963. With Verna Thayer's retirement the Sunday school curriculum for children, youth and adults was revised, and publication began on a seven-year rotation schedule. Copies of these materials are in the Archives at Atlanta Bible College.

Also during the Decade of Development, Pastor Alva Huffer authored *Systematic Theology* a book of Bible doctrines organized according to seven main areas of biblical study: Theology (God), Anthropology (Man), Harmartiology (Sin), Soteriology (Salvation), Christology (Christ), Ecclesiology (Church) and

Harold Doan
Executive Secretary of the General Conference

Eschatology (Prophecy). When *Systematic Theology* was first developed as a course at Oregon Bible College, students received their textbooks as mimeographed notebooks. The book was first published in hard cover and then paperback, and efforts were made by the Priscilla organization to put it into every library in the world. Through this effort, many people became acquainted with the truths of the Bible, and contacts were made that are still bearing fruit today.

A *Systematic Theology* correspondence course has been printed; it remains a popular course at conference headquarters in McDonough, Georgia. At the 2008 Minister's Conference, David Krogh reported the *Systematic Theology Correspondence Course* has had global impact as inquiries continue from the far reaches of the world. Students are now able to complete lessons for *Systematic Theology* over the Internet.

General Conference Building,
110 N. Third Street, Oregon, Illinois

During the Doan administration, the Gospelettes, a ladies trio from Oregon Bible College, toured America in 1961 visiting over 30 churches and camps, completing the summer tour with the production of a gospel music album. This was well-received by the members, and set the precedent for other performers to produce albums and tapes, including Lee McQuinn, The Boyers in Virginia, Oregon Bible College Chorale and many more.

Harold Doan's administration along with the vision of several members of the Board of Directors accounted for the Church of God's growth during the 20th century. With the emphasis in evangelism, churches experienced growth. The attendance at General Conference and various youth camps also increased, and conferences were moved from campgrounds to college campuses.

Harold had an understated sense of humor. At the 50th Anniversary Conference of the formation of the General Conference in Cedar Rapids, Iowa, in 1971, Harold and several board members participated in a skit written by Marge Overmeyer. This skit was part of a pageant detailing the history of the conference and highlighting key individuals who helped stabilize the work.

In the skit, Harold conducted a board meeting on the golf course with the board in tow. Real board meetings were often grueling and continued into the night, but Harold loved golf and everyone knew it. So, Marge set the board meeting on the golf course where they conducted "serious" business for the Lord as they made imaginary swings, chips, putts and holes-in-one. Board members participating in the skit included Willis Turner, Dean Urish, Wayne Lanning and S.O. Ross. Although all were amateur performers, they acted well, and Harold Doan's one-liners kept both the actors and the crowd laughing throughout the skit.

Harold's last issue of *The Restitution Herald* was June 14, 1968. After his retirement from the editor's role, the Doans moved to California where Harold entered the advertising business with his brother. In California, he assisted the Pomona church to establish ownership of a disputed property by holding regular preaching services in that church. This was enough activity to satisfy the California court that the congregation who claimed to own the building, did own it, and that ended the matter.

Harold died much too young, and his sudden and unexpected death caused grief throughout the Church of God. He rests at the Forest Lawn Cemetery in Glendale, California. Jean Doan died in Texas in 2006.

Bibliography: Ancestry.com Social Security Death List, record for Harold J. Doan; Ancestry.com. Social Security Death List, record for Bette Jean Doan, June 10, 2006; *The Restitution Herald*. March 16, 1948; JStilson "Reminiscence of Harold and Jean Doan"; Doan, Harold. "Report of Radio Work" *The Restitution Herald*, Oct. 12, 1948. Doan, Harold. Sermon collection, donated to the Archives of Oregon/Atlanta Bible College by Jean Doan, 1985.

Drabenstott, Cantwell
   b. September 24, 1888
   d. March 1967

Cantwell Drabenstott was a member of the Church of God Abrahamic Faith near Roll, Indiana. He was devoted to the message of the Gospel of the Kingdom and raised his children to believe it. J.W. Williams baptized Cantwell on March 3, 1912. Cantwell was dedicated to advancing the message throughout Indiana state; he helped stabilize the work at Plymouth, Indiana and begin it at Kokomo. He preached at Kokomo, alternating Sundays with Vaughn Long.

Cantwell's son, Herman, married Vivian Johnson of Minnesota. The couple met at Summer Bible Training Class at Oregon, Illinois.

When the Church of God General Conference was organized in 1921, Cantwell and the brethren from Roll Church of God, Lee Avenue Church of God in Cleveland, and Perryville, Kentucky, Church of God chose not to become charter members over differences in expression of doctrine.

See Long, Vaughn
Roll, Ward (19th)
Williams, J.W.

Bibliography: Ancestry.com. Social Security Death List. Record for Cantwell Drabenstott; Record of baptism of Cantwell Drabenstott, *The Restitution Herald*, March 14, 1912.

Drake, Anderson
b. July 26, 1880
d. April 24, 1959

The First World War was a time of great agitation against those who espoused pacifism as a way of life. Central Washington was no exception, and the Church of God there experienced direct opposition from the community leaders. Among the faithful was Anderson Drake, a member of the congregation at Cashmere.

There was a strong drive to have all in the community buy war bonds to support the effort in Europe. The Church of God, with its convictions that the brethren should be peacemakers, would not advocate for or purchase such bonds. When solicitors for the Fourth Liberty Loan talked with church members on October 5, 1918, they decided to force the issue and took Anderson from his home to the local hardware where they purchased yellow paint. They painted his back yellow and led him behind a truck through the town with a rope around his neck.

Government officials prosecuted the perpetrators. At trial in the over-crowded courtroom, a verdict was rendered which the newspapers remarked as amounting to, "Not guilty, but don't do it again." The ten businessmen were reprieved from conviction on the assault charge on a technicality; the jury said, "No resistance, No Assault." Anderson had not resisted being taken into custody by the businessmen, nor when they painted his back and led him through town. He implemented his conviction not to resist evil and to suffer patiently under persecution. He nearly died before brethren and family could remove the lead-based paint coating his back.

To those who knew him, including this writer, he was an example of a humble servant, being a man of a quiet, meek and gentle demeanor. The influence of his conviction encouraged the brethren and was a testimony of Christ-likeness to the community.

Arlen Rankin contributed this entry.

Bibliography: Rankin, Arlen F., *Pacifism in the Church of God of North Central Washington (1893-1920)* presented at the Second Annual History Conference, Springfield, Ohio, November 8, 2007; Bruce Mitchell, *Reform, Repression and Reaction—A Social and Political History of the Periods Preceding, During and Following the First World War*, Wenatchee, WA: The Wenatchee World, 1978; Microfilm copies of *The Wenatchee Daily World* newspaper at the North Central Washington Regional Library in Wenatchee, WA.

Drinkard, Theodore Alonzo
b. July 17, 1888
d. December 31, 1967

T.A. Drinkard was born in Van Zandt County, Texas. He married Nicy E. Ramfield on December 11, 1910. They had three children, Curtis, Annie Lee (Vaughn) and Dorothy (Randall).

Drinkard preached his first sermon at 20 and indicated to other Church of God ministers that he wished to be involved in preaching ministry. He looked after the preaching duties at several Nebraska Bible studies in 1919, including Blair, Lincoln and Arlington. Possibly, because of this experience, he was listed as a recognized minister of the Church of God beginning in 1921, the first year such a list was compiled. T.A. Drinkard continued his career as a noted preacher and writer principally throughout Iowa, Nebraska, Arkansas, Missouri and Texas.

As he began in the ministry, he was hired to be an Illinois evangelist in southern Illinois, particularly in the Eldorado community, for six weeks in 1918. S.J. Lindsay invited him to preach in Illinois, and had made an announcement in *The Restitution Herald*, "the work is too heavy for Bro. Siple and ye editor, to handle." People in southern Illinois were expecting Drinkard. He attempted to keep his appointments, but the influenza epidemic prevented him. He arrived in Illinois but had to return home. Not deterred, Drinkard steadfastly made other appointments and kept them after the public health crisis had passed.

In 1919, the Nebraska conference of the Church of God engaged Drinkard to be its evangelist. At this conference, he preached a series of meetings directed to church people instead of to the world. He admonished them to assemble together as the Day of the Lord approaches. Being scattered members, they had not often all worshipped together regularly, which made it hard

TA and Nicy Drinkard

for an evangelist or pastor to build a steady work in any community.

In November 1919, he stopped in Lincoln, Nebraska, and preached in the Advent Christian Church about the Second Coming of Christ. Nettie M. Daharsh reported this service to *The Restitution Herald*. Later that same month, Drinkard visited Stratton County, which O.J. Allard visited the previous month. Elder Allard had baptized four members. Drinkard baptized two more, after which he taught from his famous Bible chart. At this time, he was snowbound. Weather is unpredictable in the Great Plains.

The following story illustrates his dedication to serving wherever a call was made. Mrs. Susan Howard in British Columbia, Canada, requested that a Church of God minister come north to baptize her. No one stepped forward, but S.J. Lindsay asked T.A. Drinkard if he could go. He had no means to buy a ticket, so Bro. Garard of the Troy, Ohio, area loaned him $35. Evidently that was enough to get Drinkard to Canada, but not enough to buy him a berth on the train for comfortable sleeping. Bro. Robert Huggins began a fund drive and $36 more was raised so Drinkard could "have something for his time and trouble." Readers from all over the nation donated to the effort to baptize Mrs. Howard.

Pete McGinty of McGintytown Church of God remembered that T.A. Drinkard loved to engage in debates. He most notably debated Christadelphian Herbert Edwards at Waterloo, Iowa, on Resurrection in November 1921. Drinkard affirmed general resurrection, meaning that all men are raised, some to reward, the wicked to judgment. Adherents to this position differed on whether all were raised at the time of Christ's return or whether the wicked were raised a thousand years later. Herbert Edwards took the position of denying that the wicked would be raised for additional judgment. He said their judgment occurred at the time of their Adamic death, a typical Christadelphian position of that day.

Elder Drinkard would have agreed with L.E. Conner regarding the work of the Holy Spirit in the life of the believer and the church. Drinkard was a cessationist. He believed that the Comforter was sent only to the Apostles to assist them in miracles and performing the work of building the early church. He believed that the way modern Christians receive the Holy Spirit is through the reading of the Scriptures. This was a controversy discussed in the Church of God during the early 20th century; half the membership believed cessationism, and half believed the Spirit is received at baptism and works in the life of the believer to enable him to powerfully serve the Lord.

Drinkard was a prodigious writer for *The Restitution Herald* published at Oregon, Illinois, and an avid participant in various state conferences. He wrote a piece for *The Restitution Herald* stating the people of the Church of God were spiritually dead. He said God wants workers who will work all the time. God demands that we render absolute obedience to his requirements. He said it seems the closer we get to the Kingdom age the more indifferent the people become.

Grace Marsh said in an interview that when the Committee of Ten did its study during 1920 in preparation for a new General Conference organization, they found and reported that the "people of the Church of God were just too carnal." It was felt that a national conference corporation should address the issues of spirituality among the churches.

In 1921, T.A. Drinkard traveled a circuit through Iowa, Kansas, Nebraska and Oklahoma. One humorous story indicates his style. While passing through Marshalltown, Iowa, by train he disembarked spontaneously one night at midnight and called the local pastor, G.E. Marsh. Pastor Marsh got out of bed on a snowy night and came to pick him up at the station. He said G.E. Marsh was good-natured about it, and that it was the mark of western hospitality to be surprised in such a manner and still be a good host.

In 1923, Drinkard was forced to go into secular work as the evangelistic work could not support his family. Yet, in 1925, he was fulltime in the Lord's service, if he had ever left, and reports of his work at the Minnesota conference, where he preached on the subject of resurrection, can be seen in *The Restitution Herald*. In the next issue of *The Herald*, someone complained about his interpretation of the subject in a letter to the editor.

In 1925 A.S. Bradley in Texas and Elder Drinkard joined to ward off the universalism influence that was drifting south from Iowa through the evangelistic ministry of several noted preachers there, ostensibly A.J. Eychaner, G.M. Myers and W.L. Crowe. Drinkard wrote years later in *The Gospel Messenger*: "Bro. Bradley wrote me that the condition was not good through false teaching of universalism, and asked if I could attend that summer meeting, and the money was raised for the expenses. The opposition raised their cry: 'Get anybody but T.A. Drinkard.'" Their numbers at the meeting had reached almost 600, according to A.S. Bradley. While they struggled against the doctrine, it still did damage to the work. Drinkard said, "When a man takes a dose of universalist doctrine it will bring sorrow along the path of life. It never builds up the gospel work."

T.A. Drinkard continued faithful in ministry well past the mid-20th century. He met and baptized a family at McAllen, Texas, by the name of Hayse. John Hayse became active in the Texas conference and served on the Board of Directors of the Church of God General Conference. He had learned of the Church of God through his mother-in-law, Mrs. Robbins of Riviera, Texas. This is a case where a mother-in-law was highly respected because of her Christian influence. John and his family helped build the church at Harlingen, Texas, and escorted the Gospelettes trio from Oregon Bible College into Mexico during their summer tour in 1961.

T.A. Drinkard remained active in ministry as an evangelist until he began to experience bad health in 1963. During his final years he continued to publish *The Gospel Messenger* from his home in Arlington, Texas.

Sherwin Williams, pastor at Blessed Hope in Rockford, Illinois. and the Church of God at Ripley, Illinois, told of his boyhood experiences at Oklahoma/ Texas Conference. He said:

> T.A. Drinkard would play tag in the grass with the boys and they would chase him, and he, them. He'd fall in the grass and get stains on his knees. When he'd return to the church Mrs. Drinkard would say, 'How will we ever get the stains out of those trousers?' And the pastor would reply, 'Oh, mother we will figure it out somehow, and it was such great fun!'

In the pages of *The Gospel Messenger*, a small mimeographed paper in the 1960s, are some interesting tidbits of attitude and history. In more than one issue are articles in which Drinkard took exception to the publication of *Systematic Theology* written by Alva Huffer, pastor at that time in Virginia and Michigan. Drinkard's primary objection was over the issue of atonement and the nature of Christ. In *Systematic Theology* Huffer said men are redeemed through the shed blood of Christ. T.A. Drinkard held an unusual position for that day. He felt Christ could not be a man with blood descended from David for that would mean Christ was also descended from Adam who passed along original sin. Christ had no sin. Therefore, Christ had to have royal blood, as a created Son of God.

Drinkard wrote:

> We submit that the inspired apostle Paul told the truth when he said: 'By one man sin entered into the world, and death by sin; and so death passed upon all men, for that all have sinned' (Romans 5:12). This inspired statement of itself proves that every man and woman born into this world, as children; as members of Adam's and Eve's FAMILY were made sinners [emphasis by Drinkard]. Now the point is, WAS Jesus Christ a member of that family? So much has been said in the S.T. [*Systematic Theology*] about Jesus Christ being a member of the human race. Why did the author fail to call the precious Son of God a sinner, since he went that far?

In another issue regarding the nature of Christ's blood, Editor Drinkard said:

> It is interesting to say the least, to hear one try to prove that the precious blood of Jesus Christ was connected with the blood of the Adam race. IF such could be done then the human family has no redeemer. As I have heretofore said, that when I first went to the north about 1920, it was [S.J.] Lindsay who told me that he had heard one say in his sermon that the blood of Jesus Christ was not more precious than any other man's blood. Teach this doctrine to young men who want to be gospel ministers, and what will you have?

In the same issue of *The Gospel Messenger* (March/April 1961), Drinkard said:

> After Adam and Eve sinned their blood was under condemnation of sin and death. Therefore, the blood of the Son of God had to come from an unsinful source. It had to be created by the God of heaven, and had no taint of sin in it. This is the BLOOD that had no sin in it.

Drinkard had other issues with the National Bible Institute, mostly over the anticipated publication of the *Systematic Theology*. He felt the young students were being led astray, and he was quite vocal about it. He even objected to the fact that it was copyrighted. He said:

> *Systematic Theology* was printed by the National Bible Institution and copyrighted by its author in 1960....Why was this book copyrighted, if it was designed to teach the truth? Could it be possible that the copyright was to act as a shield against those who dared to point out dangerous errors that might be found therein? It is admitted that before it was printed, the MS. [manuscript] was used in the O.B.C. Did the teachers examine carefully what they were teaching the students? In fact, why was a humanized book [used] as a text book? If the teaching was true, why not use the Bible? Has the Bible, as the greatest book ever made, ever been copyrighted? If not, then how can a humanized book be lawfully copyrighted containing a large number of passages of Scripture from the Word of God?

Whereas most of the Church of God welcomed the publication of *Systematic Theology* with great joy and held its author in high esteem, T.A. Drinkard's comments seem harsh by comparison.

Pastor and Mrs. Drinkard celebrated their 50th wedding anniversary on December 11, 1960, with loved ones, and received many cards and letters. They served the Lord faithfully until death. He succumbed on the last day of 1967. Pastor Harry Goekler preached his funeral service and wrote, "His strong faith in the Word of God, and the hope of the second coming of Jesus to establish His Kingdom on the Earth marked Bro. Drinkard's ministry and life."

While researching US Census data for occupations of persons in this encyclopedia, the author learned that early preachers frequently stated "Farmer" or "Carpenter," but T.A. Drinkard gave his occupation as "Minister, Church of God." He never missed an opportunity to witness.

> See Allard, O.J. (19th)
> Bradley, A.S. (19th)
> Conner, L.E. (19th)
> Goekler, Harry
> Howard, Susan (19th)
> Huffer, Alva
> Lindsay, S.J. (19th)
> Marsh, G.E. (19th)
> Myers, G.M. (19th)

Bibliography: Ancestry.com. U.S. Census. Nebraska. Furnas. Burton Bend. Dist. 81. 1920; Drinkard, T.A. "Copywrited! Why

Copywrited?" *The Gospel Messenger,* Jan/Feb 1961; "Preaching the Word," *The Gospel Messenger,* March/April 1962; "The Redemption in Jesus Christ" *The Gospel Messenger,* July/Aug. 1963; Goekler, Harry. "Obituary of T.A. Drinkard," *The Progress Journal*, February 1968; Interview with Grace Marsh at Pinecrest Manor by Jan Stilson, *History Newsletter of the Church of God General Conference*, Summer 1992; Mattison, James; Letter to *History Newsletter,* JStilson, ed., 1992; McGinty, Pete, Interview with Jan Stilson for the *Church of God History Newsletter,* Winter 1985*; The Restitution.* Jan. 1920; *The Restitution Herald,* March 4, 1915; June 14, 1916; Oct. 30, 1918; July 7, 1919; Nov. 11, 1919; Nov. 25, 1919; Oct. 1921; Williams, Sherwin, "Memories of T.A. Drinkard, IL. Conference, E. Peoria, Nov. 6, 2010.

Driskill, (James) Leon
b. January 1930
d. September 11, 2009

Leon Driskill was born to Howard and Opal (Palmer) Driskill, in Cross Timbers, Missouri. His mother and stepfather, Howard Spencer, raised him there. Leon grew to be a slender fellow who loved the Lord, his family and the outdoors. He came to Oregon Bible College in 1947 and graduated in 1951. The ministries of Francis Burnett, Weldon McCoy and others in that state greatly influenced Leon.

Following graduation, Leon entered the ministry. He served at East Oregon, Illinois, a new work which had just been established by Mary Mae Nedrow. He met Delores Lewis while serving in that congregation. She was the daughter of Seward and Caroline Lewis. Leon and Delores married on July 2, 1950. They had three sons, Dennis who died at age 25 in 1977, Tim (Julie Vance) and Lonnie (Linda), and one daughter, Terri Emmett.

During Leon's pastoral career he and Delores served several churches: East Oregon, Illinois (1950-51); Kokomo, Indiana (1951-53); Stanhope, Iowa (1953-1956); East Peoria, Illinois (1956-1959); Niles, Michigan (1959-1962); Harlingen, Texas (1962-1965); New Lenox, Illinois (1965-1968; Tipp City, Ohio (1968-1973); Holbrook, Nebraska (1973-1987); Royal, Arkansas (1987-1991); and Eldorado, Illinois (1991-1996). Leon attended every session of the state conference meetings and every General Conference meeting. He had a sweet tenor voice and often sang solos or in men's quartets at worship services.

Leon was a good Bible student relying on various library resources to support his studies. He especially liked Campbell's *Translation of the New Testament* and Benjamin Wilson's *Emphatic Diaglott.* When he retired,

Ministers gathered at Jordan, Missouri, circa 1948, from left: John Gates, A Weldon McCoy, Roy Graham, Leon Driskill, unknown, Francis Burnett.

Leon donated many of his books to the library of Rock River Christian College in Beloit, Wisconsin.

In his senior years, Leon endured memory loss, which was relieved for several years by medicine. He was able to discuss history issues and recognize faces. A year or so before his death, he told this story, here paraphrased:

> When I was twelve years old at Cross Timbers, Missouri, my father and grandfather went out to the woods to cut down a tree. Wood was the principle way to heat homes during the winter in that part of the country. The men set up the tree so that it would fall in the direction towards which they were sawing. I was with them and was told to stay back. I stood by and watched them. As the tree gave way, much to the horror of the men, it began to fall off to the side in the same direction that I was standing. I began to run away from it. My grandfather cried out, "Oh no! We've lost our precious boy!" The tree fell full force upon me and crushed me beneath it. They sawed through its dense foliage to reach me as quickly as they could and lifted me unconscious and limp in their arms. They carried me to mother, thinking I would surely die. But the Lord was with us all for after prayer, and some time later, I revived much to everyone's joy.

Leon said that he had never shared that story before, but believed God raised him up to serve Him, and that is why he became a minister. He owed his life to the Lord.

Leon died at Manor Care, Peoria, Illinois, where he resided. Pastor Curt Rowden conducted funeral services. Leon was interred at a graveside service at the Daysville Cemetery, Daysville, Illinois, near Oregon. Many Church of God members are buried at the Daysville Cemetery.

See Burnett, Francis
McCoy, Weldon

Bibliography: Ancestry.com. U.S. Census. Missouri. Hickory. Jordan. Dist. 4; 1930; Driskill, Leon, "Story of Felling a Tree," told to Jan Stilson in Peoria, Il., April, 2004; Driskill, Delores. E-mail to JStilson, Sept. 25, 2008; *The Restitution Herald,* Sydney Magaw, ed., Oregon Il., Oct. 29, 1947; Snyder, Janet. Updated history of Maple Grove Community Church from an earlier history by Edgar Harvey, courtesy of Pastor Dale Bliss, May 1, 2010.

Dunbar, Roscoe F.
b. July 19, 1888
d. June 11, 1969

Roscoe Dunbar was born and raised in Fulton County, Ohio, near Raker Corners, west of Toledo. He married Florence B. (1889 to May 5, 1982) and they had three sons, Delbert, Dale and Glenn, and one daughter, Amy. Roscoe was a farmer near Swan Creek.

Roscoe and Flo were brought to Christ by Melville Lyon, and upon their confession of faith, they began to work in the Raker Church of God just south of Delta. In 1913, a young evangelist from Louisiana stopped by the church to preach and sing. His name was Frank Siple, and the people liked him so well, they asked him to stay. He stayed for one year as their pastor before moving north to Michigan in 1914.

The church at Raker hosted the Ohio Conference several times, and some present-day Ohio ministers remember attending conference there. Celaine Randall preached at Raker for a number of years following Frank Siple, but following Celaine's death it is thought the church closed its doors.

Dale Dunbar, right, and his airplane

Roscoe's son Dale distinguished himself through service as president of the Board of Directors of the Church of God General Conference from 1950-1954. Dale further impressed the Church of God delegates and the board by flying to General Conference in his own airplane, landing at Polo Airport. Under Dale's administration the Church of God began to wake up and show interest in home and foreign missions in obedience to the Lord's command. Leaders also searched for ways to develop Oregon Bible College to prepare it for accreditation. They began a pastoral aid program for churches struggling to pay pastors' salaries. They also endorsed the ministry of Mrs. Verna Thayer, minister and child evangelist. This administration paved the way for the ensuing Decade of Development from 1955-1965 under the leadership of President Willis Turner and directors Willard Naylor, Dean Urish, Stan Ross, Wayne Lanning and Arlie Townsend.

Each president or chairman who has served the Board of Directors signed his name in the front of a Bible held in the Archives of the Atlanta Bible College. The line of succession begins with James A. Patrick, the first president in 1921, and continues to the present.

Roscoe's daughter Amy married Frederick Puehler. They lived at Wauseon, Ohio, and had three children. Two daughters survived her. Amy lived to be 93 years old and remained firmly grounded in the Church of God.

See Lyon, Melville
 Ross, Stanley O.
 Siple, Frank E.
 Thayer, Verna
 Turner, Willis H.

Bibliography: Ancestry.com U.S. Census. Ohio. Fulton. Swan Creek. Dist. 20. 1903; Ohio Death Index. Records for Roscoe F. Dunbar and Flo Dunbar. Retrieved through Ancestry.com Jan. 5, 2010; Social Security Master Death List; Obituary of Amy Puehler, Grisier Funeral Home, Delta, Ohio, retrieved Jan. 6, 2010; Krogh, David e-mails to clarify names, Jan. 6, 2010; Cain, Rex. E-mail with information on Roscoe Dunbar and daughter Amy, Jan. 6, 2010.

Duncan, Zerden B.
b. May 29, 1921
d. March 10, 1984

Z.B. Duncan was born in Hickory, North Carolina, the eldest of Ernest Lee and Daisy Page Duncan's five children. He was the grandson of Advent Christian minister, Henry Lee Duncan, who founded Hickory Advent Christian Church in Hickory. Z.B. married Verlie Estelle Brown on December 24, 1941. They had four children, two girls and two boys: Patricia Ann (Clontz), born in 1943; David Paul, 1947; Wanda Elaine (Keller), 1952; and Timothy Wayne, 1957.

Z.B. Duncan was the pastor of Calvary Advent Christian Church in Lenoir, North Carolina, from 1952 to 1961. He then established the Church of Resurrection Hope and pastored there until his death. The family currently attends the Church of Resurrection Hope where Wanda is the pianist, Tim is choir director and a deacon, Patricia is a Sunday school teacher, and Paul is the organist and an elder. In addition to the children, Z.B.'s six grandchildren also attend and are active there. The entire family strives to serve the Lord with the vigor and reverence as Z.B. did before them. They look forward to being reunited with their beloved husband, father and grandfather in the glorious Kingdom of God.

Z.B. was laid to rest in the Woodlawn Memorial Cemetery in Lenoir on March 12, 1984.

Bibliography: Duncan family for the Atlanta Bible College Biography Project, David Krogh, compiler; Social security master death list, Record for Zerden Duncan.

Durham, David Donald
b. March 6, 1915
d. December 8, 1997

David Durham was born to George Washington and Bessie Belle Ellenburg Durham near Pelzer, South Carolina. David lived there all his life and was a member of the Guthrie Grove Church of God. He was baptized in August 1929. David married Margaret Virginia Elrod of Piedmont, South Carolina, on June 18, 1944. They enjoyed 52 years together and had two children who also became members of the Guthrie Grove church.

A well-read man, David was hard working, honest and a devoted husband and father. He was loved by all who knew him. David served Guthrie Grove Church of God as Sunday school superintendent for six years, and as a deacon for seven years. He also was active in community service. David died in 1997 and was laid to rest in Guthrie Grove Cemetery.

See Durham, Ezekiel A.
Durham, George H.
Durham, George W.

Bibliography: Comments written by wife Margaret and sons Donald and Truman for the ABC Biography Project, David Krogh, compiler.

Durham, Ezekiel Albert
b. July 14, 1912
d. February 7, 1976

Ezekiel Albert Durham was the son of George Washington and Bessie Ellenberg Durham. He was born in Anderson County, South Carolina. Ezekiel attended White Plains High School. He married Lois McCombs on September 24, 1937. Two weeks after the wedding, they bought a grocery store on Hamilton Street in Williamston, South Carolina. Ezekiel was very successful in this business. They rented an apartment from his sister, Kate Bagwell and lived there about two years. In time, they bought a farm on Mahaffey Road, constructed a nice home, and then Ezekiel put up a building on Gossett Street where he operated a grocery store until 1949. From 1949 until 1955 he operated a cattle farm where he raised Black Angus. In 1955, he went into the house construction business. He delighted in designing a home and seeing it completed. His contracting business grew until he was building homes at the rate of eight to twelve a year.

Ezekiel and Lois had three children, twin boys who died the day of their birth, and a daughter, Rebecca. She graduated from Palmetto High School and Anderson College. She married Ron Alberson.

On November 22, 1964, the Guthrie Grove Church decided to build a parsonage for Pastor T.M. Ferrell. Zeke built it in 1965. In 1969, the church needed to build again to make room for an educational building. He contracted to build these additions, which were completed in 1970.

For a number of years, Zeke served as alderman and mayor pro tem of Williamston. He served on the School District One Board of Trustees, was a member of the Home Builders Association of Anderson, South Carolina, and of the Masonic Lodge of Williamston.

Zeke was a very conscientious and kindhearted man who loved his church and church family. He generously provided monetary support for radio programs by the church pastors. He seldom missed a Sunday at church. Ezekiel and Lois once made a trip to the Holy Land. He enjoyed talking about the things he had seen there.

After a heart attack at home, Zeke was pronounced dead at the hospital that same day. He rests in Woodlawn Memorial Park in Greenville, South Carolina.

See Durham, David
Durham, George H.
Durham, George W.

Bibliography: Gaillard, Willie Pearl D, a sister. "Ezekiel Albert Durham," for the ABC Biography Project, David Krogh, compiler.

Durham, George Hulon
b. September 30, 1903
d. September 21, 1973

George Hulon Durham was the son of George Washington and Bessie Ellenberg Durham. After graduating White Plains High School in 1923, Hulon entered Spartanburg Barber School and graduated. He returned home and worked in Pelzer, South Carolina, for a number of years. Hulon became a member of Guthrie Grove Church of God in August 1924. On April 4, 1926, he married Eva Mae Bagwell. They had six children. He worked for the Anderson County Soil Conservation Services. In the early 1940s he opened his own barber shop on Highway 8 across from White Plains School. He barbered there until his death.

Hulon held several offices in the church including Sunday school superintendent and assistant adult teacher. He believed in a one-to-one approach in teaching the plan of salvation. His barbershop was a good place for teaching. Hulon was not ashamed of his faith. He talked about the Bible everywhere he went. In the late 1960s and 1970s, Hulon suffered from a heart ailment. In 1973, after a long day of barbering, he started to the drug store to buy heart medicine but died on the way.

He was buried in the Guthrie Grove Cemetery on Sunday, September 23, 1973. Walking away from his grave after his funeral services, one lady remarked, "Wisdom went down in that grave."

See Durham, David
   Durham, Ezekiel A.
   Durham, George W.

Bibliography: Durham, W.J. for the ABC Biography Project, David Krogh, compiler.

Durham, George Washington
b. February 22, 1878
d. August 3, 1973

Durham, Bessie Belle Ellenberg
b. July 18, 1880
d. December 3, 1968

George Durham was born near Pelzer, South Carolina, to Ezekiel Albert Durham and Louisa Catherine Guthrie Durham. He lived in that community all his life and was the eleventh male member of the Guthrie Grove Church of God. He was baptized in the late 1880s.

George married Bessie Ellenberg on Dec. 22, 1898. He was 21; she was 17. George farmed while Bessie remained a housewife. He was a well-read, hard-working, honest man and a devoted father. He shared his knowledge of the Bible with family and friends who often gathered on his front porch or under shade trees in the yard on Sunday afternoon. He was loved by all and many affectionately called him "Uncle George."

The Durhams celebrated 70 years together and had nine children, two of whom died at age two. The other seven became members of Guthrie Grove Church of God. Committed to education, George and Bessie educated their children not only in the Bible, but with Bessie's devotion, they all graduated from high school as well. Three daughters attended college and became teachers, teaching a total of 83 years in Anderson County schools. They also taught Sunday school and Bible classes.

Music was extremely important to the family. George played many instruments including piano, organ, guitar, accordion and harmonica. He used his music in faithful service to the Lord. One of his favorite activities was to have people gathered around him singing. George also served the church through various offices including superintendent of the Sunday school and leader of the adult class which he taught for 40 years.

When these faithful servants of the Lord fell asleep, they were laid to rest in the Guthrie Grove Cemetery to await the resurrection and life. His children offer a fitting memorial to George: "He fought a good fight, he finished his course, and he kept the faith." For Bessie, the children have said her memorial will read, "She was a wonderful mother who brought us up in the house of the Lord, where we came to know God and His Son Jesus Christ."

See Durham, Ezekiel
   Durham, George H.
   Durham, George W.

Bibliography: Ancestry.com U.S. Census. South Carolina. Anderson. Williamston. Dist. 66. 1900; Durham, Donald and Margaret son and wife, "George Washington Durham," and Martin, Bonnie Durham, daughter, "Bessie Belle Ellenberg Durham" for the ABC Biography project, David Krogh, compiler.

Durham, John Hannon
b. 1919
d. February 14, 1999

Hannon Durham was a faithful member of the Guthrie Grove Church of God in Anderson, South Carolina. He married Katie Johnson, and they had two sons, John and Charles, and one daughter, Becky. Elder Durham retired from the Williamston Lumber Company and was a member of the White Plains Masonic Lodge #321. He served the Lord with gladness.

Bibliography: Ancestry.com. U.S. Census. South Carolina. Anderson. Williamston. Dist. 52, 1930; Biography Project of Atlanta Bible College, David Krogh, compiler.

Duvall, Margaret "Peg"
b. 1904
d. November 14, 1997

Margaret Lyon was born to Judd and Loulon Lyon. She was the third child of four with one brother, Melville, and two sisters, Dorothy and Jean. Dorothy married Frank Siple, and Jean married Attorney Robert Hall who provided legal services for the Church of God General Conference until his retirement and death. Melville served the Church of God as national evangelist during the 1940s and took many wonderful movies of churches and church members. These movies have been reconditioned and are stored in the Archives of the Atlanta Bible College. It is hoped they can be transferred to digital format.

Margaret faithfully attended Church of God conferences. She loved the fellowship, and it served as an opportunity for her to reunite with her siblings. Margaret was a nurse. She lived and worked in Chicago most of her life, moving to Louisville, Kentucky, to be near family during her last ten years. She was also an artist.

When she died, her body was donated to the University of Louisville School of Medicine for research. She was survived by her sister, Dorothy; two daughters, Suzanne Nystrand and Elizabeth Patterson; and a son, David. She had six grandchildren and seven great-grandchildren.

Bibliography: ABC Biography project, David Krogh, compiler.

Eagleston, John
b. 1871
d. Unknown

John Eagleston was born in England and came to America in 1887. His wife Florence came to America a year later when he called for her. They settled near Pasadena, California, but moved to the great Northwest after 1930. While in California they worshipped with the congregation at Pomona. Eagleston worked as an English gardener in California, and met Chester A. Ferrell, Terry Ferrell's father, who came to the Church of God from a Christadelphian background. John became a naturalized US citizen in 1950.

John accepted the Gospel of the Kingdom and began to fellowship with the Church of God. He also attended the annual conferences of the Jehovah Witnesses, which were open to everybody. He also felt a strong kinship with Jewish practices. He wore a *yarmulke* or skullcap.

After moving to the Northwest, John and Florence began worshipping with the congregation at Wenatchee, Washington, while residing at Clarkston. For a number of years during the 1940s, he served as pastor at Wenatchee. He and Florence had no children.

Eagleston traveled the United States and into many Churches of God to preach. Elizabeth Ordnung wrote in her diary that he preached at East Oregon, Illinois, on Sunday morning and at Oregon Church of God on Sunday evening on February 28, 1943.

A note in a *Restitution Herald* from 1949 mentioned that John Eagleston visited the Church of God at Pomona, California and "looked as well as he did ten years ago."

Eagleston was noted for his peculiar singing style. He had a fine voice and he leaned his body into every syllable, giving those good old gospel songs an extra punch of passion. Larry Rankin of the Cashmere church, a missionary for the Church of God in the Philippine Islands, gave a fine rendition of John Eagleston's style at a History Conference at North Hills Church of God while this volume was in production.

Eagleston joined Church of God ministers at the Oregon, Illinois, conference in February 1943. He is seated, far left.

James Rencontre remembers Eagleston. As James grew up in Weiser, Idaho, Eagleston often visited with his Advent Christian friends in that regional conference. Church of God ministers and Advent Christian ministers in that area often assisted each other and fellowshipped together well into the 1990s. Emory Macy, a Church of God pastor, served the Weiser, Idaho, Advent Christian church for nearly 20 years where he followed the pastorate of Fred Sapp. According to Jim Rencontre, Eagleston traveled up and down the west coast preaching at services, camps and conferences. He always graced the congregation with one of his fine songs. Eagleston and Fred Sapp were friends.

See Macy, Emory
Sapp, Fred

Bibliography: Ancestry.com U.S. Census. California. Los Angeles. El Monte. Dist. 930. 1930; U.S. Census. California. Los Angeles. Pasadena. Dist. 504. 1920; Ancestry.com. U.S. Naturalization Records Index 1791-1992 record for John Allen Eagleston; "Notice: *The Restitution Herald*, Sydney Magaw, ed., Oregon, Il., March 22, 1949; Information on Elder Eagleston, *The Restitution Herald,* March 23, 1948; Ordnung, Elizabeth. Notes in her Diary at Golden Rule Home, Oregon, Illinois, February 28, 1943.

Edinger, Bess (Shafer)
b. March 2, 1898
d. February 20, 1990

Bessie Shafer was one of three sisters active in the Church of God in Indiana from the time of their youth. She was Hugh and Mary Shafer's youngest daughter. Her sisters were Lulu M. (Stilson) and Verna C. (Thayer).

These sisters loved the Lord's work, especially teaching. Bess was active in the National Berean Society, formed in Chicago in 1913 as the educational arm of the Church of God before the denomination had a centrally organized conference. Bess wrote for *The Restitution* and was an encourager of children and their parents. She attended many state and local conferences.

See Shafer, Hugh (19th)
Thayer, Verna

Bibliography: Berean Columns, *The Restitution,* Dates unknown; Graham. David. E-mail to JStilson. Feb. 21, 2006; Harrison, Bert. E-mail to JStilson, June 12, 2008.

English, John Craig
b. September 28, 1913
d. February 21, 1990

John English was born in Burnsville, Yancey County, North Carolina, and educated in the Yancey County school system. On February 23, 1935, he married Quanita Pryor of Henderson County. John and Quanita had two daughters, Joy English Anders and Lyn English Hensley, and two granddaughters, Andrea Anders and Allison Anders. Two sons, Jack and Mackie, died in childhood.

John was baptized in Burnsville Baptist Church in August 1928, but he began to understand the doctrines of the Church of God Abrahamic Faith at the death of the two young sons. After 40 years, John retired from the North Carolina Forest Service, where he earned many awards and commendations for outstanding service and dedication. He respected God's creation and used his knowledge to protect the mountains and grow flower gardens. He also devoted much time and care to his family. He attended Anderson Chapel in Hendersonville and continued to uphold Bible truths until his death, which came two days before their 55th anniversary.

He rests in the Lord. Psalm 121 is very fitting for his life: "I will lift up mine eyes unto the hills, from whence cometh my help. My help cometh from the LORD which made heaven and earth."

The heritage of this family continues through the faithful service of their grandchildren. Andrea Anders, an attorney, served on the Board of Directors of the Church of God General Conference 2002 to 2006.

Bibliography: ABC Biography Project, David Krogh, compiler; Ancestry.com. Social Security Death List, record for John C. English.

F

Farley, William Milroy
b. December 25, 1863
d. June 26, 1952

William Farley was born in Noble, Ohio, to Joseph and Elizabeth Matthews Farley. He was orphaned at age five, and afterward lived in a log house with his young married cousins who raised him. He dressed in front of the fireplace and slept in the attic. Sometimes the snow blew in. William grew up accustomed to being cold. He later admitted to being a drinker and smoker until he met Verna Springer (May 29, 1879-1959). They wed in 1896 and resided in West Virginia. They had five children, Elza Roy (E. Roy), Leslie Earl (d. 1923), Verna Ruth (d. 1917), Elizabeth Elanore "Betty" (b. January 17, 1921) and Endsley (b. 1899). William Farley worked in a bank.

William and Verna

William and Verna were Methodists by background, but William heard about the Gospel of the Kingdom from a man who hired him to cut corn on an island in the Ohio River. He loved the Gospel message so much he rented a hall and D.C. Robison came from Salem, Ohio, to preach there. William and Verna were baptized (possibly by D.C. Robison or William Rennie) in the Ohio River. Sadly, though, no one responded with any interest after Evangelist Robison preached. Another evangelist by the name of J.F. Wilcox came up from downstream and preached on the Faith of Abraham. They never saw him again. Wilcox may have been an Indiana evangelist who lived around Plymouth. The History Committee welcomes more information about Wilcox.

William continued to attend the Sisterville Church of Christ. He thought he might be able to teach them about the Kingdom of God. They offered communion every Sunday, which he liked. All the years that he worshipped with them, they never listened to him. If he raised a question at Bible study, the leader would say, "Next verse please," time after time. William never stopped trying to teach them about the Gospel of the Kingdom.

William prayed before every meal. One time, they had household guests for a week that spent their days out but returned for meals. One of the guests was a little girl. One day they were late in arriving to dinner, and Mr. Farley had already said grace. When they got to the table, the little girl jumped on her chair which was a box with a board across it, hit her plate with her spoon, and said, "Wait a minute, everybody! Mr. Farley has not talked to his plate!" William's daughter Betty concluded the story with, "Needless to say, she looked puzzled when everybody around the table burst out in laughter."

As time went by, William became an invalid. When their Sisterville home burned, William and Verna moved in with eldest son, Endsley in Columbus, Ohio, after Endsley's wife died. Betty Ackels wrote, "Somehow a Gospel of the Kingdom preacher, Richard Smith, I think, heard about Daddy, and came to visit him. Daddy was so pleased to get in touch with a Church of God preacher."

William wrote a letter to Betty in 1951 in which he related some details of his spiritual journey. He wrote:

> I will add a little more to the subject about the *Emphatic Diaglott*. When Bro. Benjamin Wilson died, the Jehovah Witnesses, or Russellites, bought the copyright and also [began to] publish and sell the Diaglott. That is the reason we have to purchase it from them. In 1893 I was working up near Pittsburgh, Pa. I went down to Allegheny, Pa. where Charles T. Russell lived. I visited in his home a few hours and heard him preach in the afternoon. His followers called themselves Russellites at that time. I was hunting for the truth. But, I never became a believer in his doctrine. After his death his fellowship split into two factions. Two men wanted to be the leaders. Judge Rutherford was the Head of Jehovah Witnesses, I think, and the other faction was called the Bible Students.

William's son, E. Roy, was uniquely talented in electronics. He and a friend built a radio and began broadcasting in Sisterville, West Virginia, where the family lived. The US Signal Corp hired E. Roy in 1946 to compute the distance from the earth to the moon for a project to bounce radar off the moon many years before man landed on there in 1969. E. Roy was sworn to secrecy while he was working on this project.

Jerome, Mary and William Farley

William and Verna are buried in the New Cemetery at Sisterville, West Virginia. Nephew Wellington Gallagher, a former Catholic that became a Church of Christ member, conducted their funerals. Betty Ackels said her father always talked to his two nephews about the Gospel

Betty Thibault Ackels with the Thibault children and grandchildren.

of the Kingdom, and they respected that but remained with their denomination.

Betty said she and her siblings attended the Church of Christ where she learned her Bible stories when she was growing up. They insisted that believers not take their word for it but take the Bible first. So she did. When she was an adult she began to listen to the things her father taught about the Gospel of the Kingdom, and she came to believe it, but her brothers and sister could not.

William's heritage resides in the families of Betty Thibault Ackels and her children and grandchildren. Betty has been a faithful member of the Church of God at Countryside Church of God, Peculiar, Missouri, and at Harlingen, Texas, throughout her adult life. Her son, Bill Thibault, attended Oregon Bible College in 1967 and assisted with the photos for this entry. Son Scott Thibault preaches at Peculiar when Pastor Don Ward is away.

> See Mattison, James
> Rennie, William (19th)
> Robison, D.C. (19th)
> Smith, E. Richard
> Wilson, Benjamin (19th)

Bibliography: Ackels, Elizabeth "Betty", Letter to James Mattison Nov. 2, 2010, forwarded to Jan Stilson, and Letter to Jan Stilson, Nov. 15, 2010, Nov.18, 2010, Feb. 2, 2011, March 1, 2011; Ancestry.com. Kammers Family Tree, record for William M. Farley; Ancestry.com. U.S. Census. West Virginia. Tyler. Lincoln. Dist. 11. 1900, 1920 and 1930; Thibualt, Bill. Photos sent to JStilson by e-mail, Nov. 19, 2010.

Fletcher, Joseph Arthur Franklin
b. November 6, 1931
d. May 22, 2001

Joseph Fletcher was born in Fonthill, Ontario, Canada. Joe's mother died when he was 13 and a new stepmother, Doris Fletcher, entered the home shortly thereafter. She became a much-loved mother to Joe and his brother, Art. Joe's parents raised him in the Fonthill Church of God. He loved Bible study. He also loved baseball and seemed intuitive about calling plays in the game. He could almost predict the outcome of the game.

Joe decided to study for the ministry at Oregon Bible College. There he met Shirley Van Vleet who became his wife. They had four children, Cheryl, Debbie, Jeff and Christie. While in Oregon Joe served as the student pastor at East Oregon Chapel Church of God, Shirley's home church. Upon graduating from Bible College, Joe and Shirley moved to Aurora where he completed studies at Aurora College. After graduation, Joe served churches in Baltimore and Fairfax, Virginia. He also taught school while Shirley worked in a bookstore.

He participated in the various activities of the Virginia State Conference, Church of God General Conference—where he served on the Board of Directors—and the Ministerial Association. In his final illness, Joe and Shirley resided near son Jeff in Louisiana. Joe endured great pain in the final days but was uplifted by his faith.

The Fonthill boys, from left: Ron Dilamarter, Joe Fletcher, Art Fletcher, George Peterson, Welland Holland.

> The following letter from Pastor Joe Fletcher's cousin, Betty Hummel, speaks lovingly of Church of God ministers she has respected during her life.
>
> August 30, 1994
>
> Dear Jan,
>
> My oldest sister Wilda Blackwell married Joseph Fletcher (Sr.) in Toronto in 1920. Our family were Christadelphians. My mother preferred the beliefs of the Church of God with whom she became acquainted in Fonthill (Ontario).
>
> After the death of my father, my mother brought the family to California to live in 1923. We were met by Sr. Emma Railsback who hosted us until Mama found a home. Emma at that time preached in her home until a church home was shared with the Seventh-day Baptists. She later mortgaged her home to make it possible to build a church on 103rd Street, Los Angeles. She was a tireless worker.
>
> Later, that fabulous S.J. Lindsay became our pastor. My sister Nina and I were baptized by him in 1924. At times, Bro. (L.E.) Conner preached to us. What an impressive man he was! Norman McLeod was an excellent minister as were Brother (G.E.) Marsh and a number of others.
>
> They were great influences who kept me firm during the difficult years at UCLA when there was so much criticism of the Scriptures.
>
> There were so many other great ones like Roy Graham and James McLain who I'll always remember along with David Wilsterman and Cecil Smead, and on and on.
>
> I am Aunt and Great Aunt to many Fletchers I'm happy to say.
>
> Yours in Christ
> Betty Blackwell Hummel
> Upland, California

His life served as an example to many. He is missed by his friends and family but he rests in the Lord.

See Conner, L.E. (19th)
    Graham, Roy
    Hummel, Charles M.
    Lindsay, S.J. (19th)
    Marsh, G.E.
    McLain, James
    Railsback, Emma (19th)
    Smead, Cecil

Bibliography: Fletcher, Art. "My Tribute to Joey," Part of the collection of Art Fletcher donated to the Atlanta Bible College Archives, Spring, 2008.

Ferrell, Terry M.
b. January 20, 1922

Terry Ferrell was born at Pomona, California, to Chester A. and Marjorie McLeod Ferrell, the ninth of ten children, six of whom lived to maturity: Richard, Donald, Patricia, Marilyn, Terry and Jack. Terry was raised in the William Street Chapel, later incorporated as The Church of the Open Bible. His parents, grandparents and great-grandparents on both sides were Christadelphian. There was a doctrinal disagreement and separation occurred, with the Chapel being built in 1914. By 1930 the Pomona Church was affiliated with the General Conference. There was no paid ministry, and J.E. Adamson, Norman J. McLeod and George Lichty shared the pulpit. Norman baptized Terry on August 30, 1936.

The Pomona Church sent Terry to the Summer Bible Training School at Oregon, Illinois, in 1940. He stayed on as General Conference delegate. E. Richard Smith, a member of the first class of the Winter Bible Training School, later known as Oregon Bible College, encouraged Terry to return to school. He did and graduated in 1943.

At Summer School Terry met Orpha Hoskins LeMasurier. She was widowed in 1939 and had a daughter, Diane Clare, born in 1932. Orpha was made treasurer and bookkeeper for the National Bible Institution. Orpha's office was next to the college classroom, and she was the confidante of the students. Terry's ministry began June 8, 1941, at Hickory Grove, Iowa. He preached there until WWII interfered. He pastored the Hillisburg, Indiana, church during his senior year, and received his "baptism of fire" when Billy Huffer would stand up and talk back during the sermon. Terry preached wherever he was called all through school.

Terry and Richard LeCrone were guest speakers at Virginia Conference in August 1943. When Terry was asked to pastor the three Virginia churches he went back to Oregon and married Orpha on September 7, 1943. They raised quite a few eyebrows, as Orpha was 37 and Terry 21. They were married 54 years. While on their honeymoon in Minnesota, they learned the Virginia churches had a change of mind, so they stayed in Minnesota for the winter with Orpha's mother, Ruth Hoskins.

Terry and Orpha were called to Holbrook, Nebraska, in April 1944. It was an active pastorate with services at McCook and Cozad. Terry helped build the parsonage. Their son Stephen was born there March 2, 1945. Most of the members were from early Indiana families. Terry and Orpha were called to Morning Star Church at South Bend, Indiana, and were there from 1949 to 1951. Daughter Diane married Bob Huddlestun, and they remained in South Bend. The Ferrells were at Morristown, Tennessee, in 1951-1952. This was a mission church planted by Evangelist James W. McLain with the beloved Holt families. The Ferrells were called to Brush Creek, Ohio, 1952-1956. There the sanctuary was reversed and classrooms and a social room added. Terry and Orpha pioneered in Christian camping, and continued in it for the next 25 years. How fulfilling to see many of those young campers go on to become leaders.

In 1956 Terry and Orpha were called to Los Angeles, California, where they served until 1961. They were called to Eden Valley, Minnesota, Orpha's home church, and served from 1961 to 1963. They helped build the new church. They served the Guthrie Grove, South Carolina, church from 1963 to May 1968. The parsonage was built, and they taught tithing. While at Guthrie Grove Terry learned the Ferrells were Southerners, and Orpha learned her Grandpa Asa Wilson was from South Carolina.

Terry was asked to edit *The Restitution Herald,* and did so from May 1968 until September 1971. Terry loved the publishing, but not the politics. The Ferrells returned to South Carolina, and helped found the Greenville Church of God, with the blessing of the Guthrie Grove Church, whose members formed the church. Terry founded *The Honest Truth,* and published magazines and books. Aside from short pastorates by Charles Durham and Kenneth Milne, Terry has remained pastor until the present, his 70th year in the ministry.

Besides ministry, Terry has collected and sold antiques, being a licensed dealer since January 1972. His major collection is pottery of the Edgefield District of South Carolina. He and Stephen have written for several major magazines, appeared on TV, and taught and lectured widely for years. Stephen is the official Edgefield potter, and Terry has a shop and museum in Edgefield.

Terry's true and abiding interest and joy is studying the Bible, and he loves helping people know and live the Word of God. His greatest sorrow is seeing people turn from serving God. To any young person considering the ministry, he would say, it is the highest calling in the world, and never just a job.

 See Holt, Belus
    LeCrone, J. Richard
    McLain, James
    McLeod, Norman
    Milne, Kenneth
    Smith, E. Richard
Bibliography: Ferrell, Terry. "Memoirs" April 5, 2011

Foster, Margaret Mattison
b. September 21, 1921

Margaret and second husband, Ray Foster.

Margaret was the pride and joy of her grandfather, S.J. Lindsay. When she was born to Hazel (Lindsay) and Henry Mattison, her grandfather wrote this birth announcement for *The Restitution Herald,* "born: an 8.2 pound girl. She is the picture of health, but is yet without a name. Papa and mama say that whatever her name is to be, she will likely wear it a long time, hence, a good deal of consideration should be given it."

Margaret may have been the granddaughter of a conservative minister, but she was a spirited child who delighted in testing her parents and pushing boundaries. One of Margaret's favorite stories refers to her delight in shocking her mother. One day while discussing an unusual topic, Margaret said, "What a *dastardly* act!" Her mother said, "WHAT?" thinking she'd said a bad word. Margaret laughed.

Also, Margaret didn't mind tormenting her little brother, Jim, as he writes in his memoirs. Jim includes some hilarious stories about their growing-up days in Oregon, Illinois. Here is one about his sister, "Marney" entitled "My Scars":

 My mother wanted to get a bushel of pears from a lady east of town, so she, my sister and I got into the car and drove there. While she and my sister were seeing about the pears, I noticed a barbed wire fence with wooden posts. I had just read a book where the hero placed his hand on the fence post and vaulted over. So I thought I would try that and jump the fence. I put my right hand on the post and vaulted over. However, as I was directly over the barbed wire, my hand slipped off the post and I fell on the barbed wire, tearing my shirt, and deeply cutting my right palm and under my left arm near the shoulder. I was afraid to tell my mother so I kept my hand hidden and sat in the back seat, holding my right hand with my left to keep the blood from dripping on the car. On the way to town, I asked my mother if we could stop and get some bandages in town. My sister immediately spun around to see why I said that, and saw my bloody hand. I got more sympathy from her at that moment than I ever did before or since, I think. (She was always the Chief and I was always the Indian. I never got to be Chief, and I resented that.) That scar remains on my right palm to this day.

 One time when she was telling me what to do and I was resenting it, I hit her. My mother was not far away and saw it. She came over and made me hug and kiss my sister. Ugh.

Thus, the dynamics of siblings in a well-known and dedicated Church of God family from in the 1920s and 1930s are probably not too different from families today.

As a teenager, Margaret knew she was ready to be baptized. The family lived one mile south of Oregon, and she hiked to the north end of town, a distance of nearly two miles, where her grandfather Lindsay lived, and asked him to baptize her. He heard her confession of faith, and took her to the river where he immersed her. This single act of faith impressed her brother so much that he momentarily forgot to be resentful of her. She had set a fine example for him to follow.

Margaret and Jim's parents met at the Katherine Shaw Bethea Hospital in Dixon where Henry was a patient with a broken leg and Hazel was his nurse. They got married and, having neither house nor apartment, camped on the Margaret Fuller Island in the Rock River north of Oregon for nearly a year. It must have been a warm winter.

When their first baby was due, Henry rowed Hazel across the western channel of the river, and they walked to the Lindsay home on North Sixth Street, about two blocks west of the river, where Margaret was born. Soon thereafter, the happy family moved into the remodeled barn behind the Lindsay home where *The Restitution Herald* had been published.

Margaret received a music degree from Northern Illinois Teacher's College. She was a capable pianist and cellist. She taught school and performed wherever she could with an orchestra. She met Elroy "Bud" Budrow at college and they married. He was a well known and beloved Jazz and Dixieland instrumental artist. He excelled at playing string bass and bass horn.

Being a musician did not pay well, so Henry arranged for his son-in-law to work at the Mattison Machine Works in Rockford. This was at the beginning of WWII. Mattison manufactured wooden war implements with metal parts. Elroy was unfortunately killed in a foundry accident when molten metal fell on him. He knew his

Elroy Budrow

baby daughter, Jean, for only two months before his death in 1942.

Margaret married Ray Foster at her parent's home on October 25, 1947. Ray was an accomplished musician, and together they played in area bands. Margaret and Ray started a new family and had nine children. Jean Budrow was raised by Hazel and Henry.

When Jean was a toddler, her grandmother gave her a sports whistle and she went around the house tooting on the whistle. About then, Henry's mother came to visit. She and Hazel had a strained relationship, and Mother Mattison quickly became annoyed with the whistle. Hazel drew Jean's teenaged Uncle Jim aside, and said, "I am afraid Jean's whistle might wear out. Can you pick up a new one in town?" Mother Mattison soon returned home.

Of Margaret's ten children, two married ministers, one became a minister of music and another a minister's daughter. Jean married a minister and became one herself in the Methodist fellowship. Ray and Margaret helped steady the work at the newly formed Family Bible Fellowship in Rockford, Illinois. Both participated in short mission trips to the Philippines with the Churches of God in Washington State in the early 1990s.

Ray died in February 2002 from complications after heart surgery, and Pastor Jeff Peterson of

Back, from left - Sam Foster, Ray Foster, Dan Foster, Judy Foster, Sarah Cronin, Mary Foster, Susan Brown, Nancy Rankin. Front - Elizabeth Mulli, Margaret Foster, Jean Budrow Rencontre.

Family Bible Fellowship offered words of comfort to the family and spoke of seeing Ray again in the Kingdom of God.

Margaret continues in her dedication to assist the congregation as it ministers to the poor, homeless, weak and disabled of Rockford. Margaret has a rich and charitable character, which she has generously shared with the Church of God during her lifetime.

Jean Budrow with her great-grandmother Nellie Lindsay

See Lindsay, S.J. (19th)
Mattison, Hazel Lindsay
Mattison, James

Bibliography: Foster, Margaret. Letter to, and Interview with JStilson regarding Margaret's memories of childhood. Fall 2005 and Spring 2007; Mattison, Jim. "Life of Jim (James Henry) Mattison 1924-20, Life of a Country Boy Preacher." Self published. 2005; *The Restitution Herald*, Birth Announcement. October 4, 1921; Budrow/Foster wedding announcement, *The Restitution Herald*, Sydney Magaw, ed., Oregon, IL. Oct. 28, 1947.

Ezra Railsback was a noted church leader. During the tumultuous year of controversy over the management of *The Restitution*, after which it was moved to Cleveland under the editorial guidance of Robert Huggins, Indiana people were unhappy. Ezra made this motion at the Summer Conference:

"That since *The Restitution* in transferring to its present management has violated its previous position before the Indiana people to the extent that the majority of the brethren in the state desire severance from their former relations, that motion be presented to declare *The Restitution* no longer the official organ of the Church of God in Indiana and that its place is vacant."

Ref.: *The Restitution Herald*, October 26, 1911.

Pastor Leon Driskill at Northeast Conference with his class of Juniors.
Photo provided by Rex Cain

G

Gallagher, Hazel E. (Stadden)
b. March 27, 1932
d. November 21, 1986

Hazel Stadden was born in Cleveland, Ohio, to Herbert and Frances Stadden. She attended the Golden Rule Church of God there and was baptized as a teenager. Hazel married Harold Gallagher of New York They had four children, Steve H., Dan H., Sharonlee F. and Mark H. The family lived in Dayton, Ohio, where Hazel was an LPN in the Dayton hospital pediatric intensive care unit. She cared for seriously ill infants and children. Sharonlee died in an auto accident on July 3, 1978; she was 20.

Hazel was a member of Troy View Church of God in Troy, Ohio, where she played piano and organ, and directed the choir. Hazel is also buried in Troy.

   See Stadden, Frances A.
         Stadden, Herbert W.

Bibliography: Atlanta Bible College biography project, David Krogh, compiler.

Gaspar, Joe
b. October 1, 1891
d. October 10, 1968

Gaspar, May (Mary) Hanon
b. September 11, 1890
d. July 26, 1967

Pastor James A. Patrick immersed teenager May Hanon following special meetings at a rural schoolhouse south of Lake Koromis, Paynesville, Minnesota. Soon thereafter, he also baptized Joe Gaspar and officiated at their wedding on May 16, 1916. The couple had three children, Elmo of Eden Valley, Lorraine of Minneapolis, and James of Chippewa Falls, Minnesota.

Joe and May resided in Eden Valley their entire married life. Joe owned a grocery business for 62 years with May's help. Both served in many offices of the Eden Valley Church of God and the Minnesota State Conference. Their legacy in the Church of God lives in the service of their grandchildren Bill and Bob Gaspar and their sister, Michelle "Shelly" Millard.

   See Patrick, James

Bibliography: ABC Biography project, David Krogh, compiler; Ancestry.com U.S. Census. Minnesota. Mannanah. Meeker. 1930; Social Security Death List, Records of Joseph Gaspar and Mary (May) Gaspar.

Geiselman, Nathan H.
b. March, 1858
d. 1955

Nathan Geiselman was born to Josiah and Mary Geiselman in Marshall County, Indiana. Josiah was a blacksmith. Nathan was baptized in 1874 at age 16. It is unknown who baptized him but might have been one of several evangelists working in Indiana, including John Shafer, Stedman Chaplin or Ephraim Miller. Nathan married Julia A. Miller at Elkhart, Indiana, on November 8, 1880.

Nathan was influential in beginning the North Union Church of God near Burr Oak, Indiana, in the late 1800s. North Union was a community church with a strong membership of Brethren. The Fetter family began to study their Bible at home and became convinced that the church was not teaching Bible doctrines. About that time, Nathan Geiselman arrived and was invited to preach. The Fetters found they agreed with him, and Nathan was invited to preach regularly at North Union. The Williams family also came to believe in the Gospel of the Kingdom, and in a short time, the congregation grew as people came to hear him preach. Nathan taught Kingdom of God on Earth and the sleep of the dead, and some began to call it the "Advent Church."

Soon, not wanting to be labeled Adventists, the Age-to-Come believers at North Union departed and relocated closer to Burr Oak. They built the first Church of God there, but it was a short-lived cause for celebration.

Lightning struck the church, and it burned to the ground. They rebuilt.

Pastor Geiselman lived in Baltimore, Maryland, for a time where he assisted in preaching for the Virginia churches. In 1922, Geiselman filled in as pastor for the Virginia churches after the death of Pastor J.H. Anderson's wife, a bad circumstance that forced him to make arrangements for care and raising his children. The Virginia people enjoyed Geiselman's preaching and reported on the work to *The Restitution Herald*. In 1946, Pastor J.R. LeCrone mentioned Geiselman in his Virginia history and affirmed that N.H. Geiselman had been a well-liked pastor by the Virginia brethren. After the Church of God General Conference was incorporated, a newly-created ministerial recognition list included Nathan Geiselman for 1922, and perhaps more years after that.

Nathan spent winters near Tampa, Florida. In early 1948, word came to readers of *The Restitution Herald* that N.H. Geiselman had a stroke at his home in Florida but was improving. He was nearly 90 years old at the time and lived several more years beyond that. It is not known where he was interred.

   See Anderson, J.H. (19th)
           Chaplin, Stedman (19th)
           Miller, Ephraim (19th)
           Shafer, John (19th)

Bibliography: Ancestry.com. U.S. Census. Indiana. Marshall. German. 1860; Ancestry.com. Florida Death Index, 1877-1998, Record of Nathan H. Geiselman; Ancestry.com. Indiana Marriage Collection 1800-1941 record for Nathan and Julia Geiselman; LeCrone, J.R. "Men Who Pastored in Virginia." *The Restitution Herald*. Sept. 17, 1946; *The Fiftieth Anniversary of the Burr Oak Church of God*. Dec. 10, 1951, Historical Committee of the Burr Oak; Various reports, *The Restitution Herald*, Jan. 29, 1919; Feb. 10, 1948; Oct. 12, 1948.

Gesin, Mary A.
b. August 10, 1883
d. December 1972?

Mary and Charles Gesin lived in Adeline, Maryland Township, Ogle County, Illlinois. Charles was either the brother or son of Ernest. Early Church of God circuit riders who came through Maryland Township introduced them to the Gospel of the Kingdom. Adeline was a small town that did not grow after the railroad bypassed it. The lack of railroad commerce may be one reason that Church of God moved from Adeline to Oregon, Illinois, the county seat.

Mary Gesin was a Berean who resided near Forreston but sometimes attended worship in Oregon. She and other members felt strongly about the mission of the Bereans. The Bereans believed in Bible study, and in printing study and evangelistic materials that proclaimed the Gospel.

In 1910 she wrote *Jesus, Light of the World*, a series of Bible stories for children. The foreword says:

> This little book is published because of an urgent demand on the part of many parents who love their children and wish to have them enjoy the truth of the story of Jesus in its simplicity, without error or man's theory.

The stories were short, each a page or two in length. The chapters included, "The Angel," "The Babe," "The Shepherds," "The Three Wise Men," "A Wicked Ruler," "In the Temple," "The Baptism of Jesus," "Calling His Helpers," "Feeding the Multitude" and several more.

The book is bound in dark colored parchment paper with gold print on the title page and an illustration of a lighthouse. The book is part of the archival collection at Atlanta Bible College, McDonough, Georgia.

   See Aslaksen, Martin
           Austin, Evelyn Harsh
           Gesin, Ernest

Bibliography: Ancestry.com US Census. Illinois. Ogle. Maryland. Dist. 78. 1910; Gesin. Mary. *Jesus, Light of the World*. 1910. Housed at Atlanta Bible College; Stilson. J., Book Review.

Gifford, Ezra D.
b. January 1, 1860
d. April 8, 1953

Ezra Gifford was born in Cox Creek, Iowa, to George L. and Clarinda Gifford, the fifth of seven children. He and Mary were married in Iowa, and they had two daughters, Clara, and Eudora, and a son, David. Ezra attended a nondenominational theological seminary in Hillsdale, Michigan, and majored in biblical languages. He learned about the Abrahamic Faith from his seminary studies. He served as pastor of Churches of God at Philadelphia, Grand Rapids, Dubuque, Minneapolis, Marshalltown (Iowa) and San Diego. He then moved to Spokane, Washington, to become pastor of the Church of God in Christ Jesus there.

When he moved to Spokane there was no Church of God, so he started one. He became a church planter and a church builder. He rented a hall and began to announce meetings for preaching services. With no members except his own family, he built the congregation by baptizing more than 75 believers the first four years. In 1888, when the Church of God organized a national conference work in Philadelphia, the constitution specified that new churches associated with the conference should choose the name "Church of God in Christ Jesus," or "Church of the Blessed Hope." The US Census listed his occupation as a "Minister of the Church of God in Christ Jesus."

By 1937 the Spokane congregation had grown by an additional 100 members. They purchased a church building for $4,500 and paid the mortgage within five years. Ezra was relatively isolated from other Church of God brethren. Delbert Rankin of the Church of God Archives at Belle Plaine, Iowa, wrote, "The preachers at Cashmere (Church of God) visited Gifford one time in Spokane, 180 miles to the east. [Gifford] apparently maintained independence."

Ezra was also a noted author. He published *The Way of Truth*. Having an education in biblical languages was an asset to *The Way of Truth* because Ezra's explanations had depth and clarity. *The Spokane Daily Chronicle* noted "his writings give frequent independent translations." It seemed each issue of *The Way of Truth* was devoted to one topic. Volume I carried the subtitle, "Divine Doctrine Showing Clearly the Truth Concerning the True God." In this issue he laid out the biblical teaching of the Old and New Testaments regarding the nature of God which he believed taught the oneness of God.

Ezra also authored *The Seven Churches of Revelation* from *The Way of Truth* series; *Salvation, What it is and How to Get it; The Perfect Law and the Sabbath of the Gospel; The True Church;* and *The Prophet Jonah the Sign of the Man*.

It is not known how many monthly issues of *The Way of Truth* were published. Within a few years the circulation of the periodical included nearly 2,000 Spokane, national and Canadian readers. The Atlanta Bible College Archive has at least one copy of *The Way of Truth* and would like to have more.

Gifford authored *The Life of Jesus the Christ, Studies in His Life as Teacher, Example, Lawgiver, Redeemer, Lifegiver, Priest and King*. His daughter, Clara May Gifford, published this 499-page book in Spokane in 1949. In addition, Clara May published several other titles by her father including *The True God, The True Christ, The True Holy Spirit,* hard-bound with 192 pages, a very important book according to advertisements. These titles may have been part of *The Way of Truth* series. Elder Gifford was a musician and composer. He wrote all the hymns sung at church. In time, he compiled this music into a volume of worship hymns and songs, *Songs of Grace and Truth*.

Gifford did not preach for salary nor take up collections. In those days, many churches had free-will offering boxes in the foyer for private offerings from members and guests. It is unknown if he had outside employment in addition to his writing. His books and periodicals were circulated throughout the United States and Canada and "sold by the thousands." Perhaps there was enough income from this to afford the family home.

It is thought that Ezra and Mary Gifford are interred at Greenwood Memorial Terrace in Spokane.

Bibliography: Ancestry.com, U.S. Census. Iowa. Clayton. Cox Creek. 1870; U.S. Census. Washington. Spokane. Spokane. Dist. 235. 1920; Gifford, Ezra, *The Way of Truth*, Dec. 1921 excerpt from *The Spokane Daily Chronicle* of Nov. 26, 1921;"Elder E.D. Gifford" *The Spokane Daily Chronicle*, May 1, 1937; Ancestry. com, Washington Death Index 1940-1996; Rankin, Delbert. Letter to JStilson, together with considerable Gifford material from the Belle Plaine Church of God Archives, Aug. 3, 2009.

Goekler, Harry
b. January 23, 1911
d. March 24, 1998

Harry and Thelma

Harry Goekler was born at Dolson, Clark County, Illinois, to Clarence and Mary Jane Goekler, the third of five children (two boys, three girls). The Goeklers were Church of God members at Casey, Illinois.

Harry's parents raised him to believe that one day the Jews would return to their homeland, and soon thereafter, the Lord would return to earth to establish the Kingdom of God. Harry attended Oregon Bible College graduating to serve the Lord in several pastorates. He served at Happy Woods, Louisiana, where he met Thelma Richardson. They married and had two children, Sylvia and Dennis. Harry served the Happy Woods congregation on two separate times. He also served as pastor at the Blood River Church of God at Springfield, Louisiana. Other pastoral assignments included Hector, Minnesota, Church of God; Harlingen, Texas (twice); and Oregon, Illinois.

He wrote a tract, "The Kingdom of God," a small three-fold paper that covered the location, extent, duration, ruler and people of the Kingdom. This was published at the National Bible Institute by the National Berean Society at Oregon, Illinois, and may be found in the Atlanta Bible College archival tract collection.

Harry was a good Bible student and he loved people. He had a ready smile and a strong handshake. He loved history, and when *The History Newsletter* began at Oregon Bible College in the 1980s, he regularly contributed letters, stories and photos from the work at Casey and Marshall in Illinois. Harry told the story of D.M. Hudler (1837-1909) to *The History Newsletter*. Hudler, an Iowa evangelist, worked throughout Kentucky and Tennessee during the winter and across the north in summer. Harry reported that the last time Hudler was in Harriman, Tennessee, was also his final tour of service. Because

Marshall Church of God, home church of Harry Goekler's grandparents, the Claypools.

The congregation at Marshall, Illinois.
Photo from Mildred Dennis

Hudler preached a message unpopular with the other churches in the area, he was beaten by mob action. Harry said Hudler was beaten so badly after an evening service that he died of his wounds a few days later. Hudler's obituary said he died with his "Armor on and the sword of the Spirit in his hand."

Pastor Goekler died in Harlingen and was interred there, surrounded by his loving family. His service was conducted by Kent H. Ross of Atlanta Bible College.

See Hudler, D.M. (19th)
See Also Appendix, Catalyst for Change
Bibliography: ABC Biography Project, David Krogh, compiler; Goekler, Harry, "The Kingdom of God," NBI, National Berean Society, Oregon, IL. 1938; JStilson, memories of Pastor Harry Goekler; Ross, Kent. E-mail to JStilson Sept 4, 2010.

Goit, Edward "Ed"
b. November 1, 1921

Edward "Ed" Goit was born to Emery Herbert and Ona Lee (Ackerman) Goit. Ona Lee was from Wilson, New York, and Emery from Canada. Ona met Emery when she moved to the Niagara area. Ed was the eldest of four children, with one sister, Shirley, and two half sisters, June and Sarah. They grew up in the Niagara Falls area.

As a teen, Ed went to a youth activity at the Niagara Falls Church of God. His cousin, Ruth Hill (who later married Linford Moore), invited Ed's sister Shirley to church and Ed went also. There he met Viola, the prettiest girl there. She was Linford Moore's sister. Ed and Viola have been sweethearts ever since. Pastor Clyde Randall baptized all the teenagers, and married Ed and Viola on June 5, 1942.

Viola and Ed had five children, Sharon (Kilgore), born in 1943; Edward Jr. (Margaret), 1945; Carol (Glen Swartz), 1946; Robert William, 1949, who died recently of brain cancer; and Marilyn (Keighley), 1952. Ed and Viola have been blessed with ten grandchildren and 15 great-grandchildren, one of whom died young.

Ed moved his family to Oregon, Illinois, to attend Oregon Bible College. They resided in an upstairs apartment. To support the family, Ed worked at various places, including the Locker Plant in Byron and Kable in Mt. Morris. He also delivered the *Chicago Sun Times* and *Chicago Tribune*; his route covered the whole town of Oregon. Ed graduated from college in 1945 with Harold Doan, Linford Moore and Jim Mattison. When he graduated, he had one child, Sharon, and a second on the way. Ed was ordained to the ministry that same year.

Men who greatly influenced Ed in his student years and early ministry were F.L. Austin and L.E. Conner, instructors, and Clyde Randall, his pastor, and Sydney E. Magaw, editor of *The Restitution Herald*. Ed said, "I have sat many times at the dining table in the Magaw home and enjoyed that family." Ed also commented that G.E. Marsh and Clyde Randall served as his mentors. While in Oregon, Ed and Viola worshipped at the Oregon Church of God where he filled in as needed for teaching and preaching.

After Ed's graduation, the Goit family moved to Arkansas City, Kansas, to serve the church there until 1946. They also spent a year at the Eldorado Church of God. They returned to the Niagara Falls area where Ed enrolled at Niagara University and studied business. He began to work in retail, and especially enjoyed men's clothing because he had learned the business while working at the National Clothing House in Oregon when he was a student.

In 1951 Ed took a position with Montgomery Ward in Portsmouth, New Hampshire. He also preached for the Advent Christian Church in Eliot, Maine, which was just over the state line from New Hampshire. In 1953, they were transferred to Greenville, Pennsylvania, where Ed became the Montgomery Ward store manager. There they attended a Baptist church, and Ed participated in teaching the adult class, preaching and other duties as requested. He said, "I always preached Church of God doctrine in the Baptist Church!"

The family returned to New York and settled in North Tonawanda where Ed was employed at Sattler's Department store and worked there for 28 years. During this time he served as elder of the Fonthill, Ontario, congregation and was the fill-in pastor twice. He replaced Milon Hall as interim pastor, and while serving there, began the midweek service. Ed said he has served as elder under Pastors Milon Hall, Emory Macy, Jack Hearp, Stephen Bolhous, and is an Honorary Elder at the time of this compilation. During this time he has also written for the Church of God *Adult Quarterly* and *The Restitution Herald*. Ed faced a low point in his career when he left the full-time ministry. He said churches should be more supportive of young ministers and their families. His advice to churches and ministers is "Keep your promises. The ministry should warrant that."

In 1979, Ed had major surgery to remove a portion of his stomach and esophagus because of cancer. He regained his health, and he gave God the credit for returning him to good health.

In 1981, Ed and Viola moved to Hedrick, Indiana. Ed said, "The people in Hedrick were wonderful." They were supportive and friendly and treated them like family. Ed said, "At holidays when we couldn't get home because of the distance, they invited us in at Christmas and we were like family."

When asked what aspect of his ministry impacted him the most he replied promptly about weekends in Chicago at the Pacific Garden Mission when he was a student at Oregon Bible College. He said a carload of students would go in, and it was there he learned about the human condition and its needs. He said serving in that capacity taught him how to serve humanity with love. Over the years interacting with the public, his experience at PGM helped him work with people. He said, "Students and ministers need practical experience like that." He felt it prepared him to deal with the problems that people have.

For example, Ed cited the times in Hedrick when he routinely visited three area nursing homes that had

> "Place trust in God. He works for you to mold you and use you. He touched my life. His ways are higher than mine. His way is beyond me. He gives me strength!"
>
> - Ed Goit

between 200-500 patients, all of them with troubles and needs. He visited them every week and brought them the Word of God, prayer, and a word of encouragement.

His advice to young and student ministers:
Be grounded in the faith. Preach the Bible. Know what you believe. Put your dependence on God. It means everything in situations where you are confronted. Ministers can get into bad situations, too. You have problems too, and you have no one else to turn to in many instances, but turn to God.

Ed faced his deepest crisis when his health failed. He faced it again in 2010 when he had a cancerous kidney removed. At this writing, he thrives and gives God credit for that. He said, "God is not through with me yet. He has things for me to do."

When asked about the future for children who have died without Christ, he replied quickly, "It's in God's hands. He knows what is best. I can't know that." When asked the fate of carnal Christians when Christ comes again, he replied without hesitation, "God will forgive them, but be sure that the sin will be punished." By punishment he meant that the rewards to the righteous will be less to the carnal Christians who have sinned but who have repented and stayed with the Lord. He did not see the carnal Christians as being the unjust and cast into the outer darkness. He said, "When one puts on Christ in baptism, God is faithful to forgive that person and to fulfill His promises."

In 2009, Ed donated his study library to the Atlanta Bible College which is greatly appreciated. Ed and Viola continue to serve and have been great examples to those who have benefitted from their leadership. All are grateful for their service in the Church of God.

See Austin, F.L.
Conner, L.E. (19th)
Doan, Harold
Magaw, Sydney
Marsh, G.E.
Mattison, Jim
Moore, Linford
Randall, Clyde
Siple, F.E.

Bibliography: Goit, Ed and Viola, Interview with JStilson, March 26, 2011.

Ed and Viola

Gordon, Grover
b. March 18, 1889
d. June 6, 1960

Grover Gordon was one of 14 children born to James and Emma Gordon at St. Paul, Nebraska. After James' death in 1897, Grover made his home with his sister, Mrs. Eva Phelps, near Cambridge, Nebraska. As an adult, Grover engaged in farming for several years. Grover, his mother and brother Harry united with the Church of God and were baptized by Almus Adams on October 30, 1915. Grover later attended the Bible Training Class of the Church of God at Oregon, Illinois.

On June 24, 1929, Grover married Inez G. Long at her home near Cambridge. They had no children. On August 15 that same year, he was ordained and entered the ministry for the Church of God. He served as the first regular pastor at Holbrook, Nebraska, from 1931 to 1938. During that time he also preached for the Chappell and Omaha congregations. When Grover was away from Holbrook, Arthur Hornaday filled the pulpit.

Gordon also served Los Angeles, Cleveland and Lawrenceville churches in Ohio (1943-1948), and the Church of God at Fonthill, Ontario, but his heart was in Nebraska. He and Inez stayed in Fonthill two years before moving home.

Grover and Inez Gordon

A story about Grover Gordon is recorded in the minutes of the Church of God at Ripley, Illinois. In 1935, C.E. Lapp had given notice at Ripley. The church received a letter from Grover Gordon that he was interested. Gordon said he would need $75 per month and rent money for a parsonage. The church took pledges from members, as was their usual method to finance the pastor's salary, and raised $42. The church discussed it and did not call Pastor Gordon.

On September 1, 1956, Grover Gordon moved to Chappell and was still serving this congregation when he died. Inez was at his side. At the time of Grover's death he was survived by Inez, five sisters and one brother. They were Mrs. Cora Pace, Hastings, Nebraska; Mrs. A.T. Nelson, Omaha; Mrs. Ida Pinkerton, Denver, Colorado; Mrs. William Greenlee Sr., Oshkosh, Nebraska; Mrs.

Grover Gordon, left, with Clarence Lapp

Jesse Steele, Tooele, Utah; and Harry Gordon, Auburn, Washington. When Inez was called to work at Oregon Bible College, she moved east again and settled in Oregon, Illinois. She served as the female students' matron in the Women's Dorm from 1961-1966. Inez then married Grover's brother and moved to Washington.

Harvey U. Krogh Jr. of Oregon, Illinois, conducted funeral services for Grover at the Churches of God at Chappell and Holbrook, with Elders Vivian Kirkpatrick and C.E. Randall assisting at Holbrook. Burial was in the Holbrook Cemetery. Inez rests beside him.

See Kirkpatrick, Vivian, Sr.
Krogh, Harvey U., Jr.
Lapp, C.E.

Bibliography: Ancestry.com U.S. Census. Nebraska. Furnas. Burton Bend. Dist. 81. 1920; *The Restitution Herald*. Various issues; "Inez Gordon," Atlanta Bible College Biography Project, compiled David Krogh, Autumn 2006; Photo copy of Early Records-1900s, Ripley Church of God Ripley, Illinois, copy owned by Rock River Christian College Archives, Beloit, Wisconsin; "We are pleased to honor Holbrook Church of God," *The Restitution Herald*, Oregon, Il., July, 1975.

Graham, Ernest Edwin, Jr.
b. July 7, 1919
d. February 26, 2009

Ernest "Ed" Graham was born in Fredericktown, Missouri, to Ernest and Maude Graham. Ed was born a few months after the death of his father. Maude raised Ed and his siblings, Roy and Alice, by herself. This family was instrumental in starting and building the Blush Church of God in Missouri. Roy and Ed became pastors in the Church of God.

Ernest married Lois Johnson from Minnesota. They had seven children: Steve, Judy, Dave, Dan, Joe, Mark and Elizabeth. Lois, Mark and Dan predeceased Ernest. Dan died in Colorado May 9, 2007, surrounded by his sisters and brothers. While Ed and Lois were still in college, they and their

Graham's photo of Oregon Bible College, winter 1945

The Grahams lived in this small trailer while they were students.
National Bible Institute Evangelistic Truck.

Pastors Ed Graham, back left, and J Arlen Marsh with the Golden Rule Church of God youth group, 1960.

two children resided in a small trailer because the dorms did not have accommodations for families. Evangelists Francis Burnett and Jim McLain pulled this same trailer behind the Gospel Van, Burnett across Missouri and McLain across Arkansas. While still in college, Ernest filled the pulpit at Hedrick, Indiana.

After graduation, Ernest preached in Graytown, Wisconsin, until he was called to Holbrook, Nebraska, in 1950. He and Lois also served in Golden, Colorado, and Dixon, Illinois. Lois was an excellent pianist and an asset to the music program of every church they served. She accompanied on piano or organ while Ed, and later the children, sang special musical ensembles. All the children were trained to play several instruments. They enhanced worship services at church and conference meetings with harmonious and inspiring music.

Ernest engaged in pastoral duties and had compassion for his people. He excelled in counseling others in times of trouble. He participated in the hospital chaplaincy program as many Church of God ministers have. He was able to soothe a troubled spirit by reminding a patient of the sufferings Christ endured so we might be redeemed.

Lois died at Dixon, Illinois, on April 22, 1973, bringing grief to family and friends throughout the Church of God. A few years later, Ernest remarried and moved to Florida. Altogether Ed served in pastoral ministry for 30 years. His son, David Graham, became a Church of God historian, researching the history of the Age-to-Come movement in America, especially the life and work of Joseph Marsh, early publisher of that prophecy system.

Pastor Ed died at Lakeland, Florida, after a courageous battle with cancer and was interred beside Lois at Chapel Hill Cemetery in Dixon, Illinois, where they had served in the Church of God. A moving memorial service hosted by the family with music was held at the Oregon Church of God June 13, 2009. Pastor Joe Myers of Cornerstone Bible Church of God in McDonough, Georgia, a former Dixon youth member, preached the memorial sermon.

See Bailey, Joshua (19th)
     Burnett, Francis
     Graham, Roy
     Marsh, Joseph (19th)
     McLain, James

Bibliography: *The Restitution Herald* June, 19, 1919; Aug. 6, 1919; Oct. 5, 1948; Graham, David. Graham family information by e-mail March 23, 2008, Sept 4, 2010, Feb. 10, 2011; Obituary for Ernest Graham, *Democrat News Online* as retrieved from dailyjournalonline.com March 23, 2009.

Graham, Roy Gervaise
b. November 29, 1912
d. December 1977

Roy Graham was born in Madison County, Polk Township, Missouri, son of Ernest Graham Sr. Ernest died in a tragic accident when Roy was eight. Roy's mother raised the children in the knowledge of the Lord. Roy, Ed and Alice's son, Carl Jennings, became Church of God pastors. Roy and his family were responsible for building the Blush, Missouri, church where he baptized 12 new believers. Roy also constructed the Fredericktown, Missouri, church building. Clarence Lapp preached at the dedication service and helped lay the cornerstone after the

The Brothers and Sisters of Oregon Bible College (1968-69), from left: Dan Graham, Mike Berry, Debbie Peters (Lewis), Betsy Mattison (Moore), Alice Dochstader (Railton), Valeria Smith (Berry), Joe Duncan, David Graham.

Fredericktown church under construction

service. It read "Church of God of the Faith of Abraham, 1946 A.D."

Roy was a musical protégé. When the family moved to Denver, he built a sound studio in his home. He built and sold six- and seven-string guitars and mandolins. Roy also gave lessons in his studio and furnished instruments to musicians with the Denver Mandolin Orchestra, which he helped organize. As every member of the family was musically inclined, many fine recordings were made in this studio. His collection of fine guitars and instruments was destroyed in a house fire in Phoenix in early 2011.

Roy and wife with son Gerry

The Denver Mandolin Orchestra
Photo from denvermandolin.com and used with permission.

Roy preached at the Denver Church of God and participated in many conference and ministerial activities. He invited gospel teams from Oregon Bible College to present musical programs at the Denver Church. The Brothers and Sisters, a college folk-music group, presented a program in Denver and many other Churches of God during the 1970s. David and Dan Graham, Roy's nephews, were members of this singing group.

Roy is buried at the New Masonic Cemetery in Fredericktown, Missouri.

   See Graham, Ernest Edwin, Jr.
          Lapp, Clarence

Bibliography: Ancestry.com U.S. Census. Missouri. Madison. Polk. Dist. 55. 1920; Social Security Death List record for Roy Graham; Notice of baptisms, *The Restitution Herald,* Sydney Magaw, ed., Oregon, Il., May 1, 1948; Graham, David, Information about Uncle Roy," by E-mail July 3, 2008; Graham, David. E-mail August 2009; Graham, David. "Church of God Connexion & Review" *Wisdom and Power,* Nov. 1992, pp.18,19; D. Graham made a list of burial sites of fifty Church of God leaders and pastors which has been helpful in adding detail to many entries in this encyclopedia; Photo of Denver Mandolin Orchestra used with permission.

Green, John Freeman
b. September 12, 1873
d. May 1966

Green, Lina T.
b. March 20, 1877
d. August 1976

John Green was ordained in the Church of God and preached for over 30 years. He resided in Kansas City, Missouri, with Lina faithfully at his side in ministry for more than 65 years. They read the Bible together daily and prayed together often. They gave God the glory for their longevity. They raised eight children and adopted another girl when they were past 60 years old.

Lina was a seamstress and one of her clients was Margaret "Molly" Brown—The Unsinkable Molly Brown of Titanic fame. Margaret would show Lina a picture of a dress from a magazine, and Lina could duplicate it with attention to every detail.

Their son Mark wrote that Lina applied herself to every chore from running a household to being a minister's wife. He said, "This was no small doing." Of John, Mark wrote, "Many times my father prayed in the basement of our home when he thought no one else was around. I was witness to this and it always stirred me deeply to see him doing this. To this I am indebted and it impressed me very much."

Bibliography: Green, Mark. ABC Biography Project of John and Lina Green, David Krogh, compiler.

Hall, Frederick E.
b. April 25, 1892
d. April 1966

Fred Hall was born to Eugene and Claudia Hall in Potter County, Pennsylvania. The family moved to Michigan when Fred was 11. Where or when the family came into the Church of God is unknown. Eugene may have met George Storrs or others who had been prominent in the Millerite movement of the early 19th century.

Fred wed Winnie Peck. They had two daughters, Elizabeth "Betty" (Townsend) and Zoe (Birde). Winnie died soon after Zoe's birth. Fred married Eurie Mae Retalick of Battle Creek, Michigan. They had three children, E. Milon, Iris Harriet (Burnett) and David Randolph.

Fred and Eurie lived in Grand Rapids from 1917 to 1942. They first attended the Southlawn Church of God in Grand Rapids, during which time Eurie learned about the Gospel of the Kingdom and was baptized. Fred and Eurie were good Bible students who loved to read the Scriptures. In 1935, they joined with several other Church of God faithful and became charter members of the Pennellwood Church of God in Grand Rapids. They remained active at Pennellwood until they began to winter in Tempe, Arizona, in 1942.

During the 1946 General Conference, Fred announced his intention to become a minister. He began his pastorate in Arkansas in September 1946. In the fall of 1947, they moved to Hillisburg, Indiana, where he began preaching at the Old "Plummer" Church of God, now known as Country Chapel. At that time, his son, Milon, was a student at Oregon Bible College. On one occasion they both attended homecoming at Kokomo and served communion together. D.G. Harvey commented in his report, "What a beautiful thing it was to see father and son working together in this service." Because of asthma, Fred was forced to retire again to Arizona in 1950.

Fred was known for an interest in Anglo-Israelism, the idea that the ten lost tribes of Israel may be found in America and European countries, making all descendants of European ancestry Jewish. John Wilson's, *Our Israelitish Origins,* published in England around 1850, exposed America to this teaching, but it never became a component of a statement of faith in the Church of God.

Fred and Eurie are buried at the Double Butte Cemetery in Tempe, Arizona.

See Burnett, Francis
Hall, E. Milon

Bibliography: Ancestry.com. U.S. Census. Michigan. Kent. Paris. Dist. 125. 1930. Biography project of Atlanta Bible College, David Krogh, compiler; *The Restitution Herald*, Oct. 7, 1947; Stilson, Jan, Reminiscences of Eurie and Fred Hall following a stay in their home, 1961 during a Gospelette tour; Social Security Master Death List, record for Fred Hall.

Hall, E. Milon
b. 1919
d. December 31, 1978

Milon Hall was born to Frederick and Eurie Hall, the third of five children. His siblings included half sisters, Elizabeth "Betty" (Townsend) and Zoe (Birde); and full siblings Iris and David. The family lived in Kent County, Michigan. Milon and wife Joan had five children: Ken, Ray, Connie, Gail and Kerry.

Before entering the ministry, Milon was a farmer. In 1941, the young couple packed and moved to Oregon, Illinois, where Milon attended the newly organized Oregon Bible College. He graduated in 1945. Pastorates where Milon and Joan served included Fonthill, Ontario; Pennellwood Church of God at Grand Rapids, Michigan; Blessed Hope in Rockford, Illinois; and others.

Milon loved to preach and sing. He participated in the youth movement of the Church of God by serving on camp staffs for several decades as counselor, teacher, director or sports coordinator. As teacher at one camp class, he reported to the teens that he got very motivated at Fonthill to give his best for the Lord. At Fonthill he had to drive past the fire station every day. It had a large sign that said "Fire Hall." He was inspired by it to give his very best, or the elders might "fire Hall." Milon also taught an impressive lesson on making decisions, as in making a decision for Christ. He said "even not making a decision is a decision. When confronting Christ, it's better to make a decision for him than to not decide and eventually to turn away."

When Milon died following a battle with a brain tumor, he was greatly missed by his Christian friends in the Church of God. He is interred at Kent Memorial Gardens in Kentwood, Michigan. His widow, Joan, married Edwin Smith of Oregon, Illinois. Milon and Joan's children continue in ministry through the faithful service of Connie (Dale) Ramsey and Pastor Ray (Sue Alcumbrack) Hall and their children.

Bibliography: Ancestry.com. U.S. Census. Michigan. Kent. Paris. Dist. 125. 1930; Krogh, David. E-mail to Jstilson Aug. 21, 2009.

Hanson, Leland
b. October 1899
d. September 1976

Leland Hanson was born in Lebanon, Illinois, to Chris and Asa G. Hanson. He was the youngest of six: three sons and three daughters. Leland and his sister Leota became the best known of the Hansons within the Church of God. All the Hanson children were members of the National Berean Society, but Leota and Leland were the most distinguished.

Leland frequented conference meetings in Missouri and Illinois and through this, met young Mary Austin, daughter of Mr. and Mrs. F.L. Austin. After a suitable courtship, Leland and Mary wed on June 8, 1924 at her parent's home in Oregon, Illinois. Leland taught school in Pine Creek area of Ogle County near Oregon.

Later, Leland became Assistant Superintendent of Schools for Ogle County. Later, he and Mary moved to Grand Rapids, Michigan, where they resided until his retirement. Leland died in Fort Lauderdale, Florida.

See Austin, F.L.
Hanson, Leota B.

Bibliography: Ancestry.com. U.S. Census. Il. St. Clair. Lebanon. Dist. 112. 1900; U.S. Census. Il. Ogle. Pine Creek. Dist. 14. 1920; Social Security Death List, record for Leland Hanson; *The Restitution Herald*, June 10, 1924.

Hanson, Leota B.
b. March 28, 1888
d. June 1982

Leota B. Hanson was born in Lebanon, Illinois, near St. Louis. She was a capable young woman determined to earn her way in the world. Leota was employed in a business office in St. Louis where her ability with numbers and records was an asset. In her off time, she was editor of the Berean Column in *The Restitution* and *The Restitution Herald* from 1920-1925.

Leota was an organizing member of the National Berean Society, begun principally by Illinois women in 1913. She worked with Anna Drew, Evelyn Harsh Austin and Dr. Leila Whitehead. The Bereans encouraged young adults to study God's Word, prepare for service and remain faithful. They carried on a publishing ministry, distributing tracts and educational material eight years before a national general conference was organized.

Leota was a large woman and not very pretty, but she had a heart of gold. She was so outspoken people seldom left the room without knowing her opinion. Leota was a spinster but not by choice. She was once engaged to be married, but her fiancé died, possibly during combat in WWI. She had a generous heart and engaged in a helping ministry for the poor and elderly. Leota enjoyed traveling and drove to Wyoming to visit her sister Ella and to Oregon, Illinois, to visit her brother Leland and his family.

Because of her extensive business experience and frequent visits to the area, she relocated to Oregon, Illinois, to become the Church of God General Conference's business manager. Her dedication to the General Conference went beyond being employed by it. She helped design it, and recommended it to the delegates through her position on the Committee of Ten. The Committee of Ten prayerfully studied the challenge of incorporating a not-for-profit organization from 1920 to 1921 and recommended a course of action at the 1921 annual conference at Waterloo.

Leota was an awesome figure behind her desk. When a teenager approached her to sign up for the Berean Youth

> **The Committee of Ten, 1920-21**
>
> J.W. Williams, Iowa, Chairman
> F.L. Austin, Ontario, Secretary
> James A. Patrick, Minnesota
> Grace Marsh, Iowa
> F.E. Siple, Illinois
> Alta King, Nebraska
> Judd Lyon, Alabama
> Rolla Hightower, Illinois
> Leota B. Hanson, Illinois
> D.E. Van Vactor, Indiana
>
> Ref.: "Our Conference: Its Start and Basis," *The History Newsletter* embedded in *The Restitution Herald*, October, 1985.

Fellowship annual summer camp, he or she instinctively knew not to act up around Leota.

As a faithful member of the Oregon Church of God all her life, Leota attended every service, every Illinois state conference and every General Conference. Even after she retired from the General Conference, she never missed a service. She was faithful to the message and the mission of the national work.

Leota's favorite gift for a young bride was a white Bible which she carried down the aisle with her bouquet. These Bibles were sold at the National Bible Institute bookstore, so giving them away helped the brides and the General Conference. While Leota chose not to marry after her youthful misfortune, she always helped young women celebrate their approaching wedding.

See Austin, Evelyn Harsh
Drew, Anna (19th)
Hanson, Leland
Whitehead, Leila, M.D.
Williams, J.W.

Bibliography: Ancestry.com U.S. Census. Illinois. St. Clair. Lebanon. Dist. 112. 1900; Memories of Leota Hanson by Jan Stilson, 2006; Various reports and columns, *The Restitution Herald*.

Hardesty, Robert
b. June 1918

Robert Hardesty was a pastor at Omaha and secretary of the Ministerial Association of the Church of God. As such, he drafted a set of ethical guidelines to be presented to the ministers during the annual General Conference meeting in the summer of 1948. Those guidelines for ministerial conduct are as follows:

1. The Spirit of Christ should be the guiding factor in all personal and church relationships…all conduct should be governed by Christian love (Rom. 15:52).
2. Absolute justice and fair dealing should be exercised in all business and social relationships that the proclaimed effects of Christianity may be upheld and a greater degree of evangelistic influence exerted upon the general public.
3. The biblical condemnation of gossip or harmful reports should be remembered and the Christian be first assured of the truth of all statements….that only good and no harm may result.
4. Profanity and all idle talk should be avoided as marks of carnality.
5. Every effort should be made to uphold a sound marriage.
6. Flirtations and insincere conduct in matters of friendships, love and marriage should be avoided.
7. Faith and spirituality can be maintained only by study, prayer and fellowship, church attendance and personal effort in daily Christian living are essential.
8. Attendance at dances, taverns or questionable amusements should be avoided.
9. Total abstinence from alcohol should be the accepted practice of all Christians.
10. Gambling and games of chance are not in keeping with Christian conduct. "Avoid all appearance of evil."
11. Uphold standards by avoiding use of tobacco.

Signed, Robert Hardesty, January 1948

This statement may have been commissioned by the ministers in reaction to the unethical conduct of Frank Siple, one of their own. See the Siple entry for details of the incident.

See Siple, Frank E.
Bibliography: "Ethical Guidelines," *The Restitution Herald*, Sydney Magaw, ed., Oregon, IL, May 11, 1948.

Hatch, Paul Milo
b. February 10, 1897
d. April 1986

Paul Hatch grew up in the Church of God at Plymouth, Indiana. When he was born his family had been in the denomination at least two generations. Paul was Jeremiah S. Hatch's grandson. Jeremiah was an early circuit rider from Indiana who preached throughout that state, Illinois and Wisconsin during the latter half of the 19th century. Paul's father was J.E. Hatch who left the Midwest and moved to California. J.E. helped stabilize the work in California during the early 20th century and may have worked with Benjamin Wilson to organize the California Conference.

As an adult, Paul moved to Chicago where his Indiana friend, Evelyn Harsh, lived. He worshipped with the Chicago Church of God until 1922 when he moved to Oregon, Illinois, to work on the General Conference's greenhouse farm. His move was noted in the minutes of the Chicago church that stated the congregation regretted losing a valuable teacher and preacher.

Paul never married, but his sister married Sydney Magaw, whom Paul greatly respected. Unfortunately, Paul was the driver when Margaret and Sydney were killed on slippery roads in December 1950. Paul was severely injured at that time with crushed jaws, they were wired in a half-opened position the rest of his life. Eating was a process of pushing in the food with little chewing. Having also had a crushed pelvis, he limped and remained a thin broken man the remainder of his life.

He was a scholar, a researcher and historian. In spite of his physical limitations and pain, Paul did much to locate 19th century Church of God history, and to formally document it. He wrote many papers on history and organized the Archives at the Church of God General Conference offices at Oregon during the 1950s. While his methods were simple, they were an important beginning to the establishment of a formal Archives and the authorship of denominational histories. He traveled throughout the "burned-over district" of Finger Lakes in western New York, researching the life of Joseph Marsh. Paul's notes remain in the Archives; they formed the basis for copy of *The Historical Waymarks of the Church of God* by Clyde Randall and of this encyclopedia. Paul also indexed *The Restitution Herald*, which was helpful in pre-computer days.

Paul with parents, Mr. and Mrs. JE Hatch at their California home.

When Paul returned from his six-week New York trip, he briefly reported his findings to the General Conference delegates meeting at Camp Alexander Mack. Paul had an exhibit documenting his travels that greatly influenced a younger generation of historians.

Paul was helpful to young historians. He told it like it was. At the time this volume's author was studying the Wilsons of Geneva for the first time, she could not determine what made Benjamin Wilson a member of the Church of God. He worshipped in a church called "Disciples Meeting House." Did that mean he was of Campbellite persuasion? He was friendly with Dr. John Thomas who formed the Christadelphians. Did that mean he was Christadelphian? He came from an English Baptist background. Did that mean he was Baptist? The rights to *The Emphatic Diaglott* were sold to the Jehovah's Witnesses. Did that mean he joined with them when he moved to California? So the question was put to Paul, "How do we know Benjamin Wilson was Church of God?" Paul drew himself up taller, fixed a look at the young historian, and without hesitation said, "Because he believed the Bible doctrines preached by the Church of God." While it is still doubtful that Wilson repudiated all aberrant systems of belief, he did remain in contact with the Church of God his remaining years and was a delegate at the 1888 Philadelphia General Conference.

Paul Hatch believed the doctrines, but worried that he had jeopardized his salvation. He doubted that he would inherit a place in the Kingdom of God because he felt he had "murdered" his sister's family. They had asked him to slow down, and he had not. But he *hoped* he would see them again in the Kingdom.

In his youth, Paul assisted the ministry at Oregon, Illinois. He studied at the Bible Training Class, and assisted in filling pulpits throughout the Midwest. Reports in *The Restitution Herald* demonstrate that Paul helped begin the new church work in Rockford, Illinois, in 1930; he held a series of meetings at Eldorado, Illinois, (these two works were at opposite ends of the state, 400 miles apart); and he also preached at Adeline, Illinois, the sister church of the Oregon Church of God.

Paul was active until his death, slowing with age as old injuries continued to pain him. He died peacefully in the home Margaret and Sydney Magaw had owned in Oregon. Ivan Magaw, Paul's nephew, was at his bedside.

An issue of *The History Newsletter* was dedicated to Paul Hatch because he had revealed the historical foundations of the Church of God. He is buried in the Daysville Cemetery southeast of Oregon, Illinois.

See Hatch, Jeremiah S. (19th)
Hatch, A.E. (19th)
Magaw, Sydney
Wilson, Benjamin (19th)

Bibliography: Ancestry.com. Social Security Master Death List. Record for Paul Hatch. *The Restitution Herald,* June 11, 1919; Nov. 13, 1923; Oct. 7, 1930; Oct. 21, 1930; Hatch, Paul. Numerous interviews with Jan Stilson in the 1980s; Hatch, Paul, Various drafts of Church of God history. Many of these papers are in the possession of Ivan Magaw, Oregon, Il.; Minutes of the Church of God at Chicago, 1890-1925 presently in the Atlanta Bible College Archives, McDonough, Ga.; Tribute to Paul Hatch, *The History Newsletter of the Church of God.* Oregon, Il., Spring 1986; Marsh, Grace, Interview with Ivan Magaw, Aug. 22, 1983, from the Atlanta Bible College Archives.

Hayse, Nina Jean
b. November 17, 1945
d. August 31, 1996

Nina Jean Hayse was born in Harlingen, Texas, to John G. and Opal Hayse. She had two older brothers,

Allen and Robin. Nina Jean was raised in the Church of God by Christian parents who predeceased her. She loved children, and over the years, served as Sunday school teacher and superintendent. She enjoyed working with the girl's softball league and was a faithful fan of the teams.

Nina Jean was a robust and high-spirited Texas gal; when she entered a room, every eye was on her. She loved the attention and to talk and laugh with her friends. During her teen years, her family made the long drive from Texas so that she and Robin could attend the Berean Youth Congress of the Church of God at Quaker Haven Camp and Camp Mack in Indiana.

Nina Jean died after a long illness; memorial donations were made in her name to the Diabetes Association and the Kidney Foundation. She left many friends of long-standing to mourn her loss.

Bibliography: Biography Project of Atlanta Bible College, David Krogh, compiler.

Hearp, John "Jack"
b. February 22, 1926
d. December 12, 2010

John Hearp was born in Cleveland to John T. and Louise E. Hearp. Jack, as friends knew him, served in the US Navy. After returning from duty, he graduated from Western Reserve University with a business degree and worked in Ohio and Michigan for a few years. He felt a call from the Lord to enter the ministry and gave up his successful secular employment. He moved to Oregon, Illinois, and received a B.Th. from Oregon Bible College in 1964. He entered the ministry for the Church of God in his first pastorate at Ripley, Illinois, with his new bride, Helen, by his side.

Throughout his life, Jack served his church by serving his community. He participated in community service organizations such as Lion's Club. He was chaplain at several local hospitals and well known in his community as a caring pastor. Jack experienced tragedy and sorrow in his life, yet because of his strong faith, he never wavered in the face of adversity. He set a fine example of endurance and patience to everyone who knew him.

Jack was a tall man at 6'7". When he stretched up to full height, he commanded attention. Each of his wives was much shorter than Jack, but each of them lovingly complemented him in so many ways.

As Jack grew weak in his later years, friends knew his ministry was ending. When word came of his death, pastors who had learned from him or who had worked with him began to share stories and experiences. They are excerpted here because they are so eloquent, a summary cannot improve them.

From Wally Winner:
Now Ripley was well known as the first pastorate for a number of men. This was Jack and Helen's first home in the ministry. They did not have a lot of items of furniture when they moved in, but they did have a first class turn table and sound system. He had a book collection started. I remember they used cinder blocks and boards to build a shelf system to locate their turn table, speakers and records on. I used that same system on several occasions myself.

I have a recording still of Helen playing on the saxophone. She would on occasion stand a repeat the poem "A Touch of the Master's Hands" by memory. I committed it to memory because of her touching rendition of it. I remember the heartache Helen and Jack had when Helen had a miscarriage.

It was while we were on our way to my grandparents house (they lived behind the Ripley church) on a winter night (I think it was Christmas), that my mother remarked there were no lights on at the parsonage. The Hearps were supposed to be home. It was while we were at my grandparents that Millie Laning called with the horrible news that Helen had died and the other three people were in the hospital. The accident happened near Valparaiso, Indiana when the train came from one side and hit the car Jack was driving. He was looking into an afternoon sun and there was snow on the warning lights. He never saw the train until the collision. It dragged the car for a distance before it could stop. Helen died instantly. Jack's mother died a few days later as I recall. Jack was banged up pretty good, but made it back to Ripley after a hospital stay. His first service back was a Wednesday evening prayer and Bible study time. I was up front taking the prayer requests when someone asked about the fourth passenger in the car, Ada Brooks. Ada was a member of the local congregation who was traveling with the Hearps to visit some of her family. Wayne Laning was sitting near Jack, and spoke up. Wayne said Ada had died that afternoon. I was looking right at Jack's face when that was announced and saw the pain.

The following summer at General Conference time, Rob Laning, and I rode with Jack to GC. We left Ripley four times. We would get a few miles down the road and Jack would remember something he had forgotten to bring. I didn't thing we were going to get out of the state in time to attend GC.

Jack and I were the only ones in the church sanctuary when he listened to my speech for the Men's Christian Speech contest held each year at Mack. He gave me some pointers. I won. No other male competed that year. I guess they were afraid of me.

On several occasions I saw Jack not using notes for his sermon, but using a book from his library. I watched as he flipped the pages. On at least one occasion when it came time to preach, he didn't have anything with him. He went down the back steps, over to the parsonage and retrieved what he needed while we all visited among ourselves.

He was a joiner. He was a member of several

Ministers gather on the Oregon Church of God steps in 1982. Jack Hearp is in the back row on the end.

organizations in the Rushville, Mt. Sterling, Beardstown area. Because of that he was well known in the area.

He was habitually late. We waited for many services to start because he wasn't there. Often it was because he had taken time out for somebody. He would start to visit one person from the congregation in the hospital or nursing home, and soon would be ministering to several others before he left. People would stop him on the street to get his advice. It is little wonder then that during my lifetime with the Ripley congregation, he reached its attendance zenith during his time there. We had to remodel, enlarging the sanctuary, adding classrooms and even indoor bathrooms.

He continued his interest in the congregation by his frequent visits and financial contributions. He was primarily responsible for the lift on the stairs at the Ripley church. If it had not been for that lift my mother would not have been able to continue teaching until a few weeks before her death. She would not have been able to navigate the stairs.

I guess I was his first "preacher boy." He quietly aided me through my college years. I wasn't supposed to know he was financially helping me, but leaks happen. I never let him know I knew because he intended it to be a secret.

I was excited when he found Louise. I enjoyed my visits with them. Often she would take the lead in visiting with me as the years went on because Jack was involved with some aspect of the General Conference business. She was a great match for him.

I took the opportunity on several occasions to publicly thank Jack for what I learned from being around him. As Harry Sheets had taught me Bible, Jack had taught me pastoring. Jack taught me that people are more important than schedules.

Jack, Millie and my mother had a close relationship. In just a span of a few months they all have fallen asleep awaiting the resurrection.

Yes, I'll miss knowing that Jack is around, but I know the kingdom will be made up of people such as him.

From Michael Brown:

Jack was highly thought of by the Glad Tidings brethren as he served as minister here in Fonthill (Ontario) from 1971 to 1984. He was very outgoing in the community and local ministerial association and helped to start the chaplain program at the Welland Hospital many years ago. I attended local ministerial meetings with Jack if we happened to be visiting at those times. He continued to be close to many of our members over the years since he pastored at Glad Tidings.

I remember in our pastoral works class at OBC when Bro. John Lewis, our instructor, remarked how Jack was one of the most "professional" ministers he knew in our churches.

I enjoyed the many times when we came up to the church from the states and we got together with Jack and Louise and Foots (sp?) their dog for some visits. Both of them were very hospitable.

Jack officiated at our wedding in 1973. I never said anything to him about this, but the wedding ceremony went almost without a problem except for one tiny detail: When it came time in the ceremony for the lighting of the unity candle, he completely forgot it and went on with the rest of the ceremony. I was still waiting for him to go back to it when the next thing I knew, he was pronouncing Diane and me, "husband and wife." Back then, the lighting of the unity candle was a relatively new activity in weddings, so I don't fault Jack for not remembering.

I must say, I am so honored to pastor a church where Jack once served. He left some great indelible memories at our church.

What a day it will be when Jesus comes back!

From Mark DeYoung:

Millie, Rob Laning, Wally and his mother, and sister, Peggy, told some wonderful stories. How if you were in the hospital in Rushville, Jack would come and because the hospital was small, he would often visit everyone there. How when he first came to the church he would bring several books and notes to the pulpit with him to speak.

From Jeff Fletcher:

I remember Jack's books...he had an enormous library of books in his study next to the Church in Fonthill...I think many of those books are now part of the ABC library.

From Jan Stilson:

The Hearp books are being added into the ABC library as space permits. It is a marvelous collection--every commentary and reference book a pastor might need. It had devotional material, topical material for pastors, theological material and many minister's manuals from years back. Most of the manuals were passed along to ABC students who were interested. He had many first editions and many books showed evidence of being well used. He bought them from all over: Library book sales, estate sales, garage sales, used book stores, etc.

That same fall Jack delivered a wonderful paper at the history conference held at North Hills on the history of the Cleveland Churches of God. Not only was it well researched, but it was well delivered in his usual

Jack, Louise and Foots

preaching style, and injected with personal memories that gave it impact. I will never forget when he walked up to the podium slowly, and then stretched himself up to full height and began to speak. It's a great memory.

From Curt Rowden:
Two very vivid memories of Jack Hearp stand out in my mind. The first was when he did my great-grandfather's funeral service in the Ripley church. The entrance in those days was different than now and included several wide stairs leading into the front door. Jack came out of the church and stood on the top step and paused while I was standing one step below him. I was about 10 at the time and a runt of a kid. He appeared to me a giant of a man, and as I knew him in later years, that was confirmed in more ways than one.

The second was being his roommate at CWS in Gatlinburg some years back. He had a cardboard box that served as his cassette tape container and was filled with big band/swing/jazz music. He said it helped him on his long drives.

His resonant voice, and his compassionate smile are things I will long remember.

From Jan Stilson again:
A year before Jack died, a man stopped at Atlanta Bible College. He began to ask about Church of God history at Cleveland, and I was called in to talk with him. I was working in the Archives that week. This man told the story of his youth when he had been a member of the Golden Rule Church, and Jack Hearp had been his pal. He said they chummed around to sports events, and went to church and youth group. He said Jack joined the church first and then he decided to join also. He inquired, "Is Jack well?" "Where does he live?" The old friend said he was wintering near Morrow, Georgia, but when he went back home in the spring, he'd like to stop by, and see his old friend again at Springfield. I hope they made that final connection.

Jack's funeral services were conducted from Conroy Funeral Home in Springfield, Ohio. Pastor Alan Cain officiated. Jack was interred beside Louise at the Ferncliff Cemetery in Springfield.

Bibliography: Entries from Cogpastors@googlegroups.com following the announcement of death. Used with permission; Obituary, supplied by Pastor Rex Cain.

Helenburg, Woodrow Robert
b. November 17, 1916
d. December 9, 1986

Woodrow Robert Helenburg, known as "Woody" to friends and family, was the son of Charles L. and Ruth (Finley) Helenburg. He grew up in Florida, returning to Indianapolis, Indiana, as a teenager. His last three years of high school were at the old Central High School in South Bend, Indiana. He graduated in 1936. Due to family obligations, Woody was unable to attend college. On December 24, 1937, he married Eloise Vera Dixon, a 1937 graduate of Central High School. They had three children, Woodrow "Rob" Robin, Freya Louise and Lisa Kristen. Rob served as chairman of the Board of Directors of the Church of God General Conference in 2008 to 2009.

Woody was a machinist, operating a precision surface-grinding machine at the Torrington Company in South Bend. Torrington specialized in large and special order bearings for heavy duty and high-speed applications. Woody's skills led to a draft deferment during WWII, due to the company's military contracts for critical war materials. He worked at Torrington for 43 years.

Woody's avocation was singing, especially religious music, and he did so for several churches through the years, often in a paid position. God gave him a strong tenor voice. Eloise, a soprano, was also quite talented and participated in church music. She taught piano and voice and raised the family. Woody taught voice lessons early in their marriage but did so *a cappella* as he did not play an instrument. His only instruments were the pitch pipe and his tenor voice.

Through the years, the couple sang in the First Christian Church and First Methodist Church choirs. Each of them, at different times, was soloist at the Christian Science Church in Elkhart, Indiana. Later, Woody was the soloist for several years at Christian Science Church in South Bend. During that time and throughout much of the 1950s, Woody was part-time Cantor for the Temple Beth-el Jewish Reform Synagogue in South Bend. He would have to take vacation from work to sing for special feasts such as the High Holy Days. He studied Hebrew with Rabbi Shuleman's wife, Rose, to improve his pronunciation. As might be expected, the family's church attendance was related to where the parents were singing, as opposed to a belief in a doctrine or following a denomination.

Woody had a long-standing interest in electronics and would have studied electrical engineering in college if he had been able to attend. He furthered his knowledge of electronics by completing a correspondence course with the DeVry Technical Institute. His interest also led to becoming a licensed amateur (ham) radio operator, with assistance from his father-in-law, L.B. Dixon, also an amateur radio operator (WpBBD). Woody's call sign was K9BEC and his activity related mainly around 6-Meter and 2-Meter FM operations. His real interest was in antenna systems. In the late 1950s he collaborated with two other men to devise a coil tuning method for the 6-Meter Halo mobile antenna. He was a member of the local amateur radio club and the MARS system.

Fraternally, Woody was interested in service to others and became a Mason in October 1943 in Tyrian Lodge, No. 718-F&AM in Elkhart, Indiana. This also was done with the endorsement of his father-in-law who also was a Mason. In the 1960s, Woody transferred his membership to the newly formed Mishawaka-Osceola Lodge No. 83-F&AM. He also joined the St. Joseph Valley of the Scottish Rite, Northern Jurisdiction, and subsequently the Shrine in Fort Wayne, Indiana. During the 1940s and 1950s, he was an active participant in the Scottish Rite Choir in South Bend. Their concerts culminated each year with the presentation of the complete Handel's *Messiah* with Woody performing at least one solo part. In the late 1950s and early 1960s, he participated in the South Bend Shrine Club Marching Band. He played the cymbals in the percussion section and sang selected songs during band concerts.

Woody died shortly after moving to Leesburg, Florida. This was two years, nine months after Eloise's death on April 7, 1984. He was survived by their three children and their families, and by his second wife, Arline.

Bibliography: Helenburg, Rob, Biography project of Atlanta Bible College, compiled by David Krogh.

Hess, Gordon Lewis
b. September 7, 1902
d. February 28, 1988

Gordon Hess and his family moved to Oregon, Illinois, from Renssalaer, Indiana, when he became superintendent of the Golden Rule Home. Twelve-year-old son, Harold, and seven-year-old daughter, Barbara, attended Oregon Schools the fall of 1948. Barbara had curly red hair.

The responsibilities of Gordon's position called for caring for the senior residents living at Golden Rule, cooking, cleaning, assisting with medical appointments and helping them to church if they were mobile. There were extensive grounds to mow and maintenance on the more than 100-year-old building.

The Hess family was well received by the members of the Oregon Church of God, but they returned to Indiana after a year in Oregon.

Bibliography: Ancestry.com. Social Security Master Death List. Record for Gordon L. Hess. Announcement, *The Restitution Herald*, Sydney Magaw, ed., Oregon, Il. July 27, 1948.

Hollenbeck, Janie (Richards)
b. November 25, 1897
d. November 22, 1995

Janie Richards Hollenbeck was born in Macomb, Illinois, and lived most of her life there. She was a member of the Macomb Church of God and baptized there on December 16, 1962. Her family wrote a memorial for her and noted that she was a wonderful mother, good friend and neighbor always ready to help when needed.

Janie was a nurse's aide at the local hospital for many years, and later, cared for women in her home.

Bibliography: Words of comfort from her family for the ABC Biography Project, David Krogh, compiler.

Holt, Belus E.
b. September 27, 1905
d. April 7, 1994

Belus Holt was born to Rufus and Phoebe Calfee Holt in Newport, Cocke County, Tennessee. The family relocated to Roane County, Tennessee, in 1915 in a wagon. The trip took two days, and Belus was reported to have walked most of the 100-mile trek.

Belus played football while attending high school. After graduation, he taught school for a while. He remained interested in sports and in his church. In 1928, he attended the sports events where he first saw his wife to be: Iva Mae Umphrey. She played on the high school basketball team. Iva Mae first saw Belus at Cedar Fork Baptist Church where she told her friends that "he was hers if she ever got him."

Iva Mae believed the doctrines taught by the Church of God Abrahamic Faith. Her mother Lillian Cobb Umphrey taught her. After the loss of a child, Lillian Umphrey started searching the Bible for truth. About the same time, an itinerant missionary passing through Tennessee, Mr. (J.H.) Anderson, was found preaching what Lillian had discovered herself. From him she learned about the Church of God Abrahamic Faith in Illinois.

Belus was a devout Baptist and told Iva Mae he could never marry a woman who did not believe in hell. He moved to Cleveland, Ohio, in 1929, a catastrophic year for the American economy, where he was fortunate enough to find a job delivering milk. He delivered milk to the parents of entertainer Bob Hope who gave him a milk glass sugar bowl for Christmas. Iva Mae and Belus corresponded during the following years in which they exchanged religious views and decided to become life partners. They were married August 23, 1933, in Niota, Tennessee, despite the fact that Iva Mae did not believe in "eternal torturing of souls in a fizzing fire."

The couple moved back to Morristown, Tennessee, in 1937 where they opened and operated a Western Auto Store on Main Street in downtown Morristown. During the first decade of their marriage, Belus helped several other businessmen build a Baptist church in Morristown. Once the church was completed, the builders were pushed out, including Belus. This was the catalyst giving him doubt about his Baptist faith. He attended one semester at Oregon Bible College. M.O. Williamson of South Carolina baptized him after his conversion into the Church of God.

On the third floor of the Western Auto they opened the Downtown Chapel; the first public gathering place in which the Abrahamic Faith was taught. Alva Huffer, Verna C. Thayer and David Sprinkle worked to make this a thriving congregation. Belus built and opened the Hillcrest Church of God where the children of two of the Holt brothers were reared in the faith. Walter Wiggins, Terry Ferrell and Raymond and Doris Brown served as pastors until all attending families moved away from Morristown around 1960.

Belus and Iva Mae had three children, Elroy (August 10, 1937-August 24, 1961), Petsy (1942) and Jewel (1947). Dea L. Holt's children, Lowell, Joyce, Patricia and Brenda migrated to South Carolina after high school to attend Guthrie Grove Church. Sylvia moved to Cleveland where she played the organ for Columbia Station.

Belus answered a call to pastor the Cool Spring Church of God at Browntown, Virginia, where his legacy was to institute weekly services. He served there from 1961-1963. His pearl of great price was the doctrine of the Kingdom of God to be established on earth after the resurrection. Belus died at age 78 in Sweetwater, Tennessee. His daughters and two granddaughters, Susan Bell and Lillian Rudacille, and two great-grandsons, James and John Bell, survived him.

Petsy Holt Rudacille contributed this entry.

See Anderson, J.H. (19th)
      Brown, Raymond
      Huffer, Alva
      Ferrell, Terry
      Pryor, C.F.
      Thayer, Verna C.
      Williamson, M.O.

Bibliography: Ancestry.com. U.S. Census. Ohio. Cuyahoga. Lakewood. Dist 631. 1930; U.S. Census. Tennessee. Roane. Dist. 4, Dist. 12. 1930. Rudacille, Petsy. E-mail, March, 2011.

Houser, William Graceton
    b. February 23, 1882
    d. 1966
Houser, Myrtle (Stilson)
    b. April 22, 1886
    d. 1972

Graceton Houser was born February 23, 1882. He was the son of John Houser and Elizabeth Amelia (Reed) Houser. His great-grandfather was John Houser (b. 1791), the first of the family known to have been born in America. Graceton had two brothers and two sisters: George, Emma, Oscar, and Manola. Their father was a country preacher known to like to walk down the dirt roads singing hymns at the top of his voice.

Myrtle and Graceton

Myrtle Stilson Houser was born April 22, 1886. She had three brothers and one sister: Floyd, Rolland, Forrest and Iris (Kirkley).

Graceton and Myrtle were married February 16, 1905, and had four children in order of birth, Cecil, Edna, John and Walter. The parents outlived all four children, who all died as relatively young adults: Edna at 31, Walter at 30, Cecil at 42 and John at 54. Graceton and

FL Austin, back left, with the 1927 Bible Training Class, Oregon, Illinois. John Houser was a student, back row, third from left.

Myrtle had seven grandchildren.

The family connection to the Church of God of the Abrahamic Faith comes through the Stilsons. Graceton joined the church around the time he and Myrtle married. They were loyal to the church, though not particularly active except as interested members. Myrtle took the narrow point of view of the church more seriously than Graceton did, but he was friendly towards the members.

Graceton was a pleasant and good-natured fellow. He held a number of jobs during his life, including farmer, factory worker, filling station attendant and Fuller Brush salesman. He told the story about Fuller Brush sales: When he knocked on a door and the lady of the house answered, he would open his brush case and say, "Here they are, ma'am. You know more about them than I do." With that approach, he was probably quite successful.

Graceton was a ladies' man. Before he married Myrtle, she was one of five girlfriends living within a mile of each other near Plymouth, Indiana. He used to drive his horse and buggy the eight to ten miles to Plymouth. He said the girls knew when Bill Houser was around by the sound of his horse and buggy going by. Sometimes, on the way home, he would fall asleep in the buggy, but he always got home okay because the horse knew the way.

Myrtle

Myrtle was somewhat more serious, but she was a loyal friend to all. She worked hard and her meals were legendary. When workmen were first paving Highway 31, which ran in front of the Houser farmhouse between Lakeville and La Paz, Indiana, Myrtle fixed big hot lunches every day and invited all the workmen to come in for a meal. In 1962, she had the first of two devastating strokes which debilitated her for the last ten years of her life. When she had the first stroke at the age of 76, she had spent the day working in her garden, and then painting the local clubhouse a few miles away.

Graceton died quietly at home at the age of 84. Myrtle died six years later, aged 86, in a nursing home.

Ed Houser contributed this entry and the photographs.

See Kirkley, Iris
        Stilson, Floyd
        Stilson, Rolland

Bibliography: Houser, Edward. Grandson to Graceton and Myrtle. E-mail to Jstilson, July 27, 2009.

Howe, Charles W.
b. January 6, 1892
d. December 2, 1982

Charles Howe was born in West Union, Iowa. He was a member of the Church of God at Waterloo, Iowa. From 1908 to 1943 he alternated with other ministers to preach at this church. He preached at the Gladbrook, Iowa, Church of God 50th anniversary celebration in 1944. He preached "Great Types of the Bible."

In 1968, Charles moved to Tucson, Arizona, where he took up painting. He excelled at desert scenes and his work was displayed at public buildings throughout Tucson. During this same time he mimeographed his thoughts and beliefs and sent them to people throughout the Church of God.

Charles is one of those who made the Church of God great. He contributed service in response to his faith, and in so doing made an impact upon his community.

Delbert Rankin contributed this entry.

Bibliography: Rankin, Delbert. E-mail describing Charles W. Howe. Oct. 27, 2008.

Huffer, Dr. Alva G.
b. September 1925

Alva Huffer was born in Clinton County, Indiana, to Otto A. and Bessie Huffer. He had two sisters, Hazel and Opel. Otto worked as a laborer in cabinet fastening. The family attended the Plummer Church, later known as the Hillisburg Country Chapel Church of God, at Frankfort, Indiana. Alva grew up loving the Lord and the truth.

As a teenager, Alva attended summer Bible classes conducted at Oregon, Illinois, by General Conference staff. In the summer of 1943 Alva worked for the Iowa Conference and wrote a new constitution for the Iowa Berean Society. The interesting thing about this constitution was that it provided two vice presidents. One vice president was to be the activities director. He or she would plan events and direct fundraising and communicate with the other vice president. The second vice president was to contact all Bereans and organize new local societies, receive reports from the local societies and give them to the secretary to be kept in the book.

When he was old enough, Alva enrolled in the newly established Bible College at Oregon, Illinois. While a student there, Alva met Dean Moore from California. Alva asked Dean, "Do you love the Lord?" to which Dean responded, "Yes." Then Alva invited him to return to Oregon to attend Oregon Bible College and become a minister in the Lord's service. Alva and Dean remain close friends to this day. Dean became the first missionary of the gospel message into Mexico where he served full and part time for 40 years.

Alva and Awa McMinn of North Carolina married on January 1, 1950, after which they moved to Virginia to begin their ministry. Two sons, Keith and David, were born. Alva was pastor of two rural churches, Maurertown (pronounced "Morrie-town") and Fort Valley Church of God. The Fort Valley runs 50 miles between two ranges of the Massanutten Mountains that run nearly the whole length of the Shenandoah Valley. The Fort was surveyed by George Washington, an Elizabeth Furnace in the Fort was used to smelt bullets for the Revolutionary War.

Occasionally, Alva preached at Cool Springs and Baltimore. He was influential in persuading C.F. Pryor from South Carolina to move to Browntown to assume the pastorate at Cool Springs.

Alva began to research and write his first book, *Systematic Theology,* in Virginia. He organized Church of God doctrines into the format of systematic theology, explained them and supported his explanation with Scriptures. The areas of study included God, Man, Sin, Christ, Salvation, Church and Prophecy. He researched works of theology by Chafer and other notable writers and typed a manuscript that membership could use for study. When this book was published it fired up the Church of God membership and clergy. Everyone wanted a copy to read and study. A concerted effort was made by members and the General Conference to place it in every library around the world. A correspondence course was developed for members and newcomers that was distributed and graded by local pastors. This course is now available on the Internet through the Church of God General Conference at www.abc-coggc.org. It was developed as a course for Oregon Bible College, now Atlanta Bible College.

The parsonage at Maurertown was located along Highway 11 in a large two-story house. Church members returning from a late-night community meeting said that a light still burned in Alva's office as he worked feverishly on his studies.

Alva served a newly formed church in Morristown, Tennessee, during the 1950s. After a brief time there, he gave the work to Pastor Belus Holt. Mrs. Iva Mae Holt told Alva, "Go ahead and publish that book."

Alva moved to Missouri from 1954-1957, serving the churches of Jordan, Morse Mills and Cross Timbers. Daughter Myra was born in Missouri. Alva followed A. Weldon McCoy's footsteps; McCoy was an evangelist from Indiana who worked in Missouri for several years and had established some loyal friendships.

From Missouri, the Huffers moved to Grand Rapids, Michigan, where Alva assumed the pastorate for Pennellwood Church of God. Daughter Lisa was born during this time. He served in Michigan until 1961. Living in Grand Rapids was helpful to publishing his book. There are so many Christian book publishing houses in Grand Rapids that when Alva had a question, he'd just stop by and talk to the editors.

The family moved to Tempe, Arizona. Alva became pastor of the Tempe Church of God. While there, he pursued graduate work at the University of Arizona. He completed an M.A. in history and a Ph.D. in college administration. He served as Oregon Bible College president, 1968-1975. During this time he commuted between Illinois and Arizona to teach block courses on Bible Archaeology, Bible World History and Systematic Theology, using *Systematic Theology* as a textbook.

His courses were characterized by depth of content illustrated with three-screen slide shows featuring landmarks and buildings of Europe, Egypt, Greece and the Middle East. In the summer, Alva directed foreign tours for members and friends of the Church of God and continued to travel well into his 80s. The tours throughout Europe and the Middle East facilitated his making the excellent graphics and programs. In 2003, 15 people accompanied him on a five-day land tour and three-day cruise of several Greek islands and Ephesus in Turkey.

During his years of travel Alva collected replicas of famous artifacts that became the core collection in a museum he established. He designed and organized a collection of educational panels and artifacts that traced the history of mankind, including biblical and church history through the ages. The museum collection was housed at the Lakeshore Bible Church of God in Tempe. The Bible World Museum became an educational resource not only for Church of God members, but also for students from the University of Arizona who regularly visited the museum to fulfill assignments in class.

When Alva and son David moved to be near Myra and family in Pelzer, South Carolina, in 2005, he moved the Bible World Museum also. The Pelzer Church of God provided several rooms to contain the educational panels, sculpture, photos, maps and other learning resources. Alva returned to regularly teaching college classes in his specialty at Atlanta Bible College, and transported the panels to use as visual aids in his classes. College classes also visited and studied at the museum center.

In December 2008 Alva was diagnosed with cancer and began treatment. He continued to rely on the Lord to see him through the situation, and he continued to teach. Alva assisted in graduate classes at Rock River Christian College, Beloit, Wisconsin, through independent study and lecture in the museum, and he continued to teach at Atlanta Bible College.

Alva consulted on several entries in this encyclopedia. His knowledge of church history and expertise on Church of God history were invaluable resources. He explained the dynamics of the Decade of Development in the 20th century, which contributed greatly to growth from 1955-1965. He explained the impetus leading to the interest

In 2003, Alva Huffer led the eight-day "Footsteps of Paul" tour. Here he disembarks the cruise liner for Ephesus, Turkey.
Photo by Jan Stilson

and development of educational opportunities in the Church of God. (See Appendix 16–Christian Education for Eugene Stilson's article, "History of Higher Education in the Church of God.") Alva advocated for including the Joseph Priestley entry in the 19th century section of this encyclopedia. In addition to Priestley's remarkable understanding of Bible truths, which predated the development of the Church of God by 50 years, Alva said Priestley was important to the world of knowledge because he discovered the importance of oxygen to the human body which up to his time scientists had not understood. Alva said, "Man is not made of dust. He is made of the same chemicals and elements of dust. Priestley is important because he discovered the role that oxygen plays in the human body."

Alva has been a great friend to the pastors and members of the Church of God. His book *Systematic Theology* underwent its seventh printing in 2010, celebrating 50 years of publication. He was honored at the General Conference with a lecture and book signing in the Archives. (See Appendix 24–Systematic Theology, a transcript of Dr. Huffer's remarks covering 50 years of 20th century Church of God history.)

Alva has freely shared his love and his knowledge with any who were interested. Always happy, always competent, always energetic, he set a pace for ministry that has been the prime example of excellence in the Church of God throughout the 20th and into the 21st centuries. He has exemplified the eternal youth, eternal hope, and everlasting love God gives in abundance to some. Following the example of writers, editors and publishers in the 19th century, who chiefly advanced the Gospel of the Kingdom through the written word, Alva was the chief proponent of published scholarship in the 20th century. He advanced scholarship through book writing, and set the bar so high that Church of God scholars and historians are still striving to reach the benchmark.

See Huffer, Awa Belle
Lindsay, S.J. (19th)
McCoy, A. Weldon
Priestley, Joseph (19th)
Stilson, Eugene

Bibliography: Iowa State Berean Society. 1898-1973; Stilson, J. Conversations with Alva Huffer, 2003, 2008, 2009; Stilson, Eugene, "History of Higher Education in the Church of God," 1968.

Huffer, Awa Belle
b. August 9, 1922
d. May 9, 1999

Awa Belle McMinn was born in Asheville, North Carolina, to Lola Welch and Jennie Lee McMinn. An older brother, Kirkwood, predeceased her. She had a younger brother, Jack. Awa attended Lee Edwards High School with perfect attendance, graduating in June 1939. She then attended and graduated from Blanton's Business College in Asheville. She became employed as an accountant with various companies in North Carolina. She married Alva G. Huffer

Awa and Alva Huffer with sons, Keith and David

on January 1, 1950, at Anderson Chapel in Hendersonville, North Carolina. Alva was originally from Indiana and a member of Hillisburg Church of God.

The newlyweds moved to Woodstock, Virginia, where Alva pastored two small churches in Shenandoah Valley. The couple had two sons, David and Keith. The church family at Virginia greatly enjoyed having the Huffers live in their midst. It was said that Awa complemented Alva perfectly. He could cook up a fine batch of chili, and Awa took care of the bills and the family car.

In 1954, the Huffers moved to Missouri to serve two small churches there. Their daughter Myra was born. In 1957, Awa moved her small family to Grand Rapids where Alva assumed the pastoral duties at Pennellwood Church of God. Daughter Lisa was born in Grand Rapids. In 1961 the family moved to Tempe, Arizona, where Alva became pastor of the Tempe Church of God and pursued additional education at Arizona State University. He completed his doctorate in college administration; he assumed the presidency of Oregon Bible College in 1968. Alva invented long-distance commuting. He flew between Arizona and Illinois every few weeks to teach and handle details of administration.

During this same year Awa returned to work beginning at Ambassador Company. After a brief time, she transferred to Motorola where she remained for 17 years. She retired for a year and then grew tired of retirement and returned to work for Adobe Air Company. Awa retired again in July 1998.

Awa was baptized into Christ in Asheville as a young woman. She was always active in the work of the churches where she lived and served as Bible and Sunday school teacher, deaconess, choir member and pastor's wife.

Awa died from complications following an auto accident leaving her family and the Church of God community in shock. She was survived by Alva, her children, four grandchildren and her brother, Jack.

See Huffer, Alva

Bibliography: Ancestry.com, Social Security Master Death List for Awa Huffer record; ABC Biography project, David Krogh, compiler. J Stilson, Comments on Virginia history, 1967.

Huggins, Robert Gresham
b. April 30, 1877
d. May 19, 1955

A. **Christadelphian Roots**
B. **The Illinois and Texas Connection**
C. **The Cleveland Years**
D. **Anti-Organization**

Robert Huggins was the youngest of eight children born to Lankford and Rebecca Hamilton Huggins in Cooper's Gap, North Carolina. He studied the Bible with his father and fellowshipped with Church of God evangelist, Minister Enoch Anderson. Robert was also acquainted with Enoch Anderson's son, Minister J.H. Anderson, who continued to visit Robert's parents and reported their health to him over the years. The Huggins family also fellowshipped with Robert Gresham; Robert Huggins was named after him.

Robert and Edna Huggins with Russel and Kathryn

A. Christadelphian Roots

Lankford had strong ties with members of the Christadelphian fellowship, and Robert grew up understanding both cultures. In fact, the Christadelphians claim Robert Gresham as their evangelist, but it is clear in Age-to-Come writings that Gresham also fellowshipped with the Church of God. It was common in those days for Adventists or Age-to-Come clergy to fellowship with each other's congregations and preach in their worship services. There was no clear-cut separation between the sister denominations, Church of God and Advent Christians, until after the 1870 Nathaniel Field blow-out in Indiana, or between the Church of God and Christadelphians after 1863 when Benjamin Wilson broke with Thomas.

Before Robert Huggins fellowshipped with the Church of God, he served as a Christadelphian evangelist among ecclesias in Kentucky, Arkansas, Iowa, Indiana, southern Illinois and elsewhere. His travels can be traced through the pages of the *Christadelphian Advocate*.

Robert Huggins was a talented Bible student and excellent debater. He believed in One Faith ardently. In 1906, he studied privately with S.J. Lindsay in Oregon, Illinois. Lindsay hosted summer Bible schools. These were like vacation Bible schools, only for adults and young adults. As mentoring or apprentice programs, they preceded the Church of God's Bible Training Classes and Oregon Bible College.

Walter Tomlinson of Cleveland, Ohio, had referred Huggins to Lindsay. Elder Tomlinson and Huggins first met at an Ohio Church of God conference meeting in Springfield, Ohio. Tomlinson hoped to see Huggins installed as pastor at Blessed Hope Church of God in Cleveland, where he and his family worshipped. Huggins accepted the position at Blessed Hope in 1908, after he left the *Word and Work* of Texas. This particular Church of God congregation in Cleveland showed some preference for Christadelphian interpretations, and Huggins was from that background.

B. The Illinois and Texas Connection

Huggins learned the printer's trade at Marion, Illinois, while residing at Creal Springs, Illinois, in the little Egypt area. With the Tomlinson recommendation, and knowing Huggins' printer skill, S.J. Lindsay invited Huggins to Oregon. Lindsay worked at the local newspaper and published *Bible Lessons* for Sunday school on the side. He sold the *Lessons* by subscription. Huggins assisted in the print shop probably at the local newspaper because Lindsay did not have his own a press until 1911.

Robert was invited to serve as evangelist in Illinois for the Church of God. He accepted the assignment and preached for a time at Eldorado, Illinois, planting the seed for a Church of God that remains today. This move did not seem to meet with the approval of the Christadelphian editor. From *The Christadelphian Advocate* (provided by Peter Hemingray):

> **GONE TO BABYLON**—The "Restitution," in reporting a conference held in Oregon, Ill., says, "There were present rather more than the usual number of ministerial brethren, this year. We had with us Bros. Samuel Wilson of New Jersey, Jas. W. Wilson of Chicago; L.E. Conner, now of Cleveland, Ohio, R.G. Huggins, formerly of Eldorado, Illinois, but who as our Assistant State Evangelist will now live in Oregon.
>
> The "Restitution" represents the people from whom Bro. and Sister Zilmer recently come out. [1906] R.G. Huggins will be remembered as the one who was recommended by our "amendmentist" brethren in Creal Spring, Ill., as fit to travel in the interests of "amendmentism."

This copy was undated, but it can be traced to 1906 because that year L.E. Conner assumed his pastorate at the Cleveland Church of God, which had split from the original congregation begun by McLauchlan, Joblin and Newell Bond. That same year A.H. Zilmer left the Church of God, and Huggins moved to Oregon, Illinois.

From Oregon, Huggins assumed co-editorship of a Texas Church of God journal, the *Word and Work*. This fine paper had been under the direction of William L. Gibbs, but he died unexpectedly in 1907. Gibbs was a former Church of Christ evangelist. It caused quite a stir in that denomination in Texas when Gibbs came into the Church of God. The *Word and Work* was very important in spreading the truth through a generally hostile environment in Texas. Minerva Gibbs dutifully tried to do the editor's work following her husband's death, but it was too much. Robert Huggins assisted her in that effort for the better portion of a year. From Oregon, he served as both mentor and apprentice, two aspects of the publishing business that prepared him to assume *The Restitution*'s editorial duties a few years later.

During this period Huggins attended various state conferences where he met many Church of God members and evangelists. In 1910 he attended the Nebraska Conference for the first time. Members there were happy to meet the "Editor of *The Restitution*" indicating that he had been serving in that position in Cleveland the previous two years. In 1911 he attended the Nebraska Conference again as guest speaker.

C. The Cleveland Years

On May 31, 1908, Robert Huggins, then of Oregon, Illinois, preached both morning and evening. The church minutes said, "And it is expected that Brother Huggins will come to Cleveland to be pastor of the church." When the *Word and Work* no longer needed him, Huggins left Oregon and moved to Cleveland to assume the pastorate at the Blessed Hope Church of God also known as the Lee Avenue church to distinguish it from the other Church of God Abrahamic Faith in the same city.

Robert married Edna Cowell in Cleveland on August 31, 1909. They had two children, Russel Arno and Kathryn Mae.

Within two years Robert accepted the editorship of *The Restitution* beginning with the July 12, 1911 publication, volume 60, issue 25. At that time the Church of God publishing center moved from Plymouth, Indiana, to Cleveland. It is interesting to note that Lindsay began *The Restitution Herald* in 1911 and Huggins began editing *The Restitution* the same year. Huggins put forth a very good effort to keep the paper afloat, but it continued to decline in influence. Its slant was toward Christadelphian interpretation. Huggins continued as editor until January 25, 1921, when he resigned to re-enter the pastoral ministry in New Britain, Connecticut. Throughout his editorship he continued evangelistic trips into the south, southeast and southwest. He preached at special meetings in Brumsfield, Kentucky, at the Oakland Church of God in spring of 1916 where two Carpentar daughters accepted the Lord. A reporter who covered those meetings described Huggins as having a clear and forceful voice.

It should be emphasized that S.J. Lindsay was part of the newly formed Ministerial Association that attacked A.R. Underwood's editorial and financial management of *The Restitution* during Underwood's editorship. In fact, when Lindsay, L.E. Conner and three others met to form the ministers' organization, Robert Huggins, D.C. Robison and Almus Adams were specifically ignored and omitted from the invitations. Lindsay said later in a letter to Charles Crowe, editor of *The Present Truth*, that they were omitted because they were "extremes." Lindsay

Robert Huggins with the Cleveland congregation, circa 1910. Robert is in the back row, fifth from the right.

also charged that they "dictated" the policy of the Church of God, and if that had been allowed to continue, "There would be no Church of God in ten years to dictate to." That was a searing indictment, and clear indication that the majority of the Church of God wanted to move away from Christadelphian influence to form its own identity in the image of Christ.

When Lindsay's letter was published it was inflammatory and stirred up turmoil. It is highly likely that Robert Huggins assumed ownership and editorship of *The Restitution* not only to save the paper but also to counter the new direction the Ministerial Association was taking the Church of God which *Restitution* readers interpreted as watered-down truth.

The owners and readers of *The Restitution* loved the paper and seemed to prefer the narrow doctrinal position it was taking. If this were true, the introduction of *The Restitution Herald* in 1911 represents the second great split in the Church of God, the first being when the Indiana Conference successfully avoided being overtaken by the Adventists near Jeffersonville around 1870. Each paper, the old *Restitution,* and the new *Restitution Herald,* had its loyal following of readers with a few crossover readers who hoped both papers would survive.

Huggins defended himself following Lindsay's letter to *The Present Truth,* giving credit to Lindsay for mentoring him in doctrine. Huggins said that he and Lindsay knew each other's positions very well. Yet from the beginning of his editorship, Huggins was more conservative than Lindsay in his doctrinal approach.

D. Anti-Organization

In the course of the next decade, the Churches of God moved toward organizing a national conference that was intended to help direct the work, build unity and especially to address issues of spirituality among the members. In actuality, a national organization was essential to prevent other "sister denominations" from absorbing Church of God members and whole churches into their conferences. As it developed, *The Restitution Herald* became the advocate for national organization and *The Restitution* became the critic of it. This put the two editors, once friends, on a course of permanent disagreement.

In the months leading to the organizational conference held in Waterloo, Iowa, in the summer of 1921, *The Restitution Herald* published a proposed creed as recommended by the Committee of Ten. Huggins reprinted the creed in *The Restitution* and picked it apart, piece by piece. That creed in basic form:

1. Oneness of God
2. The inspiration of scripture
3. Death, burial, resurrection of Jesus as a means for the remission of sins and salvation.
4. Immortality only through Christ
5. Resurrection of the dead.
6. Second coming of Christ followed by the establishment of the Kingdom of God.
7. Belief, repentance and baptism for remission of sins
8. A godly life.

Huggins said the whole creed was defective since it did not contain any scriptures to explain it. He said the Holy Spirit was never mentioned, and the Son of God was never mentioned. Huggins was not against a creed, as such. He said in one article:

> Is it criminal to have a creed? After all, the word is harmless. It just means you believe something, and that you are able and willing to give 'a definite summary' of your faith. Faith is the assent of the mind to a definite summary of what is believed.

Huggins' creed published in *The Restitution,* February 22, 1911:

- The Bible is the Word of God 2 Tim. 3:16, 2 Pet 1:21
- The coming of Christ is near, John 14:1-3; Acts 1:11
- In repentance and conversion, Matt. 18: 3: Luke 13:35
- In baptism as Jesus was, Mark 1:9.10 Rom 6:4
- In conditional immortality. John 3:16, Rom. 2:7
- In a day of judgment, John 12: 48, Acts 17: 31
- That the dead are unconscious, Eccl. 9:3-10
- In their literal resurrection, Dan 12:2; Isa. 26: 19
- In the destruction of the lost, 2 Pet. 2:9 Rom. 6:23
- The earth is the saints' home. Prov. 2:21, Matt 5:5, Heb. 9:8-9
- Sunday is the day of rest and worship. Mark 16:9, Acts 20:7

Where in this statement is mention of God's nature? The Holy Spirit? The Son of God? This creed is deficient by Robert Huggins' own criteria.

Contrast that list of topics with the statement of faith of the Geneva, Illinois, Church of God published by *The Herald of the Coming Kingdom and Christian Instructor* in February 1868 "Creed of Geneva Church of God":

1. One God
2. Inspiration
3. All have sinned
4. Salvation through Christ
5. Promises made to Abraham
6. Covenant to David
7. Jesus the Anointed born of a virgin
8. Jesus the sacrifice for sins of world, seated at God's right hand
9. Jesus, Mediator and High Priest in Heaven
10. Jesus coming again
11. Jesus the judge of living and the dead
12. Jesus at return will assemble outcasts of Israel on the land of their fathers with Jerusalem as its capital and the Kingdom will increase until all nations have been absorbed by it.
13. Then Jesus will be Prince of Peace
14. Men have salvation by believing in the Gospel of the Kingdom and name of Jesus and will be heirs with Abraham
15. It is the duty of those who have taken the name of Jesus to meet regularly.

The 1930 US Census shows Robert Huggins considered himself a Minister of an Interdenominational Church.

This statement was signed by Samuel Wilson, James W. Wilson, Sarah Underwood, Emma Underwood and Josephine Shaw of the Geneva church. It might be significant that Benjamin Wilson did not sign this statement, which clearly included "Jesus the Anointed born of a virgin." Wilson was not strong on that point.

By the time Huggins resigned from *The Restitution* in January 1921, the paper had been reduced in size, twice, from a 19" x 13" newspaper to a quarto size 6" x 9" due to lack of readers and donations. He had fought a brilliant battle, but he had lost the war over the papers.

In the last issue, Huggins wrote that he made friends and enemies, as anyone must who sticks to dogmatic principles. He accused some in the Church of God of having a "false gospel" and of trying to "kill" *The Restitution*. He was referring to the leaders who began a new general conference in 1921 and accepted a ten-year-old paper, *The Restitution Herald,* over *The Restitution*. Huggins and several others who believed in historical interpretation, pacifism, non-personality of Satan and limited resurrection never joined in the new national organization.

Hard feelings remained on both sides of the question for decades following the birth of the General Conference. Even S.J. Lindsay, editor of *The Restitution Herald*, felt the pressure. He stepped away from his editorial position in 1922 and spent six months of the year in the west.

During this same time, Robert Huggins published a book which is still in use in the Church of God today, *The Bible and Its Principles and Texts*. A copy, hand-signed by the author stating, "To W.J. Halls, compliments of the Author," was owned by Ruth Tomlinson Halls Overholser's family and is part of the archival collection at Atlanta Bible College, McDonough, Georgia. This book is, in effect, a statement of faith, an exposition of clear principles around which to live our Christian lives and a series of questions and his replies. Most questions came to him via *The Restitution* and the book is a reply to writers' concerns. It is very readable and a good reference book or starter text for new believers. The book began as a series of independent Bible lessons; their original publication date is unknown.

Huggins left Cleveland to assume pastoral duties at an Advent Union church in Connecticut. He lived there a few years and finally returned to Cleveland to retire. He spent his last years in Chagrin Falls, pastoring at Blessed Hope Church of God from 1929 to 1951 when he retired.

Historical Waymarks of the Church of God by Clyde Randall reported a story about Huggins being threatened by an angry husband who did not want the preacher to immerse his wife into the saving name of Jesus. Huggins proceeded to baptize her because she felt convicted it was what she must do. On the way home in the horse and buggy, the man lay in wait for Huggins with a "ten-foot rail." The horse having no blinders, saw the beam swinging toward them and jolted forward in fright. The beam missed horse, buggy and Huggins. The story illustrates Robert's devotion and dedication to serving the Lord even in the face of danger.

David Graham, Church of God historian, wrote:
Huggins and others [A.H. Zilmer] would have cheerfully rejoined the Church of God had it not been for the big Five, the Ministerial Association. Lindsay was the minister of propaganda for the Five, and he was pretty good at it. [They] were able to smooth things over [by using] the Bereans. Nevertheless, they nearly shipwrecked or destroyed the whole Age to Come effort.

Those are strong words. It is doubtful Huggins or Zilmer would have rejoined the Church of God General Conference because they disagreed with its doctrinal direction.

Graham believed the basic message of the Age to Come was lost in the turmoil of the 1920s to the extent that two generations grew up without understanding the background of either the doctrine or Joseph Marsh's struggle to publicize the doctrine. Graham laid the blame at the feet of the "Ministerial Monopoly." When David Graham came to a General Conference meeting at Rockford College in the 1980s wearing a black tee shirt emblazoned with "Age to Come" on it, people asked him what it meant.

It must be left to God to judge those tumultuous times, which resulted in the organization of a national work. It is unclear to this writer if Elder Huggins was definitely in the camp of the Christadelphians, and it may not have been clear to Huggins either. In the 1930 US Census data Robert Huggins supplied this information for the column entitled Occupation: "Minister. Interdenominational church."

See Adams, Almus (19th)
    Anderson, Enoch (19th)
    Allard, O.J. (19th)
    Brown, William (19th)
    Gibbs, William L. (19th)
    Gresham, Robert H. (19th)
    Hogarth, Jabez, E. (19th)
    Lindsay, S.J. (19th)
    Underwood, A.R. (19th)
    Wilson, Benjamin (19th)

Bibliography: Ancestry.com. North Carolina Birth Index. 1800-2000, Robert Gresham Huggins, Birth Record; Ancestry.com. U.S. Census. Ohio. Cuyahoga. East Cleveland. Dist. 600. 1930; Bender, Ed., "History of Western Nebraska Conference," a paper for History Conf. at North Hills Church of God, Springfield, Oh. Nov. 2007; Graham, David. *Wisdom and Power* Sept 1992 from research in various *Restitutions*, and interviews with T.M. Ferrell, Byron Williams, Joyce Stadden Schroth and Don Swartz.; E-mails to Stilson Spring and Summer 2006; Huggins, Robert. Co-editor of *Word and Work*, Abilene, Tx. 1907-1908; Huggins, Robert. *The Bible Its Principles and Texts*. Cleveland, Ohio. No date; Huggins, Robert. "Editorial," *The Restitution*, July 5, 1921 "About Geneva," *Herald of the Coming Kingdom and Christian Instructor* Feb. 1868; *The Restitution*, Feb. 22, 1911; April 5, 1911; April 12, 1911; March 16, 1920; Last Huggins Issue: Jan. 25, 1921; *The Restitution Herald.* March 1, 1916; "Gone to Babylon" *The Christadelphian Advocate*, circa 1906 as furnished by Peter Hemingray for inclusion in the Huggins entry; *The Christadelphian*: Vol. 39 Bd. 39.retrieved from e-ed. Birmingham: Christadelphian Magazine & Publishing Association, 2001, c1902, S. 39:335, furnished by Peter Hemingray. This entry refers to Huggin's printing experience in Marion, Illinois; Copy of Huggins Family Tree, and Index to Delayed Birth Certificates April 30, 1877, and many other documents confirming Robert Huggins' residence and ministry in Cleveland, furnished by e-mail, from Franklyne Ross, Aug. 3, 2009; *History of the Church of the Blessed Hope 1863-1963*, by the Elders, Cleveland Heights, Ohio.

Hummel, Betty Blackwell
b. 1880
d. Unknown

Betty Hummel of Fonthill, Ontario, was a faithful worker in the Church of God. In a letter sent to *The History Newsletter* in 1994 Betty said her oldest sister, Wilda Blackwell, married Joseph Fletcher in Toronto in 1920. She reported her joy at being aunt and great-great aunt to many Fletchers in the Church of God.

Betty and Wilda's mother was a Christadelphian because she preferred their doctrines. When Betty's father died in 1923, her mother moved the family to California the same year. They stayed, temporarily, with Emma Railsback, pastor of the Los Angeles Church of God.

Emma Railsback had *housechurch* in her home. Eventually, the group shared the Seventh-day Baptists' church building. The Baptists used it on Saturday, and the Church of God used it on Sunday. In time, Mrs. Railsback mortgaged her own home so the Church of God on 103rd Street in Los Angeles could be built. Betty noted that Mrs. Railsback was a tireless worker.

Shortly thereafter, S.J. Lindsay, of Oregon, Illinois, became pastor of the new church in Los Angeles. He had retired from editing *The Restitution Herald* in Oregon in 1922 and, thereafter, went west each the winter. He baptized Betty and her sister, Nina, in 1924.

Betty also mentioned L.E. Connor's preaching; he visited California on occasion, as his daughter, Corrine, lived there. Betty also mentioned the work of Norman McLeod, G.E. Marsh, Roy Graham, James McLain, Dave Wilsterman and Cecil Smead, all of whom ministered in California. Betty testified in her letter that these preachers, especially the early ones, helped to keep her firmly in faith during the difficult years when she was at UCLA.

See Graham, Roy
    Hummel, Charles M.
    Lindsay, S.J. (19th)
    Marsh, G.E.
    McLeod, Norman
    Railsback, Emma

Bibliography: *The Restitution Herald.* 1920. Letter from Betty Hummel, Archives circa 1985.

Hummel, Charles Mahlon
b. December 27, 1908
d. September 27, 1983

Charles M. Hummel was born in St. Louis, Missouri, where he was trained as a sculptor. He went to California in 1932. It was there he met Betty, his future wife. They were married and attended the Church of God together. Charles was baptized 30 years later.

During WWII Charles was employed by Lockheed as a plaster pattern maker. Later, he opened a plaster pattern business and made mock-ups and patterns for Lockheed, working up the P-38 fighter. Later he worked at motion picture studios making special effects and prop miniatures. He spent more than 20 years with the Walt Disney Studios.

Charles held church offices, including president of the Board of the Los Angeles Church of God. He and his wife had two children, Marilee Biba and Charles III, both of whom joined the Church of God.

See Biba, Marilee
    Hummel, Betty
See Also Doan, Harold

Bibliography: ABC Biography Project, David Krogh, compiler; Ancestry.com. California Death Index. 1940-1997, Record for Charles M. Hummel.

Hunt, Herman S.
b. July 30, 1878
d. May 17, 1967

Herman Hunt was born near Shell Rock, Iowa. He married LaVerne Neal of Clarksville, Iowa, in 1916 when he was 24 and she 23. They had at least one daughter. Herman and LaVerne spent their 50 years together on the farm near Clarksville.

During these years Herman served as an alternating pastor of the Gladbrook congregation and at Koszta, Iowa. He also served at the Clarksville congregation, which was formed in 1890 and closed in 1930. The Clarksville work was begun by A.J. Eychaner on March 5, 1889, with 19 members. Elder Eychaner held tent meetings at Clarksville in 1890.

Herman also participated in the Iowa Conference meetings. At one conference, he was appointed to manage the automobiles on the conference grounds. A conference meeting was hosted in June 1893. Sixty-eight people attended. Herman baptized many during 50 years of ministry. His preaching theme often centered on the word "Love." He and La Verne also loved to attend Minnesota Conferences where one summer he preached on the subject of Gideon.

Herman authored a tract entitled, "By the Grace of God I Am what I Am," in 1959. He said:
> Was it not the love of God for the man and the hate of man toward God's Son which met at the cross and slew the sacrifice which give eternal life to the slayers of that sacrifice? "As we have borne the image of the earthy we shall also bear the image of the heavenly" (I Cor. 15:49).

Herman made the point that God loves all men because of the sacrifice made by the second Adam, Christ. For as in Adam all men died, so also in Christ shall all be made alive (Romans 5:19). The grace of God covers the sin of mankind because of what Christ did at the cross.

Pastors Louis Cronbaugh and Linford Moore officiated Herman's funeral service. LaVerne died a year later. Both are interred at Clarksville.

Bibliography: Ancestry.com U.S. Census. Iowa. Butler. Butler. Dist. 8. 1930 and 1920; Hunt, H.S. "By the Grace of God I am What I Am." Self-published Cedar Falls, Iowa, 1959; Rankin, Delbert. E-mail regarding Herman Hunt, Oct. 27, 2008 and Rankin, Delbert. "The Doctrine of Universal Reconciliation Among Iowa Brethren" Church of God History Conference, North Hills Church of God, October 2008; History of the Minnesota Church of God Conference, Sydney Magaw, ed., 1931.

Huston, Pearle V.
b. December 16, 1905
d. September 1, 1993

Pearle Huston attended the Brush Creek Church of God and was a member there. She was an avid reader and Bible scholar; she believed the basic truths of the Scriptures. Her favorite doctrines were future Kingdom of God on the earth; sleep of the dead; Christ's immediate return to set up his kingdom; man is the author of his own destiny by the choices he makes for salvation, or to refuse it; and a righteous life needed to attain eternal life.

Pearle served in several offices at Brush Creek. She was a Sunday school teacher for over 50 years and church treasurer for 24 years. She wrote lessons for the Church of God Sunday School Quarterlies.

She was also supportive of the church youth. She provided tuition for the Brush Creek youth to attend local and national camps. Pearle was a faithful worker for the Lord who influenced many over the years in their walk with Christ. She died in the Lord and is buried at Curtis Cemetery beside the Brush Creek church.

Bibliography: Biographical information furnished to the Atlanta Bible College by the family. David Krogh, compiler.

There are no biographical entries for this letter.

J

Jenks, Orrin Roe
b. January 1, 1868
d. 1951

Orrin R. Jenks was born in Rockford, Minnesota, to C.C. and Adelaide Jenks when his father was 60 years old and his mother 40. His father was a laborer, but Orrin was destined to seek higher education in the Lord's service. The family was acquainted with Adventist teachings, and the religious background of his family could be considered colorful. His mother was from Ireland where her father had studied for the Catholic priesthood. At the last minute, he refused to take his vows and became a protestant. One source noted Orrin was converted as a Baptist and in 1883 at age 16 immersed in the Fox River by Dr. Kittredge Wheeler of Chicago.

Since Elder Jenks was an active member of the Minnesota Conference in 1885, the Church of God in Minnesota ordained him. While studying or working at Aurora College in 1905, Orrin Jenks pastored an Advent Christian church at 428 Augusta Street, Chicago. As part of his duties to the Advent Christian denomination he often visited their churches and campgrounds. He became a beloved brother to a great many people. One source notes, "While he is by birth a child of the 'Middle West' we are coming to feel that he belongs to the United States and especially to New England. He has become a 'fixture' at our large camp meetings and many a home has been gladdened by his presence."

He next accepted the call of the Burr Oak, Indiana, Church of God and preached there intermittently from 1910-1915. Jenks graduated from Chicago Theological Seminary in 1919. His dissertation was titled "Syriac Versions of the New Testament."

During the Chicago years he visited Minnesota as often as possible. The editor of *The Day Dawn* noted when Jenks was in the state but he could not visit all the churches, but promised to visit those he missed the next time. The editor urged the people to stay in touch with Orrin. He said, "Do not forget, that our Brother was a Church of God boy, and still holds a warm place in his heart for his people."

Jenks preached for the Advent Christians in Minneapolis for eight years. At this same time the Mendota College in Mendota, Illinois, owned by the Advent Christians, began to merge with Aurora College, Aurora, Illinois, also owned by the Advent Christians. *The Day Dawn* editor noted that money was being raised to pay for the relocation. At that writing $57,000 had come in and only $3,000 more was needed with eight months left to reach the goal. He said, "It might be interesting for our friends to know, that this success has largely been due to the faithful, energetic management of a Church of God boy, Elder O.R. Jenks of Chicago. He has been on the road for a year, and we are glad to state that his mission has not been in vain."

It was only reasonable that O.R. Jenks was called by Aurora College to assume leadership as the institution's president. During his tenure at Aurora (1911-1933) and for years afterward, there was a good relationship between Aurora College and the newer Church of God Bible Training School, and between the Advent Christians and the Church of God, which continues to this day.

In 1923 when the Bible Training School was begun— the precursor to the Oregon Bible College—President Jenks visited the Oregon Church of God with four of his students. Later they dined at the Golden Rule Home with "our young men," meaning the students of the training school, namely, Harry A. Sheets native of Blanchard, Michigan; Paul and Arthur Johnson, Sac City, Iowa; and John Railton, Fonthill, Ontario.

See Johnson, Paul
Magaw, Sydney
Sheets, Harry

Bibliography: Ancestry.com U.S. Census. Minnesota. Meeker. New Virginia. 1870; Chicago Theological Seminary Library Index of Dissertations and Theses 1895-1915; *Fiftieth Anniversary of the*

Church of God at Burr Oak, Ind. *History of the Minnesota Church of God Conference,* Sydney Magaw, ed., 1931; History Committee, 1955; *Report of Churches in Chicago.* Iltrails.org; Hatch, A.E. "Report" and "Mendota College" *The Day Dawn and Harvest Messenger,* May, 1911; "The Man Who Does Things," *The Watchtower Advent Christian Church* publication. Wallingford, Ct., Dec. 1910 as cited in *The Arian* Jonathon Ross, ed., Sunnyvale, Ca., Issue #16.

Johns, Arnold
b. August 27, 1913
d. July 20, 1983

Arnold Johns was born in New Mexico. How he learned of the Gospel of the Kingdom is unknown, but it is possible his parents learned of the message from the Arizona, Texas or California evangelists, including S.J. Lindsay, L.E. Conner, J.W. Williams and W.L. Skeels.

When Arnold was of age, he moved north and attended Oregon Bible College. He was a happy person, often smiling. He loved music, but since he didn't sing very well he offered special music through whistling. This was whistling with vibrato, a beautiful style. It was unusual and nearly like an instrument in quality. He often accompanied vocalists.

Arnold filled the pulpit wherever needed. While in college he preached at Flagg Center Community Church until 1950. His daughter Eileen related that Arnold and William Wachtel were instrumental in starting the work there. Glenn Birkey, another Church of God member, attended there, and he facilitated Bible college students preaching at the Community Church. Eventually, this church joined the General Conference Churches of God.

After graduating from Oregon Bible College in 1954, Arnold preached in Casey, Illinois, and East Oregon Chapel. Arnold met Marie Henson from Clinton, Iowa, through Mrs. Louise Kump from the East Oregon Chapel. Arnold and Marie married three months later on June 29, 1956. Marie was actively involved in evangelism for her own denomination, but when she married Arnold she became a baptized member of the Church of God. The couple had two children: Eileen (b. March 31, 1957) and David (b. November 24, 1958).

Arnold took a pastorate in St. Cloud, Minnesota, and later in Fredericktown, Missouri. While in Fredericktown, Arnold hosted a radio program on station KFTW on Sundays at 6 p.m. After he retired from preaching at Fredericktown in 1976, he and Marie moved to Lafayette, Indiana, where he resided until his death. He authored at least one tract in 1970, entitled "The Devil Question."

Eileen helped him publish. Arnold rests in the Riverview Cemetery in Oregon, Illinois.

See Conner, L.E. (19th)
Lindsay, S.J. (19th)
Skeels, W.L. (19th)
Williams, J.W. (19th)

Bibliography: Ancestry.com Social Security Master Death List. Record for Arnold Johns; Johns, Eileen. Interview with Jan Stilson, July 9, 2009.

Johnson, Arthur
b. 1902
d. 1975?

Arthur Johnson and brother Paul attended Bible Training School in 1923, its first year of operation. Arthur returned to Iowa to live and work; he married and had a family. After his first wife died, Arthur married again. He participated in General Conference and Ministerial meetings at Oregon, Illinois, and continued to preach intermittently for the congregation in Sac City, Iowa, sharing the pulpit with J.W. Williams and his son, Paul.

See Johnson, Paul C.
Williams, J.W.

Bibliography: Ancestry.com. U.S. Census. Iowa. Sac. Sac City.Ward 2. Dist. 149. 1920; Swanson, Russell "A Little History for *Searchlight Readers*" Searchlight LXIX:2 Summer 2005; Swanson, Russell, Packet of History Material relating to Sac City received July 6, 2008.

Johnson, Kimberly Sue
b. January 29, 1970
d. December 31, 1990

Kim Johnson was the daughter of Larry and Kathleen (Schmid) Johnson. She was baptized on June 23, 1985, and became an active member of the Church of God in Hector, Minnesota. Her dedication to God's work included two mission trips to Labor Vieja, Mexico. She served as a member of the State Bible quiz teams for two years and worked as a counselor and newspaper editor of the Minnesota Church of God Berean Youth Camp. Kim attended Hector public schools and was in the first graduating class of Buffalo Lake-Hector High School in 1988. While in high school, she was active in Future Homemakers of America, yearbook staff, band, choir and Pop Singers; she was Chapter Sweetheart for Buffalo Lake-Hector High School.

Kim attended Willmar Community College and Moorhead State University. Because of her deep love for children, she chose to study Early Childhood Education. She worked for a time as a typesetter at the *Buffalo Lake-Hector News Mirror*. As a community volunteer, she assisted with Early Childhood Family Education, tutored high school students and helped elementary school teachers with classroom projects. She took volleyball and basketball stats at high school games and made posters and storytime visuals for the local public library. Kim was a deserving recipient of the 1990 Southern Minnesota Sugar Cooperative "Good Neighbor" Award.

She died at age 20 in the Rice Memorial Hospital, Willmar, Minnesota, after a long illness. Her family and friends in the Church of God, especially the youth members, mourned her loss.

Bibliography: Ancestry.com. Minnesota Death Index 1908-2002; Atlanta Bible College Biography project, compiled by David Krogh.

Johnson, Paul C.
b. December 15, 1898
d. August 1977

Paul Johnson was a Sac City, Iowa, native and attended a Bible study group which met in a private home. He moved to Oregon, Illinois, in 1920 to assist S.J. Lindsay with publishing *The Restitution Herald* and to consider the ministry. Lindsay typically sent his apprentices out on preaching assignments. Paul preached at the Church of God in Blush, Missouri, in 1921.

In 1923 when the Church of God opened the Bible Training class, Paul and his brother Arthur decided to attend it, being among the first Church of God young adults to formally enroll in a pastoral training program. Part of the program included practical experience in teaching and preaching. For this, the ministers-in-training often accompanied F.E. Siple, conference evangelist, into the field to preach at local or conference services. Notices found in nearly every issue of literature show the trainees preached across the Midwest, and into the south, weather permitting, as part of their training.

Paul continued to work in the *The Restitution Herald* print shop. At this time, F.L. Austin was editing *The Herald*, as it was popularly called. Paul married the "boss's daughter," Ethel, in the summer of 1931. The ceremony was held on Governor Frank Lowden's estate known as Sinnissippi Farms. Paul and Ethel had two children, Louise (Roy) Humphreys and Robert (Diane).

Paul served as associate editor of *The Restitution Herald* and print shop manager from 1920 until 1967 when he retired. In 1925, he left that position briefly to enter the ministry after he completed the training class. Paul authored two tracts, "Rich Man and Lazarus" and "The Thief on the Cross," both published in 1921. Robert worked beside his father in the print shop for many years. Paul left the ministry and returned to work for the General Conference as manager of the print shop, printing not only *The Restitution Herald*, but also the Sunday School Quarterlies, *The Challenge* (a youth paper), *The Progress Journal, Systematic Theology* by Alva Huffer, many tracts, lesson books, manuals and much more. The shop also did job printing for local businesses.

Paul in his later years

During his tenure, the print shop upgraded from a linotype machine with hot lead type to an offset press. Later on, it transitioned to computer publishing. During the 1980s, the print shop was closed in Oregon, Illinois, and *The Restitution Herald* and other publications were computer generated and subcontracted to a local print shop. The General Conference kept its mailroom and continued to distribute the materials it outsourced to local printers. Eventually, with the transfer of college and conference operations to Georgia in 1990, Spectrum bought the old General Conference and college building at 110 N. Third Street for their computer business.

Paul and Ethel were faithful members of the Oregon Church of God. He served on the board there for many years as well as an Illinois Conference officer for several decades. In the 1930s, when the church at Plum River closed, Paul managed the sale of the church building and turned over the proceeds to the state conference work. He superintended the Oregon church's two additions to the Old Stone Church in the 1960s.

Paul and Ethel are buried at the Daysville Cemetery outside of Oregon, Illinois.

See Austin, F.L.
Huffer, Alva
Johnson, Arthur
Siple, F.E.

Bibliography: Ancestry.com. Social Security Death Index, Record for Paul Johnson; *The Restitution Herald* various issues 1921-1925; Smead, Cecil. Letters from the Smead estate furnished by John Smead, Summer 2008.

Johnson, Sidney Nathaniel
b. November 23, 1888
d. October 1972

Sidney Johnson's family immigrated to Minnesota from Sweden. Neither Sidney nor his wife spoke English well. They soon became followers of Mr. Dahlstrom of Minneapolis; he came out to Chisago County to hold Bible studies on the Gospel of the Kingdom in their home. It is not known if Elder Dahlstrom was ever affiliated with the Church of God, but he evidently preached the Kingdom of God on earth.

Sidney had 16 brothers and sisters. Some died young. Some also accepted the truth of the Gospel and became leading members of the Church of God at Hector. Two of them were Albert and Eva Johnson. Albert encouraged Sidney to send his daughters, Marge and Lois, to Oregon Bible College during the 1940s. At this time, they held beliefs similar to the Church of God and the Christadelphians, but they were not members of either organization.

Lois Johnson married Ernest Graham Jr. of Missouri in Golden, Colorado, in 1945, and together they entered the ministry and raised a family. Lois and Ernest were both talented musicians. She played instruments; he sang. They had seven children: Mark, Joe, Steve, Judy, Elizabeth, David and Dan. David and Dan attended Oregon Bible College. David became a dedicated historian and authored Church of God history. In March 2007, Dan died in Colorado after a long illness; he was surrounded by his loving siblings.

The Johnsons were railroad workers. Through this livelihood Albert and Sidney met Tom Savage; he eventually accepted the Gospel and preached for the Church of God. Other railroad workers helped start the Church of God in Eden Valley, Minnesota. Many people in that vicinity were baptized by Uncle John Foore.

See Foore, John (19th)
Graham, Ernest "Ed"
Savage, Tom

Bibliography: Ancestry.com: Social Security Death Index, Record for Sidney Johnson; David Graham, "Family Genealogy," e-mail to author, March 1, 2006, and March 23, 2008.

Jones, Arthur M.
b. September 1878
d. 1960

Pastor A.M. Jones was born in Punxsutawney, Pennsylvania, and orphaned at age seven. He worked his way through high school and paid for his younger brother's expenses, too. He then enrolled in a Methodist college to become a minister. However, he asked so many questions, especially about the relationships of the trinity and heaven at death, that he was asked to leave.

In 1896 at age 18, Jones moved to Webster City, Iowa, where he became acquainted with Church of God members and ministers, and soon after was baptized there. He became a forerunner of the work in Iowa. Jones married Mayme, and they had a daughter and three sons. The family lived at Eagle's Point, Iowa, but A.M. preached throughout the state. During the week, he was top salesman for the Grand Union Tea Company.

Arthur and Mamie

Beginning in 1899, A.M. Jones became a leader in the work at the Eagle Grove church. He helped the congregation construct the church building they used until the group disbanded in 1920. The property was then purchased by the school district for use as a playground. Elder Jones continued to lead the work with members meeting in homes at least twice a month.

Jones was among the first pastors officially recognized by the national conference. Inclusion of his name on the General Conference list authenticated his standing with his congregations and the General Conference.

Pastor and Mrs. Jones preached at Pleasant Prairie, Albert City in Iowa, and pastored churches in Lawrenceville, Ohio; St. Cloud, Minnesota; Eldorado, Illinois; and Kokomo, Indiana. A.M. Jones served the Lord faithfully for 60 years.

Arthur and Mayme's son, Delbert Jones, was a graduate of Oregon Bible College and Aurora College. Aurora College was accepted by the Board of Directors as a place for Church of God ministerial students to study during the Depression years that the Bible Training School was closed. Several Church of God students attended or graduated from Aurora including Harry Sheets; Vivian Kirkpatrick Sr.; Bud Goodwin; Art Fletcher; Bert Harrison; Welland Holland; and Jack Keenan. Delbert followed in his father's footsteps teaching school and preaching the Word throughout his life in Pomona, California. Delbert's humor will long be remembered in the Church of God.

See Jones, Delbert
Kirkpatrick, Vivian, Sr.
Sheets, Harry

Bibliography: ABC Biography Project, David Krogh, compiler. Ancestry.com U.S. Census. Iowa. Wright. Eagle Grove. Ward 4. 1920; Burnett, Francis et al history committee, *History of the Iowa Church of God and Conference 1855-1987*, printed at Belle Plaine Union, 1987. *The Restitution Herald*, Oct. 1921.

Jones, Delbert Arthur
b. November 1, 1919
d. January 5, 1997

Delbert Jones was born to Arthur M. and Mamie Jones at Eagle Grove, Iowa. According to his birth announcement, he weighed eight pounds. Arthur was a preacher. Delbert attended a summer Bible training class, hosted by the General Conference, at the Oregon Church of God in Illinois. There were 20 eager students at class in 1938. They had a great experience studying the Bible and preparing for ministry. Delbert said, "The only trouble is that the school should be at least a year long!" It was tough to say goodbye to friends at the end of summer. It operated two more summers as a Training School but opened as Oregon Bible College in autumn 1941. The summer Bible training program evolved into a summer youth camping program, managed from then on by the National Berean Society.

Delbert married Bernadene Macy of Ohio, and they had three children. Two of them, Linda and Philip, attended Oregon Bible College. Delbert attended and graduated from Aurora College, and began teaching elementary school. He also preached for the Church of God at the Hillisburg Church of God in Frankfort, Indiana, during 1943, and a few years at the Litchfield, Minnesota, Church of God. He spent the majority of his ministry at the Pomona, California, Church of God.

Delbert authored a tract, "Questions for Trinitarians," in 1957. This piece was a foldout that provided answers to questions about the nature of God and Christ.

The Jones family loved attending minister's and general conferences. Delbert was famous throughout the Church of God for his quick wit and good humor. He could have the conference dinner crowd roaring at his silly antics and funny jokes, but when he preached, he laid humor aside and spoke straight from the Word of God. He was very serious about the Kingdom of God.

Delbert died much too young and was greatly mourned throughout the Church of God. Bernadene died on December 30, 2006.

Bibliography: Ancestry.com U.S. Census. Iowa. Wright. Eagle Grove. Ward 4. 1920; Ancestry.com. California Death Index. 1940-1997; *The Restitution Herald*. November 11, 1919; *The Restitution Herald*, Sydney Magaw, ed., Oregon, Il., Oct. 2, 1947; Jones, Delbert. "Questions for Trinitarians," National Bible Institute, Oregon, Il., 1957; Obituary of Bernadene Jones, THRIVE Ministries, Kent Ross, producer retrieved on Jan. 1, 2007; Smead, Cecil. Letters from the estate furnished by John Smead Summer 2008; Randall, Clyde. *Historical Waymarks of the Church of God*. Church of God General Conference. Oregon, Il., 1976. p. 34.

Jones, Robert Loie
b. January 28, 1922
d. June 6, 1981

Robert Loie Jones was born in Oklahoma City, Oklahoma. His parents were Robert Lee from Jones Prairie, Texas, and Othello Pack Jones from Pelzer, South Carolina. Loie's formal education began at Columbus Grade School and proceeded to Stonewall Jackson Junior High, Capital Hill High School and Capital Hill Junior College in Oklahoma City. He received a Bachelor of Science from Oklahoma University at Norman in 1942. He was a member of Phi Beta Sigma. Later, he attended the University of South Carolina and Clemson University where he completed 30 hours above his Master's Degree in Mathematics.

He was drafted into the United States Armed Services in October 1942. He served in Salt Lake City, Utah; Springfield, Missouri; and Avon Park, Florida. Being a conscientious objector, he was placed in the medical corps as a laboratory technician. He was honorably discharged in 1946 with the rank of corporal.

Loie's mother taught him the Bible at home from a young age. Being isolated members, he could only attend the Guthrie Grove Church of God in the summer. His family traveled across the country to visit his mother's many relatives in South Carolina for about six weeks each summer. A week of special meetings was always held in August. To Loie, the revival meetings were the highlight of the year. But when it was over and they had to leave, it was one of the saddest times. Ties to Othello's family, the Packs, were strong. Loie's father, mother and two sisters moved to South Carolina in 1945. Upon his release from the armed forces, Loie joined the family.

Loie's teaching career began at Ellen Woodside High School in Greenville County in 1946. Later he transferred to the new consolidated Woodmost High School where he taught mathematics until his death. He was quite active in the Lord's work, serving as a Sunday school teacher and elder at Guthrie Grove. The church ordained Loie, and he served as assistant pastor for many years. Twice each month he traveled to Hendersonville, North Carolina, to preach for the Anderson Chapel Church of God. This continued for several years. He was also involved in many youth camps, besides the Southeast Conference and General Conference.

Martha Lou Holliday became Loie's wife in August 1958. They had one son, Timothy Loie, and two daughters, Melody Lee and Rebecca Lane. On June 6, 1981, Loie was stricken with a heart attack and died suddenly. His one-of-a-kind personality, influence, faith and love for his family and God and His Word will always be remembered by those who knew him best. The following tribute was written by several of his students, and given at their 39th class reunion:

> Mr. Robert Loie Jones was an ordained minister who chose to perform his ministry in the public school where he had a profound influence for good on thousands of students who were lucky enough to know him. Students in the Class of 1954 were some of those lucky ones. He played a part in every phase of our life at Ellen Woodside High School.
>
> A superb teacher, Mr. Jones taught English, Social Studies and Mathematics. It seems he was certified in almost all areas of study. He could make the dullest material exciting with his humor. We learned in his class and it was fun!
>
> He was not content to be just a teacher. Other phases of education were important to him. Could we ever forget the plays he directed? One wonders just how much time was spent in rehearsals or where the time came from for a man who also farmed, taught Bible in his church, performed other church tasks, and looked after his family?
>
> It's a good thing basketball season ended before play season began because he was also our Coach. How many of us did he pick up for practice and return home when it was over? He taught us to be competitive, to do our best, to be aggressive, but always to play fair and to be good sports.
>
> So many good lessons we learned from him because he lived them all himself. He never grew angry at us for our mistakes. He teased but always in good taste, never to hurt or embarrass. His language was always that of the Christian gentleman he was.
>
> We are better people today because he was part of our lives-a beloved teacher, beloved Coach beloved friend.

After Loie's death, Martha married retired pastor James Mattison. In 2006 Martha developed a degenerative muscular disease that caused great pain. The first symptoms appeared during her participation in an African Mission Trip. Within a few weeks after Martha's death, daughter Melody died of complications from cancer. Soon after Melody's death her husband died suddenly, leaving their children to be raised by Aunt Rebecca.

Loie and Martha are buried in the cemetery beside Guthrie Grove Church of God at Pelzer, South Carolina.

Bibliography: Atlanta Bible College Biography Project, David Krogh, compiler.

Judd, Rossell Henry
b. January 3, 1870
d. June 6, 1963

A. Sharing the New Faith
B. Judd, the Polemicist and Apologist

R.H. Judd was born in China to missionary parents who accompanied J. Hudson Taylor to establish the China Inland Mission. Dr. Taylor delivered Rossell. As an adult, Rossell resided in England and Canada. Around the turn of the century, he moved to Wicklow, Ontario, from England where he had lived for several years.

Later, he lived in Grafton, Ontario. Rossell married Rose Emma (1869-1950) and they had one daughter.

Judd was a noted author, theologian and missionary. He was not ashamed of the truth, despite having come into it by a circuitous route. Rossell once testified that he first learned of the doctrine of life in Christ, otherwise known as conditional immortality or immortality upon conditions, around 1894 while he was at Moody Bible Institute. It is not known if he attended a Bible conference there, or if he was a student. Two Moody students discussed the destiny of the wicked. He overheard the conversation and carried those ideas into study; this eventually changed his life. At that time, however, he was planning to be a missionary to China and confession of this new-found faith meant "abandoned prospects," so he did not commit to the new doctrine just then. It was new to Judd, although conditional immortality had been widely preached throughout the 19th century in America by George Storrs, Joseph Marsh and many others.

After serving in China, Rossell returned to Canada a number of years later. From there he returned to England where, one Sunday in 1902 at the Devonshire Square Baptist Church, London, he heard two sermons by G.P. McKay. These, on the subject of man's nature, once again awakened his conscience, and in spite of opposition from his church friends he visited that pastor. McKay gave Judd literature to read and Rossell soon accepted the new faith wholeheartedly. From his own little printing business in Nottingham, he published a small tract "Friendly Word." (The Church of God Archives at McDonough, Georgia, would like to have a copy of "Friendly Word.") That publication caused upheaval among his religious friends. In need of sympathy, he wrote at once to Bro. McKay, and he in turn wrote to a mutual acquaintance, Bro. Soar.

Soar became a friend, mentor and host to young Judd. When Rossell Judd was kicked out of the Deepening of Spiritual Life Convention through which he had operated bookstalls in order to propagate their teachings, Bro. Soar took him in, offered him sanction and support.

A. Sharing the New Faith

Rossell took his new faith back to his family at China Inland Mission, and they must have listened to him, for they modified their statement of faith to read, "eternal punishment" for the wicked. He said he agreed with that, but he knew they meant "eternal torment." He would have to talk with them again, and when he did, he would encourage them again to reword their statement of faith. He said he bore "love and esteem" for some of the more "noble workers" there.

His move to new faith brought Judd in contact with men whom he did not name in his writings, but certainly one of them was Eric Lewis, author of *Life and Immortality*. It is known through their correspondence in the Church of God magazine, *The Restitution,* that they were friends. Judd wrote about some of his new contacts. He said:

> Men who, for the sake of the truth, had faced trial, sorrow and loss, and who had become men who regarded the Word of God as literally of more importance than their daily food. Not only so, how eager, how glad these men and women, too, were to help others into the light that God had given them.

Continuing:

> They were not ashamed of the gospel of Christ, for they were ready by sound speech to give an answer to him that asked a reason for the hope that was in them, and it was from "the Word of the Lord" that their answer came.

At some point Judd returned to live in Canada and continued to write tracts and books. He became a member of the Church of God in 1922. He wrote profusely for *The Restitution* and *The Restitution Herald*. When he wasn't writing and preaching, Judd raised chickens and turkeys on his poultry farm. In the spring during hatching season, he worked 17 hours a day, often watching the incubators through the night.

In the September 1925 issue of *The Restitution Herald* Judd wrote that John 1:14, "Word made flesh" was a reference to the virgin birth thereby agreeing with Matthew, Luke and Mark. The Word was made flesh, and God made it so. He said that the earliest translations say "God was the Word," but as time went by translators changed the order and the intent of the verses.

Knowing the major fundamentalist scholars in America, Judd was able to critique their theology as one scholar critiques another. Of Dr. R.A. Torrey on the word "*elohim*" regarding the trinity Judd said, "Hebrew words are often plural when referring to one man." On another occasion, he refuted Torrey's teaching on eternal suffering of the wicked in hell.

B. Judd, the Polemicist and Apologist

Judd also refuted the idea held by some Church of God and Christadelphian men regarding limited resurrection. He said, "It is appointed once unto man to die, and after that the judgment." He noticed that advocates of limited resurrection usually quoted only the first part of the verse, but he asked, "Can judgment occur upon dead men?" Revelation 20:12 says "the dead stand." The first death is appointed to all men. The second death is appointed to the wicked. To him and many others this could only mean general resurrection in that all men would be raised, the righteous to reward, the wicked to judgment.

Rossell counted himself among those believers in the Church of God who denied the pre-existence of Jesus. In an article he wrote for *The Restitution Herald* entitled "Jesus Christ, Who is He?" he said, "that if Jesus had been the son of Joseph, he would have been barred forever from sitting on the throne of David, according to Jeremiah 22:30." And, "the virgin birth, in the providence of God, became an absolute necessity of historical significance, and the very wording of the genealogy of our Lord in Matthew's gospel is changed to accommodate this unique fact." Judd further added, the New Testament's writers bore witness repeatedly that Jesus was the Son of God.

In 1928 Judd authored a short book, *Jesus Christ in the Old Testament*, published by the National Bible Institute in Oregon. He proved through scriptural arguments that the promised Messiah of the Old Testament was Jesus Christ of the New Testament. Why? Because the founder of a major religion has no way of controlling what is said about him before his birth.

The most ambitious piece of writing he did on behalf of the truth of the Gospel of the Kingdom was *One God, God of the Ages*. This book and Lyman Booth's, *The Mystery of Iniquity Explained,* excited and instructed the Church of God in the early 20th century. Booth's book appeared around 1922 and may have been the first off the press of the newly organized General Conference. Judd's book was written and published by the General Conference in 1949 from Oregon, Illinois, just in time to train a new generation of Church of God ministers. Before it appeared as a book, it was published in an article series in *The Restitution Herald* from 1946 to 1948. Since its first edition, *One God* has had four printings. It is still available for sale and widely read among seekers of truth. The third book to inspire the Church of God was Dr. Alva

---

One God by R.H. Judd

"For there is One God; and there is none other but HE."
(Mark 12:32)

GOD LIVES, has lived, is living still,
And still will live while ages roll.
(Deut. 32:40)

He is "The first", He is "The Last."
(Isa. 46:11, Heb. 1:8)

For in Him is contained the whole.
(Acts 17: 28)

Before Him was no other GOD.
(Isa. 43:30)

And since, no other God could be.
(Deut. 32:39, Isa. 43:11)

The endless past, the present now,
Proclaim "ONE" GOD eternally.
(Isa. 57:15, Mark 12:32)

Huffer's *Systematic Theology* first published in 1960. The publishing legacy continued in the 20th century through the books of Sir Anthony Buzzard, too numerous to list in this entry. (Please visit www.focusonthekingdom.org for a bibliography of Buzzard publications.)

Rossell Judd never lost his enthusiasm for his newfound faith. He celebrated it his whole life. He wrote to *The Restitution Herald* at Christmas in 1925 that he had been distributing *Herald*s to libraries in Canada and the United States. He lived in Canada just over the border at Niagara Falls. He recommended that all the brethren make it a practice to put their *Herald*s into their public libraries. It was a great idea–one practiced again when Alva Huffer's book, *Systematic Theology,* was published 25 years later. The goal to place that book in every library in the world was nearly accomplished.

In 1930, an auto struck R.H. Judd, crushing his foot and breaking two bones in an ankle. He was in great pain and incapacitated for several weeks. At the time he lived in Toronto. The crippling injury left him unable to earn wages. God provided for Judd's family. Unexpectedly, his wife received a windfall inheritance that carried them through and allowed her to visit family in England while she was still able to travel and Rossell well enough to manage on his own. During convalescence, Rossell had time to write. People prayed for him, and he healed. He advanced to crutches and eventually reported being happy to be free of them, but his leg would never be the same.

After dispensing with his own crutches, Judd reported within two months that his brother, Dr. Frank H. Judd, a medical missionary for China Inland Mission, escaped with his life when radicals overran the compound, and burned the Jao-Cheo clinic and hospital. Everything in it was looted and all instruments stolen. Bro. Judd appealed for funds to assist the mission in this situation.

Bedford, Ohio, church members, Doris and Fred Schuld, visited R.H. Judd at his home before his final illness and death. They reported that he was a small, dignified British gentleman. Curiously, he had a clothesline strung across his enclosed front porch where all his correspondence was hung with clothespins! Perhaps this "filing" system was helpful to him as he hobbled about with a permanently crippled foot. When R.H. Judd died, notice appeared in *The Restitution Herald*. Pastor Emory Macy at Fonthill, Ontario, officiated the funeral service.

The accompanying tombstone photo was taken by R.H. Judd after Rose's death. The poem on the monument reads, "Life, New Life to them be given, When this Vale of Death has Passed, And, Through Glorious Resurrection, Endless Life Be Ours at Last."

See Booth, Lyman
Buzzard, Sir Anthony
Huffer, Dr. Alva
Lewis, Eric
Macy, Emory

Bibliography: Ancestry.com: 1901 England Census, and, Canada Census 1911; Cain, Rex. E-mail reporting Schuld visit to the Judd home, Feb. 1, 2010; *The Restitution* Sept. 16, 1913; Feb. 21, 1921; May 21, 1925; *The Restitution Herald* July 23, 1922; Sept. 1925; Dec. 15, 1925; Nov. 2, 1926; Oct. 14, 1930; Nov. 4, 1930; Dec. 16, 1930; Oct. 6, 1947 and several subsequent issues carrying chapters from *One God the God of the Ages;* Krogh, David, Notes on R. H. Judd. E-mail to Jstilson, March 23, 2008. Index of Records of the China Inland Mission, Collection 215. Billy Graham Center Archives, Wheaton, Illinois retrieved March 22, 2008 at wheaton.edu/bgc/archives/GUIDES/215.htm#609.

Judy, Daniel
b. December 29, 1926
d. May 1987

Daniel Judy became a California preacher at the Church of God in Glendoria, California, after he attended Oregon Bible College. This work was also known as the San Gabriel Mission. Other California Church of God members felt Daniel was not upholding the truth. His congregation dwindled and other California members referred to them as "Dan Judy and the six old ladies." Evidently the California members tried to take control of the church property; Daniel resisted. The dispute landed in the court system.

After Harold Doan moved to California in 1970, Charles Hummel of the Pomona Church of God went to him and asked if Harold could assist in obtaining the Glendoria property. Harold agreed. The court required services be held regularly there to fulfill the law. The case continued for at least a year, but because of the regularly kept worship schedule, the Church of God retained the property. The California membership always respected Harold for his assistance.

Nothing more is known about Daniel Judy.

See Doan, Harold
Hummel, Charles

Bibliography: Ancestry.com Social Security Death Index. Various sources and reports of members.

Judd still lived when this photo was taken, yet the epitaph expresses his faith in resurrection to eternal life.

Kennedy, Billie Ray
b. April 24, 1934

Billie Ray Kennedy was born near Springfield, Louisiana, where he attended school with Irene Richardson. When Billie and Irene dated in high school, her father, a member of the Blood River Church of God, said, "If you want to date my daughter, you have to go to church!" So, Billie attended church and learned about the things of God. He never looked back. Tim Pearson was his baptizing pastor at Blood River, and Billie still looks to him as the person who most greatly influenced him.

After high school graduation, Billie moved to Oregon, Illinois, to attend Oregon Bible College in 1953. On December 30, 1954, he married Irene. When they returned to Oregon, she attended college for a semester.

Following graduation in 1957, Billie and Irene moved to Harlingen, Texas, to assume the work there after the departure of Jim and Mary Helen Mattison. Billie said the people welcomed them and built a parsonage attached to the church. To supplement his income, Billie drove a school bus. The Kennedys learned of the discussions in progress in the Texas Churches of God by those who believed in Universal Salvation. Those discussions weakened the work in Texas.

In 1959, the Kennedys moved to Blanchard, Michigan, where Billie became pastor at the Church of God. Billie said the Blanchard church was "a perfect church." They were welcomed and loved throughout their years there. The members loved Irene's southern cooking, especially her gumbo, and they cared about each other. "People got along," Billie said. After eight years, they received a call from Lawrenceville, Ohio, and moved there.

In Lawrenceville, Billie developed health problems. He developed trouble with his voice and within one month, he had three surgeries on his larynx and was advised not to talk. This caused him a great deal of frustration and hindered his ministry. He continued to preach, but the problem continued. After three years, he left that work and moved to Eden Valley, Minnesota.

Billie and Irene loved the Minnesota winters. He said the people were wonderful and he didn't mind the snow at all. "You could shovel the snow and never break a sweat," he said, laughing. He and Irene came to love the people and the work grew. He mentioned the Gaspars, Mills and Edith Eades among others he remembered fondly. Billie had a good relationship with the men in the church. He went deer hunting with them, and one day, one of them indicated some land and said, "From here to here is five acres. It is yours if you will retire in Minnesota and build a house on it." Billie and Irene were touched and very tempted, but their family was in Louisiana, so they retired on the old Richardson home place in Springfield, which they bought from the family. Billie became pastor at Blood River, his home church, in 1977. As the children were grown by then and some of them had moved out, Irene worked with the Junior Church program.

During their years in ministry, Irene raised the children. She said, being a very shy woman, some people first believed she was stuck up. But when they got to know her, they realized she was just shy. She was unable to do much work in the church except to get the children ready and take them to church. She also made her famous southern cooking for church potlucks. The Kennedy children are Laurie, who lives in Branson, Missouri; Donna and Mark, both live and work in Louisiana; Brenda, who resides in Richmond, Minnesota; and Jim and Dan, who live and work in Illinois. Jim, Dan and Donna attended Oregon/Atlanta Bible College.

During his career, Billie has actively worked in the Church of God youth camp program. He also led the Louisiana State Camp for several years. Also, Billie was elected to serve on the Board of Directors of the Church of God twice. He was elected in 1974 and served as chairman from 1975-1977. He was also elected in 1994 and served until 1998.

When asked if he felt it had been a good idea to move the General Conference and college to Georgia in 1990, he stated it was and explained he hadn't been in favor of the idea, but the Board advocated for it and he agreed. In looking back, however, he saw that since moving to Atlanta good things have happened in the Korean ministry, foreign mission opportunities and the number of foreign exchange students has increased, but he also believes that more representation is needed in the Midwest. He said the southern churches never felt they had adequate access to the General Conference even when it was in Oregon, lending credence to the idea that at least one regional office placed elsewhere in the nation would give local churches access to the General Conference.

Billie said:
> The church is on the forefront. The church supplies the workers. Atlanta Bible College is not at fault if there are no Church of God students in attendance. The parents are. The parents should raise their children to attend the college in order to prepare themselves to serve. Parents need to educate their children.

Billie said his greatest challenge in ministry was the physical problem he suffered while serving in Ohio. The illness prevented him from full dedication to the labors. It was a disappointing problem for him and the congregation. Billie said that he loved each of the churches he served, and if given those same choices again, he would not change even one.

His greatest joy in the ministry has been the people. Billie felt his ministry should focus on sharing the Gospel with the people and letting the Word of God meet the people's needs. To him, it was exciting to see someone's life transformed by the preaching of the Word. Yes, he had made mistakes, but he always got up and preached the Word because the people loved it so much.

His advice to young ministers is: preach. He advises if given the choice to be President of the United States or a pastor, choose pastor. Billie notes there are ups and downs in the church, but there are more ups. He said:
> Focus on the Word. God's word does not return to Him void." He said, "Sow the Word and Work. Work. Work. If it seems like there are no results, Work. Work. Work. You are on God's side and God is a Winner!

He told the story about one member who came to him and said, "When you have preached on Sunday morning, and there are no results, what do you do?" Billie said, "I go home and eat dinner." God brings the results. Pastors are to preach the Word.

Billie's physical limitations caused him and Irene to retire from the ministry, but they have a position at the local funeral home as host and hostess or greeters, and they help plan funerals. This is something they really enjoy, and it is similar in mission to being a hospital chaplain. They meet people from all over the nation and are able to help them learn about Jesus. Occasionally, when there is no one to preach a funeral service, Billie preaches. He tells them the Gospel message, "because I preach to the living, not the dead." One member asked, "Has anyone who heard you preach at a funeral come to Blood River?" Billie replied, "No, but they have gone out having heard the Word."

Each region of the country has interesting customs, culture and foods. Ministry expectations change from area to area, too. The Kennedys have experienced a rich tapestry of ministry and culture and have loved it all, and they continue to serve the Lord with joy.

Bibliography: Kennedy, Billie and Irene interview with JStilson, 2010. Used with permission from eHerald.

Kiger, Lanie Mabel
b. November 7, 1879
d. June 15, 1969

Lanie Kiger was married to James M. Kiger. This was his first marriage and her second. They resided on Lincoln Avenue in Marengo, Iowa, and were members of the Oak Lawn Church of God at Koszta. Lanie reported in a letter to a friend that Edward Houston began the church. He preached at the Dayton schoolhouse north of Koszta in 1872, and for the next ten years, church services were held there. Lanie's uncles, Eli and Van Cronbaugh, were the first members baptized at Koszta.

Lanie reported that Elders C.C. Ramsay from Kilgore and G.E. Marsh from Marshalltown preached for this congregation. The Iowa conference also concentrated part of its tent ministry in Koszta. W.L. Crowe accompanied the tent and preached at tent meetings for a number of years at the beginning of the 20th century. Following this, O.J. Allard and A.J. Eychaner preached at Oak Lawn until October 1916. At that point, J.W. Williams began preaching and continued in that ministry until the 1930s with a brief respite between 1920 and 1921 when he moved his family to Ripley, Illinois, and then Arizona.

In a letter Lanie wrote in 1942, she reported the Sunday school at Koszta began in 1915 followed later by the formation of a Berean society.

J.M. and Lanie leased land to the congregation to erect a building beneath the hillside cemetery south of Koszta. The parties involved in the transfer of land for the site signed a 99-year lease which is still in effect. The lease includes a requirement that a member of the Cronbaugh family serve on the board through the lease's duration.

Those who remember Lanie Kiger say she was a take-charge woman. Her husband, ten years her senior and a more easy-going person, gave her free rein. He could be seen standing at her side lending quiet support. Her feisty character earned her the nickname, "Kiger the Tiger."

Over the years, the church building has been expanded, creating a lovely center for worship in a beautiful rural setting. The Oak Lawn Church of God of the 21st century is a lively and active congregation. The church is on Highway 212 halfway between Marengo and Belle Plaine, Iowa.

> See Allard, O.J. (19th)
> Crowe, W.L. (19th)
> Eychaner, A.J. (19th)
> Houston, Ed (19th)
> Marsh, G.E.
> Ramsey, C.C. (19th)
> Williams, J.W.

Bibliography: Ancestry.com U.S. Census. Iowa. Iowa. Marengo. Dist. 16. 1930; Kiger, Mrs. J.M. to unknown recipient, May 18, 1942. As recorded by Terry Ferrell in a notebook for the Iowa Conference Archives at Belle Plaine Church of God Abrahamic Faith; Social Security Master Death List, record for Lanie M. Kiger.

King, Alta
b. March 17, 1887
d. April 28, 1957

Alta King was born in Palmer, Nebraska. Her family moved there from Gifford, Iowa. She was raised in a Church of God home. Her father may have heard of the Gospel of the Kingdom from Almus Adams, an evangelist who preached for the Church of God throughout the Great Plains and had lived in Gifford, Iowa. Adams baptized Alta possibly while she was still in high school. Her neighbors knew her as someone who loved little children. By the time Alta was 13, her father had died and her mother, Mary, was left to raise five children. Eldest son, Merton, assisted the family by farming the land.

Alta faithfully wrote a series of children's stories and columns for *The Restitution Herald* and other religious magazines. Her columns were Sunday school lessons that were also published in leaflets as lesson guides. The guides were popular among Church of God Sunday schools in the early part of the 20th century. Sometimes she shared her column space with Anna Drew of Dixon, Illinois. Both ladies were active in the Berean movement.

Alta was an avid Bible student, and considered herself a lay-believer. The preface to her book *Scripture Studies* said, "These studies are sent forth with the prayers and the hope that they may help others as they have helped this lay-believer."

Even though she served on the Committee of Ten that brought the Church of God General Conference into existence in 1921, the majority of members must not have known Alta advanced the doctrine of universal reconciliation. This doctrine states that sin is temporary and will be eliminated in the future age so that all men will come to salvation and be reconciled in Christ. The majority of the Church of God did not subscribe to this teaching. Iowa seemed to be the seedbed of that thinking.

In a letter to William Wachtel dated May 12, 1950, Alta wrote:

> It is true that we must refuse any line of thought that impugns or calls in question any characteristic that is inherent in Him who is God. If we do not, we destroy God—(in our thinking). In accordance with this "must," I offer the following scriptural facts and what seems to me to be scriptural conclusions based on these facts:
> - God (is) omniscient—He knew every detail of the sin problem before it emerged into reality through Adam's sin. He knew the very core of that problem--even the strength and the rebellion of the natural will against His own will, and the pride inherent in that natural will.
> - God is absolutely supreme in power, in wisdom and in love.
> - God desires and would have men to be saved from sin and all its consequences.
> - God…sent Jesus to be the Savior of the world. He made this provision before the foundation of the world before there was sin or sinner.
> - Jesus out of His love and compassion for sinning man accepted of God's desire and purpose in Himself. He died a ransom of the sins of the whole world.
> - Since God knew every facet of the sin problem…the provision He made to meet the sin problem is adequate to solve that problem not only in wishful desire but in actual accomplished fact.

She also wrote an explanation of Ephesians 1:19-23 and Philippians 2:8-10 regarding "all things under his feet" and "every knee should bow." She said:

> This redemptive work will be finished when every knee bows at the name of Jesus Christ in His resurrection glory, and every tongue confesses that He is Lord. Since this bowing and this confessing will be to the glory of God the Father, there will be in all God's universe no enemies, no unwilling slaves bending before Him and confessing that He is Lord. God the Father will be all and in all.
>
> *Delbert Rankin provided this quote from his paper on Iowa universalism.*

Alta was an educated woman. At the beginning of her career she taught in Nebraska country schools, and after graduating with a master's degree from the University of Nebraska, she taught in Iowa city schools. Her author's biography from *Scripture Studies* reported that she moved to Palo Alto, California, in 1938 and in 1941 she joined the staff of Stanford University Library's cataloguing department. She worked there until retiring in 1955.

She wrote numerous articles in various Universalist magazines including *The Differentiator*. The March/April

1949 issue of this journal contained articles by King, Joseph Williams and E.O. Stewart, all of whom claimed to believe in the Gospel of the Kingdom. She stated in her article "that [Jesus] is the Savior of the world, an effective lesson on universal salvation, or rather on the effective, victorious working of His living power."

She also noted that "Universal salvation is usually associated with Universalism or Unitarianism that leaves out Jesus as Savior." Rankin commented:

> I think this is interesting that there is a difference. Universalism in the Church of God and that which is apart from the Unitarian-Universalist position seems at least to insist on some understandings of the nature of man and nature of God and work of Jesus saying, for instance, that there is a need at some point for Jesus and the Cross, and that, "there is no unending torment in flames." But then it takes on its own flavor of, shall we say, "wishful thinking?"

Alta King never married. After her death, her body came to Palmer, Nebraska, for burial. Her contribution to educating a generation of Church of God children through her numerous columns cannot be measured in this life, but God knows her life and remembers her in death.

See Drew, Anna (19th)
Stewart, E.O.
Wachtel, William
Williams, J.W.

Bibliography: Ancestry.com U.S. Census. Nebraska. Buffalo. Kearney. Ward 1. 1900; King, Alta. *Scripture Studies,* Greenwich Book Publishers, New York. 1957; Photo from book jacket of *Scripture Studies. The Restitution Herald,* May 10, 1916 and numerous other issues; King, Alta "Letter to William Wachtel," May 1950, furnished by Archives of Belle Plaine, Iowa Church of God Abrahamic Faith, to Jan Stilson Nov. 2008; Rankin, Delbert, pastor at Belle Plaine Church of God Abrahamic Faith, "The Doctrine of Universal Reconciliation Among Iowa Brethren," presented to the Church of God History Conference, North Hills Church of God, October, 2008.

Kirkley, Iris (Stilson)
b. August 19, 1900
d. November 17, 1993

Iris Stilson was born to Alexander Fremont Stilson and Eva McChesney Stilson in Marshall County, Indiana. She was raised in a Church of God family and remained true to the Gospel of the Kingdom all her life. She had four siblings: Floyd, Rolland, Forrest and Myrtle (Houser). Elder David E. Van Vactor baptized Iris November 28, 1915, at Plymouth, Indiana. She was active in the church work at North Salem Church of God in Plymouth and with the Indiana State Conference.

Iris was a member of the Daughters of the American Revolution because Alexander served in the Civil War. She researched the family history, and because of this, much of the Stilson family has been located and documented.

In 1920, Iris married C. Russell Kirkley; they had three daughters, Joan, Dolly and Nancy. They resided in Plymouth all their married lives. Mr. Kirkley preceded Iris in death. She rests beside her beloved husband at the Oak Hill Cemetery in Plymouth, Indiana. Their gravesite is across the road from Floyd and Lulu Stilson.

See Stilson, Alexander
Stilson, Floyd A.

Bibliography: Biography project of Atlanta Bible College, David Krogh compiler. Stilson,J., Memories of Iris Kirkley.

Kirkpatrick, Vivian, Sr.
b. February 18, 1911
d. December 17, 1990

Vivian Kirkpatrick was born in Blackduck, Minnesota, to Lester and Sarah Matheny Kirkpatrick. During his youth in the Church of God, Sydney Magaw was Vivian's pastor. He also knew Clyde Randall during those years. Vivian graduated from Oregon Bible College and Aurora College in Aurora, Illinois. He married Walcie Rhea Smith on August 30, 1942, in Dixon, Illinois. Walcie was a student at Summer Bible Training Class. She was the daughter of H. Scott Smith, evangelist and teacher from Arkansas.

Vivian and Walcie had six children, Pastor Vivian II (Paula Bolhous), Pastor Sydney (Deirdre Daley, Digby, Nova Scotia), Mrs. Judy (Gary) Myers, Mrs. Becky (Donald) Needham, Debbi Kirkpatrick and Mrs. Donna (James) Dimmick.

The State of Minnesota Church of God Conference licensed Vivian as a pastor in the Church of God Abrahamic Faith in 1939. He was ordained by the same organization in 1942. During his 45 years of active ministry, Vivian pastored a number of churches in resident, interim and supply capacities, beginning with Blanchard, Michigan, in 1939. Over the years he served churches in Morrilton, Arkansas; St. Cloud, Minnesota; Holbrook, Nebraska; Graytown, Wisconsin; Kokomo, Lafayette and Hedrick, Indiana; Hector, Minnesota; Digby, Nova Scotia, Canada; Weiser, Idaho; and Eldorado, Illinois, where his pastoral ministry ended in 1984.

While serving at Holbrook, once a month Vivian traveled to Moorefield, Nebraska. when they didn't have a pastor; to Arkansas City, Kansas, once a quarter; and he conducted regular services and or Bible studies at McCook, Cozad and other places in Nebraska. In addition to his pastoral duties, he also held superintendent, principal and teaching positions in public schools in Minnesota, Montana, Nebraska and Illinois. He taught Bible, and pastoral ministry courses at Oregon Bible College for eight years. While there, he served as librarian and organized and expanded the library by adding several hundred new and classic books to the collection.

When the Kirkpatrick family returned to Oregon, they purchased the home on Jefferson Street once owned by Otto E. Dick and family. Otto Dick was Oregon Bible College's president from 1947 until his death.

Vivian died following a long illness. His family and friends mourned their beloved husband, father and servant of the Lord. Funeral services were held on December 21, 1990, at the Oregon Church of God with Pastor Michael Hoffman officiating. His son, Sydney, gave the eulogy. Vivian was interred at Riverview Cemetery north of the city.

    See Dick, Otto E.
           Magaw, Sydney
           Randall, Clyde
           Smith, H. Scott

Bibliography: Kirkpatrick family for the ABC Biography Project, David Krogh, compiler.

Knapp, Charles
    b. July 30, 1925
    d. March 7, 2000

Charles "Chuck" Knapp was born in Paris, Michigan, to Charles L. and Marie Knapp. His father was a hardworking shop foreman. Charles grew up to love the Lord and was a baptized member of the Southlawn Church of God. He married Joyce Slocum; they enjoyed 50 years together. They had four children Steven (Norma), Lynne (David) Krogh, Paula Knapp-Haven, Janice (Tom) Mawson and six grandchildren.

Charles and Joyce Knapp

Chuck served in WWII in the Engineers Corps 361st Special Services Regiment. He was Band Master in the Reserves for the 21st Armored Division Band and the 84th Division Band of the 5th Army and a member of the 394th Station Hospital Unit in the Army Reserves. Chuck was employed by Service Metal Company of Grand Rapids. He was a member of the Grand Rapids Industrial Executives and past president and treasurer of the Grand Rapids Engineers Club. Chuck served on the Health, Welfare and Pension Board of Sheet Metal Local Zone 2. He was a member of the Knickerbocker Concert Band.

Chuck was a founding member and elder of the Garden Park Church of God in Kentwood and served on the General Conference Board of Directors. He participated in conference activities. He and Joyce attended annual conference regularly, using vacation time. He was a generous and giving man. After retirement, Chuck and Joyce traveled in a motor home. They traveled to Rockford, Illinois, and parked in the lot of the newly purchased Family Bible Fellowship on North Ridge Street. Here they lent a hand with building maintenance, making small repairs, scrubbing the floors and waxing furniture and floors. Their goal was to help a new congregation get a footing. Their help was much appreciated.

Charles died in the Lord, and he is buried at the Lawrence Hill Cemetery, Lawrence, Michigan.

Bibliography: ABC Biography Project, David Krogh, Chuck's son-in-law, compiler.

Krogh, Harvey Ulysses, Jr.
    b. November 30, 1910
    d. June 17, 1968

Harvey Krogh Jr. was born to Harvey and Birdie Mehrens Krogh in Pawnee City, Nebraska. He was the oldest of five children and raised on a farm near Blair, Nebraska. Harvey's Church of God heritage came from his maternal grandparents, Herman and Josephine Mehrens. A Church of God pastor baptized Herman in 1860. He became a faithful Church of God member, supporting its ministry with his means until his death in 1914. The Mehrens passed the faith on to their children.

Harvey attended the Church of God at Blair where his parents were very active. Elder T.A. Drinkard baptized Harvey and his sisters Dorothy and Clara in fall 1927.

After high school Harvey attended Bible Training Class In Oregon, Illinois, forerunner of Oregon/Atlanta Bible College. Sister Dorothy also attended the class. After graduation in 1933, he took the pastorate at the Plum River Church.

On September 4, 1934, Harvey wed Mary Reynolds of Oregon. Mary and her family were members of the Oregon church. Harvey and Mary continued to serve at Plum River for another year, and then they moved to pastor the Ripley, Illinois, Church of God. Harvey later served as Illinois Evangelist, living in Macomb and traveling into Missouri conducting services in both states.

For 35 years Harvey and Mary ministered at churches in the Midwest: Brush Creek, Ohio (1939-1942); Pennellwood, Grand Rapids, Michigan (1942-1947); Hope Chapel, South Bend, Indiana (1947-1954); Oregon, Illinois (1954-1960); Southlawn, Grand Rapids, Michigan (1960-1966); Brush Creek, Ohio (1966-1968).

While serving as pastor at Hope Chapel, Harvey recorded a radio broadcast every week for station WHOT. It played on Tuesdays at 3:00 p.m. as a test market. Harvey and Harold Doan, pastor of the nearby Morningstar Church of God, jointly recorded a weekly radio broadcast called the Morning Chapel. Later, while pastoring the Southlawn Church in Grand Rapids, Harvey also broadcast messages over station WOOD.

In 1966 while at Southlawn, Harvey and Milon Hall, pastor at Pennellwood Church, worked with Charles and Joyce Knapp and Dorothy Siple to start the Garden Park Church, about ten miles south of Southlawn and Pennellwood. Garden Park held worship service first at 9:30 a.m. followed by Sunday school. This allowed Harvey and Milon, who preached on alternate Sundays, to preach first at Garden Park, and then drive to their respective churches to preach an 11:00 a.m. service.

Harvey enjoyed working with his hands. He liked to fix things, and he worked as a watch repairman while with the Plum River church. This supplemented the family income. Throughout his years Harvey continued to keep the family's watches running and did repairs for friends.

Harvey enjoyed music. In 1947, he served as committee chairman for publishing the *Songs of Truth* hymnal. Evelyn Austin of Oregon, Illinois, and Evelyn Barr of Grand Rapids, Michigan, also served on the songbook committee. Titles of Church of God hymnals are *Songs of Truth*, *Songs of Truth Two* and *Psalms, Hymns and Spiritual Songs*. Harvey had a strong tenor voice and often favored the service with a solo or a duet with Rachel or David. He also sang in the choir and played the trombone. His children were encouraged to develop their musical talent as well. A favorite musical special at the Oregon Church of God was a trio of instruments played by Harvey, Rachel and David.

Harvey was a great preacher. His sermons were well-studied and presented in a lively and affable manner. He often had object lessons or charts behind him to illustrate the sermon's subject. One Sunday evening he preached on the Doomsday Clock, maintained by the directors for *The Bulletin of the Atomic Scientists* since 1947. That year the clock was set at 11:53. Harvey used the illustration that midnight represented global disaster. He then preached about the signs of the times, and why Christians should be ready to meet the Lord when he comes in the air. On another occasion he preached about the image made from several metals in Daniel 2. To illustrate his remarks he had painted a life-sized image on a board propped beside him. As he preached about the various empires corresponding to the categories of metal in the image, he talked again about prophecy and what is yet to be fulfilled.

In addition to pastoral work, Harvey served the General Conference as a member of the Board of Directors from 1945-1951. Later he chaired the Ministerial License and Ordination Board for several years.

Harvey died June 17, 1968, in Dayton, Ohio. Funeral services were conducted by his boyhood friend and fellow Bible Training Class classmate, J. Richard LeCrone, at the Oregon Church of God on June 20; burial was in the Daysville Cemetery near Oregon.

Children Rachel and David graduated from Oregon Bible College and have been active in the Church of God ministry. Rachel served as a missionary in Mexico and as Superintendent of Missions for the Church of God General Conference from 1969 until her marriage to John Carr. She and Jon worship at the Lakeshore Bible Church in Tempe, Arizona. They have one son, Jeff.

David pastored at Garden Park Church of God, Grand Rapids, Michigan. He was interim pastor at the Blessed Hope Church in Rockford, Illinois, and interim pastor at the East Oregon Chapel. He held various positions within the General Conference offices in Oregon, Illinois, and Morrow and McDonough, Georgia. He served as office manager, *The Restitution Herald* editor, Oregon/Atlanta Bible College President and General Conference Executive Director. He is married to the former Lynn Knapp of Grand Rapids. They have two children, Peter and Carrie (Briggs). Carrie was elected to serve on the Board of Directors of the General Conference in 2009.

David Krogh and Rachel Carr contributed to this entry.
See Austin, Evelyn Harsh
 Doan, Harold
 Krogh, Harvey U., Sr.
 Krogh, Mary A.
 LeCrone, John Richard
Bibliography: Ancestry.com. Ohio Deaths 1958-2002; Census. Nebraska. Washington. Blair. Dist. 126. 1900; Biographical information from Atlanta Bible College Biography project, David Krogh, compiler; Krogh, David. E-mail to J. Stilson, Feb. 16, 2006; *The Restitution Herald*, Sydney Magaw, editor, Oregon, Il., July 20, 1948.

Krogh, Harvey Ulysses, Sr.
b. December 30, 1885
d. April 26, 1967

Harvey U. Krogh Sr. was born in Deerfield, Wisconsin, near Kroghville, to Carl E. and Clara C. Krogh, both of Norwegian descent. Harvey was the eldest of three sons. The family moved to Blair, Nebraska, just after the turn of the century. Harvey worked in the hardware business with his father until 1911 when he started farming. He resided on his farm near Blair until his death. Harvey married Birdie Mehrens on December 29, 1909. Birdie's family had been Church of God members for several years. Her father Herman was baptized in 1869. Harvey and Birdie had five children: Harvey Jr., Dorothy (Paulson), Clara (Westerfield), Oakley and Kenneth.

Almus Adams baptized Harvey in November 1912; Harvey remained a faithful member of the church to the time of his death. Birdie preceded him in death by nearly 29 years. Harvey died following a brief illness at the age of 82. Pastor Clyde E. Randall of the Omaha Church of God conducted funeral services. Harvey was buried in the Blair Cemetery beside Birdie.

See Adams, Almus (19th)
Krogh, Birdie (19th)
Krogh, Carl Otto (19th)
Krogh, Harvey U., Jr.
Mehrens, Herman (19th)
Randall, Clyde E.

Bibliography: Ancestry.com U.S. Census. Nebraska. Washington. Blair. Dist. 156. 1920; Social Security Master Death List, Harvey U. Krogh record; ABC Biography project, David Krogh, compiler.

Krogh, Mary A.
b. February 22, 1913
d. May 24, 2006

Mary Adaline Reynolds was born February 22, 1913, on a farm west of Oregon, Illinois, to William Reynolds and Clara Reitzell Reynolds. Mary began attending the Oregon Church of God with her mother and sisters, Lucille and Iva, when she was a teen. Along with six others from the Oregon Church, the Reynolds sisters were baptized on April 5, 1931. Mary served as Sunday school secretary. She met Harvey U. Krogh Jr. of Blair, Nebraska, who had come to Oregon to attend Bible Training Class. They were married on September 4, 1934. Together, they served pastorates in Illinois (three churches), Michigan (two churches), Indiana and Ohio (same church twice). Harvey and Mary had two children, Rachel (John Carr) and David (Lynn Knapp) and three grandchildren, Peter Krogh, Carrie Krogh (Jerry Briggs) and Jeff Carr. Mary had three sisters, Ethel Reynolds, Lucille (Rittenhouse) and Iva (Buse).

Following Harvey's death, Mary served as housemother for female students at Oregon Bible College, 1972 to 1978. She was also a proofreader at S & S Computype Service. Mary served as a volunteer proofreader for the Oregon/Atlanta Bible College and the General Conference publishing department. She also assisted in the mailroom. She continued with these activities until a few days before her death.

Mary's life focused on the Lord's work, having served not only as a pastor's wife, but as Sunday school teacher, vacation Bible school leader and teacher and in many other positions, including deaconess. She also had a great interest in the work of Oregon/Atlanta Bible College and the General Conference. She attended nearly every summer conference held during her adult life.

Mary lived a full and active life. She enjoyed very good health and was still driving her car just three weeks prior to her death at age 93. She was mentally sharp and remembered details of things that happened both recently and in the past. She had a godly influence on the lives of her family and on many others who knew her over the years. Mary strongly believed in the truths of Scripture taught and believed by the Church of God.

She died in Morrow, Georgia, having resided near Atlanta Bible College from 1991 to 2006. Her funeral service was conducted from the Oregon Church of God, and she was interred beside her dear husband in the beautiful Daysville Cemetery.

See Krogh, Harvey U., Jr.

Bibliography: Krogh family for the Atlanta Bible College Biography Project, David Krogh, compiler.

1960 Sunday School Rally at Flagg Center Church of God, Mary Krogh is third row, center, with large white collar.

Landry, Gordon
b. March 10, 1928

Gordon Landry was born in Hammond, Louisiana, to George Gustav and Mary Addie Alexander Landry. Gordon had four brothers, Robert, Cecil, Jerry and Preston, and one sister, Mary Helen (Mattison), now deceased. When Melville Lyon visited Hammond to conduct a series of revival meetings Gordon was convinced that he needed the Lord and so 12-year-old Gordon requested baptism. Pastor Harry Goekler baptized him, and when Harry moved, Pastor Vernis Wolfe taught Gordon.

As many young people in the Church of God did, Gordon came to Oregon, Illinois, the summers of 1943 and 1944 to attend Summer Bible Training School for six weeks. Gordon said, he didn't want to be a minister, but he overheard his mother say that she wanted one of her sons to be a pastor, and she thought Gordon would make a fine minister. Gordon said when he heard her say that, he thought, "Not me."

But he loved the Lord, and he enjoyed the Summer Training Class where he was introduced to life-long friends, Norman McLeod and J. Arlen Marsh. All these factors contributed to his coming to Oregon Bible College in 1945; he graduated in 1949. He served as Sunday school superintendent and pastor of the East Oregon Chapel during his final two years at the college. He dated Barbara Kump. She attended OBC for a year while she finished high school. They married in 1949 and had eight children: Rick, Dan, David, Joel, Jarad (deceased), GiGi, Jennifer and Barry.

Gordon's first full-time pastorate was in Ripley, Illinois. While there he looked into becoming a missionary in South Africa. He applied for a visa, but they would not allow him to enter the country unless he had a job or organizational backing. He had neither. Gordon then applied for a position at a South African newspaper because he had expertise as a printer, but they had no openings. So, he turned his attention to home missions.

Gordon's next pastorate was a mission effort in Douglas, Arizona, along the Mexican border. He stayed a year and baptized one woman. Gordon said the biggest problem was the language barrier. When he received an invitation letter from Blood River Church of God at Springfield, Louisiana, he and his family moved north. They ministered at Blood River four years, and then moved to Baton Rouge, Louisiana, where he pastored for 17 years. Pastor Vernis Wolfe greatly influenced Gordon at this time.

In 1974, the General Conference called Gordon to Oregon, Illinois, to work in the print shop. He was especially gifted in producing and designing *The Restitution Herald* pages. One of his most famous artistic projects for *The Restitution Herald* was the foldout centerpiece for the 75th Anniversary issue in October 1986. The special layout, designed by David Graham and Jan Stilson, detailed the line of succession of the historic periodicals in the Church of God in America.

Jim Mattison, Gordon's brother-in-law, influenced him the most. Gordon said Jim "straightened me out on prophecy, changing me from pre-trib to post-trib." Gordon had his own print shop and he printed his materials and Jim's. They worked together in Louisiana. Pastors Harry Goekler and Vernis Wolfe also received considerable credit for helping Gordon mold his ministry. Gordon also mentioned life-long friends, Dean Moore and Alva Huffer, who were his roommates at Oregon Bible College. In fact, Gordon learned the printing industry when Dean Moore left his job in the General Conference print shop. Dean said, "I am leaving. If you want the job, I will recommend you."

Paul Johnson was Gordon's mentor. In 1974, when Gordon returned to work in the print shop, Paul Johnson's standards had not changed. He still expected perfection.

Paul taught Gordon to operate the hand-fed press, so he assigned Gordon to print Quarterly covers on that press. The "Q" was missing in the word and Gordon didn't notice it. Paul said, "Put that letter in the form by itself,

Gordon and Barbara Landry

and run the covers through again. Let's see how good you are." Gordon was proud and relieved that everything lined up on the second run.

The biggest challenge facing Gordon in his ministry involved those cases where divorced people wanted to remarry. He believed the Scriptures allow Christians to divorce under certain circumstances, but not to re-marry. He refused to re-marry such couples, and he refused to marry couples living with each other by excusing himself from the situation.

Gordon said his greatest answer to prayer was finding Barbara. He had prayed for a loving wife, and they have been married for 61 happy years. She has been a very supportive and helpful pastor's wife.

Gordon's advice for young ministers is to "Love your people and don't require too much of them. Ministers need to be the example in order to work with people." Currently, his biggest concern for the Church of God is that Atlanta Bible College is not training enough pastors, and of the ones who graduate, not many are entering the ministry. Many churches need pastors.

When Gordon was re-employed at the General Conference print shop in 1974, he took the pastorate at Flagg Center. He remained their pastor for 35 years, retiring in 2010. His friends and family threw a retirement party at the church on October 23, 2010.

After Gordon left the print shop, he took a job at Dawson in Oregon. This was a magazine jobber who supplied subscription lists to libraries around the world. Atlanta Bible College had a Dawson account for its library journals at one time. Dawson has since gone out of business.

Gordon said he wrote two novels and a book of Bible cryptograms over his lifetime, but the novels were lost when he moved from Louisiana to Illinois. Now he is planning to write another book, *The Commonwealth of Israel from the Death of Moses to the Death of Samuel*. It is anticipated to be a great book, and it will be an asset to place a copy in the Archives.

See Goekler, Harry
Huffer, Alva
Marsh, J. Arlen
Mattison, James
McLeod, Norman

Bibliography: Landry, Gordon. Interview with JStilson, 2011.

Laning, Wayne
b. November 19, 1913
d. September 26, 2004

Laning, Millie
b. May 22, 1917
d. July 5, 2010

Wayne Laning was born in Brown County, Illinois, to Frank and Tessa Laning. He was raised in the Church of God at Ripley where he met Millie Miller. F.L. Austin baptized Millie on May 22, 1932. He had also baptized Wayne. Wayne and Millie married on December 22, 1940.

Wayne was a well-known farmer in the area, and he participated in community affairs benefiting farmers. He served as director of local and state boards of the electric cooperative for 37 years. He was instrumental in bringing electricity to the rural areas of Brown County. Wayne was on the Brown County Farm Bureau Board for nine years. He served on the local school board for 12. The Church of God General Conference delegates elected him to the Board of Directors for a four-year term in the 1950s. After retirement, Wayne worked with local tax groups to lobby for lower taxes in Illinois.

Millie worked faithfully beside her husband on the farm and at church. They had one of the biggest farms in the county with hens, pigs, dairy cows and two bears in a wire cage in the back yard. During youth retreats

The Ripley congregation came together to make apple butter at the Laning farm.

at the church the bears provided entertainment for the guests who slept at the Laning residence. Millie was an excellent hostess and cook. She hosted many ministers and guests at her home. She and the ladies at Ripley made apple butter every fall. They sold it or donated it to other Churches of God, the Illinois Conference and Oregon Bible College. College students thought this was the best apple butter in Illinois, and maybe in the Midwest.

Millie taught Sunday school and youth Bible classes at Illinois Conference. She could give wonderful flannelgraph Bible stories and was a gifted soloist. She had a sweet spirit, but stood staunchly behind what she thought was right. Millie was interested in church history and wrote about the Ripley Church of God history. (See Appendix 12.)

Wayne and Millie are interred at the Ripley Cemetery. Their son Rob and his family survive them.

Rob Laning contributed to this entry.

See Austin, F.L.
Bibliography: Laning, Rob and Karen. E-mail to JStilson, Nov 15, 2010.

Lansbury, Esta (Starbuck)
b. January 14, 1905
d. February 1984

Esta Lansbury Starbuck was a member of the Moriah Church of God in Casey, Illinois. She graduated high school in 1922. In 1925 she became bookkeeper for the newly-organized National Bible Institute office in Oregon, Illinois. During her tenure there, Lyman Booth audited the conference accounts; he was a noted preacher of the Dixon Church of God, writer for *The Restitution Herald* and a businessman in Dixon. Miss Lansbury's friends included the Drew sisters, Anna and Ada, of Dixon. Esta married Harold Starbuck and moved to Rockford, Illinois, where they assisted the newly-organized Blessed Hope Church of God on the west side. This church began in 1930 as a Berean Bible Study Class for young adults.

See Booth, Lyman (19th)
Drew, Anna (19th)
Bibliography: *The Restitution Herald*. Various issues, 1922-1930.

The General Conference/Bible College building on 3rd St. Clarence Lapp's office was on the second floor behind the tree.

Lapp, Clarence E.
b. July 21, 1906
d. November 20, 1989

Lapp, Mary Louise Brewer
b. November 9, 1909

Clarence Lapp was born in Moorefield, Nebraska, to Daniel and Lucy (Stedman) Lapp. Lucy was a member of the Moorefield Church, and devoted to the Abrahamic Faith. When times grew tough, the Lapps left the family farm near Moorefield to relocate to Sunnyside, Washington. Although they became isolated Church of God members, Lucy kept in touch through visits and special meetings with Evangelist Almus Adams and other preachers who toured the west. Daniel and Lucy had three children: Clarence, Ida and Charlie who grew to be tall and stately in appearance with handsome features. The children were baptized at a church conference in Felida, Washington, around 1925, although the records give more than one date for this event. Daniel Lapp died when Clarence was a teen.

As an adult, Clarence tried banking, but he found it unfulfilling. Clarence's widow, Louise Lapp, remembered that, as a young man, Clarence fell in love with the daughter of a Brethren minister; he wanted to teach her the truth but didn't know the best way to approach the subject. He decided to give up his job and move to Oregon, Illinois, for three years to attend the new Bible Training Class. He boarded a sheep train and fed the sheep all the way to Illinois to earn his ticket.

While Clarence was away, his girlfriend married someone else. Clarence taught classes at the 1931 and 1932 General Conferences, and there he met Mary Louise Brewer, a member of the Brush Creek Church of God. They began to correspond, and eventually set a wedding date for June 7, 1933. According to the minutes of the Ripley, Illinois, Church of God, Clarence was preaching there when he married Louise. This was during the Great Depression. The Ripley congregation raised pledges to pay Clarence $35 per month. After he married, the church pledges decreased to $25 per month. Clarence reported the elders told him: "Two can live cheaper than one." Actually, an infestation of chinch bugs the summer of 1933 caused the pledges to drop. Members assisted the Lapps with meat, butter and garden produce.

After Ripley, Clarence and Louise went to college at Central Bible Institute in Springfield, Missouri. At

Central, Clarence and Louise learned a spirit of worship and service filled with enthusiasm. They were both devoted to serving the Lord, and it was common to see Clarence kneel at his pew in the front row and pray during the final song service. Clarence also took graduate studies at Arizona State University.

Louise related the story of returning to the ministry after being students to Daniel Smead:

> It was important to Clarence to live on faith; the principle of operating on faith was much stressed by Brother F.L. Austin. Austin was something of a surrogate father to Clarence, who had lost his own father at an early age.
>
> After Clarence and Louise left Central Bible Institute they went to St. Cloud, Minnesota, based on faith. Clarence had faith that if ten families in the church would tithe, this would give enough money to support the Lapps to minister there. One man in the church lost his job within a couple of months, and after a bit longer another family moved away.
>
> It was during this time that Clarence and Louise had their daughter, Elaine, in 1937. Things kept going downhill for the church and for the Lapps financially, and at Christmas the Lapps were again broke because the contributions of the church were insufficient. One of the men from the Thoms family walked to their house through the snow and gave them five dollars. Clarence said they should spend the money to have milk for their baby, Elaine, who needed it. Things weren't always that tough for them in St. Cloud, but it wasn't easy going.
>
> One year someone gave Louise enough green beans that she canned 85 quarts of them. All that winter the family's meals were green beans and bread. Their young daughter Elaine recalls asking at mealtime "Where's the beans?" – they were always there. Louise said that the couple made some friends in St. Cloud who were "as good as gold" to them – people like Tom and Madge Savage, and others as well. But these friends couldn't carry the whole load.
>
> Brother Austin commented on the situation, "Clarence's faith was good, but the people's wasn't so good." They remained for three years.

Clarence and Louise loved the pastoral ministry and went on to serve the Lord at Pennellwood Church of God in Grand Rapids; Church of God, Tempe, Arizona; Oregon, Illinois, Church of God; and Eden Valley Church of God in Minnesota.

Between Oregon and Eden Valley, Clarence and Louise taught at Oregon Bible College for 11 years during the Otto E. Dick, Sr. administration. Following Sydney Magaw's death in 1950, Oregon Bible College called Clarence to teach. He taught freshman- and sophomore-level courses of New Testament Survey, Christian Education Principles, Bible Geography and upper level Homiletics and Preaching. Louise taught Music Appreciation, Music Fundamentals, Conducting, Choir, Piano and Organ. She also planned spring choir trips to Churches of God across America for which the choir performed an Easter cantata. These programs were very popular with the students and the hosting congregations. Louise worked with student wives, and she composed hymns, some of which are included in the *Psalms, Hymns and Spiritual Songs* hymnbook.

Clarence in 1924

One of Clarence's strengths was his excellent preaching style. He captivated an audience when preaching the Word of God. He explained a difficult Bible passage in practical terms with easy-to-visualize illustrations. To illustrate how one must guard his salvation he often said "Many folks will miss eternity by 12-18 inches," that being the distance from the head to the heart. He was a good Bible student, a good speaker using humor appropriately. He was fond of giving object lessons to make his point. If a student asked Clarence a question, he would answer it with a question, and many times the student would answer his own question. He said Jesus used this method. Clarence was fond of talking about the shortest men in the Bible, "Knee-high-mi-ah," and Bildad, the "Shoe-hite," the latter being so short "he would have to jump up to catch the curb."

Clarence was a member of the Mission Board of the General Conference. In 1950, the board made it possible for him to travel to the Holy Land. The surprise of this unexpected opportunity is found here in Clarence's own words. He typed a post card to Harold and Betty Doan:

> Miracles do happen to those who believe, don't they? Plans are made for me to leave the 30th of March by plane for Paris, then on to Israel for about 10 days on a conducted tour, to be in Jerusalem on Easter Sunday, visit all the religious shrines and points of interest there, return to London for a couple of days and then back home April 16th, New York, I should say. Does that sound wonderful? Ten days ago that would have been an idle dream. Today, the $990 cost of the tour is all in and I just came home from the P.O. where I made application for my passport. The only extra expense will be my fare to New York City & return, money for film which I will take along, and incidentals on the trip. Do you wonder that I am woozy? Surely the Lord is good. Zechariah 4:6
> C.E.L.

Clarence loved music. He loved hymns, choruses, gospel songs, choir songs and good instrumentals. He played the trombone; Louise played the piano and organ. Following her parents' interests and her own, Elaine majored in piano performance at Bob Jones' University and Wheaton College.

One of Clarence's sermon outlines found in his notebooks in the Atlanta Bible College Archives is entitled "Rock Music." Every time he preached a sermon, the outline was included in this notebook and dated with the day of delivery. Clarence clearly didn't like rock music, because he said, "It was of the devil," and "it had

sensuous rhythms that took the mind and body to bawdry places." He said:
- It was rebellious and against Christ.
- Devil music becomes a religion. It is addictive.
- Give God your mind, body and spirit.
- If you want to get out there and live, live for Jesus.
- Stand for something or you will stand for nothing.
- Surrender to God, be plugged into Power.

And he quoted, "As long as he sought the Lord, God made him to prosper" (2 Chronicles 26:5).

Louise authored a small (2" x 3"), yellow, three-fold tract, "TRUTHS...the Child of God Should Know." It was so small it easily fit into a wallet. She had made a list of Bible truths for her Young Adults class at Brush Creek Church before her wedding. Her mother arranged to have it published without Louise's knowledge. It is still in print today. There were 12 truths with Scriptures, three to a page, set out in simple phrases such as "God is creator and He made man in His own image," and "The dead are unconscious and sleep." The last page had this simple admonition: "Study, Strive, Sing, Serve."

In 1955 Louise agreed to accept the Church of God Junior Quarterlies editorship. Verna Thayer edited these quarterlies the previous two decades. Verna used mimeographed material, but she wanted Louise to prepare copy and move it into a print format. Louise didn't feel she could handle the extra responsibilities until Jon turned nine, but when Verna retired, Louise accepted. From then until the 1980s the children's curriculum was printed as a regular quarterly. When Louise left the position, the General Conference outsourced the content.

In 1961, the Lapps and Jon planned a summer tour of Churches of God with the Gospelettes, a ladies' trio from Oregon Bible College. The tour visited Illinois, Missouri, Arkansas, Louisiana, Texas down to the southern tip at Harlingen, Arizona, New Mexico, the entire length of California from south to north, Oregon, Washington, Idaho, Utah, Wyoming, Colorado, Nebraska, Iowa and the full length of Illinois. In six weeks, six people covered 5200 miles in a comfortable, but non-air-conditioned, car. The Gospelettes were Martha Burnett (Mikl), Rachel Krogh (Carr) and Janet Turner (Stilson).

They visited more than 30 churches and homes one or two nights each, and spent a week at the Washington State Camp. While in Washington the group visited Charles Lapp and enjoyed fresh apricots and bing cherries from his orchard. They visited various spots of interest along the way: Mexico while in Texas, New Orleans, Carlsbad Caverns in New Mexico, Arizona's Petrified Forest and the Grand Canyon, California's Redwood Forest and Disneyland, swam in the Salt Lake of Utah, and witnessed a noon-hour organ recital at the Mormon Tabernacle in Salt Lake City. Because Louise and the Gospelettes were organists, they were privileged to sit

Clarence in his office at Oregon Bible College

in the Mormon Tabernacle Choir loft directly behind the pipe organ. What a treat it was when the organist played a toccata, his hands and feet flying across the manuals and pedals, and only those six people witnessed it due to their wonderful location in the choir loft.

Many fine Church of God members were blessed by the trio's music and Clarence's preaching. Some of those members throughout the denomination still serve the Lord. Many thanks to the Lapps for undertaking such a trip with three energetic young women who learned life lessons of service that summer.

Upon returning from the tour, Louise arranged a recording session through Rodeheaver in Winona Lake, Indiana, to press a vinyl album of Gospelette songs and distribute 500 33-1/3-rpm albums throughout the Church of God. This album has recently been converted to MP3 format and broadcast with other selections by Church of God musicians on the cogcast.org radio program sponsored by Joy Fellowship in South Carolina. Fifty years after the summer ministry tour coordinated by the Lapps, the Gospelettes' music plays again around the world via Internet radio.

After leaving Eden Valley in 1976, the Lapps retired to Troy, Ohio, where Clarence served as associate pastor at Troy View Church of God for five years until his health failed. At this writing, Louise is 101 and still serving the Lord. She relocated from Ohio to Minnesota and resides with Jon. Once again, she attends Eden Valley Church of God. Her vision is impaired, but well into her 90s she memorized the hymns at home and played them by memory for church on Sundays. She does her exercises every morning and enjoys a petite rocking chair given her by Verda Sitler, also a short woman.

Clarence died with his beloved wife at his side. Craig Wagganer, Rex Cain and David Krogh conducted services at Troy View Church of God November 23, 1994. Burial was at the Curtis Cemetery near Troy. Louise wanted him buried in the back row next to her brothers and their families. Jon considers this ironic since this is the only time Clarence was ever in the back row.

Daniel Smead contributed to this entry.

See Austin, F.L.
Brewer, Edna
Cain, Rex
Dick, Otto E., Sr.
Savage, Thomas Madison, II

Bibliography: Cline, Lois. Interview with Jan Stilson, July 15, 2009; Demmit, Greg, Comment on Cogmail. "Worthy is the Lamb." March 18, 2007; Lapp, Jon. e-mail to Jan Stilson, Summer 2006 and Summer 2009; Lapp, Clarence. Notebook of Sermons, "Rock Music" in his own handwriting, circa 1975; Lapp, C.E. Postcard to Harold and Betty Doan, no date, found in the files of Harold Doan in the Archives of Atlanta Bible College, McDonough, Ga.; Lapp, Louise (Brewer) Memories of Her Husband via e-mail with Joyce Demmitt, 2005; Lapp, Louise. "TRUTHS…the child of God should know." Restitution Herald Office, Oregon, Il., circa 1960; Lapp, Louise. Interview with Daniel Smead, March 4, 2011; Minute Book of Ripley Church of God 1888-1935; Poole. Elaine Lapp. Memories of Her Parents via e-mail, 2005; *The Restitution Herald*, April 22, 1913; May 18, 1920; Stilson, Jan (Turner) Memories of Gospelettes' Tour, 1961; Biography Project of Atlanta Bible College, David Krogh, compiler; Fredericktown Dedication report, *The Restitution Herald*, Sydney Magaw, ed., Oregon, Il., Oct. 21, 1947.

Lawrence, Stanley
b. December 1927
d. August 4, 2009

Pastor Stanley Lawrence died at his home in Washington, where he had moved following his retirement from the North Salem Church of God, Plymouth, Indiana, in 2006. Stan attended Oregon Bible College from 1950 to 1955 and received a Bachelor of Theology. He served the Cool Spring Church of God at Browntown, Virginia;

Hilda and Stan Lawrence

Churches of God at Litchfield, Minnesota; Waterloo, Iowa (two terms of service); and North Salem in Plymouth, Indiana. While living in Iowa, he served as Iowa Conference president for many years. Just before retiring from the ministry, Stan donated many books from his personal library to the libraries of Atlanta Bible College and Rock River Christian College. He was married to Hilda and they had one son, Bernie, and two granddaughters.

Bibliography: ABC Alumni Newsletter, August, 2009.

LeCrone, John Richard
b. August 25, 1909
d. April 1, 1992

LeCrone, Olive Jane
b. November 21, 1910
d. December 25, 1992

Richard "J.R." LeCrone was born to Claar and Belle LeCrone near Omaha, Nebraska, the middle child of three with an older sister, Lucille (Boyer), and younger brother, Leslie. They attended church in Blair where Richard developed a friendship with Harvey U. Krogh Jr. When Richard was in sixth grade, his family moved to Omaha where he completed school, graduating from Omaha Tech, a vocational school.

In 1928, Richard, Lucille and Harvey traveled to Oregon, Illinois, by car to attend Bible Training Class to prepare for the ministry. Other members of that early class were Clarence Lapp, Jerry Cooper, John Denchfield and Cecil Smead. J.R. LeCrone related in an interview for *The History Newsletter* that F.L. Austin, the instructor, influenced him immensely.

Following completion of his studies, J.R. took the pastorate at Lester Prairie, Minnesota. Then, remembering a beautiful young woman he had met at Omaha Tech, he returned to Nebraska to marry Olive Jane before moving on to his second pastorate at Eden Valley, Minnesota. He and Jane wed on January 5, 1935. They had three children, Faith, Martha and Arlan, who married and had families. The LeCrones had ten grandchildren and four great-grandchildren. One of Arlan's sons was an Illinois State Trooper, and then became a Secret Service agent for President George W. Bush.

J.R. and Jane served churches at Maurertown and Fort Valley, Virginia, until 1947; Oregon Church of God until 1952; Hillisburg, Indiana, Church of God from 1953 to 1967; Golden Rule Church of God in Cleveland 1968 to 1973; and East Peoria, Illinois, from 1979 until they retired to Milledgeville, Illinois.

While in Virginia, Richard initiated a Bible study in Winchester. This group met the first Friday of each month and included Austin and Cecil Railton Sr.; George Thayer; and Sr. Alice Updike. J.R. performed a great service to the church by documenting Church of God history in Virginia using resources salvaged from a fire by older members. Without Richard's writings, the region's history would be very scant.

Following the ministry in Cleveland, General Conference Board of Directors called Richard to Oregon,

JR and Jane with granddaughter

Illinois, in June 1974, to become editor of *The Restitution Herald and Progress Journal.* He served in this capacity until September 1979.

Throughout his ministry, Richard's guiding philosophy was "the pastor is for the church, and not the church for the pastor." The highlights of his ministry are found in the faces of those he baptized. Richard said once that being in the ministry was not always joyful. There were times when his family got by on $1, $2 or $3 per week. Once he drew up a pie chart of the family budget and presented it to the congregation. He said, "If you can find any way that we can cut back, let us know." It eventually became necessary to leave that congregation, but a few understood the problem, and when the new pastor came, they gave him a higher salary.

Richard LeCrone was active in projects that coincided with General Conference or state conference business. He was guest speaker for numerous conferences or special meetings, served on the Board of Directors and on the Ministerial Board of License and Ordination.

While staying abreast of numerous meetings, classes, choir practices and church responsibilities, he found time for his family, and a hobby carving miniature wooden animals that he gave to his friends.

Older church members recall J.R. LeCrone was often behind the camera at minister's conferences and youth camps, supplying photos now found in albums throughout the world. Recently, the accompanying photo surfaced and was published in the online *History Newsletter,* Kent Ross, editor. The questions posed with it: "Can you identify these people?" It happened to be a photo of the Illinois State Conference in 1957 attended by many members of the Oregon congregation and students of Oregon Bible College. Jane LeCrone was there, and Mary Krogh. Where were Richard and Harvey? The conclusion: The two shutterbugs took the photo.

In their retirement years, Richard and Jane lived in Milledgeville, Illinois, near their daughter, Faith. Richard predeceased Jane. When Jane became ill, she resided in a nursing home. She died in the Lord.

See Boyer, Lucille
Cooper, Jerry
Denchfield, John
Krogh, Harvey U., Jr.
Krogh, Mary A.
Lapp, C.E.
Railton, Albert Austin
Ross, Kent
Smead, Cecil

Bibliography: Ancestry.com. U.S. Census. Nebraska. Douglas. Omaha. Dist. 127. 1930; Social Securtiy Master Death Index.; "Summary of Historical Records from Golden Rule Church of God of Cleveland, Ohio," by Dorothy Robertson, 1976, and Martha Hobbs, 1998; Interview of Jane and J.R. by Jan Stilson, 1985 for use in the *History Newsletter;* "John Richard LeCrone," ABC Biography Project, David Krogh, compiler; *The Restitution Herald*, Sydney Magaw, ed., Oregon, Il., Oct. 28, 1947; LeCrone, J.R. "Get Into the Game," *The Restitution Herald*, 75th anniversary issue, Russell Magaw, ed., Oregon, Il., Oct. 1985.

Lewis, John Richard
b. April 18, 1936
d. April 19, 1979

Lewis, Ruth (Savage)
b. September 6, 1939
d. April 19, 1979

John Richard Lewis was born in Brown County, Illinois. His parents were Ripley Church of God members. His mother died when he was 11. John and his brother lived with various relatives. When John was in high school, his father died. John went then to live with his grandfather in Hillsdale. Another relative took his brother, separating them. His brother Lyle acted as John's guardian. John was a member of the Ripley Church of God, baptized in 1950. In 1954, he moved to Oregon, Illinois, to attend Oregon Bible College. He received a Bachelor of Theology in 1958.

September 1960 Sunday School Rally at Flagg Center Church of God. JR LeCrone, photographer.

John met Ruth Savage of St. Cloud, Minnesota, at Oregon Bible College. Within a few months they realized they wanted to commit to each other and married in November 1956. They had two children: Kathy and John Wesley.

Ruth was the daughter of Tom and Madge Savage. Tom was the pastor at the St. Cloud Church of God. Ruth's sister Sarah was also a student at Oregon Bible College. They had two brothers, Tom and Bill. Sarah married Robert See; they entered the ministry together and continue to serve the Lord in Indiana.

After graduation, John and Ruth moved to Ohio to serve the Troy View Church of God. While there, John continued his education and received a bachelor's degree from Miami University in Oxford, Ohio. He began to teach.

John and Ruth Lewis visited the Bangalore mission field, which includes this church and clinic.

John served as pastor at Eldorado, Illinois, Church of God congregations and attended classes at Southern Illinois University. In 1968, Oregon Bible College called him to teach. When Dr. Alva Huffer became college president, John was promoted to Vice President of Operations in 1969. He continued to teach preaching and ministry courses. John completed a Master of Arts degree at Northern Illinois University in 1972 with the assistance of the Lawrence Scholarship He was named Oregon Bible College President in 1975.

John and Ruth were active in lay ministry at the Oregon Church of God, teaching, serving on the board and singing in the choir. For a while, they served as youth leaders. They were gracious hosts, and many fine college and church gatherings were held at their rambling two-story home on South 8th Street in Oregon.

In 1972 John traveled throughout Europe, Turkey and Egypt. He also served on a short-term mission trip to India for eight weeks in 1977. John and Ruth participated in an India mission trip with Dr. Bill and Mardy Lawrence the summer of 1978.

On the evening of April 19, 1979, John and Ruth and Wes were involved in an auto accident that inflicted minor injuries. Wes was returned to Oregon while his parents were taken to a hospital. Russell Rye met them at the hospital, and on the return trip, the three of them died in a second auto accident.. The same evening Dave Segar of the Oregon Church of God also died in an auto accident. The Church of God national membership fell into deep grief just as it had when Sydney and Margaret Magaw died unexpectedly in 1950.

Church of God members and the people of Oregon were shocked. Oregon Bible College immediately reorganized. To fill the gap of John's loss as president, Eugene Stilson, Academic Dean of Oregon Bible College, was named Interim President throughout the summer of 1979. Stilson brought order out of chaos until people could put their grief aside and begin to function as professionals again. Following Stilson, the General Conference Executive Committee assumed control and searched for a full-time president. Dr. Charles Pryor was named President and David Krogh Executive Secretary of the General Conference. Stilson returned to full time teaching and academic administration at the college until 1988 when he left to pursue other interests.

The funeral services of all were conducted from the Oregon Church of God at the stone church on North Third Street. Hollis Partlowe officiated. Pastor Partlowe said in a 2010 interview for the online magazine *eHerald* that doing those funerals for three members was the most difficult challenge of his ministry. John and Ruth were interred at the Daysville Cemetery. As a tribute to her parents, Kathy Lewis (Kugler) proceeded with wedding plans the summer of 1979 and took Wes into her new home. Wes is now grown and married with several children.

See Huffer, Dr. Alva
    Savage, Thomas Madison, II
    Stilson, Eugene

Bibliography: Welch, Lana Gaddis. "John R. Lewis" *History Newsletter*, Jan Stilson, ed., Church of God General Conference. Oregon, Il., Spring 1988; Memories of John and Ruth, by Jan and Gene Stilson; See, Sara. Interview with Jan Stilson, July 8, 2009.

Long, Clyde
b. March 1890
d. Unknown

Clyde was born to Jacob and Ana Long near Holbrook, Nebraska. Jacob was born in Tennessee, but moved west where he met Ana. Their marriage was blessed with many children. Two of them, Clyde and Inez, were well known to the Church of God membership across America. Clyde served as pastor of the Holbrook congregation, and elsewhere across Nebraska, most of his adult life. Inez married Grover Gordon who also served in the Church of God ministry. Inez and Grover never had children, and personal family information about Clyde is scant.

See Gordon, Grover

Bibliography: Ancestry.com U.S. Census. Nebraska. Richardson. Muddy. 1900. Magaw, Joyce. Interview with JStilson, August, 2008.

Long, Vaughn
b. November 24, 1896
d. June 1, 1981

Elder Vaughn Long was one of the leading supporters and workers in the Church of God in Indiana. He was baptized into Christ on April 15, 1918. A farmer at Hartford, Indiana, he assisted many in putting on Christ. In his youth, he spent a few years in Cleveland working as a printer for *The Restitution*. He was also an effective preacher who traveled a circuit across the South.

Vaughn was drafted during WWI and served as a conscientious objector. After the war, he returned to Roll, Indiana, and served as co-pastor of the church with Cantwell Drabenstott. He visited Perryville, Kentucky, several times and preached at the church. In 1920, he preached at Arkansas City, Kansas, where he baptized Mrs. Essie Paulson in the Walnut River.

While Vaughn attended the Roll, Indiana, Church of God, the work at Kokomo began. Vaughn volunteered to help with the preaching there and alternated preaching Sundays with Cantwell Drabenstott, also of the Roll church. The group met in the O. J. Parker home at first, and later in a storefront.

In the "History of the Indiana Conference," Evelyn Austin wrote: "At the end of the first year we had outgrown our seating capacity, and Sr. Parker bought a five-room house, and offered it to the group, rent free." The study group organized as a church and established a Sunday school with 78 members. The Kokomo church began during the Great Depression, but with God's help grew and prospered.

Vaughn met Elsie Bradley at Perryville, and they married on November 28, 1935. They had no children, but they considered the members of the church their children. Vaughn pastored at Perryville for 45 years. He was a dedicated Bible prophecy student and spent many years studying Revelation and history. From this research, he wrote a verse-by-verse study guide of Revelation. If this work was ever published as a book is unkown. A copy of it exists in the notebook collection of the Atlanta Bible College Archives.

See Austin, Evelyn Harsh
    Drabenstott, Cantwell

Bibliography: Ancestry.com. U.S. Census. Kentucky. Letcher. Jenkins. Dist. 4. 1930; Austin, Evelyn. "A Brief Sketch of Indiana Church History." Written around 1930; *The Restitution Herald*, G.E. Marsh, editor, Oregon, IL. Oct. 7, 1930; *The Restitution Herald,* Sydney Magaw, editor, Oregon, Il. May 25, 1948; Yokum, Keith. E-mail with birth and death dates, August 16, 2010; Long, Vaughn, "Studies in the Book of Revelation." Perryville, Kentucky, no date.

Lyon, Melville Woodbury
b. December 23, 1899
d. June 4, 1956

Melville Lyon was born in Chicago, Illinois, to Judd Stuart Lyon and Loulou "Lon" May Turney Lyon. Possibly Melville Lyon was a descendant of Ralph Vinton Lyon, an early Age-to-Come evangelist in Canada West territory west of Buffalo, New York, but this has not been documented. Ralph V. Lyon was contemporary with Joseph Marsh and helped establish the work in Canada. Melville's parents moved to Hammond, Louisiana, and then to Citronella, Alabama, outside of Mobile. Judd Lyon ran a poultry farm with 10,000 laying hens. He also had fruit and pecan orchards.

Melville attended annual Church of God conferences as a youth. He moved to Oregon, Illinois, in 1920 to assist with publishing *The Restitution Herald*. While there he learned of the summer-school program. He enrolled in Bible Training Class in 1925. These summer schools were held annually for men and women and lasted six weeks. They were designed to attract youth and train them for service in local churches and for the ministry. As the young adults met others their own age, who also believed the precious truths, many weddings came about. Students were housed in separate dormitory quarters behind the Oregon Church of God with chaperones always present.

In this manner, the Church of God continued to thrive through marriage and biological growth during the early 20th century.

A pastoral training class began in autumn 1923 and lasted until spring. Essentially, this preceded the Church of God college movement. Some of Melville's Oregon classmates included: C. E. Lapp; Harvey Krogh Jr.; and Cecil Smead. These class sessions emphasized Bible and doctrine, pastoral studies and leadership through service. Lyon's leadership style developed through preaching assignments in Casey and Ripley, Illinois, the Missouri Conference and elsewhere. He often accompanied Frank E. Siple on these trips; Siple served as mentor providing guidance and encouragement to young ministerial students. Siple eventually became Melville's brother-in-law after Frank's second marriage to Dorothy Lyon.

Melville was a popular preacher, tall, slender and of gracious disposition. His sweet manner attracted people to him and they appreciated his preaching style. Melville began preaching at Brush Creek, Ohio, in 1925, taking an every-other-week rotation so he could preach somewhere else as well. He had a beautiful voice and often sang solos and ensembles. He also wrote articles for *The Restitution Herald* and authored tracts on Bible importance. Melville wrote the lyrics for "Shepherd of Israel" for the *Songs of Truth*. He used the melody and harmony composed by Lottie Logan Pickerl of Hope Chapel in South Bend, Indiana. The hymn is drawn from Psalms 95:6, 7 "For he is our God, and we are the people of his pasture, and the sheep of his hand." Hymn verses 1 and 4:

> "Shepherd of Israel we bow before Thee
> Bringing our thanks for this bountiful land;
> Thou art our God and to Thee give we praise,
> We are Thy people and the sheep of Thy hand."

> "Shepherd of Israel as we adore Thee;
> Help us to give Thee first place in our land;
> And now again with thanksgiving we pray,
> Keep us Thy people and the sheep of Thy hand."

After he left the Bible Training Class, Melville became the pastor of Golden Rule Church of God in Cleveland for 17 years until 1943. He left that pastorate after he agreed to become a traveling national evangelist for the General Conference. As national evangelist, Melville traveled from one end of the nation to the other, putting him in very nearly every Church of God and small Bible study group that existed at the time. He strengthened those he found by teaching and preaching a series of meetings. He reinvigorated sagging churches and, in a couple of cases, restarted stopped works. In 1948, he began a new program at Dallas/Fort Worth and left a small Bible study group in the hands of Emory Macy, the Texas evangelist.

During 1948, Melville made the entire circuit of churches again, advancing the cause of college and conference development through the Layman Campaign.

Left: Melville with his parents, Lou and Judd Lyon. Below: Melville, back row far left, with members from Cleveland at General Conference in Oregon, Illinois, August 1941.

Sixty-five laymen and ministers in Chicago spearheaded this grassroots campaign in October 1947 to counteract stinging criticism leveled at the ministers by the conference's general manager, James Watkins.

The Volunteer Layman Committee meeting devised a plan to enlist local church members' support for development through a modest donation of 50¢ a week. Melville Lyon's task was to sign up every Church of God member equal to about 3500 memberships. The plan successfully enlisted about 800 members, but failed in that only 800 members were enrolled. Some goals were met, but not all could be. Monies were used for operating expenses instead of development.

None of the problems in the program could be laid at Melville Lyon's feet. He traveled 25,000 miles by rail and auto to meet hundreds and thousands of people and he made many friends. He was not a man who made enemies, and he was probably the best ambassador the General Conference could have sent on such a mission.

While working in Nebraska during 1947-1948, he stayed a month and restarted the Palmer work; it had a nucleus of 17 people and a vacant church. When Melville left, the Palmer church was functioning with a calendar of meetings. He had a personable ability to influence people for Christ and get them to work together.

In 1948, Melville revived the work at Cleveland, Arkansas. This earlier work was going dormant. They'd had no preaching services for a long time. After Melville worked with them for a few weeks, there were eight members and several others in attendance on his last day of preaching, May 24, 1948. In 1948, he also traveled to churches in Virginia. He took his mother with him. On the way, they stopped to preach at Cleveland. Possibly during this visit the sparks flew between Melville and beautiful widow "Fairy" Smith.

During his travels in various states and churches, Melville filmed movies. These movies show congregations in and about their churches, local families and pastors and their wives or families. The reels are preserved in the Atlanta Bible College Archives, but would be better served if transferred to DVD and broadcast on eHerald.com or cogcast.org.

Melville married Elizabeth Fairy Crellin Smith on April 30, 1949, in Cleveland. Pastor G.E. Marsh, who replaced Melville in that pastorate, performed the ceremony. Melville and Fairy began the pastorate in the Omaha Church of God in 1950 and remained in that ministry about four years. From there, they went to Fonthill, Ontario, Canada, and pastored there. They were living in Fonthill when Melville died suddenly in 1956.

While Melville did not publish any books, he did write several tracts, including "We Have a Message." He also wrote the words and two hymns and one chorus in the *Psalms, Hymns and Spiritual Songs* hymnbook, including "Shepherd of Israel," "Heavenly Father, Hear Us" and "The Sunday School Chorus" ("Let's everybody go to Sunday School, laughing and singing all the way"). He collaborated with Lottie Pickerl of South Bend, Indiana, on the words and music. He also wrote poems.

Recently, retired pastor Jim Mattison, missionary to Africa, translated one of Melville's tracts for the native pastors in Africa. Pastor Jim wrote:

> Melville Lyon's "10 Lessons" have been printed and distributed, plus my "Subject Concordance" (all in Chichewa). We are happy with the way the Lord has blessed the preaching of His Word in Africa.

Melville's work lives on today.

The new Hammond organ at Oregon Bible College was dedicated to Melville Lyon's memory and ministry on January 22, 1959. Mrs. Louise Lapp gave a concert at its dedication. When the college sold the 3rd Street building and centralized its campus during the 1980s, the Hammond was donated to the East Peoria Church of God for its chapel. A few years later East Peoria donated it to the newly-planted Family Bible Fellowship on North Ridge Street in Rockford, Illinois. Just recently, 60 years after its first use, the Lyon Hammond was discarded at Family Bible in favor of a newer model.

Melville died while a young man by modern standards, and members throughout the Church of God mourned his death and the suddenness of it. He rests in Hillcrest Memorial Park at Cleveland, Ohio. His widow, Fairy, married Joseph Krejacar on October 14, 1979. She died on September 14, 1982. She had two daughters, Irene and Doris, from her first husband, Hanford Smith. Much of the information for this article came from Doris Smith Schuld, Fairy's daughter, a member of the Church of God at Bedford, Ohio.

> *See* Lapp, Clarence and Mary Louise
> Lyon, Ralph Vinton (19th)
> Pickerl, Lottie Logan
> Siple, Frank E.
> Watkins, James

Bibliography: Graham, David. "Church of God Connexion & Review," *Wisdom and Power* 6:8 November 1992; Lyon, Melville and Pickerl, Lottie Logan, "Shepherd of Israel," *Songs of Truth*, National Bible Institute. Oregon, Il., 1948; Lyon, M.W., Report from Nebraska, *The Restitution Herald*, Sydney Magaw, ed., Oregon, Il., June 1, 1948 and Cleveland, Arkansas, June 22, 1948 and Virginia travels, Aug. 7, 1948; Mattison, James. African Missions (MAM) Update, November 25, 2005; Ordnung, Elizabeth, Notes from her Diary about the new Hammond organ at OBC, Jan. 22, 1959; *Psalms, Hymns and Spiritual Songs*, Church of God General Conference, Oregon, Il., 1980. pps. 32, 558, 584; *The Restitution Herald*, Sept. 1925; March 30, 1926; Oct. 7, 1947 and various issues in 1948; Schuld, Doris. E-mail letter to Author, March 21, 2006.

1942 Ministers, left to right:
Front row - Frank Siple, Clyde Randall, FL Austin, Sydney Magaw, Melville Lyon, VE Kirkpatrick. Second row - Harry Goekler, Alan McLain, unknown, Ellen Van Vleet (Ramsey), Iris Hall (Burnett), Pat Andrew (Simpson)-?, Daniel Judy-?, Emory Macy. Third row - Robert Hardesty, JR LeCrone, Francis Burnett, Vernis Wolfe, James Watkins, James McLain. Fourth row - Terry Ferrell, unknown, CE Lapp, Walter Wiggins, Ellsworth Routson, Celaine Randall, Lyle Rankin, Linford Moore.
(Notice Clyde Randall's spats.)

M

Macy, Emory
b. October 15, 1911
d. November 17, 2007

Kent Ross, Emory's son-in-law, shared the following:

"Emory grew up in Ohio, married Mildred Puterbaugh, and set to farming, like lots of his friends around him. Emory and Mildred were active in the Brush Creek Church of God, where Louise Lapp first got him to teach a class of boys in Sunday school.

"His pastor, Sydney Magaw, encouraged him to consider ministry and cajoled him into preaching his first sermon at Brush Creek. After losing an infant son, Wendell Lee, and considering their future, he and Mildred made sale, took baby Joyce and moved to Oregon, Illinois, in 1941 to study for ministry.

"Emory worked hard, not having much formal education, and he farmed Oregon Bible College land to support his family, but in 1945 he matriculated and moved to his first church in Kokomo, Indiana. Here their second daughter, Cheryl, was born.

"He next moved to Texas where he functioned first as Texas State Evangelist, and then pastor of the Gatesville Church of God. They lived in Ater, Texas, in a small four-room teacherage, later building their own home and moving to Gatesville. It was here Emory Lee Jr. was born. During the ten years Emory and Mildred lived in Texas, he baptized 42 members by his own account."

Emory took an interest in the Texas work's history, and much of the information found for James Lord, A.J. Addington, A.S. Bradley and W.L. Gibbs is included in Emory's "Church History of the Texas Church of God" written in March 1954. Emory also collected single issues of the *Word and Work* (1904-1907) edited by Gibbs, collated them chronologically and had them bound. These volumes are part of the Atlanta Bible College Archives.

As evangelist, Emory first had to confront a doctrinal error that had crept into the Texas work. Emory summed up his philosophy of Bible study in a short autobiography. That summary is paraphrased here. Emory said he searched for truth and listened to every interpretation of the Scriptures. "I never approach a subject without first making a word by word study," he wrote. He was interested in prophecy. He said, "Prophecy (fulfillment) may be coming to pass in our day, judging from the present conflict in the Middle East."

James Mattison wrote that Church of God universalists came down to the Texas Conference and converted the president sometime in the 1930s. The specific teaching of the universalists was mentioned in *The Gospel Messenger*, July 1941, quoted here:

> [T]hat God will cast the devil, "the fearful, and unbelieving, and the abominable, and murderers, and whoremongers, and sorcerers, and idolaters, and all liars…in the lake which burneth with fire and brimstone; which is the second death," (Rev. 21:8), and burn them awhile to get the carnality out of them and then God will take them out of the lake of fire and give the devil and all the wicked eternal life.

The Arkansas-Oklahoma Conference attempted to halt the influence of universalism among its churches. In August 1939, *The Gospel Messenger* published a resolution from the delegates:

> Whereas the Conference of the Church of God of Arkansas and Oklahoma was organized for the purpose of enabling our brotherhood to do a greater work by upholding and defending the faith and the doctrines of the Church of God, and Whereas, there has been taught among us the doctrine of universalism and universal reconciliation, and Whereas, the teaching of this doctrine is contrary to the Church of God and her interests, therefore, Resolved, That the conference of the Church of God of Arkansas and Oklahoma go on record as being opposed to the teaching of such doctrine, and therefore, refuse to endorse those who teach the same.

With the Arkansas/Oklahoma conference off limits, universalists such as E.O. Stewart and J.W. Williams went south into Texas. Mattison said universalism ruined the work. By the time Emory Macy arrived in Gatesville in 1950, he nearly had to start over.

The universalism problem plagued the Texas churches and the people for a couple of decades. Richard B. Taylor noted in his "Notes on Texas History" that some of the people became unhappy with Emory's approach to the problem. Taylor noted "he sat on the fence." Circumstances of Emory's approach are not available, but it is known he preached the sure Word of the Lord.

Word must have arrived at General Conference headquarters in Oregon, Illinois, that Emory was receiving some bad criticism. Sydney Magaw wrote from the National Bible Institute that the Board of Directors wanted Emory to know they encouraged him in the work and appreciated his efforts. Magaw wrote:

> Usually the best procedure is simply to continue preaching the Word, portraying Christ, loving the brethren, and not to attempt any retaliation. In due time, people learn to know and respect you for who you are, and not for what someone has said about you.

Information from the Macy history file indicates that Elder T.A. Drinkard, editor of *The Gospel Messenger*, led the opposition against Macy. Drinkard accused Macy of preaching Russellism and universalism. Both charges were not true. The president of the Texas Conference, R.F. Robbins, diplomatically went to Editor Drinkard, supporting Macy with a resolution endorsed by the Texas Conference board, and in talking with him, Drinkard relented and stated he would support the Conference work with Macy as evangelist. The resolution was never printed because when Drinkard changed his attitude, it was not necessary. The account of the interview with Pastor Drinkard is from a letter by Macy to Sydney Magaw in response to Magaw's letter.

While in Texas, Emory participated in a writing project with James Mattison, Harry Goekler and Gordon G. Landry. In 1954, this committee of Louisiana and Texas ministers compiled a subject concordance of the Bible on behalf of the Southern Berean Society of the Church of God. The concordance was small, simple to use and designed to help youth begin earnest Bible study. The booklet was called *Words of Truth as Revealed in Holy Scripture*. The subtitle was a bit longer: *A Subject Concordance concerning God, Man, Man's Savior, His Coming Kingdom, The Immortality For His People and The Destruction of the Wicked*. The concordance is also in the Archives.

This turbulent time in Texas during the Macy years indicates the kind of problems that ministers can encounter in the field. Christians are not perfect, and sometimes offenses take great toll upon the membership and the ministers.

> Kent Ross wrote in Emory's eulogy:
> After Emory did what he could to stabilize the Texas work, he and his family moved to Litchfield, Minnesota. He was pastor at the Litchfield and the Minneapolis Churches of God. While living in Minnesota, he enjoyed being among family, his sister, June and Ellsworth Routson and their family, and Bernie & Delbert Jones and their family. Karla was born in Litchfield when Mildred was nearly fifty years old. That was quite a medical marvel in those days.
>
> From there the family went to Fonthill, Ontario, to the Glad Tidings Church. Daughter, Cheryl, remained behind at Oregon Bible College while their family moved into the parsonage at 8 Church Street, and they learned to love the people in Canada. From there he went to Omaha, then to North Salem, Indiana, and finally to the Weiser, Idaho Advent Christian church. He served there for twenty-five years, ending only when his failing health at almost 94 did not allow him to continue his ministry. Another Church of God pastor served at Weiser before Emory arrived. His name was Fred O. Sapp.
>
> For over 64 years he was faithful to God's call to him. He preached in larger churches and smaller churches; he and Mildred raised a wonderful family; and he was faithful to his call to preach the Gospel of the Kingdom. A family really cannot ask for anything more.
>
> We'll get together in the Kingdom of God and he may tell me more stories about his farming and his preaching and his family.

Kent Ross contributed to this entry.

See Drinkard, T.A.
 Goekler, Harry
 Gibbs, W.L. (19th)
 Landry, Gordon
 Magaw, Sydney
 Ross, Kent
 Sapp, Frederick O.
 Stewart, E.O.
 Taylor, Richard B (19th)
 Williams, J.W.

Bibliography: Arrington, W.H. "Will All Men be Saved?" *The Gospel Messenger*, T.A. Drinkard, ed., Russellville, Ar., July 1941; Macy, Emory. "Church History of the Texas Church of God," March 1954; Macy, Emory, Follow-up letter to Sydney Magaw, March, 1948; "Minutes of Annual Conference," Drinkard, T.A., ed., *The Gospel Messenger*, Russellville, Ar., Aug., 1939; Magaw, Sydney, Letter to Emory Macy, March 11, 1948, housed with Texas materials in the Archives of Atlanta Bible College; Mattison, James, Letter to *History Newsletter*, JStilson, ed., 1992; J. Mattison. E-mail to Jstilson. Spring 2006; Taylor, Richard B. Notes on Texas History, filed in the Archives of Atlanta Bible College with material for the Texas Conference; Macy, Mattison et al. *Words of Truth, a Subject Concordance*, Southern Berean Society. Gatesville, Tx. 1954.

Macy, Jesse
b. August 8, 1888
d. 1977

Macy, Etta Mae Wood
b. August 27, 1892
d. 1978

Jesse Macy was born to Thomas Jefferson and Rebecca Jane Knife Macy in Miami County, Ohio. Rebecca was born in Miami County in 1851 to Jonathan Jr. and Elizabeth Smith Knife. Jesse's maternal grandfather moved from Pennsylvania to Miami County in 1813 and bought a quarter section of land. His paternal grandfather,

Thomas Jefferson Macy, arrived in Massachusetts from England in 1630. By 1800, the Macy family came to Miami County through North Carolina.

Etta's mother, Mattie Alice Hines, was born in Pulaski County, Kentucky, in 1872 to Ephraim and America Young Hines. Etta's father, Thomas Wood, was born to Elias and Alice McDermont Wood. Thomas Wood was from Ireland and Alice's family was from North Carolina.

Jesse and Etta married in 1911, and they had nine children: Emory Lee who married Mildred Esther Puterbaugh; Laurel Thomas who married Ketha Maxine Vore and, later, Margaret Harmon; Olevia June who married Ellsworth Routson, a long-time pastor in the Church of God; Bernedene Peace who married Delbert A. Jones, a Church of God minister; Lorna Faith who married Leslie Paul Pearson; Bette Mae who married Henry Frederick Schwier; Mary Ellen, who married Charles George Jones, faithful workers in the local church and in the General Conference; Juanita who married Melvin Smitley; and Alice Carol who married William Schmidlapp.

Jesse was a farmer all of his life, mostly in Miami County. He had a special interest in Red Poll cattle and showed them at county fairs. Etta was a busy homemaker. Besides baking bread, canning, cooking, washing, cleaning and sewing, she liked to write poetry. She wrote hundreds of letters to her children who lived throughout the United States.

Jesse and Etta were married for 66 years. Emory Macy baptized Jesse on November 27, 1967. Sydney Magaw baptized Etta in 1937. All their children were baptized and married by Church of God ministers, and all are still active in church work. Isn't that a fitting memorial to the lives of these dedicated parents?

His mother, a member of the Brush Creek (Ohio) Church of God, influenced Jesse towards the Lord. Many of the Macy children and grandchildren have been Summer Bible Training School and Oregon Bible College (OBC) students. Those attending or graduating include Cheryl Macy (Ross), daughter of Emory and Mildred. Cheryl married Kent Ross who has been a pastor in the Church of God and taught at Oregon Bible College and Atlanta Bible College more than 20 years. Their son Seth is pastor at North Hills Church of God in Springfield, Ohio. Cheryl's younger sister Karla attended OBC also.

Ron Macy, son of Laurel and Ketha, graduated OBC and has been a minister in the Church of God. He has also served as an Advent Christian minister in Sycamore, Illinois. His sister Wanda married David Cheatwood who also graduated from OBC. They have been in the Church of God ministry together since 1963. At least three Cheatwood sons, Jon, Mark and Dennis, attended OBC; Jon serves as youth coordinator for the Church of God General Conference in McDonough, Georgia.

June married Ellsworth, an OBC graduate; their children Harold and Etta Marie also attended OBC. Etta Marie's daughter, Jennifer Siderius, serves the Lord as a librarian and attends Fair Oaks Church of God in Virginia. Ellsworth and Harold are deceased.

Bernedene married Delbert Jones, another OBC graduate, and they enjoyed a lengthy ministry in the Church of God. Their children Philip and Linda attended OBC.

Lorna and Paul's daughter Denise attended OBC and married Michael Berry, an OBC graduate and a Church of God minister. Their daughter Rita Pearson (Gillette) attended OBC and has been a steady worker for the Lord in the Blessed Hope Church of God in Rockford, Illinois.

Mary Ellen and Charles' son, Robert, graduated from OBC and from Wheaton College. He has been a minister in the Church of God and professor of Old Testament studies at Oregon Bible College and Rock River Christian College, and he is presently teaching at Atlanta Bible College. He is a Hebrew scholar. Bob's sister Kathy attended OBC as well. Carol and Bill's daughters Alane and Debbie attended OBC.

In the entire 20th century there may not be any other family who has influenced the Church of God to the same extent as the Macys. Their testimony goes forth through their grandchildren and great-grandchildren. God bless faithful families who raise their children to serve the Lord. Jesse and Etta rest in peace waiting to see the Lord at his return.

   See Jones, Delbert
          Macy, Emory
          Ross, Kent
          Routson, Ellsworth
Bibliography: ABC Biography Project, David Krogh compiler.

Macy, Mildred "Mid" Esther
b. January 9, 1913
d. July 13, 1993

Mildred Macy was born in Miami County, Ohio, to Ella Pearson and Bertis Puterbaugh. Mid married Emory Macy; they had four children, Joyce Nordstrom, Cheryl Ross, E.L. Macy and Karla Bigger. Mildred was a wonderful farmer's wife. After farming for several years Emory decided to attend Oregon Bible College. Following his graduation they pastored churches in Indiana, Texas, Minnesota, Ontario (Fonthill), Nebraska and Idaho. Mildred was beside him all the way.

In Texas she began a radio ministry through the weekly production of children's evangelistic programs, called "Aunt Mid's Bible Stories" and "Bible Quiz Kids." She also authored two books: *In the Beginning God...* and *Israel Is Mine, Sayeth the Lord.*

Her life touched thousands of people, and when some of them ended up in her home for special meetings, she was a delightful hostess, often making home-baked cinnamon rolls and other goodies for breakfast. She was always willing to go the extra mile. Her example of Christ-like living could even be heard by her caring, loving voice as it traveled across the radio airwaves.

Mid's death caused a serious gap in her family. Many friends throughout the Church of God dearly missed her. She was laid to rest in the Curtis Cemetery near Brush Creek Church. Emory joined her there in 2007.

See Macy, Emory

Bibliography: "Mildred Esther Macy" ABC Biography Project, David Krogh, compiler.

Magaw, Russell
b. February 28, 1939

Magaw, Joyce (Wilson)
b. April 8, 1939

Russell Magaw was born at home to Vivian and Ruth Magaw in Tipp City, Ohio. He attended Tipp City schools, graduating in 1957. Russ felt the call to serve the Lord through his attendance at International Berean Youth Conferences (IBYC), 1955-1957, and accepted Christ at the invitation of Clarence E. Lapp at the 1957 IBYC decision night. He was immersed at his home church, and entered Oregon Bible College (OBC) soon after. Russ is the nephew of noted Church of God editor Sydney Magaw.

Joyce is the daughter of Wayne and Ruth (Johnson) from McCook, Nebraska. Joyce learned about the Gospel of the Kingdom from the ministers who served the Nebraska churches and by attending Nebraska Conference. Some who challenged her to stronger spiritual life were Clyde E. Randall, James Mattison and Vivian Kirkpatrick. Joyce attended OBC to gain a better understanding of the Bible. Russ and Joyce were members of the same freshman class. They dated for a time and married on August 4, 1959. They had three children, Kent Lee (November 5, 1960), Sharon Ruth (May 12, 1963) and Robert Harlow (June 14, 1964).

Joyce and Russ with Kent, Sharon and Robert

On September 1, 1961, Russ and Joyce accepted a call to pastor the San Jose Church of God in Campbell, California. In 1958, the group reorganized in Campbell on a one-acre plot with a four-room parsonage attached to a new church building. Russ wrote:

While living there the church increased in attendance each of six years of the pastorate as the Lord added to the number. Vacation Bible Schools and an intensive calling campaign aided, along with a growing youth group and participation annually in Southwest Youth Camps in Arizona and southern California.

In 1967 the Magaws moved to Lafayette, Indiana, to take up the work of a newly planted congregation of 25 members. Over the next five years through the ministry of calling campaigns, vacation Bible schools, the Morrison home Bible study and Christian Life Crusades, the church grew. In 1972, Russ accepted the call to serve at the Columbia Station Church of God in Columbia Station, Ohio. This congregation was eight years old and had a church building, parsonage and historic schoolhouse on five acres. Russ and Gayle Reye served as youth leaders with 35 youth in attendance. When attendance continued to grow over the next seven years, a 64' x 44' church addition and service building were built. Home Bible studies, vacation Bible schools and revival meetings were tools God used to add to his church. In Columbia Station Russ discovered he loved to write about sports, an avocation which continues to this day. In 1977, Russ was elected to the General Conference Board of Directors.

On September 1, 1979, the family relocated to Oregon, Illinois, where Russ became the General Conference's Director of Publishing responsible for *The Restitution Herald, The Progress Journals*, books, tracts and other materials. Russ also assisted in the Outreach and Development department of the General Conference, and sponsored several groups to do house-to-house calling in Illinois, Louisiana and Michigan. He also served as instructor at Oregon Bible College. Part of his duties included traveling among the churches to encourage their growth and assisting the board with plans to relocate the General Conference to Atlanta, Georgia.

Russ wrote:

Before that move [to Atlanta], we were called along with Rick and Vickie Cooper to start a new church in St. Charles, Missouri, so the two couples relocated to Missouri on September 1, 1990. St. Charles Community Church was started on the last Sunday of October, 1990, at the St. Charles

10 Cine, using God's guidance and "The Phone's for YOU" program, attracting 249 to the first church service. Dozens of Church of God persons helped in the phone campaign that generated a mailing list of 3500 families. Attendance averaged over 100 for the first year of operation, but each year thereafter the numbers decreased, in spite of much prayer and intense personal work. Still, a few dozen persons were baptized in four years.

Associate Pastor Russell Magaw's last sermon at Oregon Church of God prior to his retirement.

Russ continued to edit the *Truth Seeker's Adult Quarterly* and also became the Pastor's Pastor for the Church of God Ministerial Association Leadership Team (MALT), a position he has held for many years.

On September 1, 1994, Russ and Joyce relocated to Eden Valley, Minnesota, to pastor the Church of God there. Russ wrote:

> God's blessings were evident during this seven-year pastorate as more members were added by prayer, Bible studies, VBS programs, public school release-time religious education classes, and youth camps of the Minnesota Conference at Long Lake Bible Camp.

He pursued community activities that took him among the people. He continued to write sports news, joined the Lion's Club and became acquainted with most families in the community.

The Magaws returned to Oregon, Illinois, in September 2001 to be near their children's families. Russ became associate pastor at Oregon Church of God working beside Pastor Michael Hoffman. In this capacity Russ interviewed most of the families in the church and published a weekly bulletin insert with this information. He also made calls, taught Sunday school, preached occasionally and baptized his four granddaughters. Also during this time Russ served as chaplain of the newly formed Rock River Christian College in Beloit, Wisconsin, for two years.

Russ and Joyce retired in September 2005 and now winter in Florida near son Robert. Russ still writes for the *Truth Seeker's Adult Quarterly*, serves as Pastor's Pastor, preaches occasionally and writes sports. Russ wrote, "God has blessed the 50-year ministry; may He be honored and glorified."

Russ Magaw contributed this entry.

See Kirkpatrick, Vivian, Sr.
    Lapp, Clarence E.
    Magaw, Vivian
    Magaw, Sydney
    Mattison, James
    Randall, Clyde E.

Bibliography: Magaw, Russ. E-mail, March 12, 2011.

Magaw, Sydney Everett
b. April 1, 1904
d. December 26, 1950

A. The Work of a Pastor
B. Interest in Church of God History
C. Statement of Faith
D. Final Years at Oregon, Illinois
E. Mission Challenge
F. Influence on the Denomination
G. Tragedy

"Sydney Magaw was a people person," Ivan Magaw said at the History Conference at North Hills Church of God in Springfield, Ohio. Sydney was born in Minnesota to Mr. and Mrs. Elmer Magaw of Lester Prairie. Elmer was pastor of the church at Bergen, Minnesota. Sydney was baptized at age 13 and began to preach occasionally at 17. He also attended conference at Waterloo and met many church leaders. This prepared him to write an excellent and definitive history of the Church of God in the February 14, 1922, issue of *The Restitution Herald*.

He married Margaret Hatch (July 14, 1904-December 26, 1950), daughter of Elder Jeremiah S. Hatch, in Harvey, Illinois, when both were 19. Elder Orrin Jenks, president at Aurora College, performed the ceremony. Sydney graduated from Aurora College. After the wedding they returned to work at Dunwoody Institute. They had five sons, Ivan, Malcolm, Milo, Sydney and Jimmy, and two daughters, Ione and Norma.

A. The Work of a Pastor

Sydney Magaw began preaching at Clear Water, Wisconsin. He baptized 17 people there. The attendance grew to 73. In 1925, he wrote an article for one of the papers, "Spread the Gospel." He believed in evangelism. Syd began the work at Graytown, Wisconsin, in the fall of 1925. By March of 1926, they had 52 members with a Berean Society of 30 young adults.

In 1927 Sydney began preaching at Eden Valley,

Sydney and Margaret Magaw and children in the backyard of their home.

Minnesota. He loved preaching, and he loved Minnesota. One winter he spent most of his time at Blackduck, a small village on a lake, but when winter ended he was back at work. He left Eden Valley to assume a pastorate at Tipp City, Ohio, at the small Brush Creek church.

Sydney loved being a pastor at Brush Creek. He preached a full hour. His favorite topic was prophecy. After each service he offered an invitation to anyone considering accepting Jesus as Savior. He preached the Kingdom of God so effectively that it impressed not only his congregation but his young son Ivan, as well. Sydney often used a chart in his preaching. He would unfold it and preach a series of sermons from it. Soon, he had invitations to preach from his chart from other Churches of God and traveled to Michigan, Nebraska and Louisiana to preach prophecy. This established him as a national figure.

B. Interest in Church of God History

Sydney brought the history of the Church of God before his readers. He also emphasized the importance of mission work throughout the world. Through the pages of *The Restitution Herald* he awakened the Church of God to the need for foreign missions, especially after Israel became a nation in 1948.

He pursued a history research project, calling on the church's older generation who had lived through the era. He knew most of these people because he had frequently attended the annual conferences held in Waterloo, Iowa. His sources included James Patrick, the General Conference's first president; Leila Whitehead, great-niece of Benjamin Wilson; Clyde E. Randall, a young man yet well informed on church matters especially from the conference in Minnesota; Dorothy Lyon, presumably descended from R.V. Lyon, one of the most outstanding and dedicated preachers of Age to Come in the 19th century; S.J. Lindsay, founder and editor of *The Restitution Herald*; Frank E. Siple, who was intimately acquainted with the developing work in Louisiana and other regions; and Thomas Wilson, who shared information about the Wilson migration to America and their religious affiliations before coming to the Church of God.

From this extensive gathering of oral history, Sydney published *History of the Minnesota Conference of the Church of God* in 1931. This small book is detailed and has become a classic reference. It was updated in 1960.

Syd Magaw and the young adults of the Ohio Conference, circa 1935.

C. Statement of Faith

Sydney gathered biographical information through his historical interviews, and he gathered opinions on doctrines. His greatest contribution to the historical body of knowledge is his summary of the statement of faith as commonly believed in 1922, as follows:

1. One true church founded upon Christ and one true name, "thy only name" Eph. 3:14, 15; John 17:12; Acts 20:28.
2. Repentance is one of the first steps to be taken to "get into the church" Lk. 3:9; 13:3.
3. Baptism of believers by immersion only Gal. 3:27; Rom. 6:3-7.
4. Conditional Immortality 1 John 5:10-13; Rom. 6:23.
5. Resurrection of all the dead John 5:27, 28; I Cor. 15:22.
6. Final destruction of all the wicked Rom. 6:23; Mal. 4:1; Rev. 20:13,14.
7. The literal, personal, visible second coming of Christ Acts 1:11; Matt 24:30.
8. The re-establishment of the Kingdom of God on earth and the restitution of all things spoken of by the prophets Acts 3:21; Ezek. 21:25-27.
9. The restoration of the natural Israel to its homeland before the restoration of the kingdom Rom. 8:9,10; Amos 9:13-15; Dan. 2:44.
10. All scripture is given by inspiration of God. 2 Tim. 3:16; 2 Pet. 1:20, 21.

These were doctrines held dear by the Minnesota conference, and Sydney Magaw demonstrated that other Churches of God were in agreement by submitting the statement of faith to the Illinois Conference. Without reporting its entirety, the Illinois Conference statement agreed on all points with two additional items:

- The immortalized saints will be joint-heirs with Christ in the government of the nations. Rom. 8:17; Rev. 5:10.
- That holy life is essential to salvation. Col. 1:22; Rom 12:1; 1 Pet. 1:15.

The reader is invited to compare these statements to those mentioned with those in the Robert G. Huggins entry. Like Huggins, Sydney Magaw was a leader in doctrinal integrity and obedience to the call of Christian service. He tried to systematize those precious truths commonly believed by the brotherhood.

> **Statement of Faith presented to the Church of God by Sydney Magaw drawn from an extensive membership survey in 1922:**
> 1. **One true church** founded upon Christ and one true name, "thy only name" Eph. 3:14,15; John 17:12; Acts 20:28.
> 2. **Repentance** is one of the first steps to be taken to "get into the church" Luke 3:9; 13:3.
> 3. **Baptism** of believers by immersion only. Gal. 3:27; Rom. 6:3-7.
> 4. **Conditional Immortality** 1 John 5:10-13; Rom. 6:23.
> 5. **Resurrection of all the dead** John 5:27, 28; I Cor. 15:22.
> 6. **Final destruction of all the wicked** Rom. 6:23; Mal. 4:1; Rev. 20:13,14.
> 7. **The literal, personal, visible second coming of Christ** Acts 1:11; Matt 24:30.
> 8. **The re-establishment of the Kingdom of God on earth** and the restitution of all things spoken of by the prophets Acts 3:21; Ezek. 21:25-27.
> 9. **The restoration of the natural Israel** to its homeland before the restoration of the kingdom Rom. 8, 9,10; Amos 9:13-15; Dan. 2:44.
> 10. **All scripture is given by inspiration of God** 2 Tim. 3:16; 2 Pet. 1:20, 21.

D. Final Years at Oregon, Illinois

Sydney moved to Oregon, Illinois, and became editor of *The Restitution Herald* beginning with the October 11, 1938, issue. He wrote stirring editorials that called people to service and emphasized cooperation, and he had a heart for evangelism and missions.

Just one year after his arrival in Oregon, the delegates wanted to begin a college. The Bible Training School had been closed during the depression years, and the delegates wanted ministerial education to be offered to Church of God students on a regular basis. Because he was a pastor and a graduate of Aurora College, Sydney was appointed as an instructor at Oregon Bible College. The new college opened its doors in August 1939. L.E. Conner was another Bible instructor. Alice Carpentar taught art. Since its inception in 1939, Oregon/Atlanta Bible College has graduated over 500 students to serve in ministry positions.

In 1943, the General Conference Education Committee wanted to buy a campus. In August the delegates voted to purchase the Spoor estate just north of Oregon. This property sat along the Rock River under the watchful eye of the Black Hawk statue. A large mansion was on the land; it provided adequate sleeping quarters on the upper level, men on one side and women on the other. There was a dining room and classroom area. The library was small and housed on the wrap-around porch that faced the river. The property was purchased for $18,000. The mortgage was retired within a year.

While in Oregon, Syd Magaw served the local congregation as pastor. They loved him, except for one. One elder clashed with him and it may have been over an issue with the American and Christian flags. This was during WWII, and Sydney did not want the flags displayed on the podium behind the pulpit. He felt that the church, having a pacifistic stand, should remain neutral. Sydney stored the flags in the storage room behind the choir loft, and the next Sunday they again were displayed on the podium. He lost the battle of the flags.

Sydney also didn't like using the church baptistery. He thought running water was better for baptisms. The baptistery was used in winter when ice covered the river. This was a practical matter, however, and he accepted its use. Being from Minnesota, cutting a hole in the ice was not a problem to Sydney, but for Illinois people it was.

Some people thought the local church work should be separate from the General Conference work. By necessity, those who worked for the General Conference also worshipped at Oregon Church of God. It was difficult to separate them into two operations. But word of it got back to the Board of Directors and the next summer the General Conference delegates voted to not allow the executive secretary and editor of the General Conference to pastor the local church. The separation happened June 1, 1943. After that, Sydney Magaw still preached, but he did not pastor a church. Ivan Magaw confided that losing this pastorate bothered Sydney Magaw, but it didn't destroy him.

E. Mission Challenge

Since Sydney grew up in Minnesota he was schooled in the importance of foreign missions. To him, mission work was as important as doctrine, the Berean work and church history to which he was devoted. It became an important part of his ministry. He emphasized missions when he compiled the Minnesota church history. He taught lessons and preached sermons about it. When he moved to Oregon and began his ministry with the headquarters church, he was in a position as local pastor and editor of *The Restitution Herald* to speak up and influence the General Conference to take a positive stance on foreign missions. In May 1942 Pastor Magaw gave an informative, inspirational sermon on the state of missions in India where Minnesota had been participating. The people listened, but there was little response.

When Israel became a nation overnight in 1948, Church of God pastors and leaders recognized the

Sydney with Arkansas and Missouri ministers during his 1945 preaching trip. From left: WR Simmons, Francis Burnett, LH Shelton-?, Viv Kirkpatrick, Syd Magaw, C Alan McLain, CF Weaver, H Scott Smith, JM Morgan.

fulfillment of prophecy. This made a goal for missions imperative. Christ must be preached to the entire world.

In 1948 Sydney wrote an editorial in *The Restitution Herald* specifically to rally readers, leaders, pastors and delegates behind mission work and to incorporate it into the General Conference program of activities. Entitled "Birth Pangs of a New Nation," this editorial drew attention to the birth of Israel that could indicate the beginning of the end (of the age). He spotlighted the Arab/Jew struggle that would only end upon Christ's return. That short editorial led to a directive from the General Conference delegates that summer to become active in foreign and home missions.

Out of that interest several things happened: a national evangelist was hired and the name of Jim McLain became recognized in every Church of God household the next few years. He was sent to work in the South and the Great Plains, and he had great success there. He was a natural musician and his ministry is still remembered by elderly members in Arkansas who loved to work with him.

The second result of the Magaw emphasis on missions was C.E. Lapp's initial Holy Land trip in 1950. When Clarence returned, he reported the state of affairs in the new nation of Israel, his observations of the Jewish-Arabic conflict and the condition of Judaism at that time.

A third effect came a few years after Sydney's death. It was a second visit to the Holy Land, this time by James Watkins as ambassador of the Church of God, with Adib Lidawi as tour guide. Watkins had been hired to replace Magaw as editor and Adib, a native of Lebanon, was a foreign exchange student at Oregon Bible College. Pictures in the Archives show Watkins and Lidawi at not only the tourist sites, but also at orphanages, clinics, schools and meetings with religious leaders.

The Minnesota conference had set the precedent for foreign mission work. For years this conference supported foreign missions in India under the direction of Pastor Charles Vedantachari in 1912, and later, John Manoah and his son S.S. Manoah of Bangalore, South India, during the latter half of the 20th century.

F. Influence on the Denomination

Sydney held a prominent position within the Church of God and thus left a great legacy. Being editor of a denominational paper is a position of national importance, and he used the position as a call to service, especially to foreign missions. Terry Ferrell, one of his students, noted Syd was always busy. His light was often on at *The Herald* office late at night working to meet a deadline.

His love for the pure Word, the pure motive and the

The Magaw Chart of Bible Events - A portion of the large chart Sydney hung at the front of the church during sermons. The oil painting is stored in the ABC Archive.

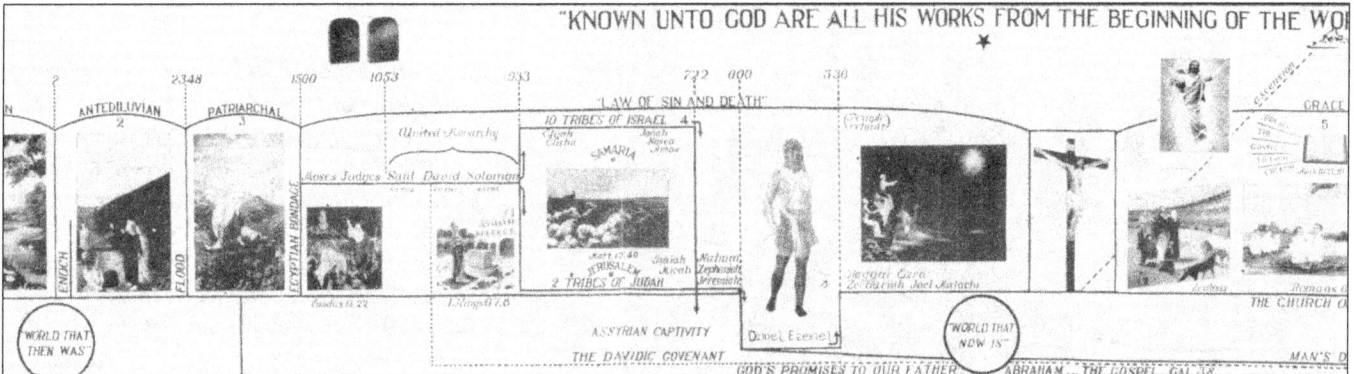

pure message seemed to be the best motivator for helping the editor stay focused on his many duties. When F.L. Austin assumed the editorship from S.J. Lindsay in 1922, and was also the executive secretary and instructor at the Bible Training School, he could not concentrate on the editorship. He was overextended in his duties. The overall attempt to forge a new organization was weakened by this, and the health of F.L. Austin was compromised. Magaw overcame all obstacles and brought the Church of God together in a mighty way.

Sydney's editorship ranks first among all the editors of *The Restitution Herald*, mirrored 30 years later by the editorship of his nephew, Russell Magaw, throughout the 1980s. Part of Syd's success may be naturally attributed to WWII. People thought it was the last Great War and that Christ would be coming soon, so they got busy and started to spread the Gospel message.

Sydney was happy and he engaged in life. He enjoyed growing roses and bird watching, and he played checkers by mail with more than 100 people. He'd make a move by post card, and a week later a return card would state the opponent's next move. Post cards were just a penny so he kept in touch with members inexpensively.

G. Tragedy

The Magaw family lived in a large two-story white house on North Sixth Street in Oregon, Illinois, that is still known today as the "Magaw house." Son Ivan and his family reside there at this writing.

At Christmas in 1950, Sydney's brilliant career ended when he and Margaret died tragically in an accident on icy roads at Minonk, Illinois. The road curved but the car went straight and struck a solitary tree in the field. They were traveling to Ivan Magaw and Marie Barnum's wedding in Hammond, Louisiana. The deaths were a great shock to Church of God members, especially to the congregation at Oregon, the staff of the General Conference and to the Magaw, Hatch and Barnum families.

On hearing the tragic news of his parents' death, Ivan was overwhelmed and talked to Pastor Vernis Wolfe about how to proceed. Vernis recommended they proceed with the wedding and deal with the tragedy later. Ivan and Marie went from their wedding to his parents' funeral. Also tragic for the family: Margaret's brother, Paul Hatch, was driving the auto. He was severely injured and disfigured in the accident. His life was extremely difficult his remaining years. Paul confided to the author in his old age that he wished he had died with them. He felt he had murdered them because they had asked him to slow down and he had not. He felt for that reason he would not be in the Kingdom of God. He could not forgive himself.

Two of the other Magaw children, Sydney and Jimmy, were also in the accident but recovered at the Streator Hospital with Paul Hatch and Ruth Hoskins who had more extensive injuries.

The news passed swiftly through the community of Oregon because anyone who worked at the General Conference was well known throughout the city. People were stunned with grief as the sad news cast a pall over their lives. Holiday joy turned suddenly bleak. Kent Ross, then age eight and living in Minnesota, related that his mother took the call, was silent, hung up the phone, and burst into sobs. It was heart wrenching, but "we sorrow not as others who have no hope" (1 Thessalonians 4:13).

The last issue of *The Restitution Herald* completed by Syd was dated December 19, 1950. Some people in the Church of God received it the day the Magaws died.

Recently, Sydney's son Milo Magaw died in Alabama. Milo had at one time been the Oregon Church of God's youth leader and helped influence this author. Ivan, the eldest of five sons, has remained a strong force in the church at Flagg Center all these years and has been active in researching church history. Much of the material used in this book has come from Ivan's files left to him by his uncle, Paul Hatch. Presently Ivan Magaw is writing the full biography of his father.

Pastors J.R. LeCrone and Grover J. Gordon of Fonthill, Ontario, Church of God conducted the Magaws' funeral services. Interment was in Daysville Cemetery. The local paper wrote, "The Magaws were among the

Sydney with students and faculty of Oregon Bible College in 1945. Seated, from left: Albert and Vena Logsdon, Otto Dick, Sydney Magaw, FL Austin, Mrs. Gesin, Alice Carpentar. Middle row: G Landry, S Logsdon (Urish), K Davis, T Pearson, Mrs. Pearson, W Sorenson, M Brown (Vadnais), R Brown, E Smith. Third row: J Johns (Haberer), A Johns, M Hall, E Barnum, H Payne, I Payne (Sorenson), unknown, B Goodwin.

best citizens of this community. When the hand of death struck them it cast a pall of sorrow on this community."

> **Sydney published the following statement 18 months prior to his death:** Yes, though Jesus went not to the burial, the disciples did bury John, (Matt. 14:12). Nor ought any Christian ever despise a parent—even in death. Burials must be, and burials of loved ones make the legitimate demands, but no excuse, no interest, no joy, no calamity dare thrust its place in front of Jesus nor in front of preaching the Kingdom of God! Preach, Young Men! Preach the Gospel of the Kingdom of God!!
>
> Ref.: Editorial, *The Restitution Herald*, May 31, 1949

See Austin, F.L.
Carpentar, Alice
Gordon, Grover J.
Hatch, Jeremiah (19th)
Hatch, Paul
Jenks, Orrin
LeCrone, J. Richard
Magaw, Russell
Wolfe, Vernis

Bibliography: Ferrell, Terry, Interview with Jan Stilson, July 14, 2009; Magaw, Ivan, *Preaching First Century Christianity, a Biography of Sydney Magaw*. Unpublished book manuscript with temporary title, Oregon, Il., 2007; Magaw, Ivan. Comments from his presentation at the 2d Annual History Conference at North Hills Church of God, Springfield, Ohio, Nov. 6, 7, 2007; Magaw, Sydney, "World Vision," *The Restitution Herald 75th anniversary Issue*, Russell Magaw, ed., Oregon, Il., Oct. 1985; Stilson, Janet Turner, "Memories of the Sydney Magaw Family"; *The Restitution Herald*, Sept. 23, 1912; February 14, 1922; Oct. 2, 1923; Nov. 10, 1925; March 9, 1926; Oct. 1, 1938; Oct. 7, 1947; May 15, 1948; May 25, 1948; June 15, 1948; May 31, 1949; Various files donated by Ivan Magaw, Oregon, Il., 2005.

Magaw, Vivian Eugene Field
b. July 4, 1908
d. June 25, 2001

Vivian Eugene was born in Lester Prairie, Minnesota, to Elmer H. and Emma Jane (Kirkpatrick) Magaw. He was the youngest of four children, one of whom died in infancy. Vivian's older brother Sydney became the executive secretary of the Church of God. Vivian adored Sydney who was outgoing and excelled at sports. At the time Syd studied at Aurora College in Illinois, Vivian attended high school and graduated.

Vivian and Ruth Magaw

Looking for something to do, Vivian and his father took a 100-mile bike ride to visit family near Eden Valley. Soon after, Viv received a letter from Sydney, now married and living in southern Ohio. Syd invited him to come to Ohio where lots of beautiful girls lived. At age 25 Vivian left Minnesota and settled in Tipp City, Ohio. He took employment with the US Postal Service delivering mail that arrived by train. His son Russell wrote, "His bid at $30 a month, by far the lowest, was accepted. He delivered and received mail at Tipp via train as it whisked through town. Then he picked up, and delivered mail to Fulton on US 40."

Vivian and Ruth

Vivian soon realized Syd had not lied. The girls in Ohio were beautiful, especially a Shellhaas girl from Kessler. Ruth Shellhaas and Vivian married on May 16, 1935, during the Great Depression. To supplement his income Vivian repaired radios. Ruth and Vivian had three sons, Russell, Harold and Larry, and a daughter, Elaine.

Spending time with family was important to Vivian. He did the grocery shopping when the family was quarantined by Larry and Elaine's scarlet fever; he taught the kids to play Monopoly, Rook and checkers. In fact, no one in the family could ever beat Viv at checkers. Russ said:

> One day I challenged Dad to a quick game. We got the board out, set up the checkers, and he offered me the first move. Dad always said that the first move determined the game's outcome. I moved a checker and it was all over. After a few more moves, Dad had his pieces lined up so that whatever move I'd make, he'd take my man.

Finally, Russ gave up and Vivian took the game.

Vivian excelled at electronics and was one of the first to work on a computer in the 1950s at Dayton Aviation Radio and Equipment (DARE). He subscribed to electronics magazines and enjoyed tinkering with radios and repair problems. Russ said when his father explained an electronic principle to him, Russ's eyes would glaze over, and his dad would regretfully shake his head.

The family joined Brush Creek Church of God where all attended Sunday school and worship, and where Vivian often taught classes, wrote Sunday school lessons and preached when the pastor was away. Vivian also served as elder, and he taught Russ how to sing tenor when they stood side by side in the worship service.

Vivian helped found the Troy View Church of God, Troy, Ohio, where he and Dewayne Demmitt became

Ruth Shellhaas Magaw

its first elders in the late 1950s. Vivian and Ruth served in this congregation for nearly 25 years.

After retirement, Viv and Ruth enjoyed travel. They attended an Elderhostel at Oregon Bible College and many church conferences as well. They visited friends and relatives in Canada and their grown children. After Russ and Joyce entered the ministry for the Church of God, Viv and Ruth visited all the churches they served. Ruth celebrated her 80th birthday at Russ and Joyce's home in St. Charles, Missouri, where Russ was the church planting pastor. Ruth died April 9, 1995, and was interred at the Curtis Cemetery beside the Brush Creek Church of God. Vivian lived to nearly 93 years old. When he died, the family was at his side. Pastor Craig Wagganer officiated at both funeral services. Vivian rests beside Ruth in Curtis Cemetery.

Russ Magaw contributed this entry.

See Magaw, Russ
      Magaw, Sydney

Bibliography: Russ Magaw, "Memories of Vivian Magaw," in honor of his 100th birthday anniversary on July 4, 2008.

Manoah, John
b. 1870?
d. 1960?

John Manoah lived in Bangalore, South India. He studied with Charles Vedantachari, who had served with Dr. Austin and Sarah Taylor in the Bible Faith Mission. This work was supported by the Advent Christians and by the Church of God Minnesota Conference. In fact, Charles Vedantachari was ordained at a Church of God Minnesota Conference in 1912 at St. Cloud, and Mrs. Taylor was ordained at their fall meeting in St. Cloud in 1914.

Elder John Manoah distributed tracts and *The Restitution Herald* in Bangalore walking from door to door and village to village. He wrote to the editor of *The Restitution Herald* and asked for prayers for the work. At that time there was no official recognition of the work by the Church of God General Conference, but everyone was aware of his labors because of the support from Minnesota.

In 1957 John had proven his steadfastness and in addition to the support from the Minnesota conference, the General Conference delegates voted to begin supporting the work in India. Up to that time the General Conference had only supported the mission work in Digby, Nova Scotia, with Roddy Pike as the missionary in residence.

Planning and managing foreign missions was new to the Church of God. It had spent over a century getting a firm hold of the work in America by sending out state, regional and national evangelists, but as interest in foreign missions became apparent at end of the 19th century, need became clear. Following WWII the incentive to send the message of the Gospel of Kingdom to foreign nations became an imperative as the signs of the times became more apparent.

The action of the United Nations to bring Israel into membership as a nation in 1948 appeared to be the handwriting on the wall. Church of God pastors agreed it was the beginning of the fulfillment of the restoration of Israel prior to the Lord's coming which the Church of God had preached from the days of Joseph Marsh in 1845 to the present.

Within the next decade, during the Decade of Development (1955-1965), the General Conference voted to support several new works. Pastor Dean Moore of Blanchard, Michigan, asked for support to enter Mexico to work with Roberto Badillo, a migrant worker at Blanchard. Dean had befriended Roberto and they had studied the Bible together. Pastor Moore's request for support was granted.

In 1960 Eleodoro Ortiguero wrote to the General Conference from the Philippine Islands requesting information. He was pastor to several churches in the province of Luzon, and he declared that he agreed with the Church of God. He said the Philippine churches needed help and spiritual direction. He had learned of the Church of God General Conference by reading Mead's *Handbook of Denominations*, a reference book which lists all denominations, their addresses, chief officers and chief doctrines. To review the history of missions within the Church of God, see Appendix 20—Missions.

When John died in India, the work passed to his son, S.S. Manoah. Dr. William and Mardy Lawrence traveled to India in 1963 and met S.S. Manoah. They felt the work in India was worthy of support so in 1964 the delegates of the General Conference voted to send support to that mission field.

In 1966, Mission Superintendent Stan Ross and travel companion Merle Patrick stopped in India after spending time in the Philippines. That summer they returned and reported to the General Conference delegates the events of their meeting with S.S. Manoah; Pastor Manoah was ordained in absentia at the annual conference meeting. A campaign was started then to raise $9,000 for a church to be built in Bangalore. This church was built with a clinic in the rear and was dedicated in 1967. Oversight of the medical clinic was given to Dr. Lawrence, who was a medical doctor along with his wife, Mardy, a nurse. They made regular visits to Bangalore to assist in the work.

Some concern arose in that work over the manner in which the money was being spent and how those expenditures were reported. Another problem of foreign missions in the Church of God was the difficulty of managing them from the States. These issues had to be worked out by the Board of Directors of the General Conference. It was felt that when generous support money was given to foreign workers whose native economy and standard of living were at poverty level or below, the native leaders could be at risk. So support money was cut modestly, and native workers were placed in charge of overseeing the foreign works with occasional visits by mission leaders from the United States.

SS Manoah replaced John Manoah in the Indian mission work. Here he is with Superintendent of Missions Stan Ross at Blessed Hope church in Rockford, Illinois.

The Foreign Missions Fellowship of Oregon Bible College brought John's son, S.S. Manoah, to the United States in 1968. He came in March and visited the college and several churches before returning home.

The Lord's Harvest International, a mission sending agency, was created by the delegates at General Conference in 1993. Judy Kirkpatrick Myers became its director. LHI is managed by a Missions Board on which Mrs. Myers serves. This mission agency has authority to work out administrative details to support foreign works.

The work begun in India by the Bible Faith Mission with Charles Vedantachari and John Manoah so long ago continues today as a native-managed mission work.

See   Doan, Harold
       Ross, Stanley O.
       Taylor, Sarah (19th)
       Vedantachari, Charles (19th)
See Also Appendix 20—Missions, ref. Ortiguero
Bibliography: Magaw, Sydney, ed., *History of the Minnesota Conference of the church of God*, 1930; Ross, S.O. Mission records available in the Archives of the Church of God General Conference.

Maple, Charles Clifford
b. 1883
d. May 10, 1963

C.C. Maple lived in North Ridgeville, Ohio. At one time he was an evangelist for the Church of God Ohio Conference. As such, he traveled throughout the state strengthening churches and holding Bible studies to begin new churches. He also served as pastor of the Delta Church at Raker, Ohio, in 1913 and at the Argos, Indiana, Church of God (1917-1925).

Throughout his travels, people asked for a Church of God songbook to use in worship and singing instruction. In one church paper C.C. reported that he had been so busy he had not had time to prepare "even a small pamphlet." He recommended making good use of a book already published called *Golden Sheafs,* by Advent Christian Publishing Company in Boston. The books cost $27.50 per one hundred copies.

In 1913 C.C. was appointed to the Music Committee with F.E. Siple and Cecil Cross. They were to compile a hymnal to express musically the Bible truths held so dear by the Church of God. If this committee was able to publish a hymnal is unknown, but C.C. Maple published one under his own name about that time, *Gospel Songs for Conference Gatherings Sunday Schools Special Meetings Berean Societies.* It included 31 gospel songs by various writers such as Fanny Crosby and Lowell Mason. The first song in the booklet was "Just Over in Eden" by W.L. Crowe of the Nebraska Conference. It had a snappy verse and happy chorus: "Just over in Eden, That beautiful city I see; Just over in Eden, A place in that city for me." The song "Beautiful Days," composed by A.J. Eychaner of the Iowa Conference, was in C.C.'s book, and later in the hymnals *Songs of Truth* and *Songs of Truth Two*, the revised edition. These small green hymnals were used in the Church of God from 1947-1980. Crowe and Eychaner's hymns were not included in the most recent hymnal, *Psalms, Hymns and Spiritual Songs* (1980).

During 1914 C.C. Maple traveled southeast into Virginia to the Shenandoah Valley and other locations within the state. The following is a report of his travels:

On October 23rd he began a series of meetings. The first began at Slate Hill, continuing three nights. The next week was spent at Dry Run (Fort Valley) a few miles from Slate Hill, both of which are in Powell's Fort in the Massanutten Mts. of Virginia. From there he went to Maurertown, across the mountains where he remained a week.

Three Miller brothers from Hagerstown, Maryland, attended the Maurertown meetings and received baptism.

The reporter continued, "It was an impressive scene to witness three noble young men surrender to Christ."

Gertrude Logan reported Maple's circuit to *The Restitution Herald*:

> The next point was Browntown in the Blue Ridge Mountains, about 18 miles from Maurertown. One addition was the result of this meeting. From there he went to Clifton Station about 20 miles from Washington D.C., where he spoke two nights. Elder Maple's sermons were clear and forceful, claiming the closest attention from a good audience at each point.

Elder Maple was a friend of the elderly H.V. Reed of Chicago. C.C. and Reed traveled to the annual conference in Iowa in 1913. Elder Maple made himself available to preach for special meetings wherever he was invited. Some members had moved to New Mexico, so in 1924, he explored the feasibility of beginning a church work there. He baptized eight souls and asked for a pastor to come, but a formal group was never started there.

Curiously, a note was published in *The Restitution* in 1913 indicating that Maple was being dropped from membership at Cleveland Church of God, and that he had resigned as evangelist of the Ohio Conference to pursue ministry in other fields. Sometimes separation from work raises questions, but clear answers aren't given in the literature to explain why one ministry ends and another begins. Historians cannot go beyond what the record says in making interpretations of history. Otherwise, history becomes fiction. One answer may be that Maple faced a conflict in his belief system. The US Census for 1910 lists him as a "Minister Church of God/Church of Christ (Disciples)." It would be difficult to represent two denominations at once. The flyer from the Argos Church uses the terminology "ecclesia" which generally is used by Christadelphians in place of the word "church." He may have been struggling with himself about which denomination best suited his beliefs and values.

C.C. Maple sent a question to *The Restitution Herald* to ask about Christ's future role as Mediator:

> Some understand that after Christ leaves his seat as mediator there can be no more salvation because there is no one to act as mediator for the sinner. I would like to ask a number of our Bible students give us their answers to this argument in a few words. Boil it down; just a direct answer.

Maple's question was not answered in future issues.

THE CHURCH OF GOD IN CHRIST JESUS

(1 Thess. 2:14.)

LOCATED ON NORTH MICHIGAN STREET

ARGOS, MARSHALL COUNTY, INDIANA

EVANGELIST C. C. MAPLE, MINISTER

A STATEMENT OF OUR POSITION

1. The Scriptures Inspired and The Christ Divine.
2. The Atonement by the Blood and Salvation by the Cross.
3. Faith, Repentance, Confession, Immersion for the Remission of Sins.
4. The Gift of Eternal Life only through Jesus Christ at His Second Coming.
5. The Personal Return of the Christ and the Establishment of the Kingdom of God.
6. The Christian Life a Manifestation of the Fruits of the Spirit by the Lord's People.

This Church is UNDENOMINATIONAL and non-sectarian.

The Bible is our rule of faith and practice, our only guide.

The New Testament is our book of Church Order and Discipline.

Lord's Day School and Bible Study upon the "First Day of the Week."

Preaching of the Word by the Minister over the Third Lord's Day, each month.

The "School of the Prophets" will begin on Thursday preceeding each Third Lord's Day.

Correspondence for the Minister should be addressed, Root Road, Elyria, Ohio.

Telegrams may be sent, Shawville Station, Ohio. All correspondence regarding local matters can be sent to Mrs. Frank Boggs, Clerk of the Ecclesia, 500 North Michigan Street, Argos, Indiana.

"Earnestly contend for the faith which was once delivered unto the saints."
—Jude 3.

THE CHURCH OF GOD, ORGANIZED JAN. 1, 1869.

We, whose names are hereunto annexed, being brought together by our mutual faith in the things concerning the Kingdom of God and the name of Jesus Christ, Acts, 8:12. Having obeyed from the heart that form of doctrine once delivered you,—Rom. 6:17, do hereby organize ourselves into a body of believers, to be known as the Church of God, of Argos, Ind., taking the Bible as our only rule of faith and practice, and making Christian character the test of friendship.

DECLARATION OF PRINCIPLES AND CONSTITUTION

Of the Indiana State Conference of the Church of God of the Abrahamic Faith, Adopted at the Annual Meeting, Held at Argos, Indiana, September 10, 1886.

Church of God in Conference Assembled at Argos, Ind., Sept. 10, 1886:

We, the members of the several churches represented by delegation, feeling deeply the necessity of closer union and better co-operation in the proclamation of the truth, and the promotion of the cause of Christ among us, as preliminary to this end, do set forth the following declaration of principles as the foundation of our faith:

We accept the Bible as the only rule of faith and practice.

We believe in the final "restitution of all things which God hath spoken by the mouth of all his Holy prophets since the world began."

As a means to this end, the establishment of the Kingdom of God on the earth, with the Christ as the King of Kings, and the immortal saints as joint heirs with Him in the government of the nations; the restoration of Israel; the literal resurrection of the dead; the immortalization of the righteous, and the final destruction of the wicked; eternal life only through Christ.

A hearty belief of the Gospel, repentance, and immersion as pre-requisites to the forgiveness of sins, and a holy life as essential for final salvation.

We believe that Jesus Christ is the son of God.

And further to secure this end we reorganize this our State Conference.

CONSTITUTION.

1. This Conference shall be known under the name of "The Indiana State Conference of the Church of God of the Abrahamic Faith."
2. It shall be composed of the organized churches of the State of Indiana, which churches shall be represented in the conference by duly authorized delegates.
3. This Conference shall, at each annual meeting, elect the following named officers: A President, First and Second Vice-President, one Secretary and one Treasurer; these officers to be an Executive Board to transact business.
4. The Secretary shall keep a record of the proceedings of each meeting; of all the business transacted, and enter the same in a book kept for the purpose of future reference; which book shall be open to the inspection of any member of the Conference.
5. The Treasurer shall keep an account of all money received, from whatever source, and of its expenditure under the direction of the Conference, or of its Executive Board; said accounts to be open to the inspection of any member of the Conference.
6. Any organized church within the State, may be admitted into the Conference upon application and approval.
7. Letters of commendation may be granted to Ministers of the Word, upon the recommendation of the local church to which each applicant belongs. Such letters shall be for one year, and may be rescinded at any time, for sufficient cause, by the Conference, if in session, or by the Executive Board, when the Conference is not in session.
8. Each church shall be entitled to one vote at all meetings of the Conference for every ten members, and one for every fraction of six, said votes to be cast by the delegates of the several churches. Each organized church, no matter how small the number, shall be entitled to one vote.
9. This Conference shall meet not less than nor more than four times a year, for the transaction of business, at such place and time as may be determined by the Executive Board, timely notice being given through THE RESTITUTION.
10. This Conference adopts THE RESTITUTION as its organ, and recommends the brethren everywhere to give it their support.
11. This Constitution may be revised, altered or amended, by a two-thirds vote of the members present at any regular meeting, notice having previously been given of the proposed change.

C.C. Maple moved west and later preached as evangelist for the Nebraska Conference. One year, he preached in Holbrook at the Thanksgiving meeting, and he conducted the double wedding of the Adam sisters in Holbrook in 1925. It is thought that Elder Maple returned to Ohio in his retirement years and likely died there.

Bibliography: Ancestry.com. U.S. Census. Ohio. Medina. Medina. Dist. 139. 1910; Ohio Death Record 1958-2002 record for C.C. Maple; Argos flyer, owned by Atlanta Bible College Archives, McDonough, Ga. *The Restitution,* May 27, 1913; July 6, 1913; *The Restitution Herald,* Dec. 2, 1914; Oct. 16, 1917; Jan. 29, 1924; Feb. 26, 1924; May 13, 1924; June 24, 1924; Nov. 10, 1925; Minute book of the Illinois State Conference of the Church of God, 1913-1914; Maple, C.C., *Gospel Songs,* Self-published. North Ridgeville, Oh., circa 1914; Krogh, Harvey U. Jr., chairman *Songs of Truth,* (1947) and *Songs of Truth* Two (1963), Church of God General Conference, Oregon,. Il; Ramsey, Dale, chairman, *Psalms, Hymns and Spiritual Songs,* Church of God General Conference, Oregon, Il., 1980.

Marlow, Augusta Victoria
b. April 11, 1912
d. April 20, 1999

Augusta was born in Browntown, Virginia, to Edward Washington and Charlotte Updike Rudacille. Edward and Charlotte were weavers at the local textile mill. Augusta married Walter Richard Marlow Jr. in 1930. Harry Sheets, pastor at Cool Spring Church of God at Browntown, baptized Augusta and her mother on September 27, 1915. They joined that church. Edward Rudacille, Augusta's father, was baptized by Earl Thayer, pastor, on April 21, 1935. Augusta was survived by son Walter, daughter Dorothy Rudacille, two sisters, Myrtle Smedley and Edith Thapre, grandchildren and great-grandchildren.

See Sheets, Harry
Thayer, Verna
Bibliography: ABC Biography Project, David Krogh, compiler.

Marsh, George Eldred
b. June 12, 1881
d. November 23, 1954

A. Marsh Lineage
B. Begins Ministry
C. Return to Iowa
D. Canadian Ministry

George E. Marsh was born in Burr Oak, Iowa. His father, Edgar, was an Advent Christian minister who died when George was a boy. At age six George quit school to help support his mother, Josephine; older brother, Oscar; and younger sister, Orrissa.

A. Marsh Lineage
George was descended from Joseph Marsh's lineage. Edgar A. Marsh's father, Julian W. Marsh, was Joseph Marsh's brother. It has not been proven that Julian Marsh and Levi Marsh, who began the Church of God at Irving, Iowa, were related, but Marsh family genealogists are researching the matter. Thomas Newman published Julian W. Marsh's obituary in *The Millennial Harbinger.* This affectionate tribute featured a poem by Jenny Marsh Parker, Joseph's daughter. This obituary proves that Joseph Marsh was G.E. Marsh's great-grand uncle.

Of note are the archival books at Atlanta Bible College that have stickers inside with the nameplate "G.E. Marsh, E.A. Marsh. O.A.Marsh."

B. Begins Ministry
Elder A.J. Eychaner greatly influenced G.E. Marsh in his youth. Eychaner baptized Marsh during the Iowa Conference at Marshalltown in 1887. Shortly thereafter, G.E. Marsh preached his first sermon at Gladbrook, Iowa. During the next several years, Marsh worked for the Iowa Conference holding tent meetings and going house to house calling with Elder Eychaner.

From Iowa G.E. moved to Minnesota where he worked with Minister O.J. Allard. Later, George was recommended to S.J. Lindsay at Oregon, Illinois, who agreed to mentor him. He moved to Oregon in 1908 to assist churches at Adeline, Plum River, Antioch, Lanark, Ripley, Marshall, Salem and Dixon under Lindsay's supervision. George served as pastor at Oregon from 1911-1913. He was self-taught, yet his lack of public school education did not hinder him. George Eldred Marsh trained himself in the classics, and probably taught Greek and Latin at the academy. Marsh may have learned a great deal from A.J. Eychaner who had been a school teacher. While in Oregon George taught at Well's Academy on North Third Street. This building later became a nuns' residence for those teaching at the Catholic school. The house burned to its foundations a few years before this publication.

On September 18, 1912, G.E. Marsh married Miss Grace Mae Williams, daughter of Joseph H. Williams of Rochelle, Illinois. Grace's father should not be confused with J.W. Williams who sat on the Committee of Ten in 1920. Grace Marsh also sat on that committee to organize the Church of God General Conference.

Grace and her parents attended the Antioch Church of God east of Washington Grove between Oregon and Rochelle. They lived in Rochelle. When the Oregon Church of God grew and became more prominent throughout the movement, Antioch closed. The automobile had been invented by then, so the Williams motored to Oregon for church.

C. Return to Iowa

Grace was 12 years younger than her husband. In fact she was the youngest student of S.J. Lindsay's Summer Bible School for young adults in 1912, the summer she married George. George and Grace had one son, J. Arlen Marsh, born in Iowa in 1914.

The Marshes moved from Oregon to Marshalltown, Iowa, where the Iowa Conference soon elected George as its president and hired him as state evangelist. He preached at five churches: Marshalltown, Stanhope, Gladbrook, Hickory Grove and Avon. In 1918, his appointment as Nebraska evangelist took him to Holbrook and several other churches that year. A good report of the meetings was given at the Nebraska Conference. Owing to all the public meetings being "forbidden or discouraged" during the flu epidemic of 1918, he returned to Marshalltown until conditions improved.

The Marshes opened their home for committee meetings to plan the organization of the Church of God General Conference. During 1920, a committee of ten men and women representing churches from many sections of the country met to design a plan to form the General Conference. The plan was presented at the August 1921 Conference held in Waterloo, Iowa; the delegates accepted it. The General Conference formally came into being after all the state conferences ratified the action at Waterloo.

Marsh supported a national conference. As soon as it was established, he had his name added to the list of recognized ministers in 1921, a new service of the General Conference that benefited ministers. Up to this time they could only be recognized or licensed through local congregations or state conferences.

The Marsh family moved to upper New York and Fonthill, Ontario, in 1922 to assume the pastorate; they remained there for seven years. George accepted the pastorate when F.L. Austin left Fonthill to become executive secretary for the newly organized Church of God General Conference, headquartered at Oregon, Illinois.

D. Canadian Ministry

From Fonthill the family moved to Los Angeles where George pastored the Los Angeles Church of God. In 1931, they returned to Illinois where, on October 13, G.E. Marsh became editor of *The Restitution Herald* and pastor of the Oregon Church of God. During this time he worked with S.J. Lindsay to establish the Bible Training Class, forerunner of Oregon and Atlanta Bible Colleges.

In 1938, Pastor Marsh moved to Grand Rapids, Michigan, where he preached at Southlawn Church of God for two years. From there, he returned to Los Angeles to preach until 1942, and then he moved to Tipp City, Ohio, to pastor the Brush Creek Church of God. From there, the Marshes moved to Cleveland and served from 1948 to 1954. This was his last place of ministry.

G.E. Marsh authored a small lesson booklet, *First Principles.* It outlined the essential Bible doctrines held dear by the Church of God in 12 lessons to use in Sunday school, Berean or Bible study groups. He also authored a tract, "Words of Comfort," for the bereaved.

George prepared meticulously for preaching or teaching. The Archives at Atlanta Bible College holds a complete set of Marsh sermons. The set includes the outlines of every sermon and lesson he prepared, and if he preached it more than once, the date and location of the sermon presentation are included at the top of the page. Survey of each year's contents yields lessons prepared for the Bible Training Class covering biblical topics as well as pastoral duties. One lesson was entitled, "The Value and Purpose of Preaching." If any scholar has interest in writing a detailed biography of any Church of God preacher, G.E. Marsh is certainly an interesting subject, and the research fruitful because of Marsh's excellent organizational skills.

In late 1953, Pastor Marsh suffered a stroke, and in 1954, he and his wife moved to Rochelle, Illinois. During his illness he enjoyed a final visit from his brother Oscar. George died near the Thanksgiving holiday.

G.E. Marsh was a short quiet man who spoke his conviction. He had a literary writing and preaching style and liked the turn of a few good words to make an interesting sentence. Like his great uncle Joseph, G.E. Marsh enjoyed writing. He authored several tracts

---

G.E. Marsh loved writing poems. This poem may be sung to the tune of "My Country 'Tis of Thee" upon which it is based.

My Country
My country 'tis of thee,
Sweet land of liberty,
Of thee I sing.
This is my song today,
For thee I still shall pray,
Until our Lord for aye
Shall reign as King!

"My country" still 'twill be
Throughout eternity,
For Christ shall reign;
He whom we now adore,
Shall rule for evermore,
All lands from shore to shore
Bless'd be His name!

Ref.: Verse provided by Lois Cline, a friend, from her files.

and many articles for *The Restitution Herald* during his extensive career. As editor of *The Restitution Herald*, George published many doctrinal articles, but for the first time, he emphasized the church's history.

Marsh wrote a series of church history articles in 1930 to educate the readership on its "faith heritage" and how the Church of God fits into the historical framework of church history including American church history. He began with "Jewish Faith in Early Church" and "Faith of Church Fathers." During 1920, he also wrote a service manual for ministers, but it was mimeographed and did not hold up well. According to his son, J. Arlen, "The book was intended to provide suggestions, not to provide complete services for all occasions."

After George's death, Grace moved to Pinecrest Manor in Mt. Morris. Dr. Leila Whitehead and Evelyn Austin lived there at that same time. Grace remained active at the Oregon Church of God well into her nineties. She researched and wrote Church of God history and wrote a historical account. Some facts from it have been used for this encyclopedia.

George is buried at the Washington Grove Cemetery on Flagg Road in Ogle County. Also buried there are Grace's parents, John Cross and his family and many other members of the Antioch Church of God.

   See Cross, John (19th)
          Marsh, Edgar A. (19th)
          Marsh, Joseph (19th)
          Marsh, Grace
          Williams, J.H. (19th)
          Williams, J.W.

Bibliography: Ancestry.com. U.S. Census. Illinois Will. Plainfield. 1850; Ancestry.com U.S. Census. Iowa. Marshall. Marshall Ward 2. Dist. 163; U.S. Census. Iowa. Marshall. Marshall. Dist. 117. 1900; Burnett, Francis et al history committee, *History of the Iowa Church of God and Conference 1855-1987,* printed at Belle Plaine, Iowa 1987; Marsh Family for the ABC Biography Project, David Krogh, Compiler; *History of the Oregon Church of God*, History Committee, 1990; Interview with Grace Marsh by Jan Stilson, Pinecrest Manor. 1985; "Notice," *The Day Dawn and Harvest Messenger*, Jas. A. Patrick, ed., Minneapolis, Mn., Jan. 1918; *The Restitution* July 6, 1913; *The Restitution Herald*, Oct. 20, 1918; Sept. 9, 1924; Oct. 14, 1925 and various history articles 1930; "Obituary of Julius W. Marsh with poem by Jenny Marsh Parker," *The Prophetic Expositor and Bible Advocate*, Joseph Marsh, ed., Rochester, NY, Aug. 1, 1857; Marsh, George E. "Minister's Service Manual," Atlanta Bible College Archives, McDonough, Ga.; Marsh, G.E. "Words of Comfort," NBI, Oregon, Illinois; Marsh, G. E. "What Shall we Do?" *The Restitution Herald 75th Anniversary Issue,* Russell Magaw, ed., Oregon, Il., Oct. 1985; Marsh, G.E., *First Principles,* National Bible Institute, Oregon, Il., circa 1935; Marsh, J. Arlen. "Comment regarding Minister's Service Manual," *The Restitution Herald,* Sydney Magaw, ed., Oregon, Il., July 13, 1948; Marsh, Grace, Interview with Ivan Magaw, Mt. Morris, Illinois, Aug. 22, 1983; Hatch, Paul, Interview with Ivan Magaw, Oregon, Il., circa 1985.

Marsh, Grace Mae
b. June 7, 1891
d. September 29, 1993

Grace Marsh was born in Rochelle, Illinois, to Joseph H. and Alice Booth Williams. She grew up in the Church of God, attending the Antioch church on Flagg Road in Ogle County. This church was the local schoolhouse so it was busy every day of the week. (Note: When the congregation moved its activities to the Oregon Church of God around 1910, the Antioch school continued operating until around 1950. When the school was discontinued, the community moved the school to a private farm down the road where it has been remodeled for use as a tenant house or mother-in-law's residence.)

Grace met George E. Marsh when he was pastor of the Oregon, Illinois, Church of God (1911-1913). At the time he also taught at Wells Academy on North Third Street. She was several years younger than he, but it didn't matter. They married in Oregon on September 18, 1912. They had one son, J. Arlen.

The Marshes were instrumental in organizing the Church of God General Conference at Waterloo, Iowa, in 1921. Grace served on the Committee of Ten the previous year. This committee drew up plans for the new organization with much prayer and correspondence. When asked why this conference organization succeeded, unlike its predecessors, and continued to operate over the decades, she responded, "It was bathed in prayer."

After George's death on November 23, 1954, Grace remained in Rochelle. As she aged, she arranged to move to Pinecrest Manor in Mt. Morris, Illinois, a senior facility owned by the Church of the Brethren. This facility was convenient to the Oregon Church of God, and Grace continued to drive herself to church well into her nineties.

During her stay at Pinecrest, she gave several interviews to Church of God historians about her family and her role in organizing the General Conference. She had always been very interested in Church of God history since George was related to one of its founders, Joseph Marsh of Rochester, New York. None of her writings were published, but all of them, including her notes, are

George and Grace Marsh

held in the Atlanta Bible College Archives. During one interview, she donated a box of letters to the Archives detailing the work of the Committee of Ten. This material has provided many insights into the issues of the day and the ensuing struggles to establish a national work with a central headquarters office.

Grace died at Pinecrest at age 102. She is still fondly remembered and greatly missed. Her son and five grandchildren mourned her. Pastor Michael Hoffman conducted memorial services at Oregon Church of God. Grace donated her body to medical science.

See Marsh, George E.
Marsh, Joseph (19th)
Marsh, Joseph Arlen

Bibliography: Biography Project of Atlanta Bible College, David Krogh, compiler; Marsh, Grace, Interview with Jan Stilson, Pinecrest Manor, 1987.

Marsh, Joseph Arlen
b. 1914
d. March 28, 1998

J. Arlen Marsh was the son of George Eldred and Grace Williams Marsh who raised him in the Church of God. Like his great-great uncle, Joseph Marsh, and his father, J. Arlen liked to write and edit magazines and journals. He served as National Berean Society secretary for several years beginning in August 1929. He edited the Berean page in *The Restitution Herald*.

In 1946, the Bereans began a new magazine, *The Guiding Star*, with Arlen as editor from January 1947 until winter 1951. The magazine was published from Rockford, Illinois, where Arlen pastored the Blessed Hope church. *The Guiding Star* began as a 5" x 7" bulletin and progressed to magazine size with 16 pages. It included news from Berean groups around the nation, and Bible-related articles written by Oregon Bible College students or by other Bereans. Arlen also edited the *Truth Seeker's Adult Quarterly* from 1946-1950 and during this time wrote two short tracts, "Jehovah is One God" and "Thus it Becometh Us" about immersion.

Arlen married Beth Hoganson Hardesty, widow of Harold Hardesty, in May 1947. Harold died in the first Battle of France in WWII. Beth had attended Oregon Bible College and worked at the post office where she met Harold. They had only been married five months, and part of that time he was overseas. Beth and Arlen had six children, five survived into adulthood: Kevin, Richard, Bill, Dorene and Cheryl (Koryta).

J. Arlen and his family moved to Cleveland where he edited industrial publications. While living in Cleveland, they attended the Golden Rule Church of God. When the Bedford core group left Golden Rule, J. Arlen served as pastor from 1955-1959. The Bedford congregation rented the lower rooms of the Masonic Temple during 1959, moving into its present building in Bedford in October 1960. J. Arlen led the dedication service and served as pastor until 1963. He served as pastor of the Golden Rule congregation from 1973-1974, and again from 1977-1984, after which he retired.

Pastor Rex Cain offered celebratory comments to honor Arlen and Beth Marsh on their 50th anniversary on May 25, 1997, at the Bedford Church of God. He said:

(Arlen) served as secretary of our General Conference Board of Directors from 1947 to 1951. Beyond that, he assisted in a lot of our churches and spoke at many of our churches around the country throughout their active years. He retired in 1978. The Marsh name among theologians in our denomination and by members of long-standing, is instantly recognized and admired. Arlen's father, G.E. Marsh, and grandfather, Edgar Marsh, were also pastors in our denomination. Joseph Marsh, a great, great uncle of Arlen's (who lived in the mid 1800s) helped start the Church of God denomination.

Arlen Marsh continues to be well respected in the Church of God, following the example of his illustrious forefathers; readers are encouraged to study all the Marsh entries in this encyclopedia to understand the legacy. Arlen rests now rests with the Lord.

See Marsh, Grace
Marsh, George Eldred
Marsh, Joseph (19th)
Marsh, Edgar A. (19th)

Bibliography: ABC Biography Project provided excerpts for this article, David Krogh, compiler; Ancestry.com. Ohio Deaths 1958-2002; Ancestry.com U.S. Census. Iowa. Marshall. Marshall Ward 2. Dist. 163; Cain, Rex, "50th Anniversary Message to Honor Beth and J. Arlen Marsh at Bedford Church of God," May 25, 1997; Marsh, J. Arlen, "Jehovah is One God," National Bible Institute, Oregon, Il., no date; Interview of Beth Marsh by Jan Stilson, October 2007. *Cleveland Plain Dealer*, Obituary, April 1, 1998. *Plain Dealer* website; "The Guiding Star," notice in *The Restitution Herald*, Sydney Magaw, ed., Oregon, Il., October 8, 1947.

Mattison, Hazel Lindsay
b. July 30, 1895
d. March 8, 1979

Hazel was the daughter of Samuel J. and Nellie Lindsay of Oregon, Illinois. As a young single woman, she was active in the church and helped begin the Berean class at Oregon which strengthened the work of the Illinois Conference. Hazel assisted her generation in growing that work. At one conference, she served on the entertainment committee.

Hazel married Henry Mattison of Oregon. In his memoirs, their son James notes that she met Henry when he was in the Katherine Shaw Bethea hospital in Dixon. Hazel had earned her nursing certificate and she was Henry's nurse. They were so poor the first year of their marriage they camped in a tent on Margaret Fuller Island in the middle of the Rock River above the Oregon dam. Henry was a carpenter but a tent was the best home he could provide at that time.

When their first child was due, Henry rowed Hazel across the river where she was met by her father who took her home for the birth. Hazel and her family had a blessed life, its antics captured in detail in Jim's memoirs. The General Conference in McDonough, Georgia, sells the memoir. Reading it brings both laughter and tears.

Hazel's home in Oregon was often the focal point for theological discussions during conference weeks at the church. The ministers staying at the Mattison home brought guests in after church. They enjoyed Hazel's famous cookies and talked "theology," as granddaughter Jean Rencontre recalled. Among Hazel's favorite guests were Jim Mattison, Melville Lyon and Raymond Brown.

Hazel's children continued in ministry. James Mattison married, had a family and served as a pastor throughout the South in Texas, Louisiana and Virginia during the latter part of the 20th century. He is now retired and living in South Carolina, but still active in the African Mission work. Margaret trained at Normal Teacher's College in DeKalb, Illinois, now Northern Illinois University, as a cellist. She was a school music teacher for many years. After Margaret's first husband, Elroy Budrow, passed away Hazel raised Margaret's daughter Jean. Margaret married a second time to Ray Foster. She is now retired; twice widowed, she lives close to her children in Rochelle, Illinois.

Henry was a successful contractor in Oregon. In their elderly years Henry and Hazel moved to Holbrook, Nebraska, to be near Jean and her pastor husband, James Rencontre, pastor at the Holbrook Church of God. Hazel died in 1979. Her funeral was held at the Oregon Church of God. She was laid to rest at Riverview Cemetery north of town. Henry has rested beside her since 1984.

 See Brown, Raymond
   Foster, Margaret
   Lindsay, S.J. (19th)
   Lyon, Melville
   Mattison, James

Bibliography: Interment.net. Riverview Cemetery. Oregon, Il.; Mattison, James. *Memoirs of a Country Preacher*. Self published. 2006; *The Restitution Herald*, May 10, 1916; Rencontre, Jean. E-mail received July 25, 2010, and Aug. 21, 2010.

Mattison, James
b. February 24, 1924

A. Pastoral Ministry
B. African Mission Work
C. African Update from the Field

James "Jim" Mattison was born in Oregon, Illinois, to Henry and Hazel Mattison. He was the grandson of Samuel J. Lindsay, one of the key leaders in the organization of the Church of God as a national denomination.

Jim was an active boy and got into the normal amount of scraps and scrapes as he grew up in Oregon. He graduated Oregon Community High School and attended Oregon Bible College to train for the ministry.

He told many funny stories in his memoirs, *The Story of a Country Preacher,* published in 2005 and available from the General Conference office in McDonough, Georgia. One story involves Jim and a friend, Ivan Magaw. The two teens were hiking on Devil's Backbone, a well-known stretch of rugged road just south of Oregon and directly across the highway from Jim's home. The hilly country ends at a rocky point near Highway 2, with a high outcropping jutting over the valley and dominating the scenery as cars heading for Oregon round the curve. They hiked on a cold wet day, and as they neared the edge of the outcropping about 80' above the highway, Ivan slipped and fell over the face of the ridge. As he dangled there yelling to Jim for help, Jim said, "Hold on while I take a picture." Jim also had many funny stories to tell of his older sister Margaret, who was the "Chief."

A. Pastoral Ministry

Jim dedicated his life to serving the Lord as a pastor. In 1948, he wrote an article for *The Restitution Herald* that was a call to missions. He said we have a living Christ for a dead world. Following this, he and his new wife, Mary Helen Landry, moved to Texas where he became the evangelist for the state. It was during his service in Texas that he planted the churches at Riviera and Harlingen, and served churches at Gatesville and Corpus Christi, all a very great distance apart.

He and Mary Helen began their family in Texas. They had eight children, Mike, Ruth, Betsy, John, Ben, Steve, Tim and Rebekah (Martin). Until 1948, they served churches at Hammond and Blood River, Louisiana.

While in Texas, Jim explored becoming a missionary to Mexico. He went to the Mexico Consulate in New Orleans to investigate entering Mexico. The Mexican envoy said if Mexico needed any preaching the Catholic priests could do it. He told Jim if he wanted to enter Mexico he must have "Proof of support, written so that he would not become a burden on the state." Jim's interest lay in missions but it was not to be at that time or place.

Jim's grandfather, S.J. Lindsay, began the Oregon Church of God from a Methodist Bible class. Jim reversed the process and built up the Methodist church from good Church of God preaching. The story follows:

Jim moved further south in Texas to work with the Mexicans north of the border. At Riviera Mrs. Robbins helped him to get an appointment to preach and teach at the local Methodist church. The Methodists and the Church of God people worshipped together. Jim wrote in a letter:

> The Methodists had no minister at that time. I was good at leading children's choruses, and in the next year and three months the children's attendance increased. Adult attendance also increased. I preached the things I believed: the coming of Kingdom of God on earth, Jesus, all the truths we hold dear. The Methodist work improved to such an extent that the Methodist Bishop decided to send a minister there.

Jim and Mary Helen spent eight years at Harlingen, Texas, just north of Matamoras, Mexico. They built a small church building and fortified the congregation, including the baptisms of several Mexican children. They found it worked well to send the children back to their families to evangelize them. While in Harlingen, Jim compiled a subject concordance to the Bible and worked with the Texas Berean Youth. He worked hand in hand with Emory Macy, the Texas evangelist at that time. They arranged for teens to attend Youth Camp in the Midwest. Other ministers who served at Harlingen included Harry Goekler, Austin Railton and Billie Kennedy.

Jim and Mary Helen also served the Church of God in Christ Jesus at Maurertown, Virginia, from 1967-1973, following Eugene Stilson in that ministry. Others who served at Maurertown and Fort Valley included Alva Huffer, Dale Ward, J.R. LeCrone, Harry Sheets, Howard Beemer and Earl Thayer.

After Mary Helen's death, Jim married Martha Jones, widow of Loie Jones from Pelzer, South Carolina.

B. African Mission Work

Jim and Martha began to serve the Lord in the missionary work in Africa. Jim tells the history of that work in the following excerpt:

> In 1992 a man from France journeying by bus through Africa, saw Ferdinand Sakala standing at the Blanyre, Malawi bus station with his Bible under his arm. The Frenchman handed him a tract, "Who is Jesus," by Sir Anthony Buzzard, saying he might find it interesting, but not to believe it for it was against the trinity. Anthony's address was on the tract and Ferdinand wrote him for more Bible materials. Anthony sent him many Bible materials and continued to write him.
>
> In 1993, Anthony flew over there and looked at the opportunity. He taught Ferdinand and Margaret Sakala the saving Bible teachings for 15 days. They believed his teachings. They had a few churches and pastors under their care. They introduced them to the new teachings and all but three pastors came to believe it. Anthony returned in 1994. He wrote a glowing report in *The Restitution Herald/Progress Journal*.

Jim reported in a letter that he had always been interested in missions but had not been able to serve, and therefore, Africa interested him deeply. He wrote to the Sakalas and they invited him to come. Matthew 24:14 impacted him greatly. "This gospel of the Kingdom shall be preached in all the world as a witness to all people, and then shall the end come." He could not get it out of his mind. He felt the Lord was calling him to this mission. The story continues in his own words:

> I wrote people that God had called me to preach salvation in Africa and without my asking, money began to come in. As the days went on I thought, "How good it would be [if] Martha could share this experience with me." When her job at the Day Care ended, she was free to accompany me.
>
> In the summer of 1994 six people flew to Malawi: Anthony, Jim, Martha, Anthony's daughters, Claire and Sarah and Brett Leininger, a friend. It was on this trip that Martha's rare muscle deterioration disease first displayed itself. She could not lift a foot to enter the bus. They propped it on a suitcase so she could balance and step up. From that point on Martha's health became an issue. She died in October 2006.

Continuing:

> Starting in 1996…the African mission work was turned over to me. Both Anthony and I began sending Bible teachings to be translated into Chichewa, and printed into tracts. Fifty Bible teachings were being circulated in Malawi and Mozambique. At this time 100,000 tracts had been distributed, and packets have been given to 167 pastors in two countries. Rebekah and Dr. Joe Martin began accompanying us on the trips that year. The last few years they have been the team leaders.
>
> We began working with the Church of God General Conference mission department, the Lord's Harvest International. They have helped in developing teams and raising money. A team goes every year now. Anthony continues to visit the work and Bob Gilbert and Don Smith have flown over to teach several times.
>
> There are now seven African Boards over the work in Malawi and Mozambique. This is helping them to take over the work and they are learning to make decision about which needs are the most important. We honor their decisions, whether it is to buy land for a church, buy a new bicycle, build a church or print tracts. At present six churches are under construction. We buy the cement and the metal roof sheets, while they make and fire the bricks, pay the mason and carpenter, the roof timbers and the nails.
>
> New African opportunities have arisen. The Swahili-speaking people of Tanzania, Kenya, Ghana and other African countries are indicating interest. Anne Mbeke from Kenya, a student at Atlanta Bible College, has translated fifty tracts into Swahili. Sarah Buzzard puts them into the computer in tract form, and Joe Martin prints them at ABC for .03 apiece.
>
> God is blessing the preaching of His Word in Africa. His name is being magnified as well as the name of His Son, the Lord Jesus. The people are given hope, as the Gospel is preached. From the beginning the two main Bible teachings have been stressed: Jesus' Gospel of the Kingdom of God and the name of Jesus (Acts 8:12).

C. African Update from the Field

To illustrate the difficulty of the African work, we include a brief excerpt from one of Pastor Mattison's updates dated January 2008:

> It has been over 5 months since last we sent a MAM update. The reason is because communication with Malawi and Mozambique is so difficult. The cell phone towers do not work well. Some of the main pastors have no address, and most of them do not understand English. We have heard from three, however, and this is what we have learned: The three churches in Mozambique are completed. Pastor Lomosi's is bricked up to the roof level. In Malawi, Christina's church, Frazer's church, the church in Daud's area, and the church in Moyo's area are completed.
>
> Prices differ in different areas. One letter stated that cement was not available in Malawi; it had to be brought in from Mozambique. Also, cement has jumped from K1500 a bag to K2,050 a bag ($10.63 to $14.53). Then there is money for transportation to the building site. The comment was made that they could not carry the cement or the iron roof sheets on their heads (and we add, on bicycles, either), which is true. The cost to build a church in these two countries now ranges from $1231.92 to $1893.62, depending on the area in which it is built and the size of the church. Presently, the Malawi kwacha is 141 to $1 American. These are two of the poorest countries on earth. Yet the people are friendly and happy. They eat mostly out of their gardens.
>
> Another printing has been made of 200 of each of the tracts on 50 major Bible teachings (total 10,000). My End-Time prophecy book has been translated and is to be printed this week. The cost of printing is our second largest expense. Some of Anthony's books are also in Chichewa. He and Don also teach here. Three bicycles were given. We've already reported before that one was given to Nyambalo's widow, and one to Namaona's wife, Gracie, who accompanies him as they visit the churches under him. She can read and write English, and is a big help to her husband in the work. He is one of the main baptizers. His river has no crocodiles. Bicycles range from $53 to $71, depending whether they are bought in the city or in the country.
>
> We have found that the 100 or so pastors truly want to serve God. It amazes me how these men become pastors. It is exactly according to 2 Timothy 2:2: a man hears the gospel, and goes and tells others, who in turn tell others. Everything we do in the mission work in Africa is centered around teaching the gospel of the Kingdom of God and the name of Jesus Christ-- helping build the churches, printing Bible teachings in Chichewa and Swahili, digging wells, helping in flood and famine, giving bicycles, paying for the food of those who come long distances to the conferences, even paying for coffins for our beloved and faithful pastors when they die.
>
> One of our greatest needs is a full-time administrator over there, to give funds for projects approved by the Board and to send us reports of the progress of the mission work. Linda has been doing that but she is so involved now with organizing the women in the churches to do good works we can't ask her to do this, too. This is a valuable work she is doing: teaching the women to pray for their pastors and the churches, carrying water to the infirm, visiting the sick, thatching roofs for invalids. She is also teaching the women how to read so they, too, can read their Bibles. And her goal is to have a "Lazarus" school for the orphans in every church as it is in Machemba's church, which takes care of 38 orphans. Several have been baptized because of this effort.

Wherever he served, Jim's ministry was characterized by dedication and energy. He worked tirelessly to serve the Lord well into his elderly years. He trusted the Lord to carry him through the difficult times and he looked forward to meeting the Lord in the air when he returns to gather his children to him.

See Foster, Margaret
　　　Huffer, Dr. Alva
　　　LeCrone, J.R.
　　　Lindsay, S.J.
　　　Mattison, Hazel
　　　Mattison, Mary Helen Landry
　　　Sheets, Harry
　　　Stilson, Eugene
　　　Ward, Dale

Bibliography: Harrison, Bert. E-mail to JStilson with Mary Helen birth and death dates, April 30, 2008; Mattison, James "A Living Christ for a Dead World," *The Restitution Herald*, Sydney Magaw, ed., Oregon, Il., March 23, 1948; Mattison, James, Letter to Jan Stilson for the *History Newsletter*, "History of Texas Work," May 14, 1994; Mattison, James, *Memoirs of a Country Boy*, Self-published. 2005; Mattison, James, "History of the African Mission Work" e-mail report Oct. 28, 2006; Mattison, James, "Malawi African Missions, Inc. Update," Jan. 31, 2008; Various e-mails to JStilson, 2006-2011.

Mattison, Mary Helen Landry

b. September 1, 1926
d. April 16, 1983

James Mattison wrote about his wife:

Mary Helen was born in Hammond, Louisiana, to Gustav and Addie Alexander Landry. There were five brothers, three older and two younger: Bob, C.G., Jerry, Gordon and Preston, and a sister who died before age two. Gustav Landry was a barber and had a shop on Thomas Street in Hammond. His brother, Warren, was also a barber. They married sisters: Addie and Elvie. All were members of the Happy Woods Church of God just outside Hammond. Two of the outstanding pastors from that time were Harry Goekler and Vernis Wolfe.

Mary Helen attended Hammond schools, walking a mile each way, and graduating in 11 years. She was baptized by Harry Goekler when a teenager. The year following graduation, Mary worked as bookkeeper for H.D. Himel, a NAPA auto parts business.

When I was a senior at Oregon Bible College, Mary Helen came to Oregon, Illinois, as a freshman. I had never met her before. Backtracking my life somewhat, when I was 16 Brother C.E. Lapp had a class for us young people at General Conference in Oregon. He said, "You young people are going to think about getting married someday, and you need to ask God's help to lead you to the right partner." I took his advice, praying for the next five years that God would lead me to the right girl for me. As I met new Church of God girls, I would wonder if this was the one God had for me. Mary Helen was God's answer. We were engaged December 3, 1944, and married Easter Sunday, April 1, 1945, by Brother Vernis Wolfe in the Happy Woods Church after the evening service.

Mary Helen was the mother of eight children: Mike, Ruth, Rebekah, Betsey, Ben, John, Steve and Tim. She loved husband and children dearly and provided for us in every way. She was an expert seamstress and made over many clothes for the children and herself. She taught our girls to sew. During the 38 years we had together, I am sure she never bought more than five or six new dresses for herself. She always looked neat and attractive, and saw to it that the children and I looked nice. As I was a carpenter as well as a pastor, it fell to her to do most of the raising of the children. She gave them a wonderful legacy of faith, love and discipline. She had such a sweet spirit. Everyone who knew her loved her. She was always so glad to see people and greeted them warmly.

Mary Helen was very active in God's service, leading Bible schools in the places we pastored: Harlingen, Texas, eight years; Louisiana, 14 years; Virginia, 11 years; Burr Oak, Indiana, six years; and until she died. After the children were older, she held women's home Bible classes in Virginia and Indiana. She converted at least two people, perhaps more.

In September 1982 doctors diagnosed melanoma in her left sinus. Despite prayers and treatments, she succumbed in April 1983. Twice before, in 1960 and 1964, through the prayers of the elders and the faithful and by the God's mercy, she had survived mortal sicknesses.

God gave us a wonderful life together. Mary Helen was the ideal wife, full of faith, happy while living on less, taking care of the family in every way. She never complained, not even while dying. She had such a wonderful sweet spirit and was loved dearly by all who knew her. This was shown during her last illness when individuals and churches from all over the country contributed more than $16,000 toward the bills for the cancer treatments. I have said many times that she was one in a million. She truly was.

James Mattison contributed this entry.

See Goekler, Harry
     Lapp, C.E.
     Mattison, James
     Wolfe, Vernis

Bibliography: Mattison, James for the Atlanta Bible College Biography Project, David Krogh, compiler.

McCall, Ralph Huston, Jr.
b. April 19, 1930
d. October 24, 1990

Ralph McCall was born in the White Plains community of Pelzer, South Carolina, the only child of Ralph Huston McCall Sr. and Annie Belle Smith McCall. He attended White Plains School, graduating in 1947.

He married Evelyn Coker on October 29, 1948. Pastor Oliver Williamson of Guthrie Grove Church of God performed the ceremony. Ralph attended that church and served as song clerk for many years. Ralph also served in the Korean War. Afterward he continued his education and graduated from Forrest College. Ralph worked with Milliken Company for 36 years while still pursuing his education. He received numerous awards of merit.

Ralph and Evelyn had two daughters and two granddaughters. He shared his faith with his co-workers and loved music. Ralph played the piano; his favorite song was "The Longer I Serve Him, the Sweeter He Grows." Ralph was active in the church where he served as deacon and chairman of deacons for a number of years, and Sunday school teacher of Adult Class No. 3.

Always ready with a smile and handshake, Ralph had love and compassion for his fellowmen and church family. He was a loving and caring husband and father. Likewise, all who knew him loved and respected him. Guthrie Grove Church building fund received more than $3,000 in memorials after his death.

Bibliography: McCall, Evelyn for the ABC Biography project, David Krogh, compiler.

McCoy, Andrew Weldon
b. March 7, 1898
d. July 7, 1987

A. Missouri Ministry
B. Relationships that Endure
C. Retirement

A. Weldon McCoy was born in Piedmont, South Carolina, and was a member of the Guthrie Grove Church of God at Pelzer, South Carolina. At some point, he left the South and became a pastor working among the churches in Indiana and Missouri.

In 1920, a notice in *The Restitution Herald* stated the South Carolina Bereans had written a statement of faith and that persons interested in obtaining a copy in tract form should write to A.W. McCoy in Piedmont. He was president of the Berean Society at that time. A couple years later, Weldon called for a card shower for Pastor A.N. Durham in celebration of his birthday on December 25, 1923.

Church of God pastors who worked throughout Indiana and across the South influenced A. Weldon McCoy. Men such as F.L. Austin, the second editor of *The Restitution Herald*; Sydney Magaw, succeeding editor after Austin; and L.E. Conner worked to influence younger men. They taught at the newly formed Bible Training School and its successor, Oregon Bible College. Records indicate A.W. McCoy attended L.E. Conner's funeral at Macy, Indiana, May 1943.

A. Missouri Ministry

Wanda Westbrook Gerullis, a little girl at the time of Weldon McCoy's ministry in Missouri, recalled in 2008 that he came to Missouri as a circuit preacher funded by the Southeast Conference.

He invigorated the work in Morse Mill, Lockwood, Doniphan, Festus, St. Louis and Fredericktown, Missouri. He visited each of the churches in rotation and preached in a radio ministry. Weldon believed in the Kingdom of God on earth and produced audiotapes from his sermons on the subject. Pastor McCoy's daughter owns these tapes and loaned them to Wanda Gerullis of St. Louis for the transcription/publication project.

Wanda wrote this in the preface to the book she published for the benefit of the youth of Missouri in the Church of God:

> In the late 40s and 50s Brother McCoy broadcast the "Voice of Bible Truth" from radio stations in Festus and Sullivan, Missouri. Many of the broadcasts were live, and he sang along with family groups from the Morse Mill (Westbrook family) and Doniphan (Roger family) congregations. In the old church building at Morse Mill, he could make the windows rattle when he sang (to the delight of the children) and some local people who would not step into a church building on a Sunday morning would gather in the churchyard just to hear him sing! He would remind those inside the building that God works in mysterious ways.
>
> One tape mentions radio station WCMR in Elkhart, Indiana. One includes the Guthrie Grove church choir of Pelzer, South Carolina singing "Coming". In most of the tapes he tells of his gratitude to supporters in Indiana and South Carolina for making the broadcasts possible.
>
> The closing prayer of programs is included as offered. During the prayer time in local worship services, Brother McCoy stood among us with right hand raised and open, palm down. With all heads bowed there was a sense of close intimacy and sheltered unity.

In the early days of radio, a preacher went to a small local station where the programs were broadcast live. The recording technology in radio stations developed first as 16" vinyl albums recorded on one side (1940s-50s), and later as reel-to-reel tapes. The master of the 16" vinyl disk was cut at the radio station usually on one side only. See the Harold Doan entry for additional impact of radio in the Church of God.

Weldon's preaching style was biblical and included many anecdotes and illustrations. The people loved him. The radio transcriptions show the message of the Gospel of the Kingdom on earth was very important to him as he shared with his radio audience how to become Christian and why it was vital. He also preached about baptism, sleep of the dead and the second coming of Jesus.

Wanda Gerullis has transcribed his radio broadcasts and published them in a book, *Voice of Bible Truth*. The book also includes copies of some of the tracts he wrote. He authored "What is the Soul," "A Change in Government is Coming," "Immortality—is it Conditional or Inherent," "The Translation of Enoch" and others. Money earned from the book sales went into the treasury of the Church of God Youth of Missouri. The following is a portion of a Weldon sermon, "Christian Baptism":

> If pouring is the correct form of baptism, then sprinkling is not. If sprinkling is the correct form, then pouring is incorrect. If baptism means "to make whelmed or fully wet," then neither pouring nor sprinkling is correct.
>
> The apostle Peter tells, in I Peter 3:10, as the eight souls were saved by water in the days of Noah that the like figure now saves us. According to this evaluation of baptism the act of being made whelmed or full wet is a very important step to take if one is to be saved. The word "whelm" means to cover or engulf in water. If the word baptize has always meant to whelm or make fully wet, why have men jeopardized the future life of millions by teaching that sprinkling or pouring is baptism?

In this manner, he evangelized the message of the Gospel of the Kingdom, thereby increasing and stabilizing the work of the church and of the Missouri Conference.

B. Relationships that Endure

Titles of other radio broadcasts of Weldon's sermons include "The Second Coming and Signs of the Times," "Sowing and Reaping" and "Does it Matter What we Believe?" Each is filled with references to the Kingdom of God on earth, which Christ is coming to establish and to begin the restitution of all things.

McCoy performs a baptism in Missouri with ministers Alva Huffer and Ellsworth Routson in attendance.

While working in Missouri, Weldon often stayed with Emmett Westbrook's family. Church members usually hosted evangelists, providing them with warm beds, good meals and Christian fellowship. Often churches sprang up around the nucleus of one Christian family who hosted visits from a circuit preacher and who invited neighbors to preaching or Bible study at their home.

Pastor McCoy baptized the three eldest Westbrook daughters, Alice, Wanda and Mary Lou, and many other members as well. He dressed comfortably for baptisms in bib overalls, because if they got wet no damage was done. Wanda described Weldon as a friendly man, outgoing and boisterous. To her he seemed "portly" in size. He had a youthful look about him, but he was balding.

Glenda Westbrook Turner said that Weldon was a great encouragement to her family. She fondly remembered vacations to the Indiana farm during the summer and shared laughs over her little radio solo of "This little light of mine" when she was four years old. Weldon loved playing that particular tape as she was growing up. He so loved working with the Missouri churches and the radio program he and wife Gertie moved to Morse Mill to be closer to the work. The Morse Mill Church of God had been closed in the 1930s, but Weldon thought it should be reopened and the work given a fresh start. He obtained a key to the building, and one day, he and the Westbrooks drove to the church. The door, badly warped and stuck shut, was forced open. It was dark and gloomy inside, spooky to the children. Everything was boarded up and they had to use flashlights. Soon, with commitment and hard work, the church was freshened up and services began again. Weldon named Wes Westbrook as elder. Wes agreed, and when Weldon wasn't preaching, Wes did. Wes and his wife Pat ran the Sunday school and soon the church was thriving.

Glenda, then a toddler, enjoyed standing beside Weldon when he preached, much to her mother's concern, but Weldon would say, "Pat, she's alright." Glenda sat inside the pulpit while he preached. She wrote, "He was truly a loving man—most of my best childhood memories include him."

C. Retirement

In 1953, Weldon McCoy left Missouri and returned to his Indiana roots on the farm near Bourbon. A youthful Alva Huffer, who was to become the foremost author in the Church of God in the 20th century, replaced him at Morse Mill.

For several years Weldon pastored at North Salem which is located along old Route 31 just north of Plymouth, Indiana. He also preached at the Kokomo church after Leon Driskill left in 1953. Weldon was well known to Harvey Krogh Jr., the pastor at Hope Chapel in

McCoy family

South Bend, and to other pastors in the state. In Missouri there had been no pastoral network.

During the Indiana years, Weldon wrote for a small mimeographed bi-monthly paper from the South, *The Gospel Messenger*, edited by Pastor T.A. Drinkard of Arlington, Texas. These articles were as short as one typed page, but the subjects were weighty and influential and included these titles: "Melchisedec," "The Spirits in Prison (I Peter 3:18-20)," "Paul's Desire to Depart and be With Christ (Philippians 1:20-24)," "Bliss or Blisters," "The Thief on the Cross" and "The Value of Your Faith." Pastor McCoy's short articles cut a wide swath, for the editor of *The Gospel Messenger* received several letters of appreciation for McCoy's writing. In October 1961 Elder Drinkard wrote:

> We are sincerely glad to have Bro. McCoy's article on the question that he presented. We regret that our short space does not allow a more lengthy article. Letters have come to us appreciating his treatise on the translation of Enoch—by faith. Even one from NE Canada from a young man in the Navy service. The subject appealed to him.

As Weldon aged, he and Della, his second wife, left the farm and retired from the ministry. They settled in South Bend. A.W. McCoy was returned to his home church for burial and lies beside his wife at the Guthrie Grove cemetery in Pelzer, South Carolina. The epitaph inscribed on their tombstone reads: At Rest.

See Austin, F.L.
 Conner, L.E. (19th)
 Doan, Harold
 Drinkard, T.A.
 Driskill, Leon
 Durham, A.N.
 Huffer, Dr. Alva
 Krogh, Harvey U., Jr.
 Westbrook, Emmett

Bibliography: Bass, Jennifer, Relative of A.W. McCoy e-mail, Jan. 3 and 6, 2011; Biography Project of Atlanta Bible College, Record of Emmett Westbrook as contributed by Glenda Turner, David Krogh, compiler; Gerullis, Wanda, transcriber, "Voice of Bible Truth," and phone interview March 14, 2008; Turner, Glenda. "Weldon McCoy" e-mail sent to Jan Stilson with more memories of Weldon, January 25, 2008; Obituary of L E. Conner lists A. Weldon McCoy as being in attendance at the funeral service, *The Restitution Herald*, 1943; North Salem Expansion project, Dedication Service booklet, June, 1985;

McCoy, A. Weldon. Several short articles in *The Gospel Messenger*, 1960-1961, and perhaps other years as well, T.A. Drinkard, ed., Arlington, Texas; McCoy, A. Weldon, "Statement of Faith," *The Restitution Herald*, Church of God General Conference, Oregon, Il., Jan. 20, 1920, March 20, 1920 and Dec. 11, 1923; Snyder, Janet, Updated History of the Maple Grove Community Church, from an earlier history by Edgar Harvey, courtesy of Pastor Dale Bliss, May 1, 2010.

McKnight, Wilsey
b. May 23, 1914
d. February 9, 2004

Wilsey McKnight was born and raised in Moorefield, Nebraska. He was distinguished within the community because his grandfather, Robert McKnight, had been Buffalo Bill's friend. In fact, Moorefield sprang up near Medicine Creek where there had been much "Wild West" and Indian activity. If there was to be a US settlement, they needed a post office. Robert McKnight became the first postmaster at Moorefield.

Wilsey learned history from his family, and he was taught Bible stories, too. The following comes from a pamphlet published after Wilsey's death: "A preacher, named Rev. Geesler (Giesler) helped him put living and dieing into perspective, telling him that life is only a test for eternity. That Jesus was soon to return to gather his faithful followers." E.E. Giesler baptized Wilsey.

Wilsey decided he wanted to become a preacher. He preached at the Minnesota Conference in 1936 and met a beautiful young woman of faith, Merelle Thoms. They soon wed, and then went off went to college in Aurora, Illinois. The Bible Training Class at Oregon, Illinois, was closed at that time due to the Great Depression; the board authorized Aurora College to train young men for the Church of God ministry. One of Wilsey's Aurora classmates was Vivian Kirkpatrick Sr. of Minnesota.

Two small rural churches benefited from Wilsey's preaching, the Burr Oak Church of God in Indiana and the Church of God at Ripley, Illinois. After graduating from Aurora College, however, Wilsey chose to preach for the Advent Christian denomination, which owned and operated Aurora College.

Moving to Kansas City, Kansas, the young family struggled financially while he preached there. Other places he preached included Sumas, Washington; Denver, Colorado; and a church planting experience in Chicago, Illinois. When Wilsey was 50, the family moved to New England where Merelle studied to become a registered nurse, and Wilsey pursued a master's degree. Not yet done with education, at age 74, he decided to pursue a doctorate and entered Gordon Cromwell seminary in New England.

Throughout Wilsey's life he maintained ties with his Church of God friends in Moorefield and Holbrook. He attended Ed Bender's graduation from Oregon Bible College in 1967 as a friend of the family, and in June 1996, he conducted David R. Bender's funeral at Moorefield.

Wilsey died after a short illness leaving many friends and family to mourn his death. Some remarked: "The boy did leave Medicine Creek, but Medicine Creek never left the boy. The skills taught by the pioneers of Medicine Creek served him well."

See Bender, David
Giesler, E.E. (19th)

Bibliography: "The boy from Medicine Creek who left home to follow Jesus" author unknown, written as a memorial to Wilsey McKnight following his death, Feb. 9, 2004, presented by Ed Bender at the 2d annual History Conference, North Hills Church of God, Springfield, Oh., Nov. 6-7, 2007.

McLain, Cecil Alan
b. 1911
d. January 2, 1976

C. Alan and James McLain were brothers born to Mr. and Mrs. Lenvil D. McLain in Brown County near Mt. Sterling. Illinois. Mr. McLain was a farmer. The family attended services at the Ripley Church of God. There they learned Bible doctrines pertaining to the coming Kingdom of God on earth. They also learned and shared beautiful music. Both men were especially talented vocalists to the delight of both congregation and community. Alan and James attended Oregon Bible College when it reopened in 1941. After college they prepared for the work of an evangelist and pastor. Alan presided at the 50th Anniversary celebration at Dixon on October 5, 1941. James became an evangelist and worked throughout Illinois and Missouri.

Within two weeks of the Dixon anniversary celebration, Alan married Virginia Lee Smith (b. December 8, 1918) on October 19, 1941 at Fredericktown, Missouri. Virginia's father was H. Scott Smith an Arkansas evangelist. The McLain's moved to Dixon, Illinois, to serve the Church of God. Virginia had several heart defects, and when she became ill with measles it proved fatal. This was a great sorrow to the young pastor.

Alan married Doris Smith. They had one daughter, Alana. Alan continued preaching at McGintytown and Russellville, Arkansas, into the 1970s until he was too old to make the trip. He usually took the bus.

During their years of service, both McLain sons thrilled Church of God members with their tireless energy and great talents for preaching and singing. Their aging parents became residents of the Golden Rule Home at Oregon, Illinois, where they lived out their retirement years in comfort and fellowship with other believers.

Pastors Dean Moore and Danny Landry conducted Alan's funeral service from the McGintytown Church of God. Alan is interred in Rest Haven Memorial Cemetery at Russellville, Arkansas.

See McLain, James Smith, H. Scott

Virginia and Alan McLain

Bibliography: Ancestry.com U.S. Census. Illinois. Brown. Cooperstown Tp. 1920. *The Restitution Herald*, "A Peek into the Golden Rule Home" date unknown. This article was found in the scrapbook of Jessie M. Wilson; Kirkpatrick, Judy. E-mail about C. Alan and James W. McLain, June 28, 2009; "We are pleased to honor McGintytown Church of God" and, "Oak Grove Church of God," *The Restitution Herald*, Oregon, Il., Oct. 1974, and Dec. 1974.

McLain, James W.

b. December 19, 1908
d. January 1, 2002

James McLain was born and raised at Ripley, Illinois, and a member of the Church of God as a youth. He was a gifted musician and successful in Chicago radio. While living in the city, he met and married a woman who proved to be worldly. He said later that she had the maturity of a 12-year-old. After a stormy and unhappy marriage, they divorced and he left the city. At that time, he turned his attention toward working with the Church of God.

Church of God General Conference appointed Jim as evangelist as part of their emphasis on evangelism beginning in 1948. He began his work under Sydney Magaw's administration. Magaw was editor and publisher of *The Restitution Herald* and instructor at Oregon Bible College. Jim organized and stabilized churches.

Jim was an excellent teacher and persuasive preacher due to his Bible study skills. He was attractive and popular, skilled at making contacts and in influencing people. He began programs and implemented them, nurturing the Churches of God, encouraging their pastors and being welcomed everywhere he went. He even conducted music classes at various churches. He pastored at the Burr Oak, Indiana, and the Delta, Ohio, Churches of God Jim served as an evangelist in nearly every Church of God from coast to coast. In 1949, he was asked to give the commencement address at OBC graduation. That year's graduating class included Kirby Davis, Gordon Landry, Ernest Graham and Arnold Johns.

Evangelist McLain often traveled with state evangelists and served as their music director. While the evangelists were gifted in preaching, not all had Jim's gift for music. He often traveled with F.L. Austin in this capacity, especially as Austin began to age.

Mr. and Mrs. Lenvil McLain of Ripley, parents of Alan and James

When Jim worked in Arkansas, he particularly influenced Pete McGinty. Pete was baptized, but he didn't fully understand the importance of the Abrahamic Faith. Jim impressed on him the importance of the Abrahamic Covenant to Jews and Christians. After that, Pete and Jim became friends. When Jim began the first Sunday school at McGintytown, he told Pete he'd have to be the superintendent. Pete said, "I ain't educated." Jim said, "You got to." Pete did it, and it's thrived ever since.

Jim retired from the pastoral ministry and, for a time, settled in Alliance, Nebraska, and finally in Pine Bluff, Wyoming, with his wife. He authored a booklet, "The Covenants of God," which was published in *The Honest Truth*, edited by Terry Ferrell in the 1970s.

In the mid-1980s Jim contacted the publisher of the Church of God General Conference's *History Newsletter* and offered rare materials to the Atlanta Bible College Archives. He had been saving the box of archival materials many years. Over two telephone interviews he relayed his joys and sorrows of serving in the Church of God ministry and negotiated the terms for donating the

McLain family

materials. When they arrived at the archives, they were examined for historical significance. The cache included tracts, books and journals that were unique, among them a single 1895 issue of *The Glad Tidings of the Kingdom*, Council Grove, Kansas, J.B. Craton, editor. This paper was previously unknown and had never been seen by historians before. This issue mentioned the names of many Church of God members and friends including W.H. Eisenhower of Abilene, Kansas, a cousin to President Dwight D. Eisenhower.

The James McLain family in 1944

Terry Ferrell, noted Church of God historian, knew James McLain as a personal friend, and related many details of McLain's ministry. When Jim died, Pastor Ferrell said he "felt he had lost half of himself." The heritage of Jim's ministry is preserved in the movies of Melville Lyon's evangelistic trips throughout the Churches of God in the 1940s. Lyon was the moviemaker, but McLain was the featured subject. Some of the movies feature Jim's sermons and others his fine solos. These movies have been restored and will be reformatted on DVD for use on Church of God broadcasts and websites.

See Austin, F.L.
 Craton, J.B. (19th)
 Graham, Ernest
 Lyon, Melville
 Magaw, Sydney
 McLain, C. Alan
 Eisenhower, W.H. (19th)

Bibliography: McLain, James, Interview with JStilson, 1985-1990; "OBC News," *The Restitution Herald*, Sydney Magaw, ed., Oregon, Il., June 2, 1949; Hummel, Betty Blackwell, Letter to Jan Stilson, Aug. 30, 1994; Ferrell, Terry. Interview with Jan Stilson, July 17, 2009, and e-mail regarding "The Covenants of God," Jan. 4, 2011; "We are pleased to honor Burr Oak Church of God," *The Restitution Herald*, Oregon, Il., Oct. 1975; Weaver, Archard and Clara, Memories of People and the Church at McGintytown, from the Anniversary celebration, Summer 2010, sent by Pastor Tom New.

McLeod, Norman
b. March 15, 1896
d. May 2, 1955

Norman McLeod was known throughout the Church of God as pastor of the new church in Los Angeles. He was the youngest of four children born to Donald and Rachel (Adamson) McLeod with an older brother Roy, and sisters Marjorie (Ferrell), Terry Ferrell's mother, and Florence (Emery). Norman attended Pomona public schools and a school operated by Bernard McFadden in Chicago. Norman aspired to become either a doctor or a concert pianist. He maintained a lifelong interest in music.

Norman served in the Army Medical Corps during WWI, training at Letterman General Hospital in San Francisco. He was a sergeant commanding a way station near the front lines in France, replacing dressings, etc., for the wounded in transit to hospitals. Upon his return from France, Norman enrolled at the University of California in Los Angeles and graduated valedictorian of his class in 1926. He majored in English with emphasis in public speaking.

In 1920, Norman attended church conference in Long Beach, California, where he met Leta Railsback. S.J. Lindsay performed their wedding ceremony on New Year's Day in 1921. The young couple settled in Los Angeles, and attended the local Church of God. Leta's parents helped to begin the Los Angeles church.

Norman and Leta had six sons, in chronological order: Kenneth, Malcolm, Duncan, Donald, John and Ross. Donald died in childhood, and John died in 1987. They also had a daughter who was stillborn. The family lived in Pomona on Norman's mother's estate. When he inherited the house and land it came with a $3,000 mortgage, and America was in the depths of the Great Depression. The mortgage was substantial in those days.

Norman was unable to work full-time due to a disability from a thyroid ailment that damaged his kidneys and required thyroid surgery. He wanted to study for a doctorate at Stanford but was denied admission because of his age. Earning income to support his family was a considerable problem. Fortunately Norman's health was good enough for him to be a substitute teacher. Leta perfected her gardening skills and nurtured the avocado orchard on their property. They gained some income from these activities, and Leta was always able to feed their growing family. She also baked bread and pies and gained customers for her baked goods. In this way, the family survived and enjoyed the pleasures of a lovely

Left - Two young men at Bible Training Class in 1947. Right - Mildred Dennis and friend await the next class at the 1947 Bible Training Class.
Photos from Mildred Dennis

home. Norman also worked as a Boy Scout Executive for in Strathmore and Porterville in the San Joaquin Valley, but he had to resign because of his health.

The McLeods and the Adamsons were very active church members. Their original affiliation was with the Christadelphians, but they were expelled from that group and joined the Church of God during the 1920s. They had a rotation of lay speakers for many years that included J.E. Adamson, George Lichty and Norman.

The church at Los Angeles invited Norman to be pastor in 1932. He was glad for the opportunity to preach, but it meant commuting from Pomona, sometimes several times a week. He earned $75 a month from the position and continued as pastor until 1938. During his tenure, he joined church activities across the nation by attending conferences and participating in evangelistic tours. In 1933, Midwest churches invited him to preach. The whole family, including Leta's parents, filled several cars and drove to Illinois and Indiana. Norman preached at Oregon, Illinois; North Salem in Plymouth, Indiana; Brush Creek, Ohio; and Holbrook, Nebraska. That summer he also preached at several state conferences.

In 1935, Norman traveled to the Northwest and participated in evangelism as a speaker for the conference at Corvallis, Oregon. Emma Railsback was instrumental in beginning the Bible group at Corvallis. Norman and Leta were excellent musicians and often performed together in musicals and plays. They also sang at church, and it was said that Norman was a natural showman and never experienced stage fright.

In 1938, Norman was appointed as Superintendent of Parks in Pomona. With their special expertise in gardening and their local reputation for such, Leta also became involved, planning a training program through the National Youth Administration. The Federal government funded this project. Through their efforts, parks were upgraded throughout Pomona and many people were taught how to plant and maintain gardens.

At the beginning of WWII Norman began to work as an arc welder at the California Shipyard in Long Beach. He also worked at other shipyards. For the first time in their lives, they became reasonably prosperous. After the war, he developed a landscaping, planting and maintenance business. This was very hard work, and he endured it only two years.

Norman supported the newly organized Oregon Bible College in every way possible. He prevailed upon his nephew Terry Ferrell to attend Summer Bible School in Oregon, the forerunner of National Youth Camp. Terry stayed and attended Oregon Bible College, becoming a Church of God minister, editor and historian after graduation. The story goes that another Summer Bible School student, Vernis Wolfe from Texas, and Norman originated the idea of developing a National Youth Camp. Vernis began the Southwest Youth Camp.

Norman had many friends from the Church of God in Arizona. The church in Tempe invited him to dedicate its parsonage in 1949. While there, he and several others collaborated and organized the Southwest Conference of the Church of God. The first conference was held in 1950 but the formal organization did not happen until 1955.

In time, Norman and Leta returned to Oregon to participate in the youth rally, an annual event becoming popular among teens and young adults throughout the Church of God. Through visits east such as this, their son Malcolm met Sybil Stilson from South Bend, Indiana, and the two eventually married. Church of God youth events often led to relationships between youths of like-precious faith. Via these marriages within the church biological growth of the denomination is sustained.

From left: Cecil Smead, John Hammond, Norman McLeod and George Lichty in Los Angeles, circa 1930.
Photo from John Smead

As the work in the Southwest developed, Norman hoped to participate in it. Unfortunately, the kidney damage he endured so many years became acute and led to his death at age 59. His sudden loss caused a great void in the family's life, especially Leta's. She had studied and received her nursing license and continued with those duties as well as church work. She was active in church camps and helped to locate a lot for a new church in Pomona. In 1960, Delbert Jones became pastor at the Church of the Open Bible. Leta was a great help to him. She remained active in the Lord's work until she was unable. She died on October 16, 1979, at age 87.

In 1961, a ladies' trio from Oregon Bible College visited California churches. The Gospelettes, consisting of Rachel Krogh (Carr), Martha Burnett (Mikl), and Janet Turner (Stilson) performed a concert at the Church of the Open Bible in Pomona and met Leta, Malcolm, Sybil and Ross McLeod. The Gospelettes also sang at the San Jose Church of God. They had the good fortune to stay with Leta's sister, Thelma Moore, and her husband, Howard, the parents of Pastor Dean Moore, at their Pacific coastal home in Eureka, California. It was wonderful fellowship. While there the McLeods served as tour guides to Disneyland and other attractions around the area.

Leta and Norman McLeod rest in the Lord waiting for His coming to retrieve them from the grave. During their lifetime, they led remarkably full and adventurous lives. Upon Norman's death, the Southwest Conference of the Church of God offered a scholarship in Norman's name that still exists at Atlanta Bible College, the successor of Oregon Bible College.

See Adamson, J.E.
Jones, Delbert
Lindsay, S.J. (19th)
Moore, Dean
Railsback, Emma
Wolfe, Vernis

Bibliography: McLeod, Malcolm, "Leta G. McLeod a Memoir" Oct. 18, 1992 from the family papers furnished by Dean Moore, Leta's nephew; Memories of the Gospelettes in California, by Jan Stilson, January 2008; Atlanta Bible College Biography Project, compiled by David Krogh.

The 1947 Bible Training Class posed in the Oregon Church of God. Norman McLeod is second from left in the front row.

McLeod, Sybil Stilson
b. September 15, 1927
d. November 27, 1997

Sybil was born in South Bend, Indiana, to Rolland and Maude Cross Stilson, the fourth of five children with siblings John Elwyn, Donald, Joy Marcell and Kenneth Hal. Sybil was educated in South Bend schools, graduating from Riley High School in 1945. Afterward, she enrolled in a lab technician training program at the local hospital. The Stilson family enjoyed outdoor recreation. Floyd and Lulu had a cabin at Diamond Lake, Michigan. Many people visited during the summer for swimming and boating. Sybil and Joy were beautiful girls and made a splashing entry into many family movies that have been preserved on DVDs.

Sybil met Malcolm McLeod when he accompanied his family to visit the Stilsons in South Bend, Indiana. At the time, Malcolm's brother had a crush on Joy, but that was not meant to be. When Malcolm saw Sybil descend the staircase, he feel in love instantly. He courted her for three years, and after WWII, Norman McLeod presided at their wedding. The couple settled in Pomona, California.

Sybil obtained work almost immediately as an office lab technician for Dr. Leigh Collins in Pomona. She held this position for a number of years and became very adept at drawing blood practically painlessly.

Children Cynthia Lane and Kathy Ann, born in 1951 and 1954, brought her to the homefront for a while. Sybil took the girls to Sunday school and stayed to teach the class. She also sang in the choir and acted as deaconess.

In 1955, the Southwest Conference of the Church of God was formed. Sybil and Malcolm worked at the Southwest Youth Camp held in Prescott, Arizona, the first year and several other beautiful spots in subsequent years. She usually served as camp nurse and also taught, cleaned, cooked and helped with crafts.

When Malcolm returned to college, she again worked to support the family. He earned a bachelor's degree from Cal Poly Pomona in 1965, and his master's from Cal State University, Fullerton in 1967. When Malcolm decided to pursue his doctorate, they moved to Tempe, Arizona. There they became active in the Tempe Church of God. In 1973, Malcolm took an assistant professorship at Cal Poly, San Luis Obispo. He started teaching the next day, and Sybil packed up the house and family and moved back to California.

In California, Sybil sought work and took a small job she liked so well she stayed for 13 years. She was a kind and gentle person, a devoted wife and mother, generous of heart and giving to many she knew and many she didn't. She loved the outdoors, being especially fond of Yosemite;

she traveled there by herself many times and with family members.

When Sybil's health declined, tests revealed multiple myeloma, cancer of the bone marrow. She lived well for another three years.

See   McLeod, Norman
      Moore, Dean
      Stilson, Rolland

Bibliography: McLeod, Malcolm, Moore family papers furnished by Dean Moore, Sybil's cousin by marriage, January 2008; ABC Biography project, David Krogh, compiler, information furnished by the family; Stilson, Eugene, "Memories of Sybil Stilson" based on many hours of family reunions and movies.

Miller, Oral Donald
b. August 1, 1927
d. August 29, 2004

From left: Mary Beth, Oral, Thelma and Vicki.

Oral Miller was born in Mt. Morris, Illinois, to Donald and Josephine Reese Miller. He had one brother, Jim. Oral graduated from Mt. Morris public schools and entered the US Merchant Marines, where he sailed around the world. Upon returning home, he opened a restaurant in Mt. Morris and met Thelma Friemuth who came in for a quick lunch from Kable News.

When the US Army drafted Oral, he was stationed at Port Townsend on Puget Sound in Washington. He served there as a cook and never saw action in Korea though most of the men who passed through the base at that time did. Thelma joined him and they were married on March 17, 1951. The had two daughters, Vicki Lynn (Dick) and Mary Beth (Bertram).

In 1952, Willis and Ida Turner led Oral and Thelma Miller to Christ while Oral was in the military at Port Townsend. After Oral left the service, he and Thelma returned to Oregon, Illinois, where they were baptized and Oral entered Oregon Bible College. Upon finishing his time there, Oral served the Lord through the Illinois State Youth Program for many years. The Millers left Oregon in 1962 and moved to Macomb, Illinois, where they worshipped at the Church of God, Hollis Partlowe, pastor. Oral worked with Willis at the Country Companies Insurance in McDonough County. At Macomb, Oral served as deacon and youth leader. In 1965, he transferred to Winchester, Illinois, as an insurance manager and from Winchester to Morton a year later. Oral, Willis Turner and Art Fletcher, all Church of God leaders, were Million Dollar Salesmen for Country Companies. They all took pride in it, but laughed it off and gave God the credit. While living in Morton, the Millers worshipped at the East Peoria Chapel Church of God. Oral was a good Bible student and he always helped with Bible discussions.

Oral and Thelma Miller with Vicki on a boat ride at Camp Mack during General Conference, 1957.

The Millers attended Illinois State Conference, General Conference and many youth camps, whether he directed them or not. Several Youth Camps Oral directed as Illinois Youth Leader included Effingham with the Thomas family, Camp Emmanuel at Astoria, Lake Bloomington for summer camps and winter retreats.

One summer when Illinois Conference was held at the old Church of God in Oregon, some teen boys whose names shall go unmentioned, tried to install sound equipment in the women's side of the old dorm behind the church. Oral caught them and grounded them. That night at the watermelon feast, the boys had to set up, cut watermelons, clean up and collect all the seeds people spat out. In retaliation, one boy named his farm pig "Thelma" which brought a laugh.

Oral brought his love for cooking into his service for the Lord. He cooked for many church and youth functions. His meal plans for youth camps and conferences were tasty, nutritious and generously portioned. He said, "If you feed them well, they will want to come back next year." The kids loved his meals, and he stayed within budget.

Oral and Thelma liked vacationing in Florida in their motor home. They were particularly fond of Key West. They swam and walked the beaches. Oral's other interests included family reunions, Bible study and model train sets. He had several model trains on a platform that filled half the basement, depicting cities from each of the foreign trips he and Thelma had taken with Country Companies and various other trips.

Oral was friendly, peppy, happy and loved everyone. His favorite blessing to family and friends, as he departed an event, was "Love your bones." Sadly, his final days were spent battling bone cancer, which he did courageously. In the hospital, he sang favorite hymns and choruses, and all joined in. It helped him forget the pain and gave him hope. He died 16 months to the day after his favorite brother-in-law Willis Turner died He was interred in Peoria. Pastor Curt Rowden conducted the services.

See   Partlowe, Hollis
      Turner, Willis

Bibliography: Dick, Vicki, Interview with cousin, Jan Stilson, Oct 3, 2010.

Milne, Kenneth
b. May 16, 1916
d. January 10, 1993

Kenneth Milne was born in Pittsburgh, Pennsylvania. As an adult he felt called to serve the Lord. To prepare, he attended and graduated from Pillar of Fire Seminary in Boundbrook, New Jersey. This organization believed in the immortality of the soul.

One day while riding the train Kenneth was reading his Bible. He came upon Romans 2:7 "To those who by patience in well-doing seek for glory and honor and immortality, he will give eternal life" (RSV). Kenneth was immediately struck by the phrase, "seek...immortality." He reasoned that if people must seek immortality, it means they do not already have it! Therefore, man does not have an immortal soul. Kenneth studied natural immortality and conditional immortality and began seeking an organization that taught conditional immortality. He found the Church of God General Conference at Oregon, Illinois, and communicated with Harold Doan, the General Conference executive secretary. Kenneth was encouraged to visit Oregon, and when he did, he accepted the new teachings.

He became a professor at Oregon Bible College in 1955 and began teaching eschatology and other Bible subjects. He especially enjoyed teaching from Dwight Pentecost's book, *Things to Come*. In this class, Kenneth contrasted Church of God teachings with Pillar of Fire teachings and further compared that to Dwight Pentecost's teachings. It was a thorough class.

Kenneth also preached for College Chapel services in rotation with others. One of his most memorable sermons was on prayer. He said:
> God answers prayers. He hears us when we pray. He knows our needs. It is not necessary to hammer Him with repeated requests of the same issue. He knows what we need *before* we pray. Pray and have faith. He will answer. He has three answers: "Yes," "No" and "Wait." Commit your prayers to him and wait for the answer. God works for us and His answers to prayer can change the world.

During this time Kenneth pastored at Blessed Hope Bible Church of God in Rockford, Illinois, he met and married F.L. Austin's granddaughter, Miss Mary Railton. Kenneth also served as pastor of the Guthrie Grove Church of God at Pelzer, South Carolina, for several years before his retirement. After his retirement, he and Mary continued to reside just around the corner from the church in a small house the church built for them.

In October 2008, cogcast.org Internet radio broadcast one of Kenneth's sermons from 1990 in which he preached about wonderful events in the Church of God. He spoke of activities and ministries conducted in several state conferences by local churches. He spoke of the possibility of the General Conference offices relocating to Atlanta, Georgia, from Oregon, Illinois. He said, "How wonderful it would be if the General Conference were located within the ministry area of the Southeast Conference." This message of hope was given with enthusiasm; it epitomized his ministry of encouragement.

Kenneth died in Indiana and was interred at the cemetery beside the Guthrie Grove Church of God. Mary still resides in the neighborhood. Pastor Wally Winner officiated at Kenneth's funeral. The church members rejoiced in this fine man's life and mourned his death.

See Austin, F.L.
Doan, Harold

Bibliography: Milne, Mary Railton. Interview with JStilson, Oct. 26, 2008. Stilson, Jan. Memories of K. Milne from our Oregon Bible College days.

Moore, Dean
b. 1927

Dean Moore was born in Los Angeles to Howard and Thelma Moore. Thelma was the daughter of Ezra and Emma Railsback, pastor of the Los Angeles Church of God. The Railsbacks moved from Indiana to California early in the 20th century. Dean's family left Los Angeles when he was a baby, but they returned to attend church at least once a year—a trip of nearly 500 miles.

Throughout the year, Thelma taught Dean and Jerry about the Gospel of the Kingdom by reading the Bible, a Bible-story book and *The Restitution Herald* children's page. When Dean was 12, his Grandma Emma baptized him. Dean said, "I remember as I searched my heart at that time, that I truly believed that Jesus was God's son."

Dean's mother and grandmother encouraged him to attend the summer session of Oregon Bible College at Oregon, Illinois, when he was 17. He wasn't very interested but agreed to go. Looking back on this years later, he was thankful he decided to go. There he met F.L. Austin who became one of his instructors. He also met Alva G. Huffer, another student, who had just accepted the Lord and was very enthusiastic about his Christian life. Beginning that summer, Alva and Dean became life-long friends. Dean attended the Oregon Church of God and enjoyed Pastor Austin's instruction, saying:
> He opened up the teachings of the Bible in a wonderful way. I remember how I felt after one of his sermons: I felt that I was not right with God, and needed forgiveness! I knew of Christ's sacrifice for me, and I was sure that God would forgive me if I asked Him. I left the church feeling a load

had been lifted off my conscience! Receiving God's mercy meant more than anything.

Dean frequently visited F.L. Austin at his home, and the elderly gentleman was very helpful in guiding Dean to "find a new life in a new environment."

Dean met Virginia in Oregon, and they decided to marry. Pastor C.E. Lapp performed the ceremony at the Pennellwood Church of God in Grand Rapids, Michigan. It was a wonderful ceremony with Louise Lapp at the organ. After the wedding, Dean and Virginia moved to Baltimore, Maryland, to help establish a new church. There were a few interested people there, but soon, they fell away. Dean and Virginia then moved to Fremont, Nebraska, where they served for a year.

When Dean decided to pursue further education, he and Virginia moved to be near Bob Jones University, and while there, they worshipped at the Hendersonville, North Carolina, Church of God and the new work at Morristown, Tennessee. The Morristown church was under Belus Holt's supervision. Belus and Dean were friends and had attended Bible College together. Morristown was a mission church, and Dean was awed by the work. He also admired the teaching of one professor at Bob Jones. This man had been a missionary, and he had a humble approach to teaching missions. Dean left his studies and accepted the pastorate at the Blanchard, Michigan, Church of God. Daughters Sharon and Eileen were born in Blanchard. Dean said of the town:

> The people of Blanchard were very friendly and supportive. They enjoyed working together. We were able to have a Sunday morning radio program out of Mt. Pleasant, Michigan. We made many close friends including Alice and Bea Aldrich. Alice later joined us when we were working in Saltillo, Mexico, as did Rachel Krogh.
>
> Many of the members of the Blanchard church were farmers and employed Mexican migrant workers each fall to harvest cucumbers. An elderly man who was originally from Mexico who was a mature Christian with a compassion for the people of Mexico, came to our church each Sunday evening to speak to the group of Mexican men, about seventy. His name was Alberto Moreno and the men really enjoyed listening to him. The meetings lasted about two hours.
>
> Mr. Moreno wondered if the people of the church might be interested in helping him, his nephew and Dean to make a trip to Mexico to visit some of the men who had attended the services. The [Blanchard] people were very happy to do this. As it turned out, everyone whom we visited [in Mexico] were very glad to we had come. Some places were in dessert country, far from any cities. The most distant location was Labor Vieja, near Rio Verde in the state of San Luis Potosi, about 550 miles south of Laredo, Texas.

On the survey trip, Dean visited Roberto and Lupe Badillo. Roberto thought it strange that Dean did not speak Spanish. As a result, Dean considered learning the language and serving in Mexico. As part of his strategy, he moved the family to Mullin, Texas, and later to Gatesville, Texas. Isolated people in Texas wanted to have meetings in places like Houston, Midland, Odessa, San Angelo, San Antonio and Abilene. Dean wanted to move to Mexico and approached the General Conference delegates for financial support. The delegates approved the Mexico work with Dean as missionary at the 1963 summer conference.

In September 1963 the Moores moved to Saltillo and began studying Spanish. They worked with Mrs. Sanchez to translate *The Systematic Theology* lessons. Mrs. Sanchez spoke fluent English and was a great help to Dean. Another encouragement came via the Moore girls. They learned Spanish so quickly Dean and Virginia frequently asked them for help with a word. Soon, because of the language immersion, Dean and Virginia began to think in Spanish and communicating with the people became easier.

Dean worked with Roberto Badillo from Labor Vieja, moving Roberto and Lupe temporarily to Saltillo where Roberto earned income by making brooms. When the farm season began, they returned to Labor Vieja and built a chapel on the Badillo compound. Lupe held Sunday school for neighborhood children. For several years vacation Bible schools have been conducted at the chapel by mission teams from the US. These teams also assist in repairs and other duties around the compound.

In 1965 the delegates appointed Rachel Krogh to assist the Mexico work. Rachel moved to Saltillo and was quite helpful with teaching and translating. In 1969, Rachel returned to Oregon, Illinois, as the Superintendent of Missions. Roberto Badillo died in 2006, but the work continues with Lupe. Rachel communicates with Lupe Badillo by telephone to encourage her in the work. Judy Myers is also an encouragement. She escorts short-term mission teams into Mexico to work and conduct Bible schools, unless the safety of the team in Mexico is in jeopardy. No team was sent in 2010 for that reason.

When the Moore girls were old enough to begin school, the family returned to the United States. From then on, Dean made frequent trips to Mexico to meet and teach people about the Gospel of the Kingdom. Being in the US also freed him to preach and teach for Churches of God north of the border. He assisted in the church work at Harlingen, Texas; Magazine and Little Rock, Arkansas. Dean has assisted with translation and logistics for many short-term trips, and has often accompanied them in his vehicle providing much needed transportation.

Dean and Virginia retired from active mission work and reside in Oregon, Illinois, to be near their daughters. The Railsback and Moore legacy carries on in the family of Sharon and Dan Bliss and in Eileen Moore's ministry.

Dean Moore contributed to this entry.

See Austin, F.L.
    Holt, Belus
    Huffer, Alva
    Railsback, Emma (19th)
See Also Appendix 20—Missions, ref. Badillo
Bibliography: Moore, Dean. "A Personal Resume," March, 2011.

Moore, Linford
b. November 14, 1922
d. April 6, 2008

Linford Moore was born in Niagara Falls, New York, to Linford W. and Cecil A. Cartwright Moore. He had two sisters, Viola (Mrs. Ed Goit) and Shirley (Hoy). He married Ruth Eleanor Hills on April 15, 1944, in Niagara Falls. Ruth died June 11, 1991. He and Ruth had two sons, Stephen and Paul, and two daughters, Cecilia and Patricia. Patricia predeceased her parents.

The General Conference licensed Pastor Moore for pastoral ministry after he graduated from Oregon Bible College, Oregon, Illinois, in 1945. His fellow graduates included James Mattison, Ed Goit and Harold Doan. He later received a Master of Arts in Education from the University of Northern Iowa. Linford pastored Churches of God in Macomb, Illinois; Waterloo, Iowa; Van Nuys, California; Fort Valley, Virginia; and Dixon, Illinois. While in Waterloo he served Conger Street Church of God from 1950-1965, and again upon his return from Virginia. He also taught in the Cedar Falls School District at Cedar Heights Elementary while in ministry.

Kent Ross, founder of THRIVE ministries, wrote:
> This weekend another older minister died. Linford Moore of Iowa died after his many years of service, most all of them in Iowa.
>
> For years he was pastor of the Church of God in Waterloo, Iowa, and after retirement, he never totally retired but was always involved in the church he loved. He preached and taught the things the Bible proclaimed and helped many in their faith.
>
> My personal involvement with him was for several years when I traveled to Waterloo, Iowa and led a Young Adult Retreat, which later became an Adult Retreat, and was moving quickly toward an Old Adult Retreat.
>
> I would get to Waterloo and Linford would meet me and we would go to dinner and talk church and the work of the Lord. I always enjoyed his positive attitude even though he was serving in a difficult situation. He always looked forward to what he hoped God might bring to pass. Then on Saturday and Sunday we would serve the people of God and seek to encourage them in their walk of faith.
>
> I've known many, like Linford, who had a serving heart. I doubted he ever asked the Lord for success, except as it would mean people coming to faith and finding a place in the Kingdom. We've had many of our ministers, humble, quiet men, who served where God planted them.
>
> We need to recognize such exemplary service and faithfulness. Many of our men have served for years, died and are shortly remembered only by their families. Their burial sites are often remote, unknown to most, BUT there is one who remembers.
>
> He writes a book of remembrance and they are part of his special treasure. These words are from Malachi 3:16-18, "Then those who feared the LORD talked with each other, and the LORD listened and heard. A scroll of remembrance was written in his presence concerning those who feared the LORD and honored his name." "They will be mine," says the LORD Almighty, "in the day when I make up my treasured possession. I will spare them, just as in compassion a man spares his son who serves him. And you will again see the distinction between the righteous and the wicked, between those who serve God and those who do not."
>
> God remembers the Linford Moores, as he remembers others who through the years were faithful with little, but will be rewarded with much. Thank you, Linford, for your faithfulness to your God and ours.

Pastor Paul Moore and Delbert Rankin officiated at his funeral. He was interred at Greenwood Cemetery, Cedar Falls, Iowa.

Kent Ross contributed to this entry.

See Doan, Harold
    Goit, Ed
    Mattison, James
    Ross, Kent
Bibliography: Krogh, David, "Obituary" retrieved from online ABC Alumni Newsletter, April 15, 2008; Ross, Kent H. "Tribute to Linford Moore," retrieved from THRIVE ministry devotional, April 7, 2008; "Linford Moore," *Searchlight,* Iowa State Berean Society, Vol.72:2 Summer 2008; *The Restitution Herald,* Sydney Magaw, ed., Oregon, Il., April 20, 1948.

Illinois ministers at Ripley Conference in 1948, from left: Francis Burnett, Celaine Randall, Linford Moore, Harvey Krogh Jr., Sydney Magaw, Harold Doan, James Watkins.

Morgan, James Manuel
b. December 25, 1868
d. 1960

James Morgan was born in Alabama but moved west into Oklahoma. In his mid-30s he wed Mary and they had one son, Luther. The Morgans resided at Bristow, Oklahoma, nearly James' whole life. Elder Morgan was a hell-fire and brimstone preacher before he learned of the

Abrahamic Faith. Children hated to see him come because he preached for two hours. James testified in 1926 that he had picked up a tract on conditional immortality, read it and thought about the new ideas it discussed. He said if a person gives up hell, but not immortal soul, that leads to Spiritism and Universalism.

He was a southern preacher who focused on Arkansas and Oklahoma ministries. While at Bristow, James produced and preached a radio program, "The Voice of Oklahoma," broadcast over the Farm and Labor station, KFRU. This station began broadcasting early in 1925. Its call letters stood for "Kind Folks Remember Us." This was the first station in Oklahoma. In 1927 it was moved to Tulsa and renamed KVOO. *Christian Science Monitor* and many newspapers reported on news of this station. Minister Morgan's radio program was a Bible study. He solicited "memberships" to the program, which may have been a means of building a mailing list for evangelism or to gain sponsors to finance the work. Such "memberships" informed him who his faithful listeners were. It was a progressive idea and one of the first radio ministries in the Church of God.

Elder Morgan's preaching style may have stirred up the community churches for Winchester Allen of the Christian church at Seven Oaks challenged him to a debate. James was described as being a "fiery preacher." The debate on "The Kingdom and the Nature of Man" was to be held at Sallisaw, Oklahoma, in the fall of 1915. Bro. Morgan was "affirmative on the Kingdom and stated that the land was promised to Abraham as the foundation which through Christ included the world." Morgan presented Allen with 12 questions on the nature of man for which Allen had no good reply. Recorder H.S. Wrett said, "Morgan proved himself a workman that needeth not be ashamed."

J.M. Morgan worked with the Arkansas, Oklahoma and Missouri Churches of God during the early 20th century. He preached at Morse Mill, Missouri, in 1914. The following year he worked with T.C. Billingsley in a tent meeting series in Oklahoma. In each of the other years he worked with other Church of God ministers throughout a four-state area. In 1926 he conducted meetings at Bristow with J.H. Self's assistance.

James Morgan was still active in the ministry in 1948, preaching at Lemard, Muskogee and Sallisaw, Oklahoma; and at London, Russellville, Morrilton, and Oak Lawn, Arkansas. The latter was a new work south of Little Rock started in 1947. James made a monthly circuit of these churches. He also continued to write well into his old age. In the winter of 1948 he authored a tract, "The Light of God's Truth Made Plain," and requested funds to publish 2,000 pieces. He was 80 years old on Christmas Day that year.

Bro. Morgan was tall and lean. He attended General Conference at Oregon, Illinois, many times and authored a study book, *The Guiding Light of God's Truth Made Plain*, which is part of the Atlanta Bible College Archives. Pete McGinty of McGintytown, Arkansas, described him as loving the Church of God doctrines, yet strangely, even though he started three churches in Bristow, Oklahoma, they all joined the Advent Christian denomination. James may have lost the deeds of the buildings, but he truly loved the Church of God. He unabashedly listed himself on the US Census as "Minister, Churches of God in Christ."

James rests in the 44 Cemetery northeast of Bristow, Oklahoma.

See Billingsley, T.C.
Self, J.H.

Bibliography: Ancestry.com. U.S. Census. Oklahoma. Creek. Bristow. Dist. 16. 1920; "Radio Station Dedicated to State," *Christian Science Monitor*. Jan. 23, 1925; McGinty, Pete, Interview with JStilson, "Formation and Early History of the McGintytown Church of God," Church of God *History Newsletter* JStilson, ed., Winter 1985; LegendsofAmerica.com/Ok-facts. Website names KFRU as Oklahoma's first radio station; Morgan, J.M. *The Guiding Light of God's Truth Made Plain*. Published during 1940s; *The Restitution Herald*, Reports from the field. Oct. 20, 1914; Sept 1, 1915; Nov. 17, 1915; May 26, 1925; Jan. 12, 1926; Aug. 10, 1926; Oct. 7, 1947; April 6, 1948; Nov. 23, 1948; Weaver, Archard and Clara, "History of People and the Church at McGintytown," from their Anniversary celebration, Summer 2010, sent by Pastor Tom New.

Morris, Rachel Anna Humphreys

b. August 30, 1908
d. July 1, 1997

Rachel was the daughter of Kittle Clyde Muncrief and Pastor Richard A. Humphreys. She was born in Arkansas into a large, loving, happy, singing, poetic, Bible-reading family. Richard Humphreys was a composer and Church of God Abrahamic Faith evangelist minister. Her grandfather, Dr. Muncrief, was a physician in the Civil War, and at his request, she was the last one to read the Holy Scriptures to him before he died.

Rachel married Ernest Manson Morris. They had seven daughters, 14 grandchildren and 13 great-grandchildren. He predeceased her on September 5, 1977.

Rachel loved history, poetry and music. She was the glue that held the big family together through tough times. She fervently taught the Kingdom of God on earth to her family, and served as the contact person for both the Humphreys and the Morris families. She was active in community service as well and created the Mike Morris Family Park in Sedro Wooley, Washington, in memory of her grandson, Michael DeBolt, who died in Vietnam. She walked the trails in the park with her dog, Fancy, and helped maintain the area around the ponds.

While she suffered with her final illness, it did not deter her from looking forward to being in God's Kingdom. She knew she would sleep in death until Jesus came for her. Rachel died in Los Angeles, but she was flown home to rest beside her beloved husband.

See Humphreys, Richard (19th)
Muncrief, Dr. Leonides (19th)
Bibliography: ABC Biography Project, David Krogh, compiler.

Morrison, Gertrude Borden McInturff
b. July 23, 1913
d. September 7, 2002
Morrison, Frank
b. September 10, 1912
d. February 18, 1989

Gertrude McInturff was the daughter of Hugh and Esta McInturff. The family resided on a farm near Woodstock, Virginia, in the heart of the Shenandoah Valley. Gertrude had two sisters and a brother. Gertrude attended and became a baptized member of the Church of God in Christ Jesus at Maurertown, Virginia. She married Frank Graham Morrison on October 23, 1937. They had one daughter, Carolyn. Carolyn married French Chapman in 1962 and joined Fair Oaks Community Church of God in Herndon, Virginia. Carolyn died in December 2006; former Pastor Gary Burnham officiated at her service.

Frank Morrison maintained membership at Emmanuel Lutheran Church in Woodstock, but Carolyn was raised in the Church of God. Frank attended church with Gertrude every Sunday. During his time at the Maurertown church, he provided transportation for other members and served as Sunday school superintendent, adult teacher and usher. Frank was always helpful to the pastor residing in the parsonage beside the church.

Frank co-owned Woodstock Garage with his brothers. This was a Plymouth/Chrysler/Dodge dealership. Frank was active in community service, following the example of his father, former mayor of Woodstock.

Gertrude had her own car, but because Frank was in the dealership, he often needed it. At these times, he gave her a loaner. One time she came to a ladies' meeting with an old Plymouth that had seen better days. The women, some of whom were nearly disabled, got into the car, and the pastor's wife drove the group north to Winchester, Virginia, for a spring luncheon. On the way home a tire blew out. Skillful driving brought the car to the side of the road where the pastor's wife began to pray and hunt for a jack. On the other side of the road, a car stopped and the driver, a lanky fellow, hippie-looking, with hair down to his waist, got out to help. Fear sprang up in the women.

But he was an angel in disguise. He removed the tire, took it two miles down the road for a quick patch, brought it back, installed it and sent the women on their way. The ladies laughed all the way home about that wonderful young man. What a lesson: when one prays for help she should never fear the messenger that God sends.

Gertrude served beside Frank as a faithful wife and mother. She was active in helping senior citizens of the congregation and community and helping the unfortunate families who lived in the county. She had a mission and goal to spread the love of Jesus. Frank taught Eugene Stilson all the intricacies of investing in the stock market, what to do and what to avoid. Gene has passed this father-son life lesson to other young men since then.

Frank and Gertrude rest together in Massanutten Cemetery in Woodstock not far from their home.

See MacInturff, Hugh (19th)
Stilson, Eugene
Bibliography: ABC Biography project, David Krogh, compiler; JStilson, Memories of Frank and Gertrude Morrison.

Munch, Cyril Homer
b. 1888
d. 1957

Cyril Munch was born and raised in Virginia's Fort Valley, which divides the Shenandoah Valley of northern Virginia nearly its full length. Cyril married Bertha, and they had three sons and three daughters. Audrey contributed information about her dad to the biography project of Atlanta Bible College, creating awareness of Cyril's story.

Cyril was baptized in 1913, probably by J.H. Anderson. Cyril entered membership with the Fort Valley Church of God in Christ Jesus at Seven Fountains, Virginia. He served there as elder from 1924-1954, and he was a trustee until his death. Cyril lived in the small community of Fort Valley his whole life and worked as a teacher for 49 years.

Audrey wrote: "I, as his daughter, remember him as a very kind and loving father, whose dedication to teaching and learning has inspired me to make a gift to our Bible College Library in his memory."

Bibliography: Ancestry.com. U.S. Census. Virginia. Shenandoah. Johnston. Dist. 75. Image 6. 1910; Atlanta Bible College Biography Project from information furnished by Audrey M. Simpson, David Krogh, compiler.

Murphy, Lucian
b. December 17, 1905
d. May 30, 1952

Lucian Murphy was born in Clarksville, Illinois. His family was very influential in establishing the Salem Church of God near Clarksville, and they continued to support it until it was destroyed by fire sometime in the 1960s. Although he became an isolated member by moving to Oklahoma in 1933, Lucian kept a torch of faith burning within his family and for others he met. He studied the Scriptures throughout his life, creating a treasured legacy. For several years family members donated scholarship money to Oregon/Atlanta Bible College in his name.

Bibliography: Atlanta Bible College Biography Project, David Krogh, compiler.

Murra, Fim F.
b. July 1874
d. 1954

Murra, Dirk J.
b. July 1876
d. 1921

The Murra family immigrated from Campen, Ostfriedland, Germany, and settled in Maryland Township of Ogle County near Adeline, Illinois. Brothers Fim and Dirk Murra joined the Church of God at Adeline. They were S.J. Lindsay's friends and neighbors when he lived in Adeline, and they remained friends for many years. They may have been his students at the old stone public school in Adeline. At this writing the school still stands as a museum. Dirk moved to Alabama and Florida. He remained single all his life and died in 1921. Notice of his death appeared in *The Restitution Herald*. Fim married Mary Alice Bayley at age 28. They had one daughter, Alice Jeanette, and one son, Wilbur Fim Murra.

After the Adeline Church of God closed, the United Brethren purchased the building. It still stands today with the cabins and dormitory behind the church. These buildings were originally used for Church of God Illinois Conference meetings. If the General Conference ever arranged to purchased this property, it would make an excellent historic site.

Fim began reading *The Restitution* and continued to fellowship with the Church of God in Oregon, Illinois. Eventually, he became acquainted with its sister denomination, the Advent Christians. He entered Aurora College in Aurora, Illinois, just two years after his conversion around 1894.

In Aurora, Fim met with considerable appreciation and success. After graduation in 1898 he served a Church of God in South Bend, Indiana, as interim pastor. This may have been the new Church of God Bible study group that began there. While in South Bend, Fim also taught public school. Moving back to Illinois, he became full-time pastor of the Advent Christian church in DeKalb, Illinois. In time, that denomination called him to serve at the mission headquarters in Boston. He lived in Boston from 1908 until 1913.

After leaving Boston, Fim compiled and edited the new Advent Christian hymnal, *The Golden Sheaf, No. 2*, in 1916. This book had 269 songs and hymns, plus the Psalms and an index. It was used in many Churches of God of that day. This hymnal is part of the songbook collection in the Atlanta Bible College Archives.

In 1918 Fim was named General Superintendent of the Advent Conference. However, while the people were enthusiastic over the appointment, things did not go well. Within a few months, Hewitt reported in *Devotion and Development* that "there was an unpaid printing bill for $30 and [Murra's] December salary was still owed." Fim wrote:

> This lack of complete cooperation, I fear, indicates indifference to the work I was asked to do by the General Conference, and the whole plan, therefore, better be dropped. Consequently I am turning my attention to other matters to support my family.

Fim served pastorates in Minneapolis, Minnesota, and Palmer, Illinois. Soon thereafter Fim was unanimously selected to preside over the Western Advent Christian Association publishing house in Mendota, Illinois, because of his former experience as business manager of the *World's Crisis*. Fim edited the magazine *Our Hope* in Mendota. Copies of *Our Hope* and *World's Crisis* are in the Atlanta Bible College Archives.

The publishing business did not go well in Mendota. This quote comes from Clyde Hewitt's book, *Responsibility and Response:*

> Ever hopeful for the advance of the Lord's work, Murra undoubtedly overreached himself in the matter of expanding the press operation in Mendota. There was not enough commercial work in that small residential community especially with the printing plant of the local newspaper competing for it, to support a large new building. Nor were there trained personnel or resources to solicit business elsewhere. With a heavy debt to the bank and to Advent Christian friends who had loaned money on unsecured notes for the new building, the financial problem was too much for Murra and in mid-1929 he felt forced to resign.

The stock market crash of October 1929 and the Great Depression took further toll upon *Our Hope* and the denomination agreed to merge it with the *World's Crisis*. The Depression also affected the Church of God's fledgling educational operation. The Bible Training Class, which had begun operating in Oregon, Illinois, in

1923, closed its doors in 1933, and did not restart until 1939. The name was changed to Oregon Bible College in 1941, and it continues today as Atlanta Bible College in McDonough, Georgia.

When Fim and Mary left Mendota, they settled in Mobile, Alabama. They remained friends with S.J. Lindsay who edited *The Restitution Herald* from 1911-1922, for the rest of their lives. The Church of God gave Fim his start, and he was grounded in the Bible.

Fim rests in the Adeline Cemetery where many Church of God founders are buried. Mary lived in Florida until she was nearly 100 years old. She was born in 1876 and died in 1976 just shy of her birthday.

See Lindsay, S.J. (19th)

Bibliography: Ancestry.com U.S. Census. Illinois. LaSalle. Mendota Ward 1. 1920; U.S. Census. Alabama. Mobile. Grand Bay. Dist. 25. 1930; Ancestry.com. Freepages.genealogy.rootsweb.ancestry.com retrieved on Feb. 16, 2009; Cramer, Roger. Information on Fim's death was furnished to rootsweb.com/ILOGLE, retrieved Feb. 16, 2009; Hewitt, Clyde E. *Responsibility and Response*. Venture Books. Charlotte, NC. 1986. 129-132; Hewitt, Clyde E. *Devotion and Development*. Venture Books. Charlotte, NC. 1990 p. 224-225; Murra, Fim, editor *The Golden Sheaf, No. 2*. Boston. Advent Christian Publishing, 1916; *The Restitution*, Oct. 1921.

Pastor James Mattison

Photo provided by Rex Cain

N

Nedrow, Mary May
b. 1892
d. 1955?

Mary May and Floyd Nedrow of Oregon, Illinois, were members of the Oregon Church of God. Mary and Floyd had four sons and a daughter. Floyd was a steam shovel engineer at the National Silica Company on Pines Road west of Oregon. Mary ran a small grocery store east of the Rock River.

East Oregon, or "Sandtown" as it was known, was a small, unincorporated settlement of southern people who had come north seeking better employment at the end of the Great Depression. Homes were small; many only shacks. The area had no parks. There was nothing for the children to do. A school was built for grades one through eight, but there was no church.

In 1937, Mary taught Bible lessons at the store for the children. She had classes each morning and afternoon throughout the summer. Things slowed once school opened in the fall. Principal Ruth Gesin Lippert of East Oregon School was a Church of God member. There was so much interest in Mary's teaching that she began a campaign to start a church and build a small chapel. Mr. and Mrs. Eugene Myers donated the land for the building. The school's administration supported the idea of having a church nearby.

The Oregon Church of God members assisted in teaching and memorization work. Visiting ministers, especially those from the state of Washington who heard of the work, offered to preach at the store/filling station when they came to Oregon. A.L. Corbaley, John Eagleston and Lyle Rankin were among their number.

Money was raised in the community and through the Oregon Church of God mission work, and a small frame building was erected on the east edge of town. This was named East Oregon Chapel. The building was dedicated on May 23, 1943. At the service, the children's Sunday school led songs and special music. Mrs. Nedrow presented church history. Pastor S.E. Magaw offered dedicatory remarks, and Robert Hardesty served as song leader. The program ended with a rousing rendition of "Onward Christian Soldiers." A large group of children attended the new Sunday school and a few adults. It was easier to attract children than adults. All who attended had great enthusiasm for the new work. The students from Oregon Bible College practiced preaching and teaching at the East Oregon Chapel. Students who served and gained experience there included Gordon Landry, Leon Driskill, Louis Kump, Alva Huffer, James Mattison, Linford Moore, Paul Shaw and many more.

Mary was well known for writing poetry. Her poems were collected into a book. She also wrote a Bible lesson book for the children. The Archives of Atlanta Bible College hold copies of both books.

See Corbaley, A.L. (19th)
Driskill, Leon
Eagleston, John
Huffer, Dr. Alva
Magaw, Sydney E.
Mattison, James
Moore, Linford
Rankin, Lyle

Bibliography: Ancestry.com. U.S. Census. Illinois. Ogle. Oregon Township. 1920 and 1930. Wilson, Jessie M., Scrapbook of Jessie M. Wilson, Golden Rule Home resident owned by Archives of Atlanta Bible College.

Netts, Charles Leonard
b. September 12, 1875
d. 1952

Netts, Mabel Gertrude Howell
b. November 18, 1880
d. 1957

Charles Netts was born in Ohio to George W. and Elizabeth Netts. His parents named him Charles Darwin Netts, but as soon as possible he legally changed his name to Charles Leonard Netts. On April 24, 1900, he wed Mabel G. Howell in Ohio. They had two sons, Benjamin C. and Walter S., and one daughter, Margaret.

Charles learned of the Gospel of the Kingdom from his father who worked with William Fish to establish the Age-to-Come work in the Springfield area. George Netts and William Fish were Mark Allen's key contacts when he visited the Dayton area in 1861. While Allen preached in southern Ohio, shots were fired on Fort Sumter.

Charles Netts and his family were members of the congregation at Springfield, Ohio, when it met on the second floor of a shop in downtown Springfield. In 1916, they purchased a one-room schoolhouse in Lawrenceville for $800 and renovated it for church use. The Lawrenceville congregation had been meeting informally since 1856. They celebrated their 150th anniversary in 2006.

Charles made miniatures. He probably learned woodworking skills from his father who was a foreman at a woodworking shop. In 1923, when the new General Conference at Oregon, Illinois, purchased the Golden Rule Home for an elderly residence, Charles began building replicas of the grand old mansion. Charles made exact scale models of the Home designed to be banks. Each was 2-1/2" tall and 4" square with a slot in the roof and a swinging door in the bottom, and 30 hand-painted windows. When the replicas/banks were finished, Charles and Mabel packed their trailer and drove to each Church of God in America and Canada to distribute them as Sunday school birthday banks. At that time there were 35 to 40 established Church of God congregations in the United States and Canada and many more home Bible study groups. The money collected was used for the upkeep of the Golden Rule Home or for missions. When the General Conference added a one-story sunroom on the east side of the Golden Rule Home, Charles made model sunrooms at home, and drove the Church of God circuit again to attach the sunroom to each model! Each sunroom had 12 windows and a door, again all hand painted. Many Churches of God still use the banks in their Sunday Schools, although some are showing wear. The bank at Lawrenceville needs a new roof. One of the Golden Rule Home models is on display in the Archives of Atlanta Bible College.

Paul Overholser and Clark Ballentine (December 24, 1902-December 5, 1990) began an ambitious project at the Lawrenceville church to gain more room for Sunday school classes. In 1940, they dug a basement under the church, by hand. They used mules to pull the dirt out. The finished basement added space for classrooms and a fellowship hall, but it had low ceilings. As this volume was written, the Lawrenceville congregation was constructing a new church building.

Mabel Howell was the daughter of Benjamin F. Howell of Springfield. She was one of seven children, and all were active in the Church of God. She was a tall, slender, take-charge kind of person, a real leader. At 5' 10", she weighed only 98 lb., and she sang as if she were much larger and with such power people gathered outside could enjoy her singing in the church. She loved to sing "His Eye is On the Sparrow" and "The Holy City."

Sylvia Ballentine Black told a story about her grandmother Mabel who attended General Conference in Oregon, Illinois. E. Richard Smith was pastor at the Lawrenceville Church of God and Mabel loved to hear him preach. At General Conference Mabel asked Richard, "Why aren't you preaching one of the evening services?" He replied that he wasn't scheduled. She said, "You must preach." She arranged for Smith to replace the scheduled speaker so he could preach the sermon she liked so well, "Bring Back the King!" No one knew how she did it, who he replaced, or what the displaced preacher thought about it.

Mabel Howell's younger sister, Carrie, wed George N.H. Peters, who authored the well-known three-volume book *The Theocratic Kingdom*. The Peters and Howells families were neighbors in Springfield, so George literally married the girl next door. It was Carrie's second marriage. His dedication to her in *The Theocratic Kingdom* is very touching. George became acquainted with Church of God teaching, referring to the members as "One Faith People." He was especially familiar with the subject of the Kingdom. In fact, he may have been inspired to write

Golden Rule Home replica bank made by Charles Netts. Several are still used for Sunday school offereings.

> **Reviews of *The Theocratic Kingdom***
>
> "The greatest work on prophetic interpretation ever written"
> - Lewis Sperry Chafer
>
> "The most important single work on biblical predictive prophecy to appear."
> - Wilbur M. Smith
>
> "...the most exhaustive, scholarly, reverent treatment of the questions of the kingdom of our Lord available today."
> - Dwight D. Pentecost
>
> Ref.: http://theocratickingdom.info

about it because his in-laws, Mabel and Charles Netts, could not stop talking about it.

In his famous work, Peters gave ample space to discussion about the people known as "The Faith" a phrase taken from Jude 3, "We must earnestly contend for the faith once delivered to the saints." "The Faith" meant the Church of God that taught Age to Come, which at the time was becoming known as One Faith or Abrahamic Faith. Peters cited the works of H.V. Reed, J.M. Stephenson and R.V Lyon. The Library at Atlanta Bible College has a full set of this valuable publication.

Charles and Mabel are interred at the Ferncliff Cemetery in Springfield, Ohio.

See Allen, Mark (19th)
Lyon, R.V. (19th)
Overholser, Paul
Peters, George N.H.
Reed, H.V. (19th)
Smith, E. Richard
Stephenson, J.M. (19th)

See Also Appendix 25—Theocratic Kingdom

Bibliography: Ancestry.com. U.S. Census. Ohio. Clark. Springfield. Dist. 47. 1880; U.S. Census. Ohio. Clark. Springfield. Dist. 47. 1900; Black, Sylvia. Presentation on Charles and Mabel Netts at the 2010 History Conference, North Hills Church of God, Springfield, Ohio. Peters, George. *The Theocratic Kingdom*, 3 vols. Springfield, Ohio, 1883. Note: The Archival papers of George N.H. Peters are housed at Dallas Theological Seminary; view them at http://library.dts.edu/Pages/TL/Special/PetersGNH_CN017.pdf.

Harold Doan presents Stan and Peg Ross with a gift of appreciation at their retirement ceremony.

Photo provided by Rex Cain

Ordnung, Elizabeth
b. August 5, 1885
d. March 1981

Elizabeth Ordnung never married, but she did devote her life to Christian service through the work of the General Conference in Oregon, Illinois. She had a sister, Ida (Orem). Elizabeth's mother, Julia Ordnung, was the daughter of J.S. Shellenberger of Ranson, Kansas. Elizabeth lived at the Golden Rule Home with her mother shortly after it opened in 1923. The home was established for Church of God's senior members who had no other place to live and needed assistance with daily chores. When J.S. Shellenberger became ill, Elizabeth and her mother went to Kansas to be with him for a year before his death in January 1925. His obituary appeared in *The Restitution Herald*. If not for that, Miss Ordnung's lineage might have been lost. Elizabeth and Julia returned to the Golden Rule Home after his estate was settled in January 1925

Elizabeth was active in the Oregon Church of God. She assisted in planning for accommodations of ministers visiting for the annual January minister's conference. To locate enough beds in the small town with only one hotel and no motels, Elizabeth went door to door to ask ordinary citizens if they would host a visiting minister. She successfully placed the ministers around the north end of town, and in doing so acquainted many residents there with various Church of God conferences and ministries. She repeated her inquiries among the good citizens of Oregon to place ministers and guests for the Illinois Conference and General Conference held for two weeks every summer from 1898 until 1957.

The Turner family assisted Elizabeth in 1946 by providing a room for Pastor C.E. Lapp and in subsequent years to many others. Impressed by the friendliness of Church of God members, the Turners sent their daughter, Janet, this book's author, to Sunday school. Myrle Claussen and Donna stopped by to accompany Janet to Vacation Bible School. Pastor Richard LeCrone and OBC student Bill Wachtel made a pastoral visit, and soon Willis and Ida Mae Turner were members of the Church of God because of a contact by Elizabeth Ordnung.

A few years later, the use of the Golden Rule as a senior citizen facility was phased out in lieu of it being a dormitory for the students of Oregon Bible College. It was first a men's dorm; in the 1960s, it became a women's dorm. Meals were served daily to all students. Elizabeth assisted in light cleaning duties at the dormitory, but as she aged assumed lighter duties. In spite of age and creaking knees, she attended church faithfully; until the last few years of her life, she walked six blocks to church. Elizabeth was a quiet, shy woman, making it difficult for her to converse. But she approached students with warmth, just as she had the Oregon residents while assisting with the conferences held there. Even a shy and retiring woman can serve the Lord in a powerful way.

Elizabeth believed in journaling. Every day for nearly 30 years she wrote simple daily entries in five-year diaries. The diaries recorded her life, its trials and joys, memories of friends and neighbors, ministers and local Church of God members. The diaries became a valuable archival resource for documenting information about other biographical entries included in this encyclopedia, including wedding dates of Oregon Bible College students, birth and death dates of ministers and members, and key information about General Conferences and Illinois Conferences held at the Oregon Church of God. She even noted sermon titles and who preached them.

The Golden Rule building continued in service with Oregon Bible College after Miss Ordnung's death until 1990 when the college moved to Morrow, Georgia. The building was sold, but the developer could not finish the project. Today, this building, once Oregon's first high school (1857), the first senior citizen home in Oregon, and the first college dormitory in Oregon, is unused and deteriorating.

Elizabeth rests in peace in Riverview Cemetery north of Oregon.

    See LeCrone, J. Richard
           Orem, William J. (19th)
           Turner, Willis H.
           Wachtel, William

Bibliography: Memories of Miss Ordnung by Janet Turner Stilson, who was an OBC alumnus, resident of the Golden Rule Dorm, and friend of Elizabeth. *The Restitution Herald*, January 27, 1925; March 17, 1925; Ordnung, Elizabeth, "Diaries," The diaries are part of the Archival collection at Atlanta Bible College covering about thirty years prior to Miss Ordnung's death.

Overholser, Helen Louise
    b. October 21, 1905
    d. December 22, 1968

Helen Louise was born to Joseph and Susie (Clemens) Linkhart in Champaign County near Urbana, Ohio. She attended local elementary schools and graduated from Enon High School in 1923. Afterward, she attended Willis Business College in Springfield, Ohio. She graduated in 1925, and then worked for the Clark County Lumber Company as a bookkeeper.

On September 15, 1926, Helen wed Paul Overholser at her parents' home. Soon after that she was baptized into the body of Christ and affiliated with the Maple Grove (now Lawrenceville) Church of God. She diligently engaged in all church, Sunday school and "Sister's Society" activities, serving as church secretary for many years. Helen and Paul had two sons and two daughters. They all accepted Christ as their Savior and were baptized, becoming members of the Lawrenceville Church of God. In 1938, the family began attending General Conference, and in 1939 took their four-month-old daughter Mary Lou with them. Since the home they stayed in had no crib, Mary Lou slept in a dresser drawer.

Also in 1938, the Overholsers and Ballentines recognized the need for more space for Sunday school classes and church activities at Maple Grove. At a short business meeting on a Sunday morning, the project was approved. According to stories, on Monday morning men and youths were at the church ready to dig a basement under the existing building. Since there were no power tools or equipment available, they used an old two-handled scoop drawn by a horse to remove the dirt. After the project was completed and the classrooms added, members noted an increase in Sunday school attendance from 17 to 42. Much of the increase was due to the interest and enthusiasm of Helen and her family. In 1941 the first Vacation Bible School was conducted at the church.

In 1945 the Overholsers moved to California where they were active in and affiliated with the Los Angeles Church of God. In 1948, they returned to Ohio and the Lawrenceville church. Helen served as deaconness, Sunday school teacher and Missionary Society secretary. She promoted the conference work throughout Ohio, now the Northeast Conference. Helen received awards, including a copy of Alva Huffer's *Systematic Theology*, for perfect attendance.

While they resided in the country, Helen and her husband operated a kennel for cocker spaniels, raised short-horned cattle and Shetland ponies. She enjoyed working with the foals and training them. While they operated the 61-acre farm, Paul worked as an electrical engineer for the Ohio Edison Company of Springfield. Children and grandchildren enjoyed life on the farm.

Among Helen and Paul's grandchildren, three grandsons, Greg, Alan and Kevin Demmitt, were Oregon Bible College graduates. Two of them married young women who also attended OBC. Two Overholser granddaughters also attended OBC as well as grandson John Demmitt.

Helen died at Christmas in 1968. The family mourned deeply. All revered her Christian character and shared her belief in the resurrection of the dead and life of immortality in the Kingdom of God.

Because of Helen's interest in children, and in OBC, it seemed right to Paul to establish a scholarship in her memory. Paul set up the "Helen L. Overholser" scholarship, which is currently awarded annually to a worthy Atlanta Bible College student. The Lawrenceville Church of God administers the scholarship. Four years after establishing the scholarship, Paul observed it would be good if there were more available for OBC students. Again, desiring to do something for the youth that Helen loved and honor her memory, he and his new wife, Ruth, decided on two more scholarships. One, known as the "Overholser, Lawrenceville" scholarship, is administered by the Lawrenceville Church of God; the other one is administered by the Troy View Church of God where Helen's daughter, Joyce, is a member. This one is known as the "Overholser, Demmitt, Troy View" scholarship. All three funds are endowment funds.

Helen's life and death truly are a testimony to her love for the Lord and her desire to serve Him.

    See Overholser, Paul H.
           Overholser, Ruth T.

Bibliography: ABC Biography Project, David Krogh compiler; Ancestry.com. U.S. Census. Ohio. Clark. Springfield. Dist. 32. 1930.

Overholser, J. Homer

b. June 18, 1914
d. March 20, 1990

J. Homer Overholser was born to Alden Earl and Nora Lucilla Overholser in Springfield, Ohio. He married Marian Lee Whalen and they had two children, James Alan and Sharyl Ann.

Mr. Overholser attended and graduated college, studying engineering and business, including business administration and management, at Wittenberg College and the University of California at Los Angeles. J.H. was a business consultant and investor with extensive experience in aeronautical engineering and business management.

He was president of the Overholser Foundation. He also served as vice-president and director of Woodlake Realty, Inc. and Lyricard Corporation of America, Inc. He held the positions of secretary, director, and finance committee chairman at Varadyne Industries, Inc. During his lifetime J.H. served as chairman of the board and/or president of 37 corporations, including Alphatec International, Inc.; National Golf Products, Inc.; and National Golf Media, Inc. He also held business partnerships in nine enterprises in commercial farming, real estate, communications and hotel management. He helped found the first Hyatt House Hotel in Los Angeles.

In his engineering career, he developed the first wing-folding method for US Navy planes, the first aircraft anti-skid braking system (Mytrol) and the first sonic altimeter. He pioneered construction of the world's first outsized cargo plane, the Pregnant Guppy, developed in close coordination with NASA's Werner Von Braun. The plane transported the major components of the Saturn space vehicle to Cape Kennedy for the moon shots. He also oversaw adoption of the Decca Navigation System in Canada, and he designed the first self-contained room air-conditioner in the United States.

Homer Overholser was a registered California Professional Engineer, and a member of the American Society of Mechanical Engineers, as well as chairman of the SAE Fuel Valve Committee. Membership in technical societies included the Institute of Aero Sciences, American Ordinance Society, American Society of Air Affairs, Society of Aerospace Engineers and Institute of Aero Sciences. Other professional affiliations included the American Institute of Management, Air Force Association, Association of the United States Army and American Society of Mechanical Engineers. He was founder, chairman and president of Woodland Savings and Loan, which he guided to a phenomenal three-year growth and success, and then sold to D.K. Ludwig, an international financier.

Homer then founded and organized Independence Bank and in 13 years it expanded to nine branches and over $100 million in deposits. In his business career, Homer founded, organized and arranged financing for over 30 companies, took eight companies public and merged seven others.

He was the author of several professional articles and holder of several patents. Mr. Overholser received many honors and awards and has been included in 27 national and international biographical references including *International Who's Who* and *Who's Who in America*.

Homer was a life-long Church of God member.

Bibliography: ABC Biography Project, David Krogh, compiler; Social Security Death Index.

Overholser, Paul H.

b. January 23, 1905
d. February 16, 2005

Paul Overholser was born in German township of Clark County, Ohio, to Alden E. and Nora L. Overholser. When Paul was five his brother Howard was born; brother, J. Homer, arrived in 1914. Paul and his siblings grew up in the Maple Grove Church of God at Springfield, Ohio. He married Helen Linkhart. They had two sons and two daughters. Helen was baptized and became a member of the body of Christ at the Lawrenceville Church of God (previously Maple Grove).

In 1938, the Overholser family began attending the annual summer General Conference meeting at Oregon, Illinois. Here they met many wonderful church members from across the country and Canada. They also learned of many ways to increase the evangelistic efforts of the local church. In 1945, the family moved to Los Angeles where Paul served as a Church of God elder. The family returned to Ohio in 1948.

After Helen died in 1968, Paul married a Christian widow from Cleveland, Ruth Tomlinson Hall. Together they advanced the cause of funding students at Oregon Bible College through several scholarships. Paul and Ruth also made a generous donation for the Golden Rule Home renovation into the OBC's Administration and Classroom building. At the restored building's dedication, an oil painting of the couple was donated to the college. It was hung in the conference room. This oil portrait is now part of the art collection in the ABC Archives.

Paul served the Lord faithfully and generously his entire life. He was a happy soul, and one felt blessed to have been in conversation with him. The Lord blessed him with long life, and he will reap the reward of eternal life in the Age to Come.

See Overholser, Helen L.
   Overholser, J. Homer
   Overholser, Ruth S.
See Also Pryor, Charles
Bibliography: Ancestry.com. U.S. Census. Ohio. Clark. German. Dist. 4 1910; U.S. Census. Ohio. Clark. Springfield Dist. 32 1930; *The Restitution Herald*, June 22, 1948; Social Security Death Index, record for Paul H. Overholser.

Overholser, Ruth S. (Tomlinson Hall)
b. June 6, 1907
d. March 22, 2001

Ruth Tomlinson was born in Cleveland to Walter and Mattie Hall Tomlinson. She was their only surviving child; two others died in childhood. She was raised in the Lee Street Church of God and enjoyed the pastorate of Robert Huggins. Her father had grown up under the teaching of Maurice Joblin, and after her father's death, Ruth donated all Joblin's handwritten sermons to the OBC/ABC Archives. Joblin was also a printer and publisher. One of his finest professional accomplishments was publishing *Cleveland Past and Present,* a high-quality photo essay that is so rare copies sell for $2,500 today.

Ruth was a dedicated member of her church. She participated in Ohio Conference activities, the Northwest Conference after Ontario and New York joined, and the national organization of the General Conference. She served on the General Conference Credentials Committee. Evelyn Austin chaired the committee for years and trained Ruth. They served together for several years, until Ruth had to retire to care for her new husband, Will Hall.

Before retiring, Ruth trained Janet Turner (Stilson) in committee work including delegate registrations for the annual meeting, counting their votes and reporting results to the delegates at the end of each business meeting so each session's information could be recorded in the minutes. The Credentials Committee gathered statistics and provided order for voting. It also determined by its rules which delegates, alternates or ministers were eligible to vote. To be a church's delegate, the church had to be chartered with the General Conference and have at least 15 members. There was one delegate for the first 15 members. Beyond 15, for every 50 members, one additional delegate was appointed. Each state conference had one delegate, and all churches and conferences could have one or more alternates who served if a delegate was absent during a session. The ministers had one vote each, and starting in the 1960s, the members of the Board of Directors had one vote each.

A young Ruth, far left in back row, and members of Golden Rule Church of God, Cleveland.

Ruth taught first grade, and her approach to teaching adults was similar to that of first-graders. She was quiet and gentle in her conversation, kind and thoughtful. If teaching a class, her explanations were basic and clear. However, when stirred up, a firm countenance overtook her gentle face. This served her well in the classroom and with the Credentials Committee.

In her 50s, Ruth wed her first husband, Will Hall, a widower. She enjoyed that relationship until his death. After a time she married Paul H. Overholser from Springfield, Ohio, also a widower. They enjoyed decades together. Paul and Ruth helped finance the Golden Rule Home's transformation into the OBC Administration and Classroom building in the 1980s.

Ruth and Paul also donated many original works by Church of God, 19th-century authors from America and Great Britain. These books are part of the collections in Atlanta and of Rock River Christian College, Beloit, Wisconsin.

See Huggins, Robert
   Joblin, Maurice (19th)
   Overholser, Paul H.
Bibliography: Ancestry.com U.S. Census. Ohio. Cuyahoga. Cleveland. Ward 26. 1910; U.S. Census. Ohio. Cuyahoga. Orange. Dist. 682. 1930; Ohio Deaths 1908-1932, 1938-1944 and 1958-2002 record for Ruth T. (Tomlinson) Overholser; Stilson, Jan. Memories of Ruth Overholser and the Credentials Committee; Joblin, Maurice, *Cleveland Past and Present*. 1887, Joblin, Maurice, *The Paternity of Jesus*, Self-published 1905.

Painter, JoAnn C.
b. December 27, 1954
d. September 8, 1993

JoAnn Coverstone Painter was born in Strasburg, Virginia, to Perry Garnett and Alva Virginia Shiley Coverstone. JoAnn was a lively little girl who loved going to church at Fort Valley Church of God in Christ Jesus. When she could, she would dash across the street and buy penny candy; it was common to see her enjoying a little piece of candy after church. Even with the extra sugar, JoAnn was thin, but she had a high-powered smile and energy to match. She married Michael Painter of Toms Brooks, Virginia, on October 4, 1975. They had one child, Alicia June.

JoAnn was always active and became involved in many projects and organizations. She attended Oregon Bible College for one year before she married, and she was a member of the Fort Valley church. Pastor James Mattison baptized her on May 3, 1970, in the little creek beside the church. JoAnn served as Fort Valley Ladies Society president and as secretary-treasurer and teacher for the Sunday school. She was chairman of the Reading Incentive Program for Sandy Hook Elementary School in Strasburg, treasurer of the Sandy Hook PTO and chosen as Sandy Hook Parent Volunteer of the Year 1992-1993. JoAnn was also a member of the OBC Alumni Association and honorary alumnus of Massanutten Military Academy in Woodstock, Virginia.

JoAnn died following a difficult, eight-year battle with cancer. However, no one ever heard her complain nor did she seem to feel sorry for herself or desirous that others should feel sorry for her. During this time her faith held firm. James 1:2-4 says:

> Consider it all joy, my brethren, when you encounter various trials, knowing that the testing of your faith produces endurance. And let endurance have its perfect result, that you may be perfect and complete, lacking in nothing.

JoAnn's faith helped her endure. She knew that even through the roughest times God would never leave her, that he was with her through it all, even to the very end. Psalm 23:4: "Even though I walk through the valley of the shadow of death, I will fear no evil, for thou art with me; Thy rod and Thy staff they comfort me." Funeral services were held on September 11, 1993, at Fort Valley Church of God by Pastor Jon T. Welch. JoAnn was 38 at the time of her death.

See Mattison, James

Bibliography: Biography Project of Atlanta Bible College, David Krogh, compiler. Memories of JoAnn Coverstone by Jan Stilson, her pastor's wife from 1963 until 1967.

Partlowe, Hollis
b. February 2, 1925

Hollis was born near Browntown, Virginia, in the mountains overlooking Front Royal. He grew up loving to hunt and fish. His father taught him to hunt. Hollis said they grew their own food, butchered cattle and hogs three times a year, plus had chickens to eat, but when he got a chance he went hunting with his father and loved it. He remarked that the flavor of wild game was a nice change. They hunted squirrels, rabbits, pheasants and grouse.

During WWII, Hollis served in the Pacific with the US Army as an amphibian on an LCN barge. They worked closely with the Navy to pick up troops, drop them on the beach, pick up more troops, back and forth. They also delivered supplies by this method. When his unit finished at New Guinea, they moved up to the next islands. While they prepared to retrieve the troops for a Philippine Island invasion, the Japanese surrendered. The invasion proceeded, but no shots were fired.

When Hollis was discharged from the Army, he returned to northern Virginia. On September 8, 1946, he married Hilda Updike, a neighbor and schoolmate. The newlyweds wanted to attend church and visited six or eight, but heard that services were being held at Cool Spring, so they went there and met Pastor Alva Huffer. Alva was preaching at Maurertown and Fort Valley churches on alternating Sundays. He preached at Cool Spring on the fifth Sunday. Alva also held Bible study at Cool Spring every Tuesday night. Hollis and Hilda began to attend. Alva Huffer baptized them on July 30, 1950.

Their daughter Rachel was born in Virginia, and soon after, Hollis and Hilda decided to attend Oregon Bible College to study for the ministry. Hollis began in the autumn of 1954 and graduated spring 1958. A second daughter, Becky, was born in Illinois. Hollis's first pastorate was at Macomb, Illinois, where he remained until 1965. That fall the family moved to Phoenix where Hollis pastored until autumn of 1976 when they returned to Illinois to assume the pastorate at the Oregon Church of God. Hollis remained at Oregon until 1988. During that time, he taught Systematic Theology at OBC for five semesters. He also edited *The Restitution Herald* from 1988-1991.

After his retirement from the Oregon church, he did not retire from preaching. He filled pulpits at Pennellwood in Grand Rapids; Naperville, Illinois; Waterloo, Iowa; and Ripley, Illinois. Finally, he took the pastorate at Dixon, Illinois, where he preached until the church closed in 2006. Hollis said his favorite aspect of the ministry was preaching. He loved to preach the Word and tell people about the Kingdom of God. He said his advice to young ministers is to "preach the Word and stick with the basics. Tell people about Jesus, his death, resurrection and coming again to establish his Kingdom." Other churches aren't preaching it. He said it was that message that attracted him to Alva's church in Virginia. He just couldn't abide the preaching of modern ministers, but Alva's Bible teaching made sense.

The second thing Hollis liked about the ministry was meeting people in their homes. He liked to call on church visitors and talk with them about their needs and their faith. He liked explaining the distinctive Bible doctrines of the Church of God. When asked if he had learned this skill at Oregon Bible College, if he had been led by the Lord to call in homes or if it was an extension of his own personality, he said, "All three." In Hollis's view, the churches he pastored grew because the laymen invited their friends and family to church, and he went out and visited them in their homes.

Hollis is a man of prayer, praying first thing every morning for the Lord's leading, and last thing at night. He said if you

Photo from Hollis & Hilda Partlowe

Macomb Church of God pastors, from left: Rex Cain, Linford Moore, Warren Sorenson, Hollis Partlowe, Roy Humphreys.
Photo from Rex Cain

want a constant relationship with the Lord, be steady in your relationship with Him morning and night. He spoke of the ministers who have had the greatest influence on him. They are Clyde Randall, Harvey U. Krogh Jr. and Alva Huffer. Hollis's deep appreciation for the friendship and the testimony of these men inspired him to be a better pastor. These men revered the message and the mission of the Church of God, and they loved people.

Baptizing and officiating for Rachel and Becky's weddings are Hollis's greatest joys along with baptizing their husbands and his two grandchildren, Kimberly and Brian Hall. Kimberly is a gemologist in southern California and Brian is a Staff Sergeant in the Air Force. As wonderful as such joys are, ministers are often faced with challenges during their ministries. Hollis said his greatest challenge was preaching the funerals of John and Ruth Lewis, Russell Reye and David Segar in April 1979; all died on the same night in three separate auto accidents. It was a tragedy which shook the Oregon community and broke the hearts of the Church of God members. Hollis said he knew that hundreds of people maybe thousands were praying for him. People called him and told him so, and he could feel it.

In talking about prophecy and how current world events might fit in, Hollis felt the strained economy, increasing natural disasters and other difficulties might be leading to the end times. He doesn't think the seven seals of Revelation have been broken yet, but notes, "we are heading in that direction." He feels the Great Tribulation is still before us and the next great event on the prophecy calendar will be the rapture of the church. He said, "We don't know the details of how that works out, but the Lord does. When the plan falls into place it will seem so evident to us that we will wonder how we could not have known it." Also, "We should live with hope and be prepared for the Lord's coming as it can't be long now."

See Huffer, Alva
     Krogh, Harvey U., Jr.
     Lewis, John
     Randall, Clyde E.
Bibliography: Interview with Hollis Partlowe, March 2010.

Patrick, Cecil A.
b. January 19, 1907
d. June 5, 1991

Cecil Patrick was born in Eden Valley, Minnesota, to James and Maud (Matheny) Patrick. His father was active in evangelistic, pastoral and editorial work for the Church of God. His instruction and example led Cecil to accept the Lord at 11. He honored this commitment throughout his life. Cecil married Mary Shirley on May 25, 1940, in Cleveland, Ohio. They had two daughters, Rebecca and Gayle.

For many years Cecil served his local church in lay ministry. He taught numerous classes and was an elder in the churches he served. He was also called on to preach and did so on many occasions in Indiana, Ohio, Illinois and Florida. While living in Indiana, Cecil was elected State Conference President, and he served on the General Conference Board of Directors in the late 1950s.

In the 1960s, Cecil was part of a core group with a vision of planting a church on the west side of Cleveland. To help this dream become a reality, Cecil applied for a ministerial license. With this license, he offered his services as a pastor of the newly formed Columbia Station Church of God. During his four-year term there, a building was constructed and the church was established. Cecil was a dedicated student of Scripture and had a heart for the teachings of the Church of God Abrahamic Faith. For 12 years he wrote lessons for the *Truth Seeker's Adult Quarterly* where he could share this marvelous truth.

In retirement, Cecil supervised an Oregon Bible College student's internship while wintering in Florida. In this Paul-Timothy relationship, he was able to impart the wisdom of his lifelong study and experience.

Cecil died in his home following a lengthy illness. He was buried in Riverview Cemetery in Oregon, Illinois. His faith was in the resurrection and he would often quote Job 19:25, 26, "For I know that my redeemer lives, and that he shall stand at the latter day upon the earth; and though after my skin worms destroy this body, yet in my flesh shall I see God."

See Patrick, James A. (19th)
Bibliography: ABC Biography Project, David Krogh, compiler.

Paulson, Dorothy Krogh
b. 1912
d. December 8, 2001

Dorothy Krogh was born in Blair, Nebraska, to Harvey and Birdie Mehrens Krogh. She was raised in the Church of God, a third generation member. A Church of God evangelist baptized her maternal grandfather, Herman Mehrens, in 1866. Dorothy's family attended the Church of God at Blair until it closed. Dorothy was the second of five children with siblings Harvey Jr., Clara, Oakley and Kenneth. She attended the Bible Training School at Oregon, Illinois, in the early 1930s along with her older brother, Harvey Jr. She married Roy Paulson and they had two sons, Bill, who attended Oregon Bible College, and Leslie. They had 14 grandchildren.

Dorothy was devoted to the truths taught by the Church of God throughout her life and died in the Lord. Pastor Scott Ross of the Jaynes Street Church of God in Omaha, Nebraska, conducted her funeral service.

See Krogh, Birdie (19th)
       Krogh, Harvey U., Jr.
Bibliography: ABC Biography project, David Krogh, compiler.

Pearson, Charles Arthur (Bob)
b. February 4, 1903
d. January 13, 1971

Bob Pearson was born in Miami County, Ohio, and died there 67 years later. Elder John H. Anderson baptized him on July 23, 1916, in Brush Creek. Bob was active in his local church and the Berean "Round Robin" group during his teen years. In 1946 he and wife Eunice moved to Oregon, Illinois, to become dormitory parents and caretakers of the property at Oregon Bible College. There Bob endeared himself to the students and became known as "Pop."

He was a faithful member of Brush Creek Church of God until 1950 when he assisted in starting the Glad Tidings Chapel Church of God of the Abrahamic Faith at Dayton, Ohio, where he served as elder until his fatal illness. The Pearson family heritage survives through the ministry of Rita Gillette of the Blessed Hope Bible Church in Rockford, Illinois, and former pastor Timothy Pearson.

See Anderson, J.H. (19th)
Bibliography: Ancestry.com. *Ohio Deaths, 1908-1932, 1938-1944, and 1958-2007*, record for Charles A. Pearson; Biography project of the Atlanta Bible College, David Krogh, compiler.

Pensyl, Frederick
b. March 24, 1918
d. May 2, 1996

Fred Pensyl was born in Greenfield, Ohio, to Jesse and Bertha Pensyl. He married Gladys "Tuttie" in Urbana, Ohio, in 1940. They had one son, Gary. Fred served as lay pastor at the new church in Urbana for a number of years. This missionary church was supported by the Northeast

Fred and Gladys Pensyl
Photo from Rex Cain

Conference and received Mission Builder's League Grant money to construct a building.

Fred worked closely in conference with E. Richard Smith, pastor of the Church of God at Lawrenceville, Ohio. In 1964, the two ministers and several laypeople met to consider planting a new church in Columbus, Ohio. The first board meeting was held April 7, 1968, to elect officers and consider a pastor. Robert Shrienk was invited to become pastor, and he began his studies at Oregon Bible College to prepare for that work. In the meantime, Fred became the regular pastor at Hope Chapel, and Tuttie served as pianist. Due to conflict over the name Church of God by another group in Columbus, the new church changed their name to Philadelphia Chapel and Abrahamic Faith Church of God. Fred served as pastor at Hope Chapel from 1964 to 1968, and co-pastored at Lawrenceville from 1971 to 1973. He helped start the Pleasant Hill Church of God and served as pastor from 1973 to 1987. Fred served as pastor at Chapel Hill in Urbana from 1987 until his death.

Pastors Jack Hearp, Rex Cain and David Krogh conducted Fred's funeral service. All the ministers of Ohio served as honorary pallbearers. Fred rests in Oak Dale Cemetery, Urbana, Ohio.

   See Cain, Rex
           Hearp, Jack
           Smith, E. Richard

Bibliography: History of the Hope Chapel Church of God, author unknown, furnished by Pastor Rex Cain, Bedford, Ohio, January 2010; Obituary of Fred Pensyl in *Urbana Citizen*, May 2, 1996.

Pickerl, Lottie Logan
   b. January 14, 1891
   d. May 1, 1999

Lottie Pickerl was born to Gideon and Eva Winrott Logan in LaPaz, Marshall County, Indiana. The family lived along Michigan Road which became US Route 31. This highway was famous for extending from Mobile, Alabama, north to Michigan. Gideon Logan owned a general store and had half-ownership of a sawmill at Teegarden, Indiana. This gave the family some income and status in the community. Lottie entered school at a younger age than her classmates, and as a result, she failed the second grade because she had difficulty with arithmetic. The teacher said if her parents would help her, she would pass. Her mother said, "Keep her in second grade until she can learn it herself." Pastor John Wince baptized Lottie in July 1909 in a creek near North Salem Church of God.

Being the daughter of an entrepreneur, Lottie learned the meaning of hard work. She chose to teach primary school as her vocation. She also completed work at Valparaiso University, but did not graduate. On October 12, 1918, she married Marion C. Pickerl. H.V. Reed, pastor of the Church of God in Chicago, performed the ceremony. Marion was a dairy farmer and Lottie helped with farm operation in many ways. Dairying is hard work, but it was a blessing Lottie knew the farm business because her husband died unexpectedly. She was widowed with children to raise and a farm to run. She worked diligently to pay the bills and raise the children, but eventually it became too difficult.

Lottie became a practical nurse and provided special care to people in their homes. Soon the family moved to South Bend where she bought a house and cared for elderly people in her home. When she received a bank loan, the banker told her she was the first widow to receive one from their institution. In time, she paid off the loan, and the family was happy. Lottie also ran a home for unwed mothers and began an adoption placement agency.

Still, Lottie was restless because she hadn't finished her college education. She went back to school in her seventies, graduated and taught for several years.

She was a member of the Hope Chapel Church of God in South Bend where she played the organ, taught Sunday school and assisted in other ministries. Her son Logan became an FBI agent, and she was quite proud of him. Daughter Jean Derbin married an architect; they also worshipped at Hope Chapel. Another daughter, Margalee, died in infancy.

Lottie Pickerl gave a testimony in *The Restitution Herald* regarding the joys of tithing. She said she had been tithing since 1932 on $5 a week, supporting two children, her father and her mother. She was a widow. She had a job when most people didn't during the Great Depression. Her income increased until it was 13 times more than when she began to work.

Lottie included a curious story about her mother in her book, *Amazing True Stories*. It obviously was a story passed down through the family. Lottie's mother, Eva, and new husband moved into their first home—the only empty house in Fizzletown near Plymouth, Indiana. The house was empty because it was said to be haunted. Eva, being a staunch member of the Church of God, did not believe in ghosts. The neighbors said the house was plagued with strange knocking and bright lights inside it. They said that within a year of moving in someone always died. The young couple moved in anyway. Strange things happened immediately including the lights and knocking. The couple noticed some of these phenomena when they returned home from an Indiana Conference meeting after dark. Within a year, Eva's first husband died of tuberculosis. Lottie concluded in her book, "No one has ever been able to solve the mystery of the haunted house." Lottie's book is in the Archives of Atlanta Bible College.

Lottie was famous throughout the Churches of God in the Midwest and some areas beyond. She was short, stout, outspoken, opinionated and stubborn. Combine these characteristics with intelligence and determination, and one discovers the widow's formula for survival. Still, these same survival traits can also make problems for pastors, and they often did. People loved Lottie, but regretted some of her outlandish and vocal misbehavior. Yet, she didn't let little things like adversity slow her down. She was an overcomer.

Pastor John Railton and Timothy Pearson served at her funeral service. She was interred in the cemetery at Edwardsburg, Michigan.

See Anderson, J.H. (19th)
Wince, John (19th)
Reed, H.V. (19th)

Bibliography: Pickerl, Lottie, "Tithing Story", *The Restitution Herald*, Sydney Magaw, editor, Oregon, Illinois, Jan. 25, 1949. Derbin, Jean. Lottie's daughter supplied information regarding her mother via e-mail, March 9, 2009; Pickerl, Lottie. *Amazing True Stories*. Self-published, circa 1990.

Poland, Earl
b. February 21, 1936
d. March 5, 2010

Earl Poland was the son of William Clarence and Anna Mae Tyree Poland. He was born in Skelton, West Virginia, but raised in Baltimore. Earl graduated from Dundalk Senior High School, and attended and graduated Oregon Bible College in Oregon, Illinois, receiving a bachelor's degree in theology. Pastor Poland or his family may have studied the Bible doctrines at the Church of God at Skelton before it closed. Circuit preacher John W. Niles of Pennsylvania evangelized this church. Earl married Deanna L. Yost in Baltimore on August 1, 1955. They had twin daughters, Lisa (Lowery) and Patricia (Bryant), and two other daughters, Dianna (Cockerham) and Dorothy (Cook).

Earl served a pastorate at Dixon, Illinois, Church of God. He lived in Hedrick, Indiana, and ministered at the Church of God for 30 years. Earl was active in the work of the Indiana State Conference and the Church of God General Conference located in McDonough, Georgia. He also served the Portland, Indiana, Church of God until his death. Earl worked as a meat cutter at the Attica IGA grocery for many years. He was a veteran of the US Navy and served in the Korean War.

Pastor Poland died at St. Vincent Hospice, Indianapolis. Pastor Joe Astolfi conducted the service.

See Niles, John W. (19th)

Bibliography: Earl Poland obituary from the Mausfuneralhome.com

Pope, E. Cedric
b. September 28, 1908
d. May 1985

E. Cedric Pope was one of the first students to attend the newly organized Bible Training Classes at Oregon, Illinois, during the 1923 to 1924 term. He was from Niagara Falls, New York, having relocated there from Ohio.

After arriving in Oregon, he fell in love with the daughter of the Golden Rule Home's matron—her name was Martha Musselman. The Golden Rule Home opened in December 1923, but since the new home was not filled with senior citizens, the Bible Training students also resided there.

Cedric and Martha were married in a ceremony at Golden Rule Home on June 5 and drove to Macy, Indiana, to visit her relatives and from there to Niagara Falls to visit his family. Their wedding may have been the first Church of God college marriage giving OBC the nickname, Oregon *Bridal* College. After leaving Oregon, Cedric and Martha settled in Dekalb, Illinois, and attended Normal School. He was available for preaching and is seen in the pages of *The Restitution Herald* filling pulpits all over Illinois in the absence of a pastor.

Bibliography: Ancestry.com U.S. Census. Ohio. Lucas. Oregon. Dist. 4, 1920; Social Security Death List, record for Cedric Pope, *The Restitution Herald*, June 10, 1924; Oct. 6, 1925.

Pryor, Dr. Charles Vernon
b. May 24, 1941

Charles Pryor was born in Hendersonville, North Carolina, the eldest child of Clayborne Franklin (C.F.) and Helen Edna Merrill Pryor. He has two sisters, Anita (Hale) and Gayle (Ross). Charles attended elementary schools in Edneyville, North Carolina, and Warren County, Virginia. In 1955 the family moved to Cleveland, Ohio, where he graduated from high school and received a bachelor's degree in Education from Baldwin-Wallace College (BW) in Berea, Ohio. Following his freshman year Charles attended one semester at Oregon Bible College, but returned to Baldwin-Wallace where he was on scholarship for four years. Charles has been a member of Churches of God in Illinois (Oregon and East Peoria) and Ohio including the Golden Rule Church of God where his father, Pastor C.F. Pryor, baptized him in 1957. Charles and Lois Stadden married at Golden Rule on December 29, 1962, with Pastor Pryor officiating. They have three children, Bryan Charles, Elizabeth Dolores (Raymond) and Todd Herbert Pryor. Charles and Lois have six grandchildren.

Upon graduation from BW, Charles became a professional educator, a journey that took him on a career path with learning and adventure around every turn. In addition to a degree from Baldwin-Wallace, his educational attainments included 30 hours in school administration at Kent State University. In 1969, he earned a Master of Science in Education (elementary school counseling) and a Doctorate in Education (counselor education) in 1974, both from Northern Illinois University (NIU).

Charles taught elementary school in Lakewood and in Berea, Ohio, (December 1963-June 1968); at the Central Office of Peoria, Illinois, Public School from 1972-1974; in Higher Education at the University of Houston, 1974-1977, which included a six-month, off-campus teaching assignment in New Delhi, India; and Northeast Louisiana University, 1977-1980. From fall, 1980 to January 1985 Charles served as Oregon Bible College president. He returned to Northeast Louisiana University (namedchanged to University of Louisiana at Monroe (ULM) in 1999) from which he retired in December 2008, marking 45 years as a professional educator.

He accepted the challenge to preside over the academic arm of Oregon Bible College after the deaths of OBC president John Lewis and wife Ruth in 1979. The Pryors moved to Oregon with Bryan and Todd. Elizabeth remained in Louisiana to complete her college degree at NLU. They were active in the Oregon church and the community. Charles served as Chamber of Commerce president and held offices in the Kiwanis Club.

During Charles' administration at Oregon Bible College, the campus relocated from North Third Street to Seventh Street. The Golden Rule Home was remodeled with administrative offices and a conference room on the ground floor and classrooms on the second. Funds provided by Paul and Ruth Overholser financed the renovation. During the Pryor administration, Kent Ross came in to teach pastoral courses, and Anthony Buzzard was hired to teach Bible courses. Both Kent and Anthony completed graduate studies under the guidelines of the Lawrence Scholarship. Eugene Stilson served as instructor and Academic Dean and directed the education of the faculty and the educational partnership with Rock Valley College. Working together, Pryor and Stilson monitored the curriculum to assure that it met quality standards for accreditation in the future, should the organization choose to go in that direction.

Oregon Bible College entered into a cooperative effort with Rock Valley College in Rockford, Illinois, to provide general education courses needed for graduation. Those courses were open to the Oregon community and OBC students toward completing their program requirements in general education. Several instructors, including the late Lloyd Hoshaw, offered those courses on the OBC campus. Hoshaw became a board member of Rock River Christian College several years later.

Working closely with the Church of God General Conference administration and engaging the services of a professional consultant, the OBC Development Foundation was established. The foundation's goal to put a million dollar endowment program in place and work with the church membership to fund it through appropriate gift instruments was successful. In 2011 the endowment's earnings meet student support and other financial needs.

During Charles' administration, foreign missions became available for OBC student participation. Jan Stilson, newly-hired Library Director at OBC, also led or coordinated several short-term mission teams to Mexico and Peru with OBC students. Students also participated in volunteer efforts with Habitat for Humanity in Americus, Georgia, in cooperation with the Oregon Church of God. Charles also sought to improve the food service for students at OBC in keeping with guidelines of other campus food service operations. Another project included the purchase of television equipment and production of 13 television programs of interest to churchmen and community-minded citizens for the local cable company. A drama team under the direction of Kent Ross also presented morality plays and skits, always popular for Oregon's Autumn on Parade festival every October.

At the University of Louisiana at Monroe, Charles was Assistant Professor of Counseling and Counselor Education, and Associate Professor of Counseling and Department Head. In addition to teaching, he has also directed the Theses and Field Studies of nearly 20 students, and sat on Dissertation Committees of another 20+ students. Through the years Charles has been a member of appropriate professional counseling organizations including the American Counseling Association, The American School Counselors' Association, the Louisiana Counseling Association and several more. He has also been a Leadership and Counseling Department Head, President of the Faculty Senate for two terms, member of the University Strategic Planning Steering Committee and the Graduate Council. He has authored or co-authored several articles for leading Counselor Education scholarly publications or grant reviews.

In Louisiana the Pryors attend the North Monroe Baptist Church where Charles teaches a class for older men in the congregation—all WWII veterans except one. Charles said, "[It is] a fantastic teaching assignment." Charles and Lois participated in the Church of God History Conference at North Hills Church of God in Springfield, Ohio, in September 2010. Charles, Anita and Gayle presented the story of their father's ministry, and Lois and her sister, Joyce Schroth, presented the history of the Stadden family's contribution to the growth and development of the Church of God in Cleveland and Columbia Station, Ohio. In his retirement years, Charles plans to pursue fishing and other outdoor adventures on his small Christmas tree farm.

   See Pryor, Clayborne Franklin
        Ross, Kent
        Stadden, Herbert W.
        Stilson, Eugene

Bibliography: Pryor, Charles, Hale, Anita and Ross, Gayle, Paper on C.F. Pryor presented at 2010 History Conference, North Hills Church of God, Springfield, Ohio; Pryor, Charles, e-mail March 29, 2011.

Pryor, Clayborne Franklin
b. March 28, 1919
d. November 1978

Clayborne Franklin Pryor was born in Henderson County, North Carolina, to Guy V. and Ida Belle Pryor. The youngest of four children, he was named for his grandfather, Clayborne Franklin Freeman. Mr. Freeman served the Confederacy for three years in the Civil War.

After the close of the Civil War, C.F. Freeman learned biblical truth from Newell Bond and Enoch M. Anderson. J.H. Anderson, son of Enoch Anderson, spoke of Mr. Freeman lovingly as he wrote an obituary published in *The Restitution Herald* on October 26, 1920. J.H. Anderson wrote, "Brother Freeman loved the truth and was willing to support it. He led his children into the truth. His daughter, Ida Belle Pryor, is one of the best workers we have at Liberty, N.C." As a result of the work and dedication of the Andersons, young Clayborne Franklin Pryor (C.F.) was raised in a dedicated Church of God family. J.H. Anderson baptized C.F. and M.O. Williamson ordained him.

C.F. Pryor was a farmer. He built a lovely home for his family at Bearwallow Mountain, North Carolina. He was discipled in the Church of God work by M.O. Williamson, pastor of two small congregations. Williamson visited Liberty church on fifth Sundays, which were also celebrated with a potluck on the church grounds. One day Verna Thayer drove over the mountain from Morristown, Tennesee, to conduct a Bible School at Liberty Church, and with her was Alva G. Huffer, a young graduate from Oregon Bible College and pastor at the new work in Morristown. Alva and C.F. Pryor became good friends. Alva married Awa McMinn, C.F.'s cousin, and moved to Virginia. Alva was instrumental in calling C.F. Pryor to preach at the Cool Spring Church of God.

In C.F. Pryor's autobiography, written in April 1957, he said:

> I was ordained as a minister of the gospel by the two Churches of God of the Abrahamic Faith in the Carolinas – Anderson Chapel Church of God, at Hendersonville, North Carolina and Guthrie Grove Church of God, near Pelzer, South Carolina. Ordination services were officiated by Bro. M.O. Williamson of Pelzer, pastor of the two churches at that time. The ordination service took place on Easter Sunday, 1950.
>
> Following ordination, I served as associate pastor of the Anderson Chapel Church until November 1951, at which time we left our home and moved to Browntown, Virginia, where we began our first active duty as a full-time pastor. While there, because the church was small, we supplemented our church income by doing secular work. The first two years spent there we continued working as a mason and carpenter, partly on actual construction work and partly in a building supply in Front Royal, Virginia. The last two years we spent as teacher and principal of the Browntown Elementary School.
>
> While serving the church in this capacity the church grew both spiritually and in number. When we received the call from the Golden Rule Church in Cleveland, Ohio, to fill the vacancy of pastor in that church, we accepted and

began full-time church work there. We have enjoyed our work in Cleveland and believe that God has blessed us in many ways.

Our personal testimony is this, that we have certainly realized a fulfillment of the promise made by Jesus when He said, "Every one that hath forsaken houses, or brethren or sisters, or father, or mother, or wife, or children, or lands, for my name's sake, shall receive a hundredfold, and shall inherit everlasting life." We find that every member of the Church of God is like a father, mother, sister, or brother to us; so therefore we have literally a hundredfold of each. We hope to be able to realize as literal a fulfillment of the last of the promises that we shall inherit everlasting life when our Lord returns to this earth.

During the pastorate in Virginia, the family met and befriended Hollis and Hilda Partlowe. They were newly married with no children, and they were very fond of Gayle Pryor (Ross), just three years old at that time. They called her their child and teasingly renamed her Ginger Frances Partlowe. Fifty-eight years later at a church conference Hollis still greeted Gayle, "Well, hello, Ginger Frances!"

In 1955, C.F. was called to pastor at the Golden Rule Church of God in Cleveland. He succeeded Robert Huggins, another son of North Carolina. C.F. Pryor especially loved working with youth groups. He taught Berean lessons published for young people on a weekly basis and saw to it that his youth group attended state and national youth conferences. He presented a paper at Minister's Conference in 1961 on the complex subject of the corporeality of Jehovah. He believed it.

During his ministry, many were influenced to attend Oregon Bible College and some have been career pastors. Pastor Pryor mentored his son-in-law, Scott Ross, in his early ministry. C.F. taught him some of the finer points of officiating at weddings and funerals, and other pastoral tasks. Charles Pryor, the Pryors eldest child, also attended OBC for one semester. Charles received his bachelor's in education from Baldwin-Wallace College in Berea, Ohio, and both his master's and doctorate from Northern Illinois University in DeKalb, Illinois. Charles served as Oregon Bible College president. During his administration, he established the Million Dollar Club. The influence and enthusiasm of C.F. Pryor endures.

The Pryor family moved to Oregon, Illinois, in 1966 to assume the pastorate. Pastor Pryor helped the church to grow and participated actively in community events. He also assisted as he could with General Conference work and the Bible college. He was a frequent chapel speaker. While in Oregon, Anita married Michael Hale, and Gayle married Scott Ross.

In 1971, C.F. and Helen Pryor moved to Columbus, Ohio, as employees of the Northeastern Conference, to pursue home mission work for five years. A nucleus of worshippers remains active in Columbus. They later moved to Springfield, Louisiana, to pastor the Blood River Church of God. This would be C.F.'s final pastorate.

Clayborne Franklin Pryor was interred in his beloved North Carolina mountains at Bearwallow. Helen relocated to Oregon, Illinois, and lived in a duplex next to Mary Krogh. The two widows were a comfort to each other. Helen later moved to Monroe, Louisiana, to be near family. After suffering with Parkinson's disease for many years, Helen now rests beside her husband.

C.F. Pryor's loving and faithful North Carolina siblings, their families and his many church friends supported him throughout his life and career. Juanita Pryor English, Jennie Reive Pryor and Freeman Pryor lived service-filled lives. They demonstrated their faithfulness to the Lord in their various communities. The family remains strong and committed to loving God, each other and to those around them.

See Anderson, Enoch (19th)
Anderson, J.H. (19th)
Duncan, Z.B.
Partlowe, Hollis
Pryor, Dr. Charles
Pryor, Guy Vernon and Ida Belle
Williamson, M.O. (19th)

Bibliography: From the family in an e-mail August 25, 2009; "We are pleased to honor Cool Spring Church of God", *The Restitution Herald*, Oregon, Il., Nov. 1975; Pryor, Charles, Hale, Anita and Ross, Gayle, Paper on C.F. Pryor presented at the 2010 History Conference, North Hills Church of God, Springfield, Ohio.

The congregation at Liberty, North Carolina, posed after Sunday service. On the right, Robert Huggins is behind the woman in the dark dress holding a child. Ida Bell Freeman (Pryor), CF Pryor's mother, is in the second row, right of center, the short woman with a round face, wearing a hat.
Photo from Anita Hale, Charles Pryor and Gayle Ross

Pryor, Guy Vernon
b. July 26, 1886
d. April 25, 1965

Pryor, Ida Belle
b. July 25, 1884
d. September 2, 1950

Guy and Ida Belle Freeman Pryor were leading forces in the establishment of the Anderson Chapel at Henderson, North Carolina. Ida Belle was a lifelong believer of the Church of God Abrahamic Faith. She grew up in Henderson County and attended church at Liberty. Bro. J.M. Lyda baptized her there in July 1899. Mrs. Pryor was a schoolteacher before her marriage teaching for eight years in the Big Willow and Liberty communities of Henderson County. After she and Guy Pryor married she talked with him about accepting Christ. A.N. Durham baptized him on August 17, 1924. Guy was a lifelong resident of Henderson County, North Carolina.

The Pryors were instrumental in starting a congregation at Gallimore Gap, North Carolina, before the effort to establish the Anderson Chapel church. Mrs. Pryor saved earnings from farm produce and eggs to contribute Anderson Chapel building construction in the mid-1940s. She was active in the establishing children's Sunday school classes because she felt very strongly that the strength of the church lay in its youth. The Pryors had four children, Juanita (English), Freeman, Jennie and Clayborne Franklin (C.F.), a long-time popular pastor. All the Pryors have been active in the work of the Church of God Abrahamic Faith.

After Ida's death, Guy left the family farm and lived with his children. He often attended General Conference and was a familiar figure to the Church of God congregations pastored by his son, C.F. Pryor. Guy and Ida Belle sleep in the Lord, side by side they await the coming of Jesus to awaken them to everlasting life.

See Durham, A.N.
Pryor, Clayborne F.
Pryor, Dr. Charles
Bibliography: ABC Biography project, David Krogh, compiler.

There are no biographical entries for this letter.

R

Railsback, Emma Charlotte
b. January 13, 1860
d. August 21, 1958

Emma Weeks was a faithful worker in the Church of God in Indiana near South Bend. She was one of eight children and grew up in the Christian church. She married Ezra Railsback on November 9, 1891, in Hammond, Indiana. Ezra was the son of Richard C. Railsback. Most members of the Railsback family lived near Argos, Indiana.

At the time Emma met Ezra, she wasn't much concerned about doctrine. One time in studying the antics of a slow child, she asked him, "Do you think that child has an immortal soul?" He said, "No one has an immortal soul." She could scarcely believe it. She began searching her Bible for verses to prove it. Ezra offered her a dollar for every one she found. She couldn't find any. She said, "Why do ministers talk about going to heaven at death?" From that point on she began attending the Church of God. L.E. Conner baptized her in 1893.

Ezra and Emma lived in Chicago in 1892 when the White City, an exhibit for the 1893 Columbia Exhibition or World's Fair, was constructed on Chicago's south side. Ezra was a carpenter on that project. When this project ended, they returned to northern Indiana, settling in South Bend where they helped establish that church and raised their four girls, Leta (McLeod), Verna (Rahn) Thelma (Moore) and Mildred (Stantial).

The South Bend, Indiana, home the Railsbacks left when they moved west.

Emma was active in youth work. She was elected president of the Indiana Berean Society in 1911. She scheduled one of the last Berean programs in the state at the Old Antioch Church of God in 1912, just one year before activities ceased there. She schooled her daughters well in Bible truths and attended summer Bible schools in Plymouth, Indiana, and Oregon, Illinois. Emma herself attended many conferences in Illinois, Michigan and Indiana. In this way, she became acquainted with many Church of God ministers. In her diary, she made notes under the heading "Church of God Ministers I have known." There were 72 names on the list, and she corresponded with many of them on matters of doctrine.

Ezra and Emma moved to California in the summer of 1919 with ten members of the Railsback family. They began a church work in Los Angeles. *The Restitution Herald* featured an entertaining travelogue made during that arduous trip. Entertaining and informative as it was, it was Thelma's diary that gave the most details about the grueling challenges the family faced driving two cars with camping equipment across muddy roads, over mountains and through deserts with canvas water bags strapped to the backs of the vehicles. Her account as a 15-year-old journalist tells the inside story of numerous broken springs, ruptured tires and leaky tents, but it also tells of fun times, great scenery, meeting other travelers, including Native Americans, and great meals of beefsteak and potatoes over a campfire.

When they arrived in Los Angeles the Railsbacks bought a house and remodeled it. This was their church home for a while. S.J. Lindsay, who spent his summers in Oregon, Illinois, was the congregation's pastor. Emma assumed the responsibilities after Lindsay retired. She preached on Sundays when there was no other preacher available. The first church property in Los Angeles was at 103rd Street and Broadway. In 1936, Emma and Ezra mortgaged their home to build the first church at that location. A friend on the city council helped get their

*Above: The Railsback family gathers for a photo just before departing Indiana to travel to California.
Below: Railsbacks camped enroute to California. They suffered so many flat tires and broken springs the trip was lengthened by several days.*

architectural plans approved. L.D. Conner, son of L.E. Conner, was the contractor. The mortgage on the home was retired by 1939. How long they owned this church property is unknown, but it was eventually sold and new property purchased in San Gabriel. The church there was called the San Gabriel Mission. Emma pastored at the Los Angeles Church on and off from 1927-1947. Other pastors who preached at 103rd Street include G.E. Marsh from 1940-1946, Roy Graham, Harry Payne, Grover Gordon and Terry Ferrell.

In March 1948, the Railsbacks returned to South Bend for several months. During that time James McLain, who had been serving as pastor or co-pastor with Mrs. Railsback since 1946, managed the Los Angeles work.

Ezra had been active in developing *The Restitution Herald*. He was a Restitution Publishing Company board member several times while the Railsbacks lived in the Midwest. This board supervised *The Restitution* operations. During the tumultuous year of controversy over the management of *The Restitution*, after which it was moved to Cleveland under the editorial guidance of Robert Huggins, Indiana people were unhappy. In fact, Ezra Railsback was the whistleblower on *The Restitution's* activities around 1910, an act for which many people have blamed L.E. Conner. At the 1911 Indiana State Conference annual meeting Ezra moved:

> That since the *Restitution* in transferring to its present management has violated its previous position before the Indiana people to the extent that the majority of the brethren in the state desire severance from their former relations, that motion be presented to declare the *Restitution* no longer the official organ of the Church of God in Indiana and that its place is vacant.

The motion carried, setting the stage for the ultimate acceptance of *The Restitution Herald* as the official voice of the Church of God. Ezra's motion appeared in *The Restitution Herald* on October 26, 1911.

After Ezra's death in 1950 Emma continued serving churches up and down the west coast. At age 88 she wrote in her journal, "The 8th Psalm I am memorizing. It is short but my memory is poor." The limitations of age were affecting her. She wrote again, "I am praying for more strength; hope to do more teaching of the Truth."

In 1958, she ordered 13 copies of Alva Huffer's *Systematic Theology,* which was not yet in print, for her grandchildren. In 1960, well after her death, they were sent to the church and distributed to her family. Her family continues to serve the Lord through the missionary ministry of Pastor Dean Moore, son of Thelma Railsback Moore. He was largely instrumental in beginning the mission to Labor Vieja in Mexico and worked with Roberto and Lupe Badillo through the General Conference and Lord's Harvest International to develop and manage that mission from 1957 to the present.

See   Conner, L.E. (19th), ref. *The Restitution* controversy
        Huggins, Robert
        Huffer, Dr. Alva
        Marsh, G.E.
        McLain, James
        Moore, Dean

See Also   Appendix 20—Missions, ref. Badillo

Bibliography: McCaslin, Ruby. E-mail to Kent Ross regarding history of Churches of God in California. Jan. 2007; Report of Indiana Bereans, *The Restitution Herald* May 29, 1912; Other Railsback reports, *The Restitution Herald*, Oct. 28, 1947; June 22, 1948; Stantial, Mildred, "Emma C. Railsback," ABC Biography Project, David Krogh, compiler; Moore, Dean, "Family Tree of David Railsback," and other family papers, furnished to Jan Stilson January 9, 2008; Indiana Conference Report, *The Restitution Herald*, Oct. 26, 1911.

Los Angeles Church of God

Railton, Albert Austin
b. September 26, 1920
d. September 24, 1990

Austin was born into John and Ruby Railton's Christian home in Fonthill, Ontario. In February 1924 the family moved to Oregon, Illinois, to work for the Church of God General Conference. Austin began public school there. His sister Mary was born in Oregon. The family later moved to Rockford when the Great Depression ended John's conference employment. The Railton family became involved in establishing the Rockford Church of God in 1930. As a youth, Austin accepted the Gospel message of Jesus Christ and the Kingdom of God. His grandfather, F.L. Austin, immersed him in baptism on August 5, 1934.

During a summer session of the General Conference in Oregon, Illinois, in 1936, Austin met a young woman from Virginia. He followed her there from Illinois, and married Cecil Baggarly on March 9, 1940. During those years in Virginia he worked at a soda fountain, as a barber, an electric appliance repairman and in a Virginia textile mill. From 1943 to 1945, Austin served in the US Navy hospital corps caring for injured Marines. He was proud that his service was spent saving lives rather than taking them. He was awarded a Purple Heart when a bullet pierced his helmet and zoomed around his head, resulting in shrapnel embedding in his shoulder. Their children Joyce and John arrived in 1946 and 1949.

In 1954, the Railtons left Winchester, Virginia, to begin pastoral studies at Oregon Bible College. While there, Austin worked as a rough piano tuner at the Cable Piano Factory. Upon graduation from OBC in 1958, he began his 30-year career in pastoral ministry. He and Cecil served Church of God congregations in Kokomo, Indiana (1958-1962); Chappell, Nebraska (1962-1965); South Bend, Indiana (1965-1971); Grand Rapids, Michigan (1971-1974); New Port Richey, Florida (1974-1976); Harlingen, Texas (1976-1984); Bedford, Ohio (1984-1989); and the Golden Rule Church in Cleveland, Ohio (1989-1990).

During his ministry Austin shared the Gospel message of Jesus and his Kingdom, added many to the body of Christ through baptism and assisted many more in the growth of Christian discipleship. He deeply appreciated the love and affection bestowed on him and Cecil by members of his congregations. For the last two years of his life, he fulfilled his long-time dream of working as a real estate agent.

Austin's personal interests and joys were varied. He loved to read; the source and subject didn't matter; there was something to be learned in everything. He spent many hours with the newspaper, entering a special world of personal concentration from which he was not easily distracted. He loved mental exercise in any form, mastering the chessboard, Rubik's cube and the dictionary, preferring to use multi-syllable words to simple ones.

He loved music—singing the hymns of faith in worship, playing his father's violin in the high school orchestra, whistling in harmony with music on the radio. He loved Boston terriers, wrestling with successive pets, feeding them treats and letting them fall asleep beside him in the chair. Austin loved his family too, and enjoyed visits from his children and grandchildren. He played games with the grandchildren and took an interest in their personal achievements. He found special pride in his children following him into pastoral ministry.

Austin loved Jesus Christ above all, watching the Middle East crisis which seemed to announce the nearness of His coming, and eagerly anticipating His return and the Kingdom age. Austin respected the Jewish nation, recognizing the special role it occupies in God's design.

Austin died two days before his 70th birthday. Everyone missed him greatly: Cecil, his wife of 50 years; their daughter Joyce Bolhous, her husband Steve and their children Marcee Turner (Jason), Adam and Aaron; son, John (Alice), and their children Jason, Amy and Joshua; Austin's sister Mary Milne (Kenneth); and his Christian brothers and sisters and many friends. He and Cecil sleep in Hillcrest Cemetery, Bedford, Ohio.

Bibliography: By Railton family for the ABC Biography Project, David Krogh, compiler.

Ramsey, Fulton A.
b. February 28, 1921
d. March 12, 1990

Fulton Alfred Ramsey was born on February 28, 1921. On August 9, 1947, he married Ellen Van Fleet of Grand Rapids, Michigan. Ellen was a graduate of Oregon Bible College and had edited the Berean column in *The Restitution Herald*. They had four children: Dale of Browntown, Virginia, and Jay, Gary and Chris of Fort Valley, Virginia.

Fulton became a member of the Fort Valley Church of God in Christ Jesus at his baptism on September 8, 1940, and served as the secretary/treasurer until his death. He was instrumental in constructing the present church building in 1949, as well as the addition in 1988. He quietly and diligently worked at keeping the church and parsonage grounds looking their best. Fulton loved people. He helped others without being asked and always smiled while he worked. If a visitor came to church, Fulton welcomed him and made him feel right at home.

Always concerned about others, he would often visit people to see how they were doing.

In March 1990, Fulton suffered a heart attack and fell into a fire he was tending on his farm. He was 69, and his death shocked the Fort Valley and the Church of God. His friendly handshake and "What do you know?" is missed even today, but not forgotten by everyone who loved him.

See Ramsay, C.C. (19th)

Bibliography: Ramsey Family for the Atlanta Bible College Biography Project, David Krogh, compiler

Randall, Celaine R.
b. July 25, 1922
d. July 30, 2008

Celaine R. "Randy" Randall was born to Clyde and Ruby Caroline Broberg Randall in Eden Valley, Minnesota. He graduated from high school in Fenwick, Ontario, and received a B.Th. degree from Oregon Bible College, Oregon, Illinois. Clyde baptized him on February 5, 1933, at Niagara Falls. Clyde was a Church of God Abrahamic Faith pastor at Niagara and Fonthill. Randy had one brother, Myron.

Randy wed Eunice Zollinger on October 9, 1941, at the Church of God in Oregon, Illinois. Clyde officiated. The couple had four children: sons David, who married Joan at Pleasant Hill, Ohio, and Mark, who married Carol at Troy, Ohio, and daughters Carol, who married John DeWolf of Westchester, Pennsylvania, and Lynda.

Celaine was granted a Church of God ministerial license in 1941. He held pastorates at South Bend, Indiana; Ripley, Illinois; Casey, Illinois; Brush Creek Church of God, Tipp City, Ohio; and Delta Raker Union Church, Delta, Ohio, where he served for 24 years. He also served as evangelist for churches in Indiana. During his career he also managed auto dealerships near his home and served in many civic organizations.

Eunice died on January 5, 2005; Randy's brother and his parents also predeceased him. He died near Troy, Ohio. Church of God Pastor Steven Zimbleman conducted the funeral service. Randy rests in Casstown Cemetery, Casstown, Ohio.

See Randall, Clyde E.

Bibliography: Obituary. "Alumni Newsletter," Atlanta Bible College/Oregon Bible College, McDonough, Ga., David Krogh, compiler, August 13, 2008.

Randall, Clyde E.
b. June 2, 1897
d. February 24, 1983

A. **Early Ministry**
B. **Involvement with Bereans**
C. **Family Man**
D. **A Pastor With Community Interests**
E. **The Editor and Author**
F. **The Future of the Church of God**

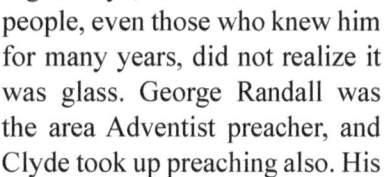

Clyde Randall was born at Eden Lake, Minnesota, to George and Lilly Chadwick Randall. He was raised in Mora, Minnesota. He had four older siblings: three brothers and a sister. The family remained close all their lives. When Clyde was little he lost an eye in an accident caused by his brother James Ernest. Clyde was fitted with a glass eye, and most people, even those who knew him for many years, did not realize it was glass. George Randall was the area Adventist preacher, and Clyde took up preaching also. His parents actively spread the Word of God around their area. Clyde was the only one of his older brothers to achieve more than an eighth grade education. His mother died while Clyde was a child, and when George remarried to a woman with a child, Clyde was old enough to be on his own.

A. Early Ministry

Elder James Patrick baptized C.E. Randall in August 1912. Clyde was licensed to the ministry in 1915 and ordained in the spring 1921. He came by preaching naturally, and approached it with vigor. He was on the go from the first chance he had, preaching at the Mora Church of God for practice, and then proceeding immediately into the Church of God national work by joining the National Berean Society. When he was only 18, he began attending state conferences around the Midwest.

Clyde also met the women who operated the Bereans' publishing ministry. In 1919 Clyde went to Chicago for a church meeting and told the congregation about the Berean work in Minnesota. The women of the Chicago congregation began the Berean society in 1913 so Chicago was its informal headquarters. Evelyn Harsh and Dr. Leila Whitehead led its publishing department. He visited their home to report the Minnesota work of the organization they had created. It showed his tremendous respect for them.

In Chicago Clyde learned about professional attire for preachers. He was always well dressed in a suit and wore "spats" over his shoes. Spats, leather covers that buttoned over the instep and ankle, protected shoes and ankles from water and mud.

Clyde Randall preached at Mora until 1925. He performed baptisms in the Snake River, often at night, with car lights pointed toward the river. He baptized his niece, Muriel Randall Haas, along with four others in such a manner.

In January 1931, Clyde and his wife, Ruby, assumed the pastorate at the Niagara Falls Church of God. Former pastor Grover Gordon returned home to Nebraska after only 1-1/2 years in the northeast. Clyde served congregations in Eldorado, Illinois; Mora, Minnesota; Tempe, Arizona; Fonthill, Ontario; and Omaha, Nebraska. He also participated in the Summer Bible Training Schools and conferences offered at the Oregon Church of God. He taught at the summer training classes from 1937 through 1940. After Oregon Bible College was organized the Bible Training School ceased but within a few years the summer camping program began. The first youth camp was held at Camp Emmaus in 1953.

B. Involvement with Bereans

While Clyde served as Minnesota Conference president the group actively promoted the Bible Faith Mission of India under the guidance of Mrs. Taylor and Pastor Charles R. Vedantachari in India. Clyde believed in missions, and for that reason, he was excited when the National Berean Society officially organized in 1913. Clyde became a spokesman and promoter of the National Berean Society from its inception. He offered to be the Bereans' emissary at other state conferences. To carry out his duties he traveled extensively to summer conferences around the country and promoted Berean organization activities. He participated in this way for several years. Muriel Haas said "He was a great public relations man."

Clyde so believed in the work of the Bereans, he wrote their mission statement in 1920. It was published in *The Restitution*. He said the organization performed an important function for the church in teaching Bible, leadership and virtue. It provided stability to young or weak church groups, as young adults met for Bible study and fellowship. It was the mission arm of the church.

C. Family Man

Clyde married Ruby on October 9, 1920, and they had two sons, Celaine and Myron, Myron died at age four. Clyde was a good husband and father, but he was occasionally absent-minded. One time Clyde and Grandpa George Randall were driving in a Model-A with little Celaine in the back seat. They hit a bump and Celaine fell out of the car. Clyde didn't notice and kept on driving. Celaine, a gutsy kid, jumped up, brushed himself off and ran after the car.

Arthritis crippled Ruby at a young age, and for a number of years before her death, she was completely disabled and in pain. She wrote a testimony about her suffering. She said, "We must have faith in order to please Him." She said she was stepping out on faith to do her part in God's service even though she was weakened in health. She acknowledged she would have difficulties but asked for prayer. Clyde cared for her at home very tenderly, looking after her needs. Theirs is one of the great love stories to emerge from the Church of God. He managed to carry on an active ministry, traveling to revival meetings and conferences as he was able to, often as guest preacher or teacher, and to provide loving care for Ruby at home.

In the early days, with Ruby already ill, Clyde took the boys on his preaching assignments, wrapped them up in a sheepskin coat, and laid them down to sleep on the floor of the meeting hall. Often this was a drafty schoolhouse with no central heat. When he was invited to preach a series of meetings, if Ruby was able to travel, she accompanied him with her caretaker, Mrs. Sword. If she was not able to travel, she received care in a nursing home until Clyde returned.

D. A Pastor with Community Interests

Ruby and Clyde moved to Arizona in 1948. When he served at the Tempe Church of God near Phoenix, he was often invited to Barry Goldwater's ranch. When Barry ran for President against Ronald Reagan, Clyde was asked to pray in Barry's home. While he was not an ecumenical man, Clyde believed in working with community ministerial activities such as the Goldwater event.

He pastored at the Omaha Church of God while this congregation was still in its old building. During his tenure in Omaha, he chaired the Billy Graham Crusade for Greater Omaha, serving on a minister's committee to help to plan the crusade and the follow-up. Clyde felt it was better to have that kind of influence in Omaha, where some of the new converts might learn the truth in a Church of God, than to not to. He thought it was important to reach people for Christ and to channel some of those good people to his congregation.

He received some criticism from other Church of God ministers for his position on Billy Graham, and it was debated at the annual Minister's Conference in January

1961 or 1962. At the time, Clyde was president of the Church of God Ministerial Association. He summed up the discussion at that meeting by challenging the brothers to accept people of other faiths as brothers. They sought salvation through the saving name of Jesus. Even Catholics accepted Jesus as the Son of God and recognized there would be a resurrection some day. He said people of other denominations are not our enemies. This inclusive language was unfamiliar to many people in the Church of God, and before his death Clyde expressed sorrow that he had been so adamant about being community-minded when he should have been counseling the young ministers to preach Bible truth.

Clyde and Ruby served the congregation at Fonthill, Ontario, for 18 years. After that, he preached at Welland and Niagara Falls, New York, just a few miles east of Fonthill. He served six years in Omaha, and 14 years in Tempe, Arizona.

E. The Editor and the Author

When he retired from the Omaha ministry, he and Ruby moved to Oregon, Illinois, where he assumed editorship of *The Restitution Herald* in October 1971. Ruby died soon after. Clyde's good friend Dean Urish was with him at the time. Clyde said he never realized how helpful it was to have someone with you during such a trying time. Clyde was deeply grateful for the company. Ruby was interred at Oakwood Cemetery in Mora, Minnesota.

While living in Oregon, Clyde preached occasionally and served as interim pastor for three months following the departure of the Oregon church's pastor. His final issue as editor of *The Restitution Herald* was in September 1973.

In his elderly years Clyde noticed a pretty widow, Mrs. Nora Anderson. She had been married to Lonnie Anderson, son of J.H. Anderson, Church of God evangelist in the Southeast. Clyde and Nora became a couple and married in the Oregon Church of God on March 30, 1973. People at the church enjoyed watching the courtship and relished having their dear friends become the newlywed couple in their midst.

Clyde and Nora continued to serve pastoral duties wherever he was asked. They traveled extensively, even to the Holy Land. Clyde was 82 at the time. They spent winters in Florida, and it was on the last trip home in early spring 1983, that he became ill while visiting a church family in Texarkana; he died there. Friends traveled there to help Nora and drive the car and trailer home. Clyde was buried in Mora, Minnesota, beside Ruby in the Oakwood Cemetery. Nora died in Rex, Georgia, at the home of her daughter, Nancy Craig. Nora's funeral was held in Oregon, Illinois, and she rests beside her first husband, Lonnie.

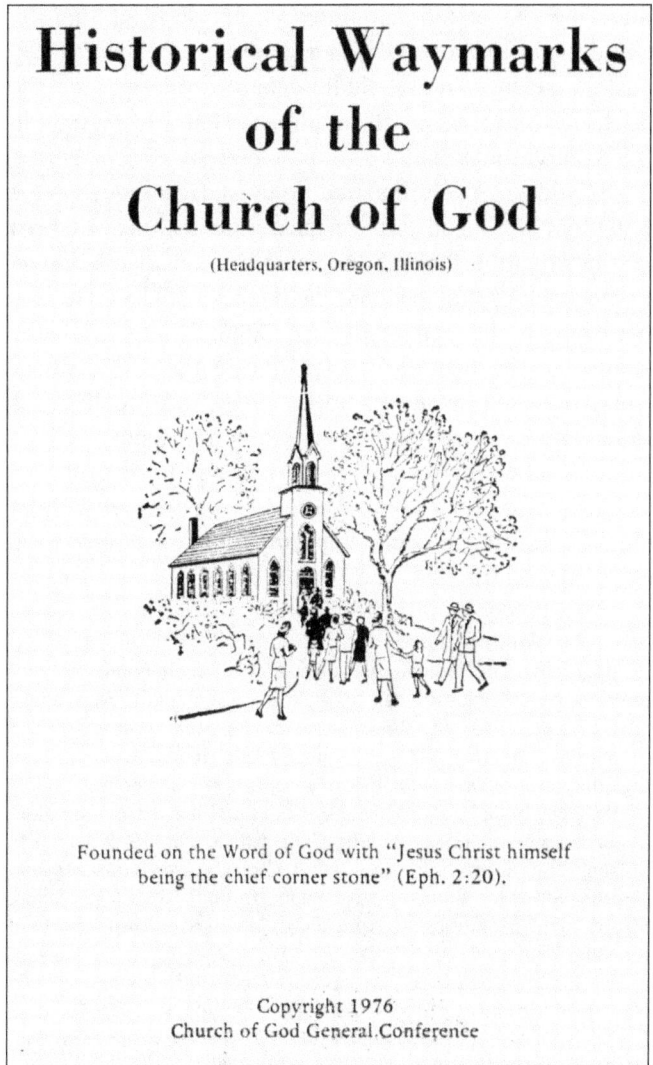

Clyde left a cherished legacy. He authored a small history book, *Historical Waymarks of the Church of God*, published by the General Conference in 1976. It was not intended to be a scholarly tome, but it covered the basics and set a precedent for the younger generation to continue researching the church's history. "Publish a better book, if you can," seemed to be its challenge. Clyde was a prolific writer, producing prophecy columns for *The Restitution Herald* for a number of years, lessons for the *Truth Seeker's Adult Quarterly*, papers for Ministerial Conferences, and many other writings for the Bereans.

F. The Future of the Church of God

In his final years, Clyde feared for Church of God ministers. He feared their level of dedication would not carry the work into the next generation. In this respect, he mirrored James Watkins who dared to express the same fear in *The Restitution Herald* as early as 1947. Clyde said, "What will happen to the work if the pastors leave the ministry?" And, "Why are the challenges to the pastors' wives and families greater today than they were in the day of the traveling evangelists?" In a videotaped interview he stated his observations showed that by comparison to those who had gone before, present-day pastors seemed more shallow and careless with the doctrines and the church traditions. That interview is in the Archives at Atlanta.

Clyde was a doctrinal traditionalist. He believed in the Kingdom of God on earth, in the second coming of Christ and in salvation through the name of Jesus. He believed in the sleep of the dead and the oneness of God. He also believed in the personality of Satan, a much-debated subject in the Church of God during the 20th century. Many believed Satan was not an entity, specifically not a fallen angel, but rather the evil within man's heart. Clyde said Christ could not have been tempted by internal sin as Christ was tempted in all points as we are, yet without sin. "Therefore," he said, "the temptation must have been external to Christ."

    See Anderson, J.H. (19th)
            Watkins, James

Bibliography: ABC Biography Project, David Krogh, compiler; Interview with Clyde Randall by J. Stilson at Oregon Bible College after Chapel, 1983; *The History of the Minnesota Church of God Conference,* Sydney Magaw, editor, 1931; Jones, Nola. E-mail regarding her lineage with a few anecdotes about her great-uncle Clyde. Oct., 2006; Ledger Minute Book of the Chicago Congregation; Letter from Muriel Haas to Julie Craig Isham, Jan. 1995 loaned to Stilson; *The Restitution,* Aug. 10, 1920; *The Restitution Herald* various entries too numerous to mention from 1910 until his death; Stilson, Jan. Memories of Minister's Conference, 1961 or 1962; Randall, Clyde, "Chiliasts" *The Restitution Herald* 75 anniversary issue, Russell Magaw, ed., Oregon, Il., Oct. 1985; Randall, Clyde, *Historical Waymarks of the Church of God,* Oregon, Il., 1976; Randall, Clyde, Notice about move to Arizona. *The Restitution Herald.* Oct. 19, 1948; Randall, Ruby, "Her Testimony," *The Restitution Herald,* G.E. Marsh, ed., Oregon, Il., March 2, 1931; Wachtel, Bill, Interview by phone regarding Clyde Randall's regrets in ministry, July, 2010.

Rankin, Edgar Daniel Lyle
    b. January 24, 1908
    d. December 23, 2004

By Boyce Photography; shared by Arlen Rankin.

Edgar Daniel Lyle Rankin was born to John C. and Emma F. Neff Rankin in Glen Elder, Kansas. The family moved to Puyallup, Washington, in 1910. Lyle received public education through eighth grade. He was an eager and lifelong learner, particularly in biblical subjects. J.M. Owens baptized Lyle's mother into the Abrahamic Faith in the 1890s. Nothing is known about Owens. The Rankins had no Church of God connections when they moved to Washington; they attended the local Christian Church.

A.L. Corbaley moved from Waterville (in central Washington) and began meetings in the Puyallup public library in 1920. On occasion, when there were no scheduled Church of God meetings, A.L. attended the Christian Church's meetings. When students there asked the teacher Bible questions and he didn't have an answer, A.L. directed them to a particular Bible passage or two. After a time, he was asked not to come back to their meetings. He then invited those he had come to know to attend his Bible studies at the public library. The Rankin family was among the number that did so. In 1927, three of the Rankin brothers—Forrest, Lyle and Everett—were discussing what they had learned from Mr. Corbaley. Forrest suggested they should be baptized, and so they sought out Corbaley and were baptized into the Abrahamic Faith. They continued to learn from their new teacher and shortly after that Lyle preached his first sermon in 1931.

In 1926, Lyle met Joyce Emma Chadbourne (b. August 8, 1907; d. November 3, 1952). They wed on January 22, 1932; they had one son, James Lyle (b. November 3, 1934; d. May 8, 2007), who followed them in the faith and ministry. Their close personal relationship and shared faith is expressed in Lyle's words as recorded in his diary when Joyce died, "A faithful wife and mother has fallen; a faithful servant of the Lord has come to rest in Jesus, to sleep until he returns." Their ministry together lasted just 20 years, but the positive impact on those they ministered still bears fruit day and will for years to come. Lyle's love and his commitment to the marriage vows moved him to unselfishly spend nine years caring for his long-ailing and eventually incapacitated second wife, Ethyl Fyfe (b. May 30, 1909; m. June 3, 1954; d. May 30, 1995), until her death.

Lyle pastored the Cashmere, Washington, Church of God Faith of Abraham from 1935 until 1968. This was not the end of his ministry, for he continued evangelism and teaching for many years. He had, since the early years of his ministry, traveled from the Northwest into the Midwest, speaking where he was invited—particularly Idaho, Montana, Kansas, Missouri, Iowa and Illinois; and of course, throughout Washington State. During those years he participated in Illinois State Conferences as a teacher; presented papers at several Ministerial Conferences and visited many isolated brethren across the US. He was instrumental in forming the Church of God Faith of Abraham in rural Lockwood, Missouri.

Lyle and seven others started the Church of God camping program in Washington in 1929 when Brethren from both sides of the Cascades met for fellowship and Bible study. That work has repeated every year since, with the exception of one when gas was rationed during WWII. The camping program continues today.

During many years of teaching, Lyle, like his mentor, drew a simple line across the chalkboard placing significant points of reference across it to show relationships of events from creation to the new heaven and new earth, as shown here:

C F S / \ (1000) NHE

In 1937, he and Joyce prepared a large cloth Chart of the Ages and hung it across the front and around the side walls of the small wood-frame church building in Cashmere. It was 3' wide x 33' long and detailed Bible events in proper succession. They prepared this from an 8.5" x 11" pencil-drawn chart borrowed from his brother Forrest. A.L. Corbaley had used this chart in his teaching. His son Jim, who later pastored the congregation when Lyle stepped aside to concentrate on evangelism, with his wife Pat and others, reformatted the chart in 1964.

In the late 1940s and early 1950s Lyle broadcast the gospel on Radio Station KPQ, Wenatchee, Washington, in conjunction with H. Gary France, pastor of the Wenatchee Church of God Faith of Abraham. Many of these programs were transcribed as articles and printed in *The Restitution Herald* during those years.

During his life Lyle committed much of the Bible to memory and taught his hearers to do so as well. He could readily recall and quote appropriate passages as occasion demanded both publicly and privately—sermons, lessons, funerals, counseling, questions, etc. He always had his Bible nearby, though he could recite passages at length without opening it. One time when asked by a young preacher how to present the message well, Lyle's reply was, "Make your mind a storehouse of the Word of God." Another young minister preached his first sermon at the home church and when he met Lyle at the back of the auditorium, Lyle said simply "That was biblical." When an older Sister overheard this, she inquired, "Lyle, is that all you can say?" His response was, "That's the best I could say." On another occasion a young preacher asked him how long it took him to prepare a sermon, Lyle said, "Thirty-five years," for that was about how long he had been in the faith and everything he had learned was foundation for each particular sermon.

In his later years Lyle continued teaching all who would listen. He had a small welding shop in Cashmere where he spoke the gospel Word to those who came in for work or just dropped by. He had a small Chart of the Ages on the shop wall along with pictures of the image and beasts of Daniel and those of Revelation, which were drawn by Julie (Dart) Pipkin. These prompted many questions which he answered with the Word of God. Lyle both sought and made opportunities to speak of spiritual and eternal matters. He traveled to the Philippine Islands in 1995 and 1998, sharing his faith through translators and enjoying fellowship with brethren.

After more than 60 years of ministry, Lyle died in the faith in 2004. He was interred at Cashmere, Washington, in what he termed "The Silent City" across the street from the church house, there to await the call of the Master to life eternal and entrance into the Kingdom of God.

Arlen Rankin contributed this entry.

See Corbaley, A.L. (19th)
       Rankin, James

Bibliography: Copy provided by nephew Arlen F. Rankin; *The Restitution Herald* Oct. 21, 1947; Rankin, Delbert. E-mail to JStilson, Oct. 13, 2009.

Rankin, James Lyle
b. November 30, 1934
d. May 8, 2007

James Lyle Rankin was born November 30, 1934, to Lyle and Joyce (Chadbourne) Rankin at Puyallup, Washington. The family moved to Cashmere in 1938, eventually purchasing property at the mouth of Woodring Canyon along Mission Creek. This is where Jim was raised and where he in turn raised his own children. He married Patricia Ann "Pat" Peters of Paynesville, Minnesota, on November 28, 1954. They had five children: Larry, Kathy, Kevin (died in infancy), Chad and Joel.

Jim began preaching in Cashmere on a fill-in basis in 1953 and became assistant pastor in 1954. He attended a local Bible training program for ministers from 1953 to 1954. His father and H. Gary France, pastor of the Wenatchee congregation, taught the class. Jim's first evangelistic outreach began in Altoona, Washington, where he shared the faith in 1954 and 1955. All through his ministry, Jim was active in organizing and teaching at the State Bible Camp. Throughout the 1950s and on into the 1960s he taught Berean youth classes, giving them a solid foundation in biblical understanding. In 1963, he began traveling regularly to Seattle and conducted meetings for the brethren of the Puget Sound area. He continued this until his cousin Arlen Rankin began pastoral work in Fall City in 1970.

In 1962, Jim taught a series of lessons on history and prophecy. This series followed the outline of Bible history beginning in Genesis and continuing into the New Testament. It then proceeded to cover post-biblical church history and consider the times of the end of the age and the Kingdom of God. This was repeated many times locally and several times in the Philippine mission field. It became his "trademark" series of lessons and included an extensive outline of historical data.

In 1964, Jim and Pat reformatted the 33' Chart of the Ages made by his parents in 1937. This currently hangs on a side wall of the Cashmere Church of God auditorium. Two years later he adapted the larger chart outline to a 2.5' x 6' chart which was more portable. This version was for use in homes, at camps and on evangelism/missions trips. It included many lists of Scriptures on relevant topics. It was then adapted for publication by the editor of *The Bible Faith* (issue #11, 1983). Jim's chart became the foundation for many other adaptations and translations into foreign languages—Ilocano, Tagalog, Hiligaynon, Cebuano, French and Spanish. It has been an effective tool for instruction and sharing the gospel.

Jim became pastor of the Cashmere Congregation in 1968 and remained until his death in 2007. In 1969 he made the first of many trips to teach Bible. Early trips took him to San Francisco, California, and Ogden, Utah. In 1971, he went to Illinois, Ohio, Indiana and Missouri. In 1972 he took a cross-country road trip with his wife and Arthur Mock, teaching in Idaho, Utah, Nebraska, Iowa, Illinois, Missouri, Indiana, Ohio, Kentucky, North Carolina, South Carolina, Virginia, Maryland and California. In 1979 the congregation purchased an airplane to assist in the evangelistic outreach.

In 1974 a completely new international ministry began. Arthur Mock brought a fellow merchant seaman to visit the local church. This man asked Jim to visit his home in Japan and teach him more of the Bible. So, in 1975, preparations were made for Jim to do so. Bill Wachtel suggested Jim also visit the brethren in the Philippines during the trip. The work in Japan did not prove to last, but the visit to the Philippines continued and enlarged in ministry. In all, Jim made 62 trips there to teach and aid the brethren. Pat accompanied him many times as she was truly "a help meet for him" in life and ministry. Jim taught many pastors' seminars, and he and Raul Javar established a year-long residential training program for young people from throughout the Islands.

During one of his trips, Jim contracted schistosomiasis (a parasitic illness). The parasite, which ordinarily settles in the liver, traveled to his brain. The effects of this life-threatening condition persisted for the remainder of his life and perhaps initiated or exacerbated Parkinson's disease which had seriously debilitated him by the time of his death. The Philippine work became a prime focus for the remainder of his ministry, though he and Pat had also traveled to Singapore, Malaysia and Australia to teach. In 2007, Jim planned one last trip to the Philippines to close some business matters and visit brethren, which he did. While at Cagayan de Oro, Misamis Oriental in Mindanao he had a heart attack and died on the mission field he loved. Jim, like those of faith who died before him, waits in the sleep of death for the awakening to life at Jesus' coming and kingdom.

Arlen Rankin contributed this entry.

See Corbaley, A.L. (19th)
Rankin, Lyle
Wachtel, William
See Also Appendix 20—Missions, ref. Ortiguero
Bibliography: Copy by Arlen F. Rankin, Jim's cousin.

Robbins, Elzie H.
b. May 7, 1884
d. December 12, 1962

Elzie Robbins was a native of Brown County, Illinois, and was a member of the Ripley Church of God. He had a missionary spirit and was one of the Ripley members who started the Church of God in Macomb, Illinois. He also spurred the Illinois Conference into action to help fund and establish a new work in East Peoria, which initially met near Metamora, Illinois, on Spring Bay Road along Illinois 116. Illinois Conference members met there regularly to help construct and finish the building. The original church still stands but is used by another congregation. This work led to the fine congregation that now owns a church building in East Peoria, Illinois. Core members of that original work included Thelma and Paul Scharer, and Jim and Carol Ring. Many Bible College students and other pastors served that congregation, including pastors J.R. LeCrone, Louis Kump, Joseph Fletcher, Darrell Cardwell and Curt Rowden, Elzie's grandson.

T.A. Drinkard wrote a brief obituary for Elzie in *The Gospel Messenger*:

> We corresponded with him for some years, and we shall never forget him attending a series of meetings in which we were engaged in Ripley, Illinois, many years ago. Among other things he said, "Brother, that teaching is what we need." Elzie died in the faith, in the hope of living with Jesus Christ when he comes again. May God comfort his loved ones along the path of life, and others who have suffered the loss of loved ones in this life.

See Drinkard, T.A.
Fletcher, Joseph
LeCrone, J. Richard
Bibliography: Ancestry.com. Social Security Master Death List, Record for Elzie Robbins; Drinkard, T.A. *The Gospel Messenger*, Jan/Feb. 1963; Rowden, Curt, Grandson of Elzie, comments made while preaching at General Conference, Oregon Church of God, July 8, 2009; JStilson, Memories of Elzie Robbins.

Robbins, W.L.
b. 1889?
d. Unknown

W.L. and Grandma Robbins resided in Riviera, Texas, during the 1940s. W.L. grew up as a Church of

Christ believer. Grandma was a Baptist. To come closer spiritually, they agreed to study the Bible together, and if one of them was wrong, he or she would change. From their studies, they realized they were both wrong. Their search led them to the Church of God Abrahamic Faith and they asked for baptism. Evangelist E.O. Stewart baptized them.

The Robbins invited Jim Mattison, a student at Oregon Bible College, to come to Texas. They provided him with a small house behind their own home in Riviera. The National Berean Society sent $50 per month for a year or so; Jim also worked out to earn his keep. This is how the work started in southern Texas. It built upon a foundation set by early believers, such as J.M. Owens, John Whitney, William Gibbs, E.W. Moses and George Waters from Corpus Christi.

Mr. and Mrs. George Waters

To learn more about the Texas work, read Jim Mattison's memoirs, *Life of a Country Preacher*, available through the Church of God General Conference in McDonough, Georgia.

See Gibbs, W.L. (19th)
      Mattison, Jim
      Stewart, E.O.

Bibliography: Mattison, James. Email to Author, April, 2006.

Robinson, Maurice
b. 1918?
d. November 1989

Maurice "Brub" Robinson married Georgia on April 17, 1938. In February 1939, he was baptized into the faith. In April 1939, their first child was born.

Brub was a dedicated church worker until his death. For many years he served as deacon for the Blood River Church of God in Springfield, Louisiana, and the Happy Woods Church of God in Hammond, Louisiana. His hope was in the coming of our Lord and Savior, a hope he passed on to his children, grandchildren and all who knew him.

Bibliography: ABC Biography Project, David Krogh, compiler.

Robinson, Orine Richardson
b. September 29, 1918
d. September 11, 1992

Orine Robinson was born to Mr. and Mrs. Samuel Richardson of Springfield, Louisiana. She was raised in a Christian family and accepted the teachings of the Bible as true and holy. Orine accepted Jesus as her personal Savior on February 21, 1937, and was baptized in the nearby Blood River. She married James A. "Dick" Robinson on May 23, 1937. He preceded her in death on November 19, 1991. They raised six children in the Lord and were blessed to see all of them educated, baptized, married and blessed with children of their own. Orine thoroughly enjoyed 12 grandchildren and three great-grandchildren.

Orine taught Sunday school for many years. She was a Junior and Senior Youth sponsor, served as a counselor and teacher at Louisiana State Camp and worked as the Louisiana Conference secretary for many years. She was a third generation member of the Church of God.

Orine accepted people as they were. She had a firm faith in God, which she exhibited in daily activities. She loved her family, and she lived her life as a shining example for them. Her spirit of love and unselfishness was shown to others throughout her life, manifesting itself daily. Orine's lingering health condition led to frequent demonstrations of unconditional love, unselfishness, patience, humility and peace. Those caring for her would often hear "thank you," "I appreciate it," "I love you" and "I'm just fine."

Bibliography: ABC Biography Project, David Krogh, compiler.

Rock, Leo E.
b. December 23, 1889
d. July 1971

Leo Rock was a preacher in the Iowa Conference. No details of his ministry exist, but this note appeared in the minutes of the Iowa Conference work: "Bro. Leo E. Rock of Avon, Iowa was granted in December 1913 a ministerial certificate and is now actively engaged in the work. Signed, G. Eldred Marsh, evangelist." Leo was a young man when he began preaching. In 1910, he resided with his parents, John and Mary Rock. He is known to the Lord and that is enough.

Bibliography: Ancestry.com U.S. Census. Iowa. Warren. Allen. Dist. 204. 1910. Rankin, Delbert. E-mail regarding Leo Rock, Oct. 27, 2008; Social Security Death List, record for Leo Rock, Des Moines, Iowa.

Rogers, Bernice
b. March 20, 1890
d. February 8, 1948

Bernice Phelps was nine years old when the Church of God at Oregon organized in 1899. The Phelps family founded Oregon in 1838. Bro. Lindsay immersed her in 1901. She married Frank T. Rogers in 1911 and they had one son, James.

Bernice was enormously talented and equipped to help a new church. She became a musician and was an especially good organist. She served on the songbook committee established by the General Conference. This led to publication of the green *Songs of Truth*. Bernice played organ for Sunday morning worship at the Church of God and often substituted for the Methodists, Lutherans and Presbyterians, as well. The latter three had pipe organs while the Church of God had an old-fashioned bellows organ.

When she was in her prime, Bernice also served on the Oregon church's remodeling committee. Their original building was a one-room limestone with high ceilings and no entryway. The remodeling committee added an entryway with vestibule and stairs leading upward to the balcony or downward to the remodeled basement. The stairway ascended in a gothic style tower, making the little stone church look like a castle. The exterior was finished in limestone to match the original building. A large amber-tone stained glass window was put in the new addition adding grace and style to the architecture and matching the smaller stained glass adjustable windows on the sides of the building.

As the stone was being laid, the mortar between them still wet, F.L. Austin, Mrs. Austin and one or two church elders gathered at the south side of the new addition, and just beneath the window outside the stairway, made thumb imprints beside their initials. This church has been sold and renovated as apartments, but those thumbprints are still visible.

As she aged, Bernice developed thyroid disease and had to curtail her activities. At that time she donated her modern organ to the church even though she was unable to play it often after that. She became unwell after attending church one Sunday evening, and upon returning home collapsed and died. It was a sad shock to the local church and the community. Frederick L. Austin preached her funeral service and she was interred southeast of Oregon in the Daysville Cemetery where many Church of God members rest.

   See Lindsay, S.J. (19th)
Bibliography: Obituary. *The Restitution Herald*, Feb. 17, 1948.

Ross, Kent H.
b. July 20, 1941

Kent Ross was born in Litchfield, Minnesota, the eldest son of Stanley O. and Peg Ross. He has a brother, Scott, and one sister, Connie. Kent grew up in an idyllic world surrounded by the safety of loving parents, a friendly neighborhood and a joyous church. He loved to play baseball with his neighborhood friends. There were just enough to play a rousing game of "work-up," and how frustrating it was to end the game when mother called him home for supper. Kent and Scottie often played cowboys and Indians with the neighborhood children and dressed the part. Everybody had a cowboy hat in those days.

Kent grew up in the Church of God where his father served in several offices. Making a commitment to accept Jesus meant walking a "mile" up the aisle to where the minister stood waiting to take his confession. Pastor William Wachtel baptized Kent, and later, was his teacher at Oregon Bible College. Kent attended the University of Minnesota for one year, but when his parents moved to Oregon, Illinois, he joined them at semester's end and studied at Oregon Bible College. Here he renewed acquaintances with Cheryl Macy. They wed on August 22, 1964. Kent and Cheryl had three sons, Seth, Kirk and Zachary. They also welcomed Natalie, Reginald, Thurman, George, Terrell, Sherrie and Cherlonika Whibbey into their family. While at Oregon Bible College, Kent served as student minister at the Flagg Center Church of God.

Kent and Cheryl entered the ministry at Moorefield, Nebraska, and experienced some of the trials and joys faced by young married couples in the ministry. At the end of the year, they moved to the Dayton, Ohio, Church of God (1966-1969). In 1969, they went to Wyoming, Michigan, and served the Pennellwood Church of God for ten years. In 1979, the Rosses relocated to Tempe, Arizona, but interrupted that ministry to return to Oregon Bible College and teach preaching and Bible subjects.

Kent served at Oregon Bible College and Atlanta Bible College (ABC) from 1981 until 2000, where he was instructor, Academic Dean, editor of various publications including *The Restitution Herald*, *History Newsletter*, *Truth Seeker's Adult Quarterly* and *The Journal from the Radical Reformation*. He also coordinated The Christian Worker's Seminar, the History Conference, Elderhostel and the popular Theological Conference. Kent oversaw the Pastoral Internship Program, and coached drama for the locally famous OBC Players who presented outstanding skits for Oregon's Autumn on Parade festival. One of Kent's favorite roles was dressing as a monk and assuming the character of "Fat Profit."

Kent has served in the Ministerial Association's

national work on the License and Ordination Board, as a member of the Ministerial Association Leadership Team (MALT) and as president of the Ministerial Association.

After Kent left ABC, he continued to serve as pastor at New Friends Bible Church in Morrow, Georgia. At this time the History Committee first planned conferences to uncover and discuss Church of God Abrahamic Faith history. Committee members were Kent, Greg Demmitt, Jan Stilson and Arlen Rankin. Jennifer Winner eventually joined the group. These conferences have always focused on the Church of God and have been open to interdenominational participation. Much has been learned from Advent Christians, Disciples, Seventh-day Baptists and Seventh-day Church of God about common religious heritage. It was Kent's idea to have a Church of God encyclopedia, a kind of biographical directory of pastors and leaders who have served to make the Church of God a tool for salvation. The various History Conferences have provided some of the data for this book.

In his retirement, Kent serves the local church at North Hills in Springfield, Ohio, and the Ohio Conference as a member and officer. He enjoys working with his pastor at North Hills, who is also his son, Seth. Kent and Cheryl enjoy playing with their grandchildren. In his spare time, Kent coordinates Sherlock Holmes mystery conventions. He writes a daily online devotional for THRIVE ministries, which he chairs, and serves presently as co-editor of the new online *e-Herald* with Pastor Wally Winner. This monthly publication is only available at www.eherald.org

Kent's greatest joy in ministry has been seeing people come to know Christ and seeing churches grow. His greatest disappointments have been some life experiences from which he had to rise and walk on. His advice to young ministers or students is to realize they must have a call from the Lord, and to find a life's partner to walk beside through the disillusionments and difficult times.

See Ross, Stanley O.
       Wachtel, William
See Also Appendix 2—Bitter Disappointment
       Appendix 18—Faith
Bibliography: Furnished for ABC Biography Project by Kent Ross.

Ross, Stanley Otto Adolph
b. March 30, 1911
d. October 24, 1992

Ross, Elna Gail "Peg" Ruhn
b. April 19, 1914
d. March 12, 2001

A. **Early Years: First Career**
B. **Second Career: Missions Director**
   1. The Philippines, Lebanon, Israel
   2. India
   3. Mexico, Australia, Africa
C. **A New Office**
D. **The Congress for the Peace of Jerusalem**
E. **Third Career: The Pastoral Ministry**

A. Early Years: First Career

Stan Ross was born to Henry and Anna Ross near Forest City, Minnesota. He was the next to the youngest child in a family of nine children. Stan dropped out of high school to work with his father on the farm, but later returned to school and received his diploma. He then enrolled in Minneapolis Business College.

While living in Forest City, the family attended a German church. As was the custom, the services were held in the German language. Several younger families requested the church board schedule one service a month in English; they declined. At that point, the Ross family left that church and looked elsewhere. They decided to attend the Lutheran church in Litchfield where they were living at the time.

After graduation from Business College, Stan worked as a bookkeeper at a construction company. It was here that he contracted tuberculosis. This made him very ill for two years. He recovered at home, a long and boring process. In those days there were no antibiotics. The treatment included rest, good food and modest exercise. When he had no strength, he sat on the porch and watched the traffic pass by.

As he began to feel better, he took daily walks to build up his strength. He was in his early twenties, but he had lost weight and strength from the illness. He walked past Elna Ruhn's house in the next block, and coincidentally, she walked past his house.

Peg and Stan Ross in 1962
Photo from Seth Ross

Soon the two became acquainted and started dating. Elna "Peg" Ruhn was a member of the Church of God in Minnesota. She was the daughter of Herman and Alda Matheny Ruhn. Alda had three sisters and several brothers. Two of the sisters were Maude and Sarah.

Peg introduced Stan to the Church of God a few miles away in Eden Valley, and he liked it. He became a man of faith. Walter Wiggins baptized him at the Eden Valley Church of God on November 10, 1940. At that time, there was no church in Litchfield. Believers from there attended services at Eden Valley.

Pastor John Denchfield wed Stan and Peg on December 15, 1939, at Eden Valley. Stan and Peg formed a Bible study group in Litchfield, and soon a church was begun. Stan had good leadership qualities that helped the small Bible study group grow into a congregation. William Wachtel was the first full-time pastor, serving from 1952-1957. Pastor Emory Macy came from Texas to preach at Litchfield from 1957 to 1962. Having a regular schedule of preaching services helped stabilize the young congregation.

Stan was deputy treasurer in the County Treasurer's office for 7-1/2 years. In 1946 he decided to run for the office of Clerk of the District Court in Meeker County and won. He was well known in the community and enjoyed meeting the people. He attended every function possible to stay in touch with the citizens. Stan was a vote-getter. In one election he received more votes than any other candidate for any office on the ballot. His daughter Connie wrote "After his first election he never had opposition, a fact of which he was quite proud!" He served District Court Clerk for 14-1/2 years.

Stan also participated in every community project available to the people. He was Meeker County Chairman of the Centennial Celebration of the State of Minnesota, May 11, 1958. He threw himself into this with great zest and grew a beard and built a float for the parade.

B. Second Career: Missions Director

The community held Stan in high esteem and his reputation drew many into the new church work. He also actively worked on the national boards for the Church of God General Conference. He was elected to the Board of Directors in 1950 and served for 11 years. He followed Willis Turner as board president in 1958. Stan's leadership and business qualities were very helpful.

At their annual meeting in 1961, the General Conference delegates voted to change the constitution regarding how directors were elected, particularly the president. They chose to elect all candidates as directors and the board itself would vote for a chairman. Stan was the last president of the Conference Board.

Harold Doan, Executive Secretary of the Church of God General Conference, made an exploratory mission trip to the Philippine Islands in 1961. On that trip he met Pastor Eleodoro Ortiguero. Because of this fact-finding trip, it became apparent that the Church of God needed a mission manager

Stan hard at work.

to direct foreign missions work for the rest of the 20th century and beyond.

Stan was invited by the Mission Board working with Harold Doan to become the Superintendent of Foreign Missions for the Church of God. He accepted that offer in May 1961. Stan and Peg had three children, Kent, Scott and Connie. Kent remained in Minnesota to attend university. The rest of the family moved to Oregon, Illinois, in the fall of 1961. Scott was a sophomore in high school. Connie was nine years old. While the idea of relocation may have been daunting to the children, Stan and Peg embraced the move with great faith.

Kent wrote in a THRIVE devotional:
But then Dad and Mom made a life-changing decision for themselves and for our family, and our family's future. He walked away from a secure position where he had been re-elected four times, the last two four year terms with no opposition. He stunned us, at least me, when he told us he and Mom had decided to move to Oregon, Illinois and work with the Church of God General Conference.

Scott Ross said, "Faith meant something to Dad." The Ross family began worshipping at the Oregon Church of God. They were well received and liked by everyone. In his position at the General Conference, Stan visited many Churches of God over his years of service.

Peg supported her husband 100%. She had a quiet but forceful ministry of support for her husband's ministry that so often took him away from home. Peg was a woman of faith. She and Stan never fought, and they shared in the decision-making. Peg was a leader in the Minnesota mission project in India. She wrote regularly to S.S. Manoah in India to encourage the work.

Peg cared for home and children and found time to work outside the home as well. Money was a concern so she worked at Warmolts Clinic in Oregon and later at Pinecrest Manor in Mt. Morris, Illinois. She supervised the mailroom at the General Conference print shop and worked tirelessly in Christian service at the local church and in the national work. In 1967, she became Director of the women's dorm at Oregon Bible College. In this capacity she influenced many women and men, many of whom still serve the Church of God. Peg accompanied Stan to state and national conferences and seldom

Left - Stan Ross visited the Philippine Islands and toured the Churches of God with Pastor Eleodoro Ortiguero. Right - Native missionary Ortiguero visited the US in 1964 and toured Churches of God with Stan.

complained in the face of exhaustion or illness. She participated in youth work. She even went around the world for the cause of missions.

1. The Philippines, Lebanon, Israel

As part of Stan's duties in the Foreign Missions office, he made three foreign trips. Twice he traveled with Merle "Pat" Patrick, his cousin, on mission fact-finding trips. In 1966 they visited Hawaii, Japan, the Philippines, Hong Kong, India, Palestine, Syria, Israel and England. In each of these places they met and talked with potential mission contacts. In 1972 Stan, Peg and Merle traveled around the world beginning in England and stopping in Germany, Turkey, Lebanon, Israel, India, the Philippines and Hawaii. Stan baptized Jamaal Suuni in Lebanon; Jamaal began a church work there. Over the years, with all the war in that region, this work has fallen out of touch with the General Conference. On this trip they also made a brief visit to Damascus in Syria. Stan later reported this city was a disaster. Once in there, Stan's group could not get out. Finally, they hired a car to take them to Jordan. Leaving Jordan they crossed through a gate to reach Israel that beyond, for half a mile, was truly a "no-man's land." Entering this area meant a visitor was on his own. One week after their return to the United States, a tourist coach was bombed, as was the Tel Aviv Airport—their arrival and departure point.

Under Stan's leadership, the work with Pastor Eleodoro Ortiguero in the Philippine Islands thrived. During their visit in the islands, Pastor Ortiguero took them into the mountains to a small village. The purpose was to dedicate a new church. Their Jitney Jeep's driver had a rough time keeping it on the road because the motor kept cutting out. It was a rough trip, and finally, they came to a river in flood stage, which they needed to cross. At this point, they turned back. They returned to the ferry just five minutes before it began its last trip of the day. If they had missed the ferry, they would have had to spend the night in the Jitney in dangerous territory. Ortiguero admitted later that it was for the best. Their village destination had never seen outsiders, and it was deep in cannibal territory.

Stan Ross introduces SS Manoah of India to the congregation at Rockford, Illinois.

2. India

On Stan's second trip in 1972, during the visit to India with S.S. Manoah, it was obvious they needed a building. Two hundred people tried to crowd into a small garage-like building, sitting on the floor or standing, with some standing outside. The work in Bangalore, led by S.S. Manoah, stabilized and expanded. A chapel and clinic were built by Church of God members. The facility offered spiritual care by Pastor Manoah and his team and medical care by local health personnel. Dr. William Lawrence and wife Mardy, from the Church of God at Scottsdale, Arizona, superintended the clinic.

3. Mexico, Australia, Africa

Stan coordinated communications with Percy Bilton in London and with others in Australia. Contacts were made in several countries but some were more fruitful than others. The mission work in Nova Scotia faded away, but new efforts began in Africa. Through his efforts three Nigerian students arrived at Oregon Bible College and gave everyone a lesson in cultural exchange. In one African location a children's school was named "The S.O. Ross School."

The mission work in Labor Vieja, Mexico, blossomed during Stan's tenure. It was under the direct supervision of Pastor Dean Moore. Pastor Roberto Badillo led Sunday school in the village. Roberto met Dean Moore when he had been a summer migrant worker at Blanchard, Michigan, where Dean pastored the Church of God.

Stan Ross with the children's Sunday school and their leaders in Labor Vieja, Mexico.

Roberto took the Spanish Bible into his village in 1961. Stan visited the churches in Mexico with Dean Moore one year at Christmas, and the airports were jammed. He had a difficult time making connections to get into Mexico and returning home.

Short-term mission trips to Labor Vieja (Spanish for "old work") began from the youth groups of local churches at Tempe, Arizona, under Pastor Jim Graham's direction, and from Oregon, Illinois, under Youth Pastor Robert Alcumbrack's direction. Oregon Bible College sent a mission team to Labor Vieja in 1986; several National Youth Caravans sponsored by the National Youth Conference also sent mission teams to Labor Vieja. Vacation Bible schools have been well received by the Labor Vieja community.

C. A New Office

Harold Doan retired as executive secretary in January 1968, but he remained until June as editor of *The Restitution Herald*, following that he moved to California. Stan became executive director of the General Conference. Several men served as editors of *The Herald* from that point: Clyde Randall, J.R. LeCrone, Terry Ferrell, Hollis Partlowe, David Krogh, Russell Magaw, Jeff Fletcher and others.

In 1969, Rachel Krogh became superintendent of missions, returning from her residence in Mexico to assume her new duties. Stan served as executive director at the General Conference until 1980. Rachel resigned her position in 1972 to marry John Carr, an Oregon Bible College student from Phoenix, Arizona. She returned to Mexico numerous times with teams and continued superintending the foreign mission work on a part-time basis from her home at Macomb, Illinois, while her husband was pastor there, and from her present home.

For several years Stan taught a Church of God history course at Oregon Bible College. At that time the archives were small but nearby in the basement of the conference building. Stan began to do research. This course resulted in several generations of OBC students receiving instruction in the Church of God heritage. After Stan's retirement, Kent Ross assumed leadership of this course. This led to the interest in Church of God history, which had been initiated by Paul Hatch and Clyde Randall.

Under the direction of Stan's office, in 1976 Clyde Randall published the denomination's first history book, *Historical Waymarks of the Church of God*. This small book set the precedent for additional study and publication of historical research from the archival collection. It also gave impetus for organizing the archival materials in a temperature-controlled room to preserve them for future generations. Jan Stilson, Library Director and Archivist of Oregon Bible College, supervised the reorganization

Oregon Bible College campus was developed by Harold Doan and administered by Stan Ross until his retirement.

effort. Also, from 1984 until 1994 the General Conference published the *History Newsletter of the Church of God*; Jan Stilson was the first editor, and Kent Ross, succeeding editor. *The Newsletter* has been scanned in pdf format and is available in the Archives. The Archives are now located at the Cornerstone Bible Church of God on Nail Road in McDonough, Georgia.

D. The Congress for the Peace of Jerusalem

In 1978, Stan led a delegation of 35 Church of God members and friends to the Congress for the Peace of Jerusalem which met in Israel. Through Stan's involvement, the Church of God General Conference was registered as a denomination participating in the worldwide peace effort. Some of the group's members had traveled to Israel during the perilous years, including Richard and Carol Eldred, Willis and Ida Mae Turner, Donald and Marge Overmyer, Charles and Nellie Mongan and many more. Upon arriving at the conference, each person was frisked and had his identity verified. The keynote speaker was Menachem Begin (1913-1992), the sixth Prime Minister of Israel. Everywhere the group toured, there were armed Israeli soldiers. It was a peace congress, but keeping the peace was the duty of the military.

Stan planned to retire from the Church of God General Conference in 1979, but tragedy struck in April that year. President John Lewis, his wife Ruth and business manager Russell Reye, died in an auto accident. That same night Dave Segar from the Oregon Church of God also died in an auto accident. The college, conference personnel, church and community were plunged into deep grief as they felt the loss of their dear friends and colleagues.

Eugene Stilson was named Interim President for the summer of 1979. He stabilized the work during the worst of the confusion, and set the academic course for the future. At summer's end, David Krogh became president and Stan Ross stayed on as General Conference executive director for one more year. In 1980, Dr. Charles Pryor

Stan Ross broadcast this five-minute radio program script over stations KLFD-Litchfield and KYRS-Wilmar:

An Ode to Summer

As we come into any summer season, we find that it is the time of year to be planning trips and vacations and winter is gone and spring is here. Then summer comes when we need to be thinking about doing all these wonderful things.

Well, even in the nice summer days there is work to be done for the Lord. I have a little item I want to share entitled:

Ain't It the Truth

This is the story of four people named Everybody, Somebody, Anybody, Nobody. There was an important job to be done and everybody was asked to do it. Anybody could have done it but nobody did it. Somebody got angry about that because it was Everybody's job. Everybody thought Anybody could do it, but Nobody realized that Everybody wouldn't do it. Consequently it wound up that Nobody told Anybody so Everybody blamed Somebody.

Well, whether it is summer or not those excuses are often used but in summer we do have so many reasons not to be available to be used in the Lord's service. It is fine to enjoy these summer months with our families and so on, but we need to also have priorities.

I have another little item I would like to share entitled:

A Psalm of Summer

Now it came to pass that spring turned to summer again. God's people raised their voices and said: "Recreation is my shepherd, I shall not stay home; he asked me to lay down in a sleeping bag; He leadeth me down the interstate each weekend. He restoreth my suntan; He leadeth me to the state park for comfort's sake. Even though I stray on the Lord's day, I will fear no recompense, for thou art with me; My rod and my reel they comfort me. I anointed my skin with oil, my gas tank runneth over; Surely my trailer shall follow me all the weekends this summer, and I will return to the house of the Lord this fall. But then it is hunting season, and that is another Psalm.

Some people wonder if a person can be a Christian without joining a church or attending worship services. The answer to this question of course is. It is possible. But it is sort of like being:

    A student who will not go to school
    A soldier who will not join the army
    A citizen who does not pay taxes or vote
    A salesman without customers
    An explorer without a base camp
    A seaman on a ship without a crew
    A businessman on a deserted island
    An author without readers
    A football player without a team
    A bee without a hive.

I think it is important for Christians to belong and to serve in a church. The members of the early church met together regularly to fellowship and worship. In the book of Acts 2:42, "And they continued steadfastly in the apostles' doctrine and fellowship, and in breaking of bread, and in prayers." And verses 46-47, "And they, continue daily with one accord in the temple, and breaking bread from house to house, did eat their meat with gladness and singleness of heart. Praising God, and having favor with all the people. And the Lord added to the church daily such as should be saved." Yes, worship is important at all times, and it is certainly important in the summer as well as other times of the year. Let us get our priorities straight and let us be about the Lord's business.

Transcript provided by the Ross family.

---

became part of the family as president of the college. David Krogh remained as executive director. Eugene Stilson continued as academic dean of the college.

E. Third Career: The Pastoral Ministry

Stan retired in 1980, and he and Peg returned to Litchfield, and he was invited to become the pastor at the Church of God. He and Peg accepted the call, and under his leadership, the church stabilized and grew. While in this position, he began a five-minute radio program; it was broadcast twice a week for 11 years. Altogether he recorded 1,100 individual broadcasts.

Since Stan was so well known in the community and his voice so distinctive, he had many listeners. He geared the program to the casual listener who needed a word of encouragement. He had a funny story in each program which he extrapolated into a spiritual lesson. When he retired from the pastorate, Stan was made an elder. He served in this way until death.

In the months after Stan's death, Peg moved in with her children. She first lived in Omaha with Scott and family, then moved to Georgia with Kent and his family where she had her own little house behind the family home, giving her independence. She moved to Freeport, Illinois, to be with daughter Connie Sorn for her remaining time. As her health declined, Peg settled in the Stephenson County Nursing Home. Stan and Peg are interred in the Ripley Cemetery at Litchfield, Minnesota.

The Ross family heritage is found today in the ministries of their children: Scott and Gayle Ross, pastoring at Omaha; daughter Christy Ross, associate pastor (Omaha); Kent Ross, former pastor at Moorefield, Nebraska, Dayton, Ohio, Pennellwood Church of God in Grand Rapids, Tempe, Arizona, and then professor and later academic dean at Oregon/Atlanta Bible College; and Seth Ross, pastor at North Hills Church of God, Springfield, Ohio.

    See Doan, Harold
           Hatch, Paul
           Moore, Dean
           Patrick, James (19th)
           Pryor, Dr. Charles V.
           Randall, Clyde   E.

Turner, Willis H.
Wachtel, William

See Also Appendix 20—Missions, ref. Ortiguero
Bibliography: Ancestry.com U.S. Census. Minnesota. Meeker. Litchfield. Dist. 18. 1930; U.S. Census. Minnesota. Meeker. Litchfield. Dist. 109. 1900; Ross, Scott, Interview with Jan Stilson at General Conference, Oregon, Illinois, July 2009; Ross, Kent. "Thriving with memories and with Hope," THRIVE online devotional Sept. 10, 2010; Sorn (Ross), Connie; E-mail interview, July 2009; Ross, Scott, Follow-up E-mails, July 2009; Krogh, David. Director's Bible which contains a list of the Presidents or Chairman of the Boards beginning with James A Patrick in 1921 and continuing through to the present. This list includes the names of Willis Turner and Stanley Ross. The Bible is maintained at the Archives of the Atlanta Bible College/General Conference office, McDonough, Ga; Ross, Stanley, "An Ode to Summer," a five-minute radio program.

When SS Manoah of India visited the US he met many Church of God leaders and members. From left: Merle Patrick, SS Manoah, Stan Ross and Cecil Patrick.

Routson, Ellsworth Otto
b. February 7, 1918
d. January 31, 1975

Ellsworth Routson was born in Dayton, Ohio. As a teen he attended the Brush Creek Church of God and was baptized by Sydney Magaw on July 6, 1934. Ellsworth entered Oregon Bible College in 1939 and graduated in 1942. He married Olevia June Macy in June 1941. They entered the ministry together after Ellsworth's graduation. They had two children, Harold "Hal" and Etta Marie (Wetzel). Both Etta Marie and Hal attended Oregon Bible College during the 1960s.

Ellsworth was the first full-time pastor at Fredericktown, Missouri, Church of God. He also pastored Churches of God at Los Angeles, California; Blanchard, Michigan; Eden Valley Minnesota; Hector, Minnesota; Burr Oak, Indiana; and Lombard, Illinois. He became ill at Lombard and died unexpectedly. Pastors and members of the Church of God were greatly saddened. He was interred at the Burr Oak Cemetery, Burr Oak, Indiana.

See Magaw, S.E.

Bibliography: ABC Biography Project, David Krogh, compiler; *The Restitution Herald,* Sydney Magaw, ed., Oregon, Il., May 4, 1948; "We are pleased to honor Fredericktown Church of God," *The Restitution Herald,* Oregon, Il., Sept. 1974.

Sapp, Frederick Olen
b. April 17, 1894
d. December 14, 1973

Fred O. Sapp was born in Mystic, Missouri. His mother died from complications of birth when he was only four weeks old. Fred's grandmother, Susannah, raised him until he was 11, and then his other grandmother, Alcinda Frazier, took responsibility for him. When the Fraziers moved to Montana young Fred went with them. He enlisted and served in the US Army in WWI, but contracting the flu kept him from shipping out. He married his third wife Martha Brown on July 2, 1928, and they had four children. Martha was 15 years younger than Fred. Little Fred Sapp Jr. was born in 1930 while the family lived in Nez Perce, Idaho.

Fred was a self-taught Bible student. He believed in the Bible as the Church of God Abrahamic Faith taught it, and he proclaimed the Gospel of the Kingdom. He was ordained, and pastored for the Church of God at Felida, Washington, in the 1940s. His license may have come through the state conference organizations of either California or Washington.

Fred Sapp, far right beside John Eagleston, fellowships with Northwest Advent Christian Conference ministers.
Photo from James Rencontre

He had a problem in Felida and left that church because he thought they had not treated him properly. The problem may have arisen over the divorce issue. Fred moved into the Advent Christian Church and preached for them at Clarkson, Washington, and Medford, Oregon. These churches were part of the Willamette Valley Advent Christian Conference of the State of Oregon.

Following his ministry in those churches, Fred went to another Advent Christian Church in Weiser, Idaho. James Rencontre, a young man from the Weiser church, testified how the new pastor mentored him.

> I was a freshman in high school and I had epilepsy. I had difficulty getting along with kids my own age. I was in a rock fight with a couple of kids in the street in front of the Advent Christian Church in Weiser when he came out and broke up the fight. He knew me because I came to church with a lady that lived next door to my grandmother. Bro. Sapp was pressing the people to invite someone to church and she asked me. Bro. Sapp took me into his house and talked to me for a while and asked me to continue coming to church which I did.
>
> He took me under his wing and I studied with him and pestered him to death for several years. I would go with him as he called on people and after a while I was teaching Adult Sunday School class and helping with a mission work in Payette, Idaho. I preached one week, and he preached the next week. My cousin and her kids came to hear us while I was preaching there. We met in the Townsend Club building and most of the people who attended were people in the club. Bro Sapp had a radio program each week. His wife and oldest daughter would sing and he would preach. I learned how to work in a time frame with the preaching at these broadcasts.

Fred Sapp conscientiously attended the Troutdale Bible Camp sponsored by the Willamette Conference. Church of God campers and pastors also attended this camp. James Rencontre attended every year once he entered high school. James loved talking Bible with Lyle Rankin, a Church of God pastor. Troutdale camp was quite famous in the area. The Troutdale Historical Society website describes baptisms in the Sandy River and the closing of the campground:

> For 55 years, beginning in 1909, the shady grounds next to the Sandy River were used for religious camp meetings with families coming to Troutdale to live for a week or two at a time, dining in a huge cookhouse, tending their needs in wash houses and spending days in worship, prayer and Bible study. Large gatherings were held in the building that is now called Sam K. Cox Hall. The climax of those camp-

outs was a baptismal service. Half of the camp choir would ascend Broughton Bluff on the east bank of the Sandy River and the other half of the choir assembled on the west shore. As people were baptized in the river, the choirs sang back and forth to each other, their notes echoing off the bluff and in the canyon walls. Use of the grounds for camp meeting purposes dwindled by the 1960s. The events stopped in 1964 when a Christmas flood swept down the Sandy, snatching the huge cookhouse and grinding it up under the Troutdale Bridge. The river tore a gap in what is now the parking lot, linking up with Beaver Creek and washing out the highway. Access was cut off and, eventually, church officials decided to sell the site.

James Rencontre graduated Oregon Bible College, married Jean Budrow, great-granddaughter of S.J. Lindsay, and then he entered the ministry in the Church of God. The Rencontres celebrated their 50th wedding anniversary in October 2010 at their home church in Ironwood, Michigan. Elder Sapp set a fine example for Jim.

In 1967, Fred wrote "The Kingdom Age" for *The Bible Student's Forum*, a Church of God publication for the Northwest members. A copy of this is in the Atlanta Bible College Archives. Following Pastor Sapp's retirement from Weiser Advent Christian Church, a pastor from the Advent Christian fellowship led that congregation for awhile. Church of God pastor Emory Macy succeeded that pastor. Emory and Mildred Macy moved there in 1979 and stayed in that pastorate for 25 years.

Fred died suddenly of a heart attack at his retirement residence in Caldwell, Idaho, at age 79. He died just before Christmas, saddening his family greatly. He is interred at the Eastside Cemetery in Midvale, Idaho.

See   Eagleston, John
      Lindsay, S.J. (19th)
      Macy, Emory
      Rankin, Lyle

Bibliography: Ancestry.com. U.S. Census. Idaho. Nez Perce. Arrow. Dist. 1. 1930; Social Security Death Index, Record for Frederick O. Sapp, Weiser, Idaho; "Descendants of Adriaen (Aert) Van Schaick," retrieved from Familytreemaker.com April 15, 2008; Rencontre, James. E-mail to JStilson, April 5, 2008; History of Troutdale Bible Camp retrieved from Troutdale Historical Society website on April 12, 2008.

Savage, Thomas Madison, II
b. June 17, 1896
d. November 13, 1966

Savage, Madge Hoskins
b. February 18, 1903
d. May 18, 1998

Tom Savage was born to Thomas Madison and Mamie Savage near St. Cloud, Minnesota. The elder T.M. Savage had moved from Canada into Minnesota where he met Mamie Dell Bowers, a Church of God member. They married in 1893. T.M. had been raised Catholic and Mamie asked him to decide where they would attend church. They had sometimes gone to the Methodist church in Waite Park. T.M. decided they should attend the Church of God in St. Cloud. He studied his Bible, and after baptism, became the minister at St. Cloud. *The History of the Minnesota Churches of God* said Elder E.E. Thoms baptized him in 1915. That same year he began assisting Pastor Thoms in the pulpit.

Tom and Madge with Tom, Ruth, Sara and Bill
Photo from Sara See

Young Thomas and his siblings were raised in the Church of God. After his father's death, Tom followed his father's example. Tom married Madge Hoskins, also a Church of God member. James A. Patrick had baptized her. Tom and Madge had four children: Thomas, Ruth, Sara and William.

While Tom pastored at the Church of God in St. Cloud, he also preached for the Church of God at Graytown, Wisconsin, once a month, and occasionally at Bergen, Emily and Mora, Minnesota. Bergen was in Hay Township east of St. Cloud near Lester Prairie. Gaslights lit the old church. Tom and his family arrived early during the winter and lit a fire in the old potbelly stove so that when worshippers arrived the church was warm. His daughter Ruth accepted Christ at Bergen.

Tom was also a full-time employee for the Great Northern Railway Car Shop in Waite Park where he had spent a good part of his youth. He chaired the car shop's wood mill department. Tom played for the Waite Park Baseball Club, and he was the local constable. In 1957 the Ford Motor Company introduced the Edsel; Tom bought one. Edsels had an unusual grill design. Critics across America joked and jested about it. Tom drove his new Edsel to General Conference at Camp Mack, Indiana, and was immediately ribbed about the car. He took the joking in good humor and even joined in.

Madge Savage was active in the national conference work. She wrote the Children's Page in *The Restitution Herald* for a number of years. She also composed a Christmas hymn, "Bethlehem's King," that was in *Songs of Truth*, the Church of God hymnal. Throughout her life she taught Sunday school for both children and youth. She also sang with two sisters-in-law, Vivian and Bernice Savage, and they called themselves "The Savage Trio."

When Brother Tom died, he was interred at the Eden Lake Cemetery in Eden Valley, Minnesota. Madge rests beside him.

Daughter Sara married Robert See while they attended Oregon Bible College. Robert entered the ministry and has served in several churches and several national offices during his career. Robert retired from the Board of Directors in 2010. Their daughter, Julie, and son-in-law, Pastor Dale Bliss, continue in the Church of God ministry. Daughter Ruth married John Lewis, president of Oregon Bible College. They died in an auto accident near Oregon, Illinois, in April 1979. Ruth and John pastored churches in Illinois and Ohio and worked in foreign missions. Their deaths were a great shock and sorrow to Church of God members.

See Lewis, John and Ruth
      Patrick, James A. (19th)
      Savage, T.M. (19th)
      Thoms, E.E. (19th)

Bibliography: See, Sara Savage e-mail March 12, 2009; Magaw, Sydney, ed., *History of the Minnesota Conference of the Churches of God*, 1930.

Shaw, Cyrus Jennings
    b. January 5, 1897
    d. September 1972

Cyrus Shaw was born to William and Mary Shaw in Little Rock, Arkansas. He had five brothers and one sister. His mother attended a Christadelphian ecclesia near their home. Cyrus and his wife, Hazel, did not attend church for some time. Across the street from their home was an independent community church. As their children were born, they began to attend services there. C.J. and Hazel had four children: David, Shirley, Paul and John. Hazel was baptized at this church, and Cyrus read and studied his Bible. Eventually, he was asked to teach adult Sunday school. This he did very capably, but the teachings he learned as a child in the Christadelphian fellowship began to enter the discussion. Soon, he was asked to give up his class. Wounded, the family left the church.

Eventually they heard of a Christadelphian ecclesia nearby and began attending. It was a small group of six to eight elderly women. When the Shaw family came with their handsome bunch of children, it made a wonderful picture. Once a month, a Church of God evangelist came to this little group and preached. Alan McLain and his father-in-law H. Scott Smith took turns preaching here.

Cyrus and Hazel liked the preaching Sundays and talked with the ministers about their teachings, which were very similar to Christadelphian ideas. One of them said, "We preach here Sunday morning, but we preach at another congregation Sunday night. You are welcome to come to our evening service." C.J. and his family went to the Oak Grove Church of God, which was started by Richard and Delia Stanton. This church was a simple frame building, not much to look at, but full of heart. The Stantons, who had donated land for the church, lived next door. Eventually the Shaws made it their home church, and soon, C.J. was asked to preach. Around 1950 they invited him to be pastor.

On one occasion, T.A. Drinkard, a fiery Church of God preacher from Texas, came to Oak Grove to preach. After services, people gathered at the Stanton home for Sunday dinner. While Mrs. Stanton brought the meal together, a knock came on the door. A neighbor came to buy eggs. Mrs. Stanton accepted the money and laid it on the table where Elder Drinkard had put his Bible. In fact, she absent-mindedly laid the money *on top of the book*. Perhaps she intended to give it to him for a donation. The whole family was startled to hear Pastor Drinkard bellow, "Get that filthy lucre off the Word of God!"

Word that Pastor Shaw preached about the Holy Spirit reached the General Conference. Some said C.J. believed in the work of the Holy Spirit. The Church of God General Conference did not wish to be confused with any of the Pentacostal Church of God denominations in the United States. The Church of God wanted to be known as a prophecy-oriented Church, one which predated the Millerite Adventist movement in New England, and one that practiced Bible teaching and holy living. Therefore, men were sent to talk with Cyrus about teaching about the Holy Spirit. The Christadelphians had taught that a Christian did not receive the Holy Spirit until Jesus comes again, and that believers then receive their full reconciliation. The Church of God taught that believers receive the Holy Spirit at baptism, and that they continue in the Holy Spirit through the reading of the Word. The Bible is living and active in the lives of believers. Cyrus taught the latter, but he also prayed for people to be healed after the service during an altar call. This form of worship was not prevalent then throughout the Church of God. Cyrus left his position as pastor over this, although everyone in the church remained friends to him.

The very next Sunday, Cyrus rented a hall, and half the church followed him there. This new congregation became known as New Hope Church of God. They met in a small building and eventually built a lovely church on Battle Road in southeastern Little Rock with a sanctuary, fellowship hall and classrooms located around a central patio and courtyard. The Oak Grove church continued until Richard Stanton's death. New Hope prospered. The congregation grew and they built a parsonage. They hired several pastors. Paul Shaw served as pastor for two years after his father died. Louis Kump, Richard Alcumbrack,

Brian J. Atra, Dean Moore and others have served the Little Rock fellowship. Joe White was elder most of the years of the life of the congregation.

Cyrus was interred at the Roselawn Cemetery in Little Rock, Arkansas. Hazel outlived Cyrus by several years and gave a guiding hand to the congregation.

See Drinkard, T.A.
     McLain, C. Alan
     Moore, Dean
     Smith, H. Scott
     White, Joe

Bibliography: Shaw, Paul, Interview with JStilson, August 17, 2009.

Sheets, Harry Albert
b. October 19, 1898
d. 1986

Harry Sheets was a native of Blanchard, Michigan, where he was a member of the Church of God. He was the eldest son of Bert Sheets. Mary Woodward, mother of F.L. Austin, baptized Harry on October 9, 1915.

Harry was one of the first young men to attend the newly formed Bible Training Class, after the Church of God General Conference formed in 1921. Harry moved to Oregon, Illinois, as a student-in-training in 1923. Students in the training class had evening classes with F.L. Austin the first year. Austin was the newly appointed secretary of the conference. Night classes allowed them to hold day jobs. In later years, morning classes were held so the students could work afternoons or evenings.

Some students assisted F.L. Austin with publishing *The Restitution Herald,* and most of them filled pulpits in Illinois and Indiana almost from the beginning of their training. They are mentioned in *The Herald* as preaching at Chicago, Oregon, Dixon, Ripley and elsewhere around the Midwest. They traveled by train to assist state conference meetings. The states that benefited most from student preachers were those that sent students including Illinois, Indiana, Missouri, Michigan, Minnesota and Iowa. In fact, so that more churches could be covered with regular preaching services, each student may have had four appointments. On the first Sunday Harry Sheets preached at Chicago, the second at North Salem in Indiana, the third at Oregon, the fourth somewhere else. In this manner many congregations benefited and the students grew steadily in their ability and confidence.

Harry's classmates in the Bible Training Class were Melville Lyon who went to southern Ohio to preach, and Paul Johnson who remained in Oregon to help publish *The Restitution Herald,* and to fill pulpits as needed. Harry testified of his experience at the Bible Training Class, saying:

> I doubt very much if I would be proclaiming God's truths from the pulpit today if it had not been for the Training Class. The Church of God will recognize some day, I believe, if it does not now, that the Training Class is its greatest work.

After finishing the Bible Class in 1925, Harry enrolled at Aurora College in Aurora, Illinois. He also worked part-time in a factory and preached every other Sunday at Burr Oak near Culver, Indiana. In October 1925 Harry accepted a pastorate in Virginia. He lived and preached at Maurertown and commuted to Fort Valley where he also preached every other week. He may have also preached at the Cool Spring Church above Front Royal.

When the Bible Training School was discontinued in 1933 due to delayed financial problems stemming from the Great Depression, the executive secretary made arrangements for Church of God men to attend Aurora College. According to Clyde Randall who lived through that era, Harry Sheets was engaged to teach Church of God students one doctrine class per week.

Harry also served churches at South Bend, Indiana, and Litchfield, Minnesota. He was a dedicated pastor and a capable preacher. He knew the Word of God intimately and was able to teach others the simple truths in an interesting fashion. Janet Stilson recalled one General Conference in Oregon, Illinois, where Pastor Sheets was assigned to teach Bible Doctrine to the youth. That is not an easy assignment on a hot summer day with no air conditioning, yet he was able to do it; he held the students' attention and answered their questions.

Harry wed Ruth Booth on June 4, 1928. They had no children of their own, but cherished and cared for others' children. Ruth and Harry were schoolteachers. Harry taught for 15 years, worked as a mechanic, and was employed by a highway transportation department. He loved to work outside in his garden and lawn. In 1945 they were invited to return to Burr Oak, he and Ruth answered the call. The congregation remodeled the parsonage behind the church for their new pastor. It wasn't long before the church paid off the debt.

Harry died while in the Lord's service at the Litchfield, Minnesota, Church of God and was laid to rest in the Litchfield Cemetery.

See Austin, F.L.
     Lyon, Melville
     Johnson, Paul
     Sheets, Ruth
     Smead, Cecil
     Woodward, Mary A. (19th)

Bibliography: ABC Biography project, David Krogh, compiler; *The Restitution Herald*, June, 1922; Oct. 18 and 25, 1925; Nov. 3, 1925. *Wisdom and Power*, Nov. 1992; "50th Anniversary of the Church of God at Burr Oak," by the History Committee, Dec. 10, 1950; Randall, Clyde, *Historical Waymarks of the Church of God*, Church of God General Conference, Oregon, Il., 1976. p. 32; Smead, Cecil, "Letter to Marj Overmyer, June 1970, shared by John Smead, June 26, 2008.

Sheets, Ruth
b. April 7, 1904
d. April 25, 1992

Ruth Mildred Booth was born in Batavia, Illinois, the only child of Glen R. and Violet West Booth. Ruth graduated from Sugar Grove High School, and from the Normal School at DeKalb. She taught for five years, and then quit to care for her mother. She accepted the Lord and was baptized at age 21 by F.L. Austin.

Ruth reconnected with Harry Sheets, her former teacher at Illinois State Conference Bible School. They married on June 4, 1928. Although they had no children, they "adopted" some through the years. One was Evelyn Holtzinger, who lost her mother as a young woman. Others who called Ruth their adopted "Mom" were Karen Wegner and Barbara Johnson.

Ruth and Harry served several churches, including Hector, Minnesota; Maurertown and Fort Valley, Virginia; Burr Oak, Indiana; and Chicago, Illinois. Harry preached and Ruth was the organist. She also taught music and piano. At one time in Hector she had 27 piano and organ students. The couple retired in Hector and built a new home there. They enjoyed many years of happy retirement. Harry died in 1986. In 1988 Ruth moved into the Good Samaritan Home in Paynesville, Minnesota. After suffering a stroke she was moved to the Koronis Manor, also in Paynesville. Ruth and Harry were faithful to the Lord in their service, and to the Church of God in their friendship and ministry.

See Austin, F.L.
Sheets, Harry

Bibliography: "Ruth Mildred (Booth) Sheets," ABC Biography Project, David Krogh, compiler.

Simmons, Will R.
b. July 13, 1895
d. June 1972

Will Simmons and wife Ruby had several children. He was a rice farmer at Haileyville, Oklahoma, about 40 miles southwest of Fort Smith, Arkansas, where his family lived. Because of the proximity, Will preached throughout Arkansas. In fact, he was instrumental in beginning a new work a few miles west of Clark's Chapel. This group erected a building and enjoyed a good attendance. To strengthen the work, Melville Lyon, national evangelist, visited to preach and teach in December 1947. Lyon returned to Oregon, Illinois, with a good report of the new work.

Will was a circuit minister with several Arkansas preachers so that no church in the state was left without regular monthly preaching. He worked with H. Scott Smith at McGintytown, and he preached at Bear Creek near Hot Springs.

Sherwin Williams, pastor at Blessed Hope in Rockford, Illinois, is an Oklahoma native who recalled that Will Simmons was a soft-spoken man but powerful in the pulpit. Williams remembered when Simmons visited the Williams family they would share a meal. Simmons had false teeth which rattled when he talked until they nearly flew out of his mouth. He would take a breath, adjust them, and keep on talking.

See Lyon, Melville
Smith, H. Scott

Bibliography: Ancestry.com. U.S. Census. Arkansas. Craigshead. Gilkerson. Dist. 13. 1930; Ancestry.com. Society Security Death List, record for Will Simmons, Craigshead; *The Restitution Herald*, June 4, 1946; Jan. 27, 1948; March 30, 1947; Williams, Sherwin, Interview. Jan. 16, 2011.

Siple, Frank E.
b. 1894
d. April 9, 1960

A. Liked By Most
B. Death of Wife
C. Crimes Overshadow Ministry

Frank Siple was born to Mr. and Mrs. Arlo Siple in Louisiana. The family attended the Church of God. The Siples had moved to Louisiana from Iowa where they had been part of the Iowa Church of God. Frank attended Pine Woods Bible Class in Hammond, Louisiana. He must have been well acquainted with the teachings of W.H. Wilson who always emphasized Gospel of the Kingdom and the second coming of Christ.

When he was a young adult, Frank went north, probably to attend a Summer Bible School at the Oregon, Illinois, Church of God, and work with S.J. Lindsay. In 1913 at age 20, Frank attended conference at Old Raker Church near Delta, Ohio. He preached and sang, exhibiting his lovely voice and captivating personality. His permanent address was still in Louisiana at that time. The Raker Church liked him so well they asked him to be their pastor and he accepted. By 1914 he had left Raker and moved north to pastor at Adrian, Michigan. In Adrian he met his future wife, Bertie

Frank and first wife, Bertie Smith Siple

Smith, a Yankee. It seemed to be a good match. The couple had five beautiful daughters

Frank moved to Oregon, Illinois, in 1915 to substitute for S.J. Lindsay who was unable to preach due to a throat condition. Lindsay's summer Bible schools at the Oregon Church of God were beginning to catch on with the young adults in the denomination. But Frank, being a summer school almnus, was given work to do and must have shown promise for he was paid $10 for each appointment. The following year he assisted S.J. Lindsay with publishing *The Restitution Herald* in Oregon. Because of Frank's steady work in publishing, and since he, Bertie and their daughters lived in Illinois, the Illinois Conference Board of Directors voted to hire him as evangelist in 1922. From 1918 to 1922 he served as pastor of the Oregon Church of God, but he traveled so much that a note in the Michigan report said, "If you cannot come to Conference, send all the delegates possible and don't forget it takes money for Bro. Siple's dear family at home to live." By 1928, daughters number four and five were born.

Illinois Conference youth enjoy an outing at Ganymede Spring just below the Black Hawk statue. Frank Siple is second from the left.

Frank, right, with James Watkins

Throughout the Church of God Frank became known as a capable and dynamic speaker. Francis Burnett, who Siple baptized at Ripley, said his preaching "reached out and touched your heart." He was coming into prominence about the time the General Conference was organized in Waterloo, Iowa, in 1921. S.J. Lindsay stood behind this young man, saying, "Frank is fast becoming a recognized strength for the gospel among us. We feel safe in sending him out, knowing that he will acquit himself in first class shape."

As part of Siple's evangelism work, he traveled the Midwest attending special meetings, conferences, funerals and weddings. He was popular among the churches and well recommended. To illustrate his popularity, in mid-1929, Siple missed so many of his regular appointments at Ripley that the minutes recorded they changed his regular Sunday from the second to the fourth, "so Bro. Siple can come." Some of his other activities are recorded as: preaching revival meetings at Casey, Illinois, 1921; president of National Berean Society, 1921; and a preaching trip to western Colorado in 1925.

Siple attended state conferences even being the principal teacher and preacher for the week. He worked at Casey, Illinois, with Melville Lyon in October 1924. Frank's ministries often resulted in several or many baptisms. His colorful exploits fill the pages of *The Restitution Herald* when S.J. Lindsay and F.L. Austin edited. Others who joined him in evangelistic travels across the United States were Bible Training School students: Harry Sheets, Michigan; Melville Lyon, Alabama; Paul Hatch, Indiana; and brothers Paul Johnson and Arthur Johnson, from Sac City, Iowa.

Frank Siple was an instructor for the Bible Training Class early in the 1920s. The students liked him as did most members of the General Conference staff.

A. Liked by Most

While Siple may have been well liked by almost everybody, F.L. Austin was less enamored with him. Austin moved to Oregon in 1922, and the two men simply did not get along. It may explain why F.E. Siple spent so much time on the road after 1922. Siple was often away from Oregon for several days or weeks at a time, often leaving his family behind. Mrs. Siple's mother often visited from Grand Rapids, helping with the chores and the children. Retired pastor Harry Goekler recalls a story about the two men who evidently came to tolerate each other's quirks:

> One year Bro. J.W. McLain was driving into Chicago and offered a ride to any who wanted to go. I had to catch a train in Chicago. Siple had some business in Chicago, as did Austin, so we all rode together to Chicago. During the ride Austin asked Siple who Bro. Randall had referred to in a sermon he had just preached at conference. Siple replied he thought Randall was reaching out to those who in the past had held ill feelings to some. Bro. Austin replied, "I don't care two hoots about the past," and Siple said, "I don't either."

Frank Siple was a member of the Committee of Ten appointed at the Waterloo, Iowa, annual conference in 1920 to study the possibility of creating a national organization. The Committee was to compile a report and recommendation for the next conference in 1921.

Siple's frequent travels were advantageous for the cause of a General Conference. He had his finger on the pulse and heart of the people and the comprehensive work. In one report he noted the Church of God was undergoing an awakening:

> And, Oh! What a relief it is. There has been more accomplished in the past several months by way of work in the Master's vineyard than in the same number of years in the past." He credited this to a "working central body where efforts could be joined together for real good.

Sometimes Siple's family traveled with him to state conferences. The Ripley minute book shows his wife and children were with him when he preached in Ripley, Illinois, in 1928 and 1929.

B. Death of Wife

On December 29, 1929, Bertie Smith Siple died in Dixon, Illinois. Her death was recorded in the Ripley Church of God minutes. It can only be surmised that the Ripley congregation was shocked by her death, because F.E. Siple had been tending this congregation regularly from 1921 until 1930. In fact, during that time no other minister baptized anyone at Ripley while Siple baptized 33 there. Loren and Francis Burnett were the last to be baptized by Siple in 1930 before he left Illinois.

Shortly after his wife's death, Frank moved to Grand Rapids and preached at the Southlawn Church of God. Few know today that he and Dorothy Lyon of Rockford, Illinois, were getting closely acquainted. In November 1930, he announced in *The Restitution Herald* that over Christmas he planned to travel to "points south." On Christmas, Frank and Dorothy were married at her parents' home in Citronelle, Alabama, one year after his first wife's death. The ceremony was announced in the next issue of *The Restitution Herald*. Most readers were surprised at the news.

Frank Siple with Dorothy, his second wife, during the trial.

Chicago Daily Tribune Photo

C. Crimes Overshadow Ministry

Frank Siple's preaching career came to an untimely and infamous end when he was tried on murder charges for the mysterious death of his first wife in 1929 and the death of one daughter in 1939. The ugly story filled local and national papers for weeks. Evidence revealed he had poisoned his wife in this manner: He was preaching, left the pulpit, came back and reported his wife was dead. This was a terrible shock to many people.

The crimes were detected after he physically attacked Elder Lyle Doan of the Southlawn Church of God in Grand Rapids, Michigan, in or about 1945. Prior to this attack Siple had sent Doan a box of poisoned Christmas candy which Doan neglected to sample. When Doan asked questions, Siple hit him on the head with a pipe while they were driving home from church. The subsequent investigation led to the horrible truth.

Although Siple's motive for attacking Doan is unknown, the act aroused police suspicion about the demise of Siple's teenaged daughter just after her graduation from high school. When Siple first admitted to having poisoned her he said, "She knew too much." By this he was referring to her knowledge of how her mother had died in Dixon several years earlier. Shortly before the daughter's death she had accused him of murdering her mother. Siple was arrested and signed a confession. He was convicted on two counts of murder and spent most of his remaining life in prison.

The members and ministers of the Church of God were grief-stricken for Frank Siple when the sordid ordeal was revealed. He was beloved by hundreds and thousands of people. His fall from grace was dramatic and unbelievable. Three witnesses living at the time this encyclopedia was written, retired pastor Francis Burnett, Ed Goit, and layman Ivan Magaw, said the church and the General Conference extended mercy to him. His ministerial license was not rescinded until he went to prison.

The Siple siblings were deeply sorrowful because of the actions of their brother. A note appeared in the church paper. It was both gentle and accusatory:

> We wish to thank those who have sent words of sympathy in regard to the things that have happened to our brother Frank which have surely brought the deepest sorrow that has ever come to the Siple family.
>
> We cannot justify what he says he did to the daughter, but those who knew even a little of what she and the family went through may not be too sure what they would have done. As for what happened at Grand Rapids, it is impossible for us to believe that anyone with his right mind would attack another with a little piece of 1¼" pipe, 14" long, deliberately and without provocation. Frank had been working beyond his strength for a long time, and we had feared a breakdown. If he did the things he is said to have done, his mind surely must have been slipping.
>
> We hope and pray that He who will not judge after the sight of His eyes, neither reprove after the hearing of His ears, may soon come and straighten out the things that have gone amiss.
>
> *(Signed)* Albert Siple, and brother and sister

Ivan Magaw has written in his yet unpublished manuscript about his father, Sydney Magaw, who was in the ministry at the time, that Frank Siple was a great help to the elder Magaw. Syd Magaw took the news of Siple's crimes hard. Ivan believes that several ministers met with Siple after the news broke, and he repented and requested forgiveness. He knew he had sinned.

Because of this repentant attitude, after he was taken to prison the Ministerial Association met at Minister's Conference in Oregon and debated whether to remove his name from the list of ministers and possibly remove his pastoral recognition. Many wanted to, but one of the ministers who also had a troubled past pleaded for mercy toward Siple. Siple's name remained on the list for that year at least. Francis Burnett said, "It was politics. [The opinion was] Let's not move too fast."

The scandal left a dark mark upon the reputation of the Conference. Many people who worked for the General Conference knew of Siple's love for another woman, but none knew how to act on it. It is a sad story, impossible to understand, except that Satan lurks about, seeking whom he may devour, and sometimes he succeeds in wedging his way into the lives of believers to cause damage.

At some point before all his trouble began Siple wrote a tract entitled, "The Thief on the Cross." As he concluded his thoughts in the brief four-page leaflet, he said, "May we, also, so understand his gospel and order our lives as to be included when that glad day shall come."

In his old age, Siple was released from prison to die of cancer. Dorothy accepted him and nursed him for the few remaining weeks of his life. It is reported she did not believe the reports of the murders.

>See Austin, F.L.
>Burnett, Francis
>Lindsay, S.J.
>Magaw, Sydney

Bibliography: Ancestry.com. U.S. Census. Louisiana. Tangpahoa. Hammond. Dist. 119. Page 9. 1910; Burnett, Frances, Interview with Jan Stilson, December 2006; "Charges Victim of Clergyman Knew Too Much," *Chicago Tribune*, February 2, 1946; Goekler, Harry, Letter to the Editor, *History Newsletter*, (Oct. Nov. 1993); Magaw, Ivan, Interview with Jan Stilson, January 2007; Krogh, David, Death date of Frank Siple, e-mail November 9, 2009; Marsh, Grace, Interview with Stilson, Pinecrest Manor, 1985; "Pastor Tells of Poisoning Own Daughter," *Chicago Tribune*, February 7, 1946; "Photo Copy of Early Records-1900s Ripley Church of God, Ripley, Il.," The copy of the minute book is part of the archival collection at Rock River Christian College, Beloit, WI. The original records are retained by the Ripley congregation; *The Restitution* July 6, 1913; *The Restitution Herald*, Nov. 18, 1914; Dec. 22, 1915; July 26, 1917 (picture); May 14, 1919; May 21, 1919; July 18, 1922; Sept. 26, 1922; Nov. 28, 1922; Sept. 22, 1925; Nov. 4, 1930; Jan. 6, 1931; Siple, Albert, "Word of Appreciation," *The Restitution Herald*, March 26, 1946; Siple. Frank E,. "The Thief on the Cross," Church of God General Conference. Oregon, Il., n.d.

Right: Black Hawk Statue by sculptor Lorado Taft, unveiled July 4, 1911, towers on the east bluff overlooking the Rock River near Oregon, Illinois.

Below: East bluff of the Rock River overlooks Margaret Fuller Island

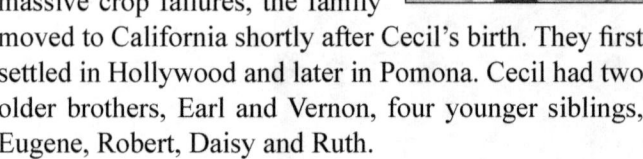

Photo of statue by Ed Graham, provided by David Graham

Smead, Cecil A.
b. January 10, 1906
d. March 8, 2003

A. The Bible Training School
B. Student Preaching Assignments
C. Student Editors
D. Family Ministry
E. The Virginia Years
F. His Senior Years

Cecil Smead was born in Chippewa County, Minnesota, to Clarence and Ruby Smead. Clarence was from Washington County, Indiana, and Ruby from Belvidere, Illinois. A.H. Zilmer baptized Ruby while he worked with the Chicago Church of God.

Due to the Dust Bowl and its massive crop failures, the family moved to California shortly after Cecil's birth. They first settled in Hollywood and later in Pomona. Cecil had two older brothers, Earl and Vernon, four younger siblings, Eugene, Robert, Daisy and Ruth.

The Smeads worshipped in a Christadelphian fellowship until the Williams Street Chapel was built. The J.E. Adamson family also worshipped there. Cecil heard bits and pieces about the Church of God, O.J. Allard being one name he remembered, but became more familiar with the church in 1922 when F.L. Austin preached at Williams

Street Chapel. Because Austin was the new executive secretary of the National Bible Institute, many Church of God people came to the meeting. This included Emma and Ezra Railsback and their extended family.

In 1929 Cecil was a truck driver for Keystone Express. He had purchased a small house in El Sereno and attended the Los Angeles Church of God where Paul Johnson was pastor. When Frank Siple came to promote the National Bible Institute and the new Bible Training Class, Cecil decided to attend. He went to Oregon, Illinois, with Paul Johnson and enrolled in the next class.

A. The Bible Training School

Cecil was 23 when he arrived in Oregon in 1929. He was a member of the sixth class. This course of study began as an experiment in August 1923 just two years after the formal organization of the General Conference. The classroom was above the *The Restitution Herald* print shop at 110 North Third Street. Each training session lasted six weeks. Students returned for more than one course. They attended morning classes and worked at the General Conference in the afternoon.

Cecil worked in the print shop as the "printer's devil"—the one who melted the old lead type and poured it into ingot molds for reuse. He also hand set the Linotype machine and ran the small press. Other students worked at the General Conference's greenhouse or helped at the Golden Rule Home. They were paid $10 a week for their work, and out of that, they paid room and board. Students paid for each class session and lived at the Golden Rule Home with the elderly residents, and they all ate dinner at the same time.

Things changed the following year, and students stayed in the dormitory behind the Oregon Church of God. This structure was heated with a wood stove in the sleeping quarters, and it was not insulated. One side of the upstairs was for women and one side for men. Members of the 1929-1930 class were J. Richard LeCrone, John L. Denchfield, Clarence Lapp, Harvey Krogh Jr., Dorothy Krogh and Cecil Smead. F.L. Austin was the Bible teacher and Mary A. Gesin taught English, history and preaching.

B. Student Preaching Assignments

In addition to Bible classes and employment, students accepted preaching assignments across the Midwest wherever a speaker was needed. Often the young ministers accompanied Frank. E. Siple or another Conference employee on the appointment. Subsequently, if that employee had to miss an appointment to preach elsewhere, the student was experienced in locating the church and understood the format of its worship service, so he could practice preaching in a real congregational setting. In this manner students learned to successfully preach sermons and conduct worship services so the congregation could benefit spiritually. Through it, the students learned and grew. Cecil student-preached at Ripley Church of God; Chicago Church of God; Oregon Church of God; Dixon Church of God, all in Illinois; and Burr Oak, Indiana, to name a few.

C. Student Editors

In a 1970 letter Cecil commented about the annual student edition of *The Restitution Herald*. The editorial committee for 1930 was Richard LeCrone, Dorothy Krogh and Cecil. Clarence Lapp, Harvey Krogh and John Denchfield made up the circulation committee. The students wrote about classes, preaching trips and shared their testimonies. The edition also featured photos of well-dressed men in three-button suits and neat-haired women in dresses below the knees.

The students enjoyed each other's fellowship. Cecil spoke of a co-ed trip to Ripley and being caught in a snowstorm on the way home. When the roads cleared, they raced back in autos prone to flat tires to meet John Denchfield's girlfriend, Cleora Randall. Cecil admitted in this same letter that he was brash. When Dorothy Krogh burned toast from holding it over a flame with a fork, he said, "You know what the recipe for toast is? Take it to the stove and burn it—take it to the sink and scrape it! She almost impaled me with the long fork! I was trying to make conversation!"

After the first three years of classes, the Board of Directors declared the "experiment" a success. The training class would continue. L.E. Conner said:

> The Training Class is no longer in the experimental stage. It has and is operating successfully, as one of the three essentials of the NBI, namely, The Publishing Plant, the Home, and the Bible Training Class, and it merits our united support in every way in which it can be given.

The program continued to educate ministers and leaders until it was forced to close after the 1931-32

Bible Training Class of 1929-1930
Cecil Smead is in the back row, third from left.

session, a casualty of the Great Depression. The school reorganized in 1939 and became Oregon Bible College in 1941.

D. Family Ministry

During the 1931 summer vacation, Cecil served as student pastor in Burr Oak, Indiana, near Culver. In January 1932, Cecil left the program in Oregon to become the first full-time pastor at Burr Oak. The congregation's history committee said in its 50th anniversary book, "It was not easy going as the church fathers had made all the decisions for thirty-two years and were not used to outside leadership."

Ministers and spouses in conference at Oregon Church of God. Cecil Smead is on the right side, wearing a checked vest.

An important part of Cecil's duties at Burr Oak was producing the radio broadcast for WMCA. This program aired three hours weekly. He wrote: "Serving as radio speaker forever changed my proficiency as a speaker. It was a beneficial experience." When WMCA was sold to an Indianapolis station WMCA was closed, ending that phase of ministry.

Cecil served as National Berean Society president in 1932, and from 1932-1939 he edited the Berean page in *The Restitution Herald*. He also contributed many articles to *The Herald*.

In the mid-1930s Cecil accepted the pastorate at Blanchard Church of God in Michigan. There he met Mildred Lesh, the postmaster. They married in 1936. Their son John was born in 1938. In 1941, Cecil left fulltime ministry to work at Dow Chemical in Midland, Michigan. During his years at Dow, Cecil remained active in the Blanchard church, and often served as guest speaker. In the early 1950s Cecil established a radio ministry in Midland. The weekly program featured discussions of Bible topics presented by Cecil, Mildred and John. Cecil's radio experience at Burr Oak helped him greatly in writing scripts. Some of the scripts were published in *The Restitution Herald*. Mildred died in May 1963. Following her death Cecil took advantage of an early retirement program at Dow and returned to fulltime ministry in Virginia.

E. The Virginia Years

Cecil accepted the pastorate at Cool Spring Church of God at Browntown above Front Royal, Virginia. When he first moved to Virginia in November 1963, he rented an apartment in Front Royal, more than an hour from the church via a winding mountain road. He described Browntown in nostalgic fashion shortly after his arrival:

> The Cool Spring church is up on the side of the Blue Ridge Mountains about 2 ½ miles south of Browntown. Gooney Creek meanders by the church to Browntown down in "the holler." It is a little white church with lovely oak pews inside, and classrooms also for the children. The community is quite scattered. It is also a resort area with many summer homes of people from Washington. People love it here.
>
> When I came two weeks ago the trees still had a great deal of color. Vistas of lovely hills and the Shenandoah Valley below open up around every curve, and although television has invaded the area, people love the simple things. I stopped at one farm home last week where apple butter making was in progress in the yard. They needed another hand to dip from the big copper kettle, which I supplied. On Sunday they rewarded me with a quart of lovely apple butter.
>
> At another home butchering was in progress, and three fires under iron kettles were burning away. They were rendering lard and cooking jowls. The neighbors all were there and I got in on supper—in relays—as some would stop their slicing of meat long enough to eat, or stop grinding sausage, or tending the rendering fires in their turn.

A few months later an old three-story farmhouse in Browntown became available for rent; Cecil moved there. The house had a "summer kitchen" on the first floor. Half the house at the ground level was built into the mountainside; even in summer the kitchen was cool. The rest of the house was on the second and third stories.

While Cecil was resident pastor at Cool Spring Church of God, some of the members from Front Royal

From left - John, Mildred and Cecil taped a weekly radio program in Blanchard, Michigan.
Photo from John Smead

planted a new church there. Cecil served as pastor in Front Royal from August 1970 to 1971, preaching Sunday evenings. In February 1971 Pastor Joe Martin came to Royal Village.

When John Smead visited Cecil in Virginia, he directed the youth in a Christmas performance of the "Second Shepherd's Play," a medieval drama depicting shepherds at Christ's birth. Such plays were used to educate churchmen during the Middle Ages before the printing press was invented. As simple men, the shepherds, dressed in period costume, created humorous scenarios. The lead shepherd role was played by Dale Ramsey who gave a credible and humorous performance. The Virginia youth performed the play at three churches, after which the performance was filmed. Cecil wed John and Shirley (Miller) Smead at the Maurertown Church of God, Shirley's hometown church. Cecil met with Eugene Stilson and Joseph Fletcher as Virginia ministers of the Church of God. The men discussed Bible, church management and Virginia Conference issues. Cecil's age and leadership skills were valuable to the other pastors.

After Virginia Cecil went to Michigan's Upper Peninsula to serve a Native American Church of God at L'Anse. This church had been a mission work of the Michigan Conference. The congregation consisted of the Brown and Curtis families. Mary Brown Vadnais served as pastor after Cecil left in 1973. He returned to Royal Village Church in Front Royal, Virginia, from 1974 until 1978. Back in Virginia, the preaching schedule changed slightly. Cecil explained it this way:

> Pastor Richard Alcumbrack was serving as our assistant pastor at Royal Village from September 5, 1971 to 1978. I preached every other week in Maurertown to help Pastor James Mattison. Pastor Alcumbrack preached every other Sunday at Royal Village and every other Sunday at Fort Valley. Bro. Mattison continued preaching the alternate Sundays at Fort Valley and Maurertown. This enabled all three churches to have preaching practically every Sunday.

Cecil served on the Board of Directors of the General Conference from 1966-1970. He attended General Conference and Minister's Conferences long after retirement and remains a valuable resource to the current generation through audio recordings of conference programs and sermons made over many years. Many of the audiotapes preserved in the Archives at McDonough were recorded by Cecil Smead. He often graced the Stilson home when attending a meeting in Oregon, Illinois. He was a great friend and a wonderful Bible student.

During the 1980s and 1990s Cecil traveled extensively, and he was often a guest speaker for churches and conferences throughout the United States. He served as interim pastor at Avondale Church of God, Harlingen, Texas, during 1982; assistant pastor at Raymore Church of God from 1978-1993; pastor to the seniors at Lakeshore, Arizona; and as guest speaker at many other locations.

Cecil recorded many details of his life and ministry in letters to his grandson, Daniel. In one letter he expressed gratitude for the people who shaped his life:

> Is my life really my own? To use as I like, use it up, drink… as long as I don't hurt anyone else? May I drive 100 mph on an empty road, with no passengers? This would be as though a person has no value but to himself.
>
> It's not my life, not completely, partly mine of course, but my parents have shaped it, my teachers, friends all have contributed to make me what I am. Even my descendants, and the people of my churches that I have pastored, have made me what I am. My wife contributed immensely to make me what I am today.
>
> Most of all, my God, my Lord, the influence of their words in my life make me what I am. I Corinthians 3:16 is the ultimate answer: The body of Christ, Christ the Head, the corporate fellowship that I am in.

F. His Senior Years

In 1996 Cecil left Arizona where he had been associate pastor for seniors at Valley View Church with Pastor James Graham, and went to Raymore, Missouri. Raymore is about an hour from Warrensburg where Dr. John Smead worked as a professor of mass communication at the University of Central Missouri. John and Shirley have two sons and one daughter. One of their sons is Daniel Smead, Technical Director of Publishing for the Church of God General Conference for nine years. Daniel and Carolyn currently serve in the ministry at Eden Valley, Minnesota. Cecil served as an assistant at Countryside Bible Church near Raymore until his death at age 97. He rests in Blanchard, Michigan, beside his dear wife.

See   Austin, F.L.
           Conner, L.E. (19th)
           Denchfield, John
           Krogh, Harvey U., Jr.
           Lapp, Clarence E.
           Fletcher, Joseph
           Siple, Frank E.

See Also Hammond, John E. (19th)

Bibliography: Ancestry.com U.S. Census. California. Los Angeles. San Jose. Dist. 353. 1910; U.S. Census. California. Los Angeles. Pomona Ward 4. Dist. 595. 1920; Krogh, David, "The Bible Training Class," a paper presented to the History Conference, North Hills Church of God, Oct. 5-7, 2008; Smead, Cecil, "Letter to Marj Overmyer," June, 1970 retrieved from John Smead, June 26, 2008; Social Security Death List, Record for Cecil Smead; *50th Anniversary of the Church of God at Burr Oak*, Dec. 10, 1950 by the History Committee; Smead, Cecil, "Letters to Daniel," March 27, 1990; March 28, 1990; November 5, 1963.

Smith, E. Richard

b. September 13, 1921
d. September 1, 2003

E. Richard "Dick" Smith was the son of Earl and Pearl Smith. His mother died when Richard was young. Earl

E Richard and Jeanne Smith

then married Dolly Smith, who became a loving stepmother. Dick married Jeanne Simpson, and they enjoyed a blessed 60-year marriage. They had four children, Bonnie, Ginnie and Jerry; son Jimmy died in infancy.

In his youth a terrible fire left Richard disfigured, scarring the left side of his face, hands and arms, yet his relationships were so notable for other reasons his scars were hardly noticed. The Lord blessed him with the ability to put people at ease and engage them in friendly conversation. From this skill, people often came to the Lord.

Richard attended Oregon Bible College where he prepared for the ministry. He graduated and served churches in Michigan, Missouri, Louisiana, Illinois, Ohio, Indiana and North Carolina, serving for 60 years.

While at Lawrenceville, Ohio, Richard and member Fred Pensyl investigated starting a new church at Columbus, Ohio. In February 1968, 12 members met with Smith and Pensyl to plan the new work. The first board meeting was held in April 1968; officers were elected. Robert Schrienk was named pastor. He enrolled at Oregon Bible College to begin preparatory studies. The new church was named Hope Chapel Church of God. Meetings began in the Seventh-day Adventist church on May 1, 1968. Fred Pensyl also served as the new group's pastor. Dick Smith, who was also instrumental in organizing the church at Hilliard, Ohio, served as New Hope's pastor beginning in April 1990. Dick left a legacy among the people he served. They often comment on his ability to "be there at the right time." Alan Cain wrote:

> I remember person after person saying, "Richard would always show up exactly at the right time." I remember one story he told me was that he was hoeing in his garden…and stood up and felt the need to go immediately to a church member's house. He did, and arrived at the same time the ambulance did.

Cain concluded:

> I call these things "nudgings of the spirit."

Alan Cain provided another example of Richard's receptivity to urging of the Spirit, this one pertinent to his father, Rex Cain, and Alan. Dick steered Rex toward Oregon Bible College, rather than military as Rex had planned. See the Rex Cain entry for more of this story. Alan called E. Richard Smith his "grandfather in the faith." Pastor Richard Smith is also remembered for the Lawrenceville Church of God's remarkable growth during his pastorate. Lawrenceville was the daughter church of Brush Creek Church of God at Tipp City; it grew from a small beginning to a mighty church. At this writing, Alan Cain serves as pastor at Lawrenceville.

Dick Smith died after a brief illness.

See Cain, Rex
    Pensyl, Fred

Bibliography: Obituary of E. Richard Smith furnished by Pastor Rex Cain; Cain, Alan. E-mail about E. Richard Smith, Jan. 14, 2010.

Smith, Homer Scott
b. April 7, 1894
d. January 3, 1955

Homer Scott Smith learned of the Kingdom of God from his father as it had been taught in his family for several generations. The first to teach those distinctive doctrines across the Southland is unknown, but may have been a combination of teachers who focused there after the Civil War, such as J.R. Ham, Dr. Leonides Muncrief, Uncle John Foore, D.M. Hudler, Levi Skeels and W.H. Wilson. These men often traveled the South preaching the Gospel of the Kingdom.

H. Scott Smith worked principally in and near Russellville, Arkansas, on a circuit with several other preachers in the region. Between them they visited about 12 small congregations and Bible study groups with at least monthly and sometimes bi-weekly preaching services. Between assignments Smith farmed and operated an orchard near Russellville. A summary of his report from *The Restitution Herald:*

> I spoke at meetings at McGintytown, Oak Grove, that was six miles south of Little Rock, at Little Rock at the Third and Center St. church. I assisted W.R. Simmons in a meeting at Brooklyn, then Cleveland. I began speaking in Little Rock on the Second and Fourth Sundays. Cyrus Shaw and family planned to attend regularly at Little Rock, attendance doubling there. Cyrus also assisted with the work at Oak Grove by conducting a Bible Study Saturday night and preaching there on Sunday night.

As preaching did not pay much, sometimes not enough to cover travel expenses, Scott taught school for $35 a month for additional income. He pastored one church for a whole year, moving his family to Magazine, Arkansas, to serve at Clark's Chapel. Eventually they returned to Russellville.

Scott was tall and slender while his wife, Eva Evants, was so short she could fit under his arm. They made a cute couple. She was Presbyterian when they married, but it wasn't long before her husband baptized her, too. Scott was a walking Bible. He knew his Scriptures inside and out and loved to preach. In all the time he preached for the Church of God he didn't have any extreme opposition from other preachers. In fact, at Russellville, where he and his family lived, the Church of God cooperated in owning and sharing a church building with the Advent Christians.

During weeks when the preacher could not be present Arkansas churches sustained an activity program. Most had Sunday schools and prayer meetings. McGintytown, and perhaps others, held a singing school to teach music and vocals. This provided neighborly fellowship and entertainment. The music was Southern Gospel before it was popular. The school taught using the shaped-notes method. Each note in the scale had a different shape. Shapes included round, square, diamond, triangle, etc. Each shape represented a position in the scale so no matter which musical key a song was in, the singer still knew how to "read" the tones. Instrumental music was taught, as well as vocal harmony for quartets and duets.

Scott Smith was instrumental in aiding the McGintytown Church of God to organize and stabilize its work. He knew they wanted him to preach, but he had not yet been asked. Little Walcie Rhea helped the situation a bit by playing an April fool joke on her dad. She told him he had received a letter from the McGintys and he became quite excited. She couldn't help but laugh and gave it away. If her joke disappointed him, he didn't suffer long, for soon after that, he began serving at McGintytown, traveling there by bus. Each trip someone met him at Conway and took him to Pete and Arlie McGinty's for the night. The next day he preached and returned home.

How did he conduct such a valuable ministry while farming, running an orchard and teaching school? Walcie remembered him being gone every weekend. When he wasn't teaching or preaching he often entertained children with stories. He was a great storyteller. Every Friday after school, children remained behind to hear him tell a good story; these were often Bible stories. One time as he talked about the New Jerusalem coming down from heaven, a little boy got so excited he exclaimed, "Oh, I can hardly wait to see it. I feel like I could just jump over the wall!" Everyone laughed.

Scott and his wife had only daughters, two of whom moved to Illinois to attend Bible college. Virginia Smith had a heart leakage problem discovered at age 15. When she was a little older, T.A. Drinkard suggested she attend the Summer Bible Training Class at Oregon, Illinois. She met Alan McLain and over the next six weeks, became engaged. She returned to Arkansas, and Alan to his pastorate at Dixon, but he didn't like the separation. He came to fetch her, stopped in Fredericktown, Missouri, and they were married. She was unable to have children because of the heart condition so they prepared to adopt. At the last minute the mother decided to keep the baby. Virginia gave her the layette she stitched for the child. Sadly, her heart failed and she died at Dixon. She was returned to Russellville, Arkansas, for burial. They had been married seven years.

Walcie Rhea Smith married Vivian Kirkpatrick. They entered the ministry and raised a family. Viv Kirkpatrick graduated from Oregon Bible College and Aurora College in Aurora, Illinois. Vivian and Walcie alternated with Francis and Iris Burnett to stabilize the mission work at Morrilton, Arkansas. When Francis had to leave in summer 1945, the young Kirkpatricks and two-year old Judy (Myers) went to Morrilton. Walcie remembered there being a few Christadelphian believers at Morrilton. Later, Vivian taught at Oregon Bible College twice and helped build the library collection. Younger sister Lila Smith married and moved to Tulsa.

In addition to being a loving family man, the people of Arkansas remember Scott as a preacher who loved the Lord and loved to preach the Gospel of the Kingdom. This fine man's ministry still reaches out through the work of Judy Myers, executive director of the Lord's Harvest International, the missionary agency of the Church of God, and through grandsons Sydney and Vivian Kirkpatrick, preachers in Minnesota, and through the testimony of daughter, Walcie Rhea Smith Kirkpatrick.

When Scott died, his family gathered around. James McLain preached his funeral at the Mill Creek Church.

See Burnett, Francis
Drinkard, T.A. (19th)
Foore, John (19th)
Ham, J.R. (19th)
Hudler, D.M. (19th)
Kirkpatrick, Vivian, Sr.
McLain, C. Alan
Muncrief, Dr. Leonides (19th)
Simmons, W.R.
Skeels, Levi (19th)
Wilson, W.H. (19th)

Bibliography: Ancestry.com. U.S. Census. Arkansas. Pope. Clark. Dist. 6. 1930; Kirkpatrick, Walcie Rhea Smith, Interview with JStilson, Oregon, Il., April 2007; *The Restitution Herald*. April 12, 1948; Oct. 5, 1948; Myers, Judy, e-mails regarding her grandfather; Weaver, Archard and Clara. Memories of People and the Church at McGintytown, for the Anniversary celebration, Summer, 2010, sent by Pastor Tom New.

Sorenson, Warren
b. July 31, 1927

Warren Sorenson is descended from Almus Adams, one of the greatest evangelists to serve in the Church of

God. Almus' son, Auguste Liesche Adams, was the father of Warren's mother, Marie Liesche. Thus, Almus was Warren's great-grandfather.

Warren was born to Clarence and Marie Sorenson, second son of three sons and a daughter, LaVonne. All Warren's siblings have predeceased him. Warren's eldest brother died in a work-related fire at age 17 when Warren was 14. The fire still haunts Warren.

The Sorensons attended the Church of God at Omaha. Pastor Robert Hardesty, who now lives in Michigan, baptized Warren as a teen. Warren attended Summer Bible School in Oregon, Illinois, in 1944 at age 17. At that time Sydney Magaw, one of the school's instructors, talked with him about attending Oregon Bible College to train for the ministry. Warren felt called to preach, so he returned to Oregon in the fall of 1946 to begin his college studies. He graduated in spring 1950.

Warren met lovely Irene Payne at the college. Irene was dedicated to serving the Lord, and when Sr. Verna Thayer asked her to be a companion and teacher in her child evangelism ministry trips, Irene accepted. She served the summers of 1947 and 1948, and for an entire year from 1949-1950. Irene and Verna traveled across the United States several times. They visited churches to conduct vacation Bible schools for children, teacher-training for adults, and to prepare lesson materials.

Irene helped do the artwork for the "Busy Bees for Jesus" lesson series. This popular series challenged the children to "Bee Loving," "Bee Faithful," "Bee Forgiving" and more. Sr. Thayer used McGintytown, Arkansas, as her headquarters; she had a little house there that the McGintys built for her. Lesson work sheets were prepared there. Copies of Verna's lesson materials are in the Archives at Atlanta Bible College. Irene said Verna was very sweet and easy to work with.

Irene and Warren married in 1951. They had two children, Ron and Leanne. Leanne is married and has a son and a daughter, and Ron is married with one daughter.

Warren and Irene Sorenson

Prior to their wedding Warren commuted between Hedrick, Indiana, and Marshall, Illinois, to pastor the Churches of God. At first, he traveled by train, but began to drive the distance once he owned a car. He was hired to be their pastor for one year. In 1952 Warren and Irene moved to Ripley, Illinois, and served until 1959. Thereafter, no matter where he served, the term lasted seven years, and then he moved on.

While at Ripley, the board decided to sell the old parsonage, a four-room house with no plumbing used as a parsonage since J.M. Stephenson was minister at Ripley in 1888. The new parsonage next door to the church had three bedrooms, a bathroom with running water, and a drive-in basement garage. In each of his pastorates thereafter, Warren conducted a building program. He felt the Lord called him to that ministry. In 1959, the Sorensons left Ripley to pastor the Burr Oak Church of God at Culver, Indiana. While there, the board agreed to remodel the church extensively. They jacked it up, removed the old foundation and laid a new one, and they added a new vestibule with a pastor's office and modern bathrooms.

From Burr Oak, Warren and Irene moved to Macomb, Illinois, in 1965. Here the congregation grew so fast, they needed a larger building. Warren worked with Willis Turner, building committee chairman, to design a large brick church with vaulted ceilings and a beautiful interior. Today that sanctuary remains as beautiful as the day it was dedicated.

When that project was finished, Warren moved on to Tempe, Arizona. At that time the congregation met in a downtown location with no room for growth. They sold their church building to the Salvation Army and built Lakeshore Bible Church. Warren noted that over the years he observed building programs represent times of difficulty in a congregation. Often it seems there are two groups with opinions on how things should be done, their positions so polarized it is hard to make any decisions. When asked how he was able to work through all those interest groups and arrive at a finished plan, he noted feeling the Lord gave him insight or discernment that allowed him to ask questions, and communicate in a manner so all parties laid aside personal preferences and arrived at a common goal. He said it is easy for special interest groups to wall themselves off, and then the other groups try to break down those walls. It is a better situation, he said, to communicate so that fears are diffused and the people pull together to negotiate and eliminate differences.

Warren learned special skills of conciliatory communication because he sought special training in hospital chaplaincy, counseling and psychology from the Chaplaincy program at South Bend Hospital. While in Indiana he served on the committee for the new Tri-State Mental Health Clinic which combined psychiatric and psychological staff to provide counseling. Warren continued to read and study in the field of counseling.

When asked what advice he would offer younger ministers, he said he didn't like to hear pastors complain

1945 Summer Bible Training Class members ready to depart for home from the Oregon depot. Warren Sorenson is the blond-haired fellow in the back row. Frank Siple is far right with second wife Dorothy behind him. Left: The Black Hawk Zephyr ran from Chicago to Minneapolis.

about their congregations. He said God gave them a congregation because He provided an area for service. A pastor should try to uphold his congregation and follow the will of the Lord. He also said if a member of the congregation made a criticism about another member, the pastor should interview the accused member to get both sides of the story. He said it is important to conduct a careful investigation to help members resolve differences. Warren said the chaplaincy training helped him conduct interviews or conversations and learn to "read between the lines" of a criticism and uncover the real problem.

In 1979 Warren left the pastorate at Tempe and enrolled at Fuller Seminary in California. Here he studied church planting. When he finished this program, he worked for the General Conference planning a series of church plantings throughout the country. He conducted calling teams to Colorado Springs, Colorado, twice; Morse Mills, Missouri; Fox Valley, Illinois; Omaha, Nebraska; and McGintytown, Arkansas. Russ Magaw also led teams to Baton Rouge, Louisiana, and Rockford, Michigan. From these calling teams, several churches were planted including one in Simi Valley, California, which continue today. Warren retired from the General Conference in 1989 and pastored the new church in Simi Valley. He continues there at the time of this writing. He is also a member of the Lord's Harvest International Board of Missions. He served on the General Conference Mission Board, taking the seat vacated by Delbert Jones in 1959. Warren was on the board when it invited and hired Stan Ross as first Superintendent of Foreign and Home Missions in 1961.

Over the years, Warren has seen the Church of God wholeheartedly enter into foreign missions and learn by doing. Sometimes, mistakes were made, and a new approach tried. Over the years, the Mission Board learned it cannot just "throw money" at a new mission opportunity. There must be investigation of both the project and the people involved before financial support is approved. In his board-member capacity, Warren traveled to Africa with Rebekah Martin and Jim Mattison to mediate a dispute between the leaders and the pastors. The mission board wanted to hear what the pastors had to say about it. Resolving that problem led to the formation of several conferences in Africa—each with many churches and pastors, and all working together to serve the Lord. To date Warren has made five trips to Africa.

See Adams, Almus (19th)
      Magaw, Russell and Joyce
      Mattison, James
      Ross, S.O.
      Thayer, Verna
      Turner, Willis H.
Bibliography: Interview with Warren and Irene, May, 2010.

Stadden, Frances A. Milburn
b. August 3, 1908
d. August 22, 1994

Frances was born to Jeffrey and Margaret Milburn in Spennymoor, County Durham, England. The family came to the United States in 1923. She married Herbert W. Stadden in the Golden Rule Church of God, Cleveland, Ohio, on November 17, 1928. They were the first couple married there. She was also baptized there in September 1929; the first at that church. Frances was a charter member of the Columbia Church of God, Columbia Station, Ohio. Herbert and Frances were members of the core group that founded this church work. They had three daughters, Hazel E. (Gallagher), Joyce A. (Schroth) and Lois M. (Pryor).

Frances worked as a cook at Columbia schools. Many of her friends remember her hospitable nature. Over the years, she opened her home to numerous friends and family. She died of a heart attack and was laid to rest in Columbia Township Cemetery, Columbia Station, Ohio, awaiting the Lord's return.

See Gallagher, Hazel
      Stadden, Herbert W.
Bibliography: ABC Biography project, David Krogh, compiler.

Stadden, Herbert W.

b. December 2, 1903
d. October 28, 1971

Herbert Stadden was born to Henry J. and Clara Belle Stadden in Cleveland, Ohio. He had a twin sister, Hazel, who died at age two. Three other sisters, Alice (Lindstrom), Doris (Reye) and Ethel (Swartz). Pastor L.E. Conner baptized Herbert in 1920 at the Glenville Baptist Church because the Church of God met in a hall on Hathaway Avenue and had no baptistery. Herbert graduated from West Technical High School in Cleveland in 1922. For 34 years he was employed as a plant electrical maintenance engineer at Cleveland Gasket Company. After retiring from Cleveland Gasket, Herbert worked as a custodian in the Columbia School System; he retired from this 11 years later.

Herbert was a charter member of the Golden Rule Church of God, Cleveland, Ohio, where he married Frances A. Milburn on November 17, 1928—the first wedding at Golden Rule. They had three daughters: Hazel E. (Gallagher), Joyce A. (Schroth) and Lois M. (Pryor). Herbert was also a charter member of the Columbia Church of God, Columbia Station, Ohio. He held many positions at both churches including Sunday school teacher and superintendent, deacon, trustee, elder, board chairman and choir member. He also worked with the Church of God Northeast and General Conferences.

He died at age 67 and rests in Columbia Township Cemetery, Columbia Station, Ohio.

See Conner, L.E. (19th)
 Gallagher, Hazel
 Stadden, Frances A.
Bibliography: ABC Biography Project, David Krogh, compiler.

Stantial, Mildred Arloa Railsback

b. January 11, 1900
d. October 26, 1998

Mildred was born in South Bend, Indiana, third of four daughters to Ezra and Emma Railsback. She attended Valparaiso University for two years, earning a teacher's certificate. She taught briefly at a country school.

In 1919 the extended Railsback family moved to California and provided a weekly diary to readers of *The Restitution Herald*. These lively columns were interesting travelogues to readers back home. The family drove a 1919 Dodge and a 1915 Ford, each with problems on the road including many ruptured and ruined tires, broken springs and a broken axle. After arriving in California, Mildred enrolled in SBUC, later called UCLA, and completed her final two years of education. Her first teaching position was in Sam Simeon during the time Hearst's Castle was under construction nearby. She soon returned to Los Angeles and taught fifth and sixth grades until she retired in 1961. Mildred married Seth Thomas Stantial soon after arriving in California. They had one daughter, Barbara Gay Weise (Simi) and one son, Thomas Dolman.

Mildred and her sister Thelma firmly believed in the Gospel of the Kingdom, and did all they could to gather California's isolated Church of God members and bring them into a Bible study or small church group. Ruby McCaslin of the current Pomona church wrote:

> We moved from Royal, Arkansas to Reseda, California, built a house and lived there nearly thirty years. I got a call from Mildred Stantial wanting to come and talk about church, or starting church up again. She pulled up in front of my house in a big Oldsmobile. She was a little woman about 4' 11" maybe. She and her car did not fit.
>
> She asked if we were interested in having Bible studies. I said, 'yes.' I offered our home for it. That was the spring of '65 and the beginning of our work in southern California again.

About six families met from that effort with someone in charge of contacting outlying members. Soon they felt able to afford a pastor. Harold Doan and family had moved to California. He contacted Mildred Stantial and asked if the church would like a part-time pastor. Mildred asked members several times, "How did we get so lucky to get Harold?" Mrs. McCaslin said, "He was a great businessman and kept things going smoothly."

Mildred loved Church of God doctrines, and she loved church history—both reading and talking about it. During the 1980s when the *History Newsletter* was published from the Archives of the General Conference at Oregon, Mrs. Stantial often wrote encouraging letters regarding certain articles. She sometimes sent information useful for the newsletter's next edition.

Mildred died peacefully and was interred at Forest Lawn next to her dear husband, Seth.

See Doan, Harold
 Moore, Dean
 Railsback, Emma
Bibliography: ABC Biography Project, David Krogh, compiler; McCaslin, Ruby. E-mail to Kent Ross in 2006 regarding the history of the California churches; Memories of Mildred Stantial by Jan Stilson.

Stewart, Eulon Oscar

b. May 18, 1885
d. September, 1972

Minister E.O. Stewart was born in Arkansas. This gentle, soft-spoken man married Ethel when he was 27. They had two children. He started preaching at the mature age of 40, preaching his way across Arkansas

 and Texas and loving the work. He pastored four churches, preaching one Sunday at each church every month. When not preaching he farmed, but his principal calling and source of income on the 1930 US Census was "Minister, Church of God." The Stewarts lived in Sweetwater, Texas. Stewart also ministered in Arkansas. He was associate editor of *The Gospel Trumpet* at Magazine, where the Church of God was the only denomination in town. Accounts reveal E.O. Stewart as highly esteemed wherever he ministered. In 1925, Elder Stewart wrote an article for *The Restitution Herald* titled, "Hope." His articles appeared in that publication frequently.

Elder Stewart was active in the General Conference and preached the annual meeting in 1922. A picture snapped at one conference shows E.O. Stewart with L.E. Conner, S.J. Lindsay and L.H. Shelton

In 1930 Stewart preached at a house church in Houston—possibly the group E.E. Brown hosted in his home. At that time, Stewart also pastored at Westbrook, Texas. He traveled from there to Riviera south of Corpus Christi, at the invitation of local resident Opal Robbins.

In time, Stewart embraced the doctrine of universal reconciliation. He may have encountered this belief by associating with J.W. Williams of Iowa. In 1926, Stewart wrote an article, presumably for a Universalist journal, entitled "The Great Barrier Removed." Delbert Rankin who has a copy of that article, quoted Stewart:

> It is evident from [Romans 5:18] that God pronounced the sentence of condemnation upon Adam's posterity because he sinned. It is also equally true that because of the obedience of Christ, God removes the sentence of condemnation upon Adam's posterity, which He pronounced upon them because of his offense; and the race stands justified in God's sight, absolutely freed from that sentence of condemnation.

Later Stewart wrote in *Bible Truth* that death is an enemy. He stated that second death is an enemy and must be abolished. He thought the only way to abolish second death was to make all alive in Christ (I Corinthians 15:22). E.O. Stewart also wrote numerous articles for Universalist magazines. In *The Differentiator*, he wrote "Adam the Figure," in which he said:

> The first fruits of that law in operation was Christ. The next to share that life are those who are Christ's at his coming. Then, the end, or the rest shall be made alive in Christ at the final consummation, when God is to become all in all (I Cor. 15:22-28). Thus the law of the Spirit of life in Christ Jesus shall finally free all mankind from the law of sin and death.

In 1948, when Elder Stewart crossed Texas preaching, he stopped at Ater where he learned that Emory Macy was coming to preach special meetings. Usually, this was a signal that the people were considering hiring that preacher, and the meetings were "trial" sermons. Stewart resigned at Ater in September that year, and Pastor Macy assumed the ministry. From that point on there was no longer a universalist message preached in Texas, but Macy endured a lot to sweep the state clean.

E.O. Stewart, J.W. Williams, W.L. Crowe and G.M. Myers tried to usurp the Western Nebraska Conference for the cause of universalism. When Stewart preached universal reconciliation at a Holbrook Conference, Almus Adams got up and walked out. One by one other dissenters left quietly until Stewart stood alone. It is no wonder he left the Church of God after being so shunned. After he left the Church of God, it's believed he fellowshipped with the Seventh-day Adventists. He rests beside Ethel at Sweetwater Cemetery, Nolan County, Texas.

See Adams, Almus (19th)
Crowe, W.L. (19th)
King, Alta
Macy, Emory
Myers, G.M. (19th)
Williams, J.W.

Bibliography: Ancestry.com. U.S. Census. Texas. Nolan. Sweetwater. Dist. 2. 1930;Interview with Pete McGinty, McGintytown, Ar., Dec.1984 as published in *Church of God History Newsletter,* J. Stilson, ed.; Winter 1985; Ferrell, Terry. Interview with JStilson regarding W. Nebr. July 30, 2009; Rankin, Delbert, pastor at Belle Plaine Church of God, from his paper, "The Doctrine of Universal Reconciliation Among Iowa Brethren," presented to the History Conference at North Hills Church of God, Oct. 2008 in which he quotes from *The Gospel Messenger*, Aug. 1, 1936, and from the *Bible Truth*, Nov. 1956; *The Restitution Herald*, Oct. 1921; Sept. 1922; Oct. 6, 1925; Dec. 9 and 16, 1930; Oct. 21, 1947; Savior of All Fellowship at saviorofall.org.; Stewart, E.O. "Adam the Figure," *The Differentiator*, March-April, 1949, pp. 70, 71; Rootsweb.Ancestry.com. Nolan, Texas Cemeteries, Record for Eulon Oscar Stewart at the Sweetwater Cemetery; Stewart E.O. listed as a debater from the Seventh-day Adventists, in T*he Encyclopedia of Religious Debates*, retrieved from www.ptc.dcs.edu/teacherpages/tthrasher/listings/Sr.htm, April 10, 2011.

Stilson, Eugene Everett
b. February 27, 1939

 Eugene Stilson was born in South Bend, Indiana, to Everett Ellsworth and Gladys Boyle Stilson of Foley, Alabama. Gene has an older sister, Sylvia. The family lived in downtown South Bend, but moved to the country when Gene was 12. At age seven Gene was struck by a car, fracturing his skull. Notice of the accident appeared in *The Restitution Herald* in April 1946:

> Bro. F.A. Stilson temporarily at Kendall, Florida, reports that his grandson, Eugene, seven-year-old son of Everett Stilson,

South Bend, Indiana, recently suffered a skull fracture from an automobile accident. An operation was required, but Eugene is returning gradually to normal strength.

Since the accident happened just after the war, surgical instruments were in scarce supply. Eugene received penicillin injections around the clock for a month until the surgical equipment arrived from Chicago. After the surgery and eventual release from the hospital, he had to learn to walk again. He repeated first grade because he had lost his math skills. Prayers of Church of God members brought Gene and his family through that trying time.

When South Bend wanted space to develop its downtown, the family sold their property and moved north to 12 acres on Auten Road, just five miles south of the Michigan/Indiana line. Here Everett and Eugene shaped the marshland and built a house on the hill.

Gene graduated from Portage Township Elementary School and from Central High School. He attended Indiana University Extension in South Bend for one year and transferred to Manchester College where he majored in Physics and Theology. After graduating from Manchester in 1961 Gene felt the call to preach for the Church of God. He attended Oregon Bible College and graduated in May 1963. He married Janet Turner that spring, and they moved to Virginia to assume the pastorate of the Maurertown and Fort Valley Churches of God. Gene and Janet have three children: Richard "Rick" (Melinda) of Morrison, Colorado; Mari Stilson-Hudson (Jeff), Atlanta, Georgia; and Randy (Brenda), Oregon, Illinois. They have five grandchildren.

During Gene's service in the Old Dominion State, he was privileged to be guest speaker at Arlington, Virginia; Baltimore, Maryland; the Kugler home in Pennsylvania; West Virginia; North Carolina; Fonthill, Ontario; and Cool Spring Church of God at Browntown, Virginia. While in Virginia, Gene enjoyed working with Cecil Smead, pastor at Cool Spring; Joe Fletcher in Arlington; and Terry Ferrell of South Carolina. For recreation, the Stilsons and Cecil Smead toured the private areas of the White House with a White House employee from the Cool Spring church. They also toured Civil War battlefields and the Luray Caverns on other excursions.

An exciting aspect of Gene's ministry came in the Virginia State Conference which lasted a week each summer. Distant members traveled to attend, sleeping in the dormitory beside the Maurertown Church. Conference guest speakers from 1963 to 1967 included Darrell Maddock, Francis Burnett, James Mattison and Emory Macy. Z.B. Duncan and Dennis Baldwin also came for special meetings. Gene spent many happy evenings in conversation with these outstanding pastors. James Mattison succeeded Eugene as pastor at Maurertown and Fort Valley.

In 1967, the Board of Directors called Gene to teach at Oregon Bible College. He answered the call and received the endorsement and friendship of Harold Doan, which continued until Harold's death. Gene served at OBC as instructor, Christian service director, academic dean and interim president in the summer of 1979 after the Lewis' deaths. Gene served at the Bible College for 21 years. He received an M.A. in Biblical and Theological Studies from Wheaton College and an M.S. from Northern Illinois University in Guidance and Counseling through the Lawrence Scholarship program.

Gene vacationing at Daytona Beach, Florida

Eugene and his family have been members of the Church of God at South Bend, the Maurertown Church of God and Oregon Church of God. Currently, he is an elder at the Winnebago New Life Bible Church in Winnebago, Illinois. This is the daughter church of Family Bible Fellowship planted in Rockford, Illinois, by the General Conference in 1988. Gene continues to write for the *Truth Seeker's Adult Quarterly,* Greg Demmitt, editor. Gene is also published in *A Journal from the Radical Reformation.* He has been an Illinois Conference board member and has participated in the History Conference in the Atlanta, Georgia, area, and North Hills Church of God, Springfield, Ohio.

In 2000 several Church of God educators from northern Illinois and southern Wisconsin initiated plans to educate ministers and lay workers. In August 2001, Rock River Christian College opened its doors in Beloit, Wisconsin. It meets on the church campus of Beloit New Life Bible Church. Dr. Brian J. Atra served as the first college president, with Eugene accepting the role when Dr. Atra left. Robert Jones served as full-time faculty until 2008 when he relocated to Atlanta Bible College, McDonough, Georgia.

In ten years of operation, RRCC has graduated 11 students, six with bachelor's degrees in Biblical Studies and five with master's degrees in Biblical Studies. Several of these graduates are involved in ministries within the Church of God today: Sherwin Williams (B.A. Bib. Studies, RRCC, 2008) originally from Oklahoma is pastor at Blessed Hope Bible Church of God in Rockford, and Ripley Church of God in Ripley, Illinois; Alan Shaw (B.Th. OBC; M.A. Bib. Studies, RRCC, 2008) formerly from Blanchard Church of God, Blanchard, Michigan, also preaches at Blessed Hope, and is board chairman at Rock River Christian College; Jan Stilson (B.Th. OBC; M.A.L.S. NIU; M.A. Bib. Studies, RRCC, 2009) is an instructor, library consultant, and author of Church of God historical material. In addition to its graduates many other pastors and students from the Church of God and the community have attended or taught at least one semester at Rock River Christian College. Eugene taught classes at Rock River after a 12-year absence from the classroom. He had built a personal library of current materials and donated the majority of this collection to the library at RRCC. Many people throughout the Church of God helped build the RRCC library of nearly 15,000 books and educational materials.

Gene's advice to young ministers is:
Read the Word, and continue to read scholarly materials about the Word. Stay current with scholarship so you can always be ready to give an answer to anyone who asks. Don't drop out. Stay in touch with God, stay in touch with believers, and stay in touch with the work of the General Conference, the other pastors, and the missionaries.

See Doan, Harold
Duncan, Z.B.
Fletcher, Joseph
Lewis, John and Ruth
Macy, Emory
Mattison, James
Pryor, Dr. Charles V.
Stilson, Floyd A.
Stilson, Janet
Smead, Cecil

See Also Appendix 6—From the JRAD-Atonement
Appendix 16—Christian Education

Bibliography: Stilson, Floyd, Report, *The Restitution Herald,* April 9, 1946; Interview with Eugene Stilson, Summer, 2010. Oregon Bible College Catalogues 1967-1988; Stilson, Eugene, "Atonement Theology in Church of God Thought," paper presented at History Conference, North Hills, Ohio, Oct. 2008 reprinted in *A Journal from the Radical Reformation,* A Buzzard, K Ross, J Fletcher, Eds., McDonough, Ga. 16:1, Sp/Smr, 2009 p.4-38.

Stilson, Floyd Arthur
b. June 17, 1882
d. November 30, 1955

Stilson, Lulu (Shafer)
b. September, 1888
d. April 22, 1965

A. The Churches in Marshall County
B. Relocation to Oregon, Illinois
C. Back Home in Indiana

Floyd was the son of Alexander Fremont and Eva McChesney Stilson. He had four siblings Rolland, Iris (Kirkley), Myrtle (Houser) and Forrest. Floyd was

educated as a businessman at the Business College in South Bend. He taught business, penmanship and calligraphy at Central High School. He was also skilled in woodworking, operated a construction enterprise and taught carpentry skills at Indiana University. He married Lulu Myrtle Shafer in Lapaz, Indiana. Lulu was the daughter of Hugh Shafer. They had three children, Everett, Arthur and Eva.

A. The Churches in Marshall County

In 1914 Floyd was president of the Indiana Conference. He recognized the need for a meeting place, and at the annual conference meeting at the old Antioch church donated land and money to the conference to assure its future. The land included a corner lot from the Stilson farm north of Plymouth near the small community of Fairmount along Indiana Highway 31. The lot was large enough for a church, parking lot and Indiana Conference dormitory. The North Salem church building was constructed on the corner giving it great visibility along a very busy route.

The first Churches of God in northern Indiana included the Pisgah church. Pisgah was near Wolf Creek Mill and was like Alexander Campbell's churches. North Salem historians called Pisgah a "Christian Advent" church. Old Antioch developed from Pisgah and was located three miles north of Argos along the Old Michigan Road (Indiana Highway 31). Another Church of God building known as North Salem was constructed or purchased on the south side of Plymouth. Unfortunately, this building burned down sometime in the 19th century. Records at the present-day North Salem church north of Plymouth indicate Antioch was disbanded around 1913 and the property sold in 1915 after the completion of the fourth church near Plymouth—the present North Salem Church of God located on the old Stilson farm.

B. Relocation to Oregon, Illinois
Due to his background in business and his devotion to the Lord, Floyd was called to Oregon, Illinois, in 1925 to serve in the newly formed National Bible Institute, the

business arm of the Church of God General Conference. To prepare for the move, Floyd and his family visited Oregon twice that summer staying at the Golden Rule Home where they enjoyed a visit with Lulu's sister, Verna Thayer. After the General Conference meeting that summer, it was announced that Floyd would become the assistant business manager at the NBI.

Floyd managed the bookstore, flower shop and greenhouse properties. His duties at the greenhouse included installation of a new heating system. He was also responsible for increasing *The Restitution Herald's* circulation. To that end, he initiated a system of premiums to new and renewal subscribers. Possibly, the premiums were bulbs from the greenhouse, as the conference printed a seed and bulb catalog and enjoyed a large mail-order business.

National Berean Society

Sample of calligraphy by F.A. Stilson

Floyd's overall responsibilities included analyzing the new organization's business practices and implementing ways to improve it, accommodating its rapid growth. He watched over operations of the Golden Rule Home for senior citizens. Lulu managed the gift and floral shop in downtown Oregon.

In 1927 Floyd began teaching an early childhood development class at the Bible Training Class in Oregon. The two youngest Stilson children, Art and Eva, graduated from Oregon High School in 1929; Everett pursued a degree at Purdue University. The Stilsons resided at 506 South Fourth Street, two houses south of Oregon Dairy.

C. Back Home in Indiana

When the Depression struck, the General Conference was forced to sell the greenhouse and flower shop. The Golden Rule Home was not sold because of contractual agreements with the residents. The Stilsons returned to Indiana in 1929, and Floyd resumed teaching business and building houses.

Bible studies had been held in South Bend since around 1900 and a nice nucleus of believers wanted to build or buy a church. The Stilsons, McChesneys and several other families purchased a church building from another congregation in South Bend during the 1930s. They named it Hope Chapel Church of God. Floyd directed the work and served as part-time pastor from 1931 to 1936. The church was located on the corner of Leer and Dayton streets in the middle of a quiet residential neighborhood on the city's southeast side. The congregation grew in that location until it called a full-time pastor. F.L. Austin, Melville Lyon, Harry Sheets, Harvey Krogh Jr., Austin Railton, Timothy Pearson, James Graham, Ed Bender, John Railton and Dustin Smith have served as pastors at Hope Chapel or Timberland. John Railton is F.L. Austin's great-grandson.

The congregation launched a new church in Roseland, Indiana, known as Morning Star. Harold Doan served this congregation in its beginning. Other pastors at Morning Star included Celaine Randall, Alva Huffer, Terry Ferrell, Harold Doan, Bud Goodwin, Daniel Fyfe, Dick Worley, Ted Arms, Ben Mattison and Bert Harrison. Eventually the two churches merged. The work continues today as Timberland Bible Church, a new facility built near Granger, Indiana.

The 1946 Summer Training Class program schedule:

9:00-9:25	Chapel
9:30-10:20	Stilson—All Students
10:30-11:20	Watkins—Business of Living
	Stilson—Types in the Bible
Lunch	
1:00-1:50	Stilson—Bible Words and Phrases
	Watkins—Working with Society
2:00-2:50	Watkins—All Students
3:00-3:50	Barnum—Music
Dinner	
7:30-8:30	Barnum—Octette
	Bible class at Church 7:30
10:00	Lights out; Friday night: 10:30

Some rules of the Class included: stay out of the kitchen except to help with dishes three times a day; no snacks from the kitchen at night; receive permission for long distance telephoning from Dean (Albert Logsden); and pay for it immediately after the call; don't stay in the bathroom to do your hair; be quiet after lights out, and no theatre attendance unless in a group.

Ref.: Floyd Stilson's Notes and Sermons.

1946 Summer Bible Training Class with Superintendent Floyd Stilson
Floyd and Lulu are in the middle of the second row.

and Texas and loving the work. He pastored four churches, preaching one Sunday at each church every month. When not preaching he farmed, but his principal calling and source of income on the 1930 US Census was "Minister, Church of God." The Stewarts lived in Sweetwater, Texas. Stewart also ministered in Arkansas. He was associate editor of *The Gospel Trumpet* at Magazine, where the Church of God was the only denomination in town. Accounts reveal E.O. Stewart as highly esteemed wherever he ministered. In 1925, Elder Stewart wrote an article for *The Restitution Herald* titled, "Hope." His articles appeared in that publication frequently.

Elder Stewart was active in the General Conference and preached the annual meeting in 1922. A picture snapped at one conference shows E.O. Stewart with L.E. Conner, S.J. Lindsay and L.H. Shelton

In 1930 Stewart preached at a house church in Houston—possibly the group E.E. Brown hosted in his home. At that time, Stewart also pastored at Westbrook, Texas. He traveled from there to Riviera south of Corpus Christi, at the invitation of local resident Opal Robbins.

In time, Stewart embraced the doctrine of universal reconciliation. He may have encountered this belief by associating with J.W. Williams of Iowa. In 1926, Stewart wrote an article, presumably for a Universalist journal, entitled "The Great Barrier Removed." Delbert Rankin who has a copy of that article, quoted Stewart:

> It is evident from [Romans 5:18] that God pronounced the sentence of condemnation upon Adam's posterity because he sinned. It is also equally true that because of the obedience of Christ, God removes the sentence of condemnation upon Adam's posterity, which He pronounced upon them because of his offense; and the race stands justified in God's sight, absolutely freed from that sentence of condemnation.

Later Stewart wrote in *Bible Truth* that death is an enemy. He stated that second death is an enemy and must be abolished. He thought the only way to abolish second death was to make all alive in Christ (I Corinthians 15:22). E.O. Stewart also wrote numerous articles for Universalist magazines. In *The Differentiator*, he wrote "Adam the Figure," in which he said:

> The first fruits of that law in operation was Christ. The next to share that life are those who are Christ's at his coming. Then, the end, or the rest shall be made alive in Christ at the final consummation, when God is to become all in all (I Cor. 15:22-28). Thus the law of the Spirit of life in Christ Jesus shall finally free all mankind from the law of sin and death.

In 1948, when Elder Stewart crossed Texas preaching, he stopped at Ater where he learned that Emory Macy was coming to preach special meetings. Usually, this was a signal that the people were considering hiring that preacher, and the meetings were "trial" sermons. Stewart resigned at Ater in September that year, and Pastor Macy assumed the ministry. From that point on there was no longer a universalist message preached in Texas, but Macy endured a lot to sweep the state clean.

E.O. Stewart, J.W. Williams, W.L. Crowe and G.M. Myers tried to usurp the Western Nebraska Conference for the cause of universalism. When Stewart preached universal reconciliation at a Holbrook Conference, Almus Adams got up and walked out. One by one other dissenters left quietly until Stewart stood alone. It is no wonder he left the Church of God after being so shunned. After he left the Church of God, it's believed he fellowshipped with the Seventh-day Adventists. He rests beside Ethel at Sweetwater Cemetery, Nolan County, Texas.

> See Adams, Almus (19th)
> Crowe, W.L. (19th)
> King, Alta
> Macy, Emory
> Myers, G.M. (19th)
> Williams, J.W.

Bibliography: Ancestry.com. U.S. Census. Texas. Nolan. Sweetwater. Dist. 2. 1930;Interview with Pete McGinty, McGintytown, Ar., Dec.1984 as published in *Church of God History Newsletter,* J. Stilson, ed.; Winter 1985; Ferrell, Terry. Interview with JStilson regarding W. Nebr. July 30, 2009; Rankin, Delbert, pastor at Belle Plaine Church of God, from his paper, "The Doctrine of Universal Reconciliation Among Iowa Brethren," presented to the History Conference at North Hills Church of God, Oct. 2008 in which he quotes from *The Gospel Messenger*, Aug. 1, 1936, and from the *Bible Truth*, Nov. 1956; *The Restitution Herald*, Oct. 1921; Sept. 1922; Oct. 6, 1925; Dec. 9 and 16, 1930; Oct. 21, 1947; Savior of All Fellowship at saviorofall.org.; Stewart, E.O. "Adam the Figure," *The Differentiator*, March-April, 1949, pp. 70, 71; Rootsweb.Ancestry.com. Nolan, Texas Cemeteries, Record for Eulon Oscar Stewart at the Sweetwater Cemetery; Stewart E.O. listed as a debater from the Seventh-day Adventists, in T*he Encyclopedia of Religious Debates*, retrieved from www.ptc.dcs.edu/teacherpages/tthrasher/listings/Sr.htm, April 10, 2011.

Stilson, Eugene Everett
b. February 27, 1939

Eugene Stilson was born in South Bend, Indiana, to Everett Ellsworth and Gladys Boyle Stilson of Foley, Alabama. Gene has an older sister, Sylvia. The family lived in downtown South Bend, but moved to the country when Gene was 12. At age seven Gene was struck by a car, fracturing his skull. Notice of the accident appeared in *The Restitution Herald* in April 1946:

> Bro. F.A. Stilson temporarily at Kendall, Florida, reports that his grandson, Eugene, seven-year-old son of Everett Stilson,

South Bend, Indiana, recently suffered a skull fracture from an automobile accident. An operation was required, but Eugene is returning gradually to normal strength.

Since the accident happened just after the war, surgical instruments were in scarce supply. Eugene received penicillin injections around the clock for a month until the surgical equipment arrived from Chicago. After the surgery and eventual release from the hospital, he had to learn to walk again. He repeated first grade because he had lost his math skills. Prayers of Church of God members brought Gene and his family through that trying time.

When South Bend wanted space to develop its downtown, the family sold their property and moved north to 12 acres on Auten Road, just five miles south of the Michigan/Indiana line. Here Everett and Eugene shaped the marshland and built a house on the hill.

Gene graduated from Portage Township Elementary School and from Central High School. He attended Indiana University Extension in South Bend for one year and transferred to Manchester College where he majored in Physics and Theology. After graduating from Manchester in 1961 Gene felt the call to preach for the Church of God. He attended Oregon Bible College and graduated in May 1963. He married Janet Turner that spring, and they moved to Virginia to assume the pastorate of the Maurertown and Fort Valley Churches of God. Gene and Janet have three children: Richard "Rick" (Melinda) of Morrison, Colorado; Mari Stilson-Hudson (Jeff), Atlanta, Georgia; and Randy (Brenda), Oregon, Illinois. They have five grandchildren.

During Gene's service in the Old Dominion State, he was privileged to be guest speaker at Arlington, Virginia; Baltimore, Maryland; the Kugler home in Pennsylvania; West Virginia; North Carolina; Fonthill, Ontario; and Cool Spring Church of God at Browntown, Virginia. While in Virginia, Gene enjoyed working with Cecil Smead, pastor at Cool Spring; Joe Fletcher in Arlington; and Terry Ferrell of South Carolina. For recreation, the Stilsons and Cecil Smead toured the private areas of the White House with a White House employee from the Cool Spring church. They also toured Civil War battlefields and the Luray Caverns on other excursions.

An exciting aspect of Gene's ministry came in the Virginia State Conference which lasted a week each summer. Distant members traveled to attend, sleeping in the dormitory beside the Maurertown Church. Conference guest speakers from 1963 to 1967 included Darrell Maddock, Francis Burnett, James Mattison and Emory Macy. Z.B. Duncan and Dennis Baldwin also came for special meetings. Gene spent many happy evenings in conversation with these outstanding pastors. James Mattison succeeded Eugene as pastor at Maurertown and Fort Valley.

In 1967, the Board of Directors called Gene to teach at Oregon Bible College. He answered the call and received the endorsement and friendship of Harold Doan, which continued until Harold's death. Gene served at OBC as instructor, Christian service director, academic dean and interim president in the summer of 1979 after the Lewis' deaths. Gene served at the Bible College for 21 years. He received an M.A. in Biblical and Theological Studies from Wheaton College and an M.S. from Northern Illinois University in Guidance and Counseling through the Lawrence Scholarship program.

Gene vacationing at Daytona Beach, Florida

Eugene and his family have been members of the Church of God at South Bend, the Maurertown Church of God and Oregon Church of God. Currently, he is an elder at the Winnebago New Life Bible Church in Winnebago, Illinois. This is the daughter church of Family Bible Fellowship planted in Rockford, Illinois, by the General Conference in 1988. Gene continues to write for the *Truth Seeker's Adult Quarterly,* Greg Demmitt, editor. Gene is also published in *A Journal from the Radical Reformation.* He has been an Illinois Conference board member and has participated in the History Conference in the Atlanta, Georgia, area, and North Hills Church of God, Springfield, Ohio.

In 2000 several Church of God educators from northern Illinois and southern Wisconsin initiated plans to educate ministers and lay workers. In August 2001, Rock River Christian College opened its doors in Beloit, Wisconsin. It meets on the church campus of Beloit New Life Bible Church. Dr. Brian J. Atra served as the first college president, with Eugene accepting the role when Dr. Atra left. Robert Jones served as full-time faculty until 2008 when he relocated to Atlanta Bible College, McDonough, Georgia.

In ten years of operation, RRCC has graduated 11 students, six with bachelor's degrees in Biblical Studies and five with master's degrees in Biblical Studies. Several of these graduates are involved in ministries within the Church of God today: Sherwin Williams (B.A. Bib. Studies, RRCC, 2008) originally from Oklahoma is pastor at Blessed Hope Bible Church of God in Rockford, and Ripley Church of God in Ripley, Illinois; Alan Shaw (B.Th. OBC; M.A. Bib. Studies, RRCC, 2008) formerly from Blanchard Church of God, Blanchard, Michigan,

In 1946 Floyd became dean for Summer Bible Training School while Lulu served as women's matron. This was offered as a program of Oregon Bible College, and it was inspiring that 43 students enrolled, the largest summer-school attendance up to that time, it was said.

S.J. Lindsay began the Summer Bible Training Schools informally by around 1906, and continued every summer until the camping program was initiated at Camp Emmaus, Mt. Morris, Illinois, in 1953. The Lindsay summer programs may be credited for keeping educational interests alive within the Church of God until the formation of the Bible Training Class in 1923 and Oregon Bible College in 1939. Even then, the summer camping program served as a feeder program to channel campers into the college to fulfill their call to prepare for Christian ministry.

Floyd was a lay preacher serving throughout Indiana and Michigan—wherever he was asked. He was an avid Bible student, believing in the work and the General Conference statement of faith. One of his favorite topics for conference lessons or sermons was the typology of the Tabernacle. People still remember him as the preacher who loved to teach about the Tabernacle.

After retirement, Floyd and Lulu traveled between Indiana and Florida. While in Florida, they resided in a trailer Floyd built, and every day, they used a small rowboat to float among the Keys. They enjoyed fishing.

In winter 1955, Floyd grew ill en route to Florida. He was hospitalized in Macon, Georgia, and suffered a fatal stroke. Everett traveled to Macon to retrieve his mother and bring Floyd's body to Indiana for services. Floyd was interred at the Oak Hill Cemetery in Plymouth, Indiana.

Lulu continued to winter in Florida for several more years and was an avid fisherwoman. When she was younger Lulu spent many weeks each summer teaching Bible school and preparing children's lesson materials for her sister Verna Thayer's child evangelism ministry. Lulu rests beside her husband.

Floyd and Lulu Stilson's heritage is seen today in the ministry of Eugene (Janet Turner) Stilson, Bert and Sylvia Harrison who pastored at Morning Star, Steve and Beth (Harrison) Mattison, Christopher and Rebecca.

 See Lindsay, S.J. (19th)
   Stilson, Alexander Fremont (19th)
   Stilson, Eugene
   Thayer, Verna

Bibliography: Ancestry.com. U.S. Census. Indiana. Marshall. Center. Dist.70. 1900. Harrison, Bert, Stilson family genealogy; *The Restitution Herald*, "Report by David Van Vactor," Dec. 23, 1914 and Sept. 1922; "Herald Receipts," Oct. 25, 1925; Dec. 29, 1925; Oct. 5, 1926; Oct. 12, 1926; Feb. 8, 1927; April 9, 1946; 1946 Summer BTS report, July 1946; Stilson, Eugene, Memories of Floyd and Lulu Stilson, Spring 2007; Cardwell, Darrell and Nancy Kirkley Mata. Interviews with Gene and Jan Stilson at North Salem Church of God, July 19, 2009; Houser, Edward, Memories of Floyd Stilson and the Tabernacle, Summer, 2005; Kirkley, Iris et al, *North Salem One Hundred Years*, Anniversary booklet, 1981.

Stilson, Janet Turner
b. June 20, 1941

Janet Ann Turner was born in Oregon, Illinois, to Willis Harvey and Ida Mae Friemuth Turner. Janet has one brother, Gary Richard Turner. Willis worked for the Ogle Service Company and Country Companies Insurance, and Ida was a homemaker. Janet grew up down the street from the Sydney Magaw family, and a few blocks west of the Oregon Church of God. She started attending Sunday and Bible schools at age five. The teachers told her primary class about Jesus coming back to earth. This sounded wonderful to Janet. She wanted to be on the side of the saints.

Janet accepted the Lord at age 12. She went forward at the end of a service and in front of many adults, requested baptism. Pastor J.R. LeCrone baptized her in the Rock River just above the dam. Since then she has been a member of the Oregon Church of God, Maurertown Church of God in Virginia and Winnebago New Life Church. Janet attended Oregon schools and after graduation she went to Oregon Bible College. She graduated in 1963 and married Eugene Stilson on May 25 of that year. They had three children: Richard "Rick" (Melinda), Marianne (Stilson-Hudson) and Randy (Brenda). Gene and Janet have five grandchildren.

Gene accepted the pastoral call to serve in the Maurertown and Fort Valley Churches of God in the Shenandoah and Massanutten Valleys respectively from 1963-1967. The Stilsons returned to Oregon when Gene was invited to teach at Oregon Bible College. He did so for the next 21 years. Janet graduated from Northern Illinois University with an M.A. in Library Science and became OBC Library Director in 1980. She served in that position for eight years and organized the General Conference's historical archives.

Janet began to edit *The History Newsletter* in 1984 under the direction of a ministerial committee who offered advice and suggestions for feature articles. The newsletter continued in Morrow, Georgia, until 1995 with Kent Ross assuming editorship its final two years. The newsletter is now available on CD. Other church historians who began teaching and writing on subjects related to Church of God history include David Graham, Kent Ross, Mark Mattison and Greg Demmitt. Jan and several others have written articles about Church of God history or the history and development of doctrinal thought for *A Journal from the Radical Reformation,* Kent Ross, Anthony Buzzard and Mark Mattison, the founding editorial board.

After OBC relocated from Illinois to Georgia, Jan became the medical librarian at Freeport Health Network, and later, newsroom librarian/information services editor at the *Rockford Register Star*. She retired from the paper in 2005. Within a year after retirement Jan published a book, *Art and Beauty in the Heartland,* the story of the Chicago artists who summered at Oregon, Illinois, and built the Black Hawk statute overlooking the Rock River Valley. The book is available on Amazon.com.

In 2000 Jan was instrumental in designing and organizing the new library at Rock River Christian College. Church of God members donated nearly 9,000 books. The collection was shelved and labeled by Jan, Nola Jones and Marcee Turner. The collection now has nearly 15,000 books. Paul and Ruth Overholser, Carl Heiser, Russ Magaw, Francis Burnett, Hollis Partlowe and several other retired Church of God pastors also donated many archival books.

In November 2006 Jan was invited to automate the library and archives of Atlanta Bible College (ABC) preparatory to the campus's relocation from Morrow to McDonough, Georgia. This was done over the next year. All titles in the ABC Library have been digitally organized. To affect an efficient move, the collection was split between the ABC campus and the ABC Korean Extension campus in Duluth, Georgia. The KE campus had a collection of Korean language books, and also accepted nearly 4,000 English language books from the main library. Recently ABC Library donations have been received from the pastoral collections of John "Jack" Hearp and Ed Goit.

About this time the History Committee formed and organized a history conference at ABC. Presenters gave papers on the history of their churches or their families, adding to the wealth of information in the ABC Archives. Guests were given tours of the archives. Kent Ross suggested the Church of God develop an encyclopedia such as the *The Encyclopedia of the Stone-Campbell Movement* published by Disciples in 2004. The *Biographical Encyclopedia: Chronicling the History of the Church of God Abrahamic Faith* was begun in 2005 using the resources of many libraries including the historical data in the Church of God Archives and oral histories from many families.

Jan vacationing at Daytona Beach, Florida

Eugene and Janet Stilson

Jan may take on other writing projects in the future as time and health permit. She is thankful for the opportunity this book has afforded her. She plans to continue volunteering in community events and enjoying her family and church. *Maranatha*.

See Austin, F.L.
      Burnett, Francis
      Buzzard, Sir Anthony
      LeCrone, John R.
      Magaw, Russell and Joyce
      Magaw, Sydney
      Overholser, Paul and Ruth
      Partlowe, Hollis
      Ross, Kent
      Stilson, Eugene
      Stilson, Floyd A.
      Turner, Willis H.

Bibliography: Autobiographical entry by Jan Turner Stilson.

Stilson, Rolland Cooly
    b. January 30, 1892
    d. November 1979

Brothers Rolland (left) and Floyd Stilson in South Bend, Indiana.

Rolland was the son of Alexander Fremont Stilson, along with siblings Floyd, Forrest, Iris (Kirkley) and Myrtle (Houser). They were born in Marshall County, Indiana, and attended the North Salem Church of God at Plymouth. Rolland was a dedicated young man who attended the summer Bible Training Class sponsored by the Church of God from 1916 until the Oregon Bible College began in 1939. While he attended the summer training, Rolland studied with L.E. Conner and S.J. Lindsay, instructors for the Bible classes. At home in South Bend Rolland worked as a production clerk at Studebaker.

He met lovely Maude Cross, daughter of John Cross, at Oregon. Mr. Cross was Superintendent of Schools for Ogle County, and attended the Church of God at Antioch east of Washington Grove. Maude was a teacher in a one-room schoolhouse near Oregon, perhaps even at the Antioch school where the church met.

The youth at Oregon had held picnics at the Ganymede Spring along the Rock River below the statue of Black Hawk. In the winter when the ice was a foot thick, they ice-skated on the Rock River. Maude said at that time people cut blocks of ice, saved it in straw in an underground cellar or ice house, and the ice kept long enough to preserve food and make ice cream nearly the whole summer. Maude also said that, when the ice went out, the riverboat "Oregon" sailed upstream and all the young people who came to Bible Training Class, including Floyd and Rolland Stilson, Benjamin Carpentar, Alice Andrew, Maude Cross, and her sister, Paul and Arthur Johnson, F.E. and Bertie Siple, and many others got on and had a merry time after class. Spending summers in Oregon was very nearly like being in a river resort town. There was much to do and much to see with several parks being nearby.

Rolland and Maude married at her parents' home in Chana, Illinois, on July 3, 1920. They had five children, John Elwyn, Donald Earl, Sybil, Joy and Kenneth "Hal". Rolland went to school and studied business. He taught industrial arts at Central High School in 1929. Seventeen years later, he earned his degree from Purdue University through night school.

In their retirement years they had a cottage at Diamond Lake, Michigan, which they built themselves. They wintered some in Sarasota, Florida, where Rolland expanded his love for fishing, adding salt-water fishing to his skills. Their later retirement years were spent near Hal in California. Rolland and Maude both died in California, she on August 2, 1991, at age 96.

See Andrew, Alice
Carpentar, Ben
Conner, L.E. (19th)
Cross, John (19th)
Kirkley, Iris
Lindsay, S.J. (19th)
Siple, F.E.
Stilson, Floyd

Bibliography: Stilson, Don. Biography project of Atlanta Bible College, compiled by David Krogh. Memories of Rolland and Maude Stilson by great-niece, Jan Stilson; *The Restitution Herald*, August 20, 1916; July 13, 1920;

Swanson, Ernest Leonard
b. April 5, 1892
d. December 30, 1982

Ernest Swanson was born near Sac City, Iowa, to Swedish immigrants Sam and Emma Johnson Swanson. Ernest was the oldest of six children with sisters: Helen, Emily, Gladys, Genevieve and Lucille. Through early homestead programs Sam acquired farmland four miles south of Sac City. Ernest was a 1910 graduate of Sac City High School. He began teaching in country schools, enrolled in a Teachers' Institute and gained a teacher's certificate. He later attended the Iowa State College. From 1916 to 1938 he was Superintendent of Schools in Defiance, Smithland and Sutherland, Iowa. He also taught manual training (shop) and science courses and coached basketball.

Ernest married Emma Sonnichsen in August 1916. Emma was the daughter of Chris and Sara Sonnichsen, a local farm family. Ernest and Emma had four children: Irene, Elaine, Russell and Marilyn. Marilyn died at age four (1936) of acute appendicitis. Irene died in 1975. Elaine and Russell reside at Bella Vista, Arkansas. Ernest bought the family farm around 1930. He hired a man to run the farm business as he still worked for the school.

Ernest retired from the superintendent position in 1938, and moved to the farm. Soon thereafter, Ernest and Emma began holding Church of God services in their home for family and neighbors. Those also sharing their home for services included Emily and John Jacobsen and Lucille and Chris Momsen and the families of Oscar and Clair Johnson, Arthur Johnson, Walter and Lavern Roose, Harvey and Ellen Wilson and Bill and Tina Klindt. J.W. Williams came from Gladbrook to conduct services. Later, his son, Paul Williams, newly ordained, also led worship. The ministers stayed with church families while in the area. On occasion Arthur Johnson preached. He had attended the Bible Training Class in Oregon and was well suited to preaching.

The Pleasant Prairie church building was located on land in the northeast section of Ernest Swanson's farm four miles south of Sac City. It had been purchased from a Church of Christ group in the late 1890s. Records show that O.J. Allard preached there in 1910. The building was idle for many years and in need of repair. The grounds were overgrown with weeds and thickets. Early in the 1940s, Ernest generated interest in renovating the building and grounds. He motivated local families to undertake the project, clearing weeds and wild plum thickets and trimming trees. He supervised the work and made repairs inside and outside including painting, refinishing the floors, window repair and treatments, and wall papering. Rural Electric Association (REA) provided electric service. Ernest wired the building with outlets and installed ceiling light fixtures. An oil-fed stove provided heat. Thereafter, from the early 1940s, Church of God services were held there. J.W. and Paul Williams continued to travel from Gladbrook as they were able. Arthur Johnson was a major supporter of the re-established church. Pastors affiliated with the Church of God from other areas came for special meetings. Ernest and Emma planned children's programs for Easter and Christmas.

Ernest also organized a board to handle the agendas, fiscal management, building and grounds maintenance and administrative details such as securing church bulletins and Sunday school lessons, and writing pertinent correspondence to secure preachers. Pleasant Prairie church continued for several years. When Ernest and Emma moved to town, church activities declined. In 1963, the "era" ended. The building was sold at auction, removed, and the land returned to farming.

Emma died on April 3, 1988. She was interred at Sac City Cemetery beside her devoted husband. Both enjoyed full and fruitful lives, supporting wholesome endeavors with civic, church, social and family activities. They were wonderful and respected parents.

Russell Swanson contributed this entry.

See   Allard, O.J. (19th)
      Johnson, Arthur
      Williams, Joseph W.

Bibliography: Burnett, Francis, et al. *History of the Iowa Church of God and Conference "Those people called Restitutionists, 1855-1987"*; Swanson, Russell, "A Little History for *Searchlight* Readers," *Searchlight.* Iowa State Berean Society Newsletter, Spring 2005; Swanson, Russell, "Brief History of E.L. Swanson, and his roles with the Church of God activities near Sac City, Iowa," June 2008; Photo of Ernest Swanson furnished by Russell Swanson.

Seniors at General Conference in 1970, including Grace Marsh, Leota Hanson, Ada Simpson, Arthur Johnson, Paul Johnson and Clyde Randall.

Photo provided by Rex Cain

Thayer, Verna Shafer (Shaffer)
b. August 26, 1893
d. April 1964

Verna was the daughter of Hugh Shafer of Plymouth, Indiana. She had two sisters, Bess and Lulu. Verna married Earl Thayer (May 21, 1897-January 1964). They resided in Hazen, Arkansas, where they began their family. They had two sons and two daughters, but only Lyle survived. Two-year-old Hugh Andrew Thayer died of pneumonia on January 30, 1922; his sisters preceded him. Hugh's funeral service was conducted in Indiana where Verna had been born. Her brother-in-law, Floyd Stilson, reported the obituary to *The Restitution Herald*. Pastor D.E. VanVactor officiated the service at North Salem Church of God in Plymouth.

Flower field for Oregon Greenhouse; Earl Thayer was greenhouse manager.

Verna and Earl's life was tumultuous after Hugh's death so they separated. Verna remained in Indiana to assist with the Indiana Conference. She earned her living as a teacher. Verna also wrote children's Sunday school lessons and the "Children's Column" for *The Restitution Herald*. It is likely that keeping busy helped her cope with the loss of her son. The couple reconciled later that year but it was not to endure. During their reconciliation she changed her column signature from Verna Thayer to Mrs. Earl Thayer.

In 1925, Verna and her small family lived in the west apartment of the newly purchased Golden Rule Home at Oregon, Illinois. She was known as "Mother Thayer," despite being young and having dark hair. At that time she was active in the National Berean work and the Berean's Children's Junior Extension. Earl was the caretaker for the Golden Rule Home and the new greenhouse. In 1931 he also pastored the newly-established Church of God in Rockford, Illinois. The church met in the WCTU building at 1904 N. Main Street.

After leaving the Rockford congregation, Earl and Verna and son Lyle moved to Virginia to pastor two churches in the Shenandoah Valley. It was here that the relationship completely disintegrated. Divorce was the result. Earl married again and Verna dedicated her life to serving the Churches of God in America as a teacher and teacher instructor. Verna returned to Illinois to work for the Conference. While in the area she also taught elementary school in New Milford, Illinois, during 1943.

Verna conducted a Bible School at Morristown, Tennessee, in 1949 when Alva Huffer was the pastor there. Alva then accompanied her across the mountain to Bearwallow Mountain, North Carolina, where he met C.F. Pryor, and Pryor's lovely cousin, Awa McMinn. Alva wanted to marry but he was leaving Morristown and didn't have a job. Verna arranged for him to become pastor at Maurertown and Fort Valley, Virginia. So Alva and Awa were married and moved to Virginia. Verna

Verna Thayer used a flannelgraph to teach Bible stories to children.

conducted a children's Bible school at the next Virginia Conference.

Mrs. Thayer went on to distinguish herself throughout the Church of God as a woman who loved little children and loved conducting teacher education classes for adult volunteers designed to improve their skills. Her workshops included instruction in the use of the materials, making crafts and handiwork, classroom procedures including discipline, and how to lead children to Christ. Verna was a pioneer in designing children's study materials and teacher's materials. She wrote Sunday school and vacation Bible school lesson series that were graded for children up to junior high. Some of the series titles were: "The Fruit of the Spirit," "The Well of Salvation" and "The Book of Life." She typed the quarterlies on mimeograph stencils and made copies. She drew the handwork materials herself. Verna's helpers also drew art for the children's handwork pages. Irene Sorenson did the art for the "Busy Bees" lesson series.

Verna and sister Lulu Stilson wrote the coursework over the winter and mimeographed it in spring, just in time for the Bible school summer season. Before beginning a tour, they printed enough books and handwork for every Bible school that summer and packed the boxes in the trunk. The mimeograph and stencils also went everywhere with them in the trunk of Verna's car. If they had miscalculated estimates of student enrollments and needed more materials, they'd bring out the mimeograph and make more copies.

The sets of lessons were designed to run for a week. Since most Bible schools were two weeks long, Verna had two series because she didn't want the children to repeat lessons. If a church didn't have a summer Bible School, they could still use the lessons. The General Conference mailed them to churches on request. One such quarterly was on the subject, "Stories Jesus Told." A copy of this lesson is part of the Atlanta Bible College Archives.

Except for the younger generation, many members recall Auntie Thayer folding her hands to lead the children's choruses during vacation Bible school, singing:

> Jesus is the Shepherd.
> Gue-ess who I am?
> Such a lovely secret.
> I'm his little lamb.

The handwork that day would be a little lamb cut out of paper with cotton balls pasted on it. The story was about Jesus, the Good Shepherd. Another chorus that everyone loved was:

The Happy Day Express
> We're going to our Bible School on
>   the Happy Day Express.
> The letters on the engine spell J-E-S-U-S.
> The guard calls "Are you ready?"
> We gladly answer, "Yes!"
> We're going to our Bible School on
>   the Happy Day Express.

The lesson accompanying that song was on the fruit of the Spirit. In order to have goodness, kindness, peace and joy, students "dug" out things that made life unhappy such as jealousy, envy, anger and pride. The handwork was coloring a picture of a man with a shovel digging unruly weeds named jealousy, envy, anger and pride from his garden. A chorus to emphasize that lesson was:

The Bunny Song
> Dig them out, get them gone;
> All the little bunnies in the field of corn;
> Jealousy, envy, malice and pride
> All the other sins that in my heart abide.
>
> Search them out; plant them in
> All the blessed virtues of the book within
> Kindness, thoughtfulness, peace and love,
> All the other likenesses of Christ above.

Verna and children at one of many summer Bible schools.

One of the children's favorite lessons was on Abraham who gathered family and flocks and moved to a new country. Abraham displayed a great deal of faith. The handwork for that lesson was a covered wagon made with a Mars candy bar. Two pipe stem cleaners were stuck in the side and taken over the top to be anchored in the other side. A pre-cut piece of white cloth was laid over the pipe cleaner arches and secured with toothpicks, and another pipe cleaner made the "tongue" of the wagon. That handwork made it home just long enough to show Mom and Dad before the child devoured it. With the Church of God emphasis on the faith of Abraham that lesson could be taught nearly every year much to the children's delight!

Verna Thayer testified one day that her mother taught her to tithe. Children did not know what tithing was. She explained it as the portion of our earnings that belongs to God for His work. She explained that she tithed all her farm produce in an egg basket for the Lord. This she would give it to the pastor for his use, or she would supply it for a conference dinner.

The children knew her as "Auntie Thayer." This

Verna and Irene Payne (Sorenson) at Lansing, Michigan.   *Verna teaches Christian Education at OBC.*

spawned a trend among pupils in churches everywhere of calling teachers "Auntie" as in "Auntie Ruby" (Ruby Railton, Rockford, Illinois), "Auntie Wince" (Roxana Wince, Pierceton, Indiana) and "Auntie Irene" (Irene Payne Sorenson). Verna's beloved friends in Arkansas called her "Annie Thayer."

Verna's strategy of discipleship was to select a female student from the Bible Training Class or the new Oregon Bible College (OBC) to accompany her during the summer tour and assist with preparing the Bible schools at each conference session she attended. Around 1959 or 1960 Verna made an exception and asked Robert See to be her driver that year. In this manner young adults learned teaching, management, travel skills, child psychology and many other skills, such as changing a tire along the road if necessary.

Verna was resourceful and frugal. Traveling was exhausting and expensive. She could not always count on having enough cash for restaurant food. She learned to attach a small lidded metal box with meat and a potato in it to the manifold of her car. By the time she drove from Oregon to Ripley her food would be cooked! This became even more manageable after the introduction of aluminum foil to consumers. An aluminum packet could be secured using a No. 1 wire cage attached to the manifold. Sources have indicated that if one did not stop every 100 miles to check the meat, it could be burned to a crisp. Kent Ross related that after she finished Bible School at Litchfield, Minnesota, on a Friday evening, Verna and her helper jumped into a previously loaded car and drove straight through to Happy Woods Church of God near Springfield, Louisiana. The Bible school at Happy Woods began on Sunday morning. This is a distance of over 1230 miles and Auntie Thayer drove on two-lane highways never faster than 50 miles an hour.

When she became older, Verna stopped traveling and retired to Arkansas. Pete McGinty built a small house for her next to the church at McGintytown. She willed her flannelgraphs and other educational materials to the church, and they are still used for the children's program by Wendy (Williamson) Johnson. Verna was invited back to Oregon, Illinois, in 1960 to teach "Principles of Christian Education" to undergraduate students at Oregon Bible College. This proved to be rewarding to the students, but taxing upon the now elderly lady. She retired again to McGintytown in the spring of 1961 where she enjoyed her quaint little home on the mountain overlooking the beautiful valley above Conway.

The Gospelettes, a ladies' trio from Oregon Bible College, stopped with Clarence, Louise and Jon Lapp for a short visit with Verna on their 1961 summer tour. Verna died almost three years later. She is greatly missed to this day by the generation of children that is now itself growing older. Strangely, while she was separated from Earl for years by mutual agreement, they both retired to Arkansas and died within three months of each other. "Annie" Thayer is buried in McGintytown Cemetery below the hill off Clinton Mountain Road.

See   Lapp, Clarence E.
　　　Shafer, Hugh (19th)
　　　Stilson, Floyd A. and Lulu

Bibliography: Ancestry.com. Social Security Master Death Index. Records for Verna Thayer and Lyle Thayer retrieved August 20, 2008; *The Restitution Herald*, April 18, 1922; Nov. 12, 1923; Sept. 1925; Dec. 1, 1925; Stilson, Jan; Memories of Gospelettes' Tour, 1961;

Verna with the Macy girls, from left, Cheryl, Karla and Joyce

Thayer, Verna, "Testimony on Tithing," *The Restitution Herald*, Sydney Magaw, ed., Oregon, Illinois, Oct. 19, 1948; Notice of Lesson Materials available, *The Restitution Herald*, Sydney Magaw, ed., Oregon, Illinois, May 3, 1949; Notice of Rockford Church, *The Restitution Herald*, G.E. Marsh, ed., Oregon, Il., Feb. 24, 1931; Shaw, Dolena (Ward), "Conversation about Auntie Thayer." Dolena grew up in Virginia and knew details of the Thayer marital problems that were not widely known, Summer, 2008 and Summer, 2009; "A Bunny Song," Author unknown, arr. By Herman Voss, *Action Songs,* Alfred B. Smith, ed., Vol. 1, 1949; "Happy Day Express," Alfred B. Smith, ed., *Singspiration,* Copyright renewed 1977 by Zondervan; Ross, Kent. "Auntie Verna Thayer—Children's Evangelist," paper for the 2010 History Conference at North Hills Church of God, Springfield, Ohio; Weaver, Archard and Clara, "History of McGintytown People and the Church," For the Anniversary celebration, Summer, 2010, sent by Pastor Tom New.

Thoms, Edwin D.
b. October 25, 1869
d. 1950?

E.D. Thoms was born to E.E. and Mary Lyde Thoms near Darwin, Minnesota. He was converted at age 17 and baptized into the faith by O.R. Jenks. In 1898, Thoms began a new publication to inform Minnesota Conference members of local church events: *The Day Dawn and Harvest Messenger*. He took the mission of the newspaper from John 4:35 "Look on the fields for they are white already to harvest." He assisted with construction of the Sylvan church in 1901 and was ordained into the ministry at Ellsworth on December 18, 1904. Thoms listed his occupation on the Minnesota Territorial and State Census 1905 as "Clergyman." After he stepped down as *The Day Dawn* editor in 1904, Elder Thoms continued serving as associate editor for most of the years the paper continued to publish.

Over the *The Day Dawn's* history two others served as editors: James Patrick from Fort Dodge, Iowa, from around 1904 to 1910; A.E. Hatch one year; and then Elder Patrick returned (after A.E. Hatch's resignation) from 1911 to September 1, 1922. During that interval, *The Day Dawn* moved to Howard Lake, Minnesota, back to Fort Dodge, then to Minneapolis, Minnesota, during 1917 and 1918, and finally back to Fort Dodge. The instability of the press may have led to the decision to cease publishing. *The Day Dawn's* mailing list was given to *The Restitution Herald* at Oregon, Illinois. The 1922 merger of these papers came one year after the General Conference's organization.

In addition to the problem *The Day Dawn* had with stability, the consensus among the General Conference membership was that all singular voices (papers or publications) in the Church of God should be silenced in favor of one recognized title: *The Restitution Herald*. See L.E. Conner and A.R. Underwood entries regarding the controversy over *The Restitution*; at one time highly-favored, it was overshadowed by the stronger *Restitution Herald*. Elder Thoms began a tradition of excellence in Minnesota publishing that lasted 24 years—a notable accomplishment for him and for the fine editors who succeeded him.

Elder Fred Daubanton preached Elder Thoms' funeral service from I Thessalonians 4:13, "We would not have you be ignorant brethren, concerning those who are asleep, that you may not grieve as others do who have no hope." His hope was in the second coming of the Lord, and in having a part in the establishment and rule of the Kingdom on earth.

See   Conner, L.E. (19th)
      Daubanton, Fred
      Hatch, A.E. (19th)
      Jenks, O.R.
      Patrick, James A. (19th)
      Thoms, E.E. (19th)
      Underwood, A.R. (19th)

Bibliography: Ancestry.com. Minnesota Territorial and State Census 1849-1905. Meeker. Swan Lake. 1875; Minnesota Territorial and State Census 1849-1905. Stearns. St. Cloud Ward. 1905; Atlanta Bible College Archival Note, *The Day Dawn and Harvest Messenger*, James A. Patrick, ed., Fort Dodge, Iowa, Nov. 1919; *The Restitution Herald,* March 3, 1924.

Turner, Willis Harvey
b. September 3, 1917
d. April 29, 2003

A. Relocation to Oregon, Illinois
B. The Influence of the Oregon Church of God
C. Joyful Service

Willis Turner was born in Henry, Illinois, to Floyd Wise and Lillian (Clement) Turner, the eldest of eight children, six boys and two girls that included two sets of fraternal twins. Willis grew up in a home filled with energy and joy—fortunate with so many children and the difficult times.

Floyd was employed in cartage. He hauled materials by wagon from community to community. Later he farmed. All the Turner boys learned many good life lessons from farm work. They learned the virtue of rising early and the value of a nickel. Willis said that once his dad splurged and gave him a nickel for a soda pop. Willis chose "cream" flavor. It was tart and burnt his tongue, and he couldn't drink it. There were no more nickels for another flavor. From that, he learned to choose wisely.

Willis attended elementary school and helped on the family farm at Wahoo, Nebraska, near Lincoln until he was 13. During the Great Depression the family moved back to Henry, Illinois. Willis graduated from Sparland High School. They lived ten miles north of Sparland, and if Willis was fortunate, he could ride the old horse; if not, he had to walk. Sometimes in winter he walked to school with holes in his shoes. He considered himself blessed to have shoes. One time he arranged to ride to Sparland with an old man in his truck. The man drove so recklessly that Willis feared for his life. He didn't ride with him again.

The Turners were Methodists. At age 17, Willis gave his life to Christ at a revival service.

A. Relocation to Oregon, Illinois

Willis moved to Ogle County, Illinois, when he was 20. He earned a certificate from the University of Illinois to test cow's milk. He traveled from dairy farm to dairy farm testing the herd's milk and testing the each cow's milk for butter fat content, amount of production, etc. He reported his results to the University County Extension office. In this way, he met many area farmers. He even tested the six herds owned by Illinois Governor Frank O. Lowden who lived in Ogle County.

In his travels, Willis met Ida Mae Friemuth, a beautiful young woman from Marion Township. After several months they decided marry, holding the ceremony at German Lutheran Church in Paynes Point, Illinois—Ida's home church. Many decades earlier Paynes Point had been the home of A.J. Eychaner, an early Church of God founder in the Midwest.

Willis and Ida attended local churches in Oregon, but they were not satisfied. They had become acquainted with the Church of God through S.J. Lindsay and Elizabeth Ordnung. The Turners' first home was a renovated barn behind the Lindsay home on North Sixth Street in Oregon. This little building was the first print shop of *The Restitution Herald*. The printing press once stood on the round flat pedestal in the middle of the living room. Ida Mae placed a rug on it and set a table there.

Board of Directors, from left: CF Pryor, Don Overmeyer, President Willis Turner, Stan Ross and Arlie Townsend at Camp Quaker Haven, circa 1955.

B. The Influence of the Oregon Church of God

The Turners noticed that the Church of God Abrahamic Faith had conference meetings at the Old Stone Church on North Third Street twice a year. On those occasions Elizabeth Ordnung went door to door asking if anyone had a room to rent or donate for a visiting minister. Ida Mae opened their home to visiting pastors. In this way the family met Clarence E. Lapp, Lucille Appleby, J.R. LeCrone and others. When J.R. LeCrone came to Oregon Church of God as pastor in 1948, seven-year-old Janet had already been attending Sunday school and Bible school for two years. Pastor LeCrone and Oregon Bible College student Bill Wachtel called on the Turners to invite them to church.

Willis and Ida Mae at their 50th Anniversary with Gary and Janet

Through these friendly overtures from the church, Willis and Ida started attending morning worship, and then Sunday school. They learned about the Kingdom of God on earth, about the return of the Jews to their homeland, and about the oneness of God. They learned that the Abrahamic Faith meant the promises made to Abraham (Genesis 12:1, 2) extended to Christians who accept Christ and are baptized. Willis loved these doctrines. He had never heard this kind of Bible teaching before. Like Paul Harvey the news commentator, Willis thought he was finally getting "the rest of the story." Ida said, "The message of the Church of God was so simple and easy to understand."

Willis loved to sing and often sang solos in his sweet, clear tenor voice. One of his favorite sacred songs was "His Eye is on the Sparrow" which Vicki Miller Dick sang for his funeral. He also loved to sing "Hold Thou my Hand, Dear Lord," "The Lord's Prayer" and "The Holy City." He sang for dozens of weddings, the most requested songs being, "I Love You Truly," "Because" and "The Lord's Prayer." Janet often accompanied him or sang with him.

Janet and Gary Turner were baptized into Christ at the Oregon Church of God and both graduated from Oregon Bible College. Gary now pastors the Winnebago New Life Church in Winnebago, Illinois. Janet is a retired librarian, writer and historian.

Willis and Ida moved to Macomb, Illinois, in 1962 and attended the Church of God there. Willis was building committee chairman. The group erected the beautiful building still being used by that congregation. Willis worked as a manager for Country Companies Insurance in McDonough County. He transferred to Winnebago County in 1966 where, after retirement, he sold farm real estate. He said, "You can take the boy off the farm, but you can't take the farm out of the boy."

Conference delegates and families at Camp Quaker Haven
Willis Turner is in the center, wearing a suit jacket.

C. Joyful Service

Willis served the Church of God with joy. He was Sunday school superintendent and teacher at Oregon. He sang in the choir, lending a strong Irish tenor to Ben Carpentar's tenor on many church anthems directed by Lea Doeden. Willis served as deacon, trustee and elder at Oregon, Macomb and Blessed Hope in Rockford. He served on the General Conference Sunday School Association board, and as Conference board president from 1954-1958. He also served on the Development Foundation board and helped with fundraising.

Willis chaired the Board of Directors that produced the Decade of Development projects from 1955-1965 in which foreign missions were strengthened; student numbers increased at OBC; Dr. Alva Huffer's *Systematic Theology* was published and promoted throughout the world; and home missions was emphasized both through free distribution of *The Restitution Herald* and through a calling campaign that used a special *Herald* called "Your Introduction to the Church of God." Members of local congregations in every city were there was a Church of God conducted this calling campaign.

Willis' signature is in the Presidents' Bible, among all the presidents and board chairmen who served with the Church of God General Conference since its inception in 1921. This Bible is housed in the Atlanta Bible College Archives. Others who have signed it include James A. Patrick, L.E. Conner, S.O. Ross, Dale Dunbar, Joe James and several more. While they were able and healthy, Willis and Ida never missed attending a General Conference or an Illinois Quarterly Conference.

In his final years Willis's legs failed due to post-polio syndrome. He was bedridden in his final year. Ida Mae kept him at home and helped him enjoy life. He sleeps now in the Emmanuel Cemetery at Paynes Point beside his in-laws, John and Pearl Friemuth, also members of the Oregon Church of God, just around the corner from A.J. Eychaner's descendents, and near many farm friends from Marion Township in Ogle County.

The heritage of this family lives through the children and grandchildren of the Stilson family, Rick, Randy and Marianne Stilson-Hudson, and Gary Turner's family, Jason (Marcee) Turner, Shelly (Tim) Spickler, John and Carmen Turner and Tera Yanni.

See Boyer, Lucille Appleby
Carpentar, Ben
Eychaner, A.J. (19th)
Huffer, Dr. Alva
LeCrone, J.R.
Lindsay, S.J. (19th)
Ordnung, Elizabeth
Ross, S.O.
Sorenson, Warren

Bibliography: Ancestry.com Social Security Master Death List, record for Willis H. Turner; Stilson, Jan, "Memories of My Dad." Huffer, Alva, Interview on 20th century COG history, especially the Decade of Development, 2008.

Turnpaugh, Kenneth
b. March 20, 1905
d. September 6, 1993

Kenneth Turnpaugh was born in Cass County, Indiana. His mother died when he was four and his father, Anson Wilta Turnpaugh, raised four boys by himself. Mr. Turnpaugh later remarried so the boys had a stepmother to help them through the rough times. Kenneth married Letha Phelps on November 12, 1941. They had three children: Joe, Myra (Hamilton) and Charlene (Smith). Kenneth committed to the Lord in March 1951, at age 46. He became an active member in the Church of God at Hedrick, Indiana, and served as a deacon and trustee among other offices. He died at age 86 and was interred in Warren County, Indiana.

Bibliography: Biography Project of Atlanta Bible College, David Krogh, compiler.

Ucañay, Bèder (Ortiz)
b. 1954
d. 2008

Bèder Ucañay was born in Villa de Eten, at Chiciayo, Peru, which is in the Department of Lambayeque in the north. He moved to Lima at age three and took schooling in public schools. He always believed in God without knowing Him. His parents took him to various family funerals and Bèder spent a lot of time thinking about death, life, God, heaven, the future. He was a timid child who didn't have many friends, but he had a good self-image and was content to spend time alone. He wanted to go to college and began applying, but every college rejected him. He worked in factories and attended the Catholic Church in which he had been raised. He became bored and lonely. He searched for a reason to keep on living and read every kind of book to look for meaning.

Bèder finally decided he should end his life and planned to do so at midnight, but a friend called and invited him to a family party. He went and met a wonderful girl. And now, in love, he set about searching for the meaning of love. The girl did not feel the same about him, but it opened a new awareness in his life.

Bèder searched for his Benefactor—Jesus Christ—but he could not find him in the Catholic Church. A friend invited him to a Protestant church nearby, which he was reluctant to attend, but finally did. He thought, "What else can happen to me?" Much to his surprise he heard the Word of God at that service. He accepted Jesus and was filled with peace. Someone gave him a little blue New Testament provided by the Gideons. It was his first Bible. For a while he attended the Catholic Church and the Protestant one, too. Eventually, as he was reading his Bible, he decided to leave the Catholic Church to be obedient to the verse that says, "Come out, my people, from Babylon the Great." (Revelation 18:4).

On April 1, 1978, Bèder was baptized. The church he attended was seriously damaged, however, when the pastor went astray. Bèder remained faithful and felt the Lord was with him, teaching him, leading him and even performing miracles in his life. He began to preach and testify wherever he was. Soon, he was asked to be a youth pastor in the church he attended. Later he transferred to the Church of Christ and came to know many of their missionaries. They offered to send him to college in Panama but Bèder didn't want to leave Peru. God was working in his life and Bèder prayed for guidance. The Lord brought him to Mario Olcese who told him about the Church of God Faith of Abraham, and invited him to attend church with him. Bèder testified that he soon began to preach for the Church of God. Mario eventually gave up the church work and moved to the United States to live with family. Bèder remained in Lima as the Church of God pastor.

Bèder met a lovely young woman and they married. They had three children, Maria Mercedes, Josue Gamaiel and Joel Baruch. Bèder gave up his full-time work as an accountant, a career he did not enjoy, and undertook many church projects in Lima. His congregation met Thursday nights from 7 to 9 p.m. and on Sundays to worship. They rented a meeting place for $50 a month. Bèder also operated a Bible training center to teach people about the Bible, ministry and evangelism. During his ministry there were 20-30 people in the congregation. Anthony Buzzard, Bill Wachtel and other mission teams from the General Conference visited Bèder Ucañay and the congregation several times. Sadly, Pastor Ucañay was diagnosed with cancer in his eye, and despite treatment, succumbed in 2008. Bèder's brothers Gaston and Joaquin carry on the pastoral work of evangelism at the church.

See Wachtel, William
Appendix 20—Missions

Bibliography: Ucañay, Bèder, "Testimony of Bèder Ucañay Ortiz," translated from the Spanish by William M. Wachtel, sent with the *Lima Newsletter*, January 2001 #1, retrieved from Jim Mattison Aug. 7, 2010.

Updike, Charles
b. July 1, 1892
d. December 30, 1957

Updike, Ada T.
b. February 10, 1895
d. July 1980

Charles, known by everyone in the congregation as "Mack," and Ada, known as "Aunt Ada," were pillars of the Cool Spring Church of God Abrahamic Faith in Browntown, Virginia. Ada was born Ada Updike to Randolph and Carrie Updike near South River, Warren County, Virginia. She was four when the Cool Spring Church was being built in 1899. Ada, her mother and little sister, Gracie, walked to the building site from home to bring lunch to workmen. The family shared the residence of Randolph's parents, John and Elizabeth Updike.

After they met and married, Mack and Ada worked in Washington, D.C. Mack was a policeman at Catholic University and Ada a dressmaker. They had one daughter, Ada M., born in 1915. Mack and Aunt Ada were Flo (Cooper) Coverstone's grandparents. The Updike's rest together in the family cemetery on the "home place" high on the mountain near Skyline Drive Parkway.

Bibliography: ABC Biography project, David Krogh, compiler; Ancestry.com U.S. Census. Virginia. Warren. So. River. Dist. 87. 1900; and U.S. Census, D.C. Washington. Washington. Dist. 249 1930; Social Security Master Death Index, Records for Charles and Ada T Updike; Coverstone, Flo. E-mail to JStilson via Dorothy Boyer, April 15, 2008.

Updike, Marie F.
b. October 18, 1912
d. September 28, 1999

Marie Manuel was born to Hilery and Annie (Swartz) Manuel. She lived at Browntown, Virginia, and was baptized into Christ at the Cool Spring Church of God by her son-in-law Hollis Partlowe in 1950. She had two daughters, Shadah (Sager) and Hilda (Partlowe). She served the Lord faithfully and gave her daughter Hilda into the service of the Lord through the pastoral ministry of Hollis from 1950 until his retirement from the Dixon Church of God in Dixon, Illinois in 2006. Marie is interred at Prospect Hill Cemetery.

See Partlowe, Hollis

Bibliography: ABC Biography project, David Krogh, compiler.

Urish, Shirley Logsdon
b. November 17, 1926
d. April 17, 1997

Shirley Logsdon was born in Kewanee, Illinois, but grew up near Ripley in Brown County, Illinois. She and sister Juanita (Gilbert) were the daughters of Albert and Vena Logsdon. The Logsdons were members of the Church of God at Ripley. Shirley attended Oregon Bible College after she graduated high school. After leaving the college, Shirley worked as a secretary for Ogle County Country Companies Insurance. It was there that she met the dashing Dean Urish, a Country Companies insurance adjuster. They soon wed in Oregon, Illinois, and had three children, John, James and Linda.

Shirley and Dean were members of the Oregon Church of God. She served as an officer in many church groups and helped found the Mary and Martha organization for young married women. She taught Sunday and Bible school year after year. Shirley served on the church board and as secretary of the Board of Directors for the Church of God General Conference from 1979 to 1983. Shirley and Dean relocated to Freeport, Illinois, and helped begin a church work there. While this work did not succeed, they remained active in conference work, and visited at the Oregon congregation when they could. Shirley became ill and had a kidney removed in Freeport. Afterward, her health was compromised. During their retirement Shirley and Dean spent winters at Port Charlotte, Florida, where she took ill and died in 1997.

Bibliography: ABC Biography Project, David Krogh, compiler.

Vadnais, Mary Brown

b. July 1, 1918
d. February 4, 2000

Mary Brown was born in Detroit, Michigan, to John and Laura Brown. John was a metal finisher in an auto factory. The Browns had two daughters and three sons. At some point the family moved to Michigan's Upper Peninsula and settled near L'Anse. Here, the children learned of the Gospel of the Kingdom from mission efforts advanced by the Churches of God in Michigan. Through contact with youth groups from Blanchard and Southlawn in Grand Rapids, and later Pennellwood in Grand Rapids, children began to assemble for regular Christian education classes at Baraga and L'Anse. This work was unique among mission works of the Church of God, for it focused on the Native American communities that made up the Ojibwa Reservation. Evangelist Benjamin Woodward had been the first to cultivate a mission work among these friendly people.

When young, Mary suffered an illness that left her voice soft and raspy. This must have made it difficult to preach, but she coped and the church prospered. When grown, Mary and brothers Raymond and Leonard made the journey to Oregon, Illinois, to enroll in classes at Oregon Bible College from 1945-1951; at that time the campus was on the river north of Oregon. Raymond was the only one to graduate, but all three entered the ministry for the Church of God.

Mary married Raymond Vadnais late in life. They had no children, but they had a little Chihuahua dog that they cared for like a child. Mary and Ray were committed to ministry, and fostered many teens and adults in their home and helped them cope in society. Mary and Ray were faithful to attend state and national conference gatherings. Mary preceded Ray in death by four years.

See Brown, Leonard
Brown, Raymond
Woodward, Benjamin (19th)

Bibliography: Ancestry.com. U.S. Census. Michigan. Wayne. Detroit. Dist. 472. 1930; Ancestry.com. Social Security Death List record for Raymond Vadnais, October 31, 2004; Rencontre, Jean. E-mail from Ironwood, Michigan, Aug. 21, 2010.

Wachtel, William
b. March 16, 1927

Bill Wachtel was born to William F. and Ruth E. Wachtel on Chicago's west side in the "Austin" neighborhood. Bill attended Hay Elementary School and Austin High School. Bill's father was Lutheran, so Bill was sprinkled as an infant and attended Lutheran Sunday school. When he was a little older, he abandoned that and attended a Baptist church. He was immersed at age 11. After high school graduation he enlisted in the US Navy in 1945, entering the service just as WWII ended. When he was discharged in 1946 he came home.

Harold Doan had just revived the old Chicago Church and started to preach at the YMCA in downtown Chicago. Bill went to church with his mother and Aunt Emma. He loved to hear Harold preach. Elder Bob Hall, an attorney, talked with Bill about the Kingdom of God and the Second Coming of Christ. About this, Bill said, "It clicked." It suddenly made sense. Harold Doan baptized him. Bill said, after baptism, he just "devoured" *The Restitution Herald*. He also became a Berean and had classes with Harold and Jean Doan.

Bill then attended the University of Illinois at Navy Pier in Chicago for two years and transferred to Elmhurst College where he received a B.A. in Spanish in 1949. Bill reports that he has always had a love for the Spanish language and had studied it all through high school. He majored in Spanish and minored in French in college. He had originally planned to be a Spanish teacher, but his plans were changed.

He felt a call to the ministry in 1949, and entered Oregon Bible College that fall. Otto E. Dick and Sydney Magaw were among his teachers. At the time, the college was located north of Oregon at what is now the Maxson Manor restaurant and motel complex. After Bill graduated from OBC in 1951, he was invited to pastor the Church of God at Litchfield, Minnesota. He moved there in September 1951 and remained until 1957. In Litchfield, he married Phyllis Rankin of the Cashmere, Washington, Church of God. Their first child was born in Litchfield. In 1957 he was called to Dixon, Illinois, to pastor the Church of God. Dixon is President Ronald Reagan's hometown. Bill remained in Dixon until 1960; he also taught Greek at OBC.

In 1960, Bill had the opportunity for further education, and entered Wheaton College Graduate School in Wheaton, Illinois, through the Lawrence Scholarship program. Wheaton College is Rev. Billy Graham's alma mater. Here, Bill majored in New Testament, along with Hebrew and Old Testament studies. He received his M.A. in New Testament Degree *Summa Cum Laude* in 1962 after completing his thesis: "The Historical Development of the Belial Concept and the Significance of Its Use by the Apostle Paul." While he was in studies at Wheaton, he pastored the Chicago church.

He began teaching full-time at Oregon Bible College in 1962; he became president two years later, after the death of Otto E. Dick. In 1968, the Wachtels moved to Washington State. Bill and Phyllis had four children. Jenice lives in Wenatchee and has three children. Jenice married Ignacio Badillo, the son of Roberto and Lupe Badillo, native missionaries in Labor Vieja, Mexico. Son Bill and wife Lyn live in Colville, Washington, and have two children. Bill is a contractor. Son Brad and wife Patricia live in Wenatchee and have three children, two of whom are in high school. Brad is a goldsmith and jeweler. Jill Wachtel married Cliff Brossard of the Eden Valley, Minnesota, Church of God. She works in a dental office in Colville, Washington, and he is a contractor and farrier. They have one son and grandson.

Bill's abilities with Spanish have been useful in his ministry. He taught Spanish at Oregon Bible College, and this opened the doors for students to enter foreign missions, particularly in Latin America. Bill led a team to Mexico while he was teaching at Oregon. He has since

development of radio ministry. He said the Church of God had no financial problems. He then described its greatest problem as lethargy and disinterest among the ministers in the field, which had spread to the general membership.

James noted salvation depends on whether we are found working when Jesus comes. "The disinterest in the opportunities provided by our national effort is…being fostered by our ministers themselves, oftentimes for no more than for personal reasons. Are we so shortsighted," he continued, "that we are failing to see the personal opportunity that is provided and can only result in the unity and success of our work as a whole? Unless we combine to build our present fields, meet their problems, and develop new opportunities, where will be the chance for the service of the minister of tomorrow?" He concluded that lack of vision and refusal to accept the values of unity and encouragement would cancel out a spirit of cooperation.

As might be imagined, these words stung the ministers and leaders. Before the month was over an announcement appeared in *The Restitution Herald* of a meeting in Chicago of the Volunteer Layman's Committee. This group invited James Watkins to join with them and several ministers on October 30, 1947, to "consider details of a complete financial, missionary and evangelism program."

At the meeting all wished to remain anonymous, a strange matter in itself; James Watkins, the invitee, served as moderator. Watkins wrote a report for members and readers of *The Restitution Herald* and assured them all meeting costs were covered by the laymen. Attorney Robert Hall most probably covered the majority of the cost. Other laymen known to have attended that meeting included Graceton Houser and Judd Lyon. The laymen felt that "we can put our church over the top as far as opportunities for advancement are concerned." They compiled a list of recommendations to take before the

James Watkins visited many Churches of God and took snapshots of each one. Right, is the Ripley, Illinois, church; below, is the Eldorado, Illinois, church.

delegates at their annual meeting. Delegates and members of the Church of God were asked to join the effort by signing pledge cards that promised 50¢ per week. Those who paid $26 up front would be members of the "Over the Top" club. At that meeting, 48 lay members signed pledge cards for the development plan.

The plan's progress was published in *The Restitution Herald* weekly for the next several years. Near the first year's end Watkins reported in *The Herald* that a few years earlier membership had dropped from 4,535, based on delegate forms for General Conference, to 3,740 in 1948, an 18% decrease in membership. The Layman's Campaign hoped to reverse that. While the campaign garnered only 800 or so contributors, that is also its strength, it enrolled over 800 to assist in developing the General Conference. The conference that year closed its financial records in the black, although the money for construction was not raised in entirety.

The large rendering is the design for a new Oregon Bible College on the rural property site north of Oregon, Illinois. This plan was scrapped in favor of moving into town.
Top inset: The old administration/ classroom building of Oregon Bible College under Jim Watkin's administration.
Bottom inset: Maxsons bought the old college building on the river and operated a popular restaurant. After a fire, the new Maxson Restaurant was built in the 1990s.

> **The Layman's Committee recommended the General Conference delegates support these actions:**
> - Advancing the Bible. Our message is Bible-centered.
> - Provide for current financial needs to support the building, publishing and youth.
> - Expand the printing and publishing for purposes of evangelism.
> - Begin a building program within a year in the city (of Oregon) in the range of $30,000, in order to be closer to postal facilities.
> - Enlarge pastoral aid to cover full-time pastors in forty-nine local churches.
> - Expand career opportunities for women. There were no Christian careers except pastor's wife.
> - Sow the seed of radio. Begin a Truth Seeker's Bible Class of the Air. Distribute *Truth Seeker's Quarterlies* to listeners. Harold Doan of Chicago would coordinate this program over WAIT. Cost of the test programs would be $65 per week.
>
> Source: *The Restitution Herald*, November 1, 1947

James Watkins and a local boy observe Jerusalem's Eastern Gate, which is now sealed.

On January 2, 1951, James became editor of *The Restitution Herald* following the tragic deaths of Sydney and Margaret Magaw the previous week. James served as editor until his resignation from the General Conference on June 7, 1955. Shortly before he ended his editorship, James visited the Holy Land to ascertain changes there since the nation's birth in 1948. Adib Lidawi, an OBC foreign exchange student from Lebanon, accompanied him on the trip. Lidawi knew the Holy Land so well he was able to get appointments with directors of orphanages, schools and clinics on behalf of the General Conference. The pictures of this trip are excellent; they are part of the Watkins photo collection in the Atlanta Bible College Archives.

In 1951, the General Conference sold the Oregon Bible College property north of Oregon and built an addition to the conference building at 110 North Third Street. Pastoral aid continued, but not to all 49 locations. A radio program in Chicago over station WAIT was undertaken as a test with several pastors contributing to the weekly quarter-hour program. After a few weeks Harold Doan took the reins.

The General Conference Board asked James to resign as editor. His last issue of *The Restitution Herald* was June 7, 1955. The Board of Directors had lost confidence in Watkin's ability to communicate the reality of corporate finances with members and delegates. The finances were, in fact, in desperate condition. People had to be apprised of the needs quickly before the Conference failed. In a 1947 chapel talk at Oregon Bible College, James Watkins said, "We do not have a financial problem," when actually the finances had been critically short all along. The money for the Layman's Campaign had been used not for development, but for operating expenses just to keep the organization viable.

James Watkins' managerial work was helpful in identifying key areas of weakness, namely financial giving, and in motivating laymen to become involved in supporting their conference. During Watkins' tenure he visited nearly every church, and often many homes within a local church's region, at least once and perhaps more. He knew and loved the people. He took their photos, and

Above: While in Israel, Watkins and his travel companion Adib Liddawi, back left, visited a local clinic.

Below: While visiting Louisiana churches, Watkins stopped at a local store, possibly owned by church members, and snapped this photo.

his collection provides a cross-section of American rural church history that is seldom seen. These photos illustrate the Church of God in the time when America was arising from the desperate war years of the 20th century to help found a new stronger nation, and to support its new ally Israel, about which the Church of God had preached since 1845. A photo essay from this collection would be both inspiring and nostalgic.

The Watkins family sold their home in Oregon, and returned to Hedrick, where all died a few years later.

   See Doan, Harold
         Houser, W. Graceton
         LeCrone, J.R.
         Lyon, Judd (19th)
         Lyon, Melville
         Magaw, Sydney
         Marsh, J. Arlen

Bibliography: *The Restitution Herald*, Oct. 7, 1947; Nov. 11, 1947; June 8, 1948; July 26, 1949; Watkins, James. "Faith of our Fathers," *The Restitution Herald 75th Anniversary Issue*, Russell Magaw, ed., Oregon, Il., Oct. 1985.

Weaver, Clarence E.
b. June 14, 1879
d. December 2, 1958

Clarence Weaver was born at Mr. Vernon, Arkansas. He married Maude Hood on December 10, 1898. Maude was a native of Mississippi, but her family moved to Arkansas when she was five. She died in October 1963. Clarence felt called to preach and moved his family from Yell County to McGintytown when their son, Archard, was seven. Elder E.O. Stewart ordained Clarence in the ministry in 1915. The Weavers conveniently lived across the road from the church.

Clarence seldom used notes when he preached and he always quoted Scripture. He raised his voice, and then dropped it softly. This held the attention of his audience. Clarence wrote out a few of his sermons; Archard owns those copies today. The sermons are bound in a leather cover made from a blacksmith's apron. They range in date from 1917 to 1954 and are indexed with titles such as "God created Psychology," "What is the Scripture?" and more. Jettie Moreland said that Clarence "was a smooth talker, but he could get really wound up and wave his arms and pound the pulpit." Clarence used visual aids while preaching and teaching. He made large cloth charts depicting ages of prophecy or lessons from Scripture, and displayed them for his audience while he talked. The charts, both letters and pictures, were drawn with crayon. Then, when the chart was finished, wax paper was ironed over the coloring so that it had a more permanent finish. He carried the charts with him from church to church, rolled up in the back of the carriage or car. There were at least eight charts. The Atlanta Bible College Archives has pictures of them. The family still owns the original charts and they are in good condition.

Clarence Weaver's legacy to the McGintytown church was one of faithful service in the Lord's work.

Bibliography: Weaver, Archard and Clara. "History of folks at McGintytown" for the anniversary celebration, 2010, sent by Pastor Tom New.

Wells, Lena Ellouise
b. April 17, 1929
d. March 29, 2006

Lena Ellouise McDaniel was born near Timewell in Brown County, Illinois, to Earnest Lelin and Lena Blanch Lewis McDaniel. She married William W. "Bill" Wells on June 9, 1951, in Bowen, Illinois. They had one son, Aaron, and a daughter, Ione.

Ellouise graduated from Bowen High School and attended the University of Illinois. She and her husband were members of the Ripley Church of God, both of them serving in offices. She worked for Schuyler County Home Extension as an assistant Youth Advisor in the 1950s. She was a member and president of Schuyler County Health Improvement Association and secretary of the Illinois Health Improvement Association. She was known as a faithful woman, loving mother and a friend to many.

Intern Pastor Brian K. Froehlich conducted her funeral service. Aaron gave a moving and humorous eulogy. Family and friends are comforted knowing they will see Bill and Ellouise again in the great resurrection morning.

Bibliography: Ellouise Wells Funeral Bulletin. Worthington Chapel, Rushville, Il., April 1, 2006.

West, Anna Mae
b. 1914
d. July 13, 2000

Anna Mae West was born in Kentucky to Charles Edwin and Mary Stoddard West. The family moved to Rockford, Illinois, to find work. Anna lived there her entire life, until the last year or so. She was a bookkeeper and treasurer of the Lanier Gardens gift shop. She taught lip-reading and Bible study, and was a member of the Blessed Hope Bible Church of God in Rockford. David Krogh baptized her. As Anna's health slowly failed she moved to Athens, Georgia, to reside with her brother,

Wayne. Both Wayne and another brother, Clyde, survived her. The Blessed Hope church keenly felt Anna's loss. She was loved by all and is greatly missed to this day.

Bibliography: ABC Biography Project, David Krogh, compiler

Westbrook, Emmett Leroy
b. May 26, 1909
d. February 5, 1994

Emmett Westbrook was born to William and Mary Westbrook in St. Francois County, Missouri. He lived in Missouri his entire life except for his WWII service in the Pacific theatre. He had younger siblings, four sisters and two brothers. The family was three-quarters Cherokee. Emmett was baptized and joined the Church of God after marrying Hattie Irene Rouse. He taught his family a love of God by his every day life. Each morning, his children would come into the kitchen to find his open Bible lying on the table after his morning devotions. This testimony of faith has been passed down through the generations.

Although Emmett was never licensed to preach that anyone can recall, he served the Lord in the pulpit many times. His ministry began through his association with Pastor Weldon McCoy. Elder McCoy often stayed with the Westbrook family as he traveled the circuit. Glenda Turner, a Westbrook daughter, wrote:

> One Saturday, he asked Emmett and Hattie to go to church with him in Morse Mill the next morning. To the surprise of the Westbrook family, Brother McCoy introduced Emmett as the new First Elder of the church who would be filling the pulpit on the Sundays when Brother McCoy was absent. As far as anyone in the family could determine, this was a complete surprise to Emmett. Brother McCoy looked at Emmett. Emmett nodded, and it was done.

Elder McCoy and the Westbrook family also had a radio ministry Sunday afternoons. Brother McCoy or Emmett preached a short sermon and the Westbrook family sang, including Emmett with his deep bass voice.

Emmett died at Salem, Missouri, and was interred to await the coming of his Lord from heaven. His family mourned their loss.

Bibliography: Ancestry.com. U.S. Census. Missouri, St. Francois, St. Francois. Dist 26. 1930; Excerpted from the Biography Project of Atlanta Bible College, information submitted by Glenda Turner, David Krogh, compiler; Social Security Master Death List, entry for Emmett L. Westbrook, retrieved from Ancestry.com, January 23, 2008.

Westlund, Chaplain Orville "Wes" A.
b. December 18, 1929

When Pastor Orville Westlund graduated from Oregon Bible College in 1952, he wondered what the next step was for him and his wife, Alice. "You won't believe how the Lord leads our lives," he declared recently. "God led us to accept the pastorate of the Church of God in Burr Oak, Indiana. From there we felt his presence and direction as our lives unfolded," he added.

God produced interesting times for the Westlunds while in Burr Oak, a small community in northern Indiana. In a short time, Sunday school attendance was more than 100, "and we had 30 in the choir on Sunday mornings," Westlund remembered. The congregation was comprised mainly of farmers from the area. They were a faithful group dedicated to serving God.

Burr Oak is just north of Culver Military Academy near Culver, Indiana. General Delmar Spivey administered the academy, but he had a problem. He needed a road into his academy. Spivey knocked on every political door he could think of to get the road built. Members of Congress, the state governor and local officials were all approached. No one could find a reason to spend tax dollars to build a road to the private academy. One day a farmer, who was a member of the Church of God, approached Pastor Westlund to suggest that if Spivey's road would also service their farms, they would help get the road through. "Great," Westlund replied. So he called Spivey on the telephone and told the adjunct that he wanted to speak to the general "about the road." Immediately Spivey was on the phone, inviting Westlund to meet him at the academy. Once in Spivey's office, Pastor Westlund informed him that several farmers would help with the road if it gave access to their farms. "You organize the farmers and I'll meet with them," Spivey replied. The meeting occurred that week in the Burr Oak church basement. The problem was solved and the road was built. Talk about cooperation between faith needs and the needs of the community! Westlund could see the hand of God working throughout the affair. And that was only the first phase of how God used Spivey and the Westlunds for the next phase of the young pastor's life.

By 1959, the work of God in the church had kept things moving, yet the Westlunds wondered how they fit in God's plans for their future. Orville was intrigued about serving the Lord through the US Navy chaplaincy program. Unfortunately, no pastor in the Church of God had ever experienced such a call and Westlund was unsure how to proceed. Orville knew he would need recommendations, but how could he receive them? After months of praying and pondering, the answer came: his old friend, General Spivey. Pastor Westlund again called the general. They met. A recommendation was requested. The general wrote a 2-1/2-page letter which helped Westlund get admitted to the Navy Chaplains Corps.

"That's how the Lord led me to the Navy through the Culver Military Academy," Orville said. And it has been one adventure after another ever since. For 22 years Chaplain Westlund conducted services, counseled Navy personnel, assisted in Navy programs and served in several dangerous locations around the world. One of his tours involved the last of the Seaplanes in Vietnam during that war. Westlund served the Navy, the Marines and the Coast Guard during his time on active duty. Since then Orville has helped produce DVDs and other presentations for the Navy. His most prized production is a 30-minute DVD about seaplanes: "In Defense of their Nation." Westlund gifted a copy of it to the Church of God General Conference.

The Westlunds retired in 1981, settling in Oak Harbor, Washington. "Oak Harbor is the site of one of the largest naval air stations in the world," Westlund noted. Retiring near such a facility has kept Westlund busy. Unfortunately, his wife died several years prior to this publication, but a son lives nearby. Orville serves on the board of the Sons of Norway, which was his mother's native land. In 1998 and 2006 Westlund visited relatives in Norway.

One of Chaplain Westlund's key messages is that the Church of God is entitled to at least one chaplain in all of the US armed services. He would be most gratified if God would move more pastors to serve in chaplaincy service. The institutional ministry is a new ministry in the Church of God. Thank God for his leading in the life of Chaplain O.A. "Wes" Westlund.

Russell Magaw contributed this entry.

Bibliography: Magaw, Russell, Interview with Chaplain Westlund, Published first in the *Church of God Pastor's Newsletter,* by Kent Ross, MALT leadership team, Nov. 2006. Used with permission.

White, Joseph Dunaway
b. June 30, 1931
d. July 26, 2008

Joe White was born in Russellville, Arkansas, to Earl Stratton and Ernestine Dunaway White. At age 14, Joe contracted polio. After three weeks in an iron lung, he could move only one thumb. His parents were told that he would probably never walk again. Joe never believed that. Not only did he walk, he golfed, camped, boated and fished while raising four children. Joe's family supported the March of Dimes by stuffing envelopes and licking stamps.

Joe married Jeanette Ussery in 1953 in the Christadelphian Chapel in North Little Rock, and went to work for K.W. LeFever during the building of Lake Maumelle. Joe came from a long line of civil engineers and developers. His great-grandfather, a civil engineer, worked on the railroad west through Kansas. His grandfather also worked on the Intracoastal Waterway along the Gulf of Mexico. Joe's father moved to Morrilton, Arkansas, to work for Mobley Construction pouring concrete streets and curbs, where he met and married Joe's mother. When Mr. LeFever died in 1956, Joe became a partner in the firm renamed Edward G. Smith & Associates. With Ed's retirement, the firm became White-Daters. Joe was very proud that his sons continued the family tradition as partners in White-Daters. Joe was blessed to love his work; he appreciated his clients and enjoyed a great relationship with the City of Little Rock. Upon his retirement in 1997, he received a plaque from the Public Works Department, City of Little Rock, which was given: "in recognition of over 40 years contributions in the development of the City of Little Rock."

Joe's joy was his God, his Savior the Lord Jesus Christ, his family and friends. Pastor C.J. Shaw ordained Joe as an Elder of New Hope Church of God of the Abrahamic Faith in 1964, and he served until his death. Former Pastor Paul Shaw described Joe as an "Elder's Elder." Pastor Richard Alcumbrack's wife, Jan, said Joe was the "best elder they ever had." Joe attended a Men's Tuesday Morning Prayer Breakfast group for 45 years. These men were his rock. Joe's favorite parting phrase to family and friends was, "See you in Jerusalem!"

Joe helped construct Camp Bradford, a youth camp associated with his church. Joe was interred by his family in a private graveside service. He rests until the joyful arrival of his Savior to awaken him to eternal life.

A Tribute to Joe White
by Paul Shaw, October 9, 2008

I had known Joe White for 45 or 50 years when he and Jeanette and family joined the church which my father pastored, the New Hope Church of God in Little Rock. He subsequently became an elder of the church, a role he held for the remainder of his life. His house was a favorite place for the young people of the church to go. It was a place of laughter, of playing ping pong and just plain fun.

When my father retired, I was in my late twenties. Dolena and I moved to Little Rock from Oregon, Illinois, and I became pastor of the church. Although I had served as a student pastor in Oregon, this was my first real pastorate and Joe was my first encounter with a functioning elder.

An Elder's Elder

Although I have known many wonderful men serving as elders in the many churches I have been associated with over the years, I have never known one that is a better example of what an elder should be than Joe White. I think of him as "an elder's elder." He was "the husband of one wife," wise, fair, apt to teach, spiritual and biblical. He modeled the wisdom that is from above, which is "first pure, then peaceable, gentle and easy to be entreated, full of mercy and good fruits, without partiality and without hypocrisy."

A Man of the Scriptures

There are not many people that have walked this earth that are impossible for me to think about or describe without biblical phrases coming to mind:

...a workman that needeth not to be ashamed.
...rich toward God.
...a good soldier of Jesus Christ.
...a man after God's own heart.
...and there is a friend that sticketh closer than a brother.
...the disciple whom Jesus loved.

Joe could certainly say with the apostle Paul "I have fought a good fight, I have finished my course, I have kept the faith. Henceforth there is laid up for me a crown of righteousness which the Lord, the righteous judge, shall give me at that day, and not to me only, but unto all those also who love His appearing."

A Lonesome Place Against the Sky

It could be said of Joe White what was said of President Lincoln at his funeral, "He went down as when a lordly cedar, green with boughs, goes down with a great shout upon the hills and leaves a lonesome place against the sky."

I knew Joe as a friend, mentor, elder and beloved brother in Christ. In my life there'll always be that "lonesome place against the sky" when I think of Joe, but on the other hand my life is infinitely richer for having known a man whose life truly made a difference.

Paul Shaw contributed to this entry.

See Shaw, Cyrus J.

Bibliography: Obituary supplied by Roller-Chenal Funeral Home, Little Rock, Ar. Shaw, Paul. "Tribute to Joe White."

Whitehead, Leila, M.D.
b. December 4, 1871
d. July 15, 1967

A. It is Well with my Soul
B. National Berean Society
C. Friendship

Leila and her mother Ruth.

Leila Whitehead was born to James P. and Ruth Wilson Whitehead in Austin, Illinois. Her parents were natives of England. Benjamin Wilson from Geneva, Illinois, was Ruth Whitehead's brother. Leila was raised in the Church of God and one wonders if she felt the awe of being a Wilson daughter. She was an unassuming Christian woman, and very likely grew up unaware of her uncle Benjamin's wonderful work translating and publishing the *Emphatic Diaglott*, an interlinear version from Greek to exact English.

Leila graduated from medical college in Chicago and became a general practitioner. This information is documented in the US Census in Chicago in 1910. By 1920, however, she had left the medical discipline and began teaching elementary school at the Nash School. During this time Evelyn Harsh and her mother Julia lived with Leila. Evelyn taught at Humboldt School. They resided on Ohio Street in Chicago. From that point on Leila practiced medicine through private consultations only. She told Eugene Stilson that she favored cases dealing with children's illnesses. It is quite possible that she became disenchanted with medicine during the horrendous national Spanish Flu epidemic of 1918-1919. In Chicago alone, 8,500 people died.

Leila had one brother, Dr. Ralph Mozart Whitehead (1867-1942), who was licensed to practice medicine in New York, having graduated as both medical doctor and surgeon from the College of Physicians and Surgeons in Chicago in 1890. He enlisted in the Merchant Marines and on a trip to South America, the S.S. Barbara was torpedoed and sank. He died at sea.

In her youthful adult years, being a single woman, Leila made friends with Evelyn Harsh of Indiana. Evelyn also was a believer who loved the Lord, the WCTU (Women's Christian Temperance Union) and The National Berean Society.

A. It is Well with my Soul

Leila's father and Horatio G. Spafford of Chicago were close friends. Spafford wrote the Gospel song, "It is Well with My Soul." After the Great Chicago Fire, Spafford and Dwight Moody worked to help the homeless. Spafford sent his wife and daughters by ship to England. He intended to join them later for vacation, and then they would all participate in one of Moody's evangelistic tours in Europe. On the way over, their ship the Ville du Harve collided with a sailing ship on the night of November 21, 1873. Spafford's four daughters died. Mrs. Spafford sent a telegram from Wales that said, "Saved alone." Mr. Whitehead helped support Mr. Spafford through his time of grief. Spafford penned the hymn on the way to England to re-join his wife.

B. National Berean Society

Leila loved to organize Bible studies, youth groups and vacation Bible schools. Whitehead, Harsh and Anna Drew of Dixon, Illinois, were the organizing members of the National Berean Society, the first formally incorporated national society within the Church of God family. It remained a viable organization from 1913 until the late 1980s. This group was organized before the Church of God developed a General Conference in 1921.

The Bereans began as small Bible study groups for youth and new members long before it was officially organized. In 1904 Ruth Whitehead, Leila's mother, wrote a note for *The Restitution*. She urged the "younger generation to pick up the load" as the older generation would soon pass away. It was advice that would be repeated at state conference meetings several times in the years to come. It may be one reason the Bereans organized when they did. They felt that to secure the future of the ministry it must be passed to subsequent generations in a stable fashion.

The National Berean Society's mission was to publish Christian education materials. They published Berean lesson books. These were printed in Chicago and mailed out to churches and isolated Berean members all over the country. They also published tracts for distribution, and they had a column in both *The Restitution* and *The Restitution Herald*. An editor for these columns was chosen from among the Bereans. The editorship changed every year when the officers were elected at the group's annual meeting. Bereans gave dues at the weekly or monthly meetings and this helped fund their publications.

The Bereans attempted to educate people on doctrine, Christian living and tithing. Through the *The Restitution Herald* Dr. Whitehead testified that her parents had believed in tithing but she had not. Then she was asked to teach a Berean lesson on it. In preparation for the lesson she tried tithing for a few weeks. When she had figured the accounts, she continued tithing.

When the General Conference formed in 1921, it assumed publishing responsibilities after a few years. The Berean group still concentrated on Christian education, having meetings most Sunday evenings before evening adult service began. The meetings consisted of singing choruses, praying, Bible study including memorization, and service projects. Bereans provided a Sunday evening service at least once a month and other programs by special request. The Bereans became less effective in the local church in favor of other more trendy names and youth camp activities. The last Berean lesson booklets published with new lessons and writers were done in the 1960s. Gene and Janet Stilson edited that series. Eventually the lessons were discontinued due to the general demise of the Berean program throughout the Church of God.

Leila often spoke extemporaneously during worship services at the Oregon Church of God, or during Wednesday night Bible studies, challenging members to be godly in their Christian conduct walking in the steps of Christ. She challenged ministers not to stray from biblical truth by buying into modern evangelical ideas that did not recognize the Abrahamic Covenant as being key to the explanation of the Gospel of the Kingdom of God. People respectfully listened to her prophecies, she being a senior matriarch in the congregation and the denomination. Leila Whitehead had a gift for memorization. She memorized whole sections of the Bible and often came to Oregon Bible College Chapels to recite scripture. Her favorite recitations at Christmas were the "Annunciation of Mary," found in Luke 1:26-45, and the "Magnificata" in Luke 1:46-56.

C. Friendship

Dr. Whitehead was the head of household and opened her home in Chicago to Evelyn Harsh for many years. After Evelyn wed F.L. Austin, Leila gave up her home and chose to live in the Austin homes in Chicago and Oregon, Illinois. After Frederick Austin died, the two elderly women maintained a home at 500 South Fourth

Leila Whitehead was one of the women who founded the National Berean Society. Left to right: Leila, Evelyn Austin and Anna Drew.

Street in Oregon, Illinois, entertaining many guests who came for general conference meetings or were guest preachers at the local church.

Leila donated an original copy of the *Emphatic Diaglott* to the archives of Oregon Bible College (now Atlanta Bible College). It was dated 1864, the only year that Benjamin Wilson, her uncle, published the work in its entirety in bound form from Geneva, Illinois. From the next year forward until 1902 it was published by Fowler and Wells in New York.

Leila and Evelyn sold their home in 1963 and moved into a modest room at Pinecrest Manor, a Church of the Brethren home for the elderly in Mt. Morris, a community near Oregon. While the Golden Rule Home did not close until Elizabeth Ordnung's death in 1981, the General Conference was no longer accepting elderly residents into the program. In effect then, there was no longer any Church of God facility to care for its senior citizens.

Dr. Whitehead was in precarious health from the time she entered Pinecrest Manor. She battled painful pressure sores. Soon she was incapacitated and bedridden. Dr. Whitehead died of her infirmities at age 96.

   See Austin, Evelyn Harsh
          Ordnung, Elizabeth
          Wilson, James W. (19th)
          Wilson, W.H.
See Also Elvey, Charles (19th)

Bibliography: Ancestry.com. U.S. Census. Illinois. Cook. Chicago. Ward 35. Dist. 1516. 1910; U.S. Census. Illinois. Cook (Chicago). Chicago. Ward 33. Dist. 2122. 1920; Bolhous, Stephen. Memories of Leila Whitehead, 2006; Retrieved from the internet on Feb. 13, 2009, Genealogytrails.com/ill/flu1918.htm; *The Restitution,* July 7, 1904; *The Restitution,* Berean columns, 1910-1920; Berean columns *The Restitution Herald,* 1910-1950; Stilson, Eugene, Interview with Leila Whitehead in the 1960s; Stilson, Jan, Memories from my Youth of Leila Whitehead. Whitehead, Leila. "Report of Berean Work," *The Restitution Herald,* Nov. 2, 1948.

Wiggins, Walter
    b. February 17, 1900
    d. December 1984

Walter was a farmer from Eldorado, Saline County, Illinois. Saline County has many salt mines, an interesting part of Illinois history. Walter married Grace; they had no children. He attended the Bible Training Class in Oregon, Illinois, from 1929 and through 1933 when the school was closed. He said he greatly benefited from the education he received at the BTC. He entered the ministry as a Church of God pastor at Eden Valley, Minnesota. He baptized Stanley O. Ross shortly after his marriage to Elna Ruhn. Walter later did evangelistic work that took him into Texas. He and Grace settled in Oregon, Illinois, and temporarily lived in a mobile home they purchased.

The Illinois Conference of the Churches of God hired Walter as state evangelist. He served in that post for several years, visiting churches for special preaching services and helping establish new churches. Walter worked with a new group meeting in New Lenox. This group's core included several families from Eldorado, Illinois. This church struggled for several years and did not survive. Walter also assisted the rural churches of Casey and Marshall south of Danville. He worked with Elzie Robbins to start and stabilize a church at East Peoria, Illinois. The work of an evangelist took him from one end of the state to the other. He preached a series of special evangelistic services at Ripley Church of God in Brown County in 1947.

In style and appearance, Walter was a southern gentleman. He was tall like Abraham Lincoln and with a beard, might have even resembled him. Walter had large hands with long fingers. He preached with a laid back and thoughtful style. As he pondered a point he ran his fingers over the edge of the pulpit. When he began to share the thought which had just come to him, he punctuated it with a graceful sweep of the hand.

Walter and Grace sold their property on South Tenth Street in Oregon to John and Pearl Friemuth in 1955. The Friemuths were locals who left the farm and moved to town. They were members of the Oregon Church of God and highly regarded Pastor and Mrs. Wiggins. Walter had added a room onto the mobile home. When the property sold, Walter removed the mobile home leaving half a house. The Friemuths built three additional rooms and a garage onto the existing structure. When the Wiggins saw it later they were very pleased with the outcome.

Walter and Grace retired to Eldorado where they lived out their days with family and friends.

Bibliography: Ancestry.com. U.S. Census. Illinois. Saline. East Eldorado. Dist. 8. 1930; Social Security Death Index, record for Walter Wiggins; "Note about Services at Ripley", *The Restitution Herald,* Sydney Magaw, ed., Oregon, Il., Nov. 4, 1947; Smead, Cecil. "Letter to Marj Overmyer," June 2, 1970, retrieved from John Smead, June 26, 2008; Memories of Walter and Grace Wiggins, JStilson.

Williams, Jess Graham
    b. March 23, 1903
    d. January 10, 1993

Jess Graham Williams was the son of James "Jim" (March 16, 1872-1954) and Julia Tuggle Williams (1875-1942). The Williams family lived in Jasper, Alabama, where they farmed, but Jim moved the family to Oklahoma in 1905 before it became a state. Jim must have heard of the message of the Gospel of the Kingdom in Alabama, but his teachers are unknown. He wanted his family to know the Bible so he used his tithe money to bring preachers from Alabama to hold preaching meetings in Oklahoma.

Jess married Ida Pitts in 1923, and they had two children, Ruby and Pauline. Ida died in 1928. Jess married Oklahoma "Okla" Myrtle Scott (1910-1990) on May 16, 1931, and they had six children, Donald, Mary, Paul, Sherwin, Sherman (Bill) and Sandra. Okla's grandfather, James Scott, had been a Methodist preacher in Oklahoma territory, but Jess and his family worshipped with the Church of God.

Jess converted an old schoolhouse at Brent, Oklahoma, into a church. Evangelists who preached in the schoolhouse included Uncle John Foore, T.J. Daniels, Jess Humphreys and T.A. Drinkard. Another evangelist who answered that call was J.M. Morgan who preached across the South for the Church of God. Morgan eventually started three churches in Bristow, Oklahoma, that were or became Advent Christian. Later, Eddie Mathews from Arkansas also came to preach. Sherwin Williams recalls a time when Pastor Morgan visited their home. Sherwin, a small boy of five or six, clearly remembered the elderly Morgan at one time tall, then bent and frail, "walking to the edge of the porch looking up to the sky and saying, 'If I could just live long enough to see my Savior coming from up there.'"

Jess Williams was a farmer but he was a talented businessman too. For a while he was the Fire Chief at the Muskogee, Oklahoma, air base during WWII. Young pilots trained to fly at this facility. After the war, Jess became a guard at the state penitentiary for two years. He left tht position to own and operate a grocery store in Sallisaw. Finally, he returned to farming the old fashioned way. He used horses because he could get closer to the fence row with a team than with a tractor.

Jess's legacy in the Church of God lives on through his children. Bill and Sherwin came north in the 1970s and settled in Rockford, Illinois, where they attended the Blessed Hope Bible Church of God. Bill married Ruth from the local church, and they returned to Oklahoma. Sherwin is pastor at the Church of God in Ripley, and the Blessed Hope Bible Church in Rockford.

Jess and Okla rest in the Sallisaw City Cemetery, Sallisaw, Oklahoma.

  See Bradley, A.S. (19th)
     Crowe, W.L. (19th)
     Daniels, T.J. (19th)
     Drinkard, T.A.
     Foore, Uncle John (19th)
     Morgan, J.M.
     Oliver, Stephen (19th)

Bibliography: Ancestry.com. Okla Scott Marriage Record attached to Jess G. Williams; Williams, Sherwin. E-mail Feb. 6, 2011, Feb. 26, 2011.

Williams, Joseph W.
 b. August 6, 1874
 d. October 20, 1963

A. An Author and a Broadcaster
B. Service on the Committee of Ten
C. Development of Universal Reconciliation
D. Williams Continues

J.W. Williams was born in Big Rock, Illinois, just west of Aurora, to David and Elizabeth Nightingale Williams. His parents heard the Gospel message from J.M. Stephenson, H.V. Reed and others who circuited through Illinois on evangelistic tours. In J.W.'s early life the family moved to Attica, Kansas, where he later graduated from the University of Kansas. He majored in English and taught for 12 years. Evidence shows he was on the cutting edge and eager to spread the word through preaching. What is known of him comes from reading his works or from reading about him in the denominational literature.

J.W. Williams and Sarah Brammel married on September 17, 1910. For a time they lived in Indiana where he pastored at Burr Oak Church of God in Culver. While in Indiana, he baptized several members including Cantwell Drabenstott. J.W. and Sarah had ten children.

In 1913 the Williams family moved to Kentucky, where he pastored the Church of God Abrahamic Faith. In a letter to William Wachtel, J.W. said that the way he was treated there caused him to leave that Church of God in 1915. The publication of a booklet, *Steps into a Higher Life,* may have troubled the Perryville congregation.

In November 1915, J.W. and the family went to Iowa by rail but they were temporarily stranded in Peoria, Illinois. Rather than sell his farm animals, J.W. decided to ship them to Iowa. He was detained in Peoria for a stock inspection so he sent his wife and children on to stay with church families in Sac City, Iowa, until he could arrive and locate a farmhouse.

Joseph Williams attended Iowa Conference as early as 1906 and from 1912 to 1946 he attended regularly. He first attended the Nebraska Conference in 1908. He did not attend Nebraska Conference again until 1912. In 1915, J.W. became the Iowa evangelist. In 1916 he held meetings at Koszta and 15 were baptized. Later, the family moved to the Koszta area and labored there several years. He continued to serve the Oak Lawn church on a rotation of Sundays until 1919 when the family relocated to Ripley, Illinois. They moved the week of November 11 after being in Iowa four years. As his final act in that conference, J.W. visited all the churches.

A. An Author and a Broadcaster

As soon as he settled his family in their Ripley home (the same house where J.M. Stephenson resided many years earlier) J.W. began writing articles for *The Restitution Herald*. His first, published January 20, 1920, was "The Nature of Man." Williams believed that the law is in us as righteousness from God. "It teaches moral virtue and is not merely a shadow...is just as good today as it ever was, provided we follow that righteousness in faith and not in ourselves." He said, "There is no command to believe (the law). It is always something to do or not to do."

He also authored several tracts that were advertised and sold by *The Restitution Herald* office in Oregon, Illinois. Some of these were "Saving Faith," "Life and Death," "Destiny of the Wicked," "Perfection, Justification," "God's Temporary Law through Moses," "God's Eternal Law," "And He Baptized Him," "Martyr or Savior," "The Forgiveness of Sins," "The Unsearchable Riches of Christ" and "What is Man?"

J.W. served in the Ripley ministry in 1920 after which they moved to Arizona. Their address in Phoenix was 807 N. Third Street. In Arizona J.W. preached at the Lakeshore Bible Church at that time located on the corner of Baseline and Dobson roads near the old Saylor farm. When S.J. Lindsay arrived in 1922 to serve that congregation, J.W. Williams returned to serve with the brethren in Iowa.

Radio was a new medium for the Gospel message in the early 1920s. Several stations were licensed in 1922 and 1923 in Iowa. J.W. Williams began to broadcast radio sermons from Eagle Point, Iowa, as soon as he was able. It is not known which stations he used, but presumably, he chose one near Dubuque or Waterloo.

B. Service on the Committee of Ten

J.W. Williams met with G.E. Marsh and F.L. Austin at the Iowa Conference in 1920 in a "casual" meeting. The discussion topic was "a General Conference of the Church of God." J.W. met again with 12 ministers in Chicago in September, and subsequently, issued invitations to all ministers and evangelists to meet in summit in November. This was the beginning of the Committee of Ten.

Joseph W. Williams was chosen to serve on the Committee of Ten in the fall of 1920 while he was still living in Arizona. Conference delegates appointed the committee to investigate the feasibility of recommending a means to organize a national General Conference. The question was to be decided at the next annual Waterloo Conference in 1921. The Committee of Ten was appointed to represent preachers and laymen, male and female, North and South, with varying views of doctrine. Other members of the committee were F.L. Austin (secretary), James A. Patrick, Grace M. Marsh, Frank E. Siple, Alta King, Judd S. Lyon, Rolla Hightower, Leota Hanson and David E. Van Vactor. The Committee chose Joseph Williams to be the Chairman. Since the members lived in various states the business was conducted by correspondence. F.L. Austin spent many hours typing letters with carbons for each member of the committee.

Their charge was to study, inform, inquire, plan and propose a plan for the next annual meeting. J.W. Williams was well suited to command the leadership of this important and dynamic committee. He had superior intelligence, vision and leadership qualities. The committee published a report, "An Effort to Discover the One True Church of God Its Architect Its Structure Its Purpose and An Appeal to Earnestly Strive to Conform to God's Instruction Pertaining Thereto in Every Particular." In an article summarizing the work of the committee one scholar wrote in "Our Conference: Its Start and Basis" that there were seven obstacles facing the committee any

---

The Committee of Ten faced seven major hurdles in their deliberations:

1. They disagreed on whether the formation of a General Assembly was the same kind of conference found in Acts 15.
2. They discussed the issue of technology. Would using modern methods of printing draw them away from the biblical example?
3. Which translation of the Bible should they recommend?
4. How to isolate and drive out the doctrine of universalism (universal salvation).
5. The controversy between strict conservative interpretation of Church of God distinctive doctrines versus a more lenient approach allowing unity in fellowship.
6. The personal discord between S.J. Lindsay, publisher of the popular *Restitution Herald* and F.L. Austin. A letter from Lindsay said, "there can be but one result to the movement and that is that if it is successful, it must win its success upon the ruins (financially) of the work in various states (the state conferences)."
7. The tract written by the Chairman, J.W. Williams, entitled "Saving Faith."

Ref.: *The Restitution Herald*, 75th Anniversary Issue, Oct., 1985

one of which would have been significant enough to sink their mission. Some of these concerns were procedural, and at least one of them was doctrinal and related to an article J.W. Williams had authored.

In this article Williams emphasized that the Pauline theology, especially I Corinthians 15:1-8, is the basis for saving faith which is in the name of Jesus Christ and his atoning death. Austin and Van Vactor agreed with him. The others felt this would promote the decline of Church of God distinctive doctrines such as the Gospel of the Kingdom of God. The discussion was so heated that Williams resigned as chairman at a November meeting in Oregon. James Patrick became the new chairman. Through the grace of God and a concerted prayer effort throughout the year, all the problems were worked out, and the Church of God General Conference was born at Waterloo, Iowa, in August 1921.

Delbert Rankin noted from that point "there seemed to develop an organizational independence of the Iowa State Conference from the General Conference. But connections and interactions between the brethren in Iowa and those of other states and the General Conference continued, and any rift to maintain organizational independence was by sufficient consensus and not unanimous." Fellowship continued and exists to this day.

C. Development of Universal Reconciliation

Rankin wrote "it was in this backdrop that the doctrine of universal reconciliation developed in Iowa and influenced the teachings of congregations at Gladbrook, Koszta, Stanhope, some in Cedar Falls/Waterloo mainly from the 1920s on."

In his book *A Primer on Predestination,* written from Tacoma during his senior years, Williams stated:

> John Calvin and his successor in doctrine Jonathan Edwards, knew the truth of predestination, but they missed the "mercy upon all" expressed in Romans 11:32, because their view of immortality of the soul and its going to heaven or hell at death as an endless destiny left no room for mercy to those who were foreordained to evil through the present life, for that view precludes the possibility of resurrection to future mercy.
>
> [It is]…error…[that] predestined evil is permanent. That predestination in evil is temporary may be seen by the word "until" in Romans 11:25, where the blindness of Israel is limited to the time during which the gentiles are being called. The blindness of the nation is the most frequently quoted…case of predestined evil in all the Bible.

Rankin concludes "[Predestination] fits the overall paradigm, God is sovereign, and man has no free will to do except to do God's will, whether for evil (temporary) or for good (permanent)."

Gordon Smith noted in "A Tribute to Joseph W. Williams," that his teaching on universal salvation stemmed from the problem of evil. He wrote:

> Because of his kindly, sympathetic nature, he came in his thinking to espouse a teaching of eventual universal salvation for the human race as the solution to the problem of evil. To this conclusion he attached and harmonized a teaching of predestination to salvation of the church in the gospel dispensation. Being convinced of the correctness of his views, he diligently presented them to groups in Iowa to which he ministered. His ability as a biblical expositor won over to his viewpoint the vast majority of the membership of the churches of God in Iowa. Because they accepted his views the churches in Iowa were alienated from the rest of the brotherhood of churches. Yet in a modest, unassuming spirit he labored on.

The writings of Williams, and those of fellow universalists Alta King and E.O. Stewart, were mostly shut out of the Church of God publications so they began to publish in noted Universalist journals. Three of these titles are *Unsearchable Riches*, *The Differentiator* and the *Roundtable of the Scriptures*. These journals are posted today on the website of "Savior of all Fellowship." Neither that website nor any of the journal titles are associated with the Church of God General Conference.

D. Williams Continues

J.W. Williams left the Committee of Ten in 1920. His adherence to the doctrine of universal reconciliation was a great problem to the majority of the members. Several others in the Church of God including L.E. Conner, A.J. Eychaner, G.M. Myers and W.L. Crowe also began to promote this doctrine. This was the same route taken by Elias Smith several decades before. The questions that arose with universal reconciliation included the place of the resurrection, and, what is the place of evangelism and missions? If one believes all people will be saved, there seems to be no need for prophecy, for judgment or reward. Iowa Universalism has taught that sin is temporary and all men will benefit from the promises made to Abraham in the Age to Come.

Alta King noted in a publication, "Universal salvation is usually associated with Universalism of Unitarianism that leaves out Jesus as Savior." She saw a difference between Unitarian Universalism and Universal Reconciliation. Rankin noted that difference as:

> Universalism in the Church of God and that which is apart from the Unitarian-Universalist position seems at least to insist on some understandings of the nature of man and the nature of God and work of Jesus, saying, for instance, that there is a need at some point for Jesus and the Cross and that "there is no unending torment in flames." But then it takes on its own flavor of shall we say, "wishful thinking?"

Joseph Williams believed in prophecy for he wrote an article for *The Day Dawn and Harvest Messenger*, edited by James Patrick, expressing that the Holy Spirit is received through reading the written and spoken words of God which reveals His spirit or mind. He also said that the fulfillment of prophecy reveals how the Spirit works among men. In other articles Williams argued against pre-existence of Christ for which William Brickley took him to task in *The Restitution Herald*. The majority of believers in the Church of God emphasize the virgin birth of Christ, which by its very nature denies pre-existence.

Williams authored the works, *The Primer on Predestination, The Mystery of Evil, Hell, A Discussion of Salvation by Grace* and *Songs in the Night*, which is a summary of 53 sermons presented as precious lessons of hope, peace and joy particularly to those who are in distress. From 1930-1946, J.W. Williams edited and published *The Sunrise Beacon* from Gladbrook, Iowa.

Joseph and Sarah Williams moved to Tacoma, Washington, in 1946; they lived there until their deaths. From there he authored many works. In his 32-page pamphlet, *Hell*, he said:

> The resurrection of the dead makes it impossible for heaven to be the endless home of the saved and hell that of the lost, for resurrection would end those endless states by taking the saved out of heaven and the others out of hell, and how could an endless tenure be ended? Shall we then accept resurrection as true, or the immortality of the soul that entails heaven and hell? Resurrection is taught in the scriptures: the other ideas are not.

In the *Mystery of Evil* he said that sin comes from within man, and that it is temporary. When Christians are resurrected there will be no more death or sin. Hell will be empty. He said, "We are saved by faith in Christ, not by knowledge of the devil."

From that point on he did not worship with Church of God, although he preached special meetings when he returned to visit in Iowa. In his later years J.W. preached a gospel of grace, a fact he said which provoked opposition in his "former denominational brethren," but that did not stop him. He was an ardent Bible student, but he turned against the Gospel of the Kingdom.

In his book, *The Gospel*, written from Tacoma in 1956, he asked:

> What message saves from sin? Does the so-called modern "gospel of the kingdom (the news of the coming kingdom), save its believers from sin? The general thought of those who advocate that this is the true gospel of the kingdom is that there is no such thing possible as righteousness in the present life....So that the true gospel may be identified as that good news about Jesus (Savior) that enables a believer like Mary, "to go and sin no more," as He said to the lame man at Bethesda. The true gospel is whatever good news about the Savior that brings the sinner to him.

Following Joseph 's death, Gordon Smith wrote:

> There is not a Church of God in Iowa which had not profited by his ministry. His quiet assurance and convincing logic was effective in leading people to Christ. Each sermon was made to fill particular needs. His opening sermon at each Iowa Conference was a theme of consecration.

See Adams, Almus (19th)
Austin, F.L.
Conner, Lincoln E. (19th)
Drabenstott, Cantwell
Eychaner, A.J. (19th)
King, Alta
Marsh, Grace M.
Stewart, E.O.
Wachtel, William

Bibliography: ABC Biography project, David Krogh, compiler; Burnett, Francis. "Firm Unto the End" Sermons by Burnett. From the Archival Collection of the Rock River Christian College, Beloit, Wisconsin; Burnett, Francis et al history committee *History of the Iowa Church of God and Conference 1855-1987*, printed at Belle Plaine Union, 1987; Smith, Gordon, "A Tribute to Joseph W. Williams," *History of the Church of God in Christ Jesus in Iowa*, no author given, no date, a mimeographed booklet of 28 pages; Interview with Grace Marsh by Jan Stilson at Pinecrest Manor Fall, 1985. At this meeting she donated all her files from the Committee of Ten. These files are part of the archives of the Church of God General Conference in Atlanta Bible College; *The Restitution Herald*, Nov. 24, 1915; April 2, 1919; April 16, 1919; November 11, 1919; January 1, 1920; "Our Conference: Its Start and Basis." *History Newsletter*, Fall 1985 as included in *The Restitution Herald, Our 75th Year.* 75:1 Oct. 1985; Williams, J.W. "Report for October," *The Day Dawn and Harvest Messenger*, James A. Patrick, editor, Fort Dodge, Iowa, Nov. 1919; "A History of the Lakeshore Bible Church of God, Tempe, Arizona" from amug.org/Lakeshore/images/History.htm; Rankin, Delbert, pastor of Belle Plaine, Iowa Church of God Abrahamic Faith, "The Doctrine of Universal Reconciliation Among Iowa Brethren", paper presented at History Conference, Oct 21-15, 2008 North Hills Church of God, Springfield, Ohio; Williams, J. W. "Nature of Man, *The Restitution Herald*, Church of God General Conference, Oregon, Il., Jan. 20, 1920; Williams, J. W. *Hell*, self published, Tacoma, Washington, no date; Williams, J.W. *The Mystery of Evil*, self published, Gladbrook, Iowa no date;Williams, J. W. *The Gospel*, self published, Tacoma, 1956; Record of baptism of Cantwell Drabenstott, *The Restitution Herald*, March 14, 1912.

Williams, Paul
b. 1919
d. December 2000

Paul Williams was born in Iowa to Joseph W. and Sarah Williams. He graduated from Oregon Bible College in Oregon, Illinois, in the early 1940s. He received a minister's license from the Iowa Conference but was active in another denomination in Washington.

Paul wed Hazel Burk (February 2, 1919 to March 14, 2005) who also graduated Oregon Bible College. It was said that he was not allowed to be Valedictorian of his graduating class because he accepted the views of Universal Reconciliation as taught through the Iowa Churches of God. Hazel lived in Tacoma, but was from the Puyallup, Washington, Church of God. Paul and Hazel had eight children, one died in infancy.

While living in Iowa, Paul served as pastor at the Sac City Church of God and later at Stanhope. While serving at Sac City he stayed with the Ernest Swanson family. Russell Swanson remembered Paul fondly, writing:

> He loved to help with the farm chores and work. His mechanical aptitude was indeed worthy; his personality and

kindness was welcomed. He helped with putting up hay, cultivating corn and so forth. We fished together on Black Hawk Lake. Although ten years my senior, I enjoyed his presence and conversation, his interest in humanity, nature and strong association with God.

One afternoon when he and I were repairing a large door on a corn crib, I called his attention to a large buildup of a cumulus cloud in the east, billowing thousands of feet upward with an "ice cap" forming against the blue background, common during Iowa summers. Paul stopped the work, sat down and took time to view that sight. I joined him as we marveled at that creative feat, reflecting on the greatness of God.

Paul and Hazel moved back to Tacoma in 1950. Both were active in their community and continued to visit friends in Iowa as they were able.

See Swanson, Ernest
Williams, Joseph W.

Bibliography: Rankin, Delbert "The Doctrine of Universal Reconciliation Among Iowa Brethren, presented to the History Conference at North Hills Church of God, Springfield, Ohio, October, 2008; Rosenberger, Ralph L. "Obituary of Paul Williams", *Searchlight*, Iowa State Berean Society Newsletter, Fall 2001; Swanson, Russell. "A Little History for *Searchlight* Readers: Reminiscence" *Searchlight*, Spring 2005.

Williamson, Martin Oliver

b. June 21, 1882
d. November 24, 1977

M.O. Williamson was a faithful worker in the Southeast Conference who preached and exercised pastoral duties at several Churches of God. He was appointed pastor of the newly reorganized church at Travelers Rest, South Carolina, in 1920. On September 12, 1948, the Anderson Chapel congregation at Hendersonville, North Carolina, dedicated its new building. M.O. Williamson preached the dedication service. Members of Bro. Williamson's family still serve the Lord in the Church of God at Pelzer, South Carolina, including Joe James and his family. Joe James, a clinical psychologist, has served on the Church of God General Conference Board of Directors as chairman and in other capacities for many years. He and his family continue to worship at the Guthrie Grove Church of God Abrahamic Faith.

See Durham, Andrew N. (19th)

Bibliography: Ancestry.com. U.S. Census. South Carolina. Beuford. Yemassee. Dist. 16. 1900. Ancestry.com. World War I Draft Registration Cards 1917-1918 record for Martin Oliver Williamson. *The Restitution*, Sept. 3, 1920; Notice of Dedication. *The Restitution Herald*, Nov. 23, 1948; Record of M.O. Williamson's interment retrieved on Oct. 23, 2010 at http://sciway3.net/scgenweb/anderson-county/cemetery-txt/a100.txt

Martin Williamson, left front holding hat, and his congregation ready to depart for General Conference.

Wolfe, Vernis

b. August 15, 1922

Vernis Wolfe was born in Texas to Alvin and Madge Myers Wolfe. He married Iris Foster on December 8, 1944, and they had two sons, David and Duain. Vernis resides now near Hammond, Louisiana, near David and his family; they share a large garden. Duain is a musician and choral director working with the Chicago Symphony, the Colorado Symphony and the Ottawa Symphony.

Vernis wrote, "I became the fourth generation of our family in the Church of God, Abrahamic Faith. That may sound like a long history in the church, but it was a case where the preceding three generations had not been in the church all that long having been converted by a pioneer Adventist preacher sometime during the years prior to my birth." While the Abrahamic faith had been in Texas since before the turn of the 20th century, the work did not become solidly organized until around the time of Vernis' birth.

In a recent correspondence, Vernis explained that unusual nature of the "church climate" in Texas. He said, "there was a great deal of cross-pollination between the churches and an unbelievable amount of debate. A person was almost compelled to know the distinctive doctrines very well in order to survive. It was a good environment for a future church professional to be reared. By the time one reached the age of maturity he had been exposed to just about every religious doctrine imagined. Perhaps it would compare to a child being inoculated against the common diseases."

Vernis gives credit to Evangelist I.A. Dykes of Goldthwaithe, Texas, for influencing him most as a young man. Vernis wrote:

> [Dykes] was an itinerant preacher that came to our church once a month and also held a lengthy revival every summer. He was the most influential minister of my youth and the one who helped me to get started preaching. While still in high school, I started filling in the three Sundays he was not there. He was a great help.

On January 1, 1941, Vernis entered the Church of God ministry at St. Cloud, Minnesota, quite a change in climate from Texas. After that he pastored the Blood River Church of God, Springfield, Louisiana; Baton Rouge Church of God, Baton Rouge, Louisiana; Tempe Church of God, Tempe, Arizona; Oregon Church of God, Oregon, Illinois; and the Happywoods Church of God, Hammond, Louisiana, where he served for 26 years.

Beginning in 1983 Vernis filled the pulpit for various churches. He primarily served as an interim pastor between one pastor leaving and another being installed. These tours of service usually lasted a year, some as long as two or three years, and one for five. Several of these churches were Presbyterian which had a program in place for such pastoral "gaps" so that Vernis' duties included preparing the congregation for the arrival of their new minister. He wrote, "This was considered a specialty and [I] received training to be intentional with a specific agenda to prepare the church for its next phase of ministry."

Other churches which Vernis assisted in this manner included the Christians (Disciples of Christ) and three Churches of God Abrahamic Faith. Vernis said, "This was both interesting and fulfilling for it gave [me] an opportunity to witness to a much broader field. Instead of having doctrinal problems there was an appreciation for my Biblical teaching and preaching. Yes, there were invitations to switch denominations, but for me they were not attractive—there is just no place like home where a common orientation of faith is important. Our distinctive Adventist faith is unique and well worth our loyalty (*hesed*)."

Vernis retired in 2005 at age 83. In retirement he has continued to be active in ministry, but he doesn't miss the deadlines and never-ending demands of the pastorate. He now has more time for in-depth Bible study and it is what he likes to do. His library, which was already "well-equipped," has grown exponentially since his retirement. He said, "I love to read, and my favorite books are biblical/theological." Vernis also loves fly fishing, and surfing the Internet. He said, "I don't spend time in spectator sports, and I don't watch TV." He does enjoy cooking, however, and specializes in Cajun.

Vernis authored a commentary on *Psalms* for the Church of God *Truth Seeker's Adult Quarterly*. He acknowledged that a few references for the lessons were URL links, but mostly his references were books. He said, "I enjoyed writing the lessons, my only frustration was not having enough time to expand, so a lot of things are abbreviated into a simple sentence." From the Preface:

> The original purpose of this series was to group together Psalms that had characteristics in common in order to identify major Biblical themes in the Psalms and to give support to those particular teachings. In the end, the great diversity of the Psalms would come into play, their unity would be manifest, and the wholeness of God's revelation would be understood. Though we have yet to reach that goal, we hope to have advanced it in some measure.

Vernis concluded, "Rather than to have studied one Psalm at a time we considered them in groups and attempted to give them continuity in order to see the Psalms as a book rather than disjointed segments. I hope you and your congregation will enjoy these Psalms."

See Bradley, A.S. (19th)
     Drinkard, T.A.
     Gibbs, W.L. (19th)
     Turner, R.O. (19th)

Bibliography: Jones, Bob. "*Hesed* is the Hebrew word for love, primarily God's loyal promise-keeping love for His people, no matter what they did. *[The] King James* normally translated it as "lovingkindness." It's a very deep and rich concept that embodies what love in the OT was all about. [It's] a great word, right up there with *agape* in the NT." Wolfe, Vernis. E-mail to Rex Cain, March 26, 2011; Wolfe, Vernis. "Psalms" *Truth Seeker's Adult Quarterly*, Church of God General Conference, McDonough, Ga.; Wolfe, Vernis. E-mail, April 9, 2011.

There are no biographical entries for this letter.

Y

Yows, Wayne
b. September 18, 1911
d. March 14, 1989

Wayne Yows was born in the Hay Valley community in Coryell County, Texas. He learned the truth at his mother's knee. He attended school in Ater and graduated. On August 2, 1930, he wed Ruby Choat in Goldthwaite. He worked for the Texas Youth Council from 1963 until his retirement in 1976. Wayne was a farmer and rancher and a member of the Church of God Faith of Abraham, where he served as an elder for more than 40 years.

Wayne died at his home in Purmela, Texas. Services were held from the Scott's Funeral Home Chapel in Gatesville. Ronnie Rhodes and Rex Tilly officiated. Wayne was interred at Ater Cemetery near Gatesville. He sleeps, awaiting the soon return of his Savior from heaven to establish the Kingdom of God in the Age to Come.

Bibliography: ABC Biography project, David Krogh, compiler; 1940 Texas Church of God Membership list located in Jessie M. Wilson's scrapbook, found in Archives in Atlanta Bible College.

Zechiel, Ferris B.
b. June 9, 1908
d. April 13, 2010

Ferris Zechiel was the eldest child of Jesse E. and Nora Pearl Hatten Zechiel. Jesse and Nora had been married six years when Ferris was born. During the next decade, they had two more children, daughters Marguarite and Elizabeth. Jesse farmed in Union Township of Marshall County, Indiana; Ferris did also.

Ferris married Leona Grosvenor (January 21, 1913-February 5, 2009) on October 13, 1933, in Tipp City, Ohio; Pastor Sydney Magaw officiated. Ferris and Leona had three children, Betty, Carol and Larry. Carol died in childhood. Ferris and Leona were members of the Community Bible Fellowship Church of God in Culver, formerly known as the Burr Oak Church of God. Ferris was active in his church and in Indiana State Conference and General Conference activities. Daughter Betty Reinhold wrote:

Dad was a very gentle, quiet, peacemaker; fun loving honest and a Godly man with a strong faith. He served God all his life and was in the Church of God since he was 15 years old.

Dad was superintendent and elder for the Burr Oak Church of God for many years. He was an officer for the Church of God State Conference. He helped with many church projects, one including helping the ladies make kettles of apple butter for many years. He believed in tithing which he practiced all of his married life.

Dad always honored his parents which scripture tells us to do in Exodus 20:12 and he attributed that for having been blessed with longevity. He quoted the 23rd Psalm daily and read the 95th Psalm daily. His bible is highlighted with many favorite scriptures that he based his faith and belief on.

Ferris and Leona lived at Culver, Indiana. He died there with his family at his side. They spent their last years together in a nursing home, celebrating their 65th anniversary with a photo and special notice by Willard Scott on the Smucker's segment of the *Today Show* on NBC. Ferris and Leona were interred at the Culver Masonic Cemetery.

Bibliography: Ancestry.com. U.S. Census. Indiana. Marshall. Union. Dist. 0114. 1910; Ancestry.com. U.S. Census. Indiana. Marshall, Union. Dist. 17. 1930; Ancestry.com. Social Security Death List, record for Ferris B. Zechiel; Ancestry.com. United States Obituary Collection, record for Leona Zechiel; Obituary for Ferris Zechiel, *South Bend Tribune*, April 15, 2010.

Appendixes

19th Century

Appendix 1—Age to Come, Literalist Interpretation 545
Appendix 2—Bitter Disappointment 551
Appendix 3—Catalyst for Change: Martyrdom 553
Appendix 4—Chronology: Pathways of Faith with Map 555
Appendix 5—Collaboration in Illinois 560
Appendix 6—From the JRAD-Atonement 562
Appendix 7—Holy Spirit 567
Appendix 8—Judgment 569
Appendix 9—Kingdom of God 571
Appendix 10—Lost Saints: Known Only to God 572
Appendix 11—Poetry and Hymns 574
Appendix 12—Second Adventism in Ripley 576
Featured Photographs 577
Appendix 13—Timeline: Periodicals 578

20th Century

Appendix 14—Atonement 580
Appendix 15—Baptism 581
Appendix 16—Christian Education 583
Appendix 17—Development Role of *The Restitution Herald* 585
Appendix 18—Faith 587
Appendix 19—Heresies: Aberrations from Scripture 588
Appendix 20—Missions 591
Appendix 21—Ohio Conference Organization 596
Appendix 22—Prophecy 597
Appendix 23—Resurrection 598
Appendix 24—Systematic Theology: Decade of Development 600
Appendix 25—Theocratic Kingdom 603
Appendix 26—Worship 604

Appendix 1
Age to Come, Literalist Interpretation
A Watershed Doctrine for the Age To Come Believers and the Millerites
by Arlen F. Rankin, BTh
Presented at the Fourth Annual History Conference, Springfield, Ohio, October 23-25, 2008.

A Watershed

There was a hermeneutical and therefore theological watershed that became apparent and separative in the thirty years between 1850 and 1880 within the Millerite Movement. Doctrinal forces were stirring both within and around the Millerite camp. The early thinkers and writers of the Church of God were at the core of the discussions in those years. The advancement of the Age-to-Come doctrine as well as the earlier Literalist teachings promoted the millennial restoration of the literal nation of Israel and with it the concept of a *probation* of living mortals and the *progression* of "the times of restitution of all things spoken by the mouth of all the holy prophets since the world began."

Julia Neuffer, under the heading Age-to Come Controversy, writes:

> Where did the age-to-come doctrine of the 1850s come from? Possibly it stemmed chiefly from the British Literalist publications that had been circulated among the Millerites. However, the name seems to have come from the title of the 1850 editorials and the 1851 book by Joseph Marsh. Certainly his paper, *The Advent Harbinger* (Rochester, N.Y.), became the sounding board for the doctrine, although other individuals had taught it before him.[1]

As we look at the divisions of thought and organizational movements following the Millerite Disappointment, we can see that the understandings regarding Israel's future remain to be the watershed that it once was. The arrival at these divergent views are the result of the differing hermaneutics[2] on each side of the discussion—the literal or the allegorical-typological. One side sees a restoration of literal, national Israel as the fulfilling of prophecies and promises; the other holds a fulfilled or replacement theology which substitutes the Church as the inheritor of Israel's promised blessings.[3] One sees the Church as becoming *sharers* in the promises by faith when Israel comes into her restoration and fullness (Eph. 3:6; Rom. 11:11, 12); the other sees the covenant promises as fulfilled or conditional, therefore, completed in Israel historically or removed from Israel as they failed to comply and had them taken away and given to the Church. It is notable that the latter applies the blessings of Israel to the Church, but not the cursings. One sees the millennial age as one of continued probation *preliminary to* the new heaven and earth; the other sees termination of all probation at the return of Jesus and all kingdom prophecies being fulfilled in the new heaven and earth which starts at that time (Advent Christian) or 1000 years later at the termination of earth's desolation and the judgment when the new heaven and earth come (Seventh-day Adventist).

We note that as time progressed there were (and are) various ways of understanding the concept of future probation in the millennial frame of reference. The Church of God and the Christadelphians most generally see the probation being applied only to the "remnant" of Israel (Isa. 10:20-22; 11:11, 12) and the "left" of the nations (Zech. 14:16; Acts 15:17) which *continue on into* the millennium in a mortal state where they "learn righteousness" (Isa. 26:9; 54:13, 14) and "learn His ways...laws" (Isa. 2:2-5) or refuse to do so. The followers of C. T. Russell see a resurrection to mortality of all those "who have never heard" to an "opportunity" or "fair chance" for hearing, acceptance and reconciliation and, some among them believe in an ultimate and universal salvation for all. The Church of God generally believes that those "who have never heard" will remain among "the rest of the dead" to be raised in the final judgment to receive an *appropriate* judgment at the hands of a *righteous* God (Gen. 18:25). Some, however, within the General Conference and its precursor membership have held to variations of the "wider hope." Christadelphians hold to a limited or partial resurrection which would leave those "who have never heard" or "cannot believe" as dead without further judgment. There was much discussion of these matters in our early periodicals.

The three-tiered nature and sequence of this historical-theological watershed is first hermeneutic, then doctrinal, and finally organizational.

Change and Development

For some of our early leaders who had been active in the Millerite Movement, change in belief was both a necessity and a reality as they renewed their efforts and immersed themselves in their study of the Word of God. Change did not come in an instant, but was rather a development in the thinking of our early leaders; a growth in understanding as they reconsidered the biblical text. Not that the truth was unknown before then, but that these men were in flux in their studies at that time.

Marsh was an example of such change. His book of 1849[4] presents his then views regarding the restoration of literal Israel—a denial of their actual restoration. He changes his position regarding this and more fully and precisely develops his theology and expresses it in his work of 1851[5] to affirm their literal restoration and the attendant ideas.

Neuffer, in *"The Gathering of Israel A Historical Study of Early Writings, pp. 74-76"* cites *The Advent Harbinger*, n.s. 1:172, 220, Nov. 17 and Dec. 29, 1849, and states:

> As late as November 1849, Marsh had restated essentially the standard Millerite position on the millennium, except for the omission of the renovation of the earth at the Advent. Yet he declared that he had never been settled on the nature of the millennium. In December, in introducing extracts from a Literalist author, he still professed disagreement with him on the literal return of the Jews to Palestine and on probation after the Second Advent.[6]

Mark Mattison[7] has written at length on the connections between Joseph Marsh and John Thomas in regard to Marsh's new views and I believe he has drawn some correct conclusions in that Thomas apparently did have at least some influence on Marsh in these things, but as Stilson points out, "Marsh had first heard of the Age to Come from Elias Smith of the Christian Connection, who published the Herald of Gospel Liberty which he had began in 1808."[8] Twenty years ago I pondered the possibility of the early seeds of Marsh's belief in the restoration of Israel to be in his previous participation in the Christian Connexion since Elias Smith's *Sermons on the Prophecies*[9] strongly emphasized the restoration of literal, natural Israel. Neuffer suggests that Marsh may also have been influenced by the writings of O. R. L. Crosier who wrote of "The Age to Come" in his *Day-Star* (1846) and who in 1847 was on the staff of *The Advent Harbinger*. Then she says, "Other possible sources of influence on Marsh's age-to-come doctrine of 1850 might be two others who set forth Literalist views in 1846 and 1848: J. B. Cook, of New England...and Henry Grew, of Philadelphia...."[10] In *The Advent Harbinger* of 1850 appeared an extended discussion series on "The Age To Come" between Literalist, J. B. Cook and Millerite, L. D. Mansfield.[11]

Elias Smith writes of Elhanan Winchester's Lectures[12] in the introduction to his sermons, "Mr. Winchester had the greatest knowledge of the prophecies, of any writer I have ever seen, and there is no doubt in my mind of his being a good man, though I think he was in error concerning the salvation of all men. His arrangement of the things which are to take place until the last judgment is, in general, according to the scriptures, and had he gone through as he set out, he would have outdone all who have written before him; but when he came to the last part of his book, his plan carried him away from the scriptures, and to make it out, he was obliged to leave what he first laid down as a rule to understand the prophecies; that is, the plain literal meaning of the scriptures."[13]

During the years of 1857-59, Marsh published Winchester's Lectures numbers 9-18 in the pages of The *Expositor & Advocate*. In the introduction to the publishing of this series Marsh says that he was indebted to one I. K. Lombard of Exeter for sending the second volume of Winchester's work–

> ...which we have long desired to obtain....On reading this Lecture, it will be seen that William Miller was indebted to Dr. Gill for his theory of the millennium, &c., which Mr. Winchester most effectually explodes. It will also be discovered why this work has nearly become extinct: It is too literal to harmonize with the mystical theories of the popular sects of the day of fables. God has had his witnesses in every age, and judging by what we have read of this work before us, none have shone more brilliantly on the millennial reign of Christ than Elhanan Winchester.[14]

We note that after having obtained on microfilm the entirety of these lectures (1740 pages in 4 volumes) we concur with Smith that Winchester moves on from the biblical view of the millennium to espouse the error of universal salvation.

Also in 1857 there was a report of a conference held in Danville submitted by Richard Corbaley and published in *The Expositor and Advocate* of June. It speaks to the importance of our literal hermeneutic. Demmitt quotes:

> In the evening, elder J. Marsh gave to an attentive audience, an exposition of the correct principle of scripture interpretation, by which Christians may come into the one faith and hope of the Gospel, and all speak, think, act and judge alike: 1 Cor. 1:10. he also showed that the different conceptions of the same doctrine, arise not from the Bible itself, nor from differing degrees of intellect, but from mystical or allegorical interpretation,—and that a oneness of faith cannot be attained by any degree of scientific or classical education, or even by a pious, sincere and prayerful study of the

Scriptures,—that the desired oneness can only be attained by making the literal element of the Bible, the basis of faith, which figurative serves to explain. Several practical rules were given, by which to be guided in Biblical investigation. The first was that,—*Whenever a person, place, or thing is made the direct subject of discourse, it is always used in a **literal** sense*. The popular error in transferring the terms, Zion, Judah, and Jerusalem to the Church, was shown, with the groundlessness and even absurdity of supposing the predicted future glory of these is to be fulfilled in the Church.[15] [Emphasis mine.]

Also in 1857, there is a two-part rebuttal by Marsh in *The Expositor and Advocate* of George Storrs' spiritualizing of the prophecies regarding Israel.[16] In the articles, "Literal Interpretations—The Bible Examiner," Marsh points out that the appellation of the terms "Zion" and "Jerusalem" as figurative of the church is an erroneous interpretation that cannot be sustained by the scrutiny of a candid mind. This was published after the Danville conference and no doubt reflects the same thesis as his presentation there.

No doubt the "Great Disappointment," among other things, gave Marsh pause to rethink the prophetic scenario he held and provoked him to restudy the Scriptures relative to the reign of Christ, God's plan concerning Israel as the seed of Abraham, including their part in the Abrahamic covenant. Marsh in the first portion of his *Age to Come, or Glorious Restitution*, disavows and refutes what he calls "William Miller's Theory" or the order of prophetic events in a series of 18 "considerations."[17] As concerning the future of the Jews, Miller likens the literality of such as being "one of the traditions of the elders" and writes:

> So, also, with the return of the Jews. That question I saw could only be sustained by denying the positive declarations of the New Testament, which assert: 'there is no difference between the Jew and the Greek;' that 'the promise that he shall be the heir of the world was not to Abraham and his seed through the law, but through the righteousness of faith;' that 'there is neither Jew nor Greek, bond nor free, male nor female;' but that 'if ye be Christ's, then are ye Abraham's seed, and heirs according to the promise.' I was, therefore, obliged to discard an objection which asserts there is a difference between the Jew and Greek; that the children of the flesh are accounted for the seed, etc.[18]

At the Albany conference of 1845 a series of statements of "important truths" were adopted. Among them was this:

> **7th.** That the promise, that Abraham should be the heir of the world, was not to him, or to his seed, through the law, but through the righteousness of faith, Rom. iv.13. That they are not all Israel which are of Israel, Rom. ix.6. That there is no difference, under the Gospel dispensation, between Jew and Gentile, Rom. x.12. That the middle wall of partition that was between them is broken down, no more to be rebuilt, Eph. ii.14, 15. That God will render to every man according to his deeds, Rom. ii.6. That if we are Christ's, then are we Abraham's seed, and heirs according to the promise, Gal. iii.29. And that *the only restoration of Israel, yet future, is the restoration of the saints to the earth, created anew, when God shall open the graves of those descendants of Abraham who died in faith*, without receiving the promise, with the believing Gentiles who have been grafted in with them into the same olive tree; and shall cause them to come up out of their graves, and bring them, with the living, who are changed, into the land of Israel, Ezek. xxxvii.12, Heb. xi.12, 13, Rom. xi.17, John v.28, 29.[19] [Emphasis mine.]

The same document, signed by William Miller as Chairman, includes some resolutions, two of which I give here in part:

> ***Resolved,*** That we consider the doctrine of the restoration of the natural Jews, as a nation, either *before* or *after* the second advent of Christ, as heirs and inheritors of the land of Canaan, as subversive of the whole Gospel system, by raising up what Christ has broken down, namely, the middle wall of partition between the Jew and Gentile.... We feel bound, therefore, as we value the fundamental principles of the gospel, to enter our most solemn protest against all such teaching.... ***Resolved,*** That...we have no fellowship for Jewish fables and commandments of men, that turn from the truth, or for any of the distinctive characteristics of modern Judaism....[20]

Opposition and Discussion

As Marsh began to promote the age to come in 1850, he faced strong and direct opposition. Joshua V. Himes labeled Marsh's views as "Judaism" and considered it a defection incompatible with Adventism.[21] Of this time, Neuffer writes, "Indeed, the winds of doctrine developed hurricane force in 1850 among the Adventists—especially the majority group—over the 'age to come'."[22]

I.C. Wellcome observes that "Judaism" was taught earlier by the "Literalists" in 1842 and calls it a "distracting influence" as he writes:

> The first question that produced a distracting influence among the hitherto united Adventists

was 'Judaism,' which taught the conversion and restoration of the natural Jews. A free and full discussion of this was permitted in the 'Signs of the times;' but after a long and wordy debate, the advocates of the Jews finding that they could not convince their opponents, and that the paper was not made subservient to their purposes, commenced the publication of the '*American Millennarian*,' in Boston, in the summer of 1842.[23]

These questions at issue were much discussed and promoted in our Age-to-Come periodicals both in articles and in dialogue. The restoration of Israel or what was called, "The Jew Question" filled many pages of print. In addition to the J.B. Cook / L.D. Mansfield discussion in *The Advent Harbinger*, there are three other series that we are aware of: 1) Hiram V. Reed / Nathaniel Field in *The Prophetic Watchman & Herald of the Kingdom* and *The Gospel Banner & Millennial Advocate*; 2) George Moyer / Nathaniel Field in *The Millennial Harbinger & Bible Expositor*; and 3) James M. Stephenson, et. al. / G.B. Stacy in *The Gospel Banner & Millennial Advocate*.

The "Age to Come" was labeled by its opposers as "heresy." One popular rebuttal to these charges was an article by H.V. Reed in an 1864 issue of *The Gospel Banner and Millennial Advocate*—"*The Age-to-Come Not A Heresy."* This was later widely circulated in leaflet format.

In my possession is a photocopy of a 109 page record of a debate on the restoration of Israel between John A. Cargile of Stevenson, Alabama (Advent Christian) and Dr. T. J. Daniel of Magazine, Arkansas (Church of God). The original is in the Atlanta Bible College archives.[24] The 1866 debate at the Old Union Church between J. M. Stephenson (Church of God) and P. T. Russell (Christian Church) covered these questions also.[25]

An address by Major J. Scott Phillips presented before the British Association of Science at Aberdeen appeared in the pages of *The Herald of the Coming Kingdom*, edited by Thomas Wilson (Vol. 1, No. 23, Dec. 1, 1868, pp. 558-565). It is concerning the millennial land inheritance of literal Israel wherein Ezekiel describes the lot of each of the twelve tribes--a division of the land among them which has never occurred in all their history. The Editor adds a note at the end that the entire text accompanied with maps and two articles he had published on "The Restoration of the Jews" (*The Herald of the Coming Kingdom*, vol. 1, no. 20, Oct. 15, 1868 and vol. 1, no. 21, Nov. 1, 1868) would be published together.[26] An extract from Philips' lecture appeared in G. M. Myers' book on the covenants.[27] After Thomas Wilson moved to California, he wrote and published a small, 24-page booklet entitled, "*A Review of Adventist Teaching on The Jew Question.*" It was subtitled, "Proving that the Return from Babylon was not a fulfillment of the Prophecies relating to their final return to the Holy Land." He advertised this in his periodical, *The Last Days*, as "A Review of Miles Grant, showing that the Restoration of Israel is still future." Wilson also advertized another booklet he wrote, "The Blindness of Adventists as to the Restoration of Israel" (16 pp.). Miles Grant was an Advent Christian and author of *Positive Theology* (464 pp., 1895) and *Two Resurrections and the Intervening Millennium* (16pp., 1886).

Among our early Age-to-Come writers of the Church of God who produced books addressing the subject of the kingdom of God which included the prophecies of the restoration of Israel in addition to Marsh, Stephenson, Myers and Thomas Wilson were Ralph V. Lyon, Wiley Jones, and Hiram V. Reed.[28] Among the Christadelphians were John Thomas, L. C. Thomas, Thos. Williams and R. C. Bingley.[29]

Two writers, in addition to Joshua V. Himes, Dr. Nathaniel Field and L. D. Mansfield, which specifically addressed what they called "Judaism" were Josiah Litch whose works were published by Joshua V. Himes and Joseph Harvey Waggoner whose works were published by *The Review & Herald*.[30] Later works putting forth the Millerite position, in addition to Hans K. LaRondelle, and Don & Julia Neuffer, Seventh Day Adventists, were Advent Christians, Miriam McKinstry, William N. Pile, Isaac C. Wellcome & Clarkson Goud and Clarence Hewitt & Orrin Roe Jenks.[31]

The opposition endeavored not only in print and pulpit to overcome the growing Age-to-Come movement, but also through organizational maneuvering and proselytizing tried to get control of the minds and devotions of men. Terry Ferrell records that "At the annual conference at 'Old Antioch' in 1875, the Advent Christian church under the leadership of Joshua Himes, made an attempt to capture the Indiana conference. Brother [Richard] Corbaley is credited with preventing the merger. One of the main points of difference was the restoration of Israel."[32]

The variant systems of hermeneutics and the resulting beliefs remain the watershed which defines organizational ties and associations. Each generation has to grapple with these issues as to how we should interpret the Scriptures and what things we should consequently believe. Our early leaders studied the biblical text thoroughly and took a stand to promote the Gospel of the Kingdom as comprehending the truths of the Age to Come, including the restoration of Israel.

Looking Back to Understand the Present

As we look at the whole of these things we see a watershed of three levels, each a result of the preceding one—the first effecting the second and the second effecting the third. These three are first, the hermeneutics which are both brought to and derive from the biblical text; second, the resultant doctrinal or theological understandings; and third, the organizational runoff of the preceding two. We illustrate it thus:

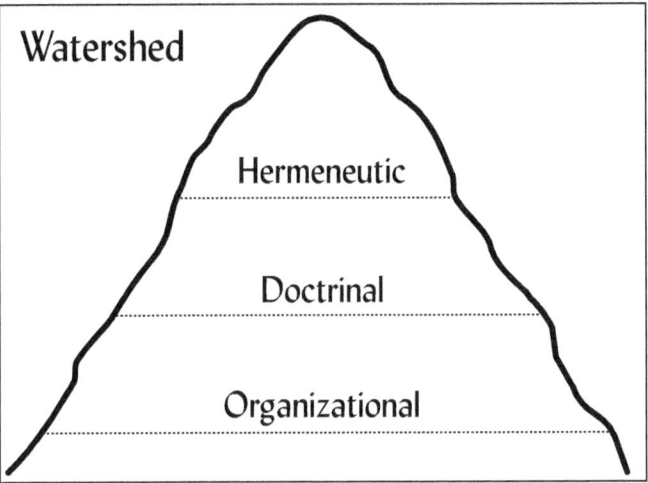

Now each of these three levels is a watershed in itself. The divide of the hermeneutic is seen in the adoption of either a predominantly allegorical or a predominantly literal system of interpretation. The resultant doctrinal positions relative to the issues of the restoration of Israel and future probation is seen in a denying or affirming of both—the allegorical denying; the literal affirming. The organizational is seen in the historical development of religious bodies or fellowships in which the points of separation can be broadly categorized within the advent movement as the Millerite versus the Age-to-Come positions. The extant groups which follow the *Millerite view* in a general way are the Advent Christians who are the closest to the original teachings of William Miller; the Seventh-day Adventists who additionally and adaptively follow the word of Ellen G. White; and the Jehovah's Witnesses who, following Rutherford, departed by 1929 from Russell's views on the age-to-come and aligned more closely to the views of Miller regarding Israel, though they are in many ways radically different in the general prophetic scenario espoused. Those extant groups which hold *Age-to-Come positions* regarding Israel, with variations relative to future probation are the Church of God Abrahamic Faith (General Conference and some independent congregations); the Christadelphians and those Abrahamic Faith brethren who are in close fellowship with them; the Church of God 7th Day (and its splinter groups—Salem, VA, Meridian, ID, Jerusalem); and those who maintain C.T. Russell's views (Dawn Bible Students, Laymen's Home Missionary Movement, Pastoral Bible Institute, etc.). These are broad and general connections, but have similar if not common origins.

The three watersheds are:

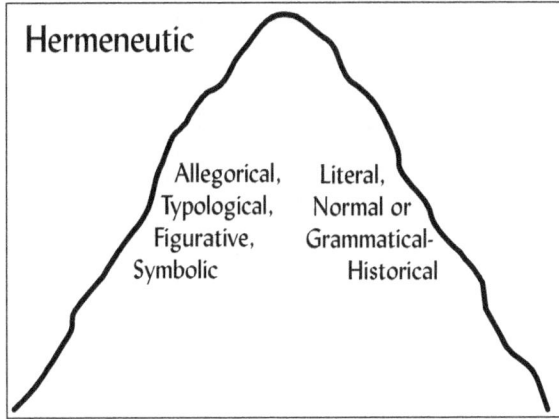

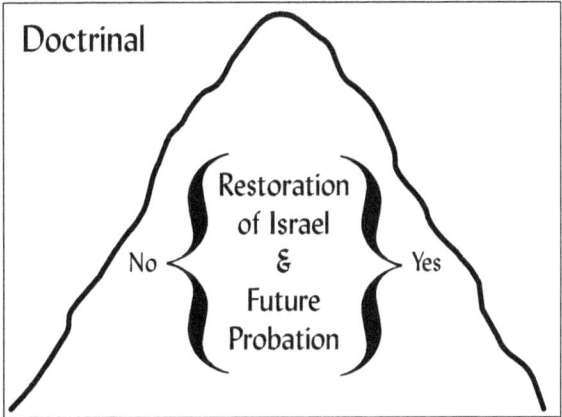

Endnotes
[1] Neuffer, Julia, *"The Gathering of Israel A Historical Study of Early Writings, pp. 74-76."* The entire text of her study can be viewed on the internet at: http://www.whiteestate.org/issues/gather.html
[2] The Church of God follows what is called the grammatical-historical or literal hermeneutic. The heirs of the Millerite tradition follow what is known as the allegorical-typological hermeneutic. One might note a like comparative distinction in hermeneutic between the dispensational-premillennial school which has a future literality for national Israel and the amillennial-preterist perspective which denies any future for Israel. The Millerite hermeneutic is explained thoroughly by LaRondelle, Hans K., *The Israel of God in Prophecy*, Berrien Springs, MI: Andrews University Press, 1978.
[3] Those who deny the literality of the restoration of Israel approach it

with one or more of the following propositions:
— Promises of restoration or inheritance are historically fulfilled;
— Promises were conditional and when conditions were not met they were nullified;
— Promises are to be spiritualized as applying to the Church who is the true "Israel of God";
— Promises will be realized through individual future resurrection.

[4] Marsh, Joseph, *The Bible Doctrine or True Gospel Faith concerning the gathering of Israel, the millennium, personal coming of Christ, resurrection, renovation of the earth, kingdom of God, and time of the second advent of Christ*, Rochester, N.Y.: The Advent Harbinger & Bible Advocate Office, 1849. A work by N. M. Catlin who affiliated with the Church of God puts forth the Church as subjects of the millennial reign--Catlin, Nicolas Mead, *The Kingdom of God: or, The Restoration of David's Throne*, 1850.

[5] Marsh, Joseph, *The Age to Come, or Glorious Restitution of all things spoken of by the mouth of all the holy prophets since the world began*, Rochester, N.Y.: The Advent Harbinger Office, 1851.

[6] Neuffer, op. cit.

[7] Mattison, Mark "Joseph Marsh's Doctrinal Development and Conflicts with Christadelphianism," *A Journal for the Radical Reformation*, Winter 1993, Vol. 2, No. 2, p. 41-50.

[8] Jan Stilson, "An Overview of the Leadership and Development of the Age to Come in the United States: 1832-1871," *A Journal for the Radical Reformation*, Fall 2001, Vol. 10, No. 1, p. 20.

[9] Smith, Elias, *Sermons Containing an Illustration of the Prophecies to be accomplished from the present time, until the new heavens and earth are created, when all the prophecies will be fulfilled*, Portsmouth, N.H.: Elias Smith; printed by Norris & Sawyer, 1808.

[10] Neuffer, op. cit.

[11] Cf. *The Advent Harbinger*, vol. 2, nos. 8, 10, 11 (August 10, 24, 31, 1850). The propositions under discussion were four:
1. There are promises of special blessings to the Jews as a people, which remain un-accomplished, but are to be fulfilled in 'The Age to Come,' or the Great Sabbath;
2. At the establishment of God's Kingdom, all the wicked of the earth will be destroyed, and the kingdom will be, from its establishment, both universal in extent and eternal in duration;
3. There will be probation in 'The Age to Come,' and men will repent and obtain pardon. 'The Age to Come,' it is agreed, begins at the Advent;
4. The New Heavens and Earth, and the New Jerusalem from Heaven, will be developed at the commencement of the millennial reign.
Cook affirmed propositions 1 and 3; Mansfield affirmed 2 and 4

[12] Winchester, Elhanan, *A Course of Lectures on the Prophecies that Remain to be Fulfilled: Delivered in the Borough of Southwark—as also, at the Chapel in Glass House Yard in the years MDCCLXXXVIII, IX, XC*, London: Philadelphia Society, 1789-1790, 4 vols. Each lecture (9-18) consisted of brief statements of introduction followed by a recitation of the Scripture texts.

[13] Smith, op. cit., p. III

[14] Marsh, Joseph, *The Expositor and Advocate*, 1857-1859. H.V. Reed later published at least one article by Elhanan Winchester in *The Millenarian*, Vol. 1, Nos. 8-9, Sept., 1874, entitled "Christ's Universal Kingdom."

[15] Cited by Greg Demmitt in "One Way or One Faith?" a paper presented at the Second Annual Church of God History Conference, Springfield, Ohio, November, 2007, p. 8.

[16] Marsh Joseph, "Literal Interpretation—The Bible Examiner," *The Expositor and Advocate*, August 15 and September 1, 1857.

[17] Cf. pp. 12-18. A copy of this work is available from the Church of God General Conference, or on-line at:
http://www.timberlandbiblechurch.org/AgeToCome/Age%20to%20Come.htm or
http://www.mun.ca/rels/restmov/texts/jmarsh/ATC.HTM

[18] Cited by Wellcome, Isaac C., *History of the Second Advent Message and Mission, Doctrine and People*, Yarmouth, ME: I. C. Wellcome; Boston: Advent Christian Publication Society, 1874. [p. 53].

[19] Ibid., p. 417.

[20] Ibid., p. 422, 423.

[21] Cf. Joseph Marsh, "The Age to Come," part 1, *Advent Harbinger*, n.s. 1:228, Jan. 5, 1851, cited by Julia Neuffer, Op. Cit. She provides an extended discussion of Marsh's views and the "Age-to-Come Controversy" and "The Adventist Reply."

[22] Neuffer, op. cit.

[23] Wellcome, op. cit., p. 385.

[24] *The Cargile-Daniel Discussion Concerning the Question of the Literal Return of the Jews to Palestine*, Boston: Advent Christian Publication Society, n.d. [John A. Cargile / T. J. Daniels].

[25] Stephenson, James M. and P. T. Russell, *A Report of a Public Discussion Between J. M. Stephenson and P. T. Russell. Subject: Kingdom of God on Earth*, Indianapolis: Downing & Brouse, 1866. Stephenson additionally writes on this in his *God's Plan of Salvation, or, His Purpose Concerning Man and Earth*, Canton, Ohio: A. D. Eshelman, 1877. Also, *The Herald of Messiah's Reign; or The Glad Tidings of the kingdom of God, as taught in the sacred oracles*, Chicago: The Office of The Herald of the Coming Kingdom, 1868.

[26] Wilson, Thomas, *Curious and Original Discoveries, Concerning the Re-Settlement of the Seed of Abraham in Syria and Arabia, with Mathematical and Geographical Proofs*, Chicago, 1879. Nathaniel West in a footnote refers to an edition of this as being published by Thos. Wilson, Chicago, in 1879. West was discussing "the redistribution and division of the Holy Land being made according to the 12 tribes of Israel" in his book, *The Thousand Years in Both Testaments*, Fincastle, Virginia: Scripture Truth Book Company, 1889.

[27] Myers, G. M., *The Covenants and Their Relationship*, Lanark, Illinois: Gazette Publishing House, 1882, pp. 28-33.

[28] Lyon, Ralph Vinton, *The Glorious Future! The Kingdom of God! Or The Reign of Christ and His Cabinet*, Suspension Bridge, N.Y.: R. V. Lyon, 186?; Lyon, R, V., *The Scattering and Restoration of Israel*, Seneca Falls, N.Y.: Office of the Millennial Harbinger, 1861; Lyon, R. V., *The Sanctuary*, Seneca Falls, N.Y.: Office of the Millennial Harbinger, 1863; Jones, Wiley, *The Gospel of the Kingdom, advocated in a series of ten discourses*, Norfolk, Va.: Virginian Steam Presses, 1879; Jones, W., *Evangelism Concerning the Reign of Christ over Israel and the Nations*, Chicago: printed at The Restitution Office, 1872; Reed, Hiram Vaughn, *The Kingdom of God or, The Reign of Christ on Earth, as Revealed in the Holy Scriptures*, Seneca Falls, N.Y.: Office of the Millennial Harbinger 1861.

[29] Thomas, John, *Elpis Israel: An Exposition of the Kingdom of God*, Birmingham: The Christadelphian, 1958 [originally written 1848-1850]; Thomas, L. C., *The law, the Covenants, and the Sabbath; also, An Epitome of the Great Salvation*, Dover, Delaware: The Author, 1883; Williams, Thomas, *The World's Redemption According to the Eternal Plan*, Richmond, Virginia: The Advocate Committee, 1953, fourth edition, [Written 1898]; Williams, T., *Seven Nights Discussion Between Mr. Clark Braden and Mr. Thos. Williams*, Englewood, Ill.: Advocate Publishing House, 1894; Bingley, R. C., *Index Rerum: A Ready Reference on Biblical Subjects*, Los Angeles: The Author, 1890.

[30] Litch, Josiah, *Judaism Overthrown: or, The Kingdom Restored to the True Israel, with the Scripture Evidence of the Epoch of the Kingdom in 1843*, Boston: J. V. Himes, 1843 (38 p.); Waggoner, Joseph Harvey, *The Kingdom of God: An Examination of the Prophecies Relative to the Time and Manner of its Establishment, or A Refutation of the Doctrine of the Age to Come*, Battle Creek, Mich.: Steam Press of the Review and Herald Office, 1859 (167 p.)

[31] Neufeld, Don F. and Julia Neuffer, *Seventh-day Adventist Bible Students' Source Book*, Washington, D.C., 1962; McKinstry, Miriam, *Fallacies of Future Probation*, Boston, Mass.: Advent Christian Publication Society, n.d. ; Pile, William N., *Israel in Prophecy, or Will the Jews be Restored as a Nation*, Boston, The Advent Christian Publication Society, 1902; Wellcome, Isaac C. and Clarkson Goud, *The Plan of Redemption by our Lord Jesus Christ*, Philadelphia: Bible Banner Office, 1879; Hewitt, Clarence & Orrin Roe Jenks, *The Two Israels* (a syllabus of 21 lessons), Aurora, Illinois: The Advent Christian General Conference, n.d.

[32] Ferrell, Terry, *A Brief History of the Church of God in America*, a series of lessons presented at the National Berean Youth Conference at Camp Reynoldswood, Dixon, Illinois, August, 1960, p. 6.

Appendix 2

Bitter Disappointment

Excerpts of
When Time Was Supposed to Be No More
by Kent H. Ross, BTh, MTh, Academic Dean (ret.), Atlanta Bible College

Background to the Millerite Movement

The entire area of upstate New York was fertile soil for the fervent, passionate message of the literal return of Jesus to this earth. The ground had been fertilized by Charles Finney, and other revivalists, in what Whitney Cross termed "The Burned-Over District." The area had been covered by evangelists since the early 1820s, culminating in the great revivals in Rochester in 1829.

Not limited to upstate New York, William Miller began his work in Low Hampton, Vermont. His local lectures caught the spirit of the area, termed "Ultraist" by Cross, where any new view was latched onto with great enthusiasm. With J. V. Himes trumpeting Miller, the cause moved on to Boston, Philadelphia and New York City.

Originally Miller was reluctant to set dates, but pressed, he finally said he felt and was confident that Jesus would return literally in the year sometime between March 21, 1843 to March 21, 1844. When that date passed there was real disappointment, but they had not yet generated the excitement and frenzy that would come later, and when they, subsequently, would fall from an even greater height.

In the February 15, 1844; issue of the *Voice of Truth* (Joseph Marsh, editor) Miller wrote, and we excerpt:

> Dear Brethren, Time rolls on his restless course. We are one year down its rapidstream towards the ocean of eternity. We have passed what the world calls the last round of 1843, and already they begin to shout (victor) over us. Are you ready to give up your hope in the blessed appearing of Jesus Christ?...Never has my faith been stronger than at this very moment. I feel confident the Savior will come and in this true Jewish year; in 2300 days in the decree given ... I have never preached nor believed in any time for Christ to come but the end of the prophetic periods, which I have always believed would end with this Jewish year; and which I still believe, and mean, with the help of God, to look for until he comes.

This citation evidences the confidence of the movement as March 21, 1844, approached. It would be the end of time, as they understood the Bible to teach, as Miller articulated. In this same issue Joseph Marsh wrote, "The Advent cause has now nearly reached the great crisis in its unparalleled history. The 'fullness' of all the prophetic 'times' will soon be complete; then all things in Christ will be gathered together in him." None will be gathered, in that glorious morn, but those who will be found 'purified, and made white, and tried.'"

As they believed the return of Jesus was just over one month away, they continued to press their case in preaching and reaching others. In this same issue is an advertisement of a Second Advent Conference to be held in Rochester at Talman Hall on the first Wednesday in March.

In the March 22, 1844, issue of the *Voice of Truth* Elon Galusha wrote, "To those who believe the end in high: Dear brethren, be watchful, be prayerful, be humble, be holy: believe all that God has spoken, do all he has commanded. Breathe a spirit of kindness to all, avoid the spirit of controversy, pray and labor for the salvation of sinners. Fix not your faith on March or April, but on the Jewish year 1843, which, should it prove to be a civil instead of sacred year, may extend to September."

Marsh himself wrote in that same issue, "We have laid over some valuable communications, which were designed for this number, to give place to Elder Galusha's article. The Lord wills, our next number will be issued immediately after this is sent out. What we now do must be done quickly, for the Lord is truly at hand. Be ready to meet him."

Immediately their world changed, by not changing! Their world had changed, but not as they had expected. Christ had not come and there was so little that they could say in response to the bitter taunts from those who just hours before had begged the Adventists to pray for their salvation. Now, with great relief, those same people who had cried for mercies became merciless in their biting sarcasm, asking "Haven't you gone up?"

The Day Passed. Jane Marsh, young daughter of Joseph Marsh, a leading Millerite editor, wrote later in "The Little Millerite" for *Century* magazine, (December 1886) that she feared as that day approached, that she had not been saved. As her father lay ill in bed, too exhausted from his labors for the Lord to rise, she clung to him in despair. "If anybody was saved I knew he would be and that he would never shake me from his arms into the fire….I meant to have a firm hold on him when the crisis arrived."

Their disappointment must have been unbearable, and for some simply unacceptable. Many kept watching the skies from day to day; desperately hoping that Miller had made a small mistake in calculation and that Jesus would come today or tomorrow.

Their disappointment and their ensuring embarrassment must have been unimaginable. To have to go out into the streets, or to the homes of relatives, or to their place of business, and face those who had not shared their hope was a burden beyond understanding.

When Marsh resumed publishing the *Voice of Truth* on November 7th, he began with an explanation copied from the *Advent Herald*:

> We have been mistaken in the belief to which we thought ourselves conducted by word and the Spirit, and Providence of God. But, the Word stands sure, however we may err; and the promise is true. We have an unwavering trust that He will cause our disappointment and trial to work for our good.

In the January issue of the *Voice of Truth*, Joseph Marsh posted the Present Principles on which the Advent cause is based.

1st The word of God teaches that the coming of Christ is yet future; that it will be personal and visible. Acts 3:20,21; Acts 1:10, Rev. 1:7

2nd It teaches that his coming is near, even at the door. Matt. 24:29-33; Mark 13:24-29; Luke 21:25-31.

3rd It teaches also that this present generation will witness his glorious appearing. Matt. 24:34; Luke 21:32.

4th The prophetic periods that reach to the cleansing of the sanctuary, and the resurrection of the saints, have nearly expired. Dan. 5:13, 14; Ezra 7:12, 13, 21; Dan. 12:11, 12, 13.

5th According to the visions of Daniel, the next great prophetical events are the coming of the Son of Man, the destruction of the brazen image representing earthly kingdoms, the burning of the fourth beast with the little horn representing Papal government, and the establishment of the kingdom of God. Dan. 2:23, 25, 44, 45; Dan. 7:7-14.

6th According to Revelations of John, the sixth trumpet has sounded, and the second woe is past; the seventh trumpet is now sounding, and the third woe cometh quickly, when the kingdoms of this world will become the kingdoms of our Lord and his Christ, and he shall reign forever. Rev. 9:13,-21; 10:5-11; 11:14-18.

Joseph Marsh and others refused to attend the Albany Conference in 1845, and began from that point on, to study, and publish their studies, on the little-known age to come and restitution of all things in Marsh's papers, and many other religious papers of the day.

The full text of this article may be read at http://www.abc-coggc.org/jrad.html. Select Spring 2003 for Part 1 and Summer 2003 for Part 2.

Additional Reading:

Ahlstrom, Sydney. *Religion in America*. Yale. 1980.

Cross, Whitney. *The Burned Over District*. Cornell University (Ithaca, NY). 1950.

Hewitt, Clyde E. *Midnight and Morning*. Venture Books. (Charlotte, NC) 1983.

Himes, Joshua V. Editor of *Advent Herald* (Boston, Ma.) 1844-1846

Marsh, Joseph. Editor of *Christian Palladium*, 1838-1843); editor of *Voice of Truth*, (1844-1847).

Parker, Jane Marsh. "The Little Millerite," *Century Illustrated Monthly Magazine*. Dec. 1886. p. 316.

Appendix 3

Catalyst for Change: Martyrdom

Excerpts of
Church History
by Lyman Booth
Reprinted from The Restitution Herald, *April 24, 1934.*

> **Annotation:** *Lyman Booth was baptized into Christ at the Antioch Church of God in Ogle County, Illinois. He wrote a Church of God history from his personal experience, including the amazing ministry and death of David M. Hudler.*

Among the ministers who visited Antioch Church in Ogle County, Illinois, I recall the names of R. Corbaley, J.T. Whitsitt, John Howell, and George Moyer. From September 21-23, 1866, a conference was held at this place in the new and unfinished church building. Brethren from eight other localities met and reported their work. Antioch had 4 members in 1860 and on this date there were 25. They had services every Sunday. Paynes Point met every two weeks, present membership 10. Silver Creek met every Sunday, with preaching every two weeks, membership 21. Pine Creek, membership 15. Lanark met every two weeks, number 9. Plum River was not reported in full, but their number was not less than 15. Twin Grove, members 10. Mt. Pleasant, Wisconsin, was not reported, although C.W. Tompkins was present. Dixon had no state preaching. Though some had moved away their membership was 10.

I obtained the above from the minutes of the meeting which were published in The Prophetic Watchman, edited by J. M. Stephenson and H. V. Reed, and published at Harvard, Illinois, Bro. Reed's home town. In some of the above locality none of the members now reside. They have either died or moved away.

> **Annotation:** *Here follows a very interesting description and interpretation of Church of God vitality from the years 1880 or so until 1892. This is especially interesting in light of the fact that a General Conference was formed in Philadelphia and sustained from 1888-1892.*

For a few years previous to 1891 the Church of God seems to have gone to sleep. No conferences were convened. Several places of worship were closed and many members scattered to various points. Most of the interest in church work seemed to have died out. But in 1892 there was a shaking of the dry bones, and awaking of the slumbering ones to action. The party who sounded the alarm that woke the brotherhood to renewed activity was none other than Brother David M. Hudler, from Davenport, Iowa, of whom it may be told, he was a devout and most earnest worker for the Master.

I will give his biography, in brief, as he gave it to me. He had been a careful and thoughtful student of the Bible, had attended other churches but could not harmonize their doctrines to the Scriptures. He struggled along for many years in this unsettled frame of mind until finally he learned of Brother Levi H. Chase's address, which he obtained from reading an article written by Brother Chase which expressed views so different from any preaching he had ever heard. Wishing to learn more about this new found doctrine, he decided to send an invitation to Brother Chase to visit him and to preach a few sermons. The arrangements were made and Brother Chase went to Davenport and to Brother Hudler's home [Muscatine, Iowa], which was a short distance from the city. Services were conducted in a near by schoolhouse. The result of the services was that Brother Hudler was immersed.

Before Brother Chase returned to his home, he gave Brother Hudler the address of Brother J.M. Glotfelty at Lanark, as the nearest member of the Church of God. Brother Hudler decided that he would go to Lanark, which he did, and there he began his preaching career. From Brother Glotfelty he learned of brethren in Dixon, Antioch, Chicago, and other localities. He visited these three places in the order given. From the brethren at these churches he learned of the past flourishing condition of the churches and the splendid conferences throughout the territory. He also learned that the zeal and activity in such matters were but a memory. Immediately he began encouraging the brotherhood to convene at some suitable place to discuss the question of organizing a state conference. The brethren (a few of them) agreed, and Lanark was the place selected. Although there were but few present the conference was organized with Brother James Wilson of Chicago as president and myself as secretary. I cannot at this time name the members of the board.

There was some discussion about employing some one as evangelist, but no decision was made on account of the means of support. I believe it was a year later arrangements were perfected and Brother Hudler was employed. He served two years, and then traveled as far south as New Orleans. In the South he met with bitter opposition to such an extent that he was boldly persecuted. But, like Paul, no opposition, no matter how bitter, no persecution, however severe, could deter him from preaching the Word. I believe, if my memory serves me correctly, that he died some place in Kentucky [Harriman, Tennessee], where his preaching aroused the animosity of some of the citizens to such a degree that it was considered by some that his death was caused by evil agencies. He became suspicious that he was being foully treated, for he wrote to a brother, (cannot recall his name) [O.J. Allard] "to come get me or they will kill me." The brother went to his aid, but found he had died. The brother had him returned to his family.

When Brother Hudler came into the state he found the church in general very feeble, but he lived to see it revived and in a growing condition. Although he has gone from among us his labors follow. His work may be compared to a pebble thrown into a pool. The wave it causes is small at first, but it continues to expand till it reaches the shore. Though his work began at Lanark, it began to grow and expand until it reached to the boundary of the states. Today the field he first began to cultivate, and in which he scattered the good seed of the kingdom, presents a striking and happy contrast, the center of attraction being at Oregon, where annually many congregate to worship Him who is the light and life of those who seek Him.

Brethren, please do not think for a moment that this glorious result has been attained by any one person. Though one made the initial move there have been others who have been loyal and labored arduously and are deserving of much credit. If the giving of a cup of water in the Master's name to a thirsty soul is worthy of a reward, how much greater shall it be for those who through years of toil and self-denial have striven to scatter sunshine and roses along life's pathway that leads to the land of promise and the home of the good of all ages. May their names be remembered and their labors richly rewarded when the King in His beauty shall crown them with victory and clothe them with the vestments of His holiness.

Appendix 4 - Chronology: Pathways of Faith
US Map

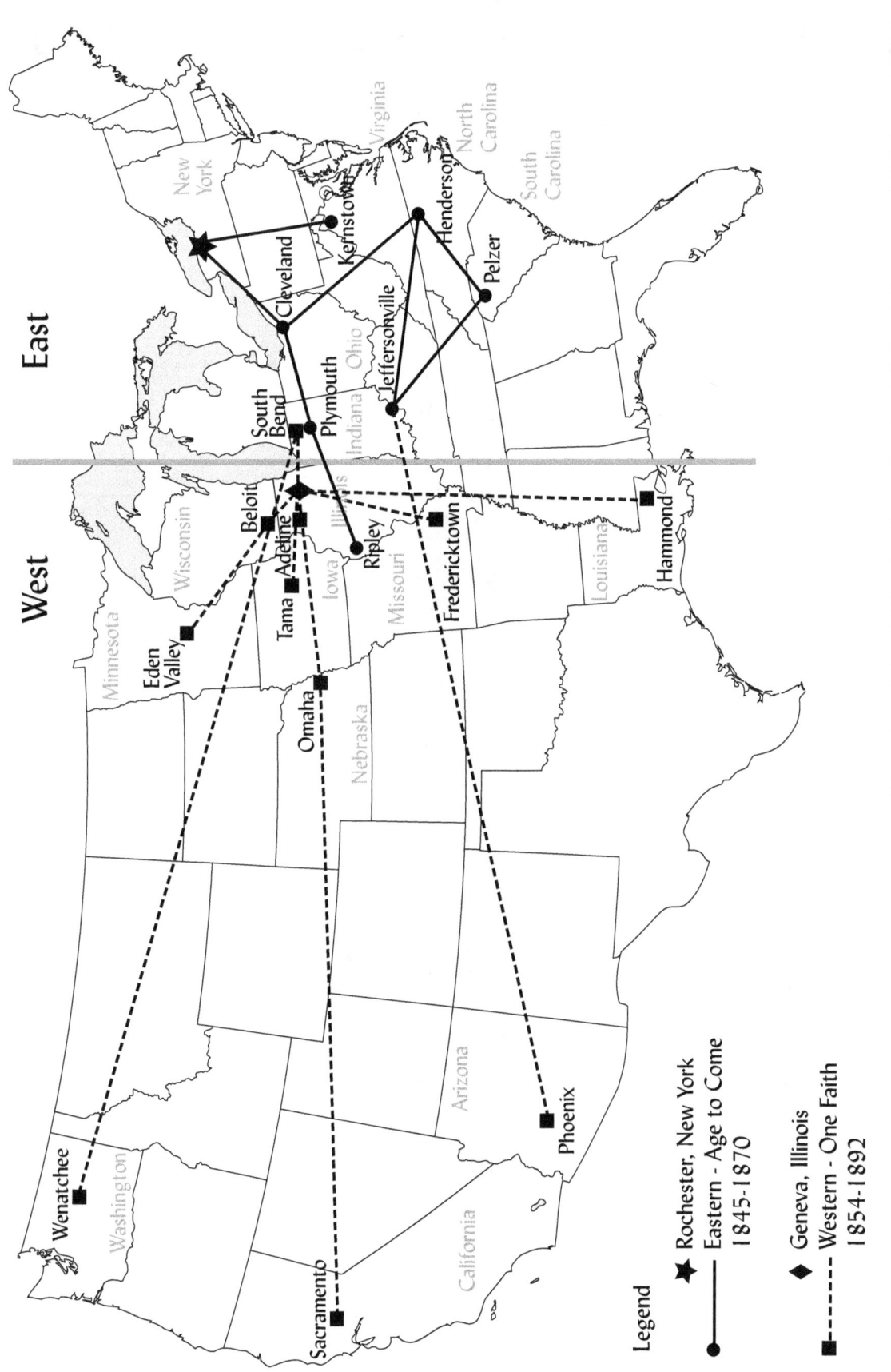

Appendix 4
Chronology: Pathways of Faith

Eastern Churches	Year	Western Churches
Joseph Priestly flees England, settles in America. Begins teaching Oneness of God and Age to Come.	1794	
Smith and Abner Jones form loose fellowship of churches known as Christian Connexion representing Oneness of God and Christian Liberty.	1803	
Elias Smith publishes *Herald of Gospel Liberty*.	1808	
Joseph Marsh begins preaching for Christian Connexion.	1818	
Marsh becomes editor of *The Christian Palladium*. Writes series on Church of God as name for the church.	1839	
George Storrs distributes *Six Sermons* that teach Conditional Immortality.	1841	
Nathaniel Field and Dr. John Thomas study Age to Come.	1843	
Marsh begins the *Voice of Truth* to advance teachings of Adventism. October 22: The Bitter Disappointment.	1844	Benjamin and James Wilson arrive in Geneva, Illinois
William Miller calls Albany Conference. Marsh, Storrs and others absent.	1845	
Marsh changes titles and begins publishing *The Advent Harbinger*.	1847	
	1850	Wilson brothers decide to leave the Restoration Movement.
April 9: Union Conference, Rochester, NY, called by Marsh/Age to Come. April 23: Union Conference, NY City, called by Weethee/Age to Come. Ephraim Miller preaches Age to Come at Old Union Church, Indiana. Marsh publishes book, *Age to Come*.	1851	
	1852	B. Wilson publishes *Guardian and Advocate* one year.
	1853	B. Wilson inquires of Marsh about providing copy for *Advent Harbinger*. B. Wilson begins translating the New Testament from Greek. B. Wilson begins *The Gospel Banner* and continues it until 1869.
Indiana State Conference forms around Adventist and Age to Come ideas.	1854	
Marsh begins publishing *The Prophetic Expositor and Bible Advocate*.	1855	
Michigan State Conference forms primarily around Age to Come and First Day worship.	1858	
Formation of Advent Christian denomination in Salem, MA.	1860	
Marsh preaches his last sermon at Indiana State Conference. September: Marsh dies.	1863	
Marsh's press is moved to Harvard, IL, and then Chicago.	1864	
	1868	Thomas Wilson begins *Herald of the Coming Kingdom* in Chicago. Letters from evangelists in Alabama, Mississippi, Arkansas and Missouri arrive at *The Gospel Banner*.
	1869	B. Wilson's *The Gospel Banner* merges with *Herald of the Coming Kingdom*. Northwest Christian Association forms in Illinois, predecessor to Church of God General Conference.
N. Field leaves Indiana Conference over Restoration of the Jews issue.	1870	B. Wilson relocates to Sacramento, CA. T. Wilson ceases publishing *Herald of the Coming Kingdom* and begins *The Restitution* in Chicago.
Chicago Fire: Marsh press, stock of bound *Heralds* and *Restitutions* lost.	1871	
The Restitution moves to Plymouth, IN; HV Reed and SA Chaplin, Editors.	1872	
Richard Corbaley and JM Stephenson block JV Himes from seizing Indiana Conference for Advent Christians.	1875	Thomas and Lillie Wilson move to Oakland, CA.
Evangelists spread the Word but local churches and state conferences languish.	1880	
Organization of The General Conference of the Churches of God in Christ Jesus in Philadelphia by delegates from eastern and western churches.	1888-1892	

Chronology: Pathways of Faith
Part 2 of 4

Eastern Churches	Year	Western Churches
	1892	Arrival of visionary DM Hudler awakens the churches. Many state conferences reorganize *new* conferences, including Michigan, Iowa, Indiana, Illinois, Ohio and Minnesota.
	1895	WH Wilson, S Oliver, J Fisk, JJ Heckman push the work across Oklahoma, Kansas and the Great Plains.
	1899	Thomas Wilson begins publishing *The Last Days*, continues for 27 years.
	1900	Almus Adams emerges as the great evangelist across the Great Plains and the western United States. Universalism begins to surface across Iowa. In Texas, AS Bradley and William Gibbs cross over to Church of God from Church of Christ and shake up Texas on issue of conditional immortality. SJ Lindsay begins mentoring young men as printers, publishers and preachers in Oregon, IL, one at a time, an early informal apprenticing program, including Robert Huggins, FE Siple, Paul Hatch, Clyde Randall and Val Mattison.
	1906	The Word spreads from Arizona to Washington through the work of WL Skeels. Gibbs, editor of *The Word and Work* in Texas, dies. Universalism begins to creep in. SJ Lindsay publishes *The Bible Lessons* and distributes them to subscribers.
	1910	Earnest attempt is made to wrest control of *The Restitution* from AR Underwood. Resentement surfaces among readers. SJ Lindsay begins The Summer Bible Training Classes of six weeks at Oregon, IL, for teenagers and young adults. The purpose is to study and serve. Attempt to organize a General Conference in Waterloo, IA, fails. The Ministerial Association forms in Cleveland, OH, under LE Conner's leadership.
	1911	*The Restitution Herald*, SJ Lindsay editor, begins publishing in Oregon, IL, with approval of The Ministerial Association.
	1913	The National Berean Society of young adults forms and begins distributing lesson materials.
Torrey, Dixon and Myers write *The Fundamentals* which becomes the voice of conservative Christians in America. The Church of God takes their basic tenets to heart excepting trinity and natural immortality. Church of God delegates begin asking for a national conference.	1917	
	1920	Committee of Ten is formed to plan a general conference organizational strategy for implementation at the 1921 Waterloo Conference.
	1921	The Church of God General Conference comes into being after ratification by all state conferences doing business at The National Bible Institute with headquarters in Oregon, IL.
	1923-1932	Bible Training Class opens at Oregon, IL. Closes due to Great Depression.
	1938	Sydney E. Magaw assumes editorship of *The Restitution Herald* and becomes General Manager of the General Conference.
	1939	Bible Training class resumes and becomes Oregon Bible College in 1941.
	1942	Ministers' wives organize as The Priscillas, an auxiliary group to plan and implement service projects.
	1943	Oregon Bible College obtains its new rural campus north of Oregon, IL.
	1946	James Watkins becomes General Manager of the National Bible Institute, business arm of the General Conference.
	1947	*Songs of Truth* hymnal is published.

Chronology: Pathways of Faith
Part 3 of 4

Eastern Churches	Year	Western Churches
	1949	Otto E. Dick Sr. becomes Instructor and Superintendent of Oregon Bible College.
	1950	Oregon Bible College Relocates to new campus on North Third St. in Oregon, IL. December 26: Sydney and Margaret Magaw die in auto accident, plunging the denomination into grief.
	1951	CE Lapp arrives at Oregon Bible College as Instructor. Otto Dick becomes President.
	1954	Harold Doan replaces James Watkins as editor and General Conference Executive Secretary.
	1955-1965	**Decade of Development:** Growth and development in many areas of the denomination.
	1956	Child Evangelist Verna Thayer retires from publishing children's quarterlies and conducting vacation Bible schools.
	1958	Mission Builders League begins to assist with fundraising for local church construction projects.
	1960	Alva Huffer publishes the first edition of *Systematic Theology*. Commitment to explore and develop foreign missions begins.
	1961	Stanley O. Ross is hired as Superintendent of Missions.
	1963	Dean Moore begins to investigate the possibility of missions in Mexico. *Songs of Truth Two* is published. Oregon Bible College builds a men's dormitory that includes a library and dining hall.
	1964-1967	Vivian Kirkpatrick Sr. becomes Instructor and Librarian at Oregon Bible College.
	1967-1988	Eugene Stilson becomes Instructor and Academic Dean at Oregon Bible College.
	1968-1975	Dr. Alva Huffer is President of Oregon Bible College.
	1969	SO Ross becomes Executive Secretary of General Conference. Rachel Krogh becomes Superintendent of Missions.
	1974	May 14: First Christian Worker's Seminar held in Tennessee.
	1975	Oregon Bible College constructs the Women's Apartment Building on campus.
	1976	Clyde Randall writes *Historical Waymarks of the Church of God*.
	1979	OBC President John and Ruth Lewis die in auto accident with Russell Reye of the General Conference; the denomination is shocked and grief-stricken. Russell Magaw becomes Director of Publishing at the General Conference.
	1980	Jan Turner Stilson becomes Librarian and Archivist at Oregon Bible College. The Golden Rule building is renovated to accommodate classrooms and administrative offices. *Psalms, Hymns and Spiritual Songs* hymnal is published.
	1980-1985	Dr. Charles Pryor serves as OBC President.
	1980-1989	Warren Sorrenson joins the General Conference as Missions Coordinator to implement church plantings and expand foreign missions.
	1980-2000	Executive Director David Krogh launches a church-planting initiative to begin new congregations and strengthen state conferences. Over 40 churches are planted.

Chronology: Pathways of Faith
Part 4 of 4

Eastern Churches	Year	Western Churches
	1980-2002	Kent Ross becomes Instructor at Oregon Bible College.
	1982	Sir Anthony Buzzard becomes Instructor at OBC, missionary and author.
	1984	First edition of *The History Newsletter* is published, Jan Turner Stilson, Editor. Later, Kent Ross becomes editor.
	1985	October: *75th Anniversary Issue of The Restitution Herald* is published, Russell Magaw, Editor.
	1985-2001	David Krogh named President of Oregon/Atlanta Bible College.
	1990	Delegates approve relocating the General Conference and Bible college to Atlanta, Georgia.
	1990-2000	Kent Ross serves as Academic Dean of Atlanta Bible College.
Bible college campus relocates to Morrow, Georgia.	1991	
Mission work in Africa opens, leading to the formation of African Malawi Mission Agency, Jim Mattison, Director.	1992	
Delegates approve formation of mission-sending agency Lord's Harvest International, Judy Myers, Director.	1993	
Ministerial License and Ordination Board is renamed Minister's Recognition Board with new guidelines for continuing education. Mission work for Haiti under direction of Pastor Lesli Bertrand becomes part of Lord's Harvest International Mission Work.	1994	
Gary Burnham becomes Controller of the General Conference. Presently, he is Operations Manager and Ministry Services Network Director.	1995	
Jon Cheatwood becomes Youth Coordinator to plan publications, retreats, conferences and adult services for youth.	1999	
US Immigration and Naturalization Service approves Atlanta Bible College to educate foreign students. ABC Korean Extension Campus begins under direction of Pastor Steve An.	2002	
Kent Ross and Jan Turner Stilson coordinate first Church of God History Conference and organize History Committee. Youth Department's RYOT program becomes FUEL program.	2003	
Atlanta Bible College campus relocates to McDonough, Georgia.	2007	
Dr. Joe Martin becomes President of Atlanta Bible College and CAO of the General Conference.	2009	.
100th Anniversary Issue of The Restitution Herald is published. *The Restitution Herald* also begins publishing in electronic format. July: Seventh edition of *Systematic Theology* is released, celebrating 50 years of publication with a book signing by Dr. Alva Huffer at the ABC Archives. Proliferation of Missions continues with African work and the addition of the Pakistan mission field. July: Two Pakistani pastors are martyred for their faith, sending their American brethren into shock and grief.	2010	
Jan Turner Stilson publishes the *Biographical Encyclopedia*, a valuable chronology for the Church of God and sister denominations. General Conference accepts two Pakistani churches into the fellowship. July: The 90th General Conference meeting is celebrated at Jaynes Street Community Church in Omaha, Nebraska.	2011	

Revised in 1992 by Jan Stilson from *Elderhostel Notes* (1986).
Redesigned for encyclopedia by Dawn Johnson, Word Edge.

Appendix 5

Collaboration in Illinois

Excerpted and Condensed from
The Advent Christian Church
by Mrs. E.S. Mansfield

The question of the near, personal coming of Christ, which was quite extensively agitated in America, and in many parts of Europe and Asia, between the years 1820 and 1842, was first introduced among the people of Mt. Sterling in the winter of 1812, by the Rev. H.A. Chittendon of New York, in a course of able lectures on the Prophetic Scriptures, which doubtless laid the foundation for more successful future work on the part of others.

In 1850 Rev. Samuel K. Chapman of Hartford, Conn, came to this State and preached more or less in different parts of the county for two or three years, when a number of adherents to the faith were gained, and worshiping assemblies were established in various localities.

In 1855 Rev. J.C. Bywater of New York preached at Buckhorn, the first sermon on the subject, known as the Life and Death Question, asserting that mankind are mortal; and that immortality is a thing to be sought for, "by a patient continuance in well doing;" and only obtained through faith and obedience to Christ, the Life-Giver, who will, by a resurrection at the last day, give eternal life and immortality to His people who serve Him; and that the dead are silent in their grave until called forth to judgment at the second coming of Christ to judge the world and reward his people.

This view so consistently blended with the doctrine of Christ's return to earth, already received by them, and in fact made that event a reasonable necessity, that, notwithstanding opposition on the part of many others, the view was generally received by those having faith in the nearness of the event.

In 1855 Rev. D.R Mansfield who held a pastoral charge at Buchanan, Mich., [was] invited to come and hold tent meetings in different parts of the country. Buildings were also opened for their use; much interest was manifested and many were added to their number.

In 1859 a church was formally organized at Mt. Pleasant, numbering at one time forty members. Churches were also organized at Ripley and at Buckhorn. Elder Larkin Scott, an esteemed citizen of Hancock County, continued to preach in those churches from 1855, more or less, for several years, encouraging and strengthening the believers, and by his earnest and faithful labor, endeared himself to the people generally; and has long been regarded as truly a Father in Israel.

During this session they were reorganized, as above stated, on the 6th of May, 1882. The denominational name, Adventist, however, embraces several distinct branches; each having separate church relations, conferences, mission societies, publishing and financial interests.

As a people they are quite generally averse to any specified creed or articles of faith; leaving the way open for a difference of opinion upon minor points of doctrine. There are, however, leading essential points, which give them their identity as a distinct people, upon which they are nearly all agreed.

A brief summary of the leading doctrines believed and taught is herein set forth:

They believe in the one, true and living God, as the creator of all things in Heaven and earth. That mankind was created upright and endowed with the power of choice. That to our first parents, Adam and Eve, was given dominion over all the earth, with only one limitation, which was to test their fidelity to God. That they were on probation for eternal life, with death as a warning and penalty for disobedience. That by transgression they lost their dominion, forfeited the only life they possessed, incurred the penalty, and thus brought death upon the entire race; were driven from the garden and shut out from the tree of life. That God still loved and pitied in their helplessness, and gave them a chance to recover from this sad condition by a promise couched in the words, "The seed of the woman shall bruise the serpent's head." That this promised seed was Christ, and that, in due time, as the only begotten Son of God, he was born of woman, and subjected to all of the temptations of humanity; yet without sin. That he offered as a sacrifice for a fallen world, a sinless, spotless life; by which act he purchased the right to redeem from a state of death all who were made subject to it by the transgression of the first man, Adam. That on the third day after the crucifixion, God raised this same Jesus from the dead; who ascended up into Heaven, and now sits at the right hand of the Father as Mediator between God and man. That we have redemption from the effects of the original sin, through his atoning sacrificial offering, and that we have pardon and justification from our individual sins only as we accept Him by faith as our Saviour, and confess and forsake sin, and yield obedience to the pure principle of his life. That in the end of the Gospel age, which they believe to be near; the Son of God shall leave the mediatorial throne and come as he went away—"in the clouds of Heaven." That there will then be a resurrection of the dead, both of the just and the unjust, and at that time and not before, shall he "reward every man as his work shall be." That evil-doers shall be cut off, and forever destroyed. That the righteous living shall be changed, and together with those who have slept in Jesus, be clothed upon with immortality and eternal life to die no more. That the curse shall be taken off from the whole earth, and the lost dominion restored, and the tree of life brought back, and the loyal subjects of Christ, the second Adam, reinstated in a purified earth, with Christ as their King and ruler; and thus the prayer of our Lord be fulfilled as taught us, "Thy kingdom come, and thy will be done on earth as it is done in Heaven;" and the long-promised blessing to the meek, of an inheritance in the earth, be given. That as the capital and great metropolis of the renewed earth, the New Jerusalem shall be brought, with its golden streets and pearly gates, open ever to the redeemed host out of every nation, kindred, tongue and people, and the Lamb shall lead them by fountains of living waters; they shall hunger no more; they shall thirst no more; and there shall be no more pain; and the fountain of tears shall be dried; and the cause of weeping be forever removed.

Annotation: *There is no teaching in this statement of faith regarding the restoration of Israel to its homeland prior to the Second Coming.*

Bibliography: The Illinois Combined Histories of Schuyler and Brown Counties, Brinks Co. Edwardsville, Illinois, 1882. In public domain.

Appendix 6

From the JRAD-Atonement

Excerpts of
The Biblical and Theological Basis of Protestant Atonement Doctrines
Biblical and Theological Data, *Revised*

by Eugene Stilson, BS (Ed.), BTh, MA (Ed.), MA (NT), President, Rock River Christian College

Conclusion from first section:

Thus far we see that atonement, in the Leviticus images, is a theme found throughout the Bible. God wants us back as his children, but sin has to go. The blood of Christ, understood from the language of Leviticus, is the key to dealing with sin. Hebrews explains how this works. When we *confess* our sins, *accept* Christ as Saviour, and are *baptized*, we come into a new standing before God. We continue to live in a sinful world, and we will experience struggles. Jesus promised his disciples, and also those in the future that would come to believe through their testimony, that *they would not be alone in the world*. Jesus will come again to this earth. Then he will begin the process of cleansing the earth. At the end of the 1000 years, the New Heavens and Earth will be established. Then there will be no more sin. Righteousness will fill the earth. At that time atonement will be an accomplished fact. We can begin to appreciate that neither the Old Testament Day of Atonement, nor the death of Christ on the Cross, is the full revelation of the Bible as to how sin is removed, and oneness with God established. We need to follow the salvation story from Genesis to Revelation. The promise was given in Genesis. The Old Testament laid the background that led us to the life and teachings of Christ, the cross, and the resurrection. It is artificial to make an analytical division of the work of God into the compartments of the objective atonement work of Christology, and the subject experience under Salvation. The Lamb of God that died in the Gospels is also the exalted Christ at the right hand of God that is the head of the church, has a presence in the lives of Christians, and ministers to us as our high priest, and mediator. All that Christ is presently doing is toward the goals of removing sin from the world, and drawing us into a son relationship with our Father. Even when Christ returns to the earth he will continue to remove sin from the world, and draw us to the Father. It is only in the New Heavens and Earth in Revelation that we see the two goals accomplished. Sin will no longer be found in the world. Satan has come to final judgment. Death is finished. Righteousness fills the earth. God walks with man upon the earth as it was so in the Garden in Genesis. (If you have not previously done so, be sure to read **Excursus Nine** which gives very important additional texts from the Psalms, Prophets, and other parts of the New Testament.)

Dialogue of Church of God and Atonement Theories in the 19th and 20th Centuries

Introduction:

Now that general outlines of Christian thought and biblical evidence have been presented, we are ready to examine six major 19th century theological issues that shape theories of atonement. In each case this will be presented in dialogue with the teachings of the Church of God. **Excursus eight** gives an overview of the teachings of the Church of God that participate in this dialogue. These are Original Sin, Free will, Conditional immortality, Christology, Age to Come, and Judgment.

Original Sin:

The 19th century was heir to all the theories to date on the nature of man and sin. There are proof texts in the Old Testament that support the idea of the sinfulness of all men. A difficulty is that an appeal is not made to Genesis 1-3 and Adam's sin at points where this might be expected. The fact that individuals are held accountable for their decisions would suggest that man is a mixture of good and evil. The idea of two impulses was well developed in the period between the Old and New Testaments. Paul revived the doctrine of Original Sin, and this was a major pillar of the theology of Augustine, and Luther. It continued as one of the fundamentals of conservative belief during the 19th and 20th centuries. The significance for atonement theology is the claim that sin separates man from relationship with God. If sin is not really a problem, then what is the purpose of atonement? Why did Christ die?

As a counter movement to the Conservatives, Liberal theology of the 19th and 20th centuries denied Original Sin, and instead considered sin in its daily occurrences. This trend began with the 17th and 18th century skepticism of Rationalism and the Enlightenment regarding theological absolutes, and the supernatural. Romanticism regarded primitive man as innocent. Liberal theology believed that man was essentially good. He could be educated, or could evolve to a higher moral state. This all goes back to the view of Plato on sin. If we know the good, we will do it. Sin is ignorance. At this same period of time, higher criticism reconstructed the Gospels, and reduced them to universal proverbs as a guide for positive living. Jesus was a religious genius. His teachings are the key to successful living. The emphasis of Liberal theology is religious experience. The focus is on the individual. The Law of the Old Testament is minimized, along with prophetic teachings. The proverbs, psalms, and the social message of the prophets are preserved. Social reform is the highest priority.

Church of God members faced these issues during the 19th and 20th centuries. It is my assessment that the doctrine of Original Sin was the prevalent position in the Church of God. Evidence of this is the belief in a literal Adam and Eve and the Fall in Genesis 3. There are questions about the mechanism by which Original Sin is transmitted. This became an issue in the birth of Jesus, and his sinlessness. Along with this is the mechanism of the virgin birth. There have been divergent views in the Church of God.

In the history of theology, the optimism of the 19th century was corrected by WWI and WWII in the 20th century. Dialectic theology, also known as Neo-Orthodox theology, recognized the reality of sin, but largely addressed the social aspects of evil. The social Gospel movement is linked with this period.

The world view of the time minimized the duality between Satan and God. In its place they worked from the personality theories and the depth psychology of Freud, which saw in the heart of man a ruthless animal, covered over with an appearance of rationality, and masked by a cultural niceness of civilized behavior. In other words, evil comes from man and not the Devil. Again, we find diversity in the Church of God on the nature of Sin and the Devil. The temptation of Christ can be viewed as an inner struggle between the will of Jesus, and the will of his Father, or between loyalty to God or Satan.

I suspect that many Church of God students that have attended the state operated schools have worked out a solution to Bible and science that is essentially Neo-Orthodox, and may include theistic evolution. The conservative alternative is Creationism. From all of this we see a movement away from the Old Time Religion of "Power in the Blood" atonement grounded in the Old Testament, and, a movement to a softer, positive view of the nature of man.

Our ministries are heavily influenced by psychology, social science, and management. This is not necessarily a bad thing, but it seems clear that the biblical foundations of atonement, and the historical positions of the past, are diminishing in emphasis.

Free Will:

The position of Augustine, represented by the acronym TULIP, was essentially followed by <u>Luther</u>, and <u>Calvin</u>. (Total depravity, Unconditional election, Limited atonement, Irresistible grace, Perseverance of the saints). Total depravity included the ideas of original sin, the denial of salvation based on merit or man's effort, and the denial of free will. <u>Pelagius</u> believed that man had to actively cooperate in receiving salvation. Catholic theology taught a balance of faith and reason, practiced penance, and believed that merit could be earned. The Reformation was a reaction to the penance, and merit system of the Catholic Church, and went back to a Pauline, and Augustinian theology.

Counter to this trend was emphasis on individualism and reason of the 17th and 18th centuries. Both democratic revolutions and radical theology flourished in this period. Immanuel Kant believed that man was more than reason. Man was a living person that had the capacity to make moral decisions. His world view included immortality of the soul. It was evident that good did not triumph over evil in present history. A future existence was necessary for justice. Hegel went on to see history as moved spiritually towards a final goal. This has parallels in the Ages of Daniel, and the Ages of Anthropology. Utopianism was present in a variety of forms during the 19th century. Modern western culture is deeply committed to freedom in every form. TULIP is counter to western thought.

The Baptists developed a middle position between grace, election, and believer's baptism. Closely akin to these influences is the congregational form of church government.

The Church of God is very similar to the Baptists on the idea of free will. We see salvation as a partnership between God and man. Huffer's *Systematic Theology* outlines this position with seven Bible images of what God is doing, and the four steps on man's part, namely, repentance, belief, baptism and a walk in newness of life.

The Church of God has generally denied the sacramental view of baptism, but agrees with the Protestant affirmation of the two ordinances based on the work of Christ on the Cross. Thus atonement is the foundation of both baptism and communion. Atonement is the significance of the Cross.

The Church of God differs from Anselm in his belief that Jesus had to be God in order to provide satisfaction.

Likewise, the Church of God disagrees with vicarious atonement in its standard evangelical form, for the same reason that it is creedal, and not fundamental to the Bible itself. The Church of God agrees with both of these in the use of the language of Leviticus, Hebrews, and the various New Testament passages that support the significance of the sacrificial blood of Christ on the cross. The Church of God believes that additional texts must also be considered that are generally excluded from the discussion of atonement, and isolated under salvation, or eschatology.

Conditional Immortality:

Adherents of immortality of the soul can be traced back to Socrates, and Plato, in their duality of body and soul. The modern biblical theology movement has increased awareness of the Hebrew concept of man as a whole. This more holistic view is more consistent with the doctrine of *resurrection of the body*. This teaching is prominent in Paul as in 1 Corinthians 15, and has recently been affirmed by the Neo-Orthodox Karl Barth, and Oscar Cullmann during the 20th century. The rationalism of the 17th and 18th centuries denied immortality of the soul, and affirmed that man was mortal. Man did not have a future hope. Immanual Kant of 19th century Germany affirmed the immortality of the soul as the means to justice and reward of the good. It was during this same period that the emphasis on the Old Testament, and its holistic view of the nature of man began. Modern personality theory is holistic, and Jewish in background. Modern medicine is essentially holistic. This trend should be contrasted with behavioral psychology and social work which places the burden on the environment. In the midst of all of this, a tradition of conditional immortality has been present from the Apostolic Fathers, down to the present time. The Church of God is part of that tradition. LeRoy Froom's *The Conditionalist Faith of Our Fathers* is essential reading for awareness of this tradition.

The relevance of all of this for atonement theory is the definition of the problem to be solved by atonement, and the way this fits in the timetable of salvation history. If man is immortal, then what is done during mortal life is merely the preface to what will ultimately be worked out in afterlife. The Catholic Church provides purgatory as the opportunity to work out what was not accomplished during life on earth. Some view the millennium as a second chance to achieve the same goal. Those that adhere to universal salvation generally hold to the immortality of the soul, or resurrection to a second period where these problems can be solved.

If man is mortal, then what is done in this life determines one's destiny. If atonement is viewed as a partnership between God and Man then at a minimum, a decision for Christ is essential for any future hope. Many would add that baptism by immersion is essential, and adherence to certain doctrines is also essential for hope of immortality. It is difficult for any two denominations to agree on what these essential doctrines are. The Church of God has certainly had a difficulty finding any uniform position on this.

All positions have a difficulty dealing with infants, and regions of the world that have never heard the Gospel. The issue is one of fairness.

Christology:

The problem here is whether Jesus is God, or man, or both. In the theology of Anselm the answer was both. In a counter position to Anselm, which was the majority position in the Middle Ages, we can object to his analysis of the problem in which debt, or punishment is seen as the primary issue. This seems to reflect the culture of the day, and its legal system. Not enough emphasis is placed on God as a person, which is the emphasis of the Old Testament prophets popular in liberal theology. What is the place of love, and forgiveness? Anselm's solution is too formal. Our relationship with God needs to be more personal. The Great Awakening, Revivalism, and even liberal Social Gospel with its emphasis on religious experience of the heart, reacted to clericalism, formalism, and sacramentalism. Thus 19th century theology moved from emphasis on the death of Christ only, to the covenant theology with its emphasis on the entire life, teachings, crucifixion, and resurrection of Christ. Liberal theology denied the deity of Christ, and Evangelical theology affirmed it.

The Church of God denied that Jesus is God, and thus rejected Anselm's theory of atonement. The Church of God has leaned towards the Evangelical vicarious atonement as evidenced certainly in its hymns and gospel songs officially issued by the Church of God General Conference. Emphasis is placed on the specific biblical images of Leviticus which have been interpreted as types of Christ. The book of Hebrews, as well as other passages throughout the New Testament, supports this idea. There are many similarities between Evangelical and Church of God interpretation of these passages in the Old and New Testament. However, it should be noted that the Church of God objects to the presentation and preaching of the idea that God died on the cross, His soul harrowed hell during the three days, and that Christ returned to his heavenly position that he had before he was incarnate during his earthly ministry. The Church of God would affirm that Jesus began at his conception. He was foreknown in the mind of God before the foundations of the earth in his role as Son of God and Messiah. Jesus was born in Adam's race, but is unique in his sinlessness. Jesus is the Son of God. From his birth He was destined to rule the world. Jesus was absolutely obedient to the will of God. Through his life and teachings Jesus is the final revelation of God to man, and the only way that man can come to God. Thus Christ is the key to atonement. What is significantly missing up to this point is the importance of the heavenly ministry of Christ at present, the second coming, the millennial work of Christ, and the Age to Come. Saying this another way, ***the Evangelical concept of atonement is mostly in the past, whereas the Church of God teaching on atonement includes the present and future in an eschatological sense.*** This will come to light in the section below.

Age to Come:

Plato divided the world into the eternal, unchanging level of perfect ideas, and the accidents of history. There is no sense of a goal in his view because there is no change possible in that which is perfect. As for history it is an illusion, and it will pass away. Eastern religions regard escape from history, and individual being as salvation. Plato looked for escape from the body, and, eternity was pure thought as salvation.

The Bible is unique in its belief that salvation is historical and involves both *man* in bodily form, and the *earth* itself. The Old Testament contrasts the *present evil age*, with the *Age to Come*. The progress of salvation is essentially a *horizontal* journey through *history* to the final goal of the *new heavens and earth*. The biblical theology movement of the 19th and 20th centuries has revived an interest in Old Testament theology of the Age to Come. Such theology was the ground in which prophetic thought developed during the 19th century. In the 20th century the Dead Sea Scrolls and similar discoveries have led to a revival of interest in apocalyptic literature, which includes Daniel and Revelation. (See **Excurses Two** for recent non-canonical literature**).**

The relevance for atonement theory is the fairly literal hermeneutic approach to the types of the tabernacle, and a literal view of the Age to Come that can be readily found in the NICOT (*New International Commentary on the Old Testament*) series. Biblical theology, and biblical archaeology have pushed back with a view that Abraham was a historical figure. Thus Moses, the Law, and the Tabernacle are more likely to be taken literally. The belief in the restoration of Israel has been confirmed by 1948. This has been widely proclaimed by the Dispensational Movement in America. N.T. Wright has advanced global awareness of the New Heavens and Earth in our times. Thus, there is a vast acceptance of Age to Come theology in our day. The Church of God lived through a transition period that flourished in the 20th century.

Judgment:

All would agree that the idea of final judgment is found in the Old Testament. The concept of it is another matter. This is included in the Apostles' Creed, and those that followed. The Jews believed judgment would occur as the transition between the present age and the Age to Come. Those that believed in resurrection likewise placed it at the transition between the two ages. The sheep and the goats in the Gospels can be interpreted along this line. The book of Daniel opens the possibility of a Great Tribulation, and a millennial reign of Christ. Some interpret Daniel 8 as fulfilled in the time of Antiochus Epiphanes IV, whereas Gleason Archer in the *Expositor's Bible Commentary,* "Daniel", develops the futurist idea of a seven-year tribulation, the return of Christ to rule for a thousand years, the final judgment, and the ew heavens and earth. A similar exposition is presented by the Dispensationalists John Walvoord and Charles Feinberg. Such a line of futurist interpretation has been present in the 20th century Church of God, and continues probably as the majority view. Also found are the historic pre-millennial position, and the historic Millerite position. I have read *The Sharpening Steel*, special issue, "The Prophecy Debate in the Church of God of the Abrahamic Faith" (August 1990), by Mark M. Mattison. Vol. 4. No. 1. Spring, 1991. Mattison notes that historical premillennialism can be divided into historicism and futurism. Historicism fulfills the 70th week of Daniel in about 33 A.D. Futurism fulfills the 70th week of Daniel right before the return of Christ to establish the millennium.

I am simply taking note that there are different views of prophecy in the history of the Church of God. Some place emphasis on the history of the church in signs leading up to the thousand year reign of Christ. Others are looking at signs in the final generation before the coming of Christ. Some are looking at the troubles that believers have experienced throughout the ages. Others are looking at a seven year Great Tribulation. The point on which the Church of God can agree is that we are not presently in the thousand year reign of Christ. We are pre-millennialists. Christ will return to earth, and will reign for a thousand years. This will be followed by the New Heavens and Earth. During the 19th century, heavy emphasis was placed in the Church of God on teaching prophecy. In the 20th century this was balanced with messages on Christian living. I see a renewed emphasis on preaching the Kingdom message in the last two decades.

As this pertains to atonement theory, the imminent possibility of the return of Christ at any moment creates an urgency to be ready. Now is the time to repent, believe, be baptized, and walk in newness of life. There is an urgency to tell the world about Jesus. It would seem to me that the

Church of God of the 19th century felt a greater level of urgency about the return of Christ, and the fulfillment of prophecy than during the last few decades. We are more inclined to listen to the ecological prophets of doom, warning us to save the planet than to John the Baptist who said "Prepare ye the way of the Lord," followed by Jesus preaching of the Gospel of the Kingdom of God.

For the Church of God, this life is the time of decision. When the resurrection comes, the final verdict is already revealed by whether we rise in the first or second resurrection. The only question is "What about those who are alive when Christ returns?" "What will happen to the nations?" Some believe that the wicked will be destroyed at the beginning of the millennium. Others believe this happens at the end of the thousand years at the Great White Throne Judgment in Revelation. It is not clear what the basis, or criteria of judgment will be. Believers are atoned by the blood of the lamb. But, what about the nations that will populate the millennium? Are they to be judged by their works, as were the sheep and the goats? There is much diversity of interpretation on this issue. It is agreed that only the righteous will inhabit the New Heavens and Earth.

(**Excursus Eight:** If you have not done this yet, see the suggested model of articles, or propositions that would seem to describe the atonement position of the Church of God. I would caution that this is my personal perception of the situation, and has not been seen by any official representative of the Church of God. I speak simply as a fifth generation member of the Church of God. The data at my disposal covers pretty much the entire organizational history of the Church of God General Conference in all of its forms. I would anticipate a certain level of dialogue, and revisions may follow this initial effort to articulate the Church of God view of Atonement in the context of the general philosophy and theology of this period. Readers should note the separate sheet entitled "Church of God Reflections on Atonement" that acknowledge some of the people that have influenced me." Eugene Stilson. October 2008.)

> **Annotation:** *The complete article with the Prologue and several Excurses may be had by ordering JRAD, Spring/Summer 2009, Church of God General Conference, 2020 Avalon Parkway Suite 4, McDonough, Ga. See http://www.abc-coggc.org.*

Bibliography: Aulen, Gustaf. *Christus Victor;* Aulen, Gustaf. *The Faith of the Christian Church,* Muhlenberg Press, 1960; Beasley-Murray, G.R. "Baptism, wash," *The New International Dictionary of New Testament Theology,* Vol. 1, Zondervan, 1975; Blendinger, C. "Might," *The New International Dictionary of New Testament Theology,* Vol. 2, Zondervan, 1976; Cairns, Earle E. *Christianity Through the Centuries.* Zondervan, 1981; Crosswalk.com Lexicons and concordances. On-line; Dodd, C.H. *The Interpretation of the Fourth Gospel.* Cambridge University Press, 1963; Dunn, James D. G. *Christology in the Making.* 2nd ed., Eerdmans, 1996; *Harper Study Bible*. Various study helps on Hebrews; Hayes, John H. and Frederick Prussner. *Old Testament Theology its history and development.* John Knox Press, 1985; Froom, LeRoy, *Conditionalist Faith of our Fathers.* 4 Vols. Advent and Review. 1950; Huffer, Alva. *Systematic Theology.* Church of God General Conf. 1960; Jewett, Paul. "Atonement," *Zondervan Pictorial Bible Encyclopedia*. Vol. 1, Eerdmans, 1976; Mattison, Mark. "The Prophecy Debate in the Church of God of the Abrahamic Faith," *The Sharpening Steel,* Gr. Rapids. (August 1990) Vol. 4. No. 1. Spring, 1991; Stumpf, Samuel Enoch. *Philosophy: History and Problems.* McGraw-Hill, 1971; Taylor, Vincent. *Jesus and His Sacrifice.* Macmillan, 1943. 3rd. ed. (1st book); Taylor, Vincent. *Forgiveness and Reconciliation.* Macmillan, 1941. (2nd book); Taylor, Vincent. *The Atonement in New Testament Teaching.* Epworth, 1958. (3rd book); Tillich, Paul. *A History of Christian Thought.* Harper & Row, 1968; Wenham, Gorgon J. *The Book of Leviticus.* (NICOT). Eerdmans, 1979; Wikipedia.com. Various links and summary articles.

Appendix 7

Holy Spirit

The Holy Spirit in the Old Testament
by Vernis Wolfe

The Holy Spirit as the power of God is operative in all areas of the cosmos and in every aspect of life. The broadcast scope envisions no power apart from divine will and no life apart from divine genesis. The Holy Spirit is God's essence in diffusion. However, for a more explicit view, when "holy" is ascribed as a condition of the Spirit it is to designate God's power operating within the realm of human history and particularly of that manifest phenomenon in which God is bringing His own influence to bear upon given situations and men for the accomplishment of His program for the salvation of the human race and the preservation of the world.

The church is very much aware that Jesus made a promise to his disciples that they should receive the Holy Spirit as Comforter during his absence from them. The way he stated the promise, and the manner in which they received and waited for the fulfillment indicates faith by prior knowledge concerning the Holy Spirit. These disciples gave credit to the operation of God's Spirit in man for the writing of the Old Testament scripture, and for the mighty acts performed in their midst at the inception of the church. These were the men that linked an awareness of the work of the Holy Spirit among their forefathers to an awareness of the working of the Holy Spirit in their own lives. The New Testament church stands in a sequence of events spawned by God's Holy Spirit that makes it expedient for the church to look at the work of the Holy Spirit prior to the beginning of this present age.

For our time and place the church is central to God's work and essential to the redemptive effort of God. This is not to say that the church is the most important object of God's concern but rather that it is the vehicle through which He is presently operating and by which He will, at least in part, bring into being the work of a new age for man. Therefore, all past time is now prologue and important to an understanding of the present or any future man may hope to enjoy.

Understanding the operation of the Holy Spirit and the involvement of the Holy Spirit in the life of men requires the establishment of a relationship to events where the Holy Spirit has been the means whereby God had intervened in the formative process of materials and life to manifest new forms. The first of these events was the creation.

The creation story as told in Genesis unveils the drama of God's intervention in the chaotic conditions of this world to bring order, life, and finally, cohesion and meaning by the intelligent agent, man. Man's failure to respond adequately to God's bidding led to a distortion of his humanity and reopened the necessity for God to intervene in man's life on some kind of a continuing basis if man were ever to realize the potential of God's intent in the original act of creation. This first episode is typical of most that follows in human history.

Man's Flight and Return

The experience of man in Eden finds man resorting to the kind of resistance he sees available, that is, simply hiding from God. Later man's acts of rebellion are more overt and God says, "My spirit shall not always strive with man" (Gen. 6:3). Man's sin was not so much the deliberate rejection of God as it was a preference for doing things according to his own imagination.

More than a little frustration and ambivalence is displayed in such expressions as Psalm 139. Here the Psalmist speaks lucidly of the attributes of God and wrestles particularly with the fact of God's omnipresence and asks: "Whither shall I go from thy spirit?" He would flee from God but finds that it is impossible, for God is inescapable. There is no hiding place either in heaven or hell. Man cannot endure the reality of what he is and therefore cannot face the God of truth who would reveal man to himself.

The Psalmist begins to see the solution available to him which is to affirm God's involvement in his life and he expresses it by saying, "I will praise thee; for I am fearfully and wonderfully made; marvelous are thy works; and that my soul knoweth right well." This backward look at what has been done gives man a readiness to align himself with God, but it is the forward look that makes reconciliation possible. Man's self-imposed alienation is recognized for the reality that it is, and he turns to seek healing from the source of all life by saying: "Search me, O God, and know my heart; try me, and know my thoughts; And see if there be any wicked way in me, and lead me in the way everlasting."

It is in the atmosphere of tension between the way of man and the Spirit of God that man's religious experience begins to emerge, and man gains the courage to be open to the resources of God and experience the healing of his distorted human spirit by the Holy Spirit of God. It is a story of God's action and man's response; God's concern and care demonstrated in the way spoken by the Psalmist: "Thou sendest forth thy spirit, they are created; and thou renewest the face of the earth (Psa. 104:30). This word may be taken as an expression of God's concern, care, action, regardless of the dispensation of time being considered.

The Spirit of God in Man

Man is regarded by the Old Testament writers in all part of his being, as an object and subject of the action of God's Spirit. In Gen. 2:7, God created man, giving him personal and intellectual life by breathing into his nostrils "the breath of life." God is spoken of as "God of the spirits of all flesh" (Numbers 16:22). Wisdom, understanding, and knowledge fills the workman for building the tabernacle (Ex.31 3; 35:31). God gives His good Spirit for instruction (Neh. 9:20), and this was probably the reason the Psalmist prayed: "Teach me to do thy will, for thou art my God; thy spirit is good" (Psa. 143:10). It was considered rebellion to take counsel apart from God's spirit (Isa. 30:1). Therefore, man had reason to be disturbed if God threatened to withdraw His Spirit (Psa. 51:11).

The experience of the prophets is that of having the Spirit as a prompter for speaking God's truth (II Pet. 1:21); Ezek. 2:1, 2); and through this Spirit they were able to speak God's Word (Heb. 1:1, 2; Zech. 7:12); and utter the frequent "thus saith the Lord." God's man, serving as His Prophet, could declare boldly: "Truly I am full of power by the spirit of the Lord, and of judgment, and of might, to declare unto Jacob his transgression, and to Israel his sin" (Mic. 3:8). The Lord was not with all men the same way as He was with the prophets (Num. 11:29), but it was by these very prophets who spoke God's message by the Spirit that God revealed Himself; and by this revelation the people had the means to develop an awareness of God and relate to Him in a religious reality.

God also manifest His special power in the rulers of Israel. The activity within the theocratic kingdom required that God be specially represented by men in whom He could manifest mental and spiritual perception and abilities, this divine activity to be extended in the judicial works of the men in positions of rulership. It was under the influence of the Spirit that Gideon (Judg. 3:10), Saul (I Sam. 11:6), David (I Sam. 16:13), and others operated as the divinely chosen men for Israel.

God also revealed the perfect king figure, in whom would abide all aspects of God's Spirit, when He spoke prophetically through such men as Isaiah of Christ's coming (Isa. 11:1, 2). The Spirit of God worked multidimensionally in and through the covenant people in order to give emergence to the new man personified by Jesus the Christ.

God or Spirit?

There seems to be a question for many about the interrelationship of the Spirit to God in the Old Testament writings. In the Old Testament the interest of the writer was in the activity of God, and they gave credit that most of what transpired in their lives were divine events. These events were apprehended as the operation of God and often were expressed as the work of God's Spirit—in fact, God and His Spirit were one. God, for the Old Testament writer, was a being with all of the supreme attributes; and His power in diffusion, operating in the channel of His holy will, was recognized as Holy Spirit.

Appendix 8

Judgment

The Nature of Judgment
by J.M. Stephenson
From the Prophetic Watchman and Herald of the Kingdom, *1:32 October 12, 1867.*

"Indeed I truly say to you, he who hears my word, and believes him who sent me, has AIONIAN life, and comes not into judgment, but is passed out of death into life."
John 5:24

There is a department of judgment into which the righteous shall not come, or else Christ's language is not true. Speaking of the same life, and the same judgment, at the 28th verse, Christ says, "And will come forth; those having done good things, to a resurrection of life (i,e, eternal life), and those having done evil things to a resurrection of judgment.

The original word is *KRISKOS* judgment. Now, if the righteous and the unrighteous come into the same judgment, the foregoing texts present the most palpable contradiction.

In judgment there are three departments 1st. The investigation. 2d. The decision. 3d. The execution. The first two are always before the same judge, that is, unless it be merely a preliminary investigation, to see whether it would be proper to bring the person accused before the legal tribunal for the alleged offense. It is manifestly proper for the judge who hears the evidence to pronounce the sentence.

God reserves to himself the right to try and decide all cases involving the everlasting destiny of man. In the Mosaic dispensation the Great God was the judge, and the high priest the advocate for the people. The people never appeared in person before the judge. They appeared in the person of their advocate, the high priest, before the great Jehovah, who appeared between the wings of the cherubim. Their cases were tried before him. The attorney communicated the decision to the people. The prerogative was granted the attorney of communicating pardon to those who had been acquitted. The judge also appointed the executioners of those whom he had condemned. So it has been since our High Priest and Advocate entered the court of heaven.

Paul referring to the typical high priest appearing in judgment for the people says, "For Christ is not entered into the holy places made with hands, which are the figures of the true; but into heaven itself, now to appear in the presence of God for us." Hebrews 9:24.

This demonstrates that our trial is now going on, and that we do not appear in our own person. John says, "My little children these things write I unto you, that you sin not. And if any many sin, we have an advocate with the Father, Jesus Christ the righteous." I John 1: 9.

But that our Advocate will succeed in procuring pardon for all whose cause he undertakes, if they shall comply with the conditions on their part, as is evident from the declaration of the inspired prophet, that "If we confess our sin, he (the Father) is faithful and just to forgive us our sins, and to cleanse us from all unrighteousness." I John 1:9.

Thus our cases are being tried before the Father and he will either Acquit or Condemn. Christians have an Advocate, but sinners who reject the Gospel, have none. Christ as the Head will advocate the cause of all members of his body. Faith in the Gospel of the Kingdom, repentance, and baptism into the name of Christ, are the divinely prescribed conditions of the remission of past sins. Confessions of our sins, and the intercession of Christ as our advocate are the only conditions of the remission of sins after having become members of the body of Christ.

Christ says, "But they which shall be accounted worthy to obtain that world (age) and the resurrection from (Ek Nekkon) among the dead, neither marry nor are given in marriage. Neither can they die any more; for they are equal unto the angels; and are the children of God, being the children of the resurrection." Luke 20:35, 36.

Ecclesia denotes a selection from among the living, and Ek Nekkon a selection from among the dead. As far as the righteous dead are concerned, the decision relative to the worth of character precedes their resurrection from among the dead. They have been accounted worthy of this distinction before they are raised. The decision must precede their resurrection. Hence, they are selected from among the rest of the dead, to reign with Christ a thousand years, while the rest of the dead remain in their graves till the thousand years are finished. Revelation 20.

That the resurrection precedes the coming of Christ is evident from the fact that when he comes, he brings the reward with him. Rev. 22:12. The reward is consequent upon the judgment. The Father decides the case and sends the reward by the Son.

The department of judgment occupied by the Son, viz: the executive department, the righteous shall not come [enter]. As far as the living nations are concerned, for one thousand years Christ and the saints will have legislative, judicial and executive power. But in all the ages past, the great God has reserved to himself the exclusive right to investigate and decide upon the cases of all responsible men.

The thrones of all kings and potentates are their judgment seats, whence they fulminate laws for the government of their kingdoms or empires. Christ's throne will be his judgment seat. The saints do not stand before the throne of Christ to be tried or to confess their sins. These will have been pardoned. Christ will confess their acts of fidelity in the face of heaven and earth and invite them to come inherit the Kingdom.

Afterwards, the unfaithful stewards are executed. They that are ready enter into the marriage feast, and the doors are closed; afterwards the foolish virgins come and are excluded. Matt. 24:1-12.

Appendix 9

Kingdom of God

The Kingdom of God
by C.E. Randall

From The Restitution Herald, *March 13, 1948, and reprinted in the 75th Anniversary issue of* The Restitution Herald, *October 1985.*

It is with deep regard that I study the views of the early Church of God writers on the subject of the "Kingdom of God." Writing on the "Age to Come," J.I. Wince said, "Glorious era in the world's history, when the last great conquest shall have been fought, and all nations shall have become one vast confederacy, one universal empire! The offspring of David upon his throne, administering a righteous government, judging with equity the meek of the earth." Yes, "glorious era" well describes the future Kingdom of God here on the earth. Our early church fathers believed the gospel of the kingdom—the good news of the "glorious era" was vital to the salvation of people. Writing to Thomas Wilson, editor of the *Herald of the Coming Kingdom and Christian Instructor* (one of our early church publications) L.H. Chase said: "I rejoice to see you take a decided stand for a ***definite*** gospel, and that all mankind ***must hear, believe, and obey the one gospel***, or they cannot be saved in the kingdom." Many such comments could be quoted.

These quotations express well the firm conviction our early church fathers held. They believed in the gospel of the kingdom, and they believed it to be essential. It was around a definite message of strong convictions of the importance of the message that our work came into being in America. Lose this conviction on the absolute importance of our message of the gospel of the kingdom, and we become just a twig in the tree of orthodox teaching.

The Kingdom of God is the central subject of the entire Bible, and, without knowledge of the kingdom, one cannot properly understand and interpret the Scriptures. We would like to give a few quotations from Bible scholars on this proposition. First quotation is from J. Orr, in *Hasting's Bible Dictionary*, on the subject of the Kingdom of God.

> "Little inquiry is necessary to convince us that this idea enters vitally into the whole texture of revelation, has its root in the fundamental ideas of the Old Testament, is paramount in the early teaching of our Lord, received further development—with special reference…in the apostolic writings, and presents deepest interest to students, both of ***doctrine and morals*** at the present day."

In his work on *The Theocratic Kingdom* George N.H. Peters' opening statement reads, "The Scriptures cannot be rightly comprehended without due knowledge of this kingdom."

The American Tract Society, in its *Bible Dictionary* says, "The ancient prophets, when describing the character of the Messiah, and even when speaking of his humiliation and sufferings, were want to intersperse hints of his power and reign." Quotations like these could be multiplied many times, but these suffice to give support to the thought that the Kingdom of God is the main subject of the Scriptures.

The gospel of the kingdom is the gospel that must be preached in all the world for a witness before the end of the age comes (Matt. 24:14). Mark says it must be "published among the nations" (13:10). This gospel that the first apostles and disciples were charged to preach was not to be given merely as, or *for*, a witness, but it was given for the primary purpose to save people from their sins. John confirmed that he came to prepare the way of the Lord. He did it by preaching, "Repent ye, for the kingdom of heaven is at hand." His message of the kingdom met the needs of all classes of sinners. These distinct groups are mentioned in Luke 3:8-14. Jesus stated that he came to "seek and to save that which was lost" (Luke 19:10). How did he do it? Through the message which he preached, and the gospel he preached throughout all Judea the Scripture calls, "the gospel of the kingdom" (Matt. 9:35).

The gospel of the kingdom had saving powers in the days of Jesus, and, according to Paul, it constituted a "great salvation" of which there is no escape if we neglect it (Heb. 2:1-3). It can be neglected in preaching as well as in hearing and believing it!

The apostles, to whom the Great Commission was given to "preach to every creature" (Mark 16:15, 16), beginning at Jerusalem, preached the message of the "kingdom of heaven" prior to the crucifixion of Christ (Matt. 10:7): and, subsequent to his resurrection and previous to his ascension, the apostles were given final instructions of "things pertaining to the kingdom of God" (Acts 1:3). This was the gospel which was to be preached in all the world for a witness, and all who believe it and are baptized according to Mark will be saved. Paul called it "God's power to salvation" (Rom. 1:16). When Paul wrote to the Romans about the gospel being the power of God to salvation, he was speaking about the gospel of the Great Commission—that great salvation which the Lord preached. Later, when Paul went to Rome, he told them about this salvation by preaching two whole years in his own hired house—"preaching the kingdom of God, and teaching those things which concern the Lord Jesus Christ" (Acts 28:30,31).

Appendix 10
Lost Saints: Known Only to God

Dassel-Cokato Enterprise Dispatch, October 4, 2010

[Excerpts]
Whatever happened to Smith Lake Cemetery?
Mel Bjur and a group of local people seemed to have figured that out
By Jennifer Kotila
Staff Writer

COKATO, MN – Mel Bjur of Cokato has been working to find Smith Lake Cemetery for about 10 years now.

This has been a difficult task because many of the people who are still alive and remember the cemetery, remember it a little differently.

Some history about Smith Lake

Smith Lake was a village that sat between Howard Lake and Cokato on what is now 49th Street Southwest. It was located next to the railroad tracks.

Today, 49th Street runs through what would have been the village of Smith Lake. Before Smith Lake disappeared, the road used to curve around the town. The road was straightened after the village disappeared.

Smith Lake was originally claimed by Eugene Smith, who located and surveyed a railroad right of way in 1858. Smith also gave his name to the village that was developed there, according to D.R. Farnham's article "Wright County History, 1880."

Smith never perfected his claim, and in 1865, W.P. Holbrook took the land by a pre-emptive claim.

Holbrook and L.W. Perkins surveyed and platted 65 acres and entered them as a town site.

The year of 1869 saw a lot of growth for Smith Lake. A railroad depot and water tank were built. Perkins built a store and a hotel that year, as well.

By 1880, Smith Lake was a bustling little village with numerous stores, a blacksmith shop, a hotel, a boardinghouse, a post office, a sawmill, an elevator, and grain houses, according to Farnham's history.

The post office moved out of Smith Lake in 1914, according to the Minnesota Historical Society.

According to the map of Smith Lake from 1901, there were two churches in the village, the **Church of God** and a Methodist church.

The cemetery that Bjur has been trying to find is thought to have been established and taken care of by the Church of God.

According to an article in the **May 12, 1910** edition of the Cokato Enterprise, **the Church of God burned to the ground in that year. The church then moved to Howard Lake,** according to Mike Worcester, director of the Cokato Museum.

After the church and the post office moved out of Smith Lake, the village slowly faded away. The cemetery slowly disappeared once it was abandoned.

So, what happened to the cemetery?

As time went on, the farmland around the cemetery slowly swallowed it up. Basically, the cemetery was plowed under.

When people learn that, their reaction is often, "They can do that? Just plow under a cemetery?" said Worcester.

At the time, they could. There are many old cemeteries from the beginning of the 20th century that were abandoned. Without a church or an association to take care of them, the cemeteries were overgrown and abandoned, said Worcester.

He went on to say that many markers in those cemeteries were made of wood and eventually disintegrated, leaving no marking for the grave sites. The graves were then lost and plowed under.

Mel Robinson also gave some insight into how Smith Lake Cemetery could have disappeared. During World War II, cemeteries were used to grow extra food for the war effort.

To make it easier to grow food on the cemetery, the grave markers were often moved aside. Anybody who did this was supposed to plot the cemetery and return the markers after the war.

If this happened at Smith Lake cemetery, the markers may not have been replaced. Robinson said there are a lot of old stones piled to the northwest of where the cemetery was.

How was the cemetery found?

Before looking for Smith Lake Cemetery, Bjur had been working to find unmarked graves at other cemeteries in the area.

He started in 1988 at Watson Cemetery, located north of Cokato off of 45th Street. He had relatives buried there.

One of the techniques that Bjur, and those working with him, used to find the graves was dowsing, or the art of finding hidden things. Dowsing is also known as "divining," "water witching," and "doodle bugging."

Bjur and his helpers used this technique at the Watson Cemetery, and Mark Peterson worked with him to prove that a grave had been found, according to both Peterson and Bjur.

They tested the technique at two sites in Watson cemetery. One of the sites was a grave, the other was not. "So it was a 50/50 deal," said Peterson.

Bjur really started working hard to find the Smith Lake Cemetery about 10 years ago.

First, he did a lot of research on the village of Smith Lake.

Bjur started his search for the cemetery by talking to all the local people mentioned above.

He also did research at the Cokato Museum, the Cokato Historical Society, the Howard Lake Historical Society, the Wright County Historical Society, and the Minnesota Historical Society.

The exact location of the cemetery was more difficult to find than expected, especially since the roads around Smith Lake had been moved after the town disappeared.

Another problem he ran into was some of the records had been burned when the Church of God burned down. There were no records of who would have been buried in the cemetery.

Since the cemetery was so difficult to pinpoint, Bjur looked to his friends for help.

Ed Reinmuth helped with a compass that he had used when working for Middleville Township. He explained it as a device that can be used to find drain tiles, old roads, or other areas that had been disturbed.

Using the compass, said Reinmuth, they were able to find the location of the cemetery.

After finding the location of the cemetery, Kenny Gausman used a dowsing stick to plot out the grave site. He learned dowsing 25 to 30 years ago, but had never put it to much use, he said.

Once they knew the location of the cemetery, plotting out the graves with a dowsing stick was fairly easy to do, Gausman said.

Lenny Kaisalahti helped find the graves with a dowsing stick and called it, "interesting work." Bill Fiedler also helped find and plot out the graves.

Wes Robertson also learned to dowse while helping plot out the cemetery. "Sometimes it brings up more questions than answers, but there is something to it," he said.

Robertson also said that each of the four men doing the dowsing would cross-check each other's work, so he said it was fairly accurate.

Mel Robinson also helped in plotting out the grave sites. After the men doing the dowsing found a grave, he would probe it to make sure it was an actual grave.

For probing, Robinson used a long stick. The stick would go down into the ground a long way, and then drop about 6 inches really easily. When it did that, they knew they had found a grave.

By using the dowsing and probing, Bjur and his friends were able to plot out more than 90 graves at Smith Lake Cemetery, according to Bjur.

Many of the people working on the project think the road may now go over some of the old cemetery.

What happens now that the cemetery has been found?

Now that the cemetery has been found, some may wonder if they can restore it. Unfortunately, that is not the case.

The land the cemetery has been found on is now private property. Bjur and his helpers had to get permission from the property owner before doing their research.

Restoring an abandoned cemetery on private property would have to be approved by the landowner. Most property owners would not agree to do that unless they also had relatives buried in the cemetery, Worcester said.

Instead, Bjur and his helpers have decided to erect a monument. They received permission from Middleville Township to place a monument near the cemetery.

Bjur is working to secure funding to complete the monument and the landscaping that will be done around it.

So far, he has received donations from the Minnesota Arts and Cultural Heritage fund, Cokato Historical Society, Cokato Township, Middleville Township, and the Wright County Historical Society. He is waiting for responses from several other organizations regarding donations for the monument.

If all goes as planned, Bjur and his helpers hope to place the monument sometime next spring.

"At least there will be a marker to show where the cemetery was when descendants of the people buried there are doing research on their ancestry, and would like to see where their relatives' graves were," said Worcester.

Reprinted with permission of Dassel-Cokato Enterprise, October 5, 2010

Appendix 11
Poetry and Hymns

There were many artists and poets in the Church of God, and every issue of The Restitution *had at least one original poem among its pages. Some of them became lyrics for hymns included in the new hymnbooks. A selection is offered here.*

The Seer
by M.P.A. Crozier (Mrs. O.R.L. Crozier)
The Restitution, March 20, 1889

I hear the stately tramp of many feet.
  The nations moving down the track of time;
Gay banners flaunting, bugles blowing sweet,
  And drum-beats measuring the march sublime.

I see where nations, fallen from the ranks,
  Lie frozen corpses, life forever fled;
And know iniquity, entrenched its law,
  Lies in their pulseless bosoms cold and dead.

I see the Judean Christ crowned King of kings,
  See earthly scepters yielded to His own;
See jeweled crowns fall humbly at His feet;
  And kings with bared brows kneel before His throne.

I see far out upon the vast plateaus,
  Of future eons, hosts of every tongue;
I hear them chanting in that high, clear air;
  The "Gloria in Excelsia" sweet and strong.

Search the Scriptures
by G.E. Marsh
The Restitution Herald, circa 1930-1934
Tune: "Marching through Georgia"

Search the Scriptures daily as Bereans did of old,
  Working ever bravely all its beauties to unfold,
Asking God to bless us as His treasures we behold,
  While we are searching the Scriptures.

Chorus:
  Onward! Onward! Forever more we'll sing!
  Onward! Onward! On het our praises ring!
  While we're marching forward, ever loyal to our King,
  Working and fighting for Jesus.
(Three more verses follow.)

Come to the Saviour
by Wiley Jones
Songs of Zion, Wiley Jones, publisher, 1877

1. Come, sinners, join the faithful band,
   And follow sin no more.
   Come journey to the Promis'd Land—
   A bright and blissful shore.

   Chorus:
     O come to the Saviour, O come to the Saviour,
     O come to the Saviour, And be forever blest.

2. Your sin may red like scarlet be,
   And as crimson glow;
   Yet Christ from all can set you free,
   And wash you white as snow.
   Chorus

3. O who can speak the joys divine
   Which Christ the Lord will give!
   His ransom'd ones like stars will shine
   And endless life receive.
   Chorus

Coming Reign of the Messiah
by Roxanna Wince

When the hoped for Messiah of ages,
Shall bring the bright mansions a-down,
And shall take as a gift from his Father,
Of earth's mighty kingdoms the crown;
When the fierce, cruel rulers of nations
To him in submission shall bow,
And the death-dealing steel of the warrior
Be changed for the sickle and plow.

The Millennial Day
by H.V. Reed
Tune: "The Thousand Years"

Cheer up the heart desponding pilgrims,
    Speak of the joys when Christ shall reign,
Preach the goodness of coming glory,
    Sound His praise with loud acclaim.

Chorus:
A thousand years earth's restitution,
    'Tis the glad day so long foretold
'Tis the bright morn of Zion's glory,
    Prophets foresaw in times of old.

Verse 2:
We have walked in tears and sadness,
    While along the earth's highway,
And have prayed in hope and gladness,
    For the light of that bright day.
    Chorus

Verse 3:
Forget your sorrows, cling to the promise,
    Hold the banner in the breeze,
He will come on that fair morrow,
    As foretold in the jubilees.
    Chorus

Verse 4:
On David's throne, on the Mt. Zion,
    We'll reign with Christ as priests and kings,
A thousand years we'll rule the nations
    While dove-like peace shall fold her wings.
    Chorus

Forgetting
The Restitution Herald October 12, 1948

If you were busy being kind,
Before you knew it, you would find
You'd soon forget to think 'twas true
That someone was unkind to you.

If you were busy being glad,
And cheering people who were sad,
Although your heart might ache a bit
You'd soon forget to notice it.

If you were busy being good
And doing just the best you could,
You'd not have time to blame some man
Who's doing just the best he can.

If you were busy being true
To what you know you ought to do,
You'd be so busy you'd forget
The blunder of the folks you've met.

If you were busy being right,
You'd find yourself too busy, quite,
To criticize your neighbor long,
Because he's busy doing wrong.

How Long, O Lord
by Roxanna Wince
Tune: "Stand Up, Stand Up for Jesus" by G.J. Webb

How long, O heav'nly Bridegroom! How long wilt thou delay?
And yet how few are grieving That Thou dost absent stay!
The very bride her portion And calling hath forgot,
And seeks for ease and glory Where Thou, her Lord, art not.

Oh, wake Thy slumbering virgins! Send forth the solemn cry,
Let all Thy saints repeat it, "The Bridegroom draweth nigh!"
May all our lamps be burning, Our loins well girded be,
Each longing heart preparing With joy Thy face to see.

Appendix 12

Second Adventism in Ripley

Excerpts of
William Greenwell and the Ripley Church of God
by Millie Laning, Mt. Sterling, Illinois
From The Restitution Herald, *Dec. 1992/Jan.1993, p.16*
Mrs. Laning referred to the History of Schuyler and Brown Counties, Illinois.

The Greenwells have been in Brown County, Illinois, since 1840. William erected a gristmill on Crooked Creek, now called Lamoine River. For many years it was the only water power mill nearer than Quincy. William Greenwell was a man of courage and conviction. He must have been rather ingenuous, too. It is said he built a cab to be used on his buggy or sled in which he installed a small stove. When he drove back and forth about the countryside, the smoke rolled cheerily out of the stove pipe, to the wonderment and amusement of the natives.

Mr. Greenwell…believed so firmly in the second coming of Christ that he built and furnished a room in his rather pretentious home so that he would be ready to receive Him. About 1840, "The Second Coming of Christ" was preached in this part of the state. Several of the earlier members by careful Bible reading and studying accepted this teaching and formed a group known then and for several years as the "Advents."

The doctrine of the Second Advent was first introduced among the people of Mt. Sterling, Illinois in the winter of 1842 by H. A. Chittendon of New York in a series of lectures on the prophetic Scriptures.

The charter or early members of the Ripley Church of God, according to an old record book, were William Greenwell, Isaiah Laning, Ellen Laning, Garrett and Mrs. Robins, Dr. Bowman and Mrs. Bowman, Emily Long, Elizabeth Cox and Jennie Cox. They obtained the building which is still used and began having services before 1865. The building had been built in 1855 and was used for church, for public meetings and as a schoolhouse.

The building originally stood south of where it is now, across the present highway which was then a deep ravine. In 1889 Isaiah Laning purchased the lots on which the church now stands, and deeded them to the trustees of the Church of God Abrahamic Faith in 1890. The church was moved across the ravine to where it now stands by means of hand-hewn logs, horses, and many men.

See Also Appendix 5–Collaboration in Illinois,
"The Advent Christian Church," by Mrs. Mansfield

**Fonthill Church of God,
looking west on Canboro Road**

**Youth at Ganymede Spring,
Oregon, Illinois**

Faithful Illinois Members
Left to right: Joe Glotfelty, Mandy Glotfelty, unknown, Anna Drew, Mary Renner, Jessie Wilson.

Hope Chapel Church of God, South Bend, Indiana

1961 Gospelettes Tour
Left to right: CE and Louise Lapp, Rachel Krogh, Janet Turner, Martha Burnett and Jon Lapp at Eldorado, Illinois, Church of God.

FL and Evelyn Austin with Kitty

Omaha Church of God, 1961

Appendix 13 - Timeline: Periodicals, 1800-1899

Decade	Col 1	Col 2	Col 3	Col 4
1800	*Herald of Gospel Liberty* Elias Smith 1809-1817 at Portsmouth, NH			
1810				
1820				
1830		*Christian Palladium* Joseph Marsh 1839-1843 at Union Mills, NY		
1840		*Voice of Truth* Joseph Marsh 1844-1847 at Rochester, NY	« *Glad Tidings of the Kingdom at Hand* LO Fleming 1830s-1843 at Rochester, NY	*Bible Examiner* George Storrs 1841-1869 at NYC & Albany, NY
1850	*Herald of Life* George Storrs 1862-?	*Advent Harbinger &* *Bible Advocate* Joseph Marsh 1847-1854 at Rochester, NY		*Gospel Banner &* *Millennial Advocate* Benjamin Wilson 1853-1865 at Geneva, IL
1860		*Prophetic Expositor &* *Bible Advocate* Joseph Marsh 1855-1860 at Rochester, NY	*Prophetic Watchman &* *Herald of the Kingdom* JM Stephenson (Editor) HV Reed (Co-editor) 1860-1867 at Chicago, IL	⌄
		The Bible Expositor Joseph Marsh (Editor/Publisher) Thomas Newman (Assist. Editor) 1860 at Seneca Falls, NY	⌄	⌄
		The Bible Teacher Joseph Marsh 1860-1863 at Rochester, NY	⌄	⌄
		Millennial Harbinger & *Bible Advocate*, 1860-1864 Joseph Marsh 1860-1862 at Rochester, NY; Thomas Newman 1862-63 at Seneca Falls, NY; Reed, Austin, Judson, Green 1864 at Seneca Falls, NY »	*Herald of the Coming Kingdom* Thomas Wilson 1868-1870 Chicago, IL ⌄	« « « «
1870		*The Millennarian/The Evangelist* HV Reed 1873-1874 at Chicago, IL	*The Restitution*, 1870-1926 Thomas Wilson 1870-74 at Chicago, IL	
		Our Rest Thomas Wilson 1874-1875 at Chicago, IL	*The Restitution* HV Reed 1874-77 at Chicago, IL	*Sunshine* JF Willcox 1876-1877 at Plymouth, IN
1880	*Our Rest* Charles Jones 1880-1891	*The Millennarian* GM Myers 1885-1890 at Lanark, IL	*The Restitution* Stedman Chaplin 1877-87 at Plymouth, IN	*Gospel Trumpet*, 1884-1915 TJ Daniel 1884-1906 at Waveland, AR
	Words of Truth Samuel Wilson 1884-1904 at Rahway, NJ			*Gospel Trumpet* « RO Turner 1906-1914 at Boynton, OK
1890	*Word & Work* William Gibbs 1896-1908 at Abilene, TX	*The Christian Inquirer* GM Myers 1890-1895 at Belle Plaine, IA	*The Restitution* AR Underwood 1887-1911 at Plymouth, IN	*Glad Tidings of the Kingdom* JB Craton 1890?-1898? at Council Grove, KS
	The Last Days Thomas Wilson 1897-1925 at Oakland, CA	*The Evangelist* GM Myers 1895-1898 at Belle Plaine, IA	*continues on next page*	*Day Dawn & Harvest Messenger* James Patrick 1898-1922 at Howard Lake, MN

NOTE: Publications grouped with gray backgrounds indicate consecutive titles by same editor(s) **OR** continuous publication by same editor(s) with publication location and/or name change **OR** hand-offs to other editors **AND/OR** title mergers by multiple editors. » Also indicates title mergers.

Based on charts by David Graham (1985) and Jan Stilson (1985, 2011). Redesigned for encyclopedia by Dawn Johnson, Word Edge.

Appendix 13 - Timeline: Periodicals, 1900-Present

1900		*Present Truth* Charles & WL Crowe 1898-1915 at St. Paul, NE ⋎	*continued from previous page*	
1910	*Way of Truth* Ezra Gifford 1916-1957(?) at Spokane, WA	*The Restitution Herald,* 1911-Present SJ Lindsay 1911-22 at Oregon, IL	*The Restitution* Robert Huggins 1911-22 at Cleveland, OH	
1920		*The Restitution Herald* FL Austin 1922-31		*Gospel Messenger* TA Drinkard 1923?-1963 at Arlington, TX
1930		*The Restitution Herald* GE Marsh 1931-38		
1940		*The Restitution Herald* SE Magaw 1938-50		
1950		*The Restitution Herald* James Watkins 1951-54	*Progress Journal*, CofGGC 1958-Present at Oregon, IL (Merged w/ *The Restitution Herald*)	
		The Restitution Herald Harold Doan 1954-68	*Challenge*, CofGGC 1957-1983 and 1985-1988 at Oregon, IL	
1960		*The Restitution Herald* TM Ferrell 1968-71		
1970	*The Honest Truth* TA Ferrell 1972-1979 at Greenville, SC	*The Restitution Herald* Clyde Randall 1971-73		
	The Bible Truth Arlen Rankin 1978-1983 at Fall City, WA	*The Restitution Herald* JR LeCrone 1973-78		
		The Restitution Herald David Krogh, Interim Editor 1978		
1980		*The Restitution Herald* Russell Magaw 1978-90	*Wisdom and Power* Charles Jones 1988-1994 at Wyoming, MI	*History Newsletter* Jan Stilson 1984-95 at Oregon, IL/Morrow, GA
1990	*Focus on the Kingdom* A Buzzard 1998-Present at McDonough, GA	*The Restitution Herald* Hollis Partlowe 1990-93		
		The Restitution Herald Kent Ross 1993-95		
		The Restitution Herald Jeff Fletcher 1995-2004		
2000	*e-Herald* (e-herald.org) Kent Ross & Wally Winner 2009-Present	*The Restitution Herald* David Riley 2005-06	*Wisdom and Power* Charles Jones 2001-Present at Pomona, CA	
2010		*The Restitution Herald* Gary Burnham 2006-Present		

LEGEND: *Publication Title*, encompassing date range (if title had multiple editors)
Editor's name
Years he or she edited (if applicable)
Years produced at city, state (if known or changed from previous location)

Based on charts by David Graham (1985) and Jan Stilson (1985, 2011). Redesigned for encyclopedia by Dawn Johnson, Word Edge.

Appendix 14

Atonement

Atonement
Editorial by F.L. Austin
Reprinted from The Restitution Herald, *April 15, 1924.*

The resurrection of Christ has largeness of meaning according as one gathers meaning of his death.

Not only is Christ "our Passover" and our High Priest, he also is our atonement. As Passover, he, through death, protected a people for the service of firstborn; as Priest, he consecrated himself unreservedly unto the service of the Priesthood. Those subjects having been referred to in previous numbers of The Herald, it is now fitting to consider his death briefly from the standpoint of the atonement.

The example in Leviticus 16 could not completely reveal the entrance of Christ, our true high priest, into the holiest of all for atonement purposes as declared in Hebrews 9:7-9.

The tabernacle was one. It was the place in the midst of God's chosen people in which he would abide among them. It was divided into two rooms. It was within the second room, upon the mercy seat, that the Father's presence was manifested. It was here that the high priest must appear that he might be in the presence of God, perhaps even at his right hand. But God is spirit; man is soul; Aaron was man. It was impossible for Aaron, or any soul to abide in the presence of God. He was permitted to enter God's secret chamber once each year, which entrance always pointed forward to the time when the true high priest should enter the holy of holies once for all, to abide continuously.

But he, too, in the days of his flesh, was like unto his brethren. He was soul. He poured his soul out unto death. To abide in the holy of holies he must lay off the soulual [sic] that he might take on the spiritual, even that he might become the new man, who in the strength of his being, and the position of his service should perform the labors of atoning the sins of his brethren, even those labors which the Aaronic priesthood prefigured, as they year by year entered the holy of holies for brief moments. For this, it was necessary that he should die, that is, lay off the old man in order that he might become the new creation.

This was prefigured by Aaron and his successors in their atonement services each year. A bullock was set aside for the high priest to make atonement for him and his house. The bullock, according to Leviticus 16:11-14, was not for the congregation of Israel, but for the priest and his co-laborers. Likewise, one phase of Christ's atonement work was that of preparing himself for an abode within the holy of holies. Having passed the veil of his flesh, according to Hebrews 10:19, he was then in position to ascend to the heavens and return; to abide on earth, to return to the heavens; in fact, he would always be in the holy of holies, in the perfected completed state. From this condition he will never return. Should he return he can then never again enter the holiest for his entrance was to be but "once."

Aaron in addition to entering the holy of holies with the blood of the bullock for himself and his own, afterward, on the same day, slew the goat, which Moses explained in Leviticus 15:16, was for the sins of the people. Aaron then did with the blood of the goat as he had previously done with the blood of the bullock. He took it within the veil to make atonement for the holy place, because of the uncleanness of the children of Israel. The blessings resulting from this atonement were afterwards announced by Aaron in the presence of the congregation.

Thus John says in his general epistle, chapter 2:1, that Christ is the "propitiation for our sins; and not for ours only, but also for the sins of the whole world."

It is thus seen that there were two labors accomplished by Christ's death; the first was that of preparing himself to enter and abide in the presence and service of God in the most holy. This work also included those who are in Christ, who, being glorified together, are to abide with him. This work of Christ's enables them to have boldness, liberty, and confidence, to enter into the holiest, into and beyond the same veil, even the veil of his flesh. None others may enter there.

The second work of the Master was to cover, cancel, forgive, [and] atone for the sins of the congregation beyond. Thus in the fulfillment, the nation of Israel, and of those who will ally themselves with Israel in the Kingdom of God, will be forgiven their iniquities, and they will dwell, not in the holy of holies with Christ, and his church, but in the uncursed, glorified earth they will plant and reap, build and inhabit, under the guidance and blessings of him and his who abide in the condition of the holiest place.

Appendix 15

Baptism

Baptism—and the Plan of Salvation

by Pastor Kenneth Milne

Reprinted from The Restitution Herald, *Oregon, Illinois, September 1975.*

The Church of God of the Abrahamic Faith is composed of those who have obtained remission of sins by virtue of the blood of the Lord Jesus Christ (Acts 20:28). Christ commanded that penitent ones must be baptized for the remission of sins; therefore, baptism is essential for one to gain the hope of salvation, and to be added to the Church of God (Acts 2:38-47).

Obedience to the gospel of Christ is essential to salvation. Paul declared, in Romans 1:16, "I am not ashamed of the gospel of Christ: for it is the power of God unto salvation to every one that believeth to the Jew first, and also to the Greek."

The Apostle Paul declared: "Seeing ye have purified your souls in obeying the truth through the Spirit unto unfeigned love of the brethren, see that ye love one another with a pure heart fervently: being born again, not of corruptible seed, but of incorruptible, by the word of God, which liveth and abideth for ever" (I Pet. 1:22,23).

From these scriptures, it may be observed that obedience to the gospel is imperative. We know that Christ, the author of salvation, made baptism a part of the gospel. Baptism is essential to salvation.

Read what Jesus said in Mark 16:15, 15: "Go ye into all the world, and preach the gospel to every creature. He that believeth and is baptized shall be saved; but he that believeth not shall be damned." Jesus predicates man's salvation upon certain conditions. "Preach the gospel…He that believeth and is baptized shall be saved." The gospel must be believed, and the believer must be baptized. In the Book of Acts, no case of conversion is recorded in which one obeyed the gospel without being baptized into Christ. When conditions are stated, those conditions must always be fully met. Baptism is definitely a condition for salvation.

In response to the question, "What shall we do? Peter commanded, "Repent and be baptized, every one of you in the name of Jesus Christ for the remission of sin; and ye shall receive the gift of the Holy Ghost."

The thrust of the question, in view of the answer, is "What shall we do for remission of sins?" They were told, "Be baptized for the remission of sins." But baptism alone is not sufficient; it must be accompanied by repentance.

At this point, it is well that we understand what the word "remission" means. It comes from the Greek word that means "release"; "pardon"; "cancellation"; or "forgiveness". In fact, this same word is translated "forgiveness" several times in the New Testament.

I need not remind you that all men have sinned. There is none righteous. All need to have their sins forgiven. In the sight of God, each has a spiritual criminal record against him. Each must clear his record. Until this is done, we are cut off form direct contact with God.

How do we clear our record with God? Baptism is the means by which this is accomplished. We are baptized, or buried, that our old selves may died figuratively. The old criminal records are destroyed in the process.

By reason of this unique experience in your life, you become spiritually clean and pure before your Creator. All previous sin is forgiven. This is why Peter commanded: "Repent, and be baptized…for the remission of sins."

How can being immersed in water clean up our total spiritual criminal record? The answer is that it doesn't. What actually makes remission of sins possible at the time of baptism is that the benefits of the shed blood of Jesus are applied to the baptized person personally (Rom. 5:9). This is what Paul meant when he said, "Know ye not that so many of us as were baptized into Jesus Christ were baptized into his death? Therefore we are buried with him by baptism into death? (Rom. 6:3,4).

These events—your baptism, the application of Jesus' blood to your record, and the remission of your sins—all come into focus at one point of time.

The Apostle Peter declared: "Baptism doth also now save us" (I Peter 3:21), Regardless of any doctrine of men to the contrary, Peter, by inspiration, affirmed that "baptism doth also now save us!"

Paul explains why baptism saves—because baptism puts one into Christ. "As many of you as have been baptized into Christ have put on Christ" (Gal. 3:27). Baptism is the act of obedience that puts one into Christ. Baptism saves because salvation is in Christ (Col. 1:13,14).

One in Christ is a new creature. "If any man be in Christ, he is a new creature; old things are passed away; behold, all things are become new" (2 Cor. 2:17).

Since redemption is in Christ, forgiveness is also in Christ. One in Christ is a new creature. It is of the utmost importance that we are ourselves in Christ. The Scriptural fact is that we are only placed in Christ by baptism. We must accept baptism as essential to salvation.

If one could receive salvation outside of Christ, he could be saved apart from redemption, with no forgiveness of sins, and without becoming a new creature in Christ Jesus. All of this is, of course, impossible. We must consult the Word of God, and listen to what He has to tell us. The Bible clearly teaches us that baptism is indispensible to our hope of eternal life!

Pastor Kenneth and Mary Milne
Photo provided by Rex Cain

Appendix 16

Christian Education

Excerpts of

Historical Documents Supporting Higher Education in the Church of God

compiled by Eugene Stilson, BS (Ed.), BTh, MA (Ed.), MA (NT), President, Rock River Christian College

Introduction

A group of delegates met at Philadelphia in 1888 to organize the first General Conference of the Church of God. A committee on Evangelism and Education presented a report on the objectives of theological education.

The delegates met for the second annual meeting in Chicago in 1889. They approved the report of the Education, Music, and Literature Committee. The detailed plan for theological education was patterned after the Chautauqua method.

The Chautauqua movement was a system of summer school and correspondence school founded at Chautauqua Lake, New York in 1874. There were also traveling groups called Tent Chautauquas. This form of education came out of the desire of a Methodist minister to offer teacher training to Sunday School teachers.

The Philadelphia Conference

Report of the First Annual Conference of the Churches of God in Christ Jesus, for the United States and Canada held at Philadelphia, November 16-26, 1888. Published for the churches by James Wilson, Corresponding Secretary, Austin, Illinois. Church of God Archives.

Committee of Evangelism and Educational work included William Brookman, Toronto; Peyton G. Bowman, Perryville, KY; George Elton, Cleveland, OH; John O. Woodruff, Elizabeth, NJ; George W. Young, Brooklyn, NY.

2. Whilst maintaining that the Church of God should edify itself in love by calling out the gifts of its members, we believe that where special aptitude for Evangelistic work is manifested by any member, it should be recognized and nourished; and whilst opposed to the principle that in general actuates the Theological School or Institute, which appears to be for the purpose of maintaining particular views, rather than a free investigation of the Truth as contained in the Holy Scriptures, yet your Committee is not opposed to the principle of training or equipping such suitable men efficiently for the service of the Lord, being convinced, as was well said by on eof old, that "if He has no need of our wisdom, He has still less need of our ignorance;" and believing in general that acceptable candidates for so great an office should be well grounded in

   I. The spirit of prayer. Acts 6:4
   II. In the principle of rightly dividing the word of truth.
   III. In the history of the church at large.
   IV. In the grace of a good delivery of words.
   V. If practicable, (instruction) of the original languages of the Scriptures.

Your Committee, therefore, would recommend to this Conference that such means to so desirable an end should form a subject for their serious and prayerful consideration; and though we have no defined plan to present to this body, yet the following letter in connection with the subject, speaks for itself and forms a suggestion upon which this Conference is asked to act.

Letter to the Chairman of the Committee on Evangelists and Educational Work:

Dear Brother:

If you decide to form a Ministerial School, at some central point like Plymouth, Indiana, with four terms of three months each in each year, under some reliable teacher, like Elder Chaplin, with three or more lessons a week on the doctrines of truth according to the Scriptures, on the unspeakable love of God in Christ, on Elocution, and, if possible, in the study of the original languages of Holy Writ, to be given to a candidate for the ministry; and that a preacher's certificate be granted by some recognized authority on the recommendation of the teacher, to such scholars passing not less than one full term there.

I will contribute the sum of five hundred dollars toward such a school, as soon as a similar amount of five hundred dollars is raised by the church at large for that object: Two hundred and fifty dollars per annum of the sum thus raised to be paid in monthly portions to such teacher or teachers; and five dollars a week to be allowed to each needy scholar for his maintenance during his term of instruction.

Signed, George F. Work

The Chicago Conference 1889

Report of the Second General Conference held at Chicago, November 15, 1889. The General Conference of the Churches of God in Christ Jesus for the United States and Canada. History, Constitution and By-laws, p. 11.

Your committee on Education, Music and Literature would respectfully report as follows: First, that an educational institution be established to be designated as the Berean Institute.

Second, that the object of this Institute shall be the instruction of its patrons in biblical, historical and philosophical learning, the original languages of the scriptural text, and to train them in the arts of composition and public speaking.

Third, that the expense of the Institute be met by the sale of scholarships or collection of tuition fees of its patrons, together with donations, and that the scale of prices shall be at the lowest margin to cover expenses.

Fourth, that certification or diplomas be issued to students who have completed the prescribed course of study in the different departments, and passed satisfactory examinations therein.

The committee recommends the appointment of a faculty to consist of a president, and professors or preceptors for each department. The following departments are suggested: Bible Study and Exegesis; History; Science of Life and Christian Literature; Greek and Hebrew; and Elocution and Rhetoric.

The Third General Conference 1921

There was a conference at Waterloo, Iowa, in 1910. This organization failed to continue. Another attempt at organization was made at Waterloo in 1921. This is the present organization of the Church of God General Conference. Two important documents came out of this conference: A Declaration of Understanding and the Constitution.

Declaration of Understanding

Working Rules pertaining to Education:

IV. The officers of this General Conference constitute a Council Board.

VI. For purposes of conducting the business of this General Conference, this Council Board shall be incorporated under the name National Bible Institute.

XI. The several officers of this Conference shall, ex-officio, exercise the duties of officers of corresponding designation in the National Bible Institute according to the terms of the Constitution governing said National Bible Institute.

XIV. The purpose for which the NBI shall be incorporated are: C. That facilities be provided to aid in the education of those desiring to prepare themselves for the ministry, Bible teaching or other religious work.

Constitution (1921)

Article 1 Section 3. The object for which this Institute is formed is to carry on religious, educational and charitable work as may be determined from time to time by the General Conference of the Church of God.

Section 4. The work undertaken by this Institute shall be divided into departments as follows: ...Educational.... each department to be provided with its own department head, all under the administration of the National Bible Institute.

Oregon Bible College Class of 1961
Clockwise from back left:
Larry Townsend, Bob See, Russ Magaw, Paul Shaw, Rex Cain, Jesse Pestle,
Betty Finney, Nancy Anderson, OE Dick.

Appendix 17

Development Role of *The Restitution Herald*

The Importance of *The Restitution Herald* in the Development of the Church of God

by Jan Stilson, BTh, BS, MALS, MA (Biblical Studies)

Reprinted with permission from the 100th Anniversary Issue of The Restitution Herald, *with revisions, Church of God General Conference, McDonough, GA. October, 2010.*

The birth of *The Restitution Herald* on October 12, 1911, set a trend in the Church of God which saved the denomination from collapse, and set it on a path of growth and development in keeping with the our forefathers' desires to teach Bible truth. To explain, the new religious paper was the product of the defeat at the 1910 Waterloo Conference to organize a national work, and the dispute between the newly formed Ministerial Association, fall 1910, with the owner of the esteemed, but aging *Restitution*, Plymouth, Indiana. Turmoil was the word of the day in 1910.

The Ministerial Association took leadership to appoint a publishing company comprising some of the men who supported the new organization and the new paper. These officers included Ezra Railsback, president, Indiana, S.J. Lindsay, secretary/treasurer, Oregon, Illinois, and Peter Jeffrey, John E. Cross and E.F. Gesin, all of Illinois as directors. They appointed S.J. Lindsay as editor and manager to begin publishing a new paper, *The Restitution Herald*. Subscription costs were $1.50 per annum, payable in advance.

This paper would reflect biblical truth, would avoid tangents, would not be a gossip sheet, but would report news of members, churches, conferences and evangelists. It would be published 50 weeks a year. It would be used for evangelism purposes. It would have a page for Bereans for which they would furnish copy, and it would also include a page for children with a children's editor. It would be a paper that members could be proud to pass along to other readers, because it would not be argumentative or radical in its approach.

Editor S.J. Lindsay was an educator at the time of the start up. He was assistant Superintendent of Schools in Ogle County, the pastor of the Oregon Church of God, and a member of the print staff of the local newspaper. He was well qualified to understand the heart and mission of the Church of God. He had helped to begin the Oregon church, and he went on from there immediately to begin organizing Summer Bible Schools for young adults at Oregon. This became the first attempt to educate teachers and ministers in the Church of God, and from it came the youth camp movement, the Bible Training Class, and the Bible Colleges we have supported the past 100 years.

The student body of these summer "camps", for which a dormitory was built behind the church, provided some of the copy for the new *Restitution Herald* and preachers for empty pulpits. One ministry supported another. Through its pages *The Herald* notified members in the field of student preaching assignments, upcoming conferences, special meetings and news. Doctrine was present in every issue and was well presented by the best writers in the Church of God.

The first issue was eight pages in length, 10" by 15" in size, and included articles by notable laymen and pastors. Peter Jeffrey of Murphysboro, Illinois wrote, "Not Far from the Kingdom," and from just up the road, Rolla Hightower of Golden, Illinois, wrote, "The Gospel." B.W. Woodward of Michigan wrote, "Fight the Good Fight."

Samuel J. Lindsay continued as editor until after the successful formation of the Church of God General Conference at Waterloo, Iowa in 1921. When F.L. Austin was hired as Executive Secretary, he also became the editor. At that time the stock and equipment was turned over to the National Bible Institute, the business arm of the General Conference.

After F.L. Austin retired, G.E. Marsh became editor. He continued serving a steady diet of doctrinal, educational and informative articles patterned after an evangelical model. Many members and pastors contributed to every page of *The Herald*. Marsh began to emphasize Church of God history. He wrote a series which began with first century church history and ended with the present-day Church of God. Readers loved it. It opened up a new area of exploration and awakened people to how the doctrines of the Church of God fit into church history, and how the Church of God began in America. It also offered ideas of where it needed to go in the 20th century.

One direction it moved to was missions. First, home missions were emphasized. Members were encouraged to strengthen their local works, and begin new ones. As ministers were being trained at Oregon, they were snapped up by congregations hungry for regular preaching services.

Second, foreign missions began to be emphasized, first in India and later other countries. Editor Sydney E. Magaw was influential in promoting missions, especially after the formation of Israel as a nation in 1948. He also continued to emphasize Church of God history.

Other editors who have contributed significantly to the stabilization of the Church of God through the ministry of *The Restitution Herald* have included James Watkins, who traveled to Israel in 1951, Harold Doan, the designer of the Decade of Development (1955-1965) who was succeeded by Stanley Ross, the foreign missions editor who traveled around the world making contacts and baptizing members. We cannot forget Terry Ferrell, editor, pastor and historian of the Church of God; Clyde Randall, author of *Historical Waymarks of the Church of God*, pastor and editor of *The Herald*; J.R. LeCrone, pastor and editor; David Krogh, executive director and editor after the deaths of John and Ruth Lewis; Hollis Partlowe, pastor, prophecy student and editor; Russell Magaw, pastor and editor; and Pastor Jeff Fletcher who headed the work after the move to Atlanta, all of whom served in editorial capacity from the 1960s-2000s.

It was under Russell Magaw's editorship that the now well-known "75th Anniversary Issue" was published (October, 1985) with Bible content, design and grace. It may be the only edition of *The Restitution Herald* to have a center fold-out! Pastor Gordon Landry, an artist at design and page layout, designed the center fold and worked many years in the print shop preparing copy for the press. Copies of the Anniversary issue are still available through the General Conference office.

Through many volumes, print shop staff worked tirelessly running the linotype and the press, and later, computers, year after year. Many worked faithfully in the publishing department including Val Mattison, Paul Johnson, Robert Johnson, Rachel Krogh Carr, Marlyn Holquist Fyfe, Jean Doan, Helen Burnett Jones, Daniel Smead, Michelle Turner, and Mary Krogh who volunteered many years as a proof reader. We especially think of student Bob Pike who couldn't remember how to tie a square knot to bundle packages for mailing, so the staff prayed for him.

Through the years, *The Restitution Herald* has truly been the "Voice of the Church of God". It culminates a long line of Kingdom of God publications beginning in 1844 with Editor Joseph Marsh and his beloved *Voice of Truth*. *The Restitution Herald* has reported our interests and it has directed our ministries. It has taught us current trends in Christian education, missions, youth work, person-to-person evangelism, and much more. It has been a leader in unifying the work and reflecting the will of the Lord through the work of the members. It has made us laugh. It has made us weep at the shocking deaths of beloved church members. It has inspired us to witness throughout our communities and throughout the world. It has always taught the truth.

In the last decade, technological changes to *The Restitution Herald* have been noticed by readers as editors have positioned the paper to enter the electronic internet age, but the message has not changed. It remains dedicated to preaching the whole truth of the Bible, especially the story of the Second Coming of Jesus to establish the Kingdom of God on earth, a message unique to the Church of God since the days of Joseph Marsh.

Appendix 18

Faith

Thriving as Signs Begin to Accumulate
by Kent H. Ross
From THRIVE Ministry, *Springfield, Ohio, Online November 9, 2009.*

In our Sunday School class, we're just coming to the last lessons in our original series that started considering the Abrahamic covenant and coming through to the hope of the Kingdom. Known once as the Church of God of the Abrahamic Faith, that title seems seldom used any more, but that God's covenant with Abraham, is still in effect And needs to be understood and appreciated by Christians today.

Studying that "old agreement" God made with Abraham is fascinating as you begin to understand why the animosity between Jews and those of the Arab world is so deep today. It goes back, first to Abraham's first son, Ishmael, albeit semi-illegitimate, and then, his legitimate son Isaac's first son, Esau, who despised his birthright and with negligence discarded his legitimate right and Jacob became the heir.

We then began studying how it was that some Gentiles became part of God's family. Of course, it was through Christ's death that we became and still become heirs of Abraham. Paul wrote all about it in Galatians 3:26-29 – ²⁶You are all sons of God through faith in Christ Jesus, ²⁷for all of you who were baptized into Christ have clothed yourselves with Christ. ²⁸There is neither Jew nor Greek, slave nor free, male nor female, for you are all one in Christ Jesus. ²⁹If you belong to Christ, then you are Abraham's seed, and heirs according to the promise."

Paul in Romans 11 illustrates this by comparing us to a wild olive branch, or branches, that have been grafted into the main tree. At that point, he said, the natural branches, the Jews, because of their unbelief, were branches cut-off.

At this point the Jewish people remain cut-off from their inheritance, but Paul says the day will come when they, some of them at least, will be re-grafted into the main tree again. He says they were cut off to give us a chance to be grafted in.

So, by faith we become children of Abraham and heirs according to those old, old promises. How fascinating to learn how God's Plan, which for so many years seemed obscure, is now become clearer as we need to end of this Age.

Daniel wrote in what we call the twelfth chapter of the book by his name, that he was to close the book, as the knowledge of when these things he prophesied about would come to pass. But as we come down to the end, some things are becoming clearer. They are not completely clear, but things are emerging to make us believe that "soon and very soon, we are going to see the King." Yes, with our own eyes, just as Job said (19:25-27).

Appendix 19

Heresies: Aberrations from Scripture

The Exclusion of Questionable Doctrine by Church of God Members in the 20th Century

by Jan Stilson, BTh, BS, MALS, MA (Biblical Studies)

These ideas were presented first to Elderhostel at Oregon Bible College in 1988.

The ideas that shaped the doctrine of the Church of God as we know it today resulted from a winnowing process. To explain, certain ideas or "heresies" crept into the Age to Come movement. While heresies might seem like a strong word, particularly when some of our most cherished leaders held the divergent views, it is intended not to judge them but to explain the importance that conference delegates and ministers attributed to deleting those views from the mainstream of denominational thought. The membership dealt with these differing and sometimes enticing views through discussion, debate and Bible study. If a new notion did not measure up to scriptural standards through several witnesses in the Bible, if it did not follow proper exegesis or hermeneutical standards, or in some cases, if it did not agree with the majority opinion, it was drummed out. The latter reason often caused a contentious state at general conference meeting, members leaving with hurt feelings. In this manner, over the decades connecting the end of the nineteenth century to the new century, a firmer doctrinal statement of faith developed.

Doctrines that were accepted as collective beliefs by the 1880s included conditional immortality, the restoration of Israel to its homeland prior to the return of Christ, the second coming of Christ to earth to establish the Millennial Kingdom, the Oneness of God, and Jesus the Son of God born of a virgin. Doctrines that were not emphasized included the nature of Christ, atonement, the nature and timing of the resurrection, and the nature and work of the Holy Spirit beyond belief that it was the power of God.

Even so, the Church of God tried to organize in 1869, 1888 and 1910 without success. Member churches could not agree upon a written statement of faith.

In fact, as other Church of God denominations developed that were pentacostal in worship style, the Church of God General Conference shied away from emphasizing the Holy Spirit in order to avoid confusion. Leaders reacted strongly against being associated with charismatic denominations. One leader was quoted as saying, "We don't know what that spirit is, but we don't want it around here." In suppressing free investigation about the teaching of the Holy Spirit, the Church of God may have weakened its development, and delayed its national organization by at least four decades.

It was said that the reason the 1921 Conference organizational attempt succeeded was, in fact, because of earnest prayer and the work of the Spirit through that prayer. So, the Church of God General Conference has never denied the work of the Spirit, but it did shy away from a pentacostal emphasis within its ranks.

In 1921 the organization was born after agreement had been reached upon a statement of faith. There were other doctrines still swirling about the heads of leaders, pastors and members, and many things were discussed privately, but were never officially brought into the General Conference dogma.

These ideas or heresies are set forth here briefly for reader review.

Josephism. This view taught that Jesus was the natural born son of Joseph and Mary. The idea promoted the natural genealogy of Jesus from the line of King David. Because of His lineage, He was eligible to set upon the Throne of David in the Kingdom. He received the Holy Spirit at baptism at which time God adopted Him and empowered Him to perform miracles. He was not sinless so there was no atonement.

Problem: The problem with this idea is that it denies the work of the Holy Spirit in the conception process. Why would it be so easy to accept the Holy Spirit in Jesus' ministry following baptism, but not accept the virgin birth? Because it repudiated a Divine nature of Christ, it also had to explain the theology of atonement. If Christ were only a mere man with no divine nature, there is also no need for atonement and that leads to universalism.

One of the most revered publishers in the Church of God came to believe Josephism in his elderly years. Benjamin Wilson's writings from 1870 onward clearly stated this position. He believed it was not necessary to have a "God-man" for atonement to occur. He believed the Greek did not support the divinity of Christ. As translator of the *Emphatic Diaglott* his opinion was respectfully considered but rejected.

Larger Hope. This doctrine stated that unbelievers and disobeyers have a larger hope of being saved during the Millennium. It was also referred to as "Fair Chance, or Second Chance." This kind of thinking was encouraged through the doctrine of Universal Reconciliation also known as Universalism. Advocates of this position state that sin is temporary and God will remove sin from the world, and, bring everyone into the Kingdom. Including Satan and the wicked who died the Adamic death.

Problem: Larger Hope seems to be the extreme presentation of the Age to come idea that not only the mortal nations but also the wicked dead will be brought into the Millennial Kingdom under the rule of Christ, given opportunity to repent, and, be saved. Joseph Marsh said the living nations would be on probation during the thousand years. Probation, however, is not the Larger Hope. Mortal Men from the nations have the freedom during probation to reject Christ. For those unrepentant mortals there will be no hope, only the second death.

Church of God advocates of Larger Hope were J.W. Williams, Alta King, Wiley Jones, and maybe H.V. Reed. This idea was promoted by C.T. Russell (founder of the Jehovah's Witnesses who studied briefly with the Advent Christians).

Partial Resurrection. This doctrine assumes the wicked die the Adamic death, and, are never raised. Job says, "If a man die, shall he live again?" (Job 14:14). They felt the Bible taught that God would not raise a wicked man only to send him to death again. The Church of God did not go along with this. This is also known as Resurrection of the Righteous only, or Limited Resurrection.

Problem. The problem with this is that it does not agree with the many verses that talk about the resurrection of the just and the unjust. If only the righteous are raised, why then are the carnal Christians called the unjust, and who are raised then at the end of the Millennium that are part of the second death? If only the righteous are raised, are the carnal Christians considered righteous? Advocates of this teaching tended to be those who leaned more toward Christadelphian doctrines, including Robert Huggins and Benjamin Wilson.

S.J. Lindsay attempted to sway people's understanding with his tract on "Universal Resurrection" in which he stated that the Bible speaks of the first resurrection in which the just and the unjust are raised, the righteous at the beginning of the Millennium and the unjust (the Christian disobeyers and the mortal wicked from the Millennium) at the end (Rev. 20:4-6). This is the second death, not the second resurrection.

Mortal Emergence. This doctrine was created by Dr. John Thomas to solve the problem of the resurrection to immortality of carnal Christians (disobeyers). If all Christians are raised immortal in the twinkling of an eye, then how could God judge the disobeyers to the second death? It was a problem he did not explain in the manner that S.J. Lindsay did in his tract mentioned above. Thomas said, that all Christians are raised mortal from the grave and THEN judged as righteous or unjust. While Benjamin Wilson believed in partial resurrection, he could not tolerate mortal emergence, and split with Dr. Thomas over this doctrine. Wilson said the just and the unjust are raised in a general or universal resurrection. The unjust were **not** the Adamic wicked; they were the Christian disobeyers. We have been told that the Christadelphians have modified this doctrine and some do not hold to it now.

Problem: The Bible doesn't speak about mortal emergence from the grave. It was an attempt by Dr. Thomas to solve an exegetical problem with a logical explanation, but exegetical issues must be solved exegetically.

Universal Reconciliation. This teaching advances the idea that God will remove sin from the world and bring all men into the Kingdom. One proof text for this is, "For as in Adam all die, even so in Christ shall all be made alive" (I Cor. 15:22). Sin is temporary. Those mortal nations still living when Christ returns, and the wicked dead will enter the Millennium with the righteous, so there is no difference in their reward.

Problem: The fallacy of this position is that it denies man's free will to accept Christ. It therefore also denies conditional immortality. The Church of God teaches that man is free to accept Christ, and, without that choice, and, without holy living, cannot receive eternal life. If God acts finally to save all men, it is the ultimate extreme in Calvinistic predestination. The effect of this on church people is a nominal Christianity in which Christians have no incentive to "Go and make disciples" as Christ commanded. Why have a missions program if all men will be saved anyway? It also denies atonement. Why would Christ need to die to save men if all men were going to be saved anyway?

This problem was prevalent in the Church of God across Iowa, Missouri and Arkansas. The principal advocates of it were J.W. Williams of Iowa, Alta King of Nebraska and E.O. Stewart from Arkansas. Howard Bradford of Clark's Chapel Church of God in Arkansas discussed the problem, and, explained that it was "routed out" of Arkansas. E.O Stewart left the fellowship over it. L.E. Conner was said to privately believe it, but not to preach it from the pulpit.

Anglo-Israelism. This idea was quite comforting. It said that if you didn't make it into the Kingdom on the merits of your Christian life, perhaps you will make it because you have Jewish heritage and were part of the lost ten tribes of Israel. It stated that several European nations and the United States as a former British colony were direct descendants from the ten tribes. Denmark, for example was Dan's mark. Israel was God's chosen people. All Israel will be saved.

Problem: It offered greater assurance of salvation, but was an empty doctrine. It was highly speculative. It was similar in comfort level to "Larger Hope". There is no other way to God than through Christ. Jesus said, "I am the way, the truth and the life" (John 14:6).

F.L. Austin was reported to be an advocate of it across America, but the literature of the Church of God does not reveal this. Elder Fred Hall was also known for believing this teaching.

Sabbatarianism. At least three sister denominations in America worship on the Seventh-day. Those who practiced Saturday worship were the Seventh-day Adventists who were influenced by a Church of God man, O.R.L. Crozier, the Seventh-day Church of God which developed simultaneously but separately from the Church of God Abrahamic Faith, and the Seventh-day Baptists, who agreed with us only on the form of baptism. Sabbatarians believe the Ten Commandments were still in force today. To them this meant Saturday worship.

Problem: Acceptance of an Old Testament Jewish principle denied the New Covenant of Christ. The early church worshipped on the first day of the week, the day that Christ was raised from the dead. It was the beginning of a new faith and a new worship form centered around the Savior.

Those in the Church of God who formerly accepted Seventh-day practices but who either recanted, or worshipped on Sunday, included J. M. Stephenson, A J. Eychaner, and G.M. Myers. All of these ideas have been discovered and studied from the writings that make up the Archives of the Church of God now at the Cornerstone Bible Church in McDonough, Georgia. Many of these ideas are discussed throughout this encyclopedia.

Appendix 20

Missions

Excerpts of
History of Missions in the Church of God General Conference
by Judy Myers, Director of Lord's Harvest International

Mission work within the Church of God (Abrahamic Faith) began in the early1900s. Dr. and Mrs. Taylor of Bridgeton, Maine were national leaders in India. Mrs. Sarah Taylor was ordained by the Minnesota Conference of the Churches of God in 1914 at their fall conference in Eden Valley. In June of 1912, Elder Charles R. Vedantachari, Madras, India, had attended the Minnesota Church of God Conference at Eden Valley, where he was ordained a minister of the Minnesota Conference. He was twenty-six years of age at this time. He had been in Boston where he had taken postgraduate work. He was a very erudite man, and could speak seven languages fluently. Under Vedantachari's leadership, the India work progressed rapidly. With the passing of Sr. Taylor and the death of Charles Vedantachari in India, the mission work gradually deteriorated and the support from America fell off.

One of the converts under the Vedantachari leadership was John Manoah who carried on the work in a limited way. At the time of his death, he had a teenage son, S.S. Manoah. During the 1940s Brother S.S. Manoah began preaching. He sought and received support from the Minnesota Conference.

The main evangelism focus of the General Conference was carried on through the direction of a Committee on Evangelism. National evangelism was for adults and children.

In 1951, the emphasis changed from evangelism to missionary work. In 1952, Ada Simpson, Grand Rapids, Michigan, was asked by the Priscillas to act as chairman and call a meeting for the purpose of organizing a National Missionary Society. At this meeting, the following motion was made and adopted by the minister's wives: "That the Department of Evangelism be called the Department of Evangelism and Missions and include departments of home and foreign missions." Officers elected were C.E. Lapp, president; Mrs. Ada Simpson, vice president; and Mrs. Stanley Ross, Secretary.

In 1954 the Department of Evangelism and Missions became incorporated into the General Conference. [Editor's note]: During that time, two trips were made to the Holy Land, one by C.E. Lapp and another by James Watkins in company with Adib Lidawi to survey the land after it became a nation in 1948.

Dr. and Mrs. William Lawrence of Phoenix, Arizona traveled in 1963 to India to survey the work. They were greatly impressed with what was being done there. Upon returning, their reports were presented to the Board of Evangelism and Missions, and the General Conference Board of Directors was directed by the delegates at the 1964 General Conference to "continue the work with Bro. S.S. Manoah in and around Bangalore, India, including financial support."

Trips were made in 1966 by Stanley O. Ross, the Superintendent of Missions, accompanied by Merle Patrick, and in January 1972, Ross, Patrick and Mrs. Stanley "Peg" Ross traveled around the world to survey the work in India and other mission field where we were working with native leaders. (Source: *Historical Waymarks of the Church of God*, C.E. Randall.)

In 1977 the Foreign Missions Board outlined a better way to conduct foreign mission work. In this document the board set forth this statement: "The goal, then, is to teach the Gospel of Christ and to make disciples who will teach others." It was thought that sending long-term missionaries to plant indigenous churches in the native land was better than sending financial support with little oversight. These native churches should become self-governing, self-propagating and self-supporting.

Therefore a recommendation was made to the delegates of the 1977 summer conference that the financial support of the pastors in various fields be reduced and eventually stopped. By delegate action, this recommendation was passed. Following the reduction and discontinuance of financial support, dissatisfaction began to surface from pastors in various fields. Financial requests were submitted and according to new policy, not granted. Some of these included requests for buildings. Following these denials, some native leaders began to disassociate with the General Conference.

Mission Fields:

Nigeria. The work in Nigeria began through a recommendation by a student of Arizona State University, who had been entertained in the home of the Church of

God pastor one evening during the Christmas holidays. When he returned home, he suggested to the native pastors that they become involved with the Church of God Abrahamic Faith in Tempe, Arizona. In 1967 Lee McQuinn visited Nigeria and brought back a favorable report. The delegates at the summer conference voted to receive ten churches and nine pastors into the General Conference.

In 1970-71 three Nigerian students enrolled in Oregon Bible College. They returned home to supervise the work there. When Steve and Pam Grant visited Nigeria in 1983, they reported that the primary interest of the pastors in that nation seemed to be financial support.

Ghana. During his visit to Africa in 1967, Lee McQuinn met Oliver K. Amani. He had established an active work. In 1970 this work was recognized and accepted into the Church of God General Conference. In 1974 the Lawrences went to Africa and made a careful evaluation of the needs, changes, and brought back a favorable report. Brother and Sr. Paul Overholser of Lawrenceville, Ohio also visited the African work and brought back a favorable report. Steve and Pam Grant visited with Bro. Amani in 1983.

Nova Scotia. This field was opened by Roddy Pike who began it largely under a nondenominational banner. He came into contact with the Church of God through tracts and literature and after much study, became affiliated with us. He was received into the ministerial body. He attended General Conference in 1957 and 1958. In the fall of 1958 he felt the call to begin work in other areas of Nova Scotia and submitted his resignation. Two of his sons attended Oregon Bible College.

In November 1958 Pastor John Denchfield began nine years of service in Digby, Nova Scotia. In September 1967, Pastor Raymond Brown took over the leadership of the work, and remained there until his sudden death in 1974. Several lay workers followed Pastor Brown's service including Mrs. Eunice Pearson, Ohio, Mrs. Nina Hatcher and son Gary from Missouri, but the members of the church were not trained to be self-sufficient, reproducing Christians, and the work languished.

Liberia. Cornelius Boykai became acquainted with the Church of God while attending the Golden Rule Church in Cleveland. He was immersed by Pastor J.R. LeCrone after he completed the Systematic Bible Study Course. Upon his return to Liberia he desired to set up a clinic to help his people. The Northeast Conference undertook his support. The Overholsers helped to build the clinic, but when they visited found it was not completed. Eventually Boykai wrote asking forgiveness for his actions over the matter.

Philippine Islands. The work in the Philippines started when Eleodoro Ortiguero heard a debate between two men on which was the correct Bible name for the church—"Church of Christ" or "Church of God". Seeking to find the truth, his study led him to believe that the biblical evidence was in favor of the Church of God. He purchased a Handbook of Denominations by Meade and found the Church of God General Conference, Oregon, Illinois.

After corresponding with Executive Secretary Harold Doan, and studying the beliefs of the Church of God, he requested baptism. Harold Doan traveled to the islands and baptized Elders Ortiguero and Bonifacio Gabanes on June 25, 1961. He presented them with licenses as ministers of the Church of God General Conference.

In the summer of 1963, Ortiguero was brought to America and visited many of the churches in the United States and Canada, preaching and meeting the people. At that time we believed him to be in good standing with the Lord. However, after some time it was learned that he turned away from the Lord. Support of him was discontinued. Many fine Christians remained in the islands, so the work was taken up by the brethren of the Washington State Conference. Their mission trips continue to this day to nurture the members there, and to expand it. [Editor's note]: Those leading and participating in this work have included Elders Jim and Larry Rankin, Arlen Rankin, Ron Rankin, Ray, Margaret and Dan Foster and many others.

India. Presently, a governing body oversees the work in India as S.S. Manoah is elderly and unable to do much work. M.R. Noel served as Pastor in one of the Indian churches for a number of years, but is now deceased. For a time a medical clinic was opened in Bangalore. This clinic was entirely supported by Dr. and Mrs. Rossman, who were interested in the physical welfare of the people of India. The Rossmans were friends of the Church of God. The clinic operated for several years and served the community well, but was discontinued in 1984 because many other clinics had been started nearby.

Mexico. In 1962, migrant workers who had become acquainted with us through the Blanchard, Michigan Church of God, indicated to the General Conference that they were desirous of starting a work in Mexico and receiving help from us. Pastor Dean Moore of Blanchard was acquainted with these workers, and he along with Alberto Moreno made a trip to Mexico to do survey work. The first work in Mexico officially began on September 9, 1963 when the Moore family moved to Mexico.

In 1965 at the annual general conference, the delegates approved the recommendation to send Miss Rachel Krogh to Mexico to help with the work. In April 1968 Miss Alice Aldrich went to Mexico at her own expense to assist with the work. Rachel continued to work in Mexico until August 1969 when she was called to Oregon Bible College as instructor, and to serve as Superintendent of Missions for the General Conference. Alice left the work in 1971 but returned with support from the General Conference in 1974.

During the summer of 1966 Paul Shaw led a Youth Caravan including Bill Wachtel, a specialist in the Spanish language. Rachel traveled with the team to Matehuala and on to Rio Verde, and returned to the States with them to attend General Conference.

Other teams that were sent to Labor Vieja, ("old work") the hometown of Roberto and Lupe Badillo, the native leaders of the work, included the Church of God youth in Scottsdale, Arizona under the direction of Pastor James Graham, and the Mission Committee teams of the Oregon Church of God under the direction of Janet Stilson, who planned the trips and Robert Alcumbrack who led them in the field.

In the summer of 1986, the Oregon Mission Committee cooperated with the Youth of East Oregon Chapel to send a team that had been trained by Mexican native, Cesar Rocha. The team conducted a Vacation Bible School in Labor Vieja. The team included members from Oregon, East Oregon and Oregon Bible College students.

In January 1987, the Oregon Mission Committee sent Pastor Robert Alcumbrack, Alane Schmidlapp, and Judy Myers, mission director for the General Conference to plan for future short term mission trips to Mexico to cultivate it as a training ground for Oregon Bible College students and others in cross-cultural mission experiences. A team was sent that summer from the Oregon Church of God, after which yearly trips were planned by Judy Myers for the General Conference missions department. Until 1992 when Roberto Badillo began having health problems, teams traveled to Labor Vieja every year to host Bible schools, refurbish the church, and, assist the Badillos in their home compound.

In 2001, the Troy View Ohio youth group made a trip to Labor Vieja under the supervision of Judy Myers, after which annual trips have been conducted by Judy through the Lord's Harvest International, the newly created mission sending agency of the General Conference. The LHI was organized at the recommendation of the Minnesota Conference, long a leader in promoting foreign missions. The Minnesota Conference would have incorporated LHI, but didn't want to take contributions away from the General Conference, so the recommendation was made to the delegates through the Board of Directors' announcement in the *Progress Journal* that a vote be taken at the upcoming annual conference. At the 1993 summer conference, the motion to create a training and sending agency was passed.

Pastor Roberto Badillo died in the fall of 2006, after many years of faithful service. Lupe Badillo is carrying on the work and has a Sunday school for the children in the church that is within the family compound.

Lebanon. In 1964 Jamal Sunna'a from Beirut, Lebanon took a correspondence course from Oregon Bible College. He was a pastor formerly of another denomination. A small amount of support was given to him. In June 1966 Stanley Ross met with Pastor Sunna'a in Beirut. After much discussion and prayer Ross baptized him in the Mediterranean Sea. Sunna'a had a home church with about thirty people in attendance. There were forty-two children in the Sunday school.

Pastor Suuna'a also translated the Systematic Theology Correspondence Course into Lebanese, but it was discovered later, that he had not been faithful to the content, but had included doctrinal material which could not be endorsed by the General Conference. It was learned also that he was supported by another denomination so support was discontinued.

Egypt. Through Jamal Sunna'a contact was made with Shaker Iskander in Cario. He was a convert of Sunna'a and support of him was begun and continued until May 1973. At one time, he was attacked by Coptic monks and burned badly. He spent thirty-seven days in the hospital.

Peru. In late 1986 contact was made through Bill Wachtel and Anthony Buzzard with Mario Olcese in Lima. Olcese seemed to share many of our doctrinal truths. Anthony traveled to Lima in January 1987 to meet him and dialogue with him. That summer the mission committee of Oregon Bible College under the direction of Janet Stilson sent a team to Lima to assist with the work there. The team included several Bible College students who trained in the language, and prepared many skits and songs that could be presented in open-air market places. Anthony Buzzard, a theologian and instructor at Oregon Bible College, accompanied the team. Bill Wachtel participated in that trip.

In 1988 Jim and Alane Day were sent to work in Lima for 2-½ months. Mario later moved to the States and turned the work over to Beder Ucañay. Pastor Ucañay had been trained by another denomination, but had studied with Mario Olcese and came to believe the Gospel of the Kingdom. In 2001 another team visited Lima to become acquainted with the work. This team included David Krogh, Alice (Aldrich) Badillo, Judy Myers and Bill Wachtel. They discovered that he desired to spread the word across South America. Beder Ucañay had begun a training school for members, teaching them deeper truths of the Bible, and how to share the message with others. There is a door-to-door ministry, and a childrens' ministry. Since 2004 no less than six trips have been made, some people returning more than once to nurture the work. Sadly, Pastor Ucañay developed cancer in the eye and lost the battle after 2-½ years of treatment. Rachel Carr reports that presently Beder's brother, Gaston Ucañay, is pastoring the church with the assistance of another brother, Joaquin, and Beder's widow, Maria.

Second and third groups have been started north of Lima. David and Lynn Krogh, Bill Wachtel and Jennifer Koryta made a trip in the Summer 2010. David and Bill returned in October 2010 and were greatly encouraged by the work.

England. In April of 1988, Warren and Irene Sorenson and Jeff Fletcher made a survey trip to England in preparation for a church-planting ministry there. They chose the location for the work, and then Jeff and Karen Fletcher moved there in August. In 1990 a youth caravan went over to assist with the Bible School. Jeff and Karen lived there a year before returning to the states. For the time, energy, money and prayers spent in beginning the work, there was never a return of interest from the people.

Russia. In 1986 Tracy Savage from Minnesota came to Oregon Bible College to train. Her desire was to become a full-time missionary. She spent one year at the college and returned home to complete her education. In 1991 she traveled to Russia as part of a women's soccer team. She felt led to the Soviet Union, and began to study the language. On her trip, she developed friendships that might provide an invitation to return and live there. She requested that the Church of God General Conference assist her with this ministry.

In August 1992 Tracy was sent to Russia to serve. She worked in orphanages to share the gospel with children. Later, that door was closed as others also desired to do that same and no one could teach Bible in a government-operated orphanage. However, she was able to develop friendships with some girls that continue to this day. Tracy returned to the States in 1994 with her friend Olya who needed medical assistance. She also returned in 1995 with the support of the Lord's Harvest International Board.

In 1996 a short-term mission team traveled to Russia to assist Tracy. They were able to work with the children. In 1998 another team went to assist in construction work on a house Tracy had purchased north of St. Petersburg. Tracy married Stepan Zhykhovich from Belarus on January 20, 1999 in her home church in Minneapolis, Minnesota. Rebekah Martin spent time with them in Russia after their first child was born.

The government cracked down on religious groups that had not been registered with them over five years. This limits what Tracy is able to do, but she still shares the gospel and continues to cultivate relationships. In 2005 she requested that financial support to her be stopped so it can be used in other missions.

Haiti. In 1994 through study of Scriptures, Pastor Lesly Bertrand came to believe that there is only one God, that man is mortal and that the Kingdom of God will be on earth. He shared these truths with others in his Mennonite group of pastors. These pastors also studied and came to understand these same truths. In 1996 they were all expelled from the Mennonite fellowship and formed their own fellowship of about thirty churches.

In 1999 after confirming these truths through correspondence with Anthony Buzzard, Lesly attended the Theological Conference at Atlanta Bible College. At the conference he met several of our pastors and invited them to come to Haiti and teach at some of his conferences. In 2000, after storms blew down one of their churches, he contacted Pastor Jack Hearp and asked about receiving financial support. Through this he came in contact with Judy Myers of the Lord's Harvest International and invited her to come to Haiti and take a look.

In February of 2001 three LHI board members went to Haiti to meet with Pastor Bertrand. It was learned that he operated an orphanage, and it was arranged for a team to visit to work with the children and to do some construction. In May 2002 the first team went to Haiti. Another trip was made in 2003. Future trips have not taken place because our government has advised against travel to Haiti. The work, however, is ongoing.

In April 2010 an earthquake hit Port au Prince, Haiti, and devastated the region. Gary Turner traveled there and located Lesly Bertrand reporting back significant damage to the compound, but no deaths. Judy and a team will travel there to ascertain how construction can be done to rebuild the work.

Malawi/Mozambique. The mission work in Malawi began in 1992 when a Sakala family in Blantyre, Malawi obtained one of Anthony Buzzard's booklets, "Who is Jesus?" They invited him to come over and teach in a conference in 1993, which he did. In 1994 Anthony, Sarah and Claire Buzzard, his daughters, and Jim and Martha Mattison traveled together to teach and work with the people there.

In 1996 Anthony, Jim and Martha, and Joe and Rebekah Martin made an additional trip. Since that time many trip have been made to teach and to share with the people. [Editor's note: The Malawi Africa Missions was organized to coordinate funds and supplies for the trips, but it also works through the auspices of the Lord's Harvest International.] Through the generosity of many, Bibles have been purchased and distributed, orphans have been fed and clothed, corn has been provided during times of famine and seed/fertilizer packets and bucket kits have been provided for the people. Several churches have been built, and several bicycles have been purchased for pastors, who use them as they spread the gospel of the kingdom of God to many people.

South Korea. Contact with the Koreans came through Pastor Steve An who studied the Abrahamic Faith and was baptized. He had come from another denomination, but after baptism requested licensure from the General Conference. This was done at the annual conference in Rockford, Illinois, 2001. Pastor An began a Korean worship service at the New Friends Church in Morrow, and a Korean college extension to the Atlanta Bible College, then in Morrow, Georgia, now in Duluth, Georgia. The Korean college is a cross-cultural ministry in cooperation with the General Conference. There are other Korean Bible colleges in the United States and also in Korea. Pastor An oversees much of that work.

As we look to the future, the purpose of the Lord's Harvest International mission agency is to continue the work of foreign missions into the future with these goals:

- to become a trained professional sending agency by understanding mission science, understanding culture, and by understanding world politics.
- to establish a training program for missionaries.
- to send trained missionaries to develop and establish mission fields.
- to carry out the responsibilities as described in the philosophy statement of the Church of God General Conference.

Standing, left to right: Gary, Todd, Steve and Judy (Kirkpatrick) Myers, Director of Lord's Harvest International. Seated front: Walcie Rhea (Smith) and Pastor Vivian Kirkpatrick.
Photo provided by Rex Cain

Appendix 21

Ohio Conference Organization

Church of God in Christ Jesus
by G.E. Marsh

This brief article was found on page 41 of a 72-page booklet entitled, "Churches in the Buckeye Country" produced for the Ohio Sesquicentennial (1803-1953) that contains the history and origins of many Ohio churches. This document was furnished to the Biographical Encyclopedia by Pastor Rex Cain of the Bedford Ohio Church of God.

ALTHOUGH the Churches of God in Christ Jesus (which is the official name of this denomination in Ohio) has maintained local organizations and district gatherings for more than a century in the state, it was not until October 29, 1857, that the first state conference was held at Fairport, Ohio.

Representative churchmen from many parts of the state were present whose names have long been associated with our denominational work. To name a few out of many: D.C. Robison, Peter Neill, Walter Tomlinson, A.R. Curtis, Nancy Barber. Elder Joseph Marsh, editor and publisher of the first Church of God journal established in the United States, gave the initial address.

At this conference the following resolution was adopted:

1. That we should, when there are three or more believers in a place, organize ourselves under the name Church of God, recognizing no other name for ourselves than Christians, and none for the church but the Church of God.
2. That we should appoint an elder or elders and a deacon or deacons.
3. That we, in our organization, should make no declarations than simply declare that we, the undersigned, do organize ourselves under the name of the Church of God in (naming the place) recognizing the New Testament as the constitution of the church, and the Bible as the only rule of faith and practice.

Owing possibly to the confusion occasioned by the approach of the Civil War, the churches of the state discontinued their united activities for several years. But, in January 1903, a meeting of the Church of God in Cleveland was called for the purpose of considering the subject of again organizing a state conference. The result of this activity was a meeting held at Salem, Ohio, beginning on August 15, 1903. Here a conference was organized with the following officers: President, Wm. Pate, Vice President, D. C. Robison, Secretary, J. C. Thompson, Treasurer, John Lehman.

In 1904 the Conference was again held in Salem, in 1905 the Cleveland church acted as host, and following year the Brush Creek church, a rural church north of Dayton, requested the gathering for 1906.

One of the first churches to organize locally was that in Springfield, Ohio, which was established in 1856. Charter members here were Wm. Fish and wife, A. B. Barnes, Alec Dean, and George Cherry and wife.

In November 1863, the group organized in Cleveland. There were twelve members at that time. Their first pastor was M. Joblin who served them in that capacity until 1908.

The distinguishing tenets of faith of the Church of God are expressed in the following statement which appeared for many years in the Restitution, its official organ:

The Restitution advocates the final "restitution of all things which God has spoken by the mouth of all his holy prophets since the world began." As a means to this end the establishment of the kingdom of God on the earth, with Christ as the King of kings, and the immortal saints as joint-heirs with Him in the government of the nations; the restoration of Israel; the literal resurrection of the dead; the immortalization of the righteous, and the final destruction of the wicked; the eternal life only through Christ, and many other kindred truths.

Appendix 22

Prophecy

The Seven Last Years of This Age
by Jim Mattison
Provided to Jan Stilson by Mr. Mattison on November 6, 2009.

Background

Jesus referred to "the abomination of desolation" that was revealed to Daniel (11:31; 12:11) as the first of six signs Jesus lists concerning "the end of the age" (Matt. 24:3-31).

They are:
1. The abomination of desolation.
2. The great tribulation.
3. The signs in the sky.
4. The appearance of the sign of Christ in the heavens and all tribes of the earth mourning.
5. The coming of Christ in Power and Glory.
6. The angels sent out with great trumpet sound to gather the Elect (resurrection).

These six happenings shall END this age.

The apostles had asked Jesus, "What will be the sign of Your coming, and "the end of the age"? (These signs were still future.)This thought of the ending of this second age (Peter lists three ages) is mentioned four times in Matthew 24: vs. 3, 6-"but that is not yet the end," 13-"the one who endures to the end...shall be saved", 14-"and then the end shall come."

The Seven Year Covenant

In God's plan for His people Israel, He told Daniel that "seventy weeks" (heptads, or seventy weeks of years—490 years), were determined for Israel and Jerusalem, the holy city, that when they were finished 6 things would be fulfilled-Dan. 9:24-27. They would be:
1. Finish the transgression.
2. Make an end of sin.
3. Make atonement for iniquity.
4. Bring in everlasting righteousness.
5. Seal up the vision and prophecy.
6. Anoint the most holy place.

From the decree to restore and build Jerusalem until "Messiah the Prince" "will be seven weeks and sixty-two weeks" (69 of these weeks of years, or 483 years, v. 25.) "after the sixty-two weeks (plus the seven) Messiah will be cut off." v. 26. "The people of the prince who is to come will destroy the city (Jerusalem) and the sanctuary (temple). And its (his, Heb.) end will come with a flood; even to the end there will be war; desolations are determined. And he will make a firm covenant with the many for one week but in the middle of the week (after 3 ½ years) he will put a stop to sacrifice and grain offering, and on the wing of abominations will come one who makes desolate, even until a complete destruction, one that is decreed, is poured out on the one who makes desolate" (26-27).

Antichus Epiphanes fulfilled this the first time around 586 B.C. But since Jesus spoke about the abomination also occuring at the time of the end of this age, we know there will be a second fulfillment just before Jesus comes. The abomination of desolation will begin the last three and a half years. "When you see it," Jesus said, "then there will be a great tribulation such as has not occurred since the beginning of the world until now, nor ever shall. And unless those days had been cut short, no life would have been saved; but for the elect's sake those days shall be cut short."

This last three and a half year period at the end of this age is mentioned numerous times in the Bible, and is described in different terms: Midst of the week, 1260 days (Jewish days, 360 a year), 42 months.

However, the covenant the evil man makes with Israel is a seven year covenant. Little is said about the first 3-½ years. It appears to be a time of security. Probably the last Jewish temple will be built in this time.

But at the halfway point in the 7 years, he will stop their sacrifices and the abomination will be put in the holy place (Matt. 24:15). This can be either an image or statue of himself, or, as Paul explains in 2 Thessalonians 2:4, "he takes his seat in the temple of God, displaying himself as being God." Not only will he blaspheme God, he will also wear out and kill the saints (Rev. 13:7; Dan. 7:25; 8:24).

Thankfully, Jesus will come and destroy him and bring in everlasting righteousness, establishing the Kingdom of God over earth. That is the day we long for. When you see a seven year covenant made with Israel, we will know the end is near.

Appendix 23
Resurrection

Rapture and Resurrection
by Sir Anthony Buzzard
Reprinted from The Restitution Herald, *December 1989/January 1990 26, 27.*

The great strength of the Adventist movement of the last century was that it recaptured the massively important doctrine of Christ's Second coming. The mistaken idea that the Christian goal is to "go to heaven when we die" had reduced the need for Christ's personal return at the end of the age to virtually zero. When the Adventists (Advent Christians, Church of God Abrahamic Faith, and Seventh-day Adventists), pointed out that Scripture describes the dead as actually unconscious, "sleeping" until resurrection day, the process of recovering lost truth was launched. The Second Coming began to receive the attention it obviously enjoys in the Bible.

Yet error inevitably interfered with this new enlightenment about the events of the end of the age. Regrettable date-setting, which has persisted to this day, tended to attract ridicule of the whole idea of the Second Coming. For example, William Miller confidently predicted that Christ would return in 1844. When Jesus did not return, some even abandoned the faith, feeling that the Bible was unreliable. Others later announced (and still announce) that the Advent occurred in 1914, 2520 years from the battle of Carchemmish, which was wrongly supposed to have happened in 607 B.C. Such calculations have proven false; yet they live on.

All such attempts to compute the end of the age are based on serious misreadings of the biblical data and were always rejected by the more careful students of Scripture. Within the past two years several other confident assertions about the Second Coming have failed, and much uncertainty persists about what the Bible says in regard to the order of events at the end of the age.

Resolving Uncertainty

There are three very simple keys to resolving this uncertainty.

1. The so-called rapture of I Thessalonians 4:13ff occurs, as all agree, at the same time as the resurrection of the faithful believers. If, therefore, we can establish when the faithful dead are to be raised to immortality, we can know where this resurrection/rapture fits into God's plan.
2. Jesus gave his disciples a very precise outline of events which would precede his coming in glory. This material is obviously primary data for understanding the order of endtime events.
3. Paul warned against systems which did not allow that certain events *must occur before* the resurrection/rapture of the Christians. In so doing, he laid out the proper sequence of events clearly.

An examination of these three points will help to dispel uncertainty.

The Resurrection/Rapture

First: the resurrection and rapture of the faithful to meet Christ as he comes to the earth.

It is crucial to remember that difference of opinion about the "pre-tribulation" or "post-tribulation rapture" is in fact a question about the pre-tribulation or post-tribulation ***resurrection*** of the Christian dead. The issue is about the moment for the resurrection of the dead. The rapture is only an incident within a whole complex of events involving the resurrection. When Jesus returns, he will raise the dead at the sound of the trumpet and catch them up, along with the surviving believers, to meet him in the air. The saints will thus accompany Jesus as he descends to earth. This is the way important dignitaries are escorted to their destination.

Fortunately, Scripture does not leave us in the dark about the place of this great resurrection/rapture event in God's purposes. In I Corinthians 15:52 we are informed that we Christians shall all be resurrected and changed "in the moment, in the twinkling of an eye, ***at the last trumpet.***" Last, of course, means last in a sequence. The faithful will be raised to life when the "last trumpet" blows. When is this?

Using the well-tested method of comparing Scripture with Scripture, we look elsewhere to see when this last trumpet is to occur. Our answer is found in the book of Revelation. Just such a sequence of trumpets is described in chapter 11. The "last trumpet" is very evidently the seventy of the sequence which ends in Revelation 11:15-18. There are no more trumpets in this series. The last is the seventh, and it is then that the resurrection occurs:

Then the seventh angel blew his trumpet....The nations raged, but thy wrath came, and the time for the dead to be judged, for rewarding your servants, the prophets and saint and for those who fear your name, both small and great, and for destroying the destroyers of the earth. (Rev. 11: 15, 18 RSV).

Just as we would expect, this seventh and last trumpet speaks, in complete harmony with Paul in I Corinthians 15:52, of the resurrection of the faithful, placing it at the moment when Christ intervenes to establish the Kingdom of God. As I Thessalonians 4:16,17 says, the rapture of the surviving saints occurs at exactly the same time—at the sound of the great trumpet which is the last, or seventh trumpet announcing the arrival of the Kingdom of God on earth. The suggestion that the last trumpet of I Corinthians 15, is not the seventh trumpet of Revelation fractures the Scripture. There can only be one last trumpet when the Bible speaks of only one sequence of seven trumpets! The last must be that seventh trumpet of Revelation.

Jesus' Great Last Discourse for the Disciples

Secondly, Jesus outlines for us in Matthew 24, Mark 13,, and Luke 21, the sequence of events leading to his return. There is no room for uncertainty about whom Jesus addresses in this famous "Olivet Discourse." He speaks to the *disciples* and through them to the *church*. This is a critically important point, sometimes overlooked. No one doubts that Jesus' instructions to the disciples to preach the gospel throughout the world are instructions to the church of subsequent generations (Matt. 28:19, 20). The case is no different in Matthew 24. We should not forget that the church is founded on the apostles and prophets—that is, on their teaching (Eph. 2:20). In Matthew 24 Jesus addresses "you" (disciples) as the ones who should not be deceived (v. 4). It is "you" disciples who will hear of wars and rumors of wars (described in Daniel 11) (Matthew 24:6). It is "You" (disciples) who are to run away to the hills when the Abomination of Desolation appears (v. 15). Jesus does not foresee an escape to heaven! "You" (disciples) are the elect who must avoid deception during the tribulation"

"If any says to you (disciples), 'Lo, here is Christ or there' don't believe it. These false prophets will deceive, if possible, the very elect (vv. 23, 24). Who are the elect? "Behold, I have told you (disciples) in advance" (v. 25).

According to the ordinary rules of language, the disciples are equated with the elect in the whole discourse. And the same elect are to be present on earth during the time of tribulation and witness the darkening of the sun just before the arrival of Jesus in glory. When the disciples, those living at the time of Christ's return, "see all these things, you know that He is near" (v. 33).

When do these elect disciples expect to be gathered together to Christ? The text is very clear. "Immediately *after the tribulation* of these days" the sign of the Son of man will appear in heaven, "and He shall send His angels with a great sound of the trumpet to gather the elect" (Matt. 24:29-31).

Once again the same trumpet marks the gathering of the faithful, exactly as Paul predicts the resurrection of the Christians at the last trumpet, and the Revelation places it at the seventh trumpet, which, as all agree, occurs after the tribulation period.

Paul's Warning Against a Competing System

Thirdly, Paul warned expressly against any disturbance of the simple pattern of events destined to precede the Second Coming and the gathering of the saints. In 2 Thessalonians 2:1 he centers the discussion of "the coming of the Lord and our gathering together to Him" (v.2). He then emphasizes the two events ***must occur before*** Christ returns to rapture and gather the faithful. First, the apostasy (rebellion against God) and secondly, the appearing of the Man of Sin. The message is simple and clear.

"Don't let any one fool you like that, because the falling away must come first. The lawless man, the son of destruction, will be revealed then" (2Thes. 2:3, Simple English Bible).

Summary

We may summarize our findings as follows:

1. The rapture/resurrection event will occur at the last trumpet. Scripture knows of only one last trumpet, the seventh trumpet of Revelation 11:15. This trumpet sounds after or "post-tribulation" (Matt. 24:29-31). This is "the resurrection of the just" (Like 14:14), when all the faithful will be rewarded.
2. Jesus spoke of the "elect," whom he equates with the disciples and their successors in the church. Matthew, who is his own best interpreter, elsewhere means, "believers," when he uses the term "elect" (Matt. 22:14): "Many are called, but few are *elect*" (Gr. 'eklectos'). It is a basic rule of good exegesis that a writer must be allowed to interpret himself.
3. Paul specifically warned against systems which would encourage belief in the arrival of Christ before the Man of Sin. He definitely stated that the Man of Sin will appear before the arrival of Christ.

The doctrine of the Second Advent, which is the special strength of Adventist groups must be freed from unnecessary complications. The last trumpet (I Cor. 15:52) really is the last trumpet! Scripture knows of only one sequence of trumpets, and the seventh-the last-blows after the tribulation. Therefore the resurrection/rapture of the saints happens after the tribulation. These simple connections provided by Scripture show a picture of the gathering of all the faithful at the seventh or last trumpet of Revelation 11.

What Scripture so joins together should not be torn asunder.

Appendix 24

Systematic Theology: Decade of Development

Fifty Years of *Systematic Theology*
by Dr. Alva G. Huffer, BTh, BA, MA, PhD

Dr. Huffer presented this lecture at the 74th Annual Meeting of the Church of God General Conference at Cornerstone Bible Church of God, McDonough, Georgia, July 7, 2010. A book signing of the new edition of the Systematic Theology *followed the lecture. Readers may view Dr. Huffer's lecture at e-herald.org. This transcript is duplicated here with Dr. Huffer's permission.*

It's really an exciting time to be here with you all, and my many friends I've known over the years to celebrate the Golden Jubilee anniversary of *Systematic Theology*. The book has been in continuous printing all 50 years. The current book is the seventh printing.

It's an anniversary year for me. In September I'm going to be 85 years old. One of the advantages of living many decades is that you have more memories. This year is my 65th year as a minister of the Church of God General Conference, starting in 1949 and during those years I have been pastor of 10 groups in 7 states, not only East Oregon Church of God, but in seven conferences. In Illinois, Indiana, Morristown, Tennessee in 1948 to help Belus and Iva Holt start a new church. In January 1, 1950 my wife Awa and I were married in Hendersonville, North Carolina. Immediately, we moved to my fourth congregation in Virginia. We lived in Virginia for five years.

"The writing of *Systematic Theology* began in Virginia 1950-1954; Missouri 1954-1957; (St. Louis/Morse Mill, Missouri,) Grand Rapids 1957-1961; Arizona 1961-1970. We were there for 42 years. I moved to South Carolina to Guthrie Grove in 2004 where Myra lives and my son-in-law in the pastor. In Virginia is where *Systematic Theology* had its start.

This is an exciting time to live in the Church of God General Conf. Our ministers graduated from the college that began again in 1939. There was a great unity among our ministers and a great feeling of brotherhood. There was emphasis upon the distinctive doctrines of the Church of God, and there was a great surge in evangelism, including home missions. Harold Doan wrote "Your Introduction to the Church of God" and local groups went out into their communities to acquaint them with the COG. They took a special issue of the Restitution Herald that Harold Doan wrote. How did you do evangelism in those days? Two ways: The written word and the other is Radio! Radio was the great medium for evangelism during this time.

When I was in Virginia there were five groups. I alternated services at Fort Valley one Sunday and Maurertown the other. Then on the fifth Sunday we went to Browntown. They had evangelistic services and vacation Bible schools. Hollis Partlowe and Hilda started coming to Browntown. They were both baptized and Hollis became one of our leading ministers. And Austin Railton also. They both went to Oregon Bible College and became ministers.

In Virginia after two years, C.F. Pryor came to pastor the Browntown church. Then on fifth Sundays, we went to Washington, D.C. Then came Joe Fletcher to pastor the church in D.C. Then, we went to Baltimore of the fifth Sunday, and here came Dean Moore to pastor Baltimore. Every year, another minister, another church, another radio program. Harvey Krogh had radio messages in the 1940s, and he with Harold Doan had radio messages. Kenneth Milne came into our church and he had great experience in radio. Mildred Macy in Texas had radio on Saturdays for all the children. In Chicago, Harold Doan had a weekly message on WAIT.

I had a radio program in Morristown in Tennessee and in Virginia we started the "Voice of Tomorrow." Every Sunday, we offered a copy of that sermon to people who would write in. Kenneth Milne broadcast it from Macomb. We had a bulletin for all five churches in the Virginia conference every week. We had bigger Virginia conferences than had been at General Conference! Harvey Krogh came as special speaker for Virginia Conference, and his message was "God's Watch." Harvey was a watchmaker.

In Virginia. I put together the first part of *Systematic Theology*. We didn't have computers. We didn't have Xerox machines, but we had the ABDick Mimeograph machine. David Krogh visited, and he helped turn the crank mimeograph as I was putting together the sections of *Systematic Theology*. He was eight years old and he was part of *Systematic Theology*. Sometimes the weekly bulletins would be eight pages long because I put a section of the *Systematic Theology* in them.

From shore to shore it was a great time of evangelism for the Church of God. During this time, I purchased books on theology and was reading and producing copy.

Also, we had a neighbor who was a retired minister of the Evangelical Reformed Church, Dr. Barley, and he had a vast library. He said, "Come and use anything you like." I did. All the time I studied and produced the written word. I became acquainted that way with the concept of systematic theology.

What is it? Systematic Theology is the apex of all theological forces. Here everything that has been learned in Bible survey, Bible doctrine has been organized in separate divisions. Throughout history, theology has been special. It is the Queen of the sciences. Systematic Theology is the Queen's crown. It connects all the syntheses of all the courses you'd study in community college. It reaches not only down into pastoral work and church history but also into history, sociology, psychology, natural sciences, and brings it all together into one beautiful whole.

I discovered that all our distinctive doctrines fit in. They are organized into a logical sequence. Start with God. Who is in the center? Jesus Christ. It emphasizes His three-fold ministry, earthly ministry in the past; heavenly ministry today and his kingly ministry in the future. Most believe that Christ is working today, heading the church, adding to it today. He is busy working in our life. Christ centered. All the leading ministers in our church believed it.

Then, Otto Dick, who had been Superintendent of Schools in Indiana became President of Oregon Bible College in 1953 while I was still in Virginia. I stayed at his house when in Oregon, and I explained Systematic Theology to him. He said, "This is great. Wouldn't it be a wonderful course for Oregon Bible College? What textbook do you recommend?" Well, there is this, but it won't work, but over here is another, but.... Otto said, "Alva, why don't you write the book as a textbook for OBC and I will see to it that it is a required course, so you always have a market." (audience laughter at this point). I said, "OK, I will." I hadn't realized that all this study and writing I had been doing for radio programs, bulletins, lessons, and here it was. All I needed was to organize it.

I wrote the book between May 5, 1953, and May 4, 1954. Clarence Lapp was to be the one to teach it at Oregon Bible College. I'd write about eight weeks' worth to be taught at OBC, and while it was being taught, I would be writing the next section and mimeographing all of these sections. At Christmas time I wrote the section of Christ. (Here, Alva shows a copy of the first mimeographed manuscript, 321 pages.) Many of the ministers said, "We'd like to have a copy. How can we get a copy?" I'd saved all the mimeos of all the sections, so there I was cranking the handle of the mimeograph for 30 more copies for my friends.

Finally, at Ministers' Conference when it was 20 below zero. I presented the concept of Systematic Theology to the ministers, and one after another stood up and said, "I think this should be published as a book." James Watkins, said, "Yes, let's do this."

The Board of Directors asked, "How shall we pay for this?" The NBI was designated to print it, but they had never printed anything this size. Let's sell pre-publication copies. Instead of $5.95 we'll offer it for $5. All the churches appointed a chairman in that congregation to promote the book and raise the money. Kenneth Brewer was the chairman at Brush Creek. The people raised the money. In Tempe, Arizona where Vernis Wolfe was pastor, the church said, we haven't seen the book yet, but we know the author! So they sent $500. The Board said, "There will be money enough to do this."

Meanwhile, in 1954 we decided to move to St. Louis and Morse Mill, Missouri. I called this the Decade of Evangelism. When Harold Doan came into the General Conference in 1954, he said, "Let's do this for the whole General Conference, and we'll change the name to Decade of Development. He was head of the conference until 1968. He was a wonderful writer. During his time the National Bible Institute name was changed to Church of God General Conference. He promoted Pastoral Aid., the Missions Builders League, The Community Crusade, and *Systematic Theology* which was to be printed with a Bible Study course based on the book, with a film strip also based on it. The delegates agreed. It was a great time.

Some people look back and say it was a Golden Age. The National Missionary society started in 1952, and all the ladies organizations were sending money to India. But let's get it coordinated. Clarence Lapp was the first president, and I became president the next year and served ten years.

So we moved to Missouri. We were there three years. I started rewriting *Systematic Theology*, getting it ready for the print shop in Oregon, Illinois. We were on call for special meetings. We went to Macomb five times under five different pastors. When Kenneth Milne was there we had fourteen baptisms. Wherever I went, I took my typewriter along typing the manuscript. I enlarged it, adding a chapter on the History of Conditional Immortality.

In 1957 we moved to Pennellwood in Grand Rapids. When we moved there, we had enough of a manuscript to send to the printer. Paul Johnson and Robert Johnson in the print shop began to set up the type on the linotype. I'll show you here, we typed it all and they set up the pages using linotype. (Here Alva shows the first line of type from the linotype.) This is the first one that started Chapter One. This is the first sentence. They had liquid lead. They had a big typewriter and the lead would drop down and make a line of type. After they printed so many copies, they had to melt the lead down so they could use it again, because they only had so much lead. They had metal strips in a tray, and they'd make a copy and send it to me. I'd check the galley proof and send it back.. Then they set up pages and they did it all the time. They were printing tracts also, and *The Restitution Herald* every week.

In Grand Rapids were Zondervans, Eerdmans, Kregels, Baker Book House, etc. What a wonderful place to be. It was the best place to be because I had access to all those books, but also to editors. I had quoted 30 different books and magazines. So I asked to the editor of Eerdmans, how do you get permission? What do you say? He said, "Just show what you want to quote, and how you want to use it and they'll be happy to give you permission to use it." Baker gave me addresses of all 30 people I needed to contact. It was a big help. Everyone gave permission to use their material.

How about the index? Authors, subject, Bible verses. We couldn't do an index until we knew what pages those things would be on. No computer. No Xerox. 1959. How do you do that? I had to just go through the book, put the info on a page and set it in the file. Then we had to alphabetize it. My wife Awa and I with a neighbor, Nathan Moore, spent hours and hours sorting out the index and eating pizza. The students used it that fall without an index.

In the next few weeks the Index was ready so when we went to the Ministers' Conference in January, the whole book was ready. I remember arriving in Oregon, Illinois at 20 below zero, we had car problems at Sycamore at a farm house, and Clarence Lapp came and towed Dean Moore all the way to Oregon. I had one copy of *Systematic Theology* which they'd given me ahead of time, and I gave it away to the farmers to thank them. The very first book was given away. It was a book to be given away. Harvey Krogh was the very first person to ask if I would autograph his book.

C.E. Randall got up at conference and announced to the ministers that finally, the book was published, and each minister gave his testimony about how thrilled he was.

People wanted to give it away. The Priscilla Organization wanted to put a copy of the book into every college and seminary library. The ministers took the books home to distribute to the people who paid ahead of time. They took them to their local library.

In London, Percy Bilton was wealthy. He did a lot of construction throughout London. He had become acquainted with *The Restitution Herald* and he used to be a Christadelphian, and he said, "The Church of God is more logical," and he bought lots of books to send all over the world. The Christadelphians also were thrilled because they believed almost everything in it. There were some things they didn't accept. But they bought it in Australia, South America, all over. The Church of God, with Christadelphians on the right hand side of it, and the Advent Christians on the left, had a book we could share with them.

In Arizona, the people spent a lot of time sending the book out. I was in San Francisco one time and I went to the library, and there it was, right on the shelf.

The theological students said, "We saw this book that Dr. "Hoofer" wrote and we fell in love with it, and we want our own copies." So the next goal was to send one to every library in the world. The librarian at the Arizona State University gave us names of English speaking contacts in every country in the world. We sent books to all these libraries. Soon we had 77 countries, and then 111 countries, and then every country in the world had a copy. The Church of God was giving out the message.

Then we started the Systematic Theology Bible Study course was started in Tempe. In 1964, Harold Doan coordinated all these things. In 1993, it was on the internet. It is available now to every person in every country in the world. I have been privileged to teach Systematic Theology at Atlanta Bible College in the fall and spring with panorama panels all around the room. In Fort Wayne, Indiana, here was a person in the Kokomo Church. "I want to put the book on the pdf format. This book should never go out of publication." He was head of a big company in Fort Wayne. He was a computer expert. So it has been done, and now this book has been reprinted in its seventh printing.

the prophets and saint and for those who fear your name, both small and great, and for destroying the destroyers of the earth. (Rev. 11: 15, 18 RSV).

Just as we would expect, this seventh and last trumpet speaks, in complete harmony with Paul in I Corinthians 15:52, of the resurrection of the faithful, placing it at the moment when Christ intervenes to establish the Kingdom of God. As I Thessalonians 4:16,17 says, the rapture of the surviving saints occurs at exactly the same time—at the sound of the great trumpet which is the last, or seventh trumpet announcing the arrival of the Kingdom of God on earth. The suggestion that the last trumpet of I Corinthians 15, is not the seventh trumpet of Revelation fractures the Scripture. There can only be one last trumpet when the Bible speaks of only one sequence of seven trumpets! The last must be that seventh trumpet of Revelation.

Jesus' Great Last Discourse for the Disciples

Secondly, Jesus outlines for us in Matthew 24, Mark 13,, and Luke 21, the sequence of events leading to his return. There is no room for uncertainty about whom Jesus addresses in this famous "Olivet Discourse." He speaks to the *disciples* and through them to the *church*. This is a critically important point, sometimes overlooked. No one doubts that Jesus' instructions to the disciples to preach the gospel throughout the world are instructions to the church of subsequent generations (Matt. 28:19, 20). The case is no different in Matthew 24. We should not forget that the church is founded on the apostles and prophets—that is, on their teaching (Eph. 2:20). In Matthew 24 Jesus addresses "you" (disciples) as the ones who should not be deceived (v. 4). It is "you" disciples who will hear of wars and rumors of wars (described in Daniel 11) (Matthew 24:6). It is "You" (disciples) who are to run away to the hills when the Abomination of Desolation appears (v. 15). Jesus does not foresee an escape to heaven! "You" (disciples) are the elect who must avoid deception during the tribulation"

"If any says to you (disciples), 'Lo, here is Christ or there' don't believe it. These false prophets will deceive, if possible, the very elect (vv. 23, 24). Who are the elect? "Behold, I have told you (disciples) in advance" (v. 25).

According to the ordinary rules of language, the disciples are equated with the elect in the whole discourse. And the same elect are to be present on earth during the time of tribulation and witness the darkening of the sun just before the arrival of Jesus in glory. When the disciples, those living at the time of Christ's return, "see all these things, you know that He is near" (v. 33).

When do these elect disciples expect to be gathered together to Christ? The text is very clear. "Immediately *after the tribulation* of these days" the sign of the Son of man will appear in heaven, "and He shall send His angels with a great sound of the trumpet to gather the elect" (Matt. 24:29-31).

Once again the same trumpet marks the gathering of the faithful, exactly as Paul predicts the resurrection of the Christians at the last trumpet, and the Revelation places it at the seventh trumpet, which, as all agree, occurs after the tribulation period.

Paul's Warning Against a Competing System

Thirdly, Paul warned expressly against any disturbance of the simple pattern of events destined to precede the Second Coming and the gathering of the saints. In 2 Thessalonians 2:1 he centers the discussion of "the coming of the Lord and our gathering together to Him" (v.2). He then emphasizes the two events ***must occur before*** Christ returns to rapture and gather the faithful. First, the apostasy (rebellion against God) and secondly, the appearing of the Man of Sin. The message is simple and clear.

"Don't let any one fool you like that, because the falling away must come first. The lawless man, the son of destruction, will be revealed then" (2Thes. 2:3, Simple English Bible).

Summary

We may summarize our findings as follows:

1. The rapture/resurrection event will occur at the last trumpet. Scripture knows of only one last trumpet, the seventh trumpet of Revelation 11:15. This trumpet sounds after or "post-tribulation" (Matt. 24:29-31). This is "the resurrection of the just" (Like 14:14), when all the faithful will be rewarded.

2. Jesus spoke of the "elect," whom he equates with the disciples and their successors in the church. Matthew, who is his own best interpreter, elsewhere means, "believers," when he uses the term "elect" (Matt. 22:14): "Many are called, but few are *elect*" (Gr. 'eklectos'). It is a basic rule of good exegesis that a writer must be allowed to interpret himself.

3. Paul specifically warned against systems which would encourage belief in the arrival of Christ before the Man of Sin. He definitely stated that the Man of Sin will appear before the arrival of Christ.

The doctrine of the Second Advent, which is the special strength of Adventist groups must be freed from unnecessary complications. The last trumpet (I Cor. 15:52) really is the last trumpet! Scripture knows of only one sequence of trumpets, and the seventh-the last-blows after the tribulation. Therefore the resurrection/rapture of the saints happens after the tribulation. These simple connections provided by Scripture show a picture of the gathering of all the faithful at the seventh or last trumpet of Revelation 11.

What Scripture so joins together should not be torn asunder.

Appendix 24

Systematic Theology: Decade of Development

Fifty Years of *Systematic Theology*
by Dr. Alva G. Huffer, BTh, BA, MA, PhD

Dr. Huffer presented this lecture at the 74th Annual Meeting of the Church of God General Conference at Cornerstone Bible Church of God, McDonough, Georgia, July 7, 2010. A book signing of the new edition of the Systematic Theology *followed the lecture. Readers may view Dr. Huffer's lecture at e-herald.org. This transcript is duplicated here with Dr. Huffer's permission.*

It's really an exciting time to be here with you all, and my many friends I've known over the years to celebrate the Golden Jubilee anniversary of *Systematic Theology*. The book has been in continuous printing all 50 years. The current book is the seventh printing.

It's an anniversary year for me. In September I'm going to be 85 years old. One of the advantages of living many decades is that you have more memories. This year is my 65th year as a minister of the Church of God General Conference, starting in 1949 and during those years I have been pastor of 10 groups in 7 states, not only East Oregon Church of God, but in seven conferences. In Illinois, Indiana, Morristown, Tennessee in 1948 to help Belus and Iva Holt start a new church. In January 1, 1950 my wife Awa and I were married in Hendersonville, North Carolina. Immediately, we moved to my fourth congregation in Virginia. We lived in Virginia for five years.

"The writing of *Systematic Theology* began in Virginia 1950-1954; Missouri 1954-1957; (St. Louis/Morse Mill, Missouri,) Grand Rapids 1957-1961; Arizona 1961-1970. We were there for 42 years. I moved to South Carolina to Guthrie Grove in 2004 where Myra lives and my son-in-law in the pastor. In Virginia is where *Systematic Theology* had its start.

This is an exciting time to live in the Church of God General Conf. Our ministers graduated from the college that began again in 1939. There was a great unity among our ministers and a great feeling of brotherhood. There was emphasis upon the distinctive doctrines of the Church of God, and there was a great surge in evangelism, including home missions. Harold Doan wrote "Your Introduction to the Church of God" and local groups went out into their communities to acquaint them with the COG. They took a special issue of the Restitution Herald that Harold Doan wrote. How did you do evangelism in those days? Two ways: The written word and the other is Radio! Radio was the great medium for evangelism during this time.

When I was in Virginia there were five groups. I alternated services at Fort Valley one Sunday and Maurertown the other. Then on the fifth Sunday we went to Browntown. They had evangelistic services and vacation Bible schools. Hollis Partlowe and Hilda started coming to Browntown. They were both baptized and Hollis became one of our leading ministers. And Austin Railton also. They both went to Oregon Bible College and became ministers.

In Virginia after two years, C.F. Pryor came to pastor the Browntown church. Then on fifth Sundays, we went to Washington, D.C. Then came Joe Fletcher to pastor the church in D.C. Then, we went to Baltimore of the fifth Sunday, and here came Dean Moore to pastor Baltimore. Every year, another minister, another church, another radio program. Harvey Krogh had radio messages in the 1940s, and he with Harold Doan had radio messages. Kenneth Milne came into our church and he had great experience in radio. Mildred Macy in Texas had radio on Saturdays for all the children. In Chicago, Harold Doan had a weekly message on WAIT.

I had a radio program in Morristown in Tennessee and in Virginia we started the "Voice of Tomorrow." Every Sunday, we offered a copy of that sermon to people who would write in. Kenneth Milne broadcast it from Macomb. We had a bulletin for all five churches in the Virginia conference every week. We had bigger Virginia conferences than had been at General Conference! Harvey Krogh came as special speaker for Virginia Conference, and his message was "God's Watch." Harvey was a watchmaker.

In Virginia. I put together the first part of *Systematic Theology*. We didn't have computers. We didn't have Xerox machines, but we had the ABDick Mimeograph machine. David Krogh visited, and he helped turn the crank mimeograph as I was putting together the sections of *Systematic Theology*. He was eight years old and he was part of *Systematic Theology*. Sometimes the weekly bulletins would be eight pages long because I put a section of the *Systematic Theology* in them.

From shore to shore it was a great time of evangelism for the Church of God. During this time, I purchased books on theology and was reading and producing copy.

Appendix 25

Theocratic Kingdom

The Theocratic Kingdom

Reprinted from The History of Fundamentalism *by George W. Dollar, as retrieved from http://www.theocratickingdom.com/MrPeters/Preaching.html.*

> **Annotation:** *Rev. Peters participated in the great Niagara Prophecy Conference organized by James H. Brookes, a friend of Peters. It was not until after* The Theocratic Kingdom *(1884) was published that Peters was invited to preach at the conference. This is an excerpt of what was recorded regarding his participation.*

The author of the *Theocratic Kingdom*, G.N.H. Peters, a Lutheran from Springfield, Ohio, spoke on the subject of the covenants and the Kingdom. Peters asked how believers should relate the promises made to Abraham, Isaac, and Jacob to the coming Kingdom. These covenants were confirmed by oath and no matter how long the time, there is absolute assurance they will be verified. Peters observed that most Christians reject the entire Davidic Covenant - it is "utterly ignored." Are we to take these promises in "their plain grammatical meaning?" His answer was an emphatic "yes."

"Is it in the nature of a covenant that embraces the vital interests of the Messiah, of believers, of the race, of the world that it should be so constructed that, instead of conveying a decisive meaning clearly expressed in its wording, it presents a hidden or typical one which requires the revolution of centuries to develop through such men as Origen, Augustine, Swedenborg and others? Would God who said (Matt. 7:9) 'what man is there of you whom, if his son as bread, will he give him a stone?' give a grammatical signification, accessible to all who read, that is deceptive and misleading that fosters a faith which can never be attained, and that leads to hopes which can never be realized?"

Peters noted that some have unfairly criticized our faith as "fanatical" and extravagant in this age "that abounds in unbelief." The believer should follow the example of Abraham, who believed the promises of God. The covenant with Abraham had to do with the earth, that it will be delivered from the curse and renewed under the all-providing creative hand of Him Who will make all things new. From the time these covenants were made by the Lord there "must be a direct and special intervention of a power exerted by the supernatural." Because of these promises there will be:

1. Inheritance of a renewed earth.
2. Effectual removal of the curse.
3. Glorious theocratic reign of His co-heirs.
4. Perpetual deliverance from suffering, sickness, tears, sorrow, and death.
5. Removal of the bondage of nature.
6. Restoration of all forfeited blessings.

If this covenant fails, then the blood of Jesus has lost its power, "its sealing efficaciousness." But we have faith in that precious blood. The death of Christ is a "requisite to a restoring to us once forfeited but now covenanted blessings of an Edenic state." It is error to "limit a portion as demanded by so-called progress to modify or change the plain grammatical sense."

Appendix 26

Worship

Worship

by Pastor Scott Ross

Originally published for the Adult Truth Seeker's Quarterly, *date unknown.*

You are responsible for your own worship experience–not the song leader, not the choir, not the organist, not the preacher. Whether or not you have a good worship experience is up to you. Worship is an aggressive act. It requires our involvement. We must put something into it.

Worship begins by focusing on God, not ourselves or others. As we focus upon God and who He is and what He has done–we begin to respond. That response is worship.

If we compare our worship experience to the theater, we usually think of the preacher as the actor, ourselves as the audience, and God as the prompter. That is all wrong. We the worshipers are the actors and God is the audience. The preacher serves the role of prompter, telling us to sing praises, confess our sins, and to bring your offering before God.

Worship is offering ourselves totally to God. It is much more than what happens from 11:00 to 12:00 on Sunday morning. It is a way of life that acknowledges God in everything we say or do or even think. Worship is the response we have when we come before God. We need to seek more encounters with God so that we will worship more.

Church of God in Macomb, Illinois
Photo provided by Rex Cain

Index

In this index the reader will not find oft-mentioned terms such as Age to Come, Oregon Bible College or *The Restitution*. Such items appear on nearly every page of the encyclopedia. Rather, this index is a simple guide to locating obscure terms, landmark activities and doctrines, references to other denominations, key names, important principles and organizations of interest to scholars and casual readers. Often, these key or unique references are found in numerous locations; sometimes in one or two. It is hoped this basic index will lead readers to locating their searched-for information among the many people and details chronicled herein.

~ A ~

abolitionist, 81, 101, 175-176, 180, 202, 210, 249, 257

academic(s), 78, 332, 418, 470, 484, 488-489, 508, 551, 558-559

accident, 30, 54, 75, 92, 132, 185, 227, 238, 342, 350, 368, 370, 376, 382, 389, 418, 430, 477, 488, 493, 507-508, 558

Advent Christians, 1, 3, 38, 57, 89, 98, 116, 124, 168, 186, 211, 233-234, 252, 255, 266, 280, 315, 390, 396, 432, 456, 485, 503, 548-549, 556, 589, 602

Adventism, 18, 20, 37-38, 42, 55, 57, 87, 101, 116, 245, 249, 278, 290, 543, 547, 556, 576

American Adventist, 1, 215

Anglo-Israelism, 17, 99, 140, 163-164, 169, 178, 241, 378, 590

Armageddon, 185, 277, 286

art, 24, 210-211, 218, 257, 280, 328, 333, 345, 365-366, 399, 420, 428, 450, 463, 465, 489, 510, 512, 516, 568, 573, 575

Articles of Faith, 10, 17-18, 105, 111, 301-302, 560

ascension robes, 235-236

auto/automobile, 11, 15, 92, 113, 132, 152, 206, 238, 342, 350, 370, 385-386, 389, 403, 418, 420, 430, 436, 441, 466, 477, 488, 493, 508, 523, 558

~ B ~

bank(s), 15, 127, 176, 217, 220, 240, 262, 267, 275, 282, 338, 341, 364, 456, 459, 463, 468, 492

beauty, 16, 53, 95, 184, 211, 217-218, 345, 512, 554

Beecher, Charles, 169, 172, 174

Berean(s). *See* National Berean Society.

Bible Faith Mission, 98, 261, 264, 273, 432-433, 478

Bible Training Class, 14, 125, 156, 331-333, 337-338, 346, 348, 350, 354, 375, 381, 386, 398, 400, 407-410, 413, 416, 419-420, 436, 445, 448-449, 456, 494, 496, 499, 501, 503, 505, 510-513, 517, 526, 534, 557, 585

Bilton, Percy, 487, 602

Bishop Crowther, 154

Bitter Disappointment, 1, 14, 20, 27, 34, 36, 46, 55, 70-71, 79, 97, 128, 130-132, 135, 163, 171-172, 174, 192, 207, 210, 246, 260, 274, 303, 551, 556

Black Hawk, 60, 76, 217, 268, 345, 347, 428, 496, 498, 505, 512-513, 539

Black Oak (Black Walnut), 121

Blood of Christ, 78, 190, 198, 334, 357, 562, 564

Bolhous, Stephen, 115, 374

breach, 189

Bregninge, Poul, 311

Brockman, William, 38

Burned-over district, 381, 551

businessman, 14, 92, 325, 413, 506, 509, 535

~ C ~

Calvinism, 178, 257

Calvinist, 245, 254

Campbell, Alexander, 3-4, 6-7, 20, 101-102, 165, 169-170, 179-180, 234, 251, 286-287, 289, 291, 303, 509

Campbellite(s), 5, 59, 73-74, 116, 123, 129, 137, 160, 170, 213, 239-240, 247-248, 263, 287, 289, 291-292, 294-295, 300, 381

Canada West, 36, 53, 132-133, 162-163, 173, 220, 419

candid, 281, 547

Cane Ridge, 153

Cannonism, 64

caravan, 222, 258, 593-594

carnal, 54, 65, 103, 117, 157, 174, 190, 229-230, 242, 290, 308, 330, 356, 374, 589

Carras, John, 284, 290, 296

chaplain, 30, 52, 382-383, 405, 426, 530-531

Chart of Bible Events, 429

Chart of the Ages, 481

charts, 2, 30, 409, 529, 578-579

Cherokee, 178, 530

Chicago Fire. *See* Great Chicago Fire.

China Inland Mission, 154, 401, 403

cholera, 54, 58, 169, 184, 254

Christadelphians, 3, 5, 7, 14, 21, 25, 40, 60, 116, 157, 165, 190, 194, 226, 234, 242, 248, 251-252, 290, 292-294, 296-297, 299, 307, 314, 321-322, 325, 330, 366, 381, 390, 393, 399, 434, 448, 493, 545, 548-549, 589, 602

Christ-centered theology, 5

Christian Connexion (Connection), 1, 3-8, 27, 45, 52, 72, 105, 143, 169-170, 174-175, 178-179, 183, 210, 235, 245-246, 262-263, 279, 546, 556

Christian education, 30, 158, 221, 304, 319, 389, 414, 509, 517, 523, 533, 543, 583-584, 586

Christian Faith Ministries, 36

Christianity, primitive, 101, 289

Christology, 4, 198, 562

Christ-yans, 143, 245

Christ-yun, 45

Church of God in Christ Jesus, 21, 38-41, 77, 188-189, 240, 335, 337-338, 349, 371, 440, 455, 465, 476, 538, 596

circulation, 15, 67, 372, 499, 510

Civil War, 1, 21, 33, 38-40, 54, 56, 60-61, 76, 81, 92, 94, 96, 101, 113, 125, 137-138, 147, 149, 153, 165, 181, 188, 191, 193-194, 196, 203, 207-208, 237, 256, 297, 304, 336, 407, 454, 471, 502, 508, 596

claim, 12, 24, 60, 67, 79, 103, 123, 191, 206, 258, 292, 316, 390, 562, 572

Cleansing of the Sanctuary, 78-79, 81, 552

clergy, 2, 36, 68, 117, 121, 224, 242, 246, 330, 336-337, 388, 390
   clergyman, 35-36, 57, 61, 87, 182, 223, 227, 235, 239, 498
   clergywomen, 337

coal, 91, 94-95, 139-140, 221, 228, 346

Cogcast Theater, 137

Cogcast(.org), 37, 137, 333, 338, 340, 343, 353, 415, 421, 451

Cogmail, 5, 242, 299, 416

Cogpastors, 242

Committee of Ten, 140, 161, 212-213, 272, 330-331, 356, 379-380, 392, 406, 435-438, 496, 535-538, 557

communion, 7, 20, 45, 66, 86, 95, 101, 103, 117, 142, 148, 178, 189, 201, 206, 240, 288, 293, 303, 309, 322, 334, 364, 378, 563

Conditional Immortality, 34, 37, 41-42, 58-59, 81, 101, 107-108, 111, 115, 117-118, 120, 143, 167, 179, 204, 207, 223-224, 241, 257, 263, 271, 275, 311, 331, 392, 401, 451, 454, 556-557, 564, 588-589, 601

Conditional Immortality Mission, 294

conduct, 21-22, 31, 68, 76, 90, 113, 117, 126, 138, 140, 232, 266, 272, 328, 332, 380, 411, 452, 471, 499, 503-505, 513, 533, 591

conscientious objector, 400, 419

consensus, 111, 290, 298, 302, 313, 518, 537

conservative, 8, 73, 124, 139, 210, 212, 229, 302, 367, 392, 536, 557, 562-563

Cook, Steve(n), 5, 292, 322

copyright, 252, 296, 309, 357, 364, 518

Correspondence School of Religion, 69

court, 14, 57, 62, 75, 85, 112, 132, 184, 191, 303, 354, 403, 486, 569

courtroom, 61, 355

covered wagon, 10, 75, 151, 184, 206, 265, 516

Cramer, 9, 94

credentials, 19, 67-68, 196, 202, 227, 326, 328, 464, 526

creed, 17, 98, 102-103, 116, 119, 126, 157, 199, 252, 293, 331, 392, 560, 565

culture, 4, 11, 123, 128, 153, 182, 325, 405, 563-564, 595

~ D ~

deacon, 40, 95, 148, 160, 189, 326, 334, 338, 346, 359-360, 442, 450, 483, 506, 520, 596

debate, 9, 12, 21, 41-43, 61, 67, 72-74, 89, 98, 100-104, 110-111, 125, 127, 157-158, 165-166, 182, 213, 218, 223-225, 239, 248, 250, 252, 275, 286, 296, 312, 454, 526, 539, 548, 565-566, 588, 592

delegate, 9, 17, 37, 50, 62, 67-68, 76, 80-82, 97, 131, 140, 193, 221, 230, 257, 278, 280-281, 293, 296, 318, 320, 328, 331, 366, 381, 464, 527, 591

devotions, 334, 530, 548

Diaglott. *See Emphatic Diaglott, The.*

dialogue, 5, 41, 67, 111, 142, 196, 198-199, 224, 230, 253, 281, 325, 525, 548, 562, 566, 593

diary, 50, 70, 76, 96-100, 169, 195, 197, 250, 262, 333, 362, 421, 474, 480, 506

diphtheria, 59

disappointment, 1, 14, 20, 27, 34, 36, 46, 55, 70-71, 79, 82, 97, 128, 130-132, 135, 163, 170-172, 174, 192, 207, 210, 246, 260, 274, 303, 485, 543, 545, 547, 551-552, 556.
See also Bitter Disappointment.

Disciples Meeting House, 287, 300, 303

Disciples of Christ, 116, 165, 170, 213, 247, 251-252, 270, 286, 299, 303

Disciples, 6-7, 14, 57, 59, 74-75, 89, 101-102, 108, 110-111, 116, 129, 160, 165, 167, 169-170, 194, 208, 213, 229, 247,

Disciples, *continued*, 251-252, 254, 262, 270, 286-287, 289, 299-300, 303, 431, 512, 562, 567, 571, 589, 591, 598-599

discipline, 10, 17, 40, 68, 105, 157, 179, 198, 302, 322, 332, 442, 516, 532

dispute, 64, 74, 123-124, 167, 180-182, 189, 202, 403, 505, 585

diversity, 4, 103, 178, 540, 563, 566

divine nature, 4-6, 56, 98, 313, 588

division, 8, 49, 80, 155, 331-332, 353, 408, 548, 550, 562

Dixon, A.C., 302

Doctrinal Statement (Atlanta Bible College), 103, 252, 588

dormitory, 26, 47, 110, 114, 153, 155-156, 189, 338, 348, 419, 456, 461-462, 467, 499, 508-509, 558, 585

Dowie, George, 292, 294, 298-300

Dust Bowl, 151-152, 498

dust, 124, 252, 284, 389

Dykes, I.A., 540

~ E ~

Eagle Creek, 48, 59, 74, 101, 119, 264, 312

earthquake, 244, 594

East bank, 492

Eastern Gate, 254, 528

ecclesia, 434, 493, 569

Eisenhower, Dwight D., 77, 94, 447

elders, 22, 30-31, 40, 66, 106, 108, 142, 160, 186, 217, 241, 244, 246, 248-249, 259, 301, 317, 375, 379, 394, 405, 413, 432, 442, 484, 525, 532, 547, 592, 596

Emphatic Diaglott, The, 44, 58, 96, 155, 174, 180, 215, 232, 248, 255, 283-286, 288, 296, 300, 304, 308-310, 358, 364, 381, 532, 534, 589

enemy, 170, 301, 507

equipment, 33, 150, 158, 214, 250, 307, 431, 450, 462, 470, 474, 508, 585

erysipelas, 59, 103

ethics, 79, 242, 298

eulogy, 22, 43, 77, 95, 133, 153, 188, 244, 274, 408, 423, 529

evangelical, 5, 101, 104, 114, 124, 135, 154, 229, 302, 321, 533, 564-565, 585, 601

Evangelicalism, 75

evolution, 81, 563

executive secretary, 57, 317, 331, 353, 418, 428, 430-431, 436, 451, 486, 488, 494, 499, 525, 558, 585, 592

exemptions, 60, 336

~ F ~

faction, 247, 364

Firm Foundation, The, 213

Fish, William, 19, 459

flu, 532

free investigation, 172, 181, 213, 279, 309, 583, 588

free will, 170, 199, 348, 537, 562-563, 589

Froom, Leroy, 79, 177, 216, 564

Fugate, Mrs., 152

Fuller, Margaret, 211, 368, 439, 498

fundamentals, 302, 414, 557, 562

furnace, 58-59, 387

furnace, 58-59, 387

futurist, 177, 565

~ G ~

Galusha, Elon, 71, 277, 551

genealogist, 14, 60, 94

genealogy, 29, 58, 70, 112, 115, 137-138, 144, 153, 159, 166, 169, 196, 223, 227, 237, 242, 255-257, 298, 300, 399, 402, 457, 511, 588

generation, 4, 25, 56, 66, 113, 136, 142, 165, 226-227, 270, 295-296, 318, 326, 329, 339, 381, 402, 407, 427, 438, 467, 479, 483, 501, 516-517, 533, 539, 548, 552, 565-566

Golden Rule Home, 26, 33, 50-51, 69, 91, 110, 113, 184, 208, 220, 238, 276, 304, 313, 318, 331-332, 346, 362, 385, 396, 446, 458-459, 461, 463-464, 469-470, 499, 510, 515, 534

Graham, David, 7, 20, 29, 52, 68, 225, 228, 245, 393, 411, 498, 512, 578-579

Grant, Ulysses S., 115, 149, 317

Great Chicago Fire, 26, 53, 147, 181, 194, 223, 225, 228, 269, 293, 295, 307, 310, 525, 533

Great Depression, The, 338, 413, 419, 431, 445, 447, 456, 458, 468, 476, 494, 500, 519, 557

Great Plains, 1, 11-12, 56, 86, 111-112, 122, 128-129, 140, 186, 193, 196, 206, 208, 219, 221, 265, 275, 280, 304, 337, 356, 406, 429, 557

Greek, 70, 78, 81, 89, 128, 144, 168, 180, 190, 214, 217, 242, 248, 283-287, 290, 296, 299-300, 308-310, 342, 388, 435, 524, 532, 547, 556, 581, 584, 587-588

greenhouse, 205, 220, 329, 331-332, 381, 499, 510, 515

gristmill, 121, 188, 240, 576

~ H ~

Ham, J.R., 137-138, 195, 275, 292, 502

Hardesty, Robert, 217, 380, 421, 458, 504

Harrison, President Benjamin, 64

Hayse, John, 356

headquarters, 58, 113, 155, 157, 161, 213, 229, 266, 272, 296, 317, 319, 327, 354, 423, 428, 438, 456, 477, 504, 557

Hebrew, 5, 70, 82, 144, 168, 214, 277-278, 384, 402, 424, 524, 540, 564, 584

heresy, 3, 66, 103, 105, 117, 142, 198, 225, 253, 270, 288, 296, 299, 525, 548

Himes, J.V., 34, 79, 102, 172, 174-175, 254, 279, 288, 300

historicist, 89, 177

history, church, 1, 3, 13, 18, 23, 43, 72, 112, 127-128, 227, 242, 250, 261-262, 273, 297, 388, 413, 419, 422-423, 428, 430, 437, 458, 481, 506, 525, 529, 553, 585, 601

Holy Land, 250, 254, 360, 414, 429, 479, 528, 548, 550, 591

Holy Spirit, 1, 8, 11, 20, 33, 56-57, 61, 65, 67, 86, 98, 105, 112, 164, 166-168, 170, 178, 198, 212, 236, 239, 252, 275, 283, 292, 297, 301, 313, 356, 372, 392, 493, 537, 543, 567-568, 588

Home Department (Berean), 33

homestead, 28, 30, 40, 151-152, 184, 186, 191, 238, 264, 315, 336, 513

hope, broader, 65

hope, larger, 17, 105, 142, 190, 201, 253-254, 296, 321, 589

horse, 12, 35, 46, 130, 134, 156, 179, 212, 237, 242, 262, 282, 386, 393, 462, 519

Hoshaw, Lloyd, 470

hymn, 44, 95, 97, 191, 237, 293, 311, 314, 420, 492, 533

hymnal, 86, 175, 180, 214, 293, 308, 409, 433, 456, 492, 557-558

hymnbook, 84, 97, 214, 288, 308, 421

~ I ~

immortality, 10, 17, 34, 37, 40-43, 52, 58-59, 61, 81, 88, 101, 103, 105-108, 111, 115, 117-118, 120, 143-144, 154, 157, 166-167, 172, 179, 194, 204, 207, 213, 223-224, 226, 229-230, 237, 241, 246, 248, 252, 257, 263, 266, 271, 275, 292, 294, 301-302, 308-309, 311, 322, 331, 344, 392, 401-402, 423, 427-428, 443, 451, 454, 462, 537-538, 556-557, 560-564, 588-589, 598, 601

income, 35, 47, 51, 58, 82, 84, 89, 96, 113, 119, 121, 147, 160, 212, 214, 271, 284, 306, 309-310, 329, 341, 349, 372, 404, 409, 431, 447, 452, 468, 471, 502, 507

inheritance, 10, 122, 274, 301, 303, 403, 548, 550, 561, 587, 603

innocent, 563

investigate, 101, 199, 439, 536, 558, 570

Israel, 4, 17, 46, 49, 54, 65, 73, 78-79, 82, 89, 98, 103, 116, 143-144, 163-164, 174, 177-179, 183, 195, 206, 216, 224, 226, 240, 249, 251-252, 255, 288, 292, 295, 301, 303, 308-310, 313, 315, 328, 378, 392, 412, 414, 420-421, 425, 427-429,

Israel, *continued*, 432, 485, 487-488, 525, 528-529, 537, 545-550, 560-561, 565, 568, 580, 586, 588, 590, 596-597

~ J ~

James, Joe, 520, 539

janitor, 16, 95

Jehovah's Witnesses, 100, 105, 296, 381, 549, 589

Jerusalem, 40, 54, 75, 103, 117, 163, 177, 194, 224, 236, 251, 253-255, 262, 288, 296, 308, 392, 414, 485, 488, 503, 525, 528, 531, 547, 550, 561, 571, 597

Jew(s), 1, 10, 19, 72-73, 75, 103, 116-117, 143-145, 172, 174, 177-178, 194, 199-200, 205, 216, 224, 235, 245, 288, 296, 305, 307, 372, 429, 446, 519, 546-548, 550, 556, 565, 581, 587

Josephism, 17-18, 98-100, 111-112, 129, 166, 190-191, 199, 226-227, 283, 296-298, 300, 588

Judaizers, 172, 174

judgment, 1, 19, 28, 70-71, 138, 143-144, 157, 173, 179, 190, 199, 216, 229, 242, 260, 290-291, 306, 308, 311, 322, 330, 356, 392, 402, 537, 543, 545-546, 560, 562, 565-566, 568-570

Judson, J.M., 177, 254

~ K ~

Kansas Colony, 84

~ L ~

Latin, 299, 435, 524

lawyer, 62, 90, 165

layman, 24, 272, 420, 497, 527-528

Leasley, Mrs., 152

legislature, 101, 207

liberal, 34, 211, 214-215, 302, 331, 562-564

liberty, 1, 52, 75, 101-103, 130, 143, 163, 167, 170, 175, 181, 214, 245-246, 262, 289, 330, 355, 436, 471-473, 546, 556, 578, 580

license, 31, 37, 63, 78, 83, 91, 97, 101, 112, 125-127, 136, 155, 196, 199, 209, 265, 332, 337, 409, 417, 449, 467, 477, 485, 491, 497, 538, 559. *See also* ministerial license.

Lichty, George, 366, 448

literal, 10, 34, 117, 169, 172, 177-178, 180, 214, 216, 226, 252, 284, 286, 289, 308, 313, 331, 392, 427-428, 472, 545-551, 563, 565, 596

Little Wild Cat Church, 13, 217

Lord's Harvest International, 185, 433, 440, 475, 503, 505, 559, 591, 593-595

Lowden, Frank O., 218, 329, 519

~ M ~

Machen, John G., 302

Maddock, Darrell, 508

Magaw, Russell, 183, 351, 417, 425-426, 430-432, 437, 480, 488, 505, 512, 529, 531, 555, 558-559, 579, 586

manifested, 5, 20, 560, 580, 583

manslaughter, 132

martyred, 136, 559

Materialist, 41

Mattison, Val, 158, 557, 586

Maxson, 351, 524, 527

McGinty, Pete, 356, 446, 454, 507, 517

mediator, 246, 252, 392, 434, 560, 562

Mediterranean, 593

memorial, 33, 72-73, 86, 313, 335, 338, 359-361, 372, 376, 379, 382, 385, 398, 421, 424, 438, 445-446

menace, 251

mental health, 253, 504

mentor, 9, 122, 195, 245, 269, 311, 391, 401, 411, 420, 435, 480, 532

Mercy Seat, 237, 274, 580

Messenger Party, The, 249

Mexico, 105, 149, 219, 244, 304, 353, 357, 387, 397, 409, 415, 432, 434, 439, 452, 470, 475, 485, 487-488, 524-525, 531, 558, 592-593

military, 40, 60, 113, 138, 187, 193, 196, 325, 344, 384, 450, 465, 488, 502, 530-531

Millenarians, 124, 172

Miller, William, 1, 27, 34, 55, 70, 78, 80, 170, 172-173, 179, 246, 254, 257, 263, 277, 279, 546-547, 549, 556

Millerite Movement, 18, 20, 27, 40, 46, 131-132, 135, 148, 153, 159, 162, 172, 177, 191, 210, 257, 263, 275-278, 280, 303, 378, 545, 551

Millerite, 18, 20, 27, 36, 40, 45-46, 49, 52, 72, 79, 89, 131-132, 135, 148, 153, 159, 162, 172, 177, 182-183, 191, 210-211, 257, 263, 275-278, 280, 303, 378, 493, 545-546, 548-549, 551-552, 565

Milton, John, 216

Ministerial Association, 16, 18, 61, 67-68, 140, 155, 157, 270, 316, 329-330, 341, 365, 380, 383, 391-393, 426, 479, 484-485, 498, 526, 557, 585

ministerial license, 126, 155, 409, 467, 477, 497, 559

missionary, 24, 29, 37, 53, 77, 96, 124-125, 145, 154, 173, 179, 211, 219, 234, 261, 266, 310, 316, 336-337, 350, 353, 362, 385, 387, 401, 403, 409, 411, 421, 432, 439-440, 452, 462, 467, 475, 482, 487, 503, 526-527, 549, 559, 591, 594, 601

mob, 101, 136, 176, 373

modern, 4, 20, 52, 124, 228, 266, 284, 356, 421, 466, 484, 504, 533, 536, 538, 547, 563-564

money, 14, 33, 36, 43, 47, 61, 76, 96, 109, 117, 131-132, 134, 172, 179, 204, 221, 250, 256-257, 261, 282, 307, 319-320, 336, 349, 356, 375, 396, 414, 433, 440, 443, 456, 458-459, 468, 486, 493, 496, 505, 509, 527-528, 535, 594, 601

Morgridge, Elder, C., 178

Mormon Waterloo, The, 84, 86

Mormon, 12, 19, 84, 86-87, 415, 525

mourn(ing), 29, 70, 191, 329, 382, 445, 597

murder, 79, 497

~ N ~

National Berean Society, 2, 13, 18, 30-33, 53, 68, 75, 82, 90-91, 95, 112-113, 131, 134, 186-187, 190-191, 194, 201, 209, 218, 221, 223, 234, 247, 258, 275, 281, 302, 304, 313, 325-329, 337, 351, 363, 371-373, 379, 382, 387, 389, 393, 397, 400, 405-406, 413, 423, 425-426, 428, 433, 436, 438, 440, 442-443, 453, 467, 472, 474-479, 481, 483, 496, 500, 514-515, 524, 532-534, 539, 550, 557, 584-585

National Bible Institute, 2, 36, 68, 74, 82-83, 86, 158, 212-213, 261, 272, 314, 327, 329-331, 357, 372, 376, 380, 400, 402, 413, 421, 423, 437-438, 499, 509, 526, 557, 584-585, 601

nations, 1, 10, 65, 67, 98, 103, 121-122, 143-144, 163, 168, 172, 177-178, 185, 195, 226, 251-253, 255, 285, 301, 313, 315, 321, 330-331, 392, 427, 432, 525, 545, 550, 566, 570-571, 574-575, 589-590, 596, 598

Native American, 501, 523

naturalization, 14, 128, 362, 559

Nazarines, 20, 60, 114, 297

Neo-Orthodox, 563-564

New Jerusalem, 163, 253, 255, 262, 503, 550, 561

newspaper, 1, 64, 75-76, 110-111, 143, 155, 157, 165, 176, 197-198, 202, 224, 245, 280, 283, 289, 334, 355, 390, 393, 397, 411, 456, 476, 518, 585

Newton, Sir Isaac, 216

Normal School, 61, 113, 122, 127, 469, 495

~ O ~

obedience, 29, 46, 86, 103, 117, 139, 162-163, 179, 226, 252, 286, 301, 356, 359, 427, 507, 560-561, 581

Ojibwa, 523

Open Door Theory, 80

open, 14, 17, 45, 49, 64, 66, 70-71, 80, 97, 105, 110, 121, 142, 147, 151, 166, 197, 217, 221, 238, 247, 271, 321-322, 325, 333, 348, 362, 366, 386, 443-444, 449, 470, 485, 500, 530, 547, 560-561, 568, 593

open/closed communion, 66

opinion, 7, 67, 80, 85, 102, 110, 212, 235, 299, 347, 379, 498, 560, 588-589, 598

ordained, 19, 30-32, 55, 106, 154, 162, 186, 212, 214, 219, 222, 245, 259, 261, 264, 273, 296, 321, 373, 375, 377, 396, 400-401, 407, 432-433, 471, 477, 491, 513, 518, 529, 531, 591

Oregon *Bridal* College, 469

Orthodoxy, 40, 75, 101, 190, 215, 249

Owens, J.M., 480, 483

~ P ~

park, 16, 33, 121, 218, 225, 227-228, 234, 341, 360, 400, 408-409, 421, 454, 489, 492

parsonage, 39, 322, 333, 338, 341, 360, 366-367, 375, 382, 388, 404, 423, 425, 448, 455, 476, 493-494, 504

peace, 59-60, 87, 114, 138, 160, 188, 204, 208, 228, 237, 280, 301, 303, 335, 392, 424, 462, 483, 485, 488, 516, 521, 538, 575

Pearson, Timothy, 467, 469, 510

Pentecostal Nazarene, 114

Pentecostalism, 65, 75

Peters, George N.H., 134, 226-227, 253, 287, 459-460, 571

Pettingill, J.H., 169

philosophy, 20, 106, 214-215, 252, 417, 422, 566, 595

photos, 3, 26, 28, 75, 134, 254, 307, 320, 365, 372, 388, 417, 448, 499, 528-529

physician, 61, 89, 115, 119, 139, 146, 167, 185, 195, 223, 227, 254, 276, 454

Pine Woods Bible Class, 7, 85, 136, 138, 200, 310-311, 326, 495

poetry, 52, 210, 424, 454, 458, 543, 574-575

poison, 189

politics, 17, 47, 61, 64, 75, 81, 98, 127, 237, 301, 315, 322, 367, 498, 595

portrait, 48, 190, 463

postmodern, 67

prairie, 61, 90, 96, 121, 139, 151-152, 185, 211, 217, 256, 264, 399-400, 416, 426, 431, 492, 513-514

Principles of Literal Interpretation, 177

prison, 52, 138, 196, 444, 497-498

Proctor, W.S., 104

profession(s), 61, 241

Protestantism, 49-50, 177

punishment, 88, 101, 118, 154, 165, 216, 225, 330, 374, 401, 564

~ R ~

radio, 37, 137, 338, 340, 342-343, 352-354, 360, 364, 384, 397, 409, 415, 424-425, 431, 443-444, 446, 451-452, 454, 476, 481, 489-491, 500, 526-528, 530, 536, 600-601

railroad, 28, 46-47, 50, 62, 64, 73, 80, 104, 114, 149, 176, 206, 220, 248-249, 278-279, 294, 304, 306, 329, 335, 371, 399, 531, 572

Rankin, Arlen, 2, 16, 18, 50, 59, 74-76, 108, 144-145, 159, 164, 219-220, 244, 275, 355, 480-482, 485, 545, 579, 592

Rankin, Delbert, 13, 73, 137, 209, 372, 387, 406, 453, 507, 537

real estate, 60, 92, 116, 265, 267, 306, 310, 341, 463, 520

re-baptism/rebaptism, 6, 20, 72, 175, 179, 249, 283, 288, 292, 322

recommendation, 34, 62-63, 272, 281, 390, 496, 531, 583, 591-593

reconciliation, 17, 61, 65, 142, 163, 180, 199, 216, 274, 330, 395, 406-407, 422, 493, 507, 515, 535, 537-539, 545, 566-567, 589

redemption, 37, 86, 144, 162-163, 190, 209, 216, 237, 358, 550, 561, 582

religion, 19, 47, 69, 129, 183, 205, 215, 237, 335, 402, 415, 552, 563

Rencontre, James, 258, 362, 439, 491-492

Resolution of 1887 (women in evangelism), 30

Resolution on Slavery, 28

Restitutionists, 59, 172, 514

Restoration Movement, 6, 40, 43, 62, 101-102, 112, 116, 179, 234, 245, 251, 287, 291, 556

revival, 40, 45, 56, 78, 109, 153, 188, 239, 266-267, 281-282, 400, 411, 425, 478, 496, 519, 540, 565

reward, 1, 33, 157, 173, 190, 194-195, 233, 236, 242, 252, 274, 290, 296, 306, 330, 356, 402, 463, 537, 554, 560-561, 564, 569-570, 589

Rock River Christian College, 25, 49, 87, 107, 154, 184, 298, 304, 358, 375, 388, 416, 424, 426, 464, 470, 498, 508-509, 512, 538, 562, 583

rural, 54, 85, 96, 157, 210, 238, 274, 281, 335, 341, 370, 387, 406, 412, 445, 480, 514, 527, 529, 534, 557, 596

Russell, Charles Taze (also C.T.), 7, 38, 100, 105, 138, 196-200, 253, 255, 271, 286, 296, 309-310, 549, 589

Russellism, 142, 271, 305, 310, 423

Russia, 234, 310, 334, 594

~ S ~

Sabbatarian, 204, 249-251

Sabbatarian Adventists, 57, 80, 82

Sabbath keeping, 122, 180, 199, 322

sail, 115, 211

San Francisco, 24, 243-244, 447, 482, 602

sanctuary, 34, 71, 78-79, 81-82, 87, 163-164, 173, 328, 335, 347-348, 353, 366, 382-383, 493, 504, 550, 552, 597

Satan, 65, 79, 99, 117, 124, 195, 199, 242, 274, 288, 310, 321, 331, 393, 480, 498, 562-563, 589

sawmill, 121, 149, 220, 274, 468, 572

Schulz, Bruce, 38, 183, 197-198, 207, 227, 255, 257, 293, 308-309

Scotland, 44, 119, 140, 185, 201, 294

Scott, Walter, 6, 234

second chance, 65, 99, 126, 190, 253, 321, 564, 589

sectarian, 7, 56, 75, 80, 101, 107, 116, 162, 170, 177, 181, 213, 246, 249, 286, 293, 309

Sectarianism, 101-103, 116-118, 279, 293, 319

See, Robert, 418, 493, 517

seminary, 78, 96, 129, 210-211, 302, 342, 371, 396, 445, 451, 460, 505, 602

Servetus, Michael (Miquel Servet), 128, 216

Seventh-day Adventist(s), 3, 20, 34, 57, 79, 163, 192, 249, 507, 549, 590, 598

Seventh-day Baptists, 225, 366, 394, 590

Seventh-day Church of God, 3, 98, 148, 163, 199, 204, 249, 298, 485, 590

seventy weeks, 81, 309, 597

shaped notes, 188, 239, 503

Shaw, Paul, 458, 493, 531-532, 555, 593

ship, 47, 77, 115, 201, 294, 334, 340, 489, 533, 535

Shipman, J.H., 36

shooting, 64

Shut Door, 71-72, 78-82

social gospel, 563-564

songbook, 32, 144, 288, 409, 433, 456, 484

Sonship, 17, 166, 297

Soul sleeper, soul-sleep, 7, 9

Spanish, 319, 452, 482, 488, 521, 524, 532, 593

"Speaking and Hearing" by Wiley Jones, 144

Spiritualism, 27, 71-72, 80, 148, 210

split, 61, 68, 73-74, 102, 141, 157, 163, 166, 172-173, 179, 189, 230, 237, 243, 270, 290, 294-295, 308, 364, 391-392, 512, 589

sprinkle, 386

sprinkling, 190, 262, 443

Statement of Faith, 3, 5, 10, 13, 17, 40, 65, 68, 84, 97-99, 116, 118-119, 126, 140, 155, 157, 172, 229, 248, 251-252, 298, 301, 312-313, 318-319, 322, 330-331, 378, 392-393, 401-402, 426-428, 443, 445, 511, 561, 588

statue, 217, 268, 345, 428, 496, 498, 513, 597

Stone, Barton, 6, 8, 153, 170, 175

Systematic Theology, 353-354, 357, 387-389, 398, 403, 452, 462, 466, 475, 520, 543, 558-559, 563, 566, 593, 600-602

~ T ~

Taft, Lorado, 217, 268, 345, 498

tent, 10, 14, 16, 18, 31, 42, 44, 46-47, 84, 97-98, 100, 109, 129, 133, 162, 179, 207, 241, 250, 257-259, 282, 310, 349, 395, 405, 435, 439, 454, 560, 583

testimony, 43, 72, 77, 87, 92, 96, 107, 123, 131, 137-138, 146, 152, 162, 187, 191, 235, 237, 239, 249, 284, 297, 302-303, 305, 311, 326, 335, 355, 424, 462, 466, 468, 472, 478, 480, 503, 518, 521, 530, 562, 602

theologian, 1, 65, 166, 204, 215, 288, 308, 313, 593

theologians, 65, 153, 242, 438

theology, 1, 5, 34, 52, 55, 71, 78, 80-82, 87, 98, 105, 163, 166, 168, 211, 214-215, 225, 242, 286, 291, 302, 314, 332, 342, 353-354, 357, 387-389, 398, 402-403, 416-417, 439, 452, 462, 466, 469, 475, 508-509, 520, 537, 543, 545-546, 548, 558-559, 562-566, 588, 593, 600-602

Thomas, Dr. John, 3, 5, 8, 14, 20-21, 56, 60, 72, 74, 103, 114, 116, 144, 154, 162, 165, 170, 173-174, 178, 190, 195, 234, 253, 263, 289-294, 381, 556, 589

THRIVE Ministry, 453, 587

throne, 1, 10, 49-50, 103, 163, 172, 178, 198, 248, 253, 262, 288, 301, 330, 402, 550, 561, 566, 570-571, 574-575, 588

tithe, 414, 516, 535

tombstone, 55, 75, 182, 191, 403, 444

Torrey, R.A., 302, 402

tours, 10, 203, 229, 238, 245, 265, 272, 388, 448, 512, 531, 533, 535, 540

tract, 17, 26, 49, 60, 88, 96, 122-123, 128, 135, 141, 158, 162-163, 177, 199, 212, 226, 230, 238, 266, 288, 291, 296-297, 299, 313-314, 328, 372, 395, 397, 400-401, 415, 436, 440, 443, 454, 498, 526, 536, 571, 589

trailer, 341, 376, 459, 479, 489, 511

travelers, 77, 474, 539

Trinitarian, 5, 342

Trinity, 5-7, 65, 105, 169, 216, 245, 292, 302, 342, 399, 402, 440, 557

trumpets, 80, 183, 598-599

Turner, Gary, 519-520, 594

twelve thrones, 178

type, 18, 79, 82, 271, 284-285, 288, 307, 313, 318, 398, 499, 601

typhoid, 29, 52, 115, 133, 169, 181, 254, 312

~ U ~

Underwood controversy, 67

Unitarian(s), 1, 5-7, 87, 183, 214-216, 224, 235, 246, 262, 302, 407, 537

universal reconciliation, 395, 406-407, 422, 507, 535, 537-539, 589

universalism, 12, 54, 65-66, 105, 111, 120, 131, 142, 178, 190, 246, 253, 274, 331, 356, 406-407, 422-423, 454, 507, 536-537, 557, 588-589

universalist, 120, 168, 216, 224, 246, 290, 322, 331, 356, 406-407, 507, 537

university, 1, 24, 33, 42, 50, 59, 61, 79, 82, 125, 127, 214-215, 217-218, 228, 276-277, 285, 334, 341-342, 351, 361, 373, 382, 388-389, 397, 400, 406, 414, 418, 439, 447, 449, 452-453, 463, 468, 470-472, 484, 486, 501, 506, 508-511, 513, 519, 522, 524, 529, 535, 549, 552, 566, 591, 602

Urish, Dean, 354, 359, 479, 522

~ V ~

Vacation Bible School, 113, 156, 410, 461-462, 516, 593

van, 13, 44, 119, 129, 133, 222, 247, 270, 272, 275, 280, 340, 355, 365, 376, 380, 405, 407, 421, 453, 476, 492, 511, 536-537

View of Atonement, 236-237, 566

violent, 160, 316

~ W ~

walk, 61-62, 95, 106, 123, 151, 172, 301, 327, 344-345, 386, 395, 453, 465, 485, 508, 519, 531, 563, 565

war. *See* Civil War, WWI or WWII.

Washington Grove, 35, 82, 84, 281-282, 435, 437, 513

Watershed, 17, 545, 548-549

weather, 11, 19, 36, 61, 126, 145, 206, 294, 320, 322, 325, 335, 348, 356, 398

Wesleyan Connection, 120

Where are the Dead?, 43

Wilcox, J.F., 277, 364

Williams, J.H., 19-20, 35

Working Rules (1910 Waterloo Conference), 10, 584

WWI (World War I), 69, 85, 302, 379, 419, 447, 491, 563

WWII/World War II, 325, 334, 336, 366, 368, 384, 394, 408, 428, 430, 432, 438, 448-449, 465, 471, 480, 524, 530, 535, 563, 572

~ Y ~

yellow paint, 355

Yom Kippur, 274

Young, Albert O., 318, 320

~ Z ~

Zion's Watch Tower, 38, 100, 197-198, 200, 296

www.ingramcontent.com/pod-product-compliance
Lightning Source LLC
Chambersburg PA
CBHW080528300426
44111CB00017B/2647